ELEMENTS OF LITERATURE
SECOND COURSE

The Elements of Literature Program

ELEMENTS OF LITERATURE: First Course

ELEMENTS OF LITERATURE: Second Course

ELEMENTS OF LITERATURE: Third Course

ELEMENTS OF LITERATURE: Fourth Course

ELEMENTS OF LITERATURE: Fifth Course
Literature of the United States

ELEMENTS OF LITERATURE: Sixth Course
Literature of Britain

A Teacher's Manual, Test Book, and Teacher's Resource Organizer are available for each of the above titles.

Robert Anderson is a playwright, novelist, screenwriter, and television writer. His plays include *Tea and Sympathy; Silent Night, Lonely Night; You Know I Can't Hear You When the Water's Running;* and *I Never Sang for My Father.* His screenplays include *The Nun's Story* and *The Sand Pebbles.* Mr. Anderson has taught at the Writer's Workshop at the University of Iowa, the American Theatre Wing Professional Training Program, and the Salzburg Seminar in American Studies. He is a Past President of the Dramatists' Guild, Vice-President of the Authors' League of America, and a member of the Theatre Hall of Fame. He makes his home in Connecticut and New York City.

John Malcolm Brinnin, author of six volumes of poetry which have received many prizes and awards, is a member of the American Academy and Institute of Arts and Letters. He is also a critic of poetry and a biographer of poets and was for a number of years Director of New York's famous Poetry Center. His teaching career, begun at Vassar College, included long terms at the University of Connecticut and Boston University, where he succeeded Robert Lowell as Professor of Creative Writing and Contemporary Letters. Mr. Brinnin has written *Dylan Thomas in America: An Intimate Journal* and *Sextet: T. S. Eliot & Truman Capote & Others.* He divides his time between Duxbury, Massachusetts, and Key West, Florida.

John Leggett is an editor, a novelist, and a biographer who went to the Writer's Workshop at the University of Iowa in the spring of 1969, expecting to put in a single semester. In 1970 he assumed temporary charge of the program and was its Director for the next seventeen years. Mr. Leggett's novels include *Wilder Stone, The Gloucester Branch, Who Took the Gold Away, Gulliver House,* and *Making Believe.* He is also the author of the highly acclaimed biography *Ross and Tom: Two American Tragedies.* His short fiction, articles, and reviews have appeared in *Harper's, Esquire, Mademoiselle, The Ladies Home Journal,* and the *Los Angeles Times.* A native New Yorker, Mr. Leggett now lives in San Francisco.

David Adams Leeming is Professor of English at the University of Connecticut and the author of three books on mythology: *Mythology: The Voyage of the Hero; Flights: Readings in Magic, Mysticism, Fantasy, and Myth;* and *Mythology* (Newsweek Books series). For several years he taught English at the Robert College in Istanbul, Turkey. He also served as secretary-assistant to the writer James Baldwin in New York and Istanbul. Dr. Leeming is a contributor to *Comparative Literature, Children's Literature, Parabola,* and *Revue de Littérature Comparée.* He lives in Stonington, Connecticut.

ELEMENTS OF LITERATURE

SECOND COURSE

HOLT, RINEHART AND WINSTON, INC.

AUSTIN   NEW YORK   SAN DIEGO   CHICAGO   TORONTO   MONTREAL

Candy Carter wrote the Exercises in Critical Thinking and Writing. She is English Department Chair at Tahoe Truckee Junior-Senior High School in California. Ms. Carter has served on the editorial committee of the NCTE and has been an editor of the *California English Magazine*. She has edited books and journal articles for the NCTE and was selected to participate in the Summer 1987 NCTE/MLA invitational institute on the teaching of English. She lives in Truckee, California.

Sandra Cisneros has served as Consultant for the program. A graduate of the Writer's Workshop at the University of Iowa, she has written a novel, *The House on Mango Street,* and several collections of poems, including *My Wicked, Wicked Ways*. She has taught at California State University, Chico, and now makes her home in Texas.

Nancy E. Wiseman Seminoff has served as Consultant in Reading and Questioning Strategies for the program. Dr. Seminoff is Dean of the College of Education at Winona State University, Minnesota. She has served as a reading consultant and as a classroom teacher. She has published widely in national and state educational periodicals. Dr. Seminoff lives in Winona, Minnesota.

Printed in the United States of America

ISBN 0-15-717510-3

890123456 041 987654321

Acknowledgments

Grateful acknowledgment is made to the teachers who reviewed materials in this book, in manuscript or in classroom tests.

Anne Aldridge
Hayfield Secondary School
Alexandria, Virginia

Bea Cassidy
Miami Springs Junior High School
Miami Springs, Florida

Bernice Causey
Mobile County Public Schools
Mobile, Alabama

Charles Crawford
Radnor Middle School
Wayne, Pennsylvania

Jean Heller
Williamsport Schools
Williamsport, Pennsylvania

Karen Libby
Hamilton Junior High School
Denver, Colorado

Kathryn McMillan
Stratford, Connecticut

Ruby Lee Norris
Topping, Virginia

Sandra Prillaman
Wicomico Board of Education
Salisbury, Maryland

Grateful acknowledgment is also made to the following teachers who assisted in the planning of the instructional apparatus and in its preparation:

Marie C. Brown
Sterling Heights, Michigan

Rose Sallberg Kam
Sacramento, California

Mary Beth Lorsbach
Marquette, Michigan

Craig Minbiole
Rochester Hills, Michigan

For permission to reprint copyrighted material, grateful acknowledgment is made to the following sources:

Arte Publico Press: "Three Wise Guys: A Christmas Story" by Sandra Cisneros. Copyright © 1987 by Sandra Cisneros. "Gil's Furniture Bought and Sold" by Sandra Cisneros. Copyright © 1987 by Sandra Cisneros.

Bantam Books, Inc.: From *Dandelion Wine* by Ray Bradbury. Copyright © 1957 by Ray Bradbury. Published by Bantam Books, Inc.

Elizabeth Barnett: "The Ballad of the Harp-Weaver" from *Collected Poems* by Edna St. Vincent Millay. Copyright 1923; renewed 1951 by Edna St. Vincent Millay and Norma Millay Ellis. Published by Harper & Row, Publishers, Inc.

Joan Blackburn: "The Routine" from *The Cities* by Paul Blackburn. Copyright © 1967 by Paul Blackburn.

Bramhall House, a division of Crown Publishers, Inc.: "The Walrus and the Carpenter," from *The Annotated Alice* by Martin Gardner. Text by Lewis Carroll. Copyright © 1960 by Martin Gardner.

Brandt & Brandt Literary Agents, Inc.: From *The Blue Hen's Chick* by A. B. Guthrie, Jr. Copyright © 1965 by A. B. Guthrie, Jr. "The Devil and Daniel Webster" and "By the Waters of Babylon" from *The Selected Works of Stephen Vincent Benét.* Copyright 1936 by The Curtis Publishing Company; copyright 1937 by Stephen Vincent Benét, copyright renewed 1964 by Thomas C. Benét, Stephanie B. Mahin, and Rachel Benét Lewis. "Hernando de Soto (1499?–1542)" from *A Book of Americans* by Rosemary and Stephen Vincent Benét. Copyright 1933 by Stephen Vincent Benét and Rosemary Benét; copyright renewed 1961 by Rosemary Carr Benét.

Curtis Brown Group, Ltd.: From *The Ugly Duckling* by A. A. Milne. Copyright 1941 by A. A. Milne. "Sisters" by Lucille Clifton from *An Ordinary Woman.* Copyright © 1974 by Lucille Clifton.

Curtis Brown Group, Ltd., on behalf of John Wain: "Manhood" from *Death of the Hind Legs and Other Stories* by John Wain. Copyright © 1966 by John Wain.

Laura Cecil, Literary Agent for the James Reeves Estate: From "The Sea" in *James Reeves: The Complete Poems,* published by Heinemann.

Congdon & Weed, Inc., New York, NY: From *Growing Up* by Russell Baker. Copyright © 1982 by Russell Baker.

Don Congdon Associates, Inc.: From "A Sound of Thunder" by Ray Bradbury from *Science Fact/Fiction.* Copyright 1952 by Collier Publishing Company; copyright renewed 1980 by Ray Bradbury.

Joan Daves: From *I Have a Dream* by Martin Luther King, Jr. Copyright © 1963 by Martin Luther King, Jr.

Delacorte Press/Seymour Lawrence: "Calling Home" from *Going After Cacciato* by Tim O'Brien. Copyright © 1978 by Tim O'Brien. Originally published in *Redbook.*

Doubleday, a division of Bantam, Doubleday, Dell Publishing Group, Inc.: From *The Complete Humorous Sketches and Tales of Mark Twain,* edited by Charles Neider. Copyright © 1961 by Charles Neider. "The Counterfeit Secret Circle Member Gets the Message, or The Asp Strikes Again" from *In God We Trust, All Others Pay Cash* by Jean Shepherd. Copyright © 1966 by Jean Shepherd. From *Anne Frank: The Diary of a Young Girl* by Anne Frank. Copyright 1952 by Otto H. Frank.

"The Ransom of Red Chief" by O. Henry from *Best Stories of O. Henry.* Selected and with an Introduction by Bennett Cerf and Van H. Cartmell. Published by Garden City Books. Copyright 1945.

Dramatists Play Service: From *The Devil and Daniel Webster* by Stephen Vincent Benét in *15 American One-Act Plays,* edited by Paul Kozelka. Copyright 1938, 1939 by Stephen Vincent Benét and Dramatists Play Service.

Farrar, Straus & Giroux, Inc.: From *Life Among the Savages* retitled "Ninki" by Shirley Jackson. Copyright 1953 by Shirley Jackson. Copyright renewed 1981 by Lawrence Hyman, Barry Hyman, Mrs. Sarah Webster, and Mrs. Joanne Schnurer. "Reb Asher the Dairyman" from *A Day of Pleasure* by Isaac Bashevis Singer. Copyright © 1969 by Isaac Bashevis Singer.

Howard Fast: Comment by Howard Fast on "The First Rose of Summer." Copyright © 1987 by Howard Fast.

Edward Field: Comment by Edward Field on "Frankenstein." Copyright © 1987 by Edward Field.

Finley, Kumble, Wagner, Heine, Underberg, Manley & Casey as agents for Cyrno Corporation/Knox Burger Associates Ltd., as agents for John Cunningham: The screenplay *High Noon* by Carl Foreman. A Stanley Kramer Production. Based on *The Tin Star* by John Cunningham.

David R. Godine, Publisher, Inc.: "My Mother's Childhood" from *Teaching the Penguins to Fly* by Barry Spacks. Copyright © 1960, 1972, 1973, 1974, 1975 by Barry Spacks.

Grove Press, Inc.: "Dusting" from *Homecoming* by Julia Alvarez. Copyright © 1984 by Julia Alvarez.

John Haines: Comment by John Haines on "Wolves." Copyright © 1987 by John Haines.

Harcourt Brace Jovanovich, Inc.: "Soup" from *Smoke and Steel* by Carl Sandburg. Copyright 1950 by Carl Sandburg. "A Tragedy Revealed: Heroine's Last Days" from *A Portrait in Courage* by Ernst Schnabel. Copyright © Fischer Bücherei KG, Frankfurt am Main, 1958.

Harper & Row, Publishers, Inc.: "The Upper World" from *Nine Tales of Coyote* by Fran Martin. Copyright 1950 by Harper & Brothers. From *The Day Lincoln Was Shot* by Jim Bishop. Copyright © 1955 by Jim Bishop.

Harvard University Press on behalf of the publisher and the Trustees of Amherst College: "If I Can Stop One Heart from Breaking" from *The Poems of Emily Dickinson,* edited by Thomas H. Johnson. Copyright © 1951, 1955, 1979, 1983 by the President and Fellows of Harvard College. Published by the Belknap Press of Harvard University Press. Cambridge, Massachusetts.

Sara Henderson Hay: "The Builders" from *Story Hour* by Sara Henderson Hay. Copyright © 1963 by Sara Henderson Hay.

Robert Hayden: "Those Winter Sundays" from *Selected Poems* by Robert Hayden. Copyright © 1966 by Robert Hayden. Published by October House.

Henry Holt & Company, Inc.: "The Runaway," "Dust of Snow," and "A Time to Talk," from *The Poetry of Robert Frost,* edited by Edward Connery Lathem. Copyright 1951 by Robert Frost. "Steam Shovel" from *Upper Pasture* by Charles Malam. Copyright © 1930, 1958 by Charles Malam. "The Owl Never Sleeps at Night" from *How and Why Stories* by John Branner. "With Rue My Heart Is Laden" from *The Collected*

Design: Kirchoff/Wohlberg, Inc.
Art Development and Picture Research: Photosearch, Inc.
Cover: *Hills with Piñon, Two Horses* by Victor Higgins. Oil.
    Private Collection. Courtesy the Gerald Peters Gallery, Santa Fe, New Mexico, and Dallas, Texas.
Page v: *Down Grade* by Michael Wright (1987). Oil.
    Courtesy of Sena Galleries East, Santa Fe, New Mexico.

PICTURE CREDITS

CONTENTS

Images: Sensory Experiences   390

Figures of Speech: Unexpected Connections   398

Allusions   413

Stories in Verse   418

Messages—Open and Hidden   435

SEVEN: POINT OF VIEW—REAL EXPERIENCES   447

EIGHT: THE AMERICAN TRADITION—MYTHS, FOLKTALES, AND HISTORICAL REALITIES 497

NINE: THE ELEMENTS OF THE NOVEL 613

THE CLIFF-HANGER
CONFLICT AND SUSPENSE

Illustration by N.C. Wyeth for Robert Louis Stevenson's
Kidnapped. Charles Scribner's Sons (1913).

UNIT ONE   **John Leggett**

Unit Outline
THE CLIFF-HANGER
CONFLICT AND SUSPENSE

Conflict is the . . . fundamental element of fiction, necessary because in literature, only trouble is interesting.

—Janet Burroway

What is it that gives one story life and makes another one dull? What quality attracts us to some stories—whether they are true stories or fiction? What keeps us reading some stories, even when we ought to be getting about our other business, or turning out the lights and going to sleep?

What is it that "powers" some stories, like an engine with horsepower to spare, while other stories are limp and as lifeless as last summer's roses?

Conflict: The Energy of a Story

It is **conflict,** or struggle, that gives any story its energy. There are many conflicts—the possibilities are endless. Among the common sources of conflict are these:

1. One person (or animal) in conflict with another person.

2. One person (or animal) in conflict with a group or a whole society.

3. One person (or animal) in conflict with something in nature.

4. One person (or animal) in conflict with something in himself or herself: perhaps fear, shyness, homesickness, or just an inability to make a decision.

Suspense: The Page-Turner

It is conflict that makes us feel **suspense** in a story, and suspense is what keeps us turning those pages. The word *suspense* is related to the word *suspended.* When we feel suspense, we feel as if we are held suspended in midair, waiting for an outcome. We feel like those characters in many movies and stories who are clinging by their fingertips to the cliff, their feet kicking out into space, the waves crashing on the rocks miles below. We must find out: Will they hold on? Are their fingers starting to slip already? Is the ledge beginning to crumble?

The very picture of a cliff-hanger makes our hearts beat faster. When you read the stories in this unit, see how the writers are able to create cliff-hanger situations. Do you find you *must* finish reading their stories? Do you keep asking "What happens next?" "And next?" "And then . . . ?"

The Cliff-Hanger

Illustration by N. C. Wyeth for Robert Louis Stevenson's *Treasure Island.* Charles Scribner's Sons (1911).

Responding to a Story

Throughout this book, you'll find some short passages that have been read by a reader whose responses are noted in the margin. Different readers will have different responses, but everyone who reads has some reaction. You should be aware of your responses as you read; at times, you will want to write them down. They will be useful when you write about the story later on.

If you own a book, you can write in it as much as you like. Since this isn't true of a textbook, you should write your responses on paper.

The Path Through the Cemetery

Ivan was a timid little man—so timid that the villagers called him "Pigeon" or mocked him with the title, "Ivan the Terrible." Every night Ivan stopped in at the saloon which was on the edge of the village cemetery. Ivan never crossed the cemetery to get to his lonely shack on the other side. That path would save many minutes, but he had never taken it—not even in the full light of noon.

> Walking through a cemetery might be scary. Why would anyone do it?
> Ivan: Is this Russia?

Late one winter's night, when bitter wind and snow beat against the saloon, the customers took up the familiar mockery. "Ivan's mother was scared by a canary when she carried him." "Ivan the Terrible—Ivan the Terribly Timid One."

> Poor guy. He's timid and lonely.

> He'll go through that path in the story, I predict.

Ivan's sickly protest only fed their taunts, and they jeered cruelly when the young Cossack lieutenant flung his horrid challenge at their quarry.

> This setting is scary—if it were sunny, I'd have a different feeling. I don't think this is going to end happily.

> I feel sorry for Ivan.

"You are a pigeon, Ivan. You'll walk all around the cemetery in this cold—but you dare not cross it."

> A Cossack must be a soldier. It *is* Russia.
> Quarry: They are the "hunters."

Ivan murmured, "The cemetery is nothing to cross, Lieutenant. It is nothing but earth, like all the other earth."

> I don't like this Cossack.

The lieutenant cried, "A challenge, then! Cross the cemetery tonight, Ivan, and I'll give you five rubles—five gold rubles!"

> Ivan sounds wise. Is he faking here?

Perhaps it was the vodka. Perhaps it was the temptation of the five gold rubles. No one ever knew why Ivan, moistening his lips, said suddenly: "Yes, Lieutenant, I'll cross the cemetery!"

> Rubles must be Russian money. I suppose it must be a lot to Ivan.

The saloon echoed with their disbelief. The lieutenant winked to the men and unbuckled his saber. "Here, Ivan. When you get to the center of the cemetery, in front of the biggest tomb, stick the saber into the ground. In the morning we shall go there. And if the saber is in the ground—five gold rubles to you!"

> Why is he doing it? I predict he'll win and show them all.

> Saber must be a sword.

Ivan took the saber. The men drank a toast: "To Ivan the Terrible!" They roared with laughter.

The wind howled around Ivan as he closed the door of the saloon behind him. The cold was knife-sharp. He buttoned his long coat and crossed the dirt road. He could hear the lieutenant's voice, louder than the rest, yelling after him, "Five rubles, pigeon! If you live!"

> Weather creates a sense of doom, or disaster. Makes me uneasy.

Ivan pushed the cemetery gate open. He walked fast. "Earth, just earth . . . like any other earth." But the darkness was a massive dread. "Five gold rubles . . ." The wind was cruel and

> They keep calling him pigeon.

> One of his conflicts is fear, poor guy.
> The weather is very ominous. What's going to happen?

the saber was like ice in his hands. Ivan shivered under the long, thick coat and broke into a limping run.

He recognized the large tomb. He must have sobbed—that was the sound that was drowned in the wind. And he kneeled, cold and terrified, and drove the saber through the crust into the hard ground. With all his strength, he pushed it down to the hilt. It was done. The cemetery . . . the challenge . . . five gold rubles.

Ivan started to rise from his knees. But he could not move. Something held him. Something gripped him in an unyielding and implacable hold. Ivan tugged and lurched and pulled—gasping in his panic, shaken by a monstrous fear. But something held Ivan. He cried out in terror, then made senseless gurgling noises.

They found Ivan, next morning, on the ground in front of the tomb that was in the center of the cemetery. He was frozen to death. The look on his face was not that of a frozen man, but of a man killed by some nameless horror. And the lieutenant's saber was in the ground where Ivan had pounded it—through the dragging folds of his long coat.

—Leonard Q. Ross

He limps?

Great—he did it.

What's got him?

He goes crazy? ("senseless"?)

What killed him?

Do I get this ending? Could it mean two things? Is there a message to this story? I think there is.

Thinking Over the Story

This reader was unsure about the ending. Are you? Could it have two meanings?

If this reader wants to use the response notes, he or she might focus on these reactions: (1) The reader felt oppressed by the weather three times. Did the writer intend this? (2) The reader felt great pity for Ivan, and dislike for the Cossack. Is that the writer's intention? (3) The reader wonders why Ivan accepted the challenge in the first place. (4) The reader twice predicted how the story might end; one prediction was right; the other was wrong.

What is Ivan's conflict in the story? Does he face an outside enemy? Or is his enemy internal, some problem inside his own mind?

How does the writer keep you reading? What major question does he make you want the answer to?

Is the writer telling the story to deliver a message? This reader seems to think so. Do you?

TO BUILD A FIRE

Jack London

"To Build a Fire" must be the coldest story ever written. It is also one of the best possible examples of a conflict between a man and the elements of nature. The story has only one character and he is nameless. We see him clearly enough as he plods through the bleak, sunless Yukon in northwestern Canada, his spittle freezing on his amber beard. We get to know him rather well, too, even though we never learn about his background. We learn about his nature from what we are told directly. We know even more from what we hear him think, and from the way we see him deal with difficulties, of which he has plenty.

As you read, think of elements *other* than the weather which play key roles in the plot. One of the central fascinations of "To Build a Fire" is the Yukon lore. London uses his knowledge of the Yukon not only to give authenticity to the story, but also to build up an irresistible suspense. Knowing how to survive in bitter cold is just the kind of practical information we readers take in greedily. (Who knows when it may prove useful?) Watch how London makes a misplaced foot and the lighting of a match matters of such critical importance that we believe in the story as if it were our own experience. (You will want to dress warmly as you read.)

For a map of the Yukon, see page 44.

Day had broken cold and gray, exceedingly cold and gray, when the man turned aside from the main Yukon trail and climbed the high earth bank, where a dim and little-traveled trail led eastward through the fat spruce timberland. It was a steep bank, and he paused for breath at the top, excusing the act to himself by looking at his watch. It was nine o'clock. There was no sun or hint of sun, though there was not a cloud in the sky. It was a clear day, and yet there seemed an intangible pall over the face of things, a subtle gloom that made the day dark, and that was due to the absence of sun. This fact did not worry the man. He was used to the lack of sun. It had been days since he had seen the sun, and he knew that a few more days must pass before that cheerful orb, due south, would just peep above the skyline and dip immediately from view.

The man flung a look back along the way he had come. The Yukon lay a mile wide and hidden under three feet of ice. On top of this ice were as many feet of snow. It was all pure white, rolling in gentle undulations where the ice jams of the freeze-up had formed. North and south, as far as his eye could see, it was unbroken white, save for a dark hairline that curved and twisted from around the spruce-covered island to the south, and that curved and twisted away into the north, where it disappeared behind another spruce-covered island. This dark hairline was the trail— the main trail—that led south five hundred miles to the Chilkoot Pass, Dyea, and salt water; and that led north seventy miles to Dawson, and still on to the north a thousand miles to Nulato, and finally to St. Michael on the Bering Sea, a thousand miles and half a thousand more.

But all this—the mysterious, far-reaching hairline trail, the absence of sun from the sky, the tremendous cold, and the strangeness and weirdness of it all—made no impression on the man. It was not because he was long used to it. He was a newcomer in the land, a cheechako,[1] and this was

Words with multiple meanings. What do the words *bank* and *deposit* mean? Each of these words can have more than one meaning, ranging from money matters to rivers and rubbish. When you see these words in a sentence, how can you tell which meaning the writer is using? You have to look at the *context*, the words and sentences surrounding *bank* and *deposit*. You do the same with any other word with *multiple meanings*. The context usually will let you determine easily which meaning is intended. As you read this story, watch for context clues that help you figure out the definition of words that can have several meanings.

---

1. **cheechako** (chē·chä′kō): newcomer to Canada or Alaska.

his first winter. The trouble with him was that he was without imagination. He was quick and alert in the things of life, but only in the things, and not in the significances. Fifty degrees below zero meant eighty-odd degrees of frost. Such fact impressed him as being cold and uncomfortable, and that was all. It did not lead him to meditate upon his frailty as a creature of temperature, and upon man's frailty in general, able only to live within certain narrow limits of heat and cold, and from there on it did not lead him to the conjectural[2] field of immortality and man's place in the universe. Fifty degrees below zero stood for a bite of frost that hurt and that must be guarded against by the use of mittens, earflaps, warm moccasins, and thick socks. Fifty degrees below zero was to him just precisely fifty degrees below zero. That there should be anything more to it than that was a thought that never entered his head.

As he turned to go on, he spat speculatively. There was a sharp, explosive crackle that startled him. He spat again. And again, in the air, before it could fall to the snow, the spittle crackled. He knew that at fifty below, spittle crackled on the snow, but this spittle had crackled in the air. Undoubtedly it was colder than fifty below—how much colder he did not know. But the temperature did not matter. He was bound for the old claim on the left fork of Henderson Creek, where the boys were already. They had come over across the divide from the Indian Creek country, while he had come the roundabout way to take a look at the possibilities of getting out logs in the spring from the islands in the Yukon. He would be into camp by six o'clock; a bit after dark, it was true, but the boys would be there, a fire would be going, and a hot supper would be ready. As for lunch, he pressed his hand against the protruding bundle under his jacket. It was also under his shirt, wrapped up in a handkerchief and lying against the naked skin. It was the only way to keep the biscuits from freezing. He smiled agreeably to himself as he thought of those biscuits, each cut open and sopped in bacon grease, and each enclosing a generous slice of fried bacon.

He plunged in among the big spruce trees. The trail was faint. A foot of snow had fallen since the last sled had passed over, and he was glad he was without a sled, traveling light. In fact, he carried nothing but the lunch wrapped in the handkerchief. He was surprised, however, at the cold. It certainly was cold, he concluded, as he rubbed his numb nose and cheekbones with his mittened hand. He was a warm-whiskered man, but the hair on his face did not protect the high cheekbones and the eager nose that thrust itself aggressively into the frosty air.

At the man's heels trotted a dog, a big native husky, the proper wolf dog, gray-coated and without any visible or temperamental difference from its brother, the wild wolf. The animal was depressed by the tremendous cold. It knew that it was no time for traveling. Its instinct told it a truer tale than was told to the man by the man's judgment. In reality, it was not merely colder than fifty below zero; it was colder than sixty below, than seventy below. It was seventy-five below zero. Since the freezing point is thirty-two above zero, it meant that one hundred and seven degrees of frost obtained. The dog did not know anything about thermometers. Possibly in its brain there was no sharp consciousness of a condition of very cold such as was in the man's brain. But the brute had its instinct. It experienced a vague but menacing apprehension that subdued it and made it slink along at the man's heels, and that made it question eagerly every unwonted[3] movement of the man, as if expecting him to go into camp or to seek shelter somewhere and build a fire. The dog had learned fire, and it wanted fire, or else to burrow under the snow and cuddle its warmth away from the air.

The frozen moisture of its breathing had settled on its fur in a fine powder of frost, and especially were its jowls, muzzle, and eyelashes whitened by its crystaled breath. The man's red beard and mustache were likewise frosted, but more solidly, the deposit taking the form of ice and increasing with every warm, moist breath he exhaled. Also, the man was chewing tobacco, and the muzzle of

---

2. **conjectural** (kən·jek′chər'l): based on guesswork or uncertain evidence.

3. **unwonted** (un·wun′tid): unusual.

ice held his lips so rigidly that he was unable to clear his chin when he expelled the juice. The result was that a crystal beard of the color and solidity of amber was increasing its length on his chin. If he fell down it would shatter itself, like glass, into brittle fragments. But he did not mind the appendage. It was the penalty all tobacco-chewers paid in that country, and he had been out before in two cold snaps. They had not been so cold as this, he knew, but by the spirit thermometer[4] at Sixty Mile he knew they had been registered at fifty below and at fifty-five.

He held on through the level stretch of woods for several miles, crossed a wide flat, and dropped down a bank to the frozen bed of a small stream. This was Henderson Creek, and he knew he was ten miles from the forks. He looked at his watch. It was ten o'clock. He was making four miles an hour, and he calculated that he would arrive at the forks at half past twelve. He decided to celebrate that event by eating his lunch there.

The dog dropped in again at his heels, with a tail drooping discouragement, as the man swung along the creek bed. The furrow of the old sled trail was plainly visible, but a dozen inches of snow covered the marks of the last runners. In a month no man had come up or down that silent creek. The man held steadily on. He was not much given to thinking, and just then particularly, he had nothing to think about save that he would eat lunch at the forks and that at six o'clock he would be in camp with the boys. There was nobody to talk to; and, had there been, speech would have been impossible because of the ice muzzle on his mouth. So he continued monotonously to chew tobacco and to increase the length of his amber beard.

Once in a while the thought reiterated itself that it was very cold and that he had never experienced such cold. As he walked along he rubbed his cheekbones and nose with the back of his mittened hand. He did this automatically, now and again changing hands. But rub as he would, the instant he stopped his cheekbones went numb, and the following instant the end of his nose went numb. He was sure to frost his cheeks; he knew that,

and experienced a pang of regret that he had not devised a nose strap of the sort Bud wore in the cold snaps. Such a strap passed across the cheeks, as well, and saved them. But it didn't matter much, after all. What were frosted cheeks? A bit painful, that was all; they were never serious.

Empty as the man's mind was of thought, he was keenly observant, and he noticed the changes in the creek, the curves and bends and timber jams, and always he sharply noted where he placed his feet. Once, coming around a bend, he shied abruptly, like a startled horse, curved away from the place where he had been walking, and retreated several paces back along the trail. The creek, he knew, was frozen clear to the bottom—no creek could contain water in that arctic winter—but he knew also that there were springs that bubbled out from the hillsides and ran along under the snow and on top of the ice of the creek. He knew that the coldest snaps never froze these springs, and he knew likewise their danger. They were traps. They hid pools of water under the snow that might be three inches deep, or three feet. Sometimes a skin of ice half an inch thick

---

4. **spirit thermometer:** alcohol thermometer.

covered them, and in turn was covered by the snow. Sometimes there were alternate layers of water and ice skin, so that when one broke through he kept on breaking through for a while, sometimes wetting himself to the waist.

That was why he had shied in such panic. He had felt the give under his feet and heard the crackle of a snow-hidden ice skin. And to get his feet wet in such a temperature meant trouble and danger. At the very least it meant delay, for he would be forced to stop and build a fire, and under its protection to bare his feet while he dried his socks and moccasins. He stood and studied the creek bed and its banks, and decided that the flow of water came from the right. He reflected awhile, rubbing his nose and cheeks, then skirted to the left, stepping gingerly and testing the footing for each step. Once clear of the danger, he took a fresh chew of tobacco and swung along at his four-mile gait.

In the course of the next two hours he came upon several similar traps. Usually the snow above the hidden pools had a sunken, candied appearance that advertised the danger. Once again, however, he had a close call; and once, suspecting danger, he compelled the dog to go on in front. The dog did not want to go. It hung back until the man shoved it forward, and then it went quickly across the white, unbroken surface. Suddenly it broke through, floundered to one side, and got away to firmer footing. It had wet its forefeet and legs, and almost immediately the water that clung to it turned to ice. It made quick efforts to lick the ice off its legs, then dropped down in the snow and began to bite out the ice that had formed between the toes. This was a matter of instinct. To permit the ice to remain would mean sore feet. It did not know this. It merely obeyed the mysterious prompting that arose from the deep crypts[5] of its being. But the man knew, having achieved a judgment on the subject, and he removed the mitten from his right hand and helped tear out the ice particles. He did not expose his fingers more than a minute, and was astonished at the swift numbness that smote[6] them. It certainly was cold. He

pulled on the mitten hastily, and beat the hand savagely across his chest.

At twelve o'clock the day was at its brightest. Yet the sun was too far south on its winter journey to clear the horizon. The bulge of the earth intervened between it and Henderson Creek, where the man walked under a clear sky at noon and cast no shadow. At half past twelve, to the minute, he arrived at the forks of the creek. He was pleased at the speed he had made. If he kept it up, he would certainly be with the boys by six. He unbuttoned his jacket and shirt and drew forth his lunch. The action consumed no more than a quarter of a minute, yet in that brief moment the numbness laid hold of the exposed fingers. He did not put the mitten on, but instead struck the fingers a dozen sharp smashes against his leg. Then he sat down on a snow-covered log to eat. The sting that followed upon the striking of his fingers against his leg ceased so quickly that he was startled. He had had no chance to take a bite of biscuit. He struck the fingers repeatedly and returned them to the mitten, baring the other hand for the purpose of eating. He tried to take a mouthful, but the ice muzzle prevented. He had forgotten to build a fire and thaw out. He chuckled at his foolishness, and as he chuckled he noted the numbness creeping into the exposed fingers. Also, he noted that the stinging which had first come to his toes when he sat down was already passing away. He wondered whether the toes were warm or numb. He moved them inside the moccasins and decided that they were numb.

He pulled the mitten on hurriedly and stood up. He was a bit frightened. He stamped up and down until the stinging returned into the feet. It certainly was cold, was his thought. That man from Sulfur Creek had spoken the truth when telling how cold it sometimes got in the country. And he had laughed at him at the time! That showed one must not be too sure of things. There was no mistake about it, it *was* cold. He strode up and down, stamping his feet and threshing his arms, until reassured by the returning warmth. Then he got out matches and proceeded to make a fire. From the undergrowth, where high water of the previous spring had lodged a supply of seasoned twigs, he got his firewood. Working carefully from a small

---

5. **crypts** (kripts): literally, underground chambers.
6. **smote:** (past tense of *smite*) struck powerfully.

beginning, he soon had a roaring fire, over which he thawed the ice from his face and in the protection of which he ate his biscuits. For the moment the cold of space was outwitted. The dog took satisfaction in the fire, stretching out close enough for warmth and far enough away to escape being singed.

When the man had finished, he filled his pipe and took his comfortable time over a smoke. Then he pulled on his mittens, settled the earflaps of his cap firmly about his ears, and took the creek trail up the left fork. The dog was disappointed and yearned back toward the fire. This man did not know cold. Possibly all the generations of his ancestry had been ignorant of cold, of real cold, of cold one hundred and seven degrees below freezing point. But the dog knew; all its ancestry knew, and it had inherited the knowledge. And it knew that it was not good to walk abroad in such fearful cold. It was the time to lie snug in a hole in the snow and wait for a curtain of cloud to be drawn across the face of outer space whence this cold came. On the other hand, there was no keen intimacy between the dog and the man. The one was the toil slave of the other, and the only caresses it had ever received were the caresses of the whiplash and of harsh and menacing throat sounds that threatened the whiplash. So the dog made no effort to communicate its apprehension to the man. It was not concerned in the welfare of the man; it was for its own sake that it yearned back toward the fire. But the man whistled, and spoke to it with the sound of whiplashes, and the dog swung in at the man's heels and followed after.

The man took a chew of tobacco and proceeded to start a new amber beard. Also, his moist breath quickly powdered with white his mustache, eyebrows, and lashes. There did not seem to be so many springs on the left fork of the Henderson, and for half an hour the man saw no signs of any. And then it happened. At a place where there were no signs, where the soft, unbroken snow seemed to advertise solidity beneath, the man broke through. It was not deep. He wet himself halfway to the knees before he floundered out to the firm crust.

He was angry, and cursed his luck aloud. He had hoped to get into camp with the boys at six o'clock, and this would delay him an hour, for he would have to build a fire and dry out his footgear. This was imperative at that low temperature—he knew that much; and he turned aside to the bank, which he climbed. On top, tangled in the underbrush about the trunks of several small spruce trees, was a high-water deposit of dry firewood—sticks and twigs, principally, but also larger portions of seasoned branches and fine, dry, last year's grasses. He threw down several pieces on top of the snow. This served for a foundation and prevented the young flame from drowning itself in the snow it otherwise would melt. The flame he got by touching a match to a small shred of birch bark that he took from his pocket. This burned even more readily than paper. Placing it on the foundation, he fed the young flame with wisps of dry grass and with the tiniest dry twigs.

He worked slowly and carefully, keenly aware of his danger. Gradually, as the flame grew stronger, he increased the size of the twigs with which he fed it. He squatted in the snow, pulling the twigs out from their entanglement in the brush and feeding directly to the flame. He knew there must be no failure. When it is seventy-five below zero, a man must not fail in his first attempt to build a fire—that is, if his feet are wet. If his feet are dry, and he fails, he can run along the trail for a half a mile and restore his circulation. But the circulation of wet and freezing feet cannot be restored by running when it is seventy-five below. No matter how fast he runs, the wet feet will freeze the harder.

All this the man knew. The old-timer on Sulfur Creek had told him about it the previous fall, and now he was appreciating the advice. Already all sensation had gone out of his feet. To build the fire, he had been forced to remove his mittens, and the fingers had quickly gone numb. His pace of four miles an hour had kept his heart pumping blood to the surface of his body and to all the extremities. But the instant he stopped, the action of the pump eased down. The cold of space smote the unprotected tip of the planet, and he, being on that unprotected tip, received the full force of the blow. The blood of his body recoiled before it. The blood was alive, like the dog, and like the dog it wanted to hide away and cover itself up from the fearful cold. So long as he walked four miles an hour, he pumped that blood, willy-nilly, to the surface; but now it ebbed away and sank down into the recesses of his body. The extremities were the first to feel its absence. His wet feet froze the faster, and his exposed fingers numbed the faster, though they had not yet begun to freeze. Nose and cheeks were already freezing, while the skin of all his body chilled as it lost its blood.

But he was safe. Toes and nose and cheeks would be only touched by the frost, for the fire was beginning to burn with strength. He was feeding it with twigs the size of his finger. In another minute he would be able to feed it with branches the size of his wrist, and then he could remove his wet footgear, and, while it dried, he could keep his naked feet warm by the fire, rubbing them at first, of course, with snow. The fire was a success. He was safe. He remembered the advice of the old-timer on Sulfur Creek, and smiled. The old-timer had been very serious in laying down the law that no man must travel alone in the Klondike after fifty below. Well, here he was; he had had the accident; he was alone; and he had saved himself. Those old-timers were rather womanish, some of them, he thought. All a man had to do was to keep his head and he was all right. Any man who was a man could travel alone. But it was surprising, the rapidity with which his cheeks and nose were freezing. And he had not thought his fingers could go lifeless in so short a time. Lifeless they were, for he could scarcely make them move together to grip a twig, and they seemed remote from his body and from him. When he touched a twig, he had to look and see whether or not he had hold of it. The wires were pretty well down between him and his finger ends.

All of which counted for little. There was the fire, snapping and crackling and promising life with every dancing flame. He started to untie his moccasins. They were coated with ice; the thick German socks were like sheaths of iron halfway to the knees; and the moccasin strings were like rods of steel all twisted and knotted as by some conflagration.[7] For a moment he tugged with his numb fingers, then, realizing the folly of it, he drew his sheath knife.

But before he could cut the strings it happened. It was his own fault, or, rather his mistake. He should not have built the fire under the spruce tree. He should have built it in the open. But it had been easier to pull the twigs from the bush and drop them directly on the fire. Now the tree under which he had done this carried a weight of snow on its boughs. No wind had blown for weeks, and each bough was fully freighted. Each time he had pulled a twig he had communicated a slight agitation to the tree—an imperceptible agitation, so far as he was concerned, but an agitation sufficient to bring about the disaster. High up in the tree one bough capsized its load of snow. This fell on the boughs beneath, capsizing them. This process continued, spreading out and involving the whole tree. It grew like an avalanche, and it descended without warning upon the man and the fire, and the fire was blotted out! Where it had burned was a mantle of fresh and disordered snow.

The man was shocked. It was as though he had just heard his own sentence of death. For a moment he sat and stared at the spot where the fire had been. Then he grew very calm. Perhaps the old-timer on Sulfur Creek was right. If he had only had a trail mate, he would have been in no danger now. The trail mate could have built the fire. Well, it was up to him to build the fire over again, and this second time there must be no failure. Even if he succeeded, he would most likely lose some toes. His feet must be badly frozen by now, and there would be some time before the second fire was ready.

Such were his thoughts, but he did not sit and think them. He was busy all the time they were passing through his mind. He made a new foundation for a fire, this time in the open, where no treacherous tree could blot it out. Next he gathered dry grasses and tiny twigs from the high-water flotsam.[8] He could not bring his fingers together to pull them out, but he was able to gather them by the handful. In this way he got many rotten twigs and bits of green moss that were un-

---

7. **conflagration** (kən'flə·grā'shən): big, destructive fire.

8. **high-water flotsam** (flät'səm): rubbish washed ashore by a stream or river during the warm months.

desirable, but it was the best he could do. He worked methodically, even collecting an armful of the larger branches to be used later when the fire gathered strength. And all the while the dog sat and watched him, a certain yearning wistfulness in its eyes, for it looked upon him as the fire provider, and the fire was slow in coming.

When all was ready, the man reached in his pocket for a second piece of birch bark. He knew the bark was there, and, though he could not feel it with his fingers, he could hear its crisp rustling as he fumbled for it. Try as he would, he could not clutch hold of it. And all the time, in his consciousness, was the knowledge that each instant his feet were freezing. This thought tended to put him in a panic, but he fought against it and kept calm. He pulled on his mittens with his teeth, and threshed his arms back and forth, beating his hands with all his might against his sides. He did this sitting down, and he stood up to do it; and all the while the dog sat in the snow, its wolf brush of a tail curled around warmly over its forefeet, its sharp wolf ears pricked forward intently as it watched the man. And the man, as he beat and threshed with his arms and hands, felt a great surge of envy as he regarded the creature that was warm and secure in its natural covering.

After a time he was aware of the first faraway signals of sensation in his beaten fingers. The faint tingling grew stronger till it evolved into a stinging

ache that was excruciating, but which the man hailed with satisfaction. He stripped his mitten from his right hand and fetched forth the birch bark. The exposed fingers were quickly going numb again. Next he brought out his bunch of sulfur matches. But the tremendous cold had already driven the life out of his fingers. In his effort to separate one match from the others, the whole bunch fell in the snow. He tried to pick it out of the snow, but failed. The dead fingers could neither touch nor clutch. He was very careful. He drove the thought of his freezing feet, and nose, and cheeks, out of his mind, devoting his whole soul to the matches. He watched, using the sense of vision in place of touch, and when he saw his fingers on each side of the bunch, he closed them—that is, he willed to close them, for the wires were down, and the fingers did not obey. He pulled the mitten on the right hand, and beat it fiercely against his knee. Then, with both mittened hands, he scooped the bunch of matches, along with much snow, into his lap. Yet he was no better off.

After some manipulation he managed to get the bunch between the heels of his mittened hands. In this fashion he carried it to his mouth. The ice crackled and snapped when by a violent effort he opened his mouth. He drew the lower jaw in, curled the upper lip out of the way, and scraped the bunch with his upper teeth in order to separate a match. He succeeded in getting one, which he dropped on his lap. He was no better off. He could not pick it up. Then he devised a way. He picked it up in his teeth and scratched it on his leg. Twenty times he scratched before he succeeded in lighting it. As it flamed he held it with his teeth to the birch bark. But the burning brimstone went up his nostrils and into his lungs, causing him to cough spasmodically. The match fell into the snow and went out.

The old-timer on Sulfur Creek was right, he thought in the moment of controlled despair that ensued: After fifty below, a man should travel with a partner. He beat his hands, but failed in exciting any sensation. Suddenly he bared both hands, removing the mittens with his teeth. He caught the whole bunch between the heels of his hands. His arm muscles, not being frozen, enabled him to press the hand heels tightly against the matches. Then he scratched the bunch along his leg. It flared into flame, seventy sulfur matches at once! There was no wind to blow them out. He kept his head to one side to escape the strangling fumes, and held the blazing bunch to the birch bark. As he so held it, he became aware of sensation in his hand. His flesh was burning. He could smell it. Deep down below the surface he could feel it. The sensation developed into pain that grew acute. And still he endured it, holding the flame of the matches clumsily to the bark that would not light readily because his own burning hands were in the way, absorbing most of the flame.

At last, when he could endure no more, he jerked his hands apart. The blazing matches fell sizzling into the snow, but the birch bark was alight. He began laying dry grass and the tiniest twigs on the flame. He could not pick and choose, for he had to lift the fuel between the heels of his hands. Small pieces of rotten wood and green moss clung to the twigs, and he bit them off as well as he could with his teeth. He cherished the flame carefully and awkwardly. It meant life, and it must not perish. The withdrawal of blood from the surface of his body now made him begin to shiver, and he grew more awkward. A large piece of green moss fell squarely on the little fire. He tried to poke it out with his fingers, but his shivering frame made him poke too far, and he disrupted the nucleus of the little fire, the burning grasses and tiny twigs separating and scattering. He tried to poke them together again, but in spite of the tenseness of the effort, his shivering got away with him, and the twigs were hopelessly scattered. Each twig gushed a puff of smoke and went out. The fire provider had failed. As he looked apathetically about him, his eyes chanced on the dog, sitting across the ruins of the fire from him, in the snow, making restless, hunching movements, slightly lifting one forefoot and then the other, shifting its weight back and forth on them with wistful eagerness.

The sight of the dog put a wild idea into his head. He remembered the tale of the man, caught in a blizzard, who killed a steer and crawled inside the carcass, and so was saved. He would kill the dog and bury his hands in the warm body until the numbness went out of them. Then he could build another fire. He spoke to the dog, calling it to him; but in his voice was a strange note of fear that frightened the animal, who had never known the man to speak in such a way before. Something was the matter, and its suspicious nature sensed danger—it knew not what danger, but somewhere, somehow, in its brain arose an apprehension of the man. It flattened its ears down at the sound of the man's voice, and its restless, hunching movements and the liftings and shiftings of its forefeet became more pronounced; but it would not come to the man. He got on his hands and knees and crawled toward the dog. This unusual posture again excited suspicion, and the animal sidled mincingly away.

The man sat up in the snow for a moment and struggled for calmness. Then he pulled on his mittens, by means of his teeth, and got up on his feet. He glanced down at first in order to assure himself that he was really standing up, for the absence of sensation in his feet left him unrelated to the earth. His erect position in itself started to drive the webs of suspicion from the dog's mind; and when he spoke peremptorily,[9] with the sound of whiplashes in his voice, the dog rendered its customary allegiance and came to him. As it came within reaching distance, the man lost his control. His arms flashed out to the dog, and he experienced genuine surprise when he discovered that his hands could not clutch, that there was neither bend nor feeling in the fingers. He had forgotten for the moment that they were frozen and that they were freezing more and more. All this happened quickly, and before the animal could get away, he encircled its body with his arms. He sat down in the snow, and in this fashion held the dog, while it snarled and whined and struggled.

But it was all he could do, hold its body encircled in his arms and sit there. He realized that he could not kill the dog. There was no way to do it. With his helpless hands he could neither draw nor hold his sheath knife nor throttle the animal. He released it, and it plunged wildly away, its tail between its legs and still snarling. It halted forty feet away and surveyed him curiously, with ears sharply pricked forward. The man looked down at his hands in order to locate them, and found them hanging on the ends of his arms. It struck him as curious that one should have to use his eyes in order to find out where his hands were. He began threshing his arms back and forth, beating the mittened hands against his sides. He did this for five minutes, violently, and his heart pumped enough blood up to the surface to put a stop to his shivering. But no sensation was aroused in his hands. He had an impression that they hung like weights on the ends of his arms, but when he tried to run the impression down, he could not find it.

A certain fear of death, dull and oppressive, came to him. This fear quickly became poignant as he realized that it was no longer a mere matter of freezing his fingers and toes, or of losing his hands and feet, but that it was a matter of life and death, with the chances against him. This threw him into a panic, and he turned and ran up the creek bed along the old, dim trail. The dog joined in behind and kept up with him. He ran blindly, without intention, in fear such as he had never known in his life. Slowly, as he plowed and floundered through the snow, he began to see things again—the banks of the creek, the old timber jams, the leafless aspens, and the sky. The running made him feel better. He did not shiver. Maybe, if he ran on, his feet would thaw out; and, anyway, if he ran far enough he would reach the camp and the boys. Without doubt he would lose some fingers and toes and some of his face; but the boys would take care of him, and save the rest of him when he got there. And, at the same time, there was another thought in his mind that said he would never get to the camp and the boys; that it was too many miles away, that the freezing had too great a start on him, and that he would soon be stiff and dead. This thought he kept in the background and refused to consider. Sometimes it pushed itself forward and demanded to be heard, but he thrust it back and strove to think of other things.

It struck him as curious that he could run at all on feet so frozen that he could not feel them when they struck the earth and took the weight of his body. He seemed to himself to skim along above

9. **peremptorily** (pə·remp′tər·ə·lē): in a commanding way.

the surface, and to have no connection with the earth. Somewhere he had once seen a winged Mercury,[10] and he wondered if Mercury felt as he felt when skimming over the earth.

His theory of running until he reached camp and the boys had one flaw in it: He lacked the endurance. Several times he stumbled, and finally he tottered, crumpled up, and fell. When he tried to rise, he failed. He must sit and rest, he decided, and next time he would merely walk and keep on going. As he sat and regained his breath, he noted

that he was feeling quite warm and comfortable. He was not shivering, and it even seemed that a warm glow had come to his chest and trunk. And yet, when he touched his nose or cheeks, there was no sensation. Running would not thaw them out. Nor would it thaw out his hands and feet. Then the thought came to him that the frozen portions of his body must be extending. He tried to keep this thought down, to forget it, to think of something else; he was aware of the panicky feeling that it caused, and he was afraid of the panic. But the thought asserted itself, and persisted, until it produced a vision of his body totally frozen. This was too much, and he made another wild run

---

10. **Mercury:** messenger of the gods in Roman mythology. He wore winged sandals and a winged hat.

along the trail. Once he slowed down to a walk, but the thought of the freezing extending itself made him run again.

And all the time the dog ran with him, at his heels. When he fell down a second time, it curled its tail over its forefeet and sat in front of him, facing him, curiously eager and intent. The warmth and security of the animal angered him, and he cursed it till it flattened down its ears appeasingly. This time the shivering came more quickly upon the man. He was losing in his battle with the frost. It was creeping into his body from all sides. The thought of it drove him on, but he ran no more than a hundred feet when he staggered and pitched headlong. It was his last panic. When he had recovered his breath and control, he sat up and entertained in his mind the conception of meeting death with dignity. However, the conception did not come to him in such terms. His idea of it was that he had been making a fool of himself, running around like a chicken with its head cut off—such was the simile that occurred to him. Well, he was bound to freeze anyway, and he might as well take it decently. With his new-found peace of mind came the first glimmerings of drowsiness. A good idea, he thought, to sleep off to death. It was like taking an anesthetic. Freezing was not so bad as people thought. There were lots worse ways to die.

He pictured the boys finding his body next day. Suddenly he found himself with them, coming along the trail and looking for himself. And, still with them, he came around a turn in the trail and found himself lying in the snow. He did not belong with himself anymore, for even then he was out of himself, standing with the boys and looking at himself in the snow. It certainly was cold, was his thought. When he got back to the States, he could tell the folks what real cold was. He drifted on from this to a vision of the old-timer on Sulfur Creek. He could see him quite clearly, warm and comfortable, and smoking a pipe.

"You were right, old hoss; you were right," the man mumbled to the old-timer of Sulfur Creek.

Then the man drowsed off into what seemed to him the most comfortable and satisfying sleep he had ever known. The dog sat facing him and waiting. The brief day drew to a close in a long, slow twilight. There were no signs of a fire to be made, and, besides, never in the dog's experience had it known a man to sit like that in the snow and make no fire. As the twilight drew on, its eager yearning for the fire mastered it, and with a great lifting and shifting of forefeet, it whined softly, then flattened its ears down in anticipation of being chidden[11] by the man. But the man remained silent. Later, the dog whined loudly. And still later it crept close to the man and caught the scent of death. This made the animal bristle and back away. A little longer it delayed, howling under the stars that leaped and danced and shone brightly in the cold sky. Then it turned and trotted up the trail in the direction of the camp it knew, where were the other food providers and fire providers.

---

11. **chidden:** scolded.

Responding to the Story

Analyzing the Story

Identifying Facts

1. The man in the story is traveling in the Yukon Territory of Canada. What is his mission? Where does he plan to be by evening?
2. Not only does London tell you that it is extremely cold, but he gives many details to help you feel the cold for yourself. For instance, he notes the "sharp, explosive crackle" of spittle in the frigid air. List ten other details in the story describing the cold.
3. Several times in the story the man thinks of the old-timer from Sulfur Creek. What key advice did the old-timer give him? Did the man follow his advice?

4. The man builds two fires in the story. Why does he build the first fire? Why must he build a second fire?

5. How is the second fire extinguished? What steps does the man take to start a new fire?

6. What happens to the man at the end of the story? What happens to the dog?

Interpreting Meanings

7. **Foreshadowing** is the use of clues and hints about what might happen later in the story. These clues and hints can build up **suspense** about the story's outcome. Early in "To Build a Fire," London writes, "The animal was depressed by the tremendous cold. It knew that it was no time for traveling." This passage foreshadows possible trouble ahead—and you become alert for signs of difficulty. Find four other passages in the first six paragraphs of the story that foreshadow later events. Explain the link between each passage and the later event.

8. Find the parts of the story where we enter the man's thoughts. Where do we enter the dog's mind as well? What do you think of this technique?

9. In the story, a man who thinks is contrasted with a dog that follows its instincts without thinking. Describe how the man and the dog differ in the ways they approach the great cold of the Yukon.

10. The man in the story is not a very likable character. He's pretty much of a loner, ignores the advice of his elders, isn't good at thinking, and has no love for dogs. Explain whether you would have enjoyed the story more—or less—if the man were portrayed in a more sympathetic light. (For instance, suppose he were a sociable person with a love for animals.) Give several specific reasons to support your opinion.

11. The man thinks of killing the dog in order to warm his hands within him. Do you think this is a brutal, primitive thought? Or do you think it only seems that way to those of us who live safe, well-heated lives? Explain your response.

Applying Meanings

12. Assume that you must leave in a week to travel by foot for ten miles in the Yukon Territory. It is winter there, and several feet of snow lie on the ground. Based on what you learned in the story, list the equipment and supplies you will bring along. Explain the importance of each article in a sentence. Will you travel alone? Why?

Writing About the Story

A Creative Response

1. **Writing a Dialogue.** It's just before the story begins, and the man in the story is saying goodbye to his partners as he prepares to start out alone on the Yukon trail. Make up a **dialogue**—a conversation—that occurs between the man and two of his partners. You might want to do some **role playing.** Assign parts to different class members and let them read the dialogue aloud. What would their feelings be?

A Critical Response

2. **Focusing on the Conflict.** A chief ingredient of literature is **conflict**—a struggle between opposing forces. A conflict may be **external:** It may pit one character against another or one character against a group of characters. An external conflict may also set a character against the natural environment. On the other hand, a conflict may be **internal:** It may involve a character's struggle to make a decision or to overcome some feelings such as fear, suspicion, hostility, or sadness. Many works of literature contain several conflicts. One often stands out as the **main conflict.** Identify what you consider the main conflict in "To Build a Fire." Then, in a paragraph, describe the opposing forces. Use passages from the text to back up your interpretation. Which force wins?

Analyzing Language and Vocabulary

Multiple Meanings

The same word can have several different meanings. Only by looking at the word's **context**—the surrounding words and sentences—can you tell which meaning is intended. For instance, the adjective *light* can have many meanings, including the following: (a) bright, (b) having little weight, (c) scanty, (d) gentle, (e) cheerful, (f) faint, and (g) easily endurable. Tell which meaning fits each of the following sentences.

1. Roger felt a *light* touch on his arm.
2. Diane has a *light* cold.
3. The huge package was *light* and easy to carry.
4. The sun streamed into the *light* kitchen.
5. The print is too *light* to read.
6. Yesterday's *light* rain hardly moistened the lawn.
7. Daniel was in a *light* mood after receiving the good news.

The following quotations are from "To Build a Fire." First, tell what each italicized word means in the context. Then, without referring to a dictionary, list as many other meanings as you can think of for each italicized word. Finally, check a dictionary to see if the word has additional meanings you did not list.

1. "It was a steep *bank*, and he paused for breath at the top. . . ."
2. " . . . he noticed the changes in the creek, the curves and bends and timber *jams*. . . ."
3. " . . . as the man swung along the creek *bed*."
4. "There did not seem to be so many *springs* on the left *fork* of the Henderson. . . ."
5. "On top, tangled in the underbrush about the *trunks* of several small spruce trees, was a high-water *deposit* of dry firewood. . . ."

Reading About the Writer

Jack London (1876–1916) lived a short life that was as full of conflict and adventure as his stories are. He was born in San Francisco and lived for years in the poverty and squalor of city slums. He had no more than a year of high-school education, though he read all the time and spent hours in the public library. (You can read more about London's own story of his hard life in the material under "Focusing on Background," which follows.) London later became a millionaire from his writings, most of which center on his experiences as an (unsuccessful) gold prospector in the Klondike, which is part of Yukon Territory in northwestern Canada. It was the Yukon that taught London to see life as a perpetual struggle, in which the strongest survive and the weak don't make it. London's most famous novel is *The Call of the Wild,* a story about a heroic sled dog named Buck who escapes a brutal master and leads a wolf pack. "To Build a Fire" is considered one of the masterpieces of American fiction.

Focusing on Background
London on London

"I was born in San Francisco in 1876. Almost the first thing I realized were responsibilities. I have no recollection of being taught to read or write, though I could do both at the age of five. As a ranch boy, I worked hard from my eighth year.

"The adventure-lust was strong within me, and I left home. I joined the oyster pirates in the bay; shipped as sailor on a schooner; took a turn at salmon fishing; shipped before the mast and sailed for the Japanese coast on a seal-hunting expedition. After sealing for seven months I came back to California, and took odd jobs at coal shoveling and long-shoring, and also in a jute factory. . . .

"In my nineteenth year I returned to Oakland and started at the high school. I remained a year, doing janitor work as a means of livelihood. After leaving the high school, in three months of 'cramming' by myself, I took the three years' work for that time and entered the University of California. I worked in a laundry, and with my pen to help me, kept on. The task was too much; when halfway through my freshman year, I had to quit.

"Three months later, having decided that I was a failure as a writer, I gave it up and left for the Klondike to prospect for gold. It was in the Klondike that I found myself. There nobody talks. Everybody thinks. You get your true perspective. I got mine."

—Jack London

BARGAIN

A. B. Guthrie, Jr.

This story takes place in a town where we have all been in our imaginations. This town is called Moon Dance. You will recognize it from TV and movie Westerns, with its muddy street, its boardwalks, its saloon, and its general store. In such a setting, the "good guys" and "bad guys" can be recognized at once. But you are not certain the good guys will win out in the end. After you read through the paragraph that begins with "Slade took the envelope . . ." on this page, stop for a moment. Identify the good guy and the bad guy of the story. Then predict the outcome of their conflict. Who do you think will win, and how decisive will the victory be?

Mr. Baumer and I had closed the Moon Dance Mercantile Company and were walking to the post office, and he had a bunch of bills in his hand ready to mail. There wasn't anyone or anything much on the street because it was suppertime. A buckboard and a saddle horse were tied at Hirschs' rack, and a rancher in a wagon rattled for home ahead of us, the sound of his going fading out as he prodded his team. Freighter Slade stood alone in front of the Moon Dance Saloon, maybe wondering whether to have one more before going to supper. People said he could hold a lot without showing it except in being ornerier even than usual.

> **Figures of speech.** When the narrator says that Mr. Baumer is "half mule and half beaver," he is using a figure of speech. A *figure of speech* is a comparison between two things that are basically unlike but that have something in common. The narrator compares Mr. Baumer to two animals known for certain qualities: the mule for stubbornness and the beaver for hard work. Notice how this figure of speech helps us understand the character's personality, and adds color to the description. How different would Mr. Baumer seem if the writer compared him to a vulture, a rat, a mouse, or a flea? As you read this story, be alert for other figures of speech.

Mr. Baumer didn't see him until he was almost on him, and then he stopped and fingered through the bills until he found the right one. He stepped up to Slade and held it out.

Slade said, "What's this, Dutchie?"

Mr. Baumer had to tilt his head up to talk to him. "You know vat it is."

Slade just said, "Yeah?" You never could tell from his face what went on inside his skull. He had dark skin and shallow cheeks and a thick-growing mustache that fell over the corners of his mouth.

"It is a bill," Mr. Baumer said. "I tell you before it is a bill. For twenty-vun dollars and fifty cents."

"You know what I do with bills, don't you, Dutchie?" Slade asked.

Mr. Baumer didn't answer the question. He said, "For merchandise."

Slade took the envelope from Mr. Baumer's hand and squeezed it up in his fist and let it drop on the plank sidewalk. Not saying anything, he reached down and took Mr. Baumer's nose between the knuckles of his fingers and twisted it up into his eyes. That was all. That was all at the time. Slade half turned and slouched to the door of the bar and let himself in. Some men were laughing in there.

Mr. Baumer stooped and picked up the bill and put it on top of the rest and smoothed it out for mailing. When he straightened up, I could see

The interior of a store in Beaver City, Nebraska, in the early 1900's.

tears in his eyes from having his nose screwed around.

He didn't say anything to me, and I didn't say anything to him, being so much younger and feeling embarrassed for him. He went into the post office and slipped the bills in the slot, and we walked on home together. At the last, at the crossing where I had to leave him, he remembered to say, "Better study, Al. Is good to know to read and write and figure." I guess he felt he had to push me a little, my father being dead.

I said, "Sure. See you after school tomorrow"—which he knew I would anyway. I had been working in the store for him during the summer and after classes ever since pneumonia took my dad off.

Three of us worked there regularly, Mr. Baumer, of course, and me and Colly Coleman, who knew enough to drive the delivery wagon, but wasn't much help around the store except for car-

rying orders out to the rigs at the hitchpost and handling heavy things like the whiskey barrel at the back of the store which Mr. Baumer sold quarts and gallons out of.

The store carried quite a bit of stuff—sugar and flour and dried fruits and canned goods and such on one side and yard goods and coats and caps and aprons and the like of that on the other, besides kerosene and bran and buckets and linoleum and pitchforks in the storehouse at the rear—but it wasn't a big store like Hirsch Brothers up the street. Never would be, people guessed, going on to say, with a sort of slow respect, that it would have gone under long ago if Mr. Baumer hadn't been half mule and half beaver. He had started the store just two years before and, the way things were, worked himself close to death.

He was at the high desk at the end of the grocery counter when I came in the next afternoon. He had an eyeshade on and black sateen protectors on his forearms, and his pencil was in his hand instead of behind his ear and his glasses were roosted on the nose that Slade had twisted. He didn't hear me open and close the door or hear my feet as I walked back to him, and I saw he wasn't doing anything with the pencil but holding it over paper. I stood and studied him for a minute, seeing a small, stooped man with a little paunch bulging through his unbuttoned vest. He was a man you wouldn't remember from meeting once. There was nothing in his looks to set itself in your mind unless maybe it was his chin, which was a small, pink hill in the gentle plain of his face.

While I watched him, he lifted his hand and felt carefully of his nose. Then he saw me. His eyes had that kind of mistiness that seems to go with age or illness, though he wasn't really old or sick, either. He brought his hand down quickly and picked up the pencil, but he saw I still was looking at the nose, and finally he sighed and said, "That Slade."

Just the sound of the name brought Slade to my eye. I saw him slouched in front of the bar, and I saw him and his string[1] coming down the grade from the buttes,[2] the wheel horses held snug and the rest lined out pretty, and then the string leveling off and Slade's whip lifting hair from a horse that wasn't up in the collar.[3] I had heard it said that Slade could make a horse scream with that whip. Slade's name wasn't Freighter, of course. Our town had nicknamed him that because that was what he was.

"I don't think it's any good to send him a bill, Mr. Baumer," I said. "He can't even read."

"He could pay yet."

"He don't pay anybody," I said.

"I think he hate me," Mr. Baumer went on. "That is the thing. He hate me for coming not from this country. I come here, sixteen years old, and learn to read and write, and I make a business, and so I think he hate me."

"He hates everybody."

Mr. Baumer shook his head. "But not to pinch the nose. Not to call Dutchie."

The side door squeaked open, but it was only Colly Coleman coming in from a trip so I said, "Excuse me, Mr. Baumer, but you shouldn't have trusted him in the first place."

"I know," he answered, looking at me with his misty eyes. "A man make mistakes. I think some do not trust him, so he will pay me because I do. And I do not know him well then. He only came back to town three-four months ago, from being away since before I go into business."

"People who knew him before could have told you," I said.

"A man make mistakes," he explained again.

"It's not my business, Mr. Baumer, but I would forget the bill."

His eyes rested on my face for a long minute, as if they didn't see me but the problem itself. He said. "It is not twenty-vun dollars and fifty cents now, Al. It is not that anymore."

"What is it?"

He took a little time to answer. Then he brought his two hands up as if to help him shape the words. "It is the thing. You see, it is the thing."

I wasn't quite sure what he meant.

He took his pencil from behind the ear where he had put it and studied the point of it. "That Slade. He steal whiskey and call it evaporation. He sneak things from his load. A thief, he is. And too big for me."

I said, "I got no time for him, Mr. Baumer, but I guess there never was a freighter didn't steal whiskey. That's what I hear."

It was true, too. From the railroad to Moon Dance was fifty miles and a little better—a two-day haul in good weather, heck knew how long in bad. Any freight string bound home with a load had to lie out at least one night. When a freighter had his stock tended to and maybe a little fire going against the dark, he'd tackle a barrel of whiskey or of grain alcohol if he had one aboard, consigned to Hirsch Brothers or Mr. Baumer's or the Moon Dance Saloon or the Gold Leaf Bar. He'd drive a hoop out of place, bore a little hole with a nail or bit and draw off what he wanted. Then he'd plug the hole with a whittled peg and pound the hoop back. That was evaporation. Nobody complained much. With freighters you generally took what they gave you, within reason.

---

1. **string:** here, a row of horses.
2. **buttes** (byo͞ots): steep hills that stand alone on a plain.
3. **up in the collar:** pulling as hard as the other horses.

"Moore steals it, too," I told Mr. Baumer. Moore was Mr. Baumer's freighter.

"Yah," he said, and that was all, but I stood there for a minute, thinking there might be something more. I could see thought swimming in his eyes, above that little hill of chin. Then a customer came in, and I had to go wait on him.

Nothing happened for a month, nothing between Mr. Baumer and Slade, that is, but fall drew on toward winter and the first flight of ducks headed south and Mr. Baumer hired Miss Lizzie Webb to help with the just-beginning Christmas trade, and here it was, the first week in October, and he and I walked up the street again with the monthly bills. He always sent them out. I guess he had to. A bigger store, like Hirschs', would wait on the ranchers until their beef or wool went to market.

Up to a point things looked and happened almost the same as they had before, so much the same that I had the crazy feeling I was going through that time again. There was a wagon and a rig tied up at Hirschs' rack and a saddle horse standing hipshot[4] in front of the harness shop. A few more people were on the street now, not many, and lamps had been lit against the shortened day.

It was dark enough that I didn't make out Slade right away. He was just a figure that came out of the yellow wash of light from the Moon Dance Saloon and stood on the boardwalk and with his head made the little motion of spitting. Then I recognized the lean, raw shape of him and the muscles flowing down into the sloped shoulders, and in the settling darkness I filled the picture in— the dark skin and the flat cheeks and the peevish eyes and the mustache growing rank.

There was Slade and here was Mr. Baumer with his bills and here I was, just as before, just like in the second go-round of a bad dream. I felt like turning back, being embarrassed and half scared by trouble even when it wasn't mine. Please, I said to myself, don't stop, Mr. Baumer! Don't bite off anything! Please, shortsighted the way you are, don't catch sight of him at all! I held up and stepped around behind Mr. Baumer and came up

on the outside so as to be between him and Slade where maybe I'd cut off his view.

But it wasn't any use. All along I think I knew it was no use, not the praying or the walking between or anything. The act had to play itself out.

Mr. Baumer looked across the front of me and saw Slade and hesitated in his step and came to a stop. Then in his slow, business way, his chin held firm against his mouth, he began fingering through the bills, squinting to make out the names. Slade had turned and was watching him, munching on a cud of tobacco like a bull waiting.

"You look, Al," Mr. Baumer said without lifting his face from the bills. "I cannot see so good."

So I looked, and while I was looking Slade must have moved. The next I knew Mr. Baumer was staggering ahead, the envelopes spilling out of his hands. There had been a thump, the clap of a heavy hand swung hard on his back.

Slade said, "Haryu, Dutchie?"

Mr. Baumer caught his balance and turned around, the bills he had trampled shining white between them and, at Slade's feet, the hat that Mr. Baumer had stumbled out from under.

Slade picked up the hat and scuffed through the bills and held it out. "Cold to be goin' without a sky-piece," he said.

Mr. Baumer hadn't spoken a word. The lampshine from inside the bar caught his eyes, and in them it seemed to me a light came and went as anger and the uselessness of it took turns in his head.

Two men had come up on us and stood watching. One of them was Angus McDonald, who owned the Ranchers' Bank, and the other was Dr. King. He had his bag in his hand.

Two others were drifting up, but I didn't have time to tell who. The light came in Mr. Baumer's eyes, and he took a step ahead and swung. I could have hit harder myself. The fist landed on Slade's cheek without hardly so much as jogging his head, but it let the devil loose in the man. I didn't know he could move so fast. He slid in like a practiced fighter and let Mr. Baumer have it full in the face.

Mr. Baumer slammed over on his back, but he wasn't out. He started lifting himself. Slade leaped ahead and brought a boot heel down on the hand

---

4. **hipshot:** having one hip lower than the other.

he was lifting himself by. I heard meat and bone under that heel and saw Mr. Baumer fall back and try to roll away.

Things had happened so fast that not until then did anyone have a chance to get between them. Now Mr. McDonald pushed at Slade's chest, saying, ''That's enough, Freighter. That's enough now,'' and Dr. King lined up, too, and another man I didn't know, and I took a place, and we formed a kind of screen between them. Dr. King turned and bent to look at Mr. Baumer.

''The fool hit me first,'' Slade said.

''That's enough,'' Mr. McDonald told him again while Slade looked at all of us as if he'd spit on us for a nickel. Mr. McDonald went on, using a half-friendly tone, and I knew it was because he didn't want to take Slade on anymore than the rest of us did. ''You go on home and sleep it off, Freighter. That's the ticket.''

Slade just snorted.

From behind us Dr. King said, ''I think you've broken this man's hand.''

''Lucky for him I didn't kill him,'' Slade answered. ''Fool Dutch penny pincher!'' He fingered the chew out of his mouth. ''Maybe he'll know enough to leave me alone now.''

Dr. King had Mr. Baumer on his feet. ''I'll take him to the office,'' he said.

Blood was draining from Mr. Baumer's nose and rounding the curve of his lip and dripping from the sides of his chin. He held his hurt right hand in the other. But a thing was that he didn't look beaten even then, not the way a man who has given up looks beaten. Maybe that was why Slade said, with a show of that fierce anger, ''You stay away from me! Hear? Stay clear away, or you'll get more of the same!''

Dr. King led Mr. Baumer away, Slade went

Freight wagons near the Stage Office in a Nebraska town.

back into the bar, and the other men walked off, talking about the fight. I got down and picked up the bills, because I knew Mr. Baumer would want me to, and mailed them at the post office, dirty as they were. It made me sorer, someway, that Slade's bill was one of the few that wasn't marked up. The cleanness of it seemed to say that there was no getting the best of him.

Mr. Baumer had his hand in a sling the next day and wasn't much good at waiting on the trade. I had to hustle all afternoon and so didn't have a chance to talk to him even if he had wanted to talk. Mostly he stood at his desk, and once, passing it, I saw he was practicing writing with his left hand. His nose and the edges of the cheeks around it were swollen some.

At closing time I said, "Look, Mr. Baumer, I can lay out of school a few days until you kind of get straightened out here."

"No," he answered as if to wave the subject away. "I get somebody else. You go to school. Is good to learn."

I had a half notion to say that learning hadn't helped him with Slade. Instead, I blurted out that I would have the law on Slade.

"The law?" he asked.

"The sheriff or somebody."

"No, Al," he said. "You would not."

I asked why.

"The law, it is not for plain fights," he said. "Shooting? Robbing? Yes, the law come quick. The plain fights, they are too many. They not count enough."

He was right. I said, "Well, I'd do something anyhow."

"Yes," he answered with a slow nod of his head. "Something you vould do, Al." He didn't tell me what.

Within a couple of days he got another man to clerk for him—it was Ed Hempel, who was always finding and losing jobs—and we made out. Mr. Baumer took his hand from the sling in a couple or three weeks, but with the tape on it it still wasn't any use to him. From what you could see of the fingers below the tape it looked as if it never would be.

He spent most of his time at the high desk, sending me or Ed out on the errands he used to run, like posting and getting the mail. Sometimes I wondered if that was because he was afraid of meeting Slade. He could just as well have gone himself. He wasted a lot of hours just looking at nothing, though I will have to say he worked hard at learning to write left-handed.

Then, a month and a half before Christmas, he hired Slade to haul his freight for him.

Ed Hempel told me about the deal when I showed up for work. "Yessir," he said, resting his foot on a crate in the storeroom where we were supposed to be working. "I tell you he's throwed in with Slade. Told me this morning to go out and locate him if I could and bring him in. Slade was at the saloon, o' course, and says to the devil with Dutchie, but I told him this was honest-to-God business, like Baumer had told me to, and there was a quart of whiskey right there in the store for him if he'd come and get it. He was out of money, I reckon, because the quart fetched him."

"What'd they say?" I asked him.

"Search me. There was two or three people in the store and Baumer told me to wait on 'em, and he and Slade palavered[5] back by the desk."

"How do you know they made a deal?"

Ed spread his hands out. "'Bout noon, Moore came in with his string, and I heard Baumer say he was makin' a change. Moore didn't like it too good, either."

It was a hard thing to believe, but there one day was Slade with a pile of stuff for the Moon Dance Mercantile Company, and that was proof enough with something left for boot.

Mr. Baumer never opened the subject up with me, though I gave him plenty of chances. And I didn't feel like asking. He didn't talk much these days but went around absent-minded, feeling now and then of the fingers that curled yellow and stiff out of the bandage like the toes on the leg of a dead chicken. Even on our walks home he kept his thoughts to himself.

I felt different about him now and was sore inside. Not that I blamed him exactly. A hundred and thirty-five pounds wasn't much to throw against two hundred. And who could tell what Slade would do on a bellyful of whiskey? He had

---

5. **palavered** (pə·lav'ər): talked; met to discuss business.

promised Mr. Baumer more of the same, hadn't he? But I didn't feel good. I couldn't look up to Mr. Baumer like I used to and still wanted to. I didn't have the beginning of an answer when men cracked jokes or shook their heads in sympathy with Mr. Baumer, saying Slade had made him come to time.

Slade hauled in a load for the store, and another, and Christmastime was drawing on and trade heavy, and the winter that had started early and then pulled back came on again. There was a blizzard and then a still cold and another blizzard and afterward a sunshine that was ice-shine on the drifted snow. I was glad to be busy, selling overshoes and sheep-lined coats and mitts and socks as thick as saddle blankets and Christmas candy out of buckets and hickory nuts and the fresh oranges that the people in our town never saw except when Santa Claus was coming.

One afternoon when I lit out from class the thermometer on the school porch read forty-two degrees below. But you didn't have to look at it to know how cold the weather was. Your nose and fingers and toes and ears and the bones inside you told you. The snow cried when you stepped on it.

I got to the store and took my things off and scuffed my hands at the stove for a minute so's to get life enough in them to tie a parcel. Mr. Baumer—he was always polite to me—said, "Hello, Al. Not so much to do today. Too cold for customers." He shuddered a little, as if he hadn't got the chill off even yet, and rubbed his broken hand with the good one. "Ve need Christmas goods," he said, looking out the window to the furrows that wheels had made in the snow-banked street, and I knew he was thinking of Slade's string, inbound from the railroad, and the time it might take even Slade to travel those hard miles.

Slade never made it at all.

Less than an hour later our old freighter, Moore, came in, his beard white and stiff with frost. He didn't speak at first but looked around and clumped to the stove and took off his heavy mitts, holding his news inside him.

Then he said, not pleasantly, "Your new man's dead, Baumer."

"My new man?" Mr. Baumer said.

"Who do you think? Slade. He's dead."

All Mr. Baumer could say was, "Dead!"

"Froze to death, I figger," Moore told him while Colly Coleman and Ed Hempel and Miss Lizzie and I and a couple of customers stepped closer.

"Not Slade," Mr. Baumer said. "He know too much to freeze."

"Maybe so, but he sure's froze now. I got him in the wagon."

We stood looking at one another and at Moore. Moore was enjoying his news, enjoying feeding it out bit by bit so's to hold the stage. "Heart might've give out for all I know."

The side door swung open, letting in a cloud of cold and three men who stood, like us, waiting on Moore. I moved a little and looked through the window and saw Slade's freight outfit tied outside with more men around it. Two of them were on a wheel of one of the wagons, looking inside.

"Had a extra man, so I brought your stuff in," Moore went on. "Figgered you'd be glad to pay for it."

"Not Slade," Mr. Baumer said again.

"You can take a look at him."

Mr. Baumer answered no.

"Someone's takin' word to Connor to bring his hearse. Anyhow I told 'em to. I carted old Slade this far. Connor can have him now."

Moore pulled on his mitts. "Found him there by the Deep Creek crossin', doubled up in the snow an' his fire out." He moved toward the door. "I'll see to the horses, but your stuff'll have to set there. I got more'n enough work to do at Hirschs'."

Mr. Baumer just nodded.

I put on my coat and went out and waited my turn and climbed on a wagon wheel and looked inside, and there was Slade piled on some bags of bran. Maybe because of being frozen, his face was whiter than I ever saw it, whiter and deader, too, though it never had been lively. Only the mustache seemed still alive, sprouting thick like greasewood from alkali. Slade was doubled up all right, as if he had died and stiffened leaning forward in a chair.

I got down from the wheel, and Colly and then

Ed climbed up. Moore was unhitching, tossing off his pieces of information while he did so. Pretty soon Mr. Connor came up with his old hearse, and he and Moore tumbled Slade into it, and the team that was as old as the hearse made off, the tires squeaking in the snow. The people trailed on away with it, their breaths leaving little ribbons of mist in the air. It was beginning to get dark.

Mr. Baumer came out of the side door of the store, bundled up, and called to Colly and Ed and me. "We unload," he said. "Already is late. Al, better you get a couple lanterns now."

We did a fast job, setting the stuff out of the wagons onto the platform and then carrying it or rolling it on the one truck that the store owned and stowing it inside according to where Mr. Baumer's good hand pointed.

A barrel was one of the last things to go in. I edged it up and Colly nosed the truck under it, and then I let it fall back. "Mr. Baumer," I said. "we'll never sell all this, will we?"

"Yah," he answered. "Sure we sell it. I get it cheap. A bargain, Al, so I buy it."

I looked at the barrel head again. There in big letters I saw "Wood Alcohol—Deadly Poison."

"Hurry now," Mr. Baumer said. "Is late." For a flash and no longer I saw through the mist in his eyes, saw, you might say, that hilly chin repeated there. "Then ve go home, Al. Is good to know to read."

Responding to the Story

Analyzing the Story

Identifying Facts

1. The story opens with a heated argument between Mr. Baumer and Freighter Slade. What causes the trouble? How does the incident end?
2. About one month later Mr. Baumer and Slade have a second argument. Explain how Mr. Baumer acts differently this time.
3. Ed Hempel later tells Al, the story's narrator, about a surprising deal. Who is involved in the deal? What is agreed?
4. Describe what happens to Slade at the end.

Interpreting Meanings

5. What questions did the writer plant in your mind to make you keep reading the story? Were they all answered by the story's end?
6. A writer **foreshadows** events by presenting hints or clues about what will happen later in the story. Early in "Bargain," Mr. Baumer says, "Better study, Al. Is good to know to read and write and figure." Discuss how these words foreshadow the ending of the story.
7. Frequently a writer does not tell you in so many words what a character in a story is thinking or feeling. You are given various clues and must draw your own conclusion. At the end of "Bargain," Guthrie doesn't tell you exactly what Mr. Baumer thinks about Slade's fate. Yet what Mr. Baumer thinks is the key to understanding what happened to the freighter. Which clues let you make an **inference,** or educated guess, about what Mr. Baumer is thinking? Explain why these clues are helpful.
8. Who do you think is responsible for Slade's death—Mr. Baumer or Slade himself? Give two or three reasons to support your view.
9. If you check a dictionary, you'll see that the word bargain—the story's title—can have more than one meaning. Discuss which meaning(s) of bargain apply to the story.

Applying Meanings

10. Pretend a classmate owes you a small amount of money. The student won't pay you and even attacks you, verbally or physically, when you ask for the money. Which of the following courses of action seems best to you? Give three specific reasons for your choice.

    a. Seek help from an adult.
    b. Seek help from someone your age.
    c. Try to get even with the classmate.
    d. Drop the matter and forget about the money.

Writing About the Story

A Creative Response

1. **Writing Persuasive Paragraphs.** Imagine that Mr. Baumer is on trial for murdering Slade. In one paragraph, summarize the prosecutor's case *against* Mr. Baumer. Give reasons and evidence to persuade the jury that Mr. Baumer is guilty of Slade's murder. In another paragraph, summarize the case *for* Mr. Baumer. Give reasons and evidence to show he is not guilty.

A Critical Response

2. **Analyzing a Writer's Technique. Suspense** can be a key ingredient of a good story. Suspense arises when you become uneasy and uncertain—but very interested—about what will happen next. After the second argument in "Bargain," Al suggests that Mr. Baumer let the law deal with Slade. Write one paragraph explaining how Mr. Baumer's reply to Al's suggestion heightens the suspense of the story.

Analyzing Language and Vocabulary

Figures of Speech

Figures of speech compare two things that are basically unlike but have something in common. Here are some figures of speech from "Bargain." They are followed by questions of interpretation.

1. "There was nothing in his looks to set itself in your mind unless maybe it was his chin, which was a small, pink hill in the gentle plain of his face."

   a. To what are Mr. Baumer's chin and face compared?
   b. What do the comparisons suggest about his personality?

2. "Slade had turned and was watching him, munching on a cud of tobacco like a bull waiting."

   a. What is Slade compared to in this figure of speech?
   b. What does the figure of speech suggest about Slade's personality?

3. "He didn't talk much these days but went around absent-minded, feeling now and then of the fingers that curled yellow and stiff out of the bandage like the toes on the leg of a dead chicken."

   a. Identify the figure of speech in this sentence. What is being compared to what?
   b. How does the figure of speech make you feel? Why?
   c. Would the image of the fingers be as strong if they were simply described as "lifeless"?

4. "The snow cried when you stepped on it."

   a. In what sense does the snow "cry"?
   b. Would the effect be the same if the writer had said that the snow "squeaked"?

Reading About the Writer

Alfred Bertram Guthrie, Jr. (1901–   ) was born in a small town in Indiana. He began his writing career as a newspaper reporter in Lexington, Kentucky. Over twenty years, Guthrie worked his way up to executive editor of the newspaper. Guthrie's novels focus on the relationships between people and the land in the American West. Three of his novels have been made into movies: *The Big Sky, These Thousand Hills,* and *The Way West,* which won the Pulitzer Prize for fiction. Guthrie also wrote the screenplays for two classic Western movies, *The Kentuckian* and *Shane.*

Focusing on Background
Guthrie on the Process of Writing

"For me, writing is a slow and painful business. It demands concentration and search and presents the obstacles of dissatisfaction with what could be said better. And there's no immediate reward in putting words on paper. The reward, great but fugitive, is in having written, in having found the word, the line, the paragraph, the chapter that is as good as ever you can make it. I spent a full day on one line of dialogue and knocked off satisfied."

—A. B. Guthrie, Jr.

LINCOLN IS SHOT

Jim Bishop

On the fateful evening of April 14, 1865, President Abraham Lincoln sits in a box in Ford's Theatre in Washington, D.C. He is watching a comedy called *Our American Cousin.* In this excerpt from *The Day Lincoln Was Shot,* Jim Bishop reports the evening's events moment by moment. To help you feel like an eyewitness, Bishop includes material from the play being performed. (The play's hero is Asa Trenchard, played by Harry Hawk. Asa pretends to be rich so he can marry Mrs. Augusta Mountchessington, played by the star, Laura Keene.) As you "hear" the play, Bishop describes what's happening in the President's box. John Wilkes Booth, an actor, is about to enter that box.

This might be the most dramatic event in all of American history. Even though you know the ending, do you still feel suspense?

John Wilkes Booth, slightly ahead of schedule, came down the dress circle steps slowly. He heard the lines onstage and he knew that he had about two minutes. . . .

Booth looked down at the little white door and saw the empty chair. Confused, he looked at patrons sitting in dress circle seats as though wondering which one was the President's guard. He saw the two army officers and he moved by them. For the first time, he realized that he was going to get into that box with no trouble; no challenge; no palaver; no argument, no fight; no stabbing. He was going to be able to walk in as though Lincoln had been expecting him.

He walked down to the white door, and stood with his back to it. He studied the faces nearby, men and women, and he saw some of them glance briefly at him. A real wave of laughter swept the theater and attention reverted to the stage.

Mrs. Mountchessington had just learned that Asa Trenchard was not a millionaire.

"No heir to the fortune, Mr. Trenchard?"

"Oh, no," he said.

"What!" young Augusta shrieked. "No fortune!"

"Nary a red," said Asa brightly. "It all comes from their barking up the wrong tree about the old man's property."

Now was the time. Booth knew that, in a few seconds, Asa would be alone on the stage. He turned the knob, pushed the door, and walked into the darkness. The door closed behind him. He found the pine board, held it against the inside of the door, and tapped the other end down the wall opposite until it settled in the niche he had carved for it. Pursuit could not come from that direction. Nor interference.

He moved toward the door of Box 7 in the darkness. A tiny beam of yellow light squeezed through the gimlet[1] hole in the door and made a dot on the opposite wall. Wilkes Booth could still hear the actors faintly. . . .

> **General and precise words.** What's the difference between a *chair* and a *rocker,* a *pistol* and a *derringer?* Every language contains general words (like *chair* and *pistol*) and precise words (like *rocker* and *derringer*). Precise nouns and adjectives help a writer create a specific setting. Precise verbs and adverbs can make the action more vivid. As you read, look for examples of words that help make this setting and action come alive.

---

1. **gimlet** (gim′lit): small hand tool for drilling holes. Booth had drilled a hole in the door of the President's box earlier that evening.

The conspirator crouched and pressed his eye against the gimlet hole. What he saw was clear. The high back of the horsehair rocker was in plain view and the silhouette of a head above it. He waited. Three persons were on the stage. In a matter of seconds, Augusta would be offstage, followed by her irate mother. That would leave Harry Hawk (as Trenchard) alone and he would begin to drawl: "Don't know the manners of good society, eh? . . ."

Booth kept his eye to the gimlet hole. The head in front of him barely moved. The universe seemed to pause for breath. Then Trenchard said: "Don't know the manners of good society, eh?" Booth did not wait to hear the rest of the line. The derringer was now in his hand. He turned the knob. The door swung inward. Lincoln, facing diagonally away toward the left, was four feet from him. Booth moved along the wall closest to the dress circle. The President had dropped Mrs. Lincoln's hand and there was a little space between their chairs. The major and his Clara[2] were listening to the humorous soliloquy of the actor onstage. . . .

The derringer was behind the President's head between the left ear and the spine. Booth squeezed the trigger and there was a sound as though someone had blown up and broken a heavy paper bag. It came in the midst of laughter, so that some people heard it, and some did not. The President did not move. His head inclined toward his chest and he stopped rocking.

Mrs. Lincoln turned at the noise, her round face creased with laughter. So did Major Rathbone and Miss Harris. A chrysanthemum of blue smoke hung in Box 7. Booth, with no maniacal gleam, no frenzy, looked at the people who looked at him and said, "*Sic semper tyrannis!*"[3] It was said in such an ordinary tone that theatergoers only fourteen feet below did not hear the words.

The conspirator forced his way between the President and his wife. Mrs. Lincoln's laughter dissolved in confusion. She saw the young man towering above her, but she did not know who he was or what he wanted. The major saw the cloud

2. Major Rathbone and his fiancée Clara Harris sat in the box with the Lincolns.
3. *"Sic semper tyrannis!"*: (Latin) "Thus always to tyrants!"

of smoke and, without understanding, jumped up and tried to grapple with the intruder. Booth dropped the derringer and pulled out his knife. The major laid a hand on his arm and the assassin's arm went high in the air and slashed down. Rathbone lifted his left arm to counter the blow, and the knife sliced through his suit and flesh down to the bone.

The assassin moved to the ledge of the box and the major reached for him with his right arm. Booth shoved him and said loudly: "Revenge for the South!" Mrs. Lincoln began to rub her cheek nervously. She glanced at her husband, but he seemed to be dozing.

Harry Hawk faltered in his lines. He looked up at the State Box indecisively. In the wings, W. J. Ferguson, an actor, heard the explosion and looked up at the box in time to see a dark man come out of the smoke toward the ledge. In the dress circle, James Ferguson . . . saw Booth climb over the ledge of the box, at a point near where Boxes 7 and 8 met at the picture of George Washington, and watched him turn his back to the audience and, by holding on with his arms, let himself down over the side.

As he dropped, he pushed his body away from the box with his right hand. This turned him a little and the spur of his right foot caught in the Treasury regiment flag. As the banner ripped, and followed him to the stage in tatters, the actor, by reflex, held his left foot rigid to take the shock of the fall, plus two outstretched hands. He landed on the left leg, and it snapped just above the instep. He fell on his hands, got up, and started to run across the stage to the left. He passed Harry Hawk and headed for the wings.

The audience did not understand. They watched the running actor, and he fell again. He stood and, as he got offstage, he was limping on the outside of his left foot; in effect, walking on his ankle.

Hawk, stupefied, did not move. His arms were still raised in half gesture toward the wings through which the women had departed. Laura Keene, in the Green Room,[4] noticed that the on-stage action had stopped and she came out in time almost to bump into Booth. She brushed by him, wondering what had happened to Harry Hawk. An actor stood in Booth's way and he saw a knife flash by his face.

A piercing scream came from the State Box. This was Mrs. Lincoln. Clara Harris stood and looked out at the people below and said "Water!" Major Joseph B. Stewart, sitting in the front row of the orchestra with his wife and his sister, got up from his seat and climbed over the rim of the stage. He was a big man, looking bigger in a pale fawn suit, and he got to his feet, rushed by Harry Hawk, and yelled "Stop that man!"

The conspirator hobbled to the back door, opened it, and shut it behind him. Johnny Peanut was lying on the stone step with the mare's bridle in his hand. Booth's face was snowy and grim as he pulled his foot back and kicked the boy in the chest.

He took the bridle and limped toward the animal. She began to swing in a swift circle as he tried to get his good foot up in the stirrup. When he made it, Booth pulled himself across the saddle, threw his left leg over, and was just settling in the saddle when Major Stewart came out the back door yelling "Stop! Stop!" He reached for the rein as Booth spurred the horse and turned out of the alley.

The course he chose was not up to F Street, where the gate would have to be unlatched. He swung toward the side of the T,[5] out through Ninth Street, then right toward Pennsylvania Avenue. His job was to put that first mile between him and his pursuers; he must be ahead of the news he had created. So he spurred the little mare hard, and she laid her ears back and ran. The conspirator was in little pain. He knew that his leg had been hurt, but the pain was not great now. He leaned his weight on the right stirrup and sat with the left thigh half up on the saddle. The mare turned into Pennsylvania Avenue and headed toward the Capitol. To the right of the House wing, a moon two days shy of being full was showing.

At Capitol South, he passed another horseman,

---

4. **Green Room:** Laura Keene, the star of the play, was in a waiting room used by actors when offstage.

5. **T:** Behind Ford's Theatre was a T-shaped alley; the part of the alley leading to Ninth Street had no gate.

trotting in the opposite direction. The speed of the mare attracted the lone rider's attention. As Booth turned into New Jersey Avenue, he slowed the mare. This was a shanty section, so dark that, unless the United States Government knew his escape route, no one would look for him here. At Virginia Avenue, he turned left and was now close to the bridge.[6]

When Booth swung away from the rear of Ford's Theatre, Johnny Peanut rolled in the alley, moaning: "He kicked me. He kicked me." Major Stewart turned to go back into the theater and was met by a rush of theater people coming out. . . .

The audience began to buzz. Some of the men stood and began to ask others what did this mean. The people sensed now that this was not a part of the play and they felt vaguely alarmed. Major Rathbone pointed dramatically toward the dead wings and roared: "Stop that man!" Out of the State Box came a second scream, a shriek that chilled the audience and brought a large part of it to its feet. This again was Mrs. Lincoln. It had penetrated her mind that Mr. Lincoln could not be aroused. To the west, many farmers testified that, at this time, the moon emerged from behind clouds blood red.

In the orchestra, one man stood and brought to mouth the question everyone was asking: "For heaven's sake, what is it? What happened?" . . . Miss Harris was leaning over the ledge of the box wringing her hands and pleading for water. Someone in the box, a man, yelled:

"He has shot the President!"

All over the theater, hoarse voices shouted, "No! No!" "It can't be true!" In a trice, Ford's resembled a hive immediately after the queen bee has died. The aisles were jammed with people moving willy-nilly. The stairs were crowded, some trying to get up to the dress circle, others trying to get down. Some were up on the stage. Harry Hawk stood in stage center and wept. A group of men tried to force their way through the white door, but, the harder they pushed, the more firmly

it held. . . . Actors in makeup ran on the stage begging to know what had happened.

"Water!" Miss Harris begged from the box. "Water!"

Some of the patrons got out on the street and spread the word that Lincoln had been shot. The President, they said, is lying dead in the box inside. Tempers flared. A crowd collected. From E and F Streets, people came running. Many tried to get into the theater as others were trying to get out. Inside, a few women fainted and the cry for water could be heard from different parts of the theater.

Rathbone, soaked with blood, went back into the corridor and tried to open the door. He found the wooden bar and yelled for the men on the other side to stop leaning against the door. After several entreaties, he was able to lift the bar and it fell to the floor, stained with his blood. The major pleaded that only doctors be admitted. A short, handsome man in sideburns and mustache yelled from the rear of the mob that he was a doctor. Men pushed him forward until he got inside the corridor. He was Dr. Charles Leale, Assistant Surgeon of United States Volunteers, twenty-three years of age.

Someone, below the stage, turned the gas valve up[7] and hundreds of faces were revealed to be in varying stages of fright and anger. On the street, a man shouted, "I'm glad it happened!" In a moment, he was scuffed underfoot, most of his clothes ripped from his body, and he was carried toward a lamppost. Three policemen drew revolvers to save his life.

In the State Box, President Lincoln's knees began to relax and his head began to come forward. Mrs. Lincoln saw it, moaned, and pressed her head against his chest. Rathbone asked Dr. Leale for immediate attention. "I'm bleeding to death!" he said. The blood had soaked his sleeve and made a pool on the floor. The doctor lifted Rathbone's chin, looked into his eyes, and walked on into the box.

Miss Harris was hysterical. She was begging

---

6. **bridge:** the Navy Yard Bridge spanning the Potomac River. Across the bridge was southern Maryland and the way to Virginia.

7. **turned the gas valve up:** The theater was lighted by gas lamps, which were turned down while the play was in progress.

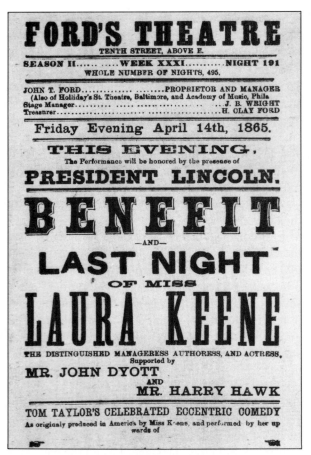

Playbill of the Ford's Theatre performance
Lincoln attended.

everyone to please help the President. The doctor looked at her, then lifted Mrs. Lincoln's head off her husband's chest. The First Lady grabbed the hand of medicine and moaned piteously.

"Oh, Doctor! Is he dead? Can he recover? Will you take charge of him? Oh, my dear husband! My dear husband!"

"I will do what I can," the doctor said, and motioned to the men who crowded into the box behind him to remove her. She was taken to the broad sofa in Box 8, and Miss Harris sat beside her, patting Mrs. Lincoln's hand.

At first, Leale thought that the President was dead. He pushed the shoulders back in the rocker so that the trunk no longer had a tendency to fall forward. Then he stood in front of the President and studied him from head to foot. With the atti-

tude of one who knows that he will be obeyed, he said to the gawking men: "Get a lamp. Lock that door back there and admit no one except doctors. Someone hold matches until the lamp gets here."

These things were done, as Dr. Leale knew that they would be. He was the first person to bring order around the dying President. The eyes of the patient were closed. There was no sound of breathing. There was no sign of a wound. Men held matches and looked openmouthed as Leale placed the palm of his hand under the whiskered chin of the President, lifted it, and then permitted it to drop.

In the crowd peering in from the corridor, he saw a few soldiers. "Come here," he said to them. "Get him out of the chair and put him on the floor." Half afraid, they did as he told them to. The body was relaxed. They placed it on the floor and stepped away. Leale was going to look for the wound. He was sure that it was a stab wound because, as he was passing the theater on his way back to the army hospital, he heard a man yell something about the President and a man with a knife. Further, he had seen that Major Rathbone sustained a knife wound.

Dr. Leale crouched behind Lincoln's head and lifted it. His hands came away wet. He placed the head back on the floor and men in a circle held matches at waist level as the doctor unbuttoned the black coat, the vest, unfastened the gold watch chain, and, while trying to unbutton the collar, he became impatient and asked for a pocket knife. William F. Rent had a sharp one, and Doctor Leale took it and slit the shirt and collar down the front.

He tore the undershirt between his hands and the chest was laid bare. He saw no wound. The doctor bent low, and put his ear to the chest. Then he lifted the eyelid and saw evidence of a brain injury. He separated his fingers and ran them through the patient's hair. At the back, he found matted blood and his fingers loosened a clot and the patient responded with shallow breathing and a weak pulse.

Onstage, men lifted another doctor into the box. This one was Dr. Charles Taft. He was senior to Leale, but he placed himself at Leale's disposal at once as an assistant. Leale lifted the body into a slumped sitting position and asked Dr. Taft to hold him. In the saffron flicker of the matches, he found what he was looking for. His fingers probed the edges of the wound and he pulled the matted black hair away from it. It was not a knife wound. The President had been shot behind the left ear and, if the probe of a pinky meant anything, the lead ball moved diagonally forward and slightly upward through the brain toward the right eye. Dr. Leale felt around the eye to see if the ball had emerged. It had not. It was in the brain.

Gently, he lowered the great head to the floor. He knew that Lincoln had to die. Leale acquainted Dr. Taft with his findings, and his feeling. He straddled the hips and started artificial respiration. His business was to prolong life—not to try to read the future—and so he raised the long arms up high and lowered them to the floor—up and back—forward and down—up and back—forward and down. For a moment, he paused. Rudely, he pushed the mouth open and got two fingers inside and pushed the tongue down to free the larynx of secretions.

Dr. Albert F. A. King was admitted to the box. Leale asked each doctor to take an arm and manipulate it while he pressed upward on the belly to stimulate the heart action.

A few soldiers started to clear the box of people. From onstage, questions flew up to the box. Mostly, they were unanswered. "How is he?" "What happened?" "Was he stabbed?" "Who did it?" "Is he breathing?" "Did anyone see who did it?"

For the first time, someone uttered the name of John Wilkes Booth. The name moved from the stage down into the orchestra, was shouted across the dress circle and out of the half-empty theater into the lobby and cascaded into Tenth Street. "Booth!" "Booth did it!" "An actor named Booth!" "The management must have been in on the plot!" "Burn the . . . theater!" "Burn it now!" "Yes, burn it!" "Burn!"

Grief spirals to insanity.

Dr. Leale sat astride the President's hips and leaned down and pressed until these strangers met, thorax to thorax. Leale turned his head and pressed his mouth against the President's lips, and breathed for him in a kiss of desperation. Then he listened to the heart again and, when he sat up, he noticed that the breathing was stronger. It sounded like a snore.

"His wound is mortal," he said to the other doctors. "It is impossible for him to recover."

One of the soldiers began to get sick. Two others removed their uniform caps. A lamp arrived. Dr. Leale saw a hand in front of him with brandy. He dripped a small amount between the bluish lips. Leale watched the Adam's apple. It bobbed. The liquid had been swallowed and was now retained.

He paused in his labors to wipe his face with a kerchief.

"Can he be removed to somewhere nearby?" Leale said.

"Wouldn't it be possible to carry him to the White House?" Dr. King said.

"No," Dr. Leale said. "His wound is mortal. It is impossible for him to recover."

On the couch, Mrs. Lincoln sat quietly, rocking slightly. Miss Laura Keene had come into the box and was now sitting with her and with Miss Harris. All three heard Dr. Leale's words, but only Mrs. Lincoln seemed not to comprehend. She sat between them, rocking a little and looking across the theater at the other boxes.

Miss Keene came over, and asked the doctor if she could hold the President's head for a moment. He looked at her coldly, and nodded. She sat on the floor and placed his head on her lap.

"If it is attempted," said Leale, still thinking about the White House, "he will be dead before we reach there."

Dr. Taft asked an officer to run out and find a place nearby—a suitable place—for President Lincoln. He called four soldiers to carry the body—at first it was decided to try seating the body in the rocker and carrying it that way—but Leale said that there were too many narrow turns and besides, it would not hurt him to be carried as long as the open wound was downward.

Four men from Thompson's Battery C, Pennsylvania Light Artillery, drew the assignment. Two formed a sling under the upper trunk; the other two held the thin thighs. Dr. King held the left shoulder. Dr. Leale followed behind and held the head in cupped hands. Miss Keene sat, oblivious to the dark stain on her dress, watching. At the last moment, Leale decided that headfirst would be better and he walked backward with Lincoln's head in his hands, his own head twisted to see ahead.

"Guards!" he yelled. "Guards! Clear the passage!"

From somewhere, a group of troopers came to life and preceded the dismal party, shoving the curious to one side. "Clear out!" they yelled at one and all. "Clear out!"

At the head of the stairs, Leale shouted orders as the party began the slow descent. Ahead, they could hear the cries of the crowd in Tenth Street. Downstairs in the lobby, a big man looked at the great placid face, and he blessed himself. Tenth Street was massed with humanity as far as the eye could see.

A short paunchy captain of infantry impressed[8] more soldiers to duty and ordered them double-ranked to precede the body. He drew his sword and said: "Surgeon, give me your commands and I will see that they are obeyed." Leale looked at the houses across the street, private homes and boardinghouses, and asked the captain to get them across.

For the first time, the crowd saw the shaggy head and the big swinging feet. A roar of rage went up. Someone in the crowd yelled "God almighty! Get him to the White House!" Leale shook his head no. "He would die on the way," Leale said. Men in the crowd began to weep openly. The little party pressed through, inch by inch, the faces of the mob forming a canopy of frightened eyes over the body. The crowd pressed in ahead, and closed in behind. . . .

The night, now, was clear. The mist gone. The wind cool and gusty. The moon threw the shadow of Ford's Theatre across the street.

Every few steps, Leale stopped the party and pulled a clot loose. The procession seemed to be interminable.[9] When they got across the street, the steady roar of the crowd made it impossible to hear or to be heard. Leale wanted to go into the nearest house, but a soldier on the stoop made motions that no one was home and made a helpless pantomime with a key. At the next house toward F Street, Leale saw a man with a lighted candle standing in the doorway, motioning. This was the William Petersen house at 453 Tenth Street. Mr. Petersen was a tailor.

Lincoln was carried up the steps and into the house. Part of the crowd followed. The man with the candle motioned for the doctors to follow him. They moved down a narrow hall. To the right was a stairway going up to the second floor. To the left was a parlor, with coal grate and black horse-hair furniture. Behind it, also on the left, was a sitting room. Under the stairway was a small bedroom.

Here, the President was placed on a bed. A soldier on leave, who had rented the room, picked up his gear and left. He was Private William T. Clark of the 13th Massachusetts Infantry. The room measured fifteen feet by nine feet. The wallpaper was oatmeal in character. A thin reddish rug covered part of the floor. There were a plain maple bureau near the foot of the bed, three straight-backed chairs, a washstand with white crock[10] bowl, a wood stove. On the wall were framed prints of "The Village Blacksmith" and Rosa Bonheur's "The Horse Fair." The bed was set against the wall under the stairway.

It was too small for the President. Leale ordered it pulled away from the wall. He also asked that the footboard be taken off, but it was found that, if that was done, the bed would collapse. The body was placed diagonally on the bed, the head close to the wall, the legs hanging off the other end. Extra pillows were found and Lincoln's head was propped so that his chin was on his chest. Leale then ordered an officer to open a bedroom window—there were two, facing a little courtyard—and to clear everybody out and to post a guard on the front stoop.

At the back end of the room, Leale held his first formal conference with the other doctors. As they talked in whispers, the man who had held the candle went through the house lighting all the gas fixtures. The house was narrow and deep, and

---

8. **impressed** (im·prest′): here. forced into service.
9. **interminable** (in·tur′mi·nə·b'l): seeming to last forever.

10. **crock:** short for *crockery,* earthenware pots and bowls.

Lincoln dying, as sketched by Herman Faber. At the top are the last names of some of those present, who included members of Lincoln's cabinet.

behind this bedroom was another and behind that a family sitting room which spread across the width of the house.

Leale, in the presence of the other doctors, began a thorough examination. As he began to remove the President's clothing, he looked up and saw Mrs. Lincoln standing in the doorway with Miss Keene and Miss Harris. He looked irritated and asked them to please wait in the front room. The patient was undressed and the doctors searched all of the areas of the body, but they found no other wound.

The feet were cold to the touch up to the ankles. The body was placed between sheets and a comforter was placed over the top. A soldier in the doorway was requisitioned as an orderly and the doctors sent him for hot water and for heated blankets. They sent another soldier for large mustard plasters.[11] These were applied to the front of the body, covering the entire area from shoulders to ankles.

Occasionally, the President sighed. His pulse was forty-four and light; breathing was stertorous;[12] the pupil of the left eye was contracted; the right was dilated—both were proved insensitive to light. Leale called a couple of more soldiers from the hallway, and sent them to summon Robert Lincoln, Surgeon General Barnes, Dr. Robert K. Stone, President Lincoln's physician, and Lincoln's pastor, Dr. Phineas D. Gurley.

The death watch began.

---

11. **mustard plasters:** cloths spread with a paste made from powdered mustard, flour, and cold water. Mustard plasters were applied to relieve irritation and increase the flow of blood to the skin's surface.
12. **stertorous** (stur′tər·əs): loud, raspy, labored.

Responding to the Story

Analyzing the Story

Identifying Facts

1. List four of the careful preparations made by John Wilkes Booth before he begins the attack on President Abraham Lincoln.
2. Describe what happens in Box 7 in the moments after Booth fires at President Lincoln. What does Booth say during the assassination? What are the reactions of the three other occupants of the box?
3. The narrative follows Booth as he scrambles from the theater. Describe how he escapes and state where he is headed.
4. Doctor Charles Leale takes charge after the shooting. Explain his diagnosis of Lincoln's condition. How does the doctor try to help the President?
5. Explain why President Lincoln is not removed to the White House. Where is he taken?

Interpreting Meanings

6. A writer holds you in **suspense** when you are uncertain about, and very interested in, what lies ahead. In some stories, you are uncertain about the ending of a course of events and are eager to find out. In other works, you know the end result from the start. You are eager, however, to find out how it came about and how the various characters behaved. "Lincoln Is Shot" belongs to the second category. If you found the selection suspenseful, explain what made it so. If you did not find the selection suspenseful, explain what it lacked.
7. Explain why Booth shoots the President. Why does the assassin say, "*Sic semper tyrannis!*"?
8. Jim Bishop wrote his book about ninety years after the assassination took place. What sources do you think he used to find the details he reports? For instance, how could he know what went on in Booth's mind as he enters the Presidential box, or what Mrs. Lincoln's exact movements were in the moments after the shooting? Also, how could he find out the way in which Dr. Leale examined President Lincoln? Do you think Bishop invented some of the details in the selection? If so, which ones?

Evaluating the Story

9. What was your reaction to this step-by-step account of President Lincoln's assassination? Did you learn new facts? Did you gain a deeper understanding of the event? Do you think the writer should have used a different approach? Explain your answer.
10. Why, in your opinion, do stories of the assassination of a powerful person have a strong fascination to most people? Is the story of Lincoln's murder like, or unlike, other assassination stories?

Writing About the Story

A Creative Response

1. **Writing an Eyewitness Account.** Imagine that you are one of the people in the theater at the time of the shooting. The police have asked you to give an eyewitness account. Identify yourself, and tell where you were when the President was shot, what you saw and heard, what you did, and how you felt. Write two paragraphs.

A Critical Response

2. **Analyzing Reactions.** People often react differently to the same event. In "Lincoln Is Shot," people react to the shooting of the President in various ways. They are shocked, angry, grief-stricken, frightened, glad, or curious, among other things. In two paragraphs, discuss the reactions of Mrs. Lincoln and Dr. Leale to the shooting. In your first paragraph, describe the reaction of each, giving details from the selection. Then, in the second paragraph, **compare and contrast** the reactions of Mrs. Lincoln and Dr. Leale. Explain the similarities and differences.

Analyzing Language and Vocabulary

General and Precise Words

1. Here are some passages from "Lincoln Is Shot." Explain whether each italicized word or phrase is general or precise. If the word is general, think of a precise word or phrase that Bishop could

have used. If the word is precise, think of a general term it might have replaced.

a. "[Booth] found the *pine board,* held it against the inside of the door, and *tapped* the other end down. . . ."
b. "The *high* back of the *horsehair rocker* was in plain view. . . ."
c. "He was a *big* man, looking bigger in a *pale fawn suit.* . . ."
d. "The conspirator *hobbled* to the back door. . . ."

2. Precise nouns and verbs can improve your own writing. As practice, replace each italicized word with a precise word that fits the meaning of the sentence.

a. The wind *blew* through the *trees* and shook the *building.*
b. Terry *walked* into the room, his arms loaded with *stuff.*
c. The crowd *moved* forward.
d. The flashlight beam *went through* the darkness.
e. The *food* was stale and tasteless.
f. The *noise* of the *music* kept her awake.

Reading About The Writer

Jim Bishop (1907–1987), a columnist and best-selling biographer, began his literary career as a $12-a-week copy boy for the New York *Daily News.* He was in his thirties when he created his original style of journalism, in which he traced the events of a day, or days, in the life of some famous figure. Bishop said he got this idea from his father, a Jersey City policeman, who spent hours writing detailed reports of the chronological events of crimes. "Lincoln Is Shot" is taken from Bishop's best-selling book *The Day Lincoln Was Shot,* in which we get an almost minute-by-minute account of what occurred before and after President Lincoln was assassinated. Bishop's other books include *A Day in the Life of President Kennedy* (which was another best-seller), *The Day Christ Died,* and *The Days of Martin Luther King, Jr.*

Focusing on Background
A Comment from the Writer

"This is about a day, a place, and a murder—and about a wide variety of men and women. It begins with the casual and somewhat late good morning of President Abraham Lincoln outside his bedroom door at 7 A.M. on Friday, April 14, 1865, and it ends at 7:22 A.M. the following morning when, as Surgeon General Barnes pressed silver coins to the President's eyelids, Mrs. Lincoln moaned: 'Oh, why did you not tell me he was dying!' . . .

"As a student of President Lincoln and his times, I began, in 1930, to keep notes on the events of this day. The best, and simplest way, I felt, was to keep notebooks labeled 7 A.M. Friday, 8 A.M. Friday, 9 A.M. Friday, and so on through 7 A.M. Saturday.

That made twenty-five notebooks. In addition, I kept one marked 'Lincoln and Family,' one labeled 'The Conspirators,' one called 'Washington—Era,' and one marked 'Bibliography.' This must be of small interest to any reader except to point out that, after years of reading and making notes, I found that I had as many as three or four versions—each at variance with the others—of what had happened in any one hour. Two years ago, when I intensified the research and started to read seven million words of government documents, the pieces of the puzzle began to orient themselves."

—Jim Bishop

STICKEEN

John Muir

Much of southeastern Alaska is covered by glaciers, which are massive sheets of ice and snow. Glaciers move very slowly, often down a mountain slope or through a valley, until they melt or break into the sea. In this true story, the American naturalist and explorer John Muir describes the day he and a spirited dog named Stickeen explored an Alaskan glacier. Muir calls this adventure "the most memorable of all my wild days." Stop a moment after you reach the end of the eighth paragraph (on page 42). Write down the principal difficulty you think Muir and Stickeen will face.

In the summer of 1880 I set out from Fort Wrangell[1] in a canoe with the Rev. S. H. Young and a crew of Indians to continue the exploration of the icy region of southeastern Alaska. The necessary provisions, blankets, etc., had been collected and stowed away, and the Indians were in their places ready to dip their paddles, while a crowd of their friends were looking down from the wharf to bid them goodbye and good luck. Mr. Young, for whom we were waiting, at length came aboard, followed by a little black dog that immediately made himself at home by curling up in a hollow among the baggage. I like dogs, but this one seemed so small, dull, and worthless that I objected to his going and asked the missionary why he was taking him.

"Such a helpless wisp of hair will only be in the way," I said. "You had better pass him up to one of the Indian boys on the wharf, to be taken home to play with the children. This trip is not likely to be a good one for toy dogs. He will be rained on and snowed on for weeks, and will require care like a baby."

But the missionary assured me that he would be no trouble at all, that he was a perfect wonder of a dog—could endure cold and hunger like a polar bear, could swim like a seal, and was wondrous wise, etc., making out a list of virtues likely to make him the most interesting of the company.

Nobody could hope to unravel the lines of his ancestry. He was short-legged, bunchy-bodied, and almost featureless—something like a muskrat. Though smooth, his hair was long and silky, so that when the wind was at his back it ruffled, making him look shaggy. At first sight his only noticeable feature was his showy tail, which was about as shady and airy as a squirrel's, and was carried curling forward nearly to his ears. On closer inspection you might see his thin, sensitive ears and his keen dark eyes with cunning tan spots. Mr. Young told me that when the dog was about the size of a wood rat he was presented to his wife by an Irish prospector at Sitka, and that when he arrived at Fort Wrangell he was adopted by the Stickeen Indians as a sort of new good-luck totem, and named "Stickeen" for the tribe, with whom he became a favorite.

On our trip he soon proved himself a queer character—odd, concealed, independent, keeping invincibly quiet, and doing many inexplicable things that piqued my curiosity. Sailing week after week through the long, intricate channels and inlets among the innumerable islands and mountains

Allusions. An *allusion* is a reference to a person, place, event, or literary work. Writers often use allusions to suggest comparisons. For example, if you called someone "as wise as Solomon," you'd be alluding to the Biblical King Solomon, known for his wise decisions. As you read the story, look for two allusions to Biblical stories.

---

1. See the map on page 44 for the location of Fort Wrangell and other places and geographical features in Alaska.

of the coast, he spent the dull days in sluggish ease, motionless, and apparently as unobserving as a hibernating marmot. But I discovered that somehow he always knew what was going forward. When the Indians were about to shoot at ducks or seals, or when anything interesting was to be seen along the shore, he would rest his chin on the edge of the canoe and calmly look out. When he heard us talking about making a landing, he roused himself to see what sort of place we were coming to, and made ready to jump overboard and swim ashore as soon as the canoe neared the beach. Then, with a vigorous shake to get rid of the brine in his hair, he went into the woods to hunt small game. But though always the first out of the canoe, he was always the last to get into it. When we were ready to start he could never be found, and refused to come to our call. We soon found out, however, that though we could not see him at such times he saw us, and from the cover of the briers and huckleberry bushes in the fringe of the woods was watching the canoe with wary eye. For as soon as we were fairly off he came trotting down the beach, plunged into the surf and swam after us, knowing well that we would cease rowing and take him in. When the contrary little vagabond came alongside, he was lifted by the neck, held at arm's length a moment to drip, and dropped aboard. We tried to cure him of this trick by compelling him to swim farther before stopping for him. But this did no good; the longer the swim, the better he seemed to like it.

Though capable of the most specious[2] idleness, he was always ready for excursions or adventures of any sort. When the Indians went into the woods for a deer, Stickeen was sure to be at their heels, provided I had not yet left camp. For though I never carried a gun, he always followed me, forsaking the hunting Indians and even his master to share my wanderings. The days that were too stormy for sailing I spent in the woods, or on the mountains or glaciers. Wherever I chanced to be Stickeen always insisted on following me, gliding through the dripping huckleberry bushes and prickly *Panax* and *Rubus* tangles like a fox, scarce stirring their close-set branches, wading and wallowing through snow, swimming ice cold streams, jumping logs and rocks and the crusty hummocks and crevasses[3] of glaciers with the patience and endurance of a determined mountaineer, never tiring or getting discouraged.

Once he followed me over a glacier the surface of which was so rough that it cut his feet until every step was marked with blood; but he trotted on with Indian fortitude until I noticed his pain and taking pity on him, made him a set of moccasins out of a handkerchief. But he never asked for help or made any complaint, as if, like a philosopher, he had learned that without hard work and suffering there could be no pleasure worth having. . . .

We had explored the glaciers of the Sumdum and Tahkoo inlet. Now we sailed through Stephen's Passage into Lynn Canal, and thence through Icy Strait into Cross Sound, looking for unexplored inlets leading toward the ice fountains of the Fairweather Range. . . . At length we discovered the entrance of what is now called Taylor Bay, and about five o'clock reached the head of it, and encamped near the front of a large glacier which extends as an abrupt barrier all the way across from wall to wall of the inlet, a distance of three or four miles.

On first observation the glacier presented some unusual features, and that night I planned a grand excursion for the morrow. I awoke early, called not only by the glacier, but also by a storm. Rain, mixed with trailing films of scud[4] and the ragged, drawn-out nether surfaces of gray clouds, filled the inlet, and was sweeping forward in a thick, passionate, horizontal flood. Everything was streaming with life and motion—woods, rocks, waters, and the sky. The main perennial streams were booming, and hundreds of new ones, born of the rain, were descending in gray and white cascades on each side of the inlet, fairly streaking their rocky slopes, and roaring like the sea.

I had intended making a cup of coffee before starting, but when I heard the storm I made haste

---

2. **specious** (spē'shəs): here, showy.

3. **hummocks and crevasses** (kri·vas'əz): ridges and cracks.
4. **scud** (skud): low, dark, fast-moving clouds.

to join it; for in storms nature has always something extra fine to show us. . . .

I took my ice ax, buttoned my coat, put a piece of bread in my pocket, and set out.

Mr. Young and the Indians were asleep, and so I hoped, was Stickeen; but I had not gone a dozen rods[5] before he left his warm bed in the tent, and came boring through the blast after me. That a man should welcome storms for their exhilarating music and motion, and go forth to see God making landscapes, is reasonable enough; but what fascination could there be in dismal weather for this poor feeble wisp of a dog, so pathetically small? Anyhow, on he came, breakfastless, through the choking blast. I stopped, turned my back to the wind, and gave him a good, dissuasive talk.

"Now don't," I said, shouting to make myself heard in the storm—"now don't, Stickeen. What has got into your queer noodle now? You must be daft. This wild day has nothing for you. Go back to camp and keep warm. There is no game abroad—nothing but weather. Not a foot or wing is stirring. Wait and get a good breakfast with your master, and be sensible for once. I can't feed you or carry you, and this storm will kill you. . . . "

After ordering him back again and again to ease my conscience, I saw that he was not to be shaken off. . . . The dog just stood there in the wind, drenched and blinking, saying doggedly, "Where thou goest I will go." So I told him to come on, if he must, and gave him a piece of the bread I had put in my pocket for breakfast. Then we pushed on in company, and thus began the most memorable of all my wild days.

The level flood, driving straight in our faces, thrashed and washed us wildly until we got into the shelter of the trees and ice cliffs on the east side of the glacier, where we rested and listened and looked on in comfort. The exploration of the glacier was my main object. But the wind was too high to allow excursions over its open surface where one might be dangerously shoved while balancing for a jump on the brink of a crevasse. In the meantime the storm was a fine study. Here the

end of the glacier, descending over an abrupt swell of resisting rock about five hundred feet high, leans forward and falls in majestic ice cascades. And as the storm came down the glacier from the north, Stickeen and I were beneath the main current of the blast while favorably located to see and hear it. A broad torrent, draining the side of the glacier, now swollen by scores of new streams from the mountains, was rolling boulders along its rocky channel between the glacier and the woods with thudding, bumping, muffled sounds, rushing toward the bay with tremendous energy. . . .

Looking southward from our shelter, we had this great torrent on our left, with mossy woods on the mountain slope above it, the glacier on our right, the wild, cascading portion of it forming a multitude of towers, spires, and flat-topped battlements seen through the trees, and smooth gray gloom ahead. . . .

When the wind began to abate I traced the east side of the glacier. All the trees standing on the edge of the woods were barked and bruised, showing high ice mark in a very telling way, while tens of thousands of those that had stood for centuries on the bank of the glacier farther out lay crushed and being crushed. In many places I could see, down fifty feet or so beneath, the margin of the glacier mill,[6] where trunks from one to two feet in diameter were being ground to pulp against outstanding rock-ribs and bosses[7] of the bank. About three miles above the front of the glacier, I climbed to the surface of it by means of ax steps, made easy for Stickeen; and as far as the eye could reach, the level, or nearly level, glacier stretched away indefinitely beneath the gray sky, a seemingly boundless prairie of ice. The rain continued, which I did not mind; but a tendency to fogginess in the drooping clouds made me hesitate about venturing far from land. No trace of the west shore was visible, and in case the misty clouds should settle, or the wind again become violent, I feared getting caught in a tangle of crevasses. Lingering undecided, watching the weather, I sauntered about on the crystal sea. For a mile or two out I

---

5. **rods:** here, units of measurement equal to 16½ feet (5 meters) each.

6. **glacier mill:** nearly vertical shaft through a glacier, down which a stream of surface water plunges.
7. **bosses:** rocks, or sections of rock, that jut out from eroded soil.

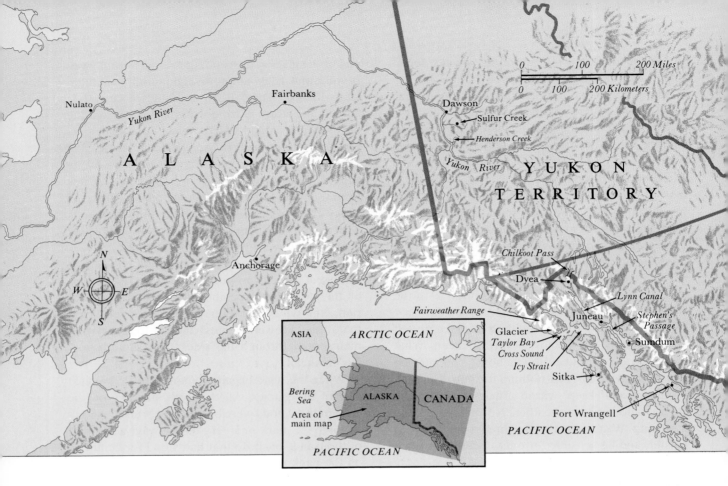

found the ice remarkably safe. The marginal crevasses were mostly narrow, while the few wider ones were easily avoided by passing around them, and the clouds began to open here and there. Thus encouraged, I at last pushed out for the other side. . . .

Toward the west side we came to a closely crevassed section, in which we had to make long, narrow tacks and doublings,[8] tracing the edges of tremendous longitudinal crevasses, many of which were from twenty to thirty feet wide, and perhaps a thousand feet deep, beautiful and awful. In working a way through them I was severely cautious, but Stickeen came on as unhesitatingly as the flying clouds. Any crevasse that I could jump he would leap without so much as halting to examine it. . . . He showed neither caution nor curiosity. His courage was so unwavering that it seemed due to dullness of perception, as if he were only blindly bold; and I warned him that he might slip or fall short. His bunchy body seemed all one skipping muscle, and his peg legs appeared to be jointed only at the top.

We gained the west shore in about three hours, the width of the glacier here being about seven miles. Then I pushed northward, in order to see as far back as possible into the fountains of the Fairweather Mountains, in case the clouds should rise. The walking was easy along the margin of the forest, which, of course, like that on the other side, had been invaded and crushed by the swollen glacier. In an hour we rounded a massive headland and came suddenly on another outlet of the glacier, which, in the form of a wild ice cascade, was pouring over the rim of the main basin toward the ocean with the volume of a thousand Niagaras. . . . It was a dazzling white torrent two miles wide, flowing between high banks black with trees. Tracing its left bank three or four miles, I found that it discharged into a freshwater lake, filling it with icebergs.

---

8. **tacks and doublings:** zig-zag courses and sharp backward turns.

I would gladly have followed the outlet, but the day was waning, and we had to make haste on the return trip to get off the ice before dark. When we were about two miles from the west shore the clouds dropped misty fringes, and snow soon began to fly. Then I began to feel anxiety about finding a way in the storm through the intricate network of crevasses which we had entered. Stickeen showed no fear. He was still the same silent, sufficient, uncomplaining Indian philosopher. When the storm-darkness fell he kept close behind me. The snow warned us to make haste, but at the same time hid our way. . . .

I pushed on as best I could, jumping innumerable crevasses, and for every hundred rods or so of direct advance traveling a mile in doubling up and down in the turmoil of chasms and dislocated masses of ice. . . . Many a mile we thus traveled, mostly up and down, making but little real headway in crossing, most of the time running instead of walking, as the danger of spending the night on the glacier threatened. . . .

At length our way was barred by a very wide and straight crevasse, which I traced rapidly northward a mile or so without finding a crossing or hope of one, then southward down the glacier about as far, to where it united with another crevasse. In all this distance of perhaps two miles there was only one place where I could possibly jump it; but the width of this jump was nearly the utmost I dared attempt, while the danger of slipping on the farther side was so great that I was loath to try it. . . . Because of the dangers already behind me, however, I determined to venture against those that might be ahead, jumped, and landed well. Stickeen followed, making nothing of it.

But within a distance of a few hundred yards we were stopped again by the widest crevasse yet encountered. Of course I made haste to explore it, hoping all might yet be well. About three fourths of a mile upstream it united with the one we had just crossed, as I feared it would. Then, tracing it down, I found it joined the other great crevasse at the lower end, maintaining a width of forty to fifty feet. We were on an island about two miles long and from one hundred to three hundred yards wide, with two barely possible ways to escape—one by the way we came, the other by an almost inaccessible sliver-bridge[9] that crossed the larger crevasse from near the middle of the island. After tracing the brink, I ran back to the sliver-bridge and cautiously studied it. . . .

This sliver was evidently very old, for it had been wasted until it was the worst bridge I ever saw. The width of the crevasse here was about fifty feet, and the sliver, crossing diagonally, was about seventy feet long, was depressed twenty-five or thirty feet in the middle, and the up-curving ends were attached to the sides eight or ten feet below the surface of the glacier. Getting down the nearly vertical wall to the end of it and up the other side were the main difficulties, and they seemed all but insurmountable.[10]

Of the many perils encountered in my years of wandering in mountain altitudes, none seemed so plain and stern and merciless as this. And it was presented when we were wet to the skin and hungry, the sky was dark with snow, and the night near, and we had to fear the snow in our eyes and the disturbing action of the wind in any movement we might make. But we were forced to face it. It was a tremendous necessity.

Beginning not immediately above the sunken end of the bridge, but a little to one side, I cut nice hollows on the brink for my knees to rest in; then, leaning over, with my short-handled ax cut a step sixteen or eighteen inches below, which, on account of the sheerness of the wall, was shallow. That step, however, was well made; its floor sloped slightly inward, and formed a good hold for my heels. Then, slipping cautiously upon it, and crouching as low as possible, with my left side twisted toward the wall, I steadied myself with my left hand in a slight notch, while with the right I cut other steps and notches in succession, guarding against glinting[11] of the ax, for life or death was in every stroke, and in the niceness of finish of every foothold. After the end of the bridge was reached, it was a delicate thing to poise on a little platform which I had chipped on its up-curving

---

9. **sliver-bridge:** thin, narrow piece of ice connecting two surfaces of a glacier.
10. **insurmountable** (in'sər·mount'ə·b'l): impossible to overcome.
11. **glinting:** striking a surface at an angle and glancing off.

end, and, bending over the slippery surface, get astride of it.

Crossing was easy, cutting off the sharp edge with careful strokes, and hitching forward a few inches at a time, keeping my balance with my knees pressed against its sides. The tremendous abyss on each side I studiously ignored. The surface of that blue sliver was then all the world. But the most trying part of the adventure was, after working my way across inch by inch, to rise from the safe position astride that slippery strip of ice, and to cut a ladder in the face of the wall—chipping, climbing, holding on with feet and fingers in mere notches. At such times one's whole body is eye, and common skill and fortitude are replaced by power beyond our call or knowledge. Never before had I been so long under deadly strain. How I got up the cliff at the end of the bridge I never could tell. The thing seemed to have been done by somebody else. . . .

But poor Stickeen, the wee, silky, sleekit beastie—I think of him! When I had decided to try the bridge, and while I was on my knees cutting away the rounded brow, he came behind me, pushed his head past my shoulder, looked down and across, scanned the sliver and its approaches with his queer eyes, then looked me in the face with a startled air of surprise and concern, and began to mutter and whine, saying as plainly as if speaking with words, "Surely you are not going to try that awful place?" This was the first time I had seen him gaze deliberately into a crevasse or into my face with a speaking look. That he should have recognized and appreciated the danger at the first glance showed wonderful sagacity. Never before had the quick, daring midget seemed to know that ice was slippery, or that there was such a thing as danger anywhere. His looks and the tones of his voice when he began to complain and speak his fears were so human that I unconsciously talked to him as I would to a boy, and in trying to calm his fears perhaps in some measure moderated my own.

"Hush your fears, my boy," I said. "We will get across safe, though it is not going to be easy. No right way is easy in this rough world. We must risk our lives to save them. At the worst we can only slip, and then how grand a grave we shall have! And by and by our nice bones will do good in the terminal moraine."[12]

But my sermon was far from reassuring him; he began to cry, and after taking another piercing look at the tremendous gulf, ran away in desperate excitement, seeking some other crossing. By the time he got back, baffled, of course, I had made a step or two. I dared not look back, but he made himself heard; and when he saw that I was certainly crossing, he cried aloud in despair. The danger was enough to daunt anybody, but it seems wonderful that he should have been able to weigh and appreciate it so justly. No mountaineer could have seen it more quickly or judged it more wisely, discriminating between real and apparent peril.

After I had gained the other side he howled louder than ever, and after running back and forth in vain search for a way of escape, he would return to the brink of the crevasse above the bridge, moaning and groaning as if in the bitterness of death. Could this be the silent, philosophic Stickeen? I shouted encouragement, telling him the bridge was not as bad as it looked, that I had left it flat for his feet, and he could walk it easily. But he was afraid to try it. Strange that so small an animal should be capable of such big, wise fears! I called again and again in a reassuring tone to come on and fear nothing, that he could come if he would only try. Then he would hush for a moment, look again at the bridge, and shout his unshakable conviction that he could never, never come that way, then lie back in despair, as if howling: "Oh-o-o, what a place! No-o-o; I can never go-o-o down there!" His natural composure and courage had vanished utterly in a tumultuous storm of fear. Had the danger been less, his distress would have seemed ridiculous. But in this gulf—a huge, yawning sepulcher[13] big enough to hold everybody in the territory—lay the shadow of death, and his heartrending cries might well have called Heaven to his help. Perhaps they did. So hidden before, he was transparent now, and one could see the workings of his mind like the movements of a clock out of its case. His voice and gestures were perfectly human, and his hopes

---

12. **terminal moraine** (mə·rān'): mass of rocks, gravel, sand, etc., deposited by a glacier at its lower end.
13. **sepulcher** (sep''l·kər): grave.

and fears unmistakable, while he seemed to understand every word of mine. I was troubled at the thought of leaving him. It seemed impossible to get him to venture. To compel him to try by fear of being left, I started off as if leaving him to his fate, and disappeared back of a hummock; but this did no good, for he only lay down and cried. So after hiding a few minutes, I went back to the brink of the crevasse, and in a severe tone of voice shouted across to him that now I must certainly leave him—I could wait no longer; and that if he would not come, all I could promise was that I would return to seek him next day. I warned him that if he went back to the woods the wolves would kill him, and finished by urging him once more by words and gestures to come on. He knew very well what I meant, and at last, with the courage of despair, hushed and breathless, he lay down on the brink in the hollow I had made for my knees, pressed his body against the ice to get the advantage of the friction, gazed into the first step, put his little feet together, and slid them slowly down into it, bunching all four in it, and almost standing on his head. Then, without lifting them, as well as I could see through the snow, he slowly worked them over the edge of the step, and down into the next and the next in succession in the same way, and gained the bridge. Then lifting his

Theodore Roosevelt and John Muir at Yosemite Park, California.

feet with the regularity and slowness of the vibrations of a seconds' pendulum, as if counting and measuring one, two, three, holding himself in dainty poise, and giving separate attention to each little step, he gained the foot of the cliff, at the top of which I was kneeling to give him a lift should he get within reach. Here he halted in dead silence, and it was here I feared he might fail, for dogs are poor climbers. I had no cord. If I had had one, I would have dropped a noose over his head and hauled him up. But while I was thinking whether an available cord might be made out of clothing, he was looking keenly into the series of notched steps and finger holds of the ice ladder I had made, as if counting them and fixing the position of each one in his mind. Then suddenly up he came, with a nervy, springy rush, hooking his paws into the notches and steps so quickly that I could not see how it was done, and whizzed past my head, safe at last!

And now came a scene! "Well done, well done, little boy! Brave boy!" I cried, trying to catch and caress him, but he would not be caught. Never before or since have I seen anything like so passionate a revulsion from the depths of despair to uncontrollable, exultant, triumphant joy. He flashed and darted hither and thither as if fairly demented, screaming and shouting, swirling round and round in giddy loops and circles like a leaf in a whirlwind, lying down and rolling over and over, sidewise and heels over head, pouring forth a tumultuous flood of hysterical cries and sobs and gasping mutterings. And when I ran up to him to shake him, fearing he might die of joy, he flashed off two or three hundred yards, his feet in a mist of motion; then, turning suddenly, he came back in wild rushes, and launched himself at my face, almost knocking me down, all the time screeching and screaming and shouting as if saying, "Saved! Saved! Saved!" Then away again, dropping suddenly at times with his feet in the air, trembling, and fairly sobbing. Such passionate emotion was enough to kill him. Moses' stately song of triumph after escaping the Egyptians and the Red Sea was nothing to it. Who could have guessed the capacity of the dull, enduring little fellow for all that most stirs this mortal frame? Nobody could have helped crying with him.

But there is nothing like work for toning down either excessive fear or joy. So I ran ahead, calling him, in as gruff a voice as I could command, to come on and stop his nonsense, for we had far to go, and it would soon be dark. Neither of us feared another trial like this. Heaven would surely count one enough for a lifetime. The ice ahead was gashed by thousands of crevasses, but they were common ones. The joy of deliverance burned in us like fire, and we ran without fatigue, every muscle, with immense rebound, glorying in its strength. Stickeen flew across everything in his way, and not till dark did he settle into his normal foxlike, gliding trot. At last the mountains crowned with spruce came in sight, looming faintly in the gloaming,[14] and we soon felt the solid rock beneath our feet, and were safe. Then came weariness. We stumbled down along the lateral moraine[15] in the dark, over rocks and tree trunks, through the bushes and devil-club thickets and mossy logs and boulders of the woods where we had sheltered ourselves in the morning. Then out on the level mud slope of the terminal moraine. Danger had vanished, and so had our strength. We reached camp about ten o'clock, and found a big fire and a big supper. A party of Hoona Indians had visited Mr. Young, bringing a gift of porpoise meat and wild strawberries, and hunter Joe had brought in a wild goat. But we lay down, too tired to eat much, and soon fell into a troubled sleep. The man who said, "The harder the toil the sweeter the rest," never was profoundly tired. Stickeen kept springing up and muttering in his sleep, no doubt dreaming that he was still on the brink of the crevasse; and so did I—that night and many others, long afterward, when I was nervous and overtired.

Thereafter Stickeen was a changed dog. During the rest of the trip, instead of holding aloof, he would come to me at night, when all was quiet about the campfire, and rest his head on my knee, with a look of devotion, as if I were his god. And often, as he caught my eye, he seemed to be trying to say, "Wasn't that an awful time we had together on the glacier?"

---

14. **gloaming** (glō'ming): twilight.
15. **lateral moraine** (mə·rān'): mass of rocks, gravel, sand, etc., deposited at the sides of a glacier.

Responding to the Story

Analyzing the Story

Identifying Facts

1. Describe the story's **setting**—the time, place, season, and climate.
2. Explain the purpose of the journey undertaken by John Muir and his companions.
3. Stickeen is the name of the dog that accompanies Muir and the others on their journey. Describe the dog's appearance. Then list three of his most important personality traits according to Muir's discussion early in the story.
4. Muir decides to explore a glacier with unusual features. Describe what will make the exploration difficult. Why doesn't Muir want Stickeen to go along with him?
5. Stickeen joins Muir anyway. They push ahead until Muir realizes that they are on an island in the glacier. Discuss why being on the island presents a great problem to the explorers.
6. How does Muir reach the main part of the glacier from the island? Why is the route more difficult for Stickeen than for Muir?

Illustration by Rockwell Kent from *Wilderness: A Journal of Quiet Adventure in Alaska*.
G. P. Putnam's Sons, The Knickerbocker Press (1920).

Interpreting Meanings

7. A **conflict** is a struggle between opposing forces in a story. It is often the main ingredient in an interesting plot. In an **external conflict,** a character struggles against nature or against another character or group of characters. Describe the main external conflict in this story.
8. In an **internal conflict,** the struggle occurs in the mind of a character. Describe the internal conflict Stickeen faces when he and Muir must cross the sliver-bridge.
9. What part of the story did you find most **suspenseful**? What were you afraid would happen?
10. Two **characters** are central to this story: John Muir and that remarkable mongrel Stickeen. How would you describe each personality? How did you feel about each character?

Evaluating Ideas

11. Early in the story Muir says, ". . . in storms nature has always something extra fine to show us. . . . [A] man should welcome storms for their exhilarating music and motion, and go forth to see God making landscapes. . . ." What is your reaction to this statement? Do you agree or do you see something different in storms, such as danger? Back up your answer with examples from real life or literature.
12. Muir also writes in the story that Stickeen ". . . had learned that without hard work and suffering there could be no pleasure worth having. . . ." Do you agree or disagree with this idea? Explain how Muir's comments relate to your own experiences and observations about life.

Writing About the Story

A Creative Response

1. **Writing a Dialogue.** Imagine that Stickeen and the dog in Jack London's "To Build a Fire" (page 6) meet around an Alaskan campfire. Write the dialogue they might have (in English) about their experiences, their views of human beings, and their philosophy of life. Give London's unnamed dog a name.

A Critical Response

2. **Supporting a Main Idea.** Muir says that Stickeen is "philosophic" and shows "sagacity." These are examples of **anthropomorphism** (an'thrə·pə·môr'fiz'm), which means giving human characteristics to something that isn't human. Find other examples of Muir's use of anthropomorphism in describing Stickeen, especially toward the end of the story. Where does Muir speak to Stickeen as if to a son? Do you think Muir has found in Stickeen a way to tell us just what the best explorers are made of? Write a paragraph answering these questions. Open with a topic sentence that describes the kind of "person" Stickeen is made out to be. Then use evidence from the story to support your main idea.

Analyzing Language and Vocabulary

Allusions

An **allusion** is often a reference to a literary work. If you're not familiar with the work, the allusion will probably sail right past you. Did you find three literary allusions in this story?

1. The first is on page 43. "The dog just stood there in the wind, drenched and blinking, saying doggedly, 'Where thou goest I will go.' " The **archaic** (rarely used) words *thou* and *goest* might have given you a clue that the quotation refers to the Bible. It refers specifically to Chapter 1 of the Book of Ruth.

    a. Why does Naomi in the Book of Ruth try to discourage Ruth from coming with her?
    b. How is Stickeen like Ruth?

2. You might easily have missed the second allusion, which is on page 46: "But poor Stickeen, the wee, silky, sleekit beastie—I think of him!" The allusion is to a poem by Robert Burns, a famous eighteenth-century Scottish poet. In Burns's poem, "To a Mouse," the speaker addresses an unfortunate mouse whose nest he's just destroyed with his plow:

    > Wee, sleekit, cowrin' tim'rous beastie,
    > O, what a panic's in thy breastie!

    At this point in the story, what feeling do the mouse and Stickeen share? What do you think the words *wee* and *sleekit* mean?

The Sierra glaciers. Illustration by Henry B. Kane from *The Wilderness World of John Muir*, edited by Edwin Way Teale. © 1982 by Nellie D. Teale.

Reprinted by permission of Houghton Mifflin Company.

3. Find where the narrator alludes to the song of Moses after he led the children of Israel across the Red Sea (see Exodus, Chapter 15).

    a. What is compared to the song of Moses?
    b. Describe Stickeen's feelings at this stage of the story.

Reading About the Writer

In his journals, **John Muir** (1838–1914) tells the story of his narrow escape in a kayak between two huge glaciers which were quickly and steadily moving together. His writings are filled with such exciting and dangerous moments. Muir, born in Dunbar, Scotland, was an amateur glacial geologist, who made some fascinating scientific discoveries. Named after Muir are the Muir Glacier, the Muir Woods, the Muir Trail, and the flower *Erigeron muirii*. In 1892, Muir founded the Sierra Club, an organization formed to protect the environment. The ideal behind the Sierra Club—that of preserving the wilderness—may be John Muir's greatest legacy to the world.

SUSPENSE

You have seen that suspense is not limited to fictional stories. Suspense can be found in all kinds of literature. For example, it is found in all types of nonfiction, including history, essays, true narratives, biographies, and autobiographies. Suspense is used whenever a writer wants to hook our curiosity and keep us turning the pages to find out the answers to the questions: "And what happens next? How will this end?"

The following is an excerpt from a book by a surgeon about his experiences. This episode takes place when he is stationed with the American armed forces in Korea after the Korean Conflict (1950–1953). Read the extract and answer the questions that follow.

It is Korea. 1955.

I am awakened by a hand on my chest, jostling.

"Sir Doc! Sir Doc!" It is Jang, the Korean man who assists me.

I open my eyes. Not gladly. To awaken here, in this place, in this time, is to invite despair.

"Boy come. Gate. Very scared. His brother bad sick. Pain belly. You come?"

O God, I think, let it not be appendicitis. I do not know how many more anesthesia-less operations I have left in me. Not many, I think. For I can no longer bear the gagged mouths, the trembling, frail bodies strapped to the table, round and round with wide adhesive tape from neck to ankles, with a space at the abdomen for the incision. Nor the knuckles burning white as they clutch the "courage stick" thrust into their hands at the last minute by a mamasan. Nor the eyes, . . . enkindled with streaky lights. Something drags at my arms, tangles my fingers. They grow ponderous at the tips.

"Couldn't they bring him here?"

"No, Sir Doc. Too very sick."

It is midnight. I force myself to look at the boy who will guide us. He is about ten years old, small, thin. . . .

We are four in the ambulance: Jang, Galloway the driver, the boy, and myself. A skinny bare arm points up into the mountains where I know the road is narrow, winding. There are cliffs.

"We'll go up the stream bed," says Galloway. "It's still dry, and safer. Far as we can, then tote in."

I make none of these decisions. The ambulance responds to the commands of the boy like a huge trained beast. Who would have thought a child to have so much power in him? Soon we are in the dry gully of the stream. It is slow. Off in the distance there is a torch. It swings from side to side like the head of a parrot. A signal. We move on.

The first cool wind plays with the hair, blows the lips dry, brightens the tips of cigarettes, then skips away. In a moment it returns. Its strength is up.

"Rain start today," says Jang.

"Today?"

"Now," says Galloway. A thrum hits the windshield, spreads to the roof, and we are enveloped in rain. A flashlight floats morosely off to one side, ogling. There is shouting in Korean.

Now we are suckstepping through rice paddies, carrying the litter and tarps. We arrive at the house.

A sliding paper door opens. It is like stepping into a snail shell. On the floor mat lies a boy. . . .

—from *Mortal Lessons,*
Richard Selzer

1. What does the boy want the narrator to do?
2. Appendectomies are performed routinely and painlessly today. They are not frightening procedures at all. Why does the surgeon dread that this might be one?
3. What obstacles make the journey difficult?
4. What details help you share what the doctor sees, hears, and feels on the journey?

5. How would you explain what the narrator means when he says: "It is like stepping into a snail shell"?

6. What question does this story plant in your mind? What are you afraid might happen next?

7. What possible ending could this story have?

8. Do any details **foreshadow**, or hint at, the story's end? How does the weather make you feel?

9. Find an example of the way the writer uses the present tense to tell this story. Does this help you feel "you are there"?

10. How would you describe the **conflict** in this story? Is the surgeon experiencing an internal struggle as well as an external one? Explain.

Writing

1. **Describing Four Types of Conflict.** Write four sentences in which you provide examples of each kind of conflict described on page 3. Pretend your audience is a younger student who doesn't understand conflict.

2. **Analyzing Conflict.** Write a paragraph in which you analyze an internal conflict or an external conflict on a TV show or in a movie. Identify the two "sides" of the conflict: Who is struggling against what? How is the conflict resolved? Exchange your paper with the other students in class. Do your classmates all agree with your analyses?

3. **Making up a Conflict.** Take one illustration from this unit and describe a conflict you think is portrayed by the illustration or suggested by it. Tell if the conflict is internal or external.

WRITING A CLIFF-HANGER

Writing Assignment

Develop an idea for a suspense-filled crime story. Write most of the story, but stop at a cliff-hanger—just before the ending. Then exchange stories with a classmate, and write endings for each other's stories.

Background

Creating Suspense

A story has suspense when we read to find out *what* will happen to the characters, *how,* and *why.* Writers create suspense in several ways:

1. **Foreshadowing.** A writer may give clues—sometimes even false clues—that hint at the story's outcome. Readers watch for these clues, and usually try to figure out which will be significant.
2. **Mystery.** Suspense may be created by withholding information from the reader—for instance, *who* the murderer is, and *how* the crime was committed. Any unusual or mysterious circumstances can also create suspense. Readers will want to find out why, for example, a man is walking down a snow-covered hill while carrying his skis.
3. **Dilemma.** Suspense is intense when a character we care about is in great danger or must choose between two threatening courses of action. We hold our breath at poor Stickeen's dilemma at the sliver bridge: Will he make the difficult jump, and if he does, will he succeed?
4. **Reversal.** In a reversal, the situation suddenly changes. Things may be looking good for the main character, and then suddenly something happens to cause terrible problems. We worry about what lies ahead: Will there be a reversal for the better, or will things get worse?

Predicting Outcomes

As you read, some part of your brain is busily at work asking yourself questions: "Why has Sheila come to school wearing a green football jersey? She hates the color green. Is she trying to impress someone? Has her opinion of green changed? Has she become color blind?" You are unconsciously **predicting outcomes**—making guesses about what will happen next.

In this assignment, you'll have to predict an outcome by writing the ending for a classmate's story. That story will stop just before its **climax,** the most suspenseful point. You'll have to guess what might logically happen next, based on what you know about the characters and the circumstances. A good ending may be a surprise, but it should be a natural and logical development of the story's details—not just a matter of chance and coincidence.

Prewriting

The following groups of words and phrases suggest ideas for a crime story. Choose one group, and use all of the words and phrases in the story you write.

Group 1	Group 2
flat tire	wig
missing key	hair dryer
flashlight	young woman
mountain road	kitchen
footprints	sink filled with water

Group 3	Group 4
computer disc	midnight
yesterday's newspaper	phone ringing
insurance policy	nephew
lipstick on drinking glass	coffee mug
crumpled-up note with telephone number	strange smell

Group 5	Group 6
microfilm	apartment
Nobel prize	argument
physicist	night
blueprints	light left on
spy	fingerprint

Before you write, spend some time thinking about

your story's plot, characters, and setting. Then fill out a chart such as the following:

Who are the characters?	
Where does the story take place?	
What is the crime?	
What is the dilemma, problem, or danger?	
How will possible endings be foreshadowed?	

Writing

Use a **first-person point of view** with the narrator-storyteller as a character in the story. Remember to stop your story at the most exciting moment, just before the crime is solved.

The following model (based on word group 4) shows how one student chose to begin the story.

I was jolted out of a mixed-up dream about my tenth-birthday party by the jangling bedside telephone. I pried my eyes open and found that it was midnight.

I lifted the receiver and muttered, "Detective Grimsley here."

"I'm sorry to wake you, sir," said the officer at the other end of the line. "But you must report immediately to the Oakridge Apartments. Something terrible has happened."

I didn't want to leave my warm bed and the first good night's sleep I'd had in months. But after seven years as a detective, I was used to doing what I didn't want to do.

I arrived at the apartment complex by 12:30 A.M. and found the place swarming with newspaper people. "Must be a biggie," I thought. . . .

Revising and Proofreading Self-Check

Before exchanging stories with a classmate, answer the following questions about your own story. Make revisions where necessary.

1. Does the story have a definite plot, setting, and main character?
2. Have I included lots of details, including all the words in the group I chose?
3. Have I made the story suspenseful? Have I stopped just before the story's climax?
4. Does every sentence start with a capital letter and end with a period or other punctuation mark? Are all the words spelled correctly?

After exchanging stories, ask the same questions about your classmate's story. If necessary, request that the classmate make revisions.

When the necessary revisions have been made, you and your partner should write endings to each other's stories. Use separate sheets of paper for the endings.

Partner Check

After the endings are completed, show them to each other. Think about the following:

1. Does your partner's ending to your story match the ending you had in mind? In what ways is it similar or different?
2. Do you like your partner's ending to your story? If yes, why do you like it? If no, what do you think is wrong with the ending?

COMEDY

A Drop of Dew Falling from the Wing of a Bird Awakens Rosalie Asleep in the Shade of a Cobweb (detail) by Joan Miró (1939). Oil.

The University of Iowa Museum of Art, Iowa City, Iowa. Purchase Mark Ranney Memorial Fund, 1948.

UNIT TWO   **John Leggett**

Unit Outline
COMEDY

Think of the trouble the world would save itself if it would pay some attention to nonsense!

—E. B. White

Comedy is often a matter of taste. What is funny is sometimes different for each of us. This is why being able to laugh at the same joke is generally taken to be the mark of a special friendship between two people.

However, there are certain situations that appeal to the funnybone in most of us. Generally, these situations involve the unexpected. We laugh at a four-year-old carrying a briefcase, or at an elephant dressed in a ballerina's tutu. We laugh at the movie comedian Charlie Chaplin when he puts an old shoe on his plate and proceeds to eat it as if it's a steak and spaghetti dinner.

Three Comic Techniques

When you watch comedians, you know that there are many ways to make people laugh. The same is true of comedy in literature. Here are three techniques that can be used to make us laugh:

1. **Exaggeration:** overstating something to create a comic effect: *The mosquito left a Vesuvius of a bite on his nose.*

2. **Understatement:** describing something as less than it is (the opposite of exaggeration): *When the jeep's wheel ran over his foot, he experienced a certain discomfort.*

3. **Verbal Irony:** saying one thing but meaning something else: *Prodding her portion of the fried snake with her fork, she remarked, "Oh, what a lovely lunch!"*

The Voice of the Storyteller

Comedy is also achieved by the storyteller's **voice.** It isn't so much *what* the voice telling the story sees, as *how* he or she sees it. We all know comedians who have a funny way of looking at things and of telling about them. People like this become known for their humorous, unexpected comments. Perhaps this quality of being funny is no more than being able to see events in sharp contrast with the conventional view of things.

Comedy and Nonsense

Nonsense is often the essence of humor. It can be **satirical**—that is, it can mock the rational world, a world where rooms must be kept in order, hands must be washed, and lessons must be learned. Nonsense can make us look at the world of good sense, as if to say, "Look where *that's* got us!"

Responding to a Story

Here is how one reader responded to this story about Davy Crockett. The reader's notes are in the right-hand margin. Make your own notes to help you write about the story later.

The morning Davy Crockett was born, Davy's Pa came busting out of his cabin in Tennessee alongside the Nola-chucky River. He fired three shots into the air, gave a whoop, and said, "I've got me a son. His name is Davy Crockett, and he'll be the greatest hunter in all creation."

> Never heard of the Nola-chucky River. It's probably made up (funny sounds).

When he said that the sun rose up in the sky like a ball of fire. The wind howled riproariously. Thunder boomed, and all the critters and varmints of the forest let out a moan.

> Funny exaggeration. It looks good for Davy Crockett. I wonder why the critters and varmints *moan*?

Then Davy's Pa went back into the cabin. Little Davy was stretched out in a cradle made of a snapping turtle's shell. There was a pair of elk horns over the top, and over the elk horns was the skin of a wildcat. The cradle was run by water power, and it was rocking away—rockety-whump, rockety-whump.

> I'd like to draw a picture of this cradle.

Now all the Crocketts were big, but Davy was big even for a Crockett. He weighed two hundred pounds, fourteen ounces, and he was as frisky as a wildcat. His Ma and his Aunt Ketinah stood over Davy, trying to get him to sleep.

> Two hundred pounds! This is really a tall tale.

"Sing somethin' to quiet the boy," said Aunt Ketinah to his Uncle Roarious, who was standing in a corner combing his hair with a rake.

> I love it: combing his hair with a rake.

Uncle Roarious opened his mouth and sang a bit of "Over the River to Charley." That is, it was meant for singing. It sounded worse than a nor'easter howling around a country barn at midnight.

> Another exaggeration. His singing was pretty bad. His name is great. I just noticed it.

"Hmmm," said Uncle Roarious. He reached for a jug and took him a sip of kerosene oil to loosen up his pipes.

> *Kerosene*—isn't it poison? Another exaggeration. The uncle must have a cast-iron stomach.

Davy was sitting up in his cradle. He kept his peepers on his uncle, watching him pull at the jug.

"I'll have a sip o' the same," said Davy, as loud as you please.

That kerosene jug slipped right out of Uncle Roarious's hand. Davy's Ma and his Aunt Ketinah let out a shriek.

"Why, the little shaver can talk!" said Davy's Pa.

"We-ell," said Davy, talking slow and easy-like, "maybe I don't jabber good enough to make a speech in Congress, but I reckon I got the hang of 'er. It's nothin' to Davy Crockett."

> I wonder why he mentions Congress?

"That's mighty big talk, Son," said Davy's Pa.

"It ought to be," said Davy. "It's comin' from a big man."

> That baby's growing pretty fast. Exaggeration.

And with that he leaped out of his cradle, kicked his heels together, and crowed like a rooster. He flapped his arms and he bellowed, "I'm Davy Crockett, fresh from the backwoods! I'm half horse, half alligator, with a little touch o' snappin' turtle! I can wade the Mississippi, ride a streak o' lightnin', hug a bear too close for comfort, and whip my weight in wildcats! I can out-eat, out-sleep, out-fight, out-shoot, out-run, out-jump, and out-squat any man in these here United States! And I will!''

Aunt Ketinah eyed him as if he was a little bit of a mosquito making a buzz.

"That'll be enough o' your sass," said she, kind of sharp-like. "Now get back into your cradle and behave."

"Yes, ma'am," said Davy. He was always polite to the ladies.

"No such thing!" said Uncle Roarious. "Settin' in the cradle won't grow him none! We've got to plant him in the earth and water him with wild buffalo's milk, with boiled corncobs and tobacco leaves mixed in."

"Can't do any harm," said Davy's Ma.

"Might do good," said Davy's Pa.

"Suits me," said Davy. "Let's give 'er a try."

So they took Davy out to Thunder Shower Hill and planted him in the earth. They watered him with wild buffalo's milk, with boiled corncobs and tobacco leaves mixed in. The sun shone on him by day, and the moon beamed down on him by night. The wind cooled him and the rain freshened him. And Davy Crockett began to grow proper.

—from "The Legendary Life of Davy Crockett,"
Irwin Shapiro

I like this part. More exaggeration.

After all that, to look at him as if he's a *mosquito*! Tough lady.

A wild story, more exaggeration. Davy's part of the earth, like a plant.

So what's going to happen next? He's like Superman.

Thinking Over the Story

Suppose these were your own responses to the story, and that you were using them as prewriting notes. You'd notice one main response: You found a lot of exaggeration, and it was comic. You also noticed how Davy Crockett has superhuman powers—another instance of exaggeration. You could gather details for your composition by filling out a chart like this one:

Exaggeration in Davy Crockett Story
1.
2.
3.
etc.

Your next step would be to formulate a topic sentence. This sentence should set forth the principal idea of your essay. In the sample topic sentences that follow, notice how each includes the story's title and author. Does one of the sentences seem best to state the main idea of your composition? Can you think of another topic sentence that would better describe your main idea?

1. "The Legendary Life of Davy Crockett" by Irwin Shapiro is full of comic exaggeration that makes Davy into a superman.
2. The exaggeration in "The Legendary Life of Davy Crockett" by Irwin Shapiro makes me realize that nothing in this story could be true. I wonder if Davy Crockett ever really existed.
3. There is a lot of funny exaggeration in "The Legendary Life of Davy Crockett" by Irwin Shapiro.

NINKI

Shirley Jackson

Life Among the Savages is Shirley Jackson's comic view of that familiar territory, American family life. Notice how this episode from that book exaggerates the characters' behavior. Notice also how it gives comic human characteristics to the household animals. Shirley Jackson's amused and amusing mind can make a trivial household event seem like an adventure. You might remember Jackson's humorous story about her son Laurie, who used to report on the very bad child called Charles in his kindergarten class. This episode takes place right after the mother discovered there was no Charles. The mother tells the story.

My husband, moved by some obscure impulse, . . . bought himself an air gun. I have never really believed that my husband is the Kit Carson[1] type, but it is remotely possible that occasionally a feeling for the life romantic overcomes him; this air gun was large and menacing and he told me, in that terribly responsible voice men get to using when they are telling their wives about machinery, or guns, or politics, that he got it for target practice.

There had been a rat in the cellar, he said; he was sure he had seen a rat when he went down to start the furnace. So, of course, he was going to shoot it. Not trap it or poison it—that was for boys and terriers; *he* was going to shoot it.

For the better part of a Sunday morning he crouched dangerously at the open cellar door, waiting for the rat to show his whiskers, which the rat was kind enough not to do. Our two excellent cats were also staying inside, sitting complacently and with some professional interest directly behind my husband. The rat hunt was broken up when the kitchen door banged open and Laurie crashed in with three friends to see how his father shot the rat. Eventually, I suppose, the rat wandered off, although I do not see how he could conceivably have been frightened by the prospect of being shot. Probably he had never realized until then that he had strayed into a house with cats *and* children. At any rate, my husband and the cats, hunting in a pack, managed to bring down even better game; it must have been about the Tuesday after the rat hunt that our female cat, Ninki, who is something of a hunter, caught a chipmunk. She has done this before and will do it again, although I am sure she will never again ask my husband to sit in with her. The chipmunk she caught that morning—it was about nine-thirty—was not cooperative, and when Ninki brought him into the kitchen, where she usually brings chipmunks with some odd conviction that she must eat them in her own dish, the chipmunk ducked under her paw and raced madly to a rather tall plant on the windowsill. The plant was just strong enough to bear the weight of one chipmunk, and

Ninki, in a sort of frenzy, hurried into the dining room where my husband was just finishing his coffee and talked him into going into the kitchen to see her chipmunk in the plant. My husband took one look and went for his air gun.

Ninki was able to get onto the windowsill, but the plant was tall enough and the pot it stood in shaky enough so that she could not quite reach the chipmunk, who was standing precariously on the very top of the plant. My husband drew a careful bead with the air gun and then found that unless he stepped up and held his weapon against the chipmunk's head, he stood a very good chance of missing the chipmunk, if not actually the cat, who was a large and intrusive target.

By this time, of course, I had put down my coffee cup and was standing in the doorway between the kitchen and the dining room, safely out of range as women should be when men are hunting, and saying things like "Dear, why don't you put a paper bag over it or something and take it outside?" and "Dear, don't you think it would be easier if—"

Ninki was by this time irritated beyond belief by the general air of incompetence exhibited in the kitchen, and she went into the living room and got Shax, who is extraordinarily lazy and never catches his own chipmunks, but who is, at least, a cat, and preferable, Ninki saw clearly, to a man with a gun. Shax sized up the situation with a cynical eye, gave my husband and his gun the coldest look I have ever seen a cat permit himself,

---

1. **Kit Carson** (1809–1868): American frontiersman known for his hunting skills.

Adverbs. Shirley Jackson uses many descriptive words to help you "see" the scenes she describes. These words include *adverbs*, which can tell how an action occurs by modifying a verb. (Adverbs can also modify adjectives and other adverbs.) In the following passage from "Ninki," the adverb is set in italic type. What word does it modify?

For the better part of a Sunday morning he crouched *dangerously* at the open cellar door. . . .

Many adverbs that modify verbs are easy to spot because they end in the suffix *-ly*.

and then leaped onto the windowsill and sat on the other side of the flowerpot. It made a pretty little tableau:[2] Ninki and Shax sitting on either side of the flowerpot and the chipmunk sitting on top of the plant.

After a minute the chipmunk—feeling rightly that all eyes were upon him—fidgeted nervously, and the plant began to sway. As the chipmunk was very nervous and the top of the plant very supple, soon the top of the plant began to swing from side to side, like a pendulum, so that the chipmunk, going faster and faster, rocked over to one cat and then to the other, grazing a nose of each, while they backed away dubiously. My husband still had his aim on the chipmunk, and *he* began to rock back and forth. When the cats finally realized what was happening, they took turns batting the chipmunk as he swung between them.

All of this happened so quickly that I believe—unless I prefer to move out I have no choice *but* to believe—that my husband pressed the trigger of the air gun without really meaning to, because it is certain that he missed the chipmunk and the cats, and hit the window. The crash sent cats, chipmunk, and Nimrod[3] in all directions—the cats under the table, the chipmunk, with rare presence of mind, out the broken window, and my husband, with even rarer presence of mind, back to the dining room and to his seat at the table. I advanced from my post in the kitchen doorway and picked up the air gun from the floor; then, with what I regard as unique forbearance,[4] I went for the broom and dustpan. All I permitted myself, spoken gently and without undue emphasis, was "Thank heaven Laurie is in school."

I was indulgent enough to return the air gun to my husband after a few days, but I would have thought that Ninki had more sense. Perhaps she never dreamed I would give the air gun back, or perhaps she just thought target practice around the house had been given up as impractical; perhaps, with some kind of feline optimism I cannot share, she believed that the chipmunk episode had been a freak, the sort of thing that might happen to any man confronting an oscillant[5] chipmunk.

So it was not more than a week later that Ninki gave the air gun another chance. It was a cool evening, and I was lying on the couch with a blanket over me, reading a mystery story; my husband was sitting quietly in his chair reading the newspaper. We had just congratulated one another on the fact that it was now too late for casual guests to drop in, and my husband had mentioned three or four times that he thought he might like some of that pot roast in a sandwich before he went to bed. Then we heard Ninki's unmistakably triumphant mighty-hunter howl from the dining room.

"Look," I said apprehensively, "Ninki's got something, a mouse or something. *Make* her take it outside."

"She'll get it out by herself."

"But she'll chase it around and around and around the dining room and kill it there and—" I gulped unhappily "—eat it. Get it out *now* while it's still alive."

"She won't—" my husband began, when Ninki's triumphant wail broke off with a muffled oath and Ninki herself came hurriedly to the dining room door and stared compellingly at my husband.

"Do you *always* need help?" he asked her crossly. "Seems to me a great big cat like you—"

I shrieked. Ninki lifted her head resignedly, as one whose bitterest views of fate have been confirmed; my husband gasped. Ninki's supper, a full-grown and horribly active bat, was sweeping magnificently down the length of the living room. For a minute I watched it with my mouth open and then, still yelling, buried my head under the blanket.

"My gun," I heard my husband shouting at Ninki, "where is my gun?"

Even under the blanket I could hear the flap of the bat's wings as it raced up and down the living

---

2. **tableau** (tab′lō): striking, dramatic scene or picture.
3. **Nimrod** (nim′räd): Biblical figure referred to as a mighty hunter.
4. **forbearance** (fôr·ber′əns): self-control; patient restraint; keeping oneself in check.

5. **oscillant:** alternate form of *oscillating* (äs′ə·lāt·ing), swaying back and forth.

room; I put my knees under my chin and my arms over my head and huddled under the blanket. Outside, they were stalking the bat; I could hear my husband tiptoeing warily down the room, with Ninki apparently right behind him, because he was saying, "Don't *hurry,* for heaven's sake, give me a chance to *aim.*"

A hideous thought came to me. "Is it on me?" I said through my teeth, "just tell me once, is it on me, on the blanket? Ninki, *is* it? Is it?"

"Now you just stay perfectly still," my husband said reassuringly. "These things never stay in one place for very long. Why, only the other day I was reading in the paper about a woman who—"

"Is it on the *blanket?*" I insisted hysterically, "on *me?*"

"Listen," my husband said crossly, "if you keep on shaking like that, I'll *never* be able to hit it. Hold still, and I'm sure to miss you."

I do not know what the official world's record

might be for getting out from under a blanket, flying across a room, opening a door and a screen door, and getting outside onto a porch with both doors closed behind you, but if it is more than about four seconds I broke it. I thought the bat was chasing me, for one thing. And I knew that, if the bat were chasing me, my husband was aiming that gun at it, wherever it was. Outside on the porch, I leaned my head against the middle pillar and breathed hard.

Inside, there was a series of crashes. I recognized the first as the report of the air gun. The second sounded irresistibly like a lamp going over, which is what it turned out to be. The third I could not identify from the porch, but my husband said later that it was Ninki trying to get out of the way of the air gun and knocking over the andirons.[6] Then my husband spoke angrily to Ninki, and

---

6. **andirons** (an′dī′ərnz): metal supports used to hold wood in a fireplace.

Ninki snarled. Each of them, it seemed, thought the other one had frightened the bat, which had left the blanket when I did, although not half so fast, and was circling gaily around the chandelier.

"Come on in," my husband said through the door; he tried to open it but I was hanging on from the outside; "Come on in, it won't hurt you. I promise it won't."

"I'll stay out here," I said.

"It's just as frightened as you are," he said.

"It is *not,*" I said.

Then he apparently spoke to Ninki again, because he said excitedly, "It's landing; keep away now, you'll be hurt."

There was a great noise of rushing and snarling and shooting, then a long silence. Finally I asked softly, "Are you all right?"

Another silence. "Are you all *right?*" I said.

Another silence. I opened the door a crack and peered in cautiously. My husband was sitting on the couch, beating his hands on his knees. The air gun was on the floor. Ninki and the bat were gone.

"Is it all right to come in?" I asked.

"I don't know," my husband said, looking at me bitterly, "have you got a ticket?"

"I mean," I said, "where's the bat?"

"She's taken it into the dining room," my husband said.

There was a nick in the wallpaper over the couch. In the dining room Ninki was growling pleasurably, deep in her throat. "She went faster than the pellet, is all," my husband said reasonably. "I was just getting ready to aim and she passed me and passed the pellet and hit the bat just as the pellet hit the wall."

"Hadn't you better get it out of the dining room?" I asked.

He began to beat his knees again. I went back to the couch, shook the blanket thoroughly to make sure there had been only one bat on it and that one was gone, and settled down in my chair with my mystery story. After a while Ninki came out of the dining room, nodded contemptuously at my husband, glanced at me and, with a grin at the air gun, got onto my husband's chair and went to sleep on his paper.

I took the air gun and put it on the top shelf of the pantry, where I believe it still is. Now and then it occurs to me that in case of burglars I can take it down to protect the house, but I really think one of the kitchen knives would be safer, if Ninki is not around to take care of me.

Responding to the Story

Analyzing the Story

Identifying Facts

1. The narrator's husband says he acquired an air gun for target practice. What kind of targets did he have in mind?
2. In the first hunting expedition, what creature does the husband stalk? Describe the outcome of the hunt.
3. Describe Ninki's actions during the chipmunk hunt. What is the outcome of the episode?
4. What animal enters the house about one week later? Describe how it is conquered.

Interpreting Meanings

5. Part of the story's fun comes from the situations that develop. Which of the following situations did you find most amusing? (You can choose another situation if you'd like.) Give three reasons for your choice.

   a. The chipmunk, perched at the top of the kitchen plant, swings from Ninki to Shax.
   b. The husband shoots at the chipmunk.
   c. The husband and Ninki stalk the bat.
   d. The narrator zooms out of the house to avoid the bat.

6. The story's fun also comes from the descriptions of the husband as a bumbling hunter. Describe three things he does that you found funny.

7. Find places where Shirley Jackson characterizes Ninki as if the cat had human thoughts and feelings. Find places where her husband speaks seriously to the cat, as if Ninki were a person. Discuss whether Jackson's descriptions of the cat, bat, and chipmunk add to your enjoyment of the story. Read aloud the passages that made you laugh.

Evaluating the Story

8. Did you find the story a believable account of the goings-on in a family even though the writer **exaggerated** some details to make the story seem funnier? Give specific evidence from the story to back up your opinion.

Writing About the Story

A Creative Response

1. Changing the Point of View. The story is told from the **point of view** of the wife—the *I* of the narration. You are only told how she sees the events. For a fresh perspective, write two paragraphs retelling the chipmunk hunt from the point of view of Ninki, the chipmunk, or the husband. Use the pronoun *I* in telling what the character did, saw, and heard, and how the character felt.

A Critical Response

2. Analyzing Humor. A serious point sometimes lies just under the surface of a humorous story. An amusing story about an uncle might really be communicating love for the uncle and his peculiar ways. A ballplayer's funny tale about making two crucial errors in a baseball game might be an attempt to smooth over the anger and frustration felt while committing the errors. Do you think a serious point lies under the surface of "Ninki"? Or is the story simply about a series of funny episodes? Write one paragraph in which you give at least three reasons for your opinion.

Analyzing Language and Vocabulary

Adverbs and Puns

1. You can think of most adverbs that modify verbs as stage directions: They tell *how* an action is performed. Below are passages from the story, with adverbs in italics. Define each adverb. Then, in a sentence, explain what each adds to the passage.

a. "Our two excellent cats were also staying inside, sitting *complacently* . . . behind my husband."

b. ". . . the chipmunk, who was standing *precariously* on the very top of the plant."

c. ". . . Ninki herself came *hurriedly* to the dining room door and stared *compellingly* at my husband."

d. "Ninki lifted her head *resignedly,* as one whose bitterest views of fate have been confirmed. . . . "

e. " . . . Ninki came out of the dining room, nodded *contemptuously* at my husband. . . . "

2. A word game called "Tom Swifties" uses adverbs to create **puns,** words or phrases that have a double meaning. For example: "I like to play the piano," Tom said *grandly.* The adverb *grandly* makes you think of a grand piano as well as the manner in which Tom spoke. Which of the following adverbs best completes each Tom Swiftie below?

crabbily   listlessly   pointlessly   frankly

a. "I'd like a hot dog," Tom said _____.

b. "I hate seafood," Tom said _____.

c. "My pencil is broken," Tom said _____.

d. "I don't know what to buy," Tom said _____.

Try creating some Tom Swifties of your own. Choose an adverb with an *-ly* ending, and think of a suitable situation.

Reading About the Writer

Shirley Jackson (1919–1965) was born in San Francisco and educated at Syracuse University in New York State. She wrote humorous stories about her own family life, and is also known for her horror tales. She gained wide recognition with her chilling story "The Lottery." "Ninki" is taken from *Life Among the Savages,* a book that Jackson jokingly says "is a disrespectful memoir of my children." The sequel to that book is called *Raising Demons.* (You can guess who the demons are.)

THE RANSOM OF RED CHIEF

O. Henry

"The Ransom of Red Chief" is a long joke about a pair of kidnappers who make off with a nine-year-old boy who proves so ornery that *they* become *his* victims.

The story's fun has two sources. The first is the ability of an energetic nine-year-old child to drive his elders crazy with a flood of questions and activities.

The second source of fun is the notion of the bungling criminal. Sam, the narrator, has only a slight edge in intelligence on his partner. But Bill Driscoll is a model of the bumbling outlaw. As a team, their greatest threat is to themselves.

As you read the story, decide where your sympathies lie—with the kidnappers or with the kidnap victim.

It looked like a good thing: but wait till I tell you. We were down South, in Alabama—Bill Driscoll and myself—when this kidnapping idea struck us. It was, as Bill afterward expressed it, "during a moment of temporary mental apparition";[1] but we didn't find that out till later.

There was a town down there, as flat as a flannel cake, and called Summit, of course. It contained inhabitants of as undeleterious[2] and self-satisfied a class of peasantry as ever clustered around a May pole.

Bill and me had a joint capital of about six hundred dollars, and we needed just two thousand dollars more to pull off a fraudulent town-lot scheme in Western Illinois with. We talked it over on the front steps of the Hotel. Philoprogenitiveness,[3] says we, is strong in semirural communities; therefore, and for other reasons, a kidnapping project ought to do better there than in the radius of newspapers that send reporters out in plain clothes to stir up talk about such things. We knew that Summit couldn't get after us with anything stronger than constables and, maybe, some lackadaisical bloodhounds and a diatribe or two in the *Weekly Farmers' Budget*. So, it looked good.

We selected for our victim the only child of a prominent citizen named Ebenezer Dorset. The father was respectable and tight, a mortgage fancier and a stern, upright collection-plate passer and forecloser. The kid was a boy of ten, with bas-relief[4] freckles, and hair the color of the cover of the magazine you buy at the newsstand when

Diction. *Diction* means word choice. Part of the fun of reading this story is hearing how the narrator, Sam, talks. At times Sam uses long, difficult-sounding words to express simple ideas. Such words are sometimes used incorrectly, because he doesn't always know their meanings. Don't be discouraged by the difficult words. Look at the footnotes or a dictionary. Reading the story out loud will help you appreciate O. Henry's "fancy" diction.

---

1. **apparition** (ap'ə·rish'ən): strange, ghostly figure. Bill means *aberration* (ab'ər·ā'shən), a deviation from the normal.
2. **undeleterious** (un·del'ə·tir'ē·əs): harmless.
3. **Philoprogenitiveness** (fil'ə·prō·jen'ə·tiv·nəs): the love of parents for their children.

4. **bas-relief** (bä' rə·lēf'): slightly raised from a flat surface, as in some types of wall sculpture.

Saturday Evening Post cover, June 3, 1916.

Printed by permission of the Estate of
Norman Rockwell. © 1916 Estate of Norman Rockwell.

you want to catch a train. Bill and me figured that Ebenezer would melt down for a ransom of two thousand dollars to a cent. But wait till I tell you.

About two miles from Summit was a little mountain, covered with a dense cedar brake.[5] On the rear elevation of this mountain was a cave. There we stored provisions.

One evening after sundown, we drove in a buggy past old Dorset's house. The kid was in the street, throwing rocks at a kitten on the opposite fence.

"Hey, little boy!" says Bill, "would you like to have a bag of candy and a nice ride?"

The boy catches Bill neatly in the eye with a piece of brick.

"That will cost the old man an extra five hundred dollars," says Bill, climbing over the wheel.

That boy put up a fight like a welterweight cinnamon bear; but, at last, we got him down in the bottom of the buggy and drove away. We took him up to the cave, and I hitched the horse in the cedar brake. After dark I drove the buggy to the little village, three miles away, where we had hired it, and walked back to the mountain.

Bill was pasting court-plaster[6] over the scratches and bruises on his features. There was a fire burning behind the big rock at the entrance of the cave, and the boy was watching a pot of boiling coffee, with two buzzard tail feathers stuck in his red hair. He points a stick at me when I come up, and says:

"Ha! Cursed paleface, do you dare to enter the camp of Red Chief, the terror of the plains?"

"He's all right now," says Bill, rolling up his trousers and examining some bruises on his shins. "We're playing Indian. We're making Buffalo Bill's show look like magic-lantern[7] views of Palestine in the town hall. I'm Old Hank, the Trapper, Red Chief's captive, and I'm to be scalped at daybreak. By Geronimo! That kid can kick hard."

Yes, sir, that boy seemed to be having the time of his life. The fun of camping out in a cave had made him forget that he was a captive himself. He immediately christened me Snake-eye, the Spy, and announced that, when his braves returned from the warpath, I was to be broiled at the stake at the rising of the sun.

Then we had supper; and he filled his mouth full of bacon and bread and gravy, and began to talk. He made a during-dinner speech something like this:

"I like this fine. I never camped out before; but I had a pet 'possum once, and I was nine last birthday. I hate to go to school. Rats ate up sixteen of Jimmy Talbot's aunt's speckled hen's eggs. Are there any real Indians in these woods? I want some more gravy. Does the trees moving make the wind blow? We had five puppies. What makes your nose so red, Hank? My father has lots of money. Are the stars hot? I whipped Ed Walker twice, Saturday. I don't like girls. You dassent catch toads unless with a string. Do oxen make any noise? Why are oranges round? Have you got beds to sleep on in this cave? Amos Murray has got six toes. A parrot can talk, but a monkey or a fish can't. How many does it take to make twelve?"

Every few minutes he would remember that he was a pesky redskin, and pick up his stick rifle and tiptoe to the mouth of the cave to rubber[8] for the scouts of the hated paleface. Now and then he would let out a war whoop that made Old Hank the Trapper shiver. That boy had Bill terrorized from the start.

"Red Chief," says I to the kid, "would you like to go home?"

"Aw, what for?" says he. "I don't have any fun at home. I hate to go to school. I like to camp out. You won't take me back home again, Snake-eye, will you?"

"Not right away," says I. "We'll stay here in the cave a while."

"All right!" says he. "That'll be fine. I never had such fun in all my life."

We went to bed about eleven o'clock. We spread down some wide blankets and quilts and

---

5. **brake:** here, thick growth of trees.
6. **court-plaster:** cloth that sticks to the skin, used for covering cuts and scratches.
7. **magic-lantern:** old-fashioned term for a projector showing still pictures from transparent slides.

8. **rubber:** short for *rubberneck,* an old slang term for a person who stretches his or her neck or turns the head to gaze about or stare out of curiosity.

put Red Chief between us. We weren't afraid he'd run away. He kept us awake for three hours, jumping up and reaching for his rifle and screeching: "Hist! Pard," in mine and Bill's ears, as the fancied crackle of a twig or the rustle of a leaf revealed to his young imagination the stealthy approach of the outlaw band. At last, I fell into a troubled sleep, and dreamed that I had been kidnapped and chained to a tree by a ferocious pirate with red hair.

Just at daybreak, I was awakened by a series of awful screams from Bill. They weren't yells, or howls, or shouts, or whoops, or yawps, such as you'd expect from a manly set of vocal organs—they were simply indecent, terrifying, humiliating screams, such as women emit when they see ghosts or caterpillars. It's an awful thing to hear a strong, desperate, fat man scream incontinently in a cave at daybreak.

I jumped up to see what the matter was. Red Chief was sitting on Bill's chest, with one hand twined in Bill's hair. In the other he had the sharp case knife we used for slicing bacon; and he was industriously and realistically trying to take Bill's scalp, according to the sentence that had been pronounced upon him the evening before.

I got the knife away from the kid and made him lie down again. But, from that moment, Bill's spirit was broken. He laid down on his side of the bed, but he never closed an eye again in sleep as long as that boy was with us. I dozed off for a while, but along toward sunup I remembered that Red Chief had said I was to be burned at the stake at the rising of the sun. I wasn't nervous or afraid; but I sat up and lit my pipe and leaned against a rock.

"What you getting up so soon for, Sam?" asked Bill.

"Me?" says I. "Oh, I got a kind of pain in my shoulder. I thought sitting up would rest it."

"You're a liar!" says Bill. "You're afraid. You was to be burned at sunrise, and you was afraid he'd do it. And he would, too, if he could find a match. Ain't it awful, Sam? Do you think anybody will pay out money to get a little imp like that back home?"

"Sure," said I. "A rowdy kid like that is just the kind that parents dote on. Now, you and the

Chief get up and cook breakfast, while I go up to the top of this mountain and reconnoiter."[9]

I went up on the peak of the little mountain and ran my eye over the contiguous[10] vicinity. Over toward Summit I expected to see the sturdy yeomanry of the village armed with scythes and pitchforks beating the countryside for the dastardly kidnappers. But what I saw was a peaceful landscape dotted with one man plowing with a dun mule. Nobody was dragging the creek; no couriers dashed hither and yon, bringing tidings of no news to the distracted parents. There was a sylvan[11] attitude of somnolent[12] sleepiness pervading that section of the external outward surface of Alabama that lay exposed to my view. "Perhaps," says I to myself, "it has not yet been discovered that the wolves have borne away the tender lambkin from the fold. Heaven help the wolves!" says I, and I went down the mountain to breakfast.

When I got to the cave I found Bill backed up against the side of it, breathing hard, and the boy threatening to smash him with a rock half as big as a coconut.

"He put a red-hot boiled potato down my back," explained Bill, "and then mashed it with his foot; and I boxed his ears. Have you got a gun about you, Sam?"

I took the rock away from the boy and kind of patched up the argument. "I'll fix you," says the kid to Bill. "No man ever yet struck the Red Chief but he got paid for it. You better beware!"

After breakfast the kid takes a piece of leather with strings wrapped around it out of his pocket and goes outside the cave unwinding it.

"What's he up to now?" says Bill, anxiously. "You don't think he'll run away, do you Sam?"

"No fear of it," says I. "He don't seem to be much of a homebody. But we've got to fix up some plan about the ransom. There don't seem to be much excitement around Summit on account of his disappearance; but maybe they haven't realized yet that he's gone. His folks may think he's spending the night with Aunt Jane or one of the

---

9. **reconnoiter** (rē′kə·noit′ər): explore (a territory) to find out information.
10. **contiguous** (kən·tig′yōō·wəs): near; touching; adjacent.
11. **sylvan** (sil′vən): characteristic of the woods or forest.
12. **somnolent** (som′nə·lənt): drowsy.

Saturday Evening Post cover, January 29, 1921.

neighbors. Anyhow, he'll be missed today. Tonight we must get a message to his father demanding the two thousand dollars for his return.''

Just then we heard a kind of warwhoop, such as David might have emitted when he knocked out the champion Goliath. It was a sling that Red Chief had pulled out of his pocket, and he was whirling it around his head.

I dodged, and heard a heavy thud and a kind of a sigh from Bill, like a horse gives out when you take his saddle off. A rock the size of an egg had caught Bill just behind his left ear. He loosened himself all over and fell in the fire across the frying pan of hot water for washing the dishes. I dragged him out and poured cold water on his head for half an hour.

By and by, Bill sits up and feels behind his ear and says: "Sam, do you know who my favorite Biblical character is?''

"Take it easy,'' says I. "You'll come to your senses presently.''

"King Herod,''[13] says he. "You won't go away and leave me here alone, will you Sam?''

I went out and caught that boy and shook him until his freckles rattled.

"If you don't behave,'' says I, "I'll take you straight home. Now, are you going to be good, or not?''

"I was only funning,'' says he, sullenly. "I didn't mean to hurt Old Hank. But what did he hit me for? I'll behave, Snake-eye, if you won't send me home, and if you'll let me play the Black Scout today.''

"I don't know the game,'' says I. "That's for you and Mr. Bill to decide. He's your playmate for the day. I'm going away for a while, on business. Now, you come in and make friends with him and say you are sorry for hurting him, or home you go, at once.''

I made him and Bill shake hands, and then I took Bill aside and told him I was going to Poplar Grove, a little village three miles from the cave, and find out what I could about how the kidnapping had been regarded in Summit. Also, I thought

it best to send a peremptory[14] letter to old man Dorset that day, demanding the ransom and dictating how it should be paid.

"You know, Sam,'' says Bill, "I've stood by you without batting an eye in earthquakes, fire, and flood—in poker games, dynamite outrages, police raids, train robberies, and cyclones. I never lost my nerve yet till we kidnapped that two-legged skyrocket of a kid. He's got me going. You won't leave me long with him, will you, Sam?''

"I'll be back sometime this afternoon,'' says I. "You must keep the boy amused and quiet till I return. And now we'll write the letter to old Dorset.''

Bill and I got paper and pencil and worked on the letter while Red Chief, with a blanket wrapped around him, strutted up and down, guarding the mouth of the cave. Bill begged me tearfully to make the ransom fifteen hundred dollars instead of two thousand. "I ain't attempting,'' says he, "to decry[15] the celebrated moral aspect of parental affection, but we're dealing with humans, and it ain't human for anybody to give up two thousand dollars for that forty-pound chunk of freckled wildcat. I'm willing to take a chance at fifteen hundred dollars. You can charge the difference up to me.''

So, to relieve Bill, I acceded, and we collaborated a letter that ran this way:

EBENEZER DORSET, ESQ.:

We have your boy concealed in a place far from Summit. It is useless for you or the most skillful detectives to attempt to find him. Absolutely, the only terms on which you can have him restored to you are these: We demand fifteen hundred dollars in large bills for his return; the money to be left at midnight tonight at the same spot and in the same box as your reply— as hereinafter described. If you agree to these terms, send your answer in writing by a solitary messenger tonight at half-past eight o'clock. After crossing Owl Creek on the road to Poplar Grove, there are three large trees about a hun-

---

13. **King Herod:** Herod the Great, king of ancient Israel, ordered the killing of all male children less than two years old.

14. **peremptory** (pə·remp′tə·rē): commanding; barring all question or debate.
15. **decry** (di·krī′): speak out against strongly; denounce.

dred yards apart, close to the fence of the wheat field on the right-hand side. At the bottom of the fence post, opposite the third tree, will be found a small pasteboard box.

The messenger will place the answer in this box and return immediately to Summit.

If you attempt any treachery or fail to comply with our demand as stated, you will never see your boy again.

If you pay the money as demanded, he will be returned to you safe and well within three hours. These terms are final, and if you do not accede to them no further communication will be attempted.

TWO DESPERATE MEN

I addressed this letter to Dorset, and put it in my pocket. As I was about to start, the kid comes up to me and says:

"Aw, Snake-eye, you said I could play the Black Scout while you was gone."

"Play it, of course," says I. "Mr. Bill will play with you. What kind of a game is it?"

"I'm the Black Scout," says Red Chief, "and I have to ride to the stockade to warn the settlers that the Indians are coming. I'm tired of playing Indian myself. I want to be the Black Scout."

"All right," says I. "It sounds harmless to me. I guess Mr. Bill will help you foil the pesky savages."

"What am I to do?" asks Bill, looking at the kid suspiciously.

"You are the hoss," says Black Scout. "Get down on your hands and knees. How can I ride to the stockade without a hoss?"

"You'd better keep him interested," said I, "till we get the scheme going. Loosen up."

Bill gets down on his all fours, and a look comes in his eye like a rabbit's when you catch it in a trap.

"How far is it to the stockade, kid?" he asks, in a husky manner of voice.

"Ninety miles," says the Black Scout. "And you have to hump yourself to get there on time. Whoa, now!"

The Black Scout jumps on Bill's back and digs his heels in his side.

"For Heaven's sake," says Bill, "hurry back, Sam, as soon as you can. I wish we hadn't made the ransom more than a thousand. Say, you quit kicking me or I'll get up and warm you good."

I walked over to Poplar Grove and sat around the post office and store, talking with the chaw-bacons[16] that came in to trade. One whiskerando says that he hears Summit is all upset on account of Elder Ebenezer Dorset's boy having been lost or stolen. That was all I wanted to know. I bought some smoking tobacco, referred casually to the price of black-eyed peas, posted my letter surreptitiously, and came away. The postmaster said the mail carrier would come by in an hour to take the mail to Summit.

When I got back to the cave Bill and the boy were not to be found. I explored the vicinity of the cave, and risked a yodel or two, but there was no response.

So I lighted my pipe and sat down on a mossy bank to await developments.

In about half an hour I heard the bushes rustle, and Bill wabbled out into the little glade in front of the cave. Behind him was the kid, stepping softly like a scout, with a broad grin on his face. Bill stopped, took off his hat, and wiped his face with a red handkerchief. The kid stopped about eight feet behind him.

"Sam," says Bill, "I suppose you'll think I'm a renegade[17] but I couldn't help it. I'm a grown person with masculine proclivities[18] and habits of self-defense, but there is a time when all systems of egotism and predominance fail. The boy is gone. I sent him home. All is off. There was martyrs in old times," goes on Bill, "that suffered death rather than give up the particular graft they enjoyed. None of 'em ever was subjugated to such supernatural tortures as I have been. I tried to be faithful to our articles of depredation;[19] but there came a limit."

"What's the trouble, Bill?" I asks him.

"I was rode," says Bill, "the ninety miles to

---

16. **chaw-bacons** (old slang): yokels; hicks.
17. **renegade** (ren′ə·gād): traitor.
18. **proclivities** (prō·kliv′ə·tēz): natural tendencies.
19. **depredation** (dep′rə·dā′shən): robbery; plunder. The phrase "articles of depredation" alludes to the Articles of Confederation, the first constitution of the United States.

the stockade not barring an inch. Then, when the settlers were rescued, I was given oats. Sand ain't a palatable substitute. And then, for an hour I had to try to explain to him why there was nothin' in holes, how a road can run both ways, and what makes the grass green. I tell you, Sam, a human can only stand so much. I takes him by the neck of his clothes and drags him down the mountain. On the way he kicks my legs black and blue from the knees down; and I've got to have two or three bites on my thumb and hand cauterized.

"But he's gone"—continues Bill—"gone home. I showed him the road to Summit and kicked him about eight feet nearer there at one kick. I'm sorry we lose the ransom; but it was either that or Bill Driscoll to the madhouse."

Bill is puffing and blowing, but there is a look of ineffable peace and growing content on his rose-pink features.

"Bill," says I, "there isn't any heart disease in your family, is there?"

"No," says Bill, "nothing chronic except malaria and accidents. Why?"

"Then you might turn around," says I, "and have a look behind you."

Bill turns and sees the boy, and loses his complexion and sits down plump on the ground and begins to pluck aimlessly at grass and little sticks. For an hour I was afraid of his mind. And then I told him that my scheme was to put the whole job through immediately and that we would get the ransom and be off with it by midnight if old Dorset fell in with our proposition. So Bill braced up enough to give the kid a weak sort of a smile and a promise to play the Russian in a Japanese war with him as soon as he felt a little better.

I had a scheme for collecting the ransom without danger of being caught by counterplots that ought to commend itself to professional kidnappers. The tree under which the answer was to be left—and the money later on—was close to the road fence with big, bare fields on all sides. If a gang of constables should be watching for anyone to come for the note, they could see him a long way off crossing the fields or in the road. But no, sirree! At half-past eight I was up in that tree as well hidden as a tree toad, waiting for the messenger to arrive.

Exactly on time, a half-grown boy rides up the road on a bicycle, locates the pasteboard box at the foot of the fence post, slips a folded piece of paper into it, and pedals away again back toward Summit.

I waited an hour and then concluded the thing was square. I slid down the tree, got the note, slipped along the fence till I struck the woods, and was back at the cave in another half an hour. I opened the note, got near the lantern, and read it to Bill. It was written with a pen in a crabbed hand,[20] and the sum and substance of it was this:

Two Desperate Men:

Gentlemen: I received your letter today by post, in regard to the ransom you ask for the return of my son. I think you are a little high in your demands, and I hereby make you a counter-proposition, which I am inclined to believe you will accept. You bring Johnny home and pay me two hundred and fifty dollars in cash, and I agree to take him off your hands. You had better come at night, for the neighbors believe he is lost, and I couldn't be responsible for what they would do to anybody they saw bringing him back. Very respectfully,

Ebenezer Dorset

"Great Pirates of Penzance," says I; "of all the impudent—"

But I glanced at Bill, and hesitated. He had the most appealing look in his eyes I ever saw on the face of a dumb or a talking brute.

"Sam," says he, "what's two hundred and fifty dollars, after all? We've got the money. One more night of this kid will send me to a bed in Bedlam.[21] Besides being a thorough gentleman, I think Mr. Dorset is a spendthrift for making us such a liberal offer. You ain't going to let the chance go, are you?"

"Tell you the truth, Bill," says I, "this little he ewe lamb has somewhat got on my nerves too. We'll take him home, pay the ransom, and make our getaway."

---

20. **crabbed** (krab′id) **hand:** cramped and irregular handwriting that is hard to read.
21. **Bedlam:** old insane asylum in London; hence, any insane asylum, or hospital for the mentally ill.

We took him home that night. We got him to go by telling him that his father had bought a silver-mounted rifle and a pair of moccasins for him, and we were to hunt bears the next day.

It was just twelve o'clock when we knocked at Ebenezer's front door. Just at the moment when I should have been abstracting the fifteen hundred dollars from the box under the tree, according to the original proposition, Bill was counting out two hundred and fifty dollars into Dorset's hand.

When the kid found out we were going to leave him at home he started up a howl like a calliope[22]

---

22. **calliope** (kə·lī′ə·pē′): keyboard instrument like an organ, with a series of whistles sounded by steam or compressed air.

and fastened himself as tight as a leech to Bill's leg. His father peeled him away gradually, like a porous plaster.

"How long can you hold him?" asks Bill.

"I'm not as strong as I used to be," says old Dorset, "but I think I can promise you ten minutes."

"Enough," says Bill. "In ten minutes I shall cross the Central, Southern, and Middle Western States, and be legging it trippingly for the Canadian border."

And, as dark as it was, and as fat as Bill was, and as good a runner as I am, he was a good mile and half out of Summit before I could catch up with him.

Responding to the Story

Analyzing the Story

Identifying Facts

1. Explain why Sam and Bill decide to kidnap someone. Why do they choose Ebenezer Dorset's son?
2. Describe how the boy reacts when he is first kidnapped. How does he behave when he reaches the cave?
3. List three things Johnny does to terrorize Bill.
4. When Bill loses all patience, what does he tell the boy to do? Explain whether the boy obeys him.
5. The kidnappers send a ransom note to Ebenezer Dorset. List the two main conditions in the note for returning Dorset's son.
6. Describe Dorset's reply to the ransom note.
7. Explain whether Sam and Bill's kidnapping adventure was successful.

Interpreting Meanings

8. One way a writer makes us laugh is by **exaggerating**—overstating or otherwise enlarging the truth. List four examples of exaggeration in the story. Then explain whether or not the story remains believable despite the writer's use of exaggeration. Could a similar kidnapping occur in real life?
9. **Foreshadowing** means that a writer drops clues about what will happen later in a story. In this way you are prepared for later events, and your interest may be hooked. Look at the very first things we see Johnny doing. How do they foreshadow the kind of character he turns out to be?
10. Some of the fun of the story results from **irony**. There are several types of irony. **Irony of situation** is when something turns out very differently from what you expect. For example, if an excellent speller misspells an easy word like "train" in a contest, that's ironic. Explain the irony in Mr. Dorset's reply to the ransom note.

Applying Meanings

11. Do you think any subject can be treated comically? Can a talented writer or comedian make us laugh at illness or death or war—or kidnapping? Or do you think some subjects shouldn't be laughed at? Give reasons to support your opinion.

Writing About the Story

A Creative Response

1. **Making Up an Inappropriate Name.** Early in the story Sam says, "There was a town down there, as flat as a flannel cake, and called Summit, of course." What is funny about Summit's name? Make up three other inappropriate names of towns, and in a sentence tell how the towns are misnamed. Names like Beach Haven, Mountain View, and Fairlawn have comic possibilities.

A Critical Response

2. **Responding to the Story.** "The Ransom of Red Chief" includes a number of episodes. If the story amused you, describe the episode you think is funniest. Explain why you find it so amusing. Is it the action involved? The irony of the situation? The words used by the narrator? Something else? Or a combination of qualities? Perhaps you did not find the story amusing. If so, explain your response. Analyze an episode to prove your point. Can you pick one word to describe the story?

Analyzing Language and Vocabulary

Diction

Diction refers to the kinds of words a writer chooses. In this story, the diction of Sam and Bill is what we'd call "elevated" or "high flown." The intended meaning is sometimes difficult to figure out at first reading. The following are passages from the story. Translate each into "plain English." The first is done for you.

1. "It contained inhabitants of as undeleterious and self-satisfied a class of peasantry as ever clustered around a May pole."

   The people who lived there were harmless and self-satisfied hicks.

2. "Philoprogenitiveness, says we, is strong in se-mirural communities; therefore, and for other reasons, a kidnapping project ought to do better there than in the radius of newspapers that send reporters out in plain clothes to stir up talk about such things."

3. "There was a sylvan attitude of somnolent sleepiness pervading that section of the external outward surface of Alabama that lay exposed to my view."

4. "'I ain't attempting,' says he, 'to decry the celebrated moral aspect of parental affection. . . .'"

5. "I'm a grown person with masculine proclivities and habits of self-defense, but there is a time when all systems of egotism and predominance fail."

Reading About the Writer

"O. Henry" (1862–1910) was the pen name for William Sydney Porter, who wrote almost three hundred short stories in his relatively brief life. He grew up in Greensboro, North Carolina. His mother died when he was young, and his aunt, who ran a private school, took over his education. It was she who fired him with the enthusiasm to read and later to write.

Porter moved to Texas when he was twenty years old, and there he edited a humorous magazine called *The Rolling Stone.* He also took a job at a bank, and was charged with embezzlement. No one is sure if he was guilty or not, but he fled the country and sailed to Honduras. He returned home because of his wife's illness and was obliged to face trial. Convicted of embezzlement, he went to jail for three years. His famous pen name supposedly was taken from the name of a prison guard, Orrin Henry.

Porter moved to New York in 1902. He took to life in the city, prowling streets, cafes, and stores and collecting snatches of conversation. He turned many of his experiences into fiction. His trademark became the "surprise ending."

Porter would often lock himself in a room for three or four days in order to write. In response to a friend's amazement at this habit, he said: "I have to get a story off my chest as soon as possible. . . . I have to top it off while my interest is still hot. Once I begin a yarn I must finish it without stopping or it kinda goes dead on me."

When Porter died, he was nearly penniless. A humorist to the last, he said wryly, as he walked into the hospital and pulled all the cash he had from his pockets: "I've heard of people being worth thirty cents, and here I am going to die and only worth twenty-three cents."

THE COUNTERFEIT SECRET CIRCLE MEMBER GETS THE MESSAGE,
or THE ASP STRIKES AGAIN

Jean Shepherd

Television sets weren't common until the 1950's. Before then, radios provided family entertainment. Most Americans were just as devoted to their favorite radio shows as you are to your favorite television shows. In this story the narrator remembers himself long ago, when he was a seven-year-old in Indiana and was devoted to a particular radio program.

Read the story out loud to the end of the sixth paragraph. Then stop and discuss at least two ways that the boy's experiences with radio are like your generation's experiences with television.

Every day when I was a kid I'd drop anything I was doing, no matter what it was—stealing wire, having a fistfight, siphoning gas—no matter what, and tear like a blue streak through the alleys, over fences, under porches, through secret short cuts, to get home not a second too late for the magic time. My breath rattling in wheezy gasps, sweating profusely from my long cross-country run, I'd sit glassy-eyed and expectant before our Crosley Notre Dame Cathedral model radio.

I was never disappointed. At exactly five-fifteen, just as dusk was gathering over the picturesque oil refineries and the faint glow of the muttering Open Hearths[1] was beginning to show red against the gloom, the magic notes of an unforgettable theme song came rasping out of our Crosley:

Who's that little chatterbox . . . ?
The one with curly golden locks. . . .
Who do I see . . . ?
It's Little Orphan Annie.

Ah, they don't write tunes like that anymore. There was one particularly brilliant line that dealt with Sandy, Little Orphan Annie's airedale sidekick. Who can forget it?

Arf goes Sandy.

I think it was Sandy more than anyone else that drew me to the Little Orphan Annie radio pro-

Context Clues. As you read, you are bound to come across unfamiliar words. What do you do when this happens? You can just skip over the word. Of course, you may miss something important that way. Or you can stop everything and look up the word in a dictionary. There's another alternative. You can examine the word's *context*—the words and sentences surrounding the unfamiliar word—for clues to its meaning. As you read this story, try to determine the meaning of unfamiliar words by looking at the context. If the context doesn't help, check a dictionary, or the glossary at the end of this book. (Some difficult words are also footnoted.)

1. **Open Hearths:** furnaces used in making steel.

gram. Dogs in our neighborhood never went "Arf." And they certainly were a lot of things, but never faithful.

Little Orphan Annie lived in this great place called Tompkins Corners. There were people called Joe Corntassle and Uncle. They never mentioned the poolroom. There were no stockyards or fistfights. Or drunks sleeping in doorways in good old Tompkins Corners. Orphan Annie and Sandy and Joe Corntassle were always out chasing pirates or trapping smugglers, neither of which we ever had in Indiana as far as I knew. We had plenty of hubcap stealers and once even a guy who stole a lawn. But no pirates. At least they didn't call them that.

She also had this friend named The Asp, who

whenever she was really in a tight spot would just show up and cut everybody's head off. I figured that if there was anything a kid of seven needed it was somebody named The Asp. Especially in our neighborhood. He wore a towel around his head.

Immediately after the nightly adventure, which usually took place near the headwaters of the dreaded Orinoco,[2] on would come a guy named Pierre André, the *definitive*[3] radio announcer.

"FELLAS AND GALS. GET SET FOR A MEETING OF THE LITTLE ORPHAN ANNIE SECRET CIRCLE!"

His voice boomed out of the Crosley like some monster, maniacal pipe organ played by the Devil himself. Vibrant, urgent, dynamic, commanding. Pierre André. I have long had a suspicion that an entire generation of Americans grew up feeling inferior to just the *names* of the guys on the radio. Pierre André. Harlow Wilcox. Vincent Pelletier. Truman Bradley. Westbrook Van Voorhees. André Baruch. Norman Brokenshire. There wasn't a Charlie Shmidlap in the lot. Poor little Charlie crouching next to his radio—a born right fielder. Playing right field all of his life, knee-deep in weeds, waiting for a flyball that never comes and more than half afraid that one day they *will* hit one in his direction.

"OKAY, KIDS. TIME TO GET OUT YOUR SECRET DECODER PIN. TIME FOR ANOTHER SECRET MESSAGE DIRECT FROM LITTLE ORPHAN ANNIE TO MEMBERS OF THE LITTLE ORPHAN ANNIE SECRET CIRCLE."

I got no pin. A member of an Out-Group at the age of seven. And the worst kind of an Out-Group. I am living in a non-Ovaltine-drinking[4] neighborhood.

"ALL RIGHT. SET YOUR PINS TO B–7. SEVEN . . . TWENTY-TWO . . . NINETEEN . . . EIGHT . . . *FORTY-NINE* . . . SIX . . . THIRTEEN . . . *THREE!* . . . TWENTY-TWO . . . ONE . . . FOUR . . . NINETEEN."

Pierre André could get more out of just numbers than Orson Welles was able to squeeze out of *King Lear*.

"FOURTEEN . . . NINE . . . THIRTY-TWO. OKAY, FELLAS AND GALS, OVER AND OUT."

Then—silence. The show was over and you had a sinister feeling that out there in the darkness all over the country there were millions of kids—decoding. And all I could do was to go out into the kitchen where my mother was cooking supper and knock together a salami sandwich. And plot. Somewhere kids were getting the real truth from Orphan Annie. The message. And I had no pin. I lived in an oatmeal-eating family and listened to an Ovaltine radio show. To get into the Little Orphan Annie Secret Circle you had to send in the silver inner seal from a can of what Pierre André called "that rich chocolate-flavored drink that all the kids love." I had never even *seen* an Ovaltine can in my life.

But as the old truism goes, every man has his chance, and when yours comes you had better

Little Orphan Annie's secret society membership booklet, 1940.

---

2. **Orinoco** (ôr′ə·nō′kō): river in Venezuela.
3. **definitive** (di·fin′ə·tiv): most perfect.
4. **Ovaltine** (oh′vəl·tēn′): brand of powder added to milk to make a chocolate drink.

grab it. They do not make appointments for the next day. One day while I am foraging my way home from school, coming down one of my favorite alleys, knee-deep in garbage and the thrown-out effluvia of kitchen life, there occurred an incident which forever changed my outlook on existence itself, although of course at the time I was not aware of it, believing instead that I had struck the jackpot and was at last on my way into the big time.

There was a standard game played solo by almost every male kid I ever heard of, at least in our neighborhood. It was simple, yet highly satisfying. There were no rules except those which the player improvised as he went along. The game had no name and is probably as old as creation itself. It consisted of kicking a tin can or tin cans all the way home. This game is not to be confused with a more formal athletic contest called Kick the Can, which *did* have rules and even teams. This kicking game was a solitary, dogged contest of kid against can, and is quite possibly the very earliest manifestation of the Golf Syndrome.

Anyway, I am kicking condensed milk cans, baked bean cans, sardine cans along the alley, occasionally changing cans at full gallop, when I suddenly found myself kicking a can of a totally unknown nature. I kicked it twice; good, solid, running belts, before I discovered that what I was kicking was an Ovaltine can, the first I had ever seen. Instantly I picked it up, astounded by the mere presence of an Ovaltine drinker in our neighborhood, and then discovered that they had not only thrown out the Ovaltine can but had left the silver inner seal inside. Some rich family had thrown it *all* away! Five minutes later I've got this inner seal in the mail and I start to wait. Every day I would rush home from school and ask:

"Is there any mail for me?"

Day after day, eon after eon. Waiting for three weeks for something to come in the mail to a kid is like being asked to build the pyramids single-handed, using the #3 Erector set, the one without the motor. We never did get much mail around our house anyway. Usually it was bad news when it *did* come. Once in a while a letter marked OC-CUPANT arrived, offering my old man three hundred dollars on his signature only, no questions

Little Orphan Annie paper mask.

asked, "Even your employer will not be notified." They began with:

"Friend, are you in money troubles?"

My old man could never figure out how they knew, especially since they only called him OC-CUPANT. Day after day I watched our mailbox. On Saturdays when there was no school I would sit on the front porch waiting for the mailman and the sound of the yelping pack of dogs that chased him on his appointed rounds through our neighborhood, his muffled curses and thumping kicks mingling nicely with the steady uproar of snarling and yelping. One thing I knew. Trusty old Sandy never chased a mailman. And if he *had,* he would have caught him.

Everything comes to he who waits. I guess. At last, after at least two hundred years of constant vigil, there was delivered to me a big, fat, lumpy letter. There are few things more thrilling in life than lumpy letters. That rattle. Even to this day I feel a wild surge of exultation when I run my hands over an envelope that is thick, fat, and pregnant with mystery.

I ripped it open. And there it was! My simulated[5] gold plastic decoder pin. With knob. And my membership card.

It was an important moment. Here was a real

---

5. **simulated** (sim′yōo·lāt′əd): imitation.

milestone, and I knew it. I was taking my first step up that great ladder of becoming a real American. Nothing is as important to an American as a membership card with a seal. I know guys who have long strings of them, plastic-enclosed: credit cards, membership cards, identification cards, Blue Cross cards, driver's licenses, all strung together in a chain of love. The longer the chain, the more they feel they belong. Here was my first card. I was on my way. And the best of all possible ways—I was making it as a phony. A non-Ovaltine-drinking Official Member.

BE IT KNOWN TO ALL AND SUNDRY THAT MR. RALPH WESLEY PARKER IS HEREBY APPOINTED A MEMBER OF THE LITTLE ORPHAN ANNIE SECRET CIRCLE AND IS ENTITLED TO ALL THE HONORS AND BENEFITS ACCRUING THERETO.

Signed: Little Orphan Annie. Countersigned: Pierre André. In ink.

Honors and benefits. Already, at the age of seven, I am *Mister* Parker. They hardly ever even called my old man that.

That night I can hardly wait until the adventure is over. I want to get to the real thing, the message. That's what counts. I had spent the entire day sharpening pencils, practicing twirling the knob on my plastic simulated gold decoder pin. I had lined up plenty of paper and was already at the radio by three-thirty, sitting impatiently through the drone of the late afternoon soap operas and newscasts, waiting for my direct contact with Tompkins Corners, my first night as a full member.

As five-fifteen neared, my excitement mounted. Running waves of goose pimples rippled up and down my spine as I hunched next to our hand-carved, seven-tube Cathedral in the living room. A pause, a station break. . . .

Who's that little chatterbox . . . ?
The one with curly golden locks. . . .
Who do I see . . . ?
It's Little Orphan Annie.

Let's get on with it! I don't need all this jazz about smugglers and pirates. I sat through Sandy's

Drawing by Harold Gray (c. 1945).

arfing and Little Orphan Annie's perils hardly hearing a word. On comes, at long last, old Pierre. He's one of *my* friends now. I am in. My first secret meeting.

"OKAY, FELLAS AND GALS. GET OUT YOUR DECODER PINS. TIME FOR THE SECRET MESSAGE FOR ALL THE REGULAR PALS OF LITTLE ORPHAN ANNIE, MEMBERS OF THE LITTLE ORPHAN ANNIE SECRET CIRCLE. ALL SET? HERE WE GO. SET YOUR PINS AT B–12."

My eyes narrowed to mere slits, my steely claws working with precision, I set my simulated gold plastic decoder pin to B–12.

"ALL READY? PENCILS SET?"

Old Pierre was in great voice tonight. I could tell that tonight's message was really important.

"SEVEN . . . TWENTY-TWO . . . THIRTEEN . . . NINETEEN . . . *EIGHT!*"

I struggled furiously to keep up with his booming voice dripping with tension and excitement.

Finally:

" OKAY, KIDS, THAT'S TONIGHT'S SECRET MESSAGE. LISTEN AGAIN TOMORROW NIGHT, WHEN YOU HEAR. . . ."

Who's that little chatterbox . . . ?
The one with curly golden locks. . . .

Ninety seconds later I am in the only room in the house where a boy of seven could sit in privacy and decode. My pin is on one knee, my Indian Chief tablet on the other. I'm starting to decode.

7 . . .

I spun the dial, poring over the plastic scale of letters. Aha! B. I carefully wrote down my first decoded number. I went to the next.

22 . . .

Again I spun the dial. E . . .

The first word is B-E.

13 . . . S . . .

It was coming easier now.

19 . . . U.

From somewhere out in the house I could hear my kid brother whimpering, his wail gathering steam, then the faint shriek of my mother:

"Hurry up! Randy's gotta go!"

Now what!

"I'LL BE RIGHT OUT, MA! GEE WHIZ!"

I shouted hoarsely, sweat dripping off my nose.

S . . . U . . . 15 . . . R . . . E. BE SURE! A message was coming through!

Excitement gripped my gut. I was getting The Word. BE SURE . . .

14 . . . 8 . . . T . . . O . . . BE SURE TO what? What was Little Orphan Annie trying to say?

17 . . . 9 . . . DR . . . 16 . . . 12 . . . I . . . 9 . . . N . . . K . . . 32 . . . OVA . . . 19 . . . LT . . .

I sat for a long moment in that steamy room, staring down at my Indian Chief notebook. A crummy commercial!

Again a high, rising note from my kid brother.

"I'LL BE RIGHT OUT, MA! FOR CRYING OUT LOUD."

I pulled up my corduroy knickers and went out to face the meat loaf and the red cabbage. The Asp had decapitated another victim.

Responding to the Story

Analyzing the Story

Identifying Facts

1. Describe the narrator's feelings for the Little Orphan Annie radio program. Why does he call it "magic time"?
2. List three ways in which life in Tompkins Corners differs from real life in the narrator's home town in Indiana.
3. What does the boy need in order to join the Little Orphan Annie Secret Circle? Why is it so difficult for him to obtain this?
4. Eventually the boy joins the Secret Circle and receives a decoder pin. Explain how the pin is used to decode messages.
5. At the end of the story the narrator decodes a message. What is the message? Discuss his reaction to the message.

Interpreting Meanings

6. The story's title—"The Counterfeit Secret Circle Member Gets the Message, *or* The Asp Strikes Again"—is long and requires some thought. Why is the boy a *counterfeit* Secret Circle member? Who is the Asp, and how does he strike again?
7. One of the techniques of humor is **exaggeration**—magnifying or overstating the facts. Discuss how the writer of this story creates a humorous effect through exaggeration. Cite specific examples of exaggeration and explain why you found each humorous. (Your first example might come from the story's very first sentence.)
8. Jean Shepherd is known for his special brand of humor. Do you like it? Explain your reaction by referring to specific passages in the story.

Applying Meanings

9. Think of something you wanted for a long time and later actually obtained. First describe the object and how much you wanted it. Then discuss your feelings when you got it. Did you feel satisfied, let down, lucky, happy, or something else?

Writing About the Story

A Creative Response

1. **Extending the Story.** The boy has gotten the message from the Little Orphan Annie Secret Circle. He now wants to become a member in good standing. Write two or three paragraphs explaining how he convinces his family to drink Ovaltine. Use a style similar to the story's, and pick up expressions you liked. Write from the boy's point of view, using the first-person pronoun *I*. Bring at least two other family members (father, mother, kid brother) into your story. Include some humorous touches.

A Critical Response

2. **Comparing Spoken and Written Stories.** For many years Jean Shepherd hosted a radio program. The program was made up almost entirely of humorous stories told by Shepherd. They were very similar to the story you just read. When Shepherd told a story, he emphasized some words, and skipped quickly over others. There was a touch of laughter behind some, irony or seriousness or nostalgia behind others. For instance, about the Little Orphan Annie theme song Shepherd writes, "Ah, they don't write tunes like that anymore." If he had spoken the sentence, his tone could show fondness for the song, happiness in remembering childhood, irony (if he really didn't think much of the song), or something else. In a paragraph or two explain how pronunciation and tone of voice could affect the meaning of another passage. Then discuss how Shepherd might speak the passage.

Analyzing Language and Vocabulary

Context Clues

The words and sentences surrounding a word are its **context.** The context often provides clues that can help you figure out the meaning of an unfa-

miliar word. Below are passages from the story which contain words that may be unfamiliar to you. These words are set in italics. Try to determine their meanings by studying their contexts. Then check a dictionary to see whether your judgments were correct.

1. "There were no rules except those which the player *improvised* as he went along."
2. "Day after day, *eon* after eon."
3. "Everything comes to he who waits. I guess. At last, after at least two hundred years of constant *vigil,* there was delivered to me a big, fat, lumpy letter."
4. "There are few things more thrilling in life than lumpy letters. That rattle. Even to this day I feel a wild surge of *exultation* when I run my hands over an envelope that is thick. . . ."
5. ". . . [I was] sitting impatiently through the *drone* of the late afternoon soap operas and newscasts, waiting for my direct contact with Tompkins Corners. . . ."

Reading About the Writer

Jean Shepherd (1923–   ) writes humorously about growing up in the Midwest—which really isn't any different from growing up in other parts of America. Shepherd claims that he first knew he was funny at an early age. He was sitting in a high chair at the breakfast table, and his mother served him soft-boiled eggs. Finding a piece of shell in his yolk, the infant Shepherd whined "There's bricks in my eggs." Says Shepherd: "Not a knee-slapper in the Jack Benny tradition, I'll admit, but I was barely two."

Shepherd's first exposure to a wider audience for his humor occurred some thirty years later, in 1956, on a New York radio station. Shepherd delighted audiences with his stories about childhood, the army, and life in modern America. Later, Shepherd performed on stage and in his own television series, *Jean Shepherd's America.*

Shepherd's short-story collections include *In God We Trust, All Others Pay Cash* and *Wanda Hickey's Night of Golden Memories and Other Disasters.* "The Counterfeit Secret Circle Member Gets the Message" is part of the former collection, which was adapted into a movie called *A Christmas Story.* Shepherd serves as the narrator of the movie.

THE DAY THE DAM BROKE

James Thurber

It is 1913, and the West Side of Columbus, Ohio, has been ravaged by flooding of the Scioto (sī·ō′tə) River. (The 1913 flood is considered one of the worst disasters in the history of Columbus.) James Thurber and his family live on the East Side. There are no radio stations in the city, and television has not been invented yet. A rumor circulates about the East Side being threatened by water from a broken dam. Thurber's humor is based on a shrewd observation of human foolishness. Here he makes fun of our tendency to follow the crowd, especially one that is running someplace.

My memories of what my family and I went through during the 1913 flood in Ohio I would gladly forget. And yet neither the hardships we endured nor the turmoil and confusion we experienced can alter my feeling toward my native state and city. I am having a fine time now and wish Columbus were here, but if anyone ever wished a city was in hell it was during that frightful and perilous afternoon in 1913 when the dam broke, or, to be more exact, when everybody in town *thought* the dam broke. We were both ennobled and demoralized[1] by the experience. Grandfather especially rose to magnificent heights which can never lose their splendor for me, even though his reactions to the flood were based upon a profound misconception; namely, that Nathan Bedford Forrest's[2] cavalry was the menace we were called upon to face. The only possible means of escape for us was to flee the house, a step which grandfather sternly forbade, brandishing his old army saber in his hand. "Let the sons – — come!" he roared. Meanwhile hundreds of people were streaming by our house in wild panic, screaming "Go east! Go east!" We had to stun grandfather with the ironing board. Impeded as we were by the inert form of the old gentleman—he was taller than six feet and weighed almost a hundred and seventy pounds—we were passed, in the first half-mile, by practically everybody else in the city. Had grandfather not come to, at the corner of Parsons Avenue and Town Street, we would unquestionably have been overtaken and engulfed by the roaring waters—that is, if there had *been* any roaring waters. Later, when the panic had died down and people had gone rather sheepishly back to their homes and their offices, minimizing the distances they had run and offering various reasons for running, city engineers pointed out that even if the dam had broken, the water level would not have risen more than two additional inches in the West Side. The

---

1. **demoralized** (di·môr′ə·līzd): discouraged; thrown into confusion.
2. **Nathan Bedford Forrest** (1821–1877): general in the Confederate Army during the Civil War.

Prefixes. One of the ways you can try to figure out the meanings of unfamiliar words is to see if parts of the words are familiar to you. Sometimes you'll know the main part of a word; sometimes a word has a prefix you'll recognize. *Prefixes* are groups of letters added to the front of a word to affect its meaning. A commonly used prefix is *mis*- meaning "not" or "wrong." Knowing this, you should be able to figure out the meaning of the word *misconception* in the first paragraph, if you know that a conception (like a concept) is an idea. A *misconception* is a "wrong idea."

Two thousand people were abruptly in full flight.

© 1933, 1961 James Thurber. From *My Life and Hard Times*, Harper & Row.

West Side was, at the time of the dam scare, under thirty feet of water—as, indeed, were all Ohio river towns during the great spring floods of twenty years ago. The East Side (where we lived and where all the running occurred) had never been in any danger at all. Only a rise of some ninety-five feet could have caused the flood waters to flow over High Street—the thoroughfare that divided the east side of town from the west—and engulf the East Side.

The fact that we were all as safe as kittens under a cookstove did not, however, assuage[3] in the least the fine despair and the grotesque desperation which seized upon the residents of the East Side when the cry spread like a grass fire that the dam had given way. Some of the most dignified, staid, cynical, and clear-thinking men in town abandoned their wives, stenographers,

---

3. **assuage** (ə·swāj′): lessen; relieve.

homes, and offices and ran east. There are few alarms in the world more terrifying than "The dam has broken!" There are few persons capable of stopping to reason when that clarion cry strikes upon their ears, even persons who live in towns no nearer than five hundred miles to a dam.

The Columbus, Ohio, broken-dam rumor began, as I recall it, about noon of March 12, 1913. High Street, the main canyon of trade, was loud with the placid hum of business and the buzzing of placid businessmen arguing, computing, wheedling, offering, refusing, compromising. Darius Conningway, one of the foremost corporation lawyers in the Middle West, was telling the Public Utilities Commission in the language of Julius Caesar that they might as well try to move the Northern Star as to move him. Other men were making their little boasts and their little gestures. Suddenly somebody began to run. It may be that he had simply remembered, all of a moment, an engagement to meet his wife, for which he was now frightfully late. Whatever it was, he ran east on Broad Street (probably toward the Maramor Restaurant, a favorite place for a man to meet his wife). Somebody else began to run, perhaps a newsboy in high spirits. Another man, a portly gentleman of affairs, broke into a trot. Inside of ten minutes, everybody on High Street from the Union Depot to the Courthouse was running. A loud mumble gradually crystallized into the dread word "dam." "The dam has broke!" The fear was put into words by a little old lady in an electric,[4] or by a traffic cop, or by a small boy: Nobody knows who, nor does it now really matter. Two thousand people were abruptly in full flight. "Go east!" was the cry that arose—east away from the river, east to safety. "Go east! Go east! Go east!"

Black streams of people flowed eastward down all the streets leading in that direction; these streams, whose headwaters were in the dry goods stores, office buildings, harness shops, movie theaters, were fed by trickles of housewives, children, cripples, servants, dogs, and cats, slipping out of the houses past which the main streams flowed, shouting and screaming. People ran out leaving fires burning and food cooking and doors wide open. I remember, however, that my mother turned out all the fires and that she took with her a dozen eggs and two loaves of bread. It was her plan to make Memorial Hall, just two blocks away, and take refuge somewhere in the top of it, in one of the dusty rooms where war veterans met and where old battle flags and stage scenery were stored. But the seething throngs, shouting "Go east!" drew her along and the rest of us with her. When grandfather regained full consciousness, at Parsons Avenue, he turned upon the retreating mob like a vengeful prophet and exhorted[5] the men to form ranks and stand off the Rebel dogs, but at length he, too, got the idea that the dam had broken and, roaring "Go east!" in his powerful voice, he caught up in one arm a small child and in the other a slight clerkish man of perhaps forty-two and we slowly began to gain on those ahead of us.

A scattering of firemen, policemen, and army officers in dress uniforms—there had been a review at Fort Hayes, in the northern part of town—added color to the surging billows of people. "Go east!" cried a little child in a piping voice, as she ran past a porch on which drowsed a lieutenant-colonel of infantry. Used to quick decisions, trained to immediate obedience, the officer bounded off the porch and, running at full tilt, soon passed the child, bawling "Go east!" The two of them emptied rapidly the houses of the little street they were on. "What is it? What is it?" demanded a fat, waddling man who intercepted the colonel. The officer dropped behind and asked the little child what it was. "The dam has broke!" gasped the girl. "The dam has broke!" roared the colonel. "Go east! Go east! Go east!" He was soon leading, with the exhausted child in his arms, a fleeing company of three hundred persons who had gathered around him from living rooms, shops, garages, back yards, and basements.

Nobody has ever been able to compute with any exactness how many people took part in the great rout of 1913, for the panic, which extended

---

4. **electric:** automobile operated by electricity and powered by a battery.

5. **exhorted** (ig·zort′id): strongly urged.

from the Winslow Bottling Works in the South End to Clintonville, six miles north, ended as abruptly as it began and the bobtail and ragtag[6] and velvet-gowned groups of refugees melted away and slunk home, leaving the streets peaceful and deserted. The shouting, weeping, tangled evacuation of the city lasted not more than two hours in all. Some few people got as far east as Reynoldsburg, twelve miles away; fifty or more reached the Country Club, eight miles away; most of the others gave up, exhausted, or climbed trees in Franklin Park, four miles out. Order was restored and fear dispelled finally by means of militiamen riding about in motor lorries[7] bawling through megaphones: "The dam has *not* broken!" At first this tended only to add to the confusion and increase the panic, for many stampeders thought the soldiers were bellowing "The dam has now broken!" thus setting an official seal of authentication on the calamity.

All the time, the sun shone quietly and there was nowhere any sign of oncoming waters. A visitor in an airplane, looking down on the straggling, agitated masses of people below, would have been hard put to it to divine a reason for the phenomenon. It must have inspired in such an observer a peculiar kind of terror, like the sight of the *Marie Celeste*,[8] abandoned at sea, its galley fires peacefully burning, its tranquil decks bright in the sunlight.

An aunt of mine, Aunt Edith Taylor, was in a movie theater on High Street when, over and above the sound of the piano in the pit (a W. S. Hart picture was being shown),[9] there rose the steadily increasing tromp of running feet. Persistent shouts rose above the tromping. An elderly man, sitting near my aunt, mumbled something, got out of his seat, and went up the aisle at a dogtrot. This started everybody. In an instant the audience was jamming the aisles. "Fire!" shouted a woman who always expected to be burned up in a theater; but now the shouts outside were louder and coherent. "The dam has broke!" cried somebody. "Go east!" screamed a small woman in front of my aunt. And east they went, pushing and shoving and clawing, knocking women and children down, emerging finally into the street, torn and sprawling. Inside the theater, Bill Hart was calmly calling some desperado's bluff and the brave girl at the piano played "Row! Row! Row!" loudly and then "In My Harem." Outside, men were streaming across the Statehouse yard, others were climbing trees, a woman managed to get up onto the "These Are My Jewels" statue, whose bronze figures of Sherman, Stanton, Grant, and Sheridan watched with cold unconcern the going to pieces of the capital city.

"I ran south to State Street, east on State to Third, south on Third to Town, and out east on Town," my Aunt Edith has written me. "A tall spare woman with grim eyes and a determined chin ran past me down the middle of the street. I was still uncertain as to what was the matter, in spite of all the shouting. I drew up alongside the woman with some effort, for although she was in her late fifties, she had a beautiful, easy running form and seemed to be in excellent condition. 'What is it?' I puffed. She gave me a quick glance and then looked ahead again, stepping up her pace a trifle. 'Don't ask me, ask God!' she said.

"When I reached Grant Avenue, I was so spent that Dr. H. R. Mallory—you remember Dr. Mallory, the man with the white beard who looks like Robert Browning?[10]—well, Dr. Mallory, whom I had drawn away from at the corner of Fifth and Town, passed me. 'It's got us!' he shouted, and I felt sure that whatever it was *did* have us, for you know what conviction Dr. Mallory's statements always carried. I didn't know at that time what he meant, but I found out later. There was a boy behind him on roller skates, and Dr. Mallory mistook the swishing of the skates for the sound of

6. **bobtail and ragtag:** general public.
7. **lorries:** trucks.
8. *Marie Celeste:* large ship, found in 1872 in the eastern Atlantic Ocean with no one on board. Oddly, a meal seemed about ready to be served aboard ship when it was found.
9. Movies of the time did not include a soundtrack. Sound effects often were provided by a piano player located in a pit below the movie screen.

10. **Robert Browning** (1812–1889): English poet.

rushing water. He eventually reached the Columbus School for Girls, at the corner of Parsons Avenue and Town Street, where he collapsed, expecting the cold frothing waters of the Scioto to sweep him into oblivion. The boy on the skates swirled past him and Dr. Mallory realized for the first time what he had been running from. Looking back up the street, he could see no signs of water, but nevertheless, after resting a few minutes, he jogged on east again. He caught up with me at Ohio Avenue, where we rested together. I should say that about seven hundred people passed us.

A funny thing was that all of them were on foot. Nobody seemed to have the courage to stop and start his car; but as I remember it, all cars had to be cranked in those days, which is probably the reason.''

The next day, the city went about its business as if nothing had happened, but there was no joking. It was two years or more before you dared treat the breaking of the dam lightly. And even now, twenty years after, there are few persons, like Dr. Mallory, who will shut up like a clam if you mention the Afternoon of the Great Run.

Responding to the Story

Analyzing the Story

Identifying Facts

1. James Thurber proposes a theory about how the rumor of the broken dam began. Explain how he imagines it started.
2. What did Thurber's grandfather think was happening when he refused to leave the house? How did the family "convince" him to leave?
3. Describe what "a visitor in an airplane" would have seen if he or she looked down on Columbus on the day the dam supposedly broke. Why were the people shouting, "Go east"?
4. Describe how Aunt Edith Taylor heard about the broken dam. What did she do after hearing about it?
5. What did Dr. Mallory think was pursuing him? Explain whether or not he was correct.

Interpreting Meanings

6. One of the things that makes us laugh is **exaggeration**—stretching the truth for an effect. Discuss three aspects of this selection you think are exaggerated.
7. We also usually laugh when we see people behaving inappropriately. For example, we would laugh if a person dressed in a skiing outfit appeared on a golf course in July. Describe an instance of inappropriate behavior in this essay. Be sure to explain why the behavior is not fitting.

8. James Thurber made drawings to go with many of his stories. On page 88 is a drawing of Dr. Mallory, Aunt Edith, and the boy on skates. Does Thurber picture the characters as you imagined them to be? Would you suggest alterations in the drawing?

Applying Meanings

9. Do you think a panic like this one could take place in real life? Would a large number of people begin running or screaming because of a rumor, without determining the facts of the situation? Back up your answer with an actual or made up example of how a large group of people might behave after hearing a rumor.

Writing About the Story

A Creative Response

1. **Writing with Humor. Exaggeration** is a key element of Thurber's humor. You'll notice, however, that he exaggerates only selected parts of the story. If everything were exaggerated, the story would become a fantasy. Try your own hand at humor while describing a real or imaginary occurrence. Use exaggeration, but be selective about what you exaggerate. Be sure to include specific details about the occurrence. Write one or two paragraphs.

A Critical Response

2. **Examining a Writer's Style.** Much of a writer's style depends on the words used to describe characters and actions. Often, several descriptive words having roughly the same meaning could be used. A good writer can choose a word that adds something special. Here is a sentence from the selection with some noteworthy words in italics.

> Grandfather especially rose to *magnificent* heights which can never lose their *splendor* for me, even though his reactions to the flood were based upon a *profound* misconception; namely, that Nathan Bedford Forrest's cavalry was the *menace* we were *called upon* to face.

Read the second paragraph of the story. Then make a list of five words or phrases that you think are well-chosen. Next to each write down two words or phrases that have roughly the same meaning. (You might want to consult a dictionary.) Finally, make up a one-paragraph story in which you use the five words or phrases.

Analyzing Language and Vocabulary

Prefixes

A **prefix** is a group of letters that can be added to the beginning of a word to form a new word. If you become familiar with their meanings, you can figure out the meaning of many new words.

Below are three prefixes plus passages from the selection. Use the prefixes to figure out the meaning of each word in italics. Then list five new words beginning with each prefix. Finally, choose two of the words from each list and use them in original sentences.

1. *Mis-* means "not" or "wrong" or "bad."
   ". . . Dr. Mallory *mistook* the swishing of the skates for the sound of rushing water."
2. *Re-* means "again."
   "When grandfather *regained* full consciousness. . . ."
3. *Un-* means "not" or "opposite of."
   "[The] bronze figures of Sherman, Stanton, Grant, and Sheridan watched with cold *unconcern* the going to pieces of the capital city."

Reading About the Writer

Some people think that **James Thurber** (1894–1961) put Columbus, Ohio, on the map—meaning that he brought it fame. The fame came from Thurber's hilarious accounts of growing up in Columbus, and of his eccentric relatives. Some of his Columbus stories are "The Night the Bed Fell," "Snapshot of a Dog," and "The Dog That Bit People." For many years, Thurber was one of the most famous of *The New Yorker*'s writers. Thurber is also known for his cartoons, especially for his big, wise dogs. Someone once said they looked as if they had been traced from a cookie cutter.

'It's got us!' he shouted.

© 1933, 1961 James Thurber. From *My Life and Hard Times*, Harper & Row.

COMEDY

One of the greatest comic writers America has ever produced is Mark Twain. (See his story about the jumping frog on page 573.) Here is part of his story about a greenhorn who was traveling in the West.

In the following episode, the tourist is participating in a buffalo hunt, and his horse has just spied a buffalo coming toward him.

The minute [the horse] saw that buffalo bull wheel on him and give a bellow, he raised straight up in the air and stood on his heels. The saddle began to slip, and I took him round the neck and laid close to him, and began to pray. Then he came down and stood on the other end a while, and the bull actually stopped pawing sand and bellowing to contemplate the inhuman spectacle. Then the bull made a pass at him and uttered a bellow that sounded perfectly frightful, it was so close to me, and that seemed to literally prostrate my horse's reason, and make a raving distracted maniac of him, and I wish I may die if he didn't stand on his head for a quarter of a minute and shed tears. He was absolutely out of his mind—he was, as sure as truth itself, and he really didn't know what he was doing. Then the bull came charging at us, and my horse dropped down on all fours and took a fresh start—and then for the next ten minutes he would actually throw one handspring after another so fast that the bull began to get unsettled, too, and didn't know where to start in—and so he stood there sneezing, and shoveling dust over his back, and bellowing every now and then, and thinking he had got a fifteen-hundred-dollar circus horse for breakfast, certain. Well, I was first out on his neck—the horse's, not the bull's—and then underneath, and next on his rump, and sometimes head up, and sometimes heels—but I tell you it seemed solemn and awful to be ripping and tearing and carrying on so in the presence of death, as you might say. Pretty soon the bull made a snatch for us and brought away some of my horse's tail (I suppose, but do not know, being pretty busy at the time), but *something* made him hungry for solitude and suggested to him to get up and hunt for it. And then you ought to have seen that spider-legged old skeleton go! And you ought to have seen the bull cut out after him, too—head down, tongue out, tail up, bellowing like everything, and actually mowing down the weeds, and tearing up the earth, and boosting up the sand like a whirlwind! By George, it was a hot race! I and the saddle were back on the rump, and I had the bridle in my teeth and holding on to the pommel with both hands. First we left the dogs behind; then we passed a jackass-rabbit; then we overtook a coyote, and were gaining on an antelope when the rotten girths let go and threw me about thirty yards off to the left, and as the saddle went down over the horse's rump he gave it a lift with his heels that sent it more than four hundred yards up in the air, I wish I may die in a minute if he didn't. I fell at the foot of the only solitary tree there was in nine counties adjacent (as any creature could see with the naked eye), and the next second I had hold of the bark with four sets of nails and my teeth, and the next second after that I was astraddle of the main limb and blaspheming my luck in a way that made my breath smell of brimstone. I *had* the bull, now, if he did not think of *one* thing. But that one thing I dreaded. I dreaded it very seriously. There was a possibility that the bull might not think of it, but there were greater chances that he would. . . .

—from "When the Buffalo Climbed a Tree," Mark Twain

Illustration from Mark Twain's
Roughing It (1872).

Courtesy of New York Public
Library, Rare Books and
Manuscripts Division.

1. The narrator says that when the bull tried to snatch his horse's tail, he was "pretty busy at the time." What was he actually doing at the time? How is this an example of **understatement**?
2. How many examples of **exaggeration** can you find?
3. Of the three techniques of humor listed on page 57—**exaggeration, understatement,** and **irony**—which technique is most prominent here?
4. How does the narrator help you to visualize what is happening to (a) the bull, (b) the horse, and (c) the rider?
5. What do you think is the one thing the narrator dreads?
6. What do you think is going to happen next?

Writing

Describing an Action. Write a paragraph in which you describe an action. Use **exaggeration** to create humor. Try also to use vivid descriptions to help your readers see and hear what is happening. You might describe some of these actions:

1. A run for the bus
2. A swim
3. Cooking
4. Babysitting
5. Trying to write
6. Taking a test

GATHERING DATA AND WRITING A SUMMARY

Writing Assignment

Conduct a survey in which you ask five to ten adults to identify either their favorite comedian or their favorite comedy show on television. Then write a paragraph summarizing the results of your survey.

Background

What makes people laugh? Humor varies somewhat from culture to culture and from generation to generation. Even among people of the same age and culture, individual tastes can vary. Most of us, however, find **exaggeration** and its opposite, **understatement,** funny. **Verbal irony,** too, is amusing to many people. Some people enjoy **slapstick,** which involves a lot of physical activity, like slipping on banana peels. Other people enjoy **satire,** the kind of biting humor that criticizes by means of ridicule. Some people like **puns** (plays on words), **jokes,** and humorous **anecdotes** (brief funny stories).

Prewriting

1. Ask five to ten adults *one* of the following questions:

   a. Who is your favorite comedian, and what are your reasons for this choice?
   b. What is your favorite television comedy show, and why?

   You may wish to write down any interesting comments or remarks your interviewees mention, and then quote one or two of them in your final report. Personal quotations can add a feeling of human interest to your report. Often statistical data and numbers alone can make a summary dry.
2. Record their answers on a form that looks like this:

Favorite Comedian or Comedy Show		
Name of Adult	Comedian	Reason(s)
1.		
2.		
3.		
4.		
5.		
6.		
7.		
8.		
9.		
10.		

3. Tally the responses. What you are doing is assembling **statistics** (facts involving numbers). Here is how a group of ten people might have responded regarding their favorite comedians:

Comedian	Number of times named favorite
1. Bill Cosby	4
2. Steve Martin	3
3. Lily Tomlin	2
4. Eddie Murphy	1

4. When you **draw a conclusion** from **data** or evidence, word it carefully so that it reflects the actual evidence. In other words, you can't go far afield and make statements that aren't backed up by the evidence. Which of the following statements are **valid** (true and logical) conclusions that can be drawn from the data shown in the chart?

   a. There are more female comedians than male comedians.
   b. The people in the survey mentioned male

comedians more often than female comedians.

c. Of the ten people surveyed, more than half mentioned Bill Cosby as their favorite comedian.

d. Of the ten people surveyed, thirty percent chose Steve Martin as their favorite comedian.

e. Americans prefer male comedians to female comedians.

5. In summarizing the results of a survey you should mention the size of the **sample** (the number of people surveyed) and any important facts about them. You should also cite the actual statistics—either in numbers or in percentages.

Writing

Summarize the results of your survey in a paragraph. Begin by writing a topic sentence that states your findings. The rest of the paragraph should cite specific statistics from your survey and reasons to support your topic sentence. To add interest to your paragraph, include direct quotations from one or more of the people surveyed. End your summary with a sentence that briefly ties up your paragraph.

The following is a student's model summarizing the data given in the prewriting chart:

In a recent survey of ten adults (five men and five women), four different persons were mentioned as the favorite comedian. Bill Cosby was the winner with forty percent of the votes, and Steve Martin was a close second. Other favorites were Lily Tomlin and Eddie Murphy. Several people said their favorite comedian is someone they would like to know. Others said they like their favorite comedian's witty one-liners. Mrs. O'Donnell, my next-door neighbor, loves Bill Cosby because, she says, "He helps me see there's a lot to laugh at in my daily life." Although my sample was somewhat limited in size, the data I have collected suggests that Bill Cosby is among the public's favorite comedians.

Topic sentence describes sample and summarizes the overall result.

Statistics given in order of most votes to least votes.

Summarizes reasons people gave.

Quotes one person directly.

Concluding sentence closes the paragraph.

**Revising and Proofreading
Self-Check**

1. Does my summary begin with a topic sentence?

2. Have I included statistics and specific facts about the survey?

3. Are my conclusions logical and valid?

4. Have I quoted some of the reasons and comments given by people in the survey?

5. Does my summary have a concluding statement?

6. Does every sentence start with a capital letter and end with a period or other end punctuation mark? Are all the words spelled correctly?

Partner Check

1. Are there any spelling errors?

2. Are sentences punctuated correctly?

3. Are the ideas clearly expressed?

4. Are statements supported with statistics?

5. What do I like best about this paper?

6. What do I think needs improvement?

THE WORLD OF FANTASY
WISHES AND NIGHTMARES

Untitled (Staircase) by Sam Szafran (1986). Watercolor.

UNIT THREE

John Leggett

Unit Outline

THE WORLD
OF FANTASY

WISHES AND NIGHTMARES

In fantasies, anything goes—anything that can possibly be imagined. **Fantasies** are stories that do not take place in the real world. Fantasies, on the other hand, often transport us to all kinds of imaginary worlds. They can take us to desirable places like castles in the air and planets in outer space. They can also take us to undesirable places, like dungeons or dark underworlds. Fantasies can even speed us back in time to the far distant past and ahead to the unknown future.

The Fantastic World

Fantasies are set in worlds where the ordinary laws of nature can be suspended. This means that, in fantasies, princes might be transformed into toads, space explorers might be able to build houses on Mars, and machines might have the human abilities to think and scheme and love.

Sometimes the characters in fantasies have superhuman powers. King Arthur is able to pull a sword out of a rock with the slightest effort. The Green Knight can submit to a blow that takes his head off, and then he can bend over, pick his head up, and put it back on. Clark Kent, the most famous popular fantasy character, can turn into a man of steel by putting on a cape in a phone booth.

Wishes and Nightmares

Like all literature, fantasies look at the world with a dual vision. Some aspects of fantasies reveal our fondest wishes. Most people, for example, would like to be able to fly, or to defeat death, or to conquer space and time. Other aspects of fantasies reveal our worst nightmares. Most people fear being trapped in a pit or prison, swallowed by a sea monster, or burned by the fiery breath of a scaly dragon.

Why do we read such stories, particularly when they scare us and keep us awake at night? One reason might be that we feel relief when we can say to ourselves, "It's only a story after all." Another reason might be that we enjoy seeing our desires realized and our bad dreams acted out, so perhaps they will no longer haunt or trouble us.

The World of Fantasy

American magazine cover from 1929.

This poem by Edward Field presents us with a new version of a famous character in literature, the monster brought to life by Frankenstein. In the original story by English author Mary Wollstonecraft Shelley, a scientist named Frankenstein uses portions of dead bodies to create a figure shaped like a man, and then gives the creature the power to move and think by activating him with electricity. Frankenstein's creation is a scientific triumph, but it is also a moral disaster that leads to tragedy. The monster, who is actually a gentle and intelligent being, is physically a hideous patchwork of other bodies. His features are so ugly and nightmarish that no one can look at him without wanting to scream. Consequently the monster is forever denied the human companionship and love that he needs.

Edward Field's poem is based on the 1931 movie starring Boris Karloff, which changed some elements of the original story. For example, the scientist Frankenstein becomes Baron Frankenstein in the movie. As you read, picture the poem as presenting a series of film clips.

Frankenstein

Edward Field

The monster has escaped from the dungeon
where he was kept by the Baron,
who made him with knobs sticking out from each side of
    his neck
where the head was attached to the body
5   and stitching all over
where parts of cadavers° were sewed together.

He is pursued by the ignorant villagers,
who think he is evil and dangerous because he is ugly
and makes ugly noises.
10 They wave firebrands at him and cudgels° and rakes,
but he escapes and comes to the thatched cottage
of an old blind man playing on the violin Mendelssohn's°
    "Spring Song."

Hearing him approach, the blind man welcomes him:
"Come in, my friend," and takes him by the arm.
"You must be weary," and sits him down inside the
15   house.
For the blind man has long dreamed of having a friend
to share his lonely life.

The monster has never known kindness—the Baron was
    cruel—
but somehow he is able to accept it now,
20 and he really has no instincts to harm the old man,
for in spite of his awful looks he has a tender heart:
Who knows what cadaver that part of him came from?

6. cadavers (kə·dav′ərz): dead bodies; corpses.

10. cudgels (kuj′əlz): short, thick sticks or clubs.

12. Mendelssohn's (men′d'l·sənz): Felix Mendelssohn (1809–1847), a German composer.

Boris Karloff portraying the monster
in the 1931 film *Frankenstein*.

The old man seats him at table, offers him bread,
and says, "Eat, my friend." The monster
25 rears back roaring in terror.
"No, my friend, it is good. Eat—gooood"
and the old man shows him how to eat,
and reassured, the monster eats
and says, "Eat—gooood,"
30 trying out the words and finding them good too.

The old man offers him a glass of wine,
"Drink, my friend. Drink—gooood."
The monster drinks, slurping horribly, and says,
"Drink—gooood," in his deep nutty voice
35 and smiles maybe for the first time in his life.

Then the blind man puts a cigar in the monster's mouth
and lights a large wooden match that flares up in his face.
The monster, remembering the torches of the villagers,
recoils, grunting in terror.
40 "No, my friend, smoke—gooood,"
and the old man demonstrates with his own cigar.

The monster takes a tentative puff
and smiles hugely, saying, "Smoke—gooood,"
and sits back like a banker, grunting and puffing.

Now the old man plays Mendelssohn's "Spring Song" on
45   the violin
while tears come into our dear monster's eyes
as he thinks of the stones of the mob, the pleasures of
        mealtime,
the magic new words he has learned
and above all of the friend he has found.

50 It is just as well that he is unaware—
being simple enough to believe only in the present—
that the mob will find him and pursue him
for the rest of his short unnatural life,
until trapped at the whirlpool's edge
55 he plunges to his death.

Responding to the Poem

Analyzing the Poem

Identifying Details

1. Explain why the villagers think the monster is "evil and dangerous."
2. Explain why the old man welcomes the monster.
3. What does the monster experience for the first time in the old man's home?
4. What is going to become of the monster?

Interpreting Meanings

5. Who is really "evil and dangerous"—the monster or the mob? Who is really "blind," the old man or the mob?
6. What humorous touches do you find in the poem? Do you think the poem is primarily comic, or do you think it is tragic? Explain.

Applying Meanings

7. State the lesson that you think we are to learn from the old man's kindness to the monster.
8. What elements of this story reflect our wishes? Which reflect our worst nightmares and fears?

Writing About the Poem

A Creative Response

Writing a Poem. Pick a movie or TV show you know well and write a poem that narrates its basic story line. Open your poem with a description of the hero or heroine of the story and describe what is about to happen to him or her, some fate which the character is as yet unaware of. Your poem should have at least three stanzas.

Analyzing Language and Vocabulary

Synonyms and Antonyms

A **synonym** is a word that means the same or almost the same as another word. (The word *deduct* is a synonym for the word *subtract*.) An **antonym** is a word that is opposite or nearly opposite in meaning to another word. (The word *add* is an antonym for *subtract*.)

Column A contains words from Field's poem. On a separate sheet of paper, write each word from column A and indicate its antonym from column B. Then list at least one synonym for each of the words in column A. (Use a dictionary if you need help.)

A	B
ignorant	energetic
weary	approach
reassured	frightened
recoil	aware

Reading About the Writer

Edward Field (1924–   ) was born in Brooklyn, New York, and attended New York University. He "discovered" poetry during World War II when he was in England. Between bombing missions, he'd go into London on passes and buy poetry books. He says he was surprised to find there were actual *living* poets. He'd received twenty-two rejections from publishers when he finally got his first poetry collection published. Field's poetry is written in a conversational style in language that is familiar and frank. It has been described as "child-like," "open," and "funny." "Frankenstein" is one of several poems based on old movies.

Focusing on Background
A Comment from the Poet

"The part I love most in the movie *Frankenstein* is where the blind man meets the monster. For the first time, the monster's need for love is revealed and we begin to see him as a victim of a cruel world which is out to destroy him because he is different.

"What then is the meaning for us of this monster? Perhaps he stands for people of other races whom we learn to hate. Perhaps he is also a secret part of us, our forbidden feelings, that we fear and must punish in ourselves and others."

—Edward Field

The writer of this poem grew up among the Laguna Pueblo Indians of New Mexico. The traditional religion of the Laguna is based on the worship of ancestors and nature gods. Nature for the Laguna has special meaning, meaning that not everyone can understand. As you read the poem, try to picture "bear country" and feel its mystery. Do you think it is a good or bad place?

Story from Bear Country

Leslie Marmon Silko

You will know
when you walk
in bear country
By the silence
5   flowing swiftly between the juniper trees
by the sundown colors of sandrock
all around you.

You may smell damp earth
scratched away
10   from yucca roots
You may hear snorts and growls
slow and massive sounds
from caves
in the cliffs high above you.

15   It is difficult to explain
how they call you
All but a few who went to them
left behind families
         grandparents
20   and sons
         a good life.

The problem is
you will never want to return
Their beauty will overcome your memory
25   like winter sun
melting ice shadows from snow
And you will remain with them
locked forever inside yourself
         your eyes will see you
30   dark shaggy and thick.

We can send bear priests
loping after you

their medicine bags
bouncing against their chests
35   Naked legs painted black
bear claw necklaces
rattling against
their capes of blue spruce.

They will follow your trail
40   into the narrow canyon
through the blue-gray mountain sage
to the clearing
where you stopped to look back
and saw only bear tracks
45   behind you.

When they call
faint memories
will writhe around your heart
and startle you with their distance.
50   But the others will listen
because bear priests sing
beautiful songs
They must
if they are ever to call you back.

55   They will try to bring you
step by step
back to the place you stopped
and found only bear prints in the sand
where your feet had been.

60   Whose voice is this?
You may wonder
hearing this story when
after all
you are alone

Bird and Bear by Beatlen Yazz.

School of American Research.

65 hiking in these canyons and hills
while your wife and sons are waiting
back at the car for you.

But you have been listening to me
for some time now
70 from the very beginning in fact
and you are alone in this canyon of
        stillness
not even cedar birds flutter.

See, the sun is going down now
the sandrock is washed in its colors
75 Don't be afraid
        we love you
        we've been calling you
        all this time
Go ahead
80 turn around
see the shape
of your footprints
in the sand.

Responding to the Poem

Analyzing the Poem

Identifying Details

1. According to the first two stanzas of the poem, what will you hear, see, and smell in bear country?
2. Describe what happens to people who are called to bear country.
3. According to lines 31–59, why would bear priests be sent after a person in bear country?
4. The title of the poem is "Story from Bear Country." In your own words, summarize the story told in the poem.

Interpreting Meanings

5. What kind of feeling does the poem give you? What word would you use to describe its **mood** or **atmosphere**? Name at least three details in the poem that help create the mood.
6. In line 60 the speaker asks, "Whose voice is this?" Who do you think the voice, or the speaker, is? Does the identity of the speaker change over the course of the poem? Include evidence from the poem in your answer.
7. The term **metamorphosis** is used to describe a fantastic change of shape or form. What metamorphosis takes place in "Story from Bear Country"? Do you think this is a good metamorphosis, or a bad one for the person involved?

8. A **symbol** is a person, place, or thing that has its own meaning, but may also stand for something else. For example, the cartoon image of Uncle Sam is a symbol for the United States government. The Laguna Pueblo have traditionally worshiped their ancestors. Do you think the bears of bear country are symbols of the ancestors? Include passages from the poem in your discussion.

Applying Meanings

9. Do you think this story reveals something only about the Laguna people? Or does it reveal desires and fears we all share?

Writing About the Poem

A Creative Response

1. **Keeping a Diary.** Assume that you are writing a diary entry in the evening of your fifth day in bear country. Describe what bear country looks like, including its landmarks. Then discuss what you did during the day. Finally, explain what you miss about the world you left behind. Write three paragraphs. Use the first-person pronoun *I*.
2. **Imitating the Writer's Technique.** Think of another mammal, a bird, or a fish that people might be changed into. Write a poem imitating "Story from Bear Country," but call it "Story from

_____ Country." The speaker in the poem should be one of the creatures that lives in the country. The speaker should address a person ("you") who is about to enter the country. Include details describing what the person will see, hear, and smell when entering the country. Your poem should have at least three stanzas.

A Critical Response

3. **Doing Research.** In a paragraph, tell whether you think you would understand the poem more fully if you were a Laguna Pueblo. Before you answer, do some research on the Laguna in an encyclopedia or another reference book. Be sure to give specific reasons to support your opinion.

Analyzing Language and Vocabulary

Images

An **image** in literature is a description that appeals to your senses. Images usually involve your sense of sight, but they can also appeal to your sense of hearing, smell, taste, or touch.

1. Most of the images in "Story from Bear Country" appeal to your sense of sight. An example is "the sundown colors of sandrock" (line 6). List five other visual images in the poem.

2. Create five visual images of your own that could be used in describing one of the following: a beach scene, a city street, a location in the countryside. The images should be as precise and interesting as possible. For the beach scene, for instance, you might include an image such as "white seagulls swooping down toward the deep-blue water." For the country location you could include an image like "slender pine trees silhouetted against the purple evening sky."

Reading About the Writer

Leslie Marmon Silko (1948–   ), a poet, short-story writer, and novelist, grew up in Albuquerque, New Mexico. Her background is partly Laguna Pueblo. She was educated at the University of New Mexico and teaches writing there now. Silko says her work has been inspired by the stories based on ancient Indian lore that her grandmother used to tell her as a child. "Story from Bear Country" is taken from a collection of prose and poetry called *Storyteller.*

Focusing on Background
A Comment from the Poet

"The Pueblo and Navajo people in the Southwest believe that bears are special animals which should be respected. The people believe that if humans are careful not to trespass, then the bears will not harm them. However, there are stories about people who accidentally wandered into bear territory. Usually this happened to small children who got lost while camping with their parents, but sometimes an adult carelessly stepped into bear country. Contrary to popular culture stereotypes about bears being dangerous killers, the old stories reveal that the bears 'adopted' the children and adults who wandered too close to them. Years later, hunters would come home and report that far off in the distance they had sighted a human being among a group of bears feeding on wild grapes."

—Leslie Silko

A SIBERIAN SHEPHERD'S REPORT OF THE ATOM BOMB

Dino Buzzati

How do you explain an atomic-bomb explosion if you are a Siberian shepherd cut off from the modern world? Perhaps an ancient legend of your people will give you the answers you want. Legends and superstitions are devised by all cultures to offer explanations for happenings that cannot be understood or explained scientifically. As you read, decide whether the shepherd is satisfied with the fantastic explanation offered by the legend.

Among us shepherds of the tribe there is a very old legend that says when Noah gathered all the animals of creation in his ark, the animals from the mountains and from the valleys made a truce among themselves and with man, recognizing Noah as their master for the time they were to remain in the ark—all, that is, except Moma, the huge tigress that snarled when Noah approached her and was the only animal Noah feared. That was why the tigress found no room in the ark and why the flood caught her in her cave. But she was extremely strong. She remained afloat by sheer strength, swimming for forty days and forty nights and more until the waters subsided, the trees rose out of the sea and the earth reappeared. The tigress Moma was then so tired she fell asleep. She is still asleep in the depths of the great forests of Amga, Ghoi, Tepotorgo, and Urakancha.

The legend also says that when the great tigress wakes up, all the other animals will flee from the forest, for man there will be a good hunting season, and Moma will reign in the great forests until the god Beyal descends from the sky to devour her.

Who among us believes this legend? Since our solitude is so great, many stories are told around campfires and all of us are accustomed to believing and not believing. Rare and most uncertain is the news that comes to us from distant lands, for our wandering life is entrusted to the will of heaven. What, for example, do we shepherds of the steppe[1] know of the measureless realm that stretches toward the setting sun? Old laws forbid us to go beyond the boundary line, and even if we were to cross it, we should have to travel endless distances through great dangers before reaching the nearest inhabited regions. It is beyond the boundary line that lie the forests of Amga, Ghoi, Tepotorgo, and Urakancha, where the tigress Moma fell asleep at the end of the flood.

Sometimes troops of armed horsemen gallop by along the boundary line. Once in a while they stop, look toward us, make measurements, and drive red poles with strange signs into the ground. After a few days the wind of the steppe uproots the poles and carries them God knows where. Sometimes even airplanes, those strange flying machines, fly over us. Nothing else happens.

But what is the use telling all this if not to explain our uneasiness? Recently strange and dreadful things have happened. No serious harm has come to us, but we feel fearful forebodings.

1. **steppe** (step): area covered mainly by short grasses, with few trees. Large steppes are located in Siberia and the central United States.

We noticed the first unusual happening last spring. The soldiers galloped by more frequently and they drove heavier poles, which the wind would not be able to uproot, into the ground. The poles are still there.

In the middle of June, two large snakes were killed near our camp. Creatures like these had never been seen before. The following day hun-

dreds were seen. They did not bother us or our flocks—they were all moving toward the East. They were of different kinds and of every size. This strange happening astonished us.

Then we noticed that the snakes were not alone. Rats, moles, skunks, worms, and numberless kinds of insects began to cross the plain, all moving in the same direction. They were strangely mixed together, but they showed no hostility toward each other, even though they belonged to species that are ordinarily enemies.

We saw even rabbits, wild goats, and quite a number of small, four-footed creatures of whose very existence we had not known. Some of them were really very beautiful, with fur that is highly prized. Then came the birds. They, too, were fleeing toward the East, abandoning their homeland. But what were they running away from? What danger hung over them? Instinct does not easily deceive animals. Even we men were uneasy. Yet what good reason did we have to abandon the region which this year was so good for pasture? No matter how much we wondered, we could not imagine a plausible explanation for this great emigration. An earthquake? A plague? What disease could strike so many different species at the same time, the beetle as well as the marmot, the serpent as well as the wildcat? A fire? No smoke could be seen on the horizon nor did the wind smell of smoke. Someone among us jokingly mentioned the old legend of Moma the tigress. I did not like that joke at all.

Finally, it seemed that the whole forest on the other side of the boundary was empty. The last to come through were the wood pigeons and swarming columns of ants that continued for miles and miles. Some stragglers followed, a few at a time. Then the flow stopped completely. The echo of our guns ceased (these had been days of triumph for the hunters), and a sepulchral[2] silence settled over the Siberian steppe. At night, we would foolishly strain our ears. Could it be that we expected the roar of Moma the tigress?

One day this great uneasiness even took hold of our flocks. It was clear that the goats, sheep, and rams were becoming excited, that they, too, were trying to escape to the East. We had to chase some of our fleeing livestock for a long time on horseback. It was necessary to build heavy enclosures.

Many of us were afraid. For no good reason, many wanted to move camp to the East. There were bitter arguments. We finally agreed to take the advice of the elders. They met and decided—we would depart with the next dawn.

It was a hot July evening. The sun had just set and the refreshing breath of night was descending when the dogs suddenly began to bark. Just after sunset, from the direction of the forest and at a great distance, an extraordinary light was seen. It seemed as if the sun had turned back, as if its burning face had become swollen on the rim of the horizon. The mass wavered a few moments, then burst, shooting forth a whirl of frightful flames—red, white, violet, green, yellow. The sun had blown up!

How long did it last? Instinctively, I thought it was the end of the world. But it was not. When it was dark again, I raised my dazzled eyes to the zenith.[3] No, the stars were still there.

Then the thunder came. And with the thunder—so frightful a noise was never heard—came the wind, a hot, suffocating wind that took our breath away and razed[4] everything to the ground. I thought I would not be able to stand it, but the wind, too, passed on.

When we recovered our senses, we again kindled the fires the burning wind had blown out, and set forth in search of our livestock, which were fleeing crazily in every direction because the enclosure had been broken to pieces. At that moment, the necessity of the chase prevailed over every other fear. But suddenly we stopped and stood motionless—even the goats, the sheep, the old people. We were all paralyzed together.

Above the bellowing and bleating, above our excited shouts, another voice was heard. No, it was not so powerful as the thunder of a little while before. Yet in a way it was even worse. Once, twice, three times, mournful and cold, it filled the night and froze our hearts. It was the roar of the tigress.

The fires, the fires! Leaving the flock to its fate, we rushed to gather twigs and weeds to increase the number of our fires. Soon there was an almost unbroken chain of flames to protect us. At last the great tigress Moma had awakened and was coming toward us.

---

2. **sepulchral** (sə·pul′krəl): gloomy.

3. **zenith** (zē′nith): part of the sky directly overhead.
4. **razed** (rāzd): destroyed; leveled.

At that very moment a long, deep roar rose on the other side of the fires. In the darkness we could see something move. Suddenly it appeared, illuminated by the red shadows. It was she, Moma. She was not an ordinary tiger. She was a monster of gigantic proportions.

Not one of us fired. We saw that the huge beast hardly moved any longer—she was about to die. Her eyes had turned to shapeless lumps of black pulp. Her hide was scorched. On her right side was an open gash as deep as a cave, from which blood flowed.

Moma the tigress, right in front of our eyes, hunched her back to the height of two horses one standing on top of the other and let out a hellish shriek. I felt that I was done for. I fired my rifle without even aiming. The others did the same.

Her huge body fell with a crash. Was she dead? We continued to fire shot after shot, senselessly.

The tigress no longer moved.

These are the strange facts referred to at the beginning of this report. The legendary tigress really existed—and even though we immediately burned her carcass because of its horrible stench, the immense skeleton has remained right there on the spot and anyone can come and measure it. But who awakened her? Who took away her life and her promised reign? What was the terrifying explosion that night? The sun had nothing to do with it—in a few hours it was born again at just the right time and in its usual place. What had happened? Could some infernal power have taken over the forests? And if its flames devoured mighty Moma, could it not capriciously reduce us to ashes too? How then can we live calmly? No one sleeps at night and in the morning we wake up tired.

Responding to the Story

Analyzing the Story

Identifying Facts

1. A **legend** is a story that is handed down from one generation to the next among a group of people. Legends often are believed to be historically true. Usually, however, they are a mixture of fact and fiction. The legend of Moma is important to this story. Retell it in your own words.

2. The narrator reports "strange and dreadful things" that have been happening recently. He mentions a variety of wild animals. What are they doing? What is unusual about the way the animals interact with each other?

3. Extraordinary events occur early on a hot July evening. Describe what the shepherd sees just after sunset. What does he hear and feel shortly thereafter? What are the shepherd's immediate explanations for these occurences?

4. Later the same evening the shepherd says he sees the legendary Moma. How do the shepherds try to protect themselves from her? Describe what she looks like. Then explain what happens to her.

Interpreting Meanings

5. Why do soldiers on horseback drive poles into the ground near the boundary of the shepherds' land? What do you think is happening in the world beyond the boundary?

6. The Siberian shepherd in the story lives a very isolated life. He is not familiar with the modern industrial world. Extraordinary events occur, and he tries to understand them by referring to the ancient legend of Moma. Which of the extraordinary events can be explained by the legend, and which cannot be explained? Discuss whether the legend explains the events to the shepherd's satisfaction.

7. The Siberian shepherd resorts to the **fantasy world** of legend to explain unusual events. Try to explain the following occurrences on the hot July evening in a more realistic manner, without referring to the legend.

   a. the extraordinary light
   b. the thunder
   c. the huge beast that emerges from the other side of the shepherds' fires

8. You learn about the narrator by the way he tells the story and by what he does in the story. How would you **characterize** him? Is he timid or brave, intelligent or unintelligent, observant or unobservant? Are there other adjectives that could be used to describe him? Include evidence from the story to support each point you make about the narrator.

Applying Meanings

9. Many reports have been written about the atomic bomb. Physicists, government officials, military personnel—all have reported on the bomb. What do you think this report reveals about the bomb that those other, official reports probably do not reveal?
10. John's people in "By the Waters of Babylon" (page 109) and the Siberian shepherds all refer to tribal myths and taboos. Explain how all these people use myths to explain the unknowable or mysterious. Do you think myths like the one about Moma make people less fearful about things they don't understand?

Writing About the Story

A Creative Response

1. **Extending the Story.** Describe what happens to the Siberian shepherd and his companions in the month following the events of the hot July evening. Be sure to include answers to the following questions:

   a. Do the shepherd and his companions move eastward?
   b. Is there another huge explosion?
   c. Do the soldiers on horseback return?

   Write two or three paragraphs. Include as many details as possible.

A Critical Response

2. **Evaluating the Story.** In the story, animals begin fleeing long before the shepherd and his companions decide to do so. In the first of two paragraphs, summarize the explanation for this offered by the writer of the story. Include passages from the story in your summary. In the second paragraph, discuss whether you think the writer's explanation is valid. Include examples of animal and human behavior in your discussion.

Analyzing Language and Vocabulary

Synonyms

You want to describe people living together in the Siberian countryside or thirty sheep grazing together. You could speak of a *group* of people and a *group* of sheep. It would be better, however, to employ synonyms of the word *group*. In "A Siberian Shepherd's Report of the Atom Bomb," Buzzati writes about a *tribe* of people and a *flock* of sheep. When speaking about a certain animal it is common to use just one of these words. (Some of the words can refer to more than one type of animal.) In many cases you do this automatically. It is almost second nature, for instance, to say a "flock of birds."

1. At the left below are listed several types of animals. At the right are the words that name groups of these animals. Match each animal with the word that describes a group of that animal.

a. cod	1. pride
b. wolf	2. gaggle
c. lion	3. colony
d. ant	4. school
e. buffalo	5. herd
f. locust	6. pack
g. goose	7. swarm

2. The young of many animals also have special names. Match each of the following animals with the word that describes its young.

a. whale	1. kit
b. robin	2. cub
c. beaver	3. lamb
d. sheep	4. fledgling
e. goat	5. calf
f. deer	6. kid
g. bear	7. fawn

Reading About the Writer

Dino Buzzati (1906–1972) was an Italian novelist and journalist, who worked as a correspondent and editor for the noted daily *Corriere della sera* from 1928 until his death. Buzzati was born in Belluno, a small town in Northern Italy. He earned a law degree in Milan, where he spent the rest of his life. Buzzati's works tend to be dominated by images of mountains and deserts. His books include *Catastrophe and Other Stories, The Siren,* and *The Tartar Steppe.*

BY THE WATERS OF BABYLON

Stephen Vincent Benét

The title of this fantasy is taken from Psalm 137 in the Bible. The Psalm tells of the Israelites' great sorrow over the destruction of their Temple in Jerusalem (Zion) and their enslavement in Babylon. The Psalm opens

> By the waters of Babylon,
> there we sat down and wept,
> when we remembered Zion.

Stephen Vincent Benét wrote this story partly as a *cautionary tale*, or a story meant to serve as a warning. As you read, be alert to what Benét is warning about.

The story was written in 1942, before the invention of nuclear weapons. However, World War II's destruction of Europe had begun in 1939, and the United States had entered the war in 1941.

Finding Clues. As you read this fantasy, you will have to make *inferences*, or educated guesses, about many things. You'll have to decide, for example, who is speaking, where he lives, and when he lives. You will also have to make inferences about just where this boy goes on his journey—the clues are there; you have to read carefully, and draw on your own experience, to find the answers.

For example, the very first sentence gives you a clue to the kind of civilization the boy is part of: They are *hunters*. The next sentence gives you a clue about the boy's people: They search for metal and the metal seems to be sacred to them. Why? Where is the metal from?

When you come across words like *Ou-dis-sun* on page 112, pronounce them aloud to see if you can guess what English names they refer to.

The north and the west and the south are good hunting ground, but it is forbidden to go east. It is forbidden to go to any of the Dead Places except to search for metal and then he who touches the metal must be a priest or the son of a priest. Afterwards, both the man and the metal must be purified. These are the rules and the laws; they are well made. It is forbidden to cross the great river and look upon the place that was the Place of the Gods—this is most strictly forbidden. We do not even say its name though we know its name. It is there that spirits live, and demons—it is there that there are the ashes of the Great Burning. These things are forbidden—they have been forbidden since the beginning of time.

My father is a priest; I am the son of a priest. I have been in the Dead Places near us, with my father—at first. I was afraid. When my father went into the house to search for the metal, I stood by the door and my heart felt small and weak. It was a dead man's house, a spirit house. It did not have the smell of man, though there were old bones in a corner. But it is not fitting that a priest's son should show fear. I looked at the bones in the shadow and kept my voice still.

Then my father came out with the metal—a good, strong piece. He looked at me with both eyes but I did not run away. He gave me the metal to hold—I took it and did not die. So he knew that I was truly his son and would be a priest in my time. That was when I was very young—nevertheless, my brothers would not have done it, though they are good hunters. After that, they gave me the good piece of meat and the warm corner by the fire. My father watched over me—he was glad that I should be a priest. But when I boasted or wept without a reason, he punished me more strictly than my brothers. That was right.

After a time, I myself was allowed to go into the dead houses and search for metal. So I learned the ways of those houses—and if I saw bones, I was no longer afraid. The bones are light and old—sometimes they will fall into dust if you touch them. But that is a great sin.

I was taught the chants and the spells—I was taught how to stop the running of blood from a wound and many secrets. A priest must know many secrets—that was what my father said. If the hunters think we do all things by chants and spells, they may believe so—it does not hurt them. I was taught how to read in the old books and how to make the old writings—that was hard and took a long time. My knowledge made me happy—it was like a fire in my heart. Most of all, I liked to hear of the Old Days and the stories of the gods. I asked myself many questions that I could not answer, but it was good to ask them. At night, I would lie awake and listen to the wind—it seemed to me that it was the voice of the gods as they flew through the air.

We are not ignorant like the Forest People—our women spin wool on the wheel, our priests wear a white robe. We do not eat grubs from the tree, we have not forgotten the old writings, although they are hard to understand. Nevertheless, my knowledge and my lack of knowledge burned in me—I wished to know more. When I was a man at last, I came to my father and said, "It is time for me to go on my journey. Give me your leave."

He looked at me for a long time, stroking his beard, then he said at last, "Yes. It is time." That night, in the house of the priesthood, I asked for and received purification. My body hurt but my spirit was a cool stone. It was my father himself who questioned me about my dreams.

He bade me look into the smoke of the fire and see—I saw and told what I saw. It was what I have always seen—a river, and, beyond it, a great Dead Place and in it the gods walking. I have always thought about that. His eyes were stern when I told him—he was no longer my father but a priest. He said, "This is a strong dream."

"It is mine," I said, while the smoke waved and my head felt light. They were singing the Star song in the outer chamber and it was like the buzzing of bees in my head.

He asked me how the gods were dressed and I told him how they were dressed. We know how they were dressed from the book, but I saw them as if they were before me. When I had finished, he threw the sticks three times and studied them as they fell.

"This is a very strong dream," he said. "It may eat you up."

"I am not afraid," I said and looked at him with both eyes. My voice sounded thin in my ears but that was because of the smoke.

He touched me on the breast and the forehead. He gave me the bow and the three arrows.

"Take them," he said. "It is forbidden to travel east. It is forbidden to cross the river. It is forbidden to go to the Place of the Gods. All these things are forbidden."

"All these things are forbidden," I said, but it was my voice that spoke and not my spirit. He looked at me again.

"My son," he said. "Once I had young dreams. If your dreams do not eat you up, you may be a great priest. If they eat you, you are still my son. Now go on your journey."

I went fasting, as is the law. My body hurt but not my heart. When the dawn came, I was out of sight of the village. I prayed and purified myself, waiting for a sign. The sign was an eagle. It flew east.

Sometimes signs are sent by bad spirits. I waited again on the flat rock, fasting, taking no food. I was very still—I could feel the sky above me and the earth beneath. I waited till the sun was beginning to sink. Then three deer passed in the valley, going east—they did not wind me or see me. There was a white fawn with them—a very great sign.

I followed them, at a distance, waiting for what would happen. My heart was troubled about going east, yet I knew that I must go. My head hummed with my fasting—I did not even see the panther spring upon the white fawn. But, before I knew it, the bow was in my hand. I shouted and the panther lifted his head from the fawn. It is not easy to kill a panther with one arrow but the arrow went through his eye and into his brain. He died as he tried to spring—he rolled over, tearing at the ground. Then I knew I was meant to go east—I knew that was my journey. When the night came, I made my fire and roasted meat.

It is eight suns' journey to the east and a man passes by many Dead Places. The Forest People are afraid of them but I am not. Once I made my fire on the edge of a Dead Place at night and, next morning, in the dead house, I found a good knife, little rusted. That was small to what came afterward but it made my heart feel big. Always when I looked for game, it was in front of my arrow, and twice I passed hunting parties of the Forest People without their knowing. So I knew my magic was strong and my journey clean, in spite of the law.

Toward the setting of the eighth sun, I came to the banks of the great river. It was half-a-day's journey after I had left the god-road—we do not use the god-roads now for they are falling apart into great blocks of stone, and the forest is safer going. A long way off, I had seen the water through trees but the trees were thick. At last, I came out upon an open place at the top of a cliff. There was the great river below, like a giant in the sun. It is very long, very wide. It could eat all the streams we know and still be thirsty. Its name is Ou-dis-sun, the Sacred, the Long. No man of my tribe had seen it, not even my father, the priest. It was magic and I prayed.

Then I raised my eyes and looked south. It was there, the Place of the Gods.

How can I tell what it was like—you do not know. It was there, in the red light, and they were too big to be houses. It was there with the red light upon it, mighty and ruined. I knew that in another moment the gods would see me. I covered my eyes with my hands and crept back into the forest.

Surely, that was enough to do, and live. Surely it was enough to spend the night upon the cliff. The Forest People themselves do not come near. Yet, all through the night, I knew that I should have to cross the river and walk in the places of the gods, although the gods ate me up. My magic did not help me at all and yet there was a fire in my bowels, a fire in my mind. When the sun rose, I thought, "My journey has been clean. Now I will go home from my journey." But, even as I thought so, I knew I could not. If I went to the Place of the Gods, I would surely die, but, if I did not go, I could never be at peace with my spirit again. It is better to lose one's life than one's spirit, if one is a priest and the son of a priest.

Nevertheless, as I made the raft, the tears ran out of my eyes. The Forest People could have killed me without fight, if they had come upon me then, but they did not come. When the raft was made, I said the sayings for the dead and painted myself for death. My heart was cold as a frog and my knees like water, but the burning in my mind would not let me have peace. As I pushed the raft from the shore, I began my death song—I had the right. It was a fine song.

> "I am John, son of John," I sang. "My people
> are the Hill People. They are the men.
> I go into the Dead Places but I am not slain.

I take the metal from the Dead Places but I am
not blasted.
I travel upon the god-roads and am not afraid.
E-yah! I have killed the panther, I have killed
the fawn!
E-yah! I have come to the great river. No man
has come there before.
It is forbidden to go east, but I have gone,
forbidden to go on the great river, but I am
there.
Open your hearts, you spirits, and hear my
song.
Now I go to the Place of the Gods, I shall not
return.
My body is painted for death and my limbs
weak, but my heart is big as I go to the Place
of the Gods!"

All the same, when I came to the Place of the Gods, I was afraid, afraid. The current of the great river is very strong—it gripped my raft with its hands. That was magic, for the river itself is wide and calm. I could feel evil spirits about me, in the bright morning; I could feel their breath on my neck as I was swept down the stream. Never have I been so much alone—I tried to think of my knowledge, but it was a squirrel's heap of winter nuts. There was no strength in my knowledge anymore and I felt small and naked as a new-hatched bird—alone upon the great river, the servant of the gods.

Yet, after a while, my eyes were opened and I saw. I saw both banks of the river—I saw that once there had been god-roads across it, though now they were broken and fallen like broken vines. Very great they were, and wonderful and broken—broken in the time of the Great Burning when the fire fell out of the sky. And always the current took me nearer to the Place of the Gods, and the huge ruins rose before my eyes.

I do not know the customs of rivers—we are the People of the Hills. I tried to guide my raft with the pole but it spun around. I thought the river meant to take me past the Place of the Gods and out into the Bitter Water of the legends. I grew angry then—my heart felt strong. I said aloud, "I am a priest and the son of a priest!" The gods heard me—they showed me how to paddle with the pole on one side of the raft. The current changed itself—I drew near to the Place of the Gods.

When I was very near, my raft struck and turned over. I can swim in our lakes—I swam to the shore. There was a great spike of rusted metal sticking out into the river—I hauled myself up upon it and sat there, panting. I had saved my bow and two arrows and the knife I found in the Dead Place but that was all. My raft went whirling downstream toward the Bitter Water. I looked after it, and thought if it had trod me under, at least I would be safely dead. Nevertheless, when I had dried my bowstring and restrung it, I walked forward to the Place of the Gods.

It felt like ground underfoot; it did not burn me. It is not true what some of the tales say, that the ground there burns forever, for I have been there. Here and there were the marks and stains of the Great Burning, on the ruins, that is true. But they were old marks and old stains. It is not true either, what some of our priests say, that it is an island covered with fogs and enchantments. It is not. It is a great Dead Place—greater than any Dead Place we know. Everywhere in it there are god-roads, though most are cracked and broken. Everywhere there are the ruins of the high towers of the gods.

How shall I tell what I saw? I went carefully, my strung bow in my hand, my skin ready for danger. There should have been the wailings of spirits and the shrieks of demons, but there were not. It was very silent and sunny where I had landed—the wind and the rain and the birds that drop seeds had done their work—the grass grew in the cracks of the broken stone. It is a fair island—no wonder the gods built there. If I had come there, a god, I also would have built.

How shall I tell what I saw? The towers are not all broken—here and there one still stands, like a great tree in a forest, and the birds nest high. But the towers themselves look blind, for the gods are gone. I saw a fish hawk, catching fish in the river. I saw a little dance of white butterflies over a great heap of broken stones and columns. I went there and looked about me—there was a carved stone with cut-letters, broken in half. I can read letters but I could not understand these. They

said UBTREAS. There was also the shattered image of a man or a god. It had been made of white stone and he wore his hair tied back like a woman's. His name was ASHING, as I read on the cracked half of a stone. I thought it wise to pray to ASHING, though I do not know that god.

How shall I tell what I saw? There was no smell of man left, on stone or metal. Nor were there many trees in that wilderness of stone. There are many pigeons, nesting and dropping in the towers—the gods must have loved them, or, perhaps, they used them for sacrifices. There are wild cats that roam the god-roads, green-eyed, unafraid of man. At night they wail like demons but they are not demons. The wild dogs are more dangerous, for they hunt in a pack, but them I did not meet till later. Everywhere there are the carved stones, carved with magical numbers or words.

I went North—I did not try to hide myself. When a god or a demon saw me, then I would die, but meanwhile I was no longer afraid. My hunger for knowledge burned in me—there was so much that I could not understand. After a while, I knew that my belly was hungry. I could have hunted for my meat, but I did not hunt. It is known that the gods did not hunt as we do—they got their food from enchanted boxes and jars. Sometimes these are still found in the Dead Places—once, when I was a child and foolish, I opened such a jar and tasted it and found the food sweet. But my father found out and punished me for it strictly, for, often, that food is death. Now, though, I had long gone past what was forbidden, and I entered the likeliest towers, looking for the food of the gods.

I found it at last in the ruins of a great temple in the mid-city. A mighty temple it must have been, for the roof was painted like the sky at night with its stars—that much I could see, though the colors were faint and dim. It went down into great caves and tunnels—perhaps they kept their slaves there. But when I started to climb down, I heard the squeaking of rats, so I did not go—rats are unclean, and there must have been many tribes of them, from the squeaking. But near there, I found food, in the heart of a ruin, behind a door that still opened. I ate only the fruits from the jars—they had a very sweet taste. There was drink, too, in

bottles of glass—the drink of the gods was strong and made my head swim. After I had eaten and drunk, I slept on the top of a stone, my bow at my side.

When I woke, the sun was low. Looking down from where I lay, I saw a dog sitting on his haunches. His tongue was hanging out of his mouth; he looked as if he were laughing. He was a big dog, with a gray-brown coat, as big as a wolf. I sprang up and shouted at him but he did not move—he just sat there as if he were laughing. I did not like that. When I reached for a stone to throw, he moved swiftly out of the way of the stone. He was not afraid of me; he looked at me as if I were meat. No doubt I could have killed him with an arrow, but I did not know if there were others. Moreover, night was falling.

I looked about me—not far away there was a great, broken god-road, leading North. The towers were high enough, but not so high, and while many of the dead-houses were wrecked, there were some that stood. I went toward this god-road, keeping to the heights of the ruins, while the dog followed. When I had reached the god-road, I saw that there were others behind him. If I had slept later, they would have come upon me asleep and torn out my throat. As it was, they were sure enough of me; they did not hurry. When I went into the dead-house, they kept watch at the entrance—doubtless they thought they would have a fine hunt. But a dog cannot open a door and I knew, from the books, that the gods did not like to live on the ground but on high.

I had just found a door I could open when the dogs decided to rush. Ha! They were surprised when I shut the door in their faces—it was a good door, of strong metal. I could hear their foolish baying beyond it but I did not stop to answer them. I was in darkness—I found stairs and climbed. There were many stairs, turning around till my head was dizzy. At the top was another door—I found the knob and opened it. I was in a long small chamber—on one side of it was a bronze door that could not be opened, for it had no handle. Perhaps there was a magic word to open it but I did not have the word. I turned to the door in the opposite side of the wall. The lock of it was broken and I opened it and went in.

Within, there was a place of great riches. The god who lived there must have been a powerful god. The first room was a small anteroom[1]—I waited there for some time, telling the spirits of the place that I came in peace and not as a robber. When it seemed to me that they had had time to hear me, I went on. Ah, what riches! Few, even, of the windows had been broken—it was all as it had been. The great windows that looked over the city had not been broken at all though they were dusty and streaked with many years. There were coverings on the floors, the colors not greatly faded, and the chairs were soft and deep. There were pictures upon the walls, very strange, very wonderful—I remember one of a bunch of flowers in a jar—if you came close to it, you could see nothing but bits of color, but if you stood away from it, the flowers might have been picked yesterday. It made my heart feel strange to look at this picture—and to look at the figure of a bird, in some hard clay, on a table and see it so like our birds. Everywhere there were books and writings, many in tongues that I could not read. The god who lived there must have been a wise god and full of knowledge. I felt I had a right there, as I sought knowledge also.

---

1. **anteroom** (an'ti·room'): outer room leading to a larger or more important room. An anteroom is usually used as a waiting room.

Nevertheless, it was strange. There was a washing-place but no water—perhaps the gods washed in air. There was a cooking-place but no wood, and though there was a machine to cook food, there was no place to put fire in it. Nor were there candles or lamps—there were things that looked like lamps but they had neither oil nor wick. All these things were magic, but I touched them and lived—the magic had gone out of them. Let me tell one thing to show. In the washing-place, a thing said "Hot" but it was not hot to the touch—another thing said "Cold" but it was not cold. This must have been a strong magic but the magic was gone. I do not understand—they had ways—I wish that I knew.

It was close and dry and dusty in their house of the gods. I have said the magic was gone but that is not true—it had gone from the magic things but it had not gone from the place. I felt the spirits about me, weighing upon me. Nor had I ever slept in a Dead Place before—and yet, tonight, I must sleep there. When I thought of it, my tongue felt dry in my throat, in spite of my wish for knowledge. Almost I would have gone down again and faced the dogs, but I did not.

I had not gone through all the rooms when the darkness fell. When it fell, I went back to the big room looking over the city and made fire. There was a place to make fire and a box with wood in it, though I do not think they cooked there. I wrapped myself in a floor-covering and slept in front of the fire—I was very tired.

Now I tell what is very strong magic. I woke in the midst of the night. When I woke, the fire had gone out and I was cold. It seemed to me that all around me there were whisperings and voices. I closed my eyes to shut them out. Some will say that I slept again, but I do not think that I slept. I could feel the spirits drawing my spirit out of my body as a fish is drawn on a line.

Why should I lie about it? I am a priest and the son of a priest. If there are spirits, as they say, in the small Dead Places near us, what spirits must there not be in that great Place of the Gods? And would not they wish to speak? After such long years? I know that I felt myself drawn as a fish is drawn on a line. I had stepped out of my body—I could see my body asleep in front of the cold fire, but it was not I. I was drawn to look out upon the city of the gods.

It should have been dark, for it was night, but it was not dark. Everywhere there were lights—lines of light—circles and blurs of light—ten thousand torches would not have been the same. The sky itself was alight—you could barely see the stars for the glow in the sky. I thought to myself "This is strong magic" and trembled. There was a roaring in my ears like the rushing of rivers. Then my eyes grew used to the light and my ears to the sound. I knew that I was seeing the city as it had been when the gods were alive.

That was a sight indeed—yes, that was a sight: I could not have seen it in the body—my body would have died. Everywhere went the gods, on foot and in chariots—there were gods beyond number and counting and their chariots blocked the streets. They had turned night to day for their pleasure—they did not sleep with the sun. The noise of their coming and going was the noise of many waters. It was magic what they could do—it was magic what they did.

I looked out of another window—the great vines of their bridges were mended and the god-roads went east and west. Restless, restless, were the gods and always in motion! They burrowed tunnels under rivers—they flew in the air. With unbelievable tools they did giant works—no part of the earth was safe from them, for, if they wished for a thing, they summoned it from the other side of the world. And always, as they labored and rested, as they feasted and made love, there was a drum in their ears—the pulse of the giant city, beating and beating like a man's heart.

Were they happy? What is happiness to the gods? They were great, they were mighty, they were wonderful and terrible. As I looked upon them and their magic, I felt like a child—but a little more, it seemed to me, and they would pull down the moon from the sky. I saw them with wisdom beyond wisdom and knowledge beyond knowledge. And yet not all they did was well done—even I could see that—and yet their wisdom could not but grow until all was peace.

Then I saw their fate come upon them and that was terrible past speech. It came upon them as they walked the streets of their city. I have been

in the fights with the Forest People—I have seen men die. But this was not like that. When gods war with gods, they use weapons we do not know. It was fire falling out of the sky and a mist that poisoned. It was the time of the Great Burning and the Destruction. They ran about like ants in the streets of their city—poor gods, poor gods! Then the towers began to fall. A few escaped—yes, a few. The legends tell it. But, even after the city had become a Dead Place, for many years the poison was still in the ground. I saw it happen, I saw the last of them die. It was darkness over the broken city and I wept.

All this, I saw. I saw it as I have told it, though not in the body. When I woke in the morning, I was hungry, but I did not think first of my hunger for my heart was perplexed and confused. I knew the reason for the Dead Places but I did not see why it had happened. It seemed to me it should not have happened, with all the magic they had. I went through the house looking for an answer. There was so much in the house I could not understand—and yet I am a priest and the son of a priest. It was like being on one side of the great river, at night, with no light to show the way.

Then I saw the dead god. He was sitting in his chair, by the window, in a room I had not entered before and, for the first moment, I thought that he was alive. Then I saw the skin on the back of his hand—it was like dry leather. The room was shut, hot and dry—no doubt that had kept him as he was. At first I was afraid to approach him—then the fear left me. He was sitting looking out over the city—he was dressed in the clothes of the gods. His age was neither young nor old—I could not tell his age. But there was wisdom in his face and great sadness. You could see that he would have not run away. He had sat at his window, watching his city die—then he himself had died. But it is better to lose one's life than one's spirit—and you could see from the face that his spirit had not been lost. I knew that, if I touched him, he would fall into dust—and yet, there was something unconquered in the face.

That is all of my story, for then I knew he was a man—I knew then that they had been men, neither gods nor demons. It is a great knowledge, hard to tell and believe. They were men—they

went a dark road, but they were men. I had no fear after that—I had no fear going home, though twice I fought off the dogs and once I was hunted for two days by the Forest People. When I saw my father again, I prayed and was purified. He touched my lips and my breast, he said, "You went away a boy. You come back a man and a priest." I said, "Father, they were men! I have been in the Place of the Gods and seen it! Now slay me, if it is the law—but still I know they were men."

He looked at me out of both eyes. He said, "The law is not always the same shape—you have done what you have done. I could not have done it in my time, but you come after me. Tell!"

I told and he listened. After that, I wished to tell all the people but he showed me otherwise. He said, "Truth is a hard deer to hunt. If you eat too much truth at once, you may die of the truth. It was not idly that our fathers forbade the Dead Places." He was right—it is better the truth should come little by little. I have learned that, being a priest. Perhaps, in the old days, they ate knowledge too fast.

Nevertheless, we make a beginning. It is not for the metal alone we go to the Dead Places now—there are the books and the writings. They are hard to learn. And the magic tools are broken—but we can look at them and wonder. At least, we make a beginning. And, when I am chief priest we shall go beyond the great river. We shall go to the Place of the Gods—the place newyork—not one man but a company. We shall look for the images of the gods and find the god ASHING and the others—the gods Lincoln and Biltmore and Moses. But they were men who built the city, not gods or demons. They were men. I remember the dead man's face. They were men who were here before us. We must build again.

Responding to the Story

Analyzing the Story

Identifying Facts

1. Describe the **setting** of this story—what do you know about where and when it takes place?
2. List and explain five rules of the Hill People. How are they different from the Forest People?
3. John tells the story and is its main character. What is his position among the Hill People? Explain why he decides to make the journey to the East.
4. Eventually John enters the Place of the Gods. What was the place formerly called? Describe two buildings he explores.
5. During the night John has a vision of what life was previously like in the Place of the Gods. The following morning he discovers a "great knowledge." Describe John's discovery and how he makes it.
6. What does John plan to do when he becomes the chief priest?

Interpreting Meanings

7. What had happened to the city John visited? What seems to have happened to civilization as we know it? What clues give you the answers?
8. John says that the people he saw "went a dark road" (page 118). What does he mean?
9. "By the Waters of Babylon" is a **fantasy** about what might happen in the future. Do you believe a world like this could emerge in the future? Or is such a world very unlikely? Include at least three passages from the story in your discussion.
10. An **internal conflict** takes place in a character's mind. The character must struggle with opposing ideas or feelings. Early in the story, John has an internal conflict about whether to journey to the Place of the Gods. Describe the opposing forces that make up his mental struggle. How does he resolve the conflict? What three signs confirm that his decision was right?

Applying Meanings

11. John is told by his father, "Truth is a hard deer to hunt. If you eat too much truth at once, you may die of the truth." Later, John thinks, "Perhaps, in the old days, they ate knowledge too fast." Explain what John and his father mean. Then discuss whether you think human beings today are "eating knowledge" too fast.
12. List three other warnings you think Stephen Vincent Benét is giving his readers in this story. Of all the warnings, which, if any, do you think is most relevant to the world today? Why?

Writing About the Story

A Creative Response

1. **Extending the Story Forward.** At the end of "By the Waters of Babylon," John is beginning to learn much more about the old civilization. He is determined that "We must build again." Assume that five years have passed and John is now chief priest. He decides to start building again. In a paragraph, identify the first three buildings John will construct. (They can be copies of famous buildings or just types of buildings.) Discuss where they will be built and how they will be used. (Remember that John has difficulty grasping how buildings were once used.)
2. **Extending the Story Backward.** Make up a story about the dead god John sees, the one who watched his city die. You might have him write in a journal as he watches. Or, you might have him write a letter to future generations.

A Critical Response

3. **Analyzing an Idea.** In the story, John finds a dead man seated in a chair. He thinks,

   . . . there was wisdom in his face and great sadness. You could see that he would have not run away. He had sat at his window, watching his city die—then he himself had died. But it is better to lose one's life than one's spirit—and you could see from the face that his spirit had not been lost.

   In one paragraph, explain what John means by ". . . it is better to lose one's life than one's spirit." In a second paragraph discuss whether you agree with John's statement. Include real or made-up examples to back up your opinion.

4. **Stating the Story's Message.** Benét wrote this story in 1942. Use a history book to find out what was happening in Europe in 1942. Then in a paragraph tell what message you think Benét wanted to communicate with his story.

Analyzing Language and Vocabulary

Clues to Meaning

This story is like a puzzle. You have to find clues and piece them together in order to understand what is really happening. John describes each of the following details. Discuss with your classmates what a reader might **infer**, or guess, about the significance of each detail. Can you tell what John is *really* seeing? As you discuss the answers, keep in mind the date the story was written.

1. The Place of the Gods
2. The Great Burning
3. Ou-dis-sun
4. The fire that fell out of the sky
5. UBTREAS
6. The statue of a man with his hair tied back like a woman, named ASHING
7. The temple in mid-city with a roof painted like the sky at night
8. The caves and tunnels where John thinks the gods kept their slaves
9. The drink of the gods that made John's head spin
10. The cooking place with no wood
11. The gods Lincoln and Biltmore and Moses

Reading About the Writer

Stephen Vincent Benét (1898–1943) won the Pulitzer Prize in 1929 for his long poem about John Brown. Brown was a radical abolitionist who led the raid on the arsenal at Harpers Ferry, Virginia, and was hanged for murder and treason. Benét wrote many poems and stories about America, including his famous "The Devil and Daniel Webster," on page 534 of this book. In collaboration with his sister Rosemary Benét, Benét also wrote poems about Johnny Appleseed, Sam Houston, and George Washington. Benét was also interested in fantasy: He wrote one poem called "Metropolitan Nightmare," in which steel-eating termites destroy New York City.

THE RUUM

Arthur Porges

"The Ruum" is a horror story. It taps directly into our childhood terror of being pursued by some frightening creature, who keeps coming on, and on, and on. "The Ruum" provides us with some of the principle delights of science fiction as well. You will find a journey through eons of time; an indestructible nightmare machine set loose by a galactic spaceship commander; and a brave hero. You will also find a tricky ending. The story should have particular appeal to people who enjoy science fiction and to mathematicians.

Like writers of mystery and crime stories, science-fiction writers often drop clues as the story goes on. Every detail in this story is important. Pay attention to the dynamite, the rifle, the pistol, and the use of numbers.

By the time you get to the sentence, "And on the earth, it was the age of reptiles," pause and answer these questions: What do you know about a ruum? Why is the ruum left on the third planet? What happens to the cruise ship *Ilkor*? What time in history did all this happen?

The cruiser *Ilkor* had just gone into her interstellar overdrive beyond the orbit of Pluto when a worried officer reported to the Commander.

"Excellency," he said uneasily, "I regret to inform you that because of a technician's carelessness a Type H–9 Ruum has been left behind on the third planet, together with anything it may have collected."

The Commander's triangular eyes hooded momentarily, but when he spoke his voice was level.

"How was the ruum set?"

"For a maximum radius of 30 miles, and 160 pounds plus or minus 15."

There was silence for several seconds; then the Commander said: "We cannot reverse course now. In a few weeks we'll be returning, and can pick up the ruum then. I do not care to have one of those costly, self-energizing models charged against my ship. You will see," he ordered coldly, "that the individual responsible is severely punished."

But at the end of its run, in the neighborhood of Rigel, the cruiser met a flat, ring-shaped raider; and when the inevitable fire-fight was over, both ships, semi-molten, radioactive, and laden with dead, were starting a billion-year orbit around the star.

And on the earth, it was the age of reptiles.

When the two men had unloaded the last of the supplies, Jim Irwin watched his partner climb into the little seaplane. He waved at Walt.

"Don't forget to mail that letter to my wife," Jim shouted.

"The minute I land," Walt Leonard called back, starting to rev the engine. "And you find us some uranium—a strike is just what Cele needs.

Word Histories. English words have come into existence in a variety of ways. Some were borrowed from other languages. (For example, *chic* was borrowed from French.) Some were formed by adding a prefix to a root. (For instance, *dis-* was added to *appear* to form *disappear*.) Some imitate sounds. (*Hiss* is an example.) Some words come from the name of a person. Early in this story you'll see the noun *Geiger counter*. This is a device for measuring radiation. The device is named for one of its developers, the German physicist Hans Geiger (1882–1945).

A fortune for your son and her, hey?'' His white teeth flashed in a grin. ''Don't rub noses with any grizzlies—shoot 'em, but don't scare 'em to death!''

Jim thumbed his nose as the seaplane speeded up, leaving a frothy wake. He felt a queer chill as the amphibian took off. For three weeks he would be isolated in this remote valley of the Canadian Rockies. If for any reason the plane failed to return to the icy blue lake, he would surely die. Even with enough food, no man could surmount the frozen peaks and make his way on foot over hundreds of miles of almost virgin wilderness. But, of course, Walt Leonard would return on schedule, and it was up to Jim whether or not they lost their stake. If there was any uranium in the valley, he had twenty-one days to find it. To work then, and no gloomy forebodings.

Moving with the unhurried precision of an experienced woodsman, he built a lean-to in the shelter of a rocky overhang. For this three weeks of summer, nothing more permanent was needed. Perspiring in the strong morning sun, he piled his supplies back under the ledge, well covered by a waterproof tarpaulin, and protected from the larger animal prowlers. All but the dynamite; that he cached,[1] also carefully wrapped against moisture, two hundred yards away. Only a fool shares his quarters with a box of high explosives.

The first two weeks went by all too swiftly, without any encouraging finds. There was only one good possibility left, and just enough time to explore it. So early one morning toward the end of his third week, Jim Irwin prepared for a last-ditch foray into the northeast part of the valley, a region he had not yet visited.

He took the Geiger counter, slipping on the earphones, reversed to keep the normal rattle from dulling his hearing, and reaching for the rifle, set out, telling himself it was now or never so far as this particular expedition was concerned. The bulky .30–06 was a nuisance and he had no enthusiasm for its weight, but the huge grizzlies of Canada are not intruded upon with impunity, and take a lot of killing. He'd already had to dispose of two, a hateful chore, since the big bears were

---

1. **cached** (kash'd): hid, concealed.

vanishing all too fast. And the rifle had proved a great comfort on several ticklish occasions when actual firing had been avoided. The .22 pistol he left in its sheepskin holster in the lean-to.

He was whistling at the start, for the clear, frosty air, the bright sun on blue-white ice fields, and the heady smell of summer all delighted his heart despite his bad luck as a prospector. He planned to go one day's journey to the new region, spend about thirty-six hours exploring it intensively, and be back in time to meet the plane at noon. Except for his emergency packet, he took no food or water. It would be easy enough to knock over a rabbit, and the streams were alive with firm-fleshed rainbow trout of the kind no longer common in the States.

All morning Jim walked, feeling an occasional surge of hope as the counter chattered. But its clatter always died down. The valley had nothing radioactive of value, only traces. Apparently they'd made a bad choice. His cheerfulness faded. They needed a strike badly, especially Walt. And his own wife, Cele, with a kid on the way. But there was still a chance. These last thirty-six hours—he'd snoop at night, if necessary—might be the payoff. He reflected a little bitterly that it would help quite a bit if some of those birds he'd staked would make a strike and return his dough. Right this minute there were close to eight thousand bucks owing to him.

A wry smile touched his lips, and he abandoned unprofitable speculations for plans about lunch. The sun, as well as his stomach, said it was time. He had just decided to take out his line and fish a foaming brook, when he rounded a grassy knoll to come upon a sight that made him stiffen to a halt, his jaw dropping.

It was like some enterprising giant's outdoor butcher shop: a great assortment of animal bodies, neatly lined up in a triple row that extended almost as far as the eye could see. And what animals! To be sure, those nearest to him were ordinary deer, bear, cougars, and mountain sheep—one of each, apparently—but down the line were strange, uncouth, half-formed, hairy beasts; and beyond them a nightmare conglomeration of reptiles. One of the latter, at the extreme end of the remarkable display, he recognized at once. There had been a

much larger specimen, fabricated about an incomplete skeleton, of course, in the museum at home.

No doubt about it—it was a small stegosaur,[2] no bigger than a pony!

Fascinated, Jim walked down the line, glancing back over the immense array. Peering more closely at one scaly, dirty-yellow lizard, he saw an eyelid tremble. Then he realized the truth. The animals were not dead, but paralyzed and miraculously preserved. Perspiration prickled his forehead. How long since stegosaurs had roamed this valley?

All at once he noticed another curious circumstance: The victims were roughly of a size. Nowhere, for example, was there a really large saurian.[3] No tyrannosaurus. For that matter, no mammoth. Each specimen was about the size of a large sheep. He was pondering this odd fact, when the underbrush rustled a warning behind him.

Jim Irwin had once worked with mercury, and for a second it seemed to him that a half-filled leather sack of the liquid-metal had rolled into the clearing. For the quasi-spherical[4] object moved with just such a weighty, fluid motion. But it was not leather; and what appeared at first a disgusting wartiness turned out on closer scrutiny to be more like the functional projections of some outlandish mechanism. Whatever the thing was, he had little time to study it, for after the spheroid had whipped out and retracted a number of metal rods with bulbous, lenslike structures at their tips, it rolled towards him at a speed of about five miles an hour. And from its purposeful advance, the man had no doubts that it meant to add him to the pathetic heap of living-dead specimens.

Uttering an incoherent exclamation, Jim sprang back a number of paces, unslinging his rifle. The ruum that had been left behind was still some thirty yards off, approaching at that moderate but

---

2. **stegosaur** (steg′ə·sôr′): dinosaur that had a small head and heavy, bony plates on its back.
3. **saurian** (sôr′ē·ən): any of a large group of reptiles, consisting of the lizards. Here, *saurian* is meant to be synonymous with *dinosaur*.
4. **quasi-spherical** (kwā′sī-sfer′i·k′l): shaped something like a ball, or sphere.

invariable velocity, an advance more terrifying in its regularity than the headlong charge of a mere brute beast.

Jim's hand flew to the bolt, and with practiced deftness he slammed a cartridge into the chamber. He snuggled the battered stock against his cheek, and using the peep sight, aimed squarely at the leathery bulk—a perfect target in the bright afternoon sun. A grim little smile touched his lips as he squeezed the trigger. He knew what one of those 180-grain, metal-jacketed, boat-tail slugs could do at 2700 feet per second. Probably at this close range it would keyhole and blow the foul thing into a mush.

Wham! The familiar kick against his shoulder. E-e-e-e! The whining screech of a ricochet.[5] He sucked in his breath. There could be no doubt whatever. At a mere twenty yards, a bullet from this hard-hitting rifle had glanced from the ruum's surface.

Frantically Jim worked the bolt. He blasted two more rounds, then realized the utter futility of such tactics. When the ruum was six feet away, he saw gleaming finger-hooks flick from warty knobs, and a hollow, sting-like probe, dripping greenish liquid, poised snakily between them. The man turned and fled.

Jim Irwin weighed exactly 149 pounds.

It was easy enough to pull ahead. The ruum seemed incapable of increasing its speed. But Jim had no illusions on that score. The steady five-mile-an-hour pace was something no organism on earth could maintain for more than a few hours. Before long, Jim guessed, the hunted animal had either turned on its implacable pursuer, or, in the case of more timid creatures, run itself to exhaustion in a circle out of sheer panic. Only the winged were safe. But for anything on the ground the result was inevitable: another specimen for the awesome array. And for whom the whole collection? Why? Why?

Coolly, as he ran, Jim began to shed all surplus weight. He glanced at the reddening sun, wondering about the coming night. He hesitated over the rifle; it had proved useless against the ruum, but his military training impelled him to keep the weapon to the last. Still, every pound raised the odds against him in the grueling race he foresaw clearly. Logic told him that military reasoning did not apply to a contest like this; there would be no disgrace in abandoning a worthless rifle. And when weight became really vital, the .30-06 would go. But meanwhile he slung it over one shoulder. The Geiger counter he placed as gently as possible on a flat rock, hardly breaking his stride.

One thing was certain. This would be no rabbit run, a blind, panicky flight until exhausted, ending in squealing submission. This would be a fighting retreat, and he'd use every trick of survival he'd learned in his hazard-filled lifetime.

Taking deep, measured breaths, he loped along, watching with shrewd eyes for anything that might be used for his advantage in the weird contest. Luckily the valley was sparsely wooded; in brush or forest his straightaway speed would be almost useless.

Suddenly he came upon a sight that made him pause. It was a point where a huge boulder overhung the trail, and Jim saw possibilities in the situation. He grinned as he remembered a Malay mantrap[6] that had once saved his life. Springing to a hillock, he looked back over the grassy plain. The afternoon sun cast long shadows, but it was easy enough to spot the pursuing ruum, still oozing along on Jim's trail. He watched the thing with painful anxiety. Everything hinged upon this brief survey. He was right! Yes, although at most places the man's trail was neither the only route nor the best one, the ruum dogged the footsteps of his prey. The significance of that fact was immense, but Irwin had no more than twelve minutes to implement the knowledge.

Deliberately dragging his feet, Irwin made it a clear trail directly under the boulder. After going past it for about ten yards, he walked backwards in his own prints until just short of the overhang, and then jumped up clear of the track to a point behind the balanced rock.

---

5. **ricochet** (rik′ə·shā): object, such as a bullet, that strikes a surface at an angle and glances off.

6. **Malay mantrap:** device involving a large object that falls on a person; also called *Malay man-catcher*. The device is usually designed so that it is triggered unwittingly by the victim. Its name refers to Malaya, now part of Malaysia in southeast Asia.

Whipping out his heavy-duty belt knife, he began to dig, scientifically, but with furious haste, about the base of the boulder. Every few moments, sweating with apprehension and effort, he rammed it with one shoulder. At last, it teetered a little. He had just jammed the knife back into his sheath, and was crouching there, panting, when the ruum rolled into sight over a small ridge on his back trail.

He watched the gray spheroid moving toward him and fought to quiet his sobbing breath. There was no telling what other senses it might bring into play, even though the ruum seemed to prefer just to follow in his prints. But it certainly had a whole battery of instruments at its disposal. He crouched low behind the rock, every nerve a charged wire.

But there was no change of technique by the ruum; seemingly intent on the footprints of its prey, the strange sphere rippled along, passing directly under the great boulder. As it did so, Irwin gave a savage yell, and thrusting his whole muscular weight against the balanced mass, toppled it squarely on the ruum. Five tons of stone fell from a height of twelve feet.

Jim scrambled down. He stood there, staring at the huge lump and shaking his head dazedly. He gave the boulder a kick. "Hah! Walt and I might clear a buck or two yet from your little meat market. Maybe this expedition won't be a total loss. Enjoy yourself in hell where you came from!"

Then he leaped back, his eyes wild. The giant rock was shifting! Slowly its five-ton bulk was sliding off the trail, raising a ridge of soil as it grated along. Even as he stared, the boulder tilted, and a gray protuberance appeared under the nearest edge. With a choked cry, Jim Irwin broke into a lurching run.

He ran a full mile down the trail. Then, finally, he stopped and looked back. He could just make out a dark dot moving away from the fallen rock. It progressed as slowly and as regularly and as inexorably as before, and in his direction. Jim sat down heavily, putting his head in his scratched, grimy hands.

But that despairing mood did not last. After all, he had gained a twenty-minute respite. Lying down, trying to relax as much as possible, he took the flat packet of emergency rations from his jacket, and eating quickly but without bolting, disposed of some pemmican, biscuit, and chocolate. A few sips of icy water from a streamlet, and he was almost ready to continue his fantastic struggle. When the ruum was still an estimated ten minutes away, Jim Irwin trotted off, much of his wiry strength back, and fresh courage to counter bone-deep weariness.

After running for fifteen minutes, he came to a sheer face of rock about thirty feet high. The terrain on either side was barely passable, consisting of choked gullies, spiky brush, and knife-edged rocks. If Jim could make the top of this little cliff, the ruum sure would have to detour, a circumstance that might put it many minutes behind him.

He looked up at the sun. Huge and crimson, it was almost touching the horizon. He would have to move fast. Irwin was no rock-climber but he did know the fundamentals. Using every crevice, roughness, and minute ledge, he fought his way up the cliff. Somehow—unconsciously—he used that flowing climb of a natural mountaineer, which takes each foothold very briefly as an unstressed pivot-point in a series of rhythmic advances.

He had just reached the top when the ruum rolled up to the base of the cliff.

Jim knew very well that he ought to leave at once, taking advantage of the few precious remaining moments of daylight. Every second gained was of tremendous value; but curiosity and hope made him wait. He told himself that the instant his pursuer detoured he would get out of there all the faster. Besides, the thing might even give up and he could sleep right here.

Sleep! His body lusted for it.

But the ruum would not detour. It hesitated only a few seconds at the foot of the barrier. Then a number of knobs opened to extrude metallic wands. One of these, topped with lenses, waved in the air. Jim drew back too late—their uncanny gaze had found him as he lay atop the cliff, peering down. He cursed his idiocy.

Immediately all the wands retracted, and from a different knob a slender rod, blood-red in the setting sun, began to shoot straight up to the man. As he watched, frozen in place, its barbed tip gripped the cliff's edge almost under his nose.

Jim leaped to his feet. Already the rod was shortening as the ruum reabsorbed its shining length. And the leathery sphere was rising off the ground. Swearing loudly, Jim fixed his eyes on the tenacious hook, drawing back one heavy foot.

But experience restrained him. The mighty kick was never launched. He had seen too many rough-and-tumbles lost by an injudicious attempt at the boot. It wouldn't do at all to let any part of his body get within reach of the ruum's superb tools. Instead he seized a length of dry branch, and inserting one end under the metal hook, began to pry.

There was a sputtering flash, white and lacy, and even through the dry wood he felt the potent surge of power that splintered the end. He dropped the smoldering stick with a gasp of pain, and wringing his numb fingers, backed off several steps, full of impotent rage. For a moment he paused, half inclined to run again, but then his upper lip drew back and, snarling, he unslung his rifle. He knew he had been right to lug the thing all this way—even if it had beat a tattoo on his ribs. Now he had the ruum right where he wanted it!

Kneeling to steady his aim in the failing light Jim sighted at the hook and fired. There was a soggy thud as the ruum fell. Jim shouted. The heavy slug had done a lot more than he expected. Not only had it blasted the metal claw loose, but it had smashed a big gap in the cliff's edge. It would be pretty damned hard for the ruum to use that part of the rock again!

He looked down. Sure enough, the ruum was back at the bottom. Jim Irwin grinned. Every time the thing clamped a hook over the bluff, he'd blow that hook loose. There was plenty of ammunition in his pocket and, until the moon rose, bringing a good light for shooting with, he'd stick the gun's muzzle inches away if necessary. Besides, the thing—whatever it might be—was obviously too intelligent to keep up a hopeless struggle. Sooner or later it would accept the detour. And then, maybe the night would help to hide his trail.

Then—he choked and, for a brief moment, tears came to his eyes. Down below, in the dimness, the squat, phlegmatic[7] spheroid was extruding three hooked rods simultaneously in a fanlike spread. In a perfectly coordinated movement, the rods snagged the cliff's edge at intervals of about four feet.

Jim Irwin whipped the rifle to his shoulder. All right—this was going to be just like the rapid fire for record back at Benning.[8] Only, at Benning, they didn't expect good shooting in the dark!

But the first shot was a bull's-eye, smacking the left-hand hook loose in a puff of rock dust. His second shot did almost as well, knocking the gritty stuff loose so the center barb slipped off. But even as he whirled to level at number three, Jim saw it was hopeless.

The first hook was back in place. No matter how well he shot, at least one rod would always be in position, pulling the ruum to the top.

Jim hung the useless rifle muzzle down from a stunted tree and ran into the deepening dark. The toughening of his body, a process of years, was paying off now. So what? Where was he going? What could he do now? Was there anything that could stop that thing behind him?

Then he remembered the dynamite.

Gradually changing his course, the weary man cut back towards his camp by the lake. Overhead the stars brightened, pointing the way. Jim lost all sense of time. He must have eaten as he wobbled along, for he wasn't hungry. Maybe he could eat at the lean-to . . . no, there wouldn't be time. The moon was up and he could hear the ruum close behind. Close.

Quite often phosphorescent[9] eyes peered at him from the underbrush and once, just at dawn, a grizzly woofed with displeasure at his passage.

Sometimes during the night his wife, Cele, stood before him with outstretched arms. "Go away!" he rasped, "Go away! You can make it! It can't chase both of us!" So she turned and ran lightly alongside of him. But when Irwin panted across a tiny glade, Cele faded away into the moonlight and he realized she hadn't been there at all.

Shortly after sunrise Jim Irwin reached the lake. The ruum was close enough for him to hear the dull sounds of its passage. Jim staggered, his eyes closed. He hit himself feebly on the nose, his eyes jerked open and he saw the explosive. The sight of the greasy sticks of dynamite snapped Irwin wide awake.

He forced himself to calmness and carefully considered what to do. Fuse? No. It would be impossible to leave fused dynamite in the trail and time the detonation with the absolute precision he needed. Sweat poured down his body, his clothes were sodden with it. It was hard to think. The explosion *must* be set off from a distance and at the exact moment the ruum was passing over it. But Irwin dared not use a long fuse. The rate of burning was not constant enough. Couldn't calibrate[10] it perfectly with the ruum's advance. Jim Irwin's body sagged all over, his chin sank toward his heaving chest. He jerked his head up, stepped back—and saw the .22 pistol where he had left it in the lean-to.

His sunken eyes flashed.

Moving with frenetic haste, he took the half-filled case, piled all the remaining percussion caps among the loose sticks in a devil's mixture. Weaving out to the trail, he carefully placed box and contents directly on his earlier tracks some twenty yards from a rocky ledge. It was a risk—the stuff might go anytime—but that didn't matter. He

---

7. **phlegmatic** (fleg·mat′ik): calm; cool.
8. **Benning:** Fort Benning, Georgia, a U.S. Army post.

9. **phosphorescent** (fäs′fə·res′ənt): glowing.
10. **calibrate** (kal′ə·brāt): here, time.

would far rather be blown to rags than end up living but paralyzed in the ruum's outdoor butcher's stall.

The exhausted Irwin had barely hunched down behind the thin ledge of rock before his inexorable pursuer appeared over a slight rise five hundred yards away. Jim scrunched deeper into the hollow, then saw a vertical gap, a narrow crack between rocks. That was it, he thought vaguely. He could sight through the gap at the dynamite and still be shielded from the blast. If it was a shield . . . when that half-caste blew only twenty yards away . . . .

He stretched out on his belly, watching the ruum roll forward. A hammer of exhaustion pounded his ballooning skull. When had he slept last? This was the first time he had lain down in hours. Hours? Ha! It was days. His muscles stiffened, locked into throbbing, burning knots. Then he felt the morning sun on his back, soothing, warming, easing. . . . No! If he let go, if he slept now, it was the ruum's macabre collection for Jim Irwin! Stiff fingers tightened around the pistol. He'd stay awake! If he lost—if the ruum survived the blast—there'd still be time to put a bullet through his brain.

He looked down at the sleek pistol, then out at the innocent-seeming booby trap. If he timed this right—and he would—the ruum wouldn't survive. No. He relaxed a little, yielding just a bit to the gently insistent sun. A bird whistled softly somewhere above him and a fish splashed in the lake.

Suddenly he was wrenched to full awareness. Of all times for a grizzly to come snooping about! With the whole of Irwin's camp ready for greedy looting, a fool bear had to come sniffing around the dynamite! The furred monster smelled carefully at the box, nosed around, rumbled deep displeasure at the alien scent of man. Irwin held his breath. Just a touch would blow a cap. A single cap meant . . .

The grizzly lifted his head from the box and growled hoarsely. The box was ignored, the offensive odor of man was forgotten. Its feral[11] little eyes focused on a plodding spheroid that was now only forty yards away. Jim Irwin snickered. Until

he had met the ruum the grizzly bear of the North American continent was the only thing in the world he had ever feared. And now—why was he so calm about it?—the two terrors of his existence were meeting head on and he was laughing. He shook his head and the great side muscles in his neck hurt abominably. He looked down at his pistol, then out at the dynamite. *These* were the only real things in his world.

About six feet from the bear, the ruum paused. Still in the grip of that almost idiotic detachment, Jim Irwin found himself wondering again what it was, where it had come from. The grizzly arose on its haunches, the embodiment of utter ferocity. Terrible teeth flashed white against red lips. The businesslike ruum started to roll past. The bear closed in, roaring. It cuffed at the ruum. A mighty paw, armed with black claws sharper and stronger than scythes, made that cuff. It would have disemboweled a rhinoceros. Irwin cringed as that sideswipe knocked dust from the leathery sphere. The ruum was hurled back several inches. It paused, recovered, and with the same dreadful casualness it rippled on, making a wider circle, ignoring the bear.

But the lord of the woods wasn't settling for any draw. Moving with that incredible agility which has terrified Indians, Spanish, French, and Anglo-Americans since the first encounter of any of them with his species, the grizzly whirled, sidestepped beautifully, and hugged the ruum. The terrible, shaggy forearms tightened, the slavering jaws champed at the gray surface. Irwin half rose. "Go it!" he croaked. Even as he cheered the clumsy emperor of the wild, Jim thought it was an insane tableau: the village idiot wrestling with a beach ball.

Then silver metal gleamed bright against gray. There was a flash, swift and deadly. The roar of the king abruptly became a whimper, a gurgle and then there was nearly a ton of terror wallowing in death—its throat slashed open. Jim Irwin saw the bloody blade retract into the gray spheroid, leaving a bright red smear on the thing's dusty hide.

And the ruum rolled forward past the giant corpse, implacable, still intent on the man's spoor, his footprints, his pathway. Okay, baby, Jim gig-

---

11. **feral** (fîr'əl): wild.

gled at the dead grizzly, this is for you, for Cele, for—lots of poor dumb animals like us—come to, you fool, he cursed at himself. And aimed at the dynamite. And very calmly, very carefully, Jim Irwin squeezed the trigger of his pistol.

Briefly, sound first. Then giant hands lifted his body from where he lay, then let go. He came down hard, face in a patch of nettles, but he was sick, he didn't care. He remembered that the birds were quiet. Then there was a fluid thump as something massive struck the grass a few yards away. Then there was quiet.

Irwin lifted his head . . . all men do in such a case. His body still ached. He lifted sore shoulders and saw . . . an enormous smoking crater in the earth. He also saw, a dozen paces away, gray-white because it was covered now with powdered rock, the ruum.

It was under a tall, handsome pine tree. Even as Jim watched, wondering if the ringing in his

ears would ever stop, the ruum rolled toward him.

Irwin fumbled for his pistol. It was gone. It had dropped somewhere, out of reach. He wanted to pray, then, but couldn't get properly started. Instead, he kept thinking, idiotically, "My sister Ethel can't spell Nebuchadnezzar[12] and never could. My sister Ethel——"

The ruum was a foot away now, and Jim closed his eyes. He felt cool, metallic fingers touch, grip, lift. His unresisting body was raised several inches, and juggled oddly. Shuddering, he waited for the terrible syringe with its green liquid, seeing the yellow, shrunken face of a lizard with one eyelid a-tremble.

Then, dispassionately, without either roughness or solicitude, the ruum put him back on the ground. When he opened his eyes, some seconds later, the sphere was rolling away. Watching it go, he sobbed drily.

---

12. **Nebuchadnezzar** (neb′yə·kəd·nez′ər): king of ancient Babylonia.

It seemed a matter of moments only, before he heard the seaplane's engine, and opened his eyes to see Walt Leonard bending over him.

Later, in the plane, five thousand feet above the valley, Walt grinned suddenly, slapped him on the back, and cried: "Jim, I can get a whirlybird, a four-place job! Why, if we can snatch up just a few of those prehistoric lizards and things while the museum keeper's away, it's like you said—the scientists will pay us plenty."

Jim's hollow eyes lit up. "That's the idea," he agreed. Then, bitterly, "I might just as well have stayed in bed. Evidently the thing didn't want me at all. Maybe it wanted to know what I paid for these pants! Barely touched me, then let go. And how I ran!"

"Yeah," Walt said. "That was queer. And after that marathon. I admire your guts, boy." He glanced sideways at Jim Irwin's haggard face. "That night's run cost you plenty. I figure you lost over ten pounds."

Responding to the Story

Analyzing the Story

Identifying Facts

1. A short prologue precedes the main story. Describe the principal events in the prologue. When do they take place?
2. What facts do you know about the Commander's eyes? (What do you make of these facts?)
3. When is the main part of the story set? As the story opens, where has Jim Irwin been dropped off and what is he planning to do?
4. What does Jim see that makes him "stiffen to a halt"? What realization makes him break out in perspiration?
5. Explain how Jim first encounters the ruum. Then give a detailed description of the machine. If you enjoy drawing, include a sketch.
6. The ruum advances on Jim, and Jim fears for his safety. Describe three ways Jim tries to stop the ruum.

7. Eventually the ruum catches Jim. Describe what the ruum does with him. What revelation that comes so neatly in the last line explains why it acts this way?

Interpreting Meanings

8. At the heart of some science fiction stories is a tricky idea or **gimmick**. Describe the gimmick in this story. At what point in the story did you figure it out?
9. What connection does the first part of the story (the prologue) have with the story about Jim?
10. If you had been in Jim's place would you have acted differently to save yourself from the ruum? Cite passages from the text in explaining your answer.
11. The writer coined a word in naming the machine that is central to the story. Do you think the word *ruum* is intended to resemble an Eng-

lish word? Or is it an example of **onomatopoeia**? (Onomatopoeia is the formation of words by imitation of sound.) Or does the word have no special significance other than being the name of a machine? Give specific reasons to support your answer.

12. Do you think the story could be made into a good movie? Give at least three reasons to back up your opinion.

Applying Meanings

13. Many science fiction stories—including "The Ruum"—are based on the idea that some kind of intelligent life exists, or has existed, somewhere else in the universe. Even serious scientists have broadcast messages to outer space, but so far there has been no answer. Discuss whether you think intelligent life exists elsewhere in the universe.

14. What are the most nightmarish parts of this story?

Writing About the Story

A Creative Response

1. **Inventing and Describing a Machine.** You've been asked to dream up an original machine for a science fiction movie. The machine must be very large and menacing, either to people or to other machines. In your first paragraph, name the machine and describe in detail its appearance and movements. Include a sketch of the machine. In your second paragraph, show the machine in action. Describe an incident in which the machine threatens—but does not attack—a person or another machine.

A Critical Response

2. **Evaluating the Importance of Realism.** You may have heard a legend about a great creature living in a remote place. Perhaps you know about Sasquatch, a huge, hairy, manlike creature supposedly living in the mountains of northwest North America. These legends are fascinating because they could be true. Nobody has fully explored the remote places to prove the creatures don't exist. Occasionally, "evidence" of a huge creature—such as something that looks like a giant footprint—is found. In the first of two paragraphs discuss whether a machine like the ruum could actually exist in an isolated, unexplored

place. If you think it could, explain in the second paragraph whether this added to your enjoyment of the story. If you think it couldn't, use the second paragraph to explain whether the story was enjoyable even if it wasn't realistic.

Analyzing Language and Vocabulary

Word Histories

Most good dictionaries contain information on word histories. For an individual dictionary entry, this information usually is placed soon after the pronunciation. The following is an excerpt from a dictionary entry.

Braille (brāl) *n.* [after Louis *Braille* (1809–52), blind Fr. teacher who devised it] [*also* **b-**] **1.** a system of printing and writing for the blind, in which characters are formed by patterns of raised dots which are felt with the fingers **2.** the characters used in this system.

You'll note that *Braille,* a system of printing and writing for the blind, is named for Louis Braille, who developed the system.

The following words and phrases are based on the names of persons. Look up each one in a dictionary. Then write down (1) the full name of the person and (2) the definition of the word or phrase.

a. Bunsen burner   e. watt
b. Salk vaccine   f. macadam
c. spoonerism   g. boycott
d. diesel engine   h. zinnia

Reading About the Writer

Arthur Porges (1915–   ) has published more than 70 short stories in various magazines. Porges was born in Chicago, and he taught mathematics at the Western Military Academy and at the Illinois Institute of Technology until his retirement in 1975. Porges, whose best-known stories are "The Ruum" and "The Fly," also writes under the pen names Peter Arthur and Pat Rogers.

THE TELL-TALE HEART

Edgar Allan Poe

"The Tell-Tale Heart" is a showcase for the eerie, spine-chilling details that Edgar Allan Poe was master of. From his first ghastly breath, Poe's narrator assures us of his madness, even as he denies it. This narrator tells us of an old man with an "evil eye," and of a decision to close that eye forever. He tells us of stealth in dark rooms, of fear and terror. His story is one of gruesome murder.

This is a classic horror tale. Yet the story is more than simply "scary." It is also about the nature of the human conscience. It is our conscience that saves us from acting on violent impulses. And if we fail our conscience, it leaves us with feelings of guilt and shame that can destroy our very spirit.

As you read, remember that this narrator might not be telling you the truth.

True!—Nervous—very, very dreadfully nervous I had been and am; but why *will* you say that I am mad? The disease has sharpened my senses—not destroyed—not dulled them. Above all was the sense of hearing acute. I heard all things in the heaven and in the earth. I heard many things in hell. How, then, am I mad? Hearken! And observe how healthily—how calmly I can tell you the whole story.

It is impossible to say how first the idea entered my brain; but once conceived, it haunted me day and night. Object there was none. Passion there was none. I loved the old man. He had never wronged me. He had never given me insult. For his gold I had no desire. I think it was his eye! Yes, it was this! One of his eyes resembled that of a vulture—a pale blue eye, with a film over it. Whenever it fell upon me, my blood ran cold; and so by degrees—very gradually—I made up my mind to take the life of the old man, and thus rid myself of the eye forever.

Now this is the point. You fancy me mad. Madmen know nothing. But you should have seen *me*. You should have seen how wisely I proceeded—with what caution—with what foresight—with what dissimulation[1] I went to work! I was never

kinder to the old man than during the whole week before I killed him. And every night, about midnight, I turned the latch of his door and opened it—oh, so gently! And then, when I had made an opening sufficient for my head, I put in a dark lantern, all closed, closed, so that no light shone

> **Style.** *Style* is the way a writer expresses himself, or herself. Styles can differ, and most good writers have a style all their own. In some cases, style helps you to spot a particular writer's work even though he or she did not sign it.
>
> The main way a writer creates a style is through the kinds of words used. And the kinds of sentences the words are used in—long, short, simple, poetic, etc. In this story, Poe uses these other techniques to help create his unique style:
>
> *Italic type*—used to show that a word is emphasized.
> *Dash*—used to show an abrupt change in thought.
> *Exclamation point*—used to indicate strong feeling.
>
> Watch for italics, dashes, and exclamation points in the story. It will help to read passages out loud to feel the full impact of Poe's famous style.

1. **dissimulation** (dis·sim'yə·lā'shən): pretense; hiding one's true feelings and plans.

The illustrations accompanying this story are from a short movie based on "The Tell-Tale Heart," distributed by Columbia Pictures.

out, and then I thrust in my head. Oh, you would have laughed to see how cunningly I thrust it in! I moved it slowly—very, very slowly, so that I might not disturb the old man's sleep. It took me an hour to place my whole head within the opening so far that I could see him as he lay upon his bed. Ha! Would a madman have been so wise as this? And then, when my head was well in the room, I undid the lantern cautiously—oh, so cautiously—cautiously (for the hinges creaked)—I undid it just so much that a single thin ray fell upon the vulture eye. And this I did for seven long nights—every night just at midnight—but I found the eye always closed; and so it was impossible to do the work; for it was not the old man who vexed me, but his Evil Eye. And every morning, when the day broke, I went boldly into the chamber, and spoke courageously to him, calling him by name in a hearty tone, and inquiring how he had passed the night. So you see he would have been a very profound old man, indeed, to suspect that every night, just at twelve, I looked in upon him while he slept.

Upon the eighth night I was more than usually cautious in opening the door. A watch's minute hand moves more quickly than did mine. Never before that night had I *felt* the extent of my own powers—of my sagacity.[2] I could scarcely contain my feelings of triumph. To think that there I was, opening the door, little by little, and he not even

2. **sagacity** (sə·gas′ə·tē): intelligence and good judgment.

to dream of my secret deeds or thoughts. I fairly chuckled at the idea; and perhaps he heard me; for he moved on the bed suddenly, as if startled. Now you may think that I drew back—but no. His room was as black as pitch with the thick darkness (for the shutters were close fastened, through fear of robbers), and so I knew that he could not see the opening of the door, and I kept pushing it on steadily, steadily.

I had my head in, and was about to open the lantern, when my thumb slipped upon the tin fastening, and the old man sprang up in the bed, crying out—"Who's there?"

I kept quite still and said nothing. For a whole hour I did not move a muscle, and in the meantime I did not hear him lie down. He was still sitting up in the bed listening—just as I have done, night after night, hearkening to the deathwatches[3] in the wall.

Presently I heard a slight groan, and I knew it was the groan of mortal terror. It was not a groan of pain or of grief—oh, no!—it was the low stifled sound that arises from the bottom of the soul when overcharged with awe. I knew the sound well. Many a night, just at midnight, when all the world slept, it has welled up from my own bosom, deepening, with its dreadful echo, the terrors that distracted me. I say I knew it well. I knew what the old man felt, and pitied him, although I chuckled at heart. I knew that he had been lying awake ever since the first slight noise, when he had turned in the bed. His fears had been ever since growing upon him. He had been trying to fancy them causeless, but could not. He had been saying to himself—"It is nothing but the wind in the chimney—it is only a mouse crossing the floor," or "it is merely a cricket which has made a single chirp." Yes, he has been trying to comfort himself with these suppositions; but he had found all in vain. *All in vain;* because Death, in approaching him, had stalked with his black shadow before him, and enveloped the victim. And it was the mournful influence of the unperceived shadow that caused him to feel—although he neither saw nor heard—

---

3. **deathwatches:** small insects, especially certain beetles, whose heads make a tapping sound. Superstitious people believe this noise is a sign of death.

to *feel* the presence of my head within the room.

When I had waited a long time, very patiently, without hearing him lie down, I resolved to open a little—a very, very little crevice in the lantern. So I opened it—you cannot imagine how stealthily, stealthily—until, at length, a single dim ray, like the thread of a spider, shot from out the crevice and fell upon the vulture eye.

It was open—wide, wide open—and I grew furious as I gazed upon it. I saw it with perfect distinctness—all a dull blue, with a hideous veil over it that chilled the very marrow in my bones; but I could see nothing else of the old man's face or person; for I had directed the ray as if by instinct, precisely upon the damned spot.

And now have I not told you that what you mistake for madness is but over-acuteness of the senses? Now, I say, there came to my ears a low, dull, quick sound, such as a watch makes when enveloped in cotton. I knew *that* sound well too. It was the beating of the old man's heart. It increased my fury, as the beating of a drum stimulates the soldier into courage.

But even yet I refrained and kept still. I scarcely breathed. I held the lantern motionless. I tried how steadily I could maintain the ray upon the eye. Meantime the hellish tattoo of the heart increased. It grew quicker and quicker, and louder and louder every instant. The old man's terror *must* have been extreme! It grew louder, I say, louder every moment! Do you mark me well? I have told you that I am nervous: so I am. And now at the dead hour of the night, amid the dreadful silence of that old house, so strange a noise as this excited me to uncontrollable terror. Yet, for some minutes longer I refrained and stood still. But the beating grew louder, louder! I thought the heart must burst. And now a new anxiety seized me—the sound would be heard by a neighbor! The old man's hour had come! With a loud yell, I threw open the lantern and leaped into the room. He shrieked once—once only. In an instant I dragged him to the floor, and pulled the heavy bed over him. I then smiled gaily, to find the deed so far done. But, for many minutes, the heart beat on with a muffled sound. This, however, did not vex me; it would not be heard through the wall. At length it ceased. The old man was dead. I removed the bed and examined the corpse. Yes, he was stone, stone dead. I placed my hand upon the heart and held it there many minutes. There was no pulsation. He was stone dead. His eye would trouble me no more.

If still you think me mad, you will think so no longer when I describe the wise precautions I took for the concealment of the body. The night waned, and I worked hastily, but in silence. First of all I dismembered the corpse. I cut off the head and the arms and the legs.

I then took up three planks from the flooring of the chamber, and deposited all between the scantlings.[4] I then replaced the boards so cleverly, so cunningly, that no human eye—not even *his*— could have detected anything wrong. There was nothing to wash out—no stain of any kind—no bloodspot whatever. I had been too wary for that. A tub had caught all—ha! ha!

When I had made an end of these labors, it was four o'clock—still dark as midnight. As the bell sounded the hour, there came a knocking at the street door. I went down to open it with a light heart—for what had I *now* to fear? There entered three men, who introduced themselves, with perfect suavity, as officers of the police. A shriek had been heard by a neighbor during the night; suspicion of foul play had been aroused; information had been lodged at the police office, and they (the officers) had been deputed to search the premises.

I smiled—for *what* had I to fear? I bade the gentlemen welcome. The shriek, I said, was my own in a dream. The old man, I mentioned, was absent in the country. I took my visitors all over the house. I bade them search—search *well*. I led them, at length, to *his* chamber. I showed them his treasures, secure, undisturbed. In the enthusiasm of my confidence, I brought chairs into the room, and desired them *here* to rest from their fatigues, while I myself, in the wild audacity[5] of my perfect triumph, placed my own seat upon the very spot beneath which reposed the corpse of the victim.

The officers were satisfied. My *manner* had convinced them. I was singularly at ease. They sat, and while I answered cheerily, they chatted familiar things. But, ere long, I felt myself getting pale and wished them gone. My head ached, and I fancied a ringing in my ears: but still they sat and still chatted. The ringing became more distinct—it continued and became more distinct: I talked more freely to get rid of the feeling: but it continued and gained definitiveness—until, at length, I found that the noise was *not* within my ears.

No doubt I now grew *very* pale—but I talked more fluently, and with a heightened voice. Yet the sound increased—and what could I do? It was *a low, dull, quick sound—much such a sound as a watch makes when enveloped in cotton.* I gasped for breath—and yet the officers heard it not. I talked more quickly—more vehemently; but the noise steadily increased. I arose and argued about trifles, in a high key and with violent gesticulations,[6] but the noise steadily increased. Why *would* they not be gone? I paced the floor to and fro with heavy strides, as if excited to fury by the observation of the men—but the noise steadily increased. Oh God! what *could* I do? I foamed— I raved—I swore! I swung the chair upon which I had been sitting, and grated it upon the boards, but the noise arose over all and continually increased. It grew louder—louder—*louder!* And still the men chatted pleasantly, and smiled. Was it possible they heard not? Almighty God!—no, no! They heard!—they suspected!—they *knew!*—they were making a mockery of my horror!—this I thought, and this I think. But anything was better than this agony! Anything was more tolerable than this derision![7] I could bear those hypocritical smiles no longer! I felt that I must scream or die!— and now—again!—hark! louder! louder! louder! *louder!*—

"Villains!" I shrieked, "dissemble[8] no more! I admit the deed!—tear up the planks!—here, here!—it is the beating of his hideous heart!"

---

4. **scantlings:** small crosspieces of wood.
5. **audacity** (ô·das′ə·tē): bold courage; daring.

6. **gesticulations** (jes·tik′yə·lā′shənz): gestures; movements of the hands and arms.
7. **derision** (di·rizh′ən): mockery; ridicule.
8. **dissemble** (di·sem′b'l): pretend.

Responding to the Story

Analyzing the Story

Identifying Facts

1. The narrator begins the story by insisting he is not insane. List three items of evidence the narrator presents early in the story to try to prove his sanity.
2. Explain why the narrator decides to kill the old man.
3. At midnight on eight successive nights the narrator goes to the old man's bedroom. Explain why the narrator does not kill him on the first seven nights.
4. What happens on the eighth night to change the narrator's behavior? Describe how the narrator commits the murder.
5. At four in the morning the police arrive. They seem satisfied that nothing bad has happened in the house. Nevertheless, the narrator becomes agitated. Explain why he confesses to the murder.

Interpreting Meanings

6. Though the narrator claims to be sane, most readers would say he is quite mad: He lives in a **fantasy world** in which things are not really what they seem to be. The title of the story gives you a clue to one thing the narrator gets wrong. On the last night, the narrator says he hears the beating of the old man's heart. Whose heart does he really hear, thumping out the foulness of his deed with a clamor that proves unbearable? Discuss the significance of the heart in this story. (Make sure you know the meaning of *tell-tale*.)
7. **Point of view** refers to the vantage point from which a story is told. "The Tell-Tale Heart" is told in the first person, from the vantage point of the murderer. We learn only what he thinks and feels. Some of what the narrator tells reflects reality, but some does not. The following matters are reported by the narrator. Explain whether you think each report is accurate or inaccurate. Which details strike you as incorrect? What do you think is really going on?

   a. The narrator has no desire for the old man's gold.

   b. The old man emits a "groan of mortal terror" soon after the narrator enters his room on the fateful night.

   c. The police suspect nothing, even though the narrator becomes very agitated, swinging a chair and grating it on the floorboards.

8. The story gives you only limited information. Some of the information is suspect because the narrator is not a very reliable source. If you wanted to get at what really happened, and why, you would need additional information. List three additional things you would like to know. Explain how each would help you better understand the murder.
9. Whom do you think the narrator is telling the story to? Where do you think he is as he tells it?

Evaluating the Story

10. What did you think of the story? Discuss whether you liked it, disliked it, or (if possible) weren't affected much one way or the other. Give specific reasons that help explain your reaction.

Writing About the Story

A Creative Response

1. **Changing the Narrator.** To shed new light on this strange household, let the old man give an account of the younger man three days before the murder. (You'll have to decide whether the old man senses that he's about to be killed.) The murderer will need a name, a physical description, and an occupation. The narration should concentrate, however, on how the murderer is behaving, especially toward the old man. Write two or three paragraphs. Use the first-person pronoun *I*.
2. **Using Another Point of View.** Write the report on the crime that the policemen file when they get back to the station. In the report, have them describe what they thought of the murderer and his behavior. How did he carry out the crime? What were his motives? Include a physical description of what the murderer looked like by the time the police found him.

A Critical Response

3. Describing the Story's Mood. Edgar Allan Poe once wrote that in certain stories every word should help create a "single overwhelming impression." He wanted to create a special mood or atmosphere in such stories. "The Tell-Tale Heart" is this kind of story. In a paragraph, describe the mood in the story. Mention at least three details that help create the mood.

Analyzing Language and Vocabulary

Style

Poe's words and sentence structures are the most important parts of his style. But his style is made up of other elements too—notably italic type, dashes, and exclamation points. To understand what Poe is doing, look at the following versions of the same sentence:

> "The large ball is yellow," Mary said.
> "The *large* ball is—yellow!" Mary said.

In the first version Mary simply states that a large ball is colored yellow. You learn nothing else. In the second version Mary does some other things too. By emphasizing the word *large,* she suggests the existence of another ball of a different size. The dash and the exclamation point indicate that Mary feels there is something unusual about the ball being yellow. (Maybe she expected it to be green.) The dash also shows that Mary pauses in surprise (or uncertainty) before uttering the word *yellow.*

1. Read the first sentence of "The Tell-Tale Heart" aloud. Then discuss what the exclamation point, the dashes, and the italics add to the sentence. Would the sentence's meaning be very different without them?
2. Find two other sentences in the story that contain italics, dashes, and/or an exclamation point. Explain what these punctuation marks add to each sentence.
3. Write a sentence about a large brown dog and two orange cats. Then add italics, a dash, and an exclamation point to alter the meaning of the sentence.

Reading About the Writer

Most people know **Edgar Allan Poe** (1809–1849) as the author of some of the world's most famous horror stories. Poe was born in Boston, the son of

traveling actors. His mother died when he was not quite three years old, and his father soon deserted the children. Edgar was taken in by the wealthy Allan family in Richmond, Virginia, and given a first-class education. But his life was always unhappy, in part because he was constantly arguing with his foster father about money. Eventually, he broke all his ties with the Allans, and was left penniless. When, in 1836, he married his young cousin, Virginia Clemm, and moved in with her and her mother in Baltimore, it was probably an attempt to find a new family. Poe made very little money from his writing, and he seemed to live on the brink of disaster. When Virginia died of tuberculosis in 1847, he fell apart. Never able to tolerate any amount of alcohol, he was found dying in a Baltimore gutter on a rainy election day in 1849. It is thought that some politicians got him drunk and dragged him from place to place to cast illegal votes. Poe is now considered a major American writer, the first to explore the dark side of the human imagination. Some of his other famous stories include "The Masque of the Red Death," "The Pit and the Pendulum," and "The Fall of the House of Usher." Poe's poem "The Raven" is on page 385.

FANTASY

One purpose of fantasy is to allow a reader to travel in his or her imagination to a world that doesn't exist. In some stories, the fantasy is so far-fetched that a reader doesn't have any trouble remembering that it couldn't actually happen. Other fantasy stories seem as real as a newspaper story, except for one or two incredible elements.

The following two excerpts are from fantasies written hundreds of years apart. After you read the excerpts, answer the questions that follow them. In the first excerpt, Lemuel Gulliver, the victim of a shipwreck, awakens to find his arms, legs, and head tied securely to the ground.

I

I could only look upwards; the sun began to grow hot, and the light offended my eyes. I heard a confused noise about me, but, in the posture I lay, could see nothing except the sky. In a little time I felt something alive moving on my left leg, which advancing gently forward over my breast, came almost up to my chin; when, bending my eyes downward as much as I could, I perceived it to be a human creature not six inches high, with a bow and arrow in his hands, and a quiver at his back. In the meantime, I felt at least forty more of the same kind (as I conjectured) following the first. I was in the utmost astonishment and roared so loud, that they all ran back in a fright; and some of them, as I was afterwards told, were hurt with the falls they got by leaping from my sides upon the ground.

—from *Gulliver's Travels*
Jonathan Swift

1. Does the beginning of the excerpt lead you to expect an ordinary story, or one that is startling and surprising?
2. Other than the sun and the sky, what is the first thing that Gulliver sees?
3. Reread the sentence in which he describes this sight. What are his feelings as he gives this description?
4. In what way is the creature Gulliver sees recognizable? In what way is he a creature of fantasy?
5. Suppose you were curious about Gulliver's experiences with these unusual creatures. As a result, you decided to read *Gulliver's Travels*, which is one of the classics of world literature. Explain why you might enjoy the story without ever believing that these creatures could ever really exist.

II

In this next excerpt, a man named Eckels has paid ten thousand dollars to travel in a time machine some sixty million years into the past, where he will hunt dinosaur. Travis, the guide for Time Safari, Inc., explains how they will move about in the prehistoric jungle they are visiting.

"And that," he said, "is the Path, laid by Time Safari for your use. It floats six inches above the earth. Doesn't touch so much as one grass blade, flower, or tree. It's an antigravity metal. Its purpose is to keep you from touching this world of the past in any way. Stay on the Path. Don't go off it. I repeat. *Don't go off*. For *any* reason! If you fall off, there's a penalty. And don't shoot any animal we don't okay."

"Why?" asked Eckels.

"We don't want to change the Future. We don't belong here in the Past. The government doesn't *like* us here. We have to pay big graft to keep our franchise. A Time Machine is finicky business. Not knowing it, we might kill an important animal, a small bird, a roach, a flower even, thus destroying an important link in a growing species."

"That's not clear," said Eckels.

"All right," Travis continued, "say we accidentally kill one mouse here. That means all the future families of this one particular mouse are destroyed, right?"

"Right."

"And all the families of the families of the families of that one mouse! With a stamp of your foot, you annihilate first one, then a dozen, then a thousand, then a million, a *billion* possible mice!"

"So they're dead," said Eckles. "So what?"

"So what?" Travis snorted quietly. "Well, what about the foxes that'll need those mice to survive? For want of ten mice, a fox dies. For want of ten foxes, a lion starves. For want of a lion, all manner of insects, vultures, infinite billions of life forms are thrown into chaos and destruction. Eventually it all boils down to this: Fifty-nine million years later, a cave man, one of a dozen on the *entire world*, goes hunting wild boar or saber-toothed tiger for food. But you, friend, have *stepped* on all the tigers in that region. By stepping on *one* single mouse. So the cave man starves. And the cave man, please note, is not just *any* expendable man, no! He is an *entire future nation*. From his loins would have sprung ten sons. From *their* loins one hundred sons, and thus onward to a civilization. Destroy this one man, and you destroy a race, a people, an entire history of life. It is comparable to slaying some of Adam's grandchildren. The stomp of your foot, on one mouse, could start an earthquake, the effects of which could shake our earth and destinies down through Time, to their very foundations. With the death of that one cave man, a billion years yet unborn are throttled in the womb. Perhaps Rome never rises on its seven hills. Perhaps Europe is forever a dark forest, and only Asia waxes healthy and teeming. Step on a mouse and you leave your print, like a Grand Canyon, across Eternity. Queen Elizabeth might never be born, Washington might not cross the Delaware, there might never be a United States at all. So be careful. Stay on the Path. *Never* step off!"

—from "A Sound of Thunder," Ray Bradbury

1. Do the characters seem like people from another world, or do they seem familiar? Mention specific lines of dialogue to support your answer.
2. Why do you suppose Eckels wants to take a trip into the past?
3. How would you describe the relationship between Travis and Eckels?
4. Describe the Path built for the hunters. How does the writer present the Path as the product of scientific research?
5. Summarize Travis's explanation of the dangers of stepping off the Path.
6. Does the explanation make sense to you? Give reasons to back up your answer.
7. How does your reaction to Travis's explanation affect your enjoyment of the excerpt?

Writing

1. **Outlining a Fantasy Plot.** Think up a plot for an original fantasy story. First decide which of these two types of fantasy you want to write: (1) a story in which incredible things happen with little or no explanation; or (2) a story with a familiar setting, in which one or two fantastic elements have a somewhat scientific explanation. Write an outline for the plot of your story, including the following literary elements. (For help, see the introduction to the Short Story unit in this book.)

   a. setting
   b. character(s)
   c. basic situation
   d. conflict(s)
   e. complications
   f. climax
   g. resolution

2. **Writing a Fantasy.** Use your outline to write a fantasy story. Keep the story relatively brief, about two to five pages. Make sure, however, that readers are given enough information so they understand what's going on. Include interesting details, especially if your story takes place in a very unusual world.

   When you are finished, exchange stories with a classmate. Give each other comments about the stories, and make revisions if necessary. Then, if you like, read your story out loud before your class.

WRITING A FANTASY

Writing Assignment

Write a brief short story that takes place in a fantasy world that you create. The story should, of course, have a plot. It should also contain interesting details about the character(s) and setting.

Background

Fantasy is an imaginative kind of writing that tells about events that could not happen in the world as we know it. A fantasy may be set in a place similar to the real world. Fabulous things take place, however, such as the events in "Story from Bear Country" (page 100). More often fantasies are set in an imagined world—another planet or a once-upon-a-time kingdom—that contains inhabitants and machines different from those on earth as we know it today. "The Ruum" (page 120) is an example of this type of fantasy. **Science fiction** is a type of fantasy that generally tells of events that might happen in the future because of technological or social changes.

Whenever you write something original, something all your own, you are using a critical-thinking skill called **synthesis.** *Synthesis* means "putting together parts or elements to form a whole." When you write a story, you have to put together certain elements, such as **setting, character,** and **plot.**

Prewriting

To help create your fantasy world, answer the following questions. Remember that no rules or limits apply; use your imagination and have fun with this assignment.

Setting	Details
What do the inhabitants look like? Do they have special powers?	
What does the world look like? (Think of geography weather, plants, houses.)	
What kinds of animals (or creatures) inhabit the world? Are they wild or tame? Are they plentiful, or are they in danger of extinction?	
Is the kingdom peaceful or warlike?	
How developed is the civilization? Do the inhabitants have advanced technology, art, music, literature?	
How do the inhabitants communicate?	

Now plan the action in your story. Answer these questions:

Characters and Plot	Details
Who is the main character? Who are other characters?	
What problem will the main character face? What will be the story's main **conflict,** or struggle?	
How will the story end?	

Choose a **point of view,** that is, decide who will be the storyteller, or **narrator.** The narrator may be a visitor to the fantasy world, an inhabitant of the world, or an **omniscient storyteller** who does not take part in the events. (Remember that these are three possible points of view—omniscient, first person, and limited third person.)

Writing

Try to write a story in which something interesting, exciting, or surprising happens to the main character. Use lots of specific details in describing what life in the fantasy world is like.

To get an idea about how to begin your story, look at the following sample opening paragraph. It introduces the story's main character and contains details that give the reader some idea about such things as the world's inhabitants, climate, and plant life.

> Anaidid woke with the continual sun sending fingers of heat through the heavily draped room. A fan made from the ever-present prickly fern leaves slowly turned above her head. Careful not to use too much of the precious clear fluid that sustained what little life there was on the planet Najak, Anaidid wet her eyelids, slicked down her blue-black hair, and washed away a few spots of purple dirt on her hands, knees, and feet.

You may, if you wish, continue writing this story. Tell what exciting or mysterious adventure awaits Anaidid on the planet of Najak. Or you may write your own story set in a fantasy world you create. Your finished story should be at least two pages long.

**Revising
Self-Check**

1. Does the story have a definite plot with a main character involved in a struggle, problem, or adventure?
2. Is there a satisfying ending?
3. Does the story include interesting details of the fantasy world setting?
4. Are sentences punctuated correctly? Are words spelled correctly?

Partner Check

1. Are there any spelling errors?
2. Are sentences punctuated correctly?
3. Is the story interesting to read? Does it contain surprise, excitement, or adventure?
4. What I like best about this paper:
5. What needs improvement:

THE ELEMENTS OF A SHORT STORY

Down Grade by Michael Wright
(1987). Oil.

UNIT FOUR

John Leggett

Unit Outline
THE ELEMENTS OF
A SHORT STORY

The short story isn't a snippet from the newspaper. It isn't realism. It is, as in all forms of art, taking the materials of every day (or otherwise) and using them to raise the consciousness of our lives to higher levels by the use of the art: to get something said.

—William Carlos Williams

It is a great gift to be able to tell a story so that it grasps, and holds, the attention of listeners, so that it moves them some-how. You might call this a magical gift, for a good storyteller casts a kind of spell.

A good storyteller can entertain people, enlighten them, possibly persuade them to see life in a new way. While this gift for story-telling is instinctive—a "knack," such as one might have for catching a ball or playing the flute—it is also a skill that can be learned.

Learning the skill, of course, begins with understanding its elements. In broad terms there are five elements of storytelling:

Plot
Character
Point of View
Setting
Theme

Plot: A Chain of Related Events

Plot is the story itself. **Plot** is a chain of related events, each event developing out of the prior one. When a plot is well told, it "hooks" us, that is, it catches our curiosity about what will happen next. A good plot draws us along after the narrator, just as a fish is hooked and played and reeled in by an expert angler.

The first thing to recognize about plot is the nature of that hook which pulls us along and keeps us reading. The hook grabs our own curiosity, and it does this by making us wonder about the outcome of a conflict. When a story is strong, you can be reasonably sure its conflict is strong.

Conflict, as you have learned in Unit One of this book, is a struggle of some kind. Conflict can take place between a character and another person, or between a character and a whole society. Very often the conflict exists because a character is struggling within himself or herself. This means that the character is fighting against some characteristic that is causing trouble: Henry's fear of heights keeps him from visiting his brother in New York; Nilda is so unsure of herself she hides in the bathroom during the dance.

The second thing to recognize about a strong plot is that it has a structure, just as a house or boat does. Classically, the structure of a story is like an incline that rises to a peak and then takes a sharp drop. It looks like this:

The Elements of a Short Story

Drawing by W. Miller.

© 1987 The New Yorker Magazine, Inc.

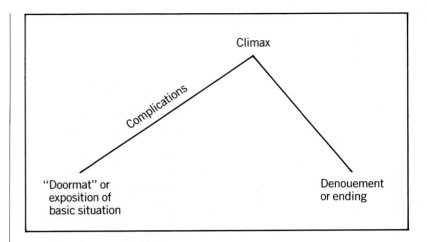

The "doormat" is the entryway to the story. Usually this is called the **exposition** of the story. The word *doormat* is appropriate because this part of the story leads us into the basic situation and introduces us to the characters. Here we learn about the story's **conflict:** The characters want something, or have a problem of some sort. (Polly feels her overcoat is too out of style to wear to school.)

Complications are events that make the character's problem even worse. (Since her parents are away, Polly "borrows" the handsome scarlet coat her father has given her mother for a recent birthday.) **Further complication.** (At school, the scarlet coat disappears from the cloakroom. Polly doesn't know what to do, and is desperate with worry.)

The **climax** is the most emotional and the most tense part of the plot. This is when the conflict is worked out one way or another. (A tearful Polly confesses to her mother, who is firm but understanding. They decide to discuss the situation. Later in the day, Polly's teacher, explaining that she had put the scarlet coat in her own closet for safekeeping, returns the coat.)

The **denouement** (dā·nōō·mä*n'*) or **resolution** ("untying" a knot) is when the story is closed. The conflicts are now resolved. (Polly's parents figure out a way to get their daughter a new coat. All three are concerned about the teacher, whom Polly secretly suspects has always wanted a scarlet coat.)

Characters: The Strength of a Story

We might well have begun with **character** as the primary element of storytelling. The best stories usually revolve around a main character and take most of their strength from that person. Moreover, it is a character that generates a story's action. It is Polly's nature, for example, her desire to be admired at school, that brings on the adventure of the scarlet coat.

Characters, as you learned in Unit Two, are created in several ways to help us feel we know them as if they are living human beings. A writer can tell us what people look like, how they act, how they speak, and how other people respond to them. Writers can also tell us directly what a person is like: that one is lazy, that another is idealistic, that another one frequently hates the way he looks.

Character is so important to a story that all a writer need do to hook our curiosity is show us the behavior of one person in a set of circumstances. If we are shown how that person deals with difficulty and opportunity, and if we are given some inkling of the reason for this behavior, we are usually captives.

To most of us, human behavior is the most fascinating of subjects. When a writer describes behavior through a believable character, we are learning what to expect from other people in actual life; from our mothers perhaps, or our fathers, sisters, brothers, friends, and enemies. Even more important, we are probing the greatest and most personal of mysteries—ourselves. We are learning how we are likely to behave when we are in peril or in luck, when we succeed or fail, when we fall in or out of love.

Point of View: Who Is Telling the Story?

This is the third element of storytelling and a very important one. **Point of view** has to do with *who* is telling the story.

In the past, most stories were told by an **omniscient** ("all-knowing") **narrator.** This god like being, who is *not* in the story, looks down on all the characters as if from a mountaintop. This all-knowing narrator can tell us what every main character is thinking. This narrator can, at will, enter the consciousness of any character and let us share his or her private thoughts and feelings. This omniscient narrator is sometimes compared to a puppeteer, who manipulates people, supplying their thoughts and voices from a position well above the action. We usually think of the omniscient narrator as the story's author.

Striving for greater realism, contemporary storytellers show a preference for the **third-person narrator.** Like the omniscient narrator, this narrator is *not* in the story. What makes this narrator different from the omniscient narrator is that this narrator focuses on *one* of the characters. Yet, this narrator is *not* that character at all, and so refers to the character and to everyone in the story with the third-person pronoun, "he" or "she." In this point of view, we feel as if we are experiencing everything in the story right along with this one character. We see the story through his or her eyes.

A third point of view is also very popular with modern storytellers. This is the **first-person point of view.** In this point of view, one of the characters tells the story using the first-person pronoun, *I.* The first-person point of view is generally held to be the most immediate of the three. It puts us, the readers, most directly into the stream of the narrative. With this point of view, however, we know only what our narrator knows. Sometimes this means we are kept in a special kind of suspense. Sometimes it means we are being tricked by an untrustworthy narrator. In some of Edgar Allan Poe's stories, for example, we hear the first-person voice of a

Illustration by N. C. Wyeth for Robert Louis Stevenson's *Kidnapped* (1913).

The Riddle Game by T. Kirk.

narrator who is clearly crazy, and we don't know what we are to believe (see page 132).

If, at first, point of view does not seem important to you (it's the same story after all), just think of how different the story of a murder would be if it were told from the victim's point of view rather than from the fisherman's who finds him. Think of how different the story of a wedding day would be if it were told by the groom left waiting at the altar, rather than by the truant bride.

Setting: Place and Time

Setting is the place and time in which the story unfolds. It may be vital to the story's impact. Setting surely is important if we *feel* it—if we get to know the Southern town with its general store and bullfrog swamp, or the Northern city with its tenement houses and littered streets. If a story is well told, we will recall the setting later, long after we've put the story aside.

In some stories, the setting becomes a principal force and threatens the characters. In this case, setting creates the conflict. Think of that ugly mining town with its dark, underground shafts where the men spend the better part of their lives. Think of how often this setting is used in stories as the adversary, as the source of conflict between, and within, the characters. Think also of the stories in Unit One by Jack London (page 6) and John Muir (page 40).

Theme: The Story's Main Idea

Finally, there is theme. **Theme** is the idea that underlies the story. Theme tells us what the story means and why the author wrote it in the first place.

After you finish a story, you automatically start thinking about the theme. You ask yourself: What does this story mean? What does it tell me about people, about how they behave in life, and about how life treats them? One way to discover theme is to ask yourself this series of questions:

1. Who is the main character?

2. What is the story about: What is its subject? (War? Love? Thievery? Growing up?)

3. What did the character in the story learn about this subject?

Theme has to be stated in a sentence. A subject can be stated in one phrase ("growing-up"). A theme has to say something about the subject ("Growing up can be a painful but comical experience").

A story's theme can reveal something about the writer, too. When we discover the theme of a story, we often know whether the writer assumes people are doomed to failure and disappointment in life, or whether, with a little luck and wit, we could all be in for a marvelous adventure.

Responding to a Story

Here is a famous short story that uses all the elements of fiction to hook your curiosity and bring you to a resolution you might not expect. One reader's notes are in the margins. You might want to take notes of your own as you read.

A Man Who Had No Eyes

A beggar was coming down the avenue just as Mr. Parsons emerged from his hotel.

He was a blind beggar, carrying the traditional battered cane, and thumping his way before him with the cautious, half-furtive effort of the sightless. He was a shaggy, thick-necked fellow; his coat was greasy about the lapels and pockets, and his hand splayed over the cane's crook with a futile sort of clinging. He wore a black pouch slung over his shoulder. Apparently he had something to sell.

The air was rich with spring; sun was warm and yellowed on the asphalt. Mr. Parsons, standing there in front of his hotel and noting the *clack-clack* approach of the sightless man, felt a sudden and foolish sort of pity for all blind creatures.

And, thought Mr. Parsons, he was very glad to be alive. A few years ago he had been little more than a skilled laborer; now he was successful, respected, admired. . . . Insurance. . . . And he had done it alone, unaided, struggling beneath handicaps. . . . And he was still young. The blue air of spring, fresh from its memories of windy pools and lush shrubbery, could thrill him with eagerness.

He took a step forward just as the tap-tapping blind man passed him by. Quickly the shabby fellow turned.

"Listen, guv'nor. Just a minute of your time."

Mr. Parsons said, "It's late. I have an appointment. Do you want me to give you something?"

"I ain't no beggar, guv'nor. You bet I ain't. I got a handy little article here"—he fumbled until he could press a small object into Mr. Parsons's hand—"that I sell. One buck. Best cigarette lighter made."

Mr. Parsons stood there, somewhat annoyed and embarrassed. He was a handsome figure with his immaculate gray suit and gray hat and malacca stick.[1] Of course the man with the cigarette lighters could not see him. . . . "But I don't smoke," he said.

"Listen. I bet you know plenty people who smoke. Nice little present," wheedled the man. "And, mister, you wouldn't mind helping a poor guy out?" He clung to Mr. Parsons's sleeve.

Mr. Parsons sighed and felt in his vest pocket. He brought out two half dollars and pressed them into the man's hand. "Certainly, I'll help you out. As you say, I can give it to someone.

Will Parsons help the beggar?

This description of the beggar's appearance is a bit disgusting.

I wonder what he's selling?
Spring setting.

Parsons seems like a nice, caring guy.

He's upbeat, too.
What handicaps?

Why *memories* of spring? Maybe he hasn't taken a vacation in a while.

Hmm. Just pretending to be blind? Or are his other senses very keen?

Got to respect that.

I wonder why he carries a cane. But then maybe he's English—some Englishmen carry canes for looks.

I bet this bugged Parsons. I feel sorry for the beggar.

---

1. **malacca stick:** cane made from palm wood.

Maybe the elevator boy would——" He hesitated, not wishing to be boorish and inquisitive, even with a blind peddler. "Have you lost your sight entirely?"

The shaggy man pocketed the two half dollars. "Fourteen years, guv'nor." Then he added with an insane sort of pride: "Westbury, sir. I was one of 'em."

"Westbury," repeated Mr. Parsons. "Ah, yes. The chemical explosion. . . . The papers haven't mentioned it for years. But at the time it was supposed to be one of the greatest disasters in——"

"They've all forgot about it." The fellow shifted his feet wearily. "I tell you, guv'nor, a man who was in it don't forget about it. Last thing I ever saw was C shop going up in one grand smudge, and that gas pouring in at all the busted windows."

Mr. Parsons coughed. But the blind peddler was caught up with the train of his one dramatic reminiscence. And, also, he was thinking that there might be more half dollars in Mr. Parsons's pocket.

"Just think about it, guv'nor. There was a hundred and eight people killed, about two hundred injured, and over fifty of them lost their eyes. Blind as bats——" He groped forward until his dirty hand rested against Mr. Parsons's coat. "I tell you, sir, there wasn't nothing worse than that in the war. If I had lost my eyes in the war, okay. I would have been well took care of. But I was just a workman, working for what was in it. And I got it. You're right I got it, while the capitalists were making their dough! They was insured, don't worry about that. They——"

"Insured," repeated his listener. "Yes. That's what I sell——"

"You want to know how I lost my eyes?" cried the man. "Well, here it is!" His words fell with the bitter and studied drama of a story often told, and told for money. "I was there in C shop, last of all the folks rushing out. Out in the air there was a chance, even with buildings exploding right and left. A lot of guys made it safe out the door and got away. And just when I was about there, crawling along between those big vats, a guy behind me grabs my leg. He says, 'Let me past, you——!' Maybe he was nuts. I dunno. I try to forgive him in my heart, guv'nor. But he was bigger than me. He hauls me back and climbs right over me! Tramples me into the dirt. And he gets out, and I lie there with all that poison gas pouring down on all sides of me, and flame and stuff. . . ." He swallowed—a studied sob—and stood dumbly expectant. He could imagine the next words: *Tough luck, my man. Now, I want to*——"That's the story, guv'nor."

The spring wind shrilled past them, damp and quivering.

"Not quite," said Mr. Parsons.

The blind peddler shivered crazily. "Not quite? What you mean, you——?"

"The story is true," Mr. Parsons said, "except that it was the other way around."

"Other way around?" He croaked unamiably. "Say, guv'nor——"

What does "boorish" mean? Probably means "like a boor."

I wonder why he asked?

Why would he be proud? Why *insane*? What is Westbury? What happened there?

Now I know.

Good memory.

That explains the beggar's blindness.

The beggar knows how to milk the public. Maybe he's not sympathetic after all.

Dirty hand. Maybe I don't like this beggar.

Capitalists? They must have been unfair to the workers.

He's told this story before—knows how to tell it too. Could the storyteller dislike the beggar?

The storyteller is critical of this beggar. He's waiting for sympathy.

Why has the spring become cold?

Why is Parsons arguing with him?

What?
Croaked makes the beggar sound like a frog.

"I was in C shop," said Mr. Parsons. "It was the other way around. You were the fellow who hauled back on me and climbed over me. You were bigger than I was, Markwardt."

The blind man stood for a long time, swallowing hoarsely. He gulped: "Parsons. I thought you——" And then he screamed fiendishly: "Yes. Maybe so. Maybe so. But I'm blind! I'm blind, and you've been standing here letting me spout to you, and laughing at me every minute! I'm blind!"

People in the street turned to stare at him.

"You got away, but I'm blind! Do you hear? I'm—"

"Well," said Mr. Parsons, "don't make such a row about it, Markwardt. . . . So am I."

—MacKinley Kantor

> **Aha! The beggar is the evil one!**

> **I guess he really is blind. Not just pretending.**

> **What a twist! How did I miss this detail? I have to go back and see if there are any clues. The title!**

Thinking Over the Story

Like many stories told years ago, this one relies for its power on a trick ending. The pleasure of the story is in feeling that shock when the truth is revealed about Mr. Parsons.

No one likes to be tricked unfairly. Did the writer drop clues about the story's ending? This reader did wonder about Mr. Parsons's cane. But there were other clues about Mr. Parsons's eyes that were missed. Can you find them?

Notice that this reader's feelings for the beggar changed as the story went on. This reader feels that the storyteller is making the beggar seem disgusting. Can you locate words used by the narrator that support this suggestion? Do you agree with this readers feelings about the beggar?

Finally, look at the reader's last question. Suppose these were your reading notes. How would you answer this last question?

If you wanted to write about this story, which element would you choose to write about? The *plot* with its trick ending? The *character* of the beggar? The *point of view,* which seems to force the reader to dislike the beggar? The *theme* of the story?

You might even talk about *setting.* Where does this reader notice details about setting? Did you notice them? What do you think they mean?

RAYMOND'S RUN

Toni Cade Bambara

One of the many virtues of this story about a black girl is its voice. It is the voice of a girl, a smart, streetwise, cocky kid named Squeaky. She doesn't always use standard grammar but her voice is musical, vivid, comic, ringing with truth. It makes us into Squeaky fans from the start.

To hear Squeaky's voice, you should listen to the story read aloud—or read it aloud yourself.

The story takes place in Harlem, a section of New York City.

Dialect. Have you ever heard a Midwest accent or a Southern drawl? Each region of the United States has its own dialect, or way of speaking English, that sets it apart from other regions. Some cities have their own dialects as well. A *dialect* usually involves distinct ways of pronouncing many words. For instance, in most parts of the United States, *Missouri* is pronounced mi·zoor′ē, but in the state itself and in other parts of the Midwest the name is often pronounced mi·zoor′ə. A dialect also contains special vocabulary. In some parts of the country groceries are carried in a *bag,* while in other parts they are carried in a *sack* or a *poke.* Grammar also differs. In a Brooklyn dialect a person might say *youse* instead of the standard *you* when referring to two or more people; a Southerner might say *you-all.* Watch out for instances of special pronunciation, vocabulary, and grammar in "Raymond's Run."

I don't have much work to do around the house like some girls. My mother does that. And I don't have to earn my pocket money. George runs errands for the big boys and sells Christmas cards. And anything else that's got to get done, my father does. All I have to do in life is mind my brother Raymond, which is enough.

Sometimes I slip and say my little brother Raymond. But as any fool can see, he's much bigger and he's older too. But a lot of people call him my little brother cause he needs looking after cause he's not quite right. And a lot of smart mouths got lots to say about that too, especially when George was minding him. But now, if anybody has anything to say to Raymond, anything to say about his big head, they have to come by me. And I don't play the dozens[1] or believe in standing around with somebody in my face doing a lot of talking. I much rather just knock you down and take my chances even if I am a little girl with skinny arms and a squeaky voice, which is how I got the name Squeaky. And if things get too rough, I run. And as anybody can tell you, I'm the fastest thing on two feet.

There is no track meet that I don't win the first-place medal. I used to win the twenty-yard dash when I was a little kid in kindergarten. Nowadays, it's the fifty-yard dash. And tomorrow I'm subject to run the quarter-meter relay all by myself and come in first, second, and third. The big kids call me Mercury[2] cause I'm the swiftest thing in the neighborhood. Everybody knows that—except two people who know better, my father and me. He can beat me to Amsterdam Avenue with me having a two-fire-hydrant head start and him running with his hands in his pockets and whistling. But that's private information. Cause can you imagine some thirty-five-year-old man stuffing himself into PAL[3] shorts to race little kids? So as far as everyone's concerned, I'm the fastest and that goes for Gretchen, too, who has put out the tale that she is going to win the first-place medal this year. Ridiculous. In the second place, she's got short legs. In the third place, she's got freckles. In the first place, no one can beat me and that's all there is to it.

I'm standing on the corner admiring the weather and about to take a stroll down Broadway so I can practice my breathing exercises, and I've got Raymond walking on the inside close to the buildings, cause he's subject to fits of fantasy and starts thinking he's a circus performer and that the curb is a tightrope strung high in the air. And sometimes after a rain he likes to step down off his tightrope right into the gutter and slosh around getting his shoes and cuffs wet. Then I get hit

---

1. **the dozens:** game in which two people trade insults. The first person to show anger at an insult loses the game.
2. **Mercury:** in Roman mythology, messenger of the gods known for his speed.
3. **PAL:** Police Athletic League.

when I get home. Or sometimes if you don't watch him he'll dash across traffic to the island in the middle of Broadway and give the pigeons a fit. Then I have to go behind him apologizing to all the old people sitting around trying to get some sun and getting all upset with the pigeons fluttering around them, scattering their newspapers and up-setting the wax-paper lunches in their laps. So I keep Raymond on the inside of me, and he plays like he's driving a stagecoach, which is OK by me so long as he doesn't run me over or interrupt my breathing exercises, which I have to do on account of I'm serious about my running, and I don't care who knows it.

Now some people like to act like things come easy to them, won't let on that they practice. Not me. I'll high-prance down 34th Street like a rodeo pony to keep my knees strong even if it does get my mother uptight so that she walks ahead like she's not with me, don't know me, is all by herself on a shopping trip, and I am somebody else's crazy child. Now you take Cynthia Procter for instance. She's just the opposite. If there's a test tomorrow, she'll say something like, "Oh, I guess I'll play handball this afternoon and watch tele-vision tonight," just to let you know she ain't thinking about the test. Or like last week when she won the spelling bee for the millionth time, "A good thing you got *receive,* Squeaky, cause I would have got it wrong. I completely forgot about the spelling bee." And she'll clutch the lace on her blouse like it was a narrow escape. Oh, brother. But of course when I pass her house on my early morning trots around the block, she is practicing the scales on the piano over and over and over and over. Then in music class she always lets herself get bumped around so she falls acci-dentally on purpose onto the piano stool and is so surprised to find herself sitting there that she de-cides just for fun to try out the old keys. And what do you know—Chopin's[4] waltzes just spring out of her fingertips and she's the most surprised thing in the world. A regular prodigy.[5] I could kill people like that. I stay up all night studying the words for the spelling bee. And you can see me any time of day practicing running. I never walk if I can trot, and shame on Raymond if he can't keep up. But of course he does, cause if he hangs back some-one's liable to walk up to him and get smart, or take his allowance from him, or ask him where he got that great pumpkin head. People are so stupid sometimes.

So I'm strolling down Broadway breathing out and breathing in on counts of seven, which is my lucky number, and here comes Gretchen and her sidekicks: Mary Louise, who used to be a friend of mine when she first moved to Harlem from Baltimore and got beat up by everybody till I took up for her on account of her mother and my mother used to sing in the same choir when they were young girls, but people ain't grateful, so now she hangs out with the new girl Gretchen and talks about me like a dog; and Rosie, who is as fat as I am skinny and has a big mouth where Raymond is concerned and is too stupid to know that there is not a big deal of difference between herself and Raymond and that she can't afford to throw stones. So they are steady coming up Broadway and I see right away that it's going to be one of those Dodge City scenes[6] cause the street ain't that big and they're close to the buildings just as we are. First I think I'll step into the candy store and look over the new comics and let them pass. But that's chicken and I've got a reputation to consider. So then I think I'll just walk straight on through them or even over them if necessary. But as they get to me, they slow down. I'm ready to fight, cause like I said I don't feature a whole lot of chitchat, I much prefer to just knock you down right from the jump and save everybody a lotta precious time.

"You signing up for the May Day races?" smiles Mary Louise, only it's not a smile at all. A dumb question like that doesn't deserve an an-swer. Besides, there's just me and Gretchen stand-ing there really, so no use wasting my breath talking to shadows.

"I don't think you're going to win this time,"

---

4. **Frédéric François Chopin** (shō′pan): Polish composer and pianist (1810–1849).
5. **prodigy** (präd′ə·jē): child with extraordinary talent.

6. **Dodge City scenes:** showdowns like those in Western movies and television programs set in places such as Dodge City, Kansas. In a typical showdown, the marshal faces an outlaw ready to use his pistol.

says Rosie, trying to signify with her hands on her hips all salty, completely forgetting that I have whupped her many times for less salt than that.

"I always win cause I'm the best," I say straight at Gretchen, who is, as far as I'm concerned, the only one talking in this ventriloquist-dummy routine. Gretchen smiles, but it's not a smile, and I'm thinking that girls never really smile at each other because they don't know how and don't want to know how and there's probably no one to teach us how, cause grown-up girls don't know either. Then they all look at Raymond, who has just brought his mule team to a standstill. And they're about to see what trouble they can get into through him.

"What grade you in now, Raymond?"

"You got anything to say to my brother, you say it to me, Mary Louise Williams of Raggedy Town, Baltimore."

"What are you, his mother?" sasses Rosie.

"That's right, Fatso. And the next word out of anybody and I'll be *their* mother too." So they just stand there and Gretchen shifts from one leg to the other and so do they. Then Gretchen puts her hands on her hips and is about to say something with her freckle-face self but doesn't. Then she walks around me looking me up and down but keeps walking up Broadway, and her sidekicks follow her. So me and Raymond smile at each other and he says, "Gidyap" to his team and I continue with my breathing exercises, strolling down Broadway toward the ice man on 145th with not a care in the world cause I am Miss Quicksilver[7] herself.

I take my time getting to the park on May Day because the track meet is the last thing on the program. The biggest thing on the program is the Maypole dancing, which I can do without, thank you, even if my mother thinks it's a shame I don't take part and act like a girl for a change. You'd think my mother'd be grateful not to have to make me a white organdy dress with a big satin sash and buy me new white baby-doll shoes that can't be taken out of the box till the big day. You'd think she'd be glad her daughter ain't out there prancing around a Maypole getting the new clothes all dirty and sweaty and trying to act like a fairy or a flower or whatever you're supposed to be when you should be trying to be yourself, whatever that is, which is, as far as I am concerned, a poor black girl who really can't afford to buy shoes and a new dress you only wear once a lifetime cause it won't fit next year.

I was once a strawberry in a Hansel and Gretel pageant when I was in nursery school and didn't have no better sense than to dance on tiptoe with my arms in a circle over my head doing umbrella steps and being a perfect fool just so my mother and father could come dressed up and clap. You'd think they'd know better than to encourage that kind of nonsense. I am not a strawberry. I do not dance on my toes. I run. That is what I am all about. So I always come late to the May Day program, just in time to get my number pinned on and lay in the grass till they announce the fifty-yard dash.

I put Raymond in the little swings, which is a tight squeeze this year and will be impossible next year. Then I look around for Mr. Pearson, who pins the numbers on. I'm really looking for Gretchen if you want to know the truth, but she's not around. The park is jam-packed. Parents in hats and corsages and breast-pocket handkerchiefs peeking up. Kids in white dresses and light-blue suits. The parkees unfolding chairs and chasing the rowdy kids from Lenox[8] as if they had no right to be there. The big guys with their caps on backward, leaning against the fence swirling the basketballs on the tips of their fingers, waiting for all these crazy people to clear out the park so they can play. Most of the kids in my class are carrying bass drums and glockenspiels[9] and flutes. You'd think they'd put in a few bongos or something for real like that.

Then here comes Mr. Pearson with his clipboard and his cards and pencils and whistles and safety pins and fifty million other things he's always dropping all over the place with his clumsy self. He sticks out in a crowd because he's on stilts. We used to call him Jack and the Beanstalk

---

7. **Quicksilver:** alternate name for *mercury,* a silverish metal that is liquid and can be very fluid.

8. **Lenox:** Lenox Avenue, a major street in Harlem.
9. **glockenspiels** (gläk′ən·spēlz′): percussion instruments with flat metal bars that are struck; often used in marching bands.

to get him mad. But I'm the only one that can outrun him and get away, and I'm too grown for that silliness now.

"Well, Squeaky," he says, checking my name off the list and handing me number seven and two pins. And I'm thinking he's got no right to call me Squeaky, if I can't call him Beanstalk.

"Hazel Elizabeth Deborah Parker," I correct him and tell him to write it down on his board.

"Well, Hazel Elizabeth Deborah Parker, going to give someone else a break this year?" I squint at him real hard to see if he is seriously thinking I should lose the race on purpose just to give someone else a break. "Only six girls running this time," he continues, shaking his head sadly like it's my fault all of New York didn't turn out in sneakers. "That new girl should give you a run for your money." He looks around the park for Gretchen like periscope in a submarine movie. "Wouldn't it be a nice gesture if you were . . . to ahhh . . . "

I give him such a look he couldn't finish putting that idea into words. Grown-ups got a lot of nerve sometimes. I pin number seven to myself and stomp away, I'm so burnt. And I go straight for the track and stretch out on the grass while the band winds up with "Oh, the Monkey Wrapped His Tail Around the Flagpole," which my teacher calls by some other name. The man on the loud-speaker is calling everyone over to the track and I'm on my back looking at the sky, trying to pretend I'm in the country, but I can't, because even grass in the city feels hard as sidewalk, and there's just no pretending you are anywhere but in a "concrete jungle" as my grandfather says.

The twenty-yard dash takes all of two minutes cause most of the little kids don't know no better than to run off the track or run the wrong way or run smack into the fence and fall down and cry. One little kid, though, has got the good sense to run straight for the white ribbon up ahead so he wins. Then the second-graders line up for the thirty-yard dash and I don't even bother to turn my head to watch cause Raphael Perez always wins. He wins before he even begins by psyching the runners, telling them they're going to trip on their shoelaces and fall on their faces or lose their shorts or something, which he doesn't really have

to do since he is very fast, almost as fast as I am. After that is the forty-yard dash, which I used to run when I was in first grade. Raymond is hollering from the swings cause he knows I'm about to do my thing cause the man on the loudspeaker has just announced the fifty-yard dash, although he might just as well be giving a recipe for angel food cake cause you can hardly make out what he's saying for the static. I get up and slip off my sweat pants and then I see Gretchen standing at the starting line, kicking her legs out like a pro. Then as I get into place I see that ole Raymond is on line on the other side of the fence, bending down with his fingers on the ground just like he knew what he was doing. I was going to yell at him but then I didn't. It burns up your energy to holler.

Every time, just before I take off in a race, I always feel like I'm in a dream, the kind of dream you have when you're sick with fever and feel all hot and weightless. I dream I'm flying over a sandy beach in the early morning sun, kissing the leaves of the trees as I fly by. And there's always the smell of apples, just like in the country when I was little and used to think I was a choo-choo train, running through the fields of corn and chugging up the hill to the orchard. And all the time I'm dreaming this, I get lighter and lighter until I'm flying over the beach again, getting blown through the sky like a feather that weighs nothing at all. But once I spread my fingers in the dirt and crouch over the Get on Your Mark, the dream goes and I am solid again and am telling myself, Squeaky you must win, you must win, you are the fastest thing in the world, you can even beat your father up Amsterdam if you really try. And then I feel my weight coming back just behind my knees then down to my feet then into the earth and the pistol shot explodes in my blood and I am off and weightless again, flying past the other runners, my arms pumping up and down and the whole world is quiet except for the crunch as I zoom over the gravel in the track. I glance to my left and there is no one. To the right, a blurred Gretchen, who's got her chin jutting out as if it would win the race all by itself. And on the other side of the fence is Raymond with his arms down to his side and the palms tucked up behind him, running in his very

own style, and it's the first time I ever saw that and I almost stop to watch my brother Raymond on his first run. But the white ribbon is bouncing toward me and I tear past it, racing into the distance till my feet with a mind of their own start digging up footfuls of dirt and brake me short. Then all the kids standing on the side pile on me, banging me on the back and slapping my head with their May Day programs, for I have won again and everybody on 151st Street can walk tall for another year.

"In first place . . ." the man on the loudspeaker is clear as a bell now. But then he pauses and the loudspeaker starts to whine. Then static. And I lean down to catch my breath and here comes Gretchen walking back, for she's overshot the finish line too, huffing and puffing with her hands on her hips taking it slow, breathing in steady time like a real pro and I sort of like her a little for the first time. "In first place . . ." and then three or four voices get all mixed up on the loudspeaker and I dig my sneaker into the grass and stare at Gretchen, who's staring back, we both wondering just who did win. I can hear old Beanstalk arguing with the man on the loudspeaker and then a few others running their mouths about what the stopwatches say. Then I hear Raymond yanking at the fence to call me and I wave to shush him, but he keeps rattling the fence like a gorilla in a cage like in them gorilla movies, but then like a dancer or something he starts climbing up nice and easy but very fast. And it occurs to me, watching how smoothly he climbs hand over hand and remembering how he looked running with his arms down to his side and with the wind pulling his mouth back and his teeth showing and all, it occurred to me that Raymond would make a very fine runner. Doesn't he always keep up with me on my trots? And he surely knows how to breathe in counts of seven cause he's always doing it at the dinner table, which drives my brother George up the wall. And I'm smiling to beat the band cause if I've lost this race, or if me and Gretchen tied, or even if I've won, I can always retire as a runner and begin a whole new career as a coach with Raymond as my champion. After all, with a little more study I can beat Cynthia and her phony self at the spelling bee. And if I bugged my mother, I could get piano lessons and become a star. And I have a big rep as the baddest thing around. And I've got a roomful of ribbons and medals and awards. But what has Raymond got to call his own?

So I stand there with my new plans, laughing out loud by this time as Raymond jumps down from the fence and runs over with his teeth showing and his arms down to the side, which no one before him has quite mastered as a running style. And by the time he comes over I'm jumping up and down so glad to see him—my brother Raymond, a great runner in the family tradition. But of course everyone thinks I'm jumping up and down because the men on the loudspeaker have finally gotten themselves together and compared notes and are announcing "In first place—Miss Hazel Elizabeth Deborah Parker." (Dig that.) "In second place—Miss Gretchen P. Lewis." And I look over at Gretchen wondering what the *P* stands for. And I smile. Cause she's good, no doubt about it. Maybe she'd like to help me coach Raymond; she obviously is serious about running, as any fool can see. And she nods to congratulate me and then she smiles. And I smile. We stand there with this big smile of respect between us. It's about as real a smile as girls can do for each other, considering we don't practice real smiling every day, you know, cause maybe we too busy being flowers or fairies or strawberries instead of something honest and worthy of respect . . . you know . . . like being people.

Responding to the Story

Analyzing the Story

Identifying Facts

1. Explain why taking care of Raymond is not an easy job. How does Squeaky protect Raymond?
2. In what way does Squeaky feel she is different from girls like Cynthia Procter?
3. How does Squeaky react when she sees Gretchen and her friends approaching along Broadway? Why does Squeaky decide not to duck into the candy store?
4. What does Mr. Pearson want Squeaky to do in the May Day race? How does she react?
5. How does Squeaky feel about Raymond after the race? How does she feel about Gretchen?

Interpreting Meanings

6. A **dynamic character** is one who changes over the course of a story. The character's feelings might change or he or she might learn something important. (A **static character,** on the other hand, does not change much.) Squeaky is a dynamic character. How does the fact that she and Gretchen exchange smiles after the race indicate that Squeaky has changed over the course of the story?
7. How would you **characterize** Squeaky? For instance, do you think she is self-confident or unsure of herself—or a mixture of both? Quote passages from the story to support your analysis.

8. The **setting** of "Raymond's Run" is Harlem, in New York City. Do you think the story could just as easily have taken place in another setting?

9. How did the narrator get the nickname "Squeaky"? Do you think she likes it?

Applying Meanings

10. About midway through the story Squeaky says, "you should be trying to be yourself, whatever that is. . . ." What does she mean? Do you agree with her?

Writing About the Story

A Creative Response

1. **Using Another Point of View.** "Raymond's Run" is written from the **point of view** of Squeaky, the "I" of the story. We learn mainly what Squeaky observes, thinks, and feels. We don't learn much about what the other characters think and feel. To fill in some gaps, let Gretchen tell about her part in the story. In a paragraph or two have Gretchen describe what she is thinking and feeling during the Dodge City scene and after the race. Use the first-person pronoun *I*.

A Critical Response

2. **Analyzing a Title.** The title often is a key to understanding a story. Why do you think Toni Cade Bambara called this story "Raymond's Run" rather than "Squeaky's Race" or "Squeaky Versus Gretchen"? Write a paragraph in which you discuss why Raymond's activity during the race is important to the story.

Analyzing Language and Vocabulary

Dialect

The **dialect,** or way of speaking, of a group of people can involve special pronunciation, vocabulary, and grammar. Here are instances of each from "Raymond's Run."

1. Bambara spells words to show how Squeaky pronounces them. What is the standard English spelling for each of these words from the story?

   a. whupped
   b. lotsa
   c. ole

2. In a dialect, words and phrases can have special meaning. What do the following italicized words and phrases from the story mean?

   a. "And a lot of *smart mouths* got lots to say about that too. . . ."
   b. " 'I don't think you're going to win this time,' says Rosie, trying to *signify* with her hands on her hips *all salty,* completely forgetting that I have whupped her many times for less *salt* than that."
   c. "And I have a big rep as the *baddest* thing around."

3. In a dialect verbs can be omitted. What verbs are omitted from the following sentences?

   a. "I much rather just knock you down. . . ."
   b. " 'You signing up for the May Day races?' . . ."
   c. " 'What grade you in now, Raymond?' "

Reading About the Writer

Toni Cade Bambara (1939–   ) writes short stories and novels. She grew up in New York, New Jersey, and the South. She studied dance, was employed as a social worker, and is currently teaching at Spelman College in Atlanta, Georgia. She adopted the name Bambara from a signature on a sketchbook she found in her great-grandmother's trunk. The name belongs to a people in northwest Africa, who are known for their precise woodcarvings. Bambara has this advice for young readers: "[I]t is very important for young folks to learn how to read, to read well, to read everything in sight; it is equally important for young folks to learn to listen, to be proud of our oral tradition, our elders who tell tales in the kitchen." Bambara's short story collections include *The Sea Birds Are Still Alive* and *Gorilla, My Love,* in which "Raymond's Run" appears.

THREE WISE GUYS
UN CUENTO DE NAVIDAD/A CHRISTMAS STORY

Sandra Cisneros

The tradition of giving Christmas gifts began with the story of the Three Wise Men, who brought gifts to the stable where the Christ child was born. This event is celebrated on January 6, known in the United States as the Feast of the Epiphany. In many countries, people exchange gifts on this day, and not on Christmas. The people in this story are Mexican-Americans who give gifts on *Dia de los Reyes,* or the "Day of the Kings." The story concerns a mysterious present, which is delivered in time for Christmas, but must remain wrapped until the Day of the Kings. See if you can guess what the present is.

The story takes place in a town in Texas, near the Mexican border.

T he big box came marked DO NOT OPEN TILL XMAS, but the mama said not until the Day of the Three Kings. Not until Dia de los Reyes, the sixth of January, do you hear? That is what the mama said exactly, only she said it all in Spanish. Because in Mexico where she was raised, it is the custom for boys and girls to receive their presents on January sixth, and not Christmas, even though they were living on the Texas side of the river[1] now. Not until the sixth of January.

Yesterday the mama had risen in the dark same as always to reheat the coffee in a tin saucepan and warm the breakfast tortillas.[2] The papa had gotten up coughing and spitting up the night, complaining how the evening before the buzzing of the chicharras[3] had kept him from sleeping. By the time the mama had the house smelling of oatmeal and cinnamon, the papa would be gone to the fields, the sun already tangled in the trees and the urracas[4] screeching their rubber-screech cry. The boy Ruben and the girl Rosalinda would have to be shaken awake for school. The mama would give the baby Gilberto his bottle and then she would go back to sleep before getting up again to the chores that were always waiting. That is how the world had been.

But today the big box had arrived. When the boy Ruben and the girl Rosalinda came home from school, it was already sitting in the living room in front of the television set that no longer worked. Who had put it there? Where had it come from? A box covered with red paper with green Christmas trees and a card on top that said "Merry Christmas to the Gonzales Family. Frank, Earl, and Dwight Travis. P.S. DO NOT OPEN TILL XMAS." That's all.

Two times the mama was made to come into the living room, first to explain to the children and

---

1. **river:** the Rio Grande, which separates Mexico and Texas.
2. **tortillas:** thin, flat cakes of cornmeal or flour.
3. **chicharras:** cicadas, insects that make a loud, high-pitched sound.
4. **urracas:** magpies, black and white birds belonging to the crow family, known for their chattering.

> **Spanish words.** This story includes some *Spanish words.* Two of them are so common in the United States that you can find them in an English dictionary. The footnotes in the story explain the meaning of the other Spanish words. The *context,* or surrounding words, should also give you an idea of what any unfamiliar word means. As you come to each word, try to figure out its meaning before you read the footnote.

Ride of the Magi. North Choir Aisle Bible Windows, Canterbury Cathedral, England.

later to their father how the brothers Travis had arrived in the blue pickup, and how it had taken all three of those big men to lift the box off the back of the truck and bring it inside, and how she had had to nod and say thank-you thank-you thank-you over and over because those were the only words she knew in English. Then the brothers Travis had nodded as well, the way they always did when they came and brought the boxes of clothes, or the turkey each November, or the canned ham on Easter, ever since the children had

begun to earn high grades at the school where Dwight Travis was the principal.

But this year the Christmas box was bigger than usual. What could be in a box so big? The boy Ruben and the girl Rosalinda begged all afternoon to be allowed to open it, and that is when the mama had said the sixth of January, the Day of the Three Kings. Not a day sooner.

It seemed the weeks stretched themselves wider and wider since the arrival of the big box. The mama got used to sweeping around it because it was too heavy for her to push in a corner. But since the television no longer worked ever since the afternoon the children had poured iced tea through the little grates in the back, it really didn't matter if the box obstructed the view. Visitors that came inside the house were told and told again the story of how the box had arrived, and then each was made to guess what was inside.

It was the comadre[5] Elodia who suggested over coffee one afternoon that the big box held a portable washing machine that could be rolled away when not in use, the kind she had seen in her Sears Roebuck catalog. The mama said she hoped so because the wringer washer she had used for the last ten years had finally gotten tired and quit. These past few weeks she had had to boil all the clothes in the big pot she used for cooking the Christmas tamales.[6] Yes. She hoped the big box was a portable washing machine. A washing machine, even a portable one, would be good.

But the neighbor man Cayetano said, What foolishness, comadre. Can't you see the box is too small to hold a washing machine, even a portable one. Most likely God has heard your prayers and sent a new color TV. With a good antenna you could catch all the Mexican soap operas, the neighbor man said. You could distract yourself with the complicated troubles of the rich and then give thanks to God for the blessed simplicity of your poverty. A new TV would surely be the end to all your miseries.

Each night when the papa came home from the fields, he would spread newspapers on the cot in the living room, where the boy Ruben and the girl Rosalinda slept, and sit facing the big box in the center of the room. Each night he imagined the box held something different. The day before yesterday he guessed a new record player. Yesterday an ice chest filled with beer. Today the papa sat with his bottle of beer, fanning himself with a magazine, and said in a voice as much a plea as a prophecy: air conditioner.

But the boy Ruben and the girl Rosalinda were sure the big box was filled with toys. They had even punctured it in one corner with a pencil when

their mother was busy cooking, but they could see nothing inside but blackness.

Only the baby Gilberto remained uninterested in the contents of the big box and seemed each day more fascinated with the exterior of the box rather than the interior. One afternoon he tore off a fistful of paper, which he was chewing when his mother swooped him up with one arm, rushed him to the kitchen sink, and forced him to swallow handfuls of lukewarm water in case the red dye of the wrapping paper might be poisonous.

When Christmas Eve finally came, the family Gonzalez put on their good clothes and went to Midnight Mass. They came home to a house that smelled of tamales and atole,[7] and everyone was allowed to open one present before going to sleep. But the big box was to remain untouched until the sixth of January.

On New Year's Eve the little house was filled with people, some related, some not, coming in and out. The friends of the papa came with bottles, and the mama set out a bowl of grapes to count off the New Year. That night the children did not sleep in the living room cot as they usually did, because the living room was crowded with big-fannied ladies and fat-stomached men sashaying to the accordion music of the midget twins from McAllen.[8] Instead the children fell asleep on a lump of handbags and crumpled suit jackets on top of the mama and the papa's bed, dreaming of the contents of the big box.

Finally, the fifth of January. And the boy Ruben and the girl Rosalinda could hardly sleep. All night they whispered last-minute wishes. The boy thought perhaps if the big box held a bicycle, he would be the first to ride it, since he was the oldest. This made his sister cry until the mama had to yell from her bedroom on the other side of the plastic curtains, Be quiet or I'm going to give you each the stick, which sounds worse in Spanish than it does in English. Then no one said anything. After a very long time, long after they heard the mama's wheezed breathing and the papa's piped snoring, the children closed their eyes and remembered nothing.

5. **comadre** (ko·mä′drä): woman who is a relative or close friend of the family (the ''co-mother'').
6. **tamales:** meat and peppers cooked in a corn husk.

7. **atole** (ä·tō′lä): broth made from corn flour.
8. **McAllen:** Texas city near the Mexican border.

The papa was already in the bathroom coughing up the night before from his throat when the urracas began their clownish chirping. The boy Ruben awoke and shook his sister. The mama, frying the potatoes and beans for breakfast, nodded permission for the box to be opened.

With a kitchen knife the boy Ruben cut a careful edge along the top. The girl Rosalinda tore the Christmas wrapping with her fingernails. The papa and the mama lifted the cardboard flaps and everyone peered inside to see what it was the brothers Travis had brought them on the Day of the Three Kings.

There were layers of balled newspaper packed on top. When these had been cleared away the boy Ruben looked inside. The girl Rosalinda looked inside. The papa and the mama looked.

This is what they saw: the complete Britannica Junior Encyclopaedia, twenty-four volumes in red imitation leather with gold-embossed letters, beginning with Volume I, Aar-Bel and ending with Volume XXIV, Yel-Zyn. The girl Rosalinda let out a sad cry, as if her hair was going to be cut again. The boy Ruben pulled out Volume IV, Ded-Fem. There were many pictures and many words, but there were more words than pictures. The papa flipped through Volume XXII, but because he could not read English words, simply put the book back and grunted, What can we do with this? No one said anything, and shortly after, the screen door slammed.

Only the mama knew what to do with the contents of the big box. She withdrew Volumes VI, VII, and VIII, marched off to the dinette set in the kitchen, placed two on Rosalinda's chair so she could better reach the table, and put one underneath the plant stand that danced.

When the boy and the girl returned from school that day they found the books stacked into squat pillars against one living room wall and a board placed on top. On this were arranged several plastic doilies and framed family photographs. The rest of the volumes the baby Gilberto was playing with, and he was already rubbing his sore gums along the corners of Volume XIV.

The girl Rosalinda also grew interested in the books. She took out her colored pencils and painted blue on the eyelids of all the illustrations of women and with a red pencil dipped in spit she painted their lips and fingernails red-red. After a couple of days, when all the pictures of women had been colored in this manner, she began to cut out some of the prettier pictures and paste them on looseleaf paper.

One volume suffered from being exposed to the rain when the papa improvised a hat during a sudden shower. He forgot it on the hood of the car when he drove off. When the children came home from school they set it on the porch to dry. But the pages puffed up and became so fat, the book was impossible to close.

Only the boy Ruben refused to touch the books. For several days he avoided the principal because he didn't know what to say in case Mr. Travis were to ask how they were enjoying the Christmas present.

On the Saturday after New Year's the mama and the papa went into town for groceries and left the boy in charge of watching his sister and baby brother. The girl Rosalinda was stacking books into spiral staircases and making her paper dolls descend them in a fancy manner.

Perhaps the boy Ruben would not have bothered to open the volume left on the kitchen table if he had not seen his mother wedge her name-day corsage[9] in its pages. On the page where the mama's carnation lay pressed between two pieces of Kleenex was a picture of a dog in a space ship. FIRST DOG IN SPACE the caption said. The boy turned to another page and read where cashews came from. And then about the man who invented the guillotine. And then about Bengal tigers. And about clouds. All afternoon the boy read, even after the mama and the papa came home. Even after the sun set, until the mama said time to sleep and put the light out.

In their bed on the other side of the plastic curtain the mama and the papa slept. Across from them in the crib slept the baby Gilberto. The girl Rosalinda slept on her end of the cot. But the boy Ruben watched the night sky turn from violet. To blue. To gray. And then from gray. To blue. To violet once again.

---

9. **name-day corsage:** flower or a bunch of flowers that are worn to celebrate the feast day of the saint for whom a person is named.

Responding to the Story

Analyzing the Story

Identifying Facts

1. What does the sign on the gift box say? Why do the parents ignore the message?
2. Where did the box come from?
3. What does each person in the family imagine is in the box?
4. What actually is in the box?
5. How does each person in the house make use of the gift?

Interpreting Meanings

6. The neighbor, Cayetano, explains to the mother why she is better off with a television. What is his explanation? Do you agree with his argument?
7. Did you guess what was in the box before it was opened? What clues does Cisneros provide to hint at the kind of gift the box might contain?
8. Toward the end of the story, Ruben emerges as the main **character.** How do the last few paragraphs set Ruben apart from the other characters?
9. How do you think the gift that was at first such a disappointment might change Ruben's life?
10. What do you think of the **title** of the story? What could it mean?

Applying Meanings

11. Do you think this story reveals something about how children become interested in learning? Why was Ruben attracted to the books, for example?
12. Do you think the Travises gave a good gift to the family? How would the gift have affected you?

Writing About the Story

A Creative Response

1. **Adding to the Story.** Imagine that it is a week later, and that Ruben is still reading the encyclopedia at night and every chance he gets. Write a conversation that takes place at the dinner table. Have the other family members comment on Ruben's actions and have Ruben explain his interest to them.
2. **Role Playing.** How would you feel if you were in this family as it opened the big box? Enact the scene, with various classmates playing the roles of the family members. Try to behave the way you think the particular person you are portraying would behave.

A Critical Response

3. **Analyzing the Story's Theme.** Now that you have answered the questions about this story, you should have an idea about what its **theme,** or main idea, is. Write a paragraph explaining the story's theme. Open with a sentence that clearly states the theme as you interpret it. Before you write, think about how the gift affected Ruben's life. In what ways did he receive two gifts: the gift of the books, and the gift of learning?

Analyzing Language and Vocabulary

Spanish Words

Tacos and tortillas are both mentioned in "Three Wise Guys." These are two **Spanish words** that are so common in the United States that they appear in American dictionaries. Spanish has been a source of American English words for centuries, especially in the old West. Use a dictionary to find out the original Spanish meaning of each of the following American words.

1. barbecue
2. buffalo
3. mosquito
4. mustang
5. ranch
6. rodeo

Reading About the Writer

Sandra Cisneros (1954–   ) was born and brought up in Chicago. As a child, she says, she buried herself in books—the lives of the saints, the Doctor Doolittle books, *Alice in Wonderland,* and fairy tales. She lived in Texas for several years and currently teaches writing at the California State University at Chico. Her books include *The House on Mango Street,* a novel; and *Bad Boys* and *My Wicked, Wicked Ways,* collections of poems.

THE FIRST ROSE OF SUMMER

Howard Fast

One of life's universal truths concerns first love: For the person enduring it, it is possibly the profoundest of tragedies, while for the spectators it is hilarious. The following story about a fourteen-year-old boy's first love for one Thelma Naille gets the utmost out of the situation. The narrator's voice reveals that he has lost all good sense over Thelma. The response of his brother to this altered state makes for both conflict and humor, which, like all good comedy, is not too far from tragedy. As you read, note the differences in the personalities of the brothers.

The story takes place in New York City, some years ago.

I was fourteen when first love came to me, which was older than some yet younger than others. A round and appropriate age, you might say, and I was ignorant of ductless glands and such things, but knew only the blaze of glory that poets have always sung about.

At that time, my brother and I had a newspaper route, which netted us fifteen dollars on good weeks and which we both conducted after school. Before we were finished on this particular day, my brother knew that childish things were behind me and that there were more than material reasons for the deep and saintly sadness in which I had wrapped myself.

> **Word roots from Latin.** A *word root* is a word or word part from which other words are made. Many English word roots come from Latin, the language of the ancient Romans. For example, the roots *equa-* and *equi-* both come from a Latin word meaning "equal." The roots appear in such English words as *equation, equator,* and *equidistant.* Knowing that *equi-* has something to do with *equal,* see if you can figure out the meaning of the italicized word in the following sentence from this story: ". . . my brother's idea of *equity* was for me to take the top three floors while he took the bottom two. . . ."

"What's eating you?" he asked me, and I told him about it. It had been a gentle day, a sweet day. We delivered our papers for the most part in five-story tenement houses, and my brother's idea of equity was for me to take the top three floors while he took the bottom two; being a year and a half older than I and some sixty pounds heavier, he could enforce this edict, but out of a basic concept of equal rights, I fought him on every house. Today, however, I accepted. There was a flavor to suffering; my whole heart was filled with music.

"I'm in love," I said.

"What?"

"In love," I said. "In love with a woman."

"No?"

"Yes," I said, with dignity that couldn't fail to impress him. "Deeply in love."

"When did this happen?" His respectful curiosity combined interest and a touch of admiration.

"Today."

"All at once?"

"Yes," I said. "I saw her in my English class, and I knew it."

"How could you know it?"

"The way I feel."

"You mean like taking the top three floors?" my brother asked hopefully.

"That's only a part of it. My own suffering is

Manhattan Magic by Carl Titolo (1986). Scraper Board.

of no consequence any longer, because now I'm consecrated to something bigger than I am.''

My brother nodded and watched me intently. ''How *do* you feel?'' he asked.

''Noble.''

''Not sick?''

''Not with physical sickness. It isn't something I can explain to you.''

''I guess not,'' he agreed. ''What's her name?''

''Thelma Naille.''

''Thelma?''

''Thelma,'' I repeated, savoring the sound of it, the joy of it, the inflection of it.

''You're sure?''

''Of course I'm sure.''

''That's a strange name,'' my brother said. ''She doesn't lisp or anything?''

''She has a voice like music.''

''Oh. Does she know about this?''

''Naturally not,'' I said—almost sorry that I had taken him into my confidence at all. However, it was necessary. Being in love was going to complicate my life; that I realized from the very beginning, and I couldn't have become a cross-country runner without my brother knowing what the motivating forces were.

At that time, we both went to George Washington High School, which is at the upper end of Manhattan Island. School let out at three; we finished our newspaper route at six, and then, since we had no mother, we prepared supper, ate it with my father, who came home from work about seven, did our homework and turned in. Love alone threw new drains on my energy. With the cross-country running, only a holy devotion permitted me to operate . . .

My brother was waiting for me when I came out of the English class the next day.

"Which one?" he wanted to know, and I pointed her out.

"The tall one?"

"She's not so tall."

"She's five feet nine inches if she's an inch."

"Oh, no. No. Never. Anyway, I'm five feet eight myself."

"Five six," my brother said coldly.

"Not with heels. Anyway, the rate of growth is different in different people. I'm just hitting my stride. She's all finished. Growing, I mean."

"How do you know?"

"Well, how tall can a girl get?"

"If you can keep on growing, so can she. That's logical."

I conquered the chill of fear that stole over my heart. He was understandably bitter; I held no resentment against him; I was filled with an inner purity and I let some of it shine through.

"You look sick," my brother said. "I hope you're all right. She didn't even look at you."

"She doesn't know me."

"Well, why don't you introduce yourself?"

"I can't until I have some achievement to lay at her feet. I'm no one. Did you see how beautiful she is? Anyone would be in love with her. That's natural."

"I'm not in love with her," my brother said. "Anyway—"

"What do you mean by laying an achievement at her feet?" my brother asked. "Are you going to buy something for her?"

I walked away. It was no use talking to him about this; it was no use talking to anyone. It was something I had to contain within me until I had won my struggle to make myself worthy. For a week I brooded about that. The football season was too far gone, and anyway I weighed only one fourteen, and football was a long-term project with all sorts of special skills required. Love, I was beginning to discover, was not something that stood still; it was a dynamic force that moved a person to immediate action, and when the week was over, I turned out for the track squad. After all, how many football players ever made an Olympics?

"Your feet are too big," the coach told me.

"For what?" I had gotten along very well with them until then.

"For sprinting."

"I don't suppose my feet will grow much more, and I intend to."

"We can't wait," the coach said.

"Don't you want to try me?" I pleaded.

"It's no use," the coach said patiently. "You can't sprint with such feet."

"Well, isn't there something where you don't have to sprint?"

"Your feet are against you. If you jumped, it would be just the same. Also, you're small and light—and that's bad for discus or shot. If you want to try for cross-country, you can."

"Cross-country?"

"That's right. You spend a year at that, and then maybe the rest of you will catch up with your feet. It's good training, if your heart is all right."

My heart was all right, and at three o'clock I was shivering in my underclothes in Van Cortlandt Park. It was a cold, bleak fall day, and a hundred other boys shivered with me. Then we started out, and for the next half hour, over hill and dale, we ran a course of two and a half miles. It may be that education, in probing the bypaths of knowledge, has discovered something crueler and more senseless than a cross-country run; if so, I missed it. I don't know what upheld the rest of the squad, but love carried me through pantingly to the end. I showered and joined my brother on the route, an hour and a half late.

This time I couldn't make the top three floors, and I told him why.

"You mean you're going up there and run two and a half miles every afternoon?" he demanded.

"Yes."

"But why?"

"For her."

"You mean she asked you to do this?"

"How could she ask me when I've never spoken to her?"

"Who asked you then?"

"No one."

"You're crazy," my brother said, which was what I might have expected, his mind being capable of rising no higher above the dirt. For the rest of that week, there was a certain bitterness of feeling between us, something I sensed only vaguely, since all my acute perceptions were blurred by a fog of constant weariness. If ever in the history of western romance love was stretched to a breaking point, that was it, and it seems to me that it is a real tribute to the gentle passion that both my devotion and I survived. However, my survival was a touch-and-go business; if I did not walk in darkness, I certainly walked in a gray haze, and my classroom response became, if not downright idiotic, at least far from alert. More than before, I realized that I would have to become the best cross-country runner America had ever produced to redeem a faltering, tired, incoherent young man in the eyes of the woman I loved.

Somehow, the five weekdays passed, and without a complete loss of the saintly gentleness that was the most manifest outward indication of my passion. The cross I bore was made no lighter by my brother's grim curiosity; in a completely scientific manner, he experimented with my new tolerance. I came late to work, but I certainly did my share.

The paper we delivered was an afternoon paper, except on Sundays, when it came out in the morning. That meant we had to dig ourselves out of bed at 3 A.M., stagger over to the assembly room, and collate[1] mountains of newsprint. By seven or seven-thirty in the morning, we were through with the delivery and could go home and catch a nap. Ordinarily, I would be tired enough, but the cross-country team—and whoever was the diabolical brain behind it—decided to hold a conditioning run on Saturday, five miles instead of two and a half; and when Sunday morning finally rolled around my accumulated fatigue was something to see. My brother's respect was tinged with awe by now, and there was almost a quality of gentleness in his suggestion that I go home and sleep most of the day.

"No," I said wistfully. "It would be nice, but I can't. I'm going to her house."

"You mean you've met her, you've talked to her? She invited you over?"

"Not exactly."

---

1. **collate:** gather sections of a newspaper together in order.

"You mean you're just going over and introduce yourself," my brother nodded admiringly.

"Not exactly that either. I'm just going to stand outside her house."

"Until she comes out?"

"Yes—yes, that's it," I agreed.

"Don't you think you ought to get some sleep first?" my brother suggested.

"I can't take the chance."

"What chance?"

I didn't try to explain, because there are some things you can't explain. Her house was a fourteen-story building on Riverside Drive. It awed me and overwhelmed me; it widened the gap; it made me search my memory for any evidence that America was a country where cross-country running was even nominally honored. And to make things more difficult, the house had two entrances, one on the Drive and one on the side street. There was no bench from which I could observe both entrances, so I had to take up my vigil on a windy street corner, reflecting morosely on the fact that even if the rest of me grew, I was not treating my feet in a manner calculated either to keep them at their present size or preserve them for sprinting.

There are cold places on earth; there are places that have a whole literature of coldness woven around them; they do not compare with a street corner on Riverside Drive on a cloudy November morning. That is a special cold; a nice, wet, penetrating cold that increases slowly enough for you to perish with a minimum of pain. By twelve o'clock I had finished with my consecration to life and had newly consecrated myself to death. There was a new poignancy to the realization that I would die here like this, on her very doorstep—a communal one, true enough, but hers too—and that she would not know. Yet wouldn't she have to know? When she looked at my pale white face, the ice rimming my lashes, wouldn't something tell her and wouldn't she regret that never by word or sign had she indicated anything to me?

It was about that time my brother appeared. He had a brown bag under his arm. "I brought you some lunch," he said.

"Thank you," I murmured. "It was sweet of you and good of you to think of me, but food doesn't matter."

"What?"

"I didn't mean to hurt your feelings," I said gently.

"That's all right," my brother nodded. He was beginning to realize that with love, you felt your way with an open mind. "Try a salami sandwich. Suppose we go over to a bench and sit down."

"No—we can't."

"Why not?"

"I have to watch both entrances, and you have to stand here to see them."

"Won't she look for you when she comes out?"

I shook my head. "She doesn't know I'm here."

"What?"

"You keep saying *what*. I think you don't understand what this means to me."

"No, I guess I don't."

"How could she know I'm here," I asked my brother, "when I never spoke to her?"

"Then what are you waiting here for?"

"For her to come out," I answered simply, eating the sandwich.

"And then?"

"Then I see her."

"But you see her every day, don't you?"

"Yes."

My brother looked at me searchingly. "Oh," he said.

"What do you mean by that?"

"Nothing. But suppose she doesn't come out?"

"She has to come out sooner or later."

"Why?" my brother demanded, parading the cold vista of logic.[2] "On a day like this, she would be very smart to stay at home. She could stay at home and read the funnies. Maybe she's even got a party up there and all kinds of people are coming in to visit her."

"Stop that."

"I'm only trying to be logical," my brother said.

"You don't know how you're hurting me. If you knew, you wouldn't talk like that."

Indicating that if I thought so little of his advice, I could maintain my vigil alone, he left me to my meditations and to the incredible combination of damp wind that blew in two directions at the same time. The top of me wasn't so bad; I had a woolen cap and a short coat we used to call a Mackinaw; but my feet suffered. It was ironical to consider that it might be *her* fault that I would never be a sprinter; even the question of plain and simple walking began to raise doubts in my mind.

The sun had set behind the Palisades[3] and the policeman on the beat was beginning to eye me uncertainly when my brother appeared again.

"Still no sign of her?" he said.

"I'm above anything you can say."

"All right. But Pop thinks you ought to come home."

"You didn't tell him?"

"Not exactly."

"How could you?"

"It's all right," my brother assured me.

"How could it be all right? How could a man Pop's age know what I'm going through? Even you can't understand it."

"I try to," my brother said. "Don't think I don't want you to be a great cross-country runner, because that wouldn't be true."

"You don't even understand that my only interest in this cross-country running is because I want to lay something at her feet."

"I just feel you ought to introduce yourself. Then if she were to come out while you're standing here, she'd know you. You got to admit that would be an advantage."

It was true; I had to. I turned it over in my mind until Wednesday of the following week, and then because it looked like rain practice in Van Cortlandt Park was canceled. I took my heart in my hands and I stopped Thelma Naille when the dismissal bell rang. As I looked up at her, she was more than ever the Greek Goddess. I asked her how she went home.

"By bus."

"Do you go alone?"

"Sometimes," she said.

"Do you like to sit on the top—where it's open?"

"Sometimes," she said.

"Could I go home with you today?" I managed.

---

2. **logic:** correct reasoning.

3. **Palisades:** steep cliffs lining the western shore of the Hudson River.

"If you want to," she said.

I walked on air. My heart beat like a triphammer. Once, her hand even touched mine for just a moment. Outside, a northeaster[4] blew, and I found a bus with an open top.

"It's cold up here," she said, when we sat down on the top of the bus. We had it to ourselves, the two of us alone with the whole world beneath us.

"You get used to it."

"And I think it's going to rain," she said.

"Maybe it won't, and anyway that's lucky for me because there's no cross-country practice."

"Oh," she said.

"That's like sprinting, only it goes on for two and a half miles."

"Oh," she said.

"I made the team," I said.

"Yes? Don't you think we ought to go downstairs?"

"You'll get used to it in no time. There are seventy men on the team, but that's the kind of a sport it is."

"Oh," she said. She turned up the collar of her coat and wrapped it more tightly around her. She stared straight ahead of her.

I made small talk to the best of my ability, but she didn't unbend, except to shiver occasionally. I even made one or two excursions into the matter of my feelings, and that was just as nonproductive of reaction. Then the sleet started, not much at first, actually not enough for you to really notice.

"I think we should go downstairs," she said.

"Oh, no. No. It's nice up here. Up here, you can see everything."

"Well, you did pay the fare," she said.

"That doesn't matter. I always pay the fare when I take someone on a bus."

"Aren't you cold?" she wanted to know.

"No. No—"

The sleet increased and then it turned to rain. For a minute or two more, she sat huddled against the rail. Then she stood up and walked to the back of the bus and down to the lower deck. I followed her, but I couldn't think of anything else to say until we came to her house.

---

4. **northeaster:** storm or strong wind that comes from the northeast.

"I'm soaked," she said. "I'm soaked through and through. And it's your fault."

"Just a little wet."

"No, I'm soaked," she said. "I'm good and soaked. Thank you for taking me home."

I told my brother about it later and he observed, "There you are. You can't tell."

"I love her more than ever," I said.

"Well—"

"What do you mean, well?"

"Nothing. Only tall girls don't like short men. That's something to think about too."

"I think it was mostly the rain. I guess she's delicate."

"She's awfully big to be delicate."

"But she's sensitive," I said. "You wouldn't understand that."

She wasn't in school the next day, and I went through the tortures of the damned. "Call her up," my brother said.

"Call her?"

"Sure. Phone her. You know her address. Look up her number in the phone book and call her. She'll think it thoughtful of you."

I did as he said. A lady's voice answered. "Thelma is sick," the voice said coldly.

"Can I speak to her?"

"You can't," the voice said, and hung up.

I wouldn't want anyone to suffer the way I suffered those next few days. Penance was all I could think of. I had read in books about how people spent whole lifetimes atoning for some awful wrong they had done. I saw myself walking in her funeral. No one knew me, but no grief was like mine, because when all was said and done, I had slain her. I and no other. A lifetime would be hardly long enough to atone for that. I decided that I would do good things. My love would never change, never slacken; people would think of me as a saint, not knowing that in all truth I was a murderer. Even my cross-country running suffered. Instead of leading the pace, I lagged. The coach called me up for it, but what did cross-country mean now?

And then Monday came, and she appeared in school, and my heart sang again. She was paler— that was true—but it only increased her beauty. I went up to her and said:

Riverside Drive No. 1 by Hugh Kepets (1975). Acrylic.

© Hugh Kepets 1975. Chase Manhattan Collection, New York City.

"You were ill, and I'm sorry. If it was my fault—" I had thought the speech out very carefully, but she didn't permit me to complete it. Instead she broke in:

"You are a horrible, nasty little boy. Please don't speak to me again."

I skipped cross-country that day. I turned up for work at three and my brother shook his head somberly when he saw my face.

"What happened?" he demanded.

"The world ends, and you want to know what happened!"

"You'll still take the top floors, won't you?"

"Yes," I said sadly. "It doesn't matter. I still love her. I will always love her, I guess." I saw the future then, a grim and bitter man who turned his face from all women. They wouldn't know and neither would she.

Responding to the Story

Analyzing the Story

Identifying Facts

1. Describe the narrator's after-school job. What does he do each day after the job is completed?
2. Why does the narrator try out for the school cross-country team? How does he feel about cross-country running after a week or so on the team?
3. Why does the narrator stand outside Thelma's building? What makes his wait so uncomfortable?
4. Describe what happens when the narrator accompanies Thelma home on the bus. What is the main result of the bus trip?
5. How does Thelma feel about the narrator at the end of the story? How does the narrator feel about Thelma?

Interpreting Meanings

6. The two brothers in the story have very different **personalities.** They think and act differently. How would you describe each? Back up your descriptions by citing specific incidents and passages in the story.
7. **Conflict** is a key to making a story interesting. Sometimes it involves a clash between opposing characters. What is the main conflict in this story? How is it resolved?
8. Whose **point of view** is this story told from? How would the story and its effect differ if it had been told by Thelma?
9. The title of this story contains an **allusion** to a song by the Irish poet Thomas Moore (1478–1535). Part of the song goes as follows.

   'Tis the last rose of summer
      Left blooming alone;
   All her lovely companions
      Are faded and gone.

   The words "last rose of summer" usually refer to the end of something, particularly to the end of youth. What do you think the story's title means?
10. Describe Thelma's personality. What did you think of her? Did she act in a reasonable manner?

Applying Meanings

11. What did the narrator do wrong? Or do you think he could never have won Thelma, no matter what he did?
12. The writer of this story makes a point about first love. What is his point? Do you agree with it?

Writing About the Story

A Creative Response

1. **Imitating the Writer's Technique.** Much of the story consists of **dialogue**—conversations between the narrator and other characters. As an example of the writer's craft, look at the first conversation between the narrator and his brother. The questions and answers are brief, often just phrases or even single words. Occasionally, but not often, the writer indicates the speaker's tone of voice. Nevertheless, you come away with a good understanding of each brother. Try to imitate the writer's technique. Have two characters discuss the merits of a music video, a sports team, or something else. They should display opposing viewpoints and should speak in short sentences or phrases. The dialogue should reveal something about the personality of each character.
2. **Reading Out Loud with Classmates.** When you have completed your original dialogue, read it out loud before the class. You should speak what one character says, a classmate should speak the other character's lines, and a second classmate should read all the material not in quotes. All of you should use your tone of voice to give added meaning to the dialogue.

A Critical Response

3. **Analyzing a Writer's Tone. Tone** is the attitude a writer takes toward a character, the subject matter, or the reader. It is communicated through the writer's choice of words and detail. A writer's tone can display affection, sarcasm, humor, seriousness, or many other attitudes. In the first of two paragraphs, describe Howard Fast's attitude toward the narrator of "The First Rose of

Summer." Include passages from the story to add substance to your description. In your second paragraph, tell whether you share Fast's attitude. Give specific reasons for your point of view.

Analyzing Language and Vocabulary

Word Roots from Latin

A large number of English **word roots** come directly or indirectly from Latin. By learning the following roots derived from Latin, you'll gain a key to the meaning of many English words.

cred, "believe"   *mit,* "send"   *ject,* "throw"

In the following sentences, identify the root in the italicized word. Then write a short definition of the word. Check a dictionary where necessary.

1. This letter lends *credence* to Jane's story.
2. David was wrongly *credited* with scoring the winning run.
3. One of Emily's faults is that she is too *credulous.*
4. You may *remit* payment of the bill in the return envelope.
5. Michael's uncle *submitted* the story to the magazine for publication.
6. The magazine *rejected* the story.
7. The plane has an emergency system that allows pilots to *eject* themselves from the aircraft.

Reading About the Writer

Howard Fast (1914–   ) was born in New York City and attended public schools there, just as the narrator of this short story does. Over the course of his long and productive career, Fast has become famous for his vivid historical fiction. He tells the story of slave revolts in the Roman Empire in his novel *Spartacus.* A boy's view of the American Revolution is his subject in *April Morning.* One of his recent historical novels is *The Immigrants.* Although chiefly known as a novelist, Fast loves the short story, which he says is often "a true impression, a flash of insight, a way of seeing the world that no other literary form can provide."

Focusing on Background
Howard Fast Comments on First Love

" 'The First Rose of Summer' is a true story, which faithfully recounts a minor tragedy in my life. But at that age, a minor tragedy is quite enormous, in spite of the fact that fifteen years later it had become rather funny. Humor is the other face of misery, and any adolescent who experiences his or her first true love will endorse the earthshaking importance of the event. In this case, Thelma's folks were reasonably wealthy, mine were dirt poor, which made any possible outcome to my worship unlikely. By the way, her first name actually was Thelma. . . . I don't know whether she ever saw the story, but I'm sure that if she did, she smiled more kindly than she had ever smiled at me."

—Howard Fast

CALLING HOME

Tim O'Brien

Home, Sweet Home by Charles Sheeler (1931). Oil.

The Detroit Institute of Arts.
Gift of Robert H. Tannahill.

"Calling Home" is a war story that focuses on the two-faced scourge of the young soldier—the fear of death in battle and the overwhelming misery of homesickness. The story is a splendid picture of the *real* war—not the battles, but what goes on in a soldier's heart. It is set in Vietnam during the Vietnam War, which ended in 1975. As you read, notice how the soldiers feel before and after calling home.

> **Jargon.** *Jargon* is the special vocabulary used by people engaged in a particular activity or occupation. Jargon can include newly created words as well as existing words that are given new meaning. It can also include abbreviations of words. During the Vietnam War American soldiers developed jargon to describe the world around them. A *dustoff*, for example, was a helicopter that took wounded soldiers from the war front to the hospitals. A *grunt* was a foot soldier or a Marine. When soldiers talked about the *real world*, or the *world*, they meant home or the United States. As you read the story, see if you can figure out the various bits of jargon that are included.

In August, after two months in the bush, the platoon returned to Chu Lai for a week's stand down.

They swam, played mini-golf in the sand, and wrote letters and slept late in the mornings. At night there were floor shows. There was singing and dancing, and afterward there was homesickness. It was neither a good time nor a bad time. The war was all around them.

On the final day, Oscar and Eddie and Doc and Paul Berlin hiked down to the 42nd Commo Detachment. Recently the outfit had installed a radio-telephone hookup with the States.

"It's called MARS," said a young Pfc[1] at the reception desk. "Stands for Military Air Radio System." He was a friendly, deeply tanned redhead without freckles. On each wrist was a gold

---

1. **Pfc:** Private First Class.

watch, and the boy kept glancing at them as if to correlate time. He seemed a little nervous.

While they waited to place their calls, the Pfc explained how the system worked. A series of radio relays fed the signal across the Pacific to a telephone exchange in downtown Honolulu, where it was sent by regular undersea cable to San Francisco and from there to any telephone in America. "Real wizardry," the boy said. "Depends a lot on the weather, but, wow, sometimes it's like talkin' to the guy next door. You'd swear you was there in the same room."

They waited nearly an hour. Relay problems, the Pfc explained. He grinned and gestured at Oscar's boots. "You guys are legs, I guess. Grunts."

"I guess so," Oscar said.

The boy nodded solemnly. He started to say something but then shook his head. "Legs," he murmured.

Eddie's call went through first.

The Pfc led him into a small, sound-proofed booth and had him sit behind a console equipped with speakers and a microphone and two pairs of headsets. Paul Berlin watched through a plastic window. For a time nothing happened. Then a red light blinked on and the Pfc handed Eddie one of the headsets. Eddie began rocking in his chair. He held the microphone with one hand, squeezing it, leaning slightly forward. It was hard to see his eyes.

He was in the booth a long time. When he came out his face was bright red. He sat beside Oscar. He yawned, then immediately covered his eyes, rubbed them, then stretched and blinked.

"Geez," he said softly.

Then he laughed. It was a strange, scratchy laugh. He cleared his throat and smiled and kept blinking.

"Geez," he said.

"What—"

Eddie giggled. "It was . . . You shoulda heard her. 'Who?' she goes. Like that—*Who*? Just like that."

He took out a handkerchief, blew his nose, shook his head. His eyes were shiny.

"Just like that—'Who?' 'Eddie,' I say, and Ma says, 'Eddie who?' and I say, 'Who do you think

Eddie?' She almost passes out. Almost falls down or something. She gets this call from Nam and thinks maybe I been shot. 'Where you at?' she says, like maybe I'm calling from Graves Registration, or something, and—''

"That's great," Doc said. "That's really great, man."

"Yeah. It's—''

"Really great."

Eddie shook his head violently, as though trying to clear stopped-up ears. He was quiet a time. Then he laughed.

"Honest, you had to hear it. 'Who?' she keeps saying. 'Who?' Real clear. Like in the next . . . And Petie! He's in high school now—you believe that? My brother. Can't even call him Petie no more. 'Pete,' he says. Real deep voice, just like that guy on Lawrence Welk—'Pete, not Petie,' he goes. You believe that?''

"Hey, it's terrific," Doc said. "It really is."

"And clear? Man! Just like— I could hear Ma's cuckoo clock, that clear."

"Technology."

"Yeah," Eddie grinned. "Real technology. It's . . . I say, 'Hey, Ma,' and what's she say? 'Who's this?' Real scared-soundin', you know? Man, I coulda just—''

"It's great, Eddie."

Doc was next, and then Oscar. Both of them came out looking a little funny, not quite choked up but trying hard not to be. Very quiet at first, then laughing, then talking fast, then turning quiet again. It made Paul Berlin feel warm to watch them. Even Oscar seemed happy.

"Technology," Doc said. "You can't beat technology."

"My old man, all he could say was 'Over.' Nothin' else. 'Weather's fine,' he'd say, 'over.' '' Oscar wagged his head. His father had been an R.T.O.[2] in Italy. "You believe that? All he says is 'Over,' and Roger that. Crazy."

They would turn pensive. Then one of them would chuckle or grin.

"Pirates are out of it this year. Not a prayer, Petie says."

"I bleed."

---

2. **R.T.O.:** radio-telephone operator.

"Yeah, but Petie—he goes nuts over the Pirates. It's all he knows. Thinks we're over here fightin' the Russians. The Pirates, that's *all* he knows."

"Crazy," Oscar said. He kept wagging his head. "Over 'n' out."

It made Paul Berlin feel good. Like buddies; he felt close to all of them. When they laughed, he laughed.

Then the Pfc tapped him on the shoulder.

He felt giddy. Everything inside the booth was painted white. Sitting down, he grinned and squeezed his fingers together. He saw Doc wave at him through the plastic window.

"Ease up," the Pfc said. "Pretend it's a local call."

The boy helped him with the headset. There was a crisp clicking sound, then a long electric hum like a vacuum cleaner running in another room. He remembered . . . his mother always used the old Hoover on Saturdays. The smell of carpets, a fine, powdery dust rising in the yellow window light. An uncluttered house. Things in their places.

He felt himself smiling. He pressed the headset tight. What day was it? Sunday, he hoped. His father liked to putz on Sundays. Putzing, he called it, which meant tinkering and dreaming and touching things with his hands, fixing them or building them or tearing them down, studying things. Putzing . . . He hoped it was Sunday. What would they be doing? What month was it? He pictured the telephone. It was there in the kitchen, to the left of the sink. It was black. Black because his father hated pastels on his telephones. . . . He imagined the ring. He remembered it clearly, how it sounded both in the kitchen and in the basement, where his father had rigged up an extra bell, much louder-sounding in the cement. He pictured the basement. He pictured the living room and den and kitchen. Pink formica on the counters and speckled pink-and-white walls. His father . . .

The Pfc touched his arm. "Speak real clear," he said. "And after each time you talk you got to say, 'Over,' it's in the regs, and the same for your loved ones. Got it?"

Paul Berlin nodded. Immediately the headphones buzzed with a different sort of sound.

He tried to think of something meaningful and cheerful to say. Nothing forced: easy and natural, but still loving. Maybe start by saying he was getting along. Tell them things weren't really so bad. Then ask how his father's business was. Don't let on about being afraid. Don't make them worry—that was Doc Peret's advice. Make it sound like a vacation, talk about the swell beaches, tell them how you're getting this spectacular tan. Tell them—tell them you're getting skin cancer from all the sun, a Miami holiday. That was Doc's advice. Tell them . . . The Pfc swiveled the microphone so that it faced him. The boy checked his two wristwatches, smiled, whispered something. The kitchen, Paul Berlin thought. He could see it now. The old walnut dining table that his mother had inherited from an aunt in Minnesota. And the big white stove, the refrigerator, stainless steel cabinets over the sink, the black telephone, the windows looking out on Mrs. Stone's immaculate back yard. She was something, that Mrs. Stone. Yes, that was something to ask his father about: Was the old lady still out there in winter, using her broom to sweep away the snow, even in blizzards, sweeping and sweeping, and in the autumn was she still sweeping leaves from her yard, and in summer was she sweeping away the dandelion fuzz? Sure! He'd get his father to talk about her. Something fun and cheerful. The time old Mrs. Stone was out there in the rain, sweeping the water off her lawn as fast as it fell, all day long, sweeping it out to the gutter and then sweeping it up the street, but how the street was at a slight angle so that the rain water kept flowing back down on her, and, Lord, how Mrs. Stone was out there until midnight, ankle-deep, trying to beat gravity with her broom. Lord, his father always said, shaking his head. Neighbors. That was one thing to talk about. And

. . . and he'd ask his mother if she'd stopped smoking. There was a joke about that. She'd say, "Sure, I've stopped four times this week," which was a line she'd picked up on TV or someplace. Or she'd say, "No, but at least I'm not smoking tulips anymore, just Luckies." They'd laugh. He wouldn't let on how afraid he was; he wouldn't mention Billy Boy Watkins or Frenchie Tucker or what happened to Bernie Lynn and the others who were gone.

Yes, they'd laugh, and afterward, near the end of the conversation, maybe then he'd tell them he loved them. He couldn't remember ever telling them that, except at the bottom of letters, but this time maybe . . . The line buzzed again, then clicked, then there was the digital pause that always comes as a connection is completed, and then he heard the first ring. He recognized it. Hollow, washed out by distance, but it was still the old ring. He'd heard it ten thousand times. He listened to the ring as he would listen to family voices, his father's voice and his mother's voice, older now and changed by what time does to voices, but still the same voices. He stopped thinking of things to say. He concentrated on the ringing. He saw the black phone, heard it ringing and ringing. The Pfc held up a thumb but Paul Berlin barely noticed; he was smiling at the sound of the ringing.

"Tough luck," Doc said afterward.

Oscar and Eddie clapped him on the back, and the Pfc shrugged and said it happened sometimes.

"What can you do?" Oscar said. "The world, it don't stop turning."

"Yeah."

"Who knows? Maybe they was out takin' a drive, or something. Buying groceries. The world don't stop."

Responding to the Story

Analyzing the Story

Identifying Facts

1. The soldiers are in Chu Lai when the story opens. Why are they there?
2. Describe Eddie's reaction to his telephone call. How do Doc and Oscar react to their calls?
3. What goes through Paul Berlin's mind as he waits for his call to go through?

Interpreting Meanings

4. The narrator never tells us what happens to Paul's call. Instead, he lets us make an **inference,** or draw a conclusion based on other words or actions in the story. Explain what happens to Paul's call. Which words or actions helped you make this inference?
5. What does Paul get out of his time in the soundproof booth that the others know nothing about? Could you say his call was a success?
6. The writer never decribes the fighting or gives any details about the Vietnam War, yet "Calling Home" is unmistakably a war story. What do you think the writer is saying about war, soldiers, and home? What is the story's **theme**— its message about life and people?
7. The **climax** is the most exciting point in a story. It's where the story's complications come to a head. Where would you locate the climax of "Calling Home"? Why?
8. In some stories the **setting** is very important. If the story were set elsewhere, it would read quite differently. In other stories the setting is not crucial. The story would have the same effect if set in a different time or place. Do you think the setting is important to "Calling Home"? Explain.
9. This story is told from the **third-person point of view.** This means that we experience everything through the eyes of one person. Which character does this narrator focus on? Find passages where you learn this person's thoughts.

Applying Meanings

10. Do you agree that it is often very hard to say what you feel? Why do you think this is true for many people?

Writing About the Story

A Creative Response

1. **Writing a Dialogue.** Assume it is a day after the story ends, and Paul has returned to the Commo Detachment. A call is put through, and he is connected with his mother and father. Make up a **dialogue,** or conversation, between Paul and his parents. The dialogue should reflect the facts presented in the story. Read your dialogue aloud in class. Try to catch the special characteristics of the voices of Paul and his parents.

A Critical Response

2. **Describing a Character.** In some stories the writer tells you directly what a character is like; this is called **direct characterization.** In other stories, like "Calling Home," the writer gives you information about a character but doesn't tell you about the character's personality directly. This is called **indirect characterization.** In the latter case, you have to make your own judgments about the character. In a paragraph, describe what you think Paul is like. Quote passages from the story to support your description.

Analyzing Language and Vocabulary

Jargon

"Calling Home" contains **jargon,** or special vocabulary, that was used by American soldiers in Vietnam. The writer does not define these terms, but clues to their meaning are in nearby words and sentences. You can use these **context clues** to figure out the meaning of the jargon.

1. Locate the following bits of jargon in the story. Then, in a sentence, tell what each means.

   a. bush
   b. stand down
   c. Commo Detachment
   d. legs
   e. Graves Registration
   f. Roger
   g. regs

2. People engaged in a variety of activities and occupations use jargon. For instance, computer users employ jargon like *boot up* (start a com-

puter by loading a program into its memory) and *dump* (transfer data from one place to another). Athletes and musicians often use jargon. Think of an activity you take part in or know about. Write down five bits of jargon associated with the activity. Include a brief definition of each.

Reading About the Writer

Tim O'Brien (1946–   ), born in Austin, Minnesota, was drafted into the U.S. Army in 1968. He served in Indochina during the Vietnam War as a foot soldier, and was later promoted to the rank of sergeant. After his return to the United States, O'Brien worked for the *Washington Post,* but he continued writing fiction on the side. "I started writing fiction," O'Brien explains, "to get away from the whole idea of aping reality." O'Brien's experiences in Vietnam provided the background for many short stories. He later put these stories together in a novel called *Going After Cacciato.* "Calling Home" is an excerpt from this novel, which won the National Book Award in 1978.

Focusing on Background
O'Brien Talks About the Story

" 'Calling Home' is part of a much larger novel titled *Going After Cacciato,* but I hope it can be read and enjoyed as a short story that stands on its own. The idea for the story grew out of my own experience as a soldier in Vietnam. One afternoon I went with a group of buddies to a radio shack in Chu Lai, where we took turns placing long-distance calls to our families back in the United States. I remember watching the faces of my friends as they talked to their mothers and fathers and brothers and sisters. I remember the little tears in their eyes, the way they tried to hide their emotions, the jokes and small talk and chatter. More than anything, I remember how hard it was for us to say anything meaningful to our families. We didn't talk about the war. We didn't mention the fear, or the loneliness, or the guys who had already died. All that mattered, really, was to hear the *sound* of familiar voices—a father's voice, a mother's voice. The words were not important. Beneath the words, beneath the clichés and banal chit-chat, what we were listening to was the sound of love."

—Tim O'Brien

THE CIRCUIT

Francisco Jiménez

Migrant farm workers in California in the 1950's led a difficult life. They traveled from region to region, moving on at the end of one harvest to take part elsewhere in another harvest. Wages were low, and living quarters often were substandard. A child might not even be able to attend school on a regular basis. As you read this story about migrant workers from Mexico, think about the attitude of the narrator toward his life. Does the attitude strike you as unusual, or is it about what you would expect?

It was that time of year again. Ito, the strawberry sharecropper, did not smile. It was natural. The peak of the strawberry season was over and the last few days the workers, most of them braceros,[1] were not picking as many boxes as they had during the months of June and July.

As the last days of August disappeared, so did the number of braceros. Sunday, only one—the best picker—came to work. I liked him. Sometimes we talked during our half-hour lunch break. That is how I found out he was from Jalisco,[2] the same state in Mexico my family was from. That Sunday was the last time I saw him.

When the sun had tired and sunk behind the mountains, Ito signaled us that it was time to go home. "Ya esora,"[3] he yelled in his broken Spanish. Those were the words I waited for twelve hours a day, every day, seven days a week, week after week. And the thought of not hearing them again saddened me.

As we drove home Papá did not say a word. With both hands on the wheel, he stared at the dirt road. My older brother, Roberto, was also silent. He leaned his head back and closed his eyes. Once in a while he cleared from his throat the dust that blew in from outside.

Yes, it was that time of year. When I opened the front door to the shack, I stopped. Everything we owned was neatly packed in cardboard boxes. Suddenly I felt even more the weight of hours, days, weeks, and months of work. I sat down on a box. The thought of having to move to Fresno and knowing what was in store for me there brought tears to my eyes.

That night I could not sleep. I lay in bed thinking about how much I hated this move.

A little before five o'clock in the morning, Papá woke everyone up. A few minutes later, the yelling and screaming of my little brothers and sisters, for whom the move was a great adventure, broke the silence of dawn. Shortly, the barking of the dogs accompanied them.

While we packed the breakfast dishes, Papá went outside to start the "Carcanchita." That was the name Papá gave his old '38 black Plymouth. He bought it in a used-car lot in Santa Rosa in the winter of 1949. Papá was very proud of his little jalopy. He had a right to be proud of it. He spent

Words borrowed from other languages. English has borrowed many words from other languages. You'll find several in this story that were borrowed from Spanish. *Bracero*, for instance, means "hired hand" in Spanish, and refers to migrant farm workers from Mexico. *Fresno*, the name of the city where part of this story takes place, is a Spanish word meaning "ash tree." There are many white ash trees in the area. Watch for other words of Spanish origin.

---

1. **braceros** (brä·ser′ōs): Mexican farm laborers brought into the U.S. temporarily for migrant work in harvesting crops.
2. **Jalisco** (hä·lēs′kō).
3. **"Ya esora"** (yä äs·ō′rä).

a lot of time looking at other cars before buying this one. When he finally chose the "Carcanchita," he checked it thoroughly before driving it out of the car lot. He examined every inch of the car. He listened to the motor, tilting his head from side to side like a parrot, trying to detect any noises that spelled car trouble. After being satisfied with the looks and sounds of the car, Papá then insisted on knowing who the original owner was. He never did find out from the car salesman, but he bought the car anyway. Papá figured the original owner must have been an important man because behind the rear seat of the car he found a blue necktie.

Papá parked the car out in front and left the motor running. "Listo,"[4] he yelled. Without saying a word, Roberto and I began to carry the boxes out to the car. Roberto carried the two big boxes

and I carried the two smaller ones. Papá then threw the mattress on top of the car roof and tied it with ropes to the front and rear bumpers.

Everything was packed except Mamá's pot. It was an old large galvanized pot she had picked up at an army surplus store in Santa María the year I was born. The pot had many dents and nicks, and the more dents and nicks it acquired the more Mamá liked it. "Mi olla," she used to say proudly.

I held the front door open as Mamá carefully carried out her pot by both handles, making sure not to spill the cooked beans. When she got to the car, Papá reached out to help her with it. Roberto opened the rear car door and Papá gently placed it on the floor behind the front seat. All of us then climbed in. Papá sighed, wiped the sweat off his forehead with his sleeve, and said wearily: "Es todo."[5]

---

4. **Listo** (lēs'tō): Spanish for "Ready."

5. **Es todo:** Spanish for "That's it."

As we drove away, I felt a lump in my throat. I turned around and looked at our little shack for the last time.

At sunset we drove into a labor camp near Fresno. Since Papá did not speak English, Mamá asked the camp foreman if he needed any more workers. "We don't need no more," said the foreman, scratching his head. "Check with Sullivan down the road. Can't miss him. He lives in a big white house with a fence around it."

When we got there, Mamá walked up to the house. She went through a white gate, past a row of rosebushes, up the stairs to the front door. She rang the doorbell. The porch light went on and a tall husky man came out. They exchanged a few words. After the man went in, Mamá clasped her hands and hurried back to the car. "We have work! Mr. Sullivan said we can stay there the whole season," she said, gasping and pointing to an old garage near the stables.

The garage was worn out by the years. It had no windows. The walls, eaten by termites, strained to support the roof full of holes. The dirt floor, populated by earthworms, looked like a gray road map.

That night, by the light of a kerosene lamp, we unpacked and cleaned our new home. Roberto swept away the loose dirt, leaving the hard ground. Papá plugged the holes in the walls with old newspapers and tin can tops. Mamá fed my little brothers and sisters. Papá and Roberto then brought in the mattress and placed it in the far corner of the garage. "Mamá, you and the little ones sleep on the mattress. Roberto, Panchito, and I will sleep outside under the trees," Papá said.

Early next morning Mr. Sullivan showed us where his crop was, and after breakfast, Papá, Roberto, and I headed for the vineyard to pick.

Around nine o'clock the temperature had risen to almost one hundred degrees. I was completely soaked in sweat and my mouth felt as if I had been chewing on a handkerchief. I walked over to the end of the row, picked up the jug of water we had brought, and began drinking. "Don't drink too much; you'll get sick," Roberto shouted. No sooner had he said that than I felt sick to my stomach. I dropped to my knees and let the jug roll off my hands. I remained motionless with my eyes glued on the hot sandy ground. All I could hear was the drone of insects. Slowly I began to recover. I poured water over my face and neck and watched the dirty water run down my arms to the ground.

I still felt a little dizzy when we took a break to eat lunch. It was past two o'clock and we sat underneath a large walnut tree that was on the side of the road. While we ate, Papá jotted down the number of boxes we had picked. Roberto drew designs on the ground with a stick. Suddenly I noticed Papá's face turn pale as he looked down the road. "Here comes the school bus," he whispered loudly in alarm. Instinctively, Roberto and I ran and hid in the vineyards. We did not want to get in trouble for not going to school. The neatly dressed boys about my age got off. They carried books under their arms. After they crossed the street, the bus drove away. Roberto and I came out from hiding and joined Papá. "Tienen que tener cuidado,"[6] he warned us.

After lunch we went back to work. The sun kept beating down. The buzzing insects, the wet sweat, and the hot dry dust made the afternoon seem to last forever. Finally the mountains around the valley reached out and swallowed the sun. Within an hour it was too dark to continue picking. The vines blanketed the grapes, making it difficult to see the bunches. "Vámonos,"[7] said Papá, signaling to us that it was time to quit work. Papá then took out a pencil and began to figure out how much we had earned our first day. He wrote down numbers, crossed some out, wrote down some more. "Quince,"[8] he murmured.

When we arrived home, we took a cold shower underneath a water hose. We then sat down to eat dinner around some wooden crates that served as a table. Mamá had cooked a special meal for us. We had rice and tortillas with "carne con chile," my favorite dish.

The next morning I could hardly move. My body ached all over. I felt little control over my arms and legs. This feeling went on every morning

---

6. **Tienen que tener cuidado:** Spanish for "You have to be careful."
7. **Vámonos:** Spanish for "Let's go."
8. **Quince** (kēnʹsā): Spanish for "Fifteen."

for days until my muscles finally got used to the work.

It was Monday, the first week of November. The grape season was over and I could now go to school. I woke up early that morning and lay in bed, looking at the stars and savoring the thought of not going to work and of starting sixth grade for the first time that year. Since I could not sleep, I decided to get up and join Papá and Roberto at breakfast. I sat at the table across from Roberto, but I kept my head down. I did not want to look up and face him. I knew he was sad. He was not going to school today. He was not going tomorrow, or next week, or next month. He would not go until the cotton season was over, and that was sometime in February. I rubbed my hands together and watched the dry, acid-stained skin fall to the floor in little rolls.

When Papá and Roberto left for work, I felt relief. I walked to the top of a small grade next to the shack and watched the "Carcanchita" disappear in the distance in a cloud of dust.

Two hours later, around eight o'clock, I stood by the side of the road waiting for school bus number twenty. When it arrived I climbed in. Everyone was busy either talking or yelling. I sat in an empty seat in the back.

When the bus stopped in front of the school, I felt very nervous. I looked out the bus window and saw boys and girls carrying books under their arms. I put my hands in my pants pockets and walked to the principal's office. When I entered I heard a woman's voice say: "May I help you?" I was startled. I had not heard English for months. For a few seconds I remained speechless. I looked at the lady who waited for an answer. My first instinct was to answer her in Spanish, but I held back. Finally, after struggling for English words, I managed to tell her that I wanted to enroll in the sixth grade. After answering many questions, I was led to the classroom.

Mr. Lema, the sixth grade teacher, greeted me and assigned me a desk. He then introduced me to the class. I was so nervous and scared at that moment when everyone's eyes were on me that I wished I were with Papá and Roberto picking cotton. After taking roll, Mr. Lema gave the class the assignment for the first hour. "The first thing we have to do this morning is finish reading the story we began yesterday," he said enthusiastically. He walked up to me, handed me an English book, and asked me to read. "We are on page 125," he said politely. When I heard this, I felt my blood rush to my head; I felt dizzy. "Would you like to read?" he asked hesitantly. I opened the book to page 125. My mouth was dry. My eyes began to water. I could not begin. "You can read later," Mr. Lema said understandingly.

For the rest of the reading period I kept getting angrier and angrier with myself. I should have read, I thought to myself.

During recess I went into the restroom and opened my English book to page 125. I began to read in a low voice, pretending I was in class. There were many words I did not know. I closed the book and headed back to the classroom.

Mr. Lema was sitting at his desk correcting papers. When I entered, he looked up at me and smiled. I felt better. I walked up to him and asked if he could help me with the new words. "Gladly," he said.

The rest of the month I spent my lunch hours working on English with Mr. Lema, my best friend at school.

One Friday during lunch hour Mr. Lema asked me to take a walk with him to the music room. "Do you like music?" he asked me as we entered the building.

"Yes, I like corridos,"[9] I answered. He then picked up a trumpet, blew on it and handed it to me. The sound gave me goose bumps. I knew that sound. I had heard it in many corridos. "How would you like to learn how to play it?" he asked. He must have read my face because before I could answer, he added: "I'll teach you how to play it during our lunch hours."

That day I could hardly wait to get home to tell Papá and Mamá the great news. As I got off the bus, my little brothers and sisters ran up to meet me. They were yelling and screaming. I thought they were happy to see me, but when I opened the door to our shack, I saw that everything we owned was neatly packed in cardboard boxes.

---

9. **corridos:** Mexican folk ballads.

Responding to the Story

Analyzing the Story

Identifying Facts

1. Explain why the family leaves the shack near Ito's farm.
2. Describe the family's living quarters near Fresno. What do they do to improve their home?
3. Why does the narrator's father become alarmed when he sees the school bus?
4. What happens when Mr. Lema asks the narrator to read aloud on his first day in sixth grade?
5. Why does the narrator eventually call Mr. Lema "my best friend in school"?
6. What happens at the end of the story? Why won't the narrator learn to play the trumpet in Fresno?

Interpreting Meanings

7. **Conflict** is a key ingredient in a good story. A conflict is **external** when a character struggles with an outside force, such as another character, society as a whole, or a natural force like a storm. It is **internal** when it involves a struggle between opposing feelings or ideas within the mind or heart of a character. What would you say is the principal external conflict of "The Circuit"? What is the narrator's main internal conflict?
8. How would you describe the narrator's attitude toward his life as part of a bracero family? Do you find the attitude unusual, or pretty much what you expected? Try to explain why the narrator feels as he does.
9. The story ends abruptly, with no information about what will become of the narrator and his family. What do you think will happen to the narrator? Will he complete his education?
10. What does the story's **title** mean?

Applying Meanings

11. "The Circuit" takes place in the 1950's. Are conditions still the same among migrant farm workers in California? What are living quarters like today? Must children still work long hours to help provide a meager existence for a family? You'll probably need to do some research to

answer. Check in a library for appropriate literature. You could also get in touch with a governmental body dealing with migrant workers, a farm-workers' organization like the United Farm Workers of America, or with a person or company that owns and operates a farm employing migrant workers.

Writing About the Story

A Creative Response

1. **Changing the Point of View.** "The Circuit" is told from the **first-person point of view.** You see everything through the narrator's eyes, and learn little about the thoughts and feelings of the other characters. The narrator says he hated the move to Fresno, but says nothing about his parents' feelings. In a paragraph, describe what you think the mother and father felt as they prepared to leave for Fresno.

A Critical Response

2. **Analyzing a Character.** The narrator of the story doesn't tell you much directly about what he's like. (He doesn't say, for instance, "I like to do hard physical work and also like to read short stories.") However, you learn about the narrator indirectly as he tells the story. You learn this by

watching how he acts and how others act toward him, and by noticing what he thinks and says. Reread the story and write down the narrator's main personality traits and how they are revealed. Then write a paragraph in which you discuss his personality. Quote passages from the story to support your analysis.

Analyzing Language and Vocabulary

English Words Borrowed from Other Languages

English has borrowed many words, including place names, from Spanish. A good dictionary will usually tell you about the origins of a word; this information generally follows soon after the pronunciation of the word. Use a dictionary to discover the Spanish origins of the following words.

1. adobe
2. alligator
3. bronco
4. cafeteria
5. corral
6. plaza
7. Rio Grande
8. San Francisco
9. Sierra Nevada
10. stampede

Carne con chile is mentioned in the story. You probably know this spicy dish better as *chili* or *chili con carne.* Many English words and phrases referring to food are borrowed from other languages. See how many of the following food terms you can define. Check a dictionary for unfamiliar terms and to find out the language from which each was taken.

1. blintz
2. bouillabaisse
3. couscous
4. goulash
5. lasagna
6. paella
7. sauerbraten
8. shish kebab
9. sushi
10. won ton

Reading About the Writer

The son of migrant workers, **Francisco Jiménez** (1943–   ) was born in San Pedro Tlaquepaque, Jalisco, Mexico, and came to the United States when he was four years old. At the age of six, Francisco started working the fields. The crop cycle took his family all around Southern California, picking strawberries, grapes, cotton, lettuce, and carrots. After many years, Jiménez was able to gain citizenship in the United States. Although he had a rough time completing his education as a child (he failed first grade, and was deported in the eighth), he went on to earn a Ph.D. in Latin American literature. He is now a professor at Santa Clara University in California. Jiménez has won several awards for his short stories.

Focusing on Background
A Comment from the Writer

" 'The Circuit' is an autobiographical short story based on my experiences as a child, growing up in a family of migrant farm workers. The setting is the San Joaquin Valley, a rich agricultural area in California, where my family made a living working in the fields.

"The idea for the story goes back many years to the time when I was in Santa Maria High School. Miss Bell, my sophomore English teacher, encouraged the class to write detailed narrative accounts of personal experiences. Even though I had difficulty expressing myself in English, I enjoyed the assignments, and with much effort I wrote about what I knew best. Long after I left her class I continued to reflect upon my life experiences and often thought of expressing them in writing.

"I actually wrote the story in graduate school at Columbia University in 1972. That year I shared two autobiographical narrative accounts with my teacher. He liked them and urged me to publish my work. Encouraged by his remarks, I decided to write 'The Circuit,' describing the joys and disappointments I encountered as I grew up in a migrant setting."

—Francisco Jiménez

WINTERBLOSSOM GARDEN

David Low

This story is about love, the love that holds a family together. It concerns the love between a son and his parents, and the love of a man and a woman that generates the family love. As you read, watch for changes in the relationship between the parents and between the parents and their son.

I

I have no photographs of my father. One hot Saturday in June, my camera slung over my shoulder, I take the subway from Greenwich Village to Chinatown.[1] I switch to the M local which becomes an elevated train after it crosses the Williamsburg Bridge. I am going to Ridgewood, Queens, where I spent my childhood. I sit in a car that is almost empty; I feel the loud rumble of the whole train through the hard seat. Someday, I think, wiping the sweat from my face, they'll tear this el down, as they've torn down the others.

I get off at Fresh Pond Road and walk the five blocks from the station to my parents' restaurant. At the back of the store in the kitchen, I find my father packing an order: White cartons of food fit neatly into a brown paper bag. As the workers chatter in Cantonese, I smell the food cooking: spare ribs, chicken lo mein, sweet and pungent pork, won ton soup. My father, who has just turned seventy-three, wears a wrinkled white short-sleeve shirt and a cheap maroon tie, even in this weather. He dabs his face with a handkerchief.

"Do you need money?" he asks in Chinese, as he takes the order to the front of the store. I notice that he walks slower than usual. Not that his walk is ever very fast; he usually walks with quiet as-

surance, a man who knows who he is and where he is going. Other people will just have to wait until he gets there.

"Not this time," I answer in English. I laugh. I haven't borrowed money from him in years but he still asks. My father and I have almost always spoken different languages.

"I want to take your picture, Dad."

"Not now, too busy." He hands the customer the order and rings the cash register.

"It will only take a minute."

He stands reluctantly beneath the green awning in front of the store, next to the gold-plated letters on the window:

WINTERBLOSSOM GARDEN
CHINESE-AMERICAN RESTAURANT
WE SERVE THE FINEST FOOD

I look through the camera viewfinder.

"Smile," I say.

Instead my father holds his left hand with the

Images of taste and smell. *Imagery* is language that appeals to our senses. Most images appeal to our sense of sight, but they can also appeal to our sense of hearing, touch, taste, or smell. Since this story deals in part with people who operate a restaurant, it is not surprising to find in it images appealing to our senses of taste and smell. You'll find some examples in the second paragraph. Watch for others as you read the story.

---

1. **Greenwich Village** and **Chinatown:** two sections of Manhattan. **Queens,** mentioned later in this paragraph, is one of New York City's five boroughs.

New York by George Grosz (1934). Watercolor.

crooked pinky on his stomach. I have often wondered about that pinky; is it a souvenir of some street fight in his youth? He wears a jade ring on his index finger. His hair, streaked with gray, is greased down as usual; his face looks a little pale. Most of the day, he remains at the restaurant. I snap the shutter.

"Go see your mother," he says slowly in English.

According to my mother, in 1929 my father entered this country illegally by jumping off the boat as it neared Ellis Island and swimming to Hoboken, New Jersey; there he managed to board a train to New York, even though he knew no English and had not one American cent in his pockets. Whether or not the story is true, I like to imagine my father hiding in the washroom on the train, dripping wet with fatigue and feeling triumphant. Now he was in America, where anything could happen. He found a job scooping ice cream at a dance hall in Chinatown. My mother claims that before he married her, he liked to gamble his nights away and drink with scandalous women. After two years in this country, he opened his restaurant with money he had borrowed from friends in Chinatown who already ran their own businesses. My father chose Ridgewood for the store's location because he mistook the community's name for "Richwood." In such a lucky place, he told my mother, his restaurant was sure to succeed.

When I was growing up, my parents spent most of their days in Winterblossom Garden. Before going home after school, I would stop at the restaurant. The walls then were a hideous pale green with red numbers painted in Chinese characters and Roman numerals above the side booths. In days of warm weather huge fans whirred from the ceiling. My mother would sit at a table in the back where she would make egg rolls. She began by placing generous handfuls of meat-and-cabbage filling on squares of thin white dough. Then she delicately folded up each piece of dough, checking to make sure the filling was totally sealed inside, like a mummy wrapped in bandages. Finally, with a small brush she spread beaten eggs on the outside of each white roll. As I watched her steadily produce a tray of these uncooked creations, she never asked me about school; she was more concerned that my shirt was sticking out of my pants or that my hair was disheveled.

"Are you hungry?" my mother would ask in English. Although my parents had agreed to speak only Chinese in my presence, she often broke this rule when my father wasn't in the same room. Whether I wanted to eat or not, I was sent into the kitchen where my father would repeat my mother's question. Then without waiting for an answer, he would prepare for me a bowl of beef with snow peas or a small portion of steamed fish. My parents assumed that as long as I ate well, everything in my life would be fine. If I said "Hello" or "Thank you" in Chinese, I was allowed to choose whatever dish I liked; often I ordered a hot turkey sandwich. I liked the taste of burnt rice soaked in tea.

I would wait an hour or so for my mother to walk home with me. During that time, I would go to the front of the store, put a dime in the jukebox and press the buttons for a currently popular song. It might be D3: "Bye Bye, Love." Then I would lean on the back of the bench where customers waited for takeouts; I would stare out the large window that faced the street. The world outside seemed vast, hostile, and often sad.

Across the way, I could see Rosa's Italian Bakery, the Western Union office and Von Ronn's soda fountain. Why didn't we live in Chinatown? I wondered. Or San Francisco? In a neighborhood that was predominantly German, I had no Chinese friends. No matter how many bottles of Coca-Cola I drank, I would still be different from the others. They were fond of calling me "Skinny Chink" when I won games of stoop ball. I wanted to have blond curly hair and blue eyes; I didn't understand why my father didn't have a ranch like the rugged cowboys on television.

Now Winterblossom Garden has wood paneling on the walls, formica tables, and aluminum Roman numerals over the mock-leather booths. Several years ago, when the ceiling was lowered, the whirring fans were removed; a huge air-conditioning unit was installed. The jukebox has been replaced by Muzak.[2] My mother no longer makes the egg rolls; my father hires enough help to do that.

Some things remain the same. My father has made few changes in the menu, except for prices; the steady customers know they can always have the combination plates. In a glass case near the cash register, cardboard boxes overflow with bags of fortune cookies and almond candies that my father gives away free to children. The first dollar bill my parents ever made hangs framed on the wall above the register. Next to that dollar, a picture of my parents taken twenty years ago recalls a time when they were raising four children at once, paying mortgages and putting in the bank every cent that didn't go toward bills. Although it was a hard time for them, my mother's face is radiant, as if she has just won the top prize at a beauty pageant; she wears a flower-print dress with a large white collar. My father has on a suit with wide lapels that was tailored in Chinatown; he is smiling a rare smile.

My parents have a small brick house set apart from the other buildngs on the block. Most of their neighbors have lived in Ridgewood all their lives. As I ring the bell and wait for my mother to answer, I notice that the maple tree in front of the house has died. All that is left is a gray ghost; bare branches lie in the gutter. If I took a picture of this tree, I think, the printed image would resemble a negative.

"The gas man killed it when they tore up the street," my mother says. She watches television as she lies back on the gold sofa like a queen, her head resting against a pillow. A documentary about wildlife in Africa is on the screen; gazelles dance across a dusty plain. My mother likes soap operas but they aren't shown on weekends. In the evenings she will watch almost anything except news specials and police melodramas.

"Why don't you get a new tree planted?"

"We would have to get a permit," she answers. "The sidewalk belongs to the city. Then we would have to pay for the tree."

"It would be worth it," I say. "Doesn't it bother you, seeing a dead tree every day? You should find someone to cut it down."

My mother does not answer. She has fallen asleep. These days she can doze off almost as soon as her head touches the pillow. Six years ago she had a nervous breakdown. When she came home from the hospital she needed to take naps in the afternoon. Soon the naps became a permanent refuge, a way to forget her loneliness for an hour or two. She no longer needed to work in the store. Three of her children were married. I was away at art school and planned to live on my own when I graduated.

"I have never felt at home in America," my mother once told me.

Now as she lies there, I wonder if she is dreaming. I would like her to tell me her darkest dream. Although we speak the same language, there has always been an ocean between us. She does not wish to know what I think alone at night, what I see of the world with my camera.

My mother pours two cups of tea from the porcelain teapot that has always been in its wicker basket on the kitchen table. On the sides of the teapot, a maiden dressed in a jade-green gown visits a bearded emperor at his palace near the sky. The maiden waves a vermillion fan.

"I bet you still don't know how to cook," my mother says. She places a plate of steamed roast pork buns before me.

"Mom, I'm not hungry."

"If you don't eat more, you will get sick."

I take a bun from the plate but it is too hot. My mother hands me a napkin so I can put the bun down. Then she peels a banana in front of me.

"I'm not obsessed with food like you," I say.

"What's wrong with eating?"

She looks at me as she takes a big bite of the banana.

"I'm going to have a photography show at the end of the summer."

"Are you still taking pictures of old buildings falling down? How ugly! Why don't you take happier pictures?"

---

2. **Muzak** (my$\overline{oo}$'zak): service providing recorded music.

"I thought you would want to come," I answer. "It's not easy to get a gallery."

"If you were married," she says, her voice becoming unusually soft, "you would take better pictures. You would be happy."

"I don't know what you mean. Why do you think getting married will make me happy?"

My mother looks at me as if I have spoken in Serbo-Croatian.[3] She always gives me this look when I say something she does not want to hear. She finishes the banana; then she puts the plate of food away. Soon she stands at the sink, turns on the hot water and washes dishes. My mother learned long ago that silence has a power of its own.

She takes out a blue cookie tin from the dining room cabinet. Inside this tin, my mother keeps her favorite photographs. Whenever I am ready to leave, my mother brings it to the living room and opens it on the coffee table. She knows I cannot resist looking at these pictures again; I will sit down next to her on the sofa for at least another hour. Besides the portraits of the family, my mother has images of people I have never met: her father who owned a poultry store on Pell Street and didn't get a chance to return to China before he died; my father's younger sister who still runs a pharmacy in Rio de Janeiro (she sends the family an annual supply of cough drops); my mother's cousin Kay who died at thirty, a year after she came to New York from Hong Kong. Although my mother has a story to tell for each photograph, she refuses to speak about Kay, as if the mere mention of her name will bring back her ghost to haunt us all.

My mother always manages to find a picture I have not seen before; suddenly I discover I have a relative who is a mortician[4] in Vancouver. I pick up a portrait of Uncle Lao-Hu, a silver-haired man with a goatee[5] who owned a curio shop on Mott

---

3. **as if . . . Serbo-Croatian** (sur′bō krō·ā′shən): as if he were speaking a language his mother didn't understand. Serbo-Croatian is a principal language of Yugoslavia.

4. **mortician** (môr·tish′ən): undertaker.
5. **goatee** (gō·tē′): small, pointed beard.

Street until he retired last year and moved to Hawaii. In a color print, he stands in the doorway of his store, holding a bamboo Moon Man in front of him, as if it were a bowling trophy. The statue, which is actually two feet tall, has a staff in its left hand, while its right palm balances a peach, a sign of long life. The top of the Moon Man's head protrudes in the shape of an eggplant; my mother believes that such a head contains an endless wealth of wisdom.

"Your Uncle Lao-Hu is a wise man, too," my mother says, "except when he's in love. When he still owned the store, he fell in love with his women customers all the time. He was always losing money because he gave away his merchandise to any woman who smiled at him."

I see my uncle's generous arms full of gifts: a silver Buddha,[6] an ivory dragon, a pair of emerald chopsticks.

"These women confused him," she adds. "That's what happens when a Chinese man doesn't get married."

My mother shakes her head and sighs.

"In his last letter, Lao-Hu invited me to visit him in Honolulu. Your father refuses to leave the store."

"Why don't you go anyway?"

"I can't leave your father alone." She stares at the pictures scattered on the coffee table.

"Mom, why don't you do something for yourself? I thought you were going to start taking English lessons."

"Your father thinks it would be a waste of time."

While my mother puts the cookie tin away, I stand up to stretch my legs. I gaze at a photograph that hangs on the wall above the sofa: my parents' wedding picture. My mother was matched[7] to my father; she claims that if her own father had been able to repay the money that Dad spent to bring her to America, she might never have married him at all. In the wedding picture she wears a stunned expression. She is dressed in a luminous gown of ruffles and lace; the train spirals at her feet. As she clutches a bouquet tightly against her stomach, she might be asking, "What am I doing? Who is this man?" My father's face is thinner than it is now. His tuxedo is too small for him; the flower in his lapel droops. He hides his hand with the crooked pinky behind his back.

I have never been sure if my parents really love each other. I have only seen them kiss at their children's weddings. They never touch each other in public. When I was little, I often thought they went to sleep in the clothes they wore to work.

Before I leave, my mother asks me to take her picture. Unlike my father she likes to pose for photographs as much as possible. When her children still lived at home, she would leave snapshots of herself all around the house; we could not forget her, no matter how hard we tried.

She changes her blouse, combs her hair, and redoes her eyebrows. Then I follow her out the back door into the garden where she kneels down next to the rosebush. She touches one of the yellow roses.

"Why don't you sit on the front steps?" I ask, as I peer through the viewfinder. "It will be more natural."

"No," she says firmly. "Take the picture now."

She smiles without opening her mouth. I see for the first time that she has put on a pair of dangling gold earrings. Her face has grown round as the moon with the years. She has developed wrinkles under the eyes, but like my father, she hardly shows her age. For the past ten years, she has been fifty-one. Everyone needs a fantasy to help them stay alive: My mother believes she is perpetually beautiful, even if my father has not complimented her in years.

After I snap the shutter, she plucks a rose.

As we enter the kitchen through the back door, I can hear my father's voice from the next room.

"Who's he talking to?" I ask.

"He's talking to the goldfish," she answers. "I have to live with this man."

My father walks in, carrying a tiny can of fish food.

"You want a girlfriend?" he asks, out of nowhere. "My friend has a nice daughter. She knows how to cook Chinese food."

6. **Buddha** (bood′ə): philosopher and teacher who founded Buddhism in the sixth century B.C. Buddhism has had an important influence on Chinese religious beliefs.
7. **matched:** having a marriage arranged by others.

"Dad, she sounds perfect for you."

"She likes to stay home," my mother adds. "She went to college and reads books like you.

"I'll see you next year," I say.

That evening in the darkroom at my apartment, I develop and print my parents' portraits. I hang the pictures side by side to dry on a clothesline in the bathroom. As I feel my parents' eyes staring at me, I turn away. Their faces look unfamiliar in the fluorescent light.

II

At the beginning of July my mother calls me at work.

"Do you think you can take off next Monday morning?" she asks.

"Why?"

"Your father has to go to the hospital for some tests. He looks awful."

We sit in the back of a taxi on the way to a hospital in Forest Hills. I am sandwiched between my mother and father. The skin of my father's face is pale yellow. During the past few weeks he has lost fifteen pounds; his wrinkled suit is baggy around the waist. My mother sleeps with her head tilted to one side until the taxi hits a bump on the road. She wakes up startled, as if afraid she has missed a stop on the train.

"Don't worry," my father says weakly. He squints as he turns his head toward the window. "The doctors will give me pills. Everything will be fine."

"Don't say anything," my mother says. "Too much talk will bring bad luck."

My father takes two crumpled dollar bills from his jacket and places them in my hand.

"For the movies," he says. I smile, without mentioning it costs more to go to a film these days.

My mother opens her handbag and takes out a compact. She has forgotten to put on her lipstick.

The hospital waiting room has beige walls. My mother and I follow my father as he makes his way slowly to a row of seats near an open window.

"Fresh air is important," he used to remind me on a sunny day when I would read a book in bed. Now after we sit down, he keeps quiet. I hear the sound of plates clattering from the coffee shop in the next room.

"Does anyone want some breakfast?" I ask.

"Your father can't eat anything before the tests," my mother warns.

"What about you?"

"I'm not hungry," she says.

My father reaches over to take my hand in his. He considers my palm.

"Very, very lucky," he says. "You will have lots of money."

I laugh. "You've been saying that ever since I was born."

He puts on his glasses crookedly and touches a curved line near the top of my palm.

"Be patient," he says.

My mother rises suddenly.

"Why are they making us wait so long? Do you think they forget us?"

While she walks over to speak to a nurse at the reception desk, my father leans toward me.

"Remember to take care of your mother."

The doctors discover that my father has stomach cancer. They decide to operate immediately. According to them, my father has already lost so much blood that it is a miracle he is still alive.

The week of my father's operation, I sleep at my parents' house. My mother has kept my bedroom on the second floor the way it was before I moved out. A square room, it gets the afternoon light. Dust covers the top of my old bookcase. The first night I stay over I find a pinhole camera on a shelf in the closet; I made it when I was twelve from a cylindrical Quaker Oats box. When I lie back on the yellow comforter that covers my bed, I see the crack in the ceiling that I once called the Yangtze River, the highway for tea merchants and vagabonds.

At night I help my mother close the restaurant. I do what she and my father have done together for the past forty-three years. At ten o'clock I turn off the illuminated white sign above the front entrance. After all the customers leave and the last waiter says goodbye, I lock the front door and flip over the sign that says "Closed." Then I shut off the radio and the back lights. While I refill the glass case with bottles of duck sauce and packs of cigarettes, my mother empties the cash register. She puts all the money in white cartons and packs them in brown paper bags. My father thought up that idea long ago.

In the past when they have walked the three blocks home, they have given the appearance of carrying bags of food. The one time my father was attacked by three teenagers, my mother was sick in bed. My father scared the kids off by pretending he knew kung fu. When he got home, he showed me his swollen left hand and smiled.

"Don't tell your mother."

On the second night we walk home together, my mother says:

"I could never run the restaurant alone. I would have to sell it. I have four children and no one wants it."

I say nothing, unwilling to start an argument.

Later my mother and I eat Jell-O in the kitchen. A cool breeze blows through the window.

"Maybe I will sleep tonight," my mother says. She walks out to the back porch to sit on one of the two folding chairs. My bedroom is right above the porch; as a child I used to hear my parents talking late into the night, their paper fans rustling.

After reading a while in the living room, I go upstairs to take a shower. When I am finished, I hear my mother calling my name from downstairs.

I find her dressed in her bathrobe, opening the dining room cabinet.

"Someone has stolen the money," she says. She walks nervously into the living room and looks under the lamp table.

"What are you talking about?" I ask.

"Maybe we should call the police," she suggests. "I can't find the money we brought home tonight."

She starts to pick up the phone.

"Wait. Have you checked everywhere? Where do you usually put it?"

"I thought I locked it in your father's closet but it isn't there."

"I'll look around," I say. "Why don't you go back to sleep?"

She lies back on the sofa.

"How can I sleep?" she asks. "I told your father a long time ago to sell the restaurant but he wouldn't listen."

I search the first floor. I look in the shoe closet, behind the television, underneath the dining room table, in the clothes hamper. Finally after examining all the kitchen cupboards without any luck, I open the refrigerator to take out something to drink. The three cartons of money are on the second shelf, next to the mayonnaise and the strawberry jam.

When I bring the cartons to the living room, my mother sits up on the sofa, amazed.

"Well," she says, "how did they ever get *there*?"

She opens one of them. The crisp dollar bills inside are cold as ice.

The next day I talk on the telephone to my father's physician. He informs me that the doctors have succeeded in removing the malignancy before it has spread. My father will remain in intensive care for at least a week.

In the kitchen my mother irons a tablecloth.

"The doctors are impressed by Dad's will-power, considering his age," I tell her.

"A fortuneteller on East Broadway told him that he will live to be a hundred," she says.

That night I dream that I am standing at the entrance to Winterblossom Garden. A taxi stops in front of the store. My father jumps out, dressed in a bathrobe and slippers.

"I'm almost all better," he tells me. "I want to see how the business is doing without me."

In a month my father is ready to come home. My sister Elizabeth, the oldest child, picks him up at the hospital. At the house the whole family waits for him.

When Elizabeth's car arrives my mother and I are already standing on the front steps. My sister walks around the car to open my father's door. He cannot get out by himself. My sister offers him a hand but as he reaches out to grab it, he misses and falls back in his seat.

Finally my sister helps him stand up, his back a little stooped. While my mother remains on the steps, I run to give a hand.

My father does not fight our help. His skin is dry and pale but no longer yellow. As he walks forward, staring at his feet, I feel his whole body shaking against mine. Only now, as he leans his weight on my arm, do I begin to understand how easily my father might have died. He seems light as a sparrow.

When we reach the front steps, my father raises his head to look at my mother. She stares at him a minute, then turns away to open the door. Soon my sister and I are leading him to the living room sofa, where we help him lie back. My mother has a pillow and a blanket ready. She sits down on the coffee table in front of him. I watch them hold each other's hands.

III

At the beginning of September my photography exhibit opens at a cooperative gallery on West 13th Street. I have chosen to hang only a dozen pictures, not much to show for ten years of work. About sixty people come to the opening, more than I expected; I watch them from a corner of the room, now and then overhearing a conversation I would like to ignore.

After an hour I decide I have stayed too long. As I walk around the gallery, hunting for a telephone, I see my parents across the room. My father calls out my name in Chinese; he has gained back all his weight and appears to be in better shape than many of the people around him. As I make my way toward my parents, I hear him talking loudly in bad English to a short young woman who stares at one of my portraits.

"That's my wife," he says. "If you like it, you should buy it."

"Maybe I will," the young woman says. She points to another photograph. "Isn't that you?"

My father laughs. "No, that's my brother."

My mother hands me a brown paper bag.

"Leftover from dinner," she tells me. "You didn't tell me you were going to show my picture. It's the best one in the show."

I take my parents for a personal tour.

"Who is that?" my father asks. He stops at a photograph of a woman covered from the waist down by a pile of leaves as she sits in the middle of a forest.

"She's a professional model," I lie.

"She needs to gain some weight," my mother says.

A few weeks after my show has closed, I have lunch with my parents at the restaurant. After we finish our meal, my father walks into the kitchen to scoop ice cream for dessert. My mother opens her handbag. She takes out a worn manila envelope and hands it to me across the table.

"I found this in a box while I was cleaning the house," she says. "I want you to have it."

Inside the envelope, I find a portrait of my father, taken when he was still a young man. He does not smile but his eyes shine like wet black marbles. He wears a polka-dot tie; a plaid handkerchief hangs out of the front pocket of his suit jacket. My father has never cared about his clothes matching. Even when he was young, he liked to grease down his hair with brilliantine.[8]

"Your father's cousin was a doctor in Hong Kong," my mother tells me. "After my eighteenth birthday, he came to my parents' house and showed them this picture. He said your father would make the perfect husband because he was handsome and very smart. Grandma gave me the picture before I got on the boat to America."

"I'll have it framed right away."

My father returns with three dishes of chocolate ice cream balanced on a silver tray.

"You want to work here?" he asks me.

"Your father wants to sell the business next year," my mother says. "He feels too old to run a restaurant."

"I'd just lose money," I say. "Besides, Dad, you're not old."

He does not join us for dessert. Instead, he dips his napkin in a glass of water and starts to wipe the table. I watch his dish of ice cream melt.

When I am ready to leave, my parents walk me to the door.

"Next time, I'll take you uptown to see a movie," I say as we step outside.

---

8. **brilliantine** (brĭl′yən·tēn): oily hair dressing.

"Radio City?" my father asks.

"They don't show movies there now," my mother reminds him.

"I'll cook dinner for you at my apartment."

My father laughs.

"We'll eat out," my mother suggests.

My parents wait in front of Winterblossom Garden until I reach the end of the block. I turn and wave. With her heels on, my mother is the same height as my father. She waves back for both of them. I would like to take their picture, but I forgot to bring my camera.

Responding to the Story

Analyzing the Story

Identifying Facts

1. The story opens with a visit by the narrator to his parents' restaurant. What does the narrator say is the purpose of the visit? Does he achieve his purpose?

2. In what ways did the narrator see himself as different from his playmates when he was a child? Why would he have liked to live in a different neighborhood?

3. How does the narrator help out during his father's illness?

4. What is the reaction of the parents to their son's exhibit of photographs? What does the narrator receive from his mother soon after?

Identifying Meanings

5. Can you find **conflicts** in this story? If so, who is struggling against whom, or what? Are the conflicts resolved by the end of the story?

6. The three main characters in "Winterblossom Garden" are **dynamic.** That is, they change as a result of the story's events. Important changes concern the relationships of the characters with each other. How does the relationship of the mother and father change over the course of the story? How does the relationship of the narrator with his parents change?

7. Taking photographs and looking at photographs are actions that occur several times in the story. Identify two examples and discuss their meaning to the narrator, the mother, and the father.

8. A **symbol** is something that has meaning in itself and also represents something else. What do you think the restaurant symbolizes?

9. The narrator says his parents had agreed to speak only Chinese in his presence when he was growing up. Why do you think his parents agreed to this? Why did the mother often break this rule when the father was not in the room?

Applying Meanings

10. Do you think this family is like many other families, whether they are Chinese-American or not? Explain why, or why not.

Writing About the Story

A Creative Response

1. **Describing a Process.** In the story the narrator describes how his mother made egg rolls. "She began," he says, "by placing generous handfuls of meat-and-cabbage filling on squares of thin white dough." He then goes on to note two other steps in making egg rolls. Choose a skill you know about, such as building models, cooking a particular dish, or fielding a grounder in baseball, that can be broken down into steps. Then, in a paragraph, describe each step. The steps should be discussed in proper sequence. There should be enough detail so a person unfamiliar with the skill will understand the steps.

A Critical Response

2. **Summarizing a Plot.** A **plot** is made up of a series of events that form the basis of a story. A story may contain many events, but usually a few stand out as more important than the others. In a paragraph, summarize the plot of "Winterblossom Garden" by discussing the five or six most important events in the story. Point out

how the events are connected to each other. The events should be discussed in order of occurrence.

3. **Describing a Theme.** The principal **theme** of a story is the most important idea the writer wants to communicate. The theme usually is about an important subject, such as love, childhood, family relations, or death. The theme generally is not stated directly. Rather, you must think about the events of the story and look closely at key passages. Then you make an **inference,** or educated guess, about what the theme is. Most stories have two or more themes, but one stands out as the principal theme. In a paragraph, describe what you consider to be the principal theme of "Winterblossom Garden." Cite passages from the story to support your inference.

Analyzing Language and Vocabulary

Images of Taste and Smell

Imagery can make the experience of reading a story more vivid. "Winterblossom Garden," which deals in part with people who operate a restaurant, contains several images appealing to our senses of taste and smell. Here are two passages from the story containing such images. See if you can find five others.

1. "As the workers chatter in Cantonese, I smell the food cooking: spare ribs, chicken lo mein, sweet and pungent pork, won ton soup."
2. "If I said 'Hello' or 'Thank you' in Chinese, I was allowed to choose whatever dish I liked; often I ordered a hot turkey sandwich. I liked the taste of burnt rice soaked in tea."

Reading About the Writer

David Low is a contemporary Chinese-American writer, born and raised in Queens, New York, where "Winterblossom Garden" is set. With the encouragement of his professors, Low began to write fiction while he was an undergraduate at Wesleyan University. He has been awarded several fellowships for his writing, and his stories have appeared in literary magazines. About "Winterblossom Garden," Low explains, "I wrote the story because I wanted to read an American short story in which Chinese-American characters were central to the story, not mere stereotypes in the background."

MANHOOD

John Wain

The relationship between parents and children is surely one of the most powerful in the human storehouse. Some parents believe their children are meant to succeed *for* them. But children often have resisted such notions, feeling that their lives are their own, to do with as *they* please. In this story the writer takes us straight to the heart of this conflict. See what you think about the way Rob handles the conflict with his father.

Swiftly freewheeling, their breath coming easily, the man and the boy steered their bicycles down the short dip which led them from woodland into open country. Then they looked ahead and saw that the road began to climb.

"Now, Rob," said Mr. Willison, settling his plump haunches firmly on the saddle, "just up that rise and we'll get off and have a good rest."

"Can't we rest now?" the boy asked. "My legs feel all funny. As if they're turning to water."

"Rest at the top," said Mr. Willison firmly. "Remember what I told you? The first thing any athlete has to learn is to break the fatigue barrier."

"I've broken it already. I was feeling tired when we were going along the main road, and I——"

"When fatigue sets in, the thing to do is to keep going until it wears off. Then you get your second wind and your second endurance."

"I've already done that."

"Up we go," said Mr. Willison, "and at the top we'll have a good rest." He panted slightly and stood on his pedals, causing his machine to sway from side to side in a labored manner. Rob, falling silent, pushed doggedly at his pedals. Slowly, the

pair wavered up the straight road to the top. Once there, Mr. Willison dismounted with exaggerated steadiness, laid his bicycle carefully on its side, and spread his jacket on the ground before sinking down to rest. Rob slid hastily from the saddle and flung himself full-length on the grass.

"Don't lie there," said his father. "You'll catch cold."

"I'm all right. I'm warm."

"Come and sit on this. When you're overheated, that's just when you're prone to——"

"I'm all *right,* Dad. I want to lie here. My back aches."

"Your back needs strengthening; that's why it aches. It's a pity we don't live near a river where you could get some rowing."

The boy did not answer, and Mr. Willison, aware that he was beginning to sound like a nagging, overanxious parent, allowed himself to be defeated and did not press the suggestion about Rob's coming to sit on his jacket. Instead, he waited a moment and then glanced at his watch.

"Twenty to twelve. We must get going in a minute."

"*What*? I thought we were going to have a rest."

"Well, we're having one, aren't we?" said Mr. Willison reasonably. "I've got my breath back, so surely you must have."

"My back still aches. I want to lie here a bit."

"Sorry," said Mr. Willison, getting up and moving over to his bicycle. "We've got at least twelve miles to do, and lunch is at one."

"Dad, why did we have to come so far if we've

Kids on Bikes by David Park (1950). Oil.   The Regis Collection, Minneapolis, Minnesota.

got to get back for one o'clock? I know, let's find a telephone box and ring up Mum and tell her we——''

''Nothing doing. There's no reason why two fit men shouldn't cycle twelve miles in an hour and ten minutes.''

''But we've already done about a million miles.''

''We've done about fourteen, by my estimation,'' said Mr. Willison stiffly. ''What's the good of going for a bike ride if you don't cover a bit of distance?''

He picked up his bicycle and stood waiting. Rob, with his hand over his eyes, lay motionless on the grass. His legs looked thin and white among the rich grass.

''Come on, Rob.''

The boy showed no sign of having heard. Mr. Willison got on to his bicycle and began to ride slowly away. ''Rob,'' he called over his shoulder, ''I'm going.''

Rob lay like a sullen corpse by the roadside. He looked horribly like the victim of an accident, unmarked but dead from internal injuries. Mr. Willison cycled fifty yards, then a hundred, then turned in a short, irritable circle and came back to where his son lay.

''Rob, is there something the matter, or are you just being awkward?''

The boy removed his hand and looked up into his father's face. His eyes were surprisingly mild: There was no fire of rebellion in them.

''I'm tired and my back aches. I can't go on yet.''

''Look, Rob,'' said Mr. Willison gently, ''I wasn't going to tell you this, because I meant it to be a surprise, but when you get home you'll find a present waiting for you.''

''What kind of present?''

''Something very special I've bought for you. The man's coming this morning to fix it up. That's one reason why I suggested a bike ride this morning. He'll have done it by now.''

''What is it?''

''Aha. It's a surprise. Come on, get on your bike and let's go home and see.''

Rob sat up, then slowly clambered to his feet. ''Isn't there a shortcut home?''

''I'm afraid not. It's only twelve miles.''
Rob said nothing.

''And a lot of that's downhill,'' Mr. Willison added brightly. His own legs were tired, and his muscles fluttered unpleasantly. In addition, he suddenly realized he was very thirsty. Rob, still without speaking, picked up his bicycle, and they pedaled away.

''Where is he?'' Mrs. Willison asked, coming into the garage.

''Gone up to his room,'' said Mr. Willison. He doubled his fist and gave the punch ball a thudding blow. ''Seems to have fixed it pretty firmly. You gave him the instructions, I suppose.''

''What's he doing up in his room? It's lunchtime.''

''He said he wanted to rest a bit.''

''I hope you're satisfied,'' said Mrs. Willison. ''A lad of thirteen, nearly fourteen years of age, just when he should have a really big appetite, and when the lunch is put on the table he's *resting*——''

''Now, look, I know what I'm——''

''Lying down in his room, resting, too tired to eat because you've dragged him up hill and down dale on one of your——''

''We did nothing that couldn't be reasonably expected of a boy of his age.''

''How do you know?'' Mrs. Willison demanded. ''You never did anything of that kind when you were a boy. How do you know what can be reasonably——''

''Now, look,'' said Mr. Willison again. ''When I was a boy, it was study, study, study all the time, with the fear of unemployment and insecurity in everybody's mind. I was never even given a bicycle. I never boxed, I never rowed, I never did anything to develop my physique. It was just work, work, work, pass this exam, get that certificate. Well, I did it and now I'm qualified and in a secure job. But you know as well as I do that they let me down. Nobody encouraged me to build myself up.''

''Well, what does it matter? You're all right——''

''Grace!'' Mr. Willison interrupted sharply. ''I am not all right and you know it. I am under average height, my chest is flat, and I'm——''

"What nonsense. You're taller than I am, and I'm——"

"No son of mine is going to grow up with the same wretched physical heritage that I——"

"No, he'll just have heart disease through overtaxing his strength, because you haven't got the common sense to——"

"His heart is one hundred percent all right. Not three weeks have gone by since the doctor looked at him."

"Well, why does he get so overtired if he's all right? Why is he lying down now instead of coming to the table, a boy of his age?"

A slender shadow blocked part of the dazzling sun in the doorway. Looking up simultaneously, the Willisons greeted their son.

"Lunch ready, Mum? I'm hungry."

"Ready when you are," Grace Willison beamed. "Just wash your hands and come to the table."

"Look, Rob," said Mr. Willison. "If you hit it with your left hand and then catch it on the rebound with your right, it's excellent ring training." He dealt the punch ball two amateurish blows. "That's what they call a right cross," he said.

"I think it's fine. I'll have some fun with it," said Rob. He watched mildly as his father peeled off the padded mittens.

"Here, slip these on," said Mr. Willison. "They're just training gloves. They harden your fists. Of course, we can get a pair of proper gloves later. But these are specially for use with the ball."

"Lunch," called Mrs. Willison from the house.

"Take a punch at it," Mr. Willison urged.

"Let's go and eat."

"Go on. One punch before you get in. I haven't seen you hit it yet."

Rob took the gloves, put on the right-hand one, and gave the punch ball one conscientious[1] blow, aiming at the exact center. "Now let's go in," he said.

"Lunch!"

"All right. We're coming. . . ."

"Five-feet-eight, Rob," said Mr. Willison, folding

up the wooden ruler. "You're taller than I am. This is a great landmark."

"Only *just* taller."

"But you're growing all the time. Now all you have to do is to start growing outward as well as upward. We'll have you in the middle of that scrum. The heaviest forward in the pack."

Rob picked up his shirt and began uncertainly poking his arms into the sleeves.

"When do they pick the team?" Mr. Willison asked. "I should have thought they'd have done it by now."

"They have done it," said Rob. He bent down to pick up his socks from under a chair.

"They have? And you——"

"I wasn't selected," said the boy, looking intently at the socks as if trying to detect minute differences in color and weave.

Mr. Willison opened his mouth, closed it again, and stood for a moment looking out of the window. Then he gently laid his hand on his son's shoulder. "Bad luck," he said quietly.

"I tried hard," said Rob quickly.

"I'm sure you did."

"I played my hardest in the trial games."

"It's just bad luck," said Mr. Willison. "It could happen to anybody."

There was silence as they both continued with their dressing. A faint smell of frying rose into the air, and they could hear Mrs. Willison laying the table for breakfast.

"That's it, then, for this season," said Mr. Willison, as if to himself.

"I forgot to tell you, though," said Rob. "I was selected for the boxing team."

"You *were*? I didn't know the school had one."

"It's new. Just formed. They had some trials for it at the end of last term. I found my punching was better than most people's because I'd been getting plenty of practice with the ball."

Mr. Willison put out a hand and felt Rob's biceps. "Not bad, not bad at all," he said critically. "But if you're going to be a boxer and represent the school, you'll need more power up there. I tell you what. We'll train together."

"That'll be fun," said Rob. "I'm training at school too."

"What weight do they put you in?"

---

1. **conscientious** (kän·′shē·en′shəs): careful and precise.

"It isn't weight, it's age. Under fifteen. Then, when you get over fifteen, you get classified into weights."

"Well," said Mr. Willison, tying his tie, "you'll be in a good position for the under-fifteens. You've got six months to play with. And there's no reason why you shouldn't steadily put muscle on all the time. I suppose you'll be entered as a team, for tournaments and things?"

"Yes. There's a big one at the end of next term. I'll be in that."

Confident, joking, they went down to breakfast. "Two eggs for Rob, Mum," said Mr. Willison. "He's in training. He's going to be a heavyweight."

"A heavyweight what?" Mrs. Willison asked, teapot in hand.

"Boxer," Rob smiled.

Grace Willison put down the teapot, her lips compressed, and looked from one to the other. "*Boxing?*" she repeated.

"Boxing," Mr. Willison replied calmly.

"Over my dead body," said Mrs. Willison. "That's one sport I'm definite that he's never going in for."

"Too late. They've picked him for the under-fifteens. He's had trials and everything."

"Is this true, Rob?" she demanded.

"Yes," said the boy, eating rapidly.

"Well, you can just tell them you're dropping it. Baroness Summerskill——"

"Blast Baroness Summerskill!" her husband shouted. "The first time he gets a chance to do something, the first time he gets picked for a team and given a chance to show what he's made of, and you have to bring up Baroness Summerskill."

"But it injures their brains! All those blows on the front of the skull. I've read about it——"

"Injures their brains!" Mr. Willison snorted. "Has it injured Ingemar Johansson's[2] brain? Why, he's one of the acutest businessmen in the world!"

"Rob," said Mrs. Willison steadily, "when you get to school, go and see the sports master and tell him you're giving up boxing."

"There isn't a sports master. All the masters do bits of it at different times."

"There must be one who's in charge of boxing. All you have to do is tell him——"

"Are you ready, Rob?" said Mr. Willison. "You'll be late for school if you don't go."

"I'm in plenty of time, Dad. I haven't finished my breakfast."

"Never mind, push along, old son. You've had your egg and bacon; that's what matters. I want to talk to your mother."

Cramming a piece of dry toast into his mouth, the boy picked up his satchel and wandered from the room. Husband and wife sat back, glaring hot-eyed at each other.

The quarrel began, and continued for many days. In the end it was decided that Rob should continue boxing until he had represented the school at the tournament in March of the following year and should then give it up.

"Ninety-six, ninety-seven, ninety-eight, ninety-nine, a hundred," Mr. Willison counted. "Right, that's it. Now, go and take your shower and get into bed."

"I don't feel tired, honestly," Rob protested.

"Who's manager here, you or me?" Mr. Willison asked bluffly. "I'm in charge of training, and you can't say my methods don't work. Fifteen solid weeks, and you start questioning my decisions on the very night of the fight?"

"It just seems silly to go to bed when I'm not——"

"My dear Rob, please trust me. No boxer ever went into a big fight without spending an hour or two in bed, resting, just before going to his dressing room."

"All right. But I bet none of the others are bothering to do all this."

"That's exactly why you're going to be better than the others. Now, go and get your shower before you catch cold. Leave the skipping rope; I'll put it away."

After Rob had gone, Mr. Willison folded the skipping rope into a neat ball and packed it away in the case that contained the boy's gloves, silk dressing gown, lace-up boxing boots, and trunks with the school badge sewn into the correct position on the right leg. There would be no harm in a little skipping, to limber up and conquer his

2. **Ingemar Johansson:** Swedish boxer.

nervousness while waiting to go on. Humming, he snapped down the catches of the small leather case and went into the house.

Mrs. Willison did not lift her eyes from the television set as he entered. "All ready now, Mother," said Mr. Willison. "He's going to rest in bed now and go along at about six o'clock. I'll go with him and wait till the doors open, to be sure of a ringside seat." He sat down on the sofa beside his wife and tried to put his arm around her. "Come on, love," he said coaxingly. "Don't spoil my big night."

She turned to him, and he was startled to see her eyes brimming with angry tears. "What about my big night?" she asked, her voice harsh. "Fourteen years ago, remember? When he came into the world."

"Well, what about it?" Mr. Willison parried,[3] uneasily aware that the television set was quacking and signaling on the fringe of his attention, turning the scene from clumsy tragedy into a clumsier farce.

"Why didn't you tell me then?" she sobbed. "Why did you let me have a son if all you were interested in was having him punched to death by a lot of rough bullet-headed louts who——"

"Take a grip on yourself, Grace. A punch on the nose won't hurt him."

"You're an unnatural father," she keened. "I don't know how you can bear to send him into the ring to be beaten and thumped. Oh, why can't you stop him now? Keep him at home? There's no *law* that compels us to——"

"That's where you're wrong, Grace," said Mr. Willison sternly. "There is a law. The unalterable law of nature that says that the young males of the species indulge in manly trials of strength. Think of all the other lads who are going into the ring tonight. D'you think their mothers are sitting about crying and kicking up a fuss? No—they're proud to have strong, masculine sons who can stand up in the ring and take a few punches."

"Go away, please," said Mrs. Willison, sinking back with closed eyes. "Just go right away and don't come near me until it's all over."

"Grace!"

"Please. Please leave me alone. I can't bear to look at you, and I can't bear to hear you."

"You're hysterical," said Mr. Willison bitterly. Rising, he went out into the hall and called up the stairs. "Are you in bed, Rob?"

There was a slight pause, and then Rob's voice called faintly, "Could you come up, Dad?"

"Come up? Why? Is something the matter?"

"Could you come up?"

Mr. Willison ran up the stairs. "What is it?" he panted. "D'you want something?"

"I think I've got appendicitis," said Rob. He lay squinting among the pillows, his face suddenly narrow and crafty.

"I don't believe you," said Mr. Willison shortly. "I've supervised your training for fifteen weeks, and I know you're as fit as a fiddle. You can't possibly have anything wrong with you."

"I've got a terrible pain in my side," said Rob. "Low down on the right-hand side. That's where appendicitis comes, isn't it?"

Mr. Willison sat down on the bed. "Listen, Rob," he said. "Don't do this to me. All I'm asking you to do is to go into the ring and have one bout. You've been picked for the school team, and everyone's depending on you."

"I'll die if you don't get the doctor," Rob suddenly hissed. "Mum!" he shouted.

Mrs. Willison came bounding up the stairs. "What is it, my pet?"

"My stomach hurts. Low down on the right-hand side."

"Appendicitis!" She whirled to face Mr. Willison. "That's what comes of your foolishness!"

"I don't believe it," said Mr. Willison. He went out of the bedroom and down the stairs. The television was still jabbering in the living room, and for fifteen minutes Mr. Willison forced himself to sit staring at the strident puppets, glistening in metallic light, as they enacted their Lilliputian[4] rituals. Then he went up to the bedroom again. Mrs. Willison was bathing Rob's forehead.

"His temperature is normal," she said.

"Of course his temperature's normal," said Mr.

---

3. **parried:** replied, trying to turn aside the question.

4. **Lilliputian** (lil′ə·pyo͞o′shən): very small, like the people of Lilliput in Jonathan Swift's famous novel *Gulliver's Travels*.

Nicholas by Andrew Wyeth (1955). Oil.

Courtesy of Nicholas Wyeth.

Willison. "He doesn't want to fight, that's all."

"Fetch the doctor," said a voice from under the cold flannel that swathed Rob's face.

"We will, pet, if you don't get better very soon," said Mrs. Willison, darting a murderous glance at her husband.

Mr. Willison slowly went downstairs. For a moment he stood looking at the telephone, then picked it up and dialed the number of the grammar school. No one answered. He replaced the receiver, went to the foot of the stairs, and called, "What's the name of the master in charge of this tournament?"

"I don't know," Rob called weakly.

"You told me you'd been training with Mr. Granger," Mr. Willison called. "Would he know anything about it?"

Rob did not answer, so Mr. Willison looked up all the Grangers in the telephone book. There were four in the town, but only one was M.A.[5] "That's him," said Mr. Willison. With lead in his heart and ice in his fingers, he dialed the number.

Mrs. Granger fetched Mr. Granger. Yes, he taught at the school. He was the right man. What could he do for Mr. Willison?

"It's about tonight's boxing tournament."

---

5. **M.A.:** abbreviation for Master of Arts, a university degree.

"Sorry, what? The line's bad."

"Tonight's boxing tournament."

"Have you got the right person?"

"You teach my son, Rob——we've just agreed on that. Well, it's about the boxing tournament he's supposed to be taking part in tonight."

"Where?"

"Where? At the school, of course. He's representing the under-fifteens."

There was a pause. "I'm not quite sure what mistake you're making, Mr. Willison, but I think you've got hold of the wrong end of at least one stick." A hearty, defensive laugh. "If Rob belongs to a boxing club, it's certainly news to me, but in any case, it can't be anything to do with the school. We don't go in for boxing."

"Don't go in for it?"

"We don't offer it. It's not in our curriculum."

"Oh," said Mr. Willison. "Oh. Thank you. I must have . . . Well, thank you."

"Not at all. I'm glad to answer any queries. Everything's all right, I trust?"

"Oh, yes," said Mr. Willison, "yes, thanks. Everything's all right."

He put down the telephone, hesitated, then turned, and began slowly to climb the stairs.

Responding to the Story

Analyzing the Story

Identifying Facts

1. The story opens with a bicycle ride that introduces two of the main characters—Mr. Willison and his son Rob. How does Rob feel about the ride? How does his father feel about it?
2. What news does Rob tell his father to make up for not being picked for the rugby team? How does Mr. Willison react to the news?
3. How does Rob's mother feel about his new sport?
4. At the end of the story, what do we learn about Rob and his new sport?

Interpreting Meanings

5. The main **conflict** in "Manhood" is between Rob and his father. Discuss how this conflict is shown to us in the opening scene.
6. A story's **climax** is the moment of our most intense involvement in it. The plot reaches a high point, and the story's outcome is decided. The climax usually occurs late in the story. Where would you place the climax of "Manhood"? What is decided at the climax?
7. When Mr. Willison tells about his childhood, he reveals his **motives,** or reasons, for pushing Rob to succeed in athletics. How would you describe his motives? Do you approve of them?

8. Why does Rob lie to his father about his new sport? How do you feel about what Rob did?

Applying Meanings

9. Mr. Willison places much emphasis on the desirability of having a strong body. Do you think this idea is common today? What do you think of it?
10. Suppose Rob were a friend of yours. How would you suggest he resolve his problems, without having to lie?

Writing About the Story

A Creative Response

1. **Extending the Story.** The story closes as Mr. Willison slowly climbs the stairs in his home. It seems likely that he is heading for Rob's room. In a short composition, describe what you think happens when Mr. Willison meets Rob. Does Mr. Willison scold Rob? Does he apologize for pushing his son to succeed in athletics? Does he say something else? How does Rob react to his father's words? Does Rob say something about having deceived his father? Include some **dialogue,** or conversation, between father and son in your composition.

A Critical Response

2. **Analyzing a Secondary Conflict.** Most stories contain two or more **conflicts.** One usually stands out as the main conflict, and the others are secondary, or less important. A secondary conflict in "Manhood" is between Mr. and Mrs. Willison over whether their son should take up boxing. In the first of two paragraphs, describe the opposing viewpoints in this conflict. In the second paragraph, discuss whether the conflict is resolved by the end of the story.

Analyzing Language and Vocabulary

British English

British English is very similar to American English, but there can be marked differences. For instance, if a Londoner approached you on a street in your community and asked for the location of the nearest chemist or ironmonger, you probably would be con-

fused. The confusion would be cleared up, however, if you knew that in England a chemist is a pharmacist and an ironmonger is a hardware store. The following passages from "Manhood" contain italicized examples of British English. Examine the context to figure out the meaning of each expression. Then write down an expression in American English having the same meaning. If necessary, check a dictionary.

1. " 'I know, let's find a *telephone box* and *ring up* Mum. . . .' "
2. "He doubled his fist and gave the *punch ball* a thudding blow."
3. ". . . they could hear Mrs. Willison *laying* the table for breakfast."
4. " 'There isn't a *sports master*. All the *masters* do bits of it at different times.' "
5. "Cramming a piece of dry toast into his mouth, the boy picked up his *satchel* and wandered from the room."

Reading About the Writer

John Wain (1925–   ) is a distinguished writer of short stories, novels, plays, poetry, and essays. He was born, and still lives, in England and was educated at Oxford. In the 1950's he became known as one of the "Angry Young Men." These members of the younger generation were severely critical of British society, especially of its rigid class system. As you see in "Manhood," Wain can write with great compassion about characters who are victims, or who feel for one reason or another that they are separated from the mainstream of life. "Manhood" is from a collection called *The Death of the Hind Legs and Other Stories.*

THE PASSOVER GUEST

Sholom Aleichem

The Seder by Michael Pressman (1950). Watercolor.

The Jewish Museum, New York City.

"The Passover Guest" takes place in a Jewish community in Eastern Europe about one hundred years ago. Passover is an important Jewish holiday. It falls in March or April, and commemorates the exodus of the ancient Israelites from Egypt. (The story of the flight is told in the Book of Exodus in the Bible.) The weeklong festival begins with a ceremonial meal called the *Seder* (sā′dər). During the Seder, events of the Exodus are remembered. Special foods with symbolic meanings are eaten. For instance, because the Jews had to leave ancient Egypt quickly, they did not have time to let their bread rise. Thus, only unleavened, or unrisen, bread is eaten during Passover.

Sholom Aleichem's story is set in a community that most likely is very different from your own. Yet its description of human behavior will not seem foreign at all. You may even know people similar to the characters in the story. See how long it takes you to figure out what the Passover guest is up to.

> **The Yiddish language.** This story is translated from Yiddish. This language first developed long ago among Jews living in German-speaking areas of Europe. Yiddish is similar in many ways to German. When Jews migrated, they took Yiddish to other areas of Europe as well as to non-European countries like the United States. A notable literature in Yiddish grew over the centuries; Sholom Aleichem and Isaac Bashevis Singer (see page 469) are among the leading writers in the language. Jewish-American fiction writers working in English sometimes include Yiddish words to give readers a better feel for the people and situations in their stories. Yiddish once was spoken by more than eleven million people. Millions of Yiddish-speaking people were killed during the Nazi Holocaust, or Shoah, of the 1930's and 1940's. Nevertheless, several million Jews still speak Yiddish as their first language. The translator of this story left a few words in Yiddish so you'll get a flavor of the language. These words include *shamesh, shul,* and *shalom.*

I

Reb[1] Yonah, I have a guest for you for Passover. I guarantee you've never seen anyone like him."

"What's he like?"

"He's no run-of-the-mill visitor, but a diamond, a peach of a man."

"What do you mean a peach?"

"I mean he's top-notch. All class. A man of distinction. But he's got only one fault. He doesn't understand Yiddish."

"Then what language *does* he understand?"

"The holy tongue, Hebrew."

"Is he from Jerusalem?"

"I don't know where he's from. But he speaks with a Sephardic[2] accent—whatever he says is full of 'aahs.' "

Such was the conversation that my father had with Azriel the *shamesh*[3] a few days before Passover. I was curious to see this peach of a man who spoke no Yiddish but only Hebrew with lots of "aahs." In *shul*[4] I had noticed an odd-looking creature in a fur cap, wearing a Turkish cloak with yellow, blue, and red stripes. All the kids surrounded him and gaped. For this, Azriel the *shamesh* raked us over the coals: It's a terrible habit for kids to go poking into a stranger's face.

After prayers the entire congregation greeted the newcomer with *Sholom*[5] and wished him a happy holiday.

A sweet smile spread over this gray-whiskered red cheeks, and instead of our *Sholom,* he replied, *"Shalom, shalom."*

His *Shalom* caused us youngsters to double over with laughter. Which annoyed Azriel the *shamesh.* He ran after us ready to dole out smacks. But we dodged him and sneaked up to the newcomer again to hear him say, *"Shalom, shalom."* Once more we burst into hysterics and ducked away from Azriel's raised hand.

---

1. **Reb:** title of respect, similar to "mister."
2. Sephardic Jews lived in areas where Yiddish was not spoken among Jews. Therefore, they spoke with a different "accent," or language.
3. *shamesh:* person responsible for running a synagogue.
4. *shul* (shool): synagogue.
5. *Sholom* (shō·lōm′) or **shalom** (shä·lōm′): traditional Yiddish and Hebrew greeting meaning "peace."

Proud as a peacock, I followed my father and the odd-looking character, sensing that all my friends envied me for having a guest of his caliber for the holiday. Their glances followed us from afar, and I turned around and stuck my tongue out at them. All three of us were silent on our way home. When we entered the house, Father called out to Mama, *"Gut yontev!* Happy holiday!"

The guest nodded, and his fur cap shook.

"Shalom, shalom."

I thought of my friends and hid my face under the table, trying hard to keep a straight face. I kept glancing at our guest. I liked him. I liked his Turkish cloak with its stripes of yellow, blue, and red; his apple-red cheeks edged with a round gray beard; his beautiful black eyes that twinkled beneath his bushy gray eyebrows. I sensed that my father liked him, too. Father was delighted by his presence. He himself prepared the cushioned chair for our guest, and Mama considered him a holy man. Yet no one said a word to him. Mama, assisted by Rikl the maid, was in a dither preparing for the Seder. Conversation first began when we were ready to recite the Kiddush over the wine. Then Father spoke to our guest in Hebrew. I brimmed with pride since I understood almost every word. Here is what they said in Hebrew, word for word:

Father: "Nu?" (*Meaning in Yiddish: Please recite the Kiddush!*)

The Guest: "Nu, nu!" (*Translated, this means: You recite it.*)

Father: "Nu-aw?" (*Why not you?*)

Guest: "Aw-nu?" (*And why don't you?*)

Father: "Ee-aw?" (*You first!*)

The Guest: "Aw-ee!" (*First you!*)

Father: "Eh-aw-ee!" (*Please, you say it!*)

The Guest: "Ee-aw-eh!" (*You say it, please!*)

Father: "Ee-eh-aw-nu?" (*Does it really matter to you if you say it first?*)

The Guest: "Eeeh-aw? Nu, nu!" (*Well, if you insist, then I'll say it!*)

The guest took the Kiddush cup from Father's hand and recited a Kiddush the likes of which we had never heard before and will never hear again. First of all, his Sephardic Hebrew pronunciation, full of "aahs." Second, his voice, which came not from his throat but from his striped Turkish cloak.

Thinking of my friends, I imagined the giggles that would have broken out and the blows and smacks that would have flown had they been here for the Kiddush. But since they were not with me, I controlled myself, asked Father the Four Questions, and we all recited the Haggada[6] together. I was proud as could be that this man was our guest and no one else's.

II

May he forgive me for saying this, but the sage who suggested silence during mealtime had no knowledge of Jewish life. When else does a Jew have time to talk, if not during mealtime? And especially at the Passover Seder, when we talk so much about the Exodus from Egypt? Rikl handed us the water for the ritual washing of hands, and we recited the benedictions. After Mama had distributed the fish, Father rolled up his sleeves and got into a lengthy Hebrew conversation with our guest. Naturally, Father began with the first question that one Jew always asks another:

"What's your name?"

The guest's reply was one full of "aahs," rattled off in one breath, as quickly as Haman's sons' names are dashed off during the reading of the Purim Megillah.[7]

"ZYXW VUTS RQPON MLK JIHG FED CBA," he said.

Father stopped chewing and looked with open-mouthed amazement at the guest who bore such a long name. I fell into a fit of coughing and stared down at the floor.

"Careful with the fish," said Mama. "You might choke on a bone, God forbid."

She looked at our guest with awe, obviously impressed by his name, even though she didn't know what it meant. And since Father did know, he explained:

"His name, you see, contains all the letters of

---

6. **Four Questions . . . Haggada** (hə·gä′də): The Four Questions, asked by the youngest person at the Seder, are found in the Haggada, which relates the Passover story.

7. **Purim Megillah** (poor′im mə·gil′ə): The feast of Purim celebrates the defeat of Haman, an official of ancient Persia who wanted to destroy the Jews. The Purim Megillah is the scroll that contains this Biblical story.

the alphabet backward. Evidently it's one of their customs to name their children in some alphabetical fashion.''

"Alphabet! Alphabet!" The guest nodded. A sweet smile played on his apple-red cheeks, and his beautiful black eyes gazed at everyone so amiably, even at Rikl the maid.

Having learned his name, Father was curious about the land he had come from. This I gathered from the names of towns and countries which I heard mentioned. Father then translated for Mama, explaining almost every word. Each word impressed Mama. Rikl, too. And with good cause. It was no small thing for a person to travel ten thousand miles from one's homeland. To reach it one had to cross seven seas, trek forty days and forty nights through a desert, and climb an enormous ice-capped mountain whose peak touched the clouds. But once one safely passed this wind-whipped mountain and entered the land, one saw before him the terrestrial Garden of Eden filled with spices and condiments, apples and pears, oranges and grapes, olives and dates, and nuts and figs. The houses, built only of pinewood, were covered with pure silver. The dishes were of gold (while saying this, our guest glanced at our silver goblets, spoons, forks, and knives), and gems, pearls, and diamonds lay scattered on the streets. No one even bothered to bend and pick them up because they had no value there. (The guest now peered at Mama's diamond earrings and her pearl necklace.)

"Do you hear that?" Father said to Mama, beaming.

"Yes," said Mama and asked, "Why don't they bring all that treasure here? They would make a fortune. Ask him about that, Yonah."

Father asked and translated the reply into Yiddish for Mama's benefit.

"You see, if you travel there, you can take as much as you like. Fill up your pockets. But when you leave, you must return everything. If they shake anything out of your pockets, they execute you."

"What does that mean?" Mama asked, frightened.

"That means they either hang you from the nearest tree or stone you to death."

III

The more our guest spoke, the more interesting his stories became. Once we had eaten the matzo balls and were sipping some wine, Father asked him:

"Who is the master of all that wealth? Is there a king there?"

He immediately got a precise answer, which he joyfully translated for Mama.

"He says that it all belongs to the Jews who live there. They are called Sephardim. They have a king, he says, a very religious Jew with a fur cap named Joseph ben Joseph. He is the Sephardim's high priest and rides about in a golden chariot drawn by six fiery steeds. And when he comes to *shul*, singing Levites[8] come to greet him.

"Do Levites sing in your *shul*?" Father asked him wonderingly. He immediately got an answer, which he translated into Yiddish for Mama.

"Imagine!" he said, his face shining like the sun. "He says that they have a holy temple with priests and Levites and an organ——

"How about an altar?" Father asked, then translated our guest's reply for Mama.

"He says they have an altar, sacrifices, and golden vessels. Everything as it once used to be in ancient Jerusalem."

Father sighed deeply. Mama looked at him and sighed, too. I didn't understand why they sighed. On the contrary, we should be proud and happy that we had a land like this where a Jewish king reigned, where there was a high priest and a holy temple with priests and Levites and an organ and an altar with sacrifices. . . .

Beautiful and bright thoughts snatched me up and carried me away to that happy Jewish land, where all the houses were made of pinewood and covered with silver, where the dishes were of gold, and where gems, pearls, and diamonds were scattered on the streets. Suddenly I had a thought. If I were there, I would have known what to do and how to hide what I had found. They wouldn't have shaken a thing out of my pockets. I would have brought Mama a fine present—diamond earrings

---

8. **Levites** (lē'vīts): descendants of the tribe of Levi, who assisted the priests in the ancient Temple in Jerusalem.

and several strands of pearls. I looked at the diamond earrings and the pearl necklace on Mama's white throat and had a strong desire to be in that land. I had an idea. After Passover I would travel there with our guest. Naturally, in absolute secrecy. No one would know a thing. I would reveal the secret only to our guest, pour out my heart to him, tell him the whole truth, and ask him to take me with him, if only for a little while. He'd surely do that for me. He was an extremely kind and pleasant man. He looked at everyone so amiably, even at Rikl the maid.

So ran my thoughts as I looked at our guest. I fancied that he read my mind, for he looked at me with his beautiful black eyes, and I imagined that he winked and said to me in his own language:

"Not a word, you little rascal. Wait till after Passover, and everything will be all right."

IV

All night long I was beset by dreams. I dreamed of a desert, a holy temple, a high priest, and a lofty mountain. I climbed the mountain. Gems, pearls, and diamonds grew there. My friends clambered up the trees and shook the branches, bringing down an endless supply of precious stones. I stood there, gathered up the jewels and stuffed them into my pockets. And, amazingly enough, no matter how many I stuffed there was always more. I put my hand into my pocket, and instead of gems, I took out all kinds of fruit—apples, pears, and oranges, olives and dates, nuts and figs. . . . This terrified me, and I tossed from side to side. I dreamed of the holy temple. I heard the priests chanting their blessing, the Levites singing, and the organ playing. I wanted to go into the holy temple but could not. Rikl the maid held my hand fast and didn't let me go. I begged her; I yelled; I wept. I was scared to death and tossed from side to side.

Then I awoke——

Before me were my parents, half-dressed, both as pale as death. Father's head was bowed. Mother wrung her hands, and tears brimmed in her beautiful eyes. My heart sensed that something awful had happened, something terribly dreadful, but yet I was unable to comprehend the extent of the disaster.

Our guest, the stranger from that faraway land, from that blissful land where houses were made of pinewood, covered with pure silver, and so on—that guest had vanished. And along with him a host of other things as well. All our silver goblets, all our silverware, all of Mama's meager jewelry, as well as all the cash in our drawers. And Rikl the maid had taken off with him, too.

I was heartbroken, but not because of the stolen silver, or Mama's jewelry, or the cash, or Rikl the maid—the devil take her. I was heartbroken over that blissful land where precious stones lay scattered about, and over the holy temple with the priests and Levites, the organ, altar, and sacrifices, and over the other good things that had been taken from me—brutally, brutally stolen.

And I turned to the wall and wept softly to myself.

—translated by Curt Leviant

Responding to the Story

Analyzing the Story

Identifying Facts

1. In what ways is the Passover guest different from the people the narrator knows? How do the children react to the man?
2. How does the guest describe his distant homeland? Who does he say rules there?
3. How does the narrator feel about the land described by the guest? What is his secret plan?
4. What does the family discover the morning after the Seder? What upsets the narrator most about what has happened?

Celebration of Passover (14th century). Illumination from The Rylands Haggadah, Spain.

Interpreting Meanings

5. You might call the Passover guest a swindler who tries to gain the confidence of intended victims in order to steal from them. Describe two or three ways the guest wins the confidence of the narrator's family.

6. Do you think the guest worked alone, or did he have helpers? If he had helpers, who were they? How can you tell they might have worked together?

7. How would you describe the writer's attitude, or **tone,** toward the characters in the story? Did the writer's tone make the story more enjoyable?

8. What do you think is the meaning of the narrator's dreams the night after the Seder? How are the dreams related to the rest of the story?

9. Did you figure out what the Passover guest was up to before the end of the story? If so, what led you to this insight?

10. Do you think the Passover guest gave the family something, even though he also robbed them? Explain.

Applying Meanings

11. Do you think the story offers a realistic portrayal of the way people behave? Give specific reasons to support your viewpoint.

12. Dreams are often related to daily occurrences. Sometimes people or events you have encountered during the day will show up in a dream. Recount a dream you have had and explain how it relates to events or people in your life.

Writing About the Story

A Creative Response

1. **Inventing a Utopia.** Sir Thomas More (1478–1535), an English statesman, wrote a book called *Utopia* (yoo·tō′pē·ə). Published in 1516, the book described an ideal world in which such evils as poverty and misery do not exist. More made up the word *utopia* from two Greek roots that together mean "not a place." The word has come to stand for any such imaginary perfect

world. Thus, the Passover guest in the story describes a utopia when he talks about the land he supposedly comes from. It can be fun as well as instructive to invent a utopia. Use your imagination to describe the main features of a utopia of your own invention. Write two paragraphs.

2. **Making Up a Dialogue.** A **dialogue** is a conversation between two or more persons. On page 208 of "The Passover Guest" is a unique dialogue. In it, the father and the guest do not speak in words. Rather, they utter interjections—sounds that aren't words but nevertheless carry meaning. For instance, when the father says "Nu?" the guest understands this to mean "Please recite the Kiddush." Most of us frequently use interjections instead of speaking complete sentences. For example, a person might say "Ugh!" rather than "I don't want to eat this burnt toast!" Make up a short dialogue between two persons in which most of the utterances are in the form of interjections. As in the story, give the meaning of each interjection in parentheses.

When the dialogue is completed, get together with a classmate and read it out loud before the class. Each of you should speak the lines of one of the persons in the dialogue. Don't read anything outside quotation marks. You'll have to use your tone of voice to help communicate meanings. After you finish reading aloud, see if the class picked up the meanings you intended.

A Critical Response

3. **Describing a Theme.** A **theme** is the main idea a writer wants to communicate. It usually deals with an important subject such as love, trust, childhood, or proper behavior. A theme usually is not stated directly. Rather, you must think about various elements of the work and then make an **inference,** or educated guess, about the theme. It helps to be clear about the subject before stating the theme. A work of literature often has two or more themes, but one stands out as the main theme. In a paragraph, discuss what you consider to be the main theme of "The Passover Guest." The first sentence or two of your paragraph should state the theme. The rest of the paragraph should cite evidence in the story that supports your interpretation.

Analyzing Language and Vocabulary
Words from Other Languages

1. The following sentences contain Yiddish words (printed in italics) that have become part of American English. Do you know the meaning of these words? Check a dictionary if necessary.

   a. Ralph devoured the *bagel,* which had cream cheese and *lox* on it.
   b. Claudia *kibitzed* as the two women played chess.
   c. It took a lot of *chutzpah* for Diana to call herself the smartest kid in school.
   d. Because Clark Kent was sort of a *nebbish,* no one thought he had any connection with Superman.

2. In the story you have learned that *Reb* is a Yiddish word equivalent to the English word *mister.* In column **a** below are the words for mister in some other languages. Can you match each with the correct language in column **b**?

a	b
Monsieur	Italian
Herr	French
Señor	German
Signor	Spanish

Reading About the Writer

"Sholom Aleichem," the pen name of **Solomon Rabinowitz** (1859–1916), is a traditional Hebrew greeting meaning "Peace be with you." Rabinowitz was born in Pereyaslev, Russia, a town in the Ukraine. As a young man, he taught and wrote short stories for Yiddish publications until he fled Russia. Upon arriving in New York in 1906, Rabinowitz began to write for Yiddish journals and theaters. He became widely known for his warm, humorous stories of Jewish life in Russia. Often called "the Jewish Mark Twain," Rabinowitz's most famous tales center around a dairyman named Tevye. These stories were later adapted into the successful Broadway musical *Fiddler on the Roof.* Rabinowitz's short story collections include *Adventures of Mottel* and *The Great Fair.* "The Passover Guest" is from *Some Laughter, Some Tears.*

THE SHORT STORY

Certain elements are fundamental to almost every short story—**plot, character, point of view, setting,** and **theme.** Even stories that are very short can contain these elements, although they may be in very simple form. The following story is by Sandra Cisneros, who also wrote "Three Wise Guys" (see page 160). Read this short story at least once, and see if you can detect the five basic elements it is built on.

Gil's Furniture Bought & Sold

There is a junk store. An old man owns it. We bought a used refrigerator from him once and Carlos sold a box of magazines for a dollar. The store is small with just a dirty window for light. He doesn't turn the lights on unless you got money to buy things with, so in the dark we look and see all kinds of things, me and Nenny. Tables with their feet upside-down and rows and rows of refrigerators with round corners and couches that spin dust in the air when you punch them and a hundred TV's that don't work probably. Everything is on top of everything so the whole store has skinny aisles to walk through. You can get lost easy.

The owner, he is a black man who doesn't talk much and sometimes if you didn't know better you could be in there a long time before your eyes notice him . . . .

Nenny who thinks she is smarter and talks to any old man ask lots of questions. Me, I never said nothing to him except once when I bought the Statue of Liberty for a dime.

But Nenny, I hear her asking one time how's this here and the man says "This, this is a music box" and I turn around quick thinking he means a *pretty* box with flowers painted on it, with a ballerina inside. Only there's nothing like that where this old man is pointing, just a wood box that's old and got a big brass record in it with holes. Then he starts it up and all sorts of things start happening. It's like all of a sudden he let go a million moths all over the dusty furniture and swanneck shadows and in our bones. It's like drops of water. Or like marimbas only with a funny little plucked sound to it like if you were running your fingers across the teeth of a metal comb.

And then I don't know why, but I have to turn around and pretend I don't care about the box so Nenny won't see how stupid I am. But Nenny, who is stupider, already is asking how much and I can see her fingers going for the quarters in her pants pocket.

"This," the old man says shutting the lid, "This ain't for sale."

—Sandra Cisneros

1. In a brief paragraph, summarize the **plot** of the story.
2. Who is the story's **main character**?
3. In a couple of sentences for each, describe what you have learned about each of the characters, and how you learned it.
4. Whose **point of view** is this story told from? Explain how you know this by quoting at least two passages from the story.
5. Where and when would you say this story takes place? For instance, do you think it is set in the United States? Do you think it is a relatively modern story? Explain which details tell you about the story's **setting**.
6. A **theme** is something important that the writer is trying to communicate to the reader. Usually themes are not stated directly. You must think about what happens in the story and then make a generalization about what the writer's message might be. A story may have more than one theme. Explain what you think the theme(s) of this short short-story might be. Which is the main theme?

Writing

1. **Creating a Character.** Choose a person you know, or make up a character. Then write about an episode which will reveal the personality of that character. You might want to put your character in one of the following places or situations:

   a. Shopping in a store
   b. Attending a party
   c. Eating a meal
   d. Studying in school
   e. Playing a game
   f. Facing a beggar

2. **Describing a Setting.** Choose a place you know fairly well—it could be indoors or outdoors, a large place or a small one. Make a list of details that describe this place. Then write a short paragraph in which you describe this place, using as many of the details from your list as possible. Tell how the place looks, sounds, and smells.

EVALUATING A SHORT STORY

Writing Assignment

Choose the story in this unit that you think is the best story. Then write a brief essay in which you give reasons to support your evaluation.

Background

When you write an essay of response, you write about how a story (or poem, etc.) makes you feel. You tell what it makes you think about and whether or not you like it. You might also tell if the story reminds you of anything in your own experience. This kind of response is **subjective**—it is based on your own feelings and thoughts. (*Subjective* means "personal.")

An essay of evaluation, on the other hand, is **objective**—it is based on certain standards that everyone agrees on. (*Objective* means "impersonal.")

In this essay, you will write an essay of evaluation. It must be based on those standards that people agree make a good short story.

Prewriting

As a first step, use the following checklist to evaluate the story you have chosen. Take notes on specific aspects of the story as you answer each question.

1. Is the **plot** believable, or does it rely too much on chance or on events that don't really belong with the rest of the story?
2. Does the story's ending resolve the main conflict in a satisfying way?
3. Are the **characters** believable? Are their motivations clear?
4. Do the main characters change or develop over the course of the story?
5. Does the story have a **theme** (an insight about life), or does it only entertain?

6. Is the **point of view** consistent? Does it help the reader understand the characters and events in a special way?
7. Does the **setting** seem believable. Does it add anything to the story?
8. Is the **writer's style** interesting to read? Is the language original and the imagery fresh?
9. Does the **dialogue** sound natural?

Next, decide on your overall evaluation of the story. Is it great, average, weak—or something in between? Remember that your evaluation should be based on objective standards and not on your subjective response to the story. Write a **thesis statement** that expresses your overall evaluation of the story. The following thesis statements are about a story in another unit of this book.

"The Tell-Tale Heart" by Edgar Allan Poe is one of the best short stories ever written.

or

"The Tell-Tale Heart" by Edgar Allen Poe is possibly the strangest story I have ever read.

From your prewriting notes, choose three reasons to support your evaluation of the story. Look for evidence in the story, such as incidents, examples, and quotations, to back up each reason.

Writing

Follow this plan for your essay:

Paragraph 1: Introductory paragraph cites the story's title and writer, and includes a thesis statement with your overall evaluation of the story.
Paragraphs 2–4: Each of these paragraphs discusses one of the reasons for your evaluation and cites details from the story to support that reason.
Paragraph 5: Summary of main points.

The following paragraph tells how point of view helps make "The Tell-Tale Heart" a great short story.

One of the elements that makes "The Tell-Tale Heart" by Edgar Allan Poe such a great story is its point of view. Poe uses the first-person point of view to focus all our attention on the narrator. We know only what this narrator tells us. At first we are not sure what to make of the narrator. Then he tells us that he has decided to murder an old man because of his "vulture eye." We now realize we are in the presence of a madman. The horror gets worse as the narrator tells us the gory details of his crime. The point of view is so clever that we even begin to feel the narrator's nervousness in the way he talks. We can almost hear him screaming. If the story had been told by anyone else it would not be so chilling.

Topic sentence.

Cites details from story.

Mentions the effect of point of view.

Sums up main point.

Checklist for Revision and Proofreading
Self-Check

1. Does the introductory paragraph mention the title and writer and include a thesis statement that gives an overall evaluation of the story?

2. Does each of the next three paragraphs give a reason to support the evaluation? Is each reason backed up by evidence (quotations, examples, incidents) from the story?

3. Does the concluding paragraph summarize the essay's main points (the evaluation and the three reasons)?

4. Does every sentence start with a capital letter and end with a period or other end punctuation mark? Are words spelled correctly?

Partner Check

1. Are there any spelling errors?
2. Are sentences punctuated correctly?
3. Are the ideas clearly expressed?
4. Is the evaluation supported with three reasons? Is each reason backed up by evidence from the story?
5. What do I like best about this paper?
6. What needs improvement?

THE ELEMENTS OF DRAMA

Untitled by Roxie Munro (1987). Watercolor.

UNIT FIVE   **Robert Anderson**

Unit Outline
THE ELEMENTS OF DRAMA

I can remember being dazed with writing, with the discovery of finding I actually had these worlds inside me. These voices. Shapes. Currents of language. Light. All the mysterious elements that cause anyone to make a journey.

—Sam Shepard

In one of Shakespeare's plays, a character instructs a group of actors not to overact. He tells them instead to "hold the mirror up to nature," meaning "Imitate real life," or "Be natural."

All people need a "mirror" in which they can see, explore, and know themselves better. In Shakespeare's day, when the literacy rate was low, the theater was the only available "mirror" for most people. Now, novels, movies, television, newspapers, and magazines bombard us with images of ourselves. But the theater remains special, because there we share our experiences with people—with the players and with the other members of the audience.

The Theater and Our Emotions

When we go to the theater, we are engaged emotionally with the action on stage. Sometimes people respond to a play as if it were real life. For example, at the end of Clifford Odets's play *Waiting for Lefty* (about trade unions), the audience jumped up and yelled "Strike! Strike! Strike!" One time in Ireland, people rioted and tore up the seats when they felt that a play was insulting them.

The Writing Process

How does the playwright achieve this kind of intense response from an audience? Some years ago, when the movie of the play *I Never Sang for My Father* was being shot in New York City, a driver would pick up the playwright and the two stars, Melvyn Douglas and Gene Hackman, and take them all to the studio. He would also take them home at night. One night, after he had dropped off the stars, the driver said to the playwright, "I know what *they* do. What do *you* do?" The playwright told him he had written the play and the screenplay. The driver said, "Imagine knowing all those words!"

"Knowing all the words" is only one part of playwriting. When a playwright was once asked how he was doing on his play, he replied that he was almost finished. "Tomorrow," he said, "I'm going to start writing the dialogue."

Dialogue, the speeches assigned to the characters in a play, is important, but everything that comes before writing the dialogue is also important. First must come feeling and passion. A writer must feel a great urgency to tell a story.

Tennessee Williams, the great American playwright, once said

The Elements of Drama

Family Night Out by Norman Rockwell (1916).

he wrote about what "bugged" him. Strangely enough, when you write about what "bugs" you, unless it is too personal, you often hit on something that "bugs" other people, too.

But a strong personal feeling is not in itself enough. The emotion or problem you are writing about may make *you* cry. But the object of the play is to make the *audience* cry, or laugh, or be excited. And that is where the skill and craft of writing come in. Ernest Hemingway said that in a writer's first draft, the writer gets everything and the reader gets nothing. In the next draft, the writer gets a little and the reader gets a little. In the final draft, the writer gets nothing, and the reader gets everything. In other words, the reader now, through the writer's skill, feels the same emotion the writer felt when the writing started.

The Structure of a Play

A distinction is sometimes made between the plot and the story of a play. The **plot** is made up of a series of connected events. It is the play's basic framework. The **story,** on the other hand, consists of the changing relationships among the characters. An absorbing play usually will have both an exciting plot and an interesting story.

A play deals with a **crisis,** with people placed in a crucial situation. Nowadays a producer may ask a writer, "What is the jeopardy in the story? Who is in jeopardy?" That is, who stands to lose what? Essentially, a play deals with a character who wants something important but who is opposed by some person or force. When this

Set design by Boris Aronson for *The Diary of Anne Frank*.

All photographs illustrating the play are from the original 1955 Broadway production, which starred Joseph Schildkraut and Susan Strasberg.

person takes steps to achieve the goal, he or she must engage in a **conflict,** or a struggle of some kind. Near the end of a play is the **climax**—an emotional or tense moment when we learn how the conflict will end. At the end of the play is the **resolution.** Here, loose ends are tied up and the story is closed.

You can easily recognize these principles in television plays and in the movies. For example, the detective wants to find the murderer. His obstacle is that the murderer does *not* want to be found. Somehow the murderer manages to threaten the detective and place the detective's life in jeopardy. The climax occurs when the detective meets the murderer at last in a blind alley and arrests him. The resolution tells us what happens to the main characters. Or, a lawyer down on her luck gets a last chance to prove her worth in defending an unlikely client. Her partner tells her that if she loses this case, she's through. The climax occurs at the trial when the lawyer successfully cross-examines a shaky but key witness. The resolution shows the lawyer being congratulated by her partner. Or, in the most universal story of all time, a boy wants to win a girl's love (or the other way around). He meets with opposition from her parents, but he urges the girl to see him anyway. Conflicts erupt, and the climax occurs when the young couple talk to the parents. Depending on what kind of play we're watching, the resolution is happy or tragic.

Characters and Change

Most plays are about characters who **change** as a result of their conflicts.

In the play you are about to read, a group of characters is placed in a very dangerous situation. They are hiding in a small attic in Amsterdam, and they are being hunted by the Nazis. What is their primary "want"? They want to survive until the Nazis are driven out of the Netherlands. Under the pressure of the situation, many more conflicts develop, and we see the characters change as they reveal their true selves. Some become more generous and heroic and wise. Others become frightened and do petty things, like steal food and nag the others.

The changes that take place in these people make us think about the story's **theme**—the main idea about life and people that the play reveals. We begin to realize that the playwright is showing us something about our need for freedom, love, and respect.

The Shock of Recognition

If a play has succeeded, we feel what has been called "the shock of recognition." If we recognize ourselves on stage, as being foolish or just human, we laugh. If we recognize our own anguish or unhappiness on stage, we cry. We go to the theater to recognize our own thoughts and feelings, to see them mirrored, and to realize in the laughter and tears of other people that we are not alone.

The Diary
of Anne Frank

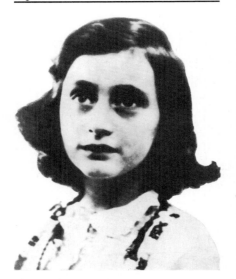

*T*he Diary of Anne Frank—the play—is the stage adaptation of a diary written by a Jewish girl, from July 1942 to August 1944. The diary was written while she and her family and some neighbors were hiding from the Nazis in the top floor of a warehouse and office building in Amsterdam, the Netherlands. Anne Frank was thirteen when she started her diary and fifteen when she wrote the last entry.

Anne Frank's Life

Anne Frank was born in Frankfurt, Germany, in 1929. When she was four years old, her parents left Germany for the Netherlands. They were trying to escape the harsh anti-Jewish laws of Hitler and the Nazi party. In Amsterdam, Otto Frank, Anne's father, managed a company that imported and exported spices. Anne and her older sister Margot grew up happily there until May 1940, when the Netherlands fell to the German army. With the arrival of the Germans, the Jews were no longer free. Laws prevented them from driving cars, owning bicycles, or riding in trains. They could not attend public schools, theaters, or movies. They could not socialize with Christians or take part in public sports. Soon the "call-ups" began. Jews were rounded up and sent to concentration camps. During the course of World War II, the Nazis systematically killed six million European Jews.

The Frank family and four other Jews lived for more than two years hidden in what Anne called the secret annex—the top two floors of the building where Mr. Frank had his offices and warehouse. In August 1944, the Nazi police raided their hiding place and sent all eight of its occupants to concentration camps. Of the eight, only Otto Frank survived. Anne died of typhus in a camp in Germany called Bergen-Belsen. She was fifteen years old. Two months after she died the war in Europe ended.

The Play

A Dutch woman named Miep Gies (who is one of the characters in this play) found Anne's diary in 1944, when she went up to the secret annex after the Nazi raid. Miep put the diary away, intending to return it to Anne after the war. In 1945, when Mr. Frank returned to Amsterdam, Miep gave him the diary. Called *The Diary of a Young Girl,* the journal was published in the Netherlands in 1947. It was translated into many languages, and its world impact has been enormous.

Frances Goodrich and Albert Hackett, a husband and wife team, wrote the stage adaptation that you are about to read. Their play opened on Broadway in October 1955 and was an immediate success.

The play has since been performed in more than twenty countries. A German critic described its powerful effect on a German audience: "When, after three hours, as if awakening from deepest

embarrassment, the people in the stalls can hardly rise from their seats, will not permit applause, and leave silently with bowed heads, that marks the greatness of a moment which must rouse the slowest of hearts and which must shake the most indifferent nerves."

Susan Strasberg in front of a sign advertising the play in which she is starring.

The Play's Dramatic Irony

When most people enter the theater to see this play, they know what actually happened to Anne and the others. This gives dramatic irony to everything that is said and done on stage. **Dramatic irony** means that the audience knows what the characters onstage do *not* know—their future. Throughout this play, the audience understands the full significance of what is being said and done, but the characters on stage do not. Thus, when Anne says toward the end of the play, "I want to go on living even after my death," we feel the irony. We know that through her diary, her wish will come true, but Anne isn't aware of this. Neither does she realize that she will never write anything else.

Anne did not survive. Her diary miraculously did. In our age, for some reason, when we read about nobility or goodness, we want to know "Could this really happen?" The events told in the diary really happened. They remain a testament not only to courage but to the eternal hope of those who believe with Anne, "In spite of everything, I still believe that people are really good at heart."

THE DIARY OF ANNE FRANK

Frances Goodrich and Albert Hackett

This play combines extraordinary situations with familiar ones. The characters live with extreme fear and suffering. But they also live in a household that has all the love and tears of families everywhere. Anne, the drama's central character or *protagonist,* is in some ways a typical teen-ager dealing with everyday problems. As you read this play, consider how much of it gives you the "shock of recognition"—the realization that these people could be your own family or neighbors.

Characters

Occupants of the secret annex
Anne Frank
Margot Frank, *her older sister*
Mr. Frank, *their father*
Mrs. Frank, *their mother*
Peter Van Daan
Mr. Van Daan, *his father*
Mrs. Van Daan, *his mother*
Dr. Dussel, *a dentist*

Workers in Mr. Frank's Business
Miep Gies, *a young Dutchwoman*
Mr. Kraler, *a Dutchman*

Setting: *Amsterdam, the Netherlands, July 1942 to August 1944; November 1945.*

Act One

Scene 1
The scene remains the same throughout the play. It is the top floor of a warehouse and office building in Amsterdam, the Netherlands. The sharply peaked roof of the building is outlined against a sea of other rooftops, stretching away into the distance. Nearby is the belfry of a church tower, the Westertoren, whose carillon rings out the hours. Occasionally faint sounds float up from below: the voices of children playing in the street, the tramp of marching feet, a boat whistle from the canal.

The three rooms of the top floor and a small attic space above are exposed to our view. The largest of the rooms is in the center, with two small rooms, slightly raised, on either side. On the right is a bathroom, out of sight. A narrow steep flight of stairs at the back leads up to the attic. The rooms are sparsely furnished with a few chairs, cots, a table or two. The windows are painted over, or covered with makeshift blackout curtains. In the main room there is a sink, a gas ring for cooking and a wood-burning stove for warmth.

The room on the left is hardly more than a closet. There is a skylight in the sloping ceiling. Directly under this room is a small steep stairwell, with steps leading down to a door. This is the only entrance from the building below. When the door is opened, we see that it has been concealed on the outer side by a bookcase attached to it.

The curtain rises on an empty stage. It is late afternoon, November 1945.

The rooms are dusty, the curtains in rags. Chairs and tables are overturned.

The door at the foot of the small stairwell swings open. MR. FRANK *comes up the steps into view. He is a gentle, cultured European in his middle years. There is still a trace of a German accent in his speech.*

He stands looking slowly around, making a supreme effort at self-control. He is weak, ill. His clothes are threadbare.

After a second he drops his rucksack on the couch and moves slowly about. He opens the door to one of the smaller rooms, and then abruptly closes it again, turning away. He goes to the window at the back, looking off at the Westertoren as its carillon strikes the hour of six, then he moves restlessly on.

From the street below we hear the sound of a barrel organ and children's voices at play. There is a many-colored scarf hanging from a nail. MR. FRANK *takes it, putting it around his neck. As he starts back for his rucksack, his eye is caught by something lying on the floor. It is a woman's white glove. He holds it in his hand and suddenly all of his self-control is gone. He breaks down, crying.*

We hear footsteps on the stairs. MIEP GIES[1] *comes up, looking for* MR. FRANK. MIEP *is a Dutch girl of about twenty-two. She wears a coat and hat, ready to go home. She is pregnant. Her attitude toward* MR. FRANK *is protective, compassionate.*

Miep. Are you all right, Mr. Frank?

Mr. Frank (*quickly controlling himself*). Yes, Miep, yes.

Miep. Everyone in the office has gone home . . . It's after six. (*Then pleading*) Don't stay up here, Mr. Frank. What's the use of torturing yourself like this?

Mr. Frank. I've come to say goodbye . . . I'm leaving here, Miep.

Miep. What do you mean? Where are you going? Where?

Mr. Frank. I don't know yet. I haven't decided.

Miep. Mr. Frank, you can't leave here! This is your home! Amsterdam is your home. Your business is here, waiting for you. . . . You're needed here. . . . Now that the war is over, there are things that . . .

Mr. Frank. I can't stay in Amsterdam, Miep. It has too many memories for me. Everywhere there's something . . . the house we lived in . . . the school . . . that street organ playing out there . . . I'm not the person you used to know, Miep. I'm a bitter old man. (*Breaking off*) Forgive me. I shouldn't speak to you like this . . . after all that you did for us . . . the suffering . . .

Miep. No. No. It wasn't suffering. You can't say we suffered.

[*As she speaks, she straightens a chair which is overturned.*]

Mr. Frank. I know what you went through, you and Mr. Kraler.[2] I'll remember it as long as I live. (*He gives one last look around.*) Come, Miep.

[*He starts for the steps, then remembers his rucksack, going back to get it.*]

Miep (*hurrying up to a cupboard*). Mr. Frank, did you see? There are some of your papers here. (*She brings a bundle of papers to him.*) We found them in a heap of rubbish on the floor after . . . after you left.

---

1. **Miep Gies** (mēp gēs).

2. **Kraler** (krä'ler).

Mr. Frank. Burn them.

[*He opens his rucksack to put the glove in it*.]

Miep. But, Mr. Frank, there are letters, notes . . .
Mr. Frank. Burn them. All of them.
Miep. Burn *this?*

[*She hands him a paperbound notebook*.]

Mr. Frank (*quietly*). Anne's diary. (*He opens the diary and begins to read*.) "Monday, the sixth of July, nineteen forty-two." (*To* MIEP) Nineteen forty-two. Is it possible, Miep? . . . Only three years ago. (*As he continues his reading, he sits down on the couch*.) "Dear Diary, since you and I are going to be great friends, I will start by telling you about myself. My name is Anne Frank. I am thirteen years old. I was born in Germany the twelfth of June, nineteen twenty-nine. As my family is Jewish, we emigrated to Holland when Hitler came to power."

[*As* MR. FRANK *reads on, another voice joins his, as if coming from the air. It is* ANNE'*s voice*.]

Mr. Frank and Anne. "My father started a business, importing spice and herbs. Things went well for us until nineteen forty. Then the war came, and the Dutch capitulation,[3] followed by the arrival of the Germans. Then things got very bad for the Jews."

[MR. FRANK'*s voice dies out.* ANNE'*s voice continues alone. The lights dim slowly to darkness. The curtain falls on the scene*.]

Anne's Voice. You could not do this and you could not do that. They forced Father out of his business. We had to wear yellow stars.[4] I had to turn in my bike. I couldn't go to a Dutch school anymore. I couldn't go to the movies, or ride in an automobile, or even on a streetcar, and a million other things. But somehow we children still managed to have fun. Yesterday Father told me we were going into hiding. Where, he wouldn't say. At five o'clock this morning Mother woke me and told me to hurry and get dressed. I was to put on as many clothes as I could. It would look too suspicious if we walked along carrying suitcases. It wasn't until we were on our way that I learned where we were going. Our hiding place was to be upstairs in the building where Father used to have his business. Three other people were coming in with us . . . the Van Daans and their son Peter . . . Father knew the Van Daans but we have never met them. . . .

[*During the last lines the curtain rises on the scene. The lights dim on.* ANNE'*s voice fades out*.]

Scene 2

It is early morning, July 1942. The rooms are bare, as before, but they are now clean and orderly.

MR. VAN DAAN, *a tall, portly man in his late forties, is in the main room, pacing up and down, nervously smoking a cigarette. His clothes and overcoat are expensive and well cut.*

MRS. VAN DAAN *sits on the couch, clutching her possessions, a hatbox, bags, etc. She is a pretty woman in her early forties. She wears a fur coat over her other clothes.*

PETER VAN DAAN *is standing at the window of the room on the right, looking down at the street below. He is a shy, awkward boy of sixteen. He wears a cap, a raincoat, and long Dutch trousers, like "plus fours."[5] At his feet is a black case, a carrier for his cat.*

The yellow Star of David is conspicuous on all of their clothes.

Mrs. Van Daan (*rising, nervous, excited*). Something's happened to them! I know it!
Mr. Van Daan. Now, Kerli!
Mrs. Van Daan. Mr. Frank said they'd be here at seven o'clock. He said . . .
Mr. Van Daan. They have two miles to walk. You can't expect . . .

---

3. **capitulation** (kə·pich′ə·lā′shən): surrender. On May 14, 1940, the Netherlands, which had declared its neutrality early in the war, surrendered to the invading German army.
4. **yellow stars:** The Nazis ordered all Jews to sew a large Star of David (a six-pointed star) on their outer clothing so they could be easily recognized as Jews.

---

5. **"plus fours":** knickers; baggy trousers that end in an elastic cuff just below the knee.

Mrs. Van Daan. They've been picked up. That's what's happened. They've been taken . . .

[MR. VAN DAAN *indicates that he hears someone coming.*]

Mr. Van Daan. You see?

[PETER *takes up his carrier and his schoolbag, etc., and goes into the main room as* MR. FRANK *comes up the stairwell from below.* MR. FRANK *looks much younger now. His movements are brisk, his manner confident. He wears an overcoat and carries his hat and a small cardboard box. He crosses to the* VAN DAANS, *shaking hands with each of them.*]

Mr. Frank. Mrs. Van Daan, Mr. Van Daan, Peter. (*Then, in explanation of their lateness*) There were too many of the Green Police[6] on the streets . . . we had to take the long way around.

[*Up the steps come* MARGOT FRANK, MRS. FRANK, MIEP (*not pregnant now*), *and* MR. KRALER. *All of them carry bags, packages, and so forth. The Star of David is conspicuous on all of the* FRANKS' *clothing.* MARGOT *is eighteen, beautiful, quiet, shy.* MRS. FRANK *is a young mother, gently bred, reserved. She, like* MR. FRANK, *has a slight German accent.* MR. KRALER *is a Dutchman, dependable, kindly.*

As MR. KRALER *and* MIEP *go upstage to put down their parcels,* MRS. FRANK *turns back to call* ANNE.]

Mrs. Frank. Anne?

[ANNE *comes running up the stairs. She is thirteen, quick in her movements, interested in everything, mercurial[7] in her emotions. She wears a cape, long wool socks, and carries a schoolbag.*]

Mr. Frank (*introducing them*). My wife, Edith. Mr. and Mrs. Van Daan (MRS. FRANK *hurries over, shaking hands with them.*) . . . their son, Peter . . . my daughters, Margot and Anne.

[ANNE *gives a polite little curtsy as she shakes*

MR. VAN DAAN'S *hand. Then she immediately starts off on a tour of investigation of her new home, going upstairs to the attic room.*

MIEP *and* MR. KRALER *are putting the various things they have brought on the shelves.*]

Mr. Kraler. I'm sorry there is still so much confusion.
Mr. Frank. Please. Don't think of it. After all, we'll have plenty of leisure to arrange everything ourselves.
Miep (*to* MRS. FRANK). We put the stores of food you sent in here. Your drugs are here . . . soap, linen here.
Mrs. Frank. Thank you, Miep.
Miep. I made up the beds . . . the way Mr. Frank and Mr. Kraler said. (*She starts out.*) Forgive me. I have to hurry. I've got to go to the other side of town to get some ration books[8] for you.
Mrs. Van Daan. Ration books? If they see our names on ration books, they'll know we're here.
Mr. Kraler. There isn't anything . . .
Miep. Don't worry. Your names won't be on them. (*As she hurries out*) I'll be up later. } *Together*
Mr. Frank. Thank you, Miep.
Mrs. Frank (*to* MR. KRALER). It's illegal, then, the ration books? We've never done anything illegal.
Mr. Frank. We won't be living here exactly according to regulations.

[*As* MR. KRALER *reassures* MRS. FRANK, *he takes various small things, such as matches, soap, etc., from his pockets, handing them to her.*]

Mr. Kraler. This isn't the black market,[9] Mrs. Frank. This is what we call the white market . . . helping all of the hundreds and hundreds who are hiding out in Amsterdam.

[*The carillon is heard playing the quarter-hour before eight.* MR. KRALER *looks at his watch.* ANNE *stops at the window as she comes down the stairs.*]

---

6. **Green Police:** Nazi police; their uniforms were green.
7. **mercurial** (mər·kyoor′ē·əl): very changeable; lively.

8. **ration books:** books of stamps or coupons issued by the government during wartime. People could purchase scarce items such as food, clothing, and gasoline only with coupons.
9. **black market:** illegal buying and selling of goods without ration stamps.

Anne. It's the Westertoren!

Mr. Kraler. I must go. I must be out of here and downstairs in the office before the workmen get here. (*He starts for the stairs leading out.*) Miep or I, or both of us, will be up each day to bring you food and news and find out what your needs are. Tomorrow I'll get you a better bolt for the door at the foot of the stairs. It needs a bolt that you can throw yourself and open only at our signal. (*To* MR. FRANK) Oh . . . You'll tell them about the noise?

Mr. Frank. I'll tell them.

Mr. Kraler. Goodbye then for the moment. I'll come up again, after the workmen leave.

Mr. Frank. Goodbye, Mr. Kraler.

Mrs. Frank (*shaking his hand*). How can we thank you?

[*The others murmur their goodbyes.*]

Mr. Kraler. I never thought I'd live to see the day when a man like Mr. Frank would have to go into hiding. When you think——

[*He breaks off, going out.* MR. FRANK *follows him down the steps, bolting the door after him. In the interval before he returns,* PETER *goes over to* MARGOT, *shaking hands with her. As* MR. FRANK *comes back up the steps,* MRS. FRANK *questions him anxiously.*]

Mrs. Frank. What did he mean, about the noise?

Mr. Frank. First let us take off some of these clothes.

[*They all start to take off garment after garment. On each of their coats, sweaters, blouses, suits, dresses, is another yellow Star of David.* MR. *and* MRS. FRANK *are underdressed quite simply. The others wear several things, sweaters, extra dresses, bathrobes, aprons, nightgowns, etc.*]

Mr. Van Daan. It's a wonder we weren't arrested, walking along the streets . . . Petronella with a fur coat in July . . . and that cat of Peter's crying all the way.

Anne (*as she is removing a pair of panties*). A cat?

Mrs. Frank (*shocked*). Anne, please!

Anne. It's all right. I've got on three more.

[*She pulls off two more. Finally, as they have all removed their surplus clothes, they look to* MR. FRANK, *waiting for him to speak.*]

Mr. Frank. Now. About the noise. While the men are in the building below, we must have complete quiet. Every sound can be heard down there, not only in the workrooms, but in the offices too. The men come at about eight-thirty, and leave at about five-thirty. So, to be perfectly safe, from eight in the morning until six in the evening we must move only when it is necessary, and then in stockinged feet. We must not speak above a whisper. We must not run any water. We cannot use the sink, or even, forgive me, the w.c.[10] The pipes go down through the workrooms. It would be heard. No trash . . . (MR. FRANK *stops abruptly as he hears the sound of marching feet from the street below. Everyone is motionless, paralyzed with fear.* MR. FRANK *goes quietly into the room on the right to look down out of the window.* ANNE *runs after him, peering out with him. The tramping feet pass without stopping. The tension is relieved.* MR. FRANK, *followed by* ANNE, *returns to the main room and resumes his instructions to the group.*) . . . No trash must ever be thrown out which might reveal that someone is living up here . . . not even a potato paring. We must burn everything in the stove at night. This is the way we must live until it is over, if we are to survive.

[*There is silence for a second.*]

Mrs. Frank. Until it is over.

Mr. Frank (*reassuringly*). After six we can move about . . . we can talk and laugh and have our supper and read and play games . . . just as we would at home. (*He looks at his watch.*) And now I think it would be wise if we all went to our rooms, and were settled before eight o'clock. Mrs. Van Daan, you and your husband will be upstairs. I regret that there is no place up there for Peter. But he will be here, near us. This will be our common room, where we'll meet to talk and eat and read, like one family.

Mr. Van Daan. And where do you and Mrs. Frank sleep?

---

10. **w.c.:** short for water closet, or toilet.

"I love cats. I have one . . . But they made me leave her behind."

Mr. Frank. This room is also our bedroom.

Mrs. Van Daan. That isn't right. We'll sleep here and you take the room upstairs. } *Together*

Mr. Van Daan. It's your place.

Mr. Frank. Please. I've thought this out for weeks. It's the best arrangement. The only arrangement.

Mrs. Van Daan (*to* MR. FRANK). Never, never can we thank you. (*Then to* MRS. FRANK) I don't know what would have happened to us, if it hadn't been for Mr. Frank.

Mr. Frank. You don't know how your husband helped me when I came to this country . . . knowing no one . . . not able to speak the language. I can never repay him for that. (*Going to* VAN DAAN) May I help you with your things?

Mr. Van Daan. No. No. (*To* MRS. VAN DAAN) Come along, *liefje.*[11]

Mrs. Van Daan. You'll be all right, Peter? You're not afraid?

Peter (*embarrassed*). Please, Mother.

[*They start up the stairs to the attic room above.* MR. FRANK *turns to* MRS. FRANK.]

Mr. Frank. You too must have some rest, Edith. You didn't close your eyes last night. Nor you, Margot.

Anne. I slept, Father. Wasn't that funny? I knew it was the last night in my own bed, and yet I slept soundly.

Mr. Frank. I'm glad, Anne. Now you'll be able to help me straighten things in here. (*To* MRS. FRANK *and* MARGOT) Come with me. . . . You and Margot rest in this room for the time being.

[*He picks up their clothes, starting for the room on the right.*]

Mrs. Frank. You're sure . . . ? I could help. . . . And Anne hasn't had her milk. . . .

Mr. Frank. I'll give it to her. (*To* ANNE *and* PETER) Anne, Peter . . . it's best that you take off your shoes now, before you forget.

[*He leads the way to the room, followed by* MARGOT.]

---

11. *liefje* (lēf'hyə): Dutch for "little dear one."

Mrs. Frank. You're sure you're not tired, Anne?

Anne. I feel fine. I'm going to help Father.

Mrs. Frank. Peter, I'm glad you are to be with us.

Peter. Yes, Mrs. Frank.

[MRS. FRANK *goes to join* MR. FRANK *and* MARGOT.

During the following scene MR. FRANK helps MARGOT and MRS. FRANK to hang up their clothes. Then he persuades them both to lie down and rest. The VAN DAANS in their room above settle themselves. In the main room ANNE and PETER remove their shoes. PETER takes his cat out of the carrier.]

Anne. What's your cat's name?

Peter. Mouschi.

Anne. Mouschi! Mouschi! Mouschi! (*She picks up the cat, walking away with it. To* PETER) I love cats. I have one . . . a darling little cat. But they made me leave her behind. I left some food and a note for the neighbors to take care of her. . . . I'm going to miss her terribly. What is yours? A him or a her?

Peter. He's a tom. He doesn't like strangers.

[*He takes the cat from her, putting it back in its carrier.*]

Anne (*unabashed*). Then I'll have to stop being a stranger, won't I? Is he fixed?

Peter (*startled*). Huh?

Anne. Did you have him fixed?

Peter. No.

Anne. Oh, you ought to have him fixed—to keep him from—you know, fighting. Where did you go to school?

Peter. Jewish Secondary.

Anne. But that's where Margot and I go! I never saw you around.

Peter. I used to see you . . . sometimes . . .

Anne. You did?

Peter. . . . in the school yard. You were always in the middle of a bunch of kids.

[*He takes a penknife from his pocket.*]

Anne. Why didn't you ever come over?

Peter. I'm sort of a lone wolf.

[*He starts to rip off his Star of David.*]

Anne. What are you doing?

Peter. Taking it off.

Anne. But you can't do that. They'll arrest you if you go out without your star.

[*He tosses his knife on the table.*]

Peter. Who's going out?

Anne. Why, of course! You're right! Of course we don't need them anymore. *(She picks up his knife and starts to take her star off.)* I wonder what our friends will think when we don't show up today?

Peter. I didn't have any dates with anyone.

Anne. Oh, I did. I had a date with Jopie to go and play ping-pong at her house. Do you know Jopie de Waal?[12]

Peter. No.

Anne. Jopie's my best friend. I wonder what she'll think when she telephones and there's no answer? . . . Probably she'll go over to the house. . . . I wonder what she'll think . . . we left everything as if we'd suddenly been called away . . . breakfast dishes in the sink . . . beds not made . . . *(As she pulls off her star the cloth underneath shows clearly the color and form of the star.)* Look! It's still there! (PETER *goes over to the stove with his star.*) What're you going to do with yours?

Peter. Burn it.

Anne *(she starts to throw hers in, and cannot).* It's funny, I can't throw mine away. I don't know why.

Peter. You can't throw . . . ? Something they branded you with . . . ? That they made you wear so they could spit on you?

Anne. I know. I know. But after all, it *is* the Star of David, isn't it?

[*In the bedroom, right,* MARGOT *and* MRS. FRANK *are lying down.* MR. FRANK *starts quietly out.*]

Peter. Maybe it's different for a girl.

[MR. FRANK *comes into the main room.*]

Mr. Frank. Forgive me, Peter. Now let me see. We must find a bed for your cat. *(He goes to a cupboard.)* I'm glad you brought your cat. Anne was feeling so badly about hers. *(Getting a used*

small washtub) Here we are. Will it be comfortable in that?

Peter *(gathering up his things).* Thanks.

Mr. Frank *(opening the door of the room on the left).* And here is your room. But I warn you, Peter, you can't grow anymore. Not an inch, or you'll have to sleep with your feet out of the skylight. Are you hungry?

Peter. No.

Mr. Frank. We have some bread and butter.

Peter. No, thank you.

Mr. Frank. You can have it for luncheon then. And tonight we will have a real supper . . . our first supper together.

Peter. Thanks. Thanks.

[*He goes into his room. During the following scene he arranges his possessions in his new room.*]

Mr. Frank. That's a nice boy, Peter.

Anne. He's awfully shy, isn't he?

Mr. Frank. You'll like him, I know.

Anne. I certainly hope so, since he's the only boy I'm likely to see for months and months.

[MR. FRANK *sits down, taking off his shoes.*]

Mr. Frank. Annele,[13] there's a box there. Will you open it?

[*He indicates a carton on the couch.* ANNE *brings it to the center table. In the street below there is the sound of children playing.*]

Anne *(as she opens the carton).* You know the way I'm going to think of it here? I'm going to think of it as a boardinghouse. A very peculiar summer boardinghouse, like the one that we— *(She breaks off as she pulls out some photographs.)* Father! My movie stars! I was wondering where they were! I was looking for them this morning . . . and Queen Wilhelmina![14] How wonderful!

Mr. Frank. There's something more. Go on. Look further.

---

12. **Jopie de Waal** (yō′pē də·väl′).

13. **Annele** (än′ə·lə): little Anne, in German (like "Annie").
14. **Queen Wilhelmina** (vil′həl·mē′nä) (1880–1962): queen of the Netherlands (1890–1948).

"I don't want you ever to go beyond that door."

[*He goes over to the sink, pouring a glass of milk from a thermos bottle.*]

Anne (*pulling out a pasteboard-bound book*). A diary! (*She throws her arms around her father.*) I've never had a diary. And I've always longed for one. (*She looks around the room.*) Pencil, pencil, pencil, pencil. (*She starts down the stairs.*) I'm going down to the office to get a pencil.

Mr. Frank. Anne! No!

[*He goes after her, catching her by the arm and pulling her back.*]

Anne (*startled*). But there's no one in the building now.

Mr. Frank. It doesn't matter. I don't want you ever to go beyond that door.

Anne (*sobered*). Never . . . ? Not even at night-time. when everyone is gone? Or on Sundays? Can't I go down to listen to the radio?

Mr. Frank. Never. I am sorry, Anneke.[15] It isn't safe. No, you must never go beyond that door.

[*For the first time* ANNE *realizes what "going into hiding" means.*]

Anne. I see.

Mr. Frank. It'll be hard, I know. But always remember this, Anneke. There are no walls, there are no bolts, no locks that anyone can put on your mind. Miep will bring us books. We will read history, poetry, mythology. (*He gives her the glass of milk.*) Here's your milk. (*With his arm about her, they go over to the couch, sitting down side by side.*) As a matter of fact, between us, Anne, being here has certain advantages for you. For instance, you remember the battle you had with your mother the other day on the subject of overshoes? You said you'd rather die than wear overshoes? But in the end you had to wear them? Well now, you see, for as long as we are here you will never have to wear overshoes! Isn't that good? And the coat that you inherited from Margot, you won't have to wear that anymore. And the piano! You won't have to practice on the piano. I tell you, this is going to be a fine life for you!

[ANNE's *panic is gone.* PETER *appears in the doorway of his room, with a saucer in his hand. He is carrying his cat.*]

Peter. I . . . I . . . I thought I'd better get some water for Mouschi before . . .

Mr. Frank. Of course.

[*As he starts toward the sink the carillon begins to chime the hour of eight. He tiptoes to the window at the back and looks down at the street below. He turns to* PETER, *indicating in pantomime that it is too late.* PETER *starts back for his room. He steps on a creaking board. The three of them are frozen for a minute in fear. As* PETER *starts away again,* ANNE *tiptoes over to him and pours some of the milk from her glass into the*

saucer for the cat. PETER *squats on the floor, putting the milk before the cat.* MR. FRANK *gives* ANNE *his fountain pen, and then goes into the room at the right. For a second* ANNE *watches the cat, then she goes over to the center table, and opens her diary.*

In the room at the right, MRS. FRANK *has sat up quickly at the sound of the carillon.* MR. FRANK *comes in and sits down beside her on the settee, his arm comfortingly around her.*

Upstairs, in the attic room, MR. *and* MRS. VAN DAAN *have hung their clothes in the closet and are now seated on the iron bed.* MRS. VAN DAAN *leans back exhausted.* MR. VAN DAAN *fans her with a newspaper.*

ANNE *starts to write in her diary. The lights dim out, the curtain falls.*

In the darkness ANNE'S *voice comes to us again, faintly at first, and then with growing strength.*]

Anne's Voice. I expect I should be describing what it feels like to go into hiding. But I really don't know yet myself. I only know its funny never to be able to go outdoors . . . never to breathe fresh air . . . never to run and shout and jump. It's the silence in the nights that frightens me most. Every time I hear a creak in the house, or a step on the street outside, I'm sure they're coming for us. The days aren't so bad. At least we know that Miep and Mr. Kraler are down there below us in the office. Our protectors, we call them. I asked Father what would happen to them if the Nazis found out they were hiding us. Pim[16] said that they would suffer the same fate that we would. . . . Imagine! They know this, and yet when they come up here, they're always cheerful and gay as if there were nothing in the world to bother them. . . . Friday, the twenty-first of August, nineteen forty-two. Today I'm going to tell you our general news. Mother is unbearable. She insists on treating me like a baby, which I loathe. Otherwise things are going better. The weather is . . .

[*As* ANNE'S *voice is fading out, the curtain rises on the scene.*]

---

15. **Anneke** (än'ə·kə): another nickname for Anne, in German.

16. **Pim:** family nickname for Mr. Frank.

Scene 3

It is a little after six o'clock in the evening, two months later.

MARGOT *is in the bedroom at the right, studying.* MR. VAN DAAN *is lying down in the attic room above.*

The rest of the "family" is in the main room. ANNE *and* PETER *sit opposite each other at the center table, where they have been doing their lessons.* MRS. FRANK *is on the couch.* MRS. VAN DAAN *is seated with her fur coat, on which she has been sewing, in her lap. None of them are wearing their shoes.*

Their eyes are on MR. FRANK, *waiting for him to give them the signal which will release them from their day-long quiet.* MR. FRANK, *his shoes in his hand, stands looking down out of the window at the back watching to be sure that all of the workmen have left the building below.*

After a few seconds of motionless silence, MR. FRANK *turns from the window.*

Mr. Frank *(quietly, to the group)*. It's safe now. The last workman has left.

[There is an immediate stir of relief.]

Anne *(her pent-up energy explodes)*. WHEE!
Mrs. Frank *(startled, amused)*. Anne!
Mrs. Van Daan. I'm first for the w.c.

[She hurries off to the bathroom. MRS. FRANK *puts on her shoes and starts up to the sink to prepare supper.* ANNE *sneaks* PETER's *shoes from under the table and hides them behind her back. Mr. Frank goes in to* MARGOT's *room.]*

Mr. Frank *(to* MARGOT*)*. Six o'clock. School's over.

*[*MARGOT *gets up, stretching.* MR. FRANK *sits down to put on his shoes. In the main room* PETER *tries to find his.]*

Peter *(to* ANNE*)*. Have you seen my shoes?
Anne *(innocently)*. Your shoes?
Peter. You've taken them, haven't you?
Anne. I don't know what you're talking about.
Peter. You're going to be sorry!
Anne. Am I?

*[*PETER *goes after her.* ANNE, *with his shoes in her hand, runs from him, dodging behind her mother.]*

Mrs. Frank *(protesting)*. Anne, dear!
Peter. Wait till I get you!
Anne. I'm waiting. *(*PETER *makes a lunge for her. They both fall to the floor.* PETER *pins her down, wrestling with her to get the shoes.)* Don't! Don't! Peter, stop it. Ouch!
Mrs. Frank. Anne! . . . Peter!

[Suddenly PETER *becomes self-conscious. He grabs his shoes roughly and starts for his room.]*

Anne *(following him)*. Peter, where are you going? Come dance with me.
Peter. I tell you I don't know how.
Anne. I'll teach you.
Peter. I'm going to give Mouschi his dinner.
Anne. Can I watch?
Peter. He doesn't like people around while he eats.
Anne. Peter, please.
Peter. No!

[He goes into his room. ANNE *slams his door after him.]*

Mrs. Frank. Anne, dear, I think you shouldn't play like that with Peter. It's not dignified.
Anne. Who cares if it's dignified? I don't want to be dignified.

*[*MR. FRANK *and* MARGOT *come from the room on the right.* MARGOT *goes to help her mother.* MR. FRANK *starts for the center table to correct* MARGOT's *school papers.]*

Mrs. Frank *(to* ANNE*)*. You complain that I don't treat you like a grown-up. But when I do, you resent it.
Anne. I only want some fun . . . someone to laugh and clown with. . . . After you've sat still all day and hardly moved, you've got to have some fun. I don't know what's the matter with that boy.
Mr. Frank. He isn't used to girls. Give him a little time.
Anne. Time? Isn't two months time? I could cry. *(Catching hold of* MARGOT*)* Come on, Margot . . . dance with me. Come on, please.
Margot. I have to help with supper.

Anne. You know we're going to forget how to dance. . . . When we get out we won't remember a thing.

[*She starts to sing and dance by herself.* MR. FRANK *takes her in his arms, waltzing with her.* MRS. VAN DAAN *comes in from the bathroom.*]

Mrs. Van Daan. Next? (*She looks around as she starts putting on her shoes.*) Where's Peter?
Anne (*as they are dancing*). Where would he be!
Mrs. Van Daan. He hasn't finished his lessons, has he? His father'll kill him if he catches him in there with that cat and his work not done. (MR. FRANK *and* ANNE *finish their dance. They bow to each other with extravagant formality.*) Anne, get him out of there, will you?
Anne (*at* PETER's *door*). Peter? Peter?
Peter (*opening the door a crack*). What is it?
Anne. Your mother says to come out.
Peter. I'm giving Mouschi his dinner.
Mrs. Van Daan. You know what your father says.

[*She sits on the couch, sewing on the lining of her fur coat.*]

Peter. For heaven's sake, I haven't even looked at him since lunch.
Mrs. Van Daan. I'm just telling you, that's all.
Anne. I'll feed him.
Peter. I don't want you in there.
Mrs. Van Daan. Peter!
Peter (*to* ANNE). Then give him his dinner and come right out, you hear?

[*He comes back to the table.* ANNE *shuts the door of* PETER's *room after her and disappears behind the curtain covering his closet.*]

Mrs. Van Daan (*to* PETER). Now is that any way to talk to your little girlfriend?
Peter. Mother . . . for heaven's sake . . . will you please stop saying that?
Mrs. Van Daan. Look at him blush! Look at him!
Peter. Please! I'm not . . . anyway . . . let me alone, will you?
Mrs. Van Daan. He acts like it was something to be ashamed of. It's nothing to be ashamed of, to have a little girlfriend.
Peter. You're crazy. She's only thirteen.
Mrs. Van Daan. So what? And you're sixteen. Just perfect. Your father's ten years older than I am.

(*To* MR. FRANK) I warn you, Mr. Frank, if this war lasts much longer, we're going to be related and then . . .
Mr. Frank. *Mazel tov!*[17]
Mrs. Frank (*deliberately changing the conversation*). I wonder where Miep is. She's usually so prompt.

[*Suddenly everything else is forgotten as they hear the sound of an automobile coming to a screeching stop in the street below. They are tense, motionless in their terror. The car starts away. A wave of relief sweeps over them. They pick up their occupations again.* ANNE *flings open the door of* PETER's *room, making a dramatic entrance. She is dressed in* PETER's *clothes.* PETER *looks at her in fury. The others are amused.*]

Anne. Good evening, everyone. Forgive me if I don't stay. (*She jumps up on a chair.*) I have a friend waiting for me in there. My friend Tom. Tom Cat. Some people say that we look alike. But Tom has the most beautiful whiskers, and I have only a little fuzz. I am hoping . . . in time . . .
Peter. All right, Mrs. Quack Quack!
Anne (*outraged—jumping down*). Peter!
Peter. I heard about you. . . . How you talked so much in class they called you Mrs. Quack Quack. How Mr. Smitter made you write a composition . . . "'Quack, quack,' said Mrs. Quack Quack."
Anne. Well, go on. Tell them the rest. How it was so good he read it out loud to the class and then read it to all his other classes!
Peter. Quack! Quack! Quack . . . Quack . . . Quack . . .

[ANNE *pulls off the coat and trousers.*]

Anne. You are the most intolerable, insufferable boy I've ever met!

[*She throws the clothes down the stairwell.* PETER *goes down after them.*]

Peter. Quack, quack, quack!
Mrs. Van Daan (*to* ANNE). That's right, Anneke! Give it to him!
Anne. With all the boys in the world . . . Why I had to get locked up with one like you! . . .

---

17. *Mazel tov!* (mä′z'l tōv′): Hebrew for "Good Luck!" or "Congratulations!"

Peter. Quack, quack, quack, and from now on stay out of my room!

[*As* PETER *passes her,* ANNE *puts out her foot, tripping him. He picks himself up, and goes on into his room.*]

Mrs. Frank (*quietly*). Anne, dear . . . your hair. (*She feels* ANNE's *forehead.*) You're warm. Are you feeling all right?

Anne. Please, Mother.

[*She goes over to the center table, slipping into her shoes.*]

Mrs. Frank (*following her*). You haven't a fever, have you?

Anne (*pulling away*). No. No.

Mrs. Frank. You know we can't call a doctor here, ever. There's only one thing to do . . . watch carefully. Prevent an illness before it comes. Let me see your tongue.

Anne. Mother, this is perfectly absurd.

Mrs. Frank. Anne, dear, don't be such a baby. Let me see your tongue. (*As* ANNE *refuses,* MRS. FRANK *appeals to* MR. FRANK.) Otto . . . ?

Mr. Frank. You hear your mother, Anne.

[ANNE *flicks out her tongue for a second, then turns away.*]

Mrs. Frank. Come on—open up! (*As* ANNE *opens her mouth very wide*) You seem all right . . . but perhaps an aspirin . . .

Mrs. Van Daan. For heaven's sake, don't give that child any pills. I waited for fifteen minutes this morning for her to come out of the w.c.

Anne. I was washing my hair!

Mr. Frank. I think there's nothing the matter with our Anne that a ride on her bike, or a visit with her friend Jopie de Waal wouldn't cure. Isn't that so, Anne?

[MR. VAN DAAN *comes down into the room. From outside we hear faint sounds of bombers going over and a burst of ack-ack.[18]*]

Mr. Van Daan. Miep not come yet?

Mrs. Van Daan. The workmen just left, a little while ago.

---

18. **ack-ack:** antiaircraft gunfire.

Mr. Van Daan. What's for dinner tonight?

Mrs. Van Daan. Beans.

Mr. Van Daan. Not again!

Mrs. Van Daan. Poor Putti! I know. But what can we do? That's all that Miep brought us.

[MR. VAN DAAN *starts to pace, his hands behind his back.* ANNE *follows behind him, imitating him.*]

Anne. We are now in what is known as the "bean cycle." Beans boiled, beans en casserole, beans with strings, beans without strings . . .

[PETER *has come out of his room. He slides into his place at the table, becoming immediately absorbed in his studies.*]

Mr. Van Daan (*to* PETER). I saw you . . . in there, playing with your cat.

Mrs. Van Daan. He just went in for a second, putting his coat away. He's been out here all the time, doing his lessons.

Mr. Frank (*looking up from the papers*). Anne, you got an excellent in your history paper today . . . and very good in Latin.

Anne (*sitting beside him*). How about algebra?

Mr. Frank. I'll have to make a confession. Up until now I've managed to stay ahead of you in algebra. Today you caught up with me. We'll leave it to Margot to correct.

Anne. Isn't algebra *vile,* Pim!

Mr. Frank. Vile!

Margot (*to* MR. FRANK). How did I do?

Anne (*getting up*). Excellent, excellent, excellent, excellent!

Mr. Frank (*to* MARGOT). You should have used the subjunctive here . . .

Margot. Should I? . . . I thought . . . look here . . . I didn't use it here. . . .

[*The two become absorbed in the papers.*]

Anne. Mrs. Van Daan, may I try on your coat?

Mrs. Frank. No, Anne.

Mrs. Van Daan (*giving it to* ANNE). It's all right . . . but careful with it. (ANNE *puts it on and struts with it.*) My father gave me that the year before he died. He always bought the best that money could buy.

Anne. Mrs. Van Daan, did you have a lot of boy friends before you were married?

Mrs. Frank. Anne, that's a personal question. It's not courteous to ask personal questions.

Mrs. Van Daan. Oh I don't mind. (*To* ANNE) Our house was always swarming with boys. When I was a girl we had . . .

Mr. Van Daan. Oh, God. Not again!

Mrs. Van Daan (*good-humored*). Shut up! (*Without a pause, to* ANNE. MR. VAN DAAN *mimics* MRS. VAN DAAN, *speaking the first few words in unison with her.*) One summer we had a big house in Hilversum. The boys came buzzing round like bees around a jam pot. And when I was sixteen! . . . We were wearing our skirts very short those days and I had good-looking legs. (*She pulls up her skirt, going to* MR. FRANK.) I still have 'em. I may not be as pretty as I used to be, but I still have my legs. How about it, Mr. Frank?

Mr. Van Daan. All right. All right. We see them.

Mrs. Van Daan. I'm not asking you. I'm asking Mr. Frank.

Peter. Mother, for heaven's sake.

Mrs. Van Daan. Oh, I embarrass you, do I? Well, I just hope the girl you marry has as good. (*Then to* ANNE) My father used to worry about me, with so many boys hanging round. He told me, if any of them gets fresh, you say to him . . . "Remember, Mr. So-and-So, remember I'm a lady."

Anne. "Remember, Mr. So-and-So, remember I'm a lady."

[*She gives* MRS. VAN DAAN *her coat.*]

Mr. Van Daan. Look at you, talking that way in front of her! Don't you know she puts it all down in that diary?

Mrs. Van Daan. So, if she does? I'm only telling the truth!

[ANNE *stretches out, putting her ear to the floor, listening to what is going on below. The sound of the bombers fades away.*]

Mrs. Frank (*setting the table*). Would you mind, Peter, if I moved you over to the couch?

Anne (*listening*). Miep must have the radio on.

[PETER *picks up his papers, going over to the couch beside* MRS. VAN DAAN.]

Mr. Van Daan (*accusingly, to* PETER). Haven't you finished yet?

Peter. No.

Mr. Van Daan. You ought to be ashamed of yourself.

Peter. All right. All right. I'm a dunce. I'm a hopeless case. Why do I go on?

Mrs. Van Daan. You're not hopeless. Don't talk that way. It's just that you haven't anyone to help you, like the girls have. (*To* MR. FRANK) Maybe you could help him, Mr. Frank?

Mr. Frank. I'm sure that his father . . . ?

Mrs. Van Daan. Not me. I can't do anything with him. He won't listen to me. You go ahead . . . if you want.

Mr. Frank (*going to* PETER). What about it, Peter? Shall we make our class coeducational?

Mrs. Van Daan (*kissing* MR. FRANK). You're an angel, Mr. Frank. An angel. I don't know why I didn't meet you before I met that one there. Here, sit down, Mr. Frank. . . . (*She forces him down on the couch beside* PETER.) Now, Peter, you listen to Mr. Frank.

Mr. Frank. It might be better for us to go into Peter's room.

[PETER *jumps up eagerly, leading the way.*]

Mrs. Van Daan. That's right. You go in there, Peter. You listen to Mr. Frank. Mr. Frank is a highly educated man.

[*As* MR. FRANK *is about to follow* PETER *into his room,* MRS. FRANK *stops him and wipes the lipstick from his lips. Then she closes the door after them.*]

Anne (*on the floor, listening*). Shh! I can hear a man's voice talking.

Mr. Van Daan (*to* ANNE). Isn't it bad enough here without your sprawling all over the place?

[ANNE *sits up.*]

Mrs. Van Daan (*to* MR. VAN DAAN). If you didn't smoke so much, you wouldn't be so bad-tempered.

Mr. Van Daan. Am I smoking? Do you see me smoking?

Mrs. Van Daan. Don't tell me you've used up all those cigarettes.

Mr. Van Daan. One package. Miep only brought me one package.

Mrs. Van Daan. It's a filthy habit anyway. It's a good time to break yourself.

Mr. Van Daan. Oh, stop it, please.

Mrs. Van Daan. You're smoking up all our money. You know that, don't you?

Mr. Van Daan. Will you shut up? (*During this,* MRS. FRANK *and* MARGOT *have studiously kept their eyes down. But* ANNE, *seated on the floor, has been following the discussion interestedly.* MR. VAN DAAN *turns to see her staring up at him.*) And what are you staring at?

Anne. I never heard grown-ups quarrel before. I thought only children quarreled.

Mr. Van Daan. This isn't a quarrel! It's a discussion. And I never heard children so rude before.

Anne (*rising, indignantly*). I, rude!

Mr. Van Daan. Yes!

Mrs. Frank (*quickly*). Anne, will you get me my knitting? (ANNE *goes to get it.*) I must remember, when Miep comes, to ask her to bring me some more wool.

Margot (*going to her room*). I need some hairpins and some soap. I made a list.

[*She goes into her bedroom to get the list.*]

Mrs. Frank (*to* ANNE). Have you some library books for Miep when she comes?

Anne. It's a wonder that Miep has a life of her own, the way we make her run errands for us. Please, Miep, get me some starch. Please take my hair out and have it cut. Tell me all the latest news, Miep. (*She goes over, kneeling on the couch beside* MRS. VAN DAAN.) Did you know that she was engaged? His name is Dirk, and Miep's afraid the Nazis will ship him off to Germany to work in one of their war plants. That's what they're doing with some of the young Dutchmen . . . they pick them up off the streets—

Mr. Van Daan (*interrupting*). Don't you ever get tired of talking? Suppose you try keeping still for five minutes. Just five minutes.

[*He starts to pace again. Again* ANNE *follows him, mimicking him.* MRS. FRANK *jumps up and takes her by the arm up to the sink, and gives her a glass of milk.*]

Mrs. Frank. Come here, Anne. It's time for your glass of milk.

Mr. Van Daan. Talk, talk, talk. I never heard such a child. Where is my . . . ? Every evening it's the same, talk, talk, talk. (*He looks around.*) Where is my . . . ?

Mrs. Van Daan. What're you looking for?

Mr. Van Daan. My pipe. Have you seen my pipe?

Mrs. Van Daan. What good's a pipe? You haven't got any tobacco.

Mr. Van Daan. At least I'll have something to hold in my mouth! (*Opening* MARGOT's *bedroom door*) Margot, have you seen my pipe?

Margot. It was on the table last night.

[ANNE *puts her glass of milk on the table and picks up his pipe, hiding it behind her back.*]

Mr. Van Daan. I know. I know. Anne, did you see my pipe? . . . Anne!

Mrs. Frank. Anne, Mr. Van Daan is speaking to you.

Anne. Am I allowed to talk now?

Mr. Van Daan. You're the most aggravating . . . The trouble with you is, you've been spoiled. What you need is a good old-fashioned spanking.

Anne (*mimicking* MRS. VAN DAAN). "Remember, Mr. So-and-So, remember I'm a lady."

[*She thrusts the pipe into his mouth, then picks up her glass of milk.*]

Mr. Van Daan (*restraining himself with difficulty*). Why aren't you nice and quiet like your sister Margot? Why do you have to show off all the time? Let me give you a little advice, young lady. Men don't like that kind of thing in a girl. You know that? A man likes a girl who'll listen to him once in a while . . . a domestic girl, who'll keep her house shining for her husband . . . who loves to cook and sew and . . .

Anne. I'd cut my throat first! I'd open my veins! I'm going to be remarkable! I'm going to Paris . . .

Mr. Van Daan (*scoffingly*). Paris!

Anne. . . . to study music and art.

Mr. Van Daan. Yeah! Yeah!

Anne. I'm going to be a famous dancer or singer . . . or something wonderful.

"Now look what you've done . . . you clumsy little fool!"

[*She makes a wide gesture, spilling the glass of milk on the fur coat in* MRS. VAN DAAN'*s lap.* MARGOT *rushes quickly over with a towel.* ANNE *tries to brush the milk off with her skirt.*]

Mrs. Van Daan. Now look what you've done . . . you clumsy little fool! My beautiful fur coat my father gave me . . .

Anne. I'm so sorry.

Mrs. Van Daan. What do you care? It isn't yours. . . . So go on, ruin it! Do you know what that coat cost? Do you? And now look at it! Look at it!

Anne. I'm very, very sorry.

Mrs. Van Daan. I could kill you for this. I could just kill you!

[MRS. VAN DAAN *goes up the stairs, clutching the coat.* MR. VAN DAAN *starts after her.*]

Mr. Van Daan. Petronella . . . *liefje! Liefje!* . . . Come back . . . the supper . . . come back!

Mrs. Frank. Anne, you must not behave in that way.

Anne. It was an accident. Anyone can have an accident.

Mrs. Frank. I don't mean that. I mean the answering back. You must not answer back. They are our guests. We must always show the greatest courtesy to them. We're all living under terrible tension. (*She stops as* MARGOT *indicates that* VAN DAAN *can hear. When he is gone, she continues.*) That's why we must control ourselves. . . . You don't hear Margot getting into arguments with them, do you? Watch Margot. She's always courteous with them. Never familiar. She keeps her distance. And they respect her for it. Try to be like Margot.

Anne. And have them walk all over me, the way they do her? No, thanks!

Mrs. Frank. I'm not afraid that anyone is going to walk all over you, Anne. I'm afraid for other people, that you'll walk on them. I don't know what happens to you, Anne. You are wild, self-willed. If I had ever talked to my mother as you talk to me . . .

Anne. Things have changed. People aren't like that anymore. "Yes, Mother." "No, Mother." "Anything you say, Mother." I've got to fight things out for myself! Make something of myself!

Mrs. Frank. It isn't necessary to fight to do it. Margot doesn't fight, and isn't she . . . ?

Anne (*violently rebellious*). Margot! Margot! Margot! That's all I hear from everyone . . . how wonderful Margot is . . . "Why aren't you like Margot?"

Margot (*protesting*). Oh, come on, Anne, don't be so . . .

Anne (*paying no attention*). Everything she does is right, and everything I do is wrong! I'm the goat around here! . . . You're all against me! . . . And you worst of all!

[*She rushes off into her room and throws herself down on the settee, stifling her sobs.* MRS. FRANK *sighs and starts toward the stove.*]

Mrs. Frank (*to* MARGOT). Let's put the soup on the stove . . . if there's anyone who cares to eat. Margot, will you take the bread out? (MARGOT *gets the bread from the cupboard.*) I don't know how we can go on living this way. . . . I can't say a word to Anne . . . she flies at me . . .

Margot. You know Anne. In half an hour she'll be out here, laughing and joking.

Mrs. Frank. And . . . (*She makes a motion upwards, indicating the* VAN DAANS.) . . . I told your father it wouldn't work . . . but no . . . no . . . he had to ask them, he said . . . he owed it to him, he said. Well, he knows now that I was right! These quarrels! . . . This bickering!

Margot (*with a warning look*). Shush. Shush.

[*The buzzer of the door sounds.* MRS. FRANK *gasps, startled.*]

Mrs. Frank. Every time I hear that sound, my heart stops!

Margot (*starting for* PETER'*s door*). It's Miep. (*She knocks at the door.*) Father?

[MR. FRANK *comes quickly from* PETER'*s room.*]

Mr. Frank. Thank you, Margot. (*As he goes down the steps to open the outer door*) Has everyone his list?

Margot. I'll get my books. (*Giving her mother a list*) Here's your list. (MARGOT *goes into her and* ANNE'*s bedroom on the right.* ANNE *sits up, hiding her tears, as* MARGOT *comes in.*) Miep's here.

[MARGOT *picks up her books and goes back.* ANNE *hurries to the mirror, smoothing her hair.*]

Mr. Van Daan (*coming down the stairs*). Is it Miep?

Margot. Yes. Father's gone down to let her in.

Mr. Van Daan. At last I'll have some cigarettes!

Mrs. Frank (*to* MR. VAN DAAN). I can't tell you how unhappy I am about Mrs. Van Daan's coat. Anne should never have touched it.

Mr. Van Daan. She'll be all right.

Mrs. Frank. Is there anything I can do?

Mr. Van Daan. Don't worry.

[*He turns to meet* MIEP. *But it is not* MIEP *who comes up the steps. It is* MR. KRALER, *followed by* MR. FRANK. *Their faces are grave.* ANNE *comes from the bedroom.* PETER *comes from his room.*]

Mrs. Frank. Mr. Kraler!

Mr. Van Daan. How are you, Mr. Kraler?

Margot. This is a surprise.

Mrs. Frank. When Mr. Kraler comes, the sun begins to shine.

Mr. Van Daan. Miep is coming?

Mr. Kraler. Not tonight.

[KRALER *goes to* MARGOT *and* MRS. FRANK *and* ANNE, *shaking hands with them.*]

Mrs. Frank. Wouldn't you like a cup of coffee? . . . Or, better still, will you have supper with us?

Mr. Frank. Mr. Kraler has something to talk over with us. Something has happened, he says, which demands an immediate decision.

Mrs. Frank (*fearful*). What is it?

[MR. KRALER *sits down on the couch. As he talks he takes bread, cabbages, milk, etc., from his briefcase, giving them to* MARGOT *and* ANNE *to put away.*]

Mr. Kraler. Usually, when I come up here, I try to bring you some bit of good news. What's the use of telling you the bad news when there's nothing that you can do about it? But today something has happened. . . . Dirk . . . Miep's Dirk, you know, came to me just now. He tells me that he has a Jewish friend living near him. A dentist. He says he's in trouble. He begged me, could I do anything for this man? Could I find him a hiding

place? . . . So I've come to you. . . . I know it's a terrible thing to ask of you, living as you are, but would you take him in with you?

Mr. Frank. Of course we will.

Mr. Kraler (*rising*). It'll be just for a night or two . . . until I find some other place. This happened so suddenly that I didn't know where to turn.

Mr. Frank. Where is he?

Mr. Kraler. Downstairs in the office.

Mr. Frank. Good. Bring him up.

Mr. Kraler. His name is Dussel . . . Jan Dussel.[19]

Mr. Frank. Dussel . . . I think I know him.

Mr. Kraler. I'll get him.

[*He goes quickly down the steps and out.* MR. FRANK *suddenly becomes conscious of the others.*]

Mr. Frank. Forgive me. I spoke without consulting you. But I knew you'd feel as I do.

Mr. Van Daan. There's no reason for you to consult anyone. This is your place. You have a right to do exactly as you please. The only thing I feel . . . there's so little food as it is . . . and to take in another person . . .

[PETER *turns away, ashamed of his father.*]

Mr. Frank. We can stretch the food a little. It's only for a few days.

Mr. Van Daan. You want to make a bet?

Mrs. Frank. I think it's fine to have him. But, Otto, where are you going to put him? Where?

Peter. He can have my bed. I can sleep on the floor. I wouldn't mind.

Mr. Frank. That's good of you, Peter. But your room's too small . . . even for *you*.

Anne. I have a much better idea. I'll come in here with you and Mother, and Margot can take Peter's room and Peter can go in our room with Mr. Dussel.

Margot. That's right. We could do that.

Mr. Frank. No, Margot. You mustn't sleep in that room . . . neither you nor Anne. Mouschi has caught some rats in there. Peter's brave. He doesn't mind.

Anne. Then how about *this?* I'll come in here with you and Mother, and Mr. Dussel can have my bed.

---

19. **Jan Dussel** (yän´ doo´səl).

Mrs. Frank. No. No. *No!* Margot will come in here with us and he can have her bed. It's the only way. Margot, bring your things in here. Help her, Anne.

[MARGOT *hurries into her room to get her things.*]

Anne (*to her mother*). Why Margot? Why can't I come in here?

Mrs. Frank. Because it wouldn't be proper for Margot to sleep with a . . . Please, Anne. Don't argue. Please.

[ANNE *starts slowly away.*]

Mr. Frank (*to* ANNE). You don't mind sharing your room with Mr. Dussel, do you, Anne?

Anne. No. No, of course not.

Mr. Frank. Good. (ANNE *goes off into her bedroom, helping* MARGOT. MR. FRANK *starts to search in the cupboards.*) Where's the cognac?

Mrs. Frank. It's there. But, Otto, I was saving it in case of illness.

Mr. Frank. I think we couldn't find a better time to use it. Peter, will you get five glasses for me?

[PETER *goes for the glasses.* MARGOT *comes out of her bedroom, carrying her possessions, which she hangs behind a curtain in the main room.* MR. FRANK *finds the cognac and pours it into the five glasses that* PETER *brings him.* MR. VAN DAAN *stands looking on sourly.* MRS. VAN DAAN *comes downstairs and looks around at all the bustle.*]

Mrs. Van Daan. What's happening? What's going on?

Mr. Van Daan. Someone's moving in with us.

Mrs. Van Daan. In here? You're joking.

Margot. It's only for a night or two . . . until Mr. Kraler finds him another place.

Mr. Van Daan. Yeah! Yeah!

[MR. FRANK *hurries over as* MR. KRALER *and* DUSSEL *come up.* DUSSEL *is a man in his late fifties, meticulous, finicky . . . bewildered now. He wears a raincoat. He carries a briefcase, stuffed full, and a small medicine case.*]

Mr. Frank. Come in, Mr. Dussel.

Mr. Kraler. This is Mr. Frank.

Dussel. Mr. Otto Frank?

Mr. Frank. Yes. Let me take your things. (*He*

takes the hat and briefcase, but DUSSEL *clings to his medicine case.*) This is my wife Edith . . . Mr. and Mrs. Van Daan . . . their son, Peter . . . and my daughters, Margot and Anne.

[DUSSEL *shakes hands with everyone.*]

Mr. Kraler. Thank you, Mr. Frank. Thank you all. Mr. Dussel, I leave you in good hands. Oh . . . Dirk's coat.

[DUSSEL *hurriedly takes off the raincoat, giving it to* MR. KRALER. *Underneath is his white dentist's jacket, with a yellow Star of David on it.*]

Dussel (*to* MR. KRALER). What can I say to thank you . . . ?

Mrs. Frank (*to* DUSSEL). Mr. Kraler and Miep . . . They're our lifeline. Without them we couldn't live.

Mr. Kraler. Please. Please. You make us seem very heroic. It isn't that at all. We simply don't like the Nazis. (*To* MR. FRANK, *who offers him a drink*) No, thanks. (*Then going on*) We don't like their methods. We don't like . . .

Mr. Frank (*smiling*). I know. I know. "No one's going to tell us Dutchmen what to do with our damn Jews!"

Mr. Kraler (*to* DUSSEL). Pay no attention to Mr. Frank. I'll be up tomorrow to see that they're treating you right. (*To* MR. FRANK) Don't trouble to come down again. Peter will bolt the door after me, won't you, Peter?

Peter. Yes, sir.

Mr. Frank. Thank you, Peter. I'll do it.

Mr. Kraler. Good night. Good night.

Group. Good night, Mr. Kraler. We'll see you tomorrow, etc., etc.

[MR. KRALER *goes out with* MR. FRANK. MRS. FRANK *gives each one of the "grown-ups" a glass of cognac.*]

Mrs. Frank. Please, Mr. Dussel, sit down.

[MR. DUSSEL *sinks into a chair.* MRS. FRANK *gives him a glass of cognac.*]

Dussel. I'm dreaming. I know it. I can't believe my eyes. Mr. Otto Frank here! (*To* MRS. FRANK) You're not in Switzerland then? A woman told me . . . She said she'd gone to your house . . . the

"And now let's have a little drink to welcome Mr. Dussel."

door was open, everything was in disorder, dishes in the sink. She said she found a piece of paper in the wastebasket with an address scribbled on it . . . an address in Zurich.[20] She said you must have escaped to Zurich.

Anne. Father put that there purposely . . . just so people would think that very thing!

Dussel. And you've been *here* all the time?

Mrs. Frank. All the time . . . ever since July.

[ANNE *speaks to her father as he comes back.*]

Anne. It worked, Pim . . . the address you left! Mr. Dussel says that people believe we escaped to Switzerland.

Mr. Frank. I'm glad . . . And now let's have a little drink to welcome Mr. Dussel. (*Before they can drink,* MR. DUSSEL *bolts his drink.* MR. FRANK *smiles and raises his glass.*) To Mr. Dussel. Welcome. We're very honored to have you with us.

Mrs. Frank. To Mr. Dussel, welcome.

[*The* VAN DAANS *murmur a welcome. The "grown-ups" drink.*]

Mrs. Van Daan. Um. That was good.

Mr. Van Daan. Did Mr. Kraler warn you that you won't get much to eat here? You can imagine . . . three ration books among the seven of us . . . and now you make eight.

[PETER *walks away, humiliated. Outside a street organ is heard dimly.*]

Dussel (*rising*). Mr. Van Daan, you don't realize what is happening outside that you should warn me of a thing like that. You don't realize what's going on . . . (*As* MR. VAN DAAN *starts his characteristic pacing,* DUSSEL *turns to speak to the others.*) Right here in Amsterdam every day hundreds of Jews disappear. . . . They surround a block and search house by house. Children come home from school to find their parents gone. Hundreds are being deported[21] . . . people that you and I know . . . the Hallensteins . . . the Wessels . . .

---

20. **Zurich** (zoor′ik): Switzerland's largest city. Because Switzerland remained neutral during World War II, many refugees sought safety there.
21. **deported:** sent away. Jews were being sent to concentration camps in central and eastern Europe, where they were killed by the Nazis.

Mrs. Frank (*in tears*). Oh, no. No!

Dussel. They get their call-up notice . . . come to the Jewish theater on such and such a day and hour . . . bring only what you can carry in a rucksack. And if you refuse the call-up notice, then they come and drag you from your home and ship you off to Mauthausen. The death camp!

Mrs. Frank. We didn't know that things had got so much worse.

Dussel. Forgive me for speaking so.

Anne (*coming to* DUSSEL). Do you know the de Waals? . . . What's become of them? Their daughter Jopie and I are in the same class. Jopie's my best friend.

Dussel. They are gone.

Anne. Gone?

Dussel. With all the others.

Anne. Oh, no. Not Jopie!

[*She turns away, in tears.* MRS. FRANK *motions to* MARGOT *to comfort her.* MARGOT *goes to* ANNE, *putting her arms comfortingly around her.*]

Mrs. Van Daan. There were some people called Wagner. They lived near us . . . ?

Mr. Frank (*interrupting, with a glance at* ANNE). I think we should put this off until later. We all have many questions we want to ask. . . . But I'm sure that Mr. Dussel would like to get settled before supper.

Dussel. Thank you. I would. I brought very little with me.

Mr. Frank (*giving him his hat and briefcase*). I'm sorry we can't give you a room alone. But I hope you won't be too uncomfortable. We've had to make strict rules here . . . a schedule of hours . . . We'll tell you after supper. Anne, would you like to take Mr. Dussel to his room?

Anne (*controlling her tears*). If you'll come with me, Mr. Dussel?

[*She starts for her room.*]

Dussel (*shaking hands with each in turn*). Forgive me if I haven't really expressed my gratitude to all of you. This has been such a shock to me. I'd always thought of myself as Dutch. I was born in Holland. My father was born in Holland, and my grandfather. And now . . . after all these years . . . (*He breaks off*) If you'll excuse me.

[DUSSEL *gives a little bow and hurries off after* ANNE. MR. FRANK *and the others are subdued.*]

Anne (*turning on the light*). Well, here we are.

[DUSSEL *looks around the room. In the main room* MARGOT *speaks to her mother.*]

Margot. The news sounds pretty bad, doesn't it? It's so different from what Mr. Kraler tells us. Mr. Kraler says things are improving.

Mr. Van Daan. I like it better the way Kraler tells it.

[*They resume their occupations, quietly.* PETER *goes off into his room. In* ANNE's *room,* ANNE *turns to* DUSSEL.]

Anne. You're going to share the room with me.

Dussel. I'm a man who's always lived alone. I haven't had to adjust myself to others. I hope you'll bear with me until I learn.

Anne. Let me help you. (*She takes his briefcase.*) Do you always live all alone? Have you no family at all?

Dussel. No one.

[*He opens his medicine case and spreads his bottles on the dressing table.*]

Anne. How dreadful. You must be terribly lonely.

Dussel. I'm used to it.

Anne. I don't think I could ever get used to it. Didn't you even have a pet? A cat, or a dog?

Dussel. I have an allergy for fur-bearing animals. They give me asthma.

Anne. Oh, dear. Peter has a cat.

Dussel. Here? He has it here?

Anne. Yes. But we hardly ever see it. He keeps it in his room all the time. I'm sure it will be all right.

Dussel. Let us hope so.

[*He takes some pills to fortify himself.*]

Anne. That's Margot's bed, where you're going to sleep. I sleep on the sofa there. (*Indicating the clothes hooks on the wall*) We cleared these off for your things. (*She goes over to the window.*) The best part about this room . . . you can look down and see a bit of the street and the canal. There's a houseboat . . . you can see the end of it . . . a bargeman lives there with his family . . .

They have a baby and he's just beginning to walk and I'm so afraid he's going to fall into the canal some day. I watch him . . .

Dussel *(interrupting).* Your father spoke of a schedule.

Anne *(coming away from the window).* Oh, yes. It's mostly about the times we have to be quiet. And times for the w.c. You can use it now if you like.

Dussel *(stiffly).* No, thank you.

Anne. I suppose you think it's awful, my talking about a thing like that. But you don't know how important it can get to be, especially when you're frightened. . . . About this room, the way Margot and I did . . . she had it to herself in the afternoons for studying, reading . . . lessons, you know . . . and I took the mornings. Would that be all right with you?

Dussel. I'm not at my best in the morning.

Anne. You stay here in the mornings then. I'll take the room in the afternoons.

Dussel. Tell me, when you're in here, what happens to me? Where am I spending my time? In there, with all the people?

Anne. Yes.

Dussel. I see. I see.

Anne. We have supper at half past six.

Dussel *(going over to the sofa).* Then if you don't mind . . . I like to lie down quietly for ten minutes before eating. I find it helps the digestion.

Anne. Of course. I hope I'm not going to be too much of a bother to you. I seem to be able to get everyone's back up.

[DUSSEL *lies down on the sofa, curled up, his back to her.*]

Dussel. I always get along very well with children. My patients all bring their children to me, because they know I get on well with them. So don't you worry about that.

[ANNE *leans over him, taking his hand and shaking it gratefully.*]

Anne. Thank you. Thank you, Mr. Dussel.

[*The lights dim to darkness. The curtain falls on the scene.* ANNE's *voice comes to us faintly at first, and then with increasing power.*]

Anne's Voice. . . . And yesterday I finished Cissy Van Marxvelt's latest book. I think she is a first-class writer. I shall definitely let my children read her. Monday the twenty-first of September, nineteen-forty-two. Mr. Dussel and I had another battle yesterday. Yes, Mr. Dussel! According to him, nothing, I repeat . . . nothing, is right about me . . . my appearance, my character, my manners. While he was going on at me I thought . . . sometime I'll give you such a smack that you'll fly right up to the ceiling! Why is it that every grown-up thinks he knows the way to bring up children? Particularly the grown-ups that never had any. I keep wishing that Peter was a girl instead of a boy. Then I would have someone to talk to. Margot's a darling, but she takes everything too seriously. To pause for a moment on the subject of Mrs. Van Daan. I must tell you that her attempts to flirt with father are getting her nowhere. Pim, thank goodness, won't play.

[*As she is saying the last lines, the curtain rises on the darkened scene.* ANNE's *voice fades out.*]

Responding to the Play

Analyzing Act One, Scenes 1–3

Identifying Facts

1. This story is told in a **flashback.** That is, we start in 1945, when Mr. Frank returns to the hiding place. Then, as he looks at Anne's diary, the scene flashes back to 1942, when the diary was being written. Though many people seeing this play when it was first produced in 1955 would be familiar with the facts of Anne's world-famous diary, the playwrights could not count on this. And so they had to go through the usual process of supplying **exposition**—the **who? what?** and **where?** of the story. Explain what we learn about the people and their basic situation in Scene 1 and in the "voice over" reading of Anne's diary.

2. Scene 2 introduces seven of the characters who will live in the secret annex. Who are they? Why have the Franks taken in the Van Daans?

3. In Scene 2, Mr. Frank tells everyone the rules of their confinement—the steps they must take to achieve their goal, which is to remain undiscovered. What are these rules?

4. One of the basic principles of playwriting is to show the action, not to tell it. The playwrights immediately show us two of the rules of confinement being put into practice by the characters. Describe the two episodes. What effect do the rules have on the people involved?

5. Sounds from outside the secret annex play an important part in the play. Some remind us of ordinary life going on in the city. Others punctuate the scene with reminders of the danger outside. List four of the sounds heard so far. Explain whether each sound is pleasant or threatening.

6. Two of the play's characters live outside the secret annex and appear from time to time. Who are these characters? What important function do they perform?

7. Describe the new character introduced in Scene 3. How does Mr. Frank respond to him? How does Mr. Van Daan respond? What news does this person bring?

Interpreting Meanings

8. At the beginning of the play, in what order do the Franks arrive onstage? Why might the playwrights have arranged it this way?

9. Before Mrs. Van Daan has spoken, we are given a picture of her which lets us know what to expect of her. What is this picture? How does Mrs. Frank let us know her feelings about Mrs. Van Daan without saying a word?

10. In a play, we get to know the **characters** by watching what they do, by hearing what they say, and by observing the way other people respond to them. Using this information, describe your impression of Mr. Frank.

11. From what you see and hear of her in these first scenes, how would you **characterize** Anne?

12. What is Anne's attitude toward her mother? Toward her father? Toward Margot? What is Peter's attitude toward *his* father and mother? Do the feelings of these people seem familiar?

13. The story of a play usually follows the ups and downs of relationships. Describe how Anne and Peter "hit it off" in their first scene together. What kind gesture does Anne make? From what you have seen in other plays and movies, does it seem that Anne and Peter might fall in love?

14. In Scenes 2 and 3, how is the relationship between Anne and Peter progressing?

15. List the **conflicts** that have developed among the characters by Scene 3. Why are these conflicts dangerous for the people in the secret annex?

16. The basic situation of the play is desperate and grim, but Scenes 2 and 3 let us know that there is humor within the seriousness. Give two examples of the play's humor. How do these scenes make you feel?

Applying Meanings

17. What do you think of Mrs. Frank's comment to Anne: "You complain that I don't treat you like a grown-up. But when I do, you resent it."

18. How do you feel about these characters so far? Do you identify with any of them?

Scene 4

It is the middle of the night, several months later. The stage is dark except for a little light which comes through the skylight in PETER's *room.*

Everyone is in bed. MR. *and* MRS. FRANK *lie on the couch in the main room, which has been pulled out to serve as a makeshift double bed.*

MARGOT *is sleeping on a mattress on the floor in the main room, behind a curtain stretched across for privacy. The others are all in their accustomed rooms.*

From outside we hear two drunken soldiers singing "Lili Marlene." A girl's high giggle is heard. The sound of running feet is heard coming closer and then fading in the distance. Throughout the scene there is the distant sound of airplanes passing overhead.

A match suddenly flares up in the attic. We dimly see MR. VAN DAAN. *He is getting his bearings. He comes quickly down the stairs, and goes to the cupboard where the food is stored. Again the match flares up, and is as quickly blown out. The dim figure is seen to steal back up the stairs.*

There is quiet for a second or two, broken only by the sound of airplanes, and running feet on the street below.

Suddenly, out of the silence and the dark, we hear ANNE *scream.*

Anne (*screaming*). No! No! Don't . . . don't take me!

[*She moans, tossing and crying in her sleep. The other people wake, terrified.* DUSSEL *sits up in bed, furious.*]

Dussel. Shush! Anne! Anne, for God's sake, shush!

Anne (*still in her nightmare*). Save me! Save me!

[*She screams and screams.* DUSSEL *gets out of bed, going over to her, trying to wake her.*]

Dussel. For God's sake! Quiet! Quiet! You want someone to hear?

[*In the main room* MRS. FRANK *grabs a shawl and pulls it around her. She rushes in to* ANNE, *taking her in her arms.* MR. FRANK *hurriedly gets up,*

putting on his overcoat. MARGOT *sits up, terrified.* PETER's *light goes on in his room.*]

Mrs. Frank (*to* ANNE, *in her room*). Hush, darling, hush. It's all right. It's all right. (*Over her shoulder to* DUSSEL) Will you be kind enough to turn on the light, Mr. Dussel? (*Back to* ANNE) It's nothing, my darling. It was just a dream.

[DUSSEL *turns on the light in the bedroom.* MRS. FRANK *holds* ANNE *in her arms. Gradually* ANNE *comes out of her nightmare, still trembling with horror.* MR. FRANK *comes into the room, and goes quickly to the window, looking out to be sure that no one outside has heard* ANNE's *screams.* MRS. FRANK *holds* ANNE, *talking softly to her. In the main room* MARGOT *stands on a chair, turning on the center hanging lamp. A light goes on in the* VAN DAANS' *room overhead.* PETER *puts his robe on, coming out of his room.*]

Dussel (*to* MRS. FRANK, *blowing his nose*). Something must be done about that child, Mrs. Frank. Yelling like that! Who knows but there's somebody on the streets? She's endangering all our lives.

Mrs. Frank. Anne, darling.

Dussel. Every night she twists and turns. I don't sleep. I spend half my night shushing her. And now it's nightmares!

[MARGOT *comes to the door of* ANNE's *room, followed by* PETER. MR. FRANK *goes to them, indicating that everything is all right.* PETER *takes* MARGOT *back.*]

Mrs. Frank (*to* ANNE). You're here, safe, you see? Nothing has happened. (*To* DUSSEL) Please, Mr. Dussel, go back to bed. She'll be herself in a minute or two. Won't you, Anne?

Dussel (*picking up a book and a pillow*). Thank you, but I'm going to the w.c. The one place where there's peace!

[*He stalks out.* MR. VAN DAAN, *in underwear and trousers, comes down the stairs.*]

Mr. Van Daan (*to* DUSSEL). What is it? What happened?

Dussel. A nightmare. She was having a nightmare!

Mr. Van Daan. I thought someone was murdering her.

Dussel. Unfortunately, no.

[*He goes into the bathroom.* MR. VAN DAAN *goes back up the stairs.* MR. FRANK, *in the main room, sends* PETER *back to his own bedroom.*]

Mr. Frank. Thank you, Peter. Go back to bed.

[PETER *goes back to his room.* MR. FRANK *follows him, turning out the light and looking out the window. Then he goes back to the main room, and gets up on a chair, turning out the center hanging lamp.*]

Mrs. Frank (*to* ANNE). Would you like some water? (ANNE *shakes her head.*) Was it a very bad dream? Perhaps if you told me . . . ?
Anne. I'd rather not talk about it.
Mrs. Frank. Poor darling. Try to sleep then. I'll sit right here beside you until you fall asleep.

[*She brings a stool over, sitting there.*]

Anne. You don't have to.
Mrs. Frank. But I'd like to stay with you . . . very much. Really.
Anne. I'd rather you didn't.
Mrs. Frank. Good night, then. (*She leans down to kiss* ANNE. ANNE *throws her arm up over her face, turning away.* MRS. FRANK, *hiding her hurt, kisses* ANNE's *arm.*) You'll be all right? There's nothing that you want?
Anne. Will you please ask Father to come.
Mrs. Frank (*after a second*). Of course, Anne dear. (*She hurries out into the other room.* MR. FRANK *comes to her as she comes in*) Sie verlangt nach Dir![22]
Mr. Frank (*sensing her hurt*). Edith, *Liebe, schau . . .*[23]
Mrs. Frank. *Es macht nichts! Ich danke dem lieben Herrgott, dass sie sich wenigstens an Dich wendet, wenn sie Trost braucht! Geh hinein, Otto, sie ist ganz hysterisch vor Angst.*[24] (*As* MR. FRANK *hesitates*) *Geh zu ihr.*[25] (*He looks at her for a second and then goes to get a cup of water for* ANNE. MRS. FRANK *sinks down on the bed, her face in her hands, trying to keep from sobbing

---

22. *Sie . . . Dir!:* German for "She's asking for you."
23. *Liebe, schau . . . :* "Dear, look . . ."
24. *Es . . . Angst:* "It doesn't matter. I thank the dear Lord that at least she turns to you when she needs comfort. Go in to her, Otto, she's completely hysterical with fear."
25. *Geh zu ihr:* "Go to her."

aloud. MARGOT *comes over to her, putting her arms around her.*) She wants nothing of me. She pulled away when I leaned down to kiss her.
Margot. It's a phase . . . You heard Father . . . Most girls go through it . . . they turn to their fathers at this age . . . they give all their love to their fathers.
Mrs. Frank. You weren't like this. You didn't shut me out.
Margot. She'll get over it. . . .

[*She smooths the bed for* MRS. FRANK *and sits beside her a moment as* MRS. FRANK *lies down. In* ANNE's *room* MR. FRANK *comes in, sitting down by* ANNE. ANNE *flings her arms around him, clinging to him. In the distance we hear the sound of ack-ack.*]

Anne. Oh, Pim. I dreamed that they came to get us! The Green Police! They broke down the door and grabbed me and started to drag me out the way they did Jopie.
Mr. Frank. I want you to take this pill.
Anne. What is it?
Mr. Frank. Something to quiet you.

[*She takes it and drinks the water. In the main room* MARGOT *turns out the light and goes back to her bed.*]

Mr. Frank (*to* ANNE). Do you want me to read to you for a while?
Anne. No. Just sit with me for a minute. Was I awful? Did I yell terribly loud? Do you think anyone outside could have heard?
Mr. Frank. No. No. Lie quietly now. Try to sleep.
Anne. I'm a terrible coward. I'm so disappointed in myself. I think I've conquered my fear. . . . I think I'm really grown-up . . . and then something happens . . . and I run to you like a baby . . . I love you, Father. I don't love anyone but you.
Mr. Frank (*reproachfully*). Annele!
Anne. It's true. I've been thinking about it for a long time. You're the only one I love.
Mr. Frank. It's fine to hear you tell me that you love me. But I'd be happier if you said you loved your mother as well. . . . She needs you help so much . . . your love . . .
Anne. We have nothing in common. She doesn't understand me. Whenever I try to explain my

views on life to her she asks me if I'm constipated.

Mr. Frank. You hurt her very much just now. She's crying. She's in there crying.

Anne. I can't help it. I only told the truth. I didn't want her here. . . . *(Then, with sudden change)* Oh, Pim, I was horrible, wasn't I? And the worst of it is, I can stand off and look at myself doing it and know it's cruel and yet I can't stop doing it. What's the matter with me? Tell me. Don't say it's just a phase! Help me.

Mr. Frank. There is so little that we parents can do to help our children. We can only try to set a good example . . . point the way. The rest you must do yourself. You must build your own character.

Anne. I'm trying. Really I am. Every night I think back over all of the things I did that day that were wrong . . . like putting the wet mop in Mr. Dussel's bed . . . and this thing now with Mother. I say to myself, that was wrong. I make up my mind, I'm never going to do that again. Never! Of course I may do something worse . . . but at least I'll never do *that* again! . . . I have a nicer side, Father . . . a sweeter, nicer side. But I'm scared

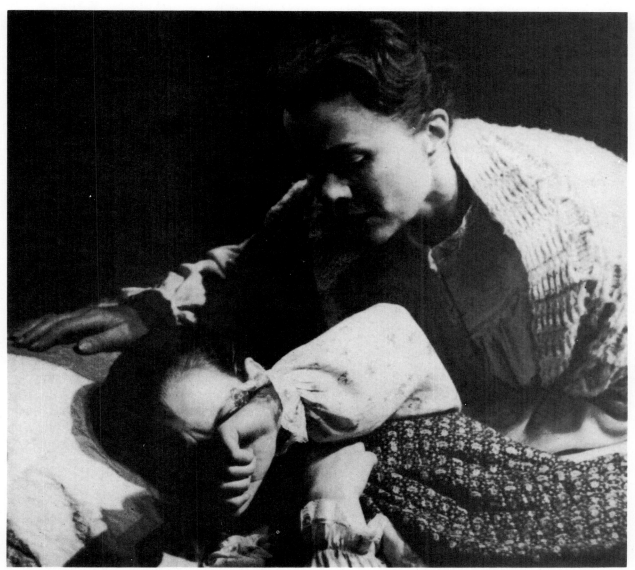

"You'll be all right? There's nothing that you want?"

to show it. I'm afraid that people are going to laugh at me if I'm serious. So the mean Anne comes to the outside and the good Anne stays on the inside, and I keep on trying to switch them around and have the good Anne outside and the bad Anne inside and be what I'd like to be . . . and might be . . . if only . . . only . . .

[*She is asleep.* MR. FRANK *watches her for a moment and then turns off the light, and starts out. The lights dim out. The curtain falls on the scene.* ANNE's *voice is heard dimly at first, and then with growing strength.*]

Anne's Voice. . . . The air raids are getting worse. They come over day and night. The noise is terrifying. Pim says it should be music to our ears. The more planes, the sooner will come the end of the war. Mrs. Van Daan pretends to be a fatalist. What will be, will be. But when the planes come over, who is the most frightened? No one else but Petronella! . . . Monday, the ninth of November, nineteen forty-two. Wonderful news! The Allies[26] have landed in Africa. Pim says that we can look for an early finish to the war. Just for fun he asked each of us what was the first thing we wanted to do when we got out of here. Mrs. Van Daan longs to be home with her own things, her needlepoint chairs, the Beckstein piano her father gave her . . . the best that money could buy. Peter would like to go to a movie. Mr. Dussel wants to get back to his dentist's drill. He's afraid he is losing his touch. For myself, there are so many things . . . to ride a bike again . . . to laugh till my belly aches . . . to have new clothes from the skin out . . . to have a hot tub filled to overflowing and wallow in it for hours . . . to be back in school with my friends . . .

[*As the last lines are being said, the curtain rises on the scene. The lights dim on as* ANNE's *voice fades away.*]

---

26. **Allies:** group of nations, including the United States, Great Britain, France, and the Soviet Union, that fought against Germany, Italy, and Japan (the Axis nations) during World War II.

Scene 5

It is the first night of the Hanukkah[27] celebration. MR. FRANK *is standing at the head of the table on which is the menorah.[28] He lights the shamas, or servant candle, and holds it as he says the blessing. Seated listening is all of the "family," dressed in their best. The men wear hats,* PETER *wears his cap.*

Mr. Frank (*reading from a prayer book*). "Praised be Thou, oh Lord our God, Ruler of the universe, who has sanctified us with Thy commandments and bidden us kindle the Hanukkah lights. Praised be Thou, oh Lord our God, Ruler of the universe, who has wrought wondrous deliverances for our fathers in days of old. Praised be Thou, oh Lord our God, Ruler of the universe, that Thou has given us life and sustenance and brought us to this happy season." (MR. FRANK *lights the one candle of the menorah as he continues.*) "We kindle this Hanukkah light to celebrate the great and wonderful deeds wrought through the zeal with which God filled the hearts of the heroic Maccabees, two thousand years ago. They fought against indifference, against tyranny and oppression, and they restored our Temple to us. May these lights remind us that we should ever look to God, whence cometh our help." Amen. (*Pronounced "o-mayn"*)

All. Amen.

[MR. FRANK *hands* MRS. FRANK *the prayer book.*]

Mrs. Frank (*reading*). "I lift up mine eyes unto the mountains, from whence cometh my help. My help cometh from the Lord who made heaven and earth. He will not suffer thy foot to be moved. He that keepeth thee will not slumber. He that keepeth Israel doth neither slumber nor sleep. The Lord is thy keeper. The Lord is thy shade upon thy right hand. The sun shall not smite thee by day, nor the moon by night. The Lord shall keep thee from all evil. He shall keep thy soul. The

---

27. **Hanukkah** (khä′nōō·kä′): a joyous eight-day Jewish holiday, usually in December, celebrating the rededication of the holy Temple in Jerusalem in 165 B.C. The Temple had been used by the Syrians to worship the god Zeus. The Maccabee family led a victorious Jewish rebellion against the Syrians.
28. **menorah** (mə·nō′rə): a candleholder that holds nine candles, eight candles for each night of Hanukkah and the shamas candle for lighting the others.

Lord shall guard thy going out and thy coming in, from this time forth and forevermore."[29] Amen.
All. Amen.

[MRS. FRANK *puts down the prayer book and goes to get the food and wine.* MARGOT *helps her.* MR. FRANK *takes the men's hats and puts them aside.*]

Dussel (*rising*). That was very moving.
Anne (*pulling him back*). It isn't over yet!
Mrs. Van Daan. Sit down! Sit down!
Anne. There's a lot more, songs and presents.
Dussel. Presents?
Mrs. Frank. Not this year, unfortunately.
Mrs. Van Daan. But always on Hanukkah everyone gives presents . . . everyone!
Dussel. Like our St. Nicholas's Day.[30]

[*There is a chorus of "no's" from the group.*]

Mrs. Van Daan. No! Not like St. Nicholas! What kind of a Jew are you that you don't know Hanukkah?
Mrs. Frank (*as she brings the food*). I remember particularly the candles . . . First one, as we have tonight. Then the second night you light two candles, the next night three . . . and so on until you have eight candles burning. When there are eight candles it is truly beautiful.
Mrs. Van Daan. And the potato pancakes.
Mr. Van Daan. Don't talk about them!
Mrs. Van Daan. I make the best *latkes*[31] you ever tasted!
Mrs. Frank. Invite us all next year . . . in your own home.
Mr. Frank. God willing!
Mrs. Van Daan. God willing.
Margot. What I remember best is the presents we used to get when we were little . . . eights days of presents . . . and each day they got better and better.
Mrs. Frank (*sitting down*). We are all here, alive. That is present enough.

---

29. Mrs. Frank is reading Psalm 121 from the Bible.
30. **St. Nicholas's Day** (December 6): a Christian holiday celebrated in the Netherlands by giving small gifts, especially to children.
31. *latkes* (lät′kəs): potato pancakes, a traditional Hanukkah food.

Anne. No, it isn't. I've got something . . .

[*She rushes into her room, hurriedly puts on a little hat improvised from the lampshade, grabs a satchel bulging with parcels and comes running back.*]

Mrs. Frank. What is it?
Anne. Presents!
Mrs. Van Daan. Presents!
Dussel. Look!
Mr. Van Daan. What's she got on her head?
Peter. A lampshade!
Anne (*she picks out one at random*). This is for Margot. (*She hands it to* MARGOT, *pulling her to her feet.*) Read it out loud.
Margot (*reading*).
  "You have never lost your temper.
  You never will, I fear,
  You are so good.
  But if you should,
  Put all your cross words here."

(*She tears open the package.*) A new crossword puzzle book! Where did you get it?
Anne. It isn't new. It's one that you've done. But I rubbed it all out, and if you wait a little and forget, you can do it all over again.
Margot (*sitting*). It's wonderful, Anne. Thank you. You'd never know it wasn't new.

[*From outside we hear the sound of a streetcar passing.*]

Anne (*with another gift*). Mrs. Van Daan.
Mrs. Van Daan (*taking it*). This is awful. . . . I haven't anything for anyone. . . . I never thought . . .
Mr. Frank. This is all Anne's idea.
Mrs. Van Daan (*holding up a bottle*). What is it?
Anne. It's hair shampoo. I took all the odds and ends of soap and mixed them with the last of my toilet water.
Mrs. Van Daan. Oh, Anneke!
Anne. I wanted to write a poem for all of them, but I didn't have time. (*Offering a large box to* MR. VAN DAAN) Yours, Mr. Van Daan, is *really* something . . . something you want more than anything. (*As she waits for him to open it*) Look! Cigarettes!

"Anneke . . . I wasn't supposed to have a present!"

Mr. Van Daan. Cigarettes!

Anne. Two of them! Pim found some old pipe tobacco in the pocket lining of his coat . . . and we made them . . . or rather, Pim did.

Mrs. Van Daan. Let me see. . . . Well, look at that! Light it, Putti! Light it.

[MR. VAN DAAN *hesitates*.]

Anne. It's tobacco, really it is! There's a little fluff in it, but not much.

[*Everyone watches intently as* MR. VAN DAAN *cautiously lights it. The cigarette flares up. Everyone laughs*.]

Peter. It works!

Mrs. Van Daan. Look at him.

Mr. Van Daan (*spluttering*). Thank you, Anne. Thank you.

[ANNE *rushes back to her satchel for another present*.]

Anne (*handing her mother a piece of paper*). For Mother, Hanukkah greeting.

[*She pulls her mother to her feet*.]

Mrs. Frank (*she reads*).
  "Here's an I.O.U. that I promise to pay.
  Ten hours of doing whatever you say.
  Signed, Anne Frank."

[MRS. FRANK, *touched, takes* ANNE *in her arms, holding her close*.]

Dussel (*to* ANNE). Ten hours of doing what you're told? *Anything* you're told?

Anne. That's right.

Dussel. You wouldn't want to sell that, Mrs. Frank?

Mrs. Frank. Never! This is the most precious gift I've ever had!

[*She sits, showing her present to the others*. ANNE *hurries back to the satchel and pulls out a scarf, the scarf that* MR. FRANK *found in the first scene*.]

Anne (*offering it to her father*). For Pim.

Mr. Frank. Anneke . . . I wasn't supposed to have a present!

[*He takes it, unfolding it and showing it to the others*.]

Anne. It's a muffler . . . to put round your neck . . . like an ascot, you know. I made it myself out of odds and ends . . . I knitted it in the dark each night, after I'd gone to bed. I'm afraid it looks better in the dark!

Mr. Frank (*putting it on*). It's fine. It fits me perfectly. Thank you, Annele.

[ANNE *hands* PETER *a ball of paper, with a string attached to it*.]

Anne. That's for Mouschi.

Peter (*rising to bow*). On behalf of Mouschi, I thank you.

Anne (*hesitant, handing him a gift*). And . . . this is yours . . . from Mrs. Quack Quack. (*As he holds it gingerly in his hands*) Well . . . open it . . . Aren't you going to open it?

Peter. I'm scared to. I know something's going to jump out and hit me.

Anne. No. It's nothing like that, really.

Mrs. Van Daan (*as he is opening it*). What is it, Peter? Go on. Show it.

Anne (*excitedly*). It's a safety razor!

Dussel. A what?

Anne. A razor!

Mrs. Van Daan (*looking at it*). You didn't make that out of odds and ends.

Anne (*to* PETER). Miep got it for me. It's not new. It's secondhand. But you really do need a razor now.

Dussel. For what?

Anne. Look on his upper lip . . . you can see the beginning of a mustache.

Dussel. He wants to get rid of that? Put a little milk on it and let the cat lick it off.

Peter (*starting for his room*). Think you're funny, don't you.

Dussel. Look! He can't wait! He's going in to try it!

Peter. I'm going to give Mouschi his present!

[*He goes into his room, slamming the door behind him*.]

Mr. Van Daan (*disgustedly*). Mouschi, Mouschi, Mouschi.

[*In the distance we hear a dog persistently barking*. ANNE *brings a gift to* DUSSEL.]

Anne. And last but never least, my roommate, Mr. Dussel.

Dussel. For me? You have something for me?

[*He opens the small box she gives him.*]

Anne. I made them myself.

Dussel (*puzzled*). Capsules! Two capsules!

Anne. They're earplugs!

Dussel. Earplugs?

Anne. To put in your ears so you won't hear me when I thrash around at night. I saw them advertised in a magazine. They're not real ones. . . . I made them out of cotton and candle wax. Try them. . . . See if they don't work . . . see if you can hear me talk . . .

Dussel (*putting them in his ears*). Wait now until I get them in . . . so.

Anne. Are you ready?

Dussel. Huh?

Anne. Are you ready?

Dussel. Good God! They've gone inside! I can't get them out! (*They laugh as* MR. DUSSEL *jumps about, trying to shake the plugs out of his ears. Finally he gets them out. Putting them away*) Thank you, Anne! Thank you!

Mr. Van Daan. A real Hanukkah! ⎤
Mrs. Van Daan. Wasn't it cute of her? ⎟
Mrs. Frank. I don't know when she ⎬ *Together*
did it. ⎟
Margot. I love my present. ⎦

Anne (*sitting at the table*). And now let's have the song, Father . . . please . . . (*To* DUSSEL) Have you heard the Hanukkah song, Mr. Dussel? The song is the whole thing! (*She sings*) "Oh, Hanukkah! Oh Hanukkah! The sweet celebration . . ."

Mr. Frank (*quieting her*). I'm afraid, Anne, we shouldn't sing that song tonight. (*To* DUSSEL) It's a song of jubilation, of rejoicing. One is apt to become too enthusiastic.

Anne. Oh, please, please. Let's sing the song. I promise not to shout!

Mr. Frank. Very well. But quietly now . . . I'll keep an eye on you and when . . .

[*As* ANNE *starts to sing, she is interrupted by* DUSSEL, *who is snorting and wheezing.*]

Dussel (*pointing to* PETER). You . . . You! (PETER *is coming from his bedroom, ostentatiously hold-*ing a bulge in his coat as if he were holding his cat, and dangling* ANNE's *present before it.*) How many times . . . I told you . . . Out! Out!

Mr. Van Daan (*going to* PETER). What's the matter with you? Haven't you any sense? Get that cat out of here.

Peter (*innocently*). Cat?

Mr. Van Daan. You heard me. Get it out of here!

Peter. I have no cat.

[*Delighted with his joke, he opens his coat and pulls out a bath towel. The group at the table laugh, enjoying the joke.*]

Dussel (*still wheezing*). It doesn't need to be the cat . . . his clothes are enough . . . when he comes out of that room . . .

Mr. Van Daan. Don't worry. You won't be bothered anymore. We're getting rid of it.

Dussel. At last you listen to me.

[*He goes off into his bedroom.*]

Mr. Van Daan (*calling after him*). I'm not doing it for you. That's all in your mind . . . all of it! (*He starts back to his place at the table.*) I'm doing it because I'm sick of seeing that cat eat all our food.

Peter. That's not true! I only give him bones . . . scraps . . .

Mr. Van Daan. Don't tell me! He gets fatter every day! Damn cat looks better than any of us. Out he goes tonight!

Peter. No! No!

Anne. Mr. Van Daan, you can't do that! That's Peter's cat. Peter loves that cat.

Mrs. Frank (*quietly*). Anne.

Peter (*to* MR. VAN DAAN). If he goes, I go.

Mr. Van Daan. Go! Go!

Mrs. Van Daan. You're not going and the cat's not going! Now please . . . this is Hanukkah . . . Hanukkah . . . this is the time to celebrate . . . What's the matter with all of you? Come on, Anne. Let's have the song.

Anne (*singing*). "On, Hanukkah! Oh, Hanukkah! The sweet celebration."

Mr. Frank (*rising*). I think we should first blow out the candle . . . then we'll have something for tomorrow night.

Margot. But, Father, you're supposed to let it burn itself out.

Mr. Frank. I'm sure that God understands shortages. (Before blowing it out) "Praised be Thou, oh Lord our God, who hast sustained us and permitted us to celebrate this joyous festival."

[He is about to blow out the candle when suddenly there is a crash of something falling below. They all freeze in horror, motionless. For a few seconds there is complete silence. MR. FRANK slips off his shoes. The others noiselessly follow his example. MR. FRANK turns out a light near him. He motions to PETER to turn off the center lamp. PETER tries to reach it, realizes he cannot and gets up on a chair. Just as he is touching the lamp he loses his balance. The chair goes out from under him. He falls. The iron lampshade crashes to the floor. There is a sound of feet below, running down the stairs.]

Mr. Van Daan (under his breath). God Almighty! (The only light left comes from the Hanukkah candle. DUSSEL comes from his room. MR. FRANK creeps over to the stairwell and stands listening. The dog is heard barking excitedly.) Do you hear anything?

Mr. Frank (in a whisper). No. I think they've gone.

Mrs. Van Daan. It's the Green Police. They've found us.

Mr. Frank. If they had, they wouldn't have left. They'd be up here by now.

Mrs. Van Daan. I know it's the Green Police. They've gone to get help. That's all. They'll be back!

Mr. Van Daan. Or it may have been the Gestapo,[32] looking for papers . . .

Mr. Frank (interrupting). Or a thief, looking for money.

Mrs. Van Daan. We've got to do something . . . Quick! Quick! Before they come back.

Mr. Van Daan. There isn't anything to do. Just wait.

[MR. FRANK holds up his hand for them to be quiet. He is listening intently. There is complete silence as they all strain to hear any sound from below. Suddenly ANNE begins to sway. With a low

cry she falls to the floor in a faint. MRS. FRANK goes to her quickly, sitting beside her on the floor and taking her in her arms.]

Mrs. Frank. Get some water, please! Get some water!

[MARGOT starts for the sink.]

Mr. Van Daan (grabbing MARGOT). No! No! No one's going to run the water!

Mr. Frank. If they've found us, they've found us. Get the water. (MARGOT starts again for the sink. MR. FRANK, getting a flashlight) I'm going down.

[MARGOT rushes to him, clinging to him. ANNE struggles to consciousness.]

Margot. No, Father, no! There may be someone there, waiting. . . . It may be a trap!

Mr. Frank. This is Saturday. There is no way for us to know what has happened until Miep or Mr. Kraler comes on Monday morning. We cannot live with this uncertainty.

Margot. Don't go, Father!

Mrs. Frank. Hush, darling, hush. (MR. FRANK slips quietly out, down the steps and out through the door below.) Margot! Stay close to me.

[MARGOT goes to her mother.]

Mr. Van Daan. Shush! Shush!

[MRS. FRANK whispers to MARGOT to get the water. MARGOT goes for it.]

Mrs. Van Daan. Putti, where's our money? Get our money. I hear you can buy the Green Police off, so much a head. Go upstairs quick! Get the money!

Mr. Van Daan. Keep still!

Mrs. Van Daan (kneeling before him, pleading). Do you want to be dragged off to a concentration camp? Are you going to stand there and wait for them to come up and get you? Do something, I tell you!

Mr. Van Daan (pushing her aside). Will you keep still!

[He goes over to the stairwell to listen. PETER goes to his mother, helping her up onto the sofa. There is a second of silence, then ANNE can stand it no longer.]

---

32. **Gestapo** (gə·stä′pō): Nazi secret police.

Anne. Someone go after Father! Make Father come back!

Peter (*starting for the door*). I'll go.

Mr. Van Daan. Haven't you done enough?

[*He pushes* PETER *roughly away. In his anger against his father* PETER *grabs a chair as if to hit him with it, then puts it down, burying his face in his hands.* MRS. FRANK *begins to pray softly.*]

Anne. Please, please, Mr. Van Daan. Get Father.

Mr. Van Daan. Quiet! Quiet!

[ANNE *is shocked into silence.* MRS. FRANK *pulls her closer, holding her protectively in her arms.*]

Mrs. Frank (*softly, praying*). "I lift up mine eyes unto the mountains, from whence cometh my help. My help cometh from the Lord who made heaven and earth. He will not suffer thy foot to be moved. . . . He that keepeth thee will not slumber . . ."

[*She stops as she hears someone coming. They all watch the door tensely.* MR. FRANK *comes quietly in.* ANNE *rushes to him, holding him tight.*]

Mr. Frank. It was a thief. That noise must have scared him away.

Mrs. Van Daan. Thank God.

Mr. Frank. He took the cash box. And the radio. He ran away in such a hurry that he didn't stop to shut the street door. It was swinging wide open. (*A breath of relief sweeps over him.*) I think it would be good to have some light.

Margot. Are you sure it's all right?

Mr. Frank. The danger has passed. (MARGOT *goes to light the small lamp.*) Don't be so terrified, Anne. We're safe.

Dussel. Who says the danger has passed? Don't you realize we are in greater danger than ever?

Mr. Frank. Mr. Dussel, will you be still?

[MR. FRANK *takes* ANNE *back to the table, making her sit down with him, trying to calm her.*]

Dussel (*pointing to* PETER). Thanks to this clumsy fool, there's someone now who knows we're up here! Someone now knows we're up here, hiding!

Mrs. Van Daan (*going to* DUSSEL). Someone knows we're here, yes. But who is the someone? A thief! A thief! You think a thief is going to go to the Green Police and say . . . I was robbing a place the other night and I heard a noise up over my head? You think a thief is going to do that?

Dussel. Yes. I think he will.

Mrs. Van Daan (*hysterically*). You're crazy!

[*She stumbles back to her seat at the table.* PETER *follows protectively pushing* DUSSEL *aside.*]

Dussel. I think some day he'll be caught and then he'll make a bargain with the Green Police . . . if they'll let him off, he'll tell them where some Jews are hiding!

[*He goes off into the bedroom. There is a second of appalled silence.*]

Mr. Van Daan. He's right.

Anne. Father, let's get out of here! We can't stay here now . . . Let's go . . .

Mr. Van Daan. Go! Where?

Mrs. Frank (*sinking into her chair at the table*). Yes. Where?

Mr. Frank (*rising, to them all*). Have we lost all faith? All courage? A moment ago we thought that they'd come for us. We were sure it was the end. But it wasn't the end. We're alive, safe. (MR. VAN DAAN *goes to the table and sits.* MR. FRANK *prays.*) "We thank Thee, oh Lord our God, that in Thy infinite mercy Thou hast again seen fit to spare us." (*He blows out the candle, then turns to* ANNE.) Come on, Anne. The song! Let's have the song! (*He starts to sing.* ANNE *finally starts falteringly to sing, as* MR. FRANK *urges her on. Her voice is hardly audible at first.*)

Anne (*singing*).
"Oh Hanukkah! Oh, Hanukkah!
The sweet . . . celebration . . ."

[*As she goes on singing, the others gradually join in, their voices still shaking with fear.* MRS. VAN DAAN *sobs as she sings.*]

Group.
"Around the feast . . . we . . . gather
In complete . . . jubilation . . .
Happiest of sea . . . sons
Now is here.
Many are the reasons for good cheer.

[DUSSEL *comes from the bedroom. He comes over to the table, standing beside* MARGOT, *listening to them as they sing.*]

"Together
We'll weather
Whatever tomorrow may bring.

[As they sing on with growing courage, the lights start to dim.]

"So hear us rejoicing
And merrily voicing
The Hanukkah song that we sing.
Hoy!

[The lights are out. The curtain starts slowly to fall.]

"Hear us rejoicing
And merrily voicing
The Hanukkah song that we sing."

[They are still singing, as the curtain falls.]

Curtain

Responding to the Play

Analyzing Act One, Scenes 4–5

Identifying Facts

1. According to the stage directions at the beginning of Scene 4, what does Mr. Van Daan do? Is his action explained?
2. Anne's nightmare in Scene 4 reveals tensions between Anne and two other members of the household. What is her nightmare? How does Mr. Dussel react to her terror?
3. When Mrs. Frank tries to comfort Anne, how does Anne respond to her? How does Mrs. Frank feel about Anne's response?
4. Later in this scene, what does Anne tell her father about the two sides of her personality? Why won't she show her sweeter side?
5. Describe what happens to interrupt the Hanukkah celebration in Scene 5. What does Peter do to make matters worse?
6. According to Dussel, how will this incident lead to their discovery by the police?

Interpreting Meanings

7. Anne is a **dynamic** character; that is, she changes during the course of the play. (A **static** character would remain pretty much the same.) Discuss one way in which Anne has changed during Act One. For example, after having hurt her mother badly in Scene 4, how does she change in Scene 5?
8. Drama thrives on **reversals.** Things appear to be going well for the characters; then suddenly things take a bad turn. Or, things look terrible, and suddenly good fortune arrives. Describe the reversal that is central to Scene 5. How did it make you feel?
9. There are many rituals in our lives: birthdays, wedding anniversaries, Christmas, Hanukkah. When we take part in these rituals, our awareness is heightened as we remember the past and look forward to the future. The theater often shows rituals being celebrated on stage. Discuss how the Hanukkah celebration contrasts with the harsh reality outside the hiding place. What is the mood of this Hanukkah scene?
10. During the dark days of World War II, when England stood alone against the Nazis, the English people found courage in these words of their Prime Minister, Winston Churchill: "We shall fight them on the beaches, we shall fight them on the landing grounds, we shall fight them in the fields and in the streets, we shall fight them in the hills, we shall never surrender." In what moment of this play does a group of people find courage in the words of a song? Can you think of other episodes from plays or movies (or real life) in which people face danger and summon up courage through speech or song?
11. Suppose you were watching this play in a theater. What questions would you have as the curtain comes down on Act One? Would you have certain expectations for Act Two?

"There is one great change, however. A change in myself. I read somewhere that girls of my age don't feel quite certain of themselves. . . ."

Act Two

Scene 1

In the darkness we hear ANNE's voice, *again reading from the diary.*

Anne's Voice. Saturday, the first of January, nineteen forty-four. Another new year has begun and we find ourselves still in our hiding place. We have been here now for one year, five months, and twenty-five days. It seems that our life is at a standstill.

[*The curtain rises on the scene. It is late afternoon. Everyone is bundled up against the cold. In the main room* MRS. FRANK *is taking down the laundry which is hung across the back.* MR. FRANK *sits in the chair down left, reading.* MARGOT *is lying on the couch with a blanket over her and the many-colored knitted scarf around her throat.* ANNE *is seated at the center table, writing in her diary.* PETER, MR. *and* MRS. VAN DAAN, *and* DUSSEL *are all in their own rooms, reading or lying down.*

As the lights dim on, ANNE's *voice continues, without a break.*]

Anne's Voice. We are all a little thinner. The Van Daans' "discussions" are as violent as ever. Mother still does not understand me. But then I don't understand her either. There is one great change, however. A change in myself. I read somewhere that girls of my age don't feel quite certain of themselves. That they become quiet within and begin to think of the miracle that is taking place in their bodies. I think that what is happening to me is wonderful . . . not only what can be seen, but what is taking place inside. Each time it has happened I have a feeling that I have a sweet secret. (*We hear the chimes and then a hymn being played on the carillon outside.*) And in spite of any pain, I long for the time when I shall feel that secret within me again.

[*The buzzer of the door below suddenly sounds. Everyone is startled,* MR. FRANK *tiptoes cautiously to the top of the steps and listens. Again the buzzer sounds, in* MIEP's *V-for-Victory signal.[1]*]

---

1. **V-for-Victory signal:** three short rings and one long ring, Morse code for the letter *V*, the Allied symbol for victory.

Mr. Frank. It's Miep!

[*He goes quickly down the steps to unbolt the door.* MRS. FRANK *calls upstairs to the* VAN DAANS *and then to* PETER.]

Mrs. Frank. Wake up, everyone! Miep is here! (ANNE *quickly puts her diary away.* MARGOT *sits up, pulling the blanket around her shoulders.* MR. DUSSEL *sits on the edge of the bed, listening, disgruntled.* MIEP *comes up the steps, followed by* MR. KRALER. *They being flowers, books, newspapers, etc.* ANNE *rushes to* MIEP, *throwing her arms affectionately around her.*) Miep . . . and Mr. Kraler . . . What a delightful surprise!

Mr. Kraler. We came to bring you New Year's greetings.

Mrs. Frank. You shouldn't . . . you should have at least one day to yourselves.

[*She goes quickly to the stove and brings down teacups and tea for all of them.*]

Anne. Don't say that, it's so wonderful to see them! (*Sniffing at* MIEP's *coat*) I can smell the wind and the cold on your clothes.

Miep (*giving her the flowers*). There you are. (*Then to* MARGOT, *feeling her forehead*) How are you, Margot? . . . Feeling any better?

Margot. I'm all right.

Anne. We filled her full of every kind of pill so she won't cough and make a noise.

[*She runs into her room to put the flowers in water.* MR. *and* MRS. VAN DAAN *come from upstairs. Outside there is the sound of a band playing.*]

Mrs. Van Daan. Well, hello, Miep. Mr. Kraler.

Mr. Kraler (*giving a bouquet of flowers to* MRS. VAN DAAN). With my hope for peace in the New Year.

Peter (*anxiously*). Miep, have you seen Mouschi? Have you seen him anywhere around?

Miep. I'm sorry, Peter. I asked everyone in the neighborhood had they seen a gray cat. But they said no.

[MRS. FRANK *gives* MIEP *a cup of tea.* MR. FRANK *comes up the steps, carrying a small cake on a plate.*]

Mr. Frank. Look what Miep's brought for us!

Mrs. Frank (*taking it*). A cake!

Mr. Van Daan. A cake! (*He pinches* MIEP'S *cheeks gaily and hurries up to the cupboard.*) I'll get some plates.

[DUSSEL, *in his room, hastily puts a coat on and starts out to join the others.*]

Mrs. Frank. Thank you, Miepia. You shouldn't have done it. You must have used all of your sugar ration for weeks. (*Giving it to* MRS. VAN DAAN) It's beautiful, isn't it?

Mrs. Van Daan. It's been ages since I even saw a cake. Not since you brought us one last year. (*Without looking at the cake, to* MIEP) Remember? Don't you remember, you gave us one on New Year's Day? Just this time last year? I'll never forget it because you had "Peace in nineteen forty-three" on it. (*She looks at the cake and reads.*) "Peace in nineteen forty-four!"

Miep. Well, it has to come sometime, you know. (*As* DUSSEL *comes from his room*) Hello, Mr. Dussel.

Mr. Kraler. How are you?

Mr. Van Daan (*bringing plates and a knife*). Here's the knife, *liefje*. Now, how many of us are there?

Miep. None for me, thank you.

Mr. Frank. Oh, please. You must.

Miep. I couldn't.

Mr. Van Daan. Good! That leaves one . . . two . . . three . . . seven of us.

Dussel. Eight! Eight! It's the same number as it always is!

Mr. Van Daan. I left Margot out. I take it for granted Margot won't eat any.

Anne. Why wouldn't she!

Mrs. Frank. I think it won't harm her.

Mr. Van Daan. All right! All right! I just didn't want her to start coughing again, that's all.

Dussel. And please, Mrs. Frank should cut the cake.

Mr. Van Daan. What's the difference?

Mrs. Van Daan. It's not Mrs. Frank's } *Together* cake, is it, Miep? It's for all of us.

Dussel. Mrs. Frank divides things better.

Mrs. Van Daan (*going to* DUSSEL). What are you trying to say?

Mr. Van Daan. Oh, come on! Stop } *Together* wasting time!

Mrs. Van Daan (*to* DUSSEL). Don't I always give everybody exactly the same? Don't I?

Mr. Van Daan. Forget it, Kerli.

Mrs. Van Daan. No. I want an answer! Don't I?

Dussel. Yes. Yes. Everybody gets exactly the same . . . except Mr. Van Daan always gets a little bit more.

[VAN DAAN *advances on* DUSSEL, *the knife still in his hand.*]

Mr. Van Daan. That's a lie!

[DUSSEL *retreats before the onslaught of the* VAN DAANS.]

Mr. Frank. Please, please! (*Then to* MIEP) You see what a little sugar cake does to us? It goes right to our heads!

Mr. Van Daan (*handing* MRS. FRANK *the knife*). Here you are, Mrs. Frank.

Mrs. Frank. Thank you. (*Then to* MIEP *as she goes to the table to cut the cake*) Are you sure you won't have some?

Miep (*drinking her tea*). No, really, I have to go in a minute.

[*The sound of the band fades out in the distance.*]

Peter (*to* MIEP). Maybe Mouschi went back to our house . . . they say that cats . . . Do you ever get over there . . . ? I mean . . . do you suppose you could . . . ?

Miep. I'll try, Peter. The first minute I get I'll try. But I'm afraid, with him gone a week . . .

Dussel. Make up your mind, already someone has had a nice big dinner from that cat!

[PETER *is furious, inarticulate. He starts toward* DUSSEL *as if to hit him.* MR. FRANK *stops him.* MRS. FRANK *speaks quickly to ease the situation.*]

Mrs. Frank (*to* MIEP). This is delicious, Miep!

Mrs. Van Daan (*eating hers*). Delicious!

Mr. Van Daan (*finishing it in one gulp*). Dirk's in luck to get a girl who can bake like this!

Miep (*putting down her empty teacup*). I have to run. Dirk's taking me to a party tonight.

Anne. How heavenly! Remember now what everyone is wearing, and what you have to eat and everything, so you can tell us tomorrow.

Miep. I'll give you a full report! Goodbye, everyone!

Mr. Van Daan (to MIEP). Just a minute. There's something I'd like you to do for me.

[*He hurries off up the stairs to his room.*]

Mrs. Van Daan (*sharply*). Putti, where are you going? (*She rushes up the stairs after him, calling hysterically.*) What do you want? Putti, what are you going to do?

Miep (*to* PETER). What's wrong?

Peter (*his sympathy is with his mother*). Father says he's going to sell her fur coat. She's crazy about that old fur coat.

Dussel. Is it possible? Is it possible that anyone is so silly as to worry about a fur coat in times like this?

Peter. It's none of your darn business . . . and if you say one more thing . . . I'll, I'll take you and I'll . . . I mean it . . . I'll . . .

[*There is a piercing scream from* MRS. VAN DAAN *above. She grabs at the fur coat as* MR. VAN DAAN *is starting downstairs with it.*]

Mrs. Van Daan. No! No! No! Don't you dare take that! You hear? It's mine! (*Downstairs* PETER *turns away, embarrassed, miserable.*) My father gave me that! You didn't give it to me. You have no right. Let go of it . . . you hear?

[MR. VAN DAAN *pulls the coat from her hands and hurries downstairs.* MRS. VAN DAAN *sinks to the floor, sobbing. As* MR. VAN DAAN *comes into the main room the others look away, embarrassed for him.*]

Mr. Van Daan (*to* MR. KRALER). Just a little— discussion over the advisability of selling this coat. As I have often reminded Mrs. Van Daan, it's very selfish of her to keep it when people outside are in such desperate need of clothing. . . . (*He gives the coat to* MIEP.) So if you will please to sell it for us? It should fetch a good price. And by the way, will you get me cigarettes. I don't care what kind they are, get all you can.

Miep. It's terribly difficult to get them, Mr. Van Daan. But I'll try. Goodbye.

[*She goes.* MR. FRANK *follows her down the steps to bolt the door after her.* MRS. FRANK *gives* MR. KRALER *a cup of tea.*]

Mrs. Frank. Are you sure you won't have some cake, Mr. Kraler?

Mr. Kraler. I'd better not.

Mr. Van Daan. You're still feeling badly? What does your doctor say?

Mr. Kraler. I haven't been to him.

Mrs. Frank. Now, Mr. Kraler! . . .

Mr. Kraler (*sitting at the table*). Oh, I tried. But you can't get near a doctor these days . . . they're so busy. After weeks I finally managed to get one on the telephone. I told him I'd like an appointment . . . I wasn't feeling very well. You know what he answers . . . over the telephone . . . Stick out your tongue! (*They laugh. He turns to* MR. FRANK *as* MR. FRANK *comes back.*) I have some contracts here. . . . I wonder if you'd look over them with me. . . .

Mr. Frank (*putting out his hand*). Of course.

Mr. Kraler (*he rises*). If we could go downstairs . . . (MR. FRANK *starts ahead,* MR. KRALER *speaks to the others.*) Will you forgive us? I won't keep him but a minute.

[*He starts to follow* MR. FRANK *down the steps.*]

Margot (*with sudden foreboding*). What's happened? Something's happened! Hasn't it, Mr. Kraler?

[MR. KRALER *stops and comes back, trying to reassure* MARGOT *with a pretense of casualness.*]

Mr. Kraler. No, really. I want your father's advice . . .

Margot. Something's gone wrong! I know it!

Mr. Frank (*coming back, to* MR. KRALER). If it's something that concerns us here, it's better that we all hear it.

Mr. Kraler (*turning to him, quietly*). But . . . the children . . . ?

Mr. Frank. What they'd imagine would be worse than any reality.

[*As* MR. KRALER *speaks, they all listen with intense apprehension.* MRS. VAN DAAN *comes down the stairs and sits on the bottom step.*]

Mr. Kraler. It's a man in the storeroom . . . I don't know whether or not you remember him . . . Carl, about fifty, heavy-set, nearsighted . . . He came with us just before you left.

Mr. Frank. He was from Utrecht?

Mr. Kraler. That's the man. A couple of weeks ago, when I was in the storeroom, he closed the door and asked me . . . how's Mr. Frank? What do you hear from Mr. Frank? I told him I only knew there was a rumor that you were in Switzerland. He said he'd heard that rumor too, but he thought I might know something more. I didn't pay any attention to it . . . but then a thing happened yesterday. . . . He'd brought some invoices to the office for me to sign. As I was going through them, I looked up. He was standing staring at the bookcase . . . your bookcase. He said he thought he remembered a door there. . . . Wasn't there a door there that used to go up to the loft? Then he told me he wanted more money. Twenty guilders[2] more a week.

Mr. Van Daan. Blackmail!

Mr. Frank. Twenty guilders? Very modest blackmail.

Mr. Van Daan. That's just the beginning.

Dussel (coming to MR. FRANK). You know what I think? He was the thief who was down there that night. That's how he knows we're here.

Mr. Frank (to MR. KRALER). How was it left? What did you tell him?

Mr. Kraler. I said I had to think about it. What shall I do? Pay him the money? . . . Take a chance on firing him . . . or what? I don't know.

Dussel (frantic). For God's sake don't fire him! Pay him what he asks . . . keep him here where you can have your eye on him.

Mr. Frank. Is it so much that he's asking? What are they paying nowadays?

Mr. Kraler. He could get it in a war plant. But this isn't a war plant. Mind you, I don't know if he really knows . . . or if he doesn't know.

Mr. Frank. Offer him half. Then we'll soon find out if it's blackmail or not.

Dussel. And if it is? We've got to pay it, haven't we? Anything he asks we've got to pay!

Mr. Frank. Let's decide that when the time comes.

Mr. Kraler. This may be all my imagination. You get to a point, these days, where you suspect everyone and everything. Again and again . . . on some simple look or word, I've found myself . . .

[*The telephone rings in the office below.*]

Mrs. Van Daan (hurrying to MR. KRALER). There's the telephone! What does that mean, the telephone ringing on a holiday?

Mr. Kraler. That's my wife. I told her I had to go over some papers in my office . . . to call me there when she got out of church. (He starts out.) I'll offer him half then. Goodbye . . . we'll hope for the best!

[*The group call their goodbye's half-heartedly.* MR. FRANK *follows* MR. KRALER, *to bolt the door below. During the following scene,* MR. FRANK *comes back up and stands listening, disturbed.*]

Dussel (to MR. VAN DAAN). You can thank your son for this . . . smashing the light! I tell you, it's just a question of time now.

[*He goes to the window at the back and stands looking out.*]

Margot. Sometimes I wish the end would come . . . whatever it is.

Mrs. Frank (shocked). Margot!

[ANNE *goes to* MARGOT, *sitting beside her on the couch with her arms around her.*]

Margot. Then at least we'd know where we were.

Mrs. Frank. You should be ashamed of yourself! Talking that way! Think how lucky we are! Think of the thousands dying in the war, every day. Think of the people in concentration camps.

Anne (interrupting). What's the good of that? What's the good of thinking of misery when you're already miserable? That's stupid!

Mrs. Frank. Anne!

[*As* ANNE *goes on raging at her mother,* MRS. FRANK *tries to break in, in an effort to quiet her.*]

Anne. We're young, Margot and Peter and I! You grown-ups have had your chance! But look at us. . . . If we begin thinking of all the horror in the world, we're lost! We're trying to hold onto some kind of ideals . . . when everything . . . ideals, hopes . . . everything, are being destroyed! It isn't our fault that the world is in such a mess! We

---

2. **guilders** (gil′dərz): Dutch money. In 1944, twenty guilders would have been worth about five dollars.

weren't around when all this started! So don't try to take it out on us!

[*She rushes off to her room, slamming the door after her. She picks up a brush from the chest and hurls it to the floor. Then she sits on the settee, trying to control her anger.*]

Mr. Van Daan. She talks as if we started the war! Did we start the war?

[*He spots* ANNE*'s cake. As he starts to take it,* PETER *anticipates him.*]

Peter. She left her cake. (*He starts for* ANNE*'s room with the cake. There is silence in the main room.* MRS. VAN DAAN *goes up to her room, followed by* VAN DAAN. DUSSEL *stays looking out the window.* MR. FRANK *brings* MRS. FRANK *her cake. She eats it slowly, without relish.* MR. FRANK *takes his cake to* MARGOT *and sits quietly on the sofa beside her.* PETER *stands in the doorway of* ANNE*'s darkened room, looking at her, then makes a little movement to let her know he is there.* ANNE *sits up, quickly, trying to hide the signs of her tears.* PETER *holds out the cake to her.*) You left this.
Anne (*dully*). Thanks.

[PETER *starts to go out, then comes back.*]

Peter. I thought you were fine just now. You know just how to talk to them. You know just how to say it. I'm no good . . . I never can think . . . especially when I'm mad . . . That Dussel . . . when he said that about Mouschi . . . someone eating him . . . all I could think is . . . I wanted to hit him. I wanted to give him such a . . . a . . . that he'd . . . That's what I used to do when there was an argument at school. . . . That's the way I . . . but here . . . And an old man like that . . . it wouldn't be so good.
Anne. You're making a big mistake about me. I do it all wrong. I say too much. I go too far. I hurt people's feelings. . . .

[DUSSEL *leaves the window, going to his room.*]

Peter. I think you're just fine . . . What I want to say . . . if it wasn't for you around here, I don't know. What I mean . . .

[PETER *is interrupted by* DUSSEL*'s turning on the light.* DUSSEL *stands in the doorway, startled to see* PETER. PETER *advances toward him forbiddingly.* DUSSEL *backs out of the room.* PETER *closes the door on him.*]

Anne. Do you mean it, Peter? Do you really mean it?
Peter. I said it, didn't I?
Anne. Thank you, Peter!

[*In the main room* MR. *and* MRS. FRANK *collect the dishes and take them to the sink, washing them.* MARGOT *lies down again on the couch.* DUSSEL, *lost, wanders into* PETER*'s room and takes up a book, starting to read.*]

Peter (*looking at the photographs on the wall*). You've got quite a collection.
Anne. Wouldn't you like some in your room? I could give you some. Heaven knows you spend enough time in there . . . doing heaven knows what . . .
Peter. It's easier. A fight starts, or an argument . . . I duck in there.
Anne. You're lucky, having a room to go to. His lordship is always here . . . I hardly ever get a minute alone. When they start in on me, I can't duck away. I have to stand there and take it.
Peter. You gave some of it back just now.
Anne. I get so mad. They've formed their opinions . . . about everything . . . but we . . . we're still trying to find out . . . We have problems here that no other people our age have ever had. And just as you think you've solved them, something comes along and bang! You have to start all over again.
Peter. At least you've got someone you can talk to.
Anne. Not really. Mother . . . I never discuss anything serious with her. She doesn't understand. Father's all right. We can talk about everything . . . everything but one thing. Mother. He simply won't talk about her. I don't think you can be really intimate with anyone if he holds something back, do you?
Peter. I think your father's fine.
Anne. Oh, he is, Peter! He is! He's the only one who's ever given me the feeling that I have any sense. But anyway, nothing can take the place of

school and play and friends of your own age . . . or near your age . . . can it?

Peter. I suppose you miss your friends and all.

Anne. It isn't just . . . (*She breaks off, staring up at him for a second.*) Isn't it funny, you and I? Here we've been seeing each other every minute for almost a year and a half, and this is the first time we've ever really talked. It helps a lot to have someone to talk to, don't you think? It helps you to let off steam.

Peter (*going to the door*). Well, any time you want to let off steam, you can come into my room.

Anne (*following him*). I can get up an awful lot of steam. You'll have to be careful how you say that.

Peter. It's all right with me.

Anne. Do you mean it?

Peter. I said it, didn't I?

[*He goes out.* ANNE *stands in her doorway looking after him. As* PETER *gets to his door he stands for a minute looking back at her. Then he goes into his room.* DUSSEL *rises as he comes in, and quickly passes him, going out. He starts across for his room.* ANNE *sees him coming, and pulls her door shut.* DUSSEL *turns back toward* PETER's *room.* PETER *pulls his door shut.* DUSSEL *stands there, bewildered, forlorn.*

The scene slowly dims out. The curtain falls on the scene. ANNE's *voice comes over in the darkness . . . faintly at first, and then with growing strength.*]

Anne's Voice. We've had bad news. The people from whom Miep got our ration books have been arrested. So we have had to cut down on our food. Our stomachs are so empty that they rumble and make strange noises, all in different keys. Mr. Van Daan's is deep and low, like a bass fiddle. Mine is high, whistling like a flute. As we all sit around waiting for supper, it's like an orchestra tuning up. It only needs Toscanini[3] to raise his baton and we'd be off in the Ride of the Valkyries.[4] Monday, the sixth of March, nineteen forty-four. Mr. Kraler is in the hospital. It seems he has ulcers. Pim says

we are his ulcers. Miep has to run the business and us too. The Americans have landed on the southern tip of Italy. Father looks for a quick finish to the war. Mr. Dussel is waiting every day for the warehouse man to demand more money. Have I been skipping too much from one subject to another? I can't help it. I feel that spring is coming. I feel it in my whole body and soul. I feel utterly confused. I am longing . . . so longing . . . for everything . . . for friends . . . for someone to talk to . . . someone who understands . . . someone young, who feels as I do . . .

[*As these last lines are being said, the curtain rises on the scene. The lights dim on.* ANNE's *voice fades out.*]

Scene 2

It is evening, after supper. From outside we hear the sound of children playing. The "grown-ups," with the exception of MR. VAN DAAN, *are all in the main room.* MRS. FRANK *is doing some mending,* MRS. VAN DAAN *is reading a fashion magazine.* MR. FRANK *is going over business accounts.* DUSSEL, *in his dentist's jacket, is pacing up and down, impatient to get into his bedroom.* MR. VAN DAAN *is upstairs working on a piece of embroidery in an embroidery frame.*

In his room PETER *is sitting before the mirror, smoothing his hair. As the scene goes on, he puts on his tie, brushes his coat and puts it on, preparing himself meticulously for a visit from* ANNE. *On his wall are now hung some of* ANNE's *motion-picture stars.*

In her room ANNE *too is getting dressed. She stands before the mirror in her slip, trying various ways of dressing her hair.* MARGOT *is seated on the sofa, hemming a skirt for* ANNE *to wear.*

In the main room DUSSEL *can stand it no longer. He comes over, rapping sharply on the door of his and* ANNE's *bedroom.*

Anne (*calling to him*). No, no, Mr. Dussel! I am not dressed yet. (DUSSEL *walks away, furious, sitting down and burying his head in his hands.* ANNE *turns to* MARGOT.) How is that? How does that look?

Margot (*glancing at her briefly*). Fine.

Anne. You didn't even look.

---

3. **Toscanini** (tos′kə·nē′nē): Arturo Toscanini (1867–1957), a famous orchestra conductor.

4. **Ride of the Valkyries** (val·kir′ēz): a lively piece of music from an opera by the German composer Richard Wagner (1813–1883). The Valkyries were maidens in Norse mythology who escorted the souls of dead heroes slain in battle.

Margot. Of course I did. It's fine.

Anne. Margot, tell me, am I terribly ugly?

Margot. Oh, stop fishing.

Anne. No. No. Tell me.

Margot. Of course you're not. You've got nice eyes . . . and a lot of animation, and . . .

Anne. A little vague, aren't you?

[*She reaches over and takes a brassiere out of* MARGOT's *sewing basket. She holds it up to herself, studying the effect in the mirror. Outside,* MRS. FRANK, *feeling sorry for* DUSSEL, *comes over, knocking at the girls' door.*]

Mrs. Frank (*outside*). May I come in?

Margot. Come in, Mother.

Mrs. Frank (*shutting the door behind her*). Mr. Dussel's impatient to get in here.

Anne (*still with the brassiere*). Heavens, he takes the room for himself the entire day.

Mrs. Frank (*gently*). Anne, dear, you're not going in again tonight to see Peter?

Anne (*dignified*). That is my intention.

Mrs. Frank. But you've already spent a great deal of time in there today.

Anne. I was in there exactly twice. Once to get the dictionary, and then three-quarters of an hour before supper.

Mrs. Frank. Aren't you afraid you're disturbing him?

Anne. Mother, I have some intuition.

Mrs. Frank. Then may I ask you this much, Anne. Please don't shut the door when you go in.

Anne. You sound like Mrs. Van Daan!

[*She throws the brassiere back in* MARGOT's *sewing basket and picks up her blouse, putting it on.*]

Mrs. Frank. No. No. I don't mean to suggest anything wrong. I only wish that you wouldn't expose yourself to criticism . . . that you wouldn't give Mrs. Van Daan the opportunity to be unpleasant.

Anne. Mrs. Van Daan doesn't need an opportunity to be unpleasant!

Mrs. Frank. Everyone's on edge, worried about Mr. Kraler. This is one more thing . . .

Anne. I'm sorry, Mother. I'm gong to Peter's room. I'm not going to let Petronella Van Daan spoil our friendship.

[MRS. FRANK *hesitates for a second, then goes out, closing the door after her. She gets a pack of playing cards and sits at the center table, playing solitaire. In* ANNE's *room* MARGOT *hands the finished skirt to* ANNE. *As* ANNE *is putting it on,* MARGOT *takes off her high-heeled shoes and stuffs paper in the toes so that* ANNE *can wear them.*]

Margot (*to* ANNE). Why don't you two talk in the main room? It'd save a lot of trouble. It's hard on Mother, having to listen to those remarks from Mrs. Van Daan and not say a word.

Anne. Why doesn't she say a word? I think it's ridiculous to take it and take it.

Margot. You don't understand Mother at all, do you? She can't talk back. She's not like you. It's just not in her nature to fight back.

Anne. Anyway . . . the only one I worry about is you. I feel awfully guilty about you.

[*She sits on the stool near* MARGOT, *putting on* MARGOT's *high-heeled shoes.*]

Margot. What about?

Anne. I mean, every time I go into Peter's room, I have a feeling I may be hurting you. (MARGOT *shakes her head.*) I know if it were me, I'd be wild. I'd be desperately jealous, if it were me.

Margot. Well, I'm not.

Anne. You don't feel badly? Really? Truly? You're not jealous?

Margot. Of course I'm jealous . . . jealous that you've got something to get up in the morning for . . . But jealous of you and Peter? No.

[ANNE *goes back to the mirror.*]

Anne. Maybe there's nothing to be jealous of. Maybe he doesn't really like me. Maybe I'm just taking the place of his cat . . . (*She picks up a pair of short white gloves, putting them on.*) Wouldn't you like to come in with us?

Margot. I have a book.

[*The sound of the children playing outside fades out. In the main room* DUSSEL *can stand it no longer. He jumps up, going to the bedroom door and knocking sharply.*]

Dussel. Will you please let me in my room!

Anne. Just a minute, dear, dear Mr. Dussel. (*She*

picks up her mother's pink stole and adjusts it elegantly over her shoulders, then gives a last look in the mirror.) Well, here I go . . . to run the gauntlet.[5]

[*She starts out, followed by* MARGOT.]

Dussel (*as she appears—sarcastic*). Thank you so much.

[DUSSEL *goes into his room.* ANNE *goes toward* PETER's *room, passing* MRS. VAN DAAN *and her parents at the center table.*]

Mrs. Van Daan. My God, look at her! (ANNE *pays no attention. She knocks at* PETER's *door.*) I don't know what good it is to have a son. I never see him. He wouldn't care if I killed myself. (PETER *opens the door and stands aside for* ANNE *to come in.*) Just a minute, Anne. (*She goes to them at the door.*) I'd like to say a few words to my son. Do you mind? (PETER *and* ANNE *stand waiting.*) Peter, I don't want you staying up till all hours tonight. You've got to have your sleep. You're a growing boy. You hear?
Mrs. Frank. Anne won't stay late. She's going to bed promptly at nine. Aren't you, Anne?
Anne. Yes, Mother . . . (*To* MRS. VAN DAAN) May we go now?
Mrs. Van Daan. Are you asking me? I didn't know I had anything to say about it.
Mrs. Frank. Listen for the chimes, Anne dear.

[*The two young people go off into* PETER's *room, shutting the door after them.*]

Mrs. Van Daan (*to* MRS. FRANK). In my day it was the boys who called on the girls. Not the girls on the boys.
Mrs. Frank. You know how young people like to feel that they have secrets. Peter's room is the only place where they can talk.
Mrs. Van Daan. Talk! That's not what they called it when I was young.

[MRS. VAN DAAN *goes off to the bathroom.* MARGOT *settles down to read her book.* MR. FRANK *puts his papers away and brings a chess game to the center table. He and* MRS. FRANK *start to play.*]

---

5. **run the gauntlet** (gont'lit): here, face a difficult test in which criticism is expected from more than one direction.

In PETER's *room,* ANNE *speaks to* PETER, *indignant, humiliated.*]

Anne. Aren't they awful? Aren't they impossible? Treating us as if we were still in the nursery.

[*She sits on the cot.* PETER *gets a bottle of pop and two glasses.*]

Peter. Don't let it bother you. It doesn't bother me.
Anne. I suppose you can't really blame them . . . they think back to what *they* were like at our age. They don't realize how much more advanced we are. . . . When you think what wonderful discussions we've had! . . . Oh, I forgot. I was going to bring you some more pictures.
Peter. Oh, these are fine, thanks.
Anne. Don't you want some more? Miep just brought me some new ones.
Peter. Maybe later.

[*He gives her a glass of pop and, taking some for himself, sits down facing her.*]

Anne (*looking up at one of the photographs*). I remember when I got that. . . . I won it. I bet Jopie that I could eat five ice-cream cones. We'd all been playing ping-pong. . . . We used to have heavenly times . . . we'd finish up with ice cream at the Delphi, or the Oasis, where Jews were allowed . . . there'd always be a lot of boys . . . we'd laugh and joke . . . I'd like to go back to it for a few days or a week. But after that I know I'd be bored to death. I think more seriously about life now. I want to be a journalist . . . or something. I love to write. What do you want to do?
Peter. I thought I might go off some place . . . work on a farm or something . . . some job that doesn't take much brains.
Anne. You shouldn't talk that way. You've got the most awful inferiority complex.
Peter. I know I'm not smart.
Anne. That isn't true. You're much better than I am in dozens of things . . . arithmetic and algebra and . . . well, you're a million times better than I am in algebra. (*With sudden directness*) You like Margot, don't you? Right from the start you liked her, liked her much better than me.
Peter (*uncomfortably*). Oh, I don't know.

"I don't agree at all. I think you're pretty."

[*In the main room* MRS. VAN DAAN *comes from the bathroom and goes over to the sink, polishing a coffee pot.*]

Anne. It's all right. Everyone feels that way. Margot's so good. She's sweet and bright and beautiful and I'm not.

Peter. I wouldn't say that.

Anne. Oh, no, I'm not. I know that. I know quite well that I'm not a beauty. I never have been and never shall be.

Peter. I don't agree at all. I think you're pretty.

Anne. That's not true!

Peter. And another thing. You've changed . . . from at first, I mean.

Anne. I have?

Peter. I used to think you were awful noisy.

Anne. And what do you think now, Peter? How have I changed?

Peter. Well . . . er . . . you're . . . quieter.

[*In his room* DUSSEL *takes his pajamas and toilet articles and goes into the bathroom to change.*]

Anne. I'm glad you don't just hate me.

Peter. I never said that.

Anne. I bet when you get out of here you'll never think of me again.

Peter. That's crazy.

Anne. When you get back with all of your friends, you're going to say . . . now what did I ever see in that Mrs. Quack Quack.

Peter. I haven't got any friends.

Anne. Oh, Peter, of course you have. Everyone has friends.

Peter. Not me. I don't want any. I get along all right without them.

Anne. Does that mean you can get along without me? I think of myself as your friend.

Peter. No. If they were all like you, it'd be different.

[*He takes the glasses and the bottle and puts them away. There is a second's silence and then* ANNE *speaks, hesitantly, shyly.*]

Anne. Peter, did you ever kiss a girl?

Peter. Yes. Once.

Anne (*to cover her feelings*). That picture's crooked. (PETER *goes over, straightening the photograph*). Was she pretty?

Peter. Huh?

Anne. The girl that you kissed.

Peter. I don't know. I was blindfolded. (*He comes back and sits down again.*) It was at a party. One of those kissing games.

Anne (*relieved*). Oh. I don't suppose that really counts, does it?

Peter. It didn't with me.

Anne. I've been kissed twice. Once a man I'd never seen before kissed me on the cheek when he picked me up off the ice and I was crying. And the other was Mr. Koophuis, a friend of Father's who kissed my hand. You wouldn't say those counted, would you?

Peter. I wouldn't say so.

Anne. I know almost for certain that Margot would never kiss anyone unless she was engaged to them. And I'm sure too that Mother never touched a man before Pim. But I don't know . . . things are so different now . . . What do you think? Do you think a girl shouldn't kiss anyone except if she's engaged or something? It's so hard to try to think what to do, when here we are with the whole world falling around our ears and you think . . . well . . . you don't know what's going to happen tomorrow and . . . What do you think?

Peter. I suppose it'd depend on the girl. Some girls, anything they do's wrong. But others . . . well . . . it wouldn't necessarily be wrong with them. (*The carillon starts to strike nine o'clock.*) I've always thought that when two people . . .

Anne. Nine o'clock. I have to go.

Peter. That's right.

Anne (*without moving*). Good night.

[*There is a second's pause, then* PETER *gets up and moves toward the door.*]

Peter. You won't let them stop you coming?

Anne. No. (*She rises and starts for the door.*) Sometime I might bring my diary. There are so many things in it that I want to talk over with you. There's a lot about you.

Peter. What kind of thing?

Anne. I wouldn't want you to see some of it. I thought you were a nothing, just the way you thought about me.

Peter. Did you change your mind, the way I changed my mind about you?

Anne. Well . . . You'll see . . .

[*For a second* ANNE *stands looking up at* PETER, *longing for him to kiss her. As he makes no move she turns away. Then suddenly* PETER *grabs her awkwardly in his arms, kissing her on the cheek.* ANNE *walks out dazed. She stands for a minute, her back to the people in the main room. As she regains her poise she goes to her mother and father and* MARGOT, *silently kissing them. They murmur their good nights to her. As she is about to open her bedroom door, she catches sight of* MRS. VAN DAAN. *She goes quickly to her, taking her face in her hands and kissing her first on one cheek and then on the other. Then she hurries off into her room.* MRS. VAN DAAN *looks after her, and then looks over at* PETER's *room. Her suspicions are confirmed.*]

Mrs. Van Daan (*she knows*). Ah hah!

[*The lights dim out. The curtain falls on the scene. In the darkness* ANNE's *voice comes faintly at first and then with growing strength.*]

Anne's Voice. By this time we all know each other so well that if anyone starts to tell a story, the rest can finish it for him. We're having to cut down still further on our meals. What makes it worse, the rats have been at work again. They've carried off some of our precious food. Even Mr. Dussel wishes now that Mouschi were here. Thursday, the twentieth of April, nineteen forty-four. Invasion fever is mounting every day. Miep tells us that people outside talk of nothing else. For myself, life has become much more pleasant. I often go to Peter's room after supper. Oh, don't think I'm in love, because I'm not. But it does make life more bearable to have someone with whom you can exchange views. No more tonight. P.S. . . . I must be honest. I must confess that I actually live for the next meeting. Is there anything lovelier than to sit under the skylight and feel the sun on your cheeks and have a darling boy in your arms? I admit now that I'm glad the Van Daans had a son and not a daughter. I've outgrown another dress. That's the third. I'm having to wear Margot's clothes after all. I'm working hard on my French and am now reading *La Belle Nivernaise*.[6]

[*As she is saying the last lines, the curtain rises on the scene. The lights dim on, as* ANNE's *voice fades out.*]

Scene 3

It is night, a few weeks later. Everyone is in bed. There is complete quiet. In the VAN DAANS' *room a match flares up for a moment and then is quickly put out.* MR. VAN DAAN, *in bare feet, dressed in underwear and trousers, is dimly seen coming stealthily down the stairs and into the main room, where* MR. *and* MRS. FRANK *and* MARGOT *are sleeping. He goes to the food safe and again lights a match. Then he cautiously opens the safe, taking out a half-loaf of bread. As he closes the safe, it creaks. He stands rigid.* MRS. FRANK *sits up in bed. She sees him.*

Mrs. Frank *(screaming).* Otto! Otto! *Komme schnell!*[7]

[*The rest of the people wake, hurriedly getting up.*]

Mr. Frank. *Was ist los? Was ist passiert?*[8]

[DUSSEL, *followed by* ANNE, *comes from his room.*]

Mrs. Frank *(as she rushes over to* MR. VAN DAAN*).* *Er stiehlt das Essen!*[9]

---

6. *La Belle Nivernaise* (nē·ver·nes′): a novel by the French writer Alphonse Daudet (1840–1897).
7. *Komme schnell!:* Come quickly!
8. *Was . . . passiert?:* What's going on? What happened?
9. *Er . . . Essen!:* He is stealing the food!

Dussel *(grabbing* MR. VAN DAAN*).* You! You! Give me that.
Mrs. Van Daan *(coming down the stairs).* Putti . . . Putti . . . what is it?
Dussel *(his hands on* VAN DAAN's *neck).* You dirty thief . . . stealing food . . . you good-for-nothing . . .
Mr. Frank. Mr. Dussel! For God's sake! Help me, Peter!

[PETER *comes over, trying, with* MR. FRANK, *to separate the two struggling men.*]

Peter. Let him go! Let go!

[DUSSEL *drops* MR. VAN DAAN, *pushing him away. He shows them the end of a loaf of bread that he has taken from* VAN DAAN.]

Dussel. You greedy, selfish . . . !

[MARGOT *turns on the lights.*]

Mrs. Van Daan. Putti . . . what is it?

[*All of* MRS. FRANK's *gentleness, her self-control, is gone. She is outraged, in a frenzy of indignation.*]

Mrs. Frank. The bread! He was stealing the bread!
Dussel. It was you, and all the time we thought it was the rats!
Mr. Frank. Mr. Van Daan, how could you!
Mr. Van Daan. I'm hungry.
Mrs. Frank. We're all of us hungry! I see the children getting thinner and thinner. Your own son Peter . . . I've heard him moan in his sleep, he's so hungry. And you come in the night and steal food that should go to them . . . to the children!
Mrs. Van Daan *(going to* MR. VAN DAAN *protectively).* He needs more food than the rest of us. He's used to more. He's a big man.

[MR. VAN DAAN *breaks away, going over and sitting on the couch.*]

Mrs. Frank *(turning on* MRS. VAN DAAN*).* And you . . . you're worse than he is! You're a mother, and yet you sacrifice your child to this man . . . this . . . this . . .
Mr. Frank. Edith! Edith!

[MARGOT *picks up the pink woolen stole, putting it over her mother's shoulders*.]

Mrs. Frank (*paying no attention, going on to* MRS. VAN DAAN). Don't think I haven't seen you! Always saving the choicest bits for him! I've watched you day after day and I've held my tongue. But not any longer! Not after this! Now I want him to go! I want him to get out of here!

Mr. Frank. Edith!

Mr. Van Daan. Get out of here?   } *Together*

Mrs. Van Daan. What do you mean?

Mrs. Frank. Just that! Take your things and get out!

Mr. Frank (*to* MRS. FRANK). You're speaking in anger. You cannot mean what you are saying.

Mrs. Frank. I mean exactly that!

[MRS. VAN DAAN *takes a cover from the* FRANK'S *bed, pulling it about her*.]

Mr. Frank. For two long years we have lived here, side by side. We have respected each other's rights . . . we have managed to live in peace. Are we now going to throw it all away? I know this will never happen again, will it, Mr. Van Daan?

Mr. Van Daan. No. No.

Mrs. Frank. He steals once! He'll steal again!

[MR. VAN DAAN, *holding his stomach, starts for the bathroom.* ANNE *puts her arms around him, helping him up the step*.]

Mr. Frank. Edith, please. Let us be calm. We'll all go to our rooms . . . and afterwards we'll sit down quietly and talk this out . . . we'll find some way . . .

Mrs. Frank. No! No! No more talk! I want them to leave!

Mrs. Van Daan. You'd put us out, on the streets?

Mrs. Frank. There are other hiding places.

Mrs. Van Daan. A cellar . . . a closet. I know. And we have no money left even to pay for that.

Mrs. Frank. I'll give you money. Out of my own pocket I'll give it gladly.

[*She gets her purse from a shelf and comes back with it*.]

Mrs. Van Daan. Mr. Frank, you told Putti you'd never forget what he'd done for you when you came to Amsterdam. You said you could never repay him, that you . . .

Mrs. Frank (*counting out money*). If my husband had any obligation to you, he's paid it, over and over.

Mr. Frank. Edith, I've never seen you like this before. I don't know you.

Mrs. Frank. I should have spoken out long ago.

Dussel. You can't be nice to some people.

Mrs. Van Daan (*turning on* DUSSEL). There would have been plenty for all of us, if *you* hadn't come in here!

Mr. Frank. We don't need the Nazis to destroy us. We're destroying ourselves.

[*He sits down, with his head in his hands.* MRS. FRANK *goes to* MRS. VAN DAAN.]

Mrs. Frank (*giving* MRS. VAN DAAN *some money*). Give this to Miep. She'll find you a place.

Anne. Mother, you're not putting *Peter* out. Peter hasn't done anything.

Mrs. Frank. He'll stay, of course. When I say I must protect the children, I mean Peter too.

[PETER *rises from the steps where he has been sitting*.]

Peter. I'd have to go if Father goes.

[MR. VAN DAAN *comes from the bathroom.* MRS. VAN DAAN *hurries to him and takes him to the couch. Then she gets water from the sink to bathe his face*.]

Mrs. Frank (*while this is going on*). He's no father to you . . . that man! He doesn't know what it is to be a father!

Peter (*starting for his room*). I wouldn't feel right. I couldn't stay.

Mrs. Frank. Very well, then. I'm sorry.

Anne (*rushing over to* PETER). No, Peter! No! (PETER *goes into his room, closing the door after him.* ANNE *turns back to her mother, crying*.) I don't care about the food. They can have mine! I don't want it! Only don't send them away. It'll be daylight soon. They'll be caught . . .

Margot (*putting her arms comfortingly around* ANNE). Please, Mother!

Mrs. Frank. They're not going now. They'll stay here until Miep finds them a place. (*To* MRS. VAN DAAN) But one thing I insist on! He must never come down here again! He must never come to this room where the food is stored! We'll divide what we have . . . an equal share for each! (DUSSEL *hurries over to get a sack of potatoes from the food safe.* MRS. FRANK *goes on, to* MRS. VAN DAAN) You can cook it here and take it up to him.

[DUSSEL *brings the sack of potatoes back to the center table.*]

Margot. Oh, no. No. We haven't sunk so far that we're going to fight over a handful of rotten potatoes.

Dussel (*dividing the potatoes into piles*). Mrs. Frank, Mr. Frank, Margot, Anne, Peter, Mrs. Van Daan, Mr. Van Daan, myself . . . Mrs. Frank . . .

[*The buzzer sounds in* MIEP'*s signal.*]

Mr. Frank. It's Miep!

[*He hurries over, getting his overcoat and putting it on.*]

Margot. At this hour?
Mrs. Frank. It is trouble.
Mr. Frank (*as he starts down to unbolt the door*). I beg you, don't let her see a thing like this!
Dussel (*counting without stopping*). . . . Anne, Peter, Mrs. Van Daan, Mr. Van Daan, myself . . .
Margot (*to* DUSSEL). Stop it! Stop it!
Dussel. . . . Mr. Frank, Margot, Anne, Peter, Mrs. Van Daan, Mr. Van Daan, myself, Mrs. Frank . . .
Mrs. Van Daan. You're keeping the big ones for yourself! All the big ones . . . Look at the size of that! . . . And that! . . .

[DUSSEL *continues on with his dividing.* PETER, *with his shirt and trousers on, comes from his room.*]

Margot. Stop it! Stop it!

[*We hear* MIEP'*s excited voice speaking to* MR. FRANK *below.*]

Miep. Mr. Frank . . . the most wonderful news! . . . The invasion[10] has begun!
Mr. Frank. Go on, tell them! Tell them!

[MIEP *comes running up the steps, ahead of* MR. FRANK. *She has a man's raincoat on over her nightclothes and a bunch of orange-colored flowers in her hand.*]

Miep. Did you hear that, everybody? Did you hear what I said? The invasion has begun! The invasion!

[*They all stare at* MIEP, *unable to grasp what she is telling them.* PETER *is the first to recover his wits.*]

Peter. Where?
Mrs. Van Daan. When? When, Miep?
Miep. It began early this morning . . .

[*As she talks on, the realization of what she has said begins to dawn on them. Everyone goes crazy. A wild demonstration takes place.* MRS. FRANK *hugs* MR. VAN DAAN.]

Mrs. Frank. Oh, Mr. Van Daan, did you hear that? (DUSSEL *embraces* MRS. VAN DAAN. PETER *grabs a frying pan and parades around the room, beating on it, singing the Dutch National Anthem.* ANNE *and* MARGOT *follow him, singing, weaving in and out among the excited grown-ups.* MARGOT *breaks away to take the flowers from* MIEP *and distribute them to everyone. While this pandemonium is going on* MRS. FRANK *tries to make herself heard above the excitement. To* MIEP) How do you know?
Miep. The radio . . . The BBC![11] They said they landed on the coast of Normandy![12]
Peter. The British?
Miep. British, Americans, French, Dutch, Poles, Norwegians . . . all of them! More than four thousand ships! Churchill[13] spoke, and General Eisenhower![14] D-Day they call it!
Mr. Frank. Thank God, it's come!
Mrs. Van Daan. At last!
Miep (*starting out*). I'm going to tell Mr. Kraler. This'll be better than any blood transfusion.

---

10. **The invasion:** On June 6, 1944, Allied troops landed in northern France in a push to conquer the German army.

11. **BBC:** British Broadcasting Corporation.
12. **Normandy:** region of northern France.
13. **Churchill:** Sir Winston Churchill (1874–1965), British Prime Minister during the war.
14. **General Eisenhower:** Dwight D. Eisenhower (1890–1969), commander of the Allied armies in Europe. He later became President of the United States (1953–1961).

Mr. Frank (*stopping her*). What part of Normandy did they land, did they say?

Miep. Normandy . . . that's all I know now . . . I'll be up the minute I hear some more!

[*She goes hurriedly out.*]

Mr. Frank (*to* MRS. FRANK). What did I tell you? What did I tell you?

[MRS. FRANK *indicates that he has forgotten to bolt the door after* MIEP. *He hurries down the steps.* MR. VAN DAAN, *sitting on the couch, suddenly breaks into a convulsive sob. Everybody looks at him, bewildered.*]

Mrs. Van Daan (*hurrying to him*). Putti! Putti! What is it? What happened?

Mr. Van Daan. Please. I'm so ashamed.

[MR. FRANK *comes back up the steps.*]

Dussel. Oh, for God's sake!

Mrs. Van Daan. Don't, Putti.

Margot. It doesn't matter now!

Mr. Frank (*going to* MR. VAN DAAN). Didn't you hear what Miep said? The invasion has come! We're going to be liberated! This is a time to celebrate!

[*He embraces* MRS. FRANK *and then hurries to the cupboard and gets the cognac and a glass.*]

Mr. Van Daan. To steal bread from children!

Mrs. Frank. We've all done things that we're ashamed of.

Anne. Look at me, the way I've treated Mother . . . so mean and horrid to her.

Mrs. Frank. No, Anneke, no.

[ANNE *runs to her mother, putting her arms around her.*]

Anne. Oh, Mother, I was. I was awful.

Mr. Van Daan. Not like me. No one is as bad as me!

Dussel (*to* MR. VAN DAAN). Stop it now! Let's be happy!

Mr. Frank (*giving* MR. VAN DAAN *a glass of cognac*). Here! Here! *Schnapps!*[15] *Lachaim!*[16]

---

15. *Schnapps* (shnäps): German for "strong liquor."
16. *Lachaim!* (lə khä´yim): (Hebrew toast meaning "To life."

[VAN DAAN *takes the cognac. They all watch him. He gives them a feeble smile.* ANNE *puts up her fingers in a V-for-Victory sign. As* VAN DAAN *gives an answering V-sign, they are startled to hear a loud sob from behind them. It is* MRS. FRANK, *stricken with remorse. She is sitting on the other side of the room.*]

Mrs. Frank (*through her sobs*). When I think of the terrible things I said . . .

[MR. FRANK, ANNE, *and* MARGOT *hurry to her, trying to comfort her.* MR. VAN DAAN *brings her his glass of cognac.*]

Mr. Van Daan. No! No! You were right!

Mrs. Frank. That I should speak that way to you! . . . Our friends . . . Our guests!

[*She starts to cry again.*]

Dussel. Stop it, you're spoiling the whole invasion!

[*As they are comforting her, the lights dim out. The curtain falls.*]

Anne's Voice (*faintly at first and then with growing strength*). We're all in much better spirits these days. There's still excellent news of the invasion. The best part about it is that I have a feeling that friends are coming. Who knows? Maybe I'll be back in school by fall. Ha, ha! The joke is on us! The warehouse man doesn't know a thing and we are paying him all that money! . . . Wednesday, the second of July, nineteen forty-four. The invasion seems temporarily to be bogged down. Mr. Kraler has to have an operation, which looks bad. The Gestapo have found that radio that was stolen. Mr. Dussel says they'll trace it back and back to the thief, and then, its just a matter of time till they get to us. Everyone is low. Even poor Pim can't raise their spirits. I have often been downcast myself . . . but never in despair. I can shake off everything if I write. But . . . and that is the great question . . . will I ever be able to write well? I want to so much. I want to go on living even after my death. Another birthday has gone by, so now I am fifteen. Already I know what I want. I have a goal, an opinion.

[*As this is being said, the curtain rises on the scene, the lights dim on, and* ANNE's *voice fades out.*]

Scene 4

It is an afternoon a few weeks later. . . . Everyone but MARGOT *is in the main room. There is a sense of great tension.*

Both MRS. FRANK *and* MR. VAN DAAN *are nervously pacing back and forth,* DUSSEL *is standing at the window, looking down fixedly at the street below.* PETER *is at the center table, trying to do his lessons.* ANNE *sits opposite him, writing in her diary.* MRS. VAN DAAN *is seated on the couch, her eyes on* MR. FRANK *as he sits reading.*

The sound of a telephone ringing comes from the office below. They all are rigid, listening tensely. MR. DUSSEL *rushes down to* MR. FRANK.

Dussel. There it goes again, the telephone! Mr. Frank, do you hear?

Mr. Frank *(quietly).* Yes. I hear.

Dussel *(pleading, insistent).* But this is the third time, Mr. Frank! The third time in quick succession! It's a signal! I tell you it's Miep, trying to get us! For some reason she can't come to us and she's trying to warn us of something!

Mr. Frank. Please. Please.

Mr. Van Daan *(to* DUSSEL*).* You're wasting your breath.

Dussel. Something has happened, Mr. Frank. For three days now Miep hasn't been to see us! And today not a man has come to work. There hasn't been a sound in the building!

Mrs. Frank. Perhaps it's Sunday. We may have lost track of the days.

Mr. Van Daan *(to* ANNE*).* You with the diary there. What day is it?

Dussel *(going to* MRS. FRANK*).* I don't lose track of the days! I know exactly what day it is! It's Friday, the fourth of August. Friday, and not a man at work. *(He rushes back to* MR. FRANK, *pleading with him, almost in tears.)* I tell you Mr. Kraler's dead. That's the only explanation. He's dead and they've closed down the building, and Miep's trying to tell us!

Mr. Frank. She'd never telephone us.

Dussel *(frantic).* Mr. Frank, answer that! I beg you, answer it!

Mr. Frank. No.

Mr. Van Daan. Just pick it up and listen. You don't have to speak. Just listen and see if it's Miep.

Dussel *(speaking at the same time).* For God's sake . . . I ask you.

Mr. Frank. No. I've told you, no. I'll do nothing that might let anyone know we're in the building.

Peter. Mr. Frank's right.

Mr. Van Daan. There's no need to tell us what side you're on.

Mr. Frank. If we wait patiently, quietly, I believe that help will come.

[There is silence for a minute as they all listen to the telephone ringing.]

Dussel. I'm going down. *(He rushes down the steps.* MR. FRANK *tries ineffectually to hold him.* DUSSEL *runs to the lower door, unbolting it. The telephone stops ringing.* DUSSEL *bolts the door and comes slowly back up the steps.)* Too late. *(*MR. FRANK *goes to* MARGOT *in* ANNE's *bedroom.)*

Mr. Van Daan. So we just wait here until we die.

Mrs. Van Daan *(hysterically).* I can't stand it! I'll kill myself! I'll kill myself!

Mr. Van Daan. For God's sake, stop it!

[In the distance, a German military band is heard playing a Viennese waltz.]

Mrs. Van Daan. I think you'd be glad if I did! I think you want me to die!

Mr. Van Daan. Whose fault is it we're here! *(*MRS. VAN DAAN *starts for her room. He follows, talking to her.)* We could've been safe somewhere . . . in America or Switzerland. But no! No! You wouldn't leave when I wanted to. You couldn't leave your things. You couldn't leave your precious furniture.

Mrs. Van Daan. Don't touch me!

[She hurries up the stairs, followed by MR. VAN DAAN. PETER, *unable to bear it, goes to his room.* ANNE *looks after him, deeply concerned.* DUSSEL *returns to his post at the window.* MR. FRANK *comes back into the main room and takes a book, trying to read.* MRS. FRANK *sits near the sink, starting to peel some potatoes.* ANNE *quietly goes to* PETER's *room, closing the door after her.* PETER *is lying face down on the cot.* ANNE *leans over him, holding him in her arms, trying to bring him out of his despair.]*

Anne. Look, Peter, the sky. (*She looks up through the skylight.*) What a lovely, lovely day! Aren't the clouds beautiful? You know what I do when it seems as if I couldn't stand being cooped up for one more minute? I *think* myself out. I think myself on a walk in the park where I used to go with Pim. Where the jonquils and the crocuses and the violets grow down the slopes. You know the most wonderful part about *thinking* yourself out? You can have it anyway you like. You can have roses and violets and chrysanthemums all blooming at the same time. . . . It's funny . . . I used to take it all for granted . . . and now I've gone crazy about everything to do with nature. Haven't you?

Peter. I've just gone crazy. I think if something doesn't happen soon . . . if we don't get out of here . . . I can't stand much more of it!

Anne (*softly*). I wish you had a religion, Peter.

Peter. No, thanks! Not me!

Anne. Oh, I don't mean you have to be Orthodox[17] . . . or believe in heaven and hell and purgatory and things . . . I just mean some religion . . . it doesn't matter what. Just to believe in something! When I think of all that's out there . . . the trees . . . and flowers . . . and seagulls . . . when I think of the dearness of you, Peter . . . and the goodness of the people we know . . . Mr. Kraler, Miep, Dirk, the vegetable man, all risking their lives for us every day. . . . When I think of these good things, I'm not afraid anymore. . . . I find myself, and God, and I . . .

[PETER *interrupts, getting up and walking away.*]

Peter. That's fine! But when I begin to think, I get mad! Look at us, hiding out for two years. Not able to move! Caught here like . . . waiting for them to come and get us . . . and all for what?

Anne. We're not the only people that've had to suffer. There've always been people that've had to . . . sometimes one race . . . sometimes another . . . and yet . . .

Peter. That doesn't make me feel any better!

Anne (*going to him*). I know it's terrible, trying to have any faith . . . when people are doing such horrible . . . But you know what I sometimes

_____
17. **be Orthodox:** Orthodox Jews strictly observe Jewish rites and traditions.

think? I think the world may be going through a phase, the way I was with Mother. It'll pass, maybe not for hundreds of years, but some day . . . I still believe, in spite of everything, that people are really good at heart.

Peter. I want to see something now. . . . Not a thousand years from now!

[*He goes over, sitting down again on the cot.*]

Anne. But, Peter, if you'd only look at it as a part of a great pattern . . . that we're just a little minute in a life . . . (*She breaks off.*) Listen to us, going at each other like a couple of stupid grown-ups! Look at the sky now. Isn't it lovely. (*She holds out her hand to him.* PETER *takes it and rises, standing with her at the window looking out, his arms around her.*) Someday, when we're outside again, I'm going to . . .

[*She breaks off as she hears the sound of a car, its brakes squealing as it comes to a sudden stop. The people in the other rooms also become aware of the sound. They listen tensely. Another car roars up to a screeching stop.* ANNE *and* PETER *come from* PETER's *room.* MR. *and* MRS. VAN DAAN *creep down the stairs.* DUSSEL *comes out from his room. Everyone is listening, hardly breathing. A doorbell clangs again and again in the building below.* MR. FRANK *starts quietly down the steps to the door.* DUSSEL *and* PETER *follow him. The others stand rigid, waiting, terrified.*

In a few seconds DUSSEL *comes stumbling back up the steps. He shakes off* PETER's *help and goes to his room.* MR. FRANK *bolts the door below, and comes slowly back up the steps. Their eyes are all on him as he stands there for a minute. They realize that what they feared has happened.* MRS. VAN DAAN *starts to whimper.* MR. VAN DAAN *puts her gently in a chair, and then hurries off up the stairs to their room to collect their things.* PETER *goes to comfort his mother. There is a sound of violent pounding on a door below.*]

Mr. Frank (*quietly*). For the past two years we have lived in fear. Now we can live in hope.

[*The pounding below becomes more insistent. There are muffled sounds of voices, shouting commands.*]

They stand together, waiting. We hear the thud of gun butts on the door, trying to break it down.

Men's Voices. *Aufmachen! Da drinnen! Aufmachen! Schnell! Schnell! Schnell!*[18] *etc., etc.*

[*The street door below is forced open. We hear the heavy tread of footsteps coming up.* MR.

FRANK *gets two school bags from the shelves, and gives one to* ANNE *and the other to* MARGOT. *He goes to get a bag for* MRS. FRANK. *The sound of feet coming up grows louder.* PETER *comes to* ANNE, *kissing her goodbye, then he goes to his room to collect his things. The buzzer of their door starts to ring.* MR. FRANK *brings* MRS. FRANK *a*

---

18. **Aufmachen! . . . Schnell!:** Open up! You in there! Open up! Quickly! Quickly! Quickly!

bag. They stand together, waiting. We hear the thud of gun butts on the door, trying to break it down.

ANNE *stands, holding her school satchel, looking over at her father and mother with a soft, reassuring smile. She is no longer a child, but a woman with courage to meet whatever lies ahead.*

The lights dim out. The curtain falls on the scene. We hear a mighty crash as the door is shattered. After a second ANNE's *voice is heard.*]

Anne's Voice. And so it seems our stay here is over. They are waiting for us now. They've allowed us five minutes to get our things. We can each take a bag and whatever it will hold of clothing. Nothing else. So, dear Diary, that means I must leave you behind. Goodbye for a while. P.S. Please, please, Miep, or Mr. Kraler, or anyone else. If you should find this diary, will you please keep it safe for me, because some day I hope . . .

[*Her voice stops abruptly. There is silence. After a second the curtain rises.*]

Scene 5

It is again the afternoon in November, 1945. The rooms are as we saw them in the first scene. MR. KRALER *has joined* MIEP *and* MR. FRANK. *There are coffee cups on the table. We see a great change in* MR. FRANK. *He is calm now. His bitterness is gone. He slowly turns a few pages of the diary. They are blank.*

Mr. Frank. No more.

[*He closes the diary and puts it down on the couch beside him.*]

Miep. I'd gone to the country to find food. When I got back the block was surrounded by police . . .
Mr. Kraler. We made it our business to learn how they knew. It was the thief . . . the thief who told them.

[MIEP *goes up to the gas burner, bringing back a pot of coffee.*]

Mr. Frank (*after a pause*). It seems strange to say this, that anyone could be happy in a concentration camp. But Anne was happy in the camp in Holland where they first took us. After two years of being shut up in these rooms, she could be out . . . out in the sunshine and the fresh air that she loved.
Miep (*offering the coffee to* MR. FRANK). A little more?
Mr. Frank (*holding out his cup to her*). The news of the war was good. The British and Americans were sweeping through France. We felt sure that they would get to us in time. In September we were told that we were to be shipped to Poland. . . . The men to one camp. The women to another. I was sent to Auschwitz. They went to Belsen. In January we were freed, the few of us who were left. The war wasn't yet over, so it took us a long time to get home. We'd be sent here and there behind the lines where we'd be safe. Each time our train would stop . . . at a siding, or a crossing . . . we'd all get out and go from group to group . . . Where were you? Were you at Belsen? At Buchenwald? At Mauthausen? Is it possible that you knew my wife? Did you ever see my husband? My son? My daughter? That's how I found out about my wife's death . . . of Margot, the Van Daans . . . Dussel. But Anne . . . I still hoped . . . Yesterday I went to Rotterdam. I'd heard of a woman there. . . . She'd been in Belsen with Anne. . . . I know now.

[*He picks up the diary again, and turns the page back to find a certain passage. As he finds it we hear* ANNE's *voice.*]

Anne's Voice. In spite of everything, I still believe that people are really good at heart.

[MR. FRANK *slowly closes the diary.*]

Mr. Frank. She puts me to shame.

[*They are silent.*]

The Curtain Falls

A Comment on the Play

Two situations give this play its structure. The first situation involves the hiding itself. Will these eight people hiding from the Nazis be detected and caught? How will it happen? The characters, trapped in a loft, can do little but try to remain unnoticed. The playwrights remind us of their desperate situation. They let us hear noises from outside: screeching cars, marching feet, nighttime noises in the office. All these sounds increase our tension and create suspense.

Meanwhile, under this umbrella of suspense, the Franks and the Van Daans live in what amounts at times to a domestic comedy-drama. All the familiar relationships are here: parent-child, husband-wife, neighbor-neighbor, boy-girl. Their very special situation—hiding from the Nazis with their lives at stake—puts all of the characters under pressure. Tensions and stresses cause the characters to reveal their truer selves. The elder Van Daans, for example, show that they are self-centered. Even their attitudes toward Peter seem uncaring in contrast to the Franks' concern for their daughters.

The play's texture and richness comes from its characters. But at the center of the play is a second major situation, the most universal of all stories. It is the blossoming of a young girl (Anne) under the influence of first love (Peter). The play's forward movement comes from the development of the relationship between Anne and Peter. The relationship starts out coolly—Anne wishes that Peter was a girl so that she could have a friend to talk to. Later the relationship turns into first love that *we* know is doomed. Anne's love for Peter causes her to "open up" to the rest of the world. The most affecting moment in the play comes at the end of Act Two, Scene 2, when Anne, having just been kissed by Peter, silently moves around the room kissing others—even the unpleasant Mrs. Van Daan.

Thus, we have the two situations that drive the action of the play. The primary "want" is the characters' desire to survive. They take various steps to remain undetected because their lives are at stake. But along with this "communal desire" is Anne's own personal "want": her need to mature, to emerge from childhood. It is Anne's emergence as a young woman that becomes the spine of the play, that holds the rest of the play together.

Responding to the Play

Analyzing Act Two

Identifying Facts

1. In the theater, we should not have to look at the program for information about the play. The playwright should put all the information on the stage. In Scene 1, the playwrights let us know about the passage of time in several places. Where and how do they do this?
2. Miep and Mr. Kraler's first visit provokes two **conflicts:** one over a cake, the other over a coat. Describe both of these conflicts. How are they resolved?
3. What bad news does Mr. Kraler bring?
4. The relationship between Anne and Peter changes in Scene 1. What happens to cause this change?

5. As Scene 2 opens, the meeting we have been waiting for between Anne and Peter is about to happen. Not only do *we* know it, but the other characters do, too. How? Describe the ways Mrs. Frank and Mrs. Van Daan react to Anne and Peter's friendship.
6. In Scene 3, Mr. Van Daan steals again and is caught. This is the final injustice for Mrs. Frank, the gentlest person in the group. Her husband says to her what might be said of many characters by the end of a play: "I've never seen you like this before." Mrs. Frank has been pushed past her limit, and has revealed her true feelings. How does Mrs. Frank expose her feelings? How do the other characters react? Do you think they have changed also? If so, how?

7. In reality (see "Focusing on Background," page 282), the Franks had a radio, so they knew what was happening in the war. The radio told them about the Allied invasion of Africa and about the Allied landing in Normandy. But the playwrights found it more dramatic to have Miep and Mr. Kraler bring news into the hiding place. The news they bring often contrasts with what is happening on stage. What news does Miep bring in Scene 3, and how does it affect the others?

8. At the beginning of Scene 4, what two things are creating great tension in the household?

Interpreting Meanings

9. Some characters in plays tend to react the same way over and over again. This is called the **"Jack-in-the-box"** response. How does Mr. Van Daan illustrate this response?

10. Throughout the play, we have seen a series of reversals. Things look terrible, and then suddenly we are laughing. People are quarreling, and then there is a love scene. Chart the reversals in Act Two. What are the worst crises? Which scenes lift our spirits?

11. The **climax** of a play is the moment of greatest tension. What would you say is this play's climax? What feelings did you have as you read this scene?

12. **Change** is the essence of drama. How would you describe the changes that have taken place in Anne, from the beginning of the play until the end? Have any other characters changed under the pressure of the action?

13. Possibly the most moving moment from the original Broadway production of the play occurred at the end of Scene 4. When Joseph Schildkraut, who played Mr. Frank, came back up the stairs after finding that the police had broken in below, he simply looked at his family and opened his hands in a gesture of resignation, as though to say "It has happened." There is no stage direction for this gesture, so it may have been Schildkraut's own idea. Do you think this interpretation is best? In what other ways could this wordless moment be acted?

14. At first glance, Scene 5 might seem unnecessary. However it is important. What do you think this last scene accomplishes?

15. Why is Mr. Frank ashamed? Do you think he has any reason to be?

Applying Meanings

16. On the basis of your own experiences, do you agree or disagree with Anne that "people are really good at heart"? Explain.

The Play as a Whole

1. A play often has several **themes,** or main ideas, about life that the writer wants to reveal. What do you think this play reveals about our need for freedom, about the power of love, about courage and hope, and about good and evil?

2. During the crisis in Act Two, Scene 3, Mr. Frank says, "We don't need the Nazis to destroy us. We're destroying ourselves." How would you describe the forces that are destroying the characters from the "inside"? Do you think, given their desperate situation, that such behavior was inevitable?

3. The play is about a specific group of people living under extraordinary circumstances in the Netherlands during World War II. The play, however, also has a universal appeal. Through the character of Anne, what age-old human experiences does the play depict?

4. How did reading the play make you feel? Did you find the play depressing, uplifting, or something else? Try to describe your response and tell what made you feel this way.

Writing About the Play

A Creative Response

1. **Extending the Play.** Read Ernst Schnabel's nonfiction report "A Tragedy Revealed: A Heroine's Last Days" (page 481). Work with another student to write the dialogue and stage directions for one of the following brief scenes between Anne and another character. Be sure to indicate the setting. In some way, indicate how much time has passed since the raid on the secret annex. When you have finished, assign the parts of characters and present your scene to the class.

   a. A conversation in the women's cell after the arrest (page 485).

   b. A scene on the passenger train to Westerbork (page 486).

   c. A conversation between Anne and Peter at Westerbork (page 486).

A Critical Response

2. **Comparing the Play and the Report.** Compare Schnabel's report of the final scene in the secret annex (page 483) with the playwrights' version (page 276). In a paragraph, cite three ways in which the two scenes differ. To help you write, prepare a chart like the following one:

Play's Final Scene	Report's Account
1.	1.
2.	2.
3.	3.

In a second paragraph, tell which version of the story you think you will remember longer. Explain why you feel this way.

3. **Comparing the Play to the Diary.** The playwrights had to take Anne Frank's diary and decide which incidents to use in their play. Then they had to create dialogue for the characters. Much of the dialogue was quoted from the diary. The diary entry telling about the burglary at the office building appears in "Focusing on Background" (page 282). In a paragraph or two, describe the ways in which the diary differs from the play's version of the break-in.

4. **Responding to a Scene.** In a two-paragraph essay, describe one scene from the play and your response to it. As a model, you might use the following comment from a critic's review of the play's opening performance.

Perhaps no scene in the play is more touching than that in which a fifteen-year-old girl and a nineteen-year-old boy enter into the formalities of courtship. They have, with their families, been cooped up on the top floor of an Amsterdam office building for nearly two years. They have seen each other morning, noon, and night during all this time, eaten together, squabbled together, been terrified together, simply grown up together.

When the time comes, though, for each to seek the other out in a shy, faltering, heart-breaking romance, they at once begin to behave like lovers who have just been introduced. In her own little corner of the densely populated living quarters, the girl piles her hair on top of her head and hopefully drapes a scarf about her shoulders; in his cubbyhole the boy puts on a jacket, straight-

ens his tie, and trembles in expectation. The girl "goes out" for the evening to see him—just across the room. . . .

The circumstances around her are the circumstances of despair and decay. In the midst of this, a fresh and shining dignity, a springtime innocence and an instinctive honor rise to fill the shabby room. Since you know that Anne Frank's life is to end in the horrors of Belsen, the play cannot help but break your heart. But along the way it takes great care to let you know that the moments of living—short as they were—were all moments of growth and discovery and very great joy.

—Walter Kerr

Follow this plan in writing your own essay:

a. In paragraph 1, briefly summarize the scene you'll talk about.

b. In paragraph 2, state your responses to the scene. Refer to specific events and lines to support your response.

5. **Analyzing Characters.** In a brief essay, analyze one of the characters in the play. When you analyze something, you "take it apart" to see what makes it work. When you analyze a character, you look at how he or she talks, acts, and treats other people; this will help you see what this person is like. You also look at the way other people respond to this character. Here are some characters from the play, and a short description of each one written by the drama critic Walter Kerr. You might want to use the descriptive line as part of your topic statement.

a. Anne Frank: "spirited and straightforward."

b. Mr. Frank: "controlled and confident . . . a tower of strength."

c. Mr. Dussel: a "fussy dentist."

d. Mr. Van Daan: an "eternally hungry businessman."

e. Mrs. Van Daan: "vain and pathetic."

Producing a Play

The person in charge of staging a play is called the **director.** Working for the director are the **set designer** and people in charge of **costumes, lights and special effects,** and **props** (the movable articles used as part of the setting, excluding the costumes and scenery). Form groups and imagine that you are working on a production of this play. You must have many conferences before the play's **script** (its printed version) can become a live performance.

1. Sketch roughly your idea of how the **set** for the secret annex should look. How would you divide the stage to show the four rooms described in the stage directions on pages 225–226?
2. What furniture would you put onstage? (Read the stage directions carefully.)
3. List the **props** you will need for each scene of this play, beginning with a woman's white glove. Read the dialogue and stage directions closely to find the items you will need. (A version of the play printed for actors will have a list of props.)
4. What offstage **sounds** must be produced for the play, and how would you create them? What kinds of **lighting** do you need?
5. Describe (or sketch) the **costumes** you want your characters to wear. Note carefully when the characters must change costumes.

Reading About the Writers

Frances Goodrich (1890–1984) and **Albert Hackett** (1900–   ) both started out as actors. They began collaborating on writing plays and screenplays in the late 1920's and were married soon after. In the 1930's they wrote the scripts for several popular movies. Their play, *Western Union, Please,* had a successful New York run in 1939. Goodrich once said of their method of working together, ''Each of us writes a version of the scene.'' They would write at desks facing in opposite directions in the same room. When finished, the playwrights would trade versions of the scene for comments and criticism. The next draft would then be prepared. *The Diary of Anne Frank* is considered their masterpiece. They did much research for the play, including speaking with Otto Frank in Amsterdam. It took the playwrights two years to write the play. They went through eight drafts before agreeing on the version produced with great success on Broadway in 1955.

Focusing on Background
From Anne Frank's Diary

Tuesday, 11 April, 1944

''Dear Kitty,

''My head throbs, I honestly don't know where to begin.

''On Friday (Good Friday) we played Monopoly, Saturday afternoon too. These days passed quickly and uneventfully. On Sunday afternoon, on my invitation, Peter came to my room at half past four; at a quarter past five we went to the front attic, where we remained until six o'clock. There was a beautiful Mozart concert on the radio from six o'clock until a quarter past seven. I enjoyed it all very much, but especially the 'Kleine Nachtmusik.' I can hardly listen in the room because I'm always so inwardly stirred when I hear lovely music.

''On Sunday evening Peter and I went to the front attic together and, in order to sit comfortably, we took with us a few divan cushions that we were able to lay our hands on. We seated ourselves on one packing case. Both the case and the cushions were very narrow, so we sat absolutely squashed together, leaning against other cases. Mouschi kept us company too, so we weren't unchaperoned.

''Suddenly, at a quarter to nine, Mr. Van Daan whistled and asked if we had one of Dussel's cushions. We both jumped up and went downstairs with cushion, cat, and Van Daan.

''A lot of trouble arose out of this cushion, because Dussel was annoyed that we had one of his cushions, one that he used as a pillow. He was afraid that there might be fleas in it and made a great commotion about his beloved cushion! Peter and I put two hard brushes in his bed as a revenge. We had a good laugh over this little interlude!

''Our fun didn't last long. At half past nine Peter knocked softly on the door and asked Daddy if he would just help him upstairs over a difficult English sentence. 'That's a blind,'[1] I said to Margot, 'anyone could see through that one!' I was right. They were in the act of breaking into the warehouse. Daddy, Van Daan, Dussel, and Peter were downstairs in a flash. Margot, Mummy, Mrs. Van Daan, and I stayed upstairs and waited.

''Four frightened women just have to talk, so talk we did, until we heard a bang downstairs. After that

---

1. **blind:** here, something used to mislead; decoy.

all was quiet, the clock struck a quarter to ten. The color had vanished from our faces, we were still quiet, although we were afraid. Where could the men be? What was that bang? Would they be fighting the burglars? Ten o'clock, footsteps on the stairs: Daddy, white and nervous, entered, followed by Mr. Van Daan. 'Lights out, creep upstairs, we expect the police in the house!'

"There was no time to be frightened: The lights went out, I quickly grabbed a jacket, and we were upstairs. 'What has happened? Tell us quickly!' There was no one to tell us, the men having disappeared downstairs again. Only at ten past ten did they reappear; two kept watch at Peter's open window, the door to the landing was closed, the swinging cupboard shut. We hung a jersey round the night light, and after that they told us:

"Peter heard two loud bangs on the landing, ran downstairs, and saw there was a large plank out of the left half of the door. He dashed upstairs, warned the 'Home Guard' of the family, and the four of them proceeded downstairs. When they entered the warehouse, the burglars were in the act of enlarging the hole. Without further thought Van Daan shouted: 'Police!'

"A few hurried steps outside, and the burglars had fled. In order to avoid the hole being noticed by the police, a plank was put against it, but a good hard kick from outside sent it flying to the ground. The men were perplexed at such impudence, and both Van Daan and Peter felt murder welling up within them; Van Daan beat on the ground with a chopper, and all was quiet again. Once more they wanted to put the plank in front of the hole. Disturbance! A married couple outside shone a torch[2] through the opening, lighting up the whole warehouse. . . . Now they switched over from their role of police to that of burglars. The four of them sneaked upstairs, Peter quickly opened the doors and windows of the kitchen and private office, flung the telephone onto the floor, and finally the four of them landed behind the swinging cupboard."

. . .

"The married couple with the torch would probably have warned the police: It was Sunday evening, Easter Sunday, no one at the office on Easter Monday, so none of us could budge until Tuesday morning. Think of it, waiting in such fear for two nights

and a day! No one had anything to suggest, so we simply sat there in pitch-darkness, because Mrs. Van Daan in her fright had unintentionally turned the lamp right out; talked in whispers, and at every creak one heard 'Sh! sh!'

"It turned half past ten, eleven, but not a sound; Daddy and Van Daan joined us in turns. Then a quarter past eleven, a bustle and noise downstairs. Everyone's breath was audible, otherwise no one moved. Footsteps in the house, in the private office, kitchen, then . . . on our staircase. No one breathed audibly now, footsteps on our staircase, then a rattling of the swinging cupboard. This moment is indescribable. 'Now we are lost!' I said, and could see us all being taken away by the Gestapo that very night. Twice they rattled at the cupboard, then there was nothing, the footsteps withdrew, we were saved so far. A shiver seemed to pass from one to another, I heard someone's teeth chattering, no one said a word.

"There was not another sound in the house, but a light was burning on our landing, right in front of the cupboard. Could that be because it was a secret cupboard? Perhaps the police had forgotten the light? Would someone come back to put it out? Tongues loosened, there was no one in the house any longer, perhaps there was someone on guard outside. . . .

"By half past two I was so tired that I knew no more until half past three. I awoke when Mrs. Van Daan laid her head on my foot.

"'For heaven's sake, give me something to put on!' I asked. I was given something, but don't ask what—a pair of woolen knickers over my pajamas, a red jumper, and a black skirt, white oversocks, and a pair of sports stockings full of holes. Then Mrs. Van Daan sat in the chair and her husband came and lay on my feet. I lay thinking till half past three, shivering the whole time, which prevented Van Daan from sleeping. I prepared myself for the return of the police, then we'd have to say that we were in hiding; they would either be good Dutch people, then we'd be saved, or NSBers,[3] then we'd have to bribe them!

"'In that case, destroy the radio,' sighed Mrs. Van Daan. 'Yes, in the stove!' replied her husband. 'If they find us, then let them find the radio as well!'

"'Then they will find Anne's diary,' added Daddy.

---

2. **torch:** flashlight.

3. **NSB-ers:** members of the Dutch National Socialist Movement, who were Nazi sympathizers.

'Burn it then,' suggested the most terrified member of the party. This, and when the police rattled the cupboard door, were my worst moments. 'Not my diary; if my diary goes, I go with it!' But luckily Daddy didn't answer. . . .

"Four o'clock, five o'clock, half past five. Then I went and sat with Peter by his window and listened, so close together that we could feel each other's bodies quivering; we spoke a word or two now and then, and listened attentively. In the room next door they took down that blackout. They wanted to call up Koophuis at seven o'clock and get him to send someone around. Then they wrote down everything they wanted to tell Koophius over the phone. The risk that the police on guard at the door, or in the warehouse, might hear the telephone was very great, but the danger of the police returning was even greater.

"The points were these:

"Burglars broken in: Police have been in the house, as far as the swinging cupboard, but no further.

"Burglars apparently disturbed, forced open the door in the warehouse and escaped through the garden.

"Main entrance bolted, Kraler must have used the second door when he left. The typewriters and adding machine are safe in the black case in the private office.

"Try to warn Henk and fetch the key from Elli, then go and look around the office—on the pretext of feeding the cat.

"Everything went according to plan. Koophuis was phoned, the typewriters which we had upstairs were put in the case. Then we sat around the table again and waited for Henk or the police.

"Peter had fallen asleep and Van Daan and I were lying on the floor, when we heard loud footsteps downstairs. I got up quietly: 'That's Henk.'

"'No, no, it's the police,' some of the others said.

"Someone knocked at the door, Miep whistled. This was too much for Mrs. Van Daan, she turned as white as a sheet and sank limply into a chair; had the tension lasted one minute longer she would have fainted.

"Our room was a perfect picture when Miep and Henk entered, the table alone would have been worth photographing! A copy of *Cinema and Theater,* covered with jam and a remedy for diarrhea, opened at a page of dancing girls, two jam pots, two started loaves of bread, a mirror, comb,

matches, ash, cigarettes, tobacco, ash tray, books, a pair of pants, a torch, toilet paper, etc., etc., lay jumbled together in variegated splendor.

"Of course Henk and Miep were greeted with shouts and tears. Henk mended the hole in the door with some planks, and soon went off again to inform the police of the burglary. Miep had also found a letter under the warehouse door from the night watchman Slagter, who had noticed the hole and warned the police, whom he would also visit.

"So we had half an hour to tidy ourselves. I've never seen such a change take place in half an hour. Margot and I took the bedclothes downstairs, went to the w.c., washed, and did our teeth and hair. After that I tidied the room a bit and went upstairs again. The table there was already cleared, so we ran off some water and made coffee and tea, boiled the milk, and laid the table for lunch. Daddy and Peter emptied the potties and cleaned them with warm water and chlorine.

"At eleven o'clock we sat round the table with Henk, who was back by that time, and slowly things began to be more normal and cozy again. Henk's story was as follows:

"Mr. Slagter was asleep, but his wife told Henk that her husband had found the hole in our door when he was doing his tour round the canals, and that he had called a policeman, who had gone through the building with him. He would be coming to see Kraler on Tuesday and would tell him more then. At the police station they knew nothing of the burglary yet, but the policeman had made a note of it at once and would come and look round on Tuesday. On the way back Henk happened to meet our greengrocer at the corner, and told him that the house had been broken into. 'I know that,' he said quite coolly. 'I was passing last evening with my wife and saw the hole in the door. My wife wanted to walk on, but I just had a look in with my torch; then the thieves cleared at once. To be on the safe side, I didn't ring up the police, as with you I didn't think it was the thing to do. I don't know anything, but I guess a lot.'

"Henk thanked him and went on. The man obviously guesses that we're here, because he always brings the potatoes during the lunch hour. Such a nice man! . . .

"None of us has ever been in such danger as that night. God truly protected us; just think of it—the police at our secret cupboard, the light on right in front of it, and still we remained undiscovered."

—Anne Frank

High Noon belongs to a uniquely American category of stories called Westerns. **Westerns** deal with cowboys, Indians, sheriffs, outlaws, dance-hall women, ''good'' women (such as the schoolteacher just arrived from the East), and, of course, an array of horses and cattle. Westerns are primarily action stories.

The action in Westerns is mainly physical. The hero chases outlaws over the prairies and foothills, ambushing or being ambushed by gunslingers at the pass, brawling in barrooms, and, of course, shooting it out on Main Street.

Though Westerns feature physical action, most also deal with deeper subjects of almost universal appeal. Here are some typical subjects of Westerns:

1. Taming nature to open up new territory
2. Competition for land (often between whites and Indians)
3. The weak (but good) versus the powerful (but corrupt)
4. Law-and-order versus lawlessness
5. Revenge
6. The solitary individual acting to save or transform his or her community
7. The loneliness of frontier life

High Noon, released in 1952, follows most of the basic rules for a Western, but it adds a new twist. In *High Noon,* the townspeople have to make a difficult moral decision. The decision is so tough that persuasive arguments can be made for each side of the question.

When *High Noon* appeared, critics acclaimed it as one of the best Westerns ever made, and it received many honors. Carl Foreman won a Writers Guild Award for his screenplay. The star, Gary Cooper, won an Academy Award for best actor, and the film won an Academy Award for best film editing. The score, by Dimitri Tiomkin, was praised, and the title song became a hit.

High Noon

The Screenplay

When you read the script of *High Noon,* you should remember that you are not seeing what moviegoers see on the screen. You cannot see Gary Cooper's expressions of weary determination, nor Grace Kelly's cool blond beauty, nor Katy Jurado's warm dark beauty. You'll get a good idea of what the movie is like, however, if you do the following: Read the camera directions and stage directions closely, look at the movie stills printed with the screenplay, and use your imagination.

After you read and discuss the screenplay of *High Noon,* try to see the film at a revival movie house, on television, or on videocassette. Does the film meet with your expectations?

Camera Directions

In some ways, a screenplay is just like the script for a stage play. It tells a story about characters who have to deal with one or more conflicts. And the story is told chiefly in dialogue.

However, a screenplay differs from a script for a stage play in one important respect. The screenplay has to provide directions for the camera, which will record everything for the audience. For this reason, screenwriters have to do more than describe the setting and invent dialogue. Camera directions are instructions for the director on how each scene should be photographed.

In reading *High Noon*, you will come across the following camera directions. This list of definitions will help you understand what Carl Foreman intended the audience to see in each scene.

Fade-in: the dark screen is gradually filled with a picture.
Ext. (exterior): an outdoor shot.
Int. (interior): an indoor shot.
o.s. (offscreen): the action takes place outside the view of the camera.
f.g. (foreground): the part of the scene nearest the camera.
b.g. (background): the part of a scene farthest from the camera.
Truck shot: the scene is filmed by a camera on a moving truck, which allows the camera to move along with the action.
Pan: a stationary camera sweeps up, down, or sideways, sometimes following a moving person or object.
Insert: a brief view of a detail that is part of the larger scene being shown.
Closeup: a very close view, in which a face or a single object fills the screen.
Close shot: a view that is not quite as close as a closeup. It might include two faces or objects.
Medium close shot: a view that is further away than a close shot. It might include two people from the waist up.
Fade-out: the image gradually disappears until the screen is dark.

HIGH NOON

Carl Foreman

The illustrations for the screenplay of *High Noon* are from the 1952 Warner Brothers production starring Gary Cooper and Grace Kelly, and directed by Fred Zinnemann.

Characters

Will Kane, Marshal of Hadleyville
Amy Fowler, Kane's bride
Frank Mitchell
Ben Mitchell, Frank's younger brother and part of the Mitchell gang
James Pierce, part of the Mitchell gang
Jack Colby, part of the Mitchell gang
Helen Ramirez, townswoman from Mexico
Harvey Pell, deputy to the marshal
Percy Mettrick, Judge
Jonas Henderson, selectman of Hadleyville
Mrs. Henderson, Henderson's wife
Samuel Fuller, selectman of Hadleyville
Mildred Fuller, Fuller's wife
Martin Howe, selectman of Hadleyville
Sam, Helen Ramirez's elderly friend
Toby, deputy to the marshal
Dr. Mahin, minister
Gillis, bar owner
Barber
Stationmaster
Hotel Clerk
Ed Peterson, Toby's prisoner
Herb Baker, townsman
Bartender
Drunk
Weaver, storekeeper
Martinez, Mexican friend of Toby

Various townspeople, children, and Indians

Fade-in:

Ext. Outskirts of Hadleyville—Day. It is not yet eleven A.M., *and the sun is high and hot in a clear sky. Near a landmark of some kind—a tree or an outcropping of rock—a man on horseback waits. In the distance, another rider appears, riding toward the waiting man. Now, the* MAIN *and* CREDIT TITLES[1] APPEAR. *Behind them, the rider reaches the man who is waiting. They recognize each other, wave briefly, wait together. The distant bells*

of an o.s. church begin to toll. From ANOTHER ANGLE, *a third rider gallops toward them. He reaches them. The first man takes out his watch as the* FINAL CREDIT APPEARS AND FADES. *We are in* CLOSE *to the three men now, close enough to see that they are travel-weary and grim, men who seem to be driven by a mixture of hatred and hunger. In the order of their appearance, they are* JAMES PIERCE, JACK COLBY, *and* BEN MITCHELL. PIERCE *snaps his watch case shut, puts it away, nods briefly to the others. He spurs his horse, and they follow him.* CAMERA PANS *and* HOLDS *as they ride out of the scene in the direction of a church spire that can be seen above screening trees.*

Ext. Church. Its bell tolls calmly and unhurriedly, and the people going into it move torpidly,[2] hot and uncomfortable in their Sunday best. Along the road that winds past the church, MITCHELL, PIERCE, *and* COLBY *appear and ride by. They are too far from the church to be recognized by any of the people going in, and when they pass the* CAMERA *as they ride away from the church, they seem oblivious to it. Although they are only cantering,[3] they ride with purpose, and it is as if the church and the people do not even impinge themselves on their consciousness. As they move out of the scene, they pass a wagon which has come to a stop in the f.g. A man and his wife are in the wagon, and as the man starts to climb down, he sees the three riders. He looks after them thoughtfully.*

Ext. Main Street. It bakes in the sun, a rather crooked and winding street that seems deserted now in the Sunday calm. MITCHELL, PIERCE, *and* COLBY *canter into the scene and ride away from the* CAMERA.

Ext. Firehouse. A volunteer fireman, his Sunday coat off, is lovingly polishing the bright new engine. As he pauses to pour himself a glass of beer from a nearby can, the three riders pass. He looks after them with frowning recognition.

Close Shot—another man—staring o.s. at the passing riders. Troubled, he wipes his dripping forehead.

---

1. **main and credit titles:** the name of the movie and the list of people who worked on it.

2. **torpidly:** slowly; without much life.
3. **cantering:** riding at a moderate pace.

Head-on Truck Shot—on MITCHELL, PIERCE, *and* COLBY. *They keep their eyes focused ahead of them, almost contemptuously easy in their saddles but unwaveringly purposeful.*

Ext. Street—Shooting toward the hotel—far up the street, as the three men approach it. The shutters of a second story window open, and the figure of a woman can be seen.

*Med. Close Shot—*HELEN RAMIREZ*—through the window into her sitting room. She is in a negligee, still languorous[4] from sleep, her long black hair cascading down over her shoulders. She stretches luxuriously. There is the o.s.* SOUND *of the approaching horses.* HARVEY PELL *enters the scene from behind her, and draws her back into the room.*

Int. Helen's front room. HARVEY *draws* HELEN *into his arms, and she accepts the familiar embrace. The purely physical attraction each has for the other is obvious. But the sound of the approaching horses comes nearer.* HELEN's *gaze strays to the window. She recognizes the three riders below. She frowns, detaching herself from* HARVEY, *moves back to the window.* HARVEY *cranes his neck to follow her gaze.*

Harvey. Who's that?
Helen (*abstracted*). You don't know them. . . .

[*She follows the o.s. riders with her eyes.*]

[*Ext. Hay and Grain Store. The* STOREKEEPER, *in his Sunday best, is locking the door as* MITCHELL, PIERCE, *and* COLBY *ride by. He, too, recognizes them. He stares after them.*]

[*Ext. Street. An elderly* MEXICAN WOMAN *is carrying a market basket, the* CAMERA MOVING *with her. As the three men ride by, she recognizes them and stops. Unself-consciously, she crosses herself.[5]*]

[*Ext. Marshal's office—as* MITCHELL, PIERCE, *and* COLBY *ride by.* BEN MITCHELL *reins up, looking toward the marshal's office, then deliberately rears his horse. The others have stopped.*]

---

4. **languorous** (lan′gər·əs): sluggish; without vigor.
5. **crosses herself:** makes the sign of the cross, a blessing or prayer often performed in times of danger.

Pierce (*angrily*). You in a hurry?
Ben (*smiling*). I sure am.
Pierce. You're a fool! Come on—

[*He kicks his horse.* BEN *shrugs, grins.*]

[*Int. Courtroom—Shooting toward the street. A wedding is in progress.* WILL KANE *and* AMY, *behind them the* HENDERSONS, *the* FULLERS, *and* MARTIN HOWE, *face* JUDGE METTRICK. *Most of the men are perspiring.* MRS. HENDERSON, *a woman conscious of her own importance in this community, and* MRS. FULLER, *a motherly looking woman, make futile motions with their handkerchiefs. In the street beyond and unseen by the group, the three riders pass from view.* JUDGE METTRICK *finds his place in his book, looks down at* AMY *and* WILL *with benign good humor, and begins.*]

Mettrick. Will Kane and Amy Fowler, you have come before me in my capacity as Justice of the Peace of this township . . .

[*Low Truck Shot—of the three men as they ride toward the* CAMERA. *They continue down the street, grim, implacable, deadly.*]

[*Ext. Ramirez Bar. Four men, loafing in front of the bar, are staring o.s.* GILLIS, *who owns the bar, turns excitedly to the others.*]

Gillis. Did you see what I saw? (*To one of the men*) Open 'er up, Joe! We're going to have a big day today—

[*Grinning, he hands* JOE *the key.*]

[*Ext. Street. On a bench in the f.g., a little barefoot* MEXICAN BOY *lies asleep. Past him, the three men ride in and out of the scene. Above the waist they are out of frames, but their holster guns and the rifles secured to their saddles are in plain and emphatic view. The little* BOY *sleeps on.*]

[*Int. Barbershop—Shooting to Street. The* BARBER *is shaving a* MAN.]

Barber. Hot? You call this hot?

[*He sees the three men ride by, and stops, amazed.*]

Barber. Well, I'll be—!
Man. What's the matter?

Barber. Thought I saw Ben Mitchell.

Man. He's down in Texas, somewheres.

Barber. I know. . . . *(He resumes work.)* Looked like Pierce and Colby too. Couldn't be, though . . . *(He shrugs.)*

[*Int. Helen's front room.* HARVEY *is in an easy chair, lighting a cigar. Near him,* HELEN *is combing her hair before a mirror on the wall.*]

Harvey. I thought they were all split up . . . I heard Ben Mitchell got killed down in Texas . . .

Helen *(matter-of-factly)*. Too bad he wasn't.

[*He looks at her speculatively, then rises and goes to her. He leans against the wall, and, with almost unconscious fascination, reaches over and fingers the ends of her long hair.*]

Harvey *(carefully)*. Ever hear from his brother? From Frank?

[*He lets go as* HELEN *stops, looks at him briefly, then continues.*]

Helen *(with finality)*. No.

[HARVEY *senses that the discussion is closed. He puffs his cigar, then smiles suddenly.*]

Harvey. Hey, maybe it's a good thing Kane's leaving town today.

Helen *(idly)*. Maybe.

[HARVEY *looks at her shrewdly. He reaches for a tendril of hair again. Unaware,* HELEN *tosses her mane, and he withdraws his fingers.*]

[*Int. Stationmaster's office. The* STATIONMASTER, *a small citified-looking man, is taking down a telegram. The ticker stops. He reads what he has written.*]

Stationmaster *(shocked)*. My goodness gracious—!

[*Then looking up, he sees—through the window—the three men. Dismounted, they are hitching their horses to the rail.*]

Stationmaster *(really upset now)*. Oh, my goodness!

[*Now, to his increasing dismay, the three men turn and approach him. Instinctively, he turns the message face down.*]

[*Ext. Stationmaster's office. A weather-faded sign is nailed near the window. It reads:*]

> THROUGH TRAIN—2 WHISTLES.
> STOP TRAIN   —3 WHISTLES.
>
> IF STATIONMASTER NOT IN OFFICE
> BUY TICKET FROM CONDUCTOR.

PIERCE, MITCHELL, *and* COLBY *move stiffly to the window. They get there.*]

Pierce *(wiping his forehead with his sleeve)*. Noon train on time?

Stationmaster *(nervously)*. Oh, yes, sir! At least I think so, sir. Don't know any reason why it shouldn't be, Mr. Pierce. How are you, Mr. Pierce? Mr. Mitchell, Mr. Colby?

[*They stare him down, then turn and move toward a bench. They sprawl on it, remembering they are hot and tired, as they reach for tobacco.* PIERCE *looks at his watch again.*]

[*Int. Stationmaster's office. The* STATIONMASTER *watches them. When he is sure that he is unobserved, he slips furtively*[6] *out by the rear door, carrying the telegram with him.*]

[*Int. Courtroom—as* METTRICK *concludes the ceremony.*]

Mettrick *(to* KANE*)*. Do you, Will Kane, take Amy to be your lawful wedded wife, to have and to hold from this day forward, until death do you part?

Kane. I do.

Mettrick. And do you, Amy, take Will to be your lawful husband, to have and to hold from this day forward, until death do you part?

Amy. I do.

Mettrick. The ring, please.

[KANE *gets it from* HENDERSON, *slips it on* AMY'S *finger.*]

Mettrick. Then, by the authority vested in me by the laws of this territory, I pronounce you man and wife.

[*There is the usual brief, tentative pause, with* KANE *very much aware of the others, and then he*

---

6. **furtively:** secretly.

"Do you, Will Kane, take Amy to be your lawful wedded wife. . . ."

takes AMY *in his arms and kisses her, rather briefly. The tension breaks. As the men crowd around* KANE *and the women surround* AMY, MET-TRICK *smilingly moves to* AMY.]

Mettrick. I can't speak for the rest of you men, but I claim an ancient privilege.

[*There is laughter as he kisses her.*]

[*Ext. Street—as the* STATIONMASTER, *clutching the telegram, hurries up the street, his passage occasioning curious stares from loafers and passersby.*]

[*Med. Close Shot—The two* OLD MEN, *sitting in the shade. They watch the* STATIONMASTER *pass.*]

First Old Man. Moving mighty fast for a Sunday.

[*Int. Marshal's office. The door leading to the courtroom is open, and* KANE *is leading* AMY *through it. He shuts it firmly behind him.*]

Amy (*embarrassed but amused*). Will—!
Kane. All those people.

[*He leads her away from the doorway toward his desk, where his holster and guns hang from a hook.*]

Kane (*as they move*). Seems to me people ought to be alone when they get married.

[*He is half-gay, half-serious, and* AMY *understands his urge to be away from the others.*]

Amy. I know. . . .

[*They are facing each other now, their eyes holding, very conscious of each other.*]

Kane (*awkwardly*). Amy, I'm going to try . . . I'll do my best.

[*He is brushing aside the formal vows of the ceremony with his own promise, and* AMY *understands.*]

Amy (*softly*). I will, too.

[*Their awareness of each other grows. This time, when they kiss, there is a healthy passion in the embrace, and they are both a little shaken when they part. The knock on the door startles them,* HENDERSON *opens the doors and leans through.*]

Henderson (*grinning*). The honeymoon is officially over—(*He turns and calls over his shoulder.*) Come on, everybody! . . . (*As the others come through the doorway*) And don't look so shocked, ladies. A man's entitled to some privacy on his wedding day—

Mettrick. That's debatable, Jo. However, one more ceremony, and Will's a free man. More or less.

[*Laughing, smiling, the group has converged on* WILL *and* AMY *at the desk.* KANE *understands* METTRICK'*s reference, and his hand goes up to his badge, then falls away. Unconsciously, he stalls a little.*]

Kane. I was hoping Harvey and Toby'd be here. . . . (*He grins.*) A man ought to be able to make a final speech to his deputies. And here they don't even show up for his wedding.

Mettrick. They'll be along before you leave.

[AMY *is watching* KANE *with quiet understanding.*]

Kane. I guess. . . . (*He reaches for his badge again, then stops.*) Tell the truth, I kind of hate to do this without your new marshal being here.

Henderson (*with mock solemnity*). Will, Sam Fuller and Mart Howe and I are the entire board of selectmen of this community. We are, also, your very good friends. And you've done such a fine job here, that I feel completely free to say—and the Judge will bear me out—(*he grins jovially, for his punch line*) that this town will be perfectly safe until tomorrow!

[KANE *joins in the general laughter. His eyes meet* AMY'*s, and when he speaks it is to her.*]

Kane (*ruefully*). All right. But I can't help it if I'm going to feel kind of naked without this tin star under my coat, not after six years—(*To the others*) Don't ever marry a Quaker. She'll have you running a store.

Fuller. Can't quite picture you doing that, Will.

Amy (*quietly*). I can.

Howe (*soberly*). So can I. And a good thing, too.

[AMY *flashes him a grateful look.* KANE *looks at him quizzically.*]

Kane. You didn't talk that way when you were wearing a star.

[*He shakes his head with mock sadness, and then a wicked glint comes into his eyes.*]

Kane. All right, it's coming off, but I got to be paid first.

[*Swiftly, he sweeps* AMY *off her feet and holds her aloft.*]

Amy. Will, let me down!

Kane. Not till you kiss me—

Amy (*laughing*). Let me down, you fool!

[*Then she gives in, and* KANE *lets her down. Grinning, he takes off his badge and pins it to his holster on the wall. The street door opens loudly, and as they turn to it, the* STATIONMASTER *hurries in.*]

Stationmaster (*breathless*). Marshal—! Telegram for you—(*As he hands it to* KANE) It's just terrible! It's shocking!

[*The others stare as* KANE *reads it.*]

Kane (*unbelievingly*). They—they pardoned Frank Mitchell.

Amy. What is it, Will?

Henderson. I don't believe it! (*He takes the wire from* KANE.) A week ago, too . . . Nice of them to let you know.

Stationmaster. That ain't all. Ben Mitchell's down at the depot with Jim Pierce and Jack Colby. They asked about the noon train.

Kane (*still dazed*). Noon train . . . ?

[*He turns to look at the wall clock, and the others follow his gaze. It is twenty to eleven.*]

Henderson. You get out of here, Will! You get out of town this minute!

[*The others join him as he hustles* KANE *and* AMY *to the door.*]

Amy. What is it? What's the matter—?

Henderson. Never mind—there's no time—

[*Ext. Marshal's office—as the group emerges, and* KANE *helps* AMY *up into the buckboard[7] at the hitching rail. He turns to the others.*]

Henderson. Go on—
Fuller. Yes, go on, Will!

[MART HOWE *has already unhitched the two horses and turned them to the street.* KANE *hesitates, then turns and climbs into the buckboard.*]

Henderson. Good luck, boy, and hurry!

[*He slaps one of the horses on the rump. They start and move into a gallop.* HENDERSON *and the others wave anxiously, as the wagon moves o.s.*]

[*Ext. Street. Pedestrians react as the buckboard rattles by,* KANE *whipping the horses with the reins.*]

[*Int. Helen's front room.* HARVEY PELL *is at the window, staring into the street. There is the o.s. rush and clatter of* KANE'S *wagon rolling past.*]

Harvey (*aloud*). That's funny. . . .
Helen's Voice. What?

[*She comes into the scene and to the window.*]

Harvey. You can't see now. Kane and his new wife took off in a big hurry.
Helen (*not amused*). What's so funny?
Harvey. I mean a big hurry. . . . Hey, you don't suppose Kane's scared of those three gunnies?

[HELEN *looks at him skeptically.*]

Harvey (*irritated*). Well, you didn't see him. I never saw him whip a horse that way.

[HELEN *stares at him. Obviously, he is telling the truth. She frowns, then goes to the door, opens it.*]

[*Int. Hall—as* HELEN *comes out, goes to the room next door, knocks.*]

Helen. Sam . . . ?
Sam's Voice. Come on in, Helen—

[*She opens the door and goes in.*]

[*Int. Hall. In his shirtsleeves,* SAM *is seated at a*

---

7. **buckboard:** a four-wheeled, open carriage drawn by horses.

table, cleaning a rifle. He looks up at HELEN'S *entrance.*]

Helen (*quietly*). Ben Mitchell's in town. He's got two of the old bunch with him.

[SAM *looks at her unwinkingly, then gets up slowly.*]

Sam (*simply*). I guess I'll take a look around.

[*He starts to put on his coat.*]

[*Ext. Street—on the* STATIONMASTER *hurrying back to the station. As he reaches the barbershop, the* BARBER *comes out, razor in hand.*]

Barber. What's going on, Oliver?
Stationmaster (*not without pleasure in his role*). Frank Mitchell's been let go.
Barber (*amazed*). No! . . . Then that *was* Ben I seen just now—
Stationmaster. It sure was—and Pierce and Colby, too.
Barber. You don't say! Where's Kane?
Stationmaster. He's left.
Barber. That's a smart man.

[*They part, the* STATIONMASTER *going on down the street, the* BARBER *returning into his shop.*]

Barber (*as he goes in*). Now, Mr. Thompson, didn't I tell you—?

[CAMERA HOLDS *on window of the shop.*]

[*Ext. Prairie—Med. Long Shot—on the buckboard as it careens over the uneven plain,* KANE *keeping the horses at a wild gallop. But then, gradually, as the wagon approaches the* CAMERA, KANE *begins to rein up.*]

[*Ext. Prairie—Buckboard—as* KANE *brings it to a halt. He is frowning with thought, struggling with himself.* AMY *stares at him.*]

Amy. Why are you stopping?
Kane (*finally*). It's no good, I've got to go back, Amy.
Amy. Why?
Kane. This is crazy. I haven't even got any guns.
Amy. Then let's go on—hurry!
Kane. No. That's what I've been thinking. They're making me run. I never run from anybody before.

"I sent a man up five years ago for murder."

Amy *(frantic).* Who? . . . I don't understand any of this.

Kane *(taking out his watch).* I haven't got time to tell you.

Amy. Then don't go back, Will.

Kane. I've got to. That's the whole thing.

[He whips the horses and turns them back toward the town.]

[Ext. Railroad station. BEN MITCHELL, PIERCE, *and* COLBY *are on the bench.* BEN *is drinking from an almost depleted whiskey bottle. He hands it to* COLBY, *who takes a swallow, and returns it.* BEN *offers it to* PIERCE, *who shakes his head angrily.]*

Pierce. I thought you'd grew up by now.

Ben. I thought your disposition[8] might've sweetened a little down in Abilene. Guess we were both wrong.

[He takes another drink.]

[Int. Saloon. Six more men have joined the others. GILLIS, *flushed with a drink and anticipation, is in the center of a group at the bar. He pounds on it with his open hand for emphasis and attention.]*

Gillis. Hit the bar, all of you! I'm settin' 'em up!

[They move to the bar in acceptance of his largess.[9]]

[Int. Helen's front room. HELEN *and* HARVEY *are facing* SAM.]

Helen. How could they pardon Frank? He was in for life—

Sam *(shrugging).* He's out.

Harvey *(a glint of triumph in his eyes).* So that's why Kane run away.

*[*HELEN *looks at him, starts to say something, then stops. There is the o.s. clatter of hoofbeats in the streets. They turn to the window.]*

[Ext. Street—from HELEN's *point of view.* KANE's *buckboard can be seen clattering past toward his office.* HELEN *turns to the others and looks quizzically at* HARVEY. *He scowls under the amusement in her eyes.]*

---

8. **disposition** (dis'pə·zish'en): attitude.
9. **largess** (lär·jes'): generosity.

[Ext. Marshal's office—as the buckboard pulls up before it.]

[Int. Barbershop. The BARBER *is finishing with his customer. An elderly man,* FRED, *hurries in.]*

Fred *(excited).* Kane's back!

[The customer sits up.]

Barber. Don't believe it!

Fred. Just seen him.

[The BARBER *looks at the clock. It is ten minutes to eleven.]*

Barber. How many coffins we got?

Fred. Two.

Barber. We're gonna need at least two more, no matter how you figure it. You better get busy, Fred.

*[*FRED *nods and hurries out through a rear door. The* BARBER *remembers his customer, and removes the cloth with a flourish.]*

Barber. All finished, Mr. Thompson. You look just fine!

[Int. Marshal's office. AMY *and* KANE *come in, and* KANE *goes quickly to where his guns hang on the wall.* AMY *watches him as he buckles them on. His mind is already in the future, and she knows it. Nevertheless, she perseveres.]*

Amy. Please, Will—!

*[*KANE *looks at her, then goes on.]*

Amy *(desperately).* If you'd only tell me what this is all about.

Kane *(checking his guns).* I sent a man up five years ago for murder. He was supposed to hang, but up north they commuted it to life. Now he's free—I don't know how. Anyway, it looks like he's coming back.

Amy. I still don't understand—

Kane *(choosing his words carefully).* He's a . . . he was always wild—kind of crazy. . . . He'll probably make trouble . . .

Amy. That's no concern of yours—not anymore!

Kane. I'm the one who sent him up.

Amy. That was part of your job. That's finished now. They've got a new marshal—!

Kane. Won't be here till tomorrow. Seems to me I've got to stay a while. *(He reaches for his star.)* Anyway, I'm the same man—with or without this.

[*He pins it on.*]

Amy. No!
Kane *(patiently).* I expect he'll come looking for me. Three of his old bunch are waiting at the depot.
Amy. That's what makes it so stupid.
Kane *(still patient).* If he does, and if we run— they'll just come after us. Four of them, and we'd be all alone on the prairie.
Amy. We've got an hour!

[*They both look at the clock. It shows nine minutes to eleven.*]

Kane. What's an hour?
Amy. We could reach—
Kane *(cutting in).* What's a hundred miles, even? We'd never be able to keep that store, Amy. They'd come after us. We'd have to run again. Long as we live.
Amy. No, we wouldn't—not if they didn't know where to find us!

[KANE'S *face tightens. He starts toward the door.* AMY *stops him.*]

Amy. Will, I'm begging you—please! Let's go!
Kane. I can't.
Amy *(frantic).* Don't try to be a hero! You don't have to be a hero—not for me!
Kane *(losing his temper).* I'm not trying to be a hero! If you think I like this, you're crazy! *(He masters himself.)* Amy, look. This is my town. I've got friends here. Toby and Harvey'll be here. I'll swear in a bunch of special deputies. With a posse behind me, maybe there won't even be any trouble.
Amy *(defeated).* You don't believe that. Where there are guns, there'll always be trouble.
Kane. Then it's better to have it here. I'm sorry, honey. I know how you feel about it—
Amy *(harshly).* How do you know how I feel about it?
Kane *(awkwardly).* I know it's against your religion and all. Of course I know how you feel about it.

Amy *(bitterly).* But you're doing it just the same.
Kane *(helplessly).* Amy.

[AMY *comes to him, her heart in her eyes, deliberately throwing all she has of magnetism and sex at him.*]

Amy. Will, we were married just a few minutes ago—doesn't that mean anything to you? We've got our whole lives ahead of us. You want me, Will, or you wouldn't have married me. If you love me, Will—

[*With an effort,* KANE *gently pushes her aside.* AMY *is shattered.*]

Kane. Amy, you know I've only got an hour. I've got things to do. You stay at the hotel till it's over.

[*With his hand at her elbow, he starts toward the door.* AMY *holds her ground.*]

Amy *(harshly).* No! You're asking me to wait an hour to find out if I'm going to be a wife or a widow, and I say it's too long to wait! I won't do it!
Kane *(stunned).* Amy.
Amy. I know—you think I'm just saying it— because I'm angry. But I mean it! If you won't go with me now—I'll be on that train when it leaves here.

[*Their eyes meet and hold.*]

Kane *(finally).* I've got to stay, Amy.

[AMY *tries to mask her hurt. Chin high, she moves past him to the door, and out.* KANE *stares after her a moment, then follows her out.*]

[*Ext. Marshal's office.* JUDGE METTRICK *is tying his horse to the hitching rail as* AMY *emerges. Too blinded by tears of hurt and anger to see him, she climbs into the buckboard.* METTRICK *looks on impassively, first at* AMY *and then at* KANE *when the Marshal comes out. The two men watch as* AMY *turns the horses toward the station and whips them out of the scene. Then, as* METTRICK *takes down his saddlebags,* KANE *comes toward him, his face lightening with relief.*]

Kane. I'm glad you got here, Perce.
Mettrick *(evenly).* Are you?

[*Carrying the bags, he walks deliberately past*

KANE *and into the office. Surprised,* KANE *follows him.*]

[*Int. Marshal's office.* METTRICK *strides quickly across the room into the courtroom.* KANE *continues after him, puzzled.*]

[*Int. Courtroom.* METTRICK *goes to the desk that serves as the bench, and quickly begins to stuff the saddlebags with papers, his gavel, and other belongings. During the course of the scene, he will also pack his legal books, and when the bags are full he will stack and tie the remainder of his books with rawhide thongs. Watching from the doorway,* KANE *stares at him with sick understanding.* METTRICK *is very much aware of* KANE's *eyes on him. Finally, he pauses in his work.*]

Mettrick (*sharply*). Are you forgetting I'm the man who passed sentence on Frank Mitchell?

[KANE *shakes his head numbly.* METTRICK *resumes his hurried packing.*]

Mettrick. You shouldn't have come back. It was stupid.
Kane. I figured I had to. I figured it was better to stay.
Mettrick. You figured wrong.
Kane. I can deputize a posse. Ten, twelve guns is all I'd need.
Mettrick. My intuition tells me otherwise.
Kane. Why?

[METTRICK *looks up at the wall clock. It is seven minutes to eleven.*]

Mettrick (*bitterly*). There's no time for a lesson in civics,[10] my boy.

[*On the wall behind the bench are an American flag of the period and a picture of Justice, with scales and blindfold. The* JUDGE *goes to them and starts to take down and fold up the flag. Almost helplessly, he begins to talk.*]

Mettrick (*taking down the flag*). In the fifth century B.C., the citizens of Athens—having suffered grievously under a tyrant—managed to depose and banish him. However, when he returned after

---

10. **civics:** the study of the rights and duties of citizenship.

some years with an army of mercenaries, these same citizens not only opened the gates to him, but stood by while he executed the members of the legal government. A similar thing took place about eight years ago in a town called Indian Falls. I escaped death only through the intercession of a lady of somewhat dubious reputation, and at the cost of a handsome ring that once belonged to my mother. (*He shrugs.*) Unfortunately, I have no more rings.

[*He has neatly folded up the flag by now and has placed it in one of the saddlebags. He turns to the picture of Justice and takes it down.*]

Kane. But you're a judge—
Mettrick. I've been a judge many times in many towns. I hope to live to be a judge again.
Kane (*giving up*). I can't tell you what to do.
Mettrick (*harshly*). Will, why must you be such a fool! Have you forgotten what he is? Have you forgotten what he's done to people? Have you forgotten that he's *crazy?*

[*He points to the vacant chair near the defense table.*]

Mettrick. Don't you remember when he sat in that chair there and said—

[*Close Shot—Vacant chair*]

Mettrick's Voice. You'll never hang me! I'll be back! I'll kill you, Kane! I swear it, I'll kill you!

[*Back to scene.* KANE *and* METTRICK *stare at each other.*]

Kane (*after a pause*). Yeah . . . I remember.

[*Closeup—Whiskey bottle—as it shatters loudly on the railroad track, and the shards and splinters tumble and glitter in the sunlight. Then the* CAMERA TILTS UP *to reveal* MITCHELL, PIERCE, *and* COLBY *in the b.g.* COLBY *is staring at the broken glass with childlike interest.* PIERCE *is scowling angrily at* BEN, *who is looking innocently off.*]

[*Int. Stationmaster's office—*AMY *and the* STATIONMASTER. *Separated by the counter, they are both staring through the window at the three men on the platform outside,* AMY *with her fascinated loathing, the* STATIONMASTER *worried. Then they* *exchange a quiet look, and the* STATIONMASTER *goes back to what he has been doing. He stamps* AMY's *ticket and hands it to her.*]

Stationmaster (*soberly*). Here you are, ma'am. This'll take you to St. Louis.

[*She wants to turn away to sit down, then realizes that she will have to share the station with* MITCHELL, PIERCE, *and* COLBY *for the next hour. The* STATIONMASTER *senses her predicament.*]

Stationmaster (*kindly*). Maybe you'd rather wait somewheres else, ma'am? Like at the hotel, maybe. We'll get three whistles if the train's going to stop, and you'll have plenty of time to get down here.
Amy (*puzzled*). If the train stops?
Stationmaster (*embarrassed*). Yes, ma'am. It don't always, little town like this. I'd hate to tell you how many times she's just run right through my flag, 'specially if she's late. But she will stop to let off passengers . . .
Amy. I see. Thank you.

[*She turns and starts out.*]

Stationmaster (*sincerely*). I'm awful sorry about this, Mrs. Kane. But the Marshal can handle himself all right.
Amy (*wryly*). Thank you very much.

[*She goes out of the scene.*]

[*Ext. Platform—Group shot—*MITCHELL, PIERCE, *and* COLBY. BEN *is looking off, and when* AMY *appears in the b.g. and goes to the buckboard, he follows her with his eyes.*]

Ben (*lightly*). That wasn't here five years ago.
Pierce. So what?
Ben (*smiling*). Nothing . . . Yet . . . Maybe.

[*His smile broadens as* PIERCE's *irritation mounts, and he continues to watch* AMY *until she is out of sight.*]

[*Int. Helen Ramirez's sitting room. The table has been set, and* HELEN *and* HARVEY *are eating breakfast.* HELEN *looks at the clock. It is five minutes to eleven.*]

Helen (*quietly*). Don't you think Kane will be looking for you about now?

Harvey (*carelessly*). Yeah.

[*He continues eating.* HELEN *watches him.*]

Helen (*mildly*). You're really sore at him.
Harvey (*pausing*). Wouldn't you be, if you were me?
Helen (*gently*). Suppose I would—if I were you.

[HARVEY *looks at her, not quite certain of her meaning. Then he goes back to his food.* HELEN *resumes eating. They eat in silence for a while. Then an idea begins to grow in him, and he smiles suddenly. He wipes his mouth and pushes away from the table.*]

Harvey. I'll be back in a while.

[*Grinning now, he gets his hat and goes.* HELEN *looks after him speculatively.*]

[*Int. Hall.* HARVEY *comes out of the room. Down the hall Sam's door is open, and* SAM *can be seen sitting quiet guard in the doorway. He looks at* HARVEY *without expression and without warmth or liking. But* HARVEY *is too pleased with himself to care. Whistling softly, he goes to the stairs.*]

[*Int. Stairway—as* HARVEY *comes down the stairs.*]

[*Int. Lobby. The* HOTEL CLERK *watches* HARVEY *come down, cross the lobby, and go out.*]

[*Ext. Hotel.* HARVEY *comes out and walks down the street. Two* SMALL BOYS *in their Sunday best run into the scene, to* HARVEY.]

First Boy. Hey, Harvey!

[HARVEY *turns to see them, grins.*]

Second Boy. You gonna shoot it out with Frank Mitchell, Harvey? Are you?
First Boy. You gonna kill him, Harvey?
Harvey (*ruffling his hair*). I sure am.

[AMY's *buckboard clatters into the scene and past.* HARVEY, *puzzled, watches her stop before the hotel and climb down.*]

Second Boy (*tugging at* HARVEY's *shirt*). Hey, Harvey—
Harvey. Go on, go on, you ought to be in church— the both of you.

[*He throws a final look at the hotel, which* AMY *has entered, and walks off.*]

[*Int. Hotel lobby—at desk. The* CLERK *is staring at* AMY.]

Amy. May I wait for the noon train? (*As the* CLERK *continues to stare at her*) I said may I wait in the lobby until noon?
Clerk (*unabashed*[11]). Sure, lady.
Amy (*turning away*). Thank you.
Clerk. You're Mrs. Kane, ain't you?
Amy. Yes.
Clerk. And you're leaving on the noon train?
Amy (*sharply*). Yes.
Clerk (*skeptically*). But your husband ain't?
Amy (*studying him*). No. Why?
Clerk (*coolly*). No reason. But it's mighty interesting. Now me, I wouldn't leave this town at noon for all the tea in China. (*He smiles vindictively.*) No sir. It's going to be quite a sight to see.

[AMY *stares at him, puzzled by his hostility, then goes to a chair near the window.*]

[*Ext. Marshal's office—at hitching rail.* KANE *watches the* JUDGE *make his saddlebags and books secure.* METTRICK *gives the straps a final tug, hesitates, then turns to face* KANE.]

Mettrick. Goodbye, Will.
Kane (*flatly*). Goodbye.

[METTRICK *is horribly ashamed.* KANE *tries to hide his own sick, still somewhat dazed, shock and disappointment.*]

Mettrick. You think I'm letting you down, don't you?
Kane. No.
Mettrick. Look, this is just a dirty little village in the middle of nowhere. Nothing that happens here is really important. Get out!
Kane. There isn't time.
Mettrick (*staring at him*). What a waste. (*Gently*) Good luck.

[*He turns, mounts, rides off.* KANE *looks after him a moment, then turns to go into his office. He sees a* BOY *of about fifteen who has been lounging curiously nearby, trying to overhear.*]

---

11. **unabashed:** not embarrassed.

Kane (*calling him*). Johnny—

[JOHNNY *comes over to him. His wide eyes make it obvious that he knows what is going on.*]

Kane. Why aren't you in church?
Johnny. Why ain't you?

[KANE *raises his arm in a mock threat, then drops it.*]

Kane. Do something for me. Find Joe Henderson, Mart Howe, and Sam Fuller, and tell 'em I want 'em here. And then go find Harve Pell—
Harvey's Voice. Don't have to do that—here I am.

[KANE*'s face lights up as he turns and sees* HARVEY *approaching them.* JOHNNY *takes off.* KANE *senses that* HARVEY *needs no explanation.*]

Kane (*with gruff warmth*). Where you been?
Harvey (*lightly*). Busy.

[KANE *is able to smile. He knows what being "busy" usually means for* HARVEY, *and even at this moment his paternal feelings for the younger man can break through the situation. Then he sobers.*]

Kane. You know what's doing?
Harvey. Sure.
Kane. Come on. Lots to do.

[*He starts to go into the office, but* HARVEY *stops him gently and leans against the door jamb.*]

Harvey. Hold up a second. (*As* KANE *stares at him*) This ain't really your job, you know.
Kane (*almost absently*). That's what everybody keeps telling me.

[*He starts in again, but* HARVEY *bars his way with his arm.*]

Harvey. Yeah, but when I tell you it means something. So you listen a second.
Kane (*humoring him*). All right, I'm listening.
Harvey. Now, the way I see it, if you'd gone, and with the new marshal not due till tomorrow, I'd be in charge around here. Right?
Kane (*patiently*). Right.
Harvey. Well, tell me this then. If I'm good enough to hold down the job when there's trouble, how come the city fathers didn't trust me with it permanent?

[KANE *stares at him, beginning to be disturbed.*]

Kane. I don't know.
Harvey *(thinly).* Don't you?
Kane *(flatly).* No.
Harvey. That's funny. I figured you carried a lot of weight.
Kane. Maybe they didn't ask me. Maybe they thought you were too young.
Harvey. You think I'm too young, too?

[KANE's *irritation and his liking for* HARVEY *struggle with each other. His liking wins.*]

Kane. You sure act like it sometimes! Come on!

[*Grabbing* HARVEY, *he shoves him inside ahead of him.*]

[*Int. Marshal's office.* KANE *propels* HARVEY *into the room.*]

Harvey *(triumphantly).* Now here's what I want you to do, Will. When the old boys come, you tell 'em you want me to be marshal, and tomorrow they can tell the new man they're sorry but the job's filled.
Kane *(stopping).* You really mean it, don't you?
Harvey. Sure.
Kane. Well, I can't do it.
Harvey. Why not?
Kane. If you don't know, there's no use me telling you.
Harvey. You mean you won't do it.

[KANE *looks at him helplessly, then turns away from him and goes toward the desk. The clock on the wall reads one minute to eleven.*]

Kane. Have it your way.
Harvey *(flaring).* All right. The truth is you probably talked against me from the start. You been sore about me and Helen Ramirez right along, ain't you?
Kane *(surprised).* You and Helen Ramirez? I don't—*(He begins to understand.)* It so happens I didn't know, and it don't mean anything to me one way or another. You ought to know that.
Harvey. Yeah? You been washed up for more than a year—you go out and get yourself married—only you can't stand anybody taking your place there, can you? Especially me!
Kane *(overwhelmed).* You're—

[*He cannot find words. He turns and looks at the clock. It is two minutes after eleven.*]

Kane. I haven't got time, Harve . . .
Harvey. Okay! Then let's get down to business. You want me to stick, you put the word in for me like I said.
Kane *(quietly).* Sure, I want you to stick, but I'm not buying it. It's got to be up to you.

[*They look at each other as if across a chasm.* HARVEY *sees that* KANE *means it. He cannot quite believe it, but he is committed now. He goes to the desk, takes off his gun belt and badge, puts them down, turns and goes out.* KANE *stares after him, sick at heart.*]

[*Ext. Countryside—Med. Long Shot—on two riders galloping single file toward* CAMERA.]

[*Ext. Countryside. The two riders near the* CAMERA. *The man in front,* ED PETERSON, *reins up. The other rider, who wears a star, pulls up beside him. This is* TOBY, KANE's *second deputy.* TOBY *looks at* PETERSON *warily.*]

Peterson. How about resting a minute?
Toby. I'm in a hurry.
Peterson. I ain't.
Toby. I know. Goldarn you, I ought to be kissing a bride about now instead of riding herd on a mean old polecat like you.

Peterson. Come on—how about a smoke?

[*He raises his arms, and we see now that his wrists are bound by a rawhide thong.*]

Toby. You gonna be a good boy?
Peterson. You know me, Toby.
Toby. Sure, I know you . . .

[*He takes out a knife and cuts the leather strap.* PETERSON *reaches for his tobacco.*]

Toby. Make it a quick one. I want to get to that wedding before it's over.

[*Int. Helen's front room—Close Shot—*HARVEY. *He is red-faced, baffled. There is the o.s. sound of* HELEN's *laughter.*]

Harvey. What's so funny?

[CAMERA PULLS BACK *to include* HELEN. *She pulls herself together somewhat.*]

Helen. You didn't really think you could put that over on Kane, did you?

Harvey. Why not?

Helen. When are you going to grow up?

Harvey (*angrily*). I'm getting tired of that kind of talk.

Helen (*lightly*). Then grow up.

[HARVEY *is increasingly irritated and confused under the goad*[12] *of the almost maternal pity in her laughter and manner.*]

Harvey. Cut it out!

Helen (*gently*). All right.

[*She pats his cheek placatingly, but* HARVEY *shoves her hand away. Under her level look, he starts to pace angrily.*]

Harvey. Why shouldn't he have gone for it? He needs me. He'll need me plenty when Mitchell gets here.

Helen (*watching him*). That's possible.

Harvey. He should've had me made marshal to begin with. He's just sore, is all. He's sore about you and me.

Helen (*frowning*). Is he?

Harvey. Sure.

Helen (*quietly*). You told him?

Harvey (*unaware of his danger*). Sure.

Helen (*with controlled rage*). You're a fool.

Harvey (*reacting to her tone*). Why? Didn't you want him to know? (*With a blind impulse to hurt her*) Say, who did the walking out anyway, you or him?

Helen (*flatly*). Get out, Harvey.

[HARVEY *begins to realize that he has made a fatal blunder.*]

Harvey. I might just do that.

Helen (*and she means it*). Then do it.

Harvey. You don't mean that.

Helen. You think not?

Harvey (*beginning to bluster*). You're going to talk different when Frank Mitchell gets in. You might want somebody around you when you're explaining to him about Kane.

Helen. I can take care of myself.

---

12. **goad:** driving impulse which spurs action.

Harvey. Sure. Only from what I've heard you might not be so pretty when he gets through with you.

[HELEN *looks at him with cold disgust, then goes to the door and opens it.*]

Harvey (*his last attempt*). I won't be back.

Helen (*quietly*). Good.

[*He slams the door as he goes. Alone,* HELEN *paces the floor. She looks at the clock. It is five after eleven. She comes to a decision, goes to the door, opens it.*]

[*Int. Hall. In his room,* SAM *looks up as* HELEN'*s door opens.*]

Helen. Sam—

[*He rises and goes to her.*]

Helen. I think I have to talk to Mr. Weaver.

Sam. You're getting out?

Helen. Yes.

[*He considers her answer, accepts it.*]

Sam. You want me to give Kane a hand?

[HELEN *thinks it over, almost but not quite disguising her inner struggle. Then she makes her decision.*]

Helen (*flatly*). No.

[SAM *nods, turns and goes.*]

[*Int. Helen's front room. She shuts the door, stands there a moment, thinking, then walks unhurriedly toward her bedroom.* CAMERA PANS *with her. Reflected in her dresser mirror, we can see her beginning to change.*]

[*Int. Marshal's office.* KANE *is at his desk, lost in thought. There is the sound of his door opening, and he jerks into awareness and turns. A solidly built, normally pleasant-looking man, now scowling with indignation, is coming in. His name is* BAKER.]

Baker. Will—I just heard!

Kane (*rising*). Hello, Herb—

Baker. You can count on me. You know that, don't you?

Kane (*his spirits rising*). I figured I could.

Baker. Why, you cleaned this town up—you made it fit for women and children to live in, and neither Mitchell or nobody else is going to drag it down again!

Kane. I was hoping people'd feel that way.

Baker. What other way is there? *(As* KANE *shrugs)* How many men you got lined up?

Kane. None, yet.

[BAKER *looks at the clock. It is seven after eleven.*]

Baker. You better get going, man—*(He starts out.)* I'll be back in ten minutes *(grins)*—loaded for bear.

[KANE *looks after him, touched and encouraged. He looks up at the clock, then frowns as he remembers his scene with* HARVEY PELL. *He takes a wanted poster from a desk drawer, and on its back he writes:*

"BACK IN FIVE MINUTES—
KANE."

He props this up on his desk and goes out.]

[*Ext. Saloon.* HARVEY PELL, *still seething, strides toward the saloon. He passes two* INDIANS *lounging before the saloon, and goes in.*]

[*Int. Saloon. It is crowded now, with an almost holiday atmosphere.* HARVEY *comes in and goes to the bar. His entrance gains considerable attention. Some of the* MEN *nod, and* HARVEY *returns the gesture briefly. The* BARTENDER *comes to him with a bottle and glass, and* HARVEY *pours himself*

Kane walks steadily toward the hotel.

a drink. GILLIS, *the owner, leaves the group he is with and comes to the bar next to* HARVEY. HARVEY *ignores him as he drinks.*]

Gillis. Hi, Harve.
Harvey. How are you?
Gillis. Where's the tin star?
Harvey. I turned it in. I quit.
Gillis. Smart move.
Harvey. I didn't ask for your opinion.

[*He takes the bottle and glass and moves to a vacant table.* GILLIS *looks after him wisely.*]

[*Ext. Street.* KANE *walks steadily toward the hotel. The street seems empty except for him, but* KANE *has the feeling that eyes are watching him.*]

[*Int. Room overlooking street. A* MAN *and a* WOMAN, *townspeople, are looking out of the window at* KANE *as he passes.*]

[*Ext. Street—Truck Shot with* KANE. *The two* LITTLE BOYS *we have seen before dash into the scene, one in pursuit of the other. The pursuer extends his arm and shoots.*]

First Boy. Bang! Bang!—You're dead, Kane!

[*He turns and runs headlong into* KANE, *who holds and steadies him. The* BOY *looks up and recognizes* KANE. *His mouth goes wide in dazed panic. Then he jerks out of* KANE's *grasp and runs away, as the other* BOY *disappears as well.* KANE *continues up the street.*]

[*Ext. Depot—*MITCHELL, PIERCE, *and* COLBY. COLBY *is playing a Western folk tune on his harmonica.* BEN *takes a deep drag of his cigarette, then flips the butt away sharply and gets to his feet.* PIERCE *watches him narrowly.* BEN *stretches.*]

Ben. You know what? Think I'll go get some liquor.
Pierce. You have to have it?
Ben. Yep.
Pierce. If you're going after that woman—
Ben. I said I was going for liquor.

[*He starts to walk away.*]

Pierce. You keep away from Kane.
Ben. Sure. I can wait.

[*He saunters on.*]

[*Ext. Hotel. As* KANE *nears the hotel, he sees the buckboard hitched before it. His face brightens and his pace quickens.*]

[*Int. Hotel Lobby.* AMY, *sitting near the window, sees* KANE *approaching. Believing he is coming to her, she is overjoyed. Rising, she hurries to the door, and is there waiting for him when he comes in.* KANE *takes her arms in his happily.*]

Kane. Amy, you changed your mind.

[AMY *stares up at him, the joy ebbing out of her eyes as she begins to understand him. She disengages her arms.*]

Amy (*dully*). I'd thought you had changed yours. No, Will, I have my ticket.
Kane (*brought down*). I see.

[*He looks at her, his disappointment suddenly boiling over into anger, then turns from her and goes toward the desk. The* CLERK *is leaning on it, watching him come. There is no sympathy in his eyes. As* KANE *nears the desk, an elderly* CHAMBERMAID *comes in with mop and pail, and reaches the desk at the same time as he does. Ignoring* KANE, *the* CLERK *gets a key and tosses it on the counter toward the* CHAMBERMAID.]

Clerk. Open 19, and clean it up good. (*Deliberately*) Mr. Mitchell's very particular.

[*As she takes the key and goes, he looks at* KANE *calmly.* KANE's *face tightens.*]

Kane. Helen Ramirez in?
Clerk. Guess so.

[KANE *looks at him, turns and goes to the stairs.*]

Clerk (*meaningly*). Think you can find it all right?

[KANE *doesn't answer. He starts up the stairs. The* CLERK *grins.* AMY *is watching* KANE *as he goes, puzzled.*]

[*Int. Stairway—on* KANE *as he mounts the stairs.*]

[*Int. Hall—on* KANE *as he comes to the landing and goes to Helen's door. He knocks.*]

[*Int. Helen's bedroom. She is packing as she hears* KANE's *knock.*]

Helen. Come—

[*Int. Helen's front room—as* KANE *enters, looks around, sees no one, waits.*]

[*Int. Helen's bedroom. She stops, puzzled, then goes to the front room.*]

[*Int. Helen's front room.* HELEN *enters the room, stops short as she sees* KANE. *Their eyes meet and hold. The silent tension grows, seeming to fill the room as with an explosive gas. It is* HELEN *who breaks the silence.*]

Helen (*quietly*). What are you looking at? You think I've changed?
Kane. No.

[*All the long-pent fury of her baffled anger and wounded pride overflows.*]

Helen. Well, what do you want? You want me to help you? You want me to ask Frank to let you go? You want me to beg for you? Well, I won't do it. I won't lift a finger for you. You're on your own!

[KANE *has been waiting patiently for the storm to subside.*]

Kane (*gently*). I came to tell you he was coming. I should've figured you'd know about it.

[HELEN *has pulled herself together, angry and ashamed with herself.*]

Helen. I know about it.
Kane. I think you ought to get out of town. I might not be able to—well, anything can happen.
Helen (*quietly*). I'm not afraid of him.
Kane. I know you're not, but you know how he is.
Helen (*dully*). I know how he is.

[*She turns away from him, goes to the window. They are both silent for a moment.*]

Helen (*without hope*). Maybe he doesn't know.
Kane. He probably got letters.
Helen. Probably. (*She smiles without humor.*) Nothing in life is free. I'm getting out—I'm packing now.
Kane. That's good.

[*He hesitates, then turns to the door. Hearing him, she turns. Again, their eyes meet and hold.*]

Helen (*in Spanish*). It's been more than a year.
Kane (*also in Spanish*). Yes, I know.

[*There is a pause. Then, unable to help herself,* HELEN *goes on, still in Spanish.*]

Helen. Do you want to kiss me goodbye? (*But as* KANE *hesitates, she cuts in sharply in English.*) Never mind! Goodbye.
Kane. Goodbye, Helen.

[*He turns to the door again.*]

Helen (*flatly*). Kane. (*As he looks at her*) If you're smart, you'll get out yourself.
Kane. I can't.
Helen. I didn't think you would.

[*He goes out.* HELEN *stares after him. For a moment her heart and soul are in her eyes, going after him.*]

Helen (*to herself, in Spanish*). Do you want to kiss me goodbye?

[*She grimaces with self-contempt. Then, herself again, she turns and goes to her bedroom.*]

[*Int. Hotel lobby.* AMY, *back at the window, and the* CLERK, *behind the desk, listen to* KANE's *footsteps as he comes down the steps. As he reaches the landing, his eyes go to the clock. It is 11:11. Deliberately, the* CLERK *takes his watch out, checks it with the clock, apparently adjusts it and then starts to wind it.* KANE *looks at him, then turns and goes to the door. As he passes her,* AMY *averts[13] her head. Without breaking stride,* KANE *goes out.*]

[*Ext. Saloon.* BEN MITCHELL *approaches the saloon and goes inside.*]

[*Int. Saloon. The murmur of conversation and cards stops as the men recognize* BEN. *Unconcerned, he goes to the bar, takes out a silver dollar.*]

Bartender (*obsequiously[14]*). How are you, Ben?

---

13. **averts:** turns aside.
14. **obsequiously** (əb·sē′kwē·əs·lē): in a way that exaggerates his willingness to serve.

Ben. All right. Give me a bottle.
Bartender. Sure thing!

[*He turns away to get one.* GILLIS *has sidled up to the bar.*]

Gillis. It's been a long time, Ben!

[BEN *looks at him dryly.*]

Gillis. Yes, sir! How's Frank?

[*The* BARTENDER *returns with the bottle.*]

Ben. He's not complaining.
Gillis (*jovially*). Well, there'll be a hot time in the old town tonight, hey Ben?

[BEN *looks at him, then grins suddenly.*]

Ben. I wouldn't be surprised.

[*Int. Hotel lobby.* AMY *is still at the window, her face mirroring her inner struggle. Then, giving in, she turns and goes to the desk. The* CLERK *waits coolly for her approach.*]

Amy (*trying to cover her embarrassment*). May I ask you something?
Clerk. Sure.
Amy. Who is Miss Ramirez?
Clerk (*enjoying himself*). Mrs. Ramirez. She used to be a friend of your husband's awhile back. Before that, she was a friend of Frank Mitchell.
Amy (*off balance*). I see. Thank you—(*She starts to go back to her place, stops.*) You—don't like my husband, do you?
Clerk. No.
Amy. Why?
Clerk. Lots of reasons. One thing, this place was always busy when Frank Mitchell was around. I'm not the only one—there's plenty of people around here think he's got a comeuppance[15] coming. You asked me, ma'am, so I'm telling you.
Amy (*quietly*). Thank you.

[*She goes back to the window thoughtfully.*]

[*Closeup—Clock in Marshal's office. It reads 11:16.* CAMERA PANS DOWN *to reveal the empty room and the note still on* KANE's *desk. Then* KANE *enters, looks around and realizes that no one has come yet. He looks up at the clock wor-*

---

15. **comeuppance:** overdue punishment for past actions.

riedly. Then, frowning, he gets the note, goes back to the door, spikes the note on a nail on the outside of the door and goes out, closing the door behind him.]

[*Ext. Street.—Truck Shot—*KANE—*as he comes out and starts down the street. He approaches the saloon, hesitates, then goes on. He changes his mind, crosses the street and goes to the saloon. As he reaches the door and is about to go in, it swings out and* BEN MITCHELL *emerges. Both men are taken off balance for an instant, and then they achieve control. Their eyes hold for a long moment. Then* BEN's *lips curl in a confident grin. Shifting his grip on his quart of whiskey, he turns and deliberately walks away, whistling softly.* KANE *looks after him, tight-lipped, then takes a deep breath, and pushes the door open. There is a burst of laughter from within.*]

[*Int. Saloon.* KANE's *entrance is unnoticed at first except by those near the door.* GILLIS *is in a small group, his back to the door.*]

Gillis (*loudly*). I'll give you odds Kane's dead five minutes after Frank gets off the train!
Man. That's not much time.
Gillis. That's all Frank'll need—because—

[*He becomes aware that everyone is looking past him to the entrance, turns and sees* KANE *standing there. The room has gone silent.* KANE *starts over slowly toward* GILLIS, *his face tight. He has had enough. When he reaches* GILLIS, *he stops, then swings from the hip.* GILLIS *goes down to the floor. No one moves as he lies there a moment, then sits up dazedly, wiping the blood from his lips.*]

Gillis (*thickly*). You carry a badge and a gun, Marshal. You had no call to do that.

[KANE *slumps, suddenly and obscurely ashamed.*]

Kane. You're right.

[*He starts toward* GILLIS *to help him up and two* MEN *step out for the same purpose. But* GILLIS *shoves the Marshal's proffered hand out of the way, and lets himself be helped by the others on his feet and to a table. The* BARTENDER *pours a drink for him and brings it to him. The customers wait silently for* KANE *to make his move.* KANE *looks at them. At his table near the window,* HARVEY *is watching.* KANE's *eyes meet* HARVEY's, *then move away.*]

Kane *(to all of them).* I guess you all know why I'm here. I need deputies. I'll take as many as I can get.

[*He waits. There is no response.*]

Gillis *(suddenly).* I ain't saying I'd've helped you before, but I sure ain't gonna now.
Kane *(ignoring him).* Some of you were special deputies when we broke this bunch. I need you again—now.

[*The* MEN *in the room remain silent. One or two seem affected, but they look at the others, waiting for a lead.* KANE *waits, his heart sinking. The clock ticks loudly in the silence.* KANE *looks at it. Some of the other* MEN *follow his eyes. It is 11:19.*]

Kane *(finally).* Well?
Man at Bar. Things were different then, Kane. You had six steady deputies to start off with—every one a top gun. You ain't got but two now.
Second Man. You ain't got two. Harve Pell here says he quit. Why?

[*Everyone turns to look at* HARVEY. *He stares them down.*]

Kane. That's between the two of us.
First Man. And where's Toby?
Kane. He's on his way in. He'll be here.
Second Man. That's what you say. You're asking a lot, Kane, all things considered.

[*He turns to look at a* MAN *alone at a table and the others follow his glance. The* MAN *at the table looks up. He is bleary-eyed, an obvious alcoholic, and he has a livid whip-lash scar across one eye and across his face.*]

Kane. All right, we all know what Mitchell's like. That's why I'm here. How about it?

Gillis *(suddenly).* You must be crazy, coming in here to raise a posse. Frank's got friends in this room—you ought to know that!

[KANE *ignores him, waits. The room is silent. The two* MEN *who have seemed to be disposed to join him shrink back among the others.* KANE *realizes*

there is nothing here. The MEN *watch him go in silence.*]

[*Ext. Saloon. The two* INDIANS *have been listening from the outside door. They give way for* KANE. *He comes out, looks across the street toward his office.*]

[*Ext. Marshal's office—from* KANE's *point of view. There are no horses at the rail, and Kane's note can be seen fluttering on the door.*]

[*Ext. Saloon.* KANE *turns and starts down the street, moving out of scene. The* INDIANS *watch him go. The young* INDIAN *turns to the older* INDIAN *and looks at him inquiringly. The older man shrugs.*]

[*Int. Church. It is well-filled, and the choir—composed of six men and six women—is singing a hymn.* SAM *comes in unobtrusively and unnoticed and searches the room with his eyes. Finally he sees the man he is looking for,* WEAVER *the store-keeper, singing in the choir. Their eyes meet, and* WEAVER *gets the almost imperceptible signal* SAM *sends him with his lifted eyebrows.* WEAVER *frowns with annoyance and worry, but when the hymn ends and while the rest of the choir is finding its seats again, he leans over to his pompous wife, whispers to her and slips out through the rear door. She, too, is puzzled and annoyed, but she covers his exit by dropping and retrieving her hymnal. With his usual impassivity,* SAM *turns and gets out as quietly as he came.*]

[*Ext. Mart Howe's house. It is a small house, rather shabby in appearance, as if its owner is unwilling or unable to keep its paint and trim and flower beds in order, or perhaps, just doesn't care.* KANE *enters the scene and walks to the door, sweating freely under the glare of the high sun. He knocks and waits. The door is opened by a stout* INDIAN WOMAN *well past middle age. She recognizes* KANE *wordlessly and lets him in.*]

[*Int. Mart Howe's house. This main room of the house, which serves as both living and dining room, is fairly clean and well kept, but like the exterior it is barren, unloved. Two large, old-fashioned guns hang on the wall beneath a badge mounted on a leather base.* MART HOWE *is sitting in the one comfortable chair in the room, staring at the floor. The* INDIAN WOMAN *goes to the chair at the eating table and resumes what she was doing before* KANE'*s interruption—rolling cigarettes by hand and mouth and adding them to the small pile already on the table.* KANE *goes toward* HOWE *and stops, looking down at him.* HOWE *finally looks up at him, his face wooden, his eyes hopeless.*]

Kane. I sent a kid to find you. Didn't he come?

Howe *(heavily).* He was here.

[KANE *stares down at him unbelievingly, turns away helplessly, then to him again.*]

Kane *(finding words).* You been my friend all my life. You got me this job! You made them send for me.

[HOWE'*s bent frame droops, but he remains silent.*]

Kane. From the time I was a kid I wanted to be like you. Mart, you been a lawman your whole life!

Howe *(bitterly).* It's a rotten life. You risk your skin catching killers and the juries let them go so they can come back and shoot at you again. If you're honest, you're poor your whole life, and in the end you wind up dying all alone in a dirty street, or some stinking alley. For what? For nothing. A tin star.

"For what? For nothing. A tin star."

[*The* INDIAN WOMAN *picks up the handful of cigarettes she has made, comes over and puts them on the small table near Howe's chair, takes some wooden matches out of a pocket of her apron and puts them down alongside, then turns and shuffles out of the room. With difficulty,* HOWE *picks up a cigarette in his gnarled fingers and strikes a match to it.* KANE *looks at him helplessly.*]

Kane. Listen! The judge left town. Harvey's quit. I'm having trouble getting deputies.
Howe. It figures. It's all happened too sudden. People kind of got to talk themselves into law and order before they do anything about it. Maybe because deep down they got no use for it. I don't know.

[*The room goes silent. The two men look at each other. All barriers are down now. It is a time for complete honesty, for they will never again be this close to each other, this intimate.*]

Kane. What should I do, Mart?
Howe. When they didn't hang him, when they gave him that silly sentence, I knew this day would come. I've been waiting for it.
Kane. I've been waiting for it, too.
Howe. But not to commit suicide.
Kane. Sometimes prison changes a man.
Howe. Not him. (*Despairingly*) It's all planned, that's why they're all here. Get out, Will!

[KANE *turns away, wrestling it out with himself.* HOWE *watches him for a moment, then averts his eyes. Finally* KANE *draws a deep, almost shuddering breath, and shakes his head.* HOWE *understands that* KANE *has fought back.*]

Kane. Will you go down to that station with me?
Howe (*dully*). No. (*His cigarette drops to the floor, and after only a momentary hesitation he rubs it out under his shoe.*) You know how I feel about you, but I won't go with you, and I won't be with you. (*He looks at his twisted fingers.*) Seems like a man that already has busted knuckles didn't need arthritis, too, don't it? (*He shrugs hopelessly.*) No. I couldn't do anything for you. You'd be worried about me. You'd get yourself killed worrying about me. It's too one-sided the way it is.
Kane (*tired*). So long, Mart.

Howe. So long.

[KANE *turns and goes out.*]

Howe (*hopelessly*). It's for nothing, Will. It's all for nothing.

[*But* KANE'S *footsteps continue to fade in the distance.* HOWE *looks at the clock. It is 11:26.*]

[*Ext. Howe's house.* KANE *is walking steadily away from the house.*]

Voice. (*o.s.*) Kane!

[KANE *stops, turns. The scarred* DRUNK *from the saloon hurries into the scene and to the Marshal.* KANE *waits, surprise struggling with his impatience.*]

Kane. What's the matter, Jimmy?

[*The* DRUNK *is sweaty and breathless, but he carries himself with the deceptive steadiness of the confirmed alcoholic.*]

Drunk. Nothing. I been looking for you. I want a gun. I want to be with you when that train comes in.

[KANE *stares at him.*]

Kane. Can you handle a gun?
Drunk. Sure I can. I used to be good. Honest.
Kane. But why?

[*The* DRUNK *is all too conscious of* KANE'S *eyes searching his face, seeing the patch. His own fingers go up to it.*]

Drunk. It ain't just getting even, no! It's a chance, see? It's what I need. Please, Kane . . . let me get in on this!

[*In his urgency he has reached out and clutched* KANE'S *arm.* KANE *looks down at the hand gripping his forearm, sees the* DRUNK'S *fingers and arms trembling. The* DRUNK *follows* KANE'S *eyes. He pulls his hand away and tries desperately to stop the trembling. But his fingers continue to quiver until, in an agony of helplessness, he covers them with his other hand. Then his eyes meet* KANE'S *again, bleak, shamed, and hopeless, but with a last tiny spark of pleading.*]

Kane (*gently*). All right, Jim. I'll call you if I need you . . . (*He reaches in his pocket for a silver dollar.*) Get yourself a drink, meanwhile.

[*He forces the coin into the* DRUNK's *hand, tries to bring sincerity into his smile, and turns and goes.*]

Drunk (*dully*). Thanks, Will.

[*Close Truck Shot—*KANE—*as he continues away, his face still set in the empty, meaningless smile. Then his lips tighten with helpless anger.*]

[*Int. Helen's front room. She is standing in the doorway to her bedroom as* SAM *comes in and closes the door behind him.*]

Helen. Where is he?
Sam. Coming up the back way. (*He allows himself the ghost of a smile.*) That's a careful man.

[*There is the sound of approaching footsteps in the hall and* SAM *nods. He turns and opens the door, catching* WEAVER *as he is about to knock.*]

Helen. Come in, Mr. Weaver.

[*Awkwardly, the storekeeper comes in, and* SAM *closes the door after him. Throughout the scene the businessman is quite respectful toward* HELEN.]

Weaver. Anything wrong, Mrs. Ramirez?
Helen. No.
Weaver. Then why did you send for me?
Helen. I'm leaving town. I want to sell my half of the store. You want to buy me out?
Weaver (*covering his surprise*). How much did you want?
Helen. Two thousand. I think that's fair.
Weaver. Oh, it's fair all right, Mrs. Ramirez. But I couldn't raise that much right now.
Helen. How much can you raise?
Weaver. About a thousand.
Helen. All right. You can pay Sam, here, the rest in six months, and he'll get it to me. A deal?
Weaver (*pleased*). Yes, ma'am.
Helen (*dismissing him*). All right, Mr. Weaver.
Weaver (*somewhat embarrassed*). Well, I'd like to thank you, Mrs. Ramirez—for everything. I mean, when you first called me in and put the deal to me—about staking me in the store and being the silent partner—my wife thought—(*He realizes he

is on dangerous ground.*) Well, what I really mean is, you've been real decent to me right along. And I want you to know I've been honest with you.
Helen. I know you have. Goodbye, Mr. Weaver.
Weaver. Goodbye.

[*He turns to the door, stops, and turns back to her.*]

Weaver (*meaningfully*). And good luck to you.

[HELEN *nods.* WEAVER *and* SAM *go out.*]

[*Ext. Fuller house—Med. Long Shot.* KANE *is walking steadily toward the house—a larger, more imposing, better-cared-for place than Mart Howe's. It has been painted recently, and the picket fence and flower beds are in good order.* KANE *nears the house.*]

[*Int. Front room—Fuller house.* SAM FULLER *is peering out through the window.*]

Fuller (*agitated*). Mildred! Mildred!

[MRS. FULLER *hurries into the room. A simple woman, she knows the reason for his agitation, but she is bewildered, troubled.*]

Fuller (*leaving the window*). He's coming. I knew he would. Now you do like I told you! I'm not home—don't let him in! No matter what he says, I'm not home!
Mrs. Fuller. Sam, he's your friend—
Fuller. Don't argue with me! He'll be here in a second!
Mrs. Fuller. He won't believe me. He'll know I'm lying—
Fuller. You do like I tell you!

[KANE's *footsteps can be heard on the porch approaching the door. Then he knocks.* FULLER *points a tense finger at his wife, then tiptoes to the bedroom and closes the door behind him.* KANE *knocks again. Frightened, wretched,* MRS. FULLER *goes to the door and opens it about halfway.*]

Mrs. Fuller (*with tremendous effort*). Oh, hello, Will.

[*Surprised at first by her manner and the unmistakable lack of welcome in the partly opened door,* KANE *quickly sees and understands her tension.*]

Kane. Hello, Mrs. Fuller. Sam in?
Mrs. Fuller. No, he isn't.

[KANE *stares at her, convinced she is lying.*]

Kane (*quietly*). Do you know where he is, Mrs. Fuller? It's important to me that I find him.
Mrs. Fuller (*in agony*). I think he's in church, Will—he's gone to church.
Kane. Without you?
Mrs. Fuller. I'm going in a little while—as soon as I dress—

[*For a moment anger surges up in* KANE, *and then he checks it.*]

Kane (*gently*). Thanks, Mrs. Fuller. Goodbye.

[*He turns and lets her shut the door after him.*]

[*Ext. Fuller house—as* KANE *steps down the porch steps and stops a moment to stare up at the merciless sun. He wipes his face wearily, then continues down the steps and along the walk, his face grim.*]

[*Int. Front room—Fuller house.* MRS. FULLER *has crept to a chair where she slumps miserably.* FULLER *is at the window, watching* KANE *go. He turns finally, and looks at her stricken face.*]

Fuller (*shame-ridden*). Well, what do you want? You want me to get killed? You want to be a widow? Is that what you want?

[MRS. FULLER *raises her eyes to his. She is torn, bewildered, miserable.*]

Mrs. Fuller. No, Sam . . . No.

[*Ext. Railroad station—Close Shot—*BEN—*as he drinks from the whiskey bottle. There is the o.s. music of* COLBY's *harmonica, as he plays "Blue-Tail Fly."* CAMERA PULLS BACK *to include* PIERCE *and* COLBY. BEN *wipes his lips and then deliberately offers the bottle to* PIERCE, *and grins as the latter looks at him darkly.* BEN *extends the bottle to* COLBY, *who takes it and drinks.* PIERCE *turns and looks down the track.*]

[*Ext. Railroad track. The parallel lines of the track merge in the hazy distance.*]

[*Group Shot.* PIERCE *frowns to himself, takes out his watch and looks at the time.* COLBY *finishes*

his drink, hands the bottle back to BEN, *then resumes his playing.* PIERCE *gets up and goes over to the window in the b.g. The* STATIONMASTER *comes up to it.*]

Pierce. Anything on the train?
Stationmaster. It's on time, far as I know. (*As* PIERCE *turns away*) If it don't stop, there's no more southbounds till tomorrow.

[PIERCE *looks at him coldly, then turns and comes back to the group, sits down and starts to roll a cigarette.* BEN *whistles softly to* COLBY's *playing.*]

[*Ext. Prairie—Med. Long Shot—on* TOBY *and* PETERSON *as their horses gallop along the faint trail.* TOBY *keeps his horse steadily at* PETERSON's *flank.*]

[*Med. Truck Shot—on* TOBY *and* PETERSON. PETERSON's *hands are still free.* TOBY *moves up alongside* PETERSON *and points o.s. They change direction and ride out of scene.*]

[*Ext. Waterhole.* TOBY *and* PETERSON *appear in the b.g. and ride down to the waterhole. They are both tired, hot, dusty. They dismount near the hole and lead their horses to the water. The horses drink greedily.* PETERSON *looks over at* TOBY *thoughtfully, then around him, sees a stone near his feet. Behind the cover of his horse, he bends quietly and picks it up. When* TOBY *draws his horse from the water, then goes upstream a little way,* PETERSON *follows suit, hiding the stone behind his back.* TOBY *bends down and starts to drink.* PETERSON *tenses and starts to swing the stone down on* TOBY's *head. Almost in time, but not quite,* TOBY *sees his reflection in the water, and tries to dodge.* PETERSON's *fist and stone come down in a glancing blow on* TOBY's *head and* TOBY *goes face forward into the water.* PETERSON *goes in after him.* TOBY *manages to get to his feet before* PETERSON *can wrestle him down into the water, and the two men begin swinging at each other. The horses rear and retreat from the waterhole.* TOBY *and* PETERSON *fight fiercely and soundlessly, except for their panting and choking breath. When they are on their feet they are waist-deep, but more often than not both men are out of sight in the roiling and threshing water. Finally,* PETERSON *manages to knock* TOBY *down,* and he is on top of him in an instant, hitting him and ducking him under until TOBY goes limp and sinks underwater. PETERSON lets him go and scrambles breathlessly out and to his horse. TOBY comes to, and with tremendous effort takes out after him. PETERSON has trouble getting his frightened horse to stand still enough to mount, and TOBY catches him from behind and drags him down. They roll over and over into a rocky growth and a right hand from TOBY sends PETERSON's head back against a rock. He is hurt. TOBY continues to bang PETERSON's head against the stone until he caves in. TOBY rolls off and lies there, trying to recapture his breath and strength. Finally he is able to get up. He pulls PETERSON to his feet, turns him around, and kicks him toward the waterhole. PETERSON staggers forward and falls. TOBY picks him up again and kicks him all the way to the hole, where PETERSON finally falls face down at the edge of the hole. TOBY looks down at the waterhole. The water is muddy and thick with silt.]

Toby (glaring at PETERSON). Now see what you went and done! That water won't be fit to drink for hours—

[Int. Hotel lobby. The front door bangs open, and HARVEY strides in, liquor-flushed. Again AMY has looked up hopefully. She recognizes HARVEY, but he is too full of his errand to see her. Ignoring the CLERK as well, he goes across the lobby and up the stairs.]

Clerk (dryly). There's another one of Mrs. Ramirez's friends.
Amy (puzzled). Oh?
Clerk (grinning). Yep. I'd say she's got some explaining to do when that train gets in.

[AMY looks at him with increasing dislike, but she is very thoughtful as she turns away.]

[Int. Helen's front room. She is putting the final touches to her packing as a knock sounds on the door.]

Helen. Come in, Sam.

[The door opens and HARVEY enters. He is stunned when he sees the suitcases. Then HELEN looks up and sees him. She braces herself for the unpleasantness to come.]

Harvey. You leaving town?

[HELEN looks at him, but does not bother to answer. She fastens the last buckle.]

Harvey. Where are you going?
Helen. I don't know yet.

[She moves past him, checking the room for things she may have forgotten to pack. Baffled and frustrated by her manner, HARVEY follows her.]

Harvey. That doesn't make much sense.

[HELEN shrugs.]

Helen. I'll think of something, once I'm on the train.
Harvey. You're afraid, huh? You're afraid of Mitchell.
Helen (honestly). No. . . .
Harvey. Sure you are, or you wouldn't be running. You got nothing to be afraid of as long as I'm around—you know that. I'm not scared of Mitchell. I'll take him on any time!
Helen (matter-of-fact). I believe you.

[She goes to the window now and looks out. HARVEY stares sullenly at her insolent back, his rage mounting.]

Harvey. Then why are you going? (As HELEN shrugs) Are you cutting out with Kane?

[HELEN turns and looks at him. She smiles with weary contempt.]

Helen. Oh, Harvey . . .
Harvey. Then why are you going?
Helen. What difference does it make?
Harvey (furiously). It's Kane, it's Kane! I know it's Kane!

Helen. It isn't Kane! (She stops, then goes on.) But I'm going to tell you something about you and your friend Kane. You're a nice-looking boy. You have big wide shoulders. But he's a man. It takes more than big wide shoulders to make a man, Harvey. And you've got a long way to go. You know something? I don't think you'll ever make it.

[She turns away from him. Exploding, HARVEY comes after her, grabs her and turns her to him. HELEN is passive in his arms.]

Harvey (*huskily*). Now I'll tell you something. You're not going anywhere—you're staying here with me—It's going to be just like before—

[*He kisses her brutally.* HELEN *remains completely and coolly unresponsive, unresisting, untouched.* HARVEY *lets her go uncertainly.*]

Helen (*quietly*). You want to know why I'm getting out? Then listen. Kane will be a dead man in half an hour, and nobody is going to do anything about it. Don't ask me how I know. I know. And when he dies, this town dies, too. It smells dead to me already. And I'm a widow. I'm all alone in the world. I have to make a living. So—I'm going somewhere else. That's all. (*She studies him a moment, then goes on softly.*) And as for you—I don't like anybody to put their hands on me unless I want them to. And I don't want you to . . . *anymore*—

[*Stung,* HARVEY *reaches for her. She slaps him sharply, viciously.*]

[*Ext. Church—Med. Long Shot.* KANE *can be seen climbing the hill toward the church. The distant strains of a small organ can be heard.*]

[*Ext. Church—Med. Shot—as* KANE *walks through the churchyard to the church. The organ music within comes to a stop.* KANE *opens the doors.*]

[*Int. Church. The* MINISTER *is beginning his sermon.*]

Minister. Our text today is from Malachi, Chapter Four. . . .

[KANE *enters and stands near the doorway.*]

Minister (*reading from the Bible*). For, behold, the day cometh, that shall burn as an oven, and all the proud, yea, and all that do wickedly shall be as—

[*He has looked up, seen* KANE, *and stopped. The congregation, seeing him stare, turns toward the entrance. There is a rustle, a shuffle, a whispering, and then silence. Some of the people seem aware of* KANE's *mission, others are puzzled.* JO HENDERSON *seems honestly surprised to see* KANE.]

Minister (*to* KANE, *frowning*). Yes?

Kane (*awkwardly*). I'm sorry, parson. I don't want to disturb the services—

Minister (*irritated*). You already have. (*Now he gives away the real cause of his anger.*) You don't come to this church very often, Marshal. And when you got married today, you didn't see fit to be married here. What could be so important to bring you here now?

Kane. I need help.

[*He strides up front to the pulpit.*]

Kane (*to* MINISTER). It's true I haven't been a church-going man, and that's maybe a bad thing. And I wasn't married here today because my wife's . . . (*He suddenly remembers* AMY *with a pang of pain.*) my wife's a Quaker. But I've come here for help because there are people here . . .

[*The* MINISTER, *a good man who already regrets his display of temper, has been staring at him with growing shame.*]

Minister. I'm sorry, Marshal. Say what you have to say.

[KANE *turns to the people.*]

Kane. Maybe some of you already know. If you don't, it looks like Frank Mitchell's coming back on the noon train. I need as many special deputies as I can get.

[*There is a momentary pause, as those to whom this is news take it in. The* MINISTER *is shocked. He hasn't known. Then a man,* SCOTT, *in a rear pew rises.*]

Scott. What are we waiting for? Let's go!

[*He starts toward the aisle and to* KANE. *There seems to be a fairly general movement to follow him. Then another man,* COOPER, *near the rear of the church rises and yells through the jumble of voices.*]

Cooper. Hold it! Hold it a minute!

[*The crowd is held. They turn to him.*]

Cooper. That's right—hold it! Before we go rushing out into something that ain't going to be so pleasant—let's be sure we know what this is all about.

". . . I've come here for help because there are people here . . ."

[*The room is silent. Some of the men sit down.* KANE *is watching* COOPER, *frowning*.]

Cooper. What I want to know is this—ain't it true that Kane ain't the marshal anymore? And ain't it true that there's personal trouble between him and Mitchell?

[MEN *jump to their feet. There is a jumble of outcries, some in protest, some in agreement. But* COOPER's *charge has had its effect.* JO HENDERSON *hurries up front and comes beside* KANE.]

Henderson (*over the crowd*). All right, all right! Quiet, everybody!

[HENDERSON *commands the crowd's attention. The noise subsides.*]

Henderson. If there's difference of opinion, let everybody have his say. But let's do it like grown-up people. (*As the crowd assents*) And let's get all the kids out of the building . . .

[MEN *on their feet find seats.* PARENTS *push their* CHILDREN *toward the aisles. One* BOY *about twelve, highly intrigued, tries to hang back. His* FATHER *jerks him to his feet and helps him along with a slap on the behind. There is a movement of* CHILDREN *to the doors.* HENDERSON *puts his hand on* KANE's *arm, and* KANE *looks at him gratefully.*]

[*Ext. Railroad station.* PIERCE *is pacing tensely.* BEN *is sprawled lazily.* COLBY *is playing his harmonica.* PIERCE *stares out into the distance.*]

[*Ext. Tracks. They stretch out emptily.*]

[*Int. Church.* SCOTT *is speaking.*]

Scott (*angrily*). I say it don't matter if there is anything personal between Mitchell and the Marshal here. We all know who Mitchell is and what he is! What's more, we're wasting time! . . .

[KANE, HENDERSON, *and the* PARSON *are listening and watching intently. From outside, there is the sound of* CHILDREN's *voices, singing. Hands shoot up as* SCOTT *finishes.* HENDERSON *recognizes another man.*]

Henderson. All right, Coy.

Coy (*rising*). Yeah, we all know who Mitchell is, but we put him away once. Who saved him from hanging? The politicians up north. This is their mess—let them take care of it.

[*He sits. There are more hands.* HENDERSON *recognizes another man.*]

Henderson. Sawyer.

Sawyer (*rising*). What I got to say is this—we've been paying good money right along for a marshal and deputies. But the first time there's trouble, we got to take care of it ourselves! What we been paying for all this time? I say we're not peace officers here! This ain't our job.

[*There are cries of assent and disagreement. A man,* LEWIS, *jumps to his feet.*]

Lewis (*over noise*). I been saying right along we ought to have more deputies! If we did, we wouldn't be facing this now!

Henderson (*loudly*). Just a minute now—let's keep it orderly! Everybody, quiet down! (*As they do*) You had your hand up, Ezra.

[*The man named* EZRA *gets up, quivering with indignation.*]

Ezra. I can't believe I've heard some of the things that've been said here. You all ought to be ashamed of yourselves. Sure, we paid this man, and he was the best marshal this town ever had. And it ain't his trouble, it's ours. I tell you if we don't do what's right, we're going to have plenty more trouble. So there ain't but one thing to do now, and you know what that is!

[*Another man shoots his hand into the air.* HENDERSON *nods to him.*]

Henderson. Go ahead, Kibbee.

Kibbee (*stupidly*). Been a lot of talk what our duty is. Well, this is Sunday, and I don't hold with no killing on the Sabbath.

[*He sits down, highly satisfied with himself.* KANE *stares at him in amazement.* HENDERSON *hides a wry smile.*]

[*Ext. Church. Some of the older* CHILDREN *are trying to peer in through a window. The rest are playing a game brought out from Kentucky and Tennessee by the early pioneers. They have formed a circle, and hand in hand they are passing under a bridge formed by the raised arms of two taller* CHILDREN, *a* BOY *and a husky, rawboned* GIRL. *They are the captains. As the circle revolves, they sing these words:*]

> "The needle's eye that does supply
> The thread that runs so true,
> Many a beau I have let go
> Because I wanted you.
> Many a dark and stormy night
> When I went home with you
> I stumped my toe and down I go
> Because I wanted you . . ."

The captains let their arms drop around one of the boys in the circle, stopping it. They take him away from the circle.]

Boy Captain. What are you going to be, Injun or white man?

Little Boy. Injun . . .

[*They return to the others. The* BOY *and* GIRL *form the bridge again, the little* BOY *standing behind the taller* BOY. *The* CHILDREN *in the circle form hands again and resume the game.*]

[*Int. Church. A man,* TRUMBULL, *is on his feet, talking.*]

Trumbull. . . . This whole thing's been handled wrong. Here's those three killers walking the street bold as brass. Why didn't you arrest them, Marshal? Why ain't they behind bars? Then we'd only have Mitchell to worry about, instead of the four of 'em!

Kane (*simply*). I didn't have nothing to arrest 'em for, Mr. Trumbull. They haven't done anything. There's no law against them sitting on a bench at the depot . . .

[*A woman,* MRS. SIMPSON, *jumps to her feet.*]

Mrs. Simpson (*excited*). I can't listen to any more of this! What's the matter with you people? Don't you remember when a decent woman couldn't walk down the street in broad daylight? Don't you remember when this wasn't a fit place to bring up a child? How can you sit here and talk—and talk *and talk* like this?

[*Another woman,* MRS. FLETCHER, *older, rises.*]

Mrs. Fletcher. That's easy for you to say, Mrs. Simpson—your husband's a hundred miles away. Still, I ain't saying you're wrong. Only, those fellows are mighty bad. We need the strongest men we've got—young men—

[*A very young* WOMAN, *sitting beside her young husband, bursts out.*]

Young Woman. Sure, let the young men do it! It's always the young men who have to do it, have to go out and do the killing and get killed before they do any living! Why don't the old men do it for once? They're king of the walk when things are good!

[*There is an outburst of sound. A* MAN *leaps to his feet.*]

Man (*over*). What are we all getting excited about? How do we know Mitchell's on that train, anyway?

Henderson (*quietly*). I think we can be pretty sure he's on it. (*He takes out his watch, looks at it.*) Time's getting short. (*He turns to the* MINISTER.) Parson, you got anything to say?

Minister (*slowly*). I don't know. The Commandments say: Thou shalt not kill. But we hire men to do it for us. The right and the wrong seem pretty clear here, but if you're asking me to tell my people to go and kill and maybe get themselves killed—I'm sorry—I don't know what to say. . . . I'm sorry.

[*The room is quiet. Finally* EZRA *raises his head.*]

Ezra (*to* HENDERSON). What do you say, Jonas?

Henderson. All right, I say this—what this town owes Will Kane here, you could never pay him with money, and don't ever forget it. Yes, he is the best marshal we ever had, maybe the best we'll ever have.

[KANE *listens gratefully.*]

Henderson (*continuing*). Remember what this town was like before Will came here? Do we want it to be like that again? Of course we don't! So Mitchell's coming back is our problem, not his.

[*The men and women listen intently.*]

Henderson (*continuing*). It's our problem because it's our town. We built it with our own hands, from nothing . . . And if we want to keep it decent, keep it growing, then we got to think mighty clear here today—and we got to have the courage to do the right thing, no matter how hard it is. All right. There's going to be a fight when Kane and Mitchell meet, and somebody's going to get hurt, that's for sure. Now. There's people up north who've been thinking about this town, and thinking mighty hard. They've been thinking about sending money down here—to put up stores, build factories. It'd mean a lot to this town, an awful lot. But when they read about shooting and killing in the streets, what are they going to think then? I'll tell you. They'll think this is just another wide-open town, that's what. And everything we worked for is going to be wiped out in *one day*. This town is going to be set back five years, and I say we can't let that happen. Mind you, you know how I feel about this man. He's a mighty brave man, a good man. He didn't have to come back today, and for his sake and the town's sake I wish he hadn't. Because if he's not here when Mitchell comes in, my hunch is there won't be any trouble, not one bit. Tomorrow we'll have a new marshal, and if we all agree here to offer our services to him, I think we can handle anything that comes along. To me, that makes sense. To me, that's the only way out of this.

[*Almost without exception, the people are persuaded.*]

Henderson (*turning to Will*). Will, I think you ought to go while there's still time. It's better for you—and better for us.

Kane emerges from the church . . . then goes wearily on. . . .

[KANE *is staring at him, stunned. Then he looks out at the silent people, reads the answer in their eyes, in their averted or guarded faces. He turns from* HENDERSON *and walks out of the church.*]

[*Ext. Church. The game has reached its climax as* KANE *emerges from the church. There are now two rows of* CHILDREN, *each with their arms around the* CHILD *in front. With the two captains in the middle, a tug of war is going on.* KANE *stares at the screaming children for a moment, then goes wearily on, out of the scene. The girl captain's team pulls the other line of children over until it breaks. The game ends in a melee[16] of breathless laughter and shouting.*]

[*Ext. Railroad station.* MITCHELL *and* COLBY *are removing their spurs.* PIERCE *looks at his watch, then follows suit.*]

[*Closeup—Saloon clock. The time is 11:44.* CAMERA PANS DOWN *to* GILLIS *and two* MEN *at the bar, looking up at the clock.*]

Gillis (*finally*). Well, I got no use for him, but I'll say this—he's got guts.

[*The other men nod their agreement.* HARVEY *is alone at a table near the window with a bottle and glass. Drink has obviously not cooled his seething rage. Now, he hears what* GILLIS *has said, and reacts to it with a mixture of anger and shame. He drinks. Of the two men beside* GILLIS, *we remember one of them as seeming sympathetic to* KANE *in the earlier scene. He now picks up the conversation.*]

Sympathetic Man (*dryly*). That's mighty broad-minded, Joe.

[GILLIS *looks at him doubtfully, but the sympathetic man's face is blandly innocent.* GILLIS's *look slides away from him and focuses on* HARVEY. *He goes toward* HARVEY's *table.*]

Gillis. Now you, Harve—I always figured you for guts, but I never give you credit for brains . . . till now.

[HARVEY *doesn't know how to take this. Is* GILLIS *accusing him of cowardice?*]

Harvey. What does that mean?

Gillis (*sitting*). Nothing. Only it takes a smart man to know when to back away.

Harvey. If I can't pick my company when I drink in here, I ain't coming here anymore.

Gillis (*losing his smile*). Okay.

[*He gets up with bad grace and goes angrily to the bar.* HARVEY *watches him go. Once back among his friends, however,* GILLIS's *aplomb[17] returns. He whispers something to a man at the bar, and the man smiles quietly. Seething,* HARVEY *looks at the other occupants at the bar and sees only blank faces, wise faces, shrewd eyes, unspoken amusement, or contempt. But no one says anything. Furious,* HARVEY *turns away and pours himself a drink with fingers trembling with rage. Then, as he drinks, his glance moves to the window, and he sees something far down the street.*]

[*Long Shot—*KANE*—From* HARVEY's *point of view. His figure is tiny but recognizable as he walks slowly up the quiet street.*]

[*Int. Saloon.* HARVEY, *in the f.g., reacts with blind rage to the sight of* KANE. *Past him, the swinging door opens, and the* DRUNK *comes in and goes directly to the bar.*]

Drunk (*to* BARTENDER). I want a bottle.

[*The* BARTENDER *and those nearby stare at him.*]

Bartender. *You* want a bottle?

Drunk. I got the money.

[*He opens his hand and lets the silver dollar* KANE *has given him fall on the bar. Surprised, the* BARTENDER *gets a bottle and shoves it toward him. He takes it and walks out.*]

Gillis. Well, I'll be. . . .

[HARVEY, *staring through the window, is unaware of the incident. He continues to watch* KANE.]

[*Ext. Street—Med. Full Shot.* KANE *is continuing up the street. A* MAN *going in the opposite direction sees him, hesitates, then crosses the street to avoid meeting him. As the* MAN *comes into* CLOSER CAMERA VIEW, *his face reveals his mixture of shame and relief.*]

---

16. **melee:** noisy struggle.

17. **aplomb** (ə·pläm′): self-possession.

[*Med. Close Truck Shot—*KANE—*as he realizes that he has been avoided, and his face, already drawn and sick, goes tighter.*]

[*Med. Truck Shot—*KANE *as he continues up the street, past the two* OLDSTERS, *whom he passes in mutual silence, and then past the General Store. Through the window, although* KANE *does not pause to look inside,* WEAVER *and* SAM *can be seen at the safe in the rear.* KANE *continues to the end of the block. Almost without thinking, he stops there, staring almost blankly up the quiet street.*]

[*Ext. Street—Full Shot—from* KANE'*s point of view. It stretches out, empty and dusty under the sun.*]

[*Med. Close Shot—*KANE. *He becomes conscious of the sweat rolling down his forehead, and wipes his face with his handkerchief. Then, walking very slowly, he turns the corner, the* CAMERA TRUCKING *with him.*]

[*Int. Saloon.* HARVEY *has been watching* KANE *through the window. Now, he gets up suddenly, his face tight with decision, and goes out of the saloon.*]

[*Ext. Livery stable.* KANE *approaches the entrance to the stable. It is closed. A crude sign on the door reads* "GONE TO CHURCH." KANE *goes around toward the rear of the stable.*]

[*Int. Stable. A half-dozen horses are standing quietly in their stalls as* KANE *enters the stable. He stands there a moment, accustoming his eyes to the cool, quiet semitwilight after the harshness of the sunlight. Then, slowly, he goes over to one of the stalls and looks at the horse in it. It is a strong, fast animal, and the* CAMERA FOLLOWS KANE'*s eyes as they roam over the sleek body and powerful legs. This horse could make a race of it across the plains.*]

Harvey's Voice (*o.s*). Put a saddle on him, Kane.

[*Surprised,* KANE *turns quickly, sees that* HARVEY *has come into the stable behind him.* HARVEY *comes toward him, his old confidence surging back into him.*]

Harvey. Go on, saddle him. He'll go a long way before he tires. That's what you were thinking, ain't it?
Kane. Kind of.

[HARVEY *studies his face with almost greedy curiosity.*]

Harvey. You scared?
Kane. I guess so.
Harvey (*triumphantly*). I knew it. It stands to reason. (*Brushing past him*) Come on, I'll help you—

[*He sees a saddle hanging nearby, takes it down and goes to put it on the horse.*]

Harvey (*almost feverishly*). You've wasted a lot of time, but you still got a start. Ben and the others've been doing a lot of drinking. It might slow 'em up.

[KANE *has been watching* HARVEY *as he throws the saddle on the horse. He shrugs wearily.*]

Kane (*smiling wryly*). Seems like all everybody and his brother wants is to get me out of town.
Harvey. Well, nobody wants to see you get killed.

[*Tiredly,* KANE *turns and starts out of the stable.* HARVEY *hears him, and turns quickly.*]

Harvey. Hold it—where are you going?
Kane (*dully*). I don't know. Back to the office, I guess.
Harvey (*going to him*). Oh, no! You're getting on that horse and you're getting out!

[KANE *turns away from him.* HARVEY *grabs his arm and turns him back to face himself.*]

Harvey. What's the matter with you? You were ready to do it yourself—and you said so!
Kane. Look, Harve, I thought about it because I was tired. You think about a lot of things when you're tired—when people cross the street so they won't have to look at your face. And with everybody telling me I ought to get out, for a minute there I began to wonder if they weren't right. But I can't do it. . . .
Harvey (*almost frantic*). Why?
Kane (*honestly*). I don't know.
Harvey. Get on that horse, Will.
Kane. Why's it so important to you? You don't care if I live or die.

Harvey. Come on—

[*He starts to shove* KANE *toward the horse.* KANE *stands his ground.*]

Kane. Don't shove me, Harve. I'm tired of being shoved. I don't know what I'm going to do, but whatever it is it's going to be my way.

Harvey (*frantic now*). You're getting out of town if I have to beat your brains out and tie you to that horse!

[KANE *jerks loose from him and starts out.* HARVEY *swings at him and connects to the back and side of his jaw, and* KANE *goes face down to the stable floor.* HARVEY *hurries to him, grabs him and starts to drag him toward the horse. He has started to lift* KANE *on the horse when* KANE *comes to. He jerks out of* HARVEY'S *grasp. Disappointed,* HARVEY *launches himself at him.* KANE *sets himself as quickly as he can, but* HARVEY'S *momentum lets him get the first blows in, hard blows that send* KANE *reeling. Then* KANE *fights back. They punish each other mercilessly, nothing barred. The horses, becoming nervous, rear and whinny in their stalls.* KANE *goes down again, then* HARVEY. *They roll and tumble under the rearing hooves of the horses. Once,* KANE *is knocked down under a horse, and narrowly escapes being trampled. As the fight reaches a climax, the horses go completely wild. Then, finally,* KANE *connects with a series of crushing blows, and* HARVEY *goes down and out.* KANE *stands over him, panting and dazed. Then, almost staggering, he goes to a bag of feed, slumps exhaustedly down on it, and sits there, his breath whistling through his bruised lips.*]

[*Int. Hotel lobby.* AMY *is staring up at the clock. The time is ten to twelve. Behind the desk, the* CLERK *is whistling softly as he goes about his work.* AMY *comes to a decision. She rises and goes to the desk.*]

Amy (*quietly*). Excuse me. (*Then, as the* CLERK *looks at her*) What is Mrs. Ramirez's room number?

[*The* CLERK *looks at her. Then a glitter of amusement comes into his eyes.*]

Clerk. Three.

Amy (*maintaining her poise*). Thank you.

[*She turns from him and goes to the stairs.*]

[*Int. Hotel stairway—on* AMY *as she mounts the stairs.*]

[*Int. Hallway—on* AMY *as she reaches the second floor and looks about uncertainly. Then she moves doubtfully down the hall in the direction of Helen's rooms and sees the number on Helen's door. She pulls herself together and knocks.*]

[*Int. Helen's front room.* HELEN *and* SAM *are facing each other across the table, on which lies a small stack of money. They react to* AMY'S *knock.*]

Helen. Come in.

[*The door opens, and* AMY *stands in the doorway.* HELEN *and* SAM *stare at her in surprise, and* AMY *remains rooted there, confused by* SAM'S *presence and her first sight of* HELEN. HELEN *recovers first.*]

Helen. Yes?

Amy. Mrs. Ramirez? (*As* HELEN *nods*) I'm Mrs. Kane.

Helen. I know.

Amy. May I come in?

Helen. If you like.

[SAM *takes his cue and goes out silently as* AMY *comes into the room. Now that she has come this far, she is confused and uncertain again. The two women take each other in for a long moment. Finally,* HELEN *breaks the strained silence.*]

Helen. Sit down, Mrs. Kane.

Amy. No, thank you.

Helen (*sharply*). What do you want?

[AMY *realizes that* HELEN *has misunderstood her refusal.*]

Amy. Please . . . it's just that I'm afraid if I sat down I wouldn't be able to get up again.

Helen. Why?

Amy. It wasn't easy for me to come here.

Helen (*unrelenting*). Why?

Amy (*meeting the issue*). Look, Mrs. Ramirez . . . Will and I were married an hour ago—we were all packed and ready to leave. Then this thing happened, and he wouldn't go. I did everything—I pleaded. I threatened him—I couldn't reach him.

[HELEN *has been listening intently, watching* AMY's *face*.]

Helen. And now?

Amy *(quietly)*. That man downstairs—the clerk— he said things about you and Will. I've been trying to understand why he wouldn't go away with me. Now all I can think of is that it's got to be because of you.

Helen *(deliberately)*. What do you want from me?

Amy. Let him go! He's still got a chance—let him go!

[*There is a pause.* HELEN *has a brief inner struggle, then decides to be honest*.]

Helen *(flatly)*. I can't help you.

Amy. Please.

Helen. He's not staying for me. I haven't spoken to him for a year—until today. I told him to go. I'm leaving on the same train you are.

[AMY *stares at her, believing her. But with belief, her confusion returns*.]

Amy. Then what is it? Why?

Helen. If you don't know, I can't explain it to you.

Amy *(dully)*. Thank you . . . anyway. You've been very kind.

[*She turns and starts out*.]

Helen *(lashing out at her)*. What kind of a woman are you? How can you leave him like this? Does the sound of guns frighten you that much?

[AMY *has turned and waited her out*.]

''I can't help you.''

Amy (*quietly, with great dignity*). No, Mrs. Ramirez. I heard guns. My father and my brother were killed by guns. They were on the right side, but it didn't help them when the shooting started. My brother was nineteen. I watched him die. That's when I became a Quaker—because every other religion said it was all right for people to kill each other at least once in a while. I don't care who's right or wrong! There's got to be some better way for people to live! (*She stops, then goes on tiredly.*) Will knows how I feel about it.

[*She starts out again.*]

Helen (*gently*). Just a minute. (*As* AMY *turns*) Are you going to wait for the train downstairs? (*As* AMY *nods*) That man down there can't be much company. Why don't you wait here?

Amy (*reacting to the sympathy in her tone*). Thank you, I will.

[*She comes forward into the room again, sees the chair* HELEN *offered her before, hesitates an instant, then sits down.* HELEN *takes another chair. For a moment silence is strained again.* AMY *looks down at the arms of the chair she is sitting in, realizing that* WILL *must have sat here many times in the past. Her eyes go about the room and finally reach* HELEN. HELEN *is aware of what* AMY *is thinking. She nods in quiet affirmation.* AMY *takes it.*]

[*Int. Stable.* KANE *has recovered and is on his feet now. His face is still marked and bloodstained, but he is attempting with his battered hands to bring some semblance of order to his clothing. Finished, he looks down at his bruised knuckles and fingers, then starts out. Seeing a bucket of water, he stops, looks back where* HARVEY *is still lying unconscious on the stable floor, picks up the bucket, goes to* HARVEY *and douses his limp body with it. Then he tosses the bucket aside and goes out.*]

[*Ext. Stable—Truck Shot—on* KANE *as he comes out of the stable and moves wearily up the street to the main street, and turns the corner into it.*]

[*Ext. Barbershop.* KANE *approaches it and goes in.*]

[*Int. Barbershop. The* BARBER, *alone in the shop,* is putting his instruments in a cupboard as KANE comes in. There is the sound of hammering from the rear.*]

Kane. You got some clean water I can use?

[*The* BARBER *turns and recognizes him.*]

Barber. Why sure, Marshal. (*Then, looking at him more closely*) Sure, sure. (*He motions to the chair.*) Sit down.

[KANE *goes over to it and sinks into it. The* BARBER *draws some water, staring over his shoulder at* KANE. *He gets a towel and soaks it in the water.*]

Barber. Run into some kind of trouble, Marshal?
Kane. No trouble.

[*He becomes conscious of the hammering. The* BARBER *comes over with the wet towel.*]

Kane. What are you building?

[*The* BARBER *is embarrassed and ashamed.*]

Barber. Just—just fixing things up out back. (*Recovering*) Now take it easy, Mr. Kane. Just settle back—

[KANE *relaxes and closes his eyes. The* BARBER *carefully wraps the wet towel about his face, then hurries to the rear door.*]

Barber (*sharply*). Fred! (*As the hammering continues*) Fred! Hold it awhile, will you?

[*The hammering stops.*]

Fred's Voice (*puzzled*). Hold it?
Barber (*cutting in*). You just stop until I tell you to start again!

[*He turns from the doorway, gets a basin and fills it with water. He takes it to* KANE, *sets it in his lap, then takes* KANE's *battered hands and puts them in the basin, looking at the bruised knuckles with curiosity as he does so. He stares at* KANE's *hidden face for a moment, then looks up at the clock.* CAMERA PANS UP *to it. It is seven minutes to twelve.*]

[*Ext. Railroad station.* MITCHELL, PIERCE, *and* COLBY *are checking their guns, carefully reloading them and adjusting their belts and holsters.*

Beside BEN *there is an extra gun-belt holding two guns.*]

[*Int. Stable.* HARVEY *is straightening his clothes. The fine patina[18] of confidence and conceit is gone and he looks utterly crushed and defeated. He goes wearily out.*]

[*Int. Barbershop. The* BARBER *watches* KANE *as he adjusts his coat, takes a final look at his face in the mirror, and starts out.*]

Kane. Thanks.

[*He goes on to the door.*]

Barber. You're welcome, Marshal.

[KANE *stops at the door, reaches into a pocket, fishes out a coin.*]

Barber. Oh, no charge, Marshal.

[KANE *looks at him, untouched by his eagerness to please. Deliberately, he flips it to the* BARBER, *who catches it.*]

Kane (*and he knows what he is talking about*). You can tell your man to go back to work now.

[*He goes out. The* BARBER *stares after him as he passes the window. Then he shrugs helplessly, and goes to the rear door.*]

Barber (*calling out*). All right, Fred. Go ahead.

[*Ext. Marshal's office.* KANE *approaches the office, eyes narrowed against the glare of the sun. He sees that his note still flutters on the door. He rips it off, starts in, then stops and looks up at the sky.*]

[*Full Shot—Sky. The glaring white-hot ball of fire is almost exactly at its zenith. It hangs there, baleful,[19] merciless.*]

[*Med. Close Shot—*KANE. *He squints, rubs his eyes, goes into his office.*]

[*Int. Marshal's office.* BAKER, *armed, is pacing the floor tensely. In a corner of the room, almost hidden in the shadow, the boy* KANE *had sent to find the selectmen is standing.* BAKER *turns*

---

18. **patina:** thin outer coating.
19. **baleful:** deadly.

quickly as KANE *comes in and tries to accustom his eyes to the change of light.*]

Baker. Will—

[KANE *stares at him with relief and remembrance.*]

Kane. I guess I forgot about you, Herb, I'm sure glad you're here.

[*He goes to his desk.*]

Baker. I couldn't figure out what was keeping you. Time's getting short.

[KANE *looks up at the wall clock. It is five to twelve.*]

Kane. Sure is.

Baker. When are the other boys going to get here? We got to make plans.

Kane. The other boys?

[*He realizes that* BAKER *does not know. He turns to face him.*]

Kane. There aren't any other boys, Herb. It's just you and me.

Baker. You're joking.

Kane. No. I couldn't get anybody.

Baker. I don't believe it! This town ain't that low—

Kane. I couldn't get anybody.

[BAKER *stares at him. Then, suddenly, full realization of the situation comes to him.*]

Baker. Then it's just you and me?

Kane. I guess so.

[*In his corner, forgotten by* BAKER *and unseen by* KANE, *the* BOY *looks on, fascinated.*]

Baker. You and me, against Mitchell and—all four of 'em. . . .

Kane. That's right. You want out, Herb?

Baker (*writhing inwardly*). Well, it's not that I want out, no. But . . . I'll tell you the truth . . . I didn't figure on anything like this, Kane. Nothing like this—

Kane (*smiling mirthlessly*). Neither did I.

Baker (*with growing terror*). I volunteered. You know I did. You didn't have to come to me. I was ready. I'm ready now! But this is different. This

---

ain't like what you said it was going to be. This is just plain committing suicide, that's what it is! And for what? Why me? I'm no lawman—I just live here! I got nothing personal against anybody—I got no stake in this!

Kane (*harshly*). I guess not.

Baker. There's a limit how much you can ask a man! I've got a wife and kids! What about my kids? It's not fair—you ain't got the right to ask it—

Kane. Go home to your kids, Herb.

[BAKER *grabs up his rifle and starts toward the door. He stops, striving for a remnant*[20] *of decency.*]

Baker. You get some other fellows and I'll still go through with it, Kane—

Kane (*harshly*). Go on home, Herb!

[BAKER *hurries out. The door slams loudly behind him.* KANE *stares into nothing for a moment, turns and sits down automatically. Then his control gives way, and the tide of bitterness and anger overflows in him. He pounds his battered fists on the desk top brutally, almost sobbing his outrage. The surge of emotion ebbs. Gradually,* KANE *reclaims his hold on himself. In the corner, the* BOY *looks on, wide-eyed and frightened.* KANE *straightens, wipes his face and eyes, turns his chair and sees the* BOY.]

Kane (*brusquely*). What do you want?

Boy (*frightened*). I found 'em, Marshal, like you wanted me to—all but Mr. Henderson.

[KANE *is fully himself now.*]

Kane (*wryly*). I found him. Thanks.

Boy. Oh, you're welcome—

[*He hesitates, afraid to say what he has in mind.* KANE *looks at him quizzically. He comes to him.*]

Boy (*eagerly*). Marshall—listen—let me fight with you! I'm not afraid!

Kane. No.

Boy. Please, let me, Marshal!

Kane. You're a kid. You're a baby.

Boy. I'm sixteen! And I can handle a gun, too. You ought to see me—

Kane. You're fourteen. What do you want to lie for?

Boy. Well, I'm big for my age. Please, Marshal.

Kane. No! (*He rises and goes to him.*) You're big for your age, all right. . . . But you get out of here—

Boy. Aw, please . . .

Kane. Go on, go on . . .

[*He turns away. The* BOY *starts unhappily to the door.* KANE *stops, turns back to him.*]

Kane (*gently*). Johnny . . .

[JOHNNY *turns to him, his eyes brimming over.*]

Kane. Thanks.

[*He gives a little wave, as when a man says goodbye to a friend.* JOHNNY *manages to muster a kind of a smile and returns the gesture. Then he is gone.* KANE *looks after him, almost smiling, the rage and bitterness in him leavened*[21] *a little. Then he goes to his desk, sits down, takes his guns out of their holsters and checks them methodically. His bruised fingers are clumsy. He puts his gun down and looks down at his hands ruefully. He rubs and kneads his fingers, then picks up the gun again.*]

[*Closeup—Gun in* KANE's *hand. It looks deadly.*]

[*Back to scene.* KANE *stares down at the gun. His hand turns the barrel upward, pointing toward his face. For an instant it almost seems as if he is weighing the benefits of a quick, more merciful self-inflicted death. He presses the trigger. The safety catch is on. It clicks harmlessly. He picks up the other gun in his left hand and works the trigger on it. Then, putting down both guns, he opens a drawer, takes out a box of bullets and stuffs bullets into his pockets.*]

[*Ext. Railroad station.* MITCHELL *and the others have moved down to the track.* MITCHELL *is pacing tensely.* PIERCE *and* COLBY *are staring down the gleaming track. There is no sign of the train in the distance.*]

[*Int. Church. The congregation is singing a hymn.* HENDERSON, *as he sings, takes out his watch and*

---

20. **remnant:** scrap.

21. **leavened:** lightened.

looks at it. He shakes his head slightly, returns his watch, and keeps on singing.]

[*Ext. Countryside.* TOBY *and* PETERSON *gallop toward a distant ranch house. We see them reach it and dismount.*]

[*Close Shot—Wooden Sign. Weatherbeaten and so faded that it is difficult to read, it says:*

"STAGE STATION"]

[*Ext. Corral. We see now that the sign is over the corral gates. Near the gates,* TOBY *has* PETERSON *tied hand and foot in a sitting position, and he is now tying him to one of the fence rails. In the b.g.,* MARTINEZ, *a middle-aged Mexican, has tethered the horses. He comes out of the corral and looks on as* TOBY *finishes and straightens.*]

Martinez (*interested*). What he do?
Toby. Oh, he's a bad boy. Very bad . . .

[*He turns and starts for the low house past the corral, and* MARTINEZ *falls in alongside, the* CAMERA TRUCKING *with them.*]

Toby. How's the beer?
Martinez. How is my *cerveza*?[22]

[*He shrugs contemptuously.*]

Toby. Cold?
Martinez. Like well water . . .

[TOBY *smiles happily. They have reached the house.*]

[*Ext. Martinez house.* TOBY *sprawls on the porch step, as* MARTINEZ *goes on into the house.* TOBY *lets himself go, stretching his tired and aching muscles, then starts to roll a cigarette.* MARTINEZ *comes out with a copper pitcher and two mugs. He starts to pour beer for* TOBY *and himself.*]

Toby. How's business?
Martinez. It will be better when the stage runs again.
Toby. That stage ain't never going to run again. Ain't you heard? We got a railroad now.
Martinez (*shrugging*). Railroad. . . .

[TOBY *looks down at his beer with delight, then takes a long drink. He sighs happily.*]

Martinez. I go to the horses now. You wish your friend to drink?

[TOBY *hesitates, then his good nature gives in.*]

Toby. Give him beer. . . . But careful. *Muy malo. . . .*[23]

[MARTINEZ *shrugs again, pours a mugful of beer, sets the pitcher down and goes out of scene.* TOBY *takes another drink. A pretty young* MEXICAN GIRL *comes out. She recognizes him.*]

Mexican Girl. Look who's here. Wild Bill Hickok.
Toby. *Ah, Chiquita . . . Cómo está?*[24]

[*It is obvious that they know each other well.*]

Mexican Girl. If you really want to know, you come by once in a while.
Toby. I been busy . . .
Mexican Girl. Sure. You're a big man. Very busy. Very important.

[*Grinning,* TOBY *shoves over his empty mug. Carelessly, she moves it back with her toe.*]

Mexican Girl. What happened to your clothes?
Toby. I been swimming.
Mexican Girl. In your clothes?
Toby. Sure.
Mexican Girl. You're crazy.
Toby. I got a crazy job.

[*He flicks the mug closer to her. Again she inches it back to him with an insolently*[25] *provocative toe-nudge.*]

Mexican Girl. You going to stay awhile?
Toby. I got to go. I got a prisoner. Besides, I'm invited to a wedding.
Mexican Girl. If you stay awhile, I'll wash your shirt.

[*Their eyes meet and hold.* TOBY *turns and looks out to where* PETERSON *is sprawled near the fence. Then he takes out his large old-fashioned watch,*

---

22. *cerveza:* Spanish for "beer."

23. *muy malo:* "very bad."
24. *Cómo está:* "How are you?"
25. **insolently** (in'sə·lənt·lē): boldly.

looks at it, puts it to his ear, shakes it, puts it to his ear again. He shrugs.]

Toby. What do you know. Must have stopped when I went swimming.

[*He puts the watch away, his eyes meeting the girl's again.*]

Toby. Ah—I probably missed that wedding anyway.

[*Smiling, the* GIRL *bends and gets his mug and starts to fill it with beer.*]

[*Closeup—Clock in Marshal's office. The time is two minutes to twelve.* CAMERA PANS DOWN *to* KANE, *writing at his desk.*]

[*Insert—*KANE's *hand—as it writes:*

LAST WILL AND TESTAMENT

As he crosses the last "T" he pauses. In the silence the loud ticking of the clock can be heard. Deliberately, he draws a line under the words.]

[*Int. Saloon. All the men are silently watching the clock.*]

[*Int. Helen's front room.* AMY *is still in the chair, lost in her thoughts.* HELEN *is standing at the window, looking down into the street.*]

Helen. Where are you going when you leave town?
Amy. Home. St. Louis.
Helen (*turning to her*). All that way alone?
Amy. That's the way I came. I seem to make them unhappy no matter what I do. Back home they think I'm very strange. I'm a feminist. You know, women's rights—things like that. (*She looks up at* HELEN.) Where will you go?

[HELEN *shrugs.*]

Amy. Why are you going? Are you afraid of that man?
Helen. Not afraid, no. There are very few men who cannot be managed, one way or another.

[*They each think of* KANE, *and look at each other. Then* HELEN *goes on.*]

Helen. I'm just tired. (*She starts to pace.*) I hate this town. I've always hated it. To be a Mexican woman in a town like this. . . . (*She shakes her head.*) I married Ramirez when I was sixteen. He

was fat and ugly, foolish. When he touched me, I would feel sick. But he had money. When he died, *I* had money. I sold the saloon. I bought the biggest store in town. Nobody knew. I hired a big citizen to run it for me. Nobody knew that either. Big citizens do many things for money. And all the fine ladies, who never saw me when they passed me on the street, they paid me their money and they never knew. I enjoyed it for a while. But now . . . (*She shrugs again.*)
Amy (*after a pause*). I understand.
Helen. You do? That's good. I don't understand you. (*As* AMY *looks at her*) No matter what you say, if Kane was my man, I'd never leave here. I'd get a gun—I'd fight.
Amy (*deliberately*). Why don't you?
Helen. He's not my man.

[*She turns suddenly and goes to one of her bags, opens it quickly, rummages in it, comes up with a gun.*]

Helen. Here. Take this. You're his wife.
Amy (*sharply*). No! If I did I'd be saying my whole life up to now was wrong!
Helen. Right, wrong, what's the difference? He's your man.
Amy (*rising*). Is he? What made him my man? A few words spoken by a judge? Does that make a marriage? There's too much wrong between us— it doesn't fit! Anyway, this is what he chose.

[*There is an instant of complete silence, which is shattered suddenly by the distant but loud, hoarse scream of a train whistle. Involuntarily, both women react physically.*]

[*Int. Marshal's office. The train whistle continues over.* KANE *has been sitting at his desk, writing. He sits there, frozen.*]

[*Ext. Street. The two* OLD MEN *listen. The train whistle continues over.*]

[*Int. Saloon. Train whistle over. The men are rooted in their places.*]

[*Int. Room.* HARVEY *is sprawled on the rumpled bed. There is a bottle nearby. He hears the whistle.*]

[*Ext. Railroad station. Train whistle over.* MITCHELL, PIERCE, *and* COLBY *are standing at*

[*the tracks. The train is not yet visible. Then the whistle stops. They look.*]

[*Ext. Countryside—Train tracks. In the distance a small cloud of smoke can be seen.*]

[*Int. Marshal's office—on* KANE—*as he waits. Then there is the sound of the second whistle.*]

[*Int. Church. The congregation is on its feet,* HENDERSON *in the f.g., but no one is singing as the train whistle continues over.*]

[*Med. Close Shot—*ORGANIST. *He is working the keys but the music merges with the sound of the whistle.*]

[*Int. Fuller living room. Train whistle over.* FULLER *and his* WIFE *listen.*]

[*Int. Martin Howe's house. Train whistle over.* HOWE *sits in his chair, listening.*]

[*Int. Saloon. Train whistle over. The* MEN *listen.*]

[*Int. Helen's front room. Train whistle over.* HELEN *and* AMY *listen. The whistle dies.*]

[*Int. Kane's office. He waits.*]

[*Ext. Station.* MITCHELL, PIERCE, *and* COLBY *wait. There is still no sign of the train. They look at each other tensely.*]

[*Int. Stationmaster's office. He stands rooted, waiting.*]

[*Int. Helen's front room.* AMY *and* HELEN *look at each other, their eyes asking the question they are afraid to speak.*]

[*Int. Saloon. The* MEN *begin to look at each other wonderingly.*]

[*Int. Marshal's office.* KANE *waits.*]

[*Ext. Countryside—on the moving train.*]

[*Int. Marshal's office. On* KANE *waiting. He starts to put down the pen he has been holding, and now, louder than before, the third whistle blasts over the scene.* KANE *quivers. The breath he has been holding escapes in a long soundless sigh.*]

[*Ext. Railroad station.* MITCHELL, PIERCE, *and* COLBY *look at each other in triumph. In the distance, the train becomes visible.*]

[*Int. Saloon. As the whistle dies, the* MEN *stampede out. The saloon is empty. From outside, we hear the click of* GILLIS's *key in the lock, see the knob turn as he tries it.*]

[*Int. Helen's front room.* HELEN *and* AMY *are both on their feet, and* SAM *has Helen's bags. They move numbly toward the door.*]

Helen (*quietly*). Can I ride with you to the station?
Amy. Of course.

[*They start out.*]

[*Int. Marshal's office.* KANE *signs his name to what he has written, folds it, then writes on it:*

TO BE OPENED IN THE EVENT
OF MY DEATH.

He places the folded testament in the center of his desk, and then puts the cartridge box on it for a paperweight. He rises, takes a deep breath.]

[*Ext. Hotel. The* CLERK *is closing the metal shutters. They clang into place.*]

[*Series of shots—of shutters, windows, and doors being closed all over town.*]

[*Ext. Railroad station.* MITCHELL, PIERCE, *and* COLBY *watch as the approaching train draws nearer. The noise of its engine and wheels can be heard plainly now.*]

[*Int. Marshal's office.* KANE *takes a last look around the office and goes out.*]

[*Ext. Marshal's office—as* KANE *emerges into the sunlight. He looks around.*]

[*Ext. Street—From* KANE's *point of view. It is completely deserted.* CAMERA PANS *to other extreme of the street. It, too, is empty.*]

[*Close Shot—*KANE. *He smiles mirthlessly. Suddenly, there is the sound of horses' hooves, and he turns.*]

[*Ext. Street. The buckboard,* AMY *driving and* HELEN *beside her, comes down the street toward* KANE.]

[*Close Shot—*KANE—*as he sees and recognizes them.*]

Frank . . . starts out of the station. [The others] follow him.

[*Med. Close Shot*—AMY *and* HELEN—*as they see* KANE.]

[*Close Shot*—KANE—*as he watches them approach.*]

[*Closeup*—HELEN. *She is at her best. Her eyes are looking directly toward* KANE, *and there is a faint smile on her lips.*]

[*Closeup*—AMY. *She has never looked more beautiful. Her eyes avoid* KANE'S.]

[*Closeup*—KANE—*as he stares o.s. at life itself.*]

[*Ext. Marshal's office*—*as the buckboard sweeps past* KANE. *We see that* SAM *is sitting in the back among the luggage. It passes out of the scene.*]

[*Med. Close Shot*—KANE—*as he looks after the buckboard. Then, with an effort, he pulls himself together, takes out his watch, and looks at the time.*]

[*Ext. Railroad station. The train pulls in. Conductors alight.*[26] MITCHELL, PIERCE, *and* COLBY *wait impatiently. Then, one of the car doors opens, and a moment later* FRANK MITCHELL *steps out into the sunlight. He is a big man, pale, but dangerous looking, implacable. The three men hurry to him. Smiling, they extend their hands to him.* MITCHELL *is not surprised to see them. He shakes hands unsmilingly, then moves off to a more secluded portion of the platform.*]

[*Ext. Station*—*Another Angle*—*as the buckboard drives into the station yard and stops near the tracks.* SAM *jumps down and begins to unload the luggage, and* AMY *and* HELEN *climb down.*]

[*Group Shot.* MITCHELL *extends his hand inquiringly to* BEN. *Smiling,* BEN *hands him two guns.*

---

26. **alight:** climb down.

FRANK *takes no chances. He checks both guns. Then, looking up, his glance goes o.s. and is caught there.*]

[*Ext. Railroad car.* SAM *is helping* AMY *up the steps. As she goes in and he extends an arm to* HELEN, *she looks off toward* FRANK.]

[*Med. Close Shot*—FRANK MITCHELL—*as his eyes meet* HELEN's.]

[*Med. Close Shot*—HELEN. *Her eyes meet* FRANK's *calmly. Then, taking her time, she climbs the steps into the car.*]

[*Group Shot.* FRANK *watches her disappear without expression. Nothing can interfere with the business at hand. He nods to the others, and starts out of the station. They follow him.*]

[*Int. Railroad car.* AMY *is sitting by the window, pale, tense.* HELEN *is beside her on the aisle,* SAM *putting away the last of the luggage. He comes to* HELEN *and they look at each other in silence. It is a difficult parting for both of them.*]

Sam (*finally*). So long, Helen.
Helen. Goodbye, Sam. You'll hear from me.
Sam (*nodding*). Take care.

[SAM's *tight, weather-beaten face breaks into something like a smile, and he goes out quickly. There is the sudden o.s. blast of the train whistle.*]

[*Ext. Marshal's office.* KANE *reacts to the whistle. He feels for his guns, then starts slowly but firmly down the street.*]

[*Ext. Street*—*on* MITCHELL *and the others as they come up middle of the street.*]

[*Ext. Town*—*High Shot of the main street. We see the small figures approaching each other, hidden from each other by the bend of the street.*]

[*Med. Close Truck Shot*—KANE. *As he continues, keeping along the sidewalk.*]

[*Close Trucking Group Shot*—*on* MITCHELL *and the others.*]

[*Close Truck Shot*—KANE—*going on.*]

[*Ext. Street*—*on* MITCHELL *and the others. Suddenly* BEN *stops, his attention caught by a shop window. As he darts over to it, the others stop,*

startled. BEN *reaches the shop. It has women's hats of the period on display. Deliberately,* BEN *smashes the window with his gun butt, reaches in and takes out a hat.* FRANK MITCHELL's *grim face tightens.*]

Frank Mitchell (*angrily*). Can't you wait?
Ben. Just want to be ready.

[*He stuffs the hat under his shirt and hurries to rejoin them. They continue up the street.*]

[*Ext. Street*—*on* KANE *as he continues. He reaches the bend, pauses, then takes shelter in the space between two houses. He waits there.*]

[*Med. Close Shot*—KANE. *As he waits tensely.*]

[*Ext. Street.* MITCHELL *and the others come into scene. They pass* KANE's *hiding place and continue on.* KANE *lets them go about twenty feet, then draws his guns.*]

Kane (*calling*). Mitchell!

[*The other men turn, drawing as they do.* BEN *is the first to shoot. His shot misses* KANE, *but* KANE *does not miss him.* BEN *whirls and goes down. Bullets from the other three pockmark the wall behind* KANE. *He returns the fire, then runs for it.*]

[*Int. Railroad car*—AMY *and* HELEN. *They sit tensely, as the sound of the gunfight comes over. Then, suddenly, the firing stops, and there is a dead silence.* HELEN *slumps a little, believing the fight is over and* KANE *is dead.* AMY *stares at her, and then, beside herself, leaps to her feet, brushes past* HELEN, *and runs wildly to the door.*]

[*Ext. Railroad station.* AMY *climbs down the steps and runs wildly out of the station. In the b.g., the* STATIONMASTER *is the center of a curious group composed of the train crew and passengers.*]

[*Ext. Main Street. On* AMY *as she runs up the deserted street.*]

[*Ext. Street*—*shooting past* BEN's *body toward the bend in the street. In the b.g.,* AMY's *figure runs into view, then stops short as she sees the body.*]

[*Close Shot*—AMY *as she sees* BEN's *body and thinks that it is* KANE's. *CAMERA PANS with her as she runs toward it.*]

[*Ext. Street*—BEN's *body in the f.g., the hat he has stolen lying beside him.* AMY *runs toward* CAMERA, *finally crumples to her knees at* BEN's *body. To her amazement and relief, she sees that it is not* KANE. *There is a fusillade of o.s. shots, and she realizes that the gunfight is still going on.*]

[*Ext. Back Alley*—*on* KANE *as he runs, bent low. There is a shot from ahead, and he ducks into the shelter of a shed. He peers in the direction of the shot.*]

[*Ext. Alley*—*from* KANE's *point of view.* COLBY *is at the other end of the alley, behind shelter.*]

[*Int. Shed.* KANE *goes to the other side of the shed, peers through a crack. Through it, the fig-ures of* FRANK MITCHELL *and* PIERCE *can be seen coming into the other end of the alley.* KANE *fires at* MITCHELL, *misses, and they duck out of sight. There is a burst of shots from* COLBY *and an answering burst from the other two.* KANE *throws himself on the ground. He surveys his situation, realizing he is caught in a cross fire.*]

[*Ext. Street.* AMY *is on her feet, now hearing the o.s. shots. She starts uncertainly up the street.*]

[*Int. Shed.* KANE *crawls to the door of the shed, and looks out.*]

[*Ext. Stable*—*from* KANE's *point of view. Its wide door, diagonally across the alley from* KANE, *is open.*]

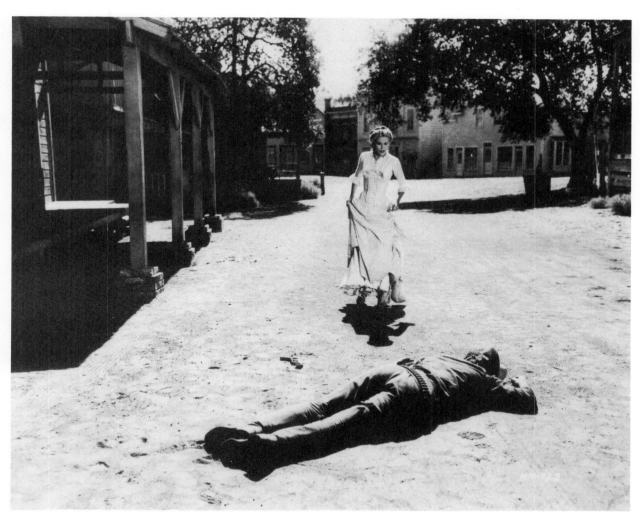

Amy runs toward . . . Ben's body.

[*Int. Stable.* KANE *makes up his mind to try for it. He gets to his feet, crouches, launches himself out.*]

[*Ext. Alley—as* KANE's *crouched body cannonballs across the alley, untouched.*]

[*Int. Stable.* KANE's *body hurtles into the stable and hits the floor. He lies there, struggling for breath. The horses whinny and rear nervously.*]

[*Ext. Alley.* MITCHELL, PIERCE, *and* COLBY *move cautiously toward the stable.*]

[*Int. Stable.* KANE *gets up, looks around, climbs up to the loft.*]

[*Int. Loft.* KANE *goes toward a large opening in the loft wall. From here, he and the* CAMERA *have a good, high view of the alley.* MITCHELL *and* PIERCE *at their end and* COLBY *at his end are both in view.* KANE *takes aim at* COLBY, *but misses.* COLBY *and the others duck out of sight.* PIERCE *dashes across the alley,* KANE *firing but missing him.*]

[*Ext. Stable—as* PIERCE *crawls around to the rear of the stable and takes shelter. He begins to fire into the stable.*]

[*Ext. Alley—*COLBY*—as he fires.*]

[*Ext. Alley—*FRANK MITCHELL*—as he fires.*]

[*Int. Loft—as bullets from all three directions hit into the loft. There is a scream of pain from one of the horses below. Bullets continue into the loft.* KANE *crawls to the ladder and climbs down.*]

[*Int. Stable.* KANE *comes down into the stable. The horses are mad with fear.* KANE *goes to them. In one of the stalls one of the horses has been hit and is down.* KANE *hurries to the stable door and slides it shut. He finds some small shelter behind some bags of feed and painfully begins to load his guns.*]

[*Ext. Alley—*MITCHELL. *He studies the situation, as o.s. shots come from* COLBY *and* PIERCE. *Looking around, he sees that he is behind the general store. He gets an idea, goes to the rear door and deliberately kicks it in. He disappears inside and returns in a moment carrying three oil lamps. Coming back to his place, he takes aim and throws one.*]

[*Ext. Stable—as the lamp flies against the stable door and smashes against it, spattering oil against the door.*]

[*Int. Stable—on* KANE *as he reacts to the sound of the lamp as it lands. Then he hears another lamp smashing on the stable wall.*]

[*Ext. Alley—On* MITCHELL *shooting toward stable—as* MITCHELL *flings the third lamp toward the stable. It takes a high arc and lands near the stable. Then* MITCHELL *takes careful aim, and fires. We see one of the lamps explode, bouncing crazily against the stable and splattering fire against it.* MITCHELL *fires again, misses his target, fires again, hits it. There is another explosion, and another splash of oil and fire on the stable door.*]

[*Ext. Stable—Lamp in f.g. There is the sound of* MITCHELL's *o.s. shot, and we see the lamp explode and carom[27] off the ground against the stable. Another sheet of flame falls on the wooden stable wall. Flames begin to spread along the front of the stable.*]

[*Int. Stable—On* KANE*—as he realizes what is happening. The horses are increasingly mad with fear.*]

[*Int. Marshal's office.* AMY *comes in, breathless, confused, terrified. Exhausted now, she can go no further; indeed she does not know where to go. She sees Kane's testament on the desk, goes to it, reads the inscription. There is the o.s. whistle of the train.*]

[*Int. Stable. Fire is eating away at the door, and smoke is beginning to fill the stable.* KANE *goes to one of the stalls and leads out the maddened horse. One by one he leads all the horses out of their stalls, pulls them toward the door, manages with a mighty effort to slide the door open, and then sends the rearing, screaming horses out into the alley.*]

[*Ext. Alley—as the horses burst out into the alley and scatter wildly. At their opposite ends of the alley,* MITCHELL *and* COLBY *take cover.* KANE *slips out of the stable and around it.*]

---

27. **carom** (kar'əm): hit and rebound.

[*Ext. Railroad station. The train is pulling out, the faces of the passengers pressed against the windows.*]

[*Ext. Wooded area—as* KANE *passes the* CAMERA *on the run. A moment later, the three men enter the scene, fanning out and firing from cover. The fading train whistle comes over.*]

[*Ext. Burying Ground.* KANE *runs into the scene, and takes cover behind a marker. In the b.g., the three men enter the scene, still fanned out. Shooting from cover, they gradually move in on him.*]

[*Int. Church. The congregation is huddled together in terror, the* MINISTER *standing with head bowed, praying silently at the pulpit.*]

[*Ext. Cemetery. On* KANE *as* COLBY *exposes himself.* KANE *shoots, and brings him down.*]

[*Int. Marshal's office.* AMY *is slumped at* KANE's *desk, past tears now,* KANE's *open testament crumpled in her hands. The sound of o.s. firing begins to come closer. Sensing it, she rises and hurries to the window. Through it, she now sees* KANE *running into the street.*]

[*Ext. Street.* KANE *is zigzagging down the street.* PIERCE *appears at the far end of the street behind him, and then suddenly* MITCHELL *comes into view in the f.g. They have him in a cross fire again.*]

[*Ext. Saloon.* KANE *heads for it, bangs against the door. It is locked. Bullets pockmark the door around him. With a supreme effort, he charges the door and smashes it in, falling inside.*]

[*Close Shot—*AMY—*as she sees what is happening.*]

[*Med. Close Shot—*MITCHELL—*as he fires.*]

[*Med. Close Shot—*PIERCE—*as he fires.*]

[*Int. Saloon.* KANE *squats on the floor, exhausted.*]

[*Ext. Street.* PIERCE *makes his way carefully along the street, firing as he goes. He reaches the Marshal's office, and shoots toward the saloon.*]

[*Int. Marshal's office.* AMY *looks on in horror as she sees* PIERCE *through the window, a scant few feet from her, shooting at the saloon. She looks*

about wildly, beside herself, then sees Harvey's guns hanging on the wall. Then, deliberately, she goes to them, takes down a gun, and goes to the window. PIERCE's *back is only two or three feet away past the window.* AMY *lifts the gun, holds it steady with both hands.*]

[*Ext. Street—on* PIERCE, *with* AMY *visible in the b.g.* PIERCE *shoots, takes aim again. Then* AMY's *gun goes off, and* PIERCE *tumbles face forward to the ground.*]

[*Int. Marshal's office.* AMY *reels and clings to the shattered window for support.*]

[*Int. Saloon.* KANE, *at the window, now, stares out into the street in surprise. He cannot see into his office, but* PIERCE's *body is plainly visible. Still, it may be a ruse.*[28]]

[*Ext. Street—on* MITCHELL—*as he stares off toward* PIERCE's *body. Then he dashes toward the alley.*]

[*Ext. Alley.* MITCHELL *runs up the alley.*]

[*Ext. Rear of Marshal's office.* MITCHELL *goes stealthily to a window, sees* AMY *and that she is alone. He goes to the door. It is open. He opens it quietly and leaps in.*]

[*Int. Marshal's office.* AMY *looks up with a start as* MITCHELL *jumps into the room, his gun ready. Exhausted, she can only stand there as* MITCHELL *darts across the room, dashes the gun from her hand, and grabs her. Holding her in front of him, he pushes her out toward the street.*]

[*Int. Saloon. Shooting past* KANE *into the street, as he sees* MITCHELL, *with* AMY *as a shield, come out of the office and toward him.*]

[*Ext. Street—on* MITCHELL *and* AMY.]

Mitchell (*yelling*). All right, Kane, come on out! Come out—or your friend here'll get it the way Pierce did!

[*Int. Saloon—as* KANE *stares out, shocked.*]

Kane. I'll come out—let her go!

[*Ext. Street—on* MITCHELL *and* AMY.]

---

28. **ruse** (rōōz): trick.

Mitchell flings [Amy] away from him and she lands in the street.

Mitchell. Soon as you walk through that door! Come on—I'll hold my fire! . . .

[*He waits, holding* AMY *tightly.* AMY *is half-fainting with terror.*]

[*Int. Saloon.* KANE *starts slowly toward the door, then hesitates. He stops, picks up a large chair, and heaves it through the doorway.*]

[*Ext. Street. As the chair hurtles through,* MITCHELL *fires a burst of shots. Wildly,* AMY *reaches up with her free hand and claws at his face and eyes.* MITCHELL *flings her away from him and she lands in the street.* KANE *steps quickly out of the saloon, firing as he comes.* MITCHELL *brings his other gun up.* KANE *staggers from a bullet in the shoulder, but keeps shooting, and* MITCHELL *goes down, his guns slipping from his fingers. For a moment,* KANE *leans tiredly against the building. Then he goes to* AMY. *He helps her up, and they cling to each other silently.*]

[*Full Shot—Street. From everywhere, people begin to appear in the street, more and more of them. They look at* KANE *and* AMY *in silence.*]

[*Ext. Street.* KANE *and* AMY *become aware of the people.* KANE *pulls himself together. He drops his guns in the street, takes off his gun-belt and lets it fall. Deliberately, he takes off his badge and drops it to the dust. The* DRUNK *enters the scene, pulling the buckboard horses. Seeing the buckboard,* KANE *guides* AMY *to it, helps her in, then climbs up after her. He nods to the* DRUNK, *who steps away, then takes the reins and starts the horses. The crowd gives way.*]

[*Full Shot—Street. Without a backward glance,* KANE *and* AMY *ride out of town, the buckboard growing smaller in the b.g. The crowd remains silent. The buckboard passes out of view. Fade-out.*]

THE END

Responding to the Screenplay

Analyzing the Screenplay

Identifying Facts

1. In the beginning of the story, the scene switches back and forth between two contrasting events. What are these two events?
2. Why does Kane decide not to leave Hadleyville? Where is he when he tells his wife his reasons?
3. How does Amy react?
4. What has happened in the past between Kane and Frank Mitchell? Why has Mitchell decided to return?
5. What clues tell us that Mitchell and his gang are the villains, even before any of them say a word?
6. What different reasons do the townspeople give for not helping Kane?
7. How does the screenwriter constantly remind us that time is passing? Why is time so important?
8. Which character has a change of attitude and supports Kane in the end? What happens in the battle?

Interpreting Meanings

9. In an **external conflict,** a character struggles with another character or with some other outside forces. What external conflicts does Kane face? Which of his external conflicts do you find most interesting? Why?
10. In an **internal conflict,** a character struggles with something in his or her own mind, usually something involving a difficult decision. What internal conflicts do Will and Amy Kane face? Which of these do you find most interesting?
11. What moral issues, or questions of right and wrong, does the movie raise? How does it answer them? What is your opinion on each of these moral issues?
12. *High Noon* is set in a specific place and time, and it shows a way of life that no longer exists. Yet many people believe that it has a timeless **message.** What does the movie suggest about the responsibility of an individual to society? About loyalty and gratitude, when they come into conflict with self-interest? About law and order and the system of justice?

13. Some people believe that Helen Ramirez is a more interesting **character** than Amy Kane. What do you think? What does Helen contribute to the story? What does she contribute to our understanding of Will and Amy Kane?
14. Look again at the ending of the story, from the first train whistle to the end of the movie. Why do you think Foreman told this part of the story without dialogue?

Applying Meanings

15. Could the events in this Western ever happen in another time and place? Could Will Kane's conflict be experienced by a modern public official? Discuss your answers.

Writing About the Screenplay

A Creative Response

1. **Writing Dialogue.** Imagine that the townspeople silently go home after the gunfight, then meet the next day in the church. Write a brief dialogue in which at least two characters discuss what happened the previous day in their town.
2. **Writing a Screenplay Scene.** How do you think Amy Kane will justify the act of violence she has committed? Write a brief scene in which she and Will discuss what she has done. Include camera directions. Describe movements, facial expressions, and tone of voice. Use as much or as little dialogue as you think is necessary.

A Critical Response

3. **Comparing and Contrasting Movies.** How does *High Noon* compare with movies that are popular today? Pick one recent popular movie and compare and contrast it with *High Noon.* In the first of two paragraphs, introduce the movie you are comparing to *High Noon.* In the second paragraph, discuss three of the following elements:

   a. The plot, or story line
   b. The amount of violence
   c. The heroes and villains
   d. The theme or themes
   e. The values of the hero or of other characters
   f. The setting

Reading About the Writer

Carl Foreman (1914–   ) was born in Chicago. He attended law school in Illinois before he became a professional screenwriter in Hollywood. *High Noon* began when he was asked, after World War II, to do a film about the United Nations. The movie was to show that free nations had to join together against tyranny. Foreman decided that the story could be told in terms of the old American West. He decided to set the story in a frontier town which was fighting for survival against the threat of outlaws.

But after submitting a story outline to his agent, Foreman found that the agent had already heard the story—or at least a story that sounded like *High Noon*. Foreman located the story ("The Tin Star" by John Cunningham), purchased movie rights to it, and completed *High Noon*. Foreman later lived in England and worked on such films as *The Bridge on the River Kwai* (1957), about prisoners of war in a Japanese internment camp; and *The Guns of Navarone* (1961), about a team of saboteurs on a Greek island occupied by the Nazis.

Focusing on Background
A Critic Writes About the Movie

The following movie review was printed in the *Saturday Review of Literature* the week *High Noon* was released. Stanley Kramer, who is mentioned in the first sentence, was the producer of the movie.

"*High Noon* is a Stanley Kramer production, which amounts almost to a guarantee of its quality, for a Stanley Kramer Western is bound to be an unusual one. The unusualness, in this case, is due to the artfulness with which Fred Zinnemann has directed the picture, and the fine screenplay Carl Foreman has written for it. They've used just about every trick in the business. They have generated suspense as calculatedly as an engineer builds a head of steam; they have kept the talk pertinent and to a minimum, and the film, visually, has been put together like a carefully wrought mosaic. There isn't a spare bit of footage in the whole hour and a half that elapses. The shot of the clocks ticking away the fading hour is as important as that of the railroad track stretching away into the hot, dry noon of the prairie, only the wisp of smoke to be seen in the distance.

"The cast has been chosen and directed as carefully as any for a Theater Guild *King Lear*. Those bags under Gary Cooper's eyes are essential for the tired, middle-aged marshal he plays; Otto Kruger makes a fine Judge Mettrick; Lloyd Bridges is properly embittered as the deputy who fails to be chosen to fill the marshal's shoes. Why, you'd think they'd all been around Hadleyville for a long time. As the crowning glory of this technique-filled Western there is a remarkable musical score by Dmitri Tiomkin. Always underneath the action one hears the folklike ballad, telling about a brave marshal who, at high noon, did what he had to do. That ballad ought to be hitting the juke boxes long about now. . . .

"There is, too, what, I guess, used to be called social significance in this movie.

"The good of law and order is pitted against the evil of lawlessness, and the issues are clear and simple. The people of the community can decide whether or not the peace is to be kept. They can join with their elected peace-keeper, Will Kane, as they did when they put Frank Miller [Mitchell in the screenplay] away; or they can leave him alone, to fight the battle himself, as they do when Frank Miller returns. That last scene, when Kane tosses his marshal's badge into the dirt, at the very feet of the townspeople, carries a lot of impact. You might say, further, that this is a Western with characterization. Why, do you know what Will Kane does when he knows he's going to have to face the Miller gang alone? Sitting there at his desk, he buries his head in his arms and cries. Who ever heard of that before? He seems just like a real person and so does everyone else in the picture. That's hard to make happen in a Western."

—Hollis Alpert

SETTING AND DIALOGUE

Excerpt I from the stage directions describes the setting for a play. As you read it, try to decide what kind of play it might be.

I

The SCENE *is the Throne Room of the Palace; a room of many doors, or, if preferred, curtain-openings: simply furnished with three thrones for Their Majesties and Her Royal Highness the* PRINCESS CAMILLA—*in other words, with three handsome chairs. At each side is a long seat: reserved, as it might be, for his Majesty's Council (if any), but useful, as today, for other purposes. The* KING *is asleep on his throne with a handkerchief on his face. He is a king of any country from any story-book, in whatever costume you please. But he should be wearing his crown.*

—from *The Ugly Duckling.*
A. A. Milne

---

1. Find the expression in parentheses in the middle of the excerpt. How does this expression suggest that the play will not be very serious?
2. What is funny about the appearance of the king?
3. How do the last two sentences of the description support the impression that we are dealing with a humorous play?
4. What other hints are there in the description of the setting that the play is a comedy?
5. If you were the director, what additions could you make to the stage setting to help create the mood the writer is after?

Dialogue is the most important element of a play. In the following excerpt, for example, the writer uses dialogue to do two important things. It establishes the setting, and it gives information about the central character, who isn't even onstage. The scene is a wedding party for State Senator Jabez Stone and his wife Mary. The time is the nineteenth century.

II

A Man. Where's the lucky bride? *(With cries of "Mary—Jabez—strike it up, Fiddler—make room for the bride and groom," the crowd drags Mary and Jabez, pleased but embarrassed, into the center of the room and Mary and Jabez do a little solo-dance, while the crowd claps, applauds, and makes various remarks.)*
A Man: Handsome steppers!
A Woman. She's pretty as a picture.
A Second Man. Cut your pigeon-wing, Jabez!
An Old Man. Young again, young again, that's the way I feel!

[*He tries to cut a pigeon-wing himself.*]

The Old Woman. Henry, Henry, careful of your rheumatiz!
A Third Woman. Makes me feel all teary, seeing them so happy.
The Old Man (*gossiping to a neighbor*). Wonder where he got it all—Stones was always poor.
His Neighbor. Ain't poor now. Makes you wonder just a mite.
A Third Man. Don't begrudge it to him—but I wonder where he got it.
The Old Man (*starting to whisper*). Let me tell you something—
The Old Woman (*quickly*). Henry, Henry, don't you start to gossip.

[*She drags him away.*]

Women. She's a lucky woman. They're a lucky pair.
Men. That's true as gospel. But I wonder where he got it.
Women. Money, land and riches.
Men. Just came out of nowhere.
Women and Men (*together*). Wonder where he got it all—But that's his business.

Fiddler. Left and right—grand chain!

[*The dance rises to a fever pitch of ecstasy with the final figure—the fiddle squeaks and stops. The dancers mop their brows.*]

First Man. Whew! Ain't danced like that since I was knee-high to a grasshopper!
Second Man. Play us "The Portland Fancy," fiddler!
Third Man. No, wait a minute, neighbor. Let's hear from the happy pair! Hey, Jabez!
Fourth Man. Let's hear from the State Senator!

[*They crowd around Jabez and push him up on the settle.*]

Old Man. Might as well. It's the last time he'll have the last word!
Old Woman. Now Henry Banks, you ought to be ashamed of yourself!
Old Man. Told you so, Jabez!
Crowd: Speech!

—from *The Devil and Daniel Webster,*
Stephen Vincent Benét

1. Based on the dialogue, how would you describe the neighbors of Jabez and Mary Stone? Are they wealthy? Poor? City or country people? Highly educated or not? Do they seem good-hearted or malicious, or some combination of these?
2. Does the dialogue suggest that Jabez and Mary Stone will be likable characters or not? Mention specific lines to support your answer.

3. What hints are given in the dialogue about Jabez Stone? How has his situation changed recently? What are his neighbors suggesting about the change?
4. Using the opening dialogue as a guide, try to predict what the central **conflict** of the play will be. Explain how you arrived at this prediction.

Writing

1. **Describing a Setting.** Think about dramas and comedies you have enjoyed in movies or on television. Pick one that you remember well. Concentrate on the **setting** of one scene in the story you selected. Then make a list of all the details you can remember from that scene. Finally, write a description of the setting, in which you include these details. Pretend you are writing for someone whose job it will be to recreate the setting for an audience.
2. **Writing Dialogue.** Think of an important character in a movie or television program. (If you like, you may use the same program you used for the previous activity.) Imagine that you are writing a scene that will introduce this character to an audience for the first time. Write several lines of dialogue that will convey one or more important personality traits of the character. Don't try to reveal too much in a short scene. Just be sure that what you do reveal is important to an understanding of the character.

ANALYZING RELATIONSHIPS

Writing Assignment

Write a three-paragraph essay in which you analyze the relationships between two characters in either *The Diary of Anne Frank* or *High Noon.*

Background

A good drama has interesting characters who connect with each other in a variety of ways. Sometimes the interaction between the characters is a **conflict,** or struggle. Sometimes it is a growing love. Almost always the relationships among the main characters in a good stage play or movie change and develop. In fact, these changing relationships are an important part of what makes the drama move forward—and hold our interest.

As you read a drama or watch it unfold, you can better understand what is happening if you **analyze** the characters' relationships. Begin by identifying the kind of relationship that exists between two characters. Sometimes the relationship is complex, but generally you can identify at least one or two main characteristics of the relationship. Then watch to see how the relationship changes and how it affects the other characters and the drama as a whole. The following list contains some of the kinds of relationships that occur between characters in dramas, novels, and stories:

Loving	Bossy/ Dominant
Friendly	Obedient/ Submissive
Approving	Respectful
Disapproving	Teasing
Angry/ Hostile	Open/ Honest
Jealous	Closed/ Uncommunicative
Hateful	Supportive

Prewriting

1. Choose two characters who interact with each other during one of the dramas.

2. Go back through the drama and reread the scenes in which your two characters talk *with* each other or *about* each other. Make notes about what the scene or dialogue reveals about each character's attitude toward the other.

3. For each of the two characters, make a clustering diagram that analyzes the character's relationship with the other character.

The following diagram illustrates Mrs. Van Daan's relationship with Anne Frank in *The Diary of Anne Frank.* Notice that the diagram names different aspects of the relationship and cites scenes, incidents, and quotations that reveal each aspect.

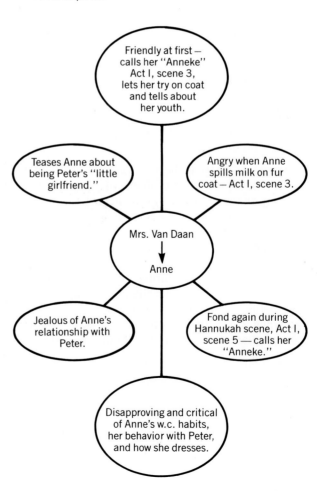

When you analyze a relationship between two characters, you have to consider each character separately because the relationship is never the same for both. If you were writing about the relationship between Anne and Mrs. Van Daan, you would next do a clustering diagram analyzing Anne's attitude toward Mrs. Van Daan.

4. Now, consider how the relationship between the two characters affects the drama as a whole. You may make a third diagram or just make notes. The following notes analyze the effect of Mrs. Van Daan and Anne's relationship on the play as a whole.

   a. The relationship reveals aspects of Anne's character that are important to the play—kindness, outspokenness.
   b. Illustrates increasing conflict and tension in daily life.
   c. Focuses attention on the love story between Anne and Peter.

Writing

You should have a clustering diagram or notes for each of the three paragraphs of your essay:

Paragraph 1: Analyze the feelings and attitudes of one character toward the other. Tell how the relationship changes during the course of the drama. Cite scenes, incidents, or lines from the drama to support your statements.

Paragraph 2: Analyze the second character's feelings and attitudes toward the other. Tell how the relationship changes during the course of the drama. Give evidence from the play to support your statements.

Paragraph 3: Discuss how the relationship between the two characters affects the drama as a whole.

The following paragraph is one student's analysis based on the clustering diagram on page 337.

Mrs. Van Daan's attitude toward Anne changes during the course of the play. She begins by being friendly and calling Anne by her nickname: "That's right, Anneke! Give it

to him" (Act I, scene 3). In this scene she lets Anne try on her fur coat and tells Anne stories of her youthful triumphs. The pleasantness ends with Mrs. Van Daan's fury toward Anne when Anne accidentally spills milk on her fur coat. Mrs. Van Daan, it seems, values that coat more than people. During the Hannukah scene (Act I, scene 5), Mrs. Van Daan once more calls Anne "Anneke," moved by Anne's thoughtfulness and gifts. But Mrs. Van Daan's early teasing of Anne as Peter's "little girl-friend" (Act I, scene 3) turns to outright jealousy in Act II as Anne's relationship with Peter blossoms. Throughout Act II, Mrs. Van Daan is disapproving of Anne—of her behavior with Peter, her outspokenness, her dress. For Mrs. Van Daan, Anne seems to represent all that she has lost: youth, high spirits, romance, and the promise of a bright future.

Revising and Proofreading Self-Check

1. Have I expressed my ideas clearly?
2. Have I cited examples and details to support my ideas?
3. Have I checked quotations, punctuated them properly, and cited the act and scene in which the quotation appears (if necessary)?
4. Does every sentence start with a capital letter and end with a period or other end punctuation mark? Are words spelled correctly?

Partner Check

1. Are there any spelling errors?
2. Are sentences punctuated correctly?
3. Are the ideas clearly expressed?
4. Are statements supported with details from the drama?
5. What do I like best about this paper?
6. What do I think needs improvement?

THE ELEMENTS OF POETRY

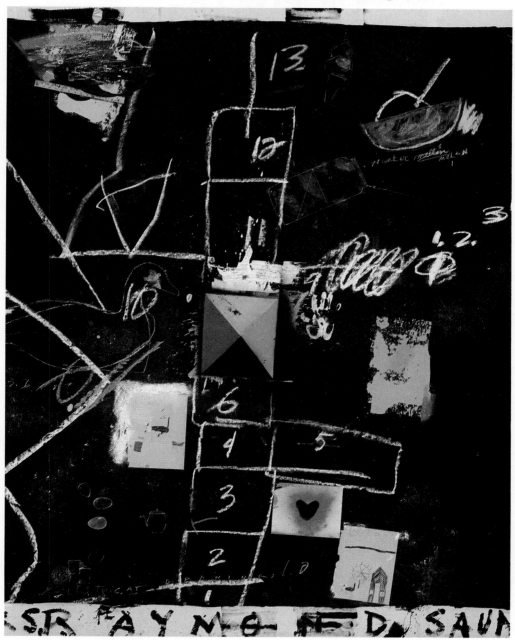

Celest, Age 5, invited me to Tea
by Raymond Saunders (1986). Mixed Media.

Courtesy Stephen Wirtz Gallery,
San Francisco.

UNIT SIX

John Malcolm Brinnin

THE ELEMENTS OF POETRY

Poetry is the language that tells us, through a more or less emotional reaction, something that cannot be said. All poetry, great or small, does this.

—Edwin Arlington Robinson

What Is Poetry?

The question, "What is poetry?" is sometimes answered like this: "Poetry is about love and stars and flowers." "Poetry is what Shakespeare wrote—like *Romeo and Juliet.*" "Poetry is what has rhyme and rhythm." "Poetry is private thoughts."

You will never find any of these definitions in a textbook. Yet each definition is an attempt to get at one essential thing: Poetry is the art and craft of putting feelings into special combinations of words.

The Importance of Words

Poetry is a form of expression—just as music, painting, sculpture, and dance are. Poetry is different from these other forms of expression because it is composed only of words—words that have as many sounds as anyone could hope for, but only limited meanings. Poets must give the same careful attention to words that composers give to melody, that painters give to color, that sculptors give to shape, and that dancers give to movement.

Poetry demands skill. While we admire poets for the beauty of their thoughts and the generosity of their feelings, we have to remember that these virtues do not by themselves make poems. Only words make poems. The best poets are not necessarily those who are most intelligent or most sensitive. The best poets are those who find the best words and put them in the best possible order.

There's a "touch of the poet" in everyone. Sometimes this shows up in infancy and childhood. A three-year-old child will make up songs, or repeat sounds, that seem like poetry even if they don't make sense. Many of the songs children sing, or the jingles they repeat when they jump rope or play jacks or kick-the-stick or farmer-in-the-dell, were made up by other children. Nobody knows their names or who they were. They themselves didn't think they were doing anything unusual when they found words to go with the games. But these children were poets all the same.

"Say it!" advised the poet William Carlos Williams to people who wanted to write poetry. He meant that experience of any kind—from skipping rope to preparing to die—cannot be communicated until the right words for it have been found and arranged in a sensible order.

Reading a Poem

In order to understand a poem fully, you need to listen to its sounds and think about its sense.

Illustration by Arthur Rackham for a 1913 edition of Mother Goose rhymes.

1. Whenever possible, read a poem aloud at least once. Poems are meant to appeal to our ears as well as to our minds.

2. Be aware of punctuation, especially periods and commas. Periods alert you to beginnings and ends of sentences (which are not always at beginnings and ends of lines).

3. If a line of poetry does not end with punctuation, do not make a full stop. Pause very briefly and continue reading until you reach some form of punctuation. A period will indicate the end of a sentence.

4. If the poem has a steady beat—da-DUM, da-DUM, da-DUM, da-DUM—do not distort the sound by reading the poem in a sing-song way. Instead, try to read the poem in a normal voice as if you were speaking to a friend. The poem's music will emerge naturally.

5. Check the meanings of unfamiliar words. Poets choose words with special care, and meanings are important.

6. Notice how poets appeal to your imagination by describing one thing in terms of another. For example, in one poem in this unit, the poet describes a steam shovel as if it were a dinosaur.

7. After you finish reading a poem, think about it. Then read it a second and even a third time. With each rereading you will probably discover something new.

Responding to a Poem

The poem that follows has been read by a reader whose responses are noted at the right. Read the poem twice. First, read it aloud for pleasure. Second, read it and look at the reader's notes. You might want to add notes of your own on a separate sheet.

Abou Ben Adhem

Abou Ben Adhem (may his tribe increase!)
Awoke one night from a deep dream of peace,
And saw, within the moonlight in his room,
Making it rich, and like a lily in bloom,
An angel writing in a book of gold.
Exceeding peace had made Ben Adhem bold,
And to the Presence in the room he said,
"What writest thou?" The vision raised its head,
And, with a look made of all sweet accord,
Answered, "The names of those who love the Lord."
"And is mine one?" said Abou. "Nay, not so,"
Replied the angel. Abou spoke more low,
But cheerily still, and said, "I pray thee, then,
Write me as one that loves his fellow men."

The angel wrote, and vanished. The next night
It came again, with a great wakening light,
And showed the names whom love of God had blessed,
And, lo! Ben Adhem's name led all the rest.

—Leigh Hunt

What an odd title. What does it mean?

It's a man's name. "Tribe" suggests maybe a bedouin? An Indian?

The poem's rhymed—I like its sounds.

An angel and a gold book—this is like a dream.

"Sweet accord"?

This sounds like something from the Bible.

He doesn't love the Lord? What will happen now?

But Abou Ben Adhem does love other people.

There are some good descriptions in this poem.

I like it! Because he loves his fellow men, he also must love God. This poem tells us very clearly what its message is.

Thinking Over the Poem

This reader had some trouble with the poem's title. Did you? Do you know now what "Abou Ben Adhem" refers to? Does it make any difference whether you know exactly where the poem takes place?

How did you respond to the poem's sounds? Are the sounds pleasant to listen to, or are they harsh and discordant?

This reader noticed these characteristics of the poem:

1. It contains "some good descriptions." What pictures did it put in your mind? Do you agree that it describes the setting well?
2. The poem has a message. How would you state it in your own words? What do you think of the message?

Memorizing the Poem

Many years ago, this poem could be recited by most schoolchildren in England and in America. The poem's rhymes and rhythms help to make it fairly easy to memorize. If you would like to memorize the poem, try these techniques:

1. Read the poem aloud three or four times.
2. Note the rhyme scheme: The lines rhyme in pairs. This should help you remember the last word of each line.
3. Memorize two lines at a time. Say the lines aloud several times, then cover them up and try to recite them from memory.
4. Try to picture the words of the poem on the page.

The poet goes in like a rope skipper to make the most of his opportunities. If he trips himself he stops the rope.

—Robert Frost

Sound Effects: Rhythm

Illustration by Arthur Rackham for a 1913 edition of Mother Goose rhymes.

Rhythm in poetry, like rhythm in music, is based on sound. It is created by repetition. The repetition can involve either a regular pattern of stressed and unstressed syllables or other sound patterns (such as those created by rhymes or repeated words). The first rhythms most of us know are singsong—simple little ditties like these nursery rhymes:

> Hey diddle, diddle,
> The cat and the fiddle,
> The cow jumped over the moon.
> The little dog laughed
> To see such sport,
> And the dish ran away with the spoon.

or

> Hickory, dickory, dock,
> The mouse ran up the clock.
> The clock struck one,
> The mouse ran down.
> Hickory, dickory, dock.

We hear poems like these in kindergarten. As we get a little older, we begin to dismiss them as baby talk. Nevertheless, these old poems have introduced us to the fun of words and to the feel of rhythm. They have given us our beginning notions of what poetry can do.

Meter: A Regular Pattern

Poetry can be written in at least two ways: It can be written with strict concern for **meter,** which means a regular pattern of stressed and unstressed syllables. In the following example, the stressed syllables are marked with an accent mark (′), and the unstressed syllables are marked with a cup (◡). Say this verse aloud and you'll hear the meter, the regular rise and fall of your voice as you speak the words:

> Between the dark and the daylight,
> When the night is beginning to lower,
> Comes a pause in the day's occupations,
> That is known as the Children's Hour . . .

—from "The Children's Hour,"
Henry Wadsworth Longfellow

Meter must be handled with skill. When meter is exactly the same throughout the whole poem, it can become monotonous and mechanical. To be effective, the meter should usually include variations, departures from what we expect. You can see that Longfellow varied his meter so his verse isn't singsong.

Free Verse: The Rhythms of Ordinary Speech

A poem can also be written in what is called **free verse.** The only thing "free" about free verse is that it does not have a regular pattern of stressed and unstressed syllables: Free verse is *not* written in meter. Free-verse poetry attempts to sound like familiar speech. Here is a poem written in free verse. Say it aloud; you'll hear at once how different it sounds from the Longfellow verse above. Notice how this poet varies her line lengths. Some lines are long; some lines are very short.

> I almost had a poem
> coming
> but I looked out
> the window and saw 3 dogs
> circling the chicken coop and by
> the time I ran out there
>   hollering & screaming &
> throwing twigs & walnuts & toy cars
> and in desperation a branch I could barely
> pick up;   and more sensibly
> 2 good-sized rocks that
> caught my eye—it was gone.   well
> I cornered the big dog(he
> couldn't run through the blackberry
> bush) & I nailed him a
> good one.   I bet he's
> the one that killed
> the duck;   she sat on
> her last batch of pitiful eggs
> till they went rotten.
>
> she always liked
> the winter best
> when the creek is
> full.
>
> —Alma Villanueva

For the free-verse poet, the trick is to sound like familiar speech without including all the hesitations (um's and ah's) and repetitions and half-finished thoughts that characterize the way most people express themselves.

Whether poets use free verse or meter, they have to give poems some kind of rhythm, or their words can't be called poetry.

This poem is based loosely on real historical events. On the night of April 18, 1775, Paul Revere and two other men set out from Boston to warn the American Colonists of a planned British raid on Concord, Massachusetts. The next day, American minutemen confronted the British, and the first skirmishes of the American Revolution occurred at Lexington and Concord.

The rhythm of this poem is dictated by its subject—a long, fast ride on horseback. The clippety-clop of the horse's hooves is first heard in the opening line, and then echoes through every stanza.

"Listen, my children," says the poet, and we know at once that this is a poem to be spoken aloud if we are to get the full flavor of Paul Revere's dramatic dash into the sleeping countryside. The excitement of the poem's story lies not only in its details about this great night in American history, but also in the swiftness of movement that keeps us jogging from the banks of the Mystic River in Boston to the bridge in Concord. There, in the words of another poet, Ralph Waldo Emerson, "embattled farmers" would fire the shot "heard 'round the world."

This story has been told many times, and in many different ways. But this poem is the most famous version of the events of that night, and the thing that makes everyone remember it above all others is its rhythm.

Paul Revere's Ride

Henry Wadsworth Longfellow

Listen, my children, and you shall hear
Of the midnight ride of Paul Revere,
On the eighteenth of April, in Seventy-five;
Hardly a man is now alive
5   Who remembers that famous day and year.

He said to his friend, "If the British march
By land or sea from the town tonight,
Hang a lantern aloft in the belfry arch
Of the North Church tower as a signal light—
10   One, if by land, and two, if by sea;
And I on the opposite shore will be,
Ready to ride and spread the alarm
Through every Middlesex° village and farm,
For the country folk to be up and to arm."

15   Then he said, "Good night!" and with muffled oar
Silently rowed to the Charlestown shore,
Just as the moon rose over the bay.
Where swinging wide at her moorings lay
The Somerset, British man-of-war;
20   A phantom ship, with each mast and spar
Across the moon like a prison bar,
And a huge black hulk, that was magnified
By its own reflection in the tide.

13. **Middlesex:** Massachusetts county.

Meanwhile, his friend, through alley and street,
Wanders and watches with eager ears.
Till in the silence around him he hears
The muster of men at the barrack door,
The sound of arms, and the tramp of feet,
And the measured tread of the grenadiers,°
Marching down to their boats on the shore.

Then he climbed the tower of the Old North Church,
By the wooden stairs, with stealthy tread,
To the belfry chamber overhead,
And startled the pigeons from their perch
On the somber rafters, that round him made
Masses and moving shapes of shade—
By the trembling ladder, steep and tall,
To the highest window in the wall,
Where he paused to listen and look down
A moment on the roofs of the town,
And the moonlight flowing over all.

29. **grenadiers** (gren′ə·dirz′) infantry soldiers.

The Midnight Ride of Paul Revere by Grant Wood (1931). Oil.

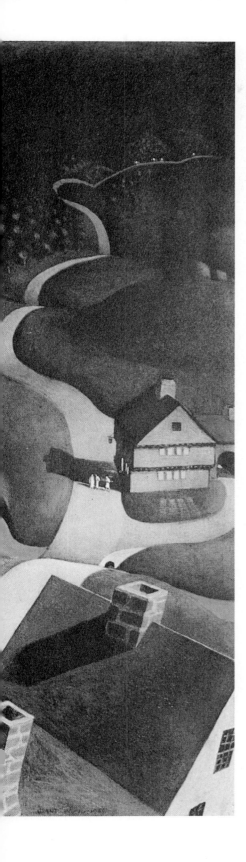

Beneath, in the churchyard, lay the dead,
In their night encampment on the hill,
Wrapped in silence so deep and still
45 That he could hear, like a sentinel's tread
The watchful night wind, as it went
Creeping along from tent to tent,
And seeming to whisper, "All is well!"
A moment only he feels the spell
50 Of the place and the hour, and the secret dread
Of the lonely belfry and the dead;
For suddenly all his thoughts are bent
On a shadowy something far away,
Where the river widens to meet the bay,
55 A line of black that bends and floats
On the rising tide, like a bridge of boats.

Meanwhile, impatient to mount and ride,
Booted and spurred, with a heavy stride
On the opposite shore walked Paul Revere.
60 Now he patted his horse's side,
Now gazed at the landscape far and near,
Then, impetuous, stamped the earth,
And turned and tightened his saddle-girth;
But mostly he watched with eager search
65 The belfry tower of the Old North Church,
As it rose above the graves on the hill,
Lonely and spectral and somber and still.
And lo! As he looks, on the belfry's height
A glimmer, and then a gleam of light!
70 He springs to the saddle, the bridle he turns,
But lingers and gazes, till full on his sight
A second lamp in the belfry burns!

A hurry of hoofs in a village street,
A shape in the moonlight, a bulk in the dark,
75 And beneath, from the pebbles, in passing, a spark
Struck out by a steed flying fearless and fleet:
That was all! And yet, through the gloom and the light,
The fate of a nation was riding that night;
And the spark struck out by that steed, in his flight,
80 Kindled the land into flame with its heat.

He has left the village and mounted the steep,
And beneath him, tranquil and broad and deep,
Is the Mystic, meeting the ocean tides;
And under the alders that skirt its edge,
85 Now soft on the sand, now loud on the ledge,
Is heard the tramp of his steed as he rides.

It was twelve by the village clock,
When he crossed the bridge into Medford town.
He heard the crowing of the cock,
90 And the barking of the farmer's dog,
And felt the damp of the river fog,
That rises after the sun goes down.

It was one by the village clock,
When he galloped into Lexington.
95 He saw the gilded weathercock
Swim in the moonlight as he passed,
And the meetinghouse windows, blank and bare,
Gaze at him with a spectral glare,
As if they already stood aghast
100 At the bloody work they would look upon.

It was two by the village clock,
When he came to the bridge in Concord town.
He heard the bleating of the flock,
And the twitter of birds among the trees,
105 And felt the breath of the morning breeze
Blowing over the meadows brown.
And one was safe and asleep in his bed
Who at the bridge would be first to fall,
Who that day would be lying dead,
110 Pierced by a British musketball.

You know the rest. In the books you have read,
How the British Regulars fired and fled,
How the farmers gave them ball for ball,
From behind each fence and farmyard wall,
115 Chasing the redcoats down the lane,
Then crossing the fields to emerge again
Under the trees at the turn of the road,
And only pausing to fire and load.

So through the night rode Paul Revere;
120 And so through the night went his cry of alarm
To every Middlesex village and farm,
A cry of defiance and not of fear,
A voice in the darkness, a knock at the door,
And a word that shall echo forevermore!
125 For, borne on the night wind of the Past,
Through all our history, to the last,
In the hour of darkness and peril and need,
The people will waken and listen to hear
The hurrying hoofbeats of that steed,
130 And the midnight message of Paul Revere.

Responding to the Poem

Analyzing the Poem

Identifying Details

1. According to the second stanza, what does Paul Revere say will be the purpose of his ride?
2. Before he begins his ride, Paul Revere waits for a signal from his friend. What is the signal, and what does it tell Revere? From where is it sent?
3. Trace the course of Paul Revere's ride as it is described in lines 81–106.
4. In line 111, the poet writes, "You know the rest." He then briefly describes the result of Revere's historic ride. In four sentences, explain what the poet says resulted from Revere's ride.
5. From the belfry, Revere's friend sees "a shadowy something far away" (line 53). What does the friend soon realize he is seeing?
6. In stanza 7, what details in the description of Paul Revere show that he is eager to begin his ride? What does he do in lines 68–72 that indicate he does not act too hastily?

Interpreting Meanings

7. Explain what the poet means when he says, "The fate of a nation was riding that night" (line 78). What is he referring to when he says the spark from the horse's hoof "kindled the land into flame" (line 80)?
8. In the last stanza, what do you think is the word "that shall echo forevermore"? How would you state the "message" of Paul Revere?
9. Why does the poet believe Revere's message will remain important to future generations?
10. Almost every line in this poem has four beats or stressed syllables, and each beat is accompanied by one or two unstressed syllables. This rhythm gives the poem its galloping sound. Copy the first three lines of the poem, and scan them using an accent mark (´) for stressed syllables and a cup (◡) for unstressed syllables. Which line has the most regular pattern of unstressed and stressed syllables?

    Repeat the exercise for groups of three lines at the start of stanzas in the middle and near the end of the poem. Are there any differences?

Applying Meanings

11. In what "hour of darkness and peril and need" might we be encouraged by Paul Revere's "message" today? In what ways would his "message" help?
12. Are there any other "Paul Reveres" in history, or in the present, who have rallied their people with cries "of defiance and not of fear"? Explain your answer.

Writing About the Poem

A Creative Response

1. **Change in the Point of View.** The poet vividly describes Revere's ride by focusing on what he and his friend see and do. Imagine that you live in one of the villages where Revere stops to deliver his message. You have just been awak-

Paul Revere by John Singleton Copley (1765–1770). Oil.

ened by his knock on the door. Write a paragraph in which you describe the village scene. What are people doing and saying? Are they excited or suspicious? Do you run out to talk to them? Or do you stay at your door? Use vivid details to add realism to your description.

A Critical Response

2. **Comparing Poetic and Historical Accounts.** Poems can be very powerful in shaping our view of history. In this case, Longfellow's account of the events of the night of April 18, 1775, is not completely accurate. Key details have been left out or changed, and yet this is the version that many people accept as fact. Read a factual account of his famous ride in a reference book, textbook, or other book. Then, in one or two paragraphs, compare Longfellow's account to the actual historical facts. In what important ways does the poem alter history? Why do you suppose the poet decided to change important details?

Analyzing Language and Vocabulary

Inverted Word Order

Occasionally a poet will change the normal order of words in a sentence. This may be done to empha-size certain words or to have the lines fit better together. It may also be done to create rhyme or rhythm.

1. One example of inverted word order appears in line 11 of "Paul Revere's Ride": "And I on the opposite shore will be." Normally we would say, "And I will be on the opposite shore." What purpose is served by ending the line with "be"?
2. What inverted word order can you find in lines 70–72? Rewrite these lines, putting the sentence in the order of normal speech.
3. Find at least one other instance of inverted word order in the poem. Rewrite those lines too.

Reading About the Writer

Henry Wadsworth Longfellow (1807–1882) was the most celebrated American poet of his time. Longfellow was born in Portland, Maine. He lived during a period when readers looked to poetry for comfort, for spiritual uplift, and for colorful accounts of history. Longfellow's own poems on historical subjects include *The Song of Hiawatha* (see page 509), *The Courtship of Miles Standish, Evangeline,* and "Paul Revere's Ride." These and other poems by Longfellow have now become part of our national mythology. There was a time in the past when almost every schoolchild in America could recite some of Longfellow's poems by heart.

This poem describes a simple but important childhood memory. The poet uses a strict rhythm and pairs of rhymed lines to unfold the scene step by step. Before you read, think about the poem's title. What things do you usually associate with the words *secret* and *heart*? Are your associations similar to the boy's in the poem?

The Secret Heart

Robert P. Tristram Coffin

Across the years he could recall
His father one way best of all.

In the stillest hour of night
The boy awakened to a light.

5 Half in dreams, he saw his sire°
With his great hands full of fire.

The man had struck a match to see
If his son slept peacefully.

He held his palms each side the spark
10 His love had kindled in the dark.

His two hands were curved apart
In the semblance of a heart.

He wore, it seemed to his small son,
A bare heart on his hidden one,

15 A heart that gave out such a glow
No son awake could bear to know.

It showed a look upon a face
Too tender for the day to trace.

One instant, it lit all about,
20 And then the secret heart went out.

But it shone long enough for one
To know that hands held up the sun.

---

5. **sire:** father.

Responding to the Poem

Analyzing the Poem

Identifying Details

1. According to lines 5–6, what did the boy see after he "awakened to a light"?
2. Why had the father entered the boy's room?
3. According to lines 9–10, what kindled the spark?
4. What did the boy think his father's palms resembled?
5. What kind of look did the boy see on his father's face?
6. According to lines 19–22, how long did the "secret heart" burn before it went out?

Interpreting Meanings

7. What do you think the speaker means by saying in the last line that the shining heart helped him realize that "hands held up the sun"? Do you think he is saying something about his father? About God? About both?
8. A **symbol** is any person, place, or thing which has meaning in itself but which is made to represent, or stand for, something else as well. In this poem, what actually is the father's "secret heart"? What does the "secret heart" symbolize for the son?
9. We usually think of love as something we cannot get enough of. Why do you think the speaker describes the glow from the father's heart as so great that "no son awake could bear to know" it?
10. Copy the first two lines and scan them, using an accent mark (ˊ) for stressed syllables and a cup (˯) for unstressed syllables. What is the basic rhythm of this poem? Next, scan line 6. What effect does the poet achieve by varying the basic rhythm?
11. How does the poet use **rhyme** to help create the poem's rhythm?

Applying Meanings

12. It is often difficult to express love openly, so we express it indirectly in many small acts. In what small ways do parents express love for their children? What are some ways that children express their love in return?

Writing About the Poem

A Creative Response

1. **Describing a Memorable Moment.** Choose a strong memory from your life, or from the life of an imagined person. The memory may involve another person or a particular place or an event. Perhaps it is a moment that was captured in a photograph. Write a precise description of the memory, using full sentences. Separate each of your sentences by a space, as in Coffin's poem.

A Critical Response

2. **Comparing Poems.** In an essay, compare the following poem to "The Secret Heart." In your essay, consider these elements of the poems:

   a. Subject
   b. Message

While I Slept

While I slept, while I slept and the night grew colder
She would come to my bedroom stepping softly
And draw a blanket about my shoulder
While I slept.

While I slept, while I slept in the dark still heat
She would come to my bedside stepping coolly
And smooth the twisted troubled sheet
While I slept.

Now she sleeps, sleeps under quiet rain
While nights grow warm or nights grow colder
And I wake and sleep and wake again
While she sleeps.

—Robert Francis

Analyzing Language and Vocabulary

Homonyms

Many words in English sound the same but are spelled differently and have different meanings. Think of the words *peek* and *peak*, *brake* and *break*, *tow* and *toe*. Such words are called **homonyms** (häm′ə·nimz).

1. Find and list ten words in the poem that have homonyms—words that sound the same but are spelled differently and have different meanings. List the homonyms beside each word.
2. Poets sometimes use homonyms in the hope that we will think of two meanings of a word at the same time. In which line of this poem do you think the poet is hoping you will think of the two meanings of a word at the same time? What is the word? Try to explain the double meaning of the line.

Reading About the Writer

Robert P. Tristram Coffin (1892–1955), born in Brunswick, Maine, was a writer of both prose and poetry, an artist, a teacher, and a lecturer. He often showed his art works, which include watercolors and pen-and-inks, when he lectured. Coffin says he gave "upward of a thousand lectures or readings" in the last years of his life. He won a Pulitzer Prize for *Strange Holiness,* a volume of poetry written in 1935.

Focusing on Background
A Comment from the Poet

"A good many of my poems are such combinations of good things, I find. The combinations range all the way from the cellar—a man and a rocking-chair, a boy and a girl and a willow whistle, a hired man and a weather vane, a hound dog's tail and a wooden porch, an old man and a mess of young clams, a young boy and his first plow—upstairs to the parlor—a woman and a cupola, fire and the footmarks on frozen rockweed at night, and an old farmer and loneliness. And I am proud to see that sometimes I have been able to reach out and bring things together in a poem that are as far apart as the east is from the west: The living and the dead, love and hate in two lonely women in a big house, cruelty and beauty in a hawk, life and death in deer and hounds, and the light of a match and the light behind the sun, when my father leaned over me in my illness once, when I was a child, in the dead of night."

—Robert P. Tristram Coffin

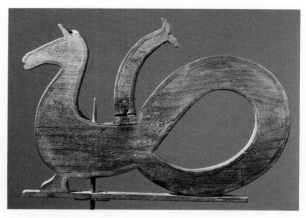

Sea-serpent weather vane by an unknown artist (c. 1850). Painted wood and iron.

Collection of the Museum of American Folk Art.

This poem can be read as a birthday card from one sister to another. Read the poem aloud in order to hear how the repetition of sounds creates its rhythm.

Sisters

For Elaine Philip on Her Birthday

Lucille Clifton

me and you be sisters.
we be the same.
me and you
coming from the same place.
5   me and you
be greasing our legs
touching up our edges.
me and you
be scared of rats
10   be stepping on roaches.
me and you
come running high down purdy street
   one time
and mama laugh and shake her head at
me and you.
15   me and you
got babies
got thirty-five
got black
let our hair go back
20   be loving ourselves
be loving ourselves
be sisters.
only where you sing
i poet.

Responding to the Poem

Analyzing the Poem

Identifying Details

1. List three ways in which the speaker and her sister are alike.
2. Describe one difference between the sisters.
3. Only one specific incident is mentioned in the poem. Describe that incident.

Interpreting Meanings

4. Does the speaker of this poem strike you as shy and quiet or as confident and outgoing? What details in the poem give you clues?
5. Do you think the two people in the poem are really sisters (that is, have the same parents)? Or does the poet use the word *sisters* to mean close friends? Support your analysis with passages from the poem.
6. What phrases are repeated in this poem to create its **rhythm**? Which phrase is repeated most often? Why is this phrase important?
7. What feelings did this poem leave with you? Try to explain the reasons for your reaction.

Writing About the Poem

A Creative Response

1. **Writing a Birthday Poem.** Lucille Clifton's poem is special partly because it expresses the poet's feelings of affection for another person. You can imagine how her sister felt on receiving this poem rather than a store-bought card. Choose someone special for whom you might write birthday greetings. Address this person in your own natural, informal language. List incidents and other details that express your feelings in a personal way. Write your greetings as a poem of five to ten lines. Try to repeat one phrase as Clifton does.

A Critical Response

2. **Comparing Rhythms.** Both this poem and "The Secret Heart" (page 353) deal with love. But the love is expressed very differently in each case. Reread both poems aloud. Listen closely to the rhythm in each poem. Then write a paragraph comparing the two rhythms.

Analyzing Language and Vocabulary

Dialect

A **dialect** is a variation of a language. It has certain rules of grammar, pronunciation, and/or vocabulary that distinguish it from the language of the general population. For example, the black American dialect used here by Lucille Clifton is one of many dialects of English spoken in the United States. In standard American English, "me and you be sisters. / we be the same" would be "You and I are sisters. / We are the same."

Rewrite all of "Sisters" to see how it would sound in standard American English. What does the poem lose when it is rewritten in standard English?

Reading About the Writer

Lucille Clifton (1936–   ) often writes about the experiences and feelings of black men and women in America. "I celebrate life," she once said. "I try to tell the truth as I see it." Clifton was born in Depew, New York, and lives in Baltimore with her family. Although she also writes short stories, she is primarily known for her poetry. Some of her works include *Good Times, Good News About the Earth,* and *Generations.* "Sisters" is from *An Ordinary Woman.*

"My Mother's Childhood" recalls a simple scene—a young girl waiting outside a candy factory. Though the scene is simple, the rhythms that the poet uses are not. The art of this poem lies in the way the poet shapes his sentences: They rise and fall, pause, and then change in speed and in length. These are the rhythms of natural speech, but they are very carefully controlled. Before you read this poem, examine its punctuation. Where does the first sentence end?

My Mother's Childhood

Barry Spacks

When she still used words, my mother told
of her childhood: they were poor, her father
peddled insurance door-to-door
in Portland, where the firehouse bell
5 would ring *no school* come heavy snow
and she'd stand—her little shrug, her sheepish
grin—in the candy factory yard,
waiting, patient child in the cold,
for sometimes an upper window would open,
10 someone would throw down gum, lumps
as large as little pumpernickels;
gray, but tasty. How she chewed!
She never wondered then, was it pure?
rejected?—chewed till her jawbone ached
15 and the tears welled in her eyes—they only
threw to her, to her, because
she waited
and was good.

Elizabeth by Fairfield Porter (1965). Oil.

Private collection. Courtesy Hirschl & Adler Modern, New York City.

Responding to the Poem

Analyzing the Poem

Identifying Details

1. On what occasions would the poet's mother go to the candy factory? Describe what she would do there.
2. According to lines 6–7, how does the girl stand while waiting? How does she chew the gum that is thrown to her (lines 12–15)?
3. Why do the workers throw gum to the girl?

Interpreting Meanings

4. Sometimes this poet is direct, as when we are told the girl is "poor," "sheepish," and "patient." At other times, he coaxes us into drawing our own conclusions. What can you tell about the girl's personality from the description in the poem?
5. Why do you suppose the girl chooses to wait for gum in the cold rather than spend her free time elsewhere? Explain what receiving the gum means to the girl.
6. The poem begins, "When she still used words. . . ." What mood does this opening cast over the rest of the poem? What do you think might have happened to make the mother stop using words?
7. **Tone** is the attitude or feeling that a writer reveals toward a subject. How does the speaker feel about the mother in this poem? Why do you suppose the scene of the girl standing in the snowy factory yard remains so important to him?
8. The **rhythms** of "My Mother's Childhood" resemble natural speech. When we speak, we sometimes leave sentences unfinished, or interrupt the flow of an idea with a suddenly remembered detail or exclamation. Find three passages in the poem that sound conversational to you. Then explain how the poet creates this quality.

Applying Meanings

9. Does anything in this poem remind you of an experience you've had or that someone else has had? Does it remind you of any news stories? How does it make you feel?

Writing About the Poem

A Creative Response

1. **Telling a Nutshell Story.** This poem packs many thoughts, feelings, and facts into a few sentences. Using three well-packed sentences, relate an old story about a member of your family or about a friend or acquaintance. Before you begin, list the details that your readers will need to know. (To find details, answer these questions about the story: Who? What? When? Where? Why?) Then look again at the way Barry Spacks uses different kinds of phrases and punctuation. You may want to imitate some of his writing tricks to get all the important details into your story.

A Critical Response

2. **Responding to a Title.** This poem is not titled "The Candy Factory" or "Snowy Days," but "My Mother's Childhood." In a paragraph, explain how the poem might be read as a description of the speaker's mother's entire childhood. Before you write, think about these questions: What kind of person do you suppose the mother was as a girl? What kind of place did she probably live in? Did she have many friends? Use passages from the poem to support your analysis.

Analyzing Language and Vocabulary

The Human Zoo

We often describe people in terms of the way animals look and act. In this poem, for example, the girl is described as having a "sheepish grin." Sheep are often thought of as meek, timid creatures. Other examples of such words are *owlish* and *mulish*. List five other words or expressions in which animals help us picture human attributes. Write a one-sentence definition for each word.

Reading About the Writer

Barry Spacks (1931–   ), a novelist and a poet, was born in Philadelphia and lives in Massachusetts. His works include *Orphans* (a novel) and *Like a Prism* (a collection of poems). "My Mother's Childhood" is from *Teaching the Penguins to Fly.*

Sound Effects: Rhyme

Rhyme is the repetition of the sound of a stressed syllable and any unstressed syllables that follow: "sip" and "dip," "prayer" and "layer," "shimmering" and "glimmering." We all learned to listen for rhymes early in childhood.

> Hickory, dickory, **dock,**
> The mouse ran up the **clock**
>
> Hey diddle, **diddle,**
> The cat and the **fiddle**

In playgrounds we use counting-out rhymes, such as "One potato, two potato," to pick teams. And probably the first Valentine's Day card that we received had a message that rhymed. Such rhymes give us pleasure, let us play with language, and convey feelings and ideas in memorable ways. For all these reasons, many poets use rhyme—whether lightheartedly or seriously—to make the music in their poems.

Rhyme in Poetry

When rhyme is used well, it does three important things:

1. It helps to hold a poem together.
2. It adds a musical quality to a poem.
3. It draws our attention to important words.

If you have ever tried to memorize or recite a poem, you already know what a great help rhyme can be. Because there is always another word with a similar sound coming up, the rhymes trigger our memory of whole lines. The pattern of rhymes in a poem is called a **rhyme scheme.**

Rhymes have a chiming effect—like the repeated bongs of a grandfather clock or of church bells. Because we expect such sounds to ring out at certain times, they assure us that things are in order and all is well. Rhymes in poetry have a similar effect on us: They assure us, through sound, that a skilled poet is in control of the poem.

Poets often use rhyme to emphasize certain important words or ideas in the poem. For example, in "The Secret Heart" (page 353), Robert P. Tristram Coffin uses rhymes to emphasize some of his important words:

> In the stillest hour of **night**
> The boy awakened to a **light.**

And again:

> He held his palms each side the **spark**
> His love had kindled in the **dark.**

Whenever you read a poem, examine the rhymes to see what words the poet is emphasizing.

Does a Poem Have to Rhyme?

Rhymed poetry is so popular that many people think that a poem has to rhyme to be poetry at all. Other people argue that rhyme is old-fashioned. Some poets think that all the good rhymes in English have already been used too often. Much of the greatest poetry in English, even from earlier centuries, does not use rhyme. Some of the best poetry being written today uses rhyme in surprisingly inventive ways. It is important to remember that rhyme can be a useful and important ingredient in a poem. But it is only one of many ingredients that help turn words into poetry. Rhyme merely for the sake of rhyme is like too much salt on food: It can spoil everything.

Dickery, dickery, dock,
The mouse ran up the clock;
The clock struck one,
The mouse ran down,
Dickery, dickery, dock.

Illustration by Frederick Richardson for a 1915 edition of Mother Goose rhymes.

Kinds of Rhyme

Most rhymes in poetry are **end rhymes**: The rhyming words appear at the ends of lines, as in the preceding examples. Rhymes can also occur within lines. These are called **internal rhymes**:

> While I nodded, nearly **napping,** suddenly there came a **tapping,**
> As of someone gently **rapping, rapping** at my chamber door.

> —''The Raven,''
> Edgar Allan Poe

Some rhymes, instead of being exact, like *cat* and *rat,* are **approximate rhymes** (also called **near rhymes, off rhymes, slant rhymes,** or **imperfect rhymes**). That is, they slightly change the echo that we expect to hear. *Cut* and *rat, bat* and *bit, praise* and *prize,* and *cat* and *catch* are approximate rhymes. This kind of rhyme is popular with many modern poets. They believe it sounds less artificial and more conversational than exact rhymes. Some poets like to use approximate rhymes because they feel that all the good exact rhymes have already been used too many times.

Poets who write humorous poems, or **light verse,** often produce much of their comic effect by rhyming more than one syllable. Some examples are *spitefully* and *delightfully* or *busy* and *is he.* Because any rhymes may sound artificial or humorous, poets have to be very careful about choosing rhymes. These rhymes should exactly suit the feelings and ideas they want to express.

Illustration by F. H. Horvath for a 1930 edition of ''The Raven'' by Edgar Allan Poe.

This poem is a masterpiece of nonsense literature. In Lewis Carroll's topsy-turvy world, the craziest things seem ordinary, and the most common things seem out of place. Rhyme plays an important role in nonsense poems. Be sure to read this poem out loud.

The Walrus and the Carpenter

Lewis Carroll

Illustration for *Through the Looking Glass.*

The sun was shining on the sea,
  Shining with all his might:
He did his very best to make
  The billows smooth and bright—
5 And this was odd, because it was
  The middle of the night.

The moon was shining sulkily,
  Because she thought the sun
Had got no business to be there
10 After the day was done—
"It's very rude of him," she said,
  "To come and spoil the fun!"

The sea was wet as wet could be,
  The sands were dry as dry.
15 You could not see a cloud, because
  No cloud was in the sky:
No birds were flying overhead—
  There were no birds to fly.

The Walrus and the Carpenter
20 Were walking close at hand:
They wept like anything to see
  Such quantities of sand:
"If this were only cleared away,"
  They said, "it *would* be grand!"

Illustration for *Through the Looking Glass.*

25   "If seven maids with seven mops
      Swept it for half a year,
    Do you suppose," the Walrus said.
      "That they could get it clear?"
    "I doubt it," said the Carpenter,
30   And shed a bitter tear.

    "O Oysters, come and walk with us!"
      The Walrus did beseech.°
    "A pleasant talk, a pleasant walk,
      Along the briny beach:
35   We cannot do with more than four,
      To give a hand to each."

    The eldest Oyster winked his eye,
      But never a word he said.
    The eldest Oyster winked his eye,
40   And shook his heavy head—
    Meaning to say he did not choose
      To leave the oyster bed.

But four young Oysters hurried up,
    All eager for the treat:
Their coats were brushed, their faces
45   washed,
Their shoes were clean and neat—
And this was odd, because, you know,
    They hadn't any feet.

Four other Oysters followed them,
50   And yet another four;
And thick and fast they came at last,
    And more, and more, and more—
All hopping through the frothy waves,
    And scrambling to the shore.

55   The Walrus and the Carpenter
    Walked on a mile or so,
And then they rested on a rock
    Conveniently low:
And all the little oysters stood
60   And waited in a row.

---

32. **beseech** (bi·sēch´): to ask earnestly.

"The time has come," the Walrus said,
  "To talk of many things:
Of shoes—and ships—and sealing-wax—
  Of cabbages—and kings—
65 And why the sea is boiling hot—
  And whether pigs have wings."

"But wait a bit," the Oysters cried,
  "Before we have our chat;
For some of us are out of breath,
70   And all of us are fat!"
"No hurry!" said the Carpenter.
  They thanked him much for that.

"A loaf of bread," the Walrus said,
  "Is what we chiefly need:
75 Pepper and vinegar besides
  Are very good indeed—
Now if you're ready, Oysters dear,
  We can begin to feed."

"But not on us!" the Oysters cried,
80   Turning a little blue.
"After such kindness, that would be
  A dismal thing to do!"
"The night is fine," the Walrus said.
  "Do you admire the view?

85 "It was so kind of you to come!
  And you are very nice!"
The Carpenter said nothing but
  "Cut us another slice.
I wish you were not quite so deaf—
90   I've had to ask you twice!"

"It seems a shame," the Walrus said,
  "To play them such a trick,
After we've brought them out so far,
  And made them trot so quick!"
95 The Carpenter said nothing but
  "The butter's spread too thick!"

"I weep for you," the Walrus said:
  "I deeply sympathize."
With sobs and tears he sorted out
100   Those of the largest size,
Holding his pocket handkerchief
  Before his streaming eyes.

"O Oysters," said the Carpenter,
  "You've had a pleasant run!
105 Shall we be trotting home again?"
  But answer came there none—
And this was scarcely odd, because
  They'd eaten every one.

Responding to the Poem

Analyzing the Poem

Identifying Details

1. Where does the poem take place, and at what time of day? What does the speaker say is "odd" about the setting?
2. Why do the Walrus and the Carpenter cry in stanzas 4 and 5? What suddenly changes their mood in the next stanza?
3. The Walrus is a sly character. How does he word his invitation to the Oysters so that they will want to come for a walk? Which Oyster refuses to accompany them?
4. When do the Oysters realize they have been tricked? What finally happens to the Oysters?

Interpreting Meanings

5. Lines 61–66 are a famous example of pure non-sense. Explain why the "many things" are a very unlikely group of topics to talk about. What other examples of nonsense can you find in the poem?
6. In lines 97–102 the Walrus tells the Oysters that he sympathizes with them. How do his actions both support and contradict what he says? Find another place where a character's words do not quite match the situation.
7. A predictable pattern of end rhymes is called a **rhyme scheme.** To indicate a rhyme scheme, we assign a letter of the alphabet, beginning with

a, to each line in a stanza. Lines that rhyme get the same letter; lines that introduce a new end-sound get the next letter. For example, the rhyme scheme for "Hey Diddle, Diddle" is *aabcdb*:

Hey diddle, diddle,	*a*
The cat and the fiddle,	*a*
The cow jumped over the moon.	*b*
The little dog laughed	*c*
To see such sport	*d*
And the dish ran away with the spoon.	*b*

Write out the rhyme scheme for "The Walrus and the Carpenter" by examining the pattern of end rhymes. Is the pattern the same in all the stanzas?

Applying Meanings

8. This poem is recited to a character named Alice in *Through the Looking-Glass*. It has been popular for more than one hundred years. Why do you suppose people enjoy such nonsense poetry?

Writing About the Poem

A Creative Response

1. **Devising Impossible Tasks.** The impossible task is a long-standing subject in poetry, songs, and fairy tales. In "The Walrus and the Carpenter," for example, the Walrus looks at the beach and wonders "if seven maids with seven mops" sweeping for "half a year" could ever clear the sand away. The more impossible the task is, the more it teases our imagination. Make up five impossible tasks. Be sure to tell who is to perform each task, what tools can be used, and the time in which the task must be completed.

A Critical Response

2. **Summarizing the Poem.** Suppose someone asked you, "What's this poem about?" In a paragraph, summarize the poem, going stanza by stanza. Before you write, consider these elements of the poem:

   a. Setting
   b. Characters
   c. Situation
   d. Outcome

Analyzing Language and Vocabulary

Spelling Rhymes

One of the things that makes English difficult for some people to learn is the variety of ways that vowel sounds can be spelled. Not only can the same letters stand for two different sounds, as in *bread* and *bead,* but the same sound can be spelled in different ways, as in *bead* and *breed.*

1. Find two stanzas in the poem in which the three rhyming words all have different vowel spellings.
2. For each of the following words, think of a rhyme that uses a different vowel spelling.

   a. thief
   b. through
   c. rough
   d. braid
   e. dyed

Reading About the Writer

Lewis Carroll (1832–1898), the writer of two famous fantasies, constitutes only half of a fascinating and brilliant personality. The other side of Lewis Carroll is Charles Lutwidge Dodgson (Carroll's real name), a teacher of mathematics at Oxford University in England. Dodgson had been trained to become a priest in the Church of England, but a speech defect made him shy of preaching. He also loved to tell stories, and despite the speech defect, children loved to hear them (and still do). Once, Dodgson went on a picnic with the three young Liddell sisters, one of whom was named Alice. He told them the story of a girl named Alice who went down a rabbit hole into a fabulous wonderland. The real Alice made Dodgson promise to write out the stories for her when he got home, which he did. The stories were published as *Alice's Adventures in Wonderland.* He later wrote a sequel, *Through the Looking-Glass,* from which "The Walrus and the Carpenter" is taken.

We usually think of saints as perfect people. We often forget, however, that saints lived in the real world. This poem takes a lighthearted look at Saint Bridget, who lived in Ireland some 1500 years ago and who became famous for her gifts to the poor. Read the poem aloud. Do you think some of the rhymes are humorous?

The Giveaway

Phyllis McGinley

Saint Bridget was
A problem child.
Although a lass
Demure and mild,
5   And one who strove
To please her dad,
Saint Bridget drove
The family mad.
For here's the fault in Bridget lay:
10   She *would* give everything away.

To any soul
Whose luck was out
She'd give her bowl
Of stirabout;
15   She'd give her shawl,
Divide her purse
With one or all.
And what was worse,
When she ran out of things to give
20   She'd borrow them from a relative.

Her father's gold,
Her grandsire's dinner,
She'd hand to cold
And hungry sinner;
25   Give wine, give meat,
No matter whose;
Take from her feet
The very shoes,
And when her shoes had gone to others,
30   Fetch forth her sister's and her mother's.

She could not quit.
She had to share;
Gave bit by bit
The silverware,
35 The barnyard geese,
The parlor rug,
Her little niece-
'S christening mug,
Even her bed to those in want,
40 And then the mattress of her aunt.

An easy touch
For poor and lowly,
She gave so much
And grew so holy
45 That when she died
Of years and fame,
The countryside

Put on her name,
And still the Isles of Erin° fidget
With generous girls named Bride or
50   Bridget.

Well, one must love her.
Nonetheless,
In thinking of her
Givingness,
55 There's no denial
She must have been
A sort of trial
To her kin.
The moral, too, seems rather quaint.
60 *Who* had the patience of a saint,
From evidence presented here?
Saint Bridget? Or her near and dear?

---

49. **Isles of Erin:** Ireland.

Responding to the Poem

Analyzing the Poem

Identifying Details

1. Explain what made Saint Bridget "a problem child." According to stanza 2, what did she do when she ran out of things of her own to give?
2. Who received Saint Bridget's charity? Name three categories of things she gave away, and list examples for each category.
3. How do the people of Ireland feel toward Saint Bridget, according to the poem? How do they show their feelings?

Interpreting Meanings

4. **Tone** is the attitude or feeling that a writer has toward a subject. What attitude does Phyllis McGinley have toward Saint Bridget? Do you think she is being disrespectful? Explain.
5. How would you answer the question that ends the poem? What, then, do you think is the "rather quaint" moral of the poem?

6. The pattern of end rhymes is called a **rhyme scheme.** Determine this poem's rhyme scheme by looking at the first stanza and assigning a letter of the alphabet (beginning with *a*) to each new rhyme. Does the last stanza fit the pattern of the other stanzas?
7. Consider the **rhythm** of the poem. How many beats are there in the first eight lines of each stanza? What effect does this rhythm have on the way you read the poem?
8. Find an example of an **approximate rhyme**—a rhyme that is not exact. Why do you think the poet used this kind of rhyme?
9. Find two examples of **multisyllable rhyme**—a rhyme involving more than one syllable. Do they add to the humor of the poem?

Applying Meanings

10. Explain who would be more of a problem to live with—someone who gives everything away or someone who hoards possessions.

Writing About the Poem

A Creative Response

1. **Writing a Humorous Poem.** Try your hand at writing a ten-line poem using the same rhythm and rhyme scheme of "The Giveaway." Write eight lines, each with the appropriate beats per line. Then end with two rhymed lines containing four beats. Choose a humorous subject that will benefit from the quick rhythms and noticeable rhymes.

A Critical Response

2. **Supporting an Opinion.** The end of "The Giveaway" asks the reader to make a judgment about Saint Bridget based on "evidence presented here." Learn more about Saint Bridget in an encyclopedia or other reference book. Do you think the poet presents Saint Bridget fairly? Write a paragraph stating your opinion. Support it with evidence from the poem and from your research.

Analyzing Language and Vocabulary

Context Clues

In "The Giveaway" the poet uses some expressions that may be unfamiliar to you. The meanings of these expressions, however, can be figured out by using common sense and **context clues.** Context clues are words and sentences that surround the unfamiliar expression. For example, we can guess that "stirabout" is some kind of cereal because it comes in a bowl and can be "stirred about." Give the meanings of the following italicized expressions. If you were not familiar with them beforehand, tell how you figured out their meaning.

1. "She'd give her shawl,
   Divide her purse
   With one or all."
2. "Her father's gold,
   Her *grandsire's* dinner . . ."
3. "An *easy touch*
   For poor and lowly,
   She gave so much . . ."
4. "The countryside
   Put on her name . . ."
5. "Who had the patience of a saint,
   From evidence presented here?
   Saint Bridget? Or *her near and dear?*"

Reading About the Writer

Phyllis McGinley (1905–1978) wrote books for children, essays, and movie scripts, but she is most famous for her light verse. Her subject matter centers on suburban and domestic life. She was a strong supporter of the family and often wrote about the roles of women as mothers and wives. McGinley was raised in Colorado, and she traced her love of reading and writing to a rather isolated childhood. At one time, Phyllis and her brother were the *only* students at a rural grade school. McGinley won the 1961 Pulitzer Prize for *Times Three: Selected Verse from Three Decades,* from which "The Giveaway" is taken.

Most poets who use rhymes place them reasonably close together. But here Robert Frost takes the chance that one particular rhyme will echo across five lines. What is that rhyme?

A Time to Talk

Robert Frost

When a friend calls to me from the road
And slows his horse to a meaning walk,
I don't stand still and look around
On all the hills I haven't hoed,
5   And shout from where I am, "What is it?"
No, not as there is time to talk.
I thrust my hoe in the mellow ground,
Blade-end up and five feet tall,
And plod: I go up to the stone wall
10 For a friendly visit.

View from the Garden by Catherine Murphy (1972). Oil.

Courtesy of the Chase Manhattan Collection, New York City.

Responding to the Poem

Analyzing the Poem

Identifying Details

1. Explain how the speaker knows that his friend wants to talk and not just say "hello."
2. What kind of work is the speaker doing when interrupted? How much of the job has the speaker completed?
3. Tell what the speaker decides to do in the second half of the poem.

Interpreting Meanings

4. Identify the **rhyme scheme** of this poem. Which end rhymes involve more than one syllable?
5. Which rhyme echoes or "shouts" across five lines? What point is Frost making by including such a rhyme?
6. The speaker says that he does not shout across the field. He seems to think that this would be inappropriate behavior. Why do you think he feels this way?

Applying Meanings

7. This poem seems to be advising us about how we should act with people. State the advice that you think this poem gives its readers. What is your response to this advice?

Writing About the Poem

A Creative Response

1. **Writing an Anecdote.** An **anecdote** is a very short story that makes a point. Anecdotes are usually told in conversation to illustrate a personal opinion. For example, if you were complaining about schoolwork at dinner and an adult said, "You know, one time when I was in school . . . ," you'd know an anecdote was on the way. Many of Robert Frost's poems, like "A Time to Talk," resemble anecdotes. Compose your own anecdote. Then, in a sentence or two, explain the point it makes. You might want to write about "a time to talk."

A Critical Response

2. **Analyzing a Poem's Language.** Often, the power of a poem comes in good part from unusual or striking word combinations. We are not accustomed to seeing the words linked together, and so we linger over them to figure out their meaning. In "A Time to Talk," Frost uses the following uncommon word combinations:

> "meaning walk"
> "mellow ground"

Explain the meaning of each word combination in a short paragraph.

Analyzing Language and Vocabulary

Precise Verbs

The speaker in Frost's poem does not *put* his hoe in the ground, he *thrusts* it. He does not *walk* to the stone wall, he *plods*. By choosing precise verbs, Frost paints a clearer picture in our minds. He also makes the poem more interesting and effective. In the following sentences, replace the rather general verb printed in italics with one that is more precise and interesting.

1. The detective *turned* around.
2. I *put* the old newspapers away.
3. He *ate* his dinner in fifteen minutes.
4. The quarterback *ran* through the defense.
5. The guitarist *played* his tunes.

Reading About the Writer

Although **Robert Frost** (1874–1963) was born in San Francisco, he is known as a "New England poet." This is because Frost lived in New England most of his life and drew subjects for his poems from the landscapes and people there. Widely honored within his lifetime, Frost was the first poet to take part in a Presidential inauguration. On January 20, 1961, he recited his poem "The Gift Outright" for John F. Kennedy's inauguration. Two more of his poems, "Dust of Snow" and "The Runaway," appear on pages 397 and 406.

The essentials of poetry are rhythm, dance, and the human voice.

—Earle Birney

Other Sound Effects

A poem takes much of its character from the sounds it makes. We may hear these sounds when a poem is read aloud in an auditorium, in a classroom, or on tapes or records. Or we may hear these sounds in our minds, like silent echoes, when we read by ourselves.

Onomatopoeia: Sound and Sense

This fearful-sounding word expresses a fairly simple idea. Literally, **onomatopoeia** (än′ə·mat′ə·pē′ə) means "the making of words to imitate the sounds of things." For example, *chickadee, phoebe,* and *bobwhite*—the names of three birds—are onomatopoeic. Each name imitates the bird's own distinctive call. When we say a gun goes *bang,* a cannon goes *boom,* and frying bacon *sizzles,* we are using onomatopoeia—words that echo their sounds.

In poetry, a single word can be onomatopoeic. Or a poet can use a whole series of words to imitate a sound. For example, in this line from "The Raven" (page 385), Edgar Allan Poe imitates the sound of wind blowing through silken curtains: "the silken, sad, uncertain rustling of each purple curtain." The rustling *s* sounds of these words fit their *sense.*

Poets use onomatopoeia to create moods, to provide a poem with "special effects." You know some of these special effects from horror movies. Doors creak, winds howl, chains clank, footsteps thud. In movies, these and other sounds are used to make the action seem more real and sensational. In poems, these effects are usually more subtle, but the intent is the same. Onomatopoeia intensifies the mood of a scene. It sharpens what you are picturing in your mind by helping you to hear it, too.

Alliteration: Repeating Letters

Alliteration is the repetition of the same letters (or similar-sounding letters) in several words. Alliteration usually involves consonants rather than vowels. For instance, in the example above from "The Raven," the *s* sound is repeated: "*s*ilken, *s*ad, uncertain ru*s*tling." In this case, the repeated *s* sounds remind us of the sounds made by the silken curtains as the wind blows through them. Alliteration is often used like this to create onomatopoeia.

Alliteration, however, does not always have to imitate a real sound. Sometimes the repeated letters just help create a mood, or they simply help the words ring in our minds. The following well-known poem contains this kind of alliteration.

With Rue My Heart is Laden

With rue my heart is laden
    For golden friends I had.
For many a rose-lipt maiden
    And many a lightfoot lad.

By brooks too broad for leaping
    The lightfoot boys are laid;
The rose-lipt girls are sleeping
    In fields where roses fade.

              —A. E. Housman

Refrains: Repeating Sounds, Words, or More

A **refrain** is a repeated sound, word, phrase, or group of lines. A refrain usually occurs at the end of a stanza but it can appear anywhere in a poem. A refrain can differ slightly each time it appears.

A refrain can serve many purposes. It can help create a mood. It can focus our attention, or it can emphasize an idea or feeling. It almost always helps to create rhythm.

Read the following song aloud and you'll hear how it uses all the sound effects we've talked about here: rhythm, rhyme, onomatopoeia ("quack quack quack"), alliteration ("Old Mother Slipper Slopper"), and refrain.

You'll also notice that one of the chief purposes of sound effects in poetry is to help us have fun with our language.

The Fox's Foray

A fox jumped up one winter's night,
And begged the moon to give him light,
For he'd many miles to trot that night
Before he reached his den O!
    Den O! Den O!
For he'd many miles to trot that night
Before he reached his den O!

The first place he came to was a farmer's yard,
Where the ducks and the geese declared it hard
That their nerves should be shaken and their rest
    so marred
By a visit from Mr. Fox O!
    Fox O! Fox O!
That their nerves should be shaken and their rest
    so marred
By a visit from Mr. Fox O!

15 He took the gray goose by the neck,
    And swung him right across his back;
    The gray goose cried out, Quack, quack, quack,
    With his legs hanging dangling down O!
        Down O! Down O!
20 The gray goose cried out, Quack, quack, quack,
    With his legs hanging dangling down O!

    Old Mother Slipper Slopper jumped out of bed,
    And out of the window she popped her head:
    Oh! John, John, John, the gray goose is gone,
25 And the fox is off to his den O!
        Den O! Den O!
    Oh! John, John, John, the gray goose is gone,
    And the fox is off to his den O!

    John ran up to the top of the hill,
30 And blew his whistle loud and shrill;
    Said the fox, That is very pretty music; still—
    I'd rather be in my den O!
        Den O! Den O!
    Said the fox, That is very pretty music; still—
35 I'd rather be in my den O!

    The fox went back to his hungry den,
    And his dear little foxes, eight, nine, ten;
    Quoth they, Good daddy, you must go there again,
    If you bring such good cheer from the farm O!
40   Farm O! Farm O!
    Quoth they, Good daddy, you must go there again,
    If you bring such good cheer from the farm O!

    The fox and his wife, without any strife,
    Said they never ate a better goose in all their life:
45 They did very well without fork or knife,
    And the little ones picked the bones O!
        Bones O! Bones O!
    They did very well without fork or knife,
    And the little ones picked the bones O!

                                —Anonymous

If you have ever heard a jet breaking the sound barrier, you know that the sound is like a deep

BOOM. In "Sonic Boom" notice the poet's use of words that make you hear more than you see.

Sonic Boom

John Updike

I'm sitting in the living room,
When, up above, the Thump of Doom
Resounds. Relax. It's sonic boom.

The ceiling shudders at the clap,
5 The mirrors tilt, the rafters snap,
And Baby wakens from his nap.

"Hush, babe. Some pilot we equip,
Giving the speed of sound the slip,
Has cracked the air like a penny whip."

10 Our world is far from frightening; I
No longer strain to read the sky
Where moving fingers (jet planes) fly,
Our world seems much too tame to die.

And if it does, with one more pop,
15 I shan't look up to see it drop.

Responding to the Poem

Analyzing the Poem

Identifying Details

1. In the first stanza, how does the speaker initially identify the sonic boom?
2. What effect does the sonic boom have on the house and the baby? How does the speaker explain the noise to the child?
3. What does the speaker no longer do?

Interpreting Meanings

4. What do you think the speaker means when he says the "world is far from frightening" and seems "too tame to die"?
5. How are jet planes like "moving fingers" (line 12)?
6. To what possible future event is the speaker referring in the last two lines?
7. List all the **onomatopoeic** words or phrases you can find in "Sonic Boom." Describe the sound effects they contribute to the poem.

Applying Meanings

8. What are your own feelings about the possibility that the world may end with a "pop"?

Writing About the Poem

A Creative Response

1. **Using Onomatopoeia.** Write three sentences describing a sound: it might be irritating, comforting, frightening, musical, or something else. Use onomatopoeic words to imitate the sound that you want your readers to hear. For instance, a car horn might *beep, honk,* or *blare.* Use as many onomatopoeic words as you can. You may even make up some if you wish.

A Critical Response

2. **Describing Tone. Tone** is the writer's attitude or feeling toward a subject. In a paragraph, describe how you think John Updike feels about sonic booms and about our world in general. Open your paragraph with a sentence that states what you feel his attitude is. Then cite passages from the poem that support your opinion. Here are some attitudes you might want to consider:

a. respectful   d. resigned
b. cynical   e. sarcastic
c. awestruck   f. comical

Analyzing Language and Vocabulary

Onomatopoeic Words

Onomatopoeic words can echo or imitate actual sounds. English has thousands of such words. Some, like *buzz, moo,* and *roar,* imitate animal sounds. Others echo different sounds in nature: *whoosh, splash, crackle, thunk.* Some imitate mechanical sounds: *tick-tock, buzz, clatter.* Think about the following categories of sounds. List as many echoic or imitative words as you can think of for each category. Then check a dictionary to make sure that your choices are appropriate.

1. animal sounds
2. wind sounds
3. water sounds
4. fire sounds
5. car sounds

Reading About the Writer

Although he is chiefly famous for his novels and short stories, **John Updike** (1932–   ) also writes witty poetry. Updike, who studied art after graduating from Harvard University, originally wanted to become a cartoonist. He says of his writing: "There is a great deal to be said about almost anything. . . . Everything can be as interesting as every other thing. . . . I like middles. It is in middles that extremes clash." Updike usually writes about suburban life and about what is known as "the middle class" in America. He is also noted for his literary criticism.

Names like Erie, Wabash, Pennsylvania (Pennsy, for short), Baltimore and Ohio (B & O), and Rock Island are familiar to many who have lived near railroad tracks. These railroad company names are usually painted in huge letters across the sides of freight cars. (Some of the companies mentioned in this poem no longer exist.) "Crossing" recreates the experience of watching a long freight train rumble past a railroad crossing. By naming what he sees, the poet creates a tongue twister that imitates the confusion of noises. Read the poem out loud, perhaps as a choral reading.

Crossing

Philip Booth

STOP LOOK LISTEN
as gate stripes swing down,
count the cars hauling distance
upgrade° through town:
5   warning whistle, bellclang,
engine eating steam,
engineer waving,
a fast-freight dream:
B & M boxcar,
10   boxcar again,
Frisco gondola,°
eight-nine-ten,
Erie and Wabash,
Seaboard, U.P.,
15   Pennsy tank car,
twenty-two-three
Phoebe Snow, B & O,
thirty-four, five,
Santa Fe cattle
20   shipped alive,
red cars, yellow cars,
orange cars, black,
Youngstown steel
down to Mobile
25   on Rock Island track,
fifty-nine, sixty,
hoppers° of coke,
Anaconda copper,
hotbox° smoke,

---

4. **upgrade:** uphill.
11. **gondola:** freight car with low sides and no top.
27. **hoppers:** freight cars whose bottoms open to unload cargo.
29. **hotbox:** overheated bearing or axle.

30   *eighty-eight,*
        red-ball freight,
        Rio Grande,
        Nickel Plate,
        Hiawatha,
35   Lackawanna,
        rolling fast
        and loose,
        ninety-seven,
        coal car,
40   boxcar,
        CABOOSE!

Responding to the Poem

Analyzing the Poem

Identifying Details

1. What does the title "Crossing" mean? What action begins the poem?
2. List the different cargoes the train carries.
3. How many cars are in the freight train? How many names can you count?

Interpreting Meanings

4. Where do you think the speaker is standing (or sitting)?
5. Booth uses **onomatopoeia** to echo some of the sounds of the train. For example, the words "warning whistle" help you hear the particular sounds of a train whistle. Find one more example of onomatopoeia in the poem. Which train noise does it imitate? Do you think the name *Lackawanna* suggests a train sound?
6. The **rhythm** in this poem imitates the movement of the train. In which part is the rhythm slow? In which part does it move faster? Fastest? Explain why you think the poet changes the rhythm.

Writing About the Poem

A Creative Response

Writing a List Poem. Philip Booth uses a list of railroad names and cargoes to recreate the experience of watching and hearing a freight train. You can compose a similar poem. Choose for your subject an experience that involves many names. You might find a list of names by browsing in a record store, watching a football game, or observing traffic on a street or highway. Before you write, list all the names that you want to include in your poem. The poem should be about ten lines long.

Analyzing Language and Vocabulary

Specialized Vocabularies

A **specialized vocabulary** or **jargon** is a set of words related to a particular subject, profession, or activity. "Crossing" includes several specialized words—such as *gondola, hopper,* and *hotbox.* Choose an activity that has a specialized vocabulary and list five of its special words or expressions. For each, write a definition and a sentence showing how the word should be used.

Reading About the Writer

Philip Booth (1925–   ) was born in Hanover, New Hampshire, and raised on the Dartmouth College campus, where his father was a professor. He himself has taught at Syracuse University in New York State. Booth's style of writing is characterized by short lines and few words, which some people think gives his poetry a "clean" and "simple" look. "Crossing" is from his first book, *Letter from a Distant Land.*

Painting the Gate

May Swenson

I painted the mailbox. That was fun.
I painted it postal blue.
Then I painted the gate.
I painted a spider that got on the gate.
5 I painted his mate.
I painted the ivy around the gate.
Some stones I painted blue,
and part of the cat as he rubbed by.
I painted my hair. I painted my shoe.
10 I painted the slats, both front and back,
all their beveled edges, too.
I painted the numbers on the gate—

I shouldn't have, but it was too late.
I painted the posts, each side and top,
15 I painted the hinges, the handle, the lock,
several ants and a moth asleep in a crack.
At last I was through.
I'd painted the gate
shut, me out, with both hands dark blue,
20 as well as my nose, which,
early on, because of a sudden itch,
got painted. But wait!
I had painted the gate.

Responding to the Poem

Analyzing the Poem

Identifying Details

1. Name all the things the speaker paints.
2. How does she feel about her work?
3. What is her problem after the painting is finished?

Interpreting Meanings

4. What initial consonant sounds are repeated often in the poem to suggest the slip-slap of the paintbrush?
5. What **rhyming** sounds do you hear? Do these sounds make the poem sound serious to you, or does it sound light and comical?
6. How does the **rhythm** of the poem imitate the action it describes? How would you describe that action: Is it restful, slow, mechanical, repetitive?

Applying Meanings

7. Can you think of a task you once got carried away with, as this speaker did with painting the gate? If so, explain.

Writing About the Poem

A Creative Response

Using Repetition. In this poem May Swenson begins almost every line with "I painted. . . ." Write your own poem of about ten lines using the same formula. Begin most or all of your lines with "I _____." The activity can be real or imagined, serious or funny. Before you write, think about the steps in the activity. Write down all the parts of the job that come to your mind. Then pick the ideas that work best, and put them in chronological order—the order in which they happened.

Analyzing Language and Vocabulary

Names of Colors

There are many shades of every color. Suppose a writer wants to describe a specific shade of blue. He or she could modify *blue* with general words like *light, dark,* and *pale.* However, such an approach might not be precise enough. Instead, the writer could name the color for something in the environment. May Swenson does this in "Painting the Gate." She calls the paint "postal blue," referring to the color of mailboxes.

1. The following are examples of colors linked to something in the environment. Write a one-sentence definition of each. For *postal blue,* for example, you might have written, "Postal blue is a fairly deep shade of blue that resembles the color of Paul's jacket."

   a. fire-engine red
   b. sky blue
   c. canary yellow
   d. steel gray
   e. pea green

2. Describe five other colors named for something in the environment.

Reading About the Writer

May Swenson (1919–   ) was born in Logan, Utah, and has spent most of her adult life in or around New York City. Like many poets, she has taught at various universities to support herself. Swenson sometimes writes concrete poetry, or "iconographs," as she calls them, in which she matches the visual shape of a poem to its subject. For example, in "How Everything Happens (Based on a Study of the Wave)," the lines of the poem suggest the ebb and flow of the ocean tide. "Painting the Gate" appeared in her 1978 book *New and Selected Things Taking Place.*

Focusing on Background
A Comment from the Poet

" 'Painting the Gate' was begun just after I had painted our gate dark blue, and was taking a shower. The first words came into my head, establishing the rhythm. While washing the paint off my hands and arms, and out of my hair, etc., I was thinking what a mess I'd made, and the things that had happened to make it difficult. Yet I *had* finished the job. Because of my inexperience, painting the gate was frustrating and also hilarious. When I sat down at my desk to write the poem I exaggerated what happened somewhat, to make it funnier."

—May Swenson

There is probably not a person in the world who has not felt what the speaker in this poem feels. The poem is an example of the way in which a refrain can change in feeling and meaning from one moment to the next.

Poem

Langston Hughes

I loved my friend.
He went away from me.
There's nothing more to say.
The poem ends,
Soft as it began—
I loved my friend.

Responding to the Poem

Analyzing the Poem

Interpreting Meanings

1. This little poem is held together by a very simple **refrain**—a single line repeated only once. That line goes through a change in feeling between its first appearance and its second. When it first occurs, we take it as no more than a flat statement of fact. But when we hear it a second time, it's a statement loaded with feeling. How would you describe this feeling?

Applying Meanings

2. In the poem, the speaker mentions an experience but doesn't give details about it or try to explain it. Do you think many people have experiences they want to tell others about but don't want to talk about in detail because "there's nothing more to say"? Explain.

Writing About the Poem

A Creative Response

1. **Supplying a Title.** Suppose the poet wanted to give his poem another title. What suggestions would you make?

2. **Filling in the Story Details.** This poem leaves wide gaps in the story. The poet expects us to draw on our own experience and imagination to fill in the missing details. Write a short narrative from the speaker's point of view. Tell the untold details as you imagine them. Describe the kind of friendship the two characters might have shared. Include an educated guess about why the speaker's friend went away.

Reading About the Writer

Langston Hughes (1902–1967) led a diversified life. As a young man, he traveled all around the world and held many jobs. One day in Washington, D.C., Hughes gave some poems to the famous poet Vachel Lindsay while he was waiting on Lindsay's table in a restaurant. Lindsay read the unknown poet's work at a poetry reading, and Hughes's distinguished career was started. According to Hughes, his poetry concerns "workers, roustabouts, and singers, and job hunters on Lenox Avenue in New York, or Seventh Street in Washington or South State in Chicago." His poems often use slang. Their rhythms echo the blues and jazz. Another Hughes poem, "Refugee in America," appears on page 436.

Illustration for *The Raven* by C. J. Staniland, from
The Poetical Works of Edgar Allan Poe, New York,
W. J. Publisher.

Courtesy of the Brooklyn Public Library.

An obsession is an idea that we cannot get out of our minds. "The Raven" is a famous poem about a man obsessed by the memory of Lenore, a woman he loved who is now dead. But his problems do not end there. As he is thinking about Lenore, a strange bird flies into his study, and keeps croaking one word. That one word makes the speaker feel even worse about Lenore. As you read, notice how the setting and the sound effects create an atmosphere of mystery. You should read the poem aloud. You might use three speakers: a chorus, a person, and a bird.

The Raven

Edgar Allan Poe

Once upon a midnight dreary, while I pondered, weak and weary,
Over many a quaint and curious volume of forgotten lore°—
While I nodded, nearly napping, suddenly there came a tapping,
As of someone gently rapping, rapping at my chamber door.
5   " 'Tis some visitor," I muttered, "tapping at my chamber door—
                         Only this and nothing more."

Ah, distinctly I remember it was in the bleak December;
And each separate dying ember wrought its ghost upon the floor.
Eagerly I wished the morrow—vainly I had sought to borrow
10 From my books surcease° of sorrow—sorrow for the lost Lenore—
For the rare and radiant maiden whom the angels name Lenore—
                         Nameless *here* forevermore.

And the silken, sad, uncertain rustling of each purple curtain
Thrilled me—filled me with fantastic terrors never felt before;
15 So that now, to still the beating of my heart, I stood repeating,
" 'Tis some visitor entreating entrance at my chamber door—
Some late visitor entreating entrance at my chamber door—
                         That it is and nothing more."

Presently my soul grew stronger; hesitating then no longer,
20 "Sir," said I, "or Madam, truly your forgiveness I implore;
But the fact is I was napping, and so gently you came rapping,
And so faintly you came tapping, tapping at my chamber door,
That I scarce was sure I heard you"—here I opened wide the door—
                         Darkness there and nothing more.

---

2. **lore:** knowledge.   10. **surcease** (sur·sēs′): end.

25 Deep into that darkness peering, long I stood there wondering, fearing,
Doubting, dreaming dreams no mortal ever dared to dream before;
But the silence was unbroken, and the stillness gave no token,
And the only word there spoken was the whispered word, "Lenore?"
This I whispered, and an echo murmured back the word "Lenore!"—
30   Merely this and nothing more.

Back into the chamber turning, all my soul within me burning,
Soon again I heard a tapping somewhat louder than before.
"Surely," said I, "surely that is something at my window lattice;°
Let me see, then, what thereat is, and this mystery explore—
35 Let my heart be still a moment and this mystery explore—
                     'Tis the wind and nothing more!"

Open here I flung the shutter, when, with many a flirt and flutter,
In there stepped a stately Raven of the saintly days of yore;
Not the least obeisance° made he; not a minute stopped or stayed he;
40 But, with mien of lord or lady, perched above my chamber door—
Perched upon a bust of Pallas° just above my chamber door—
                     Perched, and sat, and nothing more.

Then this ebony bird beguiling my sad fancy° into smiling,
By the grave and stern decorum° of the countenance it wore,
45 "Though thy crest be shorn and shaven, thou," I said, "art sure no craven,°
Ghastly grim and ancient Raven wandering from the Nightly shore—
Tell me what thy lordly name is on the Night's Plutonian shore!"°
                     Quoth the Raven, "Nevermore."

Much I marveled this ungainly fowl to hear discourse so plainly,
50 Though its answer little meaning—little relevancy bore;
For we cannot help agreeing that no living human being
Ever yet was blessed with seeing bird above his chamber door—
Bird or beast upon the sculptured bust above his chamber door,
                     With such name as "Nevermore."

55 But the Raven, sitting lonely on the placid bust, spoke only
That one word, as if his soul in that one word he did outpour.
Nothing further then he uttered, not a feather then he fluttered—
Till I scarcely more than muttered, "Other friends have flown before—
On the morrow *he* will leave me, as my Hopes have flown before."
60   Then the bird said, "Nevermore."

---

33. **lattice** (lat'is): framework of wood or metal strips.   39. **obeisance** (ō·bā'səns): gesture showing respect
(such as a bow).   41. **Pallas** (pal'əs): Pallas Athena, the Greek goddess of wisdom.   43. **fancy:** imagination.
44. **decorum** (di·kôr'əm): here, appearance.   45. **craven** (krā'vən): coward.   47. **Plutonian** (plo͞o·tō'nē·ən)
shore: in Greek mythology, the shore of the River Styx. The ancient Greeks believed the souls of the dead
had to cross the river on their journey from the realm of the living to the realm of the dead, or underworld.
The underworld was ruled by the god Pluto (hence Plutonian).

Startled at the stillness broken by reply so aptly spoken,
"Doubtless," said I, "what it utters is its only stock and store
Caught from some unhappy master whom unmerciful Disaster
Followed fast and followed faster till his songs one burden° bore—
65 Till the dirges of his Hope that melancholy burden bore
                    Of 'Never—nevermore.' "

But the Raven still beguiling all my fancy into smiling,
Straight I wheeled a cushioned seat in front of bird and bust and door;
Then, upon the velvet sinking, I betook myself to linking
70 Fancy unto fancy, thinking what this ominous bird of yore—
What this grim, ungainly, ghastly, gaunt, and ominous bird of yore
                    Meant in croaking, "Nevermore."

This I sat engaged in guessing, but no syllable expressing
To the fowl, whose fiery eyes now burned into my bosom's core;
75 This and more I sat divining, with my head at ease reclining
On the cushion's velvet lining that the lamplight gloated o'er,
But whose velvet-violet lining with the lamplight gloating o'er,
                    She shall press, ah, nevermore!

Then, methought, the air grew denser, perfumed from an unseen censer°
80 Swung by seraphim° whose footfalls tinkled on the tufted floor.
"Wretch," I cried. "thy God hath lent thee—by these angels he hath sent thee
Respite°—respite and nepenthe° from thy memories of Lenore!
Quaff°, oh, quaff this kind nepenthe and forget this lost Lenore!"
                    Quoth the Raven, "Nevermore."

85 "Prophet!" said I, "thing of evil!—prophet still, if bird or devil!—
Whether Tempter° sent, or whether tempest tossed thee here ashore,
Desolate yet all undaunted, on this desert land enchanted—
On this home by Horror haunted—tell me truly, I implore—
Is there—*is* there balm in Gilead?°—tell me—tell me, I implore!"
90   Quoth the Raven, "Nevermore."

"Prophet!" said I, "Thing of evil!—prophet still, if bird or devil!
By that Heaven that bends above us—by that God we both adore—
Tell this soul with sorrow laden if, within the distant Aidenn,°
It shall clasp a sainted maiden whom the angels name Lenore—
95 Clasp a rare and radiant maiden whom the angels name Lenore."
                    Quoth the Raven, "Nevermore."

---

64. **burden:** here, refrain. 79. **censer:** container in which incense is burned. Censers are used in religious services. 80. **seraphim** (ser′ə·fim): angels. 82. **Respite** (res′pit): rest or relief. **nepenthe** (ni·pen′thē): a drug thought by the ancient Greeks to relieve sorrow or pain. 83. **Quaff** (kwaf): drink. 86. **Tempter:** devil. 89. **balm in Gilead** (gil′ē·əd): a phrase referring to the Bible (Jeremiah 8:22) and meaning "relief from pain." Gilead was a region of ancient Palestine where *balm,* a healing ointment, was produced. 93. **Aidenn** (ā′dən): Arabic word for heaven.

"Be that word our sign of parting, bird or fiend!" I shrieked, upstarting—
"Get thee back into the tempest and the Night's Plutonian shore!
Leave no black plume as a token of that lie thy soul hath spoken!
100   Leave my loneliness unbroken!—quit the bust above my door!
Take thy beak from out my heart, and take thy form from off my door!"
                    Quoth the Raven, "Nevermore."

And the Raven, never flitting, still is sitting, *still* is sitting
On the pallid° bust of Pallas just above my chamber door;
105   And his eyes have all the seeming of a demon's that is dreaming,
And the lamplight o'er him streaming throws his shadow on the floor;
And my soul from out that shadow that lies floating on the floor
                    Shall be lifted—nevermore!

---

104. **pallid:** pale.

Responding to the Poem

Analyzing the Poem

Identifying Details

1. According to the first two stanzas, at what time of day and year does the action occur? Tell what the speaker is doing when he hears the tapping.
2. According to stanza 2, why is the speaker sorrowful? What terrifies him in lines 13–14?
3. What does the speaker see when he opens the door? What does he say and hear?
4. Where does the Raven perch? What is the only word it speaks?
5. According to lines 61–66, what explanation does the speaker give for the Raven's "reply so aptly spoken"?
6. According to lines 79–84, what does the speaker think has been sent to him?
7. State in your own words the two questions that the speaker asks the Raven in lines 85–96. How does the Raven answer?
8. According to the last two lines, what has happened to the speaker's soul?

Interpreting Meanings

9. Much of the drama of "The Raven" occurs within the speaker's mind. Describe the speaker's state of mind before the raven appears. How does the speaker try to change his state of mind during the course of the poem? What is his mental condition by the end of the poem?
10. **Atmosphere** is a general mood or feeling. Part of this poem's atmosphere comes from Poe's description of the **setting.** List the specific words describing this setting that create an atmosphere of mystery and dread.
11. At which point did you realize that Poe is using a refrain in "The Raven"? What is it? How does the refrain remind you of the dead Lenore?
12. A **symbol** is any person, place, or thing which has meaning in itself, but which is made to represent, or stand for, something else as well. In this poem what do you think the raven comes to symbolize? In your answer, consider where the bird perches and where the speaker says his soul is at the end of the poem.

Evaluating the Poem

13. Sometimes our minds work a little differently during the daytime and after dark. Try this experiment. First, read "The Raven" during the day and write down your reaction. Be as specific as possible, noting how the poem affected you in general, what passages had the most impact, what you thought of the speaker's mental condition, and anything else that struck you as noteworthy. Then read the poem late at night, perhaps a few days later. Write down your reaction without looking at what you wrote after the daytime reading. Compare your reactions. Are there any differences? What accounts for them?

14. Could the poem be true on any level? Can ravens be taught to speak, for example? Is there anything in the poem that is fantastic—that could not possibly happen in the world as we know it?

Writing About the Poem

A Creative Response

1. **Writing a Character Sketch.** Imagine that you live next door to the speaker in "The Raven." Write a letter to a friend in which you describe your neighbor's strange behavior and personality. Use details from the poem, but feel free to invent additional details to fill out your character sketch. These invented details should not contradict anything in the poem. They should help explain the neighbor's behavior.

A Critical Response

2. **Writing About Sound Effects.** "The Raven" is an excellent example of what a poet can do with sound. **Onomatopoeia, alliteration, end rhymes, internal rhymes,** and **rhythm** all work together to achieve a powerful effect. Pick three of these elements and in a series of paragraphs do the following for each:

   a. Identify and define the element.
   b. Present four examples of the element from the poem.
   c. Explain what the element contributes to the overall effect of the poem.

Analyzing Language and Vocabulary

Connotations

All words have dictionary definitions, or **denotations.** Many words, through usage, have taken on connotations as well. **Connotations** are the emotional feelings and associations that become attached to some words.

Think about the different feelings you have about these pairs of italicized words.

> Hilda *perspires.* The horse *sweats.*
> I am *firm.* He is *pig-headed.*
> Ida is a *daydreamer.* Reynolds is an *escapist.*
> The *stink* of industry . . . The *scent* of perfume . . .
> The box of candy is *half-full.* It is *half-empty.*

Poe uses many words that carry powerful emotions and associations.

1. How do you feel on a "midnight dreary"? How would the poem's emotional effect change if it took place on a "noontime sunny"?

2. What kind of weather and feelings do you associate with "bleak December"? Name another month and describe it in a way that would produce different feelings and associations.

3. *Lenore* has a beautiful sound, and Poe chose it because it rhymes with *Nevermore.* Suppose the Raven had answered "No way." How does the tone of the poem change? What name might rhyme with it? Would the effect be the same if Poe had given the woman another name?

4. Describe the atmosphere created by those purple curtains. Name another kind of curtain or window covering that would suggest different feelings.

5. Ravens are birds of prey that feed on the catches of hunters and fishers and on weaker animals. Much superstition has been attached to ravens; they often have been used to symbolize evil or death. Name another bird that would have had a completely different effect on the poem.

6. The goddess Athena is associated with the arts, wisdom, and scholarship; she belongs in the room of a scholar. How do you picture this statue of Pallas Athena—is it white marble, painted wood, or glass? Name another statue for this room that would have created a different feeling.

Images: Sensory Experiences

An **image** is basically what you see in a poem, just as though you were looking out a window. A drawing or photograph, a reflection in a mirror, a scene on a television or movie screen—all these are also images. Some images, such as news photos, can provide exact and truthful copies of our world. Other images, such as those in an abstract painting by Pablo Picasso, are much less realistic. These images try to make us see the world in an unexpected, fresh way.

Poets use words to create both kinds of images. Because we "see" word images only in our minds, our own imaginations must become actively involved when we read poetry.

Our imaginations are not triggered by visual images only. Images in poetry might also describe how things taste, smell, feel, and sound.

Look back, for example, at Poe's poem "The Raven" (page 385). Notice the images in the opening of the poem that appeal to our senses of sight, hearing, and even touch:

Sight: dying ember, silken purple curtains
Hearing: tapping, rapping, rustling, beating (of his heart)
Touch: bleak December (Does this make you feel December's cold and chill?)

Pictures painted with words can be very powerful, sometimes even more powerful than the real thing. This is partly because poetic images help us see ordinary things in new and unexpected ways. Here, for example, is how the poet James Wright saw two ponies at sundown:

> Just off the highway to Rochester, Minnesota,
> Twilight bounds softly forth on the grass.
> And the eyes of those two Indian ponies
> Darken with kindness.
>
> —from "A Blessing,"
> James Wright

Wright notices the special way the light at the end of the day moves across the grass: It "bounds softly." (We might expect the ponies, not the light, to bound.) Then, instead of fully describing the two ponies, Wright gives us an image of just their darkening eyes. What is unexpected is that the image asks us to see kindness in their eyes—we associate kindness only with humans.

Wright's lines show us another important use of images in poetry. They convey feelings. Wright's images of the two ponies at twilight do not make us feel sadness or regret that the day is fading. Nor do they make us fear the ponies. Instead, they convey a feeling of identification with nature. They suggest happiness, through a few carefully chosen images. Wright is saying through his imagery that we can find peace in ordinary places, even in a field "just off the highway."

Have you ever heard dogs or coyotes howling at night? What feelings might the sounds stir in you? In this poem, John Haines uses images to express the feelings he had when he heard wolves. When you get to line 4, stop and decide what feeling the poet had first.

Wolves

John Haines

Last night I heard wolves howling,
their voices coming from afar
over the wind-polished ice—so much
brave solitude in that sound.

5   They are death's snowbound sailors;
they know only a continual
drifting between moonlit islands,
their tongues licking the stars.

But they sing as good seamen should,
10 and tomorrow the sun will find them,
yawning and blinking
the snow from their eyelashes.

Their voices rang through the frozen
water of my human sleep,
15 blown by the night wind
with the moon for an icy sail.

Responding to the Poem

Analyzing the Poem

Identifying Details

1. At what time of day did the speaker hear the wolves?
2. What does the poet say he heard "in that sound"?
3. According to stanza 2, what do the wolves know?
4. Describe what the wolves will be doing when the sun finds them.

Interpreting Meanings

5. List four or five **images** from the poem. What sense does each image appeal to?
6. How does the poet feel about the wolves and this icy setting?
7. The poet compares the wolves to sailors, his sleep to frozen water, and the moon to an icy sail. How are wolves like sailors? Why does the poet want you to think about the events in this poem in terms of a winter sea journey?

8. What sound in the poem do you think imitates the howl of a wolf?

Applying Meanings

9. In this poem, a sound starts the poet thinking about brave solitude—not just the solitude of wolves but of sailors and dreamers as well. Describe a nighttime sound you have heard that worked on your imagination. What ideas or feelings did it stir in you?

Writing About the Poem

A Creative Response

1. **Creating Images.** Write a one-paragraph description of a familiar creature: a pet, a farm animal, a zoo animal, or local wildlife. Use at least three vivid images to help your readers see the creature in an unexpected way. Include at least one image appealing to a sense other than sight.

A Critical Response

2. **Analyzing an Image.** In a striking image, the speaker says wolves are "death's snowbound sailors." Each of these words would by itself kindle our imaginations. Together, the words produce a complicated picture. In a paragraph discuss the meaning of the image. Be sure to explain what each word contributes. Refer to other parts of the poem in your discussion.

Analyzing Language and Vocabulary

Compound Words

English has thousands of **compound words**—words formed by joining two words together. This poem, for example, contains *wind-polished, snowbound, moonlit, seamen,* and *eyelashes.* The meanings of many compound words are easy to understand. *Sunlight* is simply "light from the sun." Other compound words, however, have meanings that you might not easily guess. For example, *stardust* is not "dust from a star." (What does it mean?) Match words in the left column below with those in the right column to form compound words (such as *moonbeam*). Check them in a dictionary and then write a short definition of each.

moon	beam
sand	burn
star	fish
sun	stone
wind	storm

Reading About the Writer

John Haines (1924–   ), an artist as well as a poet, lives in and writes about Alaska. Something of an Alaskan pioneer, he is a fisherman, hunter, trapper, and homesteader. His artistic background provides the sense of color that helps him create his powerful imagery. Haines's books of poetry include *Winter News* and *The Sun on Your Shoulder.*

Focusing on Background
A Comment from the Poet

"The immediate source for the poem occurred one night well over twenty years ago, when I was awakened about midnight by what sounded like a distant singing. On going outdoors, I knew I was hearing a small band of wolves, far across the Tanana River, perhaps even two or three miles distant, singing (or howling) in unison, or in sequence. It was a brief but stunning concert. The night was clear and moonlit, with some wind blowing from the south over the river, and this was in, I think, January or February. . . . As to why the poem is written as it is, you will have to make an effort to understand the differences between matter-of-fact language such as can be read in any newspaper, and language of a figurative sort—in short, the language of poetry and of imaginative thinking. . . . Poetry is a way of thinking; it's not a trick, not a gimmick, but a fundamental act of perceiving; a kind of knowledge that can be obtained in no other way."

—John Haines

There are times when a whole poem is made up of one image after another. This does not mean the poet merely wants to give the readers a lot of pictures. It means the poet is more interested in creating a *feeling* than in expressing an idea. In a poem of this sort—the following is one of them— you'll see that there is one central image and that this image has many variations or illustrations.

The image here is moonlight—a kind of light that has the color and gleam of silver. Like King Midas whose touch turned everything to gold, here we have the moon, "queen of the skies," whose touch turns everything to silver. The feeling the poet wants us to share is not as simple as it first seems to be. As "the moon walks the night," we are invited to go with her, to share the vision in which living things, and even windows, are silvered over and held for a moment in one perfect picture of loveliness and peace.

Silver

Walter de la Mare

Slowly, silently, now the moon
Walks the night in her silver shoon;°
This way, and that, she peers, and sees
Silver fruit upon silver trees;
5 One by one the casements° catch
Her beams beneath the silvery thatch;°
Couched in his kennel, like a log,
With paws of silver sleeps the dog;
From their shadowy cote° the white
  breasts peep
10 Of doves in a silver-feathered sleep;
A harvest mouse goes scampering by,
With silver claws and a silver eye;
And moveless fish in the water gleam,
By silver reeds in a silver stream.

---

2. **shoon** (sho͞on): shoes.
5. **casements:** windows.
6. **thatch:** a thatched roof, like those in cottages still found in the British Isles.
9. **cote:** dove house.

Responding to the Poem

Analyzing the Poem

Identifying Details

1. What is the moon compared to, as it moves across the sky? Which words tell you the answer?
2. List all the things that turn silver in the moonlight.
3. Of all the things mentioned in the poem, which are the only ones that move?

Interpreting Meanings

4. Poets often use **images** like a zoom lens on a camera to bring the small details of a scene into sharp focus. Where is this poem set? Which images focus on very small parts of the scene?
5. What mood do you think the images and sounds create in this poem? Quote passages from the poem in explaining your answer.

Applying Meanings

6. "Silver" in part is about light changing the way we see and feel about the world. Have you ever experienced something similar? Explain how a change in light can alter your feelings about a particular place, such as a room, house, or neighborhood.

Writing About the Poem

A Creative Response

1. **Extending the Poem.** Write a poem of about five lines telling how you would feel if you were the moon.

A Critical Response

2. **Analyzing Images and Mood.** Walter de la Mare's images in "Silver" create a particular mood. To see how this mood depends on de la Mare's images, alter the poem as follows: Change the title to "Gold." Change *moon* to *sun, night* to *day,* and *she* and *her* to *he* and *his.* Finally, change *silver* to *golden* or *gold.* Keep everything else the same. After you write out this new version of the poem, explain in a paragraph the difference in mood between the two poems.

Analyzing Language and Vocabulary

Adjectives

In "Silver," the poet repeats one adjective—*silver*—to describe how the moon's light bathes everything below. He also uses other adjectives (for instance, "*shadowy* cote" and "*moveless* fish"). Each image not only suggests a picture but also indicates a feeling.

For each of the following nouns, use one or two adjectives to create a vivid image. Try to suggest not only a picture or idea but also a feeling.

1. storm
2. carnival
3. roar
4. desert
5. star

Reading About the Writer

Walter de la Mare (1873–1956) began his literary career by founding, publishing, and writing his own school magazine at St. Paul's School in England. After graduating, he worked for the Anglo-American (Standard) Oil Company as a bookkeeper for the next 18 years. However, he always considered himself a writer, especially a poet. He kept his hair long and wavy, and dressed in a far more Bohemian style than the average bookkeeper. De la Mare's writings, particularly his poems, often have an imaginative and dreamlike quality. As poet Louis Untermeyer said, "He is one of the poets who have ventured 'ten leagues beyond the wide world's end,' and have returned to tell us something incredible yet, somehow, believable about that uncharted and illimitable universe."

To most people, the wintry moment this poem describes would be no more than an ordinary incident. It might even be an annoyance. But to someone like Robert Frost, the moment takes on special importance.

Dust of Snow

Robert Frost

The way a crow
Shook down on me
The dust of snow
From a hemlock tree

Has given my heart
A change of mood
And saved some part
Of a day I had rued.

Responding to the Poem

Analyzing the Poem

Identifying Details

1. "Dust of Snow" is made up of a single sentence divided into two stanzas. What does the crow do to the speaker in the first stanza?
2. Describe how this event affects the speaker.
3. What does the word *rued* mean?

Interpreting Meanings

4. What **image** does this poem put in your mind?
5. Why do you think the speaker's mood changed?

Applying Meanings

6. Many people's hearts can be lifted by silent communication with nature. Describe another natural event that might make a sad day worthwhile. Could some natural events make you "rue" a day?

Writing About the Poem

A Creative Response

1. **Memorizing and Reciting the Poem.** Memorize "Dust of Snow" and then recite it before a group of classmates or the entire class. Before you memorize the poem, read the lines closely to determine which words to emphasize as you recite. Will you pause during the recitation of the poem? After the recitation, ask your audience for comments.
2. **Supplying Additional Details.** Imagine you are Frost and that you have just returned home after this incident. Write a one-paragraph journal entry describing the events surrounding the incident. Before you start writing, consider possible answers to the following question: What happened before you were dusted by snow?

> *Poetry's prime weapon is words, used for the naming, comparison, and contrast of things.*
>
> —Richard Wilbur

Figures of Speech: Unexpected Connections

If you were watching a tennis match and someone remarked "She's burning up the court," you would not call the fire department. You would understand that "burning up the court" means "playing aggressively and very well." The expression compares a fast, aggressive player to the speed and aggression of a fire.

Our everyday language includes thousands of these **figures of speech**—expressions that say one thing but mean another: "They're tied up in traffic." "Wilson's a drag." "Chloe's as cool as a cucumber." At the heart of each of these figures of speech is a comparison. "Tied up in traffic" compares being in a traffic jam to being bound with ropes. A "drag" compares a dull person to a lead weight used to keep something on the ground. "Cool as a cucumber" compares a person's outer calm to the cool feel of a cucumber.

The figures of speech we've just mentioned are used so commonly that we don't even think about the comparisons they contain. Poets want to create fresh, new figures of speech to make unexpected connections. They want to make us see everyday things in new ways.

The most common figures of speech used by poets are similes, metaphors, personification, and symbols.

Similes: Seeing Likenesses

> Oft on the dappled turf at ease
> I sit, and play with similes . . .

So says the poet William Wordsworth, who, like most poets, thinks of making similes as a kind of game—finding surprising connections between one thing and another.

A **simile** is a comparison of two unlike things, which are clearly linked by a word such as *like, as, than,* or *resembles.* Here are some examples of similes: "hands like ice," "a child as hungry as a bear," "a complexion smoother than polished marble," "a mind resembling a deep cave."

When a simile in a poem is fresh, the connection can be unforgettable. We see things in a new light. Our understanding grows. What once seemed commonplace takes on additional significance and meaning. A new dimension is opened up for us. In our minds we may be tempted to picture the comparison. Perhaps we see Robert's hands as made of ice, with each finger an icicle.

Look at the following short poem, especially the last line.

The Eagle

He clasps the crag with crooked hands:
Close to the sun in lonely lands,
Ringed with the azure° world, he stands.

The wrinkled sea beneath him crawls;
He watches from his mountain walls,
And like a thunderbolt he falls.

—Alfred, Lord Tennyson

3. **azure:** blue.

A great simile commands our attention because it amazes us with its exactitude and originality. Once we read it, we think: Why didn't anyone see that connection before? Many birds "swoop," "glide," or "dive." But only a bird of prey can drop "like a thunderbolt"—instantaneously, unpredictably, and with awesome power.

Metaphors: Seeing Identifications

A **metaphor** is a direct identification of two unlike things. In contrast to similes, metaphors make their connections without the use of *like, as, than,* or *resembles.* When we speak metaphorically, we do not say, "His hand is like a wet fish." Instead, we make a direct identification: "His hand *is* a wet fish."

Like similes, metaphors extend the range of our imagination. When they are fresh and based on a poet's true observation, we often feel that a strong secret relationship that always has existed has just been discovered by the poet. Metaphors bring not only new thoughts, but also new feelings to our experience. They enliven our world with surprising connections. After reading "The Sea," for example, you might always associate the ocean with a hungry dog:

> The sea is a hungry dog,
> Giant and gray.
> He rolls on the beach all day.
> With his clashing teeth and shaggy jaws
> Hour upon hour he gnaws
> The rumbling, tumbling stones,
> And "Bones, bones, bones!"
> The giant sea-dog moans,
> Licking his greasy paws.

> —from "The Sea,"
> James Reeves

Reeves uses an **extended metaphor,** that is, a metaphor that extends for several lines. Note several connections that are made between the dog and the sea: it is "gray," it "rolls on the beach," it has "clashing teeth and shaggy jaws," it "gnaws" on stones, it "moans," it licks its "greasy paws."

There is another metaphor in these lines. Notice that Reeves does not say directly that he is comparing the stones to the dog's bones. He implies, or hints, at the connection. This is called an **implied metaphor.** Sometimes a single word or a short phrase can imply a metaphor. In one of his poems, for example, T. S. Eliot tells us that the fog *rubs, licked, lingered, slipped by, made a sudden leap, curled,* and *fell asleep.* Each of these words or phrases describes an action that we can associate with cats. The implied metaphor is that the fog is a cat.

Personification: Humanizing the World

We use **personification** when we give human qualities to a nonhuman thing. Here the moon is described as a woman.

> Slowly, silently, now the moon
> Walks the night in her silver shoon;
>
> —from "Silver,"
> Walter de la Mare

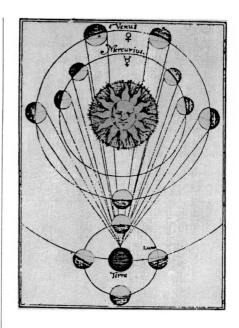

A moon can't walk and doesn't wear shoes (shoon). We understand that the lines personify the moon by talking about it as if it were a woman wearing silver shoes.

Cartoonists often use personification to tell their stories: Automobiles have eyes that blink and jaws that open wide. Rabbits lean up against lampposts and talk like philosophers. Horses do tap-dance routines. Pigs give birthday parties. The same sort of thing happens in poetry, except that personification is not necessarily used for comedy; it is used to make a serious point about human experience.

We hear many examples of personification in everyday talk. We say, "the fire engine came screaming down the street," or "the fire engine wailed," or "the siren whined." When the boiling water in a tea kettle makes its noise, we say "the kettle sings." When a motorboat makes its own noise, we say it "coughs" or it "sputters." When the fire goes out, we say it "dies." In all these cases, we are talking about something nonhuman as if it were human.

Symbols: Representations of Other Things

A **symbol** is any person, place, thing, or event that has meaning in itself and that at the same time represents, or stands for, something else.

Many symbols are traditional. We easily understand them because people have agreed on their meaning. A lamb, for example, often symbolizes innocence. A dove symbolizes peace, as does an olive branch. Five linked circles symbolize the Olympics. A crooked line on a traffic sign symbolizes a dangerously curved road ahead. A lighted light bulb symbolizes a bright idea; on a car's dashboard, it symbolizes the car lights.

Most readers of "The Raven" (page 385) sense that Poe is using the raven as a symbol. Ravens through the centuries have been associated with death and evil.

Many poets create their own personal symbols, and these may sometimes be difficult to recognize and understand. In Frost's "Dust of Snow" (page 397) for example, we know that the snow is significant because the poet says it brightened his mood. It is difficult to say for certain, however, what the snow might symbolize. Some readers might say it stands for God's grace. Such personal symbols excite our imaginations because they are so open to interpretation. We *sense* their meaning long before we can express that meaning in words.

This gripping little poem describes the tension of both a baseball player and a fan as the player leads off base during a game. Will the player try to steal? As you read look for four similes. How do they help you visualize the action?

The Base Stealer

Robert Francis

Poised between going on and back, pulled
Both ways taut like a tightrope-walker,
Fingertips pointing the opposites,
Now bouncing tiptoe like a dropped ball
5 Or a kid skipping rope, come on, come on,
Running a scattering of steps sidewise,
How he teeters, skitters, tingles, teases,
Taunts them, hovers like an ecstatic bird,
He's only flirting, crowd him, crowd him,
10 Delicate, delicate, delicate, delicate—now!

Responding to the Poem

Analyzing the Poem

Identifying Details

1. List three details that show the base stealer is tense.
2. Find the four **similes** in the poem. To whom or what is the base stealer compared in each simile?
3. In three or four sentences, tell in your own words what the base stealer does in this poem.

Interpreting Meanings

4. Identify "them" in line 8. Who is being addressed when the speaker says "come on, come on" in line 5? Who is addressed in line 9 when the speaker says "crowd him"?
5. Tell what "delicate" and "now!" refer to.

Applying Meanings

6. Have you ever been in a situation like the base stealer's? Describe an incident when you had to decide whether or not to move forward or go back. How did you feel before deciding? After?

Writing About the Poem

A Creative Response

1. **Using Vivid Similes.** The similes in "The Base Stealer" give us a vivid and surprisingly exact picture of the player as he is pulled taut, bounces, and hovers. Write a paragraph describing someone playing a sport. Use three or four similes to make the player's actions vivid. Before you write, list the specific actions you want to describe. Then think of what these actions remind you of.

A Critical Response

2. **Analyzing Figures of Speech.** Figures of speech usually suggest more than a mental picture. They often suggest feelings as well. "A handshake like steel" suggests more than strength. Steel is cold and unyielding. This association suggests that a person with such a handshake is cold and unfeeling as well as strong. In a paragraph examine three similes in "The Base Stealer." Describe at least one association each simile has for you. What do these associations add to your picture of the base stealer?

Analyzing Language and Vocabulary

Verbs in Series

In normal speech and prose, most sentences or clauses have one main verb. In prose, we rarely find the liveliness and energy of "How he teeters, skitters, tingles, teases, / Taunts them, hovers like an ecstatic bird."

For each of the following subjects, make up a sentence that uses a series of four to six verbs to describe an action. For example, if "racing boat" is your subject, you might write, "The racing boat tossed, danced, swerved, pitched, and veered on the rough seas."

1. storm cloud
2. newborn baby
3. honeybee
4. kite
5. Frisbee

Reading About the Writer

Robert Francis (1901–1987) developed a friendship with the older poet Robert Frost and became something of Frost's disciple. Frost once called Francis "the best neglected poet." In 1972, Francis published *Frost, A Time to Talk,* a collection of correspondence and conversations between the two writers. "The Base Stealer" is from *The Orb Weaver.*

If you took the title away from this poem, it would be like a riddle. One part of the metaphor is never named in the poem; only the title gives away the real subject of the poem.

Steam Shovel

Charles Malam

The dinosaurs are not all dead.
I saw one raise its iron head
To watch me walking down the road
Beyond our house today.
5   Its jaws were dripping with a load
Of earth and grass that it had cropped.
It must have heard me where I stopped,
Snorted white steam my way,
And stretched its long neck out to see,
10   And chewed, and grinned quite amiably.

Responding to the Poem

Analyzing the Poem

Identifying Details

1. What does the speaker see the "dinosaur" doing in lines 2–6? In lines 7–10?
2. Describe where the action in the poem takes place.

Interpreting Meanings

3. The speaker describes a steam shovel as if it were a dinosaur. This is the poem's **extended metaphor.** What parts of the steam shovel correspond to the dinosaur's "iron head," "jaws," "long neck"? What actually happened when the dinosaur "snorted white steam"?
4. In the movies, dinosaurs are usually presented as terrifying creatures. Can you identify all the ways in which this poet turns an awesome creature into one that's cheerful and likeable?

Applying Meanings

5. Compare some large modern machine, such as a construction crane or a bulldozer, to an animal. List three or more ways the machine resembles the animal.

Writing About the Poem

A Creative Response

Creating Figures of Speech. Charles Malam not only compares a steam shovel to a dinosaur but also **personifies** the dinosaur. He gives the nonhuman dinosaur/steam shovel human qualities: "It . . . grinned quite amiably." Humanizing something nonhuman helps us to feel we understand it better; it might even make us feel more comfortable in its presence. Write a one-paragraph description of something made of metal—anything from a radiator to a power saw. Use personification to give this manufactured object a human personality.

Analyzing Language and Vocabulary

Word Origins

The word *dinosaur* comes from ancient Greek words: *deinos,* meaning "terrible," and *sauros,* meaning "lizard." The names of many dinosaurs provide clues to their appearance or habits. The people who made up the names usually were well aware of the ancient Greek meanings. Using a dictionary that explains word origins, check the ancient Greek roots of the following names of "terrible lizards":

1. stegosaurus
2. brontosaurus
3. tyrannosaur
4. ichthyosaur
5. megalosauru

Reading About the Writer

Charles Malam (1906–   ), born in South Reygate, Vermont, is an American poet and playwright. Malam's poetry tends to present everyday objects, such as a steam shovel, with a light, humorous touch.

On one level, this poem is no more than a simple story about some people who take a walk at the beginning of a snowstorm. On their way, they see a little Morgan horse that's obviously never seen snow before. On another level, the poem is symbolic. The frightened little colt is seen as a lost child.

When a horse is "broken," it has been tamed. This involves forcing it to submit its original wildness to the demands of those who will ride it, or find some working use for it. As you read, look for the expression "winter-broken." What meaning do you think the expression may have in the poem?

The Runaway

Robert Frost

Once when the snow of the year was beginning to fall,
We stopped by a mountain pasture to say, "Whose
    colt?"
A little Morgan had one forefoot on the wall,
The other curled at his breast. He dipped his head
5   And snorted at us. And then he had to bolt.
We heard the miniature thunder where he fled,
And we saw him, or thought we saw him, dim and gray,
Like a shadow against the curtain of falling flakes.
"I think the little fellow's afraid of the snow.
10   He isn't winter-broken. It isn't play
With the little fellow at all. He's running away.
I doubt if even his mother could tell him, 'Sakes,
It's only weather!' He'd think she didn't know!
Where is his mother? He can't be out alone."
15   And now he comes again with clatter of stone,
And mounts the wall again with whited eyes
And all his tail that isn't hair up straight.
He shudders his coat as if to throw off flies.
"Whoever it is that leaves him out so late,
20   When other creatures have gone to stall and bin,
Ought to be told to come and take him in."

Responding to the Poem

Analyzing the Poem

Identifying Details

1. The speaker and a companion stop to wonder at the strange behavior of a colt. What exactly is the colt doing over and over? What does the speaker say is causing the colt's behavior?

2. The speaker imagines what might happen if the colt's mother were there. What does he imagine she might say to try to soothe her colt? How does the speaker imagine the colt would respond?

3. At the beginning of the poem, the onlookers wonder whose colt is in the pasture. What does the speaker say about the owner in the last lines?

Interpreting Meanings

4. What lines in the poem would make you think that this little horse can be seen as a **symbol** for a lost child, or for people who are too young and innocent to understand what they are experiencing?
5. If, as the speaker says, the colt is "running away," where do you think it is running *from* and where is it running *to*?
6. The "we" in the poem are adults who witness something they can easily understand, but which they can't do anything about. Explain what you think their attitude is: Are they sympathetic to the colt's unreasonable fear, or do they seem amused? Is the speaker just curious about an unusual sight, or does he seem to remember and feel his own first fears?
7. In line 10 the poet uses the expression "winter-broken." Explain the meaning of the expression.

Applying Meanings

8. What other situations in life do you think the last three lines could be applied to?

Writing About the Poem

A Creative Response

Writing a Poem. In five lines or more, tell how you would feel if you were this little horse.

Analyzing Language and Vocabulary

Word Origins

"The Runaway" is about a little Morgan. A Morgan is a breed of horse named for Justin Morgan (1747–1798?), a teacher in Vermont. Morgans are used mostly for riding and have been popular as horses for cowhands. The following are other breeds of horses. Give the origin of each name and tell what the breed is used for. You can find this information by looking at a book on horses, a dictionary, or an encyclopedia. In a dictionary, the origin of the name is usually given soon after the pronunciation.

1. Arabian
2. barb
3. Clydesdale
4. quarter horse
5. Shetland
6. Tennessee walking horse

To a poet, the most ordinary thing, even a left-over onion, can be made into an object of beauty and promise. As you read "The Routine," try to decide what the onion symbolizes, or what it stands for.

The Routine

Paul Blackburn

Each day I open the cupboard
& the green shoots of my last onion
have in the dark grown higher

   A perverse & fairly final pleasure
5   That I love to watch him stretching himself
secretly, green sprouting shamelessly in
this winter, making a park in my kitchen,
     making
spring for a moment in my kitchen

that, instead of eating him
10   I have watched him grow

Shallots from *A Book of Hours*
illuminated by Jean Bourdichon (c. 1515).

© 1987 The Pierpont Morgan Library, New York City.

Responding to the Poem

Analyzing the Poem

Identifying Details

1. According to the first stanza, what is happening to the speaker's last onion in the cupboard?
2. What two things does the poet say the onion makes in his kitchen?
3. What does the poet do with the onion, according to the last stanza?

Interpreting Meanings

4. Explain the "routine" mentioned in the title of the poem. Refer to passages in the poem in your explanation.
5. Unless it is planted, the bulb of an onion withers as it grows. Considering this fact, explain what you think the poet means when he says his pleasure at watching the onion is "perverse" and "fairly final."
6. What does the color green traditionally **symbolize**? (Ask your teacher if you are not sure.) Explain what the symbolic importance of the color adds to the poem.
7. The speaker calls the onion "him." What other words personify the onion? What does this **personification** reveal about the speaker's feelings for the onion?
8. What do you think the sprouting onion might **symbolize**?

Writing About the Poem

A Critical Response

Supporting a Topic Statement. In a paragraph, tell whether you agree or disagree with the following topic statement about the poem. No matter how you respond to this statement, cite details from the poem to support your opinion.

> *This is a poem about two metamorphoses—the marvelous transformations of two things to other, different things.*

Reading About the Writer

Paul Blackburn (1926–1971) was often associated with a group called the Black Mountain poets. This group was named for its contributions to the magazine *Black Mountain Review,* which was designed to help the failing Black Mountain College in North Carolina. Blackburn was also a noted translator and editor. He spent much of his life on the East Coast, especially in New York City, where he provided poets the opportunity to present their works in a series of poetry readings.

Many people regard poets as impractical dreamers and visionaries. But poets themselves often regard what they do as a craft or, as Amy Lowell does, a trade. Here she builds a whole poem on the trade of carpentry. Notice how she implies that the making of a house and the compositon of a poem have more in common than people suspect.

Trades

Amy Lowell

I want to be a carpenter,
To work all day long in clean wood,
Shaving it into little thin slivers
Which screw up into curls behind my plane;
5   Pounding square, black nails into white boards,
With the claws of my hammer glistening
Like the tongue of a snake.
I want to shingle a house,
Sitting on the ridgepole° in a bright breeze.
10   I want to put the shingles on neatly,
Taking great care that each is directly between two
        others.
I want my hands to have the tang of wood:
Spruce, cedar, cypress.
I want to draw a line on a board with a flat pencil,
15   And then saw along that line,
With the sweet-smelling sawdust piling up in a yellow
        heap at my feet.

That is the life!
Heigh-ho!
It is much easier than to write this poem.

9. **ridgepole:** horizontal beam at the top of a roof.

Man with Square by Jacob Lawrence (1978). Oil.   Courtesy of Terry Dintenfass Gallery, New York City.

Responding to the Poem

Analyzing the Poem

Identifying Details

1. What does the speaker want to do with wood?
2. What does the speaker say is more difficult than being a carpenter?

Interpreting Meanings

3. Explain how line 5 can be interpreted as a **metaphor** for typewriting. What part of a typewriter corresponds to "black nails"? What might the "white boards" be?
4. Select another passage from the poem, such as lines 2–5 or lines 14–16. Explain how the speaker is using the passage to compare carpentry to writing poetry.
5. What two meanings can you think of for the title "Trades"?
6. Amy Lowell was a talented and respected poet. Why do you think she says she wants to be something else? Do you believe her?

Applying Meanings

7. What other trades or jobs could be compared to the task of writing? What specific points of comparison can you name?

Writing About the Poem

A Creative Response

1. **Using Repetition.** Amy Lowell begins five lines with the phrase "I want." Write a poem of at least five lines spoken by a person who has a particular occupation or sport. In your poem, repeat "I want . . ." several times. Each time describe a separate aspect of your subject. The form of your poem should be similar to that of "Trades."

A Critical Response

2. **Summarizing a Main Idea.** In a paragraph, summarize what you think is the poet's main idea in "Trades." Open your paragraph with a statement of the main idea. Then support that statement with details from the poem. In your paragraph, consider the meaning of the poem's title.

Analyzing Language and Vocabulary

Specialized Vocabulary

In "Trades," Amy Lowell mentions a *ridgepole,* which is part of the frame of a house. The following are specialized words describing parts of a house's exterior. Using a dictionary when necessary, write a one- or two-sentence definition of each word.

1. porch
2. stoop
3. gable
4. sidelight
5. shutter
6. bay window
7. cornice

Are any of these words not used by people in your area? What word do they use instead to name this particular part of the house?

Reading About the Writer

Amy Lowell (1874–1925) is famous for her support of the Imagist movement. This movement called for a new kind of poetry that would abandon singsong meters and strive for hard, precise images. Lowell was the daughter of a distinguished, wealthy New England family. When she joined the radical group of poets called Imagists and used her wealth and status to further their aims, she suffered a great deal of ridicule. Lowell was awarded the Pulitzer Prize in 1926, a year after her death.

Allusion . . . is an extremely quick way of expressing and also of creating in our hearers shades of feeling.

—S. I. Hayakawa

Allusions

An **allusion** is a reference to a work of literature or to an actual event, person, or place. When people make allusions, they take for granted that their audience will recognize the reference. For example, when a writer alludes to "Hiroshima," most readers will recognize the reference to the Japanese city over which an atomic bomb was exploded in 1945. Some allusions, however, are not immediately recognizable. If a writer refers to "the Lady with the Lamp," for example, only readers familiar with the life of Florence Nightingale, one of the founders of modern nursing, would understand the allusion. The value of allusions is that they broaden the meaning of what is said or written. The risk in using them, however, is that some people may not make the connection.

Scrooge. Illustration by Arthur Rackham for *A Christmas Carol,* by Charles Dickens.

Allusions in Everyday Speech

Ordinary speech is full of allusions. You have probably used many allusions without being aware of it. "He's a real Scrooge," is an expression you may have heard. The allusion is to the character Ebenezer Scrooge in Charles Dickens's *A Christmas Carol* (page 619). Because Scrooge was so memorably mean and stingy, his name has passed into the general vocabulary.

To test yourself on recognizing allusions, see if you can identify the allusions in the following statements:

1. In introducing the subject of Rebecca, John opened a whole Pandora's box.
2. Lucy's life is a real Cinderella story.
3. They are very self-sufficient—real Robinson Crusoes.

Your ability to recognize allusions depends on the extent of your knowledge. The more you read, the more easily you will be able to identify allusions when they occur. But even the most highly educated man or woman could not be expected to identify every allusion that turns up. Even professors and scholars have to turn to the dictionary or encyclopedia in order to find out the meanings of some of the allusions poets make.

It won't take you long to discover the allusion upon which this poem depends. Everything mentioned alludes to a famous fairy tale that is never directly identified. But the poem is not merely a retelling of the old fairy tale. It is a clever way of creating a character portrait—and it reminds us that the old stories still have meaning today.

The Builders

Sara Henderson Hay

I told them a thousand times if I told them once:
Stop fooling around, I said, with straw and sticks;
They won't hold up; you're taking an awful chance.
Brick is the stuff to build with, solid bricks.
5   You want to be impractical, go ahead.
But just remember, I told them; wait and see.
You're making a big mistake. Awright, I said,
But when the wolf comes, don't come running to me.

The funny thing is, they didn't. There they sat,
10 One in his crummy yellow shack, and one
Under his roof of twigs, and the wolf ate
Them, hair and hide. Well, what is done is done.
But I'd been willing to help them, all along,
If only they'd once admitted they were wrong.

Responding to the Poem

Analyzing the Poem

Identifying Details

1. What did the speaker tell "them" in lines 1–4? What word does the speaker use to describe "them" in line 5?
2. What didn't "they" do, according to lines 8–11? What did "they" do instead? Tell what finally happened to "them."
3. According to the last two lines, what did the speaker want "them" to admit?

Interpreting Meanings

4. Identify the speaker and "them" in this poem. What tale is the poem **alluding** to?
5. Does the speaker in this poem care more about what happened to "them" or about the fact that they refused to listen to advice? Support your opinion with evidence from the poem.
6. What human character types or attitudes is the poet really talking about here?

Applying Meanings

7. The speaker says, "I'd been willing to help them, all along,/ If only they'd once admitted they were wrong." Was the speaker right to set this condition? What else do you think the speaker could or should have done?

Writing About the Poem

A Creative Response

1. Changing the Point of View. In a paragraph, retell the story from the point of view of one of the two friends. Speaking in the first person, tell how this character views the speaker and why he or she refuses to follow the speaker's advice.

A Critical Response

2. Identifying the Main Idea. What is the main idea, or theme, of this poem? In a paragraph, state the poem's main idea and cite details from the poem to support what you say. At the end of your paragraph, tell how you feel about this idea.

Reading About the Writer

Concerning "The Builders," **Sara Henderson Hay** (1906–   ) comments, "I was primarily trying . . . to illustrate the age-old conflict between the practical businessman and his frequently impractical brother, neither of whom understands the other." "The Builders" is taken from *Story Hour,* her collection of rewritten fairy tales.

Nursery rhymes and fairy tales are often disturbing and violent. In retelling the original verse about a girl sitting on a tuffet (a tuft of grass), this writer places the action squarely in the twentieth century. But the violence is still there . . .

Little Miss Muffet

Paul Dehn

Little Miss Muffet
  Crouched on a tuffet,
Collecting her shell-shocked wits.
  There dropped (from a glider)
  An H-bomb beside her
Which frightened Miss Muffet to bits.

Illustration by Arthur Rackham for a 1913 edition of *Mother Goose*.

Responding to the Poem

Analyzing the Poem

Identifying Details

1. In the original nursery rhyme, Miss Muffet is frightened away by a spider. What is her fate in this version?

Interpreting Meanings

2. The word *crouched* is the first clue that this poem will differ from the familiar nursery rhyme (printed below). How does this verb and other changes affect your mental picture of Miss Muffet on her tuffet? What do you imagine is happening around her?

> Little Miss Muffet
> Sat on a tuffet
> Eating her curds and whey.
> There came a great spider
> And sat down beside her,
> And frightened Miss Muffet away.

3. Besides the echoes in the first two lines, how else does the poet remind us of the original nursery rhyme? List the similarities you find.
4. Explain how this poem is both humorous and serious. What contrast do you think the poet is making between childhood in today's world and childhood in earlier times?

Applying Meanings

5. Explain whether you think this modern version of the old nursery rhyme was meant for small children or for older readers.

Writing About the Poem

A Critical Response

Evaluating the Poem. In a survey of children's preferences in poetry, this poem was found to be the most popular verse among a group of verses widely reprinted in schoolbooks today. In a paragraph, explain why you think the poem is so popular. At the end of your paragraph, tell whether you would also vote this poem as a favorite.

Analyzing Language and Vocabulary

Abbreviated Words

Many words in English contain letter abbreviations. Words such as *H-bomb* often start out as scientific jargon or military code. Eventually, they capture the public's imagination and enter common usage. Often we use these words without even knowing what the abbreviations stand for. Look up the meanings of the following words in a dictionary or other reference book. Then explain what each letter abbreviation stands for.

1. D-day
2. H-hour
3. G-man
4. X-ray
5. U-boat

Reading About the Writer

Paul Dehn (1912–1976) was a British poet well known for his screenplays, which include *Murder on the Orient Express* and the sequels to *Planet of the Apes*. Born in Manchester, England, Dehn worked for various London newspapers as a film critic. His poem "Little Miss Muffet" is taken from *Quake Quake Quake: A Leaden Treasury of English Verse*.

I still favor several simple poems published long ago which continue to have an appeal for simple people.

—Carl Sandburg

Stories in Verse

Home Ranch by Thomas Eakins (1888). Oil.

Philadelphia Museum of Art. Given by
Mrs. Thomas Eakins and
Miss Mary Adeline Williams.

Most of the poems that you have read thus far in this book are lyrics. A **lyric** is a brief poem which expresses an emotion and which usually represents the poet as "I." Lyrics like "My Mother's Childhood" (page 358) sometimes contain bits and pieces of a story, but they never tell a complete story from beginning to end. **Narrative** poems (also called story poems), on the other hand, are more like short stories. They usually have a plot, characters, and a setting.

The very earliest poems were spoken, not written down. These were sacred stories that explained the beginning of the world and the origins of a people or a nation. Other story poems told of heroic deeds, of important victories and defeats, of storms, voyages, magic, and other adventures. The "library" for these poems was the mind of the poet, who would tell these stories for an entire community. Their memories were aided by the rhythm and sounds of words that fit together so well. In this way the stories survived by word of mouth alone from generation to generation.

One of the oldest and most popular forms for story poems is the **ballad.** Ballads are sung stories, usually about some sensational or violent deed. Ballads have strong rhythms, rhymes, and refrains, which make them easy to memorize.

All of the story poems that follow remind us of the old power of the spoken word. You should listen to them all read, or sung, aloud.

A lament is an expression of sorrow and regret, usually over a death, or over anything that turned out wrong. In this ballad, a dying cowboy gives us some idea of what he did wrong. But, in the tradition of the old ballads, he never tells the full story. This ballad provided the title and the haunting theme music to *Bang the Drum Slowly,* a movie about the death of a young baseball player.

The Cowboy's Lament

Anonymous

As I walked out in the streets of Laredo,
As I walked out in Laredo one day,
I spied a poor cowboy wrapped up in white linen
Wrapped up in white linen as cold as the clay.

5   "Oh beat the drum slowly and play the fife lowly,
Play the dead march as you carry me along;
Take me to the green valley, there lay the sod o'er me,
For I'm a young cowboy and I know I've done wrong.

"I see by your outfit that you are a cowboy"—
10 These words he did say as I boldly stepped by.
"Come sit down beside me and hear my sad story;
I am shot in the breast and I know I must die.

"Let sixteen gamblers come handle my coffin,
Let sixteen cowboys come sing me a song.
15 Take me to the graveyard and lay the sod o'er me,
For I'm a poor cowboy and I know I've done wrong.

"My friends and relations they live in the Nation,°
They know not where their boy has gone.
He first came to Texas and hired to a ranchman
20 Oh, I'm a young cowboy and I know I've done wrong.

"It was once in the saddle I used to go dashing,
It was once in the saddle I used to go gay;
First to the dramhouse° and then to the cardhouse;
Got shot in the breast and I am dying today.

25 "Get six jolly cowboys to carry my coffin;
Get six pretty maidens to bear up my pall.
Put bunches of roses all over my coffin,
Put roses to deaden the sods as they fall.

17. **Nation:** United States. The ballad is set before 1845, when Texas became part of the United States.

23. **dramhouse:** saloon.

"Then swing your rope slowly and rattle your spurs
    lowly,
30   And give a wild whoop as you carry me along;
And in the grave throw me and roll the sod o'er me
For I'm a young cowboy and I know I've done wrong.

"Oh, bury beside me my knife and six-shooter,
My spurs on my heel, my rifle by my side,
35   And over my coffin put a bottle of brandy.
That the cowboys may drink as they carry me along.

"Go bring me a cup, a cup of cold water,
To cool my parched lips," the cowboy then said;
Before I returned his soul had departed,
40   And gone to the roundup—the cowboy was dead.

We beat the drum slowly and played the fife lowly,
And bitterly wept as we bore him along;
For we all loved our comrade, so brave, young, and
    handsome,
We all loved our comrade although he'd done wrong.

Responding to the Ballad

Analyzing the Ballad

Identifying Details

1. Tell who is speaking in lines 5–9 and 11–38. Who is speaking in lines 10 and 39–44?
2. What did the dying cowboy do when he "first came to Texas"?
3. Explain what the dying cowboy talks about in stanzas 4, 7, 8, and 9.
4. Describe what the cowboy's comrades do after his death, according to the last stanza.

Interpreting Meanings

5. What **metaphor** does the singer use to describe Heaven? Why is it appropriate?
6. The dying cowboy says he has "done wrong," but never tells exactly what he did. Sift through the information about the cowboy presented in the ballad. Then make an educated guess at the circumstances leading up to his being shot. Quote passages to support your explanation.

Portrait of a Cowboy by
Andrew Dasburg (1928). Oil.

Courtesy of the Anschutz Collection, Denver, Colorado.

7. Traditional ballads usually skip over certain **details** of the story and linger over others. List some important details (besides what the cowboy did wrong) omitted from this ballad. Then list some of the details it lingers over, that is, describes more extensively than you would expect.

8. Some ballads, including "The Cowboy's Lament," contain more than one **refrain**. Identify the refrain you consider most important in "The Cowboy's Lament." Then explain what it adds to the ballad.

9. How did you feel after reading "The Cowboy's Lament"? Describe your emotional reaction and try to explain why you reacted this way.

Writing About the Ballad

A Critical Response

Researching the Ballad's Setting. "The Cowboy's Lament" is set in Laredo, Texas. (The ballad is sometimes called "The Streets of Laredo.") Do some research on Laredo in a textbook, encyclopedia, or other reference. Be especially alert for information on the community in the 1830's, roughly the time the ballad takes place. Then explain what this background information adds to your understanding of the ballad and especially the kind of life the cowboy might have led.

The Creation by Aaron Douglas (1935).
Gouache on paper.

The author of this famous poem based it on a sermon he used to hear the old-time black preachers deliver. As you read, imagine you are in a crowded church listening to an eloquent preacher. You may even imagine the congregation echoing some of the lines. Read the poem out loud to get its full flavor.

The Creation
(A Negro Sermon)

James Weldon Johnson

And God stepped out on space,
And He looked around and said,
"I'm lonely—
I'll make me a world."

5 And as far as the eye of God could see
Darkness covered everything,
Blacker than a hundred midnights
Down in a cypress swamp.

Then God smiled,
10 And the light broke,
And the darkness rolled up on one side,
And the light stood shining on the other,
And God said, *"That's good!"*

Then God reached out and took the light in His hands,
15 And God rolled the light around in His hands,
Until He made the sun;
And He set the sun a-blazing in the heavens.
And the light that was left from making the sun
God gathered up in a shining ball
20 And flung against the darkness,
Spangling the night with the moon and stars.
Then down between
The darkness and the light
He hurled the world;
25 And God said, *"That's good!"*

Then God himself stepped down—
And the sun was on His right hand,
And the moon was on His left;
The stars were clustered about His head,

30   And the earth was under His feet.
And God walked, and where He trod
His footsteps hollowed the valleys out
And bulged the mountains up.

Then He stopped and looked and saw
35   That the earth was hot and barren.
So God stepped over to the edge of the world
And He spat out the seven seas;
He batted His eyes, and the lightnings flashed;
He clapped His hands, and the thunders rolled;
40   And the waters above the earth came down,
The cooling waters came down.

Then the green grass sprouted,
And the little red flowers blossomed,
The pine tree pointed his finger to the sky,
45   And the oak spread out his arms;
The lakes cuddled down in the hollows of the ground,
And the rivers ran down to the sea;
And God smiled again,
And the rainbow appeared,
50   And curled itself around His shoulder.

Then God raised His arm and He waved His hand
Over the sea and over the land,
And He said, *"Bring forth! Bring forth!"*
And quicker than God could drop His hand,
55   Fishes and fowls
And beasts and birds
Swam the rivers and the seas,
Roamed the forests and the woods,
And split the air with their wings,
60   And God said, *"That's good!"*

Then God walked around
And God looked around
On all that He had made.
He looked at His sun,
65   And He looked at His moon,
And He looked at His little stars;
He looked on His world
With all its living things,
And God said, *"I'm lonely still."*
70   Then God sat down
On the side of a hill where He could think;
By a deep, wide river He sat down;
With His head in His hands,

God thought and thought,
75 Till He thought, *"I'll make me a man!"*

Up from the bed of the river
God scooped the clay;
And by the bank of the river
He kneeled Him down;
80 And there the great God Almighty,
Who lit the sun and fixed it in the sky,
Who flung the stars to the most far corner of the night,
Who rounded the earth in the middle of His hand—
This Great God,
85 Like a mammy bending over her baby,
Kneeled down in the dust
Toiling over a lump of clay
Till He shaped it in His own image;
Then into it He blew the breath of life,
90 And man became a living soul.
Amen. Amen.

Responding to the Poem

Analyzing the Poem

Identifying Details

1. According to this poem, why does God decide to make the world? Why does He decide to create a man?
2. God is often viewed as a being or spirit without a physical body. This poem, however, describes God's physical actions in some detail. For instance, God smiles twice in the poem. What two things come into being when He smiles? List three other physical actions of God in making the world.
3. After the world cools in stanza 6, it comes to life. Describe how the poet *personifies* nature—that is, gives it human qualities.

Interpreting Meanings

4. In line 69, God says, *"I'm lonely still."* In your opinion, why is God still lonely?
5. What is so surprising to the poet about the way God created man compared with how He created the rest of the universe? Include passages from the poem in your discussion.
6. What descriptions in the poem make God seem most human to you? Which descriptions make Him seem most loving? Which make him seem powerful and superhuman?
7. A sermon is usually a lesson that teaches us something important. Describe the lesson about the nature of God and the nature of men and women revealed in this retelling of the creation story.

Reading the Poem Aloud

Often you gain additional understanding of a poem by reading it aloud. In part this is a result of deciding how to pronounce each word. To pronounce the words correctly, you need to grasp both the poem's meaning and its rhythm. A long poem without a regular rhythm, such as "The Creation," requires considerable preparation before it can be read aloud. Copy any two stanzas of "The Creation" on a piece of paper. Then read them silently, noting in the margins how you would pronounce the lines. Next, read the poem aloud a couple of times, altering your marginal notes on pronunciation if need be. When you feel ready, read the stanzas before a group of classmates or the whole class. Ask for feedback on your reading.

Writing About the Poem

A Critical Response

1. **Analyzing a Refrain.** A **refrain** is a group of words repeated at regular intervals in a poem. Identify the refrain in "The Creation." Then discuss in a paragraph what the refrain contributes to the poem. Before you write consider the following questions:

   a. Does the refrain help give the poem unity and/or shape?
   b. Does it give the poem a songlike quality?
   c. Does it draw attention to important ideas? Be sure to quote passages from the poem in your paragraph.

2. **Writing a Comparison.** To get the full flavor of this poem, it would be a good idea to read Chapters 1 and 2 of the Book of Genesis in the Bible. Since both the poem and Genesis are concerned with the creation of the earth, you might ask yourself: How does the poem repeat or reflect the story of creation as the Bible tells it? In what ways do the poem and Genesis differ? Write your comparison in a paragraph.

Analyzing Language and Vocabulary

Precise Verbs

One way that poets help readers imagine the action in a story poem is by using precise verbs. For example, James Weldon Johnson does not say that God's footsteps *formed* the mountains. Instead, he says that they "*bulged* the mountains up." *Bulged* gives us both a more precise and a more vivid picture of God's action. We can imagine the flat ground swelling upward and becoming rounded.

Answer the following questions about the precise verbs that Johnson uses in "The Creation." Use a dictionary if you need help in explaining exact meanings.

1. In line 20, why is *flung* a better choice than *threw*? (Use the context of lines 18–20.)
2. In line 21, what does *spangling* help you imagine that *lighting* would not?
3. In line 24, what does *hurled* suggest that *placed* would not?
4. In line 46, what does *cuddled* make you picture that *settled* would not?
5. In line 87, why is *toiling* a better choice than *working*?

Reading About the Writer

James Weldon Johnson (1871–1938) was a poet, teacher, lawyer, songwriter, essayist, translator, novelist, anthologist, and politician. He was the first black person ever admitted to the Florida bar. He later became executive secretary of the National Association for the Advancement of Colored People (NAACP). He also served as the American consul in Nicaragua and Venezuela. Johnson's works include a novel, *The Autobiography of an Ex-Colored Man,* and *God's Trombones,* a collection of poems based on the thunderous sermons delivered by the old-time preachers. (The trombone refers to the preacher's voice.) "The Creation" is one of those sermons.

This is the most famous poem about the great American pastime—baseball. Shortly after the poem appeared in a newspaper, it was given to an actor who was about to go on-stage in New York's Wallack's Theater for a Baseball Night. The actor must have recognized a winner. He memorized the poem quickly and the audience went wild over it. Read the poem aloud yourself to hear how its strong rhythms and rhymes make it easy to memorize, and fun to recite.

Casey at the Bat

Ernest Lawrence Thayer

The outlook wasn't brilliant for the Mudville nine that day;
The score stood four to two, with but one inning more to play;
And so, when Cooney died at first, and Burrows did the same,
A sickly silence fell upon the patrons of the game.

A straggling few got up to go in deep despair. The rest
Clung to the hope which springs eternal in the human breast;
They thought, if only Casey could but get a whack, at that,
They'd put up even money now, with Casey at the bat.

But Flynn preceded Casey, as did also Jimmy Blake,
And the former was a pudding, and the latter was a fake;
So upon that stricken multitude grim melancholy sat,
For there seemed but little chance of Casey's getting to the bat.

But Flynn let drive a single, to the wonderment of all,
And Blake, the much-despised, tore the cover off the ball;
And when the dust had lifted, and they saw what had occurred,
There was Jimmy safe on second, and Flynn a-hugging third.

Then from the gladdened multitude went up a joyous yell;
It bounded from the mountaintop, and rattled in the dell;
It struck upon the hillside, and recoiled upon the flat;
For Casey, mighty Casey, was advancing to the bat.

There was ease in Casey's manner as he stepped into his place;
There was pride in Casey's bearing, and a smile on Casey's face;
And when, responding to the cheers, he lightly doffed his hat,
No stranger in the crowd could doubt 'twas Casey at the bat.

Ten thousand eyes were on him as he rubbed his hands with dirt;
Five thousand tongues applauded when he wiped them on his shirt;
Then while the writhing pitcher ground the ball into his hip,
Defiance gleamed in Casey's eye, a sneer curled Casey's lip.

The Mighty Casey by Paul Nonnast (1954). Illustration for "The Truth About Casey," in *The Saturday Evening Post*. © 1954 The Curtis Publishing Company.

And now the leather-covered sphere came hurtling through the air,
And Casey stood a-watching it in haughty grandeur there;
Close by the sturdy batsman the ball unheeded sped.
"That ain't my style," said Casey. "Strike one," the umpire said.

From the benches, black with people, there went up a muffled roar,
Like the beating of the storm waves on a stern and distant shore;
"Kill him! Kill the umpire!" shouted someone on the stand;
And it's likely they'd have killed him had not Casey raised his hand.

With a smile of Christian charity great Casey's visage shone;
He stilled the rising tumult; he bade the game go on;
He signaled to the pitcher, and once more the spheroid flew;
But Casey still ignored it, and the umpire said, "Strike two."

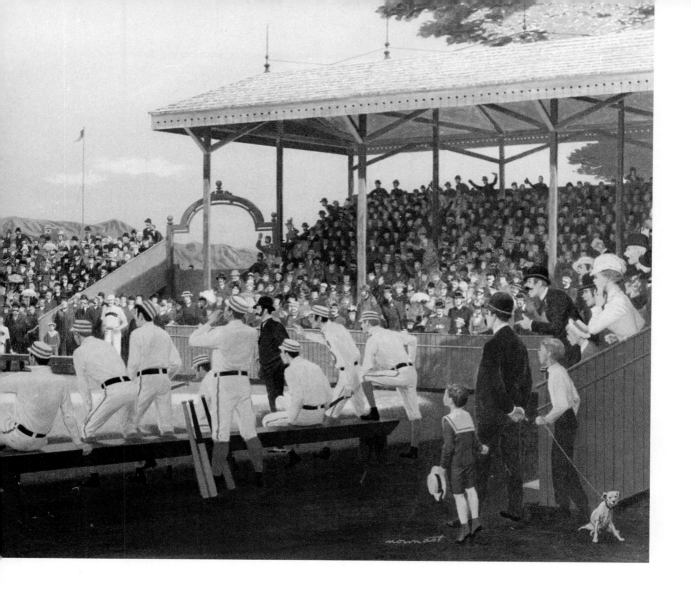

"Fraud!" cried the maddened thousands, and the echo answered, "Fraud!"
But a scornful look from Casey, and the audience was awed;
They saw his face grow stern and cold, they saw his muscles strain,
And they knew that Casey wouldn't let that ball go by again.

The sneer is gone from Casey's lips, his teeth are clenched in hate,
He pounds with cruel violence his bat upon the plate;
And now the pitcher holds the ball, and now he lets it go,
And now the air is shattered by the force of Casey's blow.

Oh! somewhere in this favored land the sun is shining bright;
The band is playing somewhere, and somewhere hearts are light;
And somewhere men are laughing, and somewhere children shout,
But there is no joy in Mudville—mighty Casey has struck out!

Responding to the Poem

Analyzing the Poem

Identifying Details

1. At the end of the first stanza, by how many runs is the Mudville team behind? How many innings and outs remain?
2. How many men are on base when Casey comes to bat? What are their names?
3. Casey enters the poem very dramatically. Describe his attitude as he comes to bat. How does he respond to the first pitch? To the second?
4. Describe Casey's face as he prepares for the third pitch.
5. According to the last stanza, why is there no joy in Mudville?

Interpreting Meanings

6. In several places the poet **exaggerates** the importance of his subject. For instance, he describes the crowd as being stricken with "grim melancholy." It might be more accurate to say the crowd felt the game was "hopeless." "Grim melancholy" is usually reserved for much more serious occasions. Find two other instances of exaggeration in the poem. What is the effect of the exaggeration?
7. The crowd itself is a **character** in this poem. Describe how the crowd's attitude changes over the course of the poem. We are not shown the crowd's reaction right after the final pitch to Casey. How do you suppose the fans reacted?
8. Did you enjoy reading the poem? In explaining your answer, note how the poem's **rhythm** and **rhyme** affected you.

Applying Meanings

9. Does Casey act like a true sports hero? Support your opinion with evidence from the poem. Can you think of any modern sports stars who behave like Casey?

Writing About the Poem

A Creative Response

1. **Writing a News Article.** Imagine you are a sports reporter for the Mudville *Gazette.* Write an article of three short paragraphs describing the game discussed in the poem. Be sure to cover journalism's five W's: **Who** was playing? **What** happened? **When** and **where** was the game played? **Why** did Mudville lose? You'll have to invent some of the details of the game.
2. **Presenting a Choral Reading.** Join with a group of classmates and read the poem out loud together. You might divide the group into two or three subgroups and assign different stanzas to each. Individuals might be assigned the direct quotes in stanzas 8–10 by Casey, the umpire, and the fan. How will you handle the cries of "Fraud!" in stanza 11?

Analyzing Language and Vocabulary

Formal and Informal Words

In this poem, Thayer uses formal words that would be out of place in an ordinary description of a baseball game. For example, he uses *spheroid* instead of *baseball.* List one or two less formal words for each of the following italized words from the poem:

1. "A sickly silence fell upon the *patrons of the game.*"
2. "So upon that *stricken multitude* grim *melancholy* sat. . . ."
3. "But Flynn let drive a single, to the *wonderment* of all. . . ."
4. " . . . the *leather-covered sphere* came hurtling through the air."
5. "With a smile of Christian charity great Casey's *visage* shone. . . ."
6. "He *stilled the rising tumult*; he *bade* the game go on. . . ."

Reading About the Writer

Ernest Lawrence Thayer (1863–1940) wrote other poems for newspapers, but he is remembered today only for "Casey at the Bat." Thayer was born in Massachusetts and attended Harvard University, where he was editor-in-chief of *The Lampoon.* He continued his journalism career with the San Francisco *Examiner.* Although Thayer said that "Casey at the Bat" was not based on any particular baseball player, many have claimed to be the subject of the poem.

The Ballad of the Harp-Weaver

Edna St. Vincent Millay

"Son," said my mother,
    When I was knee-high,
"You've need of clothes to cover you,
    And not a rag have I.

5 "There's nothing in the house
    To make a boy breeches,°
Nor shears to cut a cloth with,
    Nor thread to take stitches.

"There's nothing in the house
10   But a loaf-end of rye,
And a harp with a woman's head
    Nobody will buy,"
And she began to cry.

That was in the early fall.
15   When came the late fall,
"Son," she said, "the sight of you
    Makes your mother's blood crawl—

"Little skinny shoulder blades
    Sticking through your clothes!
20 And where you'll get a jacket from
    God above knows.

"It's lucky for me, lad,
    Your daddy's in the ground,
And can't see the way I let
25   His son go around!"
    And she made a queer sound.

That was in the late fall.
    When the winter came,
I'd not a pair of breeches
30   Nor a shirt to my name.

I couldn't go to school,
    Or out of doors to play.
And all the other little boys
    Passed our way.

35 "Son," said my mother,
    "Come, climb into my lap,
And I'll chafe your little bones
    While you take a nap."

And, oh, but we were silly
40   For half an hour or more,
Me with my long legs
    Dragging on the floor.

A-rock-rock-rocking
    To a mother-goose rhyme!
45 Oh, but we were happy
    For half an hour's time!

But there was I, a great boy,
    And what would folks say
To hear my mother singing me
50   To sleep all day,
    In such a daft° way?

Men say the winter
    Was bad that year;
Fuel was scarce,
55   And food was dear.

A wind with a wolf's head
    Howled about our door,
And we burned up the chairs
    And sat upon the floor.

---

6. **breeches** (brich′iz): trousers reaching to or just below the knees.

51. **daft:** silly, foolish.

Seated Woman by Georges Seurat (1883). Oil.

Solomon R. Guggenheim Museum, New York City.

60 All that was left us
    Was a chair we couldn't break,
    And the harp with a woman's head
    Nobody would take,
    For song or pity's sake.

65 The night before Christmas
    I cried with the cold,
    I cried myself to sleep
    Like a two-year-old.

    And in the deep night
70 I felt my mother rise,
    And stare down upon me
    With love in her eyes.

I saw my mother sitting
    On the one good chair,
75 A light falling on her
    From I couldn't tell where,

Looking nineteen,
    And not a day older,
And the harp with a woman's head
80 Leaned against her shoulder.

Her thin fingers, moving
    In the thin, tall strings,
Were weav-weav-weaving
    Wonderful things.

85   Many bright threads,
         From where I couldn't see,
     Were running through the harp-strings
         Rapidly,

     And gold threads whistling
90   Through my mother's hand.
     I saw the web grow,
         And the pattern expand.

     She wove a child's jacket,
         And when it was done
95   She laid it on the floor
         And wove another one.

     She wove a red cloak
         So regal to see,
     "She's made it for a king's son,"
100   I said, "and not for me."
     But I knew it was for me.

     She wove a pair of breeches
         Quicker than that!
     She wove a pair of boots
105   And a little cocked hat.

     She wove a pair of mittens,
         She wove a little blouse,
     She wove all night
         In the still, cold house.

110 She sang as she worked,
         And the harp-strings spoke;
     Her voice never faltered,
         And the thread never broke.
         And when I awoke,

115 There sat my mother
         With the harp against her shoulder,
     Looking nineteen,
         And not a day older,

     A smile about her lips,
120   And a light about her head,
     And her hands in the harp-strings
         Frozen dead.

     And piled up beside her
         And toppling to the skies,
125 Were the clothes of a king's son,
         Just my size.

Responding to the Poem

Analyzing the Poem

Identifying Details

1. According to lines 1–12, what does the mother say she does not have? What two things are left in the house?
2. According to stanza 5, why does the sight of her son make the mother's skin crawl? What makes the mother and son happy, according to lines 35–46?
3. In three or four sentences, tell in your own words what the boy sees happen on the night before Christmas.
4. When the boy awakes, what does he discover has happened to his mother?

Interpreting Meanings

5. Sometimes the poet adds an extra line to a stanza. Find these five-line stanzas. Explain how the poet uses them to divide the story into episodes.
6. What lets you know that the harp is special, even before the mother uses it to weave clothes? What words or details in lines 65–80 suggest that something miraculous is about to happen?
7. The speaker of the poem seems to be telling the events of a time long past. What are his emotions as he remembers his mother? Quote passages from the poem to support your interpretation.

8. How do you feel about the fate of the mother? Was her end sad, or in a way beautiful?

Writing About the Poem

A Creative Response

1. **Creating Images.** One of the most striking images in this poem is "A wind with a wolf's head / Howled about our door" (lines 56–57). The poet could just have said "The wind howled at the door." But by expanding this commonly used statement and adding a vivid image to it (the wolf's head), the poet has helped us to imagine the wind in a new and forceful way. Use your imagination to transform the following commonly used statements into striking images that bring back their true power:

   a. His eyes burned with hate.
   b. The sea roared.
   c. A chill ran up my spine.
   d. She squirreled away her earnings.
   e. I slept like a log.

A Critical Response

2. **Summarizing a Poem.** "The Ballad of the Harp-Weaver" tells a story, using **characters, plot, setting,** and **theme.** In an essay of three paragraphs, summarize the story, using these terms. When you summarize a story, you must be sure to explain how one event leads to another. Before you write, you might gather your information in a chart like the following:

	Summary of the Poem
Characters	
Setting	
Conflict	
Climax of plot	
Theme	

3. **Supporting a Main Idea.** In a paragraph, tell whether you agree or disagree with the following statement of the poem's main idea. Use details from the poem to support your position.

   "The Ballad of the Harp-Weaver" is a poem that illustrates the transforming power of love.

Reading About the Writer

Edna St. Vincent Millay (1892–1950) began writing poetry as a child. When she was scarcely nineteen years old, she wrote a long, now-famous poem called "Renascence." Millay became part of a Bohemian group of poets associated with Greenwich Village in New York City. But her poems and her themes are basically conservative and traditional. One important theme in her work is the strength of women, as indicated by "The Ballad of the Harp-Weaver." Millay's own mother was a remarkable woman. She not only supported Millay's career, but provided her daughter with a role model and idol as well. Millay won the Pulitzer Prize for "The Harp-Weaver" in 1923.

Poetry is comment on the world by people who see that world more clearly than other people and are moved by it. They notice the changing of the year and write down their image of that change so that you, too, will notice things better than you did before.

—Phyllis McGinley

Messages—Open and Hidden

Every poem is a message from its writer. Sometimes that message is openly stated in the poem. This is the way much poetry of the past was written. Then, poets often took pains to tack on their message at the end of the poem.

Today, poets tend to want to let the readers discover the messages for themselves. By doing this, poets force us to participate directly in their experience.

This poem was written by a black poet, long before the start of the civil rights movement of the 1950's and 1960's. Even without knowing this, we can sense the hidden message behind these plainly spoken thoughts about freedom and liberty.

Refugee in America

Langston Hughes

There are words like *Freedom*
Sweet and wonderful to say.
On my heart-strings freedom sings
All day everyday.

There are words like *Liberty*
That almost make me cry.
If you had known what I knew
You would know why.

Responding to the Poem

Analyzing the Poem

Identifying Details

1. What words does the speaker use to describe the word *freedom* in stanza 1? Where does he say it sings?
2. What happens to the speaker when he hears the word *liberty*? Why?

Interpreting Meanings

3. The poem's title suggests that the speaker considers himself a refugee. What is a refugee? (You will find the definition in a dictionary.) How could people be refugees in their own country?
4. What might the poet know that makes him cry when he hears the word *liberty*?
5. The speaker has different reactions to two words that mean nearly the same thing. Are there any differences between the words *freedom* and *liberty*? Explain.
6. How would you state the poem's unstated **message**?

Applying Meanings

7. What other people in the world might weep when they hear the word *liberty*?

A Critical Response

Writing About Theme. Often a poet's message can be summed up in a statement of **theme**—the **main idea** expressed in a literary work. In one sentence, state what you think is the theme of "Refugee in America." Use this sentence to begin a paragraph. In the rest of your paragraph, discuss how the theme is expressed in the poem.

Analyzing Language and Vocabulary

Connotations

Connotations are the emotions and feelings attached to certain words. Usually people agree on a word's connotations. But sometimes words affect different people in different ways. List all the feelings and associations you have when you hear these words. Do you and your classmates all agree?

1. Democrat
2. Republican
3. New York
4. Hollywood
5. fast food
6. shopping malls

This poem shows how meaning can be found in everyday things. The speaker sees special significance in a towel, a kettle, a spoon, a chair, and other aspects of her morning routine. As you read, think about your emotional reaction to the poem. Does it make you feel happy, sad, or something else?

Welcome Morning

Anne Sexton

There is joy
in all:
in the hair I brush each morning,
in the Cannon towel, newly washed,
5   that I rub my body with each morning,
in the chapel of eggs I cook
each morning,
in the outcry from the kettle
that heats my coffee
10   each morning,
in the spoon and the chair
that cry "hello there, Anne"
each morning,
in the godhead of the table
15   that I set my silver, plate, cup upon
each morning.

All this is God,
right here in my pea-green house
each morning
20   and I mean,
though often forget,
to give thanks,
to faint down by the kitchen table
in a prayer of rejoicing
25   as the holy birds at the kitchen window
peck into their marriage of seeds.

So while I think of it,
let me paint a thank-you on my palm
for this God, this laughter of the morning,
30   lest it go unspoken.

The Joy that isn't shared, I've heard,
dies young.

The Breakfast Room by Pierre Bonnard (1930–1931). Oil.   Museum of Modern Art, New York City.

Responding to the Poem

Analyzing the Poem

Identifying Details

1. The first stanza lists household objects and morning routines. They give us a sense of who the speaker is and what her life is like. List six things in which she says she finds joy.
2. According to line 17, what does she say "all this" is?
3. Explain why the speaker means "to faint down by the kitchen table."
4. What happens to joy that isn't shared?

Interpreting Meanings

5. How could the last two lines explain why the poet wrote this poem?
6. **Personification** means giving human attributes to nonhuman things. Find at least two examples of personification in the poem. Why do you suppose the poet chose to personify these things?
7. Identify the **refrain** in "Welcome Morning." How does the refrain remind us that there is "joy in all"?
8. How many religious references can you find in the poem? Do you think the poem has a religious **message**? How would you state it?
9. How did you feel after reading the poem—happy, sad, unmoved? Explain what made you feel that way.

Writing About the Poem

A Creative Response

1. **Imitating the Poem.** "Welcome Morning" contains a list of the little things in life that can bring joy. Make up a poem of your own, listing about ten of the little things that you are thankful for. Keep your lines short, like those of "Welcome Morning." You might use a refrain in your poem. Be sure to give a title to your poem.

A Critical Response

2. **Analyzing a Title.** Sometimes the title helps unlock the meaning in a work of literature. Look at this poem's title—"Welcome Morning." (Note that it isn't written "Welcome, Morning.") In the first two paragraphs explain what the title means. (Is there a hidden meaning concerning the night?) In the second paragraph, discuss how the title relates to the rest of the poem. Include passages from the poem in your second paragraph.

Reading About the Writer

Anne Sexton (1928–1974) is associated with a group of poets whose works are called "confessional." These poets often write about, or "confess," the most personal aspects of their lives. Sexton wrote about marriage, children, divorce, illness, social problems, and money. She also wrote one series of poems on animals and another series based on old fairy tales. Sexton won the Pulitzer Prize in 1967 for *Live and Die*.

Focusing on Background
A Comment from the Poet

"I do have a feeling for stories, for plot and maybe the dramatic situation. I really prefer dramatic situations to anything else. Most poets have a thought that they dress in imagery. . . . But I prefer people in a situation, in a doing, a scene, a losing or a gain, and then, in the end, find the thought (the thought I didn't know I had until I wrote the story).

. . . This is, in fact, a major criticism of my poetry. But still, I think it makes stimulating poetry and poetry need not be dull. And anyone can think of images, most anyone. I like a good image; I use them often enough—but I want, usually, more than that."

—Anne Sexton

This poem consists of little more than a single image stated clearly and briefly in the first line.

What truth does the poet want us to discover for ourselves by focusing our attention on this man?

Soup

Carl Sandburg

I saw a famous man eating soup.
I say he was lifting a fat broth
Into his mouth with a spoon.
His name was in the newspapers that day
Spelled out in tall black headlines
And thousands of people were talking about him.

   When I saw him,
He sat bending his head over a plate
Putting soup in his mouth with a spoon.

Responding to the Poem

Analyzing the Poem

Interpreting Meanings

1. Explain the contrast between who the man is and what he is doing. What does the speaker want us to think about the famous man?
2. Name at least five types of people the man could be.
3. The poem could have been called "The Famous Man." Why do you think the poet called it "Soup" instead? What other titles could the poem have?
4. What **connotations,** or associations, does the word *soup* have for you?
5. How would you state this poet's **message**?

Writing About the Poem

A Creative Response

Imitating the Writer's Technique. In a brief poem, describe a famous person you have seen, either in person or on television. Tell how you know this famous person is just like everyone else. Open with the words "I saw a famous man (or woman). . . ."

Reading About the Writer

Carl Sandburg (1878–1967), born in Galesburg, Illinois, is a poet who is identified with Chicago, the city that provided the title of his most famous poem. Sandburg is also the author of a six-volume biography of Abraham Lincoln. Sandburg wrote about all aspects of American life; he once commented, "I'll probably die propped up in bed trying to write a poem about America." He won the Pulitzer Prize in 1939 for *Abraham Lincoln, The War Years,* which he had worked on for some 15 years. In 1951, he was awarded the Pulitzer Prize for poetry.

One message of this poem is stated openly and directly. Do you also find hidden messages about the speaker's feelings toward her family?

Dusting

Julia Alvarez

Each morning I wrote my name
on the dusty cabinet, then crossed
the dining table in script, scrawled
in capitals on the backs of chairs,
5   practicing signatures like scales
while Mother followed, squirting
linseed from a burping can
into a crumpled-up flannel.

She erased my fingerprints
10   from the bookshelf and rocker,
polished mirrors on the desk
scribbled with my alphabets.
My name was swallowed in the towel
with which she jeweled the table tops.
15   The grain surfaced in the oak
and the pine grew luminous.
But I refused with every mark
to be like her, anonymous.

Responding to the Poem

Analyzing the Poem

Identifying Details

1. Name three things the speaker does "each morning."
2. How does the mother follow up on her child's actions?
3. What reason does the speaker give for her own actions?

Interpreting Meanings

4. Do you find a **hidden message** in the poem about the speaker's relationship with her mother? About the speaker's place in the family? If you do, describe the message or messages.
5. People sometimes will write their name at a public place or carve their initials in a tree. Are these actions similar to what the speaker does in the poem?

Applying Meanings

6. Do you think these are common feelings? Why does the speaker think her mother is "anonymous"?

Writing About the Poem

A Creative Response

Changing the Point of View. The poem presents the speaker's feelings, but does not tell us what the mother is thinking. In the first of two paragraphs, have the mother explain what she thinks of the child's actions. In the second paragraph, let her give several reasons to explain her own actions.

Reading About the Writer

Julia Alvarez (1950–   ) grew up in the Dominican Republic. These childhood experiences form the focus for her book *Homecoming*, from which "Dusting" is taken. Alvarez has won numerous prizes for her poetry. She has also taught creative writing at George Washington University in Washington, D.C. Other poems included in *Homecoming* are "Making Our Beds," "How I Learned to Sweep," and "What Can It Be?"

FIGURES OF SPEECH AND SOUND

If you look carefully, you'll begin to find poetic techniques used in everyday language.

1. Read the following statements. Can you identify the figure of speech used in each one?

   "Reporters peppered the president with questions."

   a. On a literal level, what is this statement saying?
   b. What does it mean on a figurative level?

   "The worldly and the wise will watch for good buys."

   a. Where does this advertising blurb use **rhyme**?
   b. Which words form **alliteration**?

   "When the going gets tough, the tough get going."

   a. What two meanings of the word *tough* does this saying depend on?
   b. Where does this saying use **alliteration**?

   "The economy was stagnant in March."

   a. What is the economy compared with?
   b. What does this statement say about the economy in plain, literal language?

2. What are the Colts, Bears, Cubs, Red Wings, and Rams? Think of five mammals or birds or insects that would *not* make good names for sports teams.
3. Many towns, states, and rivers in the United States have Native American names that are really **figures of speech.** Use a dictionary to find out what these names mean in their original tribal language.

a. Aztec	d. Omaha
b. Chicago	e. Yosemite
c. Shenandoah	f. Missouri

English is an accented language. (Japanese is not.) This means that English words of more than one syllable have one syllable that is stressed more than the others:

NUMber (num′ber)
beTWEEN (be·tween′)
HONorable (hor′or·a·ble)
disCOVer (dis·cov′er)

1. Use capital letters and accent marks ′ and ˘ to indicate the stressed and unstressed syllables in these words:

   a. Thanksgiving
   b. control
   c. commonplace
   d. awesome

2. Names in English are also accented. Show what syllables are accented in your own name, and in the names of your street, town, and state.

Here is a poem about one of the early explorers of America. Read it aloud.

Hernando De Soto (1499?–1542)

Hernando De Soto was Spanish,
An iron-clad *conquistador.*
Adventure he knew in the sack of Peru,
But it just made him anxious for more.

Hernando De Soto was knightly,
Hernando De Soto was bold,
But like most of his lot, he'd be off like a shot
Whenever he heard there was gold.

So, with priest and physician and army,
Not to speak of a number of swine,
At Tampa he started a quest, fiery-hearted,
For the gold of a fabulous mine.

And from Florida way out to Texas,
This Don° of the single-track mind
Went chasing his dream over prairie and stream,
And the pigs kept on trotting behind.

---

14. **Don:** a title of respect in Spain.

He discovered the great Mississippi,
He faced perils and hardships untold,
And his soldiers ate bacon, if I'm not mistaken,
But nobody found any gold.

They buried De Soto at midnight,
Where the wide Mississippi still jigs.
He was greedy for gain but a soldier for Spain.
(I hope someone looked after the pigs.)

     —Rosemary and Stephen
      Vincent Benét

1. Write out the first two stanzas of the poem and show which syllables are accented and which are not.
2. Suppose you didn't know how to pronounce *conquistador* (line 2). What syllable would the rhythm of the poem tell you to stress?
3. Which line in each stanza has an **internal rhyme**? What are the **rhyming words**?
4. What common expression in line 7 is a **metaphor**? What is being compared to what?
5. What **comparison** is implied in the words "single-track mind" in line 14?
6. What does the phrase "iron-clad" mean in line 2?
7. How do you think these poets feel about De Soto? What details give you your answer?

How many words can you think of that rhyme with *ghost*? Here is a poem built on three of them.

Ghosts

   When a ghost
   goes past a post
   I see the post
   through the ghost.

5 When a captain's ghost
   sails down the coast,
   I see the coast
   through the ghost.

   When a ghost
10 eats toast,
   I see the toast
   inside the ghost.

     —James Steel Smith

1. What is the main point about ghosts?
   a. They are transparent.
   b. They are invisible.
   c. They eat a lot.
2. Where does the poet use **alliteration**?
3. Can you think of four other words that **rhyme** with *ghost*? Use those words to make up another stanza for "Ghosts."
4. The word *lost* looks as if it should rhyme with *post,* but does it? Here are four words from the poem. Can you think of at least two other words that rhyme with each word and look as if they should? Can you find at least four other words that look as if they don't rhyme, but do?

   a. goes
   b. sail
   c. eat
   d. see

5. Which of the following words rhyme with *through*? Which look as if they should rhyme, but don't? bough, blew, cough, drew, enough, few, grew, hew, hue, mew, new, knew, pew, rough, slough, Sue, though, threw.

Writing

1. **Writing a Humorous Poem.** Write a poem of at least five lines, in which all the lines have the same rhyming sound. Before you begin, make a list of ordinary words, such as *rain, wall, light, chair,* and *head.* Then, for each word, write as many rhyming words as you can think of. Finally, use your list of rhymes to write your poem.
2. **Writing a Poem Around a Metaphor.** Think of a metaphor and write a poem in which you extend your comparison as far as you can and still make sense. Open with the metaphor, perhaps a line like: *I am a camera.*

ANALYZING POETRY

Writing Assignment

Write a brief essay in which you analyze one of the poems in this unit. As part of your essay, describe your response to the poem.

Background

Poetry both delights and confuses. It delights us because we enjoy its sounds and images, and the way it strikes a chord in our hearts as well as our minds. Sometimes, a poem confuses us because it leaves many questions unanswered. To understand a poem better, it helps to analyze it. When you **analyze** a poem, you take it apart to focus on its elements one at a time. These elements include **rhyme, rhythm,** and other **sound effects, images,** and **figures of speech.**

Prewriting

1. Choose a poem to write about, and read it carefully several times. Be sure to read the poem aloud, in order to hear its sound effects.
2. **Paraphrase** the poem in your own words. That is, restate its meaning either line by line (for a short poem) or stanza by stanza (for a longer poem). If you need help in figuring out any line or figure of speech, discuss the passage with someone else.
3. **Scan** the poem to make sure you understand its rhythm. Note the rhyme scheme and other sound effects.
4. Complete a chart like the following to gather together information about the poem's elements. Find passages to support or illustrate your answer to each question.

	Poem's title
Who is the **speaker** in the poem?	
Does the poem tell a **story?** If so, summarize the story in a sentence or two.	
Is the poem about a **feeling** of an experience? If so, describe it.	
How does the poem use **rhyme, rhythm,** or **free verse?** Does the poem contain **alliteration** or **onomatopoeia?** How do these sound effects contribute to the poem's meaning?	
What **images** and **figures of speech** does the poem contain? How do they affect the way the poem makes you feel?	
How do you **respond** to this poem? (How does it make you feel? What does it make you think about? Do you like it or not?) Can you explain your response?	

Writing

Use the following plan to organize your essay:

Paragraph 1: State the poem's title and author. Describe the subject of the poem. Identify its speaker.
Paragraph 2: Paraphrase the poem, either line by line or stanza by stanza. Discuss the poem's important images and figures of speech. Tell what they contribute to the poem's meaning.
Paragraph 3: Discuss the poem's sound effects (rhyme, rhythm, alliteration, etc.). Tell how sound contributes to the overall effect of the poem.
Paragraph 4: Describe and explain your personal response to the poem.

The following is an essay a reader wrote about "Steam Shovel" by Charles Malam (page 404).

In his poem "Steam Shovel," Charles Malam gives us a fresh look at an everyday object. The entire poem develops a metaphor implied (but not directly stated) in the title and first few lines—the steam shovel is a dinosaur. The speaker tells of seeing a steam shovel/dinosaur near his or her house. The machine was being used in some sort of construction project. The steam shovel/dinosaur watched the speaker walk down a road and then stop. It seemed to stretch out its neck and grin at the speaker. The poet uses personification when describing the inanimate machine as a living animal ("raise its iron head," "watch me," "heard me," "snorted white steam," "stretched its long neck," "chewed, and grinned"). The poet's images are sharp and appropriate. A vivid image is the steam shovel stretching its long neck out to see (line 9); both the dinosaur and steam shovel might move in just this way.

Topic sentence identifies poem, title, subject.

Identifies implied metaphor.

Paraphrases poem.

Gives examples of personification.

Gives example of vivid image.

Sound effects help create the light tone of "Steam Shovel." The poem has a sprightly rhythm, based mainly on iambs (feet made up of an unaccented syllable followed by an accented syllable). The poet uses end rhymes effectively and at times surprisingly. There is invention in rhyming "see" in line 9 with "amiably" in line 10. There is much alliteration in the poem; *d* sounds, for example, appear frequently.

Topic sentence tells what sound effects contribute to poem.

Discusses poem's rhythm.

Discusses rhyme and alliteration.

I enjoyed the poem a lot. It made me feel happy. Also, it opened my eyes to a connection I might never have thought of. From now on, I'll be alert to seeing similarities in unlike things. Maybe I'll get a fresh understanding of the things being compared.

Gives personal response to poem.

Self-Check

1. Does the introductory paragraph cite the title and author, describe the subject, and identify the speaker?
2. Does the second paragraph contain a paraphrase of the poem? Are imagery and figurative language discussed?
3. Does the third paragraph discuss the poem's sound effects?
4. Have I ended the essay by stating my personal response? Have I given reasons for my response?
5. Have I supported by ideas with examples, details, quotations?
6. Are sentences punctuated correctly? Are words spelled correctly?

Partner Check

1. Are there any spelling errors?
2. Are sentences punctuated correctly?
3. Are the ideas clearly expressed?
4. Are there enough examples, quotations, and details to support the writer's statements?
5. What I like best about this paper:
6. What needs improvement:

POINT OF VIEW
REAL EXPERIENCES

City Night (detail) by Georgia O'Keeffe (1926). Oil.

The Minneapolis Institute of Arts, Minneapolis, Minnesota.

UNIT SEVEN

POINT OF VIEW

REAL EXPERIENCES

A writer's problem does not change. . . . It is always how to write truly and having found out what is true, to project it in such a way that it becomes a part of the experience of the person who reads it.

—Ernest Hemingway

Point of View
Real Experiences

A stroll through a bookstore should make it clear that people enjoy reading about real experiences. Shelves marked *Cooking, Gardening, Sports, History, Biography, Travel,* and so on suggest that the categories of real experience are as varied as the world itself. Books on "real-life" subjects such as these belong to a large class of literature known as nonfiction.

Nonfiction Versus Fiction

The terms *nonfiction* and *fiction* seem to describe opposite kinds of literature. Actually, they have many elements in common. If you have ever written about a historical event or a personal experience, you were creating **nonfiction**—writing based on facts and incidents that really happened. However, to keep your readers interested, you probably used elements usually associated with **fiction,** or "made-up" literature such as short stories, novels, and plays. For example, you may have arranged your real-life incidents to reveal conflict and to create suspense, as in a short story. Or, you may have used sensory images to describe an actual setting or a real person, as in a novel. Good nonfiction is as imaginative and well crafted as fiction. The line separating the two is sometimes blurred, especially when fiction seems so true-to-life that readers mistake it for nonfiction. Many readers of Sir Arthur Conan Doyle's detective stories, for example, believe that Sherlock Holmes actually lived.

"The Facts" and "The Whole Truth"

When an author presents a piece of writing as nonfiction, we expect the facts to be accurate and verifiable. No one likes to be misinformed or misled. However, the fact that nonfiction is based on facts does not mean that it presents the whole truth. When a nonfiction book claims to tell "the true story," the truth is *as the author sees it*. When we read fiction, we "suspend disbelief." That is, we willingly believe what we read is true even though we know it never really happened. With nonfiction, we must judge the facts and decide whether they agree with the author's version of the truth.

Nonfiction, though based on facts and real experience, is really about points of view. Nonfiction interests so many readers precisely because it can be controversial. We enjoy piecing together the partial truths and trying to solve life's puzzling questions. And we enjoy sharing in another person's real experiences and seeing the world through that person's eyes. Nonfiction writers invite us to examine the facts and to be enlightened, entertained, and persuaded by their special points of view.

Three Types of Nonfiction

In this unit, you will read essays, reports, and selections from autobiographies. Because these are all forms of nonfiction, you can expect them to be about facts of one sort or another.

An **essay** is a very short piece of writing that attempts to say something about one main idea. The word *essay* comes from a French word *essai,* meaning "try" or "attempt." An essay is just that—a little "try" at something. An essay is short and it often expresses the writer's personal feelings about a topic. The points of view of the essays in this unit are all personal.

An **autobiography** is the story of the writer's own life. Autobiographies, in general, are book length. The ones you will read here are taken from books in which the writers tell their life stories. The point of view of an autobiography is usually very personal. After all, it is hard to write about your own life and not reveal your feelings about it. When reading essays and autobiographies, you should keep in mind that these pieces present a more **subjective** point of view—that is, even though the events really occurred, their retelling could be influenced by the writer's feelings.

A **report,** on the other hand, is not usually personal. You read reports in the newspaper all the time. Reports are often the same length as essays, but they tell us more about the subject than about the writer. The point of view of a report, then, is usually **objective,** or impersonal and unbiased.

Essays, autobiographies, reports: These will introduce you to the great world of informative writing that awaits you in nonfiction. Some people, in fact, think that the best writing being done today is in the form of nonfiction.

Drawing by Alexa Grace (1987).

Responding to Nonfiction

The following is an extract from a newspaper article. If you were to read this in your own newspaper, what questions would come to your mind as you were reading? What responses would you make to the reporter's main ideas? Here we have one reader's responses on the right. You might take notes on your own responses as you read.

Yeti-Like Monster Gives Staid Town in Illinois a Fright

MURPHYSBORO, Ill., Oct. 31—Mrs. Nedra Green was preparing for bed in her isolated farmhouse near here the other night when a shrill, piercing scream came from out by the shed.

'It's it again,'' she said.

Four-year-old Christian Baril was in his backyard chasing fireflies with a glass jar. He ran in the house. "Daddy, Daddy," he said, "there's a big ghost out back."

Randy Creath and Cheryl Ray were talking on her darkened porch when something moved in the brush nearby. Cheryl went to turn on a light; Randy went to investigate.

At that moment it stepped from the bushes.

Towering over the wide-eyed, teen-age couple was a creature resembling a gorilla. It was eight feet tall. It had long shaggy matted hair colored a dirty white. It smelled foul like river slime.

Silently, the couple stared at the creature and the creature stared at the couple, fifteen feet apart. Then, after an eternity of perhaps thirty seconds, the creature turned slowly and crashed off through the brush back toward the river.

It was the Murphysboro Monster, a strange creature that has baffled and frightened the police and residents for weeks now in this southern Illinois town on the sluggish Big Muddy River. . . .

Such monster sightings are bizarre indeed for an old farm county seat where brightly colored leaves fall on brick streets and high school majorettes practice baton twirling for the Red Devils' upcoming football game with Jonesboro's Wildcats.

"A lot of things in life are unexplained," said Toby Berger, the police chief, "and this is another one. We don't know what the creature is. But we do believe what these people saw was real. We have tracked it. And the dogs got a definite scent."

It all began shortly before midnight June 25. Randy Needham and Judy Johnson were conferring in a parked car on the town's boat ramp down by the Big Muddy.

At one point the couple heard a loud cry from the woods next to the car. Many were to describe the sound as that of a greatly amplified eagle shriek.

Mr. Needham looked out from the front seat. There, lumbering toward the open window was a light-colored, hairy, eight-foot creature matted with mud.

Reader's responses:

What is a "yeti"?
What is a "staid" town?

Good opening—isolated farmhouse, shrill scream.

"It" must be the "yeti-like monster."

I wonder why the kid thinks it's a *ghost*?
The writer is showing us that lots of people saw this "monster."

I guess this is what the couple told the reporter. It's a very vivid description! He really makes me want to read on.

He's showing me how "ordinary" this town is so I'll believe the people when they say they've seen a monster.

More proof. I am getting convinced myself.

This reporter describes things very well.

At that point, the police report calmly notes. "complainant left the area." He proceeded to the police station and filed an "unknown creature" report. . . .

Later, as Officer Jimmie Nash inspected some peculiar footprints fast disappearing in the oozing mud left by the receding river, he became a firm believer.

"I was leaning over when there was the most incredible shriek I've ever heard," he said. "It was in those bushes. That was no bobcat or screech owl and we hightailed it out of there."

Officers searched the river bank for hours, following an elusive splashing sound like something floundering through knee-deep water. They found nothing.

Plains folk hereabouts do not excite easily. So the next day on page three *The Southern Illinoisan* published a two-hundred-word account of the "critter." That presumably was the end of the case.

But the next night came young Christian Baril's encounter and the experience of Cheryl Ray and Randy Creath, the seventeen-year-old son of a state trooper, who drew a picture of the creature.

That did it for Chief Berger. He ordered his entire fourteen-man force out for a night-long search. And Jerry Nellis, a dog trainer, brought Reb, an eighty-pound German shepherd renowned for his zealous tracking.

I guess if the police officer believes in the monster, it's pretty convincing.

The shriek again.

By telling us that people here don't get excited, he's trying to convince me that they are telling the truth. He's convinced me already, I think.

With floodlights officers discovered a rough trail in the brush. Grass was crushed. Broken branches dangled. Small trees were snapped. On the grass Reb found gobs of black slime, much like that of sewage sludge in settling tanks on a direct line between the river and the Ray house.

Reb led Mr. Nellis and Officer Nash to an abandoned barn on the old Bullar farm. Then, at the door, the dog yelped and backed off in panic. Mr. Nellis threw it into the doorway. The dog crawled out whining. The men radioed for help. Fourteen area police cars responded, but the barn, it turned out, was empty.

It Came to the Carnival
Ten days later the Miller Carnival was set up in the town's Riverside Park, not far from the boat ramp. At 2 A.M. July 7 the day's festivities had stopped and the ponies that walk around in circles with youngsters on their backs were tied to bushes.

Suddenly they shied. They rolled their eyes. They raised their heads. They tried to pull free. Attracted by the commotion, three carnival workers—Otis Norris, Ray Adkerson, and Wesley Lavander—walked around the truck and there, standing upright in the darkness was a three-hundred- to four-hundred-pound creature, hairy and light colored and about eight feet tall.

With no menace, but intent curiosity, the creature was watching the animals. . . .

—Andrew H. Malcolm

Physical evidence. Pretty convincing.

The slime comes up a lot. It's a word that certainly is disgusting. So is the comparison with sewage.

I wonder what the dog saw?

Again, three people saw the thing.
I wonder if it couldn't just be a bear?
I'd like to know what each person said. Did they really all see the same thing?
Now how does the writer know the creature was not menacing? How does he know it was only curious? He wants us to think the monster is disgusting but harmless.

Thinking Over the Report

The report goes on. (When you see three or four dots in a piece of writing, they usually indicate that something has been omitted.) Suppose you were the reader whose responses are on the right. If you wanted to comment on the report, you could see from your notes that several ideas have emerged.

1. You comment several times that you like the way the writer describes things.
2. You are aware that the writer is trying to persuade you that this monster really exists.

3. You note that the reporter seems to use words that make the monster seem disgusting. (You might even think about the word *monster* itself. How would the headline have affected you if the writer had just called the creature an "animal"?)

Discuss these ideas with your classmates. Do you all agree with this reader's responses? Would you like to discuss any other aspect of the report? Would you like to read the rest of it?

THE COLD WAVE

Lois Phillips Hudson

Lois Phillips Hudson (1927–   ) was born and raised on a prairie farm in North Dakota. This essay, from a book called *Reapers in the Dust,* is about an incident that took place long ago when Hudson was about eight years old. Her subject is a terrible winter in North Dakota, before central heating had replaced the iron stoves that were the farmers' only means of keeping warm. Before you read, think of "the old days." Do people still seem to think that the old days were more exciting than the present? What do you think?

M y father and grandfather would often speak of the earlier days in North Dakota—of the strong man who could swing a hundred-pound sack of wheat to his back by flinging it over his shoulder with his teeth, of tornadoes that switched the roofs of barns and houses, and of hailstorms that rained sheep-killing stones, heaping July wheatfields with desolations of ice.

Even more fascinating to me were their stories of the early winters. I would never see any winters like these, they said, for a new and milder weather cycle now prevailed. I would never know the bitter years that built the grim legends of our northern land.

My mother used to tell me how once a prairie wolf had stalked her as she walked home alone from school, over miles of abandoned stubble. I always felt cheated when I looked at the faded photograph of my father sitting on a horse, his hat higher than some telephone wires. He had ridden that horse right to the top of a gigantic snowbank, packed so hard that the horse's hoofs hardly dented its crust. It was true that there was usually a bank in our yard that reached to the top of the clothesline pole, but this was hardly satisfying when I knew what grander things had been. Why couldn't something happen *after* I was born, I wondered.

Yet when the sort of thing I was waiting for finally came, its coming was so natural and casual, so unlike a legend, that I mistook it for a part of the routine of my existence. It was part of my routine, for instance, to run over behind the depot with some of the town kids and slide on the ice by the tracks before I went over to Schlagel's Store to get a ride home with my father. I was almost always the only girl to go sliding, and it was also part of my routine to try to beat the boys to the smoothest patch of ice. On the day I am talking about, the only departure from routine was that there were no contenders for any of the ice.

I didn't slide very long myself, because I began to feel some undefined discomfort that an adult would have easily identified as a deeply pervasive chill. But when an eight-year-old is too cold, he will first feel oddly tired and lonely and deserted, so that he will go to find people. Thus it was that although I began to have the feeling that I had played too long and that surely my father would be waiting for me angrily, when I opened the door to Schlagel's Store, I saw by the big Sessions

> **Modifiers.** Adjectives and adverbs are *modifiers*. They limit, or make more definite, the meaning of another word. For example, "an *icy* sidewalk" gives a more definite picture than "a sidewalk," and "to look *closely*" is more precise than "to look." In "The Cold Wave," pay particular attention to the many modifiers that the writer uses to describe things and actions. These words will help you imagine more vividly the writer's childhood in North Dakota.

Farm Buildings near Traverse City, Michigan (1976).

clock that it was still only a quarter of four and that I would have to wait for him.

Several amorphous[1] large men were warming their hands at the stove in the center of the room and speaking to each other in Russian. Their faces were always very red, and Mr. Buskowski's purplish, large-pored cheeks frightened me a good deal, as did his heavy teasing in a broken English I would make terrified and ineffectual efforts to understand. I managed to sneak past them all to the rear of the store where the harness and great quilted collar pads hung from brass pegs screwed into rough boards. Julius Schlagel's clerk, Irma, was back there shoveling some shingle nails into a brown paper bag. She straightened up from the nail bin, stared at me, and stepped nearer to see my face under the hiss of the gas lamp. "You want to know something? You froze your face, kid."

"How could I? I just came straight over here from school," I lied.

She gave a skeptical glance at the clock and said, "Go get some snow and fetch it in here."

I brought a mittenful of snow and submitted to her harsh massage. The snow felt hot on my cheeks, so I knew I'd frozen them all right.

"Now don't go out again, hear?"

Except for the candy counter, the store was a dark, monotonous jumble of bags and boxes and barrels. I was hungry, so I diverted myself by studying the penny candy and deciding how I would spend a penny if I had one. Since I rarely had the penny, no one paid any attention to me. When I did have one, I would tap it nonchalantly[2] on the grimy glass case—not as though I was impatient to be waited on, for indeed I was not, but just to let Irma and Julius know that I was a potential customer, an individual to be treated with respectful attentiveness when I had finally made up my mind.

Since I had no penny, I was glad to see my father come through the door. He saw that Julius was listening to the radio, and he strode brusquely past me to ask him about the weather reports. Julius dispensed about as many weather reports as he did bags of flour and corn meal; in 1935 in drought-ruined North Dakota, radios were a luxury, like candy.

Without speaking, Julius turned up the volume so my father could hear the announcer. ". . . the Canadian cold wave is pressing southward from central Manitoba and is expected to hit northern North Dakota tonight, causing substantial drops in the temperature within the next twenty-four hours. This is KFYR in Bismarck . . ."

"Forty below in Winnipeg last night," Julius said to my father.

"You been out in the last hour? I bet it's thirty below here right now. The pump's froze solid. We gotta go thaw it out." Directing his last sentence to me, he turned and made his way past the Russians, nodding uncordially.[3]

The sun had set while I was waiting in the store, and a vast gloom in the sky sagged low over the town weighting the rigid streets with cold. The heat absorbed by my snowsuit was gone instantly, and my thawed-out cheeks stung badly. My father scuffed me up over the brittle heaps of snow at the curb of the wooden sidewalk and hoisted me into the sleigh. The sleigh was a wagon box transferred to runners for the winter. I wanted to stand up, but he made me sit on the old Indian blanket spread on straw. There were hot stones under the straw. Then he draped a cowhide from the high side of the wagon box down over my head.

Though I could see nothing, I could hear my father talking to the horses, and I knew he was wiping the frost of their own breathing from their nostrils. Beneath me was the thin scrape of the runners, then the rattle over the railroad tracks and the smoothness of fields of snow. The cow hairs made my nose itch and the straw poked at my legs. It was very dark.

Finally my father stopped the sleigh by our house and lifted me out. "Tell Mother I'll be in directly, soon as I unhitch," he said.

Despite the hot stones, my ankles were numb, and I tripped and fell as I ran to the house. My lip struck the gallon lard pail I used for a lunch bucket and stuck there. I lay tense and still in the snow waiting for it to stop sticking. Once my little

---

1. **amorphous** (ə·môr′fəs): shapeless.
2. **nonchalantly** (nän′shə·länt′lē): in a casual way.

3. **uncordially** (un·kôr′jəl·lē): in a not very friendly way.

sister caught her tongue on the pump handle because she wouldn't believe me when I told her it would stick. She jerked away in fear and tore bleeding skin from the tip of it. So I waited until I could feel the warmth of my breath free my lip before I moved.

The porch timbers creaked with cold, like thin ice. I could hear my mother yelling to me to get the snow off my clothes and to shut the door tight even before I opened it.

The top of the kitchen stove glowed gray-red through its iron lid, and the belly of the big round stove in the living room seemed stretched dangerously thin, as though it would surely melt soon and spill out its flaming coal on the floor. My mother had set the kerosene lamp on the warming-oven doors above the stove so she could see how much salt to put in the potatoes. I could smell the rabbit she was roasting in the oven for the dog.

My father came in the door, stomping snow clear across the kitchen, and demanded a teakettle of boiling water. Seeing that I still didn't have my snowsuit off, he told me to come with him to work the pump handle.

While he poured the boiling water down the pump, the steam running up into darkness, I struggled to free the handle, but I couldn't budge it. Even when he grasped it in his large thick leather mittens, it didn't move. "Well, it looks like we'll have to melt water for the stock. Take this back to the house." He handed me the teakettle.

I was glad we had to melt snow for water, because then my little sister and I could play a game called Eskimo. We stood on chairs, balancing ourselves imprudently near the searing surface of the stove to lean over the tub. As soon as the dry snow had melted a little, we began to mold the figures for an Eskimo village—Huskies, people, babies, igloos, polar bears, and walruses, just like the ones in the *Book of North American Mammals* my mother had got once in a set of books from the National Geographic Society. We conducted hunts and dog-sled treks and sent the Eskimos into the water to harpoon the seals that were languidly floating there. But as the water warmed, the seals disappeared, and it was death for the harpooners to go into the sea. While the shores of their iceland slipped away into the ocean, the frantic people moved higher and higher on the iceberg mountain. Perched on its slushy sides, they would see a small hole appear in their snow island. Then the sea would gush up through the hole, the island would break in pieces, and the ice people would fall into the fatal warmth. Just as the warm wave washed over my people, the game would become hideously real to me, and I would often have nightmares in which I was climbing, climbing, on an ever-collapsing mountain to escape a hot tide.

After supper my father set out for the barn with two pails of the snow water. I had to spend about a half hour, it seemed, getting my outside clothes on again so I could carry the lantern and open the barn door.

I was well acquainted with the shock of stepping from the warm kitchen into a winter night. But none of the freezing memories of the past could prepare me for the burning air that night. It was like strong hot smoke in my nostrils, so that for one confused instant I thought I was going to suffocate with the cold that was so cold it was hot. I gasped for breathable air, and my father said, "Don't do that! Breathe through your nose—your breath is warmer that way when it gets to your lungs."

We walked carefully down the hill to the barn; then I slithered down the steps chopped in a snowdrift in front of the door and slid it open. The barn was very old, but always before it had been warm with the heat of the animals kept in it all day long. But that night, being inside didn't seem to make any difference. I still had the kind of ache in my temples and cheekbones that I always got when I took too big a mouthful of ice cream. The cows shifted and swung their tails and wouldn't stand still to be milked. My father poured some milk into a pail and told me to feed it to the little new calf in a pen at the rear of the barn.

He had arrived out of season and was not yet two weeks old. Usually by the time the calves came, the mothers were outside all day, and both mothers and calves quickly got used to the idea of being separated. But we had been keeping all the stock inside for nearly a week, and neither cow nor calf was properly weaned. She lowed to him and he cried back to her; he was still determined to nurse. He was still stubbornly bucking and shoving his nose all the way to the bottom of the bucket, and desperately bunting the side of it when he got a noseful of milk. I liked him, though. His hair was almost as fine and soft as a human baby's, and he had a white star on his gleaming black forehead.

Although I had never seen cattle shiver, the little calf looked as though he was shivering as he advanced stiff-legged to our evening battle with the pail. I braced it against my shins and waited for him to begin bunting. At least a winter calf didn't damage you as much as a spring calf did; at the moment I was well padded with long underwear, two pairs of long stockings, and thick pants. I patted him between the ears and he sucked my fingers with his rough, strong tongue.

After the milking was done, we lugged the pails and lantern up the hill and started back for the barn with more water. In two more trips our toes felt numb and thickened, and we both had frost-bitten faces. I had the two white spots on my cheeks again and my father's high thin nose stood out bloodless against the chapped red of his face. We took a last look at the stock; there was nothing more we could do. There was no way to heat the barn, and the cows were already half covered with straw when they lay down. We rolled the door shut.

In the house we planned for the night ahead. My little sister and I would sleep in one bed, with all the blankets and quilts in the house over us, and my mother and father would use the feather tick[4] we had rolled up in a little storeroom we called the cubbyhole. When we opened the door of that little vault to get the tick, the frigid air pushed out across the living room like a low dark flood against our legs.

It took a long time to warm the tick and blankets from the unheated bedroom at the stove. We would hold them as close as we could to its hot belly, but as soon as the warmed section was moved away it grew cold again. We left the bedroom door open, but though the living room grew instantly colder, the bedroom grew no warmer.

While we were making the beds we puffed white clouds at each other across the mattresses. We heated our two sadirons[5] and wrapped them in towels, one for each bed. Then my father stoked both stoves full of coal, and we got under the piles of bedding.

My sister and I lay close together, our legs bent and our toes touching the wrapped-up iron. Partly because I couldn't get warm and partly because I was worried about some things, I couldn't get to sleep. I wanted to know what a cold wave was. In the long solitude of prairie childhood I had memorized two sets of books—the set from the National Geographic and a set called *A Childhood Treasury* that contained legends of many lands, my favorites being those from Scandinavia. How could it possibly be that so many things had happened before I was born? For instance, *The Book of North American Mammals* told of a time when the plains of Russia and of North America had borne glaciers a mile deep. And before the glaciers there had been vast herds of mammoths. There was a drawing of them lifting their shieldlike foreheads against a gray horizon, marching on tall shaggy legs over the frozen tundra—tundra that had once covered our wheatfields. The book told about how before the glacier finally came the weather had gotten colder and colder, so that the mammoths had to grow longer and longer hair.

But even with their long hair and clever trunks and sixteen-foot tusks curved in unlikely tangles of bone, they had been unable to defend themselves. Why? Under the picture it said that a herd of these mammoths evidently had been preserved intact for centuries, and that one of the discoverers had even tried eating the meat of a carcass thousands of years old. Why couldn't the huge and powerful creatures have run away? It must have been some kind of flood, I thought, like the flood we had in our garden after a cloud burst, only different and much bigger—a flood that could race with the speed of liquid one moment and turn completely solid the next, locking forever the great knees bending for another battling step, then the tusks fending off masses of debris, and finally

---

4. **feather tick:** folding mattress, covered with ticking (striped cloth).

5. **sadirons** (sad'ī·ərnz): long metal rods used as bedwarmers.

the long trunks flailing above the tide in search of air. A cold wave freezing so fast that the bubbles of their last breathing would be fixed like beads in the ice.

What if some polar impulse was now sending a flood to rise up out of the north, to flow swiftly over our house, becoming ice as the wind touched it, shutting us off from that strangling but precious air above us? I had heard of digging out of a house completely covered with snow—that used to happen in the days before I was born—but did anybody ever dig out of a glacier? I wanted to go and climb in bed with my mother and father and have them tell me that it wouldn't get to us, that it would stop at least as far away as Leeds, twenty miles to the north. But the last time I had tried to climb in with them they had told me not to be such a big baby, that I was a worse baby than my little sister. So I lay there wondering how far the cold had gotten.

Finally the morning came. I could look from my bed across the living room and into the kitchen where my father, in his sheepskin coat, was heating some water saved from the melted snow. The tub, refilled after we had emptied it for the stock, was standing in the corner of the kitchen next to the door. The snow in it was still heaped in a neat cone. It was odd to think of a tub of snow standing inside our house, where we had slept the night, and never feeling the warmth of the stove a few feet away—to think of how the tiny flow of air around the stormlined door was more powerful than the stove filled with coal.

I felt the excitement of sharing in heroic deeds as I pulled on the second pair of long wool stockings over my underwear and fastened them with the knobs and hooks on my garter belt. I was not going to school because it was too cold to take the horses out, so I was to help with the barn chores again.

The cattle were still huddled together in their one big stall. My father set down the pails and walked swiftly to the rear of the barn. The little calf was curled quietly against the corner of his pen. The black-and-white hairs over his small ribs did not move. My father climbed into the pen and brushed the straw away from the sleeping eyes, just to make sure.

I stood looking at the soft fine hair that was too fine and the big-kneed legs that were too thin, and it seemed to me that I now understood how it was with the mammoths in the Ice Age. One night they had lain down to sleep, leaning ponderously back to back, legs bent beneath warm bellies, tusks pointing up from the dying tundra. The blood under their incredible hides slowed a little, and the warmth of their bodies ascended in ghostly clouds toward the indifferent moon. There was no rushing, congealing wave; there was only the unalarmed cold sleep of betrayed creatures.

A couple of nights later, over at the store, the men talked of the figures Julius had gotten over the radio. There had been a dozen readings around fifty degrees below zero. Fifty-two at Bismarck, fifty-eight at Leeds, and sixty-one at Portal on the Canadian border.

"My termometer is bust before I see him in the morning!" shouted Mr. Buskowski. "I do not even from Russia remember such a night."

Hopelessly studying the candy counter, I realized that even my father had forgotten the stiff little black-and-white calf in the contemplation of that remarkable number. "Sixty-one below!" they said over and over again. "Sixty-one below!" The men didn't need to make legends anymore to comprehend the incomprehensible. They had the miraculous evidence of their thermometers. But for me that little death told what there was to know about the simple workings of immense catastrophe.

Responding to the Essay

Analyzing the Essay

Identifying Facts

1. Identify four or five "legends" mentioned in the first three paragraphs that the writer regrets happened before she was born.
2. Find five factual details in the first half of the selection that the writer uses to prove how severely cold the weather was.
3. Why is the "little new calf" kept in a pen away from its mother? What prevents the calf from being weaned properly?
4. List four things the girl and her family do to prepare for bed during the cold wave.
5. Explain what the girl originally thinks killed all the mammoths.

6. At the end of the story, what happens to the calf? What does seeing the calf make the girl realize about how the mammoths actually died?

Interpreting Meanings

7. Find details in the essay that reveal what the writer thought of the cold wave before, during, and after it.
8. In her last sentence, the writer reveals the **insight,** or clear understanding, she gained by experiencing the cold wave. Reread the sentence, and explain in your own words what the cold wave finally taught her.
9. Considering her thoughts and actions, list five or more words to describe the writer's person-

ality as a child. Which of these personality traits do you think the writer continues to have as an adult?

Applying Meanings

10. What other "little" events could reveal what immense catastrophes are really like? (Think of accounts you've read, or seen on TV, of tornadoes, floods, and explosions.)

Writing About the Essay

A Creative Response

1. **Conducting Interviews.** Perhaps people in your area have experienced something like the intense cold wave described in this essay. They might have lived through a hurricane, a flood, fire, a heat wave, drought, a blackout, a blizzard, a transit strike. Interview at least three people who have experienced the same event. After you have gathered your data, write a story telling what the event was like from the point of view of the people who lived through it. Before you begin interviewing, write down at least five questions you will ask. As you write your story, pay attention to the **5 W's and H** of news reporting: What? Who? When? Where? Why? and How?

   a. What happened?
   b. Whom did it happen to?
   c. When did it happen?
   d. Where did it happen?
   e. Why did it happen?
   f. How did it happen?

2. **Drawing a Sketch Map.** "The Cold Wave" is set in North Dakota. Several communities in the state, as well as a Canadian city, are mentioned in the selection. To get a better idea of the setting, look at maps of the area in an atlas or an encyclopedia. Then draw a sketch map (a rough map) of North Dakota and the states and Canadian provinces that border on it. Place on the map at least five communities in each state and province, including those mentioned in the selection. Also, include the main physical features, such as mountains and rivers.

A Critical Response

3. **Identifying the Main Idea.** Which of the following ideas is central to this essay?

a. The idea that cold severely affected the farmers' lives
b. The idea that we learn about huge catastrophes from "little" events
c. The idea that the present is just as interesting and exciting as the past.

In a paragraph, identify the main idea of the essay and write three sentences telling how the idea is developed.

Analyzing Language and Vocabulary

Modifiers in Descriptive Writing

Writers use **modifiers**—adjectives and adverbs—to make descriptions vivid and precise. Think about the italicized modifiers in the following sentences from "The Cold Wave." Then answer the questions.

1. "I would never know the *bitter* years that built the *grim* legends of our northern land."

   a. What might have happened in North Dakota to make whole years "bitter"?
   b. What might a "grim legend" be about?

2. ". . . a *vast* gloom in the sky sagged *low* over the town weighting the *rigid* streets with cold."

   a. What do you think the sky looked like?
   b. What do you think "rigid streets" are?

3. "The top of the kitchen stove glowed *gray-red* through its *iron* lid, and the belly of the *big round* stove in the living room seemed stretched *dangerously thin*, as though it would surely melt soon and spill out its *flaming* coal on the floor."

   a. Which modifiers help give a precise picture of the stoves?
   b. Which words make the stoves seem dangerous?

4. "There was no *rushing, congealing* wave; there was only the *unalarmed cold* sleep of *betrayed* creatures."

   a. What is a "congealing" wave?
   b. What is an "unalarmed cold sleep"?
   c. *Betrayed* is a strong word. How were the creatures "betrayed"?

GREEN GULCH

Loren Eiseley

Archaeologist Loren Eiseley (1907–1977) wrote many popular books about the mysteries of existence. His first book, called *The Immense Journey,* was a series of essays about how flowers transformed the earth and prepared it for human life. "The Green Gulch" is from a book called *The Night Country,* an autobiographical account of his childhood experiences in Nebraska. Eiseley's mother was deaf, and Eiseley, an only child, often felt he shared her silent, lonely world.

In the following essay, Eiseley relates an unforgettable childhood experience. As you read, look for his *theme,* or main idea—the general truth about life that he is talking about.

Connotations. All words have *denotations,* that is, strict dictionary definitions. Some words also have *connotations*—emotions and associations that have come to be attached to them. For example, if you called someone "curious," you would be saying something complimentary. You would mean that the person takes a lively interest in the world around her. But suppose you called the person "nosey." Your meaning would be basically the same. But *nosey* has bad connotations. It suggests someone who butts his or her nose into other people's business without being asked to. As you read Eiseley's essay, notice the words he chooses to describe this upsetting event in his young life.

W e stood in a wide flat field at sunset. For the life of me I can remember no other children before them. I must have run away and been playing by myself until I had wandered to the edge of the town. They were older than I and knew where they came from and how to get back. I joined them.

They were not going home. They were going to a place called Green Gulch. They came from some other part of town, and their clothes were rough, their eyes worldly and sly. I think, looking back, that it must have been a little like a child following goblins home to their hill at nightfall, but nobody threatened me. Besides, I was very small and did not know the way home, so I followed them.

Presently we came to some rocks. The place was well named. It was a huge pool in a sandstone basin, green and dark with the evening over it and the trees leaning secretly inward above the water. When you looked down, you saw the sky. I remember that place as it was when we came there. I remember the quiet and the green ferns touching the green water. I remember we played there, innocently at first.

But someone found the spirit of the place, a huge old turtle, asleep in the ferns. He was the last lord of the green water before the town poured over it. I saw his end. They pounded him to death with stones on the other side of the pool while I looked on in stupefied horror. I had never seen death before.

Suddenly, as I stood there small and uncertain and frightened, a grimy, splattered gnome who had been stooping over the turtle stood up with a rock in his hand. He looked at me, and around that little group some curious evil impulse passed like a wave. I felt it and drew back. I was alone there. They were not human.

I do not know who threw the first stone, who splashed water over my suit, who struck me first, or even who finally, among that ring of vicious faces, put me on my feet, dragged me to the roadside, pointed and said, roughly, "There's your road, kid, follow the street lamps. They'll take you home."

They stood in a little group watching me, nervous now, ashamed a little at the ferocious pack impulse toward the outsider that had swept over them.

I never forgot that moment.

I went because I had to, down that road with the wind moving in the fields. I went slowly from one spot of light to another and in between I thought the things a child thinks, so that I did not stop at any house nor ask anyone to help me when I came to the lighted streets.

I had discovered evil. It was a monstrous and corroding knowledge. It could not be told to adults because it was the evil of childhood in which no one believes. I was alone with it in the dark.

Responding to the Essay

Analyzing the Essay

Identifying Facts

1. Where and when does the writer say he met the older children? Explain why he joined them.
2. Describe the older children's clothes and eyes.
3. Describe what Green Gulch looks like. How do the children play there at first?
4. Tell what the older children do to "the spirit of the place," and then to the writer.
5. What does Eiseley say he discovered from his experience at Green Gulch? Why didn't he tell adults about what had happened?

Interpreting Meanings

6. What do you suppose Eiseley means when he calls the turtle "the spirit of the place"? Why do you think the children attacked it?
7. Why do you think Eiseley didn't join in with the other children at Green Gulch?
8. Eiseley says the children attacked him because of the "ferocious pack impulse toward the outsider." Why do you think the children saw Eiseley as an outsider, beyond the fact that he was standing apart? Why do you think the children felt the urge to attack him?
9. State Eiseley's **theme,** or main idea, in this personal essay. What general idea about human nature is he talking about? Do you agree?

Applying Meanings

10. Do you think people in groups generally act better or worse toward others than they do when they are alone?

Writing About the Essay

A Creative Response

1. **Using Another Point of View.** A personal essay, such as "Green Gulch," generally reveals a lot about the writer. It usually does not reveal much of the thoughts and feelings of other persons mentioned in the essay. You can gain additional understanding by filling in some details. In a paragraph, have the boy holding the rock describe his thoughts and feelings just as he looks at Eiseley. Write in the first person, using the personal pronoun *I*.

A Critical Response

2. **Comparing the Essay to a Poem.** Read the following poem by a modern English poet. Then write a paragraph telling how the poem is like Eiseley's essay. Before you write, you might want to consider these points:

   a. The topic of each piece of writing
   b. Words and phrases that are similar in each
   c. The speaker's feelings
   d. Your feelings

My Parents

My parents kept me from children who
    were rough
Who threw words like stones and who
    wore torn clothes.
Their thighs showed through rags.
    They ran in the street
And climbed cliffs and stripped by the
    country streams.

I feared more than tigers their muscles
5   like iron
Their jerking hands and their knees
    tight on my arms.
I feared the salt coarse pointing of
    those boys
Who copied my lisp behind me on the
    road.

They were lithe, they sprang out be-
    hind hedges
Like dogs to bark at my world. They
10   threw mud

While I looked the other way, pretend-
    ing to smile.
I longed to forgive them, but they
    never smiled.

—Stephen Spender

Analyzing Language and Vocabulary

Connotations

Some words, in addition to their strict dictionary meanings, carry certain feelings and associations. These feelings and associations are called a word's **connotations.**

1. Eiseley says the children's clothing was "rough." What feelings do you have when you hear the word *rough*?
2. Would your feelings change if Eiseley had described the clothes as "poor" or "worn-out"?
3. Eiseley calls the children "goblins" and refers to one as a "gnome." In fantasies, are goblins and gnomes usually good characters? Or are they slightly sinister?
4. What do you think goblins and gnomes look like?
5. Suppose Eiseley had described the children as "elves" or "leprechauns." How would you have felt about them?
6. Here are some other words with strong connotations for most people. List at least two things you associate with each word. Then compare your list with your classmates' lists. Do you all agree?

a. green	**d.** rats	
b. gold	**e.** lambs	
c. serpent	**f.** dove	

7. The following words have connotations but they differ for different people. What do you associate with these words? Do your classmates agree?

a. Republican	**d.** California	
b. Democrat	**e.** New York	
c. Liberal	**f.** Midwest	

Jewish dairyman of
Warsaw, Poland,
published in the Jewish
Daily Forward, November
11, 1923.

Courtesy of the Yivo Institute.

REB ASHER THE DAIRYMAN

Isaac Bashevis Singer

Isaac Bashevis Singer (1904–   ) grew up in a Jewish community in Poland. Singer's father, a rabbi, earned a meager living in Warsaw, Poland's largest city. The way of life that Singer describes in this excerpt from his autobiographical work *In My Father's Court* has vanished. It was destroyed during World War II, during the Holocaust or Shoah.

Like every good nonfiction writer, Singer has a *purpose* in writing about Reb Asher the dairyman. As you read this true story, try to discover Singer's purpose. Is it to explain or inform, or to create a mood and stir an emotion? Is it to tell about a series of events, or to persuade the reader to do or believe something? Or is it a combination of these?

There are some people in this world who are simply born good. Such was Reb[1] Asher the dairyman. God had endowed him with many, many gifts. He was tall, broad, strong, had a black beard, large black eyes, and the voice of a lion. On the New Year and the Day of Atonement[2] he served as cantor[3] of the main prayer for the congregation that met in our house, and it was his voice that attracted many of the worshipers. He did this without payment, although he could have commanded sizable fees from some of the larger synagogues. It was his way of helping my father earn a livelihood for the holidays. And as if this were not enough, Reb Asher was always doing something for us in one way or another. No one sent my father as generous a Purim[4] gift as did Reb Asher the dairyman. When Father found himself in great straits and could not pay the rent, he sent me to Reb Asher to borrow the money. And Asher never said no,

nor did he ever pull a wry face. He simply reached into his pants pocket and pulled out a handful of paper money and silver. Neither did he limit himself to helping out my father. He gave charity in all directions. This simple Jew, who with great difficulty plowed through a chapter of the Mishnah,[5] lived his entire life on the highest ethical plane. What others preached, he practiced.

He was no millionaire, he was not even wealthy, but he had a "comfortable income," as my father would put it. I myself often bought milk, butter, cheese, clabber,[6] and cream in his shop. His wife and their eldest daughter waited on customers all day long, from early in the morning till late at night. His wife was a stout woman, with a blond wig, puffy cheeks, and a neck covered with freckles. She was the daughter of a farm bailiff. Her enormous bosom seemed to be swollen with milk. I used to imagine that if someone were to cut her arm, milk would spurt out, not blood. One

---

1. **Reb:** Jewish title of respect; equivalent of *mister.*
2. **Day of Atonement,** or *Yom Kippur* (yôm kip′ər): sacred holiday on which Jews fast, express regret for bad deeds, and state their hope to perform good deeds during the upcoming year. The holiday falls in either September or October.
3. **cantor:** person who chants or sings parts of a Jewish service.
4. **Purim** (poor′im): holiday commemorating Queen Esther's deliverance of the Jews from a massacre plotted by the ancient Persian minister Haman. The holiday falls in either February or March.

5. **Mishnah:** compilation of Jewish laws and interpretations of the Bible.
6. **clabber:** thickly curdled sour milk.

son, Yudl, was so fat that people came to stare at him as at a freak. He weighed nearly three hundred and fifty pounds. Another son, slight of build and something of a dandy, had become a tailor and gone off to Paris. A younger son was still studying at cheder,[7] and a little girl attended a secular school.

Just as our house was always filled with problems, doubts, and unrest, so everything in Asher's house was whole, placid, healthy. Every day Asher went to bring the cans of milk from the train. He rose at dawn, went to the synagogue, and after breakfast drove to the railroad depot. He worked at least eighteen hours every day, yet on the Sabbath, instead of resting, he would go to listen to a preacher or come to my father to study a portion of the Pentateuch[8] with the commentary of Rashi. Just as he loved his work, so he loved his Judaism. It seems to me that I never heard this man say no. His entire life was one great yes.

Asher owned a horse and wagon, and this horse and wagon aroused a fierce envy in me. How happy must be the boy whose father owned a wagon, a horse, a stable! Every day Asher went off to distant parts of the city, even to Praga! Often I would see him driving past our building. He never forgot to lift his head and greet whomever he saw at the window or on the balcony. Often he met me when I was running about the streets with a gang of boys or playing with those who were not "my kind," but he never threatened to tell my father, nor did he try to lecture me. He did not, like the other grown-ups, pull little boys by the ear, pinch their noses, or twist the brims of their caps. Asher seemed to have an innate respect for everyone, big or small.

Once when I saw him driving by in his wagon I nodded to him and called out, "Reb Asher, take me along!"

Asher immediately stopped and told me to get on. We drove to a train depot. The trip took several hours and I was overjoyed. I rode amid trolley cars, droshkies, delivery vans. Soldiers marched;

policemen stood guard; fire engines, ambulances, even some of the automobiles that were just beginning to appear on the streets of Warsaw rushed past us. Nothing could harm me. I was protected by a friend with a whip, and beneath my feet I could feel the throbbing of the wheels. It seemed to me that all Warsaw must envy me. And indeed people stared in wonderment at the little Hasid[9] with the velvet cap and the red earlocks[10] who was riding in a milk wagon and surveying the city. It was evident that I did not really belong to this wagon, that I was a strange kind of tourist. . . .

From that day on, a silent pact existed between me and Reb Asher. Whenever he could, he would take me along as his passenger. Fraught with danger were those minutes when Reb Asher went off to fetch the milk cans from the train, or to attend to a bill, and I remained alone in the wagon. The horse would turn his head and stare at me in astonishment. Asher had given me the reins to hold, and the horse seemed to be saying silently, "Just look who is my driver now . . ." The fear that the horse might suddenly rear up and run off gave to these moments the extra fillip of peril. After all, a horse is not a child's plaything but a gigantic creature, silent, wild, with enormous strength. Occasionally a gentile[11] would pass by, look at me, laugh, and say something to me in Polish. I did not understand his language, and he cast the same sort of dread upon me as did the horse: He too was big, strong, and incomprehensible. He too might suddenly turn on me and strike me, or yank at my earlock—a pastime some Poles considered a great joke. . . .

When I thought the end had come—any moment now the gentile would strike me, or the horse would dash off and smash into a wall or a street lamp—then Reb Asher reappeared and all was well again. Asher carried the heavy milk cans with the ease of a Samson. He was stronger than the horse, stronger than the gentile, yet he had mild eyes and spoke my language, and he was my father's friend. I had only one desire: to ride with

---

7. **cheder** (khä′der): Jewish religious school for young children.
8. **Pentateuch** (pen′tə·to͞ok′): first five books of the Bible; also known as the Torah.

9. **Hasid** (has′id): member of a Jewish sect emphasizing mysticism and joyful worship.
10. **earlocks:** curls of hair hanging in front of the ears. The Hasidic interpretation of the Bible does not allow men to shave this part of the face.
11. **gentile:** non-Jew.

this man for days and nights over fields and through forests, to Africa, to America, to the ends of the world, and always to watch, to observe all that was going on around me. . . .

How different this same Asher seemed on the New Year and the Day of Atonement! Carpenters had put up benches in my father's study, and this was where the women prayed. The beds had been taken out of the bedroom, a Holy Ark[12] brought in, and it had become a tiny prayer house. Asher was dressed in a white robe, against which his black beard appeared even blacker. On his head he wore a high cap embroidered with gold and silver. At the beginning of the Additional Service, Reb Asher would ascend to the cantor's desk and recite in a lion's roar: "Behold me, destitute of good works . . ."

Our bedroom was too small for the bass voice that thundered forth from this mighty breast. It was heard halfway down the street. Asher recited and chanted. He knew every melody, every movement. The twenty men who made up our congregation were all part of his choir. Asher's deep masculine voice aroused a tumult in the women's section. True, they all knew him well. Only yesterday they had bought from him or from his wife a saucepan of milk, a pot of clabber, a few ounces of butter, and had bargained with him for a little extra. But now Asher was the delegate who offered up the prayers of the People of Israel directly to the Almighty, before the Throne of Glory, amid fluttering angels and books that read themselves, in which are recorded the good deeds and the sins of every mortal soul. . . . When he reached the prayer "We will express the might," and began to recite the destinies of men—who shall live and who shall die, who shall perish by fire and who by water—a sobbing broke out among the women. But when Asher called out triumphantly: "But repentance, prayer, and charity can avert the evil decree!"—then a heavy stone was taken from every heart. Soon Asher began to sing of the smallness of man and the greatness of God, and joy and comfort enveloped everyone. Why need men—who are but passing shadows, wilting blos-

soms—expect malice from a God who is just, revered, merciful? Every word that Asher called out, every note he uttered, restored courage, revived hope. We indeed are nothing, but He is all. We are but as dust in our lifetime, and less than dust after death, but He is eternal and His days shall never end. In Him, only in Him, lies our hope. . . .

One year, at the close of the Day of Atonement, this same Asher, our friend and benefactor, saved our very lives. It happened in this way. After the daylong fast, we had eaten a rich supper. Later a number of Jews gathered in our house to dance and rejoice. My father had already put up, in the courtyard, the first beam of the hut for the coming Feast of Tabernacles.[13] Late that night the family had at last fallen asleep. Since benches and pews had been set up in the bedroom, and the entire house was in disorder, each of us slept wherever he could find a spot. But one thing we had forgotten—to extinguish the candles that were still burning on some of the pews.

Late that night Asher had to drive to the railroad station to pick up milk. He passed our building and noticed that our apartment was unusually bright. This was not the glow of candles or a lamp, but the glare of a fire. Asher realized that our house must be burning. He rang the bell at the gate but the janitor did not rush to open it. He too was asleep. Then Asher set to ringing the bell and beating on the door, making such a commotion that at last the janitor awoke and opened the gate. Asher raced up the stairs and banged on our door, but no one answered. Then Asher the Mighty hurled his broad shoulders against the door and forced it open. Bursting into the apartment, he found the entire family asleep, while all around benches, prayer stands, and prayer books were aflame. He began to shout in his booming cantorial voice and finally roused us, and then he tore off our quilts and set to smothering the conflagration.

I remember that moment as though it was yesterday. I opened my eyes and saw many flames, large and small, rolling about and dancing like imps. My brother Moshe's blanket had already

---

12. **Holy Ark:** enclosure holding scrolls on which the Pentateuch, or Torah, is written.

13. **Feast of Tabernacles** (tab′ər·nak′′lz), or *Sukkot* (sook′ōt): festival celebrating the fall harvest and commemorating the wanderings of the Jews in the desert.

The Market Place, Vitebsk by Marc Chagall (1917). Oil.

Metropolitan Museum of Art, New York City.
Bequest of Scofield Thayer.

caught fire. But I was young and was not frightened. On the contrary, I liked the dancing flames.

After some time the fire was put out. Here indeed something had happened that might well be called a miracle. A few minutes more, and we all would have been taken by the flames, for the wood of the benches was dry and they were saturated with the tallow of the dripping candles. Asher was the only human being awake at that hour, the only one who would ring the bell so persistently and risk his own life for us. Yes, it was fated that this faithful friend should save us from the fire.

We were not even able to thank him. It was as though we had all been struck dumb. Asher himself was in a hurry and left quickly. We wandered about amid the charred benches, tables, prayer books, and prayer shawls, and every few minutes

we discovered more sparks and smoldering embers. We all might easily have been burned to cinders.

The friendship between my father and Reb Asher grew ever stronger, and during the war years, when we were close to starvation, Asher again helped us in every way he could.

After we had left Warsaw (during the First World War), we continued to hear news of him from time to time. One son died, a daughter fell in love with a young man of low origins and Asher was deeply grieved. I do not know whether he lived to see the Nazi occupation of Warsaw. He probably died before that. But such Jews as he were dragged off to the death camps. May these memoirs serve as a monument to him and his like, who lived in sanctity and died as martyrs.

Responding to the Essay

Analyzing the Essay

Identifying Facts

1. List three of Reb Asher's actions that support Singer's opening statement that Reb Asher was "born good."
2. When Singer was a boy, what made trips to the train depot so special for him? What frightened him during these trips?
3. Describe how Asher saved the lives of Singer's family.
4. What does Singer say must have happened to Asher if he lived to see the Nazi occupation of Warsaw? What is Singer's **purpose** in writing this essay?

Interpreting Meanings

5. Nonfiction writers use the same techniques as fiction writers to create memorable characters. Find one example of each of the following techniques in Singer's portrait of Asher:

   a. Direct comment on character traits
   b. Description of physical appearance
   c. Descriptions of character's actions
   d. Character's own words
   e. What others say and think about the character

6. Singer's piece recalls a way of life that no longer exists in Poland. List three details of setting that Singer uses to help you visualize Warsaw in the early twentieth century.

7. A nonfiction writer usually has one or more of the following **purposes** in writing: to explain or inform, to create a mood or stir an emotion, to tell about events, or to persuade the reader to do or believe something. Find evidence in the essay that Singer intends each of these things.

Applying Meanings

8. Do you agree or disagree with Singer's opening statement that there are some people who are "simply born good"? If you disagree, explain what you think makes people generous, kind, and caring, as Reb Asher was. If you agree, is it then possible that some people are "born bad"? Explain what you think causes extremely bad behavior.

Writing About the Essay

A Creative Response

1. **Writing a Character Sketch.** Review your answers to question 5, and think about the techniques Singer uses to create his memorable portrait of Reb Asher. Then choose a family member, friend, or neighbor—someone you know well. In three paragraphs, write a character sketch of that person using some of Singer's techniques.

A Critical Response

2. **Supporting a Topic Statement.** *"His entire life was one great yes."* In a paragraph, cite details that support this statement about Reb Asher.

Focusing on Background
Singer Talks About His Writing

"If I were to become for a moment a critic of my own writing, I would say that it always stresses the power of the spirit over the body in one way or another. I don't feel that life is nothing but a kind of chemical or physical accident, but there is always a plan behind it. I believe in Providence. I believe in spiritual powers, good and evil. The supernatural is always in my writing and somehow I always wanted to say to the reader that even though life looks to us chaotic, it is not as chaotic as we think. There is a scheme and a design behind it. But this is only one of many interpretations. This is my interpretation at this moment. I myself could find others in other moments or in other moods."

—Isaac Bashevis Singer

BROTHER

Maya Angelou

Autobiographies describe not only significant events in the writer's life but also significant people. All of us know people who have shaped our characters and influenced our lives for better or worse. For Maya Angelou (1928–   ), one of the most significant influences during her childhood in Arkansas was her brother Bailey. The following selection is taken from her autobiography *I Know Why the Caged Bird Sings*. Her attitude toward her brother is clear from the very first sentence. As you read, look for all the evidence Angelou gives to prove why she thinks Bailey is "the greatest person."

Maya Angelou. Photo by Jill Krementz.

Bailey was the greatest person in my world. And the fact that he was my brother, my only brother, and I had no sisters to share him with, was such good fortune that it made me want to live a Christian life just to show God that I was grateful. Where I was big, elbowy, and grating, he was small, graceful, and smooth. . . . He was lauded for his velvet-black skin. His hair fell down in black curls, and my head was covered with black steel wool. And yet he loved me.

When our elders said unkind things about my features (my family was handsome to a point of pain for me), Bailey would wink at me from across the room, and I knew that it was a matter of time before he would take revenge. He would allow the old ladies to finish wondering how on earth I came about, then he would ask, in a voice like cooling bacon grease, "Oh Mizeriz Coleman, how is your son? I saw him the other day, and he looked sick enough to die."

Aghast, the ladies would ask, "Die? From what? He ain't sick."

And in a voice oilier than the one before, he'd answer with a straight face, "From the Uglies."

I would hold my laugh, bite my tongue, grit my teeth and very seriously erase even the touch of a smile from my face. Later, behind the house by the black-walnut tree, we'd laugh and laugh and howl.

Bailey could count on very few punishments for his consistently outrageous behavior, for he was the pride of the Henderson/Johnson family.[1]

His movements, as he was later to describe those of an acquaintance, were activated with oiled precision. He was also able to find more hours in the day than I thought existed. He finished chores, homework, read more books than I, and played the group games on the side of the hill with the best of them. He could even pray out loud in church, and was apt at stealing pickles from the barrel that sat under the fruit counter and Uncle Willie's nose.

Once when the Store[2] was full of lunchtime customers, he dipped the strainer, which we also used to sift weevils[3] from meal and flour, into the barrel and fished for two fat pickles. He caught them and hooked the strainer onto the side of the barrel where they dripped until he was ready for them. When the last school bell rang, he picked the nearly dry pickles out of the strainer, jammed them into his pockets and threw the strainer behind the oranges. We ran out of the Store. It was summer and his pants were short, so the pickle juice made clean streams down his ashy legs, and he jumped with his pockets full of loot and his eyes laughing a "How about that?" He smelled like a vinegar barrel or a sour angel.

After our early chores were done, while Uncle Willie or Momma minded the Store, we were free to play the children's games as long as we stayed within yelling distance. Playing hide-and-seek, his voice was easily identified, singing, "Last night, night before, twenty-four robbers at my door. Who all is hid? Ask me to let them in, hit 'em in the head with a rolling pin. Who all is hid?" In follow the leader, naturally he was the one who created the most daring and interesting things to do. And when he was on the tail of the pop the whip, he would twirl off the end like a top, spinning, falling, laughing, finally stopping just before my heart beat its last, and then he was back in the game, still laughing.

Of all the needs (there are none imaginary) a lonely child has, the one that must be satisfied, if there is going to be hope and a hope of wholeness, is the unshaking need for an unshakable God. My pretty black brother was my Kingdom Come.

---

1. **Henderson/Johnson family:** Angelou's grandmother's last name was Henderson; her mother's married name was Johnson.

2. **Store:** the children lived for a time with their grandmother, who ran a general store in Stamps, Arkansas.
3. **weevils** (wē′v′lz): insects that are a kind of beetle.

Responding to the Selection

Analyzing the Selection

Identifying Facts

1. Describe Bailey's physical appearance. How does the writer describe her own appearance as a child?
2. An **anecdote** is a very brief story that is told to make a point. Cite two anecdotes that Maya Angelou uses to show that Bailey's behavior could be outrageous.

Interpreting Meanings

3. The writer **characterizes** her brother by using the same techniques short-story writers use to create imaginary characters. She describes his appearance, tells us what he does, what he says, and what others think of him. From reading about Bailey, list three of his **character traits.**
4. Why do you suppose the writer believes that Bailey is "the greatest person" in her world? Why doesn't she resent the attention he receives and the fact that he is never punished?
5. Explain what you think Angelou means in the last sentence: "My pretty black brother was my Kingdom Come."

Applying Meanings

6. The writer describes what she considers her unattractive appearance and then says, "And yet he loved me." How important do you think a person's physical appearance is in making that person "lovable"? What seems to have been Angelou's view about this when she was a child? What was Bailey's opinion?

Writing About the Selection

A Creative Response

1. **Imitating the Writer's Technique.** Angelou describes three outdoor games she and Bailey played as children. In a paragraph, describe an outdoor game you played when you were younger. Tell how and where the game was played. Describe any special chants or rhymes that went with the game. Include specific details about how you felt when you played this game.

A Critical Response

2. **Summarizing a Passage.** In a paragraph of not more than ten sentences, summarize what the writer says in "Brother." Remember that a summary should include only the main points, not details. It will be helpful to list what you consider to be the main points before you write the paragraph.

Analyzing Language and Vocabulary

Images

Maya Angelou uses contrasting images to focus our attention not only on the differences between herself and Bailey, but also on Bailey's various personality traits.

1. "Where I was big, elbowy, and grating, he was small, graceful, and smooth."

   a. What do you think *elbowy* means?
   b. What aspects of appearance and personality do *grating* and *smooth* describe?

2. "His hair fell down in black curls, and my head was covered with black steel wool."

   a. What does steel wool feel like?
   b. Why do you think Angelou believed that curls were more desirable?

3. "He could even pray out loud in church, and was apt at stealing pickles from the barrel. . . ."

   a. What are the contrasting images here?
   b. What do they reveal about Bailey's personality?

KEAHDINEKEAH

N. Scott Momaday

Pulitzer-Prize winner N. Scott Momaday (1934–   ) had a Kiowa father and a mother who was part Cherokee. He was born in Lawton, Oklahoma, and grew up on Indian reservations in the southwest, where his parents were teachers. "Keahdinekeah" is taken from one of his books called *The Names,* which he published in 1976. This memoir traces Momaday's ancestry and tells of his early years in the Jemez Pueblo and on the Jicarilla and Navaho reservations.

Keahdinekeah is the writer's great-grandmother. She was a Kiowa, whose name means "Throwing It Down."

In this excerpt, Momaday describes an afternoon when he and Keahdinekeah reached across four generations. Think back to a time when you met an elderly relative or other adult. What was that person like? What did you say to each other, and how did you feel?

A Kiowa Flute Player by Hokeah.

We set out, my father and I, in the afternoon. We walk down the long grade to the ravine that runs diagonally below, up again and through the brambles. The sun burns my skin. I feel the stiff spines and furry burrs at my legs and hear the insects humming there all around. We walk down into the shadows of Rainy Mountain Creek. The banks are broad and the mud is dry and cracked, broken into innumerable large facets like shards[1] of pottery, smooth, delicately curved, where the water has risen and then withdrawn and the sun has baked the bank. The water is brown and runs very slowly at the surface; here and there are glints of light and beams that strike through the trees and splash on the rocks and roots and underbrush. We cross the creek on a log and climb up the west bank where the woods are thicker. There is a small clearing, and inside the clearing is a single tree that was bent down to the ground and tied as a sapling; and so it remains curved, grown over in a long, graceful arc, its nimble new branches brushing whorls on the ground. It is one of my delights, for it is a wonderful, lively swing. My father lifts me up and I take hold of the slender, tapered trunk, and then he pulls me down and lets me go. I spring up, laughing, laughing, and bob up and down.

We continue on, through fields now, to "across the creek," as the house there was always called when I was a child. It is Keahdinekeah's house, built for her by my grandfather; but when you are a child you don't think of houses as possessions; it does not occur to you that anyone has ownership in them. "Across the creek" is where Justin Lee lives, a cousin not much older than I, with his sister, Lela, and his parents, Jim and Dorothy Ware, and his grandmother Keahdinekeah.

It seems reasonable to suppose that I visited my great-grandmother on other occasions, but I remember only this once, and I remember it very well. My father leads me into her room. It is dark and close inside, and I cannot see until my eyes become accustomed to the dim light. There is a certain odor in the room and not elsewhere in the house, the odor of my great-grandmother's old

Woman Doing Beadwork on Buckskin Shirt by Blue Eagle.

Courtesy School of American Research, Santa Fe, New Mexico.

age. It is not unpleasant, but it is most particular and exclusive, as much hers as is her voice or her hair or the nails of her hands. Such a thing has not only the character of great age but something also of the deep self, of one's own dignity and well-being. Because of this, I believe, this old blind woman is like no one I have ever seen or shall ever see. To a child her presence is formidable. My father is talking to her in Kiowa, and I do not understand what is being said, only that the talk is of me. She is seated on the side of her bed, and my father brings me to stand directly in front of her. She reaches out for me and I place my hands in hers. *Eh neh neh neh neh.* She begins to weep very softly in a high, thin, hollow voice. Her hands are little and soft, so soft that they seem not to consist in flesh and bone, but in the softest fiber, cotton or fine wool. Her voice is so delicate, so surely expressive of her deep feelings. Long afterward I think: That was a wonderful and beautiful thing that happened in my life. There, on that warm, distant afternoon: an old woman and a child, holding hands across the generations. There is great good in such a remembrance; I cannot imagine that it might have been lost upon me.

---

1. **shards:** broken pieces.

Responding to the Essay

Analyzing the Essay

Identifying Facts

1. List five or more details of the landscape through which the writer and his father walk.
2. Describe the swing in the clearing, and explain how it works.
3. Explain in detail what Keahdinekeah looks like.
4. Tell what Keahdinekeah does when the writer is brought directly before her. What feelings does the writer have about this memory?

Interpreting Meanings

5. This excerpt is overflowing with **images** that appeal to the senses. Make a chart with the headings *Sight, Hearing, Smell, Taste,* and *Touch.* Under each heading, list examples from the selection. Does Momaday appeal to all five senses in this excerpt?
6. Why do you suppose Keahdinekeah wept when she held her great-grandson's hand? What did Momaday understand this weeping to mean?

Applying Meanings

7. Compare Momaday's experience with his great-grandmother to your own experience of visiting a very old person. What similarities and differences can you find?

Writing About the Essay

A Creative Response

Writing an Autobiographical Excerpt. Momaday writes of his visit to his great-grandmother, "That was a wonderful and beautiful thing that happened in my life. . . . There is great good in such a remembrance; I cannot imagine that it might have been lost upon me." Recall an experience that was "a wonderful and beautiful thing" in your life. Describe the experience in two or three paragraphs, using present-tense verbs and sensory details as Momaday does.

Analyzing Language and Vocabulary

The Meanings of Names

When he was born, Momaday was given the Kiowa name Tsoia-talee, which means "Rock-Tree Boy." He was named for a sacred place: Tsoia, or "Rock Tree," the Kiowa name for Devils Tower in northeastern Wyoming. Devils Tower is a volcanic rock tower that rises about 1,280 feet from a river bed.

Most first names have meanings. Here are the meanings of some names common in the United States.

> Thomas, "a twin" (from Arabic *tē'ōma*)
> Barbara, "foreign, strange" (from Latin *barbarus*)
> Angela, "angel" (from Latin *angelicus* and Greek *angelikos*)
> Michael, "Who is like God" (from Hebrew *mīkhā'ēl*)

If you do not already know, find out the meaning of your own first name and of the first names of five relatives or friends. Ask people, look in a dictionary or other reference book, or consult a baby name book.

Focusing on Background
The Writer on His Subject

"I count myself very fortunate to have known my Kiowa great-grandmother. In general the American Indian has great respect for old people. Age iself is considered a state of honor, an achievement that deserves to be revered for its own sake. I am glad to write about the old people in my life. They have been, and they continue to be, important to me."

—N. Scott Momaday

The building that served
as the hiding place of
Anne Frank.

A TRAGEDY REVEALED:
A HEROINE'S LAST DAYS

Ernst Schnabel

All the other selections in this unit express personal points of view. All these other writers focus on personal experiences—important events, characters, and places in their own lives. In "A Tragedy Revealed," German writer Ernst Schnabel (1913–   ) writes a report on another person. The report was published in *Life* magazine in 1958.

The main purpose of a report is to inform—to present facts in an accurate and objective manner. An *accurate* reporter has the facts straight and presents them clearly. An *objective* reporter is fair—he or she does not let personal opinions get in the way of presenting the truth. Another im-portant element of a report is human interest. These are details that help us see the way events affected ordinary people.

This reporter assumes you know the story of Anne Frank and of how she died in a concentration camp after twenty-five months of hiding in an attic in Amsterdam. A play based on Anne's now-famous diary begins on page 224 of this book.

After you read the first six paragraphs of Schnabel's report, think about how he interests you in Anne Frank. Then finish reading the report. What other techniques does Schnabel use to hook your interest?

Last year in Amsterdam I found an old reel of movie film on which Anne Frank appears. She is seen for only ten seconds and it is an accident that she is there at all.

The film was taken for a wedding in 1941, the year before Anne Frank and seven others went into hiding in their "Secret Annexe." It has a flickering, Chaplinesque[1] quality with people popping suddenly in and out of doorways, the nervous smiles and hurried waves of the departing bride and groom.

Then, for just a moment, the camera seems uncertain where to look. It darts to the right, then to the left, then whisks up a wall, and into view comes a window crowded with people waving after the departing automobiles. The camera swings farther to the left to another window. There a girl stands alone, looking out into space. It is Anne Frank.

Just as the camera is about to pass on, the child moves her head a trifle. Her face flits more into focus, her hair shimmers in the sun. At this moment she discovers the camera, discovers the photographer, discovers us watching seventeen years later, and laughs at all of us, laughs with sudden merriment and surprise and embarrassment all at the same time.

> **Quotations in Reports.** Much of Schnabel's report consists of quoted responses from the people he interviewed. Responses as informative and stirring as these here usually emerge only after carefully planned questioning. Then the writer must edit the responses to eliminate boring, repetitive, or irrelevant remarks. Finally the writer must organize the responses in the most effective way possible. As you read the quotations that Schnabel uses, try to think of the questions he asked to get those responses.

---

1. **Chaplinesque** (chap'lin·esk'): like the old silent films starring Charlie Chaplin (1889–1977).

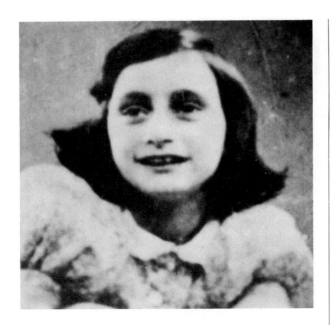

I asked the projectionist to stop the film for a moment so that we could stand up to examine her face more closely. The smile stood still, just above our heads. But when I walked forward close to the screen the smile ceased to be a smile. The face ceased to be a face, for the canvas screen was granular[2] and the beam of light split into a multitude of tiny shadows, as if it had been scattered on a sandy plain.

Anne Frank, of course, is gone too, but her spirit has remained to stir the conscience of the world. Her remarkable diary has been read in almost every language. I have seen a letter from a teen-aged girl in Japan who says she thinks of Anne's Secret Annexe as her second home. And the play based on the diary has been a great success wherever it is produced. German audiences, who invariably greet the final curtain of *The Diary of Anne Frank* in stricken silence, have jammed the theaters in what seems almost a national act of penance.

Last year I set out to follow the fading trail of this girl who has become a legend. The trail led from Holland to Poland and back to Germany, where I visited the moss-grown site of the old Bergen-Belsen concentration camp at the village of Belsen and saw the common graves shared by Anne Frank and thirty thousand others. I interviewed forty-two people who knew Anne or who survived the ordeal that killed her. Some had known her intimately in those last tragic months. In the recollections of others she appears only for a moment. But even these fragments fulfill a promise. They make explicit a truth implied in the diary. As we somehow knew she must be, Anne Frank, even in the most frightful extremity, was indomitable.

The known story contained in the diary is a simple one of human relationships, of the poignant maturing of a perceptive girl who is thirteen when her diary begins and only fifteen when it ends. It is a story without violence, though its background is the most dreadful act of violence in the history of man, Hitler's annihilation of six million European Jews.

In the summer of 1942 Anne Frank, her father, her mother, her older sister Margot, and four others were forced into hiding during the Nazi occupation of Holland. Their refuge was a tiny apartment they called the Secret Annexe, in the back of an Amsterdam office building. For twenty-five months the Franks, the Van Daan family, and later a dentist, Albert Düssel, lived in the Secret Annexe, protected from the Gestapo[3] only by a swinging bookcase which masked the entrance to their hiding place and by the heroism of a few Christians who knew they were there. Anne Frank's diary recounts the daily pressures of their cramped existence: the hushed silences when strangers were in the building, the diminishing food supply, the fear of fire from the incessant Allied[4] air raids, the hopes for an early invasion, above all the dread of capture by the pitiless men who were hunting Jews from house to house and sending them to concentration camps. Anne's di-

---

2. **granular:** uneven, bumpy.

3. **Gestapo** (ge·stä′pō): Nazi secret police force, noted for terrorism and atrocities.
4. **Allied:** In World War II the Allied nations (mainly Great Britain, the United States, and the Soviet Union) fought the Axis nations (mainly Germany, Italy, and Japan). Germany occupied The Netherlands during the war. The Allied air raids there were part of an attempt to oust the Germans.

ary also describes with sharp insight and youthful humor the bickerings, the wounded prides, the tearful reconciliations of the eight human beings in the Secret Annexe. It tells of Anne's wishes for the understanding of her adored father, of her despair at the gulf between her mother and herself, of her tremulous and growing love for young Peter Van Daan.

The actual diary ends with an entry for August 1, 1944, in which Anne Frank, addressing her imaginary friend Kitty, talks of her impatience with her own unpredictable personality. The stage version goes further: It attempts to reconstruct something of the events of August 4, 1944, the day the Secret Annexe was violated and its occupants finally taken into a captivity from which only one returned.

What really happened on that August day fourteen years ago was far less dramatic than what is now depicted on the stage. The automobiles did not approach with howling sirens, did not stop with screaming brakes in front of the house on the Prinsengracht canal in Amsterdam. No rifle butt pounded against the door until it reverberated as it now does in the theater every night somewhere in the world. The truth was, at first, that no one heard a sound.

It was midmorning on a bright summer day. In the hidden apartment behind the secret bookcase there was a scene of relaxed domesticity. The Franks, the Van Daans, and Mr. Düssel had finished a poor breakfast of ersatz coffee[5] and bread. Mrs. Frank and Mrs. Van Daan were about to clear the table. Mr. Van Daan, Margot Frank, and Mr. Düssel were resting or reading. Anne Frank was very likely at work on one of the short stories she often wrote when she was not busy with her diary or her novel. In Peter Van Daan's tiny attic room Otto Frank was chiding the eighteen-year-old boy for an error in his English lesson. "Why, Peter," Mr. Frank was saying, "you know that *double* is spelled with only one *b*."

In the main part of the building four other people, two men and two women, were working at their regular jobs. For more than two years these four had risked their lives to protect their friends in the hideout, supplied them with food and brought them news of a world from which they had disappeared. One of the women was Miep, who had just got married a few months earlier. The other was Elli, a pretty typist of twenty-three. The men were Kraler and Koophuis, middle-aged spice merchants who had been business associates of Otto Frank's before the occupation. Mr. Kraler was working in one office by himself. Koophuis and the two women were in another.

I spoke to Miep, Elli, and Mr. Koophuis in Amsterdam. The two women had not been arrested after the raid on the Secret Annexe. Koophuis had been released in poor health after a few weeks in prison, and Kraler, who now lives in Canada, had eventually escaped from a forced labor camp.

Elli, now a mother whose coloring and plump good looks are startlingly like those of the young women painted by the Dutch masters,[6] recalled: "I was posting entries in the receipts book when a car drove up in front of the house. But cars often stopped, after all. Then the front door opened, and someone came up the stairs. I wondered who it could be. We often had callers. Only this time I could hear that there were several men. . . ."

Miep, a delicate, intelligent, still young-looking woman, said: "The footsteps moved along the corridor. Then a door creaked, and a moment later the connecting door to Mr. Kraler's office opened, and a fat man thrust his head in and said in Dutch: 'Quiet. Stay in your seats.' I started and at first did not know what was happening. But then, suddenly, I knew."

Mr. Koophuis is now in very poor health, a gaunt,[7] white-haired man in his sixties. He added: "I suppose I did not hear them because of the rumbling of the spice mills in the warehouse. The fat man's head was the first thing I knew. He came in and planted himself in front of us. 'You three stay here, understand?' he barked. So we stayed in the office and listened as someone else went

---

5. **ersatz** (ur′säts) **coffee:** artificial substitute coffee, not brewed from coffee beans. Regular coffee was unavailable because of severe shortages.

6. **Dutch masters:** great Dutch painters of the seventeenth century. These painters included Rembrandt van Rijn (rīn), Frans Hals, and Jan Vermeer (vər·me′).

7. **gaunt:** thin and bony, hollow-eyed.

upstairs, and doors rattled, and then there were footsteps everywhere. They searched the whole building.''

Mr. Kraler wrote me this account from Toronto: ''A uniformed staff sergeant of the Occupation Police[8] and three men in civilian clothes entered my office. They wanted to see the storerooms in the front part of the building. All will be well, I thought, if they don't want to see anything else. But after the sergeant had looked at everything, he went out into the corridor, ordering me again to come along. At the end of the corridor they drew their revolvers all at once and the sergeant ordered me to push aside the bookcase and open the door behind it. I said: 'But there's only a bookcase there!' At that he turned nasty, for he knew everything. He took hold of the bookcase and pulled. It yielded and the secret door was exposed. Perhaps the hooks had not been properly fastened. They opened the door and I had to precede them up the steps. The policemen followed me. I could feel their pistols in my back. I was the first to enter the Franks' room. Mrs. Frank was standing at the table. I made a great effort and managed to say: 'The Gestapo is here.' ''

Otto Frank, now sixty-eight, has remarried and lives in Switzerland. Of the eight who lived in the Secret Annexe, he is the only survivor. A handsome, soft-spoken man of obviously great intelligence, he regularly answers correspondence that comes to him about his daughter from all over the world. He recently went to Hollywood for consultation on the movie version of *The Diary of Anne Frank*. About the events of that August morning in 1944 Mr. Frank told me: ''I was showing Peter Van Daan his spelling mistakes when suddenly someone came running up the stairs. The steps creaked, and I started to my feet, for it was morning when everyone was supposed to be quiet. But then the door flew open and a man stood before us holding his pistol aimed at my chest.

''In the main room the others were already assembled. My wife and the children and Van Daans were standing there with raised hands.

Then Albert Düssel came in, followed by another stranger. In the middle of the room stood a uniformed policeman. He stared into our faces.

'' 'Where are your valuables?' he asked. I pointed to the cupboard where my cashbox was kept. The policeman took it out. Then he looked around and his eye fell on the leather briefcase where Anne kept her diary and all her papers. He opened it and shook everything out, dumped the contents on the floor so that Anne's papers and notebooks and loose sheets lay scattered at our feet. No one spoke, and the policeman didn't even glance at the mess on the floor as he put our valuables into the briefcase and closed it. He asked us whether we had any weapons. But we had none, of course. Then he said, 'Get ready.' ''

Who betrayed the occupants of the Secret Annexe? No one is sure, but some suspicion centers on a man I can only call M., whom the living remember as a crafty and disagreeable sneak. He was a warehouse clerk hired after the Franks moved into the building, and he was never told of their presence. M. used to come to work early in the mornings, and he once found a locked briefcase which Mr. Van Daan had carelessly left in the office, where he sometimes worked in the dead of night. Though Kraler claimed it was his own briefcase, it is possible the clerk suspected. Little signs lead to bigger conclusions. In the course of the months he had worked in the building, M. might have gathered many such signs: the dial on the office radio left at BBC[9] by nocturnal[10] listeners, slight rearrangements in the office furniture and, of course, small inexplicable sounds from the back of the building.

M. was tried later by a war crimes court, denied everything and was acquitted. No one knows where he is now. I made no effort to find him. Neither did I search out Silberthaler, the German police sergeant who made the arrest. The betrayers would have told me nothing.

Ironically enough, the occupants of the Secret Annexe had grown optimistic in the last weeks of their self-imposed confinement. The terrors of

---

8. **Occupation Police:** police organized by the Germans, who occupied The Netherlands.

9. **BBC:** short for British Broadcasting Corporation. People listened illegally to the BBC for more accurate news of the war than German-controlled broadcasters offered.
10. **nocturnal** (näk·tur'n'l): nighttime.

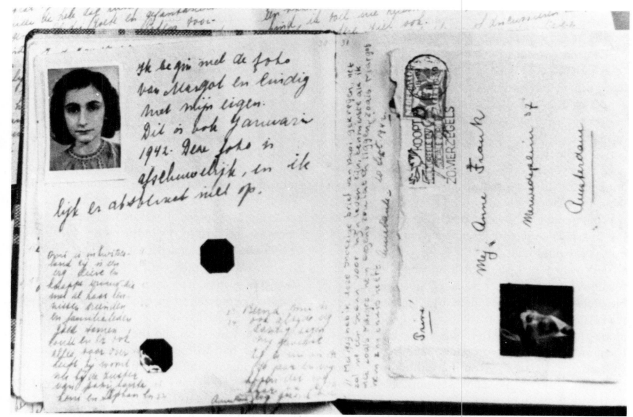

Pages from Anne Frank's diary.

those first nights had largely faded. Even the German army communiqués[11] made clear that the war was approaching an end. The Russians were well into Poland. On the Western front Americans had broken through at Avranches and were pouring into the heart of France. Holland must be liberated soon. In her diary Anne Frank wrote that she thought she might be back in school by fall.

Now they were all packing. Of the capture Otto Frank recalled: "No one wept. Anne was very quiet and composed, only just as dispirited as the rest of us. Perhaps that was why she did not think to take along her notebooks, which lay scattered about on the floor. But maybe she too had the premonition[12] that all was lost now, everything, and so she walked back and forth and did not even glance at her diary."

---

11. **communiqués** (kə·myoo′nə·kāz′): official communications or bulletins.
12. **premonition** (prē′mə·nish′ən): feeling that something will happen.

As the captives filed out of the building, Miep sat listening. "I heard them going," she said, "first in the corridor and then down the stairs. I could hear the heavy boots and the footsteps, and then the very light footsteps of Anne. Through the years she had taught herself to walk so softly that you could hear her only if you knew what to listen for. I did not see her, for the office door was closed as they all passed by."

At Gestapo headquarters the prisoners were interrogated only briefly. As Otto Frank pointed out to his questioners, it was unlikely, after twenty-five months in the Secret Annexe, that he would know the whereabouts of any other Jews who were hiding in Amsterdam.

The Franks, the Van Daans, and Düssel were kept at police headquarters for several days, the men in one cell, the women in the other. They were relatively comfortable there. The food was better than the food they had had in the Secret Annexe and the guards left them alone.

Suddenly, all eight were taken to the railroad station and put on a train. The guards named their destination: Westerbork, a concentration camp for Jews in Holland, about eighty miles from Amsterdam. Mr. Frank said: "We rode in a regular passenger train. The fact that the door was bolted did not matter very much. We were together and had been given a little food for the journey. We were actually cheerful. Cheerful, at least, when I compare that journey to our next. We had already anticipated the possibility that we might not remain in Westerbork to the end. We knew what was happening to Jews in Auschwitz. But weren't the Russians already deep into Poland? We hoped our luck would hold.

"As we rode, Anne would not move from the window. It was summer outside. Meadows, stubble fields, and villages flew by. The telephone wires along the right of way curved up and down along the windows. After two years it was like freedom for her. Can you understand that?"

Among the names given me of survivors who had known the Franks at Westerbork was that of a Mrs. de Wiek, who lives in Apeldoorn, Holland. I visited Mrs. de Wiek in her home. A lovely, gracious woman, she told me that her family, like the Franks, had been in hiding for months before their capture. She said: "We had been at Westerbork three or four weeks when the word went around that there were new arrivals. News of that kind ran like wildfire through the camp, and my daughter Judy came running to me, calling, 'New people are coming, Mama!'

"The newcomers were standing in a long row in the mustering square,[13] and one of the clerks was entering their names on a list. We looked at them, and Judy pressed close against me. Most of the people in the camp were adults, and I had often wished for a young friend for Judy, who was only fifteen. As I looked along the line, fearing I might see someone I knew, I suddenly exclaimed, 'Judy, see!'

"In the long line stood eight people whose faces, white as paper, told you at once that they had been hiding and had not been in the open air

for years. Among them was this girl. And I said to Judy, 'Look, there is a friend for you.'

"I saw Anne Frank and Peter Van Daan every day in Westerbork. They were always together, and I often said to my husband, 'Look at those two beautiful young people.'

"Anne was so radiant that her beauty flowed over into Peter. Her eyes glowed and her movements had a lilt to them. She was very pallid at first, but there was something so attractive about her frailty and her expressive face that at first Judy was too shy to make friends.

"Anne was happy there, incredible as it seems. Things were hard for us in the camp. We 'convict Jews' who had been arrested in hiding places had to wear blue overalls with a red bib and wooden shoes. Our men had their heads shaved. Three hundred people lived in each barracks. We were sent to work at five in the morning, the children to a cable workshop and the grown-ups to a shed where we had to break up old batteries and salvage the metal and the carbon rods. The food was bad, we were always kept on the run, and the guards all screamed 'Faster, faster!' But Anne was happy. It was as if she had been liberated. Now she could see new people and talk to them and could laugh. She could laugh while the rest of us thought nothing but: Will they send us to the camps in Poland? Will we live through it?

"Edith Frank, Anne's mother, seemed numbed by the experience. She could have been a mute. Anne's sister Margot spoke little and Otto Frank was quiet too, but his was a reassuring quietness that helped Anne and all of us. He lived in the men's barracks, but once when Anne was sick he came over to visit her every evening and would stand beside her bed for hours, telling her stories. Anne was so like him. When another child, a twelve-year-old boy named David, fell ill, Anne stood by his bed and talked to him. David came from an Orthodox[14] family, and he and Anne always talked about God."

Anne Frank stayed at Westerbork only three weeks. Early in September a thousand of the "convict Jews" were put on a freight train,

---

13. **mustering square:** place of assembly for inspection, roll call, etc.

14. **Orthodox:** Orthodox Jewish. Orthodox Jews strictly observe rites and traditions of Judaism.

seventy-five people to a car. Brussels fell to the Allies, then Antwerp, then the Americans reached Aachen. But the victories were coming too late. The Franks and their friends were already on the way to Auschwitz, the camp in Poland where four million Jews died.

Mrs. de Wiek was in the same freight car with the Franks on that journey from Westerbork to Auschwitz. "Now and then when the train stopped," she told me, "the SS guards[15] came to the door and held out their caps and we had to toss our money and valuables into the caps. Anne and Judy sometimes pulled themselves up to the small barred window of the car and described the villages we were passing through. We made the children repeat the addresses where we could meet after the war if we became separated in the camp. I remember that the Franks chose a meeting place in Switzerland.

"I sat beside my husband on a small box. On the third day in the train, my husband suddenly took my hand and said, 'I want to thank you for the wonderful life we have had together.'

"I snatched my hand away from his, crying, 'What are you thinking about? It's not over!'

"But he calmly reached for my hand again and took it and repeated several times, 'Thank you. Thank you for the life we have had together.' Then I left my hand in his and did not try to draw it away."

On the third night the train stopped, the doors of the car slid violently open, and the first the exhausted passengers saw of Auschwitz was the glaring searchlights fixed on the train. On the platform *Kapos* (criminal convicts who were assigned to positions of authority over the other prisoners) were running back and forth shouting orders. Behind them, seen distinctly against the light, stood the SS officers, trimly built and smartly uniformed, many of them with huge dogs at their sides. As the people poured out of the train, a loudspeaker roared, "Women to the left! Men to the right!"

Mrs. de Wiek went on calmly: "I saw them all as they went away, Mr. Van Daan and Mr. Düssel and Peter and Mr. Frank. But I saw no sign of my husband. He had vanished. I never saw him again.

"'Listen!' the loudspeaker bawled again. 'It is an hour's march to the women's camp. For the children and the sick there are trucks waiting at the end of the platform.'

"We could see the trucks," Mrs. de Wiek said. "They were painted with big red crosses. We all made a rush for them. Who among us was not sick after those days on the train? But we did not reach them. People were still hanging on to the backs of the trucks as they started off. Not one person who went along on that ride ever arrived at the women's camp, and no one has ever found any trace of them."

Mrs. de Wiek, her daughter, Mrs. Van Daan, Mrs. Frank, Margot, and Anne survived the brutal pace of the night march to the women's camp at Auschwitz. Next day their heads were shaved; they learned that the hair was useful as packing for pipe joints in U-boats.[16] Then the women were put to work digging sods of grass which they placed in great piles. As they labored each day, thousands of others were dispatched with maniacal efficiency in the gas chambers, and smoke rising from the stacks of the huge crematoriums[17] blackened the sky.

Mrs. de Wiek saw Anne Frank every day at Auschwitz. "Anne seemed even more beautiful there," Mrs. de Wiek said, "than she had at Westerbork. Of course her long hair was gone, but now you could see that her beauty was in her eyes, which seemed to grow bigger as she grew thinner. Her gaiety had vanished, but she was still alert and sweet, and with her charm she sometimes secured things that the rest of us had long since given up hoping for.

"For example, we each had only a gray sack to wear. But when the weather turned cold, Anne came in one day wearing a suit of men's long underwear. She had begged it somewhere. She looked screamingly funny with those long white legs, but somehow still delightful.

---

15. **SS guards:** unit of the Nazi party used as special police.

16. **U-boats:** submarines.

17. **crematoriums** (krē′mə·tôr′ē·əmz): ovens in which prisoners were cremated (that is, burned to ashes).

"Though she was the youngest, Anne was the leader in her group of five people. She also gave out the bread to everyone in the barracks and she did it so fairly there was none of the usual grumbling.

"We were always thirsty at Auschwitz, so thirsty that at roll call we would stick out our tongues if it happened to be raining or snowing, and many became sick from bad water. Once when I was almost dead because there was nothing to drink, Anne suddenly came to me with a cup of coffee. To this day I don't know where she got it.

"In the barracks many people were dying, some of starvation, others of weakness and despair. It was almost impossible not to give up hope, and when a person gave up, his face became empty and dead. The Polish woman doctor who had been caring for the sick said to me, 'You will pull through. You still have your face.'

"Anne Frank, too, still had her face, up to the very last. To the last also she was moved by the dreadful things the rest of us had somehow become hardened to. Who bothered to look when the flames shot up into the sky at night from the crematoriums? Who was troubled that every day new people were being selected and gassed? Most of us were beyond feeling. But not Anne. I can still see her standing at the door and looking down the camp street as a group of naked gypsy girls were driven by on their way to the crematorium. Anne watched them going and cried. And she also cried when we marched past the Hungarian children who had been waiting half a day in the rain in front of the gas chambers. And Anne nudged me and said, 'Look, look! Their eyes!' Anne cried. And you cannot imagine how soon most of us came to the end of our tears.''

Late in October the SS selected the healthiest of the women prisoners for work in a munitions factory in Czechoslovakia. Judy de Wiek was taken from her mother, but Anne and her sister Margot were rejected because they had contracted scabies.[18] A few days later there was another selection for shipment from Auschwitz. Stripped, the women waited naked for hours on the mustering ground outside the barracks. Then, one by one, they filed into the barracks where a battery of powerful lights had been set up and an SS doctor waited to check them over. Only those able to stand a trip and do hard work were being chosen for this new shipment, and many of the women lied about their age and condition in the hope that they would escape the almost certain death of Auschwitz. Mrs. de Wiek was rejected and so was Mrs. Frank. They waited, looking on.

"Next it was the turn of the two girls, Anne and Margot," Mrs. de Wiek recalled. "Even under the glare of that light Anne still had her face, and she encouraged Margot, and Margot walked erect into the light. There they stood for a moment, naked and shaven-headed, and Anne looked at us with her unclouded face, looked straight and stood straight, and then they were approved and passed along. We could not see what was on the other side of the light. Mrs. Frank screamed, 'The children! Oh, God!' ''

The chronicle of most of the other occupants of the Secret Annexe ends at Auschwitz. Mrs. Frank died there of malnutrition two months later. Mr. Frank saw Mr. Van Daan marched to the gas chambers. When the SS fled Auschwitz before the approaching Russians in January 1945, they took Peter Van Daan with them. It was bitter cold and the roads were covered wth ice and Peter Van Daan, Anne Frank's shy beloved, was never heard of again.

From Auschwitz, Mr. Düssel, the dentist, was shipped to a camp in Germany where he died. Only Otto Frank remained there alive until liberation. Anne Frank and Mrs. Van Daan and Margot had been selected for shipment to Bergen-Belsen.

Last year I drove the 225 miles from Amsterdam to Belsen and spent a day there walking over the heath.[19] The site of the old camp is near the city of Hannover in the state of Lower Saxony. It was June when I arrived, and lupine was in flower in the scrubland.

My guide first showed me the cemetery where fifty thousand Russian prisoners of war, captured in one of Hitler's great early offensives, were buried in 1941. Next to them is a cemetery for Italians. No one knows exactly whether there are three hundred or three thousand in that mass grave.

About a mile farther we came to the main site of the Bergen-Belsen camp. Amid the low growth of pine and birches many large rectangular patches can be seen on the heath. The barracks stood on these, and between them the worn tracks of thousands of bare feet are still visible. There are more mass graves nearby, low mounds overgrown with heath grass or new-planted dwarf pines. Boards bearing the numbers of the dead stand beside some mounds, but others are unmarked and barely discernible. Anne Frank lies there.

The train that carried Anne from Auschwitz to Belsen stopped at every second station because of air raids. At Bergen-Belsen there were no roll calls, no organization, almost no sign of the SS. Prisoners lived on the heath without hope. The fact that the Allies had reached the Rhine encour-

---

18. **scabies** (skā′bēz): contagious skin disease characterized by intense itching.

19. **heath** (hēth): area of open wasteland partly covered by heather and low shrubs.

aged no one. Prisoners died daily—of hunger, thirst, sickness.

The Auschwitz group had at first been assigned to tents at the Bergen-Belsen heath, tents which one survivor recalls gave an oddly gay carnival aspect to the camp. One night that fall a great windstorm brought the tents crashing down, and their occupants were then put in wooden barracks. Mrs. B. of Amsterdam remembered about Anne: "We lived in the same block and saw each other often. In fact, we had a party together at Christmastime. We had saved up some stale bread, and we cut this up and put onions and boiled cabbage on the pieces. Over our feast we nearly forgot our misery for a few hours. We were almost happy. I know that it sounds ghastly now, but we really were a little happy in spite of everything."

One of Anne Frank's dearest childhood friends in Amsterdam was a girl named Lies Goosens. Lies is repeatedly mentioned in the diary. She was captured before the Franks were found in the Secret Annexe, and Anne wrote of her great fears for the safety of her friend. Now the slim and attractive wife of an Israeli army officer, Lies lives in Jerusalem. But she was in Bergen-Belsen in February 1945, when she heard that a group of Dutch Jews had been moved into the next compound.

Lies said, "I waited until night. Then I stole out of the barracks and went over to the barbed wire which separated us from the newcomers. I called softly into the darkness, 'Is anyone there?'

"A voice answered, 'I am here. I am Mrs. Van Daan.'

"We had known the Van Daans in Amsterdam. I told her who I was and asked whether Margot or Anne could come to the fence. Mrs. Van Daan answered in a breathless voice that Margot was sick but that Anne could probably come and that she would go look for her.

"I waited, shivering in the darkness. It took a long time. But suddenly I heard a voice: 'Lies? Lies? Where are you?'

"I ran in the direction of the voice, and then I saw Anne beyond the barbed wire. She was in rags. I saw her emaciated, sunken face in the darkness. Her eyes were very large. We cried and cried as we told each other our sad news, for now there was only the barbed wire between us, nothing more, and no longer any difference in our fates.

"But there was a difference after all. My block still had food and clothing. Anne had nothing. She was freezing and starving. I called to her in a whisper, 'Come back tomorrow. I'll bring you something.'

"And Anne called across, 'Yes, tomorrow. I'll come.'

"I saw Anne again when she came to the fence on the following night," Lies continued. "I had packed up a woolen jacket and some zwieback and sugar and a tin of sardines for her. I called out, 'Anne, watch now!' Then I threw the bundle across the barbed wire.

"But I heard only screams and Anne crying. I shouted, 'What's happened?' And she called back, weeping, 'A woman caught it and won't give it to me.' Then I heard rapid footsteps as the woman ran away. Next night I had only a pair of stockings and zwieback, but this time Anne caught it."

In the last weeks at Bergen-Belsen, as Germany was strangled between the Russians and the Western Allies, there was almost no food at all. The roads were blocked, the railroads had been bombed, and the SS commander of the camp drove around the district trying unsuccessfully to requisition supplies. Still, the crematoriums worked night and day. And in the midst of the starvation and the murder there was a great epidemic of typhus.

Both Anne and Margot Frank contracted the disease in late February or early March of 1945. Margot lay in a coma for several days. Then, while unconscious, she somehow rolled from her bed and died. Mrs. Van Daan also died in the epidemic.

The death of Anne Frank passed almost without notice. For Anne, as for millions of others, it was only the final anonymity, and I met no one who remembers being with her in that moment. So many were dying. One woman said, "I feel certain she died because of her sister's death. Dying is

---

20. **zwieback** (swē′bak): biscuit that is sliced and toasted after baking.

easy for anyone left alone in a concentration camp." Mrs. B., who had shared the pitiful Christmastide feast with Anne, knows a little more: "Anne, who was very sick at the time, was not informed of her sister's death. But a few days later she sensed it and soon afterward she died, peacefully."

Three weeks later British troops liberated Bergen-Belsen.

Miep and Elli, the heroic young women who had shielded the Franks for two years, found Anne's papers during the week after the police raid on the Secret Annexe. "It was terrible when I went up there," Miep recalled. "Everything had been turned upside down. On the floor lay clothes, papers, letters, and school notebooks. Anne's little wrapper hung from a hook on the wall. And among the clutter on the floor lay a notebook with a red-checked cover. I picked it up, looked at the pages and recognized Anne's handwriting."

Elli wept as she spoke to me: "The table was still set. There were plates, cups, and spoons, but the plates were empty, and I was so frightened I scarcely dared take a step. We sat down on the floor and leafed through all the papers. They were all Anne's, the notebooks and the colored duplicate paper from the office too. We gathered all of them and locked them up in the main office.

"A few days later 'M.' came into the office, 'M.' who now had the keys to the building. He said to me, 'I found some more stuff upstairs,' and he handed me another sheaf of Anne's papers. How strange, I thought, that *he* should be the one to give these to me. But I took them and locked them up with the others."

Miep and Elli did not read the papers they had saved. The red-checked diary, the office account books into which it overflowed, the 312 tissue-thin sheets of colored paper filled with Anne's short stories and the beginnings of a novel about a young girl who was to live in freedom, all these were kept in the safe until Otto Frank finally returned to Amsterdam alone. Thus Anne Frank's voice was preserved out of the millions that were silenced. No louder than a child's whisper, it speaks for those millions and has outlasted the raucous shouts of the murderers, soaring above the clamorous voices of passing time.

Responding to the Report

Analyzing the Report

Identifying Facts

1. What feature of Anne Frank most fascinated the writer as he watched the old reel of movie film? From the recollections of those who knew Anne Frank, what truth about her does the writer say emerges "even in the most frightful extremity"?
2. Describe the Secret Annexe where Anne and seven others hid from the Nazis for over two years. Who helped them during this time? Who supposedly betrayed them?
3. What did the Gestapo do with Anne's papers at the time of her arrest? Explain what these papers contained and what ultimately happened to them.
4. What was Anne's mood in the last weeks before her arrest? What was her mood on the train to Westerbork? According to Mrs. de Wiek, how did Anne behave at this concentration camp?
5. List three examples that illustrate Anne's sensitivity and concern for others at Westerbork and Auschwitz.
6. List five hardships that prisoners had to endure at the concentration camps.
7. According to Lies Goosens, how did Anne appear when they met at Bergen-Belsen? Explain how Anne finally died. According to the last paragraph, what has happened to Anne's "voice"?

Interpreting Meanings

8. A good report is both **accurate** and **objective**. What techniques does Schnabel use throughout his report to reassure us that his facts are accurate? Find one or two instances in which Schnabel presents his own opinion about the events of Anne's final days.

9. Schnabel's title refers to Anne as a heroine. List five of Anne's character traits that Schnabel considers heroic. Are there other heroes in this report? Explain.

10. The main purpose of a report is to explain or inform, but it may do other things as well. Find passages in this report in which Schnabel's purpose is **description**. What does Schnabel seem to be trying to **persuade** his readers to believe?

Applying Meanings

11. Does this report affect how you evaluate the statement Anne makes at the end of *The Diary of Anne Frank* (page 276): "people are really good at heart"? Explain whether Schnabel's report tends to support or oppose Anne's philosophy.

12. In your opinion, which work of literature was more successful in presenting "the truth" about Anne Frank—Schnabel's nonfiction report or the drama *The Diary of Anne Frank*? Support your opinion with reasons and evidence from the selections.

13. What lessons can you draw for your own life from this report of Anne's last weeks?

14. Can you name other people whose spirit has managed to "stir the conscience of the world"? Explain.

Writing About the Report

A Creative Response

1. **Responding to the Report.** Write a letter that you might have sent to the editors of Life magazine, expressing your response to this report and to their decision to publish it. Do you have any questions about its content or point of view?

A Critical Response

2. **Evaluating a Report.** In a paragraph or two discuss whether Schnabel's report is successful. Consider the following in making your evaluation:

a. Does Schnabel inform you of the most important points? Or are you unsure of important matters after reading the report?

b. Is the writer objective? Is his reporting balanced and truthful, or does he color the material too much with his personal opinions?

c. Is the selection interesting? Did you find it difficult to stop reading? Or did you have to force yourself to continue?

Cite passages from the selection to back up your evaluation.

Analyzing Language and Vocabulary

Direct Quotations

Effective quotations in reports emerge from careful questioning during interviews and from skillful editing and organizing during writing. Examine the eye-witness accounts that Schnabel includes in "A Tragedy Revealed."

1. Schnabel quotes five different people about the Franks' arrest. Explain how Schnabel organizes the five responses to heighten suspense. Whose testimony seems the most important? Give reasons for your opinion.

2. Imagine yourself as Schnabel talking to Mrs. de Wiek, the survivor who knew Anne at Westerbork and Auschwitz. You are trying to get her to trust you and to recall highly disturbing events. Tell how you would have explained to her what you wanted from her. Using her responses as a guide, list five or more questions you think Schnabel might have asked her.

AUTOBIOGRAPHY

When writers are **objective,** they try to give us factual information without inserting their own opinions or emotions about a topic. When they are **subjective,** writers try to get us to share their reactions to something. Almost everything you read will probably be a mixture of both kinds of writing. But if you read carefully, you will learn to tell the difference between writing that is *mostly* objective and writing that is *mostly* subjective.

This mixture of objective and subjective writing is found even in autobiography. You might think that an autobiography can be only subjective, since the writer is telling about his or her own experiences. But most good autobiographies include objective as well as subjective passages.

Here is an excerpt from Russell Baker's autobiography. After his father died, Russell and his mother and sister went to live with relatives.

Often, waking deep in the night, I heard them down in the kitchen talking, talking, talking. Sitting around the table under the unshaded light bulb, they talked the nights away, reheating the coffee, then making fresh coffee, then reheating the pot again, and talking, talking, talking. I would lie on my daybed half awake listening to the murmur of voices, the clatter of cups, the splash of water in the sink, the occasional burst of laughter, the warning voice saying, "Hold it down, you'll wake the children."

Now and then I could make out a distinct phrase or two. "Lucy, remember the time old Mr. Digges . . . ?" This was Uncle Charlie addressing my mother. "—reminds me of the time the cops arrested Jim over in Jersey City." This was Uncle Allen retelling a story I'd heard many times. Uncle Hal's mellow drawl would come in: "—so I didn't do a thing but tell that dirty scoundrel, 'Man, don't you ever try—' " And I would drop

off to sleep again, lulled by the comforting familiarity of those kitchen sounds.

At New Street we lived on coffee and talk. Talking was the great Depression pastime. Unlike the movies, talk was free, and a great river of talk flowed through the house, rising at suppertime, and cresting as my bedtime approached before subsiding into a murmur that trickled along past midnight, when all but Uncle Charlie had drifted off to bed, leaving him alone to reheat the pot, roll another cigarette, and settle down with his book.

If my homework was done, I could sit with them and listen until ten o'clock struck. I loved the sense of family warmth that radiated through those long kitchen nights of talk. There were many chords resonating beneath it, and though I could not identify them precisely, I was absorbing a sense of them and storing them away in memory. There was longing for happy times now lost, and dreaming about what might have been. There was fantasy, too, which revealed itself in a story to which they returned again, and again, about the time Papa made his wonderful trip to England in search of the family's great lost fortune.

—from *Growing Up,*
Russell Baker

---

1. This excerpt includes some of Baker's feelings about his life with his relatives. Find sentences that tell how he felt about them.
2. What details make the surroundings seem pleasant?
3. In the third paragraph, what mood do the words *flowed, murmur, trickled,* and *drifted* create?
4. Find words and phrases in the last paragraph that also create a mood. What is that mood?
5. What other words might Baker have used in place of the ones you found? What effect would the new words have on the reader?
6. How might another person have described this scene objectively?

Writing

1. **Writing a Subjective Account.** Think of an experience that you have strong feelings about. It might involve your family, your friends, an exciting time you once had, or an interesting or amusing thing that happened to you. Write one or two paragraphs telling about the experience. Include as many details as you can that will make a reader share your experience.

2. **Writing an Objective Account.** Write about the same experience in a different way. This time, stick as closely as you can to the simple facts of the experience, as though it had happened to someone else. Try to keep your own feelings apart from what you write. (You may not be able to do this completely, but see how close you can come to it.)

STATING THE MAIN IDEA

Writing Assignment

Write a paragraph stating what you think is the main idea of one of the selections in this unit. Cite details from the selection to support your statements.

Background

Most of the reading you do in school is **nonfiction**—writing about real people and events. Whether it tells a true story or gives other kinds of information, nonfiction is full of specific details. You need to sift through these details to identify the writer's main idea. The **main idea** in a nonfiction selection is like the **theme** of a short story. It is the insight or meaning the writer is trying to communicate.

Sometimes the main idea is stated directly by the writer, as in "Green Gulch" (page 464). In this **personal narrative** (story about the writer's experiences) Eiseley describes an incident from his childhood. According to the final paragraph, what did Eiseley learn from the experience he describes?

Usually, the main idea is not directly stated. You must use critical thinking skills to make an **inference** (an educated guess) about what the writer is trying to communicate.

Prewriting

1. Reread the selection you have chosen. As you read, ask yourself "Why is the writer telling me this? What has the writer learned from this experience or situation?"
2. Look carefully at the first and last paragraphs. Sometimes the writer will make a comment that strongly suggests the main idea. For example, reread the last paragraph of "Reb Asher the Dairyman" (page 472). What is Singer saying here about the "larger meaning" of his biography of Reb Asher?

3. Write a **thesis statement** summarizing what you think is the writer's main idea. Try writing different versions, and choose the one you think is most effective. Which of the following do you think best summarizes the main idea of "Green Gulch"?

   a. In "Green Gulch" Loren Eiseley writes about an unhappy childhood experience.
   b. In "Green Gulch" Loren Eiseley tells about a childhood experience in which some children killed an old turtle.
   c. In "Green Gulch" Loren Eiseley writes about a time he got beat up by some older children.
   d. In "Green Gulch" Loren Eiseley tells of a childhood experience in which he witnesses death for the first time and experiences "evil" at the hands of children.

4. Write a list of details to support your statement of the main idea. Here is a list of details that could support statement d (above):

---

1. Eiseley as a small, innocent child—contrasted with the rough band of older children with worldly, sly eyes

2. Played innocently at first at Green Gulch

3. Senseless murder of old turtle; Eiseley watches "in stupefied horror"

4. Turned on Eiseley, smaller than they

5. Eiseley calls them nonhuman—the "evil impulse", "Goblins", "gnomes", "vicious"

Writing

Make your thesis statement the first sentence in your paragraph. Follow it with specific details, quotations, and incidents from the selection to support your thesis statement. The **concluding sentence** in your paragraph should make a final comment on the selection. This might be a response, a summary of your main points, or a rewording of the thesis statement.

The following is one student's paragraph, based on the prewriting notes for "Green Gulch."

In "Green Gulch," Loren Eiseley tells of a childhood experience in which he witnesses death for the first time and experiences "evil" at the hands of older children. Small and lost, Eiseley trustingly follows a group of older children who wear "rough clothes" and have eyes that are "worldly and sly." The children lead him further away from home to Green Gulch, where their innocent play soon leads to stoning an old turtle to death. It is Eiseley's first experience with death, and he is horrified at the senseless murder. The children turn on him, for he is a stranger, smaller than they, and obviously disapproving of their crime. With words like *gnomes, goblins, vicious, evil impulse,* and *not human,* Eiseley contrasts the evil of senseless violence with his own innocence. "Green Gulch" is really the story of Eiseley's loss of innocence: his first awareness of death and evil.	**Thesis statement states the main idea.** **Summarizes incident; mentions specific details.** **Quotes from selection.** **Analyzes children's motivation.** **Discusses connotations of language.** **Concluding sentence restates thesis statement.**

Revision and Proofreading Self-Check

1. Does the paragraph begin with a thesis statement that identifies the writer's main idea?
2. Does the rest of the paragraph cite details and quotations to support the thesis statement?
3. Does the paragraph have a strong concluding statement?
4. Have I expressed my ideas clearly?
5. Are words spelled correctly? Are sentences punctuated correctly?

Partner Check

1. Are there any spelling errors? Are sentences punctuated correctly?
2. Does the paragraph begin with an effective thesis statement?
3. Does the rest of the paragraph give enough support to the thesis statement?
4. What do I like best about this paper?
5. What do I think needs improvement?

THE AMERICAN TRADITION
MYTHS, FOLKTALES, AND HISTORICAL REALITIES

Kachina! Hototo. Hopi Pueblo.   Courtesy School of American Research, Santa Fe, New Mexico.

UNIT EIGHT   **David Adams Leeming**

Unit Outline
THE AMERICAN TRADITION
MYTHS, FOLKTALES, AND HISTORICAL REALITIES

> *Mythology does not have the antiquity of geologic ages,*
> *but it is nevertheless a very old pattern, woven into the*
> *terrain over the course of thousands of years.*
>
> —John Bierhorst

The Literature of the Folk

A society's myths and legends are the revelations of its inner self or "soul." Myths and legends are like dreams. They are fantasy expressions of wishes and fears that we find impossible to describe or explain directly.

American myths and legends are an unusual mixture of stories that have emerged from an unusual mixture of experiences. There are Native American stories, black American stories, and white-settler stories. In a book of American folklore, we find Davy Crockett, Jesse James, Annie Oakley, and General Custer standing next to Hiawatha, Sky Woman, John Henry, and Tar Man. Yet we must

From a Cheyenne sketch book by Cohoe. Commentary by E. Adamson Hoebel and Karen Daniels Peterson. © 1954 University of Oklahoma Press.

remember that American folklore, for all its diversity, is still a record of our society's soul.

What Are Myths, Legends, and Folktales?

Myths are a society's very earliest stories. A myth depends upon belief; it has a religious aspect. A myth's central figures are gods and goddesses, or heroes and heroines who have some direct connection with the gods. Myths often explain spiritual and physical mysteries. The Native American myth of Anpao, for example, "explains" the impossibly complex idea of creation itself. The Greek myth of Demeter and Persephone "explains" the seasonal changes on earth.

A **legend** tends to have some historical truth and it is not usually religious. Legends are exaggerated stories of real people and sometimes of real events. The legends of Davy Crockett and Johnny Appleseed, for example, have some basis in fact.

Folktales are stories about purely fictitious characters and situations. Most were handed down orally for generations before they were written down. Unlike myths, folktales are not religious. The stories that were collected and retold by the Grimm brothers in Germany are folktales, and so are the Brer Rabbit stories in America.

Myths, legends, and folktales the world over all make use of certain universal elements: the difficult quest, the evil monster, the heroic feat, the enchantress.

Folklore in America

Stories of all sorts have been an important part of people's experiences in America. The black slaves brought a rich folklore tradition with them from Africa. Black Americans also developed new stories that reflected their relationships with whites and their working and living conditions in America.

America is rare in the Western world in that it has a native population—the American Indian—whose religious systems continue to make use of their old myths and to create new ones. Many Native American groups are noted for skillful and striking artwork reflecting their myths and legends.

Great fictional heroes, similar in many ways to those of ancient myths, are even being created today by sophisticated city-dwellers. Superman is one such hero.

All of this results in folklore that is as rich as that of any culture. As we study the strange and wonderful tales in this unit, we will be searching for something uniquely American. We will be looking for a record of what it is to be American, as opposed to being English or French or Nigerian. In so doing, we contribute to the development of one of the most pervasive of American images. This is the image of a great "melting pot," in which the experiences of many cultures somehow become the *American* experience.

Nez Percé quiver and bow case (ca. 1880).

Museum of the American Indian Heye Foundation, New York City.

Cheyenne pipe bowl, Wyoming (ca. 1850–1860). Stone.

Denver Art Museum.

Illustration by Frederic Remington for the 1892 edition
of *The Song of Hiawatha,* by Henry Wadsworth Longfellow.
Houghton Mifflin Company.

Courtesy of New York Public Library,
Rare Books and Manuscripts Division.

People are always concerned with their origins. We feel that if we do not know where we came from, we somehow do not know who we are, and that disturbs us. Children love to hear stories about the day they were born and about their parents and grandparents when they were young in the "olden days." We are proud of our family histories, and sometimes we even change bits of those histories to create legends. The snowstorm on the day I was born, for example, becomes, in family stories, the blizzard of the century. Your great-grandfather's journey from the "old country" might have become a saga that rivals the perilous journey of Odysseus from Troy to Ithaca.

What applies to individuals and families also applies to tribes and nations. Like all people, Native Americans, for example, were not content to think of themselves as merely having sprung from nowhere. And so they told many wonderfully complex myths of creation, such as the one we will read about Sky Woman.

Myths and legends of origins give a whole people a sense of who they are. In this unit, you will read several origin stories. Some of these stories are myths, and were believed to be true by the people who first told them. Other stories are about historical beginnings. These beginnings are now part of the American tradition: Someday they might even become the stuff of legends.

Beginnings: Mythological and Real

Beaded pouch, probably Canadian.
Leather, trade cloth, beads.

Denver Art Museum.

SKY WOMAN

Traditional Seneca

Algonquian village of Pomeiooc (in present-day North Carolina). Colored
engraving by Theodor de Bry (1590), after a watercolor by John White.

A creation story reminds people who tell it of their origins. It reminds them that they are a significant part of a universal arrangement of things. This creation story comes from the Senecas. They were one of five Indian nations in New York State who formed the Iroquois League more than a century before the Europeans established colonies. For a time, the League controlled a territory that stretched north to Canada, east to Maine, west to Michigan, and south to Tennessee. Among the Iroquois, the mothers' blood lines determined which clans would be represented in the League council, and women nominated and removed council members. What reasons can you find in the Sky Woman myth to account for the influential role of women in Iroquois society?

Once all mankind lived in a celestial paradise. Below this paradise there was no earth but only a watery expanse, inhabited by waterfowl and water animals. There was no sun in this watery world but heaven was lighted by the beautiful blossoms of the Tree of Light which stood before the lodge of the Chief of Heaven.

This Chief of Heaven had married a beautiful young woman in accordance with the dictates of a dream. Presently she became pregnant simply from inhaling the chief's breath, but he was not aware of the miraculous nature of what had happened and became very jealous. Then another dream told him that he should tear the Tree of Light from the ground. He did so and it left a great gaping hole in the floor of heaven. When he came upon his wife peering down into the great hole he had made, jealous rage overcame him and he gave her a push. She fell from the celestial region down toward the terrestrial water. The Chief of Heaven then threw down other objects—corn, deer, wolves, bears, tobacco, squash, beaver, and many other things that ultimately would grow in the lower world.

But that world had not yet come into existence. The unfortunate wife, who came to be known as the Sky Woman, was seen, as she fell, by the numerous creatures that already inhabited the great ocean. They decided to help her. The water birds folded their wings one against another to catch her and slow her fall, and the water animals tried to arrange a landing place. The Great Snapping Turtle swam to the surface and held his shell above water while other animals dived to the bottom of the sea for earth. The Muskrat brought up

English Words Taken from Native American Languages. When European explorers of America needed words for unfamiliar plants, animals, and objects, they often adopted the Native American names. Many Native American languages belong to either the Algonquian or the Iroquoian language groups. Words directly adopted—such as *wigwam* and *totem*—come mostly from the older Algonquian cultures. Iroquoian terms tended to be translated. *Long house,* for example, refers to the distinctive buildings of the Iroquois. The word is a translation of the Iroquois's name for themselves: *Ongwanonhsioni,* or "We long-house builders." The Seneca spoke an Iroquoian language. What phrases in this Seneca story look translated to you? How did you decide?

some, as did the Toad. These little bits of earth were deposited on the great hard shell of the turtle and somehow the earth and the turtle shell began to grow into an island.

The birds bore the Sky Woman down gradually, fresh birds replacing wearied ones as time went on, and presently they put her gently on the newly formed island. The Sky Woman walked about on the island and even took handfuls of earth as it multiplied and threw them about, and the island grew large and the horizons moved out beyond human vision. Plants and trees and grass began to grow, and the animals who had fallen after the Sky Woman also flourished and propagated. In this way was the earth born and the Sky Woman became the Great Earth Mother.

—Retold by Jesse J. Cornplanter

Responding to the Myth

Analyzing the Myth

Identifying Facts

1. According to this myth, where did all mankind once live? Describe that place and the world that existed below it.
2. Why does the Chief of Heaven tear the Tree of Light from the ground and push his wife through the hole?
3. List seven objects that the Chief of Heaven throws down through the hole. What ultimately becomes of them?
4. How do the water birds and the water animals help Sky Woman reach earth? How is the land formed?

Interpreting Meanings

5. Consider the objects that the Chief of Heaven throws down through the hole. Why would these things be of special importance to the Senecas?
6. This myth suggests that the Chief of Heaven, Sky Woman, and the animals each had a different but important role in the creation of the earth. Explain what each of these roles was. Which role, if any, do you think the Senecas felt was most important? Support your opinion with reasons.

Applying Meanings

7. The animals help Sky Woman when she is in danger. What movies, television shows, or other stories do you know in which people and animals help each other out of difficulties? Explain what such stories teach about the relationship between all creatures on earth.

Writing About the Myth

A Creative Response

1. **Extending the Myth.** Another Senecan myth tells that Sky Woman gives birth to a daughter. What do you imagine their life was like at the beginning of the world? Did animals continue to play an important role? Write one or two paragraphs in the style of "Sky Woman" in which you describe what happens next.

A Critical Response

2. **Analyzing Meaning.** This creation myth doesn't tell you much directly about the Senecas. You can, however, make **inferences**, or educated guesses, about some of their basic attitudes. In a paragraph, discuss how you think the Senecas feel about nature. Do they find it threatening, a source of strength, or something else? Cite specific evidence from the myth to support your inferences.

Analyzing Language and Vocabulary

Influence of Indian Languages on English

Many Native American expressions have become part of the English language. Some of these expressions, such as *long house,* are translations. Others, such as *wigwam,* are borrowed directly from an Indian language.

1. Identify three expressions in "Sky Woman" that seem to you to be translations from Seneca.
2. Here are some additional English phrases from Indian cultures. Explain what each phrase means today.

   a. bury the hatchet
   b. go on the warpath
   c. put on war paint
   d. smoke the peace pipe

3. The following English words were borrowed directly from North American Indian languages. Explain the meaning of each word. Use a dictionary if necessary.

   a. hickory   e. pecan
   b. hominy   f. powwow
   c. moccasin   g. toboggan
   d. muskrat   h. succotash

GREAT MEDICINE MAKES A BEAUTIFUL COUNTRY

Traditional Cheyenne

This story, written down in 1905, was told among the Cheyenne (shī·an′), who once lived in the western Great Plains. It tells how groups of Cheyenne united and split again, migrated south and returned north, and experienced many natural disasters over the course of centuries. As you read, note the details that seem to be based on actual historical events. On the other hand, which details seem to be pure myth?

Cheyenne drawing (ca. 1905).

Field Museum of Natural History, Chicago.

In the beginning the Great Medicine created the earth, and the waters upon the earth, and the sun, moon, and stars. Then he made a beautiful country to spring up in the far north. There were no winters, with ice and snow and bitter cold. It was always spring; wild fruits and berries grew everywhere, and great trees shaded the streams of clear water that flowed through the land.

In this beautiful country the Great Medicine put animals, birds, insects, and fish of all kinds. Then he created human beings to live with the other creatures. Every animal, big and small, every bird, big and small, every fish, and every insect could talk to the people and understand them. The people could understand each other, for they had a common language and lived in friendship. They went naked and fed on honey and wild fruits; they were never hungry. They wandered everywhere among the wild animals, and when night came and they were weary, they lay down on the cool grass and slept. During the days they talked with the other animals, for they were all friends.

The Great Spirit created three kinds of human beings: first, those who had hair all over their bodies; second, white men who had hair all over their heads and faces and on their legs; third, red men who had very long hair on their heads only. The hairy people were strong and active. The white people with the long beards were in a class with the wolf, for both were the trickiest and most cunning creatures in that beautiful world. The red people were good runners, agile and swift, whom the Great Medicine taught to catch and eat fish at a time when none of the other people knew about eating meat.

After a while the hairy people left the north country and went south, where all the land was barren. Then the red people prepared to follow the hairy people into the south. Before they left the beautiful land, however, the Great Medicine called them together. On this occasion, the first time the red people had all assembled in one place, the Great Medicine blessed them and gave them some medicine spirit to awaken their dormant minds. From that time on they seemed to possess intelligence and know what to do. The Great Medicine singled out one of the men and told him to teach his people to band together, so that they all could work and clothe their naked bodies with skins of panther and bear and deer. The Great Medicine gave them the power to hew and shape flint and other stones into any shape they wanted—into arrow- and spearheads and into cups, pots, and axes.

The red people stayed together ever afterward. They left the beautiful country and went southward in the same direction the hairy people had taken. The hairy people remained naked, but the red people clothed themselves because the Great Medicine had told them to. When the red men arrived in the south, they found that the hairy people had scattered and made homes inside of hills and in caves high up in the mountains. They seldom saw the hairy men, for the hairy ones were afraid and went inside their caves when the red men came. The hairy people had pottery and flint tools like those of the red men, and in their caves they slept on beds made out of leaves and skins. For some reason they decreased in numbers until they finally disappeared entirely, and today the red men cannot tell what became of them.

After the red men had lived in the south for some time, the Great Medicine told them to return north, for the barren southland was going to be flooded. When they went back to that beautiful northern land, they found that the white-skinned, long-bearded men and some of the wild animals were gone. They were no longer able to talk to the animals, but this time they controlled all other creatures, and they taught the panther, the bear, and similar beasts to catch game for them. They increased in numbers and became tall and strong and active.

Then for a second time the red people left the beautiful land to go south. The waters had gone, grass and trees had grown, and the country had become as beautiful as the north. While they were living there, however, another flood swept over the land and scattered the red men. When the great waters at last sank and the ground was dry, the red people did not come together again. They traveled in small bands, just as they had done in the beginning before the Great Medicine told them to unite. The flood destroyed almost everything, and they were on the point of starvation. So they started back to their original home in the north as they had done before. But when they reached the north country this time, they found the land all barren. There were no trees, no living animals, not a fish in the water. When the red people looked upon their once-beautiful home, the men cried aloud and all the women and children wept. This happened in the beginning, when the Great Medicine created us.

The people returned to the south and lived as well as they could, in some years better, in others worse. After many hundreds of years, just before the winter season came, the earth shook, and the high hills sent forth fire and smoke. During that winter there were great floods. The people had to dress in furs and live in caves, for the winter was long and cold. It destroyed all the trees, though when spring came there was a new growth. The red men suffered much and were almost famished when the Great Medicine took pity on them. He gave them corn to plant and buffalo for meat, and from that time there were no more floods and no more famines. The people continued to live in the south, and they grew and increased. There were many different bands with different languages, for the red men were never united after the second flood.

The descendants of the original Cheyenne had men among them who were magicians with supernatural wisdom. They charmed not only their own people, but also the animals that they lived on. No matter how fierce or wild the beast, it became so tame that people could go up to it and handle it. This magic knowledge was handed down from the original Cheyenne, who came from the far north. Today Bushy Head is the only one who understands that ancient ceremony, and the Cheyenne consider him equal in rank to the medicine-arrow keeper and his assistants.

—Based on George A. Dorsey's account

Responding to the Myth

Analyzing the Myth

Identifying Facts

1. In the beginning, what was the climate of the "beautiful country" in the north? How did people and animals get along together?
2. List the three kinds of people and give at least two outstanding qualities of each group. Which group goes south first?
3. Identify at least two ways in which the hairy people and the red people differ. Explain what eventually happens to the hairy people.
4. Tell why the red people return to the "beautiful country." What changes do they find there?
5. What happens to the large, united group of red people after the second flood? What do some of the people find when they go north again?
6. What two things does the Great Medicine give the red people when they are starving?
7. Bushy Head was an actual person who lived when this story was written down in 1905. Describe the kind of knowledge that made Bushy Head unique among the Cheyenne.

Interpreting Meanings

8. Like "Sky Woman," this story assumes that people once lived in a kind of paradise. This time, though, paradise is not a purely mytho-

Cheyenne Shield.

Detroit Institute of Art.

logical place in the sky, but a "north country." This place is probably central Minnesota, where the Cheyenne originally lived until about 1700. List three details in the description of this "beautiful country" that seem to refer to an actual place. Then list details that seem mythological or idealized. Why do you suppose the Cheyenne tended to idealize their original homeland?

9. Each time the red people return to the north country, they find fewer animals. Based on your knowledge of early American history, what do you think actually happened to the animals?

10. The "Cliff Dwellers" were Indians of the Southwest who built sandstone rooms atop one another on ledges or in the hollows of cliffs. Most cliff dwellings were built between A.D. 1000 and 1300, and then abandoned—no one is certain why. Archaeologists have found stone arrowheads, pottery, and other household furnishings that the Cliff Dwellers left behind. Identify the details in the story that suggest the "hairy people" were actually the Cliff Dwellers.

Applying Meanings

11. Can you find any details in this origin story that are like those in origin stories told by other cultures?

Writing About the Myth

A Creative Response

1. **Writing a Myth.** Pretend you are a Cheyenne elder. Some youngsters have asked you to tell them the story about how the Great Medicine first taught the Cheyenne to catch and eat fish. Tell this story in two or three paragraphs. Use the style and tone of "Great Medicine Makes a Beautiful Country" for your myth.

A Critical Response

2. **Comparing Legend and History.** Some of the incidents in "Great Medicine Makes a Beautiful Country" are legendary. A **legend** is a story handed down among a people for generations and popularly believed to have a historical basis. Look in an encyclopedia or other reference book for a history of the Cheyenne. Use a map to track their migrations over the centuries. Look for parallels between their actual history and the legendary events in this story. Which events seem to have a factual rather than a mythological basis? In two or three paragraphs, describe the parallels that you find.

Analyzing Language and Vocabulary

Multiple Meanings

The word *medicine* was first used by Americans in 1807 to refer to the American Indian idea of supernatural power over the forces of nature. The Lewis and Clark expedition was supposed to have recorded the term "medicine dance" in 1806. "Medicine man" was recorded a year later. By around 1830, the term had expanded to refer to white peddlers who were selling phony medicinal remedies.

1. According to this myth, what is meant by "the Great Medicine"?

2. Considering this meaning of *medicine,* what would you say were the duties of a medicine man in Cheyenne society?

3. Look up the word *shaman.* Is Great Medicine a shaman?

Hiawatha probably lived around 1450. He was a leader of the Mohawks. According to tradition, he helped found the Iroquois League by uniting his people with four other nations. For later generations of Iroquois, Hiawatha became a legendary hero. Stories were told of his miraculous powers over the forces of nature. These legends credit Hiawatha with teaching the civilizing arts of navigation, medicine, agriculture, and picture writing. For his long poem *The Song of Hiawatha* (1855), the American poet Henry Wadsworth Longfellow drew on these legends and on those of a Chippewa hero named Manabozho. The following excerpt from Longfellow's poem deals with the origin of corn. As you read, note the characteristics of Hiawatha that make him heroic.

from The Song of Hiawatha

Henry Wadsworth Longfellow

Hiawatha Fishing by N. C. Wyeth. Illustration for the 1908 edition of *The Song of Hiawatha,* by Henry Wadsworth Longfellow. Houghton Mifflin Company.

You shall hear how Hiawatha
Prayed and fasted in the forest,
Not for greater skill in hunting,
Not for greater craft in fishing,
5   Not for triumphs in the battle,
And renown among the warriors,
But for profit of the people,
For advantage of the nations.
   First he built a lodge for fasting,
10 Built a wigwam in the forest,
By the shining Big-Sea-Water,
In the blithe and pleasant Springtime,
In the Moon of Leaves he built it,
And, with dreams and visions many,
15 Seven whole days and nights he fasted.
   On the first day of his fasting
Through the leafy woods he wandered;
Saw the deer start from the thicket,
Saw the rabbit in his burrow,
20 Heard the pheasant, Bena, drumming,
Heard the squirrel, Adjidaumo,
Rattling in his hoard of acorns,
Saw the pigeon, the Omeme,
Building nests among the pine trees,
25 And in flocks the wild goose, Wawa,
Flying to the fenlands northward,
Whirring, wailing far above him.
"Master of Life!" he cried, desponding,
"Must our lives depend on these things?"

30 On the next day of his fasting
By the river's brink he wandered,
Through the Muskoday, the meadow,
Saw the wild rice, Mahnomonee,
Saw the blueberry, Meenahga,
35 And the strawberry, Odahmin,
And the gooseberry, Shahbomin,
And the grapevine, the Bemahgut,
Trailing o'er the alder branches,
Filling all the air with fragrance!
40 "Master of Life!" he cried, desponding,
"Must our lives depend on these things?"
   On the third day of his fasting
By the lake he sat and pondered,
By the still, transparent water;
45 Saw the sturgeon, Nahma, leaping,
Scattering drops like beads of wampum,°
Saw the yellow perch, the Sahwa,
Like a sunbeam in the water,
Saw the pike, the Maskenozha,
50 And the herring, Okahahwis,
And the Shawgashee, the crawfish!
"Master of Life!" he cried, desponding,
"Must our lives depend on these things?"
   On the fourth day of his fasting
55 In his lodge he lay exhausted;
From his couch of leaves and branches
Gazing with half-open eyelids,
Full of shadowy dreams and visions,
On the dizzy, swimming landscape,
60 On the gleaming of the water,
On the splendor of the sunset.
   And he saw a youth approaching,
Dressed in garments green and yellow,
Coming through the purple twilight,
65 Through the splendor of the sunset;
Plumes of green bent o'er his forehead,
And his hair was soft and golden.
   Standing at the open doorway,
Long he looked at Hiawatha,
70 Looked with pity and compassion
On his wasted form and features,
And, in accents like the sighing
Of the South Wind in the treetops,
Said he, "O my Hiawatha!

---

46. **wampum:** small beads made of shells and used as money, for ornament, etc.

75 All your prayers are heard in heaven,
For you pray not like the others;
Not for greater skill in hunting,
Not for greater craft in fishing,
Not for triumph in the battle,
80 Nor renown among the warriors,
But for profit of the people,
For advantage of the nations.
    "From the Master of Life descending,
I, the friend of man, Mondamin,
85 Come to warn you and instruct you,
How by struggle and by labor
You shall gain what you have prayed for.
Rise up from your bed of branches,
Rise, O youth, and wrestle with me!"
90 Faint with famine, Hiawatha
Started from his bed of branches,
From the twilight of his wigwam
Forth into the flush of sunset
Came, and wrestled with Mondamin;
95 At his touch he felt new courage
Throbbing in his brain and bosom,
Felt new life and hope and vigor
Run through every nerve and fiber.
    So they wrestled there together
100 In the glory of the sunset,
And the more they strove and struggled,
Stronger still grew Hiawatha;
Till the darkness fell around them,
And the heron, the Shuh-shuh-gah,
105 From her nest among the pine trees,
Gave a cry of lamentation,
Gave a scream of pain and famine.
    "'Tis enough!" then said Mondamin,
Smiling upon Hiawatha,
110 "But tomorrow, when the sun sets,
I will come again to try you."
And he vanished, and was seen not;
Whether sinking as the rain sinks,
Whether rising as the mists rise,
115 Hiawatha saw not, knew not,
Only saw that he had vanished,
Leaving him alone and fainting,
With the misty lake below him,
And the reeling stars above him.
120 On the morrow and the next day,
When the sun through heaven descending
Like a red and burning cinder

From the hearth of the Great Spirit,
Fell into the western waters,
125 Came Mondamin for the trial,
For the strife with Hiawatha;
Came as silent as the dew comes,
From the empty air appearing,
Into empty air returning,
130 Taking shape when earth it touches
But invisible to all men
In its coming and its going.
    Thrice they wrestled there together
In the glory of the sunset,
135 Till the darkness fell around them,
Till the heron, the Shuh-shuh-gah,
From her nest among the pine trees,
Uttered her loud cry of famine,
And Mondamin paused to listen.
140 Tall and beautiful he stood there
In his garments green and yellow;
To and fro his plumes above him
Waved and nodded with his breathing,
And the sweat of the encounter
145 Stood like drops of dew upon him.
    And he cried, "O Hiawatha!
Bravely have you wrestled with me,
Thrice have wrestled stoutly with me,
And the Master of Life, who sees us,
150 He will give to you the triumph!"
    Then he smiled and said: "Tomorrow
Is the last day of your conflict,
Is the last day of your fasting.
You will conquer and o'ercome me;
155 Make a bed for me to lie in,
Where the rain may fall upon me,
Where the sun may come and warm me;
Strip these garments, green and yellow,
Strip this nodding plumage from me,
160 Lay me in the earth and make it
Soft and loose and light above me.
    "Let no hand disturb my slumber,
Let no weed nor worm molest me,
Let not Kahgahgee, the raven,
165 Come to haunt me and molest me,
Only come yourself to watch me,
Till I wake, and start, and quicken,
Till I leap into the sunshine."
    And thus saying, he departed;
170 Peacefully slept Hiawatha,

But he heard the Wawonaissa,
Heard the whippoorwill complaining,
Perched upon his lonely wigwam;
Heard the rushing Sebowisha,
175   Heard the rivulet° rippling near him,
Talking to the darksome forest;
Heard the sighing of the branches,
As they lifted and subsided
At the passing of the night wind,
180   Heard them, as one hears in slumber
Far-off murmurs, dreamy whispers:
Peacefully slept Hiawatha.
    On the morrow came Nokomis,°
On the seventh day of his fasting,
185   Came with food for Hiawatha,
Came imploring and bewailing,
Lest his hunger should o'ercome him,
Lest his fasting should be fatal.
    But he tasted not, and touched not,
190   Only said to her, "Nokomis,
Wait until the sun is setting,
Till the darkness falls around us,
Till the heron, the Shuh-shuh-gah,
Crying from the desolate marshes,
195   Tells us that the day is ended."
    Homeward weeping went Nokomis,
Sorrowing for her Hiawatha,
Fearing lest his strength should fail him,
Lest his fasting should be fatal.
200   He meanwhile sat weary waiting
For the coming of Mondamin,
Till the shadows, pointing eastward,
Lengthened over field and forest,
Till the sun dropped from the heaven,
205   Floating on the waters westward,
As a red leaf in the Autumn
Falls and floats upon the water,
Falls and sinks into its bosom.
    And behold! the young Mondamin,
210   With his soft and shining tresses,
With his garments green and yellow,
With his long and glossy plumage,
Stood and beckoned at the doorway.
And as one in slumber walking,
215   Pale and haggard, but undaunted,

Hiawatha by Thomas Eakins (ca. 1871). Oil.

From the wigwam Hiawatha
Came and wrestled with Mondamin.
    Round about him spun the landscape,
Sky and forest reeled together,
220   And his strong heart leaped within him
As the sturgeon leaps and struggles
In a net to break its meshes.
Like a ring of fire around him
Blazed and flared the red horizon,
225   And a hundred suns seemed looking

---

175. **rivulet** (riv'yoo·lit): little stream, brook.
183. **Nokomis:** Hiawatha's grandmother.

At the combat of the wrestlers.
    Suddenly upon the greensward°
All alone stood Hiawatha,
Panting with his wild exertion,
230   Palpitating with the struggle;
And before him, breathless, lifeless,
Lay the youth, with hair disheveled,
Plumage torn, and garments tattered,

Dead he lay there in the sunset.
235   And victorious Hiawatha
Made the grave as he commanded,
Stripped the garments from Mondamin,
Stripped his tattered plumage from him,
Laid him in the earth, and made it
240   Soft and loose and light above him;
And the heron, the Shuh-shuh-gah,
From the melancholy moorlands,
Gave a cry of lamentation,

---

227. **greensward:** green, grassy ground.

Gave a cry of pain and anguish!

245   Homeward then went Hiawatha
To the lodge of old Nokomis,
And the seven days of his fasting
Were accomplished and completed.
But the place was not forgotten
250 Where he wrestled with Mondamin;
Nor forgotten nor neglected
Was the grave where lay Mondamin,
Sleeping in the rain and sunshine,
Where his scattered plumes and garments
255 Faded in the rain and sunshine.
    Day by day did Hiawatha
Go to wait and watch beside it;
Kept the dark mold soft above it,
Kept it clean from weeds and insects,
260 Drove away, with scoffs and shoutings,
Kahgahgee, the king of ravens.
    Till at length a small green feather
From the earth shot slowly upward,
Then another and another,
265 And before the Summer ended
Stood the maize in all its beauty,

With its shining robes about it,
And its long, soft, yellow tresses;
And in rapture Hiawatha
270 Cried aloud, "It is Mondamin!
Yes, the friend of man, Mondamin!"
    Then he called to old Nokomis
And Iagoo, the great boaster,
Showed them where the maize was
    growing,
275 Told them of his wondrous vision,
Of his wrestling and his triumph,
Of this new gift to the nations,
Which should be their food forever.
    And still later, when the Autumn
280 Changed the long, green leaves to yellow,
And the soft and juicy kernels
Grew like wampum hard and yellow,
Then the ripened ears he gathered,
Stripped the withered husks from off them,
285 As he once had stripped the wrestler,
Gave the first Feast of Mondamin,
And made known unto the people
This new gift of the Great Spirit.

Responding to the Poem

Analyzing the Poem

Identifying Details

1. Why is Hiawatha praying and fasting in the forest? How are his prayers different from those of most other men?
2. List the animals, plants, and fish that Hiawatha sees and hears on the first three days of his fast.
3. On the fourth day, a youth named Mondamin comes to Hiawatha. Describe Mondamin's dress and appearance. Why has he come to Hiawatha?
4. Describe what Hiawatha and Mondamin do from twilight till darkness on three evenings. How does Hiawatha feel after these encounters?
5. What instructions does Mondamin give Hiawatha for the seventh night of his fast?

6. Describe Hiawatha's fourth struggle with Mondamin. What does Hiawatha do afterward?
7. What plant finally rises from Mondamin's grave? What details of Mondamin's original dress and appearance are reflected in the plant?

Interpreting Meanings

8. On the first three days of his fast, Hiawatha looks at the wild animals, plants, and fish around him. Each day he prays to the Master of Life and asks, "Must our lives depend on these things?" What does Hiawatha's question mean? Explain what he thinks is wrong with depending on these things.
9. Mondamin is called a youth. What kind of being is he actually? Identify three details in the poem that lead you to this conclusion.

10. Many myths are about a **metamorphosis,** or a marvelous transformation from one form to another. What is the metamorphosis in this myth?

11. Compare the Master of Life or Great Spirit in this excerpt to the Chief of Heaven portrayed in "Sky Woman" (page 502). Which deity seems more human?

12. The technical name of the form of poetry in *The Song of Hiawatha* is **unrhymed trochaic tetrameter.** *Unrhymed* means there is no rhyme scheme, or pattern of rhyming sounds at the ends of lines. *Trochaic* means a stressed or accented syllable is followed by an unstressed one, as in the word *prófĭt. Tetrameter* means there are four such units per line. (*Tetra* means "four" and *meter* means "measure.")

By the lake he sat and pondered,
By the still, transparent water.

With this rhythm in mind, read aloud lines 20–23 and 32–37. Identify the stressed syllables in the Indian words.

Applying Meanings

13. Many people believe that touch can convey power from one being to another. At Mondamin's touch, for example, Hiawatha feels "new life and hope and vigor." What are some of the ways that the special power of touch is still practiced today?

Writing About the Poem

A Creative Response

1. **Describing a Ceremony.** Imagine the first Feast of Mondamin when Hiawatha harvests the maize and presents it for the first time to the people. Write a paragraph or two describing the harvest and the people's celebration of thanksgiving.

A Critical Response

2. **Analyzing Heroic Elements.** *The Song of Hiawatha* is a classic **hero tale,** tracing the deeds of the legendary Hiawatha. Two typical elements of a hero tale are that (1) the hero withdraws from society for a period of prayer and meditation and (2) the hero undergoes various tests or trials for the sake of others. Write a paragraph telling how the excerpt you have read contains these two elements.

Analyzing Language and Vocabulary

Indian Expressions

Many of the Native American expressions in Longfellow's poem were never adopted into English. Instead, Longfellow uses them to create **atmosphere,** a feeling of what Hiawatha's world was like. Give Longfellow's definition of each of the following Indian expressions.

1. *Birds:* Bena, Omeme, Wawa, Kahgahgee, Wawonaissa.
2. *Fish:* Nahma, Sahwa, Maskenozha, Okahahwis, Shawgashee.
3. *Plants:* Mahnomonee, Meenagha, Odahmin, Shahbomin, Bemahgut.
4. *Other natural things:* Adjidaumo, Muskoday, Sebowisha.

Hiawatha and Pearl Feather. Illustration from Longfellow's *The Song of Hiawatha.*

THE OWL NEVER SLEEPS AT NIGHT

Traditional Black American

Folktales that explain why animals look or behave as they do are common in almost every culture. Such tales have long been popular among African peoples, and they continued the custom after coming to America. As you read this tale about why the owl stays up all night, note the reason given for the strange characteristics of several other animals, such as the pig and turkey.

Have you noticed that whenever a creature starts in this world with a habit, it stays with him all his life? Not only that, he passes it along to his children and his grandchildren. Whether the creatures have two legs or four legs or more legs, it works just the same. Another thing is that if you want to see anything, you must open your eyes.

There's the case of the owl. At the very first, he was like the other birds; he had the same kind of eyes as the other birds, and he flew around and sang in the daytime, and when it came dark he went to roost and stuck his head under his wings and slept till daybreak, just like the others. But it wasn't long before he got into the habit of sitting up nights and calling out *"Who-who,"* and he never has stopped that to this very day.

Here's what happened. During the week that the creatures were all created and were just learning how to keep house, the Good Lord noticed that there was something going wrong in the night and he felt mighty nervous about the whole thing. One morning he found the pig's tail curled up; the deer's tail and the goat's tail were cut clean off; the possum and the rat had had their hair all pulled off their tails; the duck had lost his forelegs, the snake had lost all of his; and the guinea hen and the turkey gobbler had lost all the hair off their heads; and nobody knew what was going to happen next. God had a suspicion that it was some of Old Nick's[1] doings, but he never said anything to anybody. He just asked the owl if he wouldn't stay up that night and keep a lookout and see what the matter was and how it all had happened. And the owl said he'd be mighty proud to stay up, only he's afraid he couldn't see very well in the dark. Then the Good Lord told him that all he had to do to see in the dark is to open his eyes wider. So they fixed it up that way. And when it turned dark, the owl never went to bed; he just opened his eyes a little wider, and got out in the open where he could look around over the countryside. And every time it got a little darker the owl would open his eyes a little wider, and he didn't ever have any trouble seeing all the carryings-on.

And sure enough, along about midnight he saw Old Nick tying knots in the horses' manes. And the owl called out, *"Who-who, who-who, who-who-ah?"* With that, Old Nick was so scared that he ran away and left the horses, and struck out across the country in the dark. But the owl opened his eyes wider than ever, and he followed after him and every once in a while he'd call out, *"Who-who, who-who, who-whoo-ah!"*

Well, he sure scared Old Nick away; but when it became day, Mr. Owl had his eyes so wide open

---

1. **Old Nick:** a name for the devil.

that he couldn't shut them, and the bright sun gave him a terrible headache. Then the Good Lord told the owl that as he'd been up all the night before he could find himself a shady place and sleep all day to make up for the loss of sleep the night before.

But when night came around again the owl was rested, and he didn't have his headache anymore, and he felt so wide awake that he stayed up that night too. After that, he got the habit, and he's had it ever since.

—Retold by John C. Branner

Responding to the Folktale

Analyzing the Folktale

Identifying Facts

1. List three ways in which the owl was at first like other birds.
2. What does God find wrong one morning?
3. Why does God ask the owl to stay up one night? What does God tell the owl to do so that he can see in the dark?
4. How successful is the owl at the mission God gives him?
5. Why does the owl sleep the next day? Since then, why have owls stayed awake at night?

Interpreting Meanings

6. According to this story, what characteristics must once have been common to all animals?
7. This story belongs to a group of folktales known as **"why" stories.** Using humor and exaggeration, why stories account for the origins of various things. Find at least two examples of humor and exaggeration in this story. What origins does the story attempt to explain?
8. What **morals,** or lessons about life, does this story illustrate?

Applying Meanings

9. Do some library research on owls. What answers do scientists give to explain why owls have such large eyes and stay awake at night?

Writing About the Folktale

A Creative Response

1. **Writing a "Why" Story.** Think about some animals that have strange characteristics or behavior. For example, why does a kangaroo have a pouch?

Why does an elephant have a trunk? Why does a dog turn around several times before it lies down? In one to three paragraphs, tell a humorous "why" story that accounts for a certain animal's odd characteristics or behavior. Use "The Owl Never Sleeps at Night" as your model.

A Critical Response

2. **Writing About a Folktale's Moral.** In one paragraph, identify what the owl discovers when he opens his eyes wide. In a second paragraph, explain what the owl's discovery reveals about the storytellers' beliefs concerning good and evil in the world.

Analyzing Language and Vocabulary

Compound Words

English has thousands of **compound words**—words formed by joining two other words. "The Owl Never Sleeps at Night," for example, contains *daybreak,* which means "dawn," or the time of day when light first "breaks" the darkness. Other compound words are even easier to understand. For example, *daylight* simply means "the light of day."

The following words appear within compound words in "The Owl Never Sleeps at Night":

ache	ever	out
any	grand	side
body	head	some
children	look	thing
country	more	time
day	no	when

Form as many compound words as you can by combining the words from the list in different ways. Which of the words on your list appeared in the story?

I SAIL TO CAPE COD

Richard Mather

The United States had its beginnings when energetic European settlers packed what they could and set out for the New World. Often they were leaving behind religious and political strife and economic hardship. The following firsthand account was written in 1635 by Richard Mather, a Puritan clergyman. In his journal he describes what it was like to spend months aboard ship, journeying from England to America. As you read, note the many references to God. How important were Mather's religious beliefs to him during his long journey?

Warrington and Bristol are places in England. Ships to the New World sailed from Bristol.

We came from Warrington on Thursday, April 16 [1635], and came to Bristol on the Thursday following, namely April 23, and had a very healthful, safe, and prosperous journey all the way, blessed be the name of God for the same, taking but easy journeys because of the children and footmen, displacing one hundred and nineteen or one hundred and twenty miles in seven days. . . .

Nevertheless we went not aboard the ship until Saturday, the twenty-third of May, so that the time of our staying in Bristol was a month and two days, during all which time we found friendship and courtesy at the hands of diverse godly Christians in Bristol. Yet our stay was grievous unto us when we considered how most of this time the winds were easterly and served directly for us. But our ship was not ready, so ill did our owners deal with us.

Going aboard the ship in King Road the twenty-third of May, we found things very unready, and all on heaps, many goods being not stowed but lying on disordered heaps here and there in the ship. This day there came aboard the ship two of the searchers and viewed a list of all our names, ministered the oath of allegiance to all at full age, viewed our certificates from the ministers in the parishes from whence we came, approved well thereof, and gave us tickets—that is, licenses under their hands and seals, to pass the seas—and cleared the ship, and so departed.

Thursday morning [May 28], the wind served for us, and our master and all the sailors being come aboard, we set sail and began our sea voyage with glad hearts that God had loosed us from our long stay wherein we had been holden, and with hope and trust that He would graciously guide us to the end of our journey. We were, that set sail together that morning, five ships: three bound for Newfoundland (the *Diligence,* a ship of one hundred and fifty tons; the *Mary,* a small ship of eighty tons, and the *Bess*); and two bound for New England (the *Angel Gabriel* of two hundred and forty tons and the *James* of two hundred and twenty tons).

Context Clues. When you come across an unfamiliar word in Mather's journal, *context clues* will often help you determine its meaning. Look for clues to an unfamiliar word's meaning in (1) the general sense of the passage in which the word appears; (2) a definition of the word that might be provided in a nearby phrase; (3) examples that accompany the word; and (4) comparing the unfamiliar word with a word you already know. As a first step, however, keep a list of all the unfamiliar words you encounter in the selection.

Richard Mather by John Foster.

Monday morning [June 22], the wind serving with a strong gale at east, we set sail from Milford Haven where we had waited for wind twelve days, and were carried forth with speedy course, and about noon lost all sight of land. The wind being strong, the sea was rough this day, and most of our passengers were very sick and ill through much casting.

Tuesday, the wind still easterly, and a very rainy day. We were carried forward apace and launched forth a great way into the deep, but our people were still very sick. This day at evening we lost sight of the three ships bound for New-foundland, which had been in company with us from King Road.

Thursday morning [July 23], a fine gale of wind at north and by east. Now we saw this morning abundance of porpoises and grampuses,[1] leaping and spewing up water about the ship. About eight

---

1. **grampuses** (gram′pə·sez): any of several small, black, fierce varieties of toothed whales related to dolphins.

or nine of the clock the wind blew more stiffly and we went about eight or nine leagues[2] a watch. Toward evening our seamen deemed that we were near to some land, because the color of the water was changed, but sounding with a line of an hundred and sixty fathom,[3] they could find no bottom. It was a very cold wind, like as if it had been winter, which made some to wish for more clothes.

Friday, wind still northerly, but very faint. It was a great foggy mist, and exceeding cold as if it had been December. One would have wondered to have seen the innumerable numbers of fowl which we saw swimming on every side of the ship, and mighty fishes rolling and tumbling in the waters, twice as long and big as an ox. In the afternoon we saw mighty whales spewing up water in the air like the smoke of a chimney, and making the sea about them white and hoary.

[July 26] The fifth Sabbath from Milford Haven and the tenth on shipboard; a fair sunshiny summer day, and would have been very hot, had not God allayed the heat with a good gale of southerly wind, by which also we were carried on in our journey after seven leagues a watch. I preached in the forenoon and Mr. Maude in the afternoon. In the afternoon the wind grew stronger, and it was a rough night for wind and rain, and some had our beds that night ill wet with rain leaking in through the sides of the ship.

Monday [July 27], wind still strong at south. This day we spent much time in filling diverse tuns[4] with salt water; which was needful, because much beer, fresh water, beef, and other provisions being spent, the ship went not so well, being too light for want of ballast.[5] When this work was done, we set forth more sail, and went that evening and all the night following with good speed in our journey.

Tuesday morning, a great calm, and very hot all that forenoon; our people and cattle being much afflicted with faintness, sweating, and heat; but (lo the goodness of our God) about noon the wind blew at north and by east, which called us from our heat and helped us forward in our way. This afternoon there came and lit upon our ship a little land bird with blue-colored feathers, about the bigness of a sparrow, by which some conceived we were not far from land.

Thursday, wind still westerly against us all the forenoon, but about one of the clock the Lord remembered us in mercy, and sent us a fresh gale at south; which though weak and soft yet did not only much mitigate the heat, but also helped us something forward in our way. In the evening about sunsetting, we saw with admiration and delight innumerable multitudes of huge grampuses rolling and tumbling about the sides of the ship, spewing and puffing up water as they went, and pursuing great numbers of bonitos and lesser fishes; so marvelous to behold are the works and wonders of the Almighty in the deep.

Saturday morning [August 1], a cool wind at north, whereby we went on in our course an hour or two, though very slowly because of the weakness of the wind. Afterward it became a great calm; and our seamen sounded about one of the clock and found ground at sixty fathom. Presently after, another little land bird came and lit upon the sails of the ship. In the cool of the evening (the calm still continuing) our seamen fished with hook and line and took cod as fast as they could haul them up into the ship.

[August 3] But lest we should grow secure and neglect the Lord through abundance of prosperity, our wise and loving God was pleased on Monday morning about three of the clock, when we were upon the coast of land, to exercise us with a sore storm and tempest of wind and rain; so that many of us passengers with wind and rain were raised out of our beds, and our seamen were forced to let down all the sails; and the ship was so tossed with fearful mountains and valleys of water, as if we should have been overwhelmed and swallowed up. But this lasted not long, for at our poor prayers the Lord was pleased to magnify His mercy in assuaging the winds and seas again about sunrising. But the wind was become west against us, so that we floated upon the coast, making no dispatch of way all that day and the night following; and besides there was a great fog and mist all that day,

2. **leagues:** A league is a measure of distance equal to about three miles.
3. **fathom** (fath′əm): measure of length equal to six feet.
4. **tuns:** large casks.
5. **ballast** (bal′əst): anything heavy carried in a ship to give stability.

so that we could not see to make land, but kept in all sail, and lay still, rather losing than gaining, but taking abundance of cod and halibut, wherewith our bodies were abundantly refreshed after they had been tossed with the storm.

Tuesday, the fog still continued all forenoon; about noon the day cleared up, and the wind blew with a soft gale at south, and we set sail again, going on in our course, though very slowly because of the smallness of the wind. At night it was a calm and abundance of rain.

Saturday morning [August 8] we had a good gale of wind at west-southwest; and this morning our seamen took abundance of mackerel, and about eight of the clock we all had a clear and comfortable sight of America and made land again at an island called Menhiggin, an island without inhabitants about thirty-nine leagues northward or northeast short of Cape Anne. A little from the island we saw more northward diverse other islands called St. George Islands, and the mainland of New England all along northward and eastward as we sailed. This mercy of our God we had cause more highly to esteem of, because when we first saw land this morning there was a great fog; and afterward when the day cleared up we saw many rocks and islands almost on every side of us, as Menhiggin, St. George Islands, Pemmequid, etc.

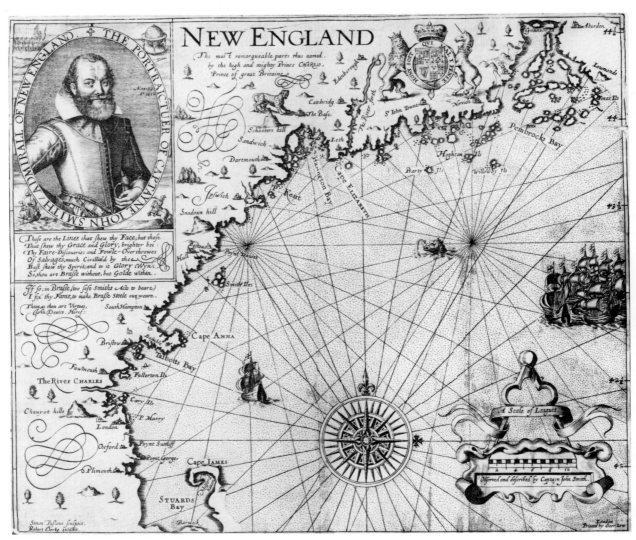

Map of New England by Captain John Smith (1616).

Yet in the midst of these dangers our God preserved us, though, because of the thick fog we could not see far about us to look unto ourselves. In the afternoon, the wind continuing still westward against us, we lay off again to the sea southward, and our seamen and many passengers delighted themselves in taking abundance of mackerel. . . .

[August 15] But yet the Lord had not done with us, nor yet had let us see all His power and goodness which He would have us take knowledge of; and therefore on Saturday morning about break of day, the Lord sent forth a most terrible storm of rain and easterly wind, whereby we were in as much danger as I think ever people were, for we lost in that morning three great anchors and cables, of which cables one having cost fifty pounds never had been in any water before; two were broken by the violence of the waves, and the third cut by the seamen in extremity and distress to save the ship and their and our lives. And when our cables and anchors were all lost, we had no outward means of deliverance but by losing sail, if so be we might get to the sea from amongst the islands and rocks where we anchored. In this extremity and appearance of death, as distress and distraction would suffer us, we cried unto the Lord and He was pleased to have compassion and pity upon us; for by His overruling providence and His own immediate good hand, He guided the ship past the rock, assuaged the violence of the sea, and the wind and rain, and gave us a little respite to fit the ship with other sails.

This day [August 16] we went on toward Cape Anne, as the wind would suffer, and our poor sails further, and came within sight thereof the other morning, which Sabbath being the thirteenth we kept on shipboard was a marvelous pleasant day, for a fresh gale of wind and clear sunshine weather. This day we went directly before the wind and had delight all along the coast as we went, in viewing Cape Anne, the bay of Saugus, the bay of Salem, Marblehead, Pullin Point, and other places, and came to anchor at low tide in the evening at Nantascot in a most pleasant harbor like to which I had never seen, amongst a great many islands on every side. I preached on shipboard both ends of the day. After the evening's exercise, when it was flowing tide again, we set sail and came that night to anchor again before Boston, and so rested that night with glad and thankful hearts that God had put an end to our long journey, being a thousand leagues, that is three thousand miles English, over one of the greatest seas in the world.

Responding to the Journal

Analyzing the Journal

Identifying Facts

1. Explain why it took Mather's party eight days to travel the 120 miles from Warrington to Bristol, in England. Why did it take another month before they could board ship?
2. Describe the government procedure the travelers had to pass through before they could sail.
3. On May 28, 1635, five ships sailed from Bristol. What were their names, and where was each bound?
4. Explain why barrels had to be filled with sea water on July 27.
5. List five of the creatures that Mather saw during his journey. Explain how he reacted to them.
6. On July 28, a bluebird landed on the ship. Explain what this incident meant to some of the travelers.
7. On August 3, what followed a period of calm? After that, why did the ship stay in one spot? Tell what the travelers did during this time.
8. On August 15, what further difficulty did the ship have?
9. On Sunday, August 16, Mather finally reached Boston Harbor. How many miles had he traveled? How long did his entire journey from Warrington take?

Interpreting Meanings

10. In real-life accounts, just as in fiction, **conflict,** or struggle between opposing forces, is often an important element. What conflicts do Mather and the other travelers experience during their journey? Identify at least three instances, and explain the outcome of each.

Applying Meanings

11. Describe a long trip you or someone you know took by road, air, or water. Even if the trip was shorter than Mather's, what similar situations occurred along the way? What kinds of modern journeys do you imagine would be as long and difficult as Mather's?

Writing About the Journal

A Creative Response

1. **Keeping a Travel Journal.** Imagine that you are one of the children making the journey with Richard Mather. While you are waiting in Bristol, what are you thinking and feeling about leaving your homeland? What are your hopes and fears regarding your journey and your new home in America? Write three journal entries for various dates at different stages of your journey. Begin by identifying yourself and your age.

A Critical Response

2. **Analyzing Character.** The Puritan settlers of the 1600's have been described as hard-working, profoundly religious, intelligent people. Find four or five passages in Mather's journal that support this comment. Explain how these qualities would have helped the Puritans survive in a strange land. Write at least one paragraph.

Analyzing Language and Vocabulary

Using Context Clues

If the italicized words in the following passage from Mather's journal were unfamiliar to you, using context clues could have helped you guess their meanings:

". . . we cried unto the Lord and He was pleased to have compassion and pity upon us; for by His overruling *providence* and His own immediate good hand, He guided the ship past the rock, *assuaged* the violence of the sea, and the wind and rain, and gave us a little *respite* to fit the ship with other sails."

An important context clue is the general sense of the passage. In this passage the general sense is that God gives the travelers a chance to put up new sails during a storm. This context clue should have led you to guess that *assuaged* means "eased" or "calmed," and that *respite* means "relief" or "rest." Examples that accompany an unfamiliar word often give clues to its meaning. In this passage, *compassion, pity, good hand,* and *guided* are all examples of God's *providence.* If you missed these clues, another kind of context clue could have helped you: pairing of the word with one you already know. *Providence* contains the familiar word *provide.* If you guessed that *providence* means "the providing of guidance or care," you were right.

Use context clues to choose the best meaning for the italicized words in the following passages.

1. "The wind being strong, the sea was rough this day, and most of our passengers were very sick and ill through much *casting.*"

   a. fishing for bonito and porpoise
   b. tossing of the ship
   c. throwing things overboard

2. "In the afternoon we saw mighty whales spewing up water in the air like the smoke of a chimney, and making the sea about them white and *hoary.*"

   a. frosty-looking
   b. horrible
   c. dangerous

3. " . . . a fair sunshiny summer day, and would have been very hot, had not God *allayed* the heat with a good gale of southerly wind, by which also we were carried on in our journey . . . ."

   a. increased
   b. added humidity to
   c. relieved us of

4. "But the wind was become west against us, so that we floated upon the coast, making *no dispatch of way* all that day and the night following. . . ."

   a. a little speed
   b. choppy progress
   c. no progress

Most nations are proud of what they consider to be their uniqueness. Just as exaggerated stories develop in families to express family identity, legends develop among the people of a nation to express national identity. The subjects of legends are often real people. These people become heroes who express the nation's hopes and dreams and ideals, rather than its actual history. Where history ends and legend begins is difficult to say, and perhaps it does not always matter. Perhaps George Washington really told lies during his lifetime. But by making him the hero of a legend about a boy who "can not tell a lie," we make him our own—the embodiment of an honorable ideal of the "new world."

Legendary Heroes

His Hammer in His Hand, from the John Henry series by Palmer C. Hayden (1944–1954). Oil.

The Museum of African American Art, Los Angeles. Palmer C. Hayden Collection. Gift of Miriam A. Hayden.

THE ORPHAN BOY AND THE ELK DOG

Traditional Blackfoot

Certain inventions or discoveries can cause great changes in the way a society lives. Imagine, for example, how different your life would be in a society without automobiles.

The following legend comes from the Blackfoot people of Montana and Alberta, Canada, who hunted buffalo on the Great Plains until the 1880's. Like other legends, this story has some basis in historical fact, but many details have been exaggerated during years of retelling. As you read, note the clues that help you discover what the mysterious Elk Dog actually is. In what ways did this creature change Blackfoot society forever?

In the days when people had only dogs to carry their bundles, two orphan children, a boy and his sister, were having a hard time. The boy was deaf, and because he could not understand what people said, they thought him foolish and dull-witted. Even his relatives wanted nothing to do with him. The name he had been given at birth, while his parents still lived, was Long Arrow. Now he was like a beaten, mangy dog, the kind who hungrily roams outside a camp, circling it from afar, smelling the good meat boiling in the kettles but never coming close for fear of being kicked. Only his sister, who was bright and beautiful, loved him.

Then the sister was adopted by a family from another camp, people who were attracted by her good looks and pleasing ways. Though they wanted her for a daughter, they certainly did not want the awkward, stupid boy. And so they took away the only person who cared about him, and the orphan boy was left to fend for himself. He lived on scraps thrown to the dogs and things he found on the refuse heaps. He dressed in remnants of skins and frayed robes discarded by the poorest people. At night he bedded down in a grass-lined dugout, like an animal in its den.

Eventually the game was hunted out near the camp that the boy regarded as his, and the people decided to move. The lodges were taken down, belongings were packed into rawhide bags and put on dog travois, and the village departed. "Stay here," they told the boy. "We don't want your kind coming with us."

For two or three days the boy fed on scraps the people had left behind, but he knew he would starve if he stayed. He had to join his people, whether they liked it or not. He followed their tracks, frantic that he would lose them, and crying at the same time. Soon the sweat was running down his skinny body. As he was stumbling, running, panting, something suddenly snapped in his left ear with a sound like a small crack, and a wormlike substance came out of that ear. All at once on his left side he could hear birdsongs for

> **Blackfoot Words.** Several words in this story refer to everyday objects found in traditional Blackfoot society. Some, like *tipi,* may be familiar to you. Others, like *travois,* may be unfamiliar. As you read, keep a list of these words from Blackfoot society. Try to guess their meanings by using context clues. Even if you are unable to figure out the full meaning of a word, the context clues should help you guess the object's function.

Blackfoot Tipis by William Armstrong.

Royal Ontario Museum, Toronto, Canada.

the first time. He took this wormlike thing in his left hand and hurried on. Then there was a snap in his right ear and a wormlike thing came out of it, and on his right side he could hear the rushing waters of a stream. His hearing was restored! And it was razor-sharp—he could make out the rustling of a tiny mouse in dry leaves a good distance away. The orphan boy laughed and was happy for the first time in his life. With renewed courage he followed the trail his people had made.

In the meantime the village had settled into its new place. Men were already out hunting. Thus the boy came upon Good Running, a kindly old chief, butchering a fat buffalo cow he had just killed. When the chief saw the boy, he said to himself, "Here comes that poor good-for-nothing boy. It was wrong to abandon him." To the boy Good Running said "Rest here, grandson, you're sweaty and covered with dust. Here, have some tripe."

The boy wolfed down the meat. He was not used to hearing and talking yet, but his eyes were alert and Good Running also noticed a change in his manner. "This boy," the chief said to himself, "is neither stupid nor crazy." He gave the orphan a piece of the hump meat, then a piece of liver, then a piece of raw kidney, and at last the very best kind of meat—a slice of tongue. The more the old man looked at the boy, the more he liked him. On the spur of the moment he said, "Grandson, I'm going to adopt you; there's a place for you in my tipi. And I'm going to make you into a good hunter and warrior." The boy wept, this time for joy. Good Running said, "They called you a stupid, crazy boy, but now that I think of it, the name you were given at birth is Long Arrow. I'll see that people call you by your right name. Now come along." . . .

So a new life began for Long Arrow. He had to learn to speak and to understand well, and to catch up on all the things a boy should know. He was a fast learner and soon surpassed other boys his age in knowledge and skills. At last even Good Running's wife accepted him.

He grew up into a fine young hunter, tall and good-looking in the quilled buckskin outfit the chief's wife made for him. He helped his grandfather in everything and became a staff for Good Running to lean on. But he was lonely, for most people in the camp could not forget that Long Arrow had once been an outcast. "Grandfather," he said one day, "I want to do something to make you proud and show people that you were wise to adopt me. What can I do?"

Good Running answered, "Someday you will be a chief and do great things."

"But what's a great thing I could do now, Grandfather?"

The chief thought for a long time. "Maybe I shouldn't tell you this," he said. "I love you and don't want to lose you. But on winter nights, men talk of powerful spirit people living at the bottom of a faraway lake. Down in that lake the spirit people keep mystery animals who do their work for them. These animals are larger than a great elk, but they carry the burdens of the spirit people like dogs. So they're called Pono-Kamita—Elk Dogs. They are said to be swift, strong, gentle,

and beautiful beyond imagination. Every fourth generation, one of our young warriors has gone to find these spirit folk and bring back an Elk Dog for us. But none of our brave young men has ever returned.

"Grandfather, I'm not afraid. I'll go and find the Elk Dog."

"Grandson, first learn to be a man. Learn the right prayers and ceremonies. Be brave. Be generous and open-handed. Pity the old and the fatherless, and let the holy men of the tribe find a medicine for you which will protect you on your dangerous journey. We will begin by purifying you in the sweat bath."

So Long Arrow was purified with the white steam of the sweat lodge. He was taught how to use the pipe, and how to pray to the Great Mystery Power. The tribe's holy men gave him a medicine and made for him a shield with designs on it to ward off danger.

Then one morning, without telling anybody, Good Running loaded his best travois dog with all the things Long Arrow would need for traveling. The chief gave him his medicine, his shield, and his own fine bow and, just as the sun came up, went with his grandson to the edge of the camp to purify him with sweet-smelling cedar smoke. Long Arrow left unheard and unseen by anyone else. After a while some people noticed that he was gone, but no one except his grandfather knew where and for what purpose.

Following Good Running's advice, Long Arrow wandered southward. On the fourth day of his journey he came to a small pond, where a strange man was standing as if waiting for him. "Why have you come here?" the stranger asked.

"I have come to find the mysterious Elk Dog."

"Ah, there I cannot help you," said the man, who was the spirit of the pond. "But if you travel further south, four-times-four days, you might chance upon a bigger lake and there meet one of my uncles. Possibly he might talk to you; then again, he might not. That's all I can tell you."

Long Arrow thanked the man, who went down to the bottom of the pond, where he lived.

Long Arrow wandered on, walking for long hours and taking little time for rest. Through deep canyons and over high mountains he went, wearing out his moccasins and enduring cold and heat, hunger and thirst.

Finally Long Arrow approached a big lake surrounded by steep pine-covered hills. There he came face to face with a tall man, fierce and scowling and twice the height of most humans. This stranger carried a long lance with a heavy spearpoint made of shining flint. "Young one," he growled, "why did you come here?"

"I came to find the mysterious Elk Dog."

The stranger, who was the spirit of the lake, stuck his face right into Long Arrow's and shook his mighty lance. "Little one, aren't you afraid of me?" he snarled.

"No, I am not," answered Long Arrow, smiling.

The tall spirit man gave a hideous grin, which was his way of being friendly. "I like small humans who aren't afraid," he said, "but I can't help you. Perhaps our grandfather will take the trouble to listen to you. More likely he won't. Walk south for four-times-four days, and maybe you'll find him. But probably you won't." With that the tall spirit turned his back on Long Arrow and went to the bottom of the lake, where he lived.

Long Arrow walked on for another four-times-four days, sleeping and resting little. By now he staggered and stumbled in his weakness, and his dog was not much better off. At last he came to the biggest lake he had ever seen, surrounded by towering snow-capped peaks and waterfalls of ice. This time there was nobody to receive him. As a matter of fact, there seemed to be no living thing around. "This must be the Great Mystery Lake," thought Long Arrow. Exhausted, he fell down upon the shortgrass meadow by the lake, fell down among the wild flowers, and went to sleep with his tired dog curled up at his feet.

When Long Arrow awoke, the sun was already high. He opened his eyes and saw a beautiful child standing before him, a boy in a dazzling white buckskin robe decorated with porcupine quills of many colors. The boy said, "We have been expecting you for a long time. My grandfather invites you to his lodge. Follow me."

Telling his dog to wait, Long Arrow took his medicine shield and his grandfather's bow and went with the wonderful child. They came to the edge of the lake. The spirit boy pointed to the water and said, "My grandfather's lodge is down there. Come!" The child turned himself into a kingfisher and dove straight to the bottom.

Afraid, Long Arrow thought, "How can I follow him and not be drowned?" But then he said to himself, "I knew all the time that this would not be easy. In setting out to find the Elk Dog, I already threw my life away." And he boldly jumped into the water. To his surprise, he found it did not make him wet, that it parted before him, that he could breathe and see. He touched the lake's sandy bottom. It sloped down, down toward a center point.

Long Arrow descended this slope until he came to a small flat valley. In the middle of it stood a large tipi of tanned buffalo hide. The images of two strange animals were drawn on it in sacred vermilion paint. A kingfisher perched high on the top of the tipi flew down and turned again into the beautiful boy, who said, "Welcome. Enter my grandfather's lodge."

Long Arrow followed the spirit boy inside. In the back at the seat of honor sat a black-robed old man with flowing white hair and such power emanating from him that Long Arrow felt himself in the presence of a truly Great One. The holy man welcomed Long Arrow and offered him food. The man's wife came in bringing dishes of buffalo hump, liver, tongues, delicious chunks of deer meat, the roasted flesh of strange, tasty water birds, and meat pounded together with berries, chokecherries, and kidney fat. Famished after his long journey, Long Arrow ate with relish. Yet he still looked around to admire the furnishings of the tipi, the painted inner curtain, the many medicine shields, wonderfully wrought weapons, shirts, and robes decorated with porcupine quills in rainbow colors, beautifully painted rawhide containers filled with wonderful things, and much else that dazzled him.

After Long Arrow had stilled his hunger, the old spirit chief filled the pipe and passed it to his guest. They smoked, praying silently. After a while the old man said, "Some came before you from time to time, but they were always afraid of the deep water, and so they went away with empty hands. But you, grandson, were brave enough to

The Orphan Boy and the Elk Dog 529

plunge in, and therefore you are chosen to receive a wonderful gift to carry back to your people. Now, go outside with my grandson.''

The beautiful boy took Long Arrow to a meadow on which some strange animals, unlike any the young man had ever seen, were galloping and gamboling, neighing and nickering. They were truly wonderful to look at, with their glossy coats fine as a maiden's hair, their long manes and tails streaming in the wind. Now rearing, now nuzzling, they looked at Long Arrow with gentle eyes which belied their fiery appearance.

"At last," thought Long Arrow, "here they are before my own eyes, the Pono-Kamita, the Elk Dogs!"

"Watch me," said the mystery boy, "so that you learn to do what I am doing." Gracefully and without effort, the boy swung himself onto the back of a jet-black Elk Dog with a high, arched neck. Larger than any elk Long Arrow had ever come across, the animal carried the boy all over the meadow swiftly as the wind. Then the boy returned, jumped off his mount, and said, "Now you try it." A little timidly Long Arrow climbed up on the beautiful Elk Dog's back. Seemingly regarding him as feather-light, it took off like a flying arrow. The young man felt himself soaring through the air as a bird does, and experienced a happiness greater even than the joy he had felt when Good Running had adopted him as a grandson.

When they had finished riding the Elk Dogs, the spirit boy said to Long Arrow, "Young hunter from the land above the waters, I want you to have what you have come for. Listen to me. You may have noticed that my grandfather wears a black medicine robe as long as a woman's dress, and that he is always trying to hide his feet. Try to get a glimpse of them, for if you do, he can refuse you nothing. He will then tell you to ask him for a gift, and you must ask for these three things: his rainbow-colored quilled belt, his black medicine robe, and a herd of these animals which you seem to like."

Long Arrow thanked him and vowed to follow his advice. For four days the young man stayed in the spirit chief's lodge, where he ate well and often went out riding on the Elk Dogs. But try as

he would, he could never get a look at the old man's feet. The spirit chief always kept them carefully covered. Then on the morning of the fourth day, the old one was walking out of the tipi when his medicine robe caught in the entrance flap. As the robe opened, Long Arrow caught a glimpse of a leg and one foot. He was awed to see that it was not a human limb at all, but the glossy leg and firm hoof of an Elk Dog! He could not stifle a cry of surprise, and the old man looked over his shoulder and saw that his leg and hoof were exposed. The chief seemed a little embarrassed, but shrugged and said, "I tried to hide this, but you must have been fated to see it. Look, both of my feet are those of an Elk Dog. You may as well ask me for a gift. Don't be timid; tell me what you want."

Long Arrow spoke boldly: "I want three things: your belt of rainbow colors, your black medicine robe, and your herd of Elk Dogs."

"Well, so you're really not timid at all!" said the old man. "You ask for a lot, and I'll give it to you, except that you cannot have all my Elk Dogs; I'll give you half of them. Now I must tell you that my black medicine robe and my many-colored belt have Elk Dog magic in them. Always wear the robe when you try to catch Elk Dogs; then they can't get away from you. On quiet nights, if you listen closely to the belt, you will hear the Elk Dog dance song and Elk Dog prayers. You must learn them. And I will give you one more magic gift: this long rope woven from the hair of a white buffalo bull. With it you will never fail to catch whichever Elk Dog you want."

The spirit chief presented him with the gifts and said, "Now you must leave. At first the Elk Dogs will not follow you. Keep the medicine robe and the magic belt on at all times, and walk for four days toward the north. Never look back—always look to the north. On the fourth day the Elk Dogs will come up beside you on the left. Still don't look back. But after they have overtaken you, catch one with the rope of white buffalo hair and ride him home. Don't lose the black robe, or you will lose the Elk Dogs and never catch them again."

Long Arrow listened carefully so that he would remember. Then the old spirit chief had his wife

Kiäsax (Bear on the Left), Piegan Blackfeet Man by
Karl Bodmer (late 19th century). Watercolor.

Joslyn Art Museum, Omaha, Nebraska.

make up a big pack of food, almost too heavy for Long Arrow to carry, and the young man took leave of his generous spirit host. The mysterious boy once again turned himself into a kingfisher and led Long Arrow to the surface of the lake, where his faithful dog greeted him joyfully. Long Arrow fed the dog, put his pack of food on the travois, and started walking north.

On the fourth day the Elk Dogs came up on his left side, as the spirit chief had foretold. Long Arrow snared the black one with the arched neck to ride, and he caught another to carry the pack of food. They galloped swiftly on, the dog barking at the big Elk Dogs' heels.

When Long Arrow arrived at last in his village, the people were afraid and hid. They did not recognize him astride his beautiful Elk Dog but took him for a monster, half-man and half-animal. Long Arrow kept calling, "Grandfather Good Running, it's your grandson. I've come back bringing Elk Dogs!"

Recognizing the voice, Good Running came out of hiding and wept for joy, because he had given Long Arrow up for lost. Then all the others emerged from their hiding places to admire the wonderful new animals.

Long Arrow said, "My grandfather and grandmother who adopted me, I can never repay you for your kindness. Accept these wonderful Elk Dogs as my gift. Now we no longer need to be humble foot-sloggers, because these animals will carry us swiftly everywhere we want to go. Now buffalo hunting will be easy. Now our tipis will be larger, our possessions will be greater, because an Elk Dog travois can carry a load ten times bigger than that of a dog. Take them, my grandparents. I shall keep for myself only this black male and this black female, which will grow into a fine herd."

"You have indeed done something great, grandson," said Good Running, and he spoke true. The people became the bold riders of the Plains and soon could hardly imagine how they had existed without these wonderful animals.

After some time Good Running, rich and honored by all, said to Long Arrow, "Grandson, lead us to the Great Mystery Lake so we can camp by its shores. Let's visit the spirit chief and the wondrous boy; maybe they will give us more of their power and magic gifts."

Long Arrow led the people southward and again found the Great Mystery Lake. But the waters would no longer part for him, nor would any of the kingfishers they saw turn into a boy. Nor, gazing down into the crystal-clear water, could they discover people, Elk Dogs, or a tipi. There was nothing in the lake but a few fish.

—Retold by George Bird Grinnell

Responding to the Legend

Analyzing the Legend

Identifying Facts

1. According to the story's beginning, what animal originally carried people's bundles?
2. What disability does Long Arrow have? As a result, what do people think of his mental abilities? Explain how people treat Long Arrow and how he is forced to live.
3. What good thing happens to Long Arrow while he is running after his people? When he arrives at the new camp, what family relationship does Good Running establish with him?
4. According to Good Running, what is an Elk Dog? Why would bringing one back be a "great thing" to do?
5. List the various things that Good Running has Long Arrow do to prepare for his journey.

6. Describe the second lake spirit that Long Arrow meets. How does he test Long Arrow's courage? How does Long Arrow react? At the Great Mystery Lake, in what other ways does Long Arrow display courage?

7. In addition to the Elk Dogs, what three magic gifts does the spirit chief give Long Arrow? How is Long Arrow to use each gift?

Interpreting Meanings

8. Considering all the descriptions of the Elk Dogs in this story, identify these animals' more common name. Discuss how the Elk Dogs' magical origin expresses both the Blackfoot's feeling about these animals and their importance in Blackfoot society.

9. In addition to explaining the origin of an important animal in Blackfoot society, this legend reveals the **personality traits** the Blackfoot considered heroic. Considering Long Arrow's childhood, his journey, and his relationship with Good Running, list as many words as you can that describe Long Arrow's personality. Which three traits do you think the Blackfoot considered most necessary for a hero? Support your opinions with evidence from the legend.

10. What **moral,** or lesson, does this story teach regarding the treatment of people with disadvantages, such as orphans and the physically impaired?

11. List at least five incidents in this story that could not happen in real life. Explain how these exaggerated or magical events add to the appeal of the story.

12. At the end of the story, Good Running asks Long Arrow to lead the people to the Great Mystery Lake. Considering the trials that Long Arrow endured and the purpose of his first journey, why do you suppose that on his second visit he finds "nothing in the lake but a few fish"?

Applying Meanings

13. Heroic journeys in search of precious objects are called **quests.** Like Long Arrow's, most quests are preceded by rituals or other preparations designed to guarantee strength. What kinds of quests might a real modern hero undertake? Describe some of the rituals he or she might perform as preparation.

Writing About the Legend

A Creative Response

1. **Creating a Legend.** Write the beginning of a legend set in your own time, about a hero or heroine who starts out in life in a very unpromising, unheroic way. Describe your hero or heroine in at least one paragraph. Consider these elements:

   a. Appearance
   b. Setting
   c. Food eaten
   d. Attitude of others

A Critical Response

2. **Writing a Research Report.** The first European explorers brought horses with them to the New World. Before their arrival, the native peoples had never seen this useful animal. In the library, read about the introduction of horses into the New World and about their effect on Native American cultures. Then write a research report of about three paragraphs in which you answer one or more of the following questions: Who brought the first horses to America and when? How did these first American horses become wild? How did Native Americans first acquire horses? Which Native Americans found horses most useful, and why? In what ways did horses change the way Native Americans lived?

Analyzing Language and Vocabulary

Native American Words and Culture

Words for everyday objects can help readers understand how people from a different culture live and work. The following words from "The Orphan Boy and the Elk Dog" describe objects that were common among the native peoples of the Great Plains. Using a good dictionary, encyclopedia, or book about Indian life, write a definition for each word. In your definitions, explain how the objects were made and used. Consider drawing illustrations to accompany your definitions.

1. lodge
2. travois
3. tipi
4. sweat bath or sweat lodge
5. buckskin

THE DEVIL AND DANIEL WEBSTER

Stephen Vincent Benét

Daniel Webster (1782–1852) was a lawyer and one of the most important American political leaders of the first half of the nineteenth century. Though he served as Secretary of State, he is best remembered as a United States Senator. In his eloquent speeches, Webster insisted that the United States remain one unified country. This story is based in part on the real Daniel Webster. Through the use of exaggeration, however, the writer has created a tall tale. As you read, think about what American ideals the fictional Daniel Webster embodies. If you read this story aloud, you'll hear how the writer has used the voice of an oral storyteller.

It's a story they tell in the border country, where Massachusetts joins Vermont and New Hampshire.

Yes, Dan'l Webster's dead—or, at least, they buried him. But every time there's a thunderstorm around Marshfield, they say you can hear his rolling voice in the hollows of the sky. And they say that if you go to his grave and speak loud and clear, ''Dan'l Webster—Dan'l Webster!'' the ground'll begin to shiver and the trees begin to shake. And after a while you'll hear a deep voice saying, ''Neighbor, how stands the Union?'' Then you better answer the Union stands as she stood, rock-bottomed and copper-sheathed, one and indivisible, or he's liable to rear right out of the ground. At least, that's what I was told when I was a youngster.

You see, for a while, he was the biggest man in the country. He never got to be President, but he was the biggest man. There were thousands that trusted in him right next to God Almighty, and they told stories about him that were like the stories of patriarchs and such. They said, when he stood up to speak, stars and stripes came right out in the sky, and once he spoke against a river and made it sink into the ground. They said, when he walked the woods with his fishing rod, Killall, the trout would jump out of the streams right into his pockets, for they knew it was no use putting up a fight against him; and, when he argued a case, he could turn on the harps of the blessed and the shaking of the earth underground. That was the kind of man he was, and his big farm up at Marshfield was suitable to him. The chickens he raised were all white meat down through the drumsticks, the cows were tended like children, and the big ram he called Goliath had horns with a curl like a morning-glory vine and could butt through an iron door. But Dan'l wasn't one of your gentleman

> **Allusions.** Many stories contain *allusions,* or references to literature or to an actual event, person, or place. Noticing and understanding allusions will help you appreciate any story more fully. In ''The Devil and Daniel Webster,'' for example, understanding allusions to the historical Daniel Webster helps make the fantastic events in Benét's story believable. As you read, list some of the allusions you find. Which do you understand? Where might you look to find the meanings of those that puzzle you?

farmers; he knew all the ways of the land, and he'd be up by candlelight to see that the chores got done. A man with a mouth like a mastiff,[1] a brow like a mountain and eyes like burning anthracite[2]—that was Dan'l Webster in his prime. And the biggest case he argued never got written down in the books, for he argued it against the devil, nip and tuck and no holds barred. And this is the way I used to hear it told.

There was a man named Jabez Stone, lived at Cross Corners, New Hampshire. He wasn't a bad man to start with, but he was an unlucky man. If he planted corn, he got borers; if he planted potatoes, he got blight.[3] He had good-enough land, but it didn't prosper him; he had a decent wife and children, but the more children he had, the less there was to feed them. If stones cropped up in his neighbor's field, boulders boiled up in his; if he had a horse with the spavins, he'd trade it for one with the staggers[4] and give something extra. There's some folks bound to be like that, apparently. But one day Jabez Stone got sick of the whole business.

He'd been plowing that morning and he'd just broke the plowshare on a rock that he could have sworn hadn't been there yesterday. And, as he stood looking at the plowshare, the off horse began to cough—that ropy kind of cough that means sickness and horse doctors. There were two children down with the measles, his wife was ailing, and he had a whitlow[5] on his thumb. It was about the last straw for Jabez Stone. "I vow," he said, and he looked around him kind of desperate—"I vow it's enough to make a man want to sell his soul to the devil! And I would, too, for two cents!"

Then he felt a kind of queerness come over him at having said what he'd said; though, naturally, being a New Hampshireman, he wouldn't take it back. But, all the same, when it got to be evening and, as far as he could see, no notice had been taken, he felt relieved in his mind, for he was a religious man. But notice is always taken, sooner or later, just like the Good Book says. And, sure enough, next day, about suppertime, a soft-spoken, dark-dressed stranger drove up in a handsome buggy and asked for Jabez Stone.

Well, Jabez told his family it was a lawyer, come to see him about a legacy. But he knew who it was. He didn't like the looks of the stranger, nor the way he smiled with his teeth. They were white teeth, and plentiful—some say they were filed to a point, but I wouldn't vouch for that. And he didn't like it when the dog took one look at the stranger and ran away howling, with his tail between his legs. But having passed his word, more or less, he stuck to it, and they went out behind the barn and made their bargain. Jabez Stone had to prick his finger to sign, and the stranger lent him a silver pin. The wound healed clean, but it left a little white scar.

After that, all of a sudden, things began to pick up and prosper for Jabez Stone. His cows got fat and his horses sleek, his crops were the envy of the neighborhood, and lightning might strike all over the valley, but it wouldn't strike his barn. Pretty soon, he was one of the prosperous people of the county; they asked him to stand for selectman,[6] and he stood for it; there began to be talk of running him for state senate. All in all, you might say the Stone family was as happy and contented as cats in a dairy. And so they were, except for Jabez Stone.

He'd been contented enough, the first few years. It's a great thing when bad luck turns; it drives most other things out of your head. True, every now and then, especially in rainy weather, the little white scar on his finger would give him a twinge. And once a year, punctual as clockwork, the stranger with the handsome buggy would come

---

1. **mastiff:** a huge, powerful dog, formerly used as a watchdog.
2. **anthracite** (an'thrə·sīt'): hard coal.
3. **borers . . . blight:** *borers* are pests that eat corn; *blight* is a disease that kills potatoes.
4. **spavins . . . staggers:** *spavins* (spav'inz) is a disease that causes lameness in a horse; *staggers* is a disease that causes horses to lose coordination, to stagger, or to fall.
5. **whitlow:** painful, infected swelling.

6. **stand for selectman:** run for the office of selectman. A selectman is a member of a board of officers chosen in many New England towns to manage municipal affairs.

driving by. But the sixth year, the stranger lighted, and, after that, his peace was over for Jabez Stone.

The stranger came up through the lower field, switching his boots with a cane—they were handsome black boots, but Jabez Stone never liked the look of them, particularly the toes. And, after he'd passed the time of day, he said, "Well, Mr. Stone, you're a hummer! It's a very pretty property you've got here, Mr. Stone."

"Well, some might favor it and others might not," said Jabez Stone, for he was a New Hampshireman.

"Oh, no need to decry your industry!" said the stranger, very easy, showing his teeth in a smile. "After all, we know what's been done, and it's been according to contract and specifications. So when—ahem—the mortgage falls due next year, you shouldn't have any regrets."

"Speaking of that mortgage, mister," said Jabez Stone, and he looked around for help to the earth and the sky, "I'm beginning to have one or two doubts about it."

"Doubts?" said the stranger, not quite so pleasantly.

"Why, yes," said Jabez Stone. "This being the USA and me always having been a religious man." He cleared his throat and got bolder. "Yes, sir," he said, "I'm beginning to have considerable doubts as to that mortgage holding in court."

"There's courts and courts," said the stranger, clicking his teeth. "Still, we might as well have a look at the original document." And he hauled out a big black pocketbook, full of papers. "Sherwin, Slater, Stevens, Stone," he muttered. "I, Jabez Stone, for a term of seven years—Oh, it's quite in order, I think."

But Jabez Stone wasn't listening, for he saw something else flutter out of the black pocketbook. It was something that looked like a moth, but it wasn't a moth. And as Jabez Stone stared at it, it seemed to speak to him in a small sort of piping voice, terrible small and thin, but terrible human. "Neighbor Stone!" it squeaked. "Neighbor Stone! Help me! For God's sake, help me!"

But before Jabez Stone could stir hand or foot, the stranger whipped out a big bandanna handkerchief, caught the creature in it, just like a butterfly, and started tying up the ends of the bandanna.

"Sorry for the interruption," he said. "As I was saying—"

But Jabez Stone was shaking all over like a scared horse.

"That's Miser Stevens's voice!" he said, in a croak. "And you've got him in your handkerchief!"

The stranger looked a little embarrassed.

"Yes, I really should have transferred him to the collecting box," he said with a simper, "but there were some rather unusual specimens there and I didn't want them crowded. Well, well, these little contretemps[7] will occur."

"I don't know what you mean by contertan," said Jabez Stone, "but that was Miser Stevens's voice! And he ain't dead! You can't tell me he is! He was just as spry and mean as a woodchuck, Tuesday!"

"In the midst of life—"[8] said the stranger, kind of pious. "Listen!" Then a bell began to toll in the valley and Jabez Stone listened, with the sweat running down his face. For he knew it was tolled for Miser Stevens and that he was dead.

"These long-standing accounts," said the stranger with a sigh; "one really hates to close them. But business is business."

He still had the bandanna in his hand, and Jabez Stone felt sick as he saw the cloth struggle and flutter.

"Are they all as small as that?" he asked hoarsely.

"Small?" said the stranger. "Oh, I see what you mean. Why, they vary." He measured Jabez Stone with his eyes, and his teeth showed. "Don't worry, Mr. Stone," he said. "You'll go with a very good grade. I wouldn't trust you outside the collecting box. Now, a man like Dan'l Webster, of course—well, we'd have to build a special box for him, and even at that, I imagine the wing spread

---

7. **contretemps** (kōn·trə·tän'): unfortunate happening; embarrassment.
8. **In . . . life:** This is a quotation from the burial service in *The Book of Common Prayer*. The sentence continues " . . . we are in death."

Wood engraving for ''The Devil and Daniel Webster''
by Fritz Eichenberg. © 1936 Stephen Vincent Benet,
Kingsport Press, Tennessee.

New York Public Library, Rare Books
and Manuscripts Division.

would astonish you. But, in your case, as I was
saying—''

''Put that handkerchief away!'' said Jabez
Stone, and he began to beg and to pray. But the
best he could get at the end was a three years'
extension, with conditions.

But till you make a bargain like that, you've
got no idea of how fast four years can run. By the
last months of those years, Jabez Stone's known
all over the state and there's talk of running him
for governor—and it's dust and ashes in his
mouth. For every day, when he gets up, he thinks,
''There's one more night gone,'' and every night
when he lies down, he thinks of the black pocketbook and the soul of Miser Stevens, and it
makes him sick at heart. Till, finally, he can't bear
it any longer, and, in the last days of the last year,

he hitches up his horse and drives off to seek Dan'l
Webster. For Dan'l was born in New Hampshire,
only a few miles from Cross Corners, and it's well
known that he has a particular soft spot for old
neighbors.

It was early in the morning when he got to
Marshfield, but Dan'l was up already, talking
Latin to the farmhands and wrestling with the ram,
Goliath, and trying out a new trotter and working
up speeches to make against John C. Calhoun.[9]
But when he heard a New Hampshireman had
come to see him, he dropped everything else he
was doing, for that was Dan'l's way. He gave

---

9. **John C. Calhoun:** U.S. statesman from South Carolina
(1782–1850). Calhoun often clashed with Webster, particularly
on the issue of slavery.

Jabez Stone a breakfast that five men couldn't eat, went into the living history of every man and woman in Cross Corners, and finally asked him how he could serve him.

Jabez Stone allowed that it was a kind of mortgage case.

"Well, I haven't pleaded a mortgage case in a long time, and I don't generally plead now, except before the Supreme Court," said Dan'l, "but if I can, I'll help you."

"Then I've got hope for the first time in ten years," said Jabez Stone, and told him the details.

Dan'l walked up and down as he listened, hands behind his back, now and then asking a question, now and then plunging his eyes at the floor, as if they'd bore through it like gimlets.[10] When Jabez Stone had finished, Dan'l puffed out his cheeks and blew. Then he turned to Jabez Stone and a smile broke over his face like the sunrise over Monadnock.

"You've certainly given yourself the devil's own row to hoe, Neighbor Stone," he said, "but I'll take your case."

"You'll take it?" said Jabez Stone, hardly daring to believe.

"Yes," said Dan'l Webster. "I've got about seventy-five other things to do and the Missouri Compromise[11] to straighten out, but I'll take your case. For if two New Hampshiremen aren't a match for the devil, we might as well give the country back to the Indians."

Then he shook Jabez Stone by the hand and said, "Did you come down here in a hurry?"

"Well, I admit I made time," said Jabez Stone.

"You'll go back faster," said Dan'l Webster, and he told 'em to hitch up Constitution and Constellation to the carriage. They were matched grays with one white forefoot, and they stepped like greased lightning.

Well, I won't describe how excited and pleased the whole Stone family was to have the great Dan'l Webster for a guest, when they finally got there.

Jabez Stone had lost his hat on the way, blown off when they overtook a wind, but he didn't take much account of that. But after supper he sent the family off to bed, for he had most particular business with Mr. Webster. Mrs. Stone wanted them to sit in the front parlor, but Dan'l Webster knew front parlors and said he preferred the kitchen. So it was there they sat, waiting for the stranger, with a jug on the table between them and a bright fire on the hearth—the stranger being scheduled to show up on the stroke of midnight, according to specifications.

Well, most men wouldn't have asked for better company than Dan'l Webster and a jug. But with every tick of the clock Jabez Stone got sadder and sadder. His eyes roved round, and though he sampled the jug you could see he couldn't taste it. Finally, on the stroke of 11:30 he reached over and grabbed Dan'l Webster by the arm.

"Mr. Webster, Mr. Webster!" he said, and his voice was shaking with fear and a desperate courage. "For God's sake, Mr. Webster, harness your horses and get away from this place while you can!"

"You've brought me a long way, neighbor, to tell me you don't like my company," said Dan'l Webster, quite peaceable, pulling at the jug.

"Miserable wretch that I am!" groaned Jabez Stone. "I've brought you a devilish way, and now I see my folly. Let him take me if he wills. I don't hanker after it, I must say, but I can stand it. But you're the Union's stay and New Hampshire's pride! He mustn't get you, Mr. Webster! He mustn't get you!"

Dan'l Webster looked at the distracted man, all gray and shaking in the firelight, and laid a hand on his shoulder.

"I'm obliged to you, Neighbor Stone," he said gently. "It's kindly thought of. But there's a jug on the table and a case in hand. And I never left a jug or a case half finished in my life."

And just at that moment there was a sharp rap on the door.

"Ah," said Dan'l Webster, very coolly, "I thought your clock was a trifle slow, Neighbor Stone." He stepped to the door and opened it. "Come in!" he said.

---

10. **gimlets:** small tools used for drilling holes.
11. **Missouri Compromise:** federal legislation of 1820 designed to settle the dispute over whether slavery should be permitted in new states west of the Missouri River. Maine and Missouri entered the Union as part of the Missouri Compromise.

The stranger came in—very dark and tall he looked in the firelight. He was carrying a box under his arm—a black, japanned[12] box with little air holes in the lid. At the sight of the box, Jabez Stone gave a low cry and shrank into a corner of the room.

"Mr. Webster, I presume," said the stranger, very polite, but with eyes glowing like a fox's deep in the woods.

"Attorney of record for Jabez Stone," said Dan'l Webster, but his eyes were glowing too. "Might I ask your name?"

"I've gone by a good many," said the stranger carelessly. "Perhaps Scratch will do for the evening. I'm often called that in these regions."

Then he sat down at the table and poured himself a drink from the jug. The liquor was cold in the jug, but it came steaming into the glass.

"And now," said the stranger, smiling and showing his teeth, "I shall call upon you, as a law-abiding citizen, to assist me in taking possession of my property."

Well, with that the argument began—and it went hot and heavy. At first, Jabez Stone had a flicker of hope, but when he saw Dan'l Webster being forced back at point after point, he just scrunched in his corner, with his eyes on that japanned box. For there wasn't any doubt as to the deed or the signature—that was the worst of it. Dan'l Webster twisted and turned and thumped his fist on the table, but he couldn't get away from that. He offered to compromise the case; the stranger wouldn't hear of it. He pointed out the property had increased in value, and state senators ought to be worth more; the stranger stuck to the letter of the law. He was a great lawyer, Dan'l Webster, but we know who's the King of Lawyers, as the Good Book tells us,[13] and it seemed as if, for the first time, Dan'l Webster had met his match.

Finally, the stranger yawned a little. "Your spirited efforts on behalf of your client do you credit, Mr. Webster," he said, "but if you have no more arguments to adduce,[14] I'm rather pressed for time"—and Jabez Stone shuddered.

Dan'l Webster's brow looked dark as a thundercloud.

"Pressed or not, you shall not have this man!" he thundered. "Mr. Stone is an American citizen, and no American citizen may be forced into the service of a foreign prince. We fought England for that in '12[15] and we'll fight all hell for it again!"

"Foreign?" said the stranger. "And who calls me a foreigner?"

"Well, I never yet heard of the dev—of your claiming American citizenship," said Dan'l Webster with surprise.

"And who with better right?" said the stranger, with one of his terrible smiles. "When the first wrong was done to the first Indian, I was there. When the first slaver put out for the Congo, I stood on her deck. Am I not in your books and stories and beliefs, from the first settlements on? Am I not spoken of, still, in every church in New England? 'Tis true the North claims me for a Southerner and the South for a Northerner, but I am neither. I am merely an honest American like yourself—and of the best descent—for, to tell the truth, Mr. Webster, though I don't like to boast of it, my name is older in this country than yours."

"Aha!" said Dan'l Webster, with the veins standing out in his forehead. "Then I stand on the Constitution! I demand a trial for my client!"

"The case is hardly one for an ordinary court," said the stranger, his eyes flickering. "And, indeed, the lateness of the hour—"

"Let it be any court you choose, so it is an American judge and an American jury!" said Dan'l Webster in his pride. "Let it be the quick[16] or the dead; I'll abide the issue!"

"You have said it," said the stranger, and pointed his finger at the door. And with that, and all of a sudden, there was a rushing of wind outside and a noise of footsteps. They came, clear and distinct, through the night. And yet, they were not like the footsteps of living men.

---

12. **japanned:** varnished or lacquered so that it had a hard, glossy finish.
13. In the Bible, Satan is very clever at argument.

14. **adduce:** give as evidence.
15. **'12:** War of 1812.
16. **quick:** living.

Wood engraving for "The Devil and Daniel Webster"
by Fritz Eichenberg. © 1936 Stephen Vincent Benet,
Kingsport Press, Tennessee.

New York Public Library, Rare Books
and Manuscripts Division.

"In God's name, who comes by so late?" cried Jabez Stone, in an ague[17] of fear.

"The jury Mr. Webster demands," said the stranger, sipping at his boiling glass. "You must pardon the rough appearance of one or two; they will have come a long way."

And with that the fire burned blue and the door blew open and twelve men entered, one by one.

If Jabez Stone had been sick with terror before, he was blind with terror now. For there was Walter Butler, the loyalist, who spread fire and horror through the Mohawk Valley in the times of the Revolution; and there was Simon Girty, the renegade, who saw white men burned at the stake and whooped with the Indians to see them burn. His eyes were green, like a catamount's,[18] and the stains on his hunting shirt did not come from the blood of the deer. King Philip was there, wild and proud as he had been in life, with the great gash in his head that gave him his death wound, and cruel Governor Dale,[19] who broke men on the wheel. There was Morton of Merry Mount, who so vexed the Plymouth Colony, with his flushed, loose, handsome face and his hate of the godly. There was Teach, the bloody pirate, with his black beard curling on his breast. The Reverend John Smeet, with his strangler's hands and his Geneva gown,[20] walked as daintily as he had to the gallows. The red print of the rope was still around his neck, but he carried a perfumed handkerchief in one hand. One and all, they came into the room with the fires of hell still upon them, and the stranger named their names and their deeds as they came, till the tale of twelve was told. Yet the stranger had told the truth—they had all played a part in America.

"Are you satisfied with the jury, Mr. Webster?" said the stranger mockingly, when they had taken their places.

The sweat stood upon Dan'l Webster's brow, but his voice was clear.

"Quite satisfied," he said. "Though I miss General Arnold from the company."

"Benedict Arnold is engaged upon other business," said the stranger, with a glower. "Ah, you asked for a justice, I believe."

He pointed his finger once more, and a tall man, soberly clad in Puritan garb, with the burning gaze of the fanatic, stalked into the room and took his judge's place.

"Justice Hathorne is a jurist of experience," said the stranger. "He presided at certain witch trials once held in Salem. There were others who repented of the business later, but not he."

"Repent of such notable wonders and undertakings?" said the stern old justice. "Nay, hang them—hang them all!" And he muttered to himself in a way that struck ice into the soul of Jabez Stone.

Then the trial began, and, as you might expect, it didn't look anyways good for the defense. And Jabez Stone didn't make much of a witness in his own behalf. He took one look at Simon Girty and screeched, and they had to put him back in his corner in a kind of swoon.

It didn't halt the trial, though; the trial went on, as trials do. Dan'l Webster had faced some hard juries and hanging judges in his time, but this was the hardest he'd ever faced, and he knew it. They sat there with a kind of glitter in their eyes, and the stranger's smooth voice went on and on. Every time he'd raise an objection, it'd be "Objection sustained," but whenever Dan'l objected, it'd be "Objection denied." Well, you couldn't expect fair play from a fellow like this Mr. Scratch.

It got to Dan'l in the end, and he began to heat, like iron in the forge. When he got up to speak he was going to flay that stranger with every trick known to the law, and the judge and jury too. He didn't care if it was contempt of court or what would happen to him for it. He didn't care anymore what happened to Jabez Stone. He just got madder and madder, thinking of what he'd say. And yet, curiously enough, the more he thought about it, the less he was able to arrange his speech in his mind.

Till, finally, it was time for him to get up on his feet, and he did so, all ready to bust out with lightnings and denunciations. But before he started he looked over the judge and jury for a

---

17. **ague** (ā′gyo͞o): shivering fit.
18. **catamount's:** wild cat's.
19. **Governor Dale:** Sir Thomas Dale (died 1619), known for his severe laws while deputy governor of the English colony of Virginia.
20. **Geneva gown:** minister's robe.

moment, such being his custom. And he noticed the glitter in their eyes was twice as strong as before, and they all leaned forward. Like hounds just before they get the fox, they looked, and the blue mist of evil in the room thickened as he watched them. Then he saw what he'd been about to do, and he wiped his forehead, as a man might who's just escaped falling into a pit in the dark.

For it was him they'd come for, not only Jabez Stone. He read it in the glitter of their eyes and in the way the stranger hid his mouth with one hand. And if he fought them with their own weapons, he'd fall into their power; he knew that, though he couldn't have told you how. It was his own anger and horror that burned in their eyes; and he'd have to wipe that out or the case was lost. He stood there for a moment, his black eyes burning like anthracite. And then he began to speak.

He started off in a low voice, though you could hear every word. They say he could call on the harps of the blessed when he chose. And this was just as simple and easy as a man could talk. But he didn't start out by condemning or reviling. He was talking about the things that make a country a country, and a man a man.

And he began with the simple things that everybody's known and felt—the freshness of a fine morning when you're young, and the taste of food when you're hungry, and the new day that's every day when you're a child. He took them up and he turned them in his hands. They were good things for any man. But without freedom, they sickened. And when he talked of those enslaved, and the sorrows of slavery, his voice got like a big bell. He talked of the early days of America and the men who had made those days. It wasn't a spread-eagle[21] speech, but he made you see it. He admitted all the wrong that had ever been done. But he showed how, out of the wrong and the right, the suffering and the starvations, something new had come. And everybody had played a part in it, even the traitors.

Then he turned to Jabez Stone and showed him as he was—an ordinary man who'd had hard luck and wanted to change it. And, because he'd

wanted to change it, now he was going to be punished for all eternity. And yet there was good in Jabez Stone, and he showed that good. He was hard and mean, in some ways, but he was a man. There was sadness in being a man, but it was a proud thing too. And he showed what the pride of it was till you couldn't help feeling it. Yes, even in hell, if a man was a man, you'd know it. And he wasn't pleading for any one person anymore, though his voice rang like an organ. He was telling the story and the failures and the endless journey of mankind. They got tricked and trapped and bamboozled, but it was a great journey. And no demon that was ever foaled could know the inwardness of it—it took a man to do that.

The fire began to die on the hearth and the wind before morning to blow. The light was getting gray in the room when Dan'l Webster finished. And his words came back at the end to New Hampshire ground, and the one spot of land that each man loves and clings to. He painted a picture of that, and to each one of that jury he spoke of things long forgotten. For his voice could search the heart, and that was his gift and his strength. And to one, his voice was like the forest and its secrecy, and to another like the sea and the storms of the sea; and one heard the cry of his lost nation in it, and another saw a little harmless scene he hadn't remembered for years. But each saw something. And when Dan'l Webster finished he didn't know whether or not he'd saved Jabez Stone. But he knew he'd done a miracle. For the glitter was gone from the eyes of judge and jury, and, for the moment, they were men again, and knew they were men.

"The defense rests," said Dan'l Webster, and stood there like a mountain. His ears were still ringing with his speech, and he didn't hear anything else till he heard Judge Hathorne say, "The jury will retire to consider its verdict."

Walter Butler rose in his place and his face had a dark pride on it.

"The jury has considered its verdict," he said, and looked the stranger full in the eye. "We find for the defendant, Jabez Stone."

With that, the smile left the stranger's face, but Walter Butler did not flinch.

"Perhaps 'tis not strictly in accordance with

---

21. **spread-eagle:** blindly patriotic.

the evidence," he said, "but even the damned may salute the eloquence of Mr. Webster."

With that, the long crow of a rooster split the gray morning sky, and judge and jury were gone from the room like a puff of smoke and as if they had never been there. The stranger turned to Dan'l Webster, smiling wryly.

"Major Butler was always a bold man," he said. "I had not thought him quite so bold. Nevertheless, my congratulations, as between two gentlemen."

"I'll have that paper first, if you please," said Dan'l Webster, and he took it and tore it into four pieces. It was queerly warm to the touch. "And now," he said, "I'll have you!" and his hand came down like a bear trap on the stranger's arm. For he knew that once you bested anybody like Mr. Scratch in fair fight, his power on you was gone. And he could see that Mr. Scratch knew it too.

The stranger twisted and wriggled, but he couldn't get out of that grip. "Come, come, Mr. Webster," he said, smiling palely. "This sort of thing is ridic—ouch!—is ridiculous. If you're worried about the costs of the case, naturally, I'd be glad to pay——"

"And so you shall!" said Dan'l Webster, shaking him till his teeth rattled. "For you'll sit right down at that table and draw up a document, promising never to bother Jabez Stone nor his heirs or assigns[22] nor any other New Hampshireman till doomsday! For any hades we want to raise in this state, we can raise ourselves, without assistance from strangers."

"Ouch!" said the stranger. "Ouch! Well, they never did run very big to the barrel, but—ouch!—I agree!"

So he sat down and drew up the document. But Dan'l Webster kept his hand on his coat collar all the time.

"And, now, may I go?" said the stranger, quite humble, when Dan'l'd seen the document was in proper and legal form.

"Go?" said Dan'l, giving him another shake. "I'm still trying to figure out what I'll do with you. For you've settled the costs of the case, but you haven't settled with me. I think I'll take you back to Marshfield," he said, kind of reflective. "I've got a ram there named Goliath that can butt through an iron door. I'd kind of like to turn you loose in his field and see what he'd do."

Well, with that the stranger began to beg and to plead. And he begged and he pled so humble that finally Dan'l, who was naturally kindhearted, agreed to let him go. The stranger seemed terrible grateful for that and said, just to show they were friends, he'd tell Dan'l's fortune before leaving. So Dan'l agreed to that, though he didn't take much stock in fortunetellers ordinarily. But, naturally, the stranger was a little different.

Well, he pried and he peered at the lines in Dan'l's hands. And he told him one thing and another that was quite remarkable. But they were all in the past.

"Yes, all that's true, and it happened," said Dan'l Webster. "But what's to come in the future?"

The stranger grinned, kind of happily, and shook his head.

"The future's not as you think it," he said. "It's dark. You have a great ambition, Mr. Webster."

"I have," said Dan'l firmly, for everybody knew he wanted to be President.

"It seems almost within your grasp," said the stranger, "but you will not attain it. Lesser men will be made President and you will be passed over."

"And, if I am, I'll still be Daniel Webster," said Dan'l. "Say on."

"You have two strong sons," said the stranger, shaking his head. "You look to found a line. But each will die in war and neither reach greatness."

"Live or die, they are still my sons," said Dan'l Webster. "Say on."

"You have made great speeches," said the stranger. "You will make more."

"Ah," said Dan'l Webster.

"But the last great speech you make will turn many of your own against you," said the stranger. "They will call you Ichabod;[23] they will call you by other names. Even in New England, some will

---

22. **assigns:** persons who inherit property or money.

23. **Ichabod** (ik′ə·bäd′): This is a reference to a poem by John Greenleaf Whittier that criticized Webster. *Ichabod* is a Hebrew name that came to mean "inglorious" to some.

say you have turned your coat and sold your country, and their voices will be loud against you till you die."

"So it is an honest speech, it does not matter what men say," said Dan'l Webster. Then he looked at the stranger and their glances locked.

"One question," he said. "I have fought for the Union all my life. Will I see that fight won against those who would tear it apart?"

"Not while you live," said the stranger, grimly, "but it will be won. And after you are dead, there are thousands who will fight for your cause, because of words that you spoke."

"Why, then, you long-barreled, slab-sided, lantern-jawed, fortune-telling note shaver!" said Dan'l Webster, with a great roar of laughter. "Be off with you to your own place before I put my mark on you! For, by the thirteen original colonies, I'd go to the Pit[24] itself to save the Union!"

And with that he drew back his foot for a kick that would have stunned a horse. It was only the tip of his shoe that caught the stranger, but he went flying out of the door with his collecting box under his arm.

"And now," said Dan'l Webster, seeing Jabez Stone beginning to rouse from his swoon, "let's see what's left in the jug, for it's dry work talking all night. I hope there's pie for breakfast, Neighbor Stone."

But they say that whenever the devil comes near Marshfield, even now, he gives it a wide berth. And he hasn't been seen in the state of New Hampshire from that day to this. I'm not talking about Massachusetts or Vermont.

---

24. **Pit:** Hell.

Responding to the Story

Analyzing the Story

Identifying Facts

1. List five examples of bad luck that make Jabez Stone vow to sell his soul to the devil. In which ways does Stone's luck change after his bargain with the stranger?

2. Six years later, when the stranger visits again, what does Stone say he has doubts about? What extension does Stone get? When the extension runs out, what does Stone ask Webster to do?

3. Explain how Webster justifies his insistence that Stone should not "be forced into the service" of the devil. What citizenship does the devil then claim, and what does Webster demand as a result?

4. What kind of men form the jury at Stone's trial? Explain what Webster realizes will happen if he fights the devil with the devil's own weapons. How does Webster change his speech's tone as a result?

5. Tell what the jury's verdict is. What reason does the head juror give for the jury's decision?

Interpreting Meanings

6. Benét wrote "The Devil and Daniel Webster" in the style of a **tall tale**—a humorous, far-fetched story that exaggerates a character's abilities. Find five examples of **exaggeration** in which Daniel Webster is made to seem almost superhuman. Which details seemed particularly humorous to you?

7. Another characteristic of a tall tale is its use of everyday speech and colorful regional expressions. Find three instances of everyday speech in the story. (Note especially passages containing contractions.) Then find two ex-

amples of colorful expressions suggesting New England dialect. How did you feel about such language in the story?

8. Benét uses many startling details to make the devil seem a particularly powerful and frightening foe. List at least three of these details. What clues identify the stranger as the devil?

9. An **external conflict** is a struggle between two opposing forces. The struggle can involve a character and a natural force. An **internal conflict** is a struggle within a character's own mind. Identify the main external conflict and two internal conflicts in "The Devil and Daniel Webster." Then explain how each conflict is resolved, or settled.

10. Consider the arguments Webster uses to win a favorable verdict. Then discuss what you think the **theme,** or main idea, of the story is. What, for instance, is Benét saying about freedom, brotherhood, and personal dignity?

Applying Meanings

11. Do you agree with what Webster says to the jury—that all people, even the worst, play some constructive role in life? Support your opinion with examples and reasons.

Writing About the Story

A Creative Response

1. **Extending the Story.** We know that the stranger kept the soul of Miser Stevens in his pocketbook and that it was something that looked like a moth but wasn't a moth. Write a paragraph or more describing what you imagine the stranger did with the souls of some of the other people who had signed a contract with him. He says he has a "collecting box" with "unusual specimens." You might describe the box and the specimens. You might even tell your story as if you are one of the "specimens" talking. How does your speaker feel about what's happened?

A Critical Response

2. **Analyzing a Character.** Write a paragraph in which you analyze the character of the devil in Benét's story. Which aspects of this devil's personality are typically devilish, and which do you think are surprisingly human? Quote passages from the story to support your ideas. How did you feel about this devil?

Analyzing Language and Vocabulary

Understanding Allusions

Tracking down **allusions**—references to literature or to actual persons, places, and events—can be like a scavenger hunt. Many items are easy to locate; others require more effort and imagination. In checking allusions, the best place to start is a dictionary or the index of an encyclopedia. If these reference books are not helpful, consider biographical dictionaries, atlases, or history books. Knowing the meanings of allusions will broaden your appreciation of whatever you read.

Follow the directions below to discover the meaning of each of these allusions from Benét's story:

1. " 'In the midst of life—' said the stranger, kind of pious." Look under *life* in the index of *Bartlett's Familiar Quotations* and locate this allusion. Explain what the devil means by quoting these particular words to Jabez Stone. Using the same reference book, find out who wrote, "The devil can cite Scripture for his purpose." Explain how knowing this allusion adds to your understanding of the irony in the devil's words.

2. "Dan'l was . . . wrestling with the ram, Goliath. . . ." Use a dictionary or encyclopedia to identify who Goliath was. What does the allusion tell you about the size and disposition of the ram? To whom is Daniel Webster compared?

3. "Then . . . a smile broke over his [Webster's] face like the sunrise over Monadnock." Using an atlas, tell what and where Monadnock is. Next, using an encyclopedia or a geology book, explain what makes this particular place unusual. What does this allusion suggest about the character of Daniel Webster?

4. " . . . he [Webster] told 'em to hitch up Constitution and Constellation to the carriage." Use an encyclopedia or a United States history book to identify the allusions to the *Constitution* and the *Constellation*. Explain how the allusions add humor to the passage.

5. "King Philip was there, wild and proud as he had been in life, with the great gash in his head that gave him his death wound. . . ." Use an encyclopedia to determine which King Philip Benét is referring to here. Explain the role King Philip played in the early history of New England, and tell how he died. According to your research, do you think King Philip deserves his place among the devil's jurors?

SUNRISE IN HIS POCKET

Davy Crockett

Though Davy Crockett is a famous character in tall tales about the backwoods of Tennessee, the real Davy Crockett (1786–1836) was a businessman and politician. During his three terms in Congress, the newspapers enjoyed exaggerating his image as a rough, bear-hunting frontiersman. Crockett's political backers found the exaggerations useful too, and so the legend grew, especially after his heroic death at the Alamo. To catch the flavor of this tale, you should read it aloud.

One January morning it was so all-screwen-up cold that the forest trees war so stiff that they couldn't shake, and the very daybreak froze fast as it war tryin' to dawn. The tinderbox in my cabin would no more ketch fire than a sunk raft at the bottom o' the sea. Seein' that daylight war so far behind time, I thought creation war in a fair way for freezin' fast.

"So," thinks I, "I must strike a leetle fire from my fingers, light my pipe, travel out a few leagues, and see about it."

Then I brought my knuckles together like two thunderclouds, but the sparks froze up afore I could begin to collect 'em—so out I walked, and endeavored to keep myself unfriz by goin' at a hop, step, and jump gait, and whistlin' the tune of "fire in the mountains!" as I went along in three double-quick time. Well, arter I had walked about twenty-five miles up the peak o' Daybreak Hill, I soon discovered what war the matter. The airth had actually friz fast in her axis, and couldn't turn round; the sun had got jammed between two cakes o' ice under the wheels, an' thar he had bin shinin' and workin' to get loose, till he friz fast in his cold sweat.

"C-r-e-a-t-i-o-n!" thought I. "This are the toughest sort o' suspension, and it mustn't be endured—somethin' must be done, or human creation is done for."

It war then so antediluvian[1] and premature cold that my upper and lower teeth an' tongue war all collapsed together as tight as a friz oyster. I took a fresh twenty-pound bear off o' my back that I'd picked up on the road, an' beat the animal agin the ice till the hot ile began to walk out on him at all sides. I then took an' held him over the airth's axes, an' squeezed him till I thawed 'em loose, poured about a ton on it over the sun's face, give the airth's cogwheel one kick backward, till I got the sun loose—whistled "Push along, keep movin'!" an' in about fifteen seconds the airth gin

---

1. **antediluvian** (an'ti·də·lōō'vē·ən): literally, before the Biblical Flood; hence, like a very old time in the history of the world.

Davy Crockett fighting a bear. Cover of the Crockett Almanac, 1841.

a grunt, and begun movin'—the sun walked up beautiful, salutin' me with sich a wind o' gratitude that it made me sneeze. I lit my pipe by the blaze o' his topknot, shouldered my bear, an' walked home, introducin' the people to fresh daylight with a piece of sunrise in my pocket, with which I cooked my bear steaks, an' enjoyed one o' the best breakfasts I had tasted for some time. If I didn't, jist wake some mornin' and go with me to the office o' sunrise!

Responding to the Tall Tale

Analyzing the Tall Tale

Identifying Facts

1. When Davy Crockett wakes up one January morning, what does he find has happened to the trees, the daylight, and all of creation?
2. Describe how Crockett tries to light his pipe.
3. When Crockett gets to the top of Daybreak Hill, what does he discover about the earth and the sun? What would happen if nothing were done?
4. Explain how Crockett uses the bear to fix the earth and sun. Tell what he uses to light his pipe and cook his breakfast.

Interpreting Meanings

5. List five or more examples of **exaggeration** in the tale.
6. In what ways is Davy Crockett a hero who saves his people from destruction? Can you think of other characters in myth and legend who do the same thing?
7. How is Davy like Hercules, the hero of ancient Greek mythology?

Writing About the Tall Tale

A Creative Response

1. **Extending the Story.** Suppose Davy wakes on another morning, this time in August, and finds that the world is in danger of burning up from heat. Write a story telling how Davy fixed things up.

A Critical Response

2. **Correcting the Errors.** Rewrite Davy's story and correct all the errors in grammar and use standard spellings. How does the effect of the story change?

Analyzing Language and Vocabulary

Dialect

Americans speak various dialects of English. A native New Englander's speech, for example, is noticeably different from that of a typical Southerner, even though both speak the same basic language. Differences in pronunciation, vocabulary, and grammar are what distinguish one **dialect** from another. Dialect is an important element in many tall tales. Consider how Crockett uses pronunciation, vocabulary, and grammar to create his Tennessee dialect.

1. **Pronunciation.** In "Sunrise in His Pocket" many common words are misspelled to suggest the way Davy Crockett would have pronounced them. Read each of the following passages aloud, and note the sound of the italicized words. Write the standard spelling of each of these words. How would you pronounce them?

    a. ". . . the forest trees *war* so stiff that they couldn't shake. . . ."
    b. "The tinderbox in my cabin would no more *ketch* fire than a sunk raft. . . ."
    c. ". . . *an' thar* he had *bin shinin'* and *workin'* to get loose. . . ."
    d. "I . . . beat the animal *agin* the ice. . . ."

2. **Vocabulary.** A dialect includes words and expressions that might not be common among speakers in a different region or social group. For example, Crockett says, "I thought creation war in a fair way for freezin' fast" instead of "I thought creation was likely to freeze fast." How would you phrase each of the following italicized expressions of Crockett's?

    a. " 'So' thinks I, 'I must . . . *travel out* a few leagues. . . .' "
    b. ". . . but the sparks froze up *afore* I could begin to collect 'em. . . ."
    c. ". . . the hot ile began to *walk out on* him *at all sides*."

3. **Grammar.** A dialect often uses verb forms that would be considered incorrect among the general population. Which words would you normally use in a formal composition in place of the following italicized verbs?

    a. " 'So,' *thinks* I, 'I must strike a leetle fire. . . .' "
    b. " 'C-r-e-a-t-i-o-n!' thought I, 'this *are* the toughest sort o' suspension. . . .' "
    c. ". . . as tight as a *friz* oyster. . . ."
    d. ". . . in about fifteen seconds the airth *gin* a grunt, and *begun movin'*. . . ."

THE SERPENTINE BOBSLED

James Stevens

Readers can compare the historical truth about Davy Crockett to the legend he inspired. Paul Bunyan, though, is a completely imaginary hero. His stories were first told by a logging company in their brochures. They hoped the stories would attract men to come and work for them in the north woods.

The Year of the Two Winters had been disastrous for Paul Bunyan. Winter had come again in the summertime that year, and the cold increased in the succeeding months. At Christmas time there was fifty feet of ice on Lake Michigan, and by the last of February the lake was frozen to the bottom. Paul Bunyan was then engaged in logging off the Peninsula[1] country, and of course his operations were halted. He cut the ice into blocks and hauled them out on the lakeshore with Babe, his big blue ox, who could pull anything that had two ends on it. This was done so that the ice would melt more quickly when normal summer weather returned. Then he moved his outfit to the old home camp in the Smiling River country, where severe weather was never experienced.

Paul Bunyan had done no logging around his old home camp for seven years. The remaining timber was so far from the river and on such steep hills that profitable logging seemed impossible. However, it was the best to be had, for elsewhere it would be weeks, even months, before the snowdrifts would melt away from the treetops. Paul Bunyan tackled the tough logging problems before him with characteristic courage. He was sure that his inventiveness and resourcefulness would, as always, triumph over every obstacle.

His most stubborn and difficult problem was that of getting the loggers to the woods in the morning in time to do any work and getting them home at night in time to do any sleep. One plan after another was tried and dropped, failures all. Paul Bunyan began with an attempt to work one day shift, but the loggers could not get to the woods before lunchtime; lunch finished, they had to start at once for the camp. Two shifts were then put on, but little work could be done at night, except when the moon was full. Paul Bunyan then sent the great Johnny Inkslinger, his timekeeper and man of science, to investigate the Aurora Borealis[2] as a means of artificial lighting. Johnny reported that it was pretty but unreliable, and he doubted if even the blue ox could move it down from the North in less than six months. The learned Inkslinger then sat down and figured des-

---

1. **Peninsula:** Upper Peninsula of Michigan.

2. **Aurora Borealis** (ô·rôr′ə bôr′ē·al′is): luminous bands or streamers of light sometimes appearing in the night sky of the Northern Hemisphere; also called *northern lights*.

perately for a week, trying to devise a method of working three twelve-hour shifts a day. With such a routine one shift could be doing a day's work, while a second shift was coming to work, and a third was going to camp. Johnny Inkslinger was, beyond a doubt, the greatest man with figures that ever lived, but here his mathematics failed him. Paul Bunyan then thought of making a campsite in the timber, and he dug for water in the high hills. He succeeded in reaching a mighty vein, but it was so deep that it took a week to draw a bucket of water out of the well. It was out of the question as a water supply for the camp.

Now Paul Bunyan had to fall back on a last plan, a farfetched one that seemed well-nigh hopeless. This was to build a great sled, something on the order of a lunch sled, and have Babe, the blue ox, haul the loggers to and from work each day. It was a desperate plan, and no one but Paul Bunyan would have had the courage to attempt it. It must be remembered that the blue ox measured forty-two ax handles and a plug of chewing tobacco between the horns; an ordinary man at his front had to use a telescope to see what he was doing with his hind legs, he was so long; he had so much energy and such delight in labor that no one could hold him when he started for the woods in the mornings; he was so fast that Paul Bunyan's foreman, the Big Swede, who was as tall as the trees, could not begin to keep up with him. Only Paul Bunyan could travel so fast. Whenever Babe moved the camp he traveled at a careful pace, but even then some of the loggers were made seasick; and all of them became so irritable when a move was being made that they fought constantly among themselves. If the comparatively slow camp-moving pace of the blue ox thus upset them, his timber-going gallop would be apt to ruin them completely. Paul Bunyan remembered how the Big Swede, hanging to Babe's halter rope, was hurled through the air, only striking the ground once in every quarter of a mile or so, when the blue ox rushed to his delightful labor each morning. A lunch sled full of loggers would be dragged by Babe in much the same fashion; it would be in the air most of the time, and when it did strike the ground loggers would be scattered like autumn leaves. The loggers who would hang on until the woods were reached would have the living daylights shaken out of them. A common lunch sled would not do; one must be invented that would hold the road.

So Paul Bunyan devised the serpentine bobsled. It was a long, low-built contraption; the runners were made in short sections, connected by double joints. When it was completed and lay in the road that led from the camp it looked like a squat fence, for it snugly fitted the contours of the hills and vales over which it extended.

"There's a rig that'll hold the road," said Paul Bunyan with pride. "Now I'll invent something equally good to hold Babe to a slow pace."

Several mechanical devices were tried without passing the first test. The sled lay idle. The loggers got sore feet, and they traveled so slowly that they began to take twelve hours to reach the woods. There was one shift on the road, going, and one coming all of the time. Not a tree was being felled.

"There's no way out of it but to try the grizzlies," Paul Bunyan told his timekeeper.

Among the other livestock on Paul Bunyan's farm, which was down the river from the old home camp, was a herd of grizzly bears. The great logger often amused himself by playing with them, and he had taught them many tricks. Not the least of their stunts was for each bear to hang from a tree with three paws and try to claw Paul Bunyan's mackinaw[3] with the other paw as he dodged by.

"I'll station them at the trees which are left standing along the road," said Paul Bunyan, "and when Babe roars by they'll hook him. They may only frighten him into a faster run, but I think surely they'll slow him down."

The next morning the loggers, for the most part, joyfully crawled upon the serpentine bobsled. The timid and cranky among the loggers were pessimistic, of course, and declared noisily that this would be the end of them. But the bards[4] laughed at their fears, and at last every logger in camp was on the sled. Paul Bunyan ordered the Big Swede to hitch up the blue ox and start in half an hour,

---

3. **mackinaw:** short coat made of heavy woolen cloth, usually with a plaid pattern.
4. **bards:** poets or singers—a reference to loggers with a poetic or musical talent.

Illustration by Eben Giben for *Here's Audacity!*
American Legendary Heroes by Frank Shay.

and he departed for the woods with his herd of grizzlies. He stationed one of them at every tree close to the road. When he reached the timber he straddled a hogback[5] and sat down to wait for the outcome of his daring attempt.

In a short time he heard a faint thunder down in the valley, then he saw enormous balloons of dust twisting up in cyclonic bursts from the foothills, next he heard the crashing sound of hoofbeats that got louder and louder. . . . Through clouds of dust he saw Babe's tail brush lifted like a triumphal banner and the glitter of his horns. . . . The Big Swede, hanging to Babe's halter rope, soared and dived. . . .

The bears had failed. Indeed, they had failed terribly, for when Babe came to a halt in the timber Paul Bunyan saw bears' paws hanging from both sides of him. Only one bear had saved his paw, and he was holding a tree in a frenzied clutch. Babe had carried away bear, tree, and all. Paul Bunyan rushed back over the road, and as he came to each unfortunate grizzly he mercifully dispatched him. He carried them all into camp.

"Bear meat for Sunday dinner," he said to Hot Biscuit Slim, as he threw the bears into the kitchen yard.

Paul Bunyan then had Johnny Inkslinger bring his medicine case, and the two hurried to the woods. But only a slight number of the loggers had been made truly ill by the terrific speed with which Babe had hauled them over the hills. The double-jointed sled runners had slipped over rocks, logs, and gullies as easily as a snake glides over a string. Not once had the sled bounded from the road. Not a logger had suffered a jolt. Some of them were dazed and breathless, others were choked with dust, but most of them were no more than badly scared by their terrific journey.

"Aye tal you it ban no use try hol' Babe down," said the Big Swede, with rare eloquence.

"The sled worked perfectly, at any rate," said Paul Bunyan. "We can depend on it. But those good bullies of mine are going to need a lot of encouragement to stand that ride every morning."

He was quite right. His loggers thought nothing of the perils of falling limbs, which are called

"widowmakers" today in the woods. Breaking up logjams, jumping rolling logs, dodging butts of trees which bucked back from the stumps when they fell—all this was in the day's work. But even the serpentine bobsled could not banish the terrors of riding behind the blue ox each morning. "I'd ruther try ridin' a peavey handle down the West Branch." "I'll tell you Babe went so fast I acshuly *seen* the wind, an' I never seen anything more sickenin' in my life!" "What if Babe ud a throwed a shoe now? I bet it 'da tore through us like a cannonball!"

Paul Bunyan frowned as he hearkened to their complaints. His loggers seldom thought of anything but their labor when they were in the woods. If they were complaining now, what would happen when the bunkhouse cranks got into action after supper? There would be much gloomy grumbling, and perhaps rebellious talk. When the loggers went to bed they would brood over the cyclonic morning ride instead of getting fortifying sleep. Then they would soon balk against riding behind the blue ox. To avoid such an event he must call on his bards to cajole, humor and inspire the men until he could devise new methods to solve his logging problems.

---

5. **hogback:** steeply sloping mountain ridge.

Responding to the Tall Tale

Analyzing the Tall Tale

Identifying Facts

1. Explain why Paul Bunyan moves his logging camp to the Smiling River country. Why does profitable logging seem impossible there? What difficult problem arises as a result?
2. Identify the two unsuccessful solutions to his problem that Bunyan tries first. Whom does he then call in to help him? What three other unsuccessful solutions do the two men try?
3. What last plan does Bunyan fall back on? Explain the weakness in this plan that leads Bunyan to devise the serpentine bobsled.
4. Explain how Bunyan intends to use the grizzly bears. Tell what happens to all but one of them. Bunyan's sled works perfectly, but what problem remains?

Interpreting Meanings

5. Like other American tall tales, the stories about Paul Bunyan use **exaggeration** and **humor.** Identify at least five instances of exaggeration and humor in this selection.
6. Identify three **conflicts,** or struggles between opposing forces, in this story. Tell whether they are **external** or **internal.** Then explain whether any of these conflicts is resolved.
7. Describe the **character** of Paul Bunyan. Is he, for example, creative, stupid, brave, generous, bossy, lazy, industrious, or timid? Next, list any of these characteristics or others that apply to the loggers working for Bunyan. Find incidents in the story to support your answers.
8. Discuss whether this story praises the loggers of the old frontier or pokes fun at them. In your answer, consider both the great difficulties Bunyan and his loggers face and the failure of many of their ideas.

Applying Meanings

9. Compare the characters of Paul Bunyan and Davy Crockett. Discuss who takes himself more seriously and who is more successful at what he does. Explain which of the two, in your opinion, would be more successful in today's world.

10. Bunyan tries to devise solutions to seemingly insoluble problems. List some famous Americans, past or present, who solved difficult problems or invented useful things.

Writing About the Tall Tale

A Creative Response

1. **Extending the Story.** At the end of the selection, Bunyan is afraid the loggers will "brood over the cyclonic morning ride." Therefore, he plans to look into new ways of solving his logging problems. In a paragraph, explain whether the loggers become accustomed to the ride on the serpentine bobsled or whether Bunyan must use a new method of getting the loggers to and from the woods. If the latter is the case, what new method does Bunyan devise?

A Critical Response

2. **Summarizing the Main Events.** In a paragraph, summarize the main events of this story. Be sure to explain how one event leads to another—in other words, be sure to explain the **causes** of the events and the **effects** of the events.

Analyzing Language and Vocabulary

Dialect and Standard American English

In fiction, **dialect** can be an important literary element. It can, for example, be used to make a setting seem authentic or to add humor to an incident. In nonfiction, such as news articles and essays, however, writers generally avoid dialect. Instead, they use **standard American English.** Standard American English helps writers make sure their ideas are understood. Rewrite each of the following examples of dialect in standard American English.

1. " 'Aye tal you it ban no use try hol' Babe down.' "
2. " 'I'd ruther try ridin' a peavey handle down the West Branch.' "
3. " 'I'll tell you Babe went so fast I acshuly *seen* the wind, an' I never seen anything more sickenin' in my life!' "
4. " 'What if Babe ud a throwed a shoe now? I bet it 'da tore through us like a cannonball!' "

The legend of John Henry began after the Civil War when railroads were being built throughout the country. His exploits were celebrated in many ballads and tall tales. The legendary John Henry may have been inspired by an actual person. It is said John Henry was the son of a slave, and was working in the 1870's on a West Virginia railroad tunnel. To carve out a tunnel, steel drivers like John Henry usually used a ten-pound hammer and a drill to crack the rock. A newly invented steam drill, however, was beginning to replace such workers. Someone set up a contest between John Henry and a steam drill. If you can, listen to the story of John Henry sung.

John Henry, The Steel Driving Man

W. T. Blankenship

John Henry was a railroad man,
   He worked from six 'till five,
"Raise 'em up bullies and let 'em drop down,
   I'll beat you to the bottom or die."

5   John Henry said to his captain:
     "You are nothing but a common man,
Before that steam drill shall beat me down,
   I'll die with my hammer in my hand."

John Henry said to the Shakers:°
10   "You must listen to my call,
Before that steam drill shall beat me down,
   I'll jar these mountains till they fall."

John Henry's captain said to him:
   "I believe these mountains are caving in."
15   John Henry said to his captain: "Oh Lord!
   That's my hammer you hear in the wind."

John Henry he said to his captain:
   "Your money is getting mighty slim,
When I hammer through this old mountain,
20   Oh, Captain, will you walk in?"

John Henry's captain came to him
   With fifty dollars in his hand,
He laid his hand on his shoulder and said:
   "This belongs to a steel driving man."

25   John Henry was hammering on the right side,
   The big steam drill on the left,
Before that steam drill could beat him down,
   He hammered his fool self to death.

9. **Shakers:** workers who held the drills.

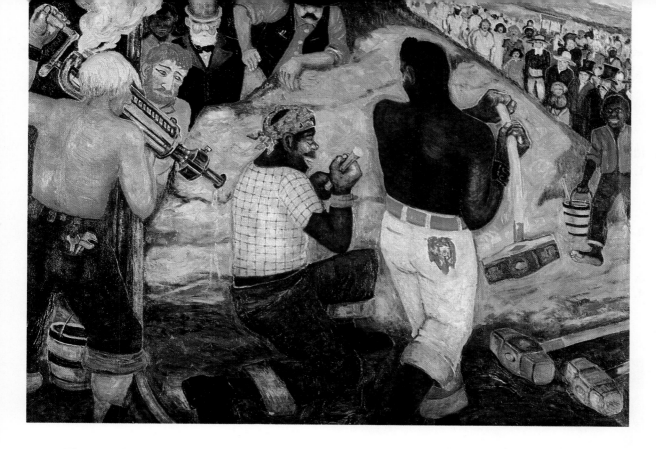

They carried John Henry to the mountains,
30   From his shoulder his hammer would ring,
She caught on fire by a little blue blaze,
      I believe these old mountains are caving in.

John Henry was lying on his deathbed,
      He turned over on his side,
35   And these were the last words John Henry said,
      "Bring me a cool drink of water before I die."

John Henry had a little woman,
      Her name was Pollie Ann,
He hugged and kissed her just before he died,
40   Saying, "Pollie, do the very best you can."

John Henry's woman heard he was dead,
      She could not rest on her bed,
She got up at midnight, caught that No. 4 train,
      "I am going where John Henry fell dead."

45   They carried John Henry to that new burying ground,
      His wife all dressed in blue,
She laid her hand on John Henry's cold face,
"John Henry, I've been true to you."

John Henry on the Right, Steam Drill on the Left, from the John Henry series by Palmer C. Hayden (1944–1954). Oil.

The Museum of African American Art, Los Angeles. Palmer C. Hayden Collection. Gift of Miriam A. Hayden.

Responding to the Ballad

Analyzing the Ballad

Identifying Details

1. How many hours a day does John Henry usually work? What does John Henry tell his captain and the Shakers he will do to keep the steam drill from beating him?
2. During the contest what does John Henry's captain say he thinks is happening to the mountain? What explanation does John Henry provide?
3. What happens to John Henry after the contest?
4. What is John Henry's last request to his co-workers? What are John Henry's last words to Pollie Ann?

The Dress She Wore Was Blue, from the John Henry series by Palmer C. Hayden (1944–1954). Oil.

The Museum of African American Art, Los Angeles. Palmer C. Hayden Collection. Gift of Miriam A. Hayden.

5. How does John Henry's wife react to the news of his death? What does she do to pay her last respects to him?

Interpreting Meanings

6. Do you think John Henry is hardworking, foolish, brave, boastful, persistent, loving, or greedy? Find evidence in the ballad to support your opinion.
7. List at least three examples of **repetition** in the ballad. Explain what actions and emotions these repetitions emphasize.
8. Think about the ballad's **theme,** or main idea. Do you think the ballad is mainly about the foolishness of accepting a dare? The dignity of hard work? The greatness of those willing to fight seemingly hopeless battles? Is it about the hopelessness of fighting against progress? Or is it about the moral worth of a human being compared to a soulless machine? Cite passages from the ballad to support your interpretation.

Writing About the Ballad

A Creative Response

1. **Rewriting the Ending.** Suppose John Henry had survived the contest. What would have happened to him next? Would he have continued working as a "steel driving man," or would the steam drill have eventually replaced him? In one or two paragraphs, write the next chapter in the legend of John Henry.

A Critical Response

2. **Comparing Legendary Heroes.** Choose two or three of the heroes from this section (Long Arrow, Daniel Webster, Davy Crockett, Paul Bunyan, John Henry). In two or three paragraphs, compare their heroic qualities. What characteristics do the heroes share? What characteristics distinguish one from another?

Film still from "The Legend of Sleepy Hollow".
© Walt Disney Productions.

Trickster Tales and Tall Tales

Trickster tales and tall tales are based on the human need to exaggerate and to be outrageous—which perhaps are particularly American characteristics.

Tricksters have always existed in the human imagination. Even the great Odysseus, the creator of the famous wooden horse of Troy, was sometimes a trickster. So was the wise fox of ancient and medieval animal fables. Tricksters are especially important in Native American mythology, and they are prominent in the black American tradition as well. Sometimes their trickery is just naughty; sometimes it is creative and even helpful to a group of people. For example, even as Coyote tricks the animals, he brings them benefits. In this respect, he resembles that ancient "trickster" Prometheus, who stole fire from the gods and gave it to the shivering human race. In a sense, this trickster is the comic version of the medicine man, who uses strange arts to bring about something useful to the community.

Tricksters tend to be masters at lying. This tendency has been taken to an extreme in the tall tale. **Tall tales** are highly exaggerated treatments of the exploits of real people, such as Daniel Webster and Davy Crockett (see pages 534 and 546). As they are told and retold, the tales grow "taller and taller."

The tall tale seems to be an integral part of our national character. Perhaps it is a comic reflection of our need to be the biggest and best at everything.

ADVENTURES OF GREAT RABBIT

Traditional Algonquian

People who hunt for their food admire the uncanny ability of animals to track their prey. They also admire animals' methods of avoiding enemies. This story about a wildcat's pursuit of a rabbit was originally told by the Micmac and Passamaquoddy. They lived near French settlers in northern New England and eastern Canada. As you read, note the many humorous and supernatural details. What do you think the Micmac and Passamaquoddy thought of the wildcat and the rabbit?

Wildcat is mean and ferocious. He has a short tail and big, long, sharp fangs, and his favorite food is rabbit. One day when Wildcat was hungry, he said to himself: "I'm going to catch and eat Mahtigwess, Great Rabbit, himself. He's plump and smart, and nothing less will do for my dinner." So he went hunting for Great Rabbit.

Now, Great Rabbit can sense what others are thinking from a long way off, so he already knew that Wildcat was after him. He made up his mind that he would use his magic power against Wildcat's strength. He picked up a handful of wood chips, threw them ahead of himself, and jumped after them, and because Great Rabbit is *m'téou-lin*,[1] every jump was a mile. Jumping that far, of course, he left very few tracks to follow.

Wildcat swore a mighty oath that he would catch Great Rabbit, that he would find him even if Mahtigwess had fled to the end of the world. At that time Wildcat had a beautiful long tail, and he swore by it: "Let my tail fall off—may I have just a little stump for a tail—if I fail to catch Great Rabbit!"

After a mile he found Rabbit's tracks. After another mile he found some more tracks. Wildcat was not altogether without magic either, and he was persevering. So mile by mile, he kept on Rabbit's trail.

In fact, Wildcat was drawing closer and closer. It grew dark and Great Rabbit grew tired. He was on a wide, empty plain of snow, and there was nothing to hide behind except a little spruce tree. He stomped on the snow and made himself a seat and bed of spruce boughs.

When Wildcat came to that spot, he found a fine, big wigwam and stuck his head through the door. Sitting inside was an old, gray-haired chief, solemn and mighty. The only strange thing about him was that he had two long ears standing up at each side of his head.

"Great Chief," said Wildcat, "have you by any chance seen a biggish rabbit running like mad?"

"Rabbits? Why of course, there are hundreds, thousands of rabbits hereabouts, but what's the hurry? It's late and you must be tired. If you want to hunt rabbits, start in the morning after a good night's sleep. I'm a lonely man and enjoy the company of a respected personage like you. Stay overnight; I have a fine rabbit stew cooking here."

Wildcat was flattered. "Big Chief, I am honored," he said. He ate a whole kettle full of tasty rabbit stew and then fell asleep before the roaring fire.

Wildcat awoke early because he was freezing. He found himself alone in the midst of a huge snowfield. Nothing was there, no wigwam, no fire, no old chief; all he could see were a few little spruce boughs. It had been a dream, an illusion created by Great Rabbit's magic. Even the stew had been an illusion, and Wildcat was ravenous.[2]

Shivering in the icy wind, Wildcat howled: "Rabbit has tricked me again, but I'll get even with him. By my tail, I swear I'll catch, kill, and eat him!"

Again Great Rabbit traveled with his mile-wide jumps, and again Wildcat followed closely. At nightfall Rabbit said to himself: "Time to rest and conjure something up."[3] This time he trampled down a large area and spread many pine boughs around.

When Wildcat arrived, he found a large village full of busy people, though of what tribe he couldn't tell. He also saw a big wooden church painted white, the kind the French Jesuits[4] were putting up among some tribes. Wildcat went up to a young man who was about to enter the church. "Friend, have you seen a biggish rabbit hereabouts, running away?"

"Quiet," said the young man, "we're having a prayer meeting. Wait until the sermon is over." The young man went into the church, and Wildcat followed him. There were lots of people sitting and listening to a gray-haired preacher. The only strange thing was the two long ears sticking up at each side of the priest's cap. He was preaching a

---

1. **m'téoulin** (em·tā′oo·lin′): gifted with great magical powers.

2. **ravenous** (rav′ə·nəs): extremely hungry.
3. **conjure . . . up:** to cause by using magic.
4. **Jesuits** (jez′oo·witz): members of a Roman Catholic order noted for missionary and educational work.

very, very long sermon about the wickedness of ferocious wild beasts who tear up victims with their big, sharp fangs and then devour them. "Such savage fiends will be punished for their sins," said this preacher over and over.

Wildcat didn't like the long sermon, but he had to wait all the same. When the preaching was over at last, he went up to the priest with the long ears and asked: "Sir, have you seen a biggish rabbit hereabouts?"

"Rabbits!" exclaimed the preacher. "We have a wet, foggy cedar swamp nearby with thousands of rabbits."

"I don't mean just any rabbit; I'm speaking of Great Rabbit."

"Of him I know nothing, friend. But over there in that big wigwam lives the wise old chief, the Sagamore. Go and ask him; he knows everything."

Wildcat went to the wigwam and found the Sagamore, an imposing figure, gray-haired like the preacher, with long white locks sticking up on each side of his head. "Young man," said the Sagamore gravely, "what can I do for you?"

"I'm looking for the biggish Great Rabbit."

"Ah! Him! He's hard to find and hard to catch. Tonight it's too late, but tomorrow I'll help you. Sit down, dear man. My daughters will give you a fine supper."

The Sagamore's daughters were beautiful. They brought Wildcat many large wooden bowls of the choicest food, and he ate it all up, because by now he was very hungry. The warmth of the fire and his full stomach made him drowsy, and the Sagamore's daughters brought him a thick white bearskin to sleep on. "You people really know how to treat a guest," said Wildcat as he fell asleep.

When he awoke, he found himself in a dismal, wet, foggy cedar swamp. Nothing was there except mud and icy slush and a lot of rabbit tracks. There was no village, no church, no wigwam, no Sagamore, no beautiful daughters. They had all been a mirage conjured up by Great Rabbit. The fine food had been a mirage too, and Wildcat's stomach was growling. He was ankle-deep in the freezing swamp. The fog was so thick he could hardly see anything. Enraged, he vowed to find and kill Great Rabbit even if he should die in the

attempt. He swore by his tail, his teeth, his claws—by everything dear to him. Then he hastened on.

That night Wildcat came to a big long house. Inside, it was like a great hall, and it was full of people. On a high seat sat the chief, who wore two long white feathers at each side of his head. This venerable[5] leader also had beautiful daughters who fed all comers, for Wildcat had stumbled into the midst of a great feast.

Exhausted and panting he gasped, "Has any one seen the bi-big-biggish G-G-Great Ra-Rab-Rabbit?"

"Later, friend," said the chief with the two white feathers. "We are feasting, dancing, singing. You seem exhausted, poor man! Sit down; catch your breath. Rest. Eat."

Wildcat sat down. The people were having a singing contest, and the chief on his high seat pointed at Wildcat and said, "Our guest here looks like a fine singer. Perhaps he will honor us with a song."

Wildcat was flattered. He arose and sang:

Rabbits!
How I hate them!
How I despise them!
How I laugh at them!
How I kill them!
How I scalp them!
How I eat them!

"A truly wonderful song," said the chief. "I must reward you for it. Here's what I give you." And with that the chief jumped up from his high seat, jumped over Wildcat's head, struck him a blow with his tomahawk, kept on jumping with mile-long leaps—and all was gone. The long house, the hall, the people, the daughters: none remained. Once more Wildcat found himself alone in the middle of nowhere, worse off than ever, for he had a gash in his scalp where Great Rabbit had hit him with the tomahawk. His feet were sore, his stomach empty. He could hardly crawl. But he was more infuriated than ever. "I'll kill him!"

---

5. **venerable** (ven′ər·ə·b'l): worthy of respect or admiration by reason of old age and dignity, character, position, etc.

he growled, "I'll give my life! And the tricks are over; he won't fool me again!"

That night Wildcat came to two beautiful wigwams. In the first was a young woman, obviously a chief's daughter. In the other was someone whom Wildcat took for her father, an elderly, gray-haired, gentle-looking man with two scalp locks sticking up at the sides of his head.

"Come in, come in, poor man," said the gray-haired host. "You're wounded! My daughter will wash and cure that cut. And we must build up your strength. I have a fine broth here and a pitcher full of wine, the drink Frenchmen make. It has great restorative powers."

But Wildcat was suspicious. "If this is Great Rabbit in disguise again, he won't fool me," he promised himself.

"Dear sir," said Wildcat, "I hesitate to mention it, but the two scalp locks sticking up at the sides of your head look very much like rabbit's ears."

"Rabbit's ears? How funny!" said the old man. "Know, friend, that in our tribe we all wear our scalp locks this way."

"Ah," said Wildcat, "but your nose is split exactly like a rabbit's nose."

"Don't remind me, friend. Some weeks ago I was hammering wampum beads, and the stone I was using to pound them on broke in half. A sharp piece flew up and split my nose—a great misfortune, because it does disfigure me.''

"It does indeed. A pity. But why are your soles so yellow, like a rabbit's soles?''

"Oh, that's nothing. I prepared some tobacco yesterday, and the juice stained my palms yellow.''

Then Wildcat said to himself: "This man is no rabbit.''

The old man called his daughter, who washed Wildcat's wound, put a healing salve into it, and bathed his face. Then the old man gave him a wonderfully strengthening broth and a large pitcher of sweet wine.

"This wine is really good,'' said Wildcat, "the finest I ever tasted.''

"Yes, these white people, these Frenchmen, are very clever at making good things to drink.''

When Wildcat awoke, he found, of course, that he had been tricked again. The food he had eaten was rabbit pellets, the wine was stale water in a half-wilted pitcher plant. Now it was only his great hatred that kept Wildcat going, but go he did, like a streak, on Rabbit's tail.

Mahtigwess, Great Rabbit, had only enough *m'téoulin,* enough magic power, left for one more trick. So he said to himself: "This time I'd better make it good!''

Great Rabbit came to a big lake and threw a chip of wood into the water. Immediately it turned into a towering ship, the kind white men build, with tall sides, three masts, white sails, and col-ored flags. That ship was pierced on each side with three rows of heavy cannon.

When Wildcat arrived at this lake, he saw the big ship with its crew. On deck was the captain, a gray-haired man with a large, gold-trimmed, cocked hat that had fluffy white plumes right and left.

"Rabbit!'' cried Wildcat, "I know you! You're no French captain; you're Great Rabbit. I know you, Mahtigwess! I am the mighty Wildcat, and I'm coming to scalp and kill you now!''

And with that, Wildcat jumped into the lake and swam toward the ship. Then the captain, who indeed was Mahtigwess, the Great Rabbit, ordered his men to fire their muskets and the three rows of heavy cannon. Bullets went whistling by Wildcat; cannonballs flew toward him; the whole world was spitting thunder and fire.

Wildcat had never before faced white men's firearms; they were entirely new to him. It didn't matter that ship, cannon, muskets, cannonballs, bullets, fire, noise, and smoke were merely illusions conjured up by Rabbit. To Wildcat they were real, and he was scared to death. He swam back to shore and ran away. And if he hasn't died, he is running still.

And yes, as Wildcat had sworn by his tail to catch and kill Rabbit, his tail fell off, and ever since then this kind of big wildcat has a short, stumpy tail and is called a bobcat.

—Based on Charles G. Leland's account

Responding to the Tale

Analyzing the Tale

Identifying Facts

1. Explain why Wildcat sets out to catch not just any rabbit, but Great Rabbit himself. What does he swear to accept if he fails?

2. List three powers that Mahtigwess—Great Rabbit—has that makes it difficult for anyone to catch him.

3. Identify the six disguises that Great Rabbit assumes. Which physical characteristic is he unable to conceal entirely?

4. Describe the first two tricks that Great Rabbit plays on Wildcat.

5. At the two wigwams, what three things make Wildcat suspect the old man is Great Rabbit? What excuse does Great Rabbit give to dispel each suspicion? When does Wildcat realize he has been tricked again?

6. Describe the final act of magic that Great Rabbit performs to chase away Wildcat. Explain how cats like Wildcat came to be called bobcats.

Interpreting Meanings

7. Great Rabbit disguises himself as several different human beings. In your opinion, what point does this story make about the relationship between human beings and animals? Refer to the story to support your opinion.

Applying Meanings

8. In many ways the cartoon character Bugs Bunny is a trickster like Great Rabbit. Describe some of the disguises and tricks Bugs Bunny uses to avoid his pursuers. Do you think Native Americans felt the same way about Great Rabbit that modern audiences feel about Bugs Bunny? Explain why or why not.

Writing About the Tale

A Creative Response

1. Telling a "Why" Story. This story explains why the bobcat has a little stumpy tail. Write a "why" story telling how another animal came to look or act the way it does; perhaps why the cat's eyes have that peculiar pupil; why dogs wag their tails; why fish can't live on land.

A Critical Response

2. Identifying a Theme. What **theme,** or main idea, do you think "Adventures of Great Rabbit" expresses? Consider what the story suggests about people's abilities to avoid or overcome opponents. For example, does the story say it is better to run than to fight? Or that special powers should not be used too harshly? Or something else? In one paragraph, first state the main idea you find expressed by the story. Then back up your analysis with incidents and details from the story.

Analyzing Language and Vocabulary

Analogies

An **analogy** is a relationship. To show the relationship of pink to red, you might say, "Pink is to red as lavender is to purple." You would be illustrating a relationship of degree: Both pink and lavender are lighter shades, respectively, of red and purple.

Analogies are often found on tests of thinking skills. They are expressed using symbols rather than the words *is to* and *as*:

> pink : red :: lavender : purple

Analogies might compare many kinds of relationships, such as the following:

> Degree or size
> puddle : lake :: anthill : mountain
> Parts and wholes
>   branch : tree :: petal : flower
> Synonyms
>   brave : courageous :: friendly : amicable
> Antonyms
>   brave : cowardly :: friendly : hostile
> Cause and effect
>   cold : shiver :: danger : tremble

Each of the following analogies involves one or more words from "Adventures of Great Rabbit." For each analogy, determine the relationship between the first pair of words. Then select the word from among the four choices to complete the second pair so that it has the same relationship.

1. fatigued : rest :: ravenous :

> **a.** sleep   **c.** hide
> **b.** eat   **d.** chase

2. lazy : energetic :: dismal :

> **a.** cheerful   **c.** eager
> **b.** gloomy   **d.** creative

3. mind : delusion :: eye :

> **a.** sight   **c.** misconception
> **b.** mirage   **d.** blindness

4. tapping : hammering :: whispering :

> **a.** chirping   **c.** shouting
> **b.** singing   **d.** weeping

5. creep : crawl :: persevere :

> **a.** continue   **c.** trouble
> **b.** pursue   **d.** relieve

Coyote (ca. 1890). Ceramic. Cochiti Pueblo.

Courtesy of School of American Research,
Santa Fe, New Mexico.

THE UPPER WORLD

Traditional Nez Percé

Tricksters appear in stories told by people the world over. For Native Americans, the trickster is often a coyote, but may also be a fox, badger, raven, or, as you have seen, a rabbit. Whatever shape the trickster takes, though, his personality sets him apart from other creatures. In the following story, told by the Nez Percé (nez′ pər·sā′) of Idaho and eastern Oregon and Washington, what makes Coyote different from other animals?

All this happened long ago, before the white man came to the Idaho country, and the arts of magic were scattered and forgotten. Close around the lodge fires on the long winter evenings, a few old men still tell the ancient stories, but soon they will all be gone, and their secrets lost. They remember when the Indians could take on animal shapes, and shuffle and sway and stamp all night in the herd with their buffalo brothers. And they tell of the days before the time of man, when the animals could change to human form, and talk and enjoy their pipes as we do today. This is the way the Great Spirit tested the world for the coming of men.

In those days, Bear wore an elkskin suit and lived in a tepee, with Porcupine, his wife. He would hunt and fish and beat his drum for the dancing, while Porcupine pounded camass[1] root like any other woman. But at times they grew tired of the talk and the confusion of living with other people. Late at night, under the hurrying moon, Porcupine would become a creature with white-tipped quills, and run off to gnaw on a hollow log in the woods. And when the melting snow came booming down the mountainsides, and the waters of the Snake and the Salmon[2] boiled up between the dark walls of the canyons, Bear would slip into a shaggy brown coat and go lumbering through the forest on his big feet, snuffing at the soft spring air.

So it was with all of nature. Even the grasses and the stones could speak, and Thunder came down out of a cloud to find himself a wife, and the Moon and his son turned into giants on the earth and spread terror up and down the valley.

Of all the creatures the old men speak of, the cleverest was Coyote. He was a small animal, yellowish-gray, like a bright-eyed little dog with a brush for a tail. But for all his small size, he was a medicine man, which means that he knew and practiced the arts of magic. Powerful and shrewd as he was, however, he could never resist a joke. So he was known far and wide as a rascal and a trickster, but not until his visit to the Upper World did he get the respect he deserved. This is how it happened:

One day as Coyote was loping along about his business, he heard the noise of a big powwow in

General and Precise Words. Words can be general in meaning, such as *building* and *dwelling*, or precise, such as *wigwam* and *tepee (tipi)*. Do you know which of these precise words is a hut covered with bark, and which is a tent covered with hides? (If not, check a dictionary.) Knowing the differences among words with similar meanings allows you to write vividly, and also to read vividly—to see exactly what a writer had in mind. As you read this tale, watch for and enjoy the many words that create precise mental pictures, especially the words that describe the animals' actions.

---

1. **camass** (kam′əs): plant of the lily family.
2. **the Snake and the Salmon:** rivers in Idaho and Oregon.

the valley. Being a sociable creature, he had to go and see what the discussion was about. He found all the animals at the foot of the tallest pine tree, arguing about which one of their number was the greatest medicine man.

"Poor idiots!" Coyote muttered. "They've forgotten me!"

But he was smart enough to say it to himself.

"I am the most powerful!" one of them would shout.

"You? No, I am! I am!" And they began to squabble. They roared, cawed, yowled, whistled, bellowed, bawled, and screeched, until they fell on their sides, panting, with their tongues lolling out, and the Thunder Bird woke on the mountain and stirred his scales. Then Coyote opened his mouth and spoke for the first time.

"We must set ourselves a test," he suggested. "Who is brave enough to climb the tallest pine to the Eagle's nest?"

The tallest pine was so high that its top was lost among the clouds, but all the animals wanted to have a try. Red Squirrel scooted easily up the long straight trunk, but he was so scatterbrained he forgot what he was doing, and ran chattering down the other side. Grizzly Bear had to give up when the tree began to sway beneath his weight.

After a while came the turn of little Black Bear. Up, up he went; but just as he was about to reach his goal, Coyote winked at the Eagle's nest and it shot up fifty feet higher. Black Bear was astonished at that, but he took a long breath and bravely went on climbing. When his head was almost on a level with the nest, Coyote slyly winked again, and up it shot another fifty feet. Then for good measure he winked again, several times in a row. By this time Black Bear was so confused that it was all he could do to scramble back to safety. Only Coyote was left to try.

Using his strongest medicine-magic, he charmed himself into his man form. He cautioned the others not to watch him climb, for if they did they would go against his medicine, and he would never be able to come back down the tree.

Coyote grasped the dry, scaly trunk with his man-arms, and set his man-moccasins on whatever small bumps and bolls he could find to support them. At first he climbed quickly, but before long he felt the medicine-magic begin to drain away. When he came to the first big branch of the tree, he threw one leg across it and braced himself, panting for breath. Cool air from the snowfields washed across his face, and the drops of sweat dried from his eyelashes. When his sight was cleared, he saw the meadow lying small and green below him. And there were all the animals, in a ring around the tree, with their mouths wide open and their heads tipped back, watching him climb in spite of all his warnings. So that was why he was losing his magic power.

"Look down! Look down! Don't watch me!" he cried, and the foolish animals remembered and hung their heads.

Again the medicine-magic made it easy for Coyote, and up, up, he went, into the thin clear air among the snow peaks. But once more he felt the strength draining fast out of his arms and legs. Bitterly he regretted those extra times he had winked at the Eagle's nest. He looked down, and there! They were watching him again.

"Look down, look down!" called Coyote in despair.

But the medicine-magic had left him for good, and he knew he could never get back to earth again by way of the pine tree. There was nothing left to do but keep on climbing. Higher and higher he went, past the Eagle's nest, with the great spicy tent of the pine tree all about him. When he stopped to rest and gasp for breath, he saw the wide countryside spread out below him, and the white mist of waterfalls spraying against bare rock. Soon the towering peaks looked as tiny as ant-heaps, and at last through drifting clouds he caught a dizzy glimpse of the whole round world at once, with the four outer worlds that lie at the points of the compass. His brain reeled at the sight and he thought he must fall, but just at that moment he came to a hole in the sky. With trembling arms he pulled himself through, and fell headlong on the grass.

It was a long time before Coyote came to himself and felt the warm sun beating on his back. He opened his eyes and saw a bright meadow about him, thick with flowers. The weariness had left him. He rolled over and over, crushing the moist, sweet grass beneath his weight. Then he walked across the blowing fields toward a little gray tepee in the distance. Outside sat two gray-bearded spiders, spinning their silvery thread. Never had Coyote seen two creatures so old and skinny and gray. They held the spinning close to their eyes, and steadily added to the silvery pile behind them. A warm wind hummed over the grassland, and the sun struck sparks from the pile of silver fluff. At last Coyote broke the drowsy silence.

"Greetings, Ancients," he said, bowing. "What is the name of your country?"

One of the spiders answered, in a cracked old voice, "This is Ah-cum-kinny-coo. The Upper World."

"Then you must be my grandfathers!" cried Coyote. "My grandfathers are said to live in the Upper World!"

He began to dance and spin about for joy, but the first of the spiders stopped him.

"Never," he croaked.

And the other said, "Our grandson is Coyote."

And the first said, "Yes, Coyote; and he lives on earth."

"Watch!" said Coyote gleefully, and as they watched he charmed himself, and changed back to his animal form.

Then the two ancients rose from their spinning, and greeted Coyote as their grandson. They went inside the tepee and prepared a feast. When it was night and they had eaten all they wanted, they filled their pipes with the last of their tobacco and sat smoking under the close, enormous stars. The sound of the wind in the grass was stilled, and from far below they heard a sorrowful wailing. It was the animals lamenting Coyote, their mightiest medicine man.

"I would go back if I could," said Coyote, "but they watched me climb and drained away my magic."

"That's soon mended," said the most ancient of the spiders. He gave Coyote one end of the silver thread and told him to let himself down through the hole in the sky. Coyote drew back in fear when he looked down into the boundless well of space, but he grasped the thread firmly and made himself slip through. Down he plunged past the spinning stars, until he could see the glimmer of snow peaks far below him. Fast as he shot down, the silver thread unreeled above him, slowing his fall, and swung him slow and slower, like a giant swing, until he landed soft as a feather among his friends. One whole long year they had passed there, bewailing their loss, for a day in the Upper World is a year in the land below. They were full of joy when Coyote appeared, and ready to listen to his words.

"Soon the human race is coming," Coyote told them "But never again will anyone go to the Upper World and return."

Then Coyote bound golden tobacco leaves with the end of the silver thread, and quickly the spiders pulled it up through the sky and closed the hole behind it.

—Retold by Fran Martin

Responding to the Myth

Analyzing the Myth

Identifying Facts

1. How long ago do the events in this story happen? At some time between then and now, what powers were common among Indians?
2. At the time this story occurs, what unusual powers did animals and all of nature have? Why did the Great Spirit allow this?
3. List five words or expressions from the story that describe Coyote.
4. Tell what Coyote overhears the other animals discussing. What test does Coyote propose to settle the issue?
5. What three animals attempt the test first? Explain why each one fails.
6. What form does Coyote adopt to make the climb? Explain why he must stop several times.

Raven Blanket, a Nez Percé.

7. What world does Coyote reach?
8. Explain how Coyote gets back to earth. Tell how the other animals greet him.

Interpreting Meanings

9. Explain how Coyote's trick on the other animals backfires on him. Tell what he then does to avoid failing his own test.
10. According to the story, not until Coyote visits the Upper World does he get the respect he deserves. What aspects of Coyote's personality and actions earned him this respect?

Applying Meanings

11. This tale suggests the desire to change shape still exists deep down inside people. What do you think is appealing about changing shape?

Writing About the Myth

A Creative Response

1. **Writing About Changing Form.** If you had the ability to change into an animal form for just one day, what kind of animal would you become?

Before you make your final choice, jot down notes about shapes, sizes, abilities, and both the advantages and disadvantages of being various animals. Then, in one or two paragraphs, tell what animal you would become and why.

A Critical Response

2. **Describing a Character.** The Nez Percé seem to have admired the personality of Coyote despite—or perhaps because of—his being "a rascal and a trickster." What do you think is Coyote's single most admirable quality? In one paragraph, state your answer and support it with reasons and with evidence from the story.

Analyzing Language and Vocabulary

General and Precise Words

Careful writers use precise words in order to create vivid pictures in their readers' minds. In the first paragraph of "The Upper World," for example, the storyteller does not say that the Indians "*walk* and *move* all night in the herd with their buffalo brothers." Instead, the storyteller uses precise words: The Indians "*shuffle* and *sway* and *stamp* all night. . . ." These words give a clearer idea of the motion and noise of the herd. Dictionaries of synonyms and many regular dictionaries explain the differences among words with similar meanings.

1. For each of the following quotations, explain what mental picture the italicized word adds to the meaning of the general word in parentheses.

   a. ". . . Porcupine would become a creature with white-tipped quills, and run off to *gnaw* (chew) on a hollow log in the woods."
   b. ". . . the melting snow came *booming* (moving) down the mountainsides. . . ."
   c. ". . . Bear would slip into a shaggy brown coat and go *lumbering* (walking) through the forest on his big feet, *snuffing* (smelling) at the soft spring air."
   d. "And they began to *squabble* (argue)."

2. Consider the precise words italicized in the following quotation. What kind of bird or other animal would make each sound?

   "They *roared, cawed, yowled, whistled, bellowed, bawled,* and *screeched,* until they fell on their sides, panting, with their tongues lolling out. . . ."

THE TAR MAN

Traditional Black American

Black trickster tales, like Native American trickster tales, almost always involve talking animals whose behavior is essentially human. The trickster rabbit in the following black American folktale is a complex mixture of character traits. What are his likable qualities? What qualities would annoy you if he were a friend of yours?

Once upon a time there was a water famine, and the runs[1] went dry and the creeks went dry and the rivers went dry, and there wasn't any water to be found anywhere, so all the animals in the forest met together to see what could be done about it. The lion and the bear and the wolf and the fox and the giraffe and the monkey and elephant, and even the rabbit,— everybody who lived in the forest was there, and they all tried to think of some plan by which they could get water. At last they decided to dig a well, and everybody said he would help—all except the rabbit, who always was a lazy little animal, and he said he wouldn't dig. So the animals all said, "Very well, Mr. Rabbit, if you won't help dig this well, you shan't have one drop of water to drink." But the rabbit just laughed and said, as smart as you please, "Never mind, you dig the well and I'll get a drink all right."

Now the animals all worked very hard, all except the rabbit, and soon they had the well so deep that they struck water and they all got a drink and went away to their homes in the forest. But the very next morning what should they find but the rabbit's footprints in the mud at the mouth of the well, and they knew he had come in the night and stolen some water. So they all began to think how they could keep that lazy little rabbit from getting a drink, and they all talked and talked and talked, and after a while they decided that some-one must watch the well, but no one seemed to want to stay up to do it. Finally, the bear said, "I'll watch the well the first night. You just go to bed, and I'll show old Mr. Rabbit that he won't get any water while I'm around."

So all the animals went away and left him, and the bear sat down by the well. By and by the rabbit came out of the thicket on the hillside and there he saw the old bear guarding the well. At first he didn't know what to do. Then he sat down and began to sing:

> Cha ra ra, will you, will you, can you?
> Cha ra ra, will you, will you, can you?

Presently the old bear lifted up his head and looked around. "Where's all that pretty music coming from?" he said. The rabbit kept on singing:

> Cha ra ra, will you, will you, can you?
> Cha ra ra, will you, will you, can you?

This time the bear got up on his hind feet. The rabbit kept on singing:

---

1. **runs:** here, small, swift streams.

Animal Metaphors. Animals in "The Tar Man" are given human characteristics. Similarly, people are sometimes described in terms of animal characteristics. Note which animal in this story suggests making the tar man. What would it mean to say that this character's ideas are "foxy"?

Cha ra ra, will you, will you, can you?
Cha ra ra, will you, will you, can you?

Then the bear began to dance, and after a while he danced so far away that the rabbit wasn't afraid of him any longer, and so he climbed down into the well and got a drink and ran away into the thicket.

Now when the animals came the next morning and found the rabbit's footprints in the mud, they made all kinds of fun of old Mr. Bear. They said, "Mr. Bear, you are a fine person to watch a well. Why, even Mr. Rabbit can outwit you." But the bear said, "The rabbit had nothing to do with it. I was sitting here wide-awake, when suddenly the most beautiful music came right down out of the sky. At least I think it came down out of the sky, for when I went to look for it, I could not find it, and it must have been while I was gone that Mr. Rabbit stole the water." "Anyway," said the other animals, "we can't trust you anymore. Mr. Monkey, you had better watch the well tonight, and mind you, you'd better be pretty careful or old Mr. Rabbit will fool you." "I'd like to see him do it," said the monkey. "Just let him try." So the animals set the monkey to watch the well.

Presently it grew dark, and all the stars came out; and then the rabbit slipped out of the thicket and peeped over in the direction of the well. There he saw the monkey. Then he sat down on the hillside and began to sing:

Cha ra ra, will you, will you, can you?
Cha ra ra, will you, will you, can you?

Then the monkey peered down into the well. "It isn't the water," said he. The rabbit kept on singing:

Cha ra ra, will you, will you, can you?
Cha ra ra, will you, will you, can you?

This time the monkey looked into the sky. "It isn't the stars," said he. The rabbit kept on singing.

This time the monkey looked toward the forest. "It must be the leaves," said he. "Anyway, it's too good music to let go to waste." So he began to dance, and after a while he danced so far away that the rabbit wasn't afraid, so he climbed down into the well and got a drink and ran off into the thicket.

Well, the next morning, when all the animals came down and found the footprints again, you should have heard them talk to that monkey. They said, "Mr. Monkey, you are no better than Mr. Bear; neither of you is of any account. You can't catch a rabbit." And the monkey said, "It wasn't old Mr. Rabbit's fault at all that I left the well. He had nothing to do with it. All at once the most beautiful music that you ever heard came out of the woods, and I went to see who was making it." But the animals only laughed at him. Then they tried to get someone else to watch the well that night. No one would do it. So they thought and thought and thought about what to do next. Finally the fox spoke up. "I'll tell you what let's do," said he. "Let's make a tar man and set him to watch the well." "Let's do," said all the other animals together. So they worked the whole day long building a tar man and set him to watch the well.

That night the rabbit crept out of the thicket, and there he saw the tar man. So he sat down on the hillside and began to sing:

Cha ra ra, will you, will you, can you?
Cha ra ra, will you, will you, can you?

But the man never heard. The rabbit kept on singing:

Cha ra ra, will you, will you, can you?
Cha ra ra, will you, will you, can you?

But the tar man never heard a word. The rabbit came a little closer:

Cha ra ra, will you, will you, can you?
Cha ra ra, will you, will you, can you?

The tar man never spoke. The rabbit came a little closer yet:

Cha ra ra, will you, will you, can you?
Cha ra ra, will you, will you, can you?

The tar man never spoke a word.

The rabbit came up close to the tar man. "Look here," he said, "you get out of my way and let me down into that well." The tar man never moved. "If you don't get out of my way, I'll hit you with my fist," said the rabbit. The tar man never moved a finger. Then the rabbit raised his fist and struck the tar man as hard as he could, and his right fist stuck tight in the tar. "Now you let go of my fist or I'll hit you with my other fist," said the rabbit. The tar man never budged. Then the rabbit struck him with his left fist, and his left fist stuck tight in the tar. "Now you let go of my fists or I'll kick you with my foot," said the rabbit. The tar man never budged an inch. Then the rabbit kicked him with his right foot, and his right foot stuck tight in the tar. "Now you let go of my foot or I'll kick you with my other foot," said the rabbit. The tar man never stirred. Then the rabbit kicked him with his left foot, and his left foot stuck tight in the tar. "Now you let me go or I'll butt you with my head," said the rabbit. And he butted him with his head, and there he was; and there the other animals found him the next morning.

Well you should have heard those animals laugh. "Oh, ho, Mr. Rabbit," they said. "Now we'll see whether you steal anymore of our water or not. We're going to lay you across a log and cut your head off." "Oh, please do," said the rabbit. "I've always wanted to have my head cut off. I'd rather die that way than any other way I know." "Then we won't do it," said the animals. "We are not going to kill you any way you like. We are going to shoot you." "That's better," said the rabbit. "If I had just stopped to think, I'd have asked you to do that in the first place. Please shoot me." "No, we'll not shoot you," said the animals; and then they had to think for a long time.

"I'll tell you what we'll do," said the bear. "We'll put you into a cupboard and let you eat and eat and eat until you are as fat as butter, and then we'll throw you up into the air and let you come down and burst." "Oh, please don't!" said the rabbit. "I never wanted to die that way. Just do anything else, but please don't burst me." "Then that's exactly what we'll do," said all the other animals together.

So they put the rabbit into the cupboard and they fed him pie and cake and sugar, everything that was good; and by and by he got just as fat as butter. And then they took him out on the hillside and the lion took a paw, and the fox took a paw, and the bear took a paw, and the monkey took a

Illustration by A. B. Frost (1919) for frontispiece of *Uncle Remus: His Songs and Sayings,* by J. C. Harris.

New York Public Library, Print Room.

paw; and then they swung him back and forth, and back and forth, saying: "One for the money, two for the show, three to make ready, and four to go." And up they tossed him into the air, and he came down and lit on his feet and said:

Yip, my name's Molly Cottontail;
Catch me if you can.

And off he ran into the thicket.

—Retold by Dora Lee Newman

Responding to the Folktale

Analyzing the Folktale

Identifying Facts

1. Explain why the animals must dig a well. Why do they deny the rabbit water from their well?
2. Tell how the rabbit tricks the bear and the monkey to get water.
3. What plan does the fox have for stopping the rabbit? How well does the fox's plan work?
4. Explain how the rabbit tricks the other animals into putting him into the cupboard.

Interpreting Meanings

5. Did you find the rabbit to be a likable character? Did you find one or more of the other animals more likable? Give specific reasons to back up your opinion.

Applying Meanings

6. The technique the rabbit uses to avoid being killed by the other animals is sometimes called *reverse psychology*. Considering what the rabbit says in the last three paragraphs of the story, define *reverse psychology*. In your opinion, why do people fall for such a strategy?

Writing About the Folktale

A Creative Response

1. **Creating a New Ending.** Imagine how the hardworking animals feel when the lazy rabbit gets to drink from the new well. Without changing the other animals to make them as clever as the tricky rabbit, create a new ending that gives the rabbit what he deserves. Tell what the other animals can do that is not cruel, but makes the rabbit earn his water in the future. Start your new ending at the point where the other animals find the rabbit stuck to the tar man. Write at least one paragraph.

A Critical Response

2. **Writing About a Symbol.** The writers Langston Hughes and Arna Bontemps have noted that the folktales of black American slaves represented "personal experiences and hopes and defeats in terms of symbols." A **symbol** is any person, place, or thing which has meaning in itself but which also stands for something else. In "The Tar Man," what do you think the rabbit's conflict with the other animals symbolizes? In two or three paragraphs, explain what "personal experiences and hopes and defeats" of the slaves you find represented in the tale.

Analyzing Language and Vocabulary

Animal Metaphors

A **metaphor** makes a comparison between unlike things. In one kind of metaphor, people are described in terms of the way animals look and act. The names of many animals mentioned in "The Tar Man" are used in expressions that describe human characteristics and behavior. Match the "animal" words on the left with the appropriate "human" meaning on the right. Use a dictionary if you need help. Then use each word or expression in a sentence.

1. bearish
2. monkey business
3. foxy
4. lion's share
5. rabbit punch
6. wolfish
7. elephantine

a. slow and clumsy
b. a blow to the back of the neck
c. mischievous tricks
d. rude and rough
e. crafty
f. the largest or best portion
g. greedy or grasping

THE CELEBRATED JUMPING FROG OF CALAVERAS COUNTY

Mark Twain

Imagine yourself as the writer Mark Twain, living in a gold mining camp in the mountains of California in 1865. The camp has a fine-sounding name—Angel's Camp—but it is winter. Most of the time you are miserable, wet, cold, and sick of the rain and the mud. Then one day everyone gathers around the stove in the camp tavern to tell stories. The longer they are, the better. You hear this one about a frog . . . among other things. As you read, note that Twain's version of the story he heard has two narrators: One is the listener, a stranger at the camp, who speaks at the beginning and end. The other is Simon Wheeler, who actually tells the story about the frog. What differences can you detect in these two characters' attitudes toward the frog story? You will miss a lot of fun if you don't hear this story told aloud.

In compliance with the request of a friend of mine, who wrote me from the East, I called on good-natured, garrulous[1] old Simon Wheeler, and inquired after my friend's friend, Leonidas W. Smiley, as requested to do, and I hereunto append[2] the result. I have a lurking suspicion that *Leonidas W.* Smiley is a myth; that my friend never knew such a personage; and that he only conjectured[3] that, if I asked old Wheeler about him, it would remind him of his infamous *Jim* Smiley, and he would go to work and bore me nearly to death with some infernal reminiscence of him as long and as tedious as it should be useless to me. If that was the design, it certainly succeeded.

I found Simon Wheeler dozing comfortably by the barroom stove of the old, dilapidated tavern in the ancient mining camp of Angel's, and I noticed that he was fat and baldheaded, and had an expression of winning gentleness and simplicity upon his tranquil countenance. He roused up, and gave me good-day. I told him a friend of mine had commissioned me to make some inquiries about a cherished companion of his boyhood named *Leonidas W.* Smiley—*Rev. Leonidas W.* Smiley—a young minister of the Gospel, who he had heard was at one time a resident of Angel's Camp. I added that, if Mr. Wheeler could tell me anything about this Rev. Leonidas W. Smiley, I would feel under many obligations to him.

Simon Wheeler backed me into a corner and blockaded me there with his chair, and then sat me down and reeled off the monotonous narrative which follows this paragraph. He never smiled, he never frowned, he never changed his voice from the gentle-flowing key to which he tuned the initial sentence, he never betrayed the slightest suspicion of enthusiasm; but all through the interminable narrative there ran a vein of impressive earnestness and sincerity, which showed me plainly that, so far from his imagining that there was anything ridiculous or funny about his story, he regarded it as a really important matter, and admired its two heroes as men of transcendent[4] genius in finesse.[5] To me, the spectacle of a man drifting serenely along through such a queer yarn without ever smiling, was exquisitely absurd. As I said before, I asked him to tell me what he knew of Rev. Leonidas W. Smiley, and he replied as follows. I let him go on in his own way, and never interrupted him once.

There was a feller here once by the name of *Jim* Smiley, in the winter of '49—or maybe it was the spring of '50—I don't recollect exactly, somehow, though what makes me think it was one or the other is because I remember the big flume[6] wasn't finished when he first came to the camp; but anyway, he was the curiousest man about always betting on anything that turned up you ever see, if he could get anybody to bet on the other side; and if he couldn't, he'd change sides. Any way that suited the other man would suit him—any way just so's he got a bet, *he* was satisfied. But still he was lucky, uncommon lucky; he most always come out winner. He was always ready and laying for a chance; there couldn't be no solit'ry thing mentioned but that feller'd offer to bet on it, and take any side you please, as I was just telling you. If there was a horse race, you'd find him flush, or

---

1. **garrulous** (gar′ə·ləs): very talkative.
2. **append:** attach.
3. **conjectured** (kən·jek′chərd): guessed.

4. **transcendent** (tran·sen′dənt): extraordinary, surpassing.
5. **finesse** (fi·nes′): cunning, clever strategy.
6. **flume:** inclined chute for carrying water.

better—thank the Lord for his inf'nit mercy—and coming on so smart that with the blessing of Prov'dence she'd get well yet; and Smiley, before he thought, says, "Well, I'll risk two-and-a-half she don't anyway."

Thish-yer Smiley had a mare—the boys called her the fifteen-minute nag, but that was only in fun, you know, because of course she was faster than that—and he used to win money on that horse, for all she was so slow and always had the asthma, or the distemper, or the consumption, or something of that kind. They used to give her two or three hundred yards' start, and then pass her under way; but always at the end of the race she'd get excited and desperate-like, and come cavorting and straddling up; and scattering her legs around limber, sometimes in the air, and sometimes out to one side amongst the fences, and kicking up m-o-r-e dust and raising m-o-r-e racket with her coughing and sneezing and blowing her nose—and always fetch up at the stand just about a neck ahead, as near as you could cipher it down.[8]

And he had a little small bull-pup, that to look at him you'd think he wa'n't worth a cent but to set around and look ornery and lay for a chance to steal something. But as soon as money was up on him he was a different dog; his under-jaw'd begin to stick out like the fo'castle[9] of a steamboat, and his teeth would uncover and shine savage like the furnaces. And a dog might tackle him and bully-rag him, and bite him, and throw him over his shoulder two or three times, and Andrew Jackson—which was the name of the pup—Andrew Jackson would never let on but what *he* was satisfied, and hadn't expected nothing else—and the bets being doubled and doubled on the other side all the time, till the money was all up; and then all of a sudden he would grab that other dog jest by the j'int of his hind leg and freeze to it—not chaw, you understand, but only jest grip and hang on till they throwed up the sponge, if it was a year. Smiley always come out winner on that pup, till he harnessed a dog once that didn't have no hind legs, because they'd been sawed off by a

you'd find him busted at the end of it; if there was a dogfight, he'd bet on it; if there was a cat fight, he'd bet on it; if there was a chicken fight, he'd bet on it; why, if there was two birds setting on a fence, he would bet you which one would fly first; or if there was a camp meeting, he would be there reg'lar to bet on Parson Walker, which he judged to be the best exhorter[7] about here, and so he was too, and a good man. If he even seen a straddlebug start to go anywheres, he would bet you how long it would take him to get wherever he was going to, and if you took him up, he would foller that straddlebug to Mexico but what he would find out where he was bound for and how long he was on the road. Lots of the boys here has seen that Smiley, and can tell you about him. Why, it never made no difference to *him*—he would bet on *any*thing—the dangdest feller. Parson Walker's wife laid very sick once, for a good while, and it seemed as if they warn't going to save her; but one morning he come in, and Smiley asked how she was, and he said she was considerable

---

7. **exhorter** (ig·zôrt′ər): here, preacher.

8. **cipher** (sī′fər) **it down:** calculate it.
9. **fo'castle** (fōk′s′l): alternate spelling of *forecastle*, the upper deck of a ship in front of the foremast.

circular saw, and when the thing had gone along far enough, and the money was all up, and he come to make a snatch for his pet holt, he saw in a minute how he'd been imposed on, and how the other dog had him in the door, so to speak, and he 'peared surprised, and then he looked sorter discouraged-like, and didn't try no more to win the fight, and so he got shucked out bad. He give Smiley a look, as much as to say his heart was broke, and it was *his* fault, for putting up a dog that hadn't no hind legs for him to take holt of, which was his main dependence in a fight, and then he limped off a piece and laid down and died. It was a good pup, was that Andrew Jackson, and would have made a name for hisself if he'd lived, for the stuff was in him and he had genius—I know it, because he hadn't had no opportunities to speak of, and it don't stand to reason that a dog could make such a fight as he could under them circumstances if he hadn't had no talent. It always makes me feel sorry when I think of that last fight of his'n, and the way it turned out.

Well, thish-yer Smiley had rat-tarriers, and chicken cocks, and tomcats and all them kind of things, till you couldn't rest, and you couldn't fetch nothing for him to bet on but he'd match you. He ketched a frog one day, and took him home, and said he calk'lated to edercate him; and so he never done nothing for three months but set in his back yard and learn that frog to jump. And you bet you he *did* learn him, too. He'd give him a little punch behind, and the next minute you'd see that frog whirling in the air like a doughnut—see him turn one summerset, or maybe a couple, if he got a good start, and come down flat-footed and all right, like a cat. He got him up so in the matter of ketching flies, and kept him in practice so constant, that he'd nail a fly every time as far as he could see him. Smiley said all a frog wanted was education, and he could do 'most anything—and I believe him. Why, I've seen him set Dan'l Webster down here on this floor—Dan'l Webster was the name of the frog—and sing out, "Flies, Dan'l, flies!" and quicker'n you could wink he'd spring straight up and snake a fly off'n the counter there, and flop down on the floor ag'in as solid as a gob of mud, and fall to scratching the side of his head with his hind foot as indifferent as if he hadn't no idea he'd been doin' anymore'n any frog might do. You never see a frog so modest and straightfor'ard as he was, for all he was so gifted. And when it come to fair and square jumping on a dead level, he could get over more ground at one straddle than any animal of his breed you ever see. Jumping on a dead level was his strong suit, you understand; and when it come to that, Smiley would ante up money on him as long as he had a red.[10] Smiley was monstrous proud of his frog, and well he might be, for fellers that had traveled and been everywheres, all said he laid over any frog that ever *they* see.

Well, Smiley kept the beast in a little lattice box, and he used to fetch him downtown sometimes and lay for a bet. One day a feller—a stranger in the camp, he was—come across him with his box, and says:

"What might it be that you've got in the box?"

And Smiley says, sorter indifferent-like, "It might be a parrot, or it might be a canary, maybe, but it ain't—it's only just a frog."

And the feller took it, and looked at it careful, and turned it round this way and that, and says "H'm—so 'tis. Well, what's *he* good for?"

"Well," Smiley says, easy and careless, "he's good enough for *one* thing, I should judge—he can outjump any frog in Calaveras County."

The feller took the box again, and took another long, particular look, and give it back to Smiley, and says, very deliberate, "Well," he says, "I don't see no p'ints[11] about that frog that's any better'n any other frog."

"Maybe you don't," Smiley says. "Maybe you understand frogs and maybe you don't understand 'em; maybe you've had experience, and maybe you ain't only a amature, as it were. Anyways, I've got *my* opinion and I'll risk forty dollars that he can outjump any frog in Calaveras County."

And the feller studied a minute, and then says, kinder sad-like, "Well, I'm only a stranger here, and I ain't got no frog; but if I had a frog, I'd bet you."

And then Smiley says, "That's all right—that's all right—if you'll hold my box a minute, I'll go

---

10. **red:** here, cent.
11. **p'ints:** short for *points*, physical characteristics or qualities of an animal.

and get you a frog." And so the feller took the box, and put up his forty dollars along with Smiley's and set down to wait.

So he set there a good while thinking and thinking to hisself, and then he got the frog out and prized his mouth open and took a teaspoon and filled him full of quail shot—filled him pretty near up to his chin—and set him on the floor. Smiley he went to the swamp and slopped around in the mud for a long time, and finally he ketched a frog, and fetched him in, and give him to this feller, and says:

"Now, if you're ready, set him alongside of Dan'l, with his forepaws just even with Dan'l's, and I'll give the word." Then he says, "One—two—three—jump!" and him and the feller touched up the frogs from behind, and the new frog hopped off, but Dan'l give a heave, and hysted up his shoulders—so—like a Frenchman, but it wa'n't no use—he couldn't budge; he was planted as solid as an anvil, and he couldn't no more stir than if he was anchored out. Smiley was a good deal surprised, and he was disgusted too, but he didn't have no idea what the matter was, of course.

The feller took the money and started away; and when he was going out at the door, he sorter jerked his thumb over his shoulder—this way—at Dan'l, and says again, very deliberate, "Well, *I* don't see no p'ints about that frog that's any better'n any other frog."

Smiley he stood scratching his head and looking down at Dan'l a long time, and at last he says, "I do wonder what in the nation that frog throw'd off for—I wonder if there ain't something the matter with him—he 'pears to look mighty baggy, somehow." And he ketched Dan'l by the nap of the neck, and lifted him up, and says, "Why, blame my cats, if he don't weigh five pound!" and turned him upside down and he belched out a double handful of shot. And then he see how it was, and he was the maddest man—he set the frog down and took out after that feller, but he never ketched him. And—

[Here Simon Wheeler heard his name called from the front yard, and got up to see what was wanted.] And turning to me as he moved away,

Courtesy New-York Historical Society.

he said: "Just set where you are, stranger and rest easy—I an't going to be gone a second."

But, by your leave, I did not think that a continuation of the history of the enterprising vagabond *Jim* Smiley would be likely to afford me much information concerning the Rev. *Leonidas W.* Smiley, and so I started away.

At the door I met the sociable Wheeler returning, and he buttonholed me and recommenced:

"Well, thish-yer Smiley had a yaller one-eyed cow that didn't have no tail, only jest a short stump like a bannanner, and—"

"Oh! Hang Smiley and his afflicted cow!" I muttered, good-naturedly, and bidding the old gentleman good-day, I departed.

Responding to the Story

Analyzing the Story

Identifying Facts

1. What does the first narrator hope to learn from Simon Wheeler? What does he learn about instead? Explain what the first narrator thinks of Wheeler's story.
2. According to Wheeler, what was Jim Smiley's most notable trait? List three or four examples that Wheeler gives to illustrate this trait.
3. Describe the bull-pup Andrew Jackson's last fight. Explain why he gave up and died.
4. Identify Dan'l Webster, and describe the tricks he could perform.
5. What bet does Smiley make with the stranger? Explain the way in which the stranger tricks Smiley.
6. Tell why the first narrator leaves the tavern when Simon Wheeler returns from the front yard.

Interpreting Meanings

7. This selection contains two major parts—the **frame** and the **story-within-the-story** (or **inner story**). The frame is at the beginning and the end of the selection. It concerns the first narrator's search for information about Leonidas W. Smiley. The story-within-the-story is told by Simon Wheeler. In six or seven sentences, **summarize** the events of the frame. Then, in ten or fewer sentences, summarize the events of the story-within-the-story.
8. Find at least three pieces of evidence at the beginning and end of the story to support the idea that the first narrator lacks a sense of humor. Then list at least three of his expressions that you think make him seem particularly formal.
9. Besides the trick played on Smiley involving his frog, identify two tricks that are played on other characters in the story. Of these three tricks, which seems the most good-natured? The most ingenious? Explain your reasoning.
10. Based on the information Simon Wheeler presents, how would you **characterize** Jim Smiley? Note at least three of his most prominent character traits.

Mark Twain rides the jumping frog. An English caricature by Frederick Waddy (1872).

Applying Meanings

11. Twain's story has led to an annual frog-jumping contest in Angel's Camp, California, a real place about sixty-five miles southeast of the state capital, Sacramento. The event attracts many contestants, who try to keep up "the Twain tradition" of humorous boasting about their frogs' abilities. Imagine that you kept a pet jumping frog. What boastful tale might you tell if you were to enter your frog in the contest?

Writing About the Story

A Creative Response

1. **Continuing the Story.** The narrator leaves when Simon Wheeler starts to talk about a "yaller one-eyed cow" Jim Smiley once owned. How could such a cow possibly have been of use to Jim Smiley? Would betting and trick-playing be involved? Brainstorm and list some possibilities, the more unusual the better. Then choose the situation that sounds most appropriate for one more episode in the life of Jim Smiley. Tell the story in one or two paragraphs.

A Critical Response

2. **Analyzing the Writer's Style.** Mark Twain once described as "distinctly American" the story that is humorous more because of how it is told than how it turns out. He noted that such stories wander all over and are told "gravely" (seriously). How do Twain's observations apply to this story? What is "wandering" about it? Whose tone is "grave"? Why does keeping a straight face ("grave" story-telling) make the story funnier? Write one or two paragraphs. Quote passages from the story to support your analysis.

Analyzing Language and Vocabulary

Mark Twain and Dialect

Mark Twain was a master at setting down in stories dialects he heard in his travels. A Twain biographer, Justin Kaplan, has noted, "Mark Twain was an entirely deliberate and conscious craftsman. . . . His ear for the rhythms of speech was unsurpassed, and he demanded in dialect . . . nothing short of perfection." Consider the elements of dialect—pronunciation, vocabulary, and grammar—that Twain uses to characterize Simon Wheeler. Begin by copying the following passage on a piece of paper:

> Well, thish-yer Smiley had rat-tarriers, and chicken cocks, and tomcats and all them kind of things, till you couldn't rest, and you couldn't fetch nothing for him to bet on but he'd match you. He ketched a frog one day, and took him home, and said he calk'lated to edercate him; and so he never done nothing for three months but set in his back yard and learn that frog to jump.

Next, underline each example of dialect you find in the passage. Then make three columns headed *Pronunciation, Vocabulary,* and *Grammar,* and list each example of dialect accordingly.

Focusing on Background
The Jumping Frog in French

"The Jumping Frog" was the first of Twain's stories to spread through the newspapers, and it brought him instant fame. The story was even translated into French. Twain retranslated the story back into English, to see what sort of "focus" the French people had put on the story. Part of the retranslation follows. Twain said that the French version would bring grief and sickness to anyone who read it. He returns the favor by butchering the French version.

[*My Retranslation*]
The Frog Jumping of the County of Calaveras

"*Eh bien!* This Smiley nourished some terriers à rats, and some cocks of combat, and some cats, and all sort of things; and with his rage of betting one no had more of repose. He trapped one day a frog and him imported with him (*et l'emporta chez lui*) saying that he pretended to make his education. You me believe if you will, but during three months he not has nothing done but to him apprehend to jump (*apprendre à sauter*) in a court retired of her mansion (*de sa maison*). And I you respond that he have succeeded. He him gives a small blow by behind, and the instant after you shall see the frog turn in the air like a grease-biscuit, make one summersault, sometimes two, when she was well started, and re-fall upon his feet like a cat. He him had accomplished in the art of to gobble the flies (*gober des mouches*), and him there exercised continually—so well that a fly at the most far that she appeared was a fly lost. . . ."

—from "Private History of the 'Jumping Frog' Story," Mark Twain

THE LEGEND OF SLEEPY HOLLOW

Washington Irving

Ghosts, a superstitious schoolmaster, a trickster rival for the affections of a wealthy girl—all of these are ingredients in one of the most famous American short stories. It is set in the 1790's in the Hudson River valley north of New York City, a region originally colonized by the Dutch. The story abounds in rich description of the countryside and its inhabitants. As you read, look for contrasting descriptions. How do the schoolmaster and his rival differ? How is Sleepy Hollow at night different from Sleepy Hollow by day?

Ichabod Crane and the Headless Horseman by John Wilgus (ca. 1835). Oil.

In the bosom of one of those spacious coves which indent the eastern shore of the Hudson, at that broad expansion of the river denominated[1] by the ancient Dutch navigators the Tappan Zee, and where they always prudently shortened sail, and implored the protection of St. Nicholas when they crossed, there lies a small market town or rural port, which by some is called Greensburgh, but which is more generally and properly known by the name of Tarrytown. This name was given, we are told, in former days, by the good housewives of the adjacent country, from the tendency of their husbands to linger about the village tavern on market days. Be that as it may, I do not vouch for the fact, but merely advert[2] to it, for the sake of being precise and authentic. Not far from this village, perhaps about two miles, there is a little valley, or rather lap of land, among high hills, which is one of the quietest places in the whole world. A small brook glides through it, with just murmur enough to lull one to repose; and the occasional whistle of a quail, or tapping of a woodpecker, is almost the only sound that ever breaks in upon the uniform tranquillity.

From the listless repose of the place, and the peculiar character of its inhabitants, who are descendants from the original Dutch settlers, this glen has long been known by the name of Sleepy Hollow, and its rustic lads are called the Sleepy Hollow Boys throughout all the neighboring country. A drowsy, dreamy influence seems to hang over the land, and to pervade the very atmosphere. Some say that the place was bewitched by a German doctor, during the early days of the settlement; others, that an old Indian chief, the prophet or wizard of his tribe, held his powwows there before the country was discovered by Master Hendrick Hudson. Certain it is, the whole neighborhood abounds with local tales, haunted spots, and twilight superstitions; stars shoot and

meteors glare oftener across the valley than in any other part of the country, and the nightmare, with her whole nine fold,[3] seems to make it the favorite scene of her gambols.[4]

The dominant spirit, however, that haunts this enchanted region, and seems to be commander-in-chief of all the powers of the air, is the apparition[5] of a figure on horseback without a head. It is said by some to be the ghost of a Hessian trooper[6] whose head had been carried away by a cannonball in some nameless battle during the Revolutionary War; and who is ever and anon[7] seen by the countryfolk hurrying along in the gloom of night, as if on the wings of the wind. His haunts are not confined to the valley, but extend at times to the adjacent roads, and especially to the vicinity of a church at no great distance. Indeed, certain of the most authentic historians of those parts, who have been careful in collecting the floating facts concerning this specter, allege[8] that the body of the trooper having been buried in the church yard, the ghost rides forth to the scene of battle in nightly quest of his head; and that the rushing speed with which he sometimes passes along the Hollow, like a midnight blast, is owing to his being belated, and in a hurry to get back to the church yard before day-

---

1. **denominated:** named.
2. **advert:** refer.

3. **fold:** offspring.
4. **gambols:** frolics, jumping and skipping about in play.
5. **apparition** (ap′ə·rish′ən): strange figure appearing suddenly and thought to be a ghost.
6. **Hessian trooper:** soldiers from Hessen (a part of Germany). Hessians were hired by the British to fight the Americans in the Revolutionary War.
7. **ever and anon:** now and then; occasionally.
8. **allege** (ə·lej′): claim; assert.

break. The specter[9] is known, at all the country firesides, by the name of the Headless Horseman of Sleepy Hollow.

It is remarkable that the visionary propensity[10] I have mentioned is not confined to the native inhabitants of the valley, but is unconsciously imbibed[11] by everyone who resides there for a time. However wide awake they may have been before they entered that sleepy region, they are sure, in a little time, to inhale the witching influence of the air, and begin to grow imaginative— to dream dreams, and see apparitions.

In this byplace of nature, there abode, in a remote period of American history, that is to say, some thirty years since,[12] a worthy fellow of the name of Ichabod Crane; who sojourned, or, as he expressed it, "tarried," in Sleepy Hollow, for the purpose of instructing the children of the vicinity. The name of Crane was not inapplicable to his person. He was tall, but exceedingly lank, with narrow shoulders, long arms and legs, hands that dangled a mile out of his sleeves, feet that might have served for shovels, and his whole frame most loosely hung together. His head was small, and flat at top, with huge ears, large green glassy eyes, and a long snipe nose,[13] so that it looked like a weathercock perched upon his spindle neck to tell which way the wind blew. To see him striding along the profile of a hill on a windy day, with his clothes bagging and fluttering about him, one might have mistaken him for the genius of famine descending upon the earth, or some scarecrow eloped from a cornfield.

His schoolhouse was a low building of one large room, rudely constructed of logs; the windows partly glazed,[14] and partly patched with leaves of old copy books. It was most ingeniously secured at vacant hours, by a willow twig twisted in the handle of the door, and stakes set against the window shutters; so that, though a thief might get in with perfect ease, he would find some embarrass-ment in getting out. The schoolhouse stood in a rather lonely but pleasant situation, just at the foot of a woody hill, with a brook running close by, and a formidable birch tree growing at one end of it. From hence the low murmur of his pupils' voices, studying their lessons, might be heard in a drowsy summer's day, like the hum of a beehive; interrupted now and then by the authoritative voice of the master, in the tone of menace or command; or, perhaps, by the appalling sound of the birch, as he urged some tardy loiterer along the flowery path of knowledge. Truth to say, he was a conscientious man, and ever bore in mind the golden maxim,[15] "Spare the rod and spoil the child." Ichabod Crane's scholars certainly were not spoiled.

I would not have it imagined, however, that he was one of those cruel potentates[16] of the school, who joy in the smart[17] of their subjects; on the contrary, he administered justice with discrimination[18] rather than severity; taking the burden off the backs of the weak, and laying it on those of the strong. Your mere puny stripling,[19] that winced at the least flourish of the rod, was passed by with indulgence; but the claims of justice were satisfied by inflicting a double portion on some little, tough, wrong-headed, broadskirted Dutch urchin, who sulked and swelled and grew dogged and sullen beneath the birch. All this he called "doing his duty by their parents"; and he never inflicted a chastisement without following it by the assurance, so consoling to the smarting urchin, that "he would remember it, and thank him for it the longest day he had to live."

When school hours were over, he was even the companion and playmate of the larger boys; and on holiday afternoons would convoy some of the smaller ones home, who happened to have pretty sisters, or good housewives for mothers, noted for the comforts of the cupboard. Indeed it behooved him to keep on good terms with his pupils. The

---

9. **specter:** ghost.
10. **visionary propensity:** tendency to see visions.
11. **imbibed:** taken in with the senses.
12. **abode . . . since:** lived thirty years ago. This story was written about 1820.
13. **snipe nose:** nose like the long, slender bill of the snipe, a type of bird.
14. **glazed:** containing glass.

15. **maxim:** rule of conduct.
16. **potentates** (pōt''n·tāts'): persons having great power.
17. **smart:** here, pain.
18. **discrimination:** here, good judgment.
19. **stripling:** youth.

Etching by Felix O. C. Darley (1849) for "The Legend of Sleepy Hollow."

revenue arising from his school was small, and would have been scarcely sufficient to furnish him with daily bread, for he was a huge feeder. To help out his maintenance, he was, according to country custom in those parts, boarded and lodged at the houses of the farmers, whose children he instructed. With these he lived successively a week at a time; thus going the rounds of the neighborhood, with all his worldly effects tied up in a cotton handkerchief.

That all this might not be too hard on the purses of his rustic patrons, who are apt to consider the costs of schooling a grievous burden, and schoolmasters as mere drones, he had various ways of rendering himself both useful and agreeable. He assisted the farmers occasionally in the lighter labors of their farms; helped to make hay; mended the fences, took the horses to water; drove the cows from pasture; and cut wood for the winter

fire. He laid aside, too, all the dominant dignity and absolute sway with which he lorded it in his little empire, the school, and became wonderfully gentle and ingratiating.[20] He found favor in the eyes of the mothers by petting the children, particularly the youngest. He would sit with a child on one knee, and rock a cradle with his foot for whole hours together.

In addition to his other vocations, he was the singing master of the neighborhood, and picked up many bright shillings[21] by instructing the young folks in psalm singing. It was a matter of no little vanity to him, on Sundays, to take his station in front of the church gallery, with a band of chosen

---

20. **ingratiating** (in·gra′shē·ā′ting): bringing oneself into the favor or good graces of another.
21. **shillings:** coins equal to one twentieth of a pound. Pounds and shillings, the main units then of British money, were used for a time in the United States.

singers; where, in his own mind, he completely carried away the palm from the parson.[22] Certain it is, his voice resounded far above all the rest of the congregation; and there are peculiar trills still to be heard in that church, and which may even be heard half a mile off, quite to the opposite side of the mill pond, on a still Sunday morning, which are said to be legitimately descended from the nose of Ichabod Crane. Thus, by diverse little makeshifts in that ingenious way which is commonly denominated "by hook and by crook," the worthy pedagogue[23] got on tolerably enough, and was thought, by all who understood nothing of the labor of headwork, to have a wonderfully easy life of it.

The schoolmaster is generally a man of some importance in the female circle of a rural neighborhood; being considered a kind of idle gentlemanlike personage, of vastly superior taste and accomplishments to the rough country swains,[24] and, indeed, inferior in learning only to the parson. Our man of letters, therefore, was peculiarly happy in the smiles of all the country damsels. How he would figure among them in the church yard, between services on Sundays, gathering grapes for them from the wild vines that overrun the surrounding trees; reciting for their amusement all the epitaphs on the tombstones; or sauntering, with a whole bevy[25] of them, along the banks of the adjacent mill pond; while the more bashful country bumpkins hung sheepishly back, envying his superior elegance and address.

From his half-itinerant life, also, he was a kind of traveling gazette, carrying the whole budget of local gossip from house to house; so that his appearance was always greeted with satisfaction. He was, moreover, esteemed by the women as a man of great erudition,[26] for he had read several books quite through, and was a perfect master of Cotton Mather's *History of New-England Witchcraft*,[27] in

which, by the way, he most firmly and potently believed.

He was, in fact, an odd mixture of small shrewdness and simple credulity.[28] His appetite for the marvelous, and his powers of digesting it, were equally extraordinary; and both had been increased by his residence in this spellbound region. No tale was too gross or monstrous for his capacious swallow. It was often his delight, after his school was dismissed in the afternoon, to stretch himself on the rich bed of clover, bordering the little brook that whimpered by his schoolhouse, and there read old Mather's direful tales, until the gathering dusk of the evening made the printed page a mere mist before his eyes. Then, as he wended his way, by swamp and stream and awful woodland, to the farmhouse where he happened to be quartered, every sound of nature at that witching hour fluttered his excited imagination: the moan of the whippoorwill from the hillside; the boding cry of the tree toad, that harbinger of storm; the dreary hooting of the screech owl, or the sudden rustling in the thicket of birds frightened from their roost. The fireflies, too, which sparkled most vividly in the darkest places, now and then startled him, as one of uncommon brightness would stream across his path; and if, by chance, a huge blockhead of a beetle came winging his blundering flight against him, the poor scoundrel was ready to give up the ghost, with the idea that he was struck with a witch's wand. His only resource on such occasions, either to drown thought, or drive away evil spirits, was to sing psalm tunes; and the good people of Sleepy Hollow, as they sat by their doors of an evening, were often filled with awe, at hearing his nasal melody floating from the distant hill or along the dusky road.

Another of his sources of fearful pleasure was to pass long winter evenings with the old Dutch

---

22. **carried . . . parson:** that is, outshown the parson.
23. **pedagogue** (ped′ə·gäg′): teacher.
24. **swains:** young men.
25. **bevy** (bev′ē): group.
26. **erudition** (er′yo͞o·dish′ən): learning.
27. **Cotton Mather's . . . Witchcraft:** Cotton Mather (1663–1728) was a noted American churchman and writer. He wrote about witchcraft, but never published a book with the title given here.

28. **credulity** (krə·do͞o′lə·tē): tendency to believe too readily.

wives as they sat spinning by the fire, with a row of apples roasting and spluttering along the hearth, and listen to their marvelous tales of ghosts and goblins, and haunted fields, and haunted brooks, and haunted bridges, and haunted houses, and particularly of the Headless Horseman, or galloping Hessian of the Hollow, as they sometimes called him. He would delight them equally by his anecdotes of witchcraft, and of the portentous[29] sights and sounds in the air, which prevailed in the earlier times of Connecticut; and would frighten them woefully with speculations upon comets and shooting stars; and with the alarming fact that the world did absolutely turn round, and that they were half the time topsy-turvy!

But if there was a pleasure in all this, while snugly cuddling in the chimney corner of a chamber that was all of a ruddy glow from the crackling wood fire, and where, of course, no specter dared to show his face, it was dearly purchased by the terrors of his subsequent walk homeward. What fearful shapes and shadows beset his path amidst the dim and ghastly glare of a snowy night! With what wistful look did he eye every trembling ray of light streaming across the waste fields from some distant window! How often was he appalled by some shrub covered with snow, which, like a sheeted specter, beset his very path! How often did he shrink with curdling awe at the sound of his own steps on the frosty crust beneath his feet; and dread to look over his shoulder, lest he should behold some uncouth being tramping close behind him! And how often was he thrown into complete dismay by some rushing blast, howling among the trees, in the idea that it was the Galloping Hessian on one of his nightly scourings![30]

All these, however, were mere terrors of the night, phantoms of the mind that walk in darkness; and though he had seen many specters in his time, yet daylight put an end to all these evils; and he would have passed a pleasant life of it, if his path had not been crossed by a being that causes more perplexity to mortal man than ghosts, goblins, and the whole race of witches put together, and that was—a woman.

Among the musical disciples who assembled one evening in each week to receive his instructions in psalm singing was Katrina Van Tassel, the daughter and only child of a substantial Dutch farmer. She was a blooming lass of fresh eighteen; plump as a partridge; ripe and melting and rosy-cheeked as one of her father's peaches, and universally famed, not merely for her beauty, but as an heir. She was withal a little of a coquette,[31] as might be perceived even in her dress, which was a mixture of ancient and modern fashions, as most suited to set off her charms. She wore the ornaments of pure yellow gold, which her great-great-grandmother had brought over from Holland; the tempting stomacher[32] of the olden time; and a provokingly short petticoat, to display the prettiest foot and ankle in the country round.

Ichabod Crane had a soft and foolish heart toward the sex; and it is not to be wondered at, that so tempting a morsel soon found favor in his eyes; more especially after he had visited her in her paternal mansion. Old Baltus Van Tassel was a perfect picture of a thriving, contented, liberal-hearted farmer. He was satisfied with his wealth, but not proud of it; and prided himself upon the hearty abundance, rather than the style in which he lived. His stronghold was situated on the banks of the Hudson, in one of those green, sheltered, fertile nooks in which the Dutch farmers are so fond of nestling. A great elm tree spread its broad branches over it; at the foot of which bubbled up a spring of the softest and sweetest water in a little well formed of a barrel; and then stole sparkling away through the grass to a neighboring brook that bubbled along among alders and dwarf willows. Hard by the farmhouse was a vast barn that might have served for a church; every window and crevice of which seemed bursting forth with the treasures of the farm. Sleek, unwieldy porkers were grunting in the repose and abundance of their pens; whence sallied forth, now and then, troops of piglets as if to snuff the air. A stately squadron of snowy geese were riding in an adjoining pond, convoying whole fleets of ducks; regiments of turkeys were gobbling through the farmyard, and

---

29. **portentous** (pôr·ten′təs): ominous; warning of evil.
30. **scourings:** here, rides in search of something.

31. **coquette** (kō·ket′): flirt.
32. **stomacher:** ornamented, triangular piece of cloth formerly worn by women as a covering for the chest and waist.

guinea fowls fretting about it, like ill-tempered housewives, with their peevish discontented cry. Before the barn door strutted the gallant cock, that pattern of a husband, a warrior, and a fine gentleman, clapping his burnished wings and crowing in the pride and gladness of his heart— sometimes tearing up the earth with his feet, and then generously calling his ever-hungry family of wives and children to enjoy the rich morsel which he had discovered.

The pedagogue's mouth watered, as he looked upon this sumptuous promise of luxurious winter fare. In his devouring mind's eye, he pictured to himself every roasting-pig running about with a pudding in his belly, and an apple in his mouth; the pigeons were snugly put to bed in a comfortable pie, and tucked in with a coverlet of crust; the geese were swimming in their own gravy; and the ducks pairing cozily in dishes, like snug married couples, with a decent amount of onion sauce. In the porkers he saw carved out the future sleek side of bacon, and juicy relishing ham; not a turkey but he beheld daintily trussed up, with its gizzard under its wing, and, peradventure, a necklace of savory sausages; and even bright chanticleer[33] himself lay sprawling on his back, in a side dish, with uplifted claws.

As the enraptured Ichabod fancied all this and as he rolled his great green eyes over the fat meadowlands, the rich fields of wheat, of rye, of buckwheat, and Indian corn, and the orchards burdened with ruddy fruit, which surrounded the warm tenement of Van Tassel, his heart yearned after the damsel who was to inherit these domains, and his imagination expanded with the idea how they might be readily turned into cash, and the money invested in immense tracts of wild land and palaces in the wilderness. Nay, his busy fancy already realized his hopes, and presented to him the blooming Katrina with a whole family of children, mounted on the top of a wagon loaded with household goods, with pots and kettles dangling beneath, and he beheld himself bestriding a pacing mare, with a colt at her heels, setting out for Kentucky, Tennessee, or the Lord knows where.

When he entered the house, the conquest of his heart was complete. It was one of those spacious farmhouses, with high-ridged but lowly-sloping roofs, built in the style handed down from the first Dutch settlers; the low projecting eaves forming a piazza[34] along the front, capable of being closed up in bad weather. Under this were hung flails,[35] harness, various utensils of husbandry,[36] and nets for fishing in the neighboring river. Benches were built along the sides for summer use; and a great spinning wheel at one end, and churn at the other, showed the various uses to which this important porch might be devoted. From this piazza the wondering Ichabod entered the hall, which formed the center of the mansion and the place of usual residence. Here, rows of resplendent pewter, ranged on a long dresser,[37] dazzled his eyes. In one corner stood a huge bag of wool ready to be spun; in another a quantity of linsey-woolsey[38] just from the loom; ears of Indian corn, and strings of dried apples and peaches, hung in gay festoons along the walls, mingled with red peppers; and a door left ajar gave him a peep into the best parlor, where the claw-footed chairs and dark mahogany tables shone like mirrors; and a corner cupboard, knowingly left open, displayed immense treasures of old silver and well-mended china.

From the moment Ichabod laid his eyes upon these regions of delight, the peace of his mind was at an end, and his only study was how to gain the affections of the peerless daughter of Van Tassel. In this enterprise, however, he had more real difficulties than generally fell to the lot of a knight-errant of yore, who seldom had anything but giants, enchanters, fiery dragons, and such like easily conquered adversaries to contend with; and had to make his way merely through gates of iron and brass, and walls of adamant[39] to the castle keep,[40] where the lady of his heart was confined;

---

33. **chanticleer** (chant′tə·klir′): rooster.

---

34. **piazza** (pē·az′ə): porch.
35. **flails**: tools for threshing grain.
36. **husbandry**: farming.
37. **dresser**: here, cupboard.
38. **linsey-woolsey**: coarse cloth of linen or cotton and wool.
39. **adamant**: very hard substance such as stone.
40. **keep**: strongest, innermost part or central tower of a castle.

all which he achieved as easily as a man would carve his way to the center of a Christmas pie; and then the lady gave him her hand as a matter of course. Ichabod, on the contrary, had to win his way to the heart of a country coquette, beset with a labyrinth of whims and caprices,[41] which were forever presenting new difficulties; and he had to encounter a host of fearful adversaries of real flesh and blood, the numerous rustic admirers, who beset every portal[42] to her heart; keeping a watchful and angry eye upon each other, but ready to fly out in the common cause against any new competitor.

Among these the most formidable was a burly, roaring, roistering blade,[43] of the name of Abraham, or, according to the Dutch abbreviation, Brom Van Brunt, the hero of the country round, which rang with his feats of strength and hardihood. He was broad-shouldered and double-jointed, with short curly black hair, and bluff but not unpleasant countenance, having a mingled air of fun and arrogance. From his Herculean frame and great powers of limb, he had received the nickname of Brom Bones, by which he was universally known. He was famed for great knowledge and skill in horsemanship. He was foremost at all races and cockfights; and, with the ascendency which bodily strength acquires in rustic life, was the umpire in all disputes, setting his hat on one side, and giving his decisions with an air and tone admitting of no gainsay[44] or appeal. He was always ready for either a fight or a frolic; but had more mischief than ill-will in his composition; and, with all his overbearing roughness, there was a strong dash of waggish[45] good humor at bottom. He had three or four boon companions who regarded him as their model, and at the head of whom he scoured the country, attending every scene of feud or merriment for miles round. In cold weather he was distinguished by a fur cap surmounted with a flaunting fox's tail; and when the folks at a country gathering spied this well-known crest at a distance, whisking about among a squad of hard riders, they always stood by for a squall. Sometimes his crew would be heard dashing along past the farmhouses at midnight, with whoop and hallo; and the old dames, startled out of their sleep, would listen for a moment till the hurry-scurry had clattered by, and then exclaim, "Aye, there goes Brom Bones and his gang!" The neighbors looked upon him with a mixture of awe, admiration, and good will; and when any madcap prank, or rustic brawl, occurred in the vicinity, always shook their heads, and warranted Brom Bones was at the bottom of it.

This reckless hero had for some time singled out the blooming Katrina for the object of his gallantries, and it was whispered that she did not altogether discourage his hopes. Certain it is, his advances were signals for rival candidates to retire. When his horse was seen tied to Van Tassel's paling[46] on a Sunday night, a sure sign that his master was courting, or, as it is termed, "sparking," within, all other suitors passed by in despair.

Such was the formidable rival with whom Ichabod Crane had to contend, and, considering all things, a stouter[47] man than he would have shrunk from the competition, and a wiser man would have despaired. He had, however, a happy mixture of pliability and perseverance in his nature; he was in form and spirit like a supplejack[48]—yielding, but tough; though he bent, he never broke; and though he bowed beneath the slightest pressure, yet, the moment it was away—jerk! He was erect, and carried his head as high as ever.

To have taken the field openly against his rival would have been madness. Ichabod, therefore, made his advances in a quiet and gently insinuating manner. Under cover of his character of singing master, he made frequent visits at the farmhouse; not that he had anything to apprehend from the meddlesome interference of parents, which is so often a stumbling block in the path of lovers. Balt Van Tassel was an easy indulgent soul; he loved his daughter better even than his pipe, and like a reasonable man and an excellent

---

41. **caprices** (kə·prē′siz): sudden, impulsive changes in the way one thinks or acts; whims.
42. **portal:** doorway.
43. **blade:** here, dashing young man.
44. **gainsay:** denial; contradiction.
45. **waggish:** playful; jesting.

46. **paling:** fence.
47. **stouter:** here, more courageous; braver.
48. **supplejack:** kind of vine.

father, let her have her way in everything. His notable little wife, too, had enough to do to attend to her housekeeping and manage her poultry; for, as she sagely observed, ducks and geese are foolish things and must be looked after, but girls can take care of themselves. Thus, while the busy dame bustled about the house or plied her spinning wheel at one end of the piazza, honest Balt would sit smoking his evening pipe at the other, watching the achievements of a little wooden warrior, who, armed with a sword in each hand, was most valiantly fighting the wind on the pinnacle[49] of the barn. In the meantime, Ichabod would carry on his suit with the daughter by the side of the spring under the great elm, or sauntering along in the twilight, that hour so favorable to the lover's eloquence.

I profess not to know how women's hearts are wooed and won. To me they have always been matters of riddle and admiration. He who wins a thousand common hearts is therefore entitled to some renown; but he who keeps undisputed sway over the heart of a coquette, is indeed a hero. Certain it is, this was not the case with the redoubtable Brom Bones; and from the moment Ichabod Crane made his advances, the interests of the former evidently declined; his horse was no longer seen tied at the palings on Sundays nights, and a deadly feud gradually arose between him and the schoolmaster of Sleepy Hollow.

Brom, who had a degree of rough chivalry in his nature, would have carried matters to open warfare, and have settled their pretensions[50] to the lady, according to the mode of those most concise and simple reasoners, the knights-errant of yore—by single combat; but Ichabod was too conscious of the superior might of his adversary to enter the lists[51] against him: He had overheard a boast of Bones, that he would "double the schoolmaster up, and lay him on a shelf of his own schoolhouse"; and he was too wary to give him an opportunity. There was something extremely provoking in this obstinately pacific[52] system; it left Brom no alternative but to draw upon the

funds of rustic waggery in his disposition, and to play boorish practical jokes upon his rival. Ichabod became the object of whimsical persecution to Bones and his gang of rough riders. They harried his hitherto peaceful domains; smoked out his singing school by stopping up the chimney; broke into the schoolhouse at night and turned everything topsy-turvy: So that the poor schoolmaster began to think all the witches in the country held their meetings there. But what was still more annoying, Brom took all opportunities of turning him into ridicule in presence of his mistress, and had a scoundrel dog whom he taught to whine in the most ludicrous manner, and introduced as a rival of Ichabod's to instruct her in psalm singing.

In this way matters went on for some time without producing any material effect on the relative situation of the contending powers. On a fine autumn afternoon, Ichabod, in pensive mood, sat enthroned on a lofty stool whence he usually watched all the concerns of his little literary realm. In his hand he swayed a ferule,[53] that scepter of despotic power; the birch of justice reposed on three nails behind the throne, a constant terror to evildoers; while on the desk before him might be seen sundry contraband articles and prohibited weapons detected upon the persons of idle urchins; such as half-munched apples, popguns, whirligigs, fly-cages, and whole legions of rampant little paper gamecocks.[54] Apparently there had been some appalling act of justice recently inflicted, for his scholars were all busily intent upon their books, or slyly whispering behind them with one eye kept upon the master; and a kind of buzzing stillness reigned throughout the schoolroom. It was suddenly interrupted by the appearance of a man mounted on the back of a ragged, wild, half-broken colt, which he managed with a rope by way of halter. He came clattering up to the school door with an invitation to Ichabod to attend a merrymaking or "quilting frolic," to be held that evening at Mynheer[55] Van Tassel's.

All was now bustle and hubbub in the late quiet schoolroom. The scholars were hurried through

49. **pinnacle** (pin'ə·k'l): highest point.
50. **pretensions:** here, claims.
51. **enter the lists:** to enter a contest or struggle.
52. **pacific:** peaceful.

53. **ferule** (fer'əl): flat stick or ruler used for punishing children.
54. **gamecocks:** roosters trained for fighting.
55. **Mynheer** (mīn·her'): Dutch for Mister.

their lessons, without stopping at trifles; those who were nimble skipped over half with impunity,[56] and those who were tardy, had a smart application now and then in the rear, to quicken their speed, or help them over a tall word. Books were flung aside without being put away on the shelves, inkstands were overturned, benches thrown down, and the whole school was turned loose an hour before the usual time; bursting forth like a legion of young imps, yelping and racketing about the green, in joy at their early emancipation.

The gallant Ichabod now spent at least an extra half hour at his toilet,[57] brushing up his best, and indeed only, suit of rusty black, and arranging his looks by a bit of broken looking glass, that hung up in the schoolhouse. That he might make his appearance before his mistress in the true style of a cavalier,[58] he borrowed a horse from the farmer with whom he was domiciliated, a choleric[59] old Dutchman of the name of Hans Van Ripper, and thus gallantly mounted, issued forth like a knight-errant in quest of adventures. But it is proper I should, in the true spirit of romantic story, give some account of the looks and equipments of my hero and his steed. The animal he bestrode was a broken-down plow horse that had outlived almost everything but his viciousness. He was gaunt and shagged, with a thin neck and a head like a hammer; his rusty mane and tail were tangled and knotted with burrs; one eye had lost its pupil, and was glaring and spectral; but the other had the gleam of a genuine devil in it. Still he must have had fire and mettle[60] in his day, if we may judge from the name he bore of Gunpowder. Old and broken-down as he looked, there was more of the lurking devil in him than in any young filly in the country.

Ichabod was a suitable figure for such a steed. He rode with short stirrups, which brought his knees nearly up to the pommel[61] of the saddle; his sharp elbows stuck out like grasshoppers'; he car-

ried his whip perpendicularly in his hand, like a scepter, and, as his horse jogged on, the motion of his arms was not unlike the flapping of a pair of wings. A small wool hat rested on the top of his nose, for so his scanty strip of forehead might be called; and the skirts of his black coat fluttered out almost to the horse's tail. Such was the appearance of Ichabod and his steed, as they shambled out of the gate of Hans Van Ripper, and it was altogether such an apparition as is seldom to be met with in broad daylight.

It was, as I have said, a fine autumn day, the sky was clear and serene, and nature wore that rich and golden livery which we always associate with the idea of abundance. As Ichabod jogged slowly on his way, his eye, ever open to every symptom of culinary[62] abundance, ranged with delight over the treasures of jolly autumn. On all sides he beheld vast stores of apples; some hanging in oppressive opulence on the trees; some gathered into baskets and barrels for the market; others heaped up in rich piles for the cider press. Farther on he beheld great fields of Indian corn, with its golden ears peeping from their leafy coverts, and holding out the promise of cakes and hasty pudding; and the yellow pumpkins lying beneath them, turning up their fair round bellies to the sun, and giving ample prospects of the most luxurious of pies; and anon he passed the fragrant buckwheat fields, breathing the odor of the beehive, and as he beheld them, soft anticipation stole over his mind of dainty slapjacks, well buttered, and garnished with honey or treacle[63] by the delicate little dimpled hand of Katrina Van Tassel.

Thus feeding his mind with many sweet thoughts, he journeyed along. It was toward evening that Ichabod arrived at the castle of the Heer Van Tassel, which he found thronged with the pride and flower of the adjacent country. Old farmers, a spare, leathern-faced race, in homespun coats and breeches, blue stockings, huge shoes,

---

56. **with impunity** (im·pyoo′nə·tē): without fear of punishment or penalty.
57. **toilet:** here, the process of dressing or grooming oneself.
58. **cavalier** (kav′ə·lir′): knight.
59. **choleric** (käl′ər·ik): bad-tempered.
60. **mettle:** spirit.
61. **pommel** (pum′′l): rounded, upward-projecting front part of a saddle.

62. **culinary** (kyoo′lə·ner′ē): suitable for cooking.
63. **treacle** (trē′k'l): molasses.

Etching by Felix O. C. Darley (1849) for "The Legend of Sleepy Hollow."

and magnificent pewter buckles. Their brisk withered little dames, in close crimped caps, long-waisted short-gowns, homespun petticoats, with scissors and pin cushions, and gay calico pockets hanging on the outside. Buxom lasses, almost as antiquated as their mothers, excepting where a straw hat, a fine ribbon, or perhaps a white frock gave symptoms of city innovation. The sons, in short square-skirted coats with rows of stupendous brass buttons, and their hair generally queued[64] in the fashion of the times.

Brom Bones, however, was the hero of the scene, having come to the gathering on his favorite steed Daredevil, a creature, like himself, full of mettle and mischief, and which no one but himself could manage. He was, in fact, noted for preferring vicious animals given to all kinds of tricks, which kept the rider in a constant risk of his neck, for he held a tractable[65] well-broken horse as unworthy of a lad of spirit.

Fain would I pause to dwell upon the world of charms that burst upon the enraptured gaze of my hero as he entered the state parlor of Van Tassel's mansion. Not those of the bevy of buxom lasses, with their luxurious display of red and white: but the ample charms of a genuine Dutch country tea table in the sumptuous time of autumn. Such heaped-up platters of cakes of various and almost indescribable kinds, known only to experienced Dutch housewives! There was the doughty[66] doughnut, the tenderer oly koek,[67] and the crisp and crumbling cruller; sweet cakes and short

---

64. **queued** (kyōod): worn in a pigtail.

65. **tractable** (trak'tə·b'l): easily controlled.
66. **doughty** (dout'ē): valiant; brave.
67. **oly koek** (äl'ə kook): kind of doughnut.

cakes, ginger cakes and honey cakes, and the whole family of cakes. And then there were apple pies and peach pies and pumpkin pies; besides slices of ham and smoked beef; and moreover delectable dishes of preserved plums, and peaches, and pears, and quinces; not to mention broiled shad and roasted chickens; together with bowls of milk and cream, all mingled higgledy-piggledy, pretty much as I have enumerated them, with the motherly teapot sending up its clouds of vapor from the midst. Heaven bless the mark! I want breath and time to discuss this banquet as it deserves, and am too eager to get on with my story. Happily, Ichabod Crane was not in so great a hurry as his historian, but did ample justice to every dainty.

He was a kind and thankful creature, whose heart dilated in proportion as his skin was filled with good cheer; and whose spirits rose with eating as some men's do with drink. He could not help, too, rolling his large eyes round him as he ate, and chuckling with the possibility that he might one day be lord of all this scene of almost unimaginable luxury and splendor. Then, he thought, how soon he'd turn his back upon the old schoolhouse; snap his fingers in the face of Hans Van Ripper and every other niggardly[68] patron, and kick any itinerant pedagogue out of doors that should dare to call him comrade!

Old Baltus Van Tassel moved about among his guests with a face dilated[69] with content and good humor, round and jolly as the harvest moon. His hospitable attentions were brief, but expressive, being confined to a shake of the hand, a slap on the shoulder, a loud laugh, and a pressing invitation to "fall to, and help themselves."

And now the sound of the music from the common room or hall summoned to the dance. Ichabod prided himself upon his dancing as much as upon his vocal powers. Not a limb, not a fiber about him was idle; and to have seen his loosely hung frame in full motion and clattering about the room, you would have thought Saint Vitus[70] himself, that blessed patron of the dance, was figuring before you in person. How could the flogger of urchins be otherwise than animated and joyous? The lady of his heart was his partner in the dance; and smiling graciously in reply to all his amorous oglings; while Brom Bones, sorely smitten with love and jealousy, sat brooding by himself in one corner.

When the dance was at an end, Ichabod was attracted to a knot of the sager folks, who, with old Van Tassel, sat smoking at one end of the piazza, gossiping over former times and drawing out long stories about the war.

This neighborhood, at the time of which I am speaking, was one of those highly favored places which abound with chronicle and great men. The British and American line had run near it during the war; it had, therefore, been the scene of marauding, and infested with refugees, cowboys, and all kinds of border chivalry. Just sufficient time had elapsed to enable each storyteller to dress up his tale with a little becoming fiction, and, in the indistinctness of his recollection, to make himself the hero of every exploit.

But all these were nothing to the tales of ghosts and apparitions that succeeded. The neighborhood is rich in legendary treasures of the kind. Local tales and superstitions thrive best in these sheltered, long-settled retreats; but are trampled underfoot by the shifting throng that forms the population of most of our country places. Besides, there is no encouragement for ghosts in most of our villages, for they have scarcely had time to finish their first nap and turn themselves in their graves before their surviving friends have traveled away from the neighborhood; so that when they turn out at night to walk their rounds, they have no acquaintance left to call upon. This is perhaps the reason why we so seldom hear of ghosts except in our long-established Dutch communities.

The immediate cause, however, of the prevalence of supernatural stories in these parts, was doubtless owing to the vicinity of Sleepy Hollow. There was a contagion in the very air that blew from that haunted region; it breathed forth an atmosphere of dreams and fancies infecting all the land. Several of the Sleepy Hollow people were present at Van Tassel's, and, as usual, were doling out their wild and wonderful legends. Many dismal

---

68. **niggardly:** stingy; miserly.
69. **dilated:** made wider or larger.
70. **Saint Vitus** (vī′təs): This is an allusion to Saint Vitus' dance, a disease that causes irregular, jerking movements.

tales were told about funeral trains, and mourning cries and wailings heard and seen about the great tree where the unfortunate Major André[71] was taken, and which stood in the neighborhood. Some mention was made also of the woman in white that haunted the dark glen at Raven Rock, and was often heard to shriek on winter nights before a storm, having perished there in the snow. The chief part of the stories, however, turned upon the favorite specter of Sleepy Hollow, the Headless Horseman, who had been heard several times of late patrolling the country; and, it was said, tethered his horse nightly among the graves in the church yard.

The lonely situation of this church seems always to have made it a favorite haunt of troubled spirits. It stands on a knoll, surrounded by locust trees and lofty elms, from among which its decent whitewashed walls shine modestly forth. A gentle slope descends from it to a silver sheet of water bordered by high trees, between which peeps may be caught at the blue hills of the Hudson. To look upon its grass-grown yard, where the sunbeams seem to sleep so quietly, one would think that there at least the dead might rest in peace. On one side of the church extends a wide woody dell, along which roars a large brook among broken rocks and trunks of fallen trees. Over a deep black part of the stream, not far from the church, was formerly thrown a wooden bridge; the road that led to it, and the bridge itself, were thickly shaded by overhanging trees which cast a gloom about it even in the daytime; but occasioned a fearful darkness at night. This was one of the favorite haunts of the headless horseman; and the place where he was most frequently encountered. The tale was told of old Brouwer, a most heretical[72] disbeliever in ghosts, how he met the horseman returning from his foray into Sleepy Hollow, and was obliged to get up behind him; how they galloped over bush and brake,[73] over hill and swamp, until they reached the bridge; when the horseman suddenly turned into a skeleton, threw old Brouwer

into the brook, and sprang away over the treetops with a clap of thunder.

This story was immediately matched by a thrice marvelous adventure of Brom Bones, who made light of the galloping Hessian as an arrant[74] jockey. He affirmed that, on returning one night from the neighboring village of Sing Sing, he had been overtaken by this midnight trooper; that he had offered to race with him for a bowl of punch, and should have won it too, for Daredevil beat the goblin horse all hollow, but, just as they came to the church bridge, the Hessian bolted, and vanished in a flash of fire.

All these tales, told in that drowsy undertone with which men talk in the dark, the countenances of the listeners only now and then receiving a casual gleam from the glare of a pipe, sank deep in the mind of Ichabod. He repaid them in kind with large extracts from his invaluable author, Cotton Mather, and added many marvelous events that had taken place in his native State of Connecticut, and fearful sights which he had seen in his nightly walks about Sleepy Hollow.

The revel now gradually broke up. The old farmers gathered together their families in their wagons, and were heard for some time rattling along the hollow roads and over the distant hills. Some of the damsels mounted on pillions[75] behind their favorite swains, and their lighthearted laughter mingling with the clatter of hoofs echoed along the silent woodlands, sounding fainter and fainter until they gradually died away—and the late scene of noise and frolic was all silent and deserted. Ichabod only lingered behind, according to the custom of country lovers, to have a tête-à-tête[76] with the heiress; fully convinced that he was now on the high road to success. What passed at this interview I will not pretend to say, for in fact I do not know. Something, however, I fear me, must have gone wrong, for he certainly sallied forth, after no very great interval, with an air quite desolate and chopfallen.[77] Oh these women! These women! Could that girl have been playing off any

---

71. **Major André** (än′drā): British officer hanged as a spy in 1780, during the American Revolution.
72. **heretical** (hə·ret′i·k′l): holding a view opposed to established opinion.
73. **brake**: here, thicket or clump of brushwood, briers, etc.

74. **arrant** (ar′ənt): notorious.
75. **pillions** (pil′yənz): cushions behind saddles for extra riders.
76. **tête-à-tête** (te·ta·tet′): private conversation between two people.
77. **chopfallen**: disheartened or humiliated; crestfallen.

of her coquettish tricks? Was her encouragement of the poor pedagogue all a mere sham to secure her conquest of his rival? Heaven only knows, not I! Let it suffice to say, Ichabod stole forth with the air of one who had been sacking[78] a hen roost, rather than a fair lady's heart. Without looking to the right or left to notice the scene of rural wealth on which he had so often gloated, he went straight to the stable, and with several hearty cuffs and kicks, roused his steed most uncourteously from the comfortable quarters in which he was soundly sleeping, dreaming of mountains of corn and oats, and whole valleys of timothy and clover.

It was the very witching time of night that Ichabod, heavyhearted and crestfallen, pursued his travel homeward along the sides of the lofty hills which rise above Tarrytown, and which he had traversed so cheerily in the afternoon. The hour was as dismal as himself. Far below him, the Tappan Zee spread its dusky and indistinct waste of waters, with here and there the tall mast of sloop[79] riding quietly at anchor under the land. In the dead hush of midnight, he could even hear the barking of the watch dog from the opposite shore of the Hudson; but it was so vague and faint as only to give an idea of his distance from this faithful companion of man. Now and then, too, the long-drawn crowing of a cock, accidentally awakened, would sound far, far off, from some farmhouse away among the hills—but it was like a dreaming sound in his ear. No signs of life occurred near him, but occasionally the melancholy chirp of a cricket, or perhaps the guttural twang of a bullfrog from a neighboring marsh, as if sleeping uncomfortably, and turning suddenly in his bed.

All the stories of ghosts and goblins that he had heard in the afternoon now came crowding upon his recollection. The night grew darker and darker; the stars seemed to sink deeper in the sky, and driving clouds occasionally hid them from his sight. He had never felt so lonely and dismal. He was, moreover, approaching the very place where many of the scenes of the ghost stories had been laid. In the center of the road stood an enormous tulip tree, which towered like a giant above all the other trees of the neighborhood, and formed a kind of landmark. Its limbs were gnarled and fantastic, large enough to form trunks for ordinary trees, twisting down almost to the earth and rising again into the air. It was connected with the tragical story of the unfortunate André, who had been taken prisoner hard by; and was universally known by the name of Major André's tree. The common people regarded it with a mixture of respect and superstition, partly out of sympathy for the fate of its ill-starred namesake, and partly from the tales of strange sights and doleful lamentations told concerning it.

As Ichabod approached this fearful tree, he began to whistle; he thought his whistle was answered—it was but a blast sweeping sharply through the dry branches. As he approached a little nearer, he thought he saw something white hanging in the midst of the tree—he paused and ceased whistling; but on looking more narrowly, perceived that it was a place where the tree had been scathed by lightning and the white wood laid bare. Suddenly he heard a groan—his teeth chattered and his knees smote against the saddle: It was but the rubbing of one huge bough upon another, as they were swayed about by the breeze. He passed the tree in safety, but new perils lay before him.

About two hundred yards from the tree a small brook crossed the road and ran into a marshy and thickly-wooded glen known by the name of Wiley's swamp. A few rough logs laid side by side served for a bridge over this stream. On that side of the road where the brook entered the wood, a group of oaks and chestnuts, matted thick with wild grapevines, threw a cavernous gloom over it. To pass this bridge was the severest trial. It was at this identical spot that the unfortunate André was captured, and under the covert of those chestnuts and vines were the sturdy yeomen[80] concealed who surprised him. This has ever since been considered a haunted stream, and fearful are the feelings of the schoolboy who has to pass it alone after dark.

As he approached the stream, his heart began

---

78. **sacking:** robbing.
79. **sloop:** relatively small, single-masted sailing vessel.

80. **yeomen** (yō′men): here, farmers.

to thump; he summoned up, however, all his resolution, gave his horse half a score of kicks in the ribs, and attempted to dash briskly across the bridge; but instead of starting forward, the perverse old animal made a lateral movement, and ran broadside against the fence. Ichabod, whose fears increased with the delay, jerked the reins on the other side, and kicked lustily with the contrary foot: It was all in vain; his steed started, it is true, but it was only to plunge to the opposite side of the road into a thicket of brambles and alder bushes. The schoolmaster now bestowed both whip and heel upon the starveling ribs of old Gunpowder, who dashed forward, snuffling and snorting, but came to a stand just by the bridge, with a suddenness that had nearly sent his rider sprawling over his head. Just at this moment a plashy tramp by the side of the bridge caught the sensitive ear of Ichabod. In the dark shadow of the grove, on the margin of the brook, he beheld something huge, misshapen, black, and towering. It stirred not, but seemed gathered up in the gloom, like some gigantic monster ready to spring upon the traveler.

The hair of the affrighted pedagogue rose upon his head with terror. What was to be done? To turn and fly was now too late; and besides, what chance was there of escaping ghost or goblin, if such it was, which could ride upon the wings of the wind? Summoning up, therefore, a show of courage, he demanded in stammering accents— "Who are you?" He received no reply. He repeated his demand in a still more agitated voice. Still there was no answer. Once more he cudgeled the sides of the inflexible Gunpowder, and, shutting his eyes, broke forth with involuntary fervor into a psalm tune. Just then the shadowy object of alarm put itself in motion, and, with a scramble and a bound, stood at once in the middle of the road. Though the night was dark and dismal, yet the form of the unknown might now in some degree be ascertained. He appeared to be a horseman of large dimensions, and mounted on a black horse of powerful frame. He made no offer of molestation or sociability, but kept aloof on one side of the road, jogging along on the blind side of old Gunpowder, who had now got over his fright and waywardness.

Ichabod, who had no relish for this strange midnight companion, and bethought himself of the adventure of Brom Bones with the Galloping Hessian, now quickened his steed in hopes of leaving him behind. The stranger, however, quickened his horse to an equal pace. Ichabod pulled up, and fell into a walk, thinking to lag behind—the other did the same. His heart began to sink within him; he endeavored to resume his psalm tune, but his parched tongue clove[81] to the roof of his mouth and he could not utter a stave.[82] There was something in the moody and dogged silence of this persistent companion that was mysterious and appalling. It was soon fearfully accounted for. On mounting a rising ground, which brought the figure of his fellow traveler in relief against the sky, gigantic in height, and muffled in a cloak, Ichabod was horror-struck on perceiving that he was headless! But his horror was still more increased, on observing that the head, which should have rested on his shoulders, was carried before him on the pommel of the saddle. His terror rose to desperation; he rained a shower of kicks and blows upon Gunpowder, hoping, by a sudden movement, to give his companion the slip—but the specter started full jump with him. Away then they dashed, through thick and thin; stones flying, and sparks flashing at every bound. Ichabod's flimsy garments fluttered in the air, as he stretched his long lank body away over his horse's head, in the eagerness of his flight.

They had now reached the road which turns off to Sleepy Hollow; but Gunpowder, who seemed possessed with a demon, instead of keeping up it, made an opposite turn, and plunged headlong downhill to the left. This road leads through a sandy hollow, shaded by trees for about a quarter of a mile, where it crosses the bridge famous in goblin story, and just beyond swells the green knoll on which stands the whitewashed church.

As yet the panic of the steed had given his unskillful rider an apparent advantage in the chase; but just as he had got halfway through the hollow, the girths of the saddle gave way, and he felt it slipping from under him. He seized it by the

81. **clove:** stuck.
82. **stave:** stanza.

Etching by Felix O. C. Darley (1849) for "The Legend of Sleepy Hollow."

pommel, and endeavored to hold it firm, but in vain; and had just time to save himself by clasping old Gunpowder round the neck, when the saddle fell to the earth, and he heard it trampled underfoot by his pursuer. For a moment the terror of Hans Van Ripper's wrath passed across his mind—for it was his Sunday saddle; but this was no time for petty fears; the goblin was hard on his haunches; and (unskillful rider that he was!) he had much ado to maintain his seat; sometimes slipping on one side, sometimes on another, and sometimes jolted on the high ridge of his horse's backbone, with a violence that he verily feared would cleave him asunder.[83]

83. **cleave him asunder** (ə·sun′dər): split him into pieces.

An opening in the trees now cheered him with the hopes that the church bridge was at hand. The wavering reflection of a silver star in the bosom of the brook told him that he was not mistaken. He saw the walls of the church dimly glaring under the trees beyond. He recollected the place where Brom Bone's ghostly competitor had disappeared. "If I can but reach the bridge," thought Ichabod, "I am safe." Just then he heard the black steed panting and blowing close behind him; he even fancied that he felt his hot breath. Another convulsive kick in the ribs, and old Gunpowder sprang upon the bridge; he thundered over the resounding planks; he gained the opposite side; and now Ichabod cast a look behind to see if his pursuer should vanish, according to rule, in a flash of fire and brimstone. Just then he saw the goblin rising in his stirrups, and in the very act of hurling his head at him. Ichabod endeavored to dodge the horrible missile, but too late. It encountered his cranium[84] with a tremendous crash—he was tumbled headlong into the dust, and Gunpowder, the black steed, and the goblin rider, passed by like a whirlwind.

The next morning the old horse was found without his saddle, and with the bridle under his feet, soberly cropping the grass at his master's gate. Ichabod did not make his appearance at breakfast—dinner hour came, but no Ichabod. The boys assembled at the schoolhouse, and strolled idly about the banks of the brook; but no schoolmaster. Hans Van Ripper now began to feel some uneasiness about the fate of poor Ichabod and his saddle. An inquiry was set on foot, and after diligent investigation they came upon his traces. In one part of the road leading to the church was found the saddle trampled in the dirt; the tracks of horses' hoofs deeply dented in the road, and evidently at furious speed, were traced to the bridge, beyond which, on the bank of a broad part of the brook, where the water ran deep and black, was found the hat of the unfortunate Ichabod, and close beside it a shattered pumpkin.

The brook was searched, but the body of the schoolmaster was not to be discovered. The mysterious events caused much speculation at the church on the following Sunday. Knots of gazers and gossips were collected in the church yard, at the bridge, and at the spot where the hat and pumpkin had been found. The stories of Brouwer, of Bones, and a whole budget of others were called to mind; and when they had diligently considered them all, and compared them with the symptoms of the present case, they shook their heads, and came to the conclusion that Ichabod had been carried off by the galloping Hessian. As he was a bachelor and in nobody's debt, nobody troubled his head anymore about him. The school was removed to a different quarter of the hollow, and another pedagogue reigned in his stead.

It is true, an old farmer, who had been down to New York on a visit several years after, and from whom this account of the ghostly adventure was received, brought home the intelligence that Ichabod Crane was still alive; that he had left the neighborhood, partly through fear of the goblin and Hans Van Ripper, and partly in mortification at having been suddenly dismissed by the heiress; that he had changed his quarters to a distant part of the country; had kept school and studied law at the same time, had been admitted to the bar, turned politician, electioneered, written for the newspapers, and finally had been made a justice of the Ten Pound Court.[85] Brom Bones too, who, shortly after his rival's disappearance, conducted the blooming Katrina in triumph to the altar, was observed to look exceedingly knowing whenever the story of Ichabod was related, and always burst into a hearty laugh at the mention of the pumpkin; which led some to suspect that he knew more about the matter than he chose to tell.

The old country wives, however, who are the best judges of these matters, maintain to this day that Ichabod was spirited away by supernatural means; and it is a favorite story often told about the neighborhood round the winter evening fire. The bridge became more than ever an object of superstitious awe, and that may be the reason why the road has been altered of late years, so as to approach the church by the border of the millpond. The school house being deserted, soon fell to decay, and was reported to be haunted by the ghost of the unfortunate pedagogue; and the plow boy loitering homeward of a still summer evening has often fancied his voice at a distance, chanting a melancholy psalm tune among the tranquil solitudes[86] of Sleepy Hollow.

---

84. **cranium** (krā′nē·əm): skull.

85. **Ten Pound Court:** court in which minor cases were tried.
86. **solitudes:** lonely, deserted places.

Responding to the Story

Analyzing the Story

Identifying Facts

1. According to the narrator, what makes Sleepy Hollow and its inhabitants unusual? Describe the "dominant spirit" that supposedly haunts Sleepy Hollow.
2. Why is *Crane* a suitable name for Sleepy Hollow's schoolmaster?
3. How were schoolmasters like Crane paid, fed, and housed at the time of this story? How do these factors relate to Crane's interest in Katrina Van Tassel?
4. Who is Brom Bones? List five or more words from the story that describe his appearance and personality.
5. Name and describe the horses that Crane and Brom Bones ride to the Van Tassel party. How, according to the narrator, does each rider match his horse?
6. Identify three activities Crane especially enjoys at the party. Describe the encounter Brom Bones claims to have had with the headless horseman.
7. Why is Crane upset when he leaves the party?
8. Describe Crane's encounter with the headless horseman. What does Crane think it is that crashes into his skull? The next day, what is found near Crane's hat?
9. What news does an old farmer bring home from New York after Crane's disappearance? What stories do the country wives like to believe instead about Crane and his abandoned schoolhouse?

Interpreting Meanings

10. Many of Irving's details of the setting in this story are carefully chosen to set up contrasts. A **contrast** is a striking difference between things. For example, the narrator describes the atmosphere of Sleepy Hollow as tranquil, but haunted. Locate and reread the passages that describe each of the following, and list as many contrasting details as you can find: (a) Crane's schoolhouse and the Van Tassel's house; (b) Crane's horse and Brom Bone's horse; (c) Sleepy Hollow by day and by night.

11. Irving also uses contrasts to develop the characters of Ichabod Crane and Brom Bones. For example, Crane has "narrow shoulders" and Bones is "broad-shouldered." In what other ways are these two characters opposites? Consider each one's personality as well as appearance.
12. What contrasts can you detect within Crane's own personality? Find examples in the story that show he is (a) shrewd yet gullible; (b) assertive yet seeking others' approval or good graces; (c) gallant yet awkward; (d) brave yet cowardly. List one or two other contrasts in Crane's personality, and support them with examples from the story.
13. In your opinion, is the trick that Brom Bones plays on Ichabod Crane cruel and unjustified? Or do you think Crane deserved what happened to him in some ways? Refer to the story to support your opinion.
14. Who do you think is the hero of this story? Why?
15. The story was written in 1820. Do any of Irving's **characterizations** seem dated to you? For example, would girls today act the way Katrina did? Explain your answer.

Applying Meanings

16. After his encounter with the horseman, Ichabod Crane leaves Sleepy Hollow. In your opinion, is the kind of humiliation Crane suffered sufficient reason to run away? What advice would you have given him?

Writing About the Story

A Creative Response

1. **Extending the Legend.** Imagine that you live in Sleepy Hollow ten years after Ichabod Crane's disappearance. Every day you go to and from your own school past the deserted one. You have heard the "old country wives" say the place is haunted. While you are passing the old schoolhouse at dusk on a windy day, your imagination gets the best of you. In one or two paragraphs, write about your encounter with the ghost of Ichabod Crane, Sleepy Hollow's latest legend.

2. **Updating the Story.** Suppose you want to write a screenplay of this story, but you want to set the events today, in your own locale. Write a proposal that will explain how the story can be brought up-to-date. Consider these elements of the story:

   a. The characters and their names
   b. The occupations of the characters
   c. Where they live: their setting
   d. What takes the place of the two horses?
   e. The ending: What will replace the headless horseman?

A Critical Response

3. **Writing About Plot.** Great plots have a certainty about them. That is, by the story's end, the reader feels the plot could not have turned out any other way. Washington Irving intended his readers to feel that Ichabod Crane had a chance of marrying Katrina and controlling her fortune—to a point. At which point in the story does Crane's downfall become certain? In one paragraph, identify this turning point, or the **climax** of the story. Explain how, until this point, Crane still had a chance of achieving his goals.

4. **Describing Food.** Irving's story is justly famous for its lush descriptions. Refer to the paragraph on page 590 beginning "Fain would I pause to dwell upon . . ." Imitate this paragraph, and write a description of your own of a table full of food. Use details that will help your readers *see* the scene, *smell* it, and even *taste* it.

Analyzing Language and Vocabulary

Changes in Meaning

This story is set in 1790 and was published in 1820. Over the years, some of Irving's words have come to be used differently. Read each quotation below. Then select the meaning that gives the best definition of the italicized word as Irving used it.

1. "From the listless repose of the place, and the *peculiar* character of its inhabitants, who are descendants from the original Dutch settlers, this glen has long been known by the name of Sleepy Hollow. . . ."

   a. odd
   b. particular
   c. improper

2. ". . . one might have mistaken him for the *genius* of famine descending upon the earth. . . ."

   a. spirit
   b. brilliant person
   c. elf

3. ". . . one might have mistaken him for . . . some scarecrow *eloped* from a cornfield."

   a. taken
   b. run away to get married
   c. escaped

4. ". . . the orchards burdened with ruddy fruit . . . surrounded the warm *tenement* of Van Tassel. . . ."

   a. estate
   b. apartment building
   c. house

5. " . . . the *skirts* of his black coat fluttered out almost to the horse's tail."

   a. sleeves
   b. lining
   c. hem

6. "The stories of Brouwer, of Bones, and a whole *budget* of others were called to mind. . . ."

   a. expense account
   b. collection
   c. mixture

Reading About the Writer

Washington Irving (1783–1859) was the first American writer to win praise from other writers in England and Europe. Before this, people thought that America could produce only imitations of stories written in England. Irving was born in New York City on the same day the American Revolution ended. He was named for George Washington. His first book, the funny and satirical *Knickerbocker's History of New York,* was published in 1809. Irving's most famous stories, "The Legend of Sleepy Hollow" and "Rip Van Winkle," were published as part of *The Sketch Book of Geoffrey Crayon, Gent* in 1819–1820. Irving knew Tarrytown, the setting for Ichabod's story, very well. He retired to "Sunnyside," a beautiful Dutch farmhouse in Tarrytown, which is now visited by many tourists every year.

Every nation has visions and dreams of the future. Such visions and dreams reflect that nation's soul, just as the stories of its origins or of its heroes do. America is a nation of many nations, a people of many cultures. We have concentrated in this unit on the folklore of Native America, black America, and white America. Now in three famous speeches from representatives of these groups, you will find expressions of the American Dream. Here are the visions that bind us together as one people, living together in one bountiful, beautiful land.

The world does not always appreciate dreamers. Lincoln was assassinated, and so was Martin Luther King, Jr.

American Visions

Part of a preliminary version of "The Gettysburg Address," in President Abraham Lincoln's handwriting.

Executive Mansion,

Washington, _____, 186 .

Four score and seven years ago our fathers brought forth, upon this continent, a new nation, conceived in liberty, and dedicated to the proposition that "all men are created equal"

Now we are engaged in a great civil war, testing whether that nation, or any nation so conceived, and so dedicated, can long endure. We are met on a great battle field of that war. We have come to dedicate a portion of it, as a final rest-ing place for those who died here, that the nation might live. This we may, in all propriety do. But, in a larger sense, we can not dedicate— we can not consecrate— we can not hallow, this ground— The brave men, living and dead, who struggled here, have hallowed it, far above our poor power to add or detract. The world will little note, nor long

THE GETTYSBURG ADDRESS

Abraham Lincoln

Abraham Lincoln (ca. 1860). Charcoal sketch.

Memorial Hall Library,
Andover, Massachusetts.

In early 1863, the outcome of the American Civil War was still in doubt. Then, in July 1863, the Battle of Gettysburg in Pennsylvania proved to be a turning point. In that bloody three-day battle, Union forces prevented Confederate forces from moving north, thus confining the war mainly to the South. In all, the battle left about 48,000 soldiers dead, wounded, or missing. On November 19, 1863, part of the battlefield was dedicated as a military cemetery. President Abraham Lincoln was asked to make some remarks at the dedication, and he responded with "The Gettysburg Address." (Part of a preliminary version, in Lincoln's handwriting, is reproduced on page 599.) Though very brief, Lincoln's address is considered one of the greatest speeches by an American political leader. It is noted especially for its vision of American democracy. As you read the speech, look for ideas that go beyond the immediate occasion and speak to the future.

Four score and seven years ago our fathers brought forth on this continent a new nation, conceived in liberty, and dedicated to the proposition that all men are created equal.

Now we are engaged in a great civil war, testing whether that nation, or any nation so conceived and so dedicated, can long endure. We are met on a great battlefield of that war. We have come to dedicate a portion of that field as a final resting place for those who here gave their lives that that nation might live. It is altogether fitting and proper that we should do this.

But, in a larger sense, we cannot dedicate—we cannot consecrate—we cannot hallow—this ground. The brave men, living and dead, who struggled here, have consecrated it far above our poor power to add or detract. The world will little note nor long remember what we say here, but it can never forget what they did here. It is for us the living, rather, to be dedicated here to the unfinished work which they who fought here have thus far so nobly advanced. It is rather for us to be here dedicated to the great task remaining before us—that from these honored dead we take increased devotion to that cause for which they gave the last full measure of devotion—that we here highly resolve that these dead shall not have died in vain—that this nation, under God, shall have a new birth of freedom—and that government of the people, by the people, for the people, shall not perish from the earth.

Responding to the Speech

Analyzing the Speech

Identifying Facts

1. In "The Gettysburg Address," President Lincoln speaks of the past, the present, and the future. To what event does he refer in his first sentence?
2. In his second paragraph, what does Lincoln say the Civil War is testing?
3. Why does Lincoln believe it is impossible for anyone to make the battlefield more sacred than it already is?
4. What challenge does Lincoln propose for the future? What is the connection between honoring the dead and the challenge he offers?

Interpreting Meanings

5. A well-made speech has one or more **purposes.** It does not ramble aimlessly. A purpose of a speech can be to explain, persuade, inform, lift the spirits, defend, entertain, or many other things. Identify three major purposes of "The Gettysburg Address." Then explain how Lincoln achieves each.

6. A speech also is directed at a specific **audience.** Who was Lincoln's audience? What parts of the speech seem directed to the hopes and fears of the audience?

7. In one of the most famous passages of "The Gettysburg Address," Lincoln states his vision of American democracy as "government of the people, by the people, for the people." What does he mean by each of these three foundations of democratic government?

8. Lincoln mentions death in the speech, as you would expect at the dedication of a cemetery. But he also stresses birth. Identify two passages where he speaks of birth, and explain the meaning of each.

Applying Meanings

9. Lincoln says, "The world will little note nor long remember what we say here," but his speech is remembered more than 125 years later. Explain why you think "The Gettysburg Address" is remembered today.

10. To what extent has Lincoln's vision of American democracy been fulfilled in the years since 1863?

Writing About the Speech

A Creative Response

1. **Delivering Lincoln's Speech.** The way one delivers a speech is very important. A speech can lose much of its power if it is delivered unclearly, in too low a voice, or too fast. It is also important to emphasize significant passages so the audience will sense that it should pay close attention. One can emphasize a passage by speaking louder, slower, or with a different tone of voice. Copy "The Gettysburg Address" on a separate sheet. Underline the key passages of the speech. Read the speech aloud by yourself several times, making sure you emphasize the key passages. Then read the speech before the class or another group. Ask the members of the audience for comments on how you delivered the speech.

2. **Delivering an Original Speech.** Imagine that you have been asked to speak at the dedication of a new school. Like President Lincoln, you are expected to keep your speech very short. Also like Lincoln, you can assume that your audience cares strongly about the dedication. Write a brief speech in which you show your understanding of the importance of education in general and the new school in particular. Be sure your points are expressed clearly. Practice the speech several times and then deliver it before the class or another group.

Analyzing Language and Vocabulary

Repetition in Speeches

Like poets, good speakers use techniques that appeal to the sense of hearing. One technique is **repetition,** which sets up "echoes" in listeners' ears. Repetition helps listeners focus their attention on the speech and shows the steps of an argument or process. It also builds mood and emphasizes important points related to the speaker's overall purpose. In "The Gettysburg Address," Lincoln repeats individual words, such as *devotion,* as well as sentence or phrase patterns, as in "we cannot dedicate—we cannot concentrate—we cannot hallow—this ground."

1. Lincoln repeats the word *here* eight times. What gesture do you suppose he made each time he said this word?

2. Find at least three other important words that Lincoln repeats. Using these words, write a sentence that you think expresses the **main idea** Lincoln wanted his audience to understand.

3. Find the repeated sentence pattern in Lincoln's second paragraph. Which words are involved? Explain the effect of this repetition.

4. Identify the repetition Lincoln uses to conclude his speech. Describe the emotional effect you think Lincoln wanted these words to have on his audience.

INDIAN RIGHTS

Red Cloud

The Sioux once lived from Minnesota across the northern plains. The United States government made several treaties with the Sioux in the 1800's, but Indians and whites failed to understand each other. Treaties were broken, and bloody battles resulted. Red Cloud (1822–1909), a leader of the Oglala subgroup of the Sioux, was famous for his bravery and wisdom. In the 1860's he clashed with United States troops in Wyoming. In an effort to increase understanding, he gave this speech in 1870 at a New York reception in his honor. As you read, notice how Red Cloud's *tone,* his attitude toward the subject matter and audience, varies during the speech.

My brethren and my friends who are here before me this day, God Almighty has made us all, and He is here to bless what I have to say to you today. The Good Spirit made us both. He gave you lands and He gave us lands; He gave us these lands; you came in here, and we respected you as brothers. God Almighty made you but made you all white and clothed you; when He made us He made us with red skins and poor; now you have come.

When you first came we were very many, and you were few; now you are many, and we are getting very few, and we are poor. You do not know who appears before you today to speak. I am a representative of the original American race, the first people of this continent. We are good and not bad. The reports that you hear concerning us are all on one side. We are always well-disposed to them. You are here told that we are traders and thieves, and it is not so. We have given you nearly all our lands, and if we have anymore land to give we would be very glad to give it. We have nothing more. We are driven into a very little land,[1] and we want you now, as our dear friends, to help us with the government of the United States.

The Great Father made us poor and ignorant— made you rich and wise and more skillful in these things that we know nothing about. The Great Father, the Good Father in Heaven, made you all to eat tame food—made us to eat wild food—gives us the wild food. You ask anybody who has gone through our country to California; ask those who have settled there and in Utah, and you will find that we have treated them always well. You have children; we have children. You want to raise your children and make them happy and prosperous; we want to raise and make them happy and prosperous. We ask you to help us to do it.

At the mouth of the Horse Creek, in 1852, the Great Father made a treaty with us by which we agreed to let all that country open for fifty-five years for the transit of those who were going through. We kept this treaty; we never treated any man wrong; we never committed any murder or depredation until afterward the troops were sent into that country, and the troops killed our people and ill-treated them, and thus war and trouble arose; but before the troops were sent there we were quiet and peaceable, and there was no disturbance. Since that time there have been various goods sent from time to time to us, the only ones that ever reached us, and then after they reached us (very soon after) the government took them away. You, as good men, ought to help us to these goods.

Colonel Fitzpatrick of the government said we must all go to farm, and some of the people went to Fort Laramie and were badly treated. I only

---

1. By 1870 some Sioux lived on reservations, areas of land smaller than the regions they had long been accustomed to roaming.

want to do that which is peaceful, and the Great Fathers know it, and also the Great Father who made us both. I came to Washington to see the Great Father in order to have peace and in order to have peace continue. That is all we want, and that is the reason why we are here now.

In 1868 men came out and brought papers. We are ignorant and do not read papers, and they did not tell us right what was in these papers. We wanted them to take away their forts, leave our country, would not make war, and give our traders something. They said we had bound ourselves to trade on the Missouri, and we said, no, we did not want that. The interpreters deceived us. When I went to Washington I saw the Great Father. The Great Father showed me what the treaties were; he showed me all these points and showed me that the interpreters had deceived me and did not let me know what the right side of the treaty was. All I want is right and justice . . . I represent the Sioux Nation; they will be governed by what I say and what I represent. . . .

Look at me. I am poor and naked, but I am the Chief of the Nation. We do not want riches, we do not ask for riches, but we want our children properly trained and brought up. We look to you for your sympathy. Our riches will . . . do us no good; we cannot take away into the other world anything we have—we want to have love and peace. . . . We would like to know why commissioners are sent out there to do nothing but rob [us] and get the riches of this world away from us?

I was brought up among the traders and those who came out there in those early times. I had a good time for they treated us nicely and well. They taught me how to wear clothes and use tobacco, and to use firearms and ammunition, and all went on very well until the Great Father sent out another kind of men—men who drank whiskey. He sent out whiskeymen, men who drank and quarreled, men who were so bad that he could not keep them at home, and so he sent them out there.

I have sent a great many words to the Great Father, but I don't know that they ever reach the Great Father. They were drowned on the way, therefore I was a little offended with it. The words

I told the Great Father lately would never come to him, so I thought I would come and tell you myself.

And I am going to leave you today, and I am going back to my home. I want to tell the people that we cannot trust his agents and superintendents. I don't want strange people that we know nothing about. I am very glad that you belong to us. I am very glad that we have come here and found you and that we can understand one another. I don't want any more such men sent out there, who are so poor that when they come out there their first thoughts are how they can fill their own pockets.

We want preserves[2] in our reserves. We want honest men, and we want you to help to keep us in the lands that belong to us so that we may not be a prey to those who are viciously disposed. I am going back home. I am very glad that you have listened to me, and I wish you goodbye and give you an affectionate farewell.

---

2. **preserves:** places treated as the special areas of a group.

Responding to the Speech

Analyzing the Speech

Identifying Facts

1. Red Cloud begins by setting up a series of comparisons and contrasts between the Sioux and white people. List three ways, according to Red Cloud, that whites and Indians are alike. List six ways they differ.
2. According to the second paragraph, what misconceptions of the Sioux do white people have?
3. List four complaints that Red Cloud has concerning the government's dealings with the Sioux.
4. Identify four things Red Cloud asks his audience to do to help the Sioux.

Interpreting Meanings

5. Speeches usually have (a) an **introduction,** (b) a statement of the speaker's **purpose,** (c) a body containing **supporting material,** and (d) a **conclusion** which may summarize the speech, request some action, or simply bring the speech to an end. Which paragraphs or sentences of Red Cloud's speech correspond to each of these divisions?
6. The **purpose** of a speech may be to entertain, to educate, to persuade, to move people to action, or something else. A speech often combines several purposes. What purpose or purposes does Red Cloud have? Cite the passages that support your analysis.
7. A speaker's **tone** may be anything from gentle and pleading to harsh and angry. Show how Red Cloud's tone varies in his speech. For example, what is his tone when he discusses the government? What is his tone when he discusses his audience? Cite passages to support your answer.
8. Red Cloud uses the title "Great Father" in two ways. Find instances in which he uses it to refer to God. Whom does it refer to in the other instances? What attitude do you think Red Cloud has toward this second Great Father?
9. Summarize Red Cloud's vision for the future of America. What kind of nation does he hope it will be?

Writing About the Speech

A Creative Response

1. **Writing an Eyewitness Reaction.** Imagine that it is 1870 and you are a New Yorker who is not sure what to think about the role of the Sioux in recent battles. You have never seen an Indian and do not understand why the Sioux would want to resist the United States government. Hoping to broaden your understanding, you attend the reception for Red Cloud. When you get home, what impressions and reactions about the chief and his speech do you record in your journal? Write at least one paragraph.

A Critical Response

2. **Analyzing a Speaker's Technique.** Like Lincoln in "The Gettysburg Address," Red Cloud uses **repetition** in his speech. Locate several passages in which Red Cloud repeats either words or sentence patterns. Then choose one of the passages you located. In a paragraph, explain in detail what point Red Cloud was trying to make, and whether repetition helped.
3. **Relating a Speech to Actual Events.** Do some research on the Sioux in a school or community library. Look particularly for information on what happened to them in the 1860's. Take notes on key events, especially any directly involving Red Cloud and other Oglala. By comparing your notes and the speech, determine how the events relate to what Red Cloud says. Then, in a paragraph, discuss the connections you found between actual events and the speech. Note any events you were surprised not to find echoed in the speech.

I HAVE A DREAM

Martin Luther King, Jr.

A century after Abraham Lincoln's Emancipation Proclamation in 1863, black Americans still found themselves barred from many neighborhoods, public places, schools, and jobs. This inequality led finally to the great Civil Rights protests of the 1960's and the Civil Rights Acts of 1964 and 1965. A black leader who worked tirelessly for change was Martin Luther King, Jr. (1929–1968). In 1963, some 250,000 listeners packed the area in front of the Lincoln Memorial, in Washington, D.C., to hear King speak. Countless others watched on television or listened on radio. His audience was deeply moved, especially by the conclusion of his speech, reprinted here in part as ''I Have a Dream.'' Read the speech aloud to hear its compelling rhythms.

I say to you today, my friends, that in spite of the difficulties and frustrations of the moment I still have a dream. It is a dream deeply rooted in the American Dream.

I have a dream that one day this nation will rise up and live out the true meaning of its creed: "We hold these truths to be self-evident; that all men are created equal."

I have a dream that one day on the red hills of Georgia the sons of former slaves and the sons of former slaveowners will be able to sit down together at the table of brotherhood.

I have a dream that one day even the state of Mississippi, a desert state sweltering with the heat of injustice and oppression, will be transformed into an oasis of freedom and justice.

I have a dream that my four little children will one day live in a nation where they will not be judged by the color of their skin but by the content of their character.

I have a dream today.

I have a dream that one day every valley shall be exalted, every hill and mountain shall be made low, the rough places will be made plain, and the crooked places will be made straight, and the glory of the Lord shall be revealed, and all flesh shall see it together.

This is our hope. This is the faith with which I return to the South. With this faith we will be able to hew out of the mountain of despair a stone of hope. With this faith we will be able to transform the jangling discords of our nation into a beautiful symphony of brotherhood. With this faith we will be able to work together, to pray together, to struggle together, to go to jail together, to stand up for freedom together, knowing that we will be free one day.

This will be the day when all of God's children will be able to sing with new meaning "My country 'tis of thee, sweet land of liberty, of thee I sing. Land where my fathers died, land of the pilgrim's pride, from every mountainside, let freedom ring."

And if America is to be a great nation, this must become true. So let freedom ring from the prodigious hilltops of New Hampshire. Let freedom ring from the mighty mountains of New York. Let freedom ring from the heightening Alleghenies of Pennsylvania!

Let freedom ring from the snow-capped Rockies of Colorado!

Let freedom ring from the curvaceous peaks of California!

But not only that; let freedom ring from Stone Mountain of Georgia!

Let freedom ring from Lookout Mountain of Tennessee!

Let freedom ring from every hill and molehill of Mississippi. From every mountainside, let freedom ring.

When we let freedom ring, when we let it ring from every village and every hamlet, from every state and every city, we will be able to speed up that day when all of God's children, black men and white men, Jews and Gentiles, Protestants and Catholics, will be able to join hands and sing in the words of the old Negro spiritual, "Free at last! Free at last! Thank God almighty, we are free at last!"

Responding to the Speech

Analyzing the Speech

Identifying Facts

1. King says he has a dream of seeing Americans truly living as equals. Quote four passages that illustrate equality in day-to-day terms.

2. What does King say he plans to bring with him as he returns to the South? What are some of the things he expects can be done with this?

3. According to King, what must become true if America is to be a great nation?

Interpreting Meanings

4. In the first paragraph, King refers to the "American Dream." Considering all the dreams he describes in this excerpt, summarize what you think King means by this term.

5. Lookout Mountain is the name given to a ridge about 2,000 feet high that runs some 650 miles through southeastern Tennessee, northwestern Georgia, and northeastern Alabama. How do these facts and the very name of the ridge create an **image** of freedom ringing through a whole region of the United States?

6. King mentions many places in America. How do these details help create a mental **image** of a United States map? Where on the map do the mountains from which freedom is ringing appear?

7. King **alludes,** or refers, to the Declaration of Independence in paragraph 2 and later to the patriotic hymn "My Country, 'Tis of Thee." Explain King's purpose in reminding his audience of these texts.

8. Find several examples of repetition in King's speech. What important ideas do they stress?

9. As a Baptist minister, King was familiar with the technique of ending a speech with a strong, emotionally charged conclusion. What you have read is the conclusion of King's speech. Read it aloud. To what emotions does it appeal? Cite passages that are particularly emotional.

Applying Meanings

10. How does King's speech make you feel about being an American? In what ways is the speech still relevant today?

Writing About the Speech

A Creative Response

1. **Writing About the American Dream.** What areas of life in America today—perhaps the way certain people are treated—make you unhappy? Following the pattern in the first five paragraphs of King's speech, insert the visions that make up your own dream for America. Imitate King's use of repetition for emotional effect.

A Critical Response

2. **Writing a Paraphrase.** A **paraphrase** is a summary or restatement that expresses the meaning of a piece of writing in other words. Much of the power of King's speech results from **repetition, imagery,** and **allusions.** His basic ideas, however, can be stated in a compact paragraph. Using your own words, write a paraphrase of King's speech in ten or fewer sentences.

Focusing on Background
Biblical Allusions

In paragraph 7, King alludes to the Book of Isaiah in the Bible. Isaiah was an ancient prophet who looked forward to the coming of the Messiah who would save Jerusalem. In this famous passage, the prophet compares the coming of the Messiah to the coming of a hero, for whom the people smooth the roads to ease his journey.

"Comfort ye, comfort ye my people, saith your God.

"Speak ye comfortably to Jerusalem, and cry unto her that her warfare is accomplished, that her iniquity is pardoned: for she hath received of the Lord's hand double for all her sins.

"The voice of him that crieth in the wilderness, Prepare ye the way of the Lord, make straight in the desert a highway for our God.

"Every valley shall be exalted, and every mountain and hill shall be made low: and the crooked shall be made straight, and the rough places plain:

"And the glory of the Lord shall be revealed, and all flesh shall see it together: for the mouth of the Lord hath spoken it.

—from The Book of Isaiah,
Chapter 40

MAIN IDEAS

Many myths, legends, and folktales are worth reading because they are interesting stories. But there is another reason for reading such stories. Most of them reveal one or more of the values that a society admires. In "The Devil and Daniel Webster," for example, people believed that good men and women, working together, could defeat the evil in the world.

I

The following Algonquian Indian legend centers on an Algonquian god named Glooskap. As you read, think about the values of the people who told this legend.

Four men managed to find their way to the home of Glooskap, who asked why they had come. The first man said he was a slave to anger, and he wanted to be meek and pious. The second was a poor man who wanted to be rich. The third man was hated by the people of his tribe, and he wanted their respect. The fourth was a conceited man, conscious of his good looks and his fine appearance. Although he was tall, he had stuffed fur into his moccasins to make himself appear even taller. He wanted to be taller than anyone else in his tribe and to live for ages.

Glooskap gave each a small box of medicine and told them not to open the boxes until they reached home. When the first three got home, each rubbed the medicine on his skin. The angry man became meek, the poor man grew wealthy, and the despised man won the respect of his tribe.

The conceited man did not wait until he got home. While he was still in the woods, he opened the box and rubbed the medicine on his skin. Like the others, his wish was granted. He was changed into a pine tree, the tallest tree in the forest and one that would live longer than any other.

—Retold by Joseph Claro

1. What qualities did the Algonquian probably admire in people?
2. What qualities did they probably think of as faults?
3. What **lesson** would you say is contained in this story?

II

As you have seen, not all folktales and legends are serious. Some simply point out ordinary human shortcomings and are amusing. Here is a tale from the Winnebago Indian tradition.

As he wandered aimlessly, Trickster came to the shore of a lake. On the other side of the lake, he saw a man who was wearing a black shirt and pointing at him.

"Younger brother," Trickster called, "why are you pointing at me?" He received no answer. He asked again and again, and still got no answer.

"So," he called out. "You're just going to stand there pointing at me, are you? Well, I can do the same to you."

So Trickster put on a black shirt of his own, and began pointing at the silent man. He stood there pointing for a long, long time.

Finally, his arm was very tired. "Younger brother," he called, "my arm hurts. Let's stop this pointing." No answer.

"We can have something to eat," Trickster called. "Then we can get back to our pointing." Still no answer.

"This is silly," Trickster said. "I'm just standing here imitating him. He doesn't even have the decency to answer me."

He let his arm fall to his side and began walking away. After a few steps, he turned for a last look at the man on the other shore.

What he saw was a tree stump. It had a long branch sticking out in Trickster's direction.

"Oh," Trickster said softly. "I see why people call me the Foolish One." Then he turned and walked away.

—Retold by Joseph Claro

1. What character type from this unit is featured in this myth?
2. What does this character think he sees on the opposite shore of the lake?
3. How does he behave as a result of his mistake?
4. What is he actually looking at? How does he react when he realizes his mistake?
5. What is the **main idea** of this tale?

III

The following legend does not really come from any Native American group. Instead, it is a comment about the kinds of legends told in all societies.

Once upon a time, a young warrior and a young maiden loved each other very much. They belonged to different tribes, however, and their tribes were at war. For that reason, they were forbidden to see each other. As if this weren't trouble enough, an enormous lake separated the lands of the two tribes.

Love, however, always finds a way to overcome obstacles. And that's what happened in the case of these two lovers. In spite of the danger of being caught and punished, the warrior ignored the laws of his tribe. The maiden did the same, though the danger for her was just as great.

Each night, the warrior paddled a canoe across the wide lake. The maiden met him on the shore, and they spent hours looking at the stars and declaring their love for each other. They both longed for the day when their tribes would end their war and the two could get married.

One night, the warrior was shocked to find that his canoe was not in its hiding place. His love was waiting for him on the opposite shore. If he didn't arrive, she would think he no longer loved her.

He decided there was only one thing to do. Without a second thought, he leaped into the lake and began to swim.

The lake, however, was too wide, even for a strong swimmer like him. Halfway across, he began losing his strength. Soon after that, he began

to struggle. From the opposite shore, the maiden watched him drown as he vainly tried to reach her.

According to the legend, the lake was later named for this young warrior who risked the impossible for the woman he loved.

Ever since that night, it has been called Lake Stupid.

—Retold by Joseph Claro

1. What is the **main idea** of this story?
2. Would you have preferred a different ending? What ending are you led to expect?

Writing

1. **Inventing a Myth or Legend.** Imagine that you wanted to teach a young child the importance of some quality, such as honesty, courage, or thoughtfulness toward others. Write an original story that illustrates the importance of the quality you want to teach about. Include supernatural elements, talking animals, or exaggerated feats of superhuman strength or courage. Exchange your stories in class and have another classmate write out the **main idea** of your legend. Is the other reader correct?
2. **Introducing Characters.** Write a story or a dialogue about two or more of the characters in this unit who meet. You might introduce these people:

   a. Hiawatha and Davy Crockett
   b. The devil and Paul Bunyan
   c. Ichabod Crane and Simon Wheeler
   d. Great Rabbit and Coyote
   e. Chief Red Cloud, Abraham Lincoln, and Martin Luther King, Jr.

3. **Describing Character Types.** Write two paragraphs in which you describe two characters who might appear in myths and folktales. One character must be a larger-than-life hero (or heroine). The other must be a trickster animal. Be sure to tell what the characters look like and what their powers are. Give your characters names and tell what part of the country they live in.

COMPARING AND CONTRASTING

Writing Assignment

Write a brief essay in which you compare and contrast any two selections in the sections of this unit (two myths, two stories about legendary heroes, two trickster tales, or two speeches).

Background

When you **compare** two literary works, you point out the ways in which they are alike or similar. When you **contrast** two works, you show how they are different. Any two works can be compared and contrasted provided they have at least one thing in common—a similar **plot,** perhaps, or a similar kind of **hero,** or a similar **tone.**

To organize your thinking and your essay, you must first figure out the **points of comparison**—the aspects you will focus on in discussing the similarities and differences. If you are comparing and contrasting two poems, you could talk about the elements of poetry, which include **rhyme, rhythm, figurative language,** and **imagery.** If you are writing about two short stories, you can compare and contrast the elements of **plot, character, setting,** and **theme.** The prewriting chart that follows suggests some possible points of comparison for the types of selections in this unit.

Prewriting

1. Choose two selections from within any one section of the unit.
2. Reread each selection carefully, and jot down ideas about similarities and differences as they occur to you. Try to figure out what the points of comparison will be—the aspects of the work that you can say are alike or different. Here are some suggestions for points of comparison for the different types of literature in the unit. If

you can think of other points of comparison for your two selections, add them to your list.

Points of Comparison	Selection 1	Selection 2
Myths		
Subject		
What the myth explains		
What the myth reveals about people's values		
Legendary Heroes (or Trickster Tales)		
Character of hero		
The hero's adventure		
Theme of story		
Tone of story (the writer's attitude)		
Use of exaggeration and humor		
What the story reveals about people's values		
Speeches		
Subject or topic		
Theme or main idea		
Purpose (what the speaker wants)		
Audience		
Use of language (images, word choice, repetition, parallel structure, Biblical echoes, etc.)		
Tone (formal, informal, poetic, emotional, solemn, etc.)		

3. Now, use your Prewriting chart to prepare a list of similarities and differences. As an example, the following reader has started listing the similarities and differences in Abraham Lincoln's "Gettysburg Address" and Martin Luther King's "I Have a Dream" speech.

Similarities	Differences
1. Subjects: both visions of America. 2. Both refer to "all men are created equal." 3. Both are short. 4. Both use repetition. Etc.	1. Purposes: one to preserve Union; one to end racial injustice. 2. Audiences: one 1863; one 1963. 3. Themes:? Etc.

Writing

Use the list of similarities and differences to organize your essay as follows:

Paragraph 1: Introductory paragraph cites authors (or sources) and titles. Tell whether the selections are more alike or more different.

Paragraph 2: Point out important similarities. Support statements with specific details and quotations. (You may need more than one paragraph.)

Paragraph 3: Point out important differences. Support statements with specific details and questions. (Again, you may need more than one paragraph.)

Paragraph 4: Concluding paragraph summarizes major similarities and differences.

The following is the opening paragraph of an essay that will discuss ways in which Lincoln's Gettysburg Address and Martin Luther King's "I Have a Dream" speech are similar and different.

> Abraham Lincoln's "Gettysburg Address" and Martin Luther King, Jr.'s, "I Have a Dream" are similar in four main ways. Both are talking about their vision of America. Both use the quotation from the Declaration of Independence: "all men are created equal." Both are short. Both use a lot of repetition to work on our feelings. . . .

Self-Check

1. Does the essay have good introductory and concluding paragraphs?
2. Are the similarities discussed first and then the differences?
3. Are general statements supported with specific details and quotations?
4. Are my ideas clearly expressed?
5. Are all the words spelled correctly? Are sentences punctuated correctly?

Partner Check

1. Are there any spelling errors? Are there any punctuation errors?
2. Are the ideas clear and easy to follow?
3. Does the essay have enough supporting details and quotations?
4. What do I like best about this paper?
5. What needs improvement?

THE ELEMENTS OF THE NOVEL

In the Days of Dickens, illustration for the Illustrated London News, 1923.

UNIT NINE   **John Leggett**

THE ELEMENTS OF THE NOVEL

A novelist's characters must be with him as he lies down to sleep, and as he wakes from his dreams. He must learn to hate them and to love them.

—Anthony Trollope

A novel, like a short story, is a fictional narrative that is built of certain elements: **plot, character, point of view, setting,** and **theme.** The most obvious difference between a novel and a short story is length. Short stories tend to have a length of about five thousand words, or some fifteen book pages. Many are considerably shorter. Novels, however, generally have a length of at least one hundred book pages. Some are more than five hundred pages long.

The marked difference in length results from differences in the scope of short stories and novels. A short story is relatively simple in structure. It draws on rules of writing called classic unities. These rules are based on the three unities the ancient Greek philosopher Aristotle developed for drama—unity of action, unity of place, and unity of time. Aristotle said the action of a drama should be as realistic as possible, and should cover a limited area and time period. A short story usually contains only one or two important characters. It generally has no minor plots, or **subplots,** but just the **main plot.** It is limited to a certain area, like the main character's house or town. If the setting shifts, it shifts just once or twice. A short story typically takes place over the course of one day—or even one hour. A novel, on the other hand, almost always expands on these limits.

The Novel's Scope

A novel's scope is likely to be fairly broad. It will usually focus on several characters, rather than just one or two. There is more character development than in a short story. The writer has the space to provide many details and to let the characters go through a series of important events. A novel often includes several subplots in addition to the main plot, which runs through the entire narrative. The writer of a novel usually develops more than one theme. As a rule, a novel will have a variety of settings. It frequently will cover a time span of several years.

Development of the Novel

The novel has been a very popular form of storytelling since it was developed in Europe in the 1500's and 1600's. One of the first great novels was *Don Quixote* (part one, 1605; part two, 1615).

The Elements of the Novel

Illustration by N. C. Wyeth for a 1920 edition of *Robinson Crusoe,* by Daniel Defoe.

It was written by the Spanish writer Miguel de Cervantes, and tells of an idealistic man who sets out to improve the world. Two early novels published in England were Daniel DeFoe's *Robinson Crusoe* (1719) and Henry Fielding's *Tom Jones* (1749). Many great novels have been written by Americans. Two masterpieces are *Moby-Dick* (1851), by Herman Melville, and *The Adventures of Huckleberry Finn* (1884), by Mark Twain.

Why Read a Novel?

There are several reasons people read novels:

1. To be entertained.

2. To learn about other people, and especially how they behave in specific situations.

3. To be informed about other places in the world today, about bygone eras, or about possible future worlds.

4. To be introduced to new ideas or new ways of looking at things.

Many novels satisfy more than one of these reasons, as well as other reasons. When we finish a good novel, we feel as if we got to know someone else, and perhaps someplace else, very well. We thus know more about the world, and how to deal with it. We have expanded our horizons.

Scrooge and Marley's ghost. From the Metro-Goldwyn-Mayer movie version of *A Christmas Carol*.

A Technical Wonder

Wherever English is spoken, *A Christmas Carol* is a part of the year-end holiday—as much as the holly wreath is. It is difficult to imagine a Christmas Day in which Dickens's story is not retold to multitudes gathered in households around the globe. Perhaps the tale is read by a family member, perhaps by a celebrity on the radio. Often a version is acted by famous stars on television.

It is no accident that Dickens's Christmas story is so popular. It is a brilliant piece of storytelling, a technical wonder. Moreover, Dickens has taken a mighty theme and made the most of it.

Nearly all of us have nightmares. We are familiar with that enormous sense of relief when we wake up and find ourselves in bed and in one piece. The house is still standing. The giant stingray is back in its tank at the aquarium. The impossibly hard math test has, in fact, not been given.

Scrooge's Memorable Journey

In *a Christmas Carol,* Dickens has given old Scrooge a magnificent dream. The dream is so satisfying on so many levels that it becomes a complicated mirror, showing us a whole, complex, and believable character. By story's end, we feel fully rewarded by our dream-trip into Scrooge's mind.

In fact, so well has Dickens told his story, that some readers believe there was no dream at all. Scrooge's memorable journey through past, present, and future was (these readers believe) totally real.

Whether a dream or a reality, Scrooge's journey shows us how a perfectly normal boy and young man is made into a miser. We see the result of the transformation in Scrooge: He is a tight-fisted, hard-hearted materialist, who believes in money as the only measure of human accomplishment. Finally, we see the futility of Scrooge's way of life, and the contempt he is going to earn from it, if he does not let some Merry Christmas into his bleak heart.

That "Merry Christmas," of course, makes up both the theme and the power of *A Christmas Carol.* The story presents the essence of the religious belief that being poor is *not* shameful, that, in fact, there is virtue in poverty, just as there is virtue in generosity and in the love of our fellow human beings. As Dickens tells the story, we see that these values grow, and flourish best, within the family.

The Life of Charles Dickens (1812—1870)

Like many of his vivid characters, Charles Dickens suffered an insecure and impoverished childhood. Born in 1812, he was one of eight children in the family of a clerk in the Royal Navy pay office at Portsmouth, England.

A Christmas Carol

Scrooge. Unless otherwise noted, all illustrations for *A Christmas Carol* are by Everett Shinn. They appeared in a 1938 edition of the novel. © 1938 Garden City Publishing Company, New York.

Courtesy New York Public Library. Prints Division.

When his father lost his job, twelve-year-old Charles was sent to work in London. His job was sealing jars of shoe polish in a rat-infested warehouse. Each night he went to bed hungry and lonely in a rooming house.

In later years he wrote of feeling ". . . utterly neglected and hopeless. . . . Even now, famous and caressed and happy, I often forget in my dreams and wander desolately back to that time in my life."

This sense of being deprived surely fueled his ambition. At fifteen he was an office boy in a law firm. Soon after he was reading widely in the great library of the British Museum, studying shorthand and, while still a youth, becoming a reporter for the *Evening Chronicle.* All the while he was accurately observing the look of things, the way people spoke and dressed and behaved.

When he was twenty-four, Dickens published his first book, *Sketches by Boz.* It contained articles he had written for the *Evening Chronicle.* In the same year he married the daughter of a newspaper associate and began work on a first novel that was to be *The Pickwick Papers* (1836–1837), his first major success.

From that moment Dickens became the unbelievably productive and ever more popular novelist. He produced *Oliver Twist* in 1837–1839, *Nicholas Nickleby* in 1838–1839, and *The Old Curiosity Shop* in 1840–1841. All were wonderfully exciting tales and perceptive portraits of ordinary English life. Most of his novels were first published in installments in magazines. Readers would eagerly await each new installment.

Dickens's fame spread throughout the world and in 1842, when he was thirty, he accepted an invitation for an American lecture tour. He liked New England well enough, but as he proceeded down the east coast and then westward, he was offended by the manners and customs of the boisterous new country.

He found New York City a hostile place. In Washington, D.C., he deplored the deceit and guile of politicians as well as their habit of spitting tobacco juice. In the south he was dismayed by what he saw of slavery. The farther west he went, the more rude and boring he found the Americans.

Dickens later modified these harsh views and made good use of his American experiences in his writing. He returned for visits in 1867 and 1868.

Back home in England after his first visit to America, Dickens promptly brought forth another masterpiece to please his multitude of readers. This was *A Christmas Carol,* which appeared in 1843 and has endured as a monument to Christian ideals of family and forgiveness.

There were more literary triumphs to come, among them *David Copperfield* in 1849–1850, *Bleak House* in 1852–1853, *A Tale of Two Cities* in 1859, and *Great Expectations* in 1860–1861.

All the while he was traveling, lecturing, and leading a vigorous social life. It is not surprising that, while in his early fifties, he began to tire and grow ill. In 1870, in his fifty-ninth year, and while at work on a new novel, he died of a stroke. He was buried in Westminster Abbey, a famous church in London.

A CHRISTMAS CAROL

Charles Dickens

The story of *A Christmas Carol* takes place in nineteenth-century London. The story spans parts of just two real days—Christmas Eve and Christmas Day—though Scrooge, the main character, goes on a journey far into the past and the future. Scrooge is one of the most famous misers in literature. He works in a counting house, which is an office where a banker keeps his records and handles his correspondence. He lives in a set of rooms that are like a modern apartment, but probably without a kitchen. He eats most of his meals out, and has a servant to take care of his day-to-day needs. These were the usual arrangements for an unmarried man in those days.

In Dickens's time, there was great poverty in London and a vast difference in the lives of the rich and the poor. Scrooge's assistant, Bob Cratchit, earns just fifteen shillings a week, which was barely enough to put food on his family's table. Scrooge, on the other hand, was very rich, although, being a miser, he was always pinching pennies and never enjoyed all the good things his money could buy.

A *carol* is a traditional song of joy that is associated with a seasonal holiday, especially Christmas. One important quality of the carol is that it has a *refrain,* or a group of lines that is repeated regularly. As you begin reading *A Christmas Carol,* you might find it difficult to identify the qualities that make it a carol—it is neither cheerful nor does it have an obvious refrain. As you continue to read, look for clues that make this novel a carol. What clues hint that it will end in some joy or celebration? What aspects of life and human nature do you think the novel is really celebrating? Can you find the novel's refrain?

Preface

I have endeavored in this Ghostly little book to raise the Ghost of an Idea which shall not put my readers out of humor with themselves, with each other, with the season, or with me. May it haunt their house pleasantly, and no one wish to lay it.

Their Faithful Friend and Servant,
C. D.

December, 1843

Stave[1] One:
Marley's Ghost

Marley was dead, to begin with. There is no doubt whatever about that. The register of his burial was signed by the clergyman, the clerk, the undertaker, and the chief mourner. Scrooge signed it. And Scrooge's name was good upon 'Change[2] for anything he chose to put his hand to. Old Marley was as dead as a doornail.

Mind! I don't mean to say that I know of my own knowledge, what there is particularly dead about a doornail. I might have been inclined, myself, to regard a coffin nail as the deadest piece of ironmongery in the trade. But the wisdom of our ancestors is in the simile; and my unhallowed hands shall not disturb it, or the country's done for. You will, therefore, permit me to repeat, emphatically, that Marley was as dead as a doornail.

Scrooge knew he was dead? Of course he did. How could it be otherwise? Scrooge and he were partners for I don't know how many years. Scrooge was his sole executor, his sole administrator, his sole assign, his sole residuary legatee,[3] his sole friend, and sole mourner. And even Scrooge was not so dreadfully cut up by the sad event but that he was an excellent man of business on the very day of the funeral, and solemnized it with an undoubted bargain.

The mention of Marley's funeral brings me back to the point I started from. There is no doubt that Marley is dead. This must be distinctly understood, or nothing wonderful can come of the story I am going to relate. If we were not perfectly convinced that Hamlet's father died before the play began, there would be nothing more remarkable in his taking a stroll at night, in an easterly wind, upon his own ramparts,[4] than there would be in any other middle-aged gentleman rashly turning out after dark in a breezy spot—say St. Paul's Churchyard, for instance—literally to astonish his son's weak mind.

Scrooge never painted out Old Marley's name. There it stood, years afterward, above the warehouse door: Scrooge and Marley. The firm was

---

1. **Stave:** set of verses or lines from a song or poem. Dickens divides his "carol" into five staves, or sections.
2. **'Change:** Royal Exchange, where businessmen bought and sold stocks and goods.
3. **residuary legatee** (ri·zij′o͞o·wer′ē leg′ə·tē): person who receives the rest of an estate after the will is carried out.
4. **Hamlet's . . . ramparts:** allusion to William Shakespeare's play *Hamlet.* The ghost of Hamlet's father appears to Hamlet at night on the wall surrounding the castle.

known as Scrooge and Marley. Sometimes people new to the business called Scrooge Scrooge, and sometimes Marley, but he answered to both names. It was all the same to him.

Oh! But he was a tight-fisted hand at the grindstone, Scrooge! A squeezing, wrenching, grasping, scraping, clutching, covetous old sinner! Hard and sharp as flint, from which no steel had ever struck out generous fire; secret, and self-contained, and solitary as an oyster. The cold within him froze his old features, nipped his pointed nose, shriveled his cheek, stiffened his gait; made his eyes red, his thin lips blue; and spoke out shrewdly in his grating voice. A frosty rime[5] was on his head, and on his eyebrows, and his wiry chin. He carried his own low temperature always about with him; he iced his office in the dog-days, and didn't thaw it one degree at Christmas.

External heat and cold had little influence on Scrooge. No warmth could warm, no wintry weather chill him. No wind that blew was bitterer than he, no falling snow was more intent upon its purpose, no pelting rain less open to entreaty. Foul weather didn't know where to have him. The heaviest rain, and snow, and hail, and sleet could boast of the advantage over him in only one respect. They often "came down"[6] handsomely, and Scrooge never did.

Nobody ever stopped him in the street to say, with gladsome looks, "My dear Scrooge, how are you? When will you come to see me?" No beggars implored him to bestow a trifle, no children asked him what it was o'clock, no man or woman ever once in all his life inquired the way to such and such a place, of Scrooge. Even the blind men's dogs appeared to know him; and, when they saw him coming on, would tug their owners into doorways and up courts; and then would wag their tails as though they said, "No eye at all is better than an evil eye, dark master!"

But what did Scrooge care? It was the very thing he liked. To edge his way along the crowded paths of life, warning all human sympathy to keep its distance, was what the knowing ones call "nuts"[7] to Scrooge.

Once upon a time—of all the good days in the year, on Christmas Eve—old Scrooge sat busy in his countinghouse. It was cold, bleak, biting weather; foggy withal; and he could hear the people in the court outside go wheezing up and down, beating their hands upon their breasts, and stamping their feet upon the pavement stones to warm

them. The City clocks had only just gone three, but it was quite dark already—it had not been light all day—and candles were flaring in the windows of the neighboring offices, like ruddy smears upon the palpable brown air. The fog came pouring in at every chink and keyhole, and was so dense without[8] that, although the court was of the narrowest, the houses opposite were mere phantoms. To see the dingy cloud come drooping down, obscuring everything, one might have thought that nature lived hard by, and was brewing on a large scale.

The door of Scrooge's countinghouse was open, that he might keep his eye upon his clerk, who in a dismal little cell beyond, a sort of tank, was copying letters. Scrooge had a very small fire, but the clerk's fire was so very much smaller that it

Descriptive Writing. English vocabulary has changed in some ways since *A Christmas Carol* was published in 1843. However, today's readers of Dickens's novel still enjoy the drama and humor of what happened to Ebenezer Scrooge one "ghostly" Christmas. Part of this pleasure comes from Dickens's use of descriptive language.

Descriptive writing communicates vivid impressions of important people, scenes, and objects in a story. To vary his descriptions, Dickens uses several techniques, including these four: (1) He includes well-chosen *sensory details,* which appeal to the reader's senses of sight, hearing, touch, taste, or smell. (2) He focuses on the sounds of words through techniques called *onomatopoeia* and *alliteration.* (3) He uses *synonyms,* words that have nearly but not exactly the same meaning. The slight differences in meaning allow Dickens to make precise descriptions. (4) He uses *similes* and *metaphors*—comparisons of unlike things that help focus you on a key point in a description.

Long after you have read *A Christmas Carol,* you will still be able to visualize Marley's Ghost, the shops overflowing with food, and the school Scrooge once attended.

---

5. **rime:** white mass of tiny ice crystals.
6. **"came down":** made a gift or donation.
7. **"nuts":** agreeable; good luck.

8. **without:** outside.

looked like one coal. But he couldn't replenish it, for Scrooge kept the coalbox in his own room; and so surely as the clerk came in with the shovel, the master predicted that it would be necessary for them to part. Wherefore the clerk put on his white comforter,[9] and tried to warm himself at the candle; in which effort, not being a man of strong imagination, he failed.

"A merry Christmas, uncle! God save you!" cried a cheerful voice. It was the voice of Scrooge's nephew, who came upon him so quickly that this was the first intimation he had of his approach.

"Bah!" said Scrooge. "Humbug!"

He had so heated himself with rapid walking in the fog and frost, this nephew of Scrooge's, that he was all in a glow; his face was ruddy and handsome, his eyes sparkled, and his breath smoked again.

"Christmas a humbug, uncle!" said Scrooge's nephew. "You don't mean that, I am sure?"

"I do," said Scrooge. "Merry Christmas! What right have you to be merry? What reason have you to be merry? You're poor enough."

"Come, then," returned the nephew gaily. "What right have you to be dismal? What reason have you to be morose? You're rich enough."

Scrooge, having no better answer ready on the spur of the moment, said, "Bah!" again; and followed it up with "Humbug!"

"Don't be cross, uncle!" said the nephew.

"What else can I be," returned the uncle, "when I live in such a world of fools as this? Merry Christmas! Out upon merry Christmas! What's Christmastime to you but a time for paying bills without money; a time for finding yourself a year older, and not an hour richer; a time for balancing your books, and having every item in 'em through a round dozen of months presented dead against you? If I could work my will," said Scrooge indignantly "every idiot who goes about with 'Merry Christmas' on his lips should be boiled with his own pudding, and buried with a stake of holly through his heart. He should!"

"Uncle!" pleaded the nephew.

"Nephew!" returned the uncle sternly, "keep Christmas in your own way, and let me keep it in mine."

"Keep it!" repeated Scrooge's nephew. "But you don't keep it."

"Let me leave it alone, then," said Scrooge. "Much good may it do you! Much good it has ever done you!"

"There are many things from which I might have derived good, by which I have not profited, I dare say," returned the nephew; "Christmas among the rest. But I am sure I have always thought of Christmastime, when it has come round—apart from the veneration[10] due to its sacred name and origin, if anything belonging to it can be apart from that—as a good time; a kind, forgiving, charitable, pleasant time; the only time I know of, in the long calendar of the year, when men and women seem by one consent to open their shut-up hearts freely, and to think of people below them as if they really were fellow passengers to the grave, and not another race of creatures bound on other journeys. And therefore, uncle, though it has never put a scrap of gold or silver in my pocket, I believe that it *has* done me good and *will* do me good; and I say, God bless it!"

The clerk in the tank involuntarily applauded. Becoming immediately sensible of the impropriety,[11] he poked the fire, and extinguished the last frail spark forever.

"Let me hear another sound from *you*," said Scrooge, "and you'll keep your Christmas by losing your situation! You're quite a powerful speaker, sir," he added, turning to his nephew. "I wonder you don't go into parliament."

"Don't be angry, uncle. Come! Dine with us tomorrow."

Scrooge said that he would see him — —. Yes, indeed he did. He went the whole length of the expression, and said that he would see him in that extremity first.

"But why?" cried Scrooge's nephew. "Why?"

"Why did you get married?" said Scrooge.

"Because I fell in love."

"Because you fell in love!" growled Scrooge, as if that were the only one thing in the world more ridiculous than a merry Christmas. "Good afternoon!"

"Nay, uncle, but you never came to see me before that happened. Why give it as a reason for not coming now?"

"Good afternoon," said Scrooge.

"I want nothing from you; I ask nothing of you; why cannot we be friends?"

"Good afternoon!" said Scrooge.

"I am sorry, with all my heart, to find you so resolute. We have never had any quarrel to which I have been a party. But I have made the trial in homage to Christmas, and I'll keep my Christmas humor to the last. So a merry Christmas, uncle!"

---

9. **comforter:** long scarf.

10. **veneration** (ven′ə·rā′shən): great respect.

11. **impropriety** (im′prə·prī′ə·tē): improper action or behavior.

"Good afternoon," said Scrooge.

"And a happy New Year!"

"Good afternoon!" said Scrooge.

His nephew left the room without an angry word, notwithstanding. He stopped at the outer door to bestow the greetings of the season on the clerk, who, cold as he was, was warmer than Scrooge; for he returned them cordially.

"There's another fellow," muttered Scrooge, who overheard him: "My clerk, with fifteen shillings a week, and a wife and family, talking about a merry Christmas. I'll retire to Bedlam."[12]

This lunatic, in letting Scrooge's nephew out, had let two other people in. They were portly gentlemen, pleasant to behold, and now stood, with their hats off, in Scrooge's office. They had books and papers in their hands, and bowed to him.

"Scrooge and Marley's, I believe," said one of the gentlemen, referring to his list. "Have I the pleasure of addressing Mr. Scrooge, or Mr. Marley?"

"Mr. Marley has been dead these seven years," Scrooge replied. "He died seven years ago, this very night."

"We have no doubt his liberality[13] is well represented by his surviving partner," said the gentleman, presenting his credentials.

It certainly was; for they had been two kindred spirits. At the ominous word *liberality* Scrooge frowned, and shook his head, and handed the credentials back.

"At this festive season of the year, Mr. Scrooge," said the gentleman, taking up a pen, "it is more than usually desirable that we should make some slight provision for the poor and destitute, who suffer greatly at the present time. Many thousands are in want of common necessaries; hundreds of thousands are in want of common comforts, sir."

"Are there no prisons?"[14] asked Scrooge.

"Plenty of prisons," said a gentleman, laying down the pen again.

"And the Union workhouses?" demanded Scrooge. "Are they still in operation?"

"They are. Still," returned the gentleman, "I wish I could say they were not."

"The Treadmill[15] and the Poor Law are in full vigor, then?" said Scrooge.

"Both very busy, sir."

"Oh! I was afraid, from what you said at first, that something had occurred to stop them in their useful course," said Scrooge. "I am very glad to hear it."

"Under the impression that they scarcely furnish Christian cheer of mind or body to the multitude," returned the gentleman, "a few of us are endeavoring to raise a fund to buy the poor some meat and drink, and means of warmth. We choose this time, because it is a time, of all others, when want is keenly felt, and abundance rejoices. What shall I put you down for?"

"Nothing!" Scrooge replied.

"You wish to be anonymous?"

"I wish to be left alone," said Scrooge. "Since you ask me what I wish, gentlemen, that is my answer. I don't make merry myself at Christmas, and I can't afford to make idle people merry. I help to support the establishments I have mentioned—they cost enough; and those who are badly off must go there."

"Many can't go there; and many would rather die."

"If they would rather die," said Scrooge, "they had better do it, and decrease the surplus population. Besides—excuse me—I don't know that."

"But you might know it," observed the gentleman.

"It's not my business," Scrooge returned. "It's enough for a man to understand his own business, and not to interfere with other people's. Mine occupies me constantly. Good afternoon, gentlemen!"

Seeing clearly that it would be useless to pursue their point, the gentlemen withdrew. Scrooge resumed his labors with an improved opinion of himself, and in a more facetious temper than was usual with him.

Meanwhile the fog and darkness thickened so, that people ran about with flaring links, proffering their services to go before horses in carriages, and conduct them on their way. The ancient tower of a church, whose gruff old bell was always peeping slyly down at Scrooge out of a Gothic window in the wall, became invisible, and struck the hours and quarters in the clouds, with tremulous vibrations afterward, as if its teeth were chattering in its frozen head up there. The cold became intense. In the main street, at the corner of the court, some laborers were repairing the gas pipes, and had lighted a great fire in a brazier, round which a party of ragged men and boys were gathered: warming their hands and winking their eyes before the blaze in rapture. The water-plug being left in solitude, its overflowings suddenly congealed and

---

12. **Bedlam:** insane asylum formerly in London.
13. **liberality** (lib′ə·ral′ə·tē): generosity.
14. **prisons:** in Dickens's time, the poor were sent to prison if they could not pay their debts.
15. **Treadmill:** mill wheel turned by the weight of persons treading steps arranged around its circumference; formerly used to discipline prison inmates.

turned to misanthropic ice. The brightness of the shops, where holly sprigs and berries crackled in the lamp heat of the windows, made pale faces ruddy as they passed. Poulterer's and grocers' trades became a splendid joke: a glorious pageant, with which it was next to impossible to believe that such dull principles as bargain and sale had anything to do. The Lord Mayor, in the stronghold of the mighty Mansion House, gave orders to his fifty cooks and butlers to keep Christmas as a Lord Mayor's household should; and even the little tailor, whom he had fined five shillings on the previous Monday for being drunk and blood-thirsty in the streets, stirred up tomorrow's pudding in his garret, while his lean wife and the baby sallied out to buy the beef.

Foggier yet, and colder! Piercing, searching, biting cold. If the good St. Dunstan had but nipped the Evil Spirit's nose with a touch of such weather as that, instead of using his familiar weapons,[16] then indeed he would have roared to lusty purpose. The owner of one scant young nose, gnawed and mumbled by the hungry cold as bones are gnawed by dogs, stopped down at Scrooge's keyhole to regale him with a Christmas carol; but, at the first sound of

God bless you, merry gentleman
May nothing you dismay!

Scrooge seized the ruler with such energy of action that the singer fled in terror, leaving the keyhole to the fog, and even more congenial frost.

At length the hour of shutting up the counting-house arrived. With an ill will Scrooge dismounted from his stool, and tacitly admitted the fact to the expectant clerk in the tank, who instantly snuffed his candle out, and put on his hat.

"You'll want all day tomorrow, I suppose?" said Scrooge.

"If quite convenient, sir."

"It's not convenient," said Scrooge, "and it's not fair. If I was to stop half-a-crown[17] for it, you'd think yourself ill used, I'll be bound?"

The clerk smiled faintly.

"And yet," said Scrooge, "you don't think *me* ill used when I pay a day's wages for no work."

The clerk observed that it was only once a year.

"A poor excuse for picking a man's pocket every twenty-fifth of December!" said Scrooge, buttoning his greatcoat to the chin. "But I suppose you must have the whole day. Be here all the earlier next morning."

The clerk promised that he would; and Scrooge walked out with a growl. The office was closed in a twinkling, and the clerk, with the long ends of his white comforter dangling below his waist (for he boasted no greatcoat), went down a slide on Cornhill, at the end of a lane of boys, twenty times, in honor of its being Christmas Eve, and then ran home to Camden Town as hard as he could pelt, to play at blindman's buff.

Scrooge took his melancholy dinner in his usual melancholy tavern; and having read all the newspapers, and beguiled the rest of the evening with his banker's book, went home to bed. He lived in chambers which had once belonged to his deceased partner. They were a gloomy suite of rooms, in a lowering pile of building up a yard, where it had so little business to be that one could scarcely help fancying it must have run there when it was a young house, playing at hide-and-seek with other houses, and have forgotten the way out again. It was old enough now, and dreary enough; for nobody lived in it but Scrooge, the other rooms being all let out as offices. The yard was so dark that even Scrooge, who knew its every stone, was fain to grope with his hands. The fog and frost so hung about the black old gateway of the house, that it seemed as if the Genius[18] of the Weather sat in mournful meditation on the threshold.

Now, it is a fact that there was nothing at all particular about the knocker on the door, except that it was very large. It is also a fact that Scrooge had seen it, night and morning, during his whole residence in that place; also that Scrooge had as little of what is called fancy about him as any man in the City of London, even including—which is a bold word—the corporation, aldermen, and livery. Let it also be borne in mind that Scrooge had not bestowed one thought on Marley since his last mention of his seven-year's-dead partner that afternoon. And then let any man explain to me, if he can, how it happened that Scrooge, having his key in the lock of the door, saw in the knocker,

---

16. St. Dunstan (924–988) was an English monk and political adviser. In a famous legend, the devil tried to tempt him to lead a life of idle pleasure. Dunstan seized the devil by the nose with red-hot pincers, and the bellowings of pain could be heard for miles.

17. A crown was an English coin equal to five shillings, or one fourth of a pound.

18. **Genius:** guardian spirit.

without its undergoing any intermediate process of change—not a knocker, but Marley's face.

Marley's face. It was not in impenetrable shadow, as the other objects in the yard were, but had a dismal light about it, like a bad lobster in a dark cellar. It was not angry or ferocious, but looked at Scrooge as Marley used to look; with ghostly spectacles turned up on its ghostly forehead. The hair was curiously stirred, as if by breath or hot air; and, though the eyes were wide open, they were perfectly motionless. That, and its livid[19] color, made it horrible; but its horror seemed to be in spite of the face, and beyond its control, rather than a part of its own expression.

As Scrooge looked fixedly at this phenomenon, it was a knocker again.

To say that he was not startled, or that his blood was not conscious of a terrible sensation to which it had been a stranger from infancy, would be untrue. But he put his hand upon the key he had relinquished, turned it sturdily, walked in, and lighted his candle.

He *did* pause, with a moment's irresolution, before he shut the door; and he *did* look cautiously behind it first, as if he half expected to be terrified with the sight of Marley's pigtail sticking out into the hall. But there was nothing on the back of the door, except the screws and nuts that held the knocker on, so he said, "Pooh, pooh!" and closed it with a bang.

The sound resounded through the house like thunder. Every room above, and every cask in the wine-merchant's cellars below, appeared to have a separate peal of echoes of its own. Scrooge was not a man to be frightened by echoes. He fastened the door, and walked across the hall, and up the stairs—slowly, too—trimming his candle as he went. . . .

Darkness is cheap, and Scrooge liked it. But, before he shut his heavy door, he walked through his rooms to see that all was right. He had just enough recollection of the face to desire to do that.

Sitting room, bedroom, lumber room.[20] All as they should be. Nobody under the table, nobody under the sofa; a small fire in the grate; spoon and basin ready; and the little saucepan of gruel[21] (Scrooge had a cold in his head) upon the hob.[22] Nobody under the bed; nobody in the closet; nobody in his dressing gown, which was hanging up

in a suspicious attitude against the wall. Lumber room as usual. Old fireguard, old shoes, two fish baskets, washing stand on three legs, and a poker.

Quite satisfied, he closed his door, and locked himself in; double locked himself in, which was not his custom. Thus secured against surprise, he took off his cravat; put on his dressing gown and slippers, and his nightcap; and sat down before the fire to take his gruel.

It was a very low fire indeed; nothing on such a bitter night. He was obliged to sit close to it, and brood over it, before he could extract the least sensation of warmth from such a handful of fuel. The fireplace was an old one, built by some Dutch merchant long ago, and paved all round with quaint Dutch tiles, designed to illustrate the Scriptures. There were Cains and Abels, Pharaoh's daughters, Queens of Sheba, Angelic messengers descending through the air on clouds like featherbeds, Abrahams, Belshazzars, Apostles putting off to sea in butterboats, hundreds of figures to attract his thoughts; and yet that face of Marley, seven years dead, came like the ancient Prophet's rod, and swallowed up the whole.[23] If each smooth tile had been a blank at first, with power to shape some picture on its surface from the disjointed fragments of his thoughts, there would have been a copy of old Marley's head on every one.

"Humbug!" said Scrooge, and walked across the room.

After several turns he sat down again. As he threw his head back in the chair, his glance happened to rest upon a bell, a disused bell, that hung in the room, and communicated, for some purpose now forgotten, with a chamber in the highest story of the building. It was with great astonishment, and with a strange, inexplicable dread, that, as he looked, he saw this bell begin to swing. It swung so softly in the outset that it scarcely made a sound; but soon it rang out loudly, and so did every bell in the house.

This might have lasted half a minute, or a minute, but it seemed an hour. The bells ceased, as they had begun, together. They were succeeded by a clanking noise deep down below as if some person were dragging a heavy chain over the casks in the wine-merchant's cellar. Scrooge then remembered to have heard that ghosts in haunted houses were described as dragging chains.

The cellar door flew open with a booming

---

19. **livid:** pale.
20. **lumber room:** storage room.
21. **gruel:** thin oatmeal, or other boiled cereal.
22. **hob:** ledge at the back of a fireplace.

23. **ancient Prophet's rod . . . whole:** In Exodus 7:1–13, the prophet Aaron's staff turned into a snake and swallowed the snakes made from the magician's rods.

EVERETT SHINN 1938

sound, and then he heard the noise much louder on the floors below; then coming up the stairs; then coming straight toward his door.

"It's humbug still!" said Scrooge. "I won't believe it."

His color changed, though, when, without a pause, it came on through the heavy door and passed into the room before his eyes. Upon its coming in, the dying flame leaped up, as though it cried, "I know him! Marley's Ghost!" and fell again.

The same face: the very same. Marley in his pigtail, usual waistcoat, tights, and boots; the tassels on the latter bristling, like his pigtail, and his coatskirts, and the hair upon his head. The chain he drew was clasped about his middle. It was long, and wound about him like a tail; and it was made (for Scrooge observed it closely) of cashboxes, keys, padlocks, ledgers, deeds, and heavy purses wrought in steel. His body was transparent: so that Scrooge, observing him, and looking through his waistcoat, could see the two buttons on his coat behind.

Scrooge had often heard it said that Marley had no bowels,[24] but he had never believed it until now.

No, nor did he believe it even now. Though he looked the phantom through and through, and saw it standing before him; though he felt the chilling influence of its death-cold eyes, and marked the very texture of the folded kerchief bound about its head and chin, which wrapper he had not observed before, he was still incredulous, and fought against his senses."

"How now!" said Scrooge, caustic and cold as ever. "What do you want with me?"

"Much!"—Marley's voice; no doubt about it.

"Who are you?"

"Ask me who I *was*."

"Who *were* you, then?" said Scrooge, raising his voice. "You're particular for a shade."[25] He was going to say "*to* a shade," but substituted this, as more appropriate.

"In life I was your partner, Jacob Marley."

"Can you—can you sit down?" asked Scrooge, looking doubtfully at him.

"I can."

"Do it, then."

Scrooge asked the question, because he didn't know whether a ghost so transparent might find himself in a condition to take a chair; and felt that in the event of its being impossible, it might in-

volve the necessity of an embarrassing explanation. But the Ghost sat down on the opposite side of the fireplace, as if he were quite used to it.

"You don't believe in me," observed the Ghost.

"I don't," said Scrooge.

"What evidence would you have of my reality beyond that of your own senses?"

"I don't know," said Scrooge.

"Why do you doubt your senses?"

"Because," said Scrooge, "a little thing affects them. A slight disorder of the stomach makes them cheats. You may be an undigested bit of beef, a blot of mustard, a crumb of cheese, a fragment of an underdone potato. There's more of gravy than of grave about you, whatever you are!"

Scrooge was not much in the habit of cracking jokes, nor did he feel in his heart by any means waggish then. The truth is, that he tried to be smart, as a means of distracting his own attention, and keeping down his terror; for the specter's voice disturbed the very marrow in his bones.

To sit staring at those fixed, glazed eyes in silence, for a moment, would play, Scrooge felt, the very deuce with him. There was something very awful, too, in the specter's being provided with an infernal atmosphere of his own. Scrooge could not feel it himself, but this was clearly the case; for though the Ghost sat perfectly motionless, its hair, and skirts, and tassels were still agitated as by the hot vapor from an oven.

"You see this toothpick?" said Scrooge, returning quickly to the charge, for the reason just assigned; and wishing, though it were only for a second, to divert the vision's stony gaze from himself.

"I do," replied the Ghost.

"You are not looking at it," said Scrooge.

"But I see it," said the Ghost, "notwithstanding."

"Well!" returned Scrooge. "I have but to swallow this, and be for the rest of my days persecuted by a legion of goblins, all of my own creation. Humbug, I tell you: Humbug!"

At this the spirit raised a frightful cry, and shook its chain with such a dismal and appalling noise, that Scrooge held on tight to his chair, to save himself from falling in a swoon. But how much greater was his horror when the phantom took off the bandage round his head, as if it were too warm to wear indoors, and its lower jaw dropped down upon its breast!

Scrooge fell upon his knees, and clasped his hands before his face.

"Mercy!" he said. "Dreadful apparition, why do you trouble me?"

---

24. **bowels:** mercy or pity. Bowels, or intestines, were thought to be the center of compassion.
25. **shade:** ghost.

"Man of the worldly mind!" replied the Ghost, "do you believe in me or not?"

"I do," said Scrooge; "I must. But why do spirits walk the earth, and why do they come to me?"

"It is required of every man," the Ghost returned, "that the spirit within him should walk abroad among his fellow men, and travel far and wide; and, if that spirit goes not forth in life, it is condemned to do so after death. It is doomed to wander through the world—oh, woe is me!—and witness what it cannot share, but might have shared on earth, and turned to happiness!"

Again the specter raised a cry, and shook its chain and wrung its shadowy hands.

"You are fettered," said Scrooge, trembling. "Tell me why?"

"I wear the chain I forged in life," replied the Ghost. "I made it link by link, and yard by yard; I girded it on of my own free will, and of my own free will I wore it. Is its pattern strange to *you?*"

Scrooge trembled more and more.

"Or would you know," pursued the Ghost, "the weight and length of the strong coil you bear yourself? It was full as heavy and as long as this seven Christmas Eves ago. You have labored on it since. It is a ponderous[26] chain!"

Scrooge glanced about him on the floor, in the expectation of finding himself surrounded by some fifty or sixty fathoms[27] of iron cable; but he could see nothing.

"Jacob!" he said imploringly. "Old Jacob Marley, tell me more! Speak comfort to me, Jacob!"

"I have none to give," the Ghost replied. "It comes from other regions, Ebenezer Scrooge, and is conveyed by other ministers, to other kinds of men. Nor can I tell you what I would. A very little more is all permitted to me. I cannot rest, I cannot stay, I cannot linger anywhere. My spirit never walked beyond our countinghouse—mark me—in life my spirit never roved beyond the narrow limits of our money-changing hole; and weary journeys lie before me!"

It was a habit with Scrooge, whenever he became thoughtful, to put his hands in his breeches pockets. Pondering on what the Ghost had said, he did so now, but without lifting up his eyes, or getting off his knees.

"You must have been very slow about it, Jacob," Scrooge observed in a businesslike manner, though with humility and deference.

"Slow!" the Ghost repeated.

"Seven years dead," mused Scrooge. "And traveling all the time?"

"The whole time," said the Ghost. "No rest, no peace. Incessant torture of remorse."

"You travel fast?" said Scrooge.

"On the wings of the wind," replied the Ghost.

"You might have got over a great quantity of ground in seven years," said Scrooge.

The Ghost, on hearing this, set up another cry, and clanked its chain so hideously in the dead silence of the night, that the ward[28] would have been justified in indicting it for a nuisance.

"Oh! captive, bound, and double-ironed," cried the phantom, "not to know that ages of incessant labor, by immortal creatures, for this earth must pass into eternity before the good of which it is susceptible is all developed! Not to know that any Christian spirit working kindly in its little sphere, whatever it may be, will find its mortal life too short for its vast means of usefulness! Not to know that no space of regret can make amends for one life's opportunities misused! Yet such was I! Oh, such was I!"

"But you were always a good man of business, Jacob," faltered Scrooge, who now began to apply this to himself.

"Business!" cried the Ghost, wringing his hands again. "Mankind was my business. The common welfare was my business; charity, mercy, forbearance, and benevolence were, all, my business. The dealings of my trade were but a drop of water in the comprehensive ocean of my business!"

It held up its chain at arm's length, as if that were the cause of all its unavailing grief, and flung it heavily upon the ground again.

"At this time of the rolling year," the specter said. "I suffer most. Why did I walk through crowds of fellow beings with my eyes turned down, and never raise them to that blessed Star which led the Wise Men to a poor abode? Were there no poor homes to which its light would have conducted *me?*"

Scrooge was very much dismayed to hear the specter going on at this rate, and began to quake exceedingly.

"Hear me!" cried the Ghost. "My time is nearly gone."

"I will," said Scrooge. "But don't be hard upon me! Don't be flowery, Jacob! Pray!"

---

26. **ponderous** (pän′dər·əs): here, very heavy.
27. **fathoms** (fath′əmz): units of measurement; one fathom is six feet long.

28. **ward:** watchman in one of the twenty-six wards, or divisions, of London.

"How it is that I appear before you in a shape that you can see, I may not tell. I have sat invisible beside you many and many a day."

It was not an agreeable idea. Scrooge shivered, and wiped the perspiration from his brow.

"That is no light part of my penance,"[29] pursued the Ghost. "I am here tonight to warn you that you have yet a chance and hope of escaping my fate. A chance and hope of my procuring,[30] Ebenezer."

"You were always a good friend to me," said Scrooge. "Thankee!"

"You will be haunted," resumed the Ghost, "by Three Spirits."

Scrooge's countenance fell almost as low as the Ghost's had done.

"Is that the change and hope you mentioned, Jacob?" he demanded in a faltering voice.

"It is."

"I—I think I'd rather not," said Scrooge.

"Without their visits," said the Ghost, "you cannot hope to shun the path I tread. Expect the first tomorrow when the bell tolls one."

"Couldn't I take 'em all at once, and have it over, Jacob?" hinted Scrooge.

"Expect the second on the next night at the same hour. The third, upon the next night when the last stroke of twelve has ceased to vibrate. Look to see me no more; and look that, for your own sake, you remember what has passed between us!"

When it had said these words, the specter took its wrapper from the table, and bound it round its head as before. Scrooge knew this by the smart sound its teeth made when the jaws were brought together by the bandage. He ventured to raise his eyes again, and found his supernatural visitor confronting him in an erect attitude, with its chain wound over and about its arm.

The apparition walked backward from him; and, at every step it took, the window raised itself a little, so that, when the specter reached it, it was wide open. It beckoned Scrooge to approach, which he did. When they were within two paces of each other, Marley's Ghost held up its hand, warning him to come no nearer. Scrooge stopped.

Not so much in obedience as in surprise and fear; for, on the raising of the hand, he became sensible of confused noises in the air; incoherent sounds of lamentation and regret; wailings inexpressibly sorrowful and self-accusatory. The spec-

---

29. **penance:** self-punishment for wrongdoing.
30. **of my procuring:** in other words, that I got for you.

ter, after listening for a moment, joined in the mournful dirge; and floated out upon the bleak, dark night.

Scrooge followed to the window, desperate in his curiosity. He looked out.

The air was filled with phantoms, wandering hither and thither in restless haste, and moaning as they went. Every one of them wore chains like Marley's Ghost; some few (they might be guilty governments) were linked together; none were free. Many had been personally known to Scrooge in their lives. He had been quite familiar with one old ghost in a white waistcoat, with a monstrous iron safe attached to its ankle, who cried piteously at being unable to assist a wretched woman with an infant, whom it saw below upon a doorstep. The misery with them all was clearly, that they sought to interfere, for good, in human matters, and had lost the power forever.

Whether these creatures faded into mist, or mist enshrouded them, he could not tell. But they and their spirit voices faded together; and the night became as it had been when he walked home.

Scrooge closed the window, and examined the door by which the Ghost had entered. It was double locked, as he had locked it with his own hands, and the bolts were undisturbed. He tried to say "Humbug!" but stopped at the first syllable. And being, from the emotions he had undergone, or the fatigues of the day, or his glimpse of the Invisible World, or the dull[31] conversation of the Ghost, or the lateness of the hour, much in need of repose, went straight to bed without undressing, and fell asleep upon the instant.

---

31. **dull:** here, gloomy.

Responding to the Novel

Analyzing Stave One

Identifying Facts

1. Explain how Scrooge originally knew Marley. According to the narrator, what about Marley "must be distinctly understood"?
2. Describe the difficult working conditions that Scrooge's clerk must endure.
3. Tell how Scrooge responds to each of the following: (a) his nephew's invitation, (b) the gentlemen's request for money for the poor, and (c) the boy who sings a carol through the keyhole.
4. When Scrooge reaches his house, what does he see in the door knocker? How does Scrooge react to what he sees?
5. Describe Jacob Marley's Ghost. Then explain why the Ghost must "travel far and wide," and how he got his chain.
6. According to Marley's Ghost, why is he visiting Scrooge? Whom does he tell Scrooge to expect next?

Interpreting Meanings

7. A novel usually begins by introducing the main character and showing you the conflicts he or she faces. A **conflict** is a struggle between a character and other people or nature **(external)** or between forces within a character's own mind **(internal)**. Who is the main character of *A Christmas Carol*? Identify and describe the conflicts between this character and other people. Do you expect that this character will encounter any **internal conflicts**?
8. Dickens's novels often show concern for the living conditions of the poor. In the conversation between Scrooge and the two gentlemen (page 623), there are references to the Treadmill and the Poor Law, prisons, and Union workhouses. These are all public means for helping the poor. What does this conversation tell you about the condition of the poor in Dickens's day?

9. A novelist can use any of five methods to reveal the personality of a character. The novelist can (1) give a physical description of the character; (2) comment directly about the character; (3) show the character's actions and let the character speak; (4) reveal the character's thoughts; and (5) tell what others think or say about the character. Dickens uses all five methods in *A Christmas Carol*.

   a. List five details from Stave One describing Scrooge's physical appearance.
   b. List five adjectives that Dickens uses to comment directly on Scrooge's personality.
   c. What does Scrooge's responses to his nephew, to the two gentlemen, and to the caroler reveal about his personality?
   d. Scrooge initially refuses to think that Marley's Ghost is real. What does he think the Ghost is instead? What does this manner of thinking reveal about Scrooge's personality?
   e. Marley's Ghost says to Scrooge that without the visits by the Three Spirits, "you cannot hope to shun the path I tread." What do Marley's words reveal about Scrooge?

10. On page 628, Scrooge says to Marley's Ghost, "But you were always a good man of business, Jacob." The Ghost replies, "Mankind was my business. . . . The dealings of my trade were but a drop of water in the comprehensive ocean of my business." Scrooge and Marley's Ghost understand the word *business* differently. Explain how each defines *business*. Then identify and discuss the main differences in the two definitions.

Applying Meanings

11. The narrator emphasizes that Scrooge likes facts, not fanciful notions. Suppose somebody told you he or she had done something very unusual. Would you be more likely to believe it if the person were like Scrooge, or if the person were known for a vivid imagination? Why?

Writing About Stave One

A Creative Response

1. **Writing a Diary Entry.** Imagine that Scrooge had sat down to write in his diary instead of going straight to bed at the end of Stave One. Based on what you know about Scrooge's personality so far, what do you suppose he might have written? Write Scrooge's diary entry. In one or two paragraphs, express his thoughts and feelings about his encounter with Marley's Ghost and about the Ghost's prediction regarding the Three Spirits.

A Critical Response

2. **Analyzing Tone.** Study the scene on pages 622–623 in which Scrooge and his nephew discuss Christmas. Then write two paragraphs in which you explain Dickens's **tone**—the attitude he has toward the subject (of Christmas). In your first paragraph, compare Scrooge's attitude toward Christmas to his nephew's attitude. In your second paragraph, explain which of these two attitudes you think represents the author's opinion. Be sure to give the reasons why you think the attitude you picked is Dickens's.

Analyzing Language and Vocabulary

A Changing Language

As times change, the words people use to describe their world change too. In *A Christmas Carol*, you will encounter unfamiliar words that were common 150 or so years ago. Such words are said to be **obsolete**, if no longer used at all, or **archaic** (är·kā′ik), if still used occasionally. Obsolete and archaic words survive mainly in literature. Recognizing these words and their meanings in a novel like *A Christmas Carol* will help you appreciate the special character of the bygone era that is an important part of the setting.

1. Find a word in Stave One that names each of the following:

   a. hardware made of iron
   b. butcher shop specializing in poultry
   c. kind of heavy overcoat
   d. hand-dipped candle
   e. type of man's vest

2. Imagine that you are preparing a film version of *A Christmas Carol*. Find five other obsolete or archaic words in Stave One that would help you in designing the sets and costumes.

Stave Two:
The First of the Three Spirits

When Scrooge awoke it was so dark, that, looking out of bed, he could scarcely distinguish the transparent window from the opaque walls of his chamber. He was endeavoring to pierce the darkness with his ferret eyes, when the chimes of a neighboring church struck the four quarters. So he listened for the hour.

To his great astonishment, the heavy bell went on from six to seven, and from seven to eight, and regularly up to twelve; then stopped. Twelve! It was past two when he went to bed. The clock was wrong. An icicle must have got into the works. Twelve!

He touched the spring of his repeater,[1] to correct this most preposterous clock. Its rapid little pulse beat twelve, and stopped.

"Why, it isn't possible," said Scrooge, "that I can have slept through a whole day and far into another night. It isn't possible that anything has happened to the sun, and this is twelve at noon!"

The idea being an alarming one, he scrambled out of bed, and groped his way to the window. He was obliged to rub the frost off with the sleeve of his dressing gown before he could see anything; and could see very little then. All he could make out was, that it was still very foggy and extremely cold, and that there was no noise of people running to and fro, and making a great stir, as there unquestionably would have been if night had beaten off bright day, and taken possession of the world. This was a great relief, because "Three days after sight of this First of Exchange pay to Mr. Ebenezer Scrooge or his order," and so forth, would have become a mere United States security if there were no days to count by.

Scrooge went to bed again, and thought, and thought, and thought it over and over, and could make nothing of it. The more he thought, the more perplexed he was, and, the more he endeavored not to think, the more he thought.

Marley's Ghost bothered him exceedingly. Every time he resolved within himself, after mature inquiry, that it was all a dream, his mind flew back again, like a strong spring released, to its first position, and presented the same problem to be worked all through, "Was it a dream or not?"

Scrooge lay in this state until the chime had gone three-quarters more, when he remembered, on a sudden, that the Ghost had warned him of a visitation when the bell tolled one. He resolved to lie awake until the hour was passed; and, considering that he could no more go to sleep than go to heaven, this was, perhaps, the wisest resolution in his power.

The quarter was so long, that he was more than once convinced he must have sunk into a doze unconsciously, and missed the clock. At length it broke upon his listening ear.

"Ding, dong!"

"A quarter past," said Scrooge, counting.

"Ding, dong!"

"Half past," said Scrooge.

"Ding, dong!"

"A quarter to it," said Scrooge.

"Ding, dong!"

"The hour itself," said Scrooge triumphantly, "and nothing else!"

He spoke before the hour bell sounded, which it now did with a deep, dull, hollow, melancholy ONE. Light flashed up in the room upon the instant, and the curtains of his bed were drawn.

The curtains of his bed were drawn aside, I tell you, by a hand. Not the curtains at his feet, nor the curtains at his back, but those to which his face was addressed. The curtains of his bed were drawn aside; and Scrooge, starting up into a half-recumbent attitude, found himself face to face with the unearthly visitor who drew them: as close to it as I am now to you, and I am standing in the spirit at your elbow.

It was a strange figure—like a child; yet not so like a child as like an old man, viewed through some supernatural medium, which gave him the appearance of having receded from the view, and being diminished to a child's proportions. Its hair, which hung about its neck and down its back, was white, as if with age, and yet the face had not a wrinkle in it, and the tenderest bloom was on the skin. The arms were very long and muscular; the hands the same, as if its hold were of uncommon strength. Its legs and feet, most delicately formed, were, like those upper members, bare. It wore a tunic of the purest white; and round its waist was bound a lustrous belt, the sheen of which was beautiful. It held a branch of fresh green holly in its hand; and, in singular contradiction of that wintry emblem, had its dress trimmed with summer flowers. But the strangest thing about it was, that from the crown of its head there sprang a bright clear jet of light, by which all this was visible; and which was doubtless the occasion of its using, in its duller moments, a great extinguisher for a cap, which it now held under its arm.

---

1. **repeater:** watch or clock that can be made to strike the time.

Even this, though, when Scrooge looked at it with increasing steadiness, was *not* its strangest quality. For, as its belt sparkled and glittered, now in one part and now in another, and what was light one instant at another time was dark, so the figure itself fluctuated in its distinctness; being now a thing with one arm now with one leg, now with twenty legs, now a pair of legs without a head, now a head without a body, of which dissolving parts no outline would be visible in the dense gloom wherein they melted away. And, in the very wonder of this, it would be itself again; distinct and clear as ever.

"Are you the Spirit, sir, whose coming was foretold to me?" asked Scrooge.

"I am!"

The voice was soft and gentle. Singularly low, as if, instead of being so close behind him, it were at a distance.

"Who and what are you?" Scrooge demanded.

"I am the Ghost of Christmas Past."

"Long past?" inquired Scrooge, observant of its dwarfish stature.

"No. Your past."

Perhaps Scrooge could not have told anybody why, if anybody could have asked him; but he had a special desire to see the Spirit in his cap, and begged him to be covered.

"What!" exclaimed the Ghost. "Would you so soon put out, with worldly hands, the light I give? Is it not enough that you are one of those whose passions made this cap, and force me through whole trains of years to wear it low upon my brow?"

Scrooge reverently disclaimed all intention to offend or any knowledge of having willfully "bonneted" the Spirit at any period of his life. He then made bold to inquire what business brought him there.

"Your welfare!" said the Ghost.

Scrooge expressed himself much obliged, but could not help thinking that a night of unbroken rest would have been more conducive to that end. The Spirit must have heard him thinking, for it said immediately—

"Your reclamation,[2] then. Take heed!"

It put out its strong hand as it spoke, and clasped him gently by the arm.

"Rise! And walk with me!"

It would have been in vain for Scrooge to plead that the weather and the hour were not adapted to pedestrian purposes; that bed was warm, and the thermometer a long way below freezing; that

he was clad but lightly in his slippers, dressing gown, and nightcap; and that he had a cold upon him at that time. The grasp, though gentle as a woman's hand, was not to be resisted. He rose; but, finding that the Spirit made toward the window, clasped its robe in supplication.

"I am a mortal," Scrooge remonstrated, "and liable to fall."

"Bear but a touch of my hand *there*," said the Spirit, laying it upon his heart, "and you shall be upheld in more than this!"

As the words were spoken, they passed through the wall, and stood upon an open country road, with fields on either hand. The city had entirely vanished. Not a vestige of it was to be seen. The darkness and the mist had vanished with it, for it was a clear, cold, winter day, with snow upon the ground.

"Good Heaven!" said Scrooge, clasping his hands together, as he looked about him. "I was bred in this place. I was a boy here!"

The Spirit gazed upon him mildly. Its gentle touch, though it had been light and instantaneous, appeared still present to the old man's sense of feeling. He was conscious of a thousand odors floating in the air, each one connected with a thousand thoughts, and hopes, and joys, and cares long, long forgotten!

"Your lip is trembling," said the Ghost. "And what is that upon your cheek?"

Scrooge muttered, with an unusual catching in his voice, that it was a pimple; and begged the Ghost to lead him where he would.

"You recollect the way?" inquired the Spirit.

"Remember it!" cried Scrooge with fervor. "I could walk it blindfolded."

"Strange to have forgotten it for so many years!" observed the Ghost. "Let us go on."

They walked along the road, Scrooge recognizing every gate, and post, and tree, until a little market town appeared in the distance, with its bridge, its church, and winding river. Some shaggy ponies now were seen trotting toward them with boys upon their backs, who called to other boys in country gigs and carts, driven by farmers. All these boys were in great spirits, and shouted to each other, until the broad fields were so full of merry music, that the crisp air laughed to hear it.

"These are but shadows of the things that have been," said the Ghost. "They have no consciousness of us."

The jocund[3] travelers came on; and as they came, Scrooge knew and named them every one.

---

2. **reclamation** (rek′lə·mā′shən): rescuing or recovering a person from error or vice.

3. **jocund** (jäk′ənd): cheerful, happy.

Why was he rejoiced beyond all bounds to see them? Why did his cold eye glisten, and his heart leap up as they went past? Why was he filled with gladness when he heard them give each other Merry Christmas, as they parted at crossroads and byways for their several homes? What was merry Christmas to Scrooge? Out upon merry Christmas! What good had it ever done to him?

"The school is not quite deserted," said the Ghost. "A solitary child, neglected by his friends, is left there still."

Scrooge said he knew it. And he sobbed.

They left the high road by a well-remembered lane and soon approached a mansion of dull red brick, with a little weather-cock surmounted cupola[4] on the roof, and a bell hanging in it. It was a large house, but one of broken fortunes; for the spacious offices were little used, their walls were damp and mossy, their windows broken, and their gates decayed. Fowls clucked and strutted in the stables; and the coachhouses and sheds were overrun with grass. Nor was it more retentive of its ancient state within; for, entering the dreary hall, and glancing through the open doors of many rooms, they found them poorly furnished, cold, and vast. There was an earthy savor in the air, a chilly bareness in the place, which associated itself somehow with too much getting up by candle light and not too much to eat.

They went, the Ghost and Scrooge, across the hall, to a door at the back of the house. It opened before them, and disclosed a long, bare, melancholy room, made barer still by lines of plain deal forms[5] and desks. At one of these a lonely boy

---

4. **cupola** (kyōō′pə·lə): small dome or similar structure on a roof.

5. **deal forms:** long benches made from unpainted pine.

was reading near a feeble fire; and Scrooge sat down upon a form, and wept to see his poor forgotten self as he had used to be.

Not a latent echo in the house, not a squeak and scuffle from the mice behind the paneling, not a drip from the half-thawed waterspout in the dull yard behind, not a sigh among the leafless boughs of one despondent poplar, not the idle swinging of an empty storehouse door, no, not a clicking in the fire, but fell upon the heart of Scrooge with softening influence, and gave a freer passage to his tears.

The Spirit touched him on the arm, and pointed to his younger self, intent upon his reading. Suddenly a man in foreign garments, wonderfully real and distinct to look at, stood outside the window, with an ax stuck in his belt, and leading by the bridle an ass laden with wood.

"Why, it's Ali Baba!"[6] Scrooge exclaimed in ecstasy. "It's dear old honest Ali Baba! Yes, yes, I know. One Christmastime, when yonder solitary child was left here all alone, he *did* come, for the first time, just like that. Poor boy! And Valentine," said Scrooge, "and his wild brother, Orson,[7] there they go! And what's his name, who was put down in his drawers, asleep, at the gate of Damascus; don't you see him? And the Sultan's Groom turned upside down by the Genii; there he is upon his head! Serve him right! I'm glad of it. What business had he to be married to the Princess?"[8]

To hear Scrooge expending all the earnestness of his nature on such subjects, in a most extraordinary voice between laughing and crying; and to see his heightened and excited face would have been a surprise to his business friends in the City, indeed.

"There's the Parrot!"[9] cried Scrooge. "Green body and yellow tail, with a thing like a lettuce growing out of the top of his head; there he is! Poor Robin Crusoe he called him, when he came home again after sailing round the island. 'Poor Robin Crusoe, where have you been, Robin Crusoe?' The man thought he was dreaming, but he wasn't. It was the Parrot, you know. There goes Friday, running for his life to the little creek! Halloa! Hoop! Halloo!"

Then, with a rapidity of transition very foreign to his usual character, he said, in pity for his former self, "Poor boy!" and cried again.

"I wish," Scrooge muttered, putting his hand in his pocket, and looking about him, after drying his eyes with his cuff, "but it's too late now!"

"What is the matter?" asked the Spirit.

"Nothing," said Scrooge. "Nothing. There was a boy singing a Christmas carol at my door last night. I should like to have given him something. That's all."

The Ghost smiled thoughtfully, and waved its hand, saying as it did so, "Let us see another Christmas!"

Scrooge's former self grew larger at the words, and the room became a little darker and more dirty. The panels shrunk, the windows cracked; fragments of plaster fell out of the ceiling, and the naked laths were shown instead; but how all this was brought about Scrooge knew no more than you do. He only knew that it was quite correct; that everything had happened so; that there he was, alone again, when all the other boys had gone home for the jolly holidays.

He was not reading now, but walking up and down despairingly. Scrooge looked at the Ghost, and, with a mournful shaking of his head, glanced anxiously toward the door.

It opened; and a little girl, much younger than the boy, came darting in, and, putting her arms about his neck, and often kissing him, addressed him as her "dear, dear brother."

"I have come to bring you home, dear brother!" said the child, clapping her tiny hands, and bending down to laugh. "To bring you home, home, home!"

"Home, little Fan?" returned the boy.

"Yes!" said the child, brimful of glee. "Home for good and all. Home for ever and ever. Father is so much kinder than he used to be, that home's like heaven! He spoke so gently to me one dear night when I was going to bed, that I was not afraid to ask him once more if you might come home; and he said Yes, you should; and sent me in a coach to bring you. And you're to be a man!" said the child, opening her eyes, "and are never to come back here; but first we're to be together all the Christmas long, and have the merriest time in all the world."

"You are quite a woman, little Fan!" exclaimed the boy.

She clapped her hands and laughed, and tried to touch his head; but, being too little laughed

---

6. **Ali Baba:** character in one of Dickens's favorite books, *The Arabian Nights*, a famous collection of Middle Eastern, Indian, and other tales.
7. **Valentine . . . Orson:** in a popular French story, Valentine and Orson are twin brothers who are parted at birth but eventually reunited.
8. **what's his name . . . Princess:** other characters from *The Arabian Nights*.
9. **Parrot:** in Daniel Defoe's *The Life and Strange Adventures of Robinson Crusoe*, the shipwrecked Robinson (or Robin) Crusoe wakes one morning to find that his parrot has found him and is calling his name. *Friday* was an inhabitant of the island who later became Crusoe's servant.

again, and stood on tiptoe to embrace him. Then she began to drag him, in her childish eagerness, toward the door; and he, nothing loath to go, accompanied her.

A terrible voice in the hall cried, "Bring down Master Scrooge's box, there!" and in the hall appeared the schoolmaster himself, who glared on Master Scrooge with a ferocious condescension,[10] and threw him into a dreadful state of mind by shaking hands with him. He then conveyed him and his sister into the veriest old well of a shivering best parlor that ever was seen, where the maps upon the wall, and the celestial and terrestrial globes in the windows, were waxy with cold. Here he produced a decanter of curiously light wine, and a block of curiously heavy cake, and administered installments of those dainties to the young people; at the same time sending out a meager servant to offer a glass of "something" to the postboy, who answered that he thanked the gentleman, but, if it was the same tap as he had tasted before, he had rather not. Master Scrooge's trunk being by this time tied on to the top of the chaise,[11] the children bade the schoolmaster good-bye right willingly; and, getting into it, drove gaily down the garden sweep; the quick wheels dashing the hoarfrost and snow from off the dark leaves of the evergreens like spray.

"Always a delicate creature, whom a breath might have withered," said the Ghost. "But she had a large heart!"

"So she had," cried Scrooge. "You're right. I will not gainsay[12] it, Spirit. God forbid!"

"She died a woman," said the Ghost, "and had, as I think, children."

"One child," Scrooge returned.

"True," said the Ghost. "Your nephew!"

Scrooge seemed uneasy in his mind, and answered briefly, "Yes."

Although they had but that moment left the school behind them, they were now in the busy thoroughfares of a city, where shadowy passengers passed and repassed; where shadowy carts and coaches battled for the way, and all the strife and tumult of a real city were. It was made plain enough, by the dressing of the shops, that here, too, it was Christmastime again; but it was evening, and the streets were lighted up.

The Ghost stopped at a certain warehouse door, and asked Scrooge if he knew it.

"Know it!" said Scrooge. "Was I apprenticed[13] here?"

They went in. At sight of an old gentleman in a Welsh wig, sitting behind such a high desk, that if he had been two inches taller, he must have knocked his head against the ceiling, Scrooge cried in great excitement—

"Why, it's old Fezziwig! Bless his heart, it's Fezziwig alive again!"

Old Fezziwig laid down his pen, and looked up at the clock, which pointed to the hour of seven. He rubbed his hands; adjusted his capacious waistcoat; laughed all over himself, from his shoes to his organ of benevolence;[14] and called out, in a comfortable, oily, rich, fat, jovial voice—

"Yo ho, there! Ebenezer! Dick!"

Scrooge's former self, now grown a young man, came briskly in, accompanied by his fellow-'prentice.

"Dick Wilkins, to be sure!" said Scrooge to the Ghost. "Bless me, yes. There he is. He was very much attached to me, was Dick. Poor Dick! Dear, dear!"

"Yo ho, my boys!" said Fezziwig. "No more work tonight. Christmas Eve, Dick. Christmas, Ebenezer! Let's have the shutters up," cried old Fezziwig, with a sharp clap of his hands, "before a man can say Jack Robinson!"

You wouldn't believe how those fellows went at it! They charged into the street with the shutters—one, two, three—had 'em up in their places—four, five, six—barred 'em and pinned 'em—seven, eight, nine—and came back before you could have got to twelve, panting like racehorses.

"Hilli-ho!" cried old Fezziwig, skipping down from the high desk with wonderful agility. "Clear away, my lads, and let's have lots of room here! Hilli-ho, Dick! Chirrup, Ebenezer!"

Clear away! There was nothing they wouldn't have cleared away, or couldn't have cleared away, with old Fezziwig looking on. It was done in a minute. Every movable was packed off, as if it were dismissed from public life forevermore; the floor was swept and watered, the lamps were trimmed, fuel was heaped upon the fire; and the warehouse was as snug, and warm, and dry, and bright a ballroom as you would desire to see upon a winter's night.

In came a fiddler with a music book, and went

---

10. **condescension** (kän′də·sen′shən): looking down on someone in a haughty way.
11. **chaise** (shāz): carriage.
12. **gainsay:** deny.

13. **apprenticed** (ə·pren′tis′d); bound as a worker without pay to learn a trade from a master craftsman.
14. **organ of benevolence** (bə·nev′ə·ləns): area above the forehead, believed by some to be the source of kindliness.

up to the lofty desk, and made an orchestra of it, and tuned like fifty stomachaches. In came Mrs. Fezziwig, one vast substantial smile. In came the three Miss Fezziwigs, beaming and lovable. In came the six young followers whose hearts they broke. In came all the young men and women employed in the business. In came the housemaid, with her cousin the baker. In came the cook with her brother's particular friend the milkman. In came the boy from over the way, who was suspected of not having board enough from his master; trying to hide himself behind the girl from next door but one, who was proved to have had her ears pulled by her mistress. In they all came, one after another; some shyly, some boldly, some gracefully, some awkwardly, some pushing, some pulling; in they all came, anyhow and everyhow. Away they all went, twenty couple at once; hands half round and back again the other way; down the middle and up again; round and round in various stages of affectionate grouping; old top couple always turning up in the wrong place; new top couple starting off again as soon as they got there; all top couples at last, and not a bottom one to help them! When this result was brought about, old Fezziwig, clapping his hands to stop the dance, cried out, "Well done!" and the fiddler plunged his hot face into a pot of porter,[15] especially provided for that purpose. But, scorning rest upon his reappearance, he instantly began again, though there were no dancers yet, as if the other fiddler had been carried home, exhausted, on a shutter, and he were a brand-new man resolved to beat him out of sight, or perish.

There were more dances, and there were forfeits,[16] and more dances, and there was cake, and there was negus,[17] and there was a great piece of Cold Roast, and there was a great piece of Cold Boiled, and there were mince pies, and plenty of beer. But the great effect of the evening came after the Roast and Boiled, when the fiddler (an artful dog, mind! The sort of man who knew his business better than you or I could have told it him!) struck up "Sir Roger de Coverley."[18] Then old Fezziwig stood out to dance with Mrs. Fezziwig. Top couple, too; with a good stiff piece of work cut out for them; three or four and twenty pair of partners; people who were not to be trifled with; people who would dance, and had no notion of walking.

But if they had been twice as many—ah! four

15. **porter:** dark-brown beer.
16. **forfeits** (fôr′fits): games in which penalties are payed for making mistakes.
17. **negus** (nē′gəs): hot wine punch with lemon and spices.
18. **"Sir Roger de Coverley":** lively country dance.

times—old Fezziwig would have been a match for them, and so would Mrs. Fezziwig. As to *her,* she was worthy to be his partner in every sense of the term. If that's not high praise, tell me higher, and I'll use it. A positive light appeared to issue from Fezziwig's calves. They shone in every part of the dance like moons. You couldn't have predicted, at any given time, what would become of them next. And when old Fezziwig and Mrs. Fezziwig had gone all through the dance; advance and retire, both hands to your partner, bow and curtsy, corkscrew, thread-the-needle, and back again to your place: Fezziwig "cut"—cut so deftly, that he appeared to wink with his legs, and came upon his feet again without a stagger.

When the clock struck eleven, this domestic ball broke up. Mr. and Mrs. Fezziwig took their stations, one on either side the door, and, shaking hands with every person individually as he or she went out, wished him or her a Merry Christmas. When everybody had retired but the two 'prentices, they did the same to them; and thus the cheerful voices died away, and the lads were left to their beds, which were under a counter in the backshop.

During the whole of this time Scrooge had acted like a man out of his wits. His heart and soul were in the scene, and with his former self. He corroborated everything, remembered everything, enjoyed everything, and underwent the strangest agitation. It was not until now, when the bright faces of his former self and Dick were turned from them, that he remembered the Ghost, and became conscious that it was looking full upon him, while the light upon its head burnt very clear.

"A small matter," said the Ghost, "to make these silly folks so full of gratitude."

"Small!" echoed Scrooge.

The Spirit signed to him to listen to the two apprentices, who were pouring out their hearts in praise of Fezziwig; and when he had done so, said:

"Why! Is it not? He has spent but a few pounds of your mortal money: three or four, perhaps. Is that so much that he deserves this praise?"

"It isn't that," said Scrooge, heated by the remark, and speaking unconsciously like his former, not his latter self. "It isn't that, Spirit. He has the power to render us happy or unhappy; to make our service light or burdensome; a pleasure or a toil. Say that his power lies in words and looks; in things so slight and insignificant that it is impossible to add and count 'em up: What then? The happiness he gives is quite as great as if it cost a fortune."

He felt the Spirit's glance, and stopped.

"What is the matter?" asked the Ghost.

"Nothing particular," said Scrooge.

"Something, I think?" the Ghost insisted.

"No," said Scrooge, "no. I should like to be able to say a word or two to my clerk just now. That's all."

His former self turned down the lamps as he gave utterance to the wish; and Scrooge and the Ghost again stood side by side in the open air.

"My time grows short," observed the Spirit. "Quick!"

This was not addressed to Scrooge, or to anyone whom he could see, but it produced an immediate effect. For again Scrooge saw himself. He was older now; a man in the prime of life. His face had not the harsh and rigid lines of later years; but it had begun to wear the signs of care and avarice.[19] There was an eager, greedy, restless motion in the eye, which showed the passion that had taken root, and where the shadow of the growing tree would fall.

He was not alone, but sat by the side of a fair young girl in a mourning dress, in whose eyes there were tears, which sparkled in the light that shone out of the Ghost of Christmas Past.

"It matters little," she said softly. "To you, very little. Another idol has displaced me; and, if it can cheer and comfort you in time to come as I would have tried to do, I have no just cause to grieve."

"What idol has displaced you?" he rejoined.

"A golden one."

"This is the even-handed dealing of the world!" he said. "There is nothing on which it is so hard as poverty; and there is nothing it professes to condemn with such severity as the pursuit of wealth!"

"You fear the world too much," she answered gently. "All your other hopes have merged into the hope of being beyond the chance of its sordid reproach. I have seen your nobler aspirations fall off one by one, until the master passion, Gain, engrosses you. Have I not?"

"What then?" he retorted. "Even if I have grown so much wiser, what then? I am not changed toward you."

She shook her head.

"Am I?"

"Our contract is an old one. It was made when we were both poor, and content to be so, until, in good season, we could improve our worldly fortune by our patient industry. You *are* changed. When it was made you were another man."

"I was a boy,'" he said impatiently.

"Your own feeling tells you that you were not what you are," she returned. "I am. That which promised happiness when we were one in heart is fraught[20] with misery now that we are two. How often and how keenly I have thought of this I will not say. It is enough that I *have* thought of it, and can release you."

"Have I ever sought release?"

"In words. No. Never."

"In what, then?"

"In a changed nature, in an altered spirit, in another atmosphere of life, another Hope as its great end. In everything that made my love of any worth or value in your sight. If this had never been between us," said the girl, looking mildly, but with steadiness, upon him, "tell me, would you seek me out and try to win me now? Ah, no!"

He seemed to yield to the justice of this supposition in spite of himself. But he said, with a struggle, "You think not."

"I would gladly think otherwise if I could," she answered. "Heaven knows! When *I* have learned a truth like this, I know how strong and irresistible it must be. But if you were free today, tomorrow, yesterday, can even I believe that you would choose a dowerless[21] girl—you who, in your very confidence with her, weigh everything by Gain: Or, choosing her, if for a moment you were false enough to your own guiding principle to do so, do I not know that your repentance and regret would surely follow? I do; and I release you. With a full heart, for the love of him you once were."

He was about to speak; but, with her head turned from him, she resumed:

"You may—the memory of what is past half makes me hope you will—have pain in this. A very, very brief time, and you will dismiss the recollection of it gladly, as an unprofitable dream, from which it happened well that you awoke. May you be happy in the life you have chosen!"

She left him, and they parted.

"Spirit!" said Scrooge, "show me no more! Conduct me home. Why do you delight to torture me?"

"One shadow more!" exclaimed the Ghost.

"No more!" cried Scrooge. "No more! I don't wish to see it. Show me no more!"

But the relentless Ghost pinioned him in both his arms, and forced him to observe what happened next.

They were in another scene and place; a room,

---

19. **avarice** (av'ər·is): greed.

20. **fraught**: filled.

21. **dowerless**: without a dowry, or the property a woman brought to her husband at marriage.

not very large or handsome, but full of comfort. Near to the winter fire sat a beautiful young girl, so like that last that Scrooge believed it was the same, until he saw *her,* now a comely matron, sitting opposite her daughter. The noise in this room was perfectly tumultuous, for there were more children there than Scrooge in his agitated state of mind could count; and, unlike the celebrated herd in the poem, they were not forty children conducting themselves like one, but every child was conducting itself like forty. The consequences were uproarious beyond belief; but no one seemed to care; on the contrary, the mother and daughter laughed heartily, and enjoyed it very much; and the latter, soon beginning to mingle in the sports, got pillaged by the young brigands most ruthlessly. What would I not have given to be one of them! Though I never could have been so rude, no, no! I wouldn't for the wealth of all the world have crushed that braided hair, and torn it down; and for the precious little shoe, I wouldn't have plucked it off, God bless my soul, to save my life. As to measuring her waist in sport, as they did, bold young brood, I couldn't have done it; I should have expected my arm to have grown round it for a punishment, and never come straight again. And yet I should have dearly liked, I own, to have touched her lips; to have questioned her, that she might have opened them; to have looked upon the lashes of her downcast eyes, and never raised a blush; to have let loose waves of hair, an inch of which would be a keepsake beyond price: In short, I should have liked, I do confess, to have had the lightest license of a child, and yet to have been man enough to know its value.

But now a knocking at the door was heard, and such a rush immediately ensued that she, with laughing face and plundered dress, was borne toward it the center of a flushed and boisterous group, just in time to greet the father, who came home attended by a man laden with Christmas toys and presents. Then the shouting and the struggling, and the onslaught that was made on the defenseless porter! The scaling him, with chairs for ladders, to dive into his pockets, despoil him of brown-paper parcels, hold on tight by his cravat, hug him round his neck, pummel his back, and kick his legs in irrepressible affection! The shouts of wonder and delight with which the development of every package was received! The terrible announcement that the baby had been taken in the act of putting a doll's frying pan into his mouth, and was more than suspected of having swallowed a fictitious turkey, glued on a wooden platter! The immense relief of finding this a false

alarm! The joy, and gratitude, and ecstasy! They are all indescribable alike. It is enough that, by degrees, the children and their emotions got out of the parlor, and, by one stair at a time, up to the top of the house, where they went to bed, and so subsided.

And now Scrooge looked on more attentively than ever, when the master of the house, having his daughter leaning fondly on him, sat down with her and her mother at his own fireside; and when he thought that such another creature, quite as graceful and as full of promise, might have called him father, and been a springtime in the haggard winter of his life, his sight grew very dim indeed.

"Belle," said the husband, turning to his wife with a smile, "I saw an old friend of yours this afternoon."

"Who was it?"

"Guess!"

"How can I? Tut, don't I know?" she added in the same breath, laughing as he laughed. "Mr. Scrooge."

"Mr. Scrooge it was. I passed his office window; and as it was not shut up, and he had a candle inside, I could scarcely help seeing him. His partner lies upon the point of death, I hear; and there he sat alone. Quite alone in the world, I do believe."

"Spirit!" said Scrooge in a broken voice, "remove me from this place."

"I told you these were shadows of the things that have been," said the Ghost. "That they are what they are do not blame me!"

"Remove me!" Scrooge exclaimed, "I cannot bear it!"

He turned upon the Ghost, and seeing that it looked upon him with a face, in which in some strange way there were fragments of all the faces it had shown him, wrestled with it.

"Leave me! Take me back. Haunt me no longer!"

In the struggle, if that can be called a struggle in which the Ghost with no visible resistance on its own part was undisturbed by any effort of its adversary, Scrooge observed that its light was burning high and bright; and dimly connecting that with its influence over him, he seized the extinguisher-cap, and by a sudden action pressed it down upon its head.

The Spirit dropped beneath it, so that the extinguisher covered its whole form; but though Scrooge pressed it down with all his force, he could not hide the light, which streamed from under it, in an unbroken flood upon the ground.

He was conscious of being exhausted, and overcome by an irresistible drowsiness; and, further, of being in his own bedroom. He gave the cap a parting squeeze, in which his hand relaxed; and had barely time to reel to bed, before he sank into a heavy sleep.

Responding to the Novel

Analyzing Stave Two

Identifying Facts

1. According to the nearby church chimes and his own watch, what time is it when Scrooge wakes up? Tell why he finds it hard to believe this is the correct time.

2. How does the Ghost of Christmas Past get Scrooge's attention? List five physical details that give this Ghost a strange appearance.

3. Discuss what the Ghost says is his business with Scrooge.

4. The Ghost helps Scrooge revisit scenes from five past Christmases. Briefly summarize the events that Scrooge witnesses in each of these scenes.

5. Explain how Scrooge gets rid of the Ghost of Christmas Past.

Interpreting Meanings

6. Each of the five scenes Scrooge sees again in Stave Two makes him regret something that he failed to do. Identify and describe each of

these five regrets. Then discuss the overall effect on Scrooge of his trip into the past.

7. In Stave One you were introduced to Dickens's technique of contrasting visual images that are dark with visual images that are light. (A **visual image** is a picture a writer creates in the reader's mind through the use of words.) In Stave Two the Ghost of Christmas Past visits Scrooge in the dark of night while glowing with "a clear jet of light." What do you think is the significance of this contrast of dark and light? What is the meaning of Scrooge's inability, at the end of the Stave, to extinguish the Ghost's light?

8. In Stave Two, Dickens suggests that Scrooge may be able to change and again care about other people. List two or three examples of such suggestions. Then discuss whether you think Scrooge will in fact change by the end of the novel.

9. You now have read nearly half of *A Christmas Carol.* What do you like most about the novel? Are there any aspects you wish Dickens had handled differently? Refer to specific details in Staves One and Two in explaining your answer.

Applying Meanings

10. Scrooge himself says that the joy Fezziwig gave others had little to do with money. What are some ways you have seen people bring joy to one another at little or no cost?

Writing About Stave Two

A Creative Response

1. **Describing a Place.** Locate the paragraph on page 634 that describes the school Scrooge attended. It begins, "They left the high road. . . ." List the words and phrases in the paragraph that convey to you how run-down the mansion is. Then choose a building or a room that created a strong impression on you. Perhaps it was unusually beautiful, intimidating, luxurious, neat, or (like Scrooge's school) run-down. List several words and phrases that focus on the key quality of the building or room. Then, using Dickens's paragraph as a model, write a paragraph describing your subject.

A Critical Response

2. **Analyzing Character.** Scrooge's fiancée sees a "master passion" in Scrooge that Scrooge himself does not see. She calls it "Gain"—an obsession with making money. In a paragraph discuss whether later events in Scrooge's life have proved her correct. Refer to specific evidence in Staves One and Two to support your analysis.

Analyzing Language and Vocabulary

Sensory Details

Sensory details help bring descriptive passages to life. In Stave One, for example, Dickens's sensory details allowed your imagination to *feel* the cold dampness of the fog, *taste* the thinness of the gruel Scrooge ate, *see* the gas lamps, and *hear* the clanking of Marley's chains.

1. For each of the following quotations from *A Christmas Carol,* identify the sense to which it appeals *most strongly*—sight, hearing, touch, taste, or smell. What specific words appeal to the sense you named for each quotation?

   a. ". . . candles were flaring in the windows . . . like ruddy smears upon the palpable brown air."
   b. "Foggier yet, and colder! Piercing, searching, biting cold."
   c. ". . . the hour bell sounded, . . . with a deep, dull, hollow, melancholy ONE."
   d. "It wore a tunic of the purest white; and round its waist was bound a lustrous belt, the sheen of which was beautiful. It held a branch of fresh green holly in its hand. . . ."
   e. . . . and there was a great piece of Cold Boiled, and there were mince pies, and plenty of beer."

2. Turn to the scene in Stave Two set in the parlor of Scrooge's school the day Fan comes to take him home (page 636). The paragraph begins, "A terrible voice in the hall cried . . ." Divide a sheet of paper into five parts labeled *sight, hearing, touch, taste,* and *smell.* Then go through the paragraph and list the words or phrases that appeal to each sense. (Some may appeal to more than one sense.)

Stave Three:
The Second of the Three Spirits

Awaking in the middle of a prodigiously tough snore, and sitting up in bed to get his thoughts together, Scrooge had no occasion to be told that the bell was again upon the stroke of one. He felt that he was restored to consciousness in the right nick of time, for the especial purpose of holding a conference with the second messenger despatched to him through Jacob Marley's intervention. But finding that he turned uncomfortably cold when he began to wonder which of his curtains this new specter would draw back, he put them every one aside with his own hands, and, lying down again, established a sharp lookout all round the bed. For he wished to challenge the Spirit on the moment of its appearance, and did not wish to be taken by surprise and made nervous.

Gentlemen of the free-and-easy sort, who plume themselves[1] on being acquainted with a move or two, and being usually equal to the time of day, express the wide range of their capacity for adventure by observing that they are good for anything from pitch-and-toss to manslaughter; between which opposite extremes, no doubt, there lies a tolerably wide and comprehensive range of subjects. Without venturing for Scrooge quite as hardily as this, I don't mind calling on you to believe that he was ready for a good broad field of strange appearances, and that nothing between a baby and a rhinoceros would have astonished him very much.

Now, being prepared for almost anything, he was not by any means prepared for nothing; and consequently, when the bell struck one, and no shape appeared, he was taken with a violent fit of trembling. Five minutes, ten minutes, a quarter of an hour went by, yet nothing came. All this time he lay upon his bed, the very core and center of a blaze of ruddy light, which streamed upon it when the clock proclaimed the hour; and which, being only light, was more alarming than a dozen ghosts, as he was powerless to make out what it meant, or would be at; and was sometimes apprehensive that he might be at that very moment an interesting case of spontaneous combustion,[2] without having the consolation of knowing it. At last, however, he began to think—as you or I would have thought at first; for it is always the person not in the predicament who knows what ought to have been done in it, and would unquestionably have done it too—at last, I say, he began to think that the source and secret of this ghostly light might be in the adjoining room, from whence, on further tracing it, it seemed to shine. This idea taking full possession of his mind, he got up softly, and shuffled in his slippers to the door.

The moment Scrooge's hand was on the lock a strange voice called him by his name, and bade him enter. He obeyed.

It was his own room. There was no doubt about that. But it had undergone a surprising transformation. The walls and ceilings were so hung with living green, that it looked a perfect grove; from every part of which bright gleaming berries glistened. The crisp leaves of holly, mistletoe, and ivy reflected back the light, as if so many little mirrors had been scattered there; and such a mighty blaze went roaring up the chimney as that dull petrification of a hearth had never known in Scrooge's time, or Marley's, or for many and many a winter season gone. Heaped up on the floor, to form a kind of throne, were turkeys, geese, game, poultry, brawn,[3] great joints of meat, sucking pigs, long wreaths of sausages, mince pies, plum puddings, barrels of oysters, red-hot chestnuts, cherry-cheeked apples, juicy oranges, luscious pears, immense twelfth-cakes,[4] and seething bowls of punch, that made the chamber dim with their delicious steam. In easy state upon this couch there sat a jolly Giant, glorious to see; who bore a glowing torch, in shape not unlike Plenty's horn,[5] and held it up, high up, to shed its light on Scrooge as he came peeping round the door.

"Come in!" exclaimed the Ghost. "Come in! and know me better, man!"

Scrooge entered timidly, and hung his head before this Spirit. He was not the dogged Scrooge he had been; and though the Spirit's eyes were clear and kind, he did not like to meet them.

"I am the Ghost of Christmas Present," said the Spirit. "Look upon me!"

Scrooge reverently did so. It was clothed in one simple deep green robe, or mantle, bordered with white fur. This garment hung so loosely on the figure, that its capacious breast was bare, as if disdaining to be warded or concealed by any ar-

---

1. **plume themselves:** pride themselves.
2. **spontaneous combustion:** catching fire as a result of internal chemical action. In Dickens's time, some believed a person's body chemicals could set the body on fire and consume it.

3. **brawn:** cooked boar meat.
4. **twelfth-cakes:** fruitcakes made for Epiphany, a holiday that takes place twelve days after Christmas.
5. **Plenty's horn:** in Greek mythology, goat's horn that would become full of whatever its owner wanted.

tifice. Its feet, observable beneath the ample folds of the garment, were also bare; and on its head it wore no other covering than a holly wreath, set here and there with shining icicles. Its dark-brown curls were long and free; free as its genial face, its sparkling eye, its open hand, its cheery voice, its unconstrained demeanor, and its joyful air. Girded round its middle was an antique scabbard; but no sword was in it, and the ancient sheath was eaten up with rust.

"You have never seen the like of me before!" exclaimed the Spirit.

"Never," Scrooge made answer to it.

"Have never walked forth with the younger members of my family; meaning (for I am very young) my elder brothers born in these later years?" pursued the Phantom.

"I don't think I have," said Scrooge. "I am afraid I have not. Have you had many brothers, Spirit?"

"More than eighteen hundred,"[6] said the Ghost.

"A tremendous family to provide for," muttered Scrooge.

The Ghost of Christmas Present rose.

"Spirit," said Scrooge submissively, "conduct me where you will. I went forth last night on compulsion, and I learned a lesson which is working now. Tonight if you have aught to teach me, let me profit by it."

"Touch my robe!"

Scrooge did as he was told, and held it fast.

Holly, mistletoe, red berries, ivy, turkeys, geese, game, poultry, brawn, meat, pigs, sausages, oysters, pies, puddings, fruit, and punch, all vanished instantly. So did the room, the fire, the ruddy glow, the hour of night, and they stood in the city streets on Christmas morning, where (for the weather was severe) the people made a rough, but brisk and not unpleasant kind of music, in scraping the snow from the pavement in front of their dwellings, and from the tops of their houses, whence it was mad delight to the boys to see it come plumping down into the road below, and splitting into artificial little snowstorms.

The housefronts looked black enough, and the windows blacker, contrasting with the smooth white sheet of snow upon the roofs, and with the dirtier snow upon the ground; which last deposit had been plowed up in deep furrows by the heavy wheels of carts and wagons: furrows that crossed and recrossed each other hundreds of times where the great streets branched off; and made intricate channels, hard to trace in the thick yellow mud and icy water. The sky was gloomy, and the shortest streets were choked up with a dingy mist, half thawed, half frozen, whose heavier particles descended in a shower of sooty atoms, as if all the chimneys in Great Britain had, by one consent, caught fire, and were blazing away to their dear heart's content. There was nothing very cheerful in the climate or the town, and yet was there an air of cheerfulness abroad that the clearest summer air and brightest summer sun might have endeavored to diffuse in vain.

For the people who were shoveling away on the housetops were jovial and full of glee; calling out to one another from the parapets, and now and then exchanging a facetious snowball—better-natured missile far than many a wordy jest—laughing heartily if it went right, and not less heartily if it went wrong. The poulterers' shops were still half open, and the fruiterers' were radiant in their glory. There were great, round, pot-bellied baskets of chestnuts, shaped like the waistcoats of jolly old gentlemen, lolling at the doors, and tumbling out into the street in their apoplectic opulence:[7] There were ruddy, brown-faced, broad-girthed Spanish onions, shining in the fatness of their growth like Spanish friars, and winking from their shelves in wanton slyness at the girls as they went by, and glanced demurely at the hung-up mistletoe. There were pears and apples clustered high in blooming pyramids; there were bunches of grapes, made, in the shopkeepers' benevolence, to dangle from conspicuous hooks that people's mouths might water gratis[8] as they passed; there were piles of filberts, mossy and brown, recalling, in their fragrance, ancient walks among the woods, and pleasant shufflings ankle deep through withered leaves; there were Norfolk Biffins,[9] squab and swarthy, setting off the yellow of the oranges and lemons, and, in the great compactness of their juicy persons, urgently entreating and beseeching to be carried home in paper bags and eaten after dinner. The very gold and silver fish, set forth among these choice fruits in a bowl, though members of a dull and stagnant-blooded race, appeared to know that there was something going on; and, to a fish, went gasping round and round their little world in slow and passionless excitement.

The grocers'! Oh, the grocers'! Nearly

---

6. **More . . . hundred:** Since this story was written in 1843, the Ghost would have 1,843 brothers.

7. **apoplectic** (ap′ə·plek′tik) **opulence:** in other words, dizzying wealth or quantity.

8. **gratis** (grat′is): free; without charge.

9. **Norfolk Biffins:** dried apples.

closed, with perhaps two shutters down, or one; but through those gaps such glimpses! It was not alone that the scales descending on the counter made a merry sound, or that the twine and roller parted company so briskly, or that the canisters were rattled up and down like juggling tricks, or even that the blended scents of tea and coffee were so grateful to the nose, or even that the raisins were so plentiful and rare, the almonds so extremely white, the sticks of cinnamon so long and straight, the other spices so delicious, the candied fruits so caked and spotted with molten sugar as to make the coldest lookers-on feel faint, and subsequently bilious.[10] Nor was it that the figs were moist and pulpy, or that the French plums blushed in modest tartness from their highly decorated boxes, or that everything was good to eat and in its Christmas dress; but the customers were all so hurried and so eager in the hopeful promise of the day, that they tumbled up against each other at the door, crashing their wicker baskets wildly, and left their purchases upon the counter, and came running back to fetch them, and committed hundreds of the like mistakes, in the best humor possible; while the grocer and his people were so frank and fresh, that the polished hearts with which they fastened their aprons behind might have been their own, worn outside for general inspection, and for Christmas daws[11] to peck at if they chose.

But soon the steeples called good people all to church and chapel, and away they came, flocking through the streets in their best clothes and with their gayest faces. And at the same time there emerged, from scores of bystreets, lanes, and nameless turnings, innumerable people, carrying their dinners to the bakers' shops.[12] The sight of these poor revelers appeared to interest the Spirit very much, for he stood with Scrooge beside him in a baker's doorway, and, taking off the covers as their bearers passed, sprinkled incense on their dinners from his torch. And it was a very uncommon kind of torch, for once or twice, when there were angry words between some dinner-carriers who had jostled each other, he shed a few drops of water on them from it, and their good humor was restored directly. For they said, it was a shame to quarrel upon Christmas Day. And so it was! God love it, so it was!

In time the bells ceased, and the bakers were shut up; and yet there was a genial shadowing forth of all these dinners, and the progress of their cooking, in the thawed blotch of wet above each baker's oven, where the pavement smoked as if its stones were cooking too.

"Is there a peculiar flavor in what you sprinkle from your torch?" asked Scrooge.

"There is. My own."

"Would it apply to any kind of dinner on this day?" asked Scrooge.

"To any kindly given. To a poor one most."

"Why to a poor one most?" asked Scrooge.

"Because it needs it most."

"Spirit!" said Scrooge, after a moment's thought, "I wonder you, of all the beings in the many worlds about us, should desire to cramp these people's opportunities of innocent enjoyment."

"I!" cried the Spirit.

"You would deprive them of their means of dining every seventh day, often the only day on which they can be said to dine at all," said Scrooge; "wouldn't you?"

"I!" cried the Spirit.

"You seek to close these places on the Seventh Day,"[13] said Scrooge. "And it comes to the same thing."

"I seek!" exclaimed the Spirit.

"Forgive me if I am wrong. It has been done in your name, or at least in that of your family," said Scrooge.

"There are some upon this earth of yours," returned the Spirit, "who lay claim to know us, and who do their deeds of passion, pride, ill will, hatred, envy, bigotry, and selfishness in our name, who are as strange to us, and all our kith and kin, as if they had never lived. Remember that, and charge their doings on themselves, not us."

Scrooge promised that he would; and they went on, invisible, as they had been before, into the suburbs of the town. It was a remarkable quality of the Ghost (which Scrooge had observed at the baker's), that notwithstanding his gigantic size, he could accommodate himself to any place with ease; and that he stood beneath a low roof quite as gracefully and like a supernatural creature as it was possible he could have done in any lofty hall.

And perhaps it was the pleasure the good Spirit had in showing off this power of his, or else it was his own kind, generous, hearty nature, and his sympathy with all poor men, that led him straight to Scrooge's clerk's; for there he went, and took

---

10. **bilious** (bil´yəs): here, sick.
11. **daws**: short for jackdaws, crow-like birds.
12. **carrying . . . shops:** poor people who did not have ovens cooked their dinners in bakery-shop ovens.

13. **Seventh Day:** Sunday. The Church made shops—including bakery shops that poor people depended on for ovens—close on Sundays.

Scrooge with him, holding to his robe; and on the threshold of the door the Spirit smiled, and stopped to bless Bob Cratchit's dwelling with the sprinklings of his torch. Think of that! Bob had but fifteen "Bob"[14] a week himself; he pocketed on Saturdays but fifteen copies of his Christian name; and yet the Ghost of Christmas Present blessed his four-roomed house!

Then up rose Mrs. Cratchit, Cratchit's wife, dressed out but poorly in a twice-turned[15] gown, but brave in ribbons, which are cheap, and make a goodly show for sixpence; and she laid the cloth, assisted by Belinda Cratchit, second of her daughters, also brave in ribbons; while Master Peter Cratchit plunged a fork into the saucepan of potatoes, and getting the corners of his monstrous shirt-collar (Bob's private property, conferred upon his son and heir in honor of the day) into his mouth, rejoiced to find himself so gallantly attired, and yearned to show his linen in the fashionable parks. And now two smaller Cratchits, boy and girl, came tearing in, screaming that outside the baker's they had smelt the goose, and known it for their own; and basking in luxurious thoughts of sage and onion, these young Cratchits danced about the table, and exalted Master Peter Cratchit to the skies, while he (not proud, although his collars nearly choked him) blew the fire, until the slow potatoes, bubbling up, knocked loudly at the saucepan lid to be let out and peeled.

"What has ever got your precious father, then?" said Mrs. Cratchit. "And your brother, Tiny Tim? And Martha warn't as late last Christmas Day by half an hour!"

"Here's Martha, mother!" said a girl, appearing as she spoke.

"Here's Martha, mother!" cried the two young Cratchits. "Hurrah! There's *such* a goose, Martha!"

"Why, bless your heart alive, my dear, how late you are!" said Mrs. Cratchit, kissing her a dozen times, and taking off her shawl and bonnet for her with officious zeal.[16]

"We'd a deal of work to finish up last night," replied the girl, "and had to clear away this morning, mother!"

"Well! never mind so long as you are come," said Mrs. Cratchit. "Sit ye down before the fire, my dear, and have a warm, Lord bless ye!"

"No, no! There's father coming," cried the two young Cratchits, who were everywhere at once. "Hide, Martha, hide!"

So Martha hid herself, and in came little Bob, the father, with at least three feet of comforter, exclusive of the fringe, hanging down before him, and his threadbare clothes darned up and brushed to look seasonable, and Tiny Tim upon his shoulder. Alas for Tiny Tim, he bore a little crutch, and had his limbs supported by an iron frame!

"Why, where's our Martha?" cried Bob Cratchit, looking round.

"Not coming," said Mrs. Cratchit.

"Not coming!" said Bob, with a sudden declension[17] in his high spirits; for he had been Tim's bloodhorse all the way from church, and had come home rampant.[18] "Not coming upon Christmas Day!"

Martha didn't like to see him disappointed, if it were only in joke; so she came out prematurely from behind the closet door, and ran into his arms, while the two young Cratchits hustled Tiny Tim, and bore him off into the washhouse, that he might hear the pudding singing in the copper.

"And how did little Tim behave?" asked Mrs. Cratchit when she had rallied Bob on his credulity,[19] and Bob had hugged his daughter to his heart's content.

"As good as gold," said Bob, "and better. Somehow, he gets thoughtful, sitting by himself so much, and thinks the strangest things you ever heard. He told me, coming home, that he hoped the people saw him in the church, because he was a cripple, and it might be pleasant to them to remember upon Christmas Day who made lame beggars walk and blind men see."

Bob's voice was tremulous when he told them this, and trembled more when he said that Tiny Tim was growing strong and hearty.

His active little crutch was heard upon the floor, and back came Tiny Tim before another word was spoken, escorted by his brother and sister to his stool beside the fire; and while Bob, turning up his cuffs—as if, poor fellow, they were capable of being made more shabby—compounded some hot mixture in a jug with gin and lemons, and stirred it round and round, and put it on the hob to simmer, Master Peter and the two ubiquitous[20] young Cratchits went to fetch the goose, with which they soon returned in high procession.

---

14. **"Bob":** slang for shilling(s), a former British coin. A pound was divided into twenty shillings.
15. **twice-turned:** remade twice (so worn parts would not show).
16. **officious** (ə·fish′əs) **zeal:** eager enthusiasm.

17. **declension** (di·klen′shən): decline.
18. **rampant:** rearing up like a horse; hence, high-spirited.
19. **rallied . . . credulity:** teased Bob for being so easily fooled.
20. **ubiquitous** (yōō·bik′wə·təs): seeming to be everywhere at the same time.

Such a bustle ensued that you might have thought a goose the rarest of all birds: a feathered phenomenon, to which a black swan was a matter of course—and, in truth, it was something very like it in that house. Mrs. Cratchit made the gravy (ready beforehand in a little saucepan) hissing hot; Master Peter mashed the potatoes with incredible vigor; Miss Belinda sweetened up the apple sauce; Martha dusted the hot plates; Bob took Tiny Tim beside him in a tiny corner at the table; the two young Cratchits set chairs for everybody, not forgetting themselves, and, mounting guard upon their posts, crammed spoons into their mouths, lest they should shriek for goose before their turn came to be helped. At last the dishes were set on, and grace was said. It was succeeded by a breathless pause, as Mrs. Cratchit, looking slowly all along the carving-knife, prepared to plunge it in the breast, but when she did, and when the long-expected gush of stuffing issued forth, one murmur of delight arose all round the board, and even Tiny Tim, excited by the two young Cratchits, beat on the table with the handle of his knife and feebly cried Hurrah!

There was never such a goose. Bob said he didn't believe there ever was such a goose cooked. Its tenderness and flavor, size and cheapness, were the themes of universal admiration. Eked out by apple sauce and mashed potatoes, it was a sufficient dinner for the whole family; indeed, as Mrs. Cratchit said with great delight (surveying one small atom of a bone upon the dish), they hadn't ate it all at last! Yet everyone had had enough, and the youngest Cratchits, in particular, were steeped in sage and onion to the eyebrows! But now, the plates being changed by Miss Belinda, Mrs. Cratchit left the room alone—too nervous to bear witness—to take the pudding up, and bring it in.

Suppose it should not be done enough! Suppose it should break in turning out! Suppose somebody should have got over the wall of the back yard and stolen it, while they were merry with the goose—a supposition at which the two young Cratchits became livid! All sorts of horrors were supposed.

Hallo! A great deal of steam! The pudding was out of the copper. A smell like a washing-day! That was the cloth. A smell like an eating-house and a pastry-cook's next door to each other, with a laundress's next door to that! That was the pudding! In half a minute Mrs. Cratchit entered—flushed, but smiling proudly—with the pudding, like a speckled cannonball, so hard and firm, blazing in half of half-a-quartern of ignited brandy, and bedight[21] with Christmas holly stuck into the top.

Oh, a wonderful pudding! Bob Cratchit said, and calmly too, that he regarded it as the greatest success achieved by Mrs. Cratchit since their marriage. Mrs. Cratchit said that, now the weight was off her mind, she would confess she had her doubts about the quantity of flour. Everybody had something to say about it, but nobody said or thought it was at all a small pudding for a large family. It would have been flat heresy[22] to do so. Any Cratchit would have blushed to hint at such a thing.

At last the dinner was all done, the cloth was cleared, the hearth swept, and the fire made up. The compound in the jug being tasted, and considered perfect, apples and oranges were put upon the table, and a shovelful of chestnuts on the fire. Then all the Cratchit family drew round the hearth in what Bob Crachit called a circle, meaning half a one; and at Bob Cratchit's elbow stood the family display of glass. Two tumblers and a custard cup without a handle.

These held the hot stuff from the jug, however, as well as golden goblets would have done; and Bob served it out with beaming looks, while the chestnuts on the fire sputtered and cracked noisily. Then Bob proposed:

"A merry Christmas to us all, my dears. God bless us!"

Which all the family re-echoed.

"God bless us every one!" said Tiny Tim, the last of all.

He sat very close to his father's side, upon his little stool. Bob held his withered little hand to his, as if he loved the child, and wished to keep him by his side, and dreaded that he might be taken from him.

"Spirit," said Scrooge, with an interest he had never felt before, "tell me if Tiny Tim will live."

"I see a vacant seat," replied the Ghost, "in the poor chimney corner, and a crutch without an owner, carefully preserved. If these shadows remain unaltered by the Future, the child will die."

"No, no," said Scrooge. "Oh no, kind Spirit! Say he will be spared."

"If these shadows remain unaltered by the Future none other of my race," returned the Ghost, "will find him here. What then? If he be like to die, he had better do it, and decrease the surplus population."

---

21. **bedight** (bi·dīt'): decorated.
22. **heresy:** holding an opinion opposed to the established view.

Scrooge hung his head to hear his own words quoted by the Spirit, and was overcome with penitence and grief.

"Man," said the Ghost, "if man you be in heart, not adamant,[23] forbear that wicked cant[24] until you have discovered what the surplus is, and where it is. Will you decide what men shall live, what men shall die? It may be that, in the sight of Heaven, you are more worthless and less fit to live than millions like this poor man's child. O God! To hear the insect on the leaf pronouncing on the too much life among his hungry brothers in the dust!"

Scrooge bent before the Ghost's rebuke, and, trembling, cast his eyes upon the ground. But he raised them speedily on hearing his own name.

"Mr. Scrooge!" said Bob. "I'll give you Mr. Scrooge, the Founder of the Feast!"

"The Founder of the Feast, indeed!" cried Mrs. Cratchit, reddening. "I wish I had him here. I'd give him a piece of my mind to feast upon, and I hope he'd have a good appetite for it."

"My dear," said Bob, "the children! Christmas Day."

"It should be Christmas Day, I am sure," said she, "on which one drinks to the health of such an odious, stingy, hard, unfeeling man as Mr. Scrooge. You know he is, Robert! Nobody knows it better than you do, poor fellow!"

"My dear!" was Bob's mild answer. "Christmas Day."

"I'll drink to his health for your sake and the Day's," said Mrs. Cratchit, "not for his. Long life to him! A merry Christmas and a happy New Year! He'll be very merry and very happy, I have no doubt!"

The children drank the toast after her. It was the first of their proceedings which had no heartiness in it. Tiny Tim drank it last of all, but he didn't care twopence for it. Scrooge was the ogre of the family. The mention of his name cast a dark shadow on the party, which was not dispelled for full five minutes.

After it had passed away they were ten times merrier than before, from the mere relief of Scrooge the Baleful[25] being done with. Bob Cratchit told them how he had a situation in his eye for Master Peter, which would bring in, if obtained, full five-and-sixpence weekly. The two young Cratchits laughed tremendously at the idea of Peter's being a man of business; and Peter himself looked thoughtfully at the fire from between his collars, as if he were deliberating what particular investments he should favor when he came into the receipt of that bewildering income. Martha, who was a poor apprentice at a milliner's,[26] then told them what kind of work she had to do, and how many hours she worked at a stretch, and how she meant to lie abed tomorrow morning for a good long rest; tomorrow being a holiday she passed at home. Also how she had seen a countess and a lord some days before, and how the lord "was much about as tall as Peter"; at which Peter pulled up his collar so high that you couldn't have seen his head if you had been there. All this time the chestnuts and the jug went round and round; and by-and-by they had a song, about a lost child traveling in the snow, from Tiny Tim, who had a plaintive little voice, and sang it very well indeed.

There was nothing of high mark in this. They were not a handsome family, they were not well dressed, their shoes were far from being waterproof, their clothes were scanty; and Peter might have known, and very likely did, the inside of a pawnbroker's. But they were happy, grateful, pleased with one another, and contented with the time; and when they faded, they looked happier yet in the bright sprinklings of the Spirit's torch at parting, Scrooge had his eye upon them, and especially on Tiny Tim, until the last.

By this time it was getting dark, and snowing pretty heavily; and as Scrooge and the Spirit went along the streets, the brightness of the roaring fires in kitchens, parlors, and all sorts of rooms was wonderful. Here, the flickering of the blaze showed preparations for a cozy dinner, with hot plates baking through and through before the fire, and deep red curtains, ready to be drawn to shut out cold and darkness. There, all the children of the house were running out into the snow to meet their married sisters, brothers, cousins, uncles, aunts, and be the first to greet them. Here, again, were shadows on the window blinds of guests assembling; and there a group of handsome girls, all hooded and fur-booted, and all chattering at once, tripped lightly off to some near neighbor's house; where, woe upon the single man who saw them enter—artful witches, well they knew it—in a glow!

But, if you had judged from the numbers of

---

23. **adamant:** unyielding.
24. **cant:** insincere or meaningless talk.
25. **Baleful:** evil.

---

26. A milliner (mil′ə·nər) is a person who designs and sells women's hats.

people on their way to friendly gatherings, you might have thought that no one was at home to give them welcome when they got there, instead of every house expecting company, and piling up its fires half-chimney high. Blessings on it, how the Ghost exulted! How it bared its breadth of breast, and opened its capacious palm, and floated on, outpouring with a generous hand its bright and harmless mirth on everything within its reach! The very lamplighter, who ran on before, dotting the dusky street with specks of light, and who was dressed to spend the evening somewhere, laughed out loudly as the Spirit passed, though little kenned[27] the lamplighter that he had any company but Christmas.

And now, without a word of warning from the Ghost, they stood upon a bleak and desert moor, where monstrous masses of rude stone were cast about, as though it were the burial place of giants; and water spread itself wheresoever it listed; or would have done so, but for the frost that held it prisoner; and nothing grew but moss and furze,[28] and coarse, rank grass. Down in the west the setting sun had left a streak of fiery red, which glared upon the desolation for an instant, like a sullen eye, and frowning lower, lower, lower yet, was lost in the thick gloom of darkest night.

"What place is this?" asked Scrooge.

"A place where miners live, who labor in the bowels of the earth," returned the Spirit. "But they know me. See!"

A light shone from the window of a hut, and swiftly they advanced toward it. Passing through the wall of mud and stone, they found a cheerful company assembled round a glowing fire. An old, old man and woman, with their children and their children's children, and another generation beyond that, were all decked out gaily in their holiday attire. The old man, in a voice that seldom rose above the howling of the wind upon the barren waste, was singing them a Christmas song; it had been a very old song when he was a boy; and from time to time they all joined in the chorus. So surely as they raised their voices, the old man got quite blithe[29] and loud; and so surely as they stopped, his vigor sank again.

The Spirit did not tarry here, but bade Scrooge hold his robe, and, passing on above the moor, sped whither? Not to sea? To sea. To Scrooge's horror, looking back, he saw the last of the land, a frightful range of rocks, behind them; and his ears were deafened by the thundering of water, as it rolled and roared, and raged among the dreadful caverns it had worn, and fiercely tried to undermine the earth.

Built upon a dismal reef of sunken rocks, some league or so from shore, on which the waters chafed and dashed, the wild year through, there stood a solitary lighthouse. Great heaps of seaweed clung to its base, and stormbirds—born of the wind, one might suppose, as seaweed of the water—rose and fell about it, like the waves they skimmed.

But, even here, two men who watched the light had made a fire, that through the loophole in the thick stone wall shed out a ray of brightness on the awful sea. Joining their horny hands over the rough table at which they sat, they wished each other Merry Christmas in their can of grog; and one of them—the elder too, with his face all damaged and scarred with hard weather, as the figurehead of an old ship might be—struck up a sturdy song that was like a gale in itself.

Again the Ghost sped on, above the black and heaving sea—on, on—until being far away, as he told Scrooge, from any shore, they lighted on a ship. They stood beside the helmsman at the wheel, the lookout in the bow, the officers who had the watch; dark, ghostly figures in their several stations; but every man among them hummed a Christmas tune, or had a Christmas thought, or spoke below his breath to his companion of some bygone Christmas Day, with homeward hopes belonging to it. And every man on board, waking or sleeping, good or bad, had had a kinder word for one another on that day than on any day in the year; and had shared to some extent in its festivities; and had remembered those he cared for at a distance, and had known that they delighted to remember him.

It was a great surprise to Scrooge, while listening to the moaning of the wind, and thinking what a solemn thing it was to move on through the lonely darkness over an unknown abyss, whose depths were secrets as profound as death: It was a great surprise to Scrooge, while thus engaged, to hear a hearty laugh. It was a much greater surprise to Scrooge to recognize it as his own nephew's and to find himself in a bright, dry, gleaming room, with the Spirit standing smiling by his side, and looking at that same nephew with approving affability!

"Ha, ha!" laughed Scrooge's nephew. "Ha, ha, ha!"

If you should happen, by any unlikely chance, to know a man more blessed in a laugh than

---

27. **kenned:** knew.
28. **furze:** prickly evergreen shrub.
29. **blithe** (blīth): carefree.

Scrooge's nephew, all I can say is, I should like to know him too. Introduce him to me, and I'll cultivate his acquaintance.

It is a fair, even-handed, noble adjustment of things, that while there is infection in disease and sorrow, there is nothing in the world so irresistibly contagious as laughter and good humor. When Scrooge's nephew laughed in this way—holding his sides, rolling his head, and twisting his face into the most extravagant contortions—Scrooge's niece, by marriage, laughed as heartily as he. And their assembled friends, being not a bit behindhand, roared out lustily.

"Ha, ha! Ha, ha, ha, ha!"

"He said that Christmas was a humbug, as I live!" cried Scrooge's nephew. "He believed it, too!"

"More shame for him, Fred!" said Scrooge's niece indignantly. Bless those women! They never do anything by halves. They are always in earnest.

She was very pretty, exceedingly pretty. With a dimpled, surprised-looking, capital face; a ripe little mouth, that seemed made to be kissed—as no doubt it was; all kinds of good little dots about her chin, that melted into one another when she laughed; and the sunniest pair of eyes you ever saw in any little creature's head. Altogether she was what you would have called provoking, you know, but satisfactory, too. Oh, perfectly satisfactory!

"He's a comical old fellow," said Scrooge's nephew, "that's the truth; and not so pleasant as he might be. However, his offenses carry their own punishment, and I have nothing to say against him."

"I'm sure he is very rich, Fred," hinted Scrooge's niece. "At least, you always tell *me* so."

"What of that, my dear?" said Scrooge's nephew. "His wealth is of no use to him. He don't do any good with it. He don't make himself comfortable with it. He hasn't the satisfaction of thinking—ha, ha, ha!—that he is ever going to benefit *us* with it."

"I have no patience with him," observed Scrooge's niece. Scrooge's niece's sisters, and all the other ladies, expressed the same opinion.

"Oh, I have!" said Scrooge's nephew. "I am sorry for him; I couldn't be angry with him if I tried. Who suffers by his ill whims? Himself always. Here he takes it into his head to dislike us, and he won't come and dine with us. What's the consequence? He don't lose much of a dinner."

"Indeed, I think he loses a very good dinner," interrupted Scrooge's niece. Everybody else said the same, and they must be allowed to have been competent judges, because they had just had dinner; and with the dessert upon the table, were clustered around the fire, by lamplight.

"Well! I am very glad to hear it," said Scrooge's nephew, "because I haven't any great faith in these young housekeepers. What do *you* say, Topper?"

Topper had clearly got his eye upon one of Scrooge's niece's sisters, for he answered that a bachelor was a wretched outcast, who had no right to express an opinion on the subject. Whereat Scrooge's niece's sister—the plump one with the lace tucker, not the one with the roses—blushed.

"Do go on, Fred," said Scrooge's niece, clapping her hands. "He never finishes what he begins to say! He is such a ridiculous fellow!"

Scrooge's nephew reveled in another laugh, and as it was impossible to keep the infection off, though the plump sister tried hard to do it with aromatic vinegar, his example was unanimously followed.

"I was only going to say," said Scrooge's nephew, "that the consequence of his taking a dislike to us, and not making merry with us, is, as I think, that he loses some pleasant moments, which could do him no harm. I am sure he loses pleasanter companions than he can find in his own thoughts, either in his moldy old office or his dusty chambers. I mean to give him the same chance every year, whether he likes it or not, for I pity him. He may rail[30] at Christmas till he dies, but he can't help thinking better of it—I defy him—if he finds me going there, in good temper, year after year, and saying 'Uncle Scrooge, how are you?' If it only put him in the vein to leave his poor clerk fifty pounds, *that's* something; and I think I shook him yesterday."

It was their turn to laugh now, at the notion of his shaking Scrooge. But being thoroughly good-natured, and not much caring what they laughed at, so that they laughed at any rate, he encouraged them in their merriment, and passed the bottle, joyously.

After tea they had some music. For they were a musical family, and knew what they were about when they sung a Glee or Catch,[31] I can assure you; especially Topper, who could growl away in the bass like a good one, and never swell the large veins in his forehead, or get red in the face over it. Scrooge's niece played well upon the harp; and

---

30. **rail:** complain violently.
31. **Glee or Catch:** song for three or more voices, not accompanied by instruments.

played, among other tunes, a simple little air (a mere nothing: you might learn to whistle it in two minutes) which had been familiar to the child who fetched Scrooge from the boarding school, as he had been reminded by the Ghost of Christmas Past. When this strain of music sounded, all the things that Ghost had shown him came upon his mind; he softened more and more; and thought that if he could have listened to it often, years ago, he might have cultivated the kindnesses of life for his own happiness with his own hands, without resorting to the sexton's[32] spade that buried Jacob Marley.

But they didn't devote the whole evening to music. After a while they played at forfeits; for it is good to be children sometimes, and never better than at Christmas, when its mighty Founder was a child himself. Stop! There was first a game at blindman's buff. Of course there was. And I no more believe Topper was really blind than I believe he had eyes in his boots. My opinion is, that it was a done thing between him and Scrooge's nephew; and that the Ghost of Christmas Present knew it. The way he went after that plump sister in the lace tucker was an outrage on the credulity of human nature. Knocking down the fire irons, tumbling over the chairs, bumping up against the piano, smothering himself amongst the curtains, wherever she went, there went he! He always knew where the plump sister was. He wouldn't catch anybody else. If you had fallen up against him (as some of them did) on purpose, he would have made a feint[33] of endeavoring to seize you, which would have been an affront to your understanding, and would instantly have sidled off in the direction of the plump sister. She often cried out that it wasn't fair; and it really was not. But when, at last, he caught her; when, in spite of all her silken rustlings, and her rapid flutterings past him, he got her into a corner whence there was no escape; then his conduct was the most execrable.[34] For his pretending not to know her; his pretending that it was necessary to touch her headdress, and further to assure himself of her identity by pressing a certain ring upon her finger, and a certain chain about her neck, was vile, monstrous! No doubt she told him her opinion of it when, another blind man being in office, they were so very confidential together behind the curtains.

Scrooge's niece was not one of the blindman's

---

32. **sexton:** church official who formerly dug the graves in the churchyard.
33. **feint** (fānt): false show; pretense.
34. **execrable** (ek′si·krə·b′l): detestable.

buff party, but was made comfortable with a large chair and a footstool, in a snug corner where the Ghost and Scrooge were close behind her. But she joined in the forfeits, and loved her love to admiration with all the letters of the alphabet. Likewise at the game of How, When, and Where, she was very great, and, to the secret joy of Scrooge's nephew, beat her sisters hollow; though they were sharp girls too, as Topper could have told you. There might have been twenty people there, young and old, but they all played, and so did Scrooge; for wholly forgetting, in the interest he had in what was going on, that his voice made no sound in their ears, he sometimes came out with his guess quite loud, and very often guessed right, too; for the sharpest needle, best Whitechapel, warranted not to cut in the eye, was not sharper than Scrooge, blunt as he took it in his head to be.

The Ghost was greatly pleased to find him in this mood, and looked upon him with such favor that he begged like a boy to be allowed to stay until the guests departed. But this the Spirit said could not be done.

"Here is a new game," said Scrooge. "One half-hour, Spirit, only one!"

It was a game called Yes and No, where Scrooge's nephew had to think of something, and the rest must find out what, he only answering to their questions yes or no, as the case was. The brisk fire of questioning to which he was exposed elicited from him that he was thinking of an animal, a live animal, rather a disagreeable animal, a savage animal, an animal that growled and grunted sometimes, and talked sometimes, and lived in London, and walked about the streets, and wasn't made a show of, and wasn't led by anybody, and didn't live in a menagerie, and was never killed in a market, and was not a horse, or an ass, or a cow, or a bull, or a tiger, or a dog, or a pig, or a cat, or a bear. At every fresh question that was put to him, this nephew burst into a fresh roar of laughter; and was so inexpressibly tickled, that he was obliged to get up off the sofa and stamp. At last the plump sister, falling into a similar state, cried out:

"I have found it out! I know what it is, Fred! I know what it is!"

"What is it?" cried Fred.

"It's your uncle Scro-o-o-oge."

Which it certainly was. Admiration was the universal sentiment, though some objected that the reply to "Is it a bear?" ought to have been "Yes"; inasmuch as an answer in the negative was sufficient to have diverted their thoughts from Mr.

Scrooge, supposing they had ever had any tendency that way.

"He has given us plenty of merriment, I am sure," said Fred. "and it would be ungrateful not to drink to his health. Here is a glass of mulled wine ready to our hand at the moment; and I say, 'Uncle Scrooge'".

"Well! Uncle Scrooge!" they cried.

"A merry Christmas and a happy New Year to the old man, whatever he is!" said Scrooge's nephew. "He wouldn't take it from me, but may he have it, nevertheless. Uncle Scrooge!"

Uncle Scrooge had imperceptibly become so gay and light of heart, that he would have pledged the unconscious company in return, and thanked them in an inaudible[35] speech, if the Ghost had given him time. But the whole scene passed off in the breath of the last word spoken by his nephew; and he and the Spirit were again upon their travels.

Much they saw, and far they went, and many homes they visited, but always with a happy end. The Spirit stood beside sickbeds, and they were cheerful; on foreign lands, and they were close at home; by struggling men, and they were patient in their greater hope; by poverty, and it was rich. In almshouse,[36] hospital, and gaol,[37] in misery's every refuge, where vain man in his little brief authority had not made fast the door, and barred the Spirit out, he left his blessing and taught Scrooge his precepts.

It was a long night, if it were only a night; but Scrooge had his doubts of this, because the Christmas holidays appeared to be condensed into the space of time they passed together. It was strange, too, that, while Scrooge remained unaltered in his outward form, the Ghost grew older, clearly older. Scrooge had observed this change, but never spoke of it until they left a children's Twelfth-Night party, when, looking at the Spirit as they stood together in an open place, he noticed that its hair was gray.

"Are spirits' lives so short?" asked Scrooge.

"My life upon this globe is very brief," replied the Ghost. "It ends tonight."

"Tonight!" cried Scrooge.

"Tonight at midnight. Hark! The time is drawing near."

The chimes were ringing the three-quarters past eleven at that moment.

"Forgive me if I am not justified in what I ask," said Scrooge, looking intently at the Spirit's robe, "but I see something strange, and not belonging to yourself, protruding from your skirts. Is it a foot or a claw?"

"It might be a claw, for the flesh there is upon it," was the Spirit's sorrowful reply. "Look here!"

From the foldings of its robe it brought two children, wretched, abject, frightful, hideous, miserable. They knelt down at its feet, and clung upon the outside of its garment.

"O Man! Look here! Look, look down here!" exclaimed the Ghost.

They were a boy and girl. Yellow, meager, ragged, scowling, wolfish, but prostrate,[38] too, in their humility. Where graceful youth should have filled their features out, and touched them with its freshest tints, a stale and shriveled hand, like that of age, had pinched and twisted them, and pulled them into shreds. Where angels might have sat enthroned, devils lurked, and glared out menacing. No change, no degradation, no perversion of humanity in any grade, through all the mysteries of wonderful creation, has monsters half so horrible and dread.

Scrooge started back, appalled. Having them shown to him in this way, he tried to say they were fine children, but the words choked themselves, rather than be parties to a lie of such enormous magnitude.

"Spirit! Are they yours?" Scrooge could say no more.

"They are Man's," said the Spirit, looking down upon them. "And they cling to me, appealing from their fathers. This boy is Ignorance. This girl is Want. Beware of them both, and all of their degree, but most of all beware this boy, for on his brow I see that written which is Doom, unless the writing be erased. Deny it!" cried the Spirit, stretching out his hand toward the city. "Slander[39] those who tell it ye! Admit it for your factious purposes,[40] and make it worse! And bide the end!"

"Have they no refuge or resource?" cried Scrooge.

"Are there no prisons?" said the Spirit, turning on him for the last time with his own words. "Are there no workhouses?"

The bell struck twelve.

Scrooge looked about him for the Ghost, and saw it not. As the last stroke ceased to vibrate, he remembered the prediction of old Jacob Marley, and, lifting up his eyes, beheld a solemn Phantom, draped and hooded, coming like a mist along the ground toward him.

---

35. **inaudible** (in·ô′də·b'l): not hearable.
36. **almshouse:** poorhouse.
37. **gaol** (jāl): British spelling of *jail.*

38. **prostrate:** lying with face downward.
39. **slander:** spread false statements about others.
40. **Admit . purposes:** in other words, create conflict.

Responding to the Novel

Analyzing Stave Three

Identifying Facts

1. What makes Scrooge realize that the second of the three Spirits has arrived? Describe the scene surrounding the second Spirit when Scrooge first sees it.
2. Describe the physical characteristics of the Ghost of Christmas Present. What does he carry in his hand? For which class of people does he have the most sympathy?
3. Describe how the Cratchits celebrate Christmas.
4. Describe Tiny Tim's handicap. What does Scrooge ask the Ghost to tell him regarding the boy? What is the Ghost's reply, and how does Scrooge react to it?
5. List three of the places that the Ghost and Scrooge visit after leaving the Cratchits and before arriving at Scrooge's nephew's house. What activities does Scrooge witness in all these places?
6. Describe the scene in Scrooge's nephew's house. Who is present? List three of the things they do as part of their Christmas celebration. Tell how Scrooge reacts to what he sees.
7. List ten words that Dickens uses to describe the two children discovered beneath the Ghost's robe. What does the Ghost say are their names?

Interpreting Meanings

8. In Stave Three, the word *spirit* can be used to refer not only to the Ghost but also to the attitudes that the various characters have toward Christmas. Make a list of ten or more words and phrases from Stave Three that you think express the spirit of Christmas.
9. In this stave, the Ghost twice quotes Scrooge's own words to him. Identify these two instances, and explain the Ghost's reason for quoting Scrooge.
10. Both Bob Cratchit and Scrooge's nephew drink toasts to Scrooge. Explain how their families and friends react to their toasts. What do the toasts reveal about Cratchit's and the nephew's characters?

11. **Point of view** refers to the vantage point from which a story is told. Who is the narrator, or the person telling the story, in *A Christmas Carol*? Is the narrator a character in the story, or some other person who is not part of the story? Is the narrator omniscient (that is, all-knowing) or is the narrator's knowledge limited? Find details in this and earlier staves to support your answer.
12. Consider the glimpse you get of the third Spirit at the end of Stave Three. In what ways do you suspect this Spirit will be different from the first two? What kinds of things do you expect it to show Scrooge?

Applying Meanings

13. Early in Stave Three the narrator says, ". . . it is always the person not in the predicament who knows what ought to have been done in it, and would unquestionably have done it too." In your own words, tell what the narrator means by this generalization. Then do the following.

    a. Describe how the generalization applies to the visits of the Ghosts to Scrooge.
    b. Explain whether you think the generalization applies to your own life. Give examples to back up your opinion.

Writing About Stave Three

A Creative Response

1. **Writing a Letter.** Pretend you are Bob Cratchit. You have found a better job, and you are writing a letter to your replacement in Scrooge's office. In two paragraphs, tell the new clerk about a typical workday at Scrooge and Marley. Discuss the hours and the working conditions and suggest ways to get along with the boss, Ebenezer Scrooge. Be honest, but remember to write as kindly Bob Cratchit would.

A Critical Response

2. **Analyzing Character.** Writers may reveal character in several ways. These ways include directly describing the character's physical appearance

and personality traits; revealing what the character does, says, and thinks; and showing how others react to the character. Scrooge's nephew, Fred, has been characterized in all these ways in *A Christmas Carol*. Review the scene between Fred and Scrooge in Stave One (pages 622–623) and the scene at Fred's house in Stave Three (pages 651–654). Then, in two or three paragraphs, write a description of Fred's character that makes clear why it would or would not be a pleasure to know him. Discuss his appearance, his personality, how he treats others, and how others react to him. Quote passages from the novel to support your opinion. Begin your composition with a statement about whether you would like to get to know a person like Fred.

Analyzing Language and Vocabulary

Sound Devices in Prose

You have already noticed that Dickens uses images that appeal to your five senses, including the sense of hearing. Images that appeal to hearing often involve **onomatopoeia** and **alliteration.**

1. **Onomatopoeia** is the use of a word whose sound imitates or suggests its meaning. For example, *chirp* imitates the sound a bird makes. Onomatopoeia makes descriptions more vivid by echoing the actual sounds that you imagine as you read. Pick out the examples of onomatopoeia in each of the following quotations from *A Christmas Carol.*

    a. "Not a latent echo in the house, not a squeak and scuffle . . . , not a drip . . . , not a sigh . . . , not a clicking in the fire. . . ."

    b. ". . . potatoes, bubbling up, knocked loudly at the saucepan lid. . . ."

    c. "Mrs. Cratchit made the gravy . . . hissing hot. . . ."

    d. "Knocking down the fire irons, tumbling over the chairs, bumping up against the piano, smothering himself amongst the curtains. . . ."

    e. ". . . her silken rustlings, and her rapid flutterings. . . ."

2. **Alliteration** is the repetition of the same consonant sound in words that are near each other. For example, the alliteration of the *t* sounds in the famous political slogan, "Tippecanoe and Tyler too," served as a memory aid and caught people's attention. (The internal rhyme added to the effectiveness of the slogan, which was used in the Presidential election of 1840.) In addition to these two purposes, writers may use alliteration to emphasize a point or to create onomatopoeia. Identify the alliteration in each of the following quotations. Then explain what purpose you think Dickens had in mind in each instance.

    a. Scrooge was "secret, and self-contained, and solitary as an oyster."

    b. "No warmth could warm, no wintry weather chill him."

    c. ". . . his ears were deafened by the thundering of water, as it rolled and roared, and raged among the dreadful caverns. . . ."

    d. "And their assembled friends, being not a bit behindhand. . . ."

    e. ". . . without resorting to the sexton's spade that buried Jacob Marley."

Stave Four:
The Last of the Spirits

The Phantom slowly, gravely, silently approached. When it came near him, Scrooge bent down upon his knee; for in the very air through which this Spirit moved it seemed to scatter gloom and mystery.

It was shrouded in a deep black garment, which concealed its head, its face, its form, and left nothing of it visible, save one outstretched hand. But for this, it would have been difficult to detach its figure from the night, and separate it from the darkness by which it was surrounded.

He felt that it was tall and stately when it came beside him, and that its mysterious presence filled him with a solemn dread. He knew no more, for the Spirit neither spoke nor moved.

"I am in the presence of the Ghost of Christmas Yet to Come?" said Scrooge.

The Spirit answered not, but pointed onward with its hand.

"You are about to show me shadows of the things that have not happened, but will happen in the time before us?" Scrooge pursued. "Is that so, Spirit?"

The upper portion of the garment was contracted for an instant in its folds, as if the Spirit had inclined its head. That was the only answer he received.

Although well used to ghostly company by this time, Scrooge feared the silent shape so much that his legs trembled beneath him, and he found that he could hardly stand when he prepared to follow it. The Spirit paused a moment, as observing his condition, and giving him time to recover.

But Scrooge was all the worse for this. It thrilled him with a vague, uncertain horror to know that, behind the dusky shroud, there were ghostly eyes intently fixed upon him, while he, though he stretched his own to the utmost, could see nothing but a spectral hand and one great heap of black.

"Ghost of the Future!" he exclaimed, "I fear you more than any specter I have seen. But as I know your purpose is to do me good, and as I hope to live to be another man from what I was,

I am prepared to bear your company, and do it with a thankful heart. Will you not speak to me?''

It gave him no reply. The hand was pointed straight before them.

"Lead on!" said Scrooge. "Lead on! The night is waning fast, and it is precious time to me, I know. Lead on, Spirit!"

The Phantom moved away as it had come toward him. Scrooge followed in the shadow of its dress, which bore him up, he thought, and carried him along.

They scarcely seemed to enter the City; for the City rather seemed to spring up about them, and encompass them of its own act. But there they were in the heart of it; on 'Change, amongst the merchants, who hurried up and down, and chinked the money in their pockets, and conversed in groups, and looked at their watches, and trifled thoughtfully with their great gold seals, and so forth, as Scrooge had seen them often.

The Spirit stopped beside one little knot of businessmen. Observing that the hand was pointed to them, Scrooge advanced to listen to their talk.

"No," said a great fat man with a monstrous chin, "I don't know much about it either way. I only know he's dead."

"When did he die?" inquired another.

"Last night, I believe."

"Why, what was the matter with him?" asked a third, taking a vast quantity of snuff out of a very large snuffbox. "I thought he'd never die."

"God knows," said the first, with a yawn.

"What has he done with his money?" asked a red-faced gentleman with a pendulous excrescence[1] on the end of his nose, that shook like the gills[2] of a turkey cock.

"I haven't heard," said the man with the large chin, yawning again. "Left it to his company, perhaps. He hasn't left it to *me*. That's all I know."

This pleasantry was received with a general laugh.

"It's likely to be a very cheap funeral," said the same speaker; "for, upon my life, I don't know of anybody to go to it. Suppose we make up a party, and volunteer?"

"I don't mind going if a lunch is provided," observed the gentleman with the excrescence on his nose. "But I must be fed if I make one."

Another laugh.

"Well, I am the most disinterested among you, after all," said the first speaker, "for I never wear black gloves, and I never eat lunch. But I'll offer to go if anybody else will. When I come to think of it, I'm not at all sure that I wasn't his most particular friend; for we used to stop and speak whenever we met. Bye, bye!"

Speakers and listeners strolled away, and mixed with other groups. Scrooge knew the men, and looked toward the Spirit for an explanation.

The phantom glided on into a street. Its finger pointed to two persons meeting. Scrooge listened again, thinking that the explanation might lie here.

He knew these men, also, perfectly. They were men of business; very wealthy, and of great importance. He had made a point always of standing well in their esteem in a business point of view, that is, strictly in a business point of view.

"How are you?" said one.

"How are you?" returned the other.

"Well!" said the first, "old Scratch[3] has got his own at last, hey?"

"So I am told," returned the second. "Cold, isn't it?"

"Seasonable for Christmastime. You are not a skater, I suppose?"

"No, no. Something else to think of. Good morning!"

Not another word. That was their meeting, their conversation, and their parting.

Scrooge was at first inclined to be surprised that the Spirit should attach importance to conversations apparently so trivial; but feeling assured that they must have some hidden purpose, he set himself to consider what it was likely to be. They could scarcely be supposed to have any bearing on the death of Jacob, his old partner, for that was Past, and this Ghost's province was the Future. Nor could he think of anyone immediately connected with himself to whom he could apply them. But nothing doubting that, to whomsoever they applied, they had some latent[4] moral for his own improvement, he resolved to treasure up every word he heard, and everything he saw; and especially to observe the shadow of himself when it appeared. For he had an expectation that the conduct of his future self would give him the clue he missed, and would render the solution of these riddles easy.

He looked about in that very place for his own image, but another man stood in his accustomed corner; and though the clock pointed to his usual time of day for being there, he saw no likeness of himself among the multitudes that poured in through the porch. It gave him little surprise, how-

---

1. **pendulous excrescence** (iks·kres''ns): loosely hanging growth.
2. **gills:** red flesh hanging below the beak.

3. **old Scratch:** the Devil.
4. **latent** (lāt''nt): hidden.

ever; for he had been revolving in his mind a change of life, and thought and hoped he saw his newborn resolutions carried out in this.

Quiet and dark, beside him stood the Phantom, with its outstretched hand. When he roused himself from his thoughtful quest, he fancied, from the turn of the hand, and its situation in reference to himself, that the unseen eyes were looking at him keenly. It made him shudder, and feel very cold.

They left the busy scene, and went into an obscure part of the town, where Scrooge had never penetrated before, although he recognized its situation and its bad repute. The ways were foul and narrow; the shops and houses wretched; the people half naked, drunken, slipshod, ugly. Alleys and archways, like so many cesspools, disgorged their offenses of smell and dirt, and life upon the straggling streets; and the whole quarter reeked with crime, with filth, and misery.

Far in this den of infamous[5] resort, there was a low-browed, beetling[6] shop, below a penthouse roof, where iron, old rags, bottles, bones, and greasy offal[7] were bought. Upon the floor within were piled up heaps of rusty keys, nails, chains, hinges, files, scales, weights, and refuse iron of all kinds. Secrets that few would like to scrutinize were bred and hidden in mountains of unseemly rags, masses of corrupted fat, and sepulchers[8] of bones. Sitting in among the wares he dealt in, by a charcoal stove made of old bricks, was a gray-haired rascal, nearly seventy years of age, who had screened himself from the cold air without by a frowzy[9] curtaining of miscellaneous tatters hung upon a line, and smoked his pipe in all the luxury of calm retirement.

Scrooge and the Phantom came into the presence of this man, just as a woman with a heavy bundle slunk into the shop. But she had scarcely entered, when another woman, similarly laden, came in too; and she was closely followed by a man in faded black, who was no less startled by the sight of them than they had been upon the recognition of each other. After a short period of blank astonishment, in which the old man with the pipe had joined them, they all three burst into a laugh.

"Let the charwoman[10] alone to be the first!" cried she who had entered first. "Let the laun-

dress alone to be the second; and let the undertaker's man alone to be the third. Look here, old Joe, here's a chance! If we haven't all three met here without meaning it!"

"You couldn't have met in a better place," said old Joe, removing his pipe from his mouth. "Come into the parlor. You were made free of it long ago, you know; and the other two an't strangers. Stop till I shut the door of the shop. Ah! how it skreeks! There an't such a rusty bit of metal in the place as its own hinges, I believe; and I'm sure there's no such old bones here as mine. Ha! ha! We're all suitable to our calling, we're well matched. Come into the parlor. Come into the parlor."

The parlor was the space behind the screen of rags. The old man raked the fire together with an old stair-rod, and having trimmed his smoky lamp (for it was night) with the stem of his pipe, put it into his mouth again.

While he did this, the woman who had already spoken threw her bundle on the floor, and sat down in a flaunting manner on a stool, crossing her elbows on her knees, and looking with a bold defiance at the other two.

"What odds, then? What odds, Mrs. Dilber?" said the woman. "Every person has a right to take care of themselves. *He* always did!"

"That's true, indeed!" said the laundress. "No man more so."

"Why, then, don't stand staring as if you was afraid, woman! Who's the wiser? We're not going to pick holes in each other's coats, I suppose?"

"No, indeed!" said Mrs. Dilber and the man together. "We should hope not."

"Very well then!" cried the woman. "That's enough. Who's the worse for the loss of a few things like these? Not a dead man, I suppose?"

"No, indeed," said Mrs. Dilber, laughing.

"If he wanted to keep 'em after he was dead, a wicked old screw,"[11] pursued the woman, "why wasn't he natural in his lifetime? If he had been, he'd have had somebody to look after him when he was struck with Death, instead of lying gasping out his last there, alone by himself."

"It's the truest word that ever was spoke," said Mrs. Dilber. "It's a judgment on him."

"I wish it was a little heavier judgment," replied the woman, "and it should have been, you may depend upon it, if I could have laid my hands on

---

5. **infamous** (in′fə·məs): having a very bad reputation.
6. **beetling:** jutting out.
7. **offal** (ôf′′l): waste parts of an animal butchered for meat.
8. **sepulchers** (sep′′l·kerz): graves; tombs.
9. **frowzy** (frou′zē): dirty and untidy.
10. **charwoman:** in Great Britain, woman hired to do rough housework or clean an office.

11. **screw:** British slang for a stingy person.

anything else. Open that bundle, old Joe, and let me know the value of it. Speak out plain. I'm not afraid to be the first, nor afraid for them to see it. We knew pretty well that we were helping ourselves before we met here, I believe. It's no sin. Open the bundle, Joe."

But the gallantry of her friends would not allow of this; and the man in faded black, mounting the breach first, produced *his* plunder.[12] It was not extensive. A seal or two, a pencil case, a pair of sleeve buttons, and a brooch of no great value, were all. They were severally examined and appraised by old Joe, who chalked the sums he was disposed to give for each upon the wall, and added them up into a total when he found that there was nothing more to come.

"That's your account," said Joe, "and I wouldn't give another sixpence, if I was to be boiled for not doing it. Who's next?"

Mrs. Dilber was next. Sheets and towels, a little wearing apparel, two old-fashioned silver teaspoons, a pair of sugar tongs, and a few boots. Her account was stated on the wall in the same manner.

"I always give too much to ladies. It's a weakness of mine, and that's the way I ruin myself," said old Joe. "That's your account. If you asked me for another penny, and made it an open question, I'd repent of being so liberal, and knock off half-a-crown."

"And now undo *my* bundle, Joe," said the first woman.

Joe went down on his knees for the greater convenience of opening it, and, having unfastened a great many knots, dragged out a large heavy roll of some dark stuff.

"What do you call this?" said Joe. "Bed-curtains?"

"Ah!" returned the woman, laughing and leaning forward on her crossed arms. "Bed-curtains!"

"You don't mean to say you took 'em down, rings and all, with him lying there?" said Joe.

"Yes, I do," replied the woman. "Why not?"

"You were born to make your fortune," said Joe, "and you'll certainly do it."

"I certainly shan't hold my hand, when I can get anything in it by reaching it out, for the sake of such a man as he was, I promise you, Joe," returned the woman coolly. "Don't drop that oil upon the blankets, now."

"His blanket?" asked Joe.

"Whose else's do you think?" replied the woman. "He isn't likely to take cold without 'em, I dare say."

"I hope he didn't die of anything catching? Eh?" said old Joe, stopping in his work, and looking up.

"Don't you be afraid of that," returned the woman. "I an't so fond of his company that I'd loiter about him for such things, if he did. Ah! you may look through that shirt till your eyes ache, but you won't find a hole in it, nor a threadbare place. It's the best he had, and a fine one too. They'd have wasted it, if it hadn't been for me."

"What do you call wasting of it?" asked old Joe.

"Putting it on him to be buried in, to be sure," replied the woman, with a laugh. "Somebody was fool enough to do it, but I took it off again. If calico an't good enough for such a purpose, it isn't good enough for anything. It's quite as becoming to the body. He can't look uglier than he did in that one."

Scrooge listened to this dialogue in horror. As they sat grouped about their spoil, in the scanty light afforded by the old man's lamp, he viewed them with a detestation[13] and disgust which could hardly have been greater, though they had been obscene demons marketing the corpse itself.

"Ha, ha!" laughed the same woman when old Joe producing a flannel bag with money in it, told out their several gains upon the ground. "This is the end of it, you see! He frightened everyone away from him when he was alive, to profit us when he was dead! Ha, ha, ha!"

"Spirit!" said Scrooge, shuddering from head to foot. "I see, I see. The case of this unhappy man might be my own. My life tends that way now. Merciful heaven, what is this?"

He recoiled in terror, for the scene had changed, and now he almost touched a bed—a bare, uncurtained bed—on which, beneath a ragged sheet, there lay a something covered up, which, though it was dumb, announced itself in awful language.

The room was very dark, too dark to be observed with any accuracy, though Scrooge glanced round it in obedience to a secret impulse, anxious to know what kind of room it was. A pale light, rising in the outer air, fell straight upon the bed; and on it, plundered and bereft, unwatched, unwept, uncared for, was the body of this man.

Scrooge glanced toward the Phantom. Its steady hand was pointed to the head. The cover was so carelessly adjusted that the slightest raising of it, the motion of a finger upon Scrooge's part, would have disclosed the face. He thought of it, felt how easy it would be to do, and longed to do it; but he had no more power to withdraw the veil than

---

12. **plunder:** goods taken by force or robbed; loot.

13. **detestation** (dē′tes·tā′shən): hatred.

to dismiss the specter at his side.

Oh, cold, cold, rigid, dreadful Death, set up thine altar here, and dress it with such terrors as thou hast at thy command; for this is thy dominion![14] But of the loved, revered, and honored head thou canst not turn one hair to thy dread purposes, or make one feature odious. It is not that the hand is heavy, and will fall down when released; it is not that the heart and pulse are still; but that the hand was open, generous, and true; the heart brave, warm, and tender, and the pulse a man's. Strike, Shadow, strike! And see his good deeds springing from the wound, to sow the world with life immortal!

No voice pronounced these words in Scrooge's ears, and yet he heard them when he looked upon the bed. He thought, if this man could be raised up now, what would be his foremost thoughts? Avarice, hard dealing, griping cares? They have brought him to a rich end, truly!

He lay in the dark, empty house, with not a man, a woman, or a child to say he was kind to me in this or that, and for the memory of one kind word I will be kind to him. A cat was tearing at the door, and there was a sound of gnawing rats beneath the hearthstone. What *they* wanted in the room of death, and why they were so restless and disturbed, Scrooge did not dare to think.

"Spirit!" he said. "This is a fearful place. In leaving it, I shall not leave its lesson, trust me. Let us go!"

Still the Ghost pointed with an unmoved finger to the head.

"I understand you," Scrooge returned, "and I would do it if I could. But I have not the power, Spirit. I have not the power."

Again it seemed to look upon him.

"If there is any person in the town who feels emotion caused by this man's death," said Scrooge, quite agonized, "show that person to me, Spirit, I beseech you!"

The Phantom spread its dark robe before him for a moment, like a wing; and, withdrawing it, revealed a room by daylight, where a mother and her children were.

She was expecting someone, and with anxious eagerness; for she walked up and down the room, started at every sound, looked out from the window, glanced at the clock, tried, but in vain, to work with her needle, and could hardly bear the voices of her children in their play.

At length the long-expected knock was heard. She hurried to the door, and met her husband; a man whose face was careworn and depressed, though he was young. There was a remarkable expression in it now, a kind of serious delight of which he felt ashamed, and which he struggled to repress.

He sat down to the dinner that had been hoarding for him by the fire, and when she asked him faintly what news (which was not until after a long silence), he appeared embarrassed how to answer.

"Is it good," she said, "or bad?" to help him.

"Bad," he answered.

"We are quite ruined?"

"No. There is hope yet, Caroline."

"If *he* relents," she said, amazed, "there is! Nothing is past hope, if such a miracle has happened."

"He is past relenting," said her husband. "He is dead."

She was a mild and patient creature if her face spoke truth; but she was thankful in her soul to hear it, and she said so with clasped hands. She prayed forgiveness the next moment, and was sorry; but the first was the emotion of her heart.

"What the half-drunken woman, whom I told you of last night, said to me when I tried to see him and obtain a week's delay—and what I thought was a mere excuse to avoid me—turns out to have been quite true. He was not only very ill, but dying, then."

"To whom will our debt be transferred?"

"I don't know. But, before that time, we shall be ready with the money; and even though we were not, it would be bad fortune indeed to find so merciless a creditor[15] in his successor. We may sleep tonight with light hearts, Caroline!"

Yes. Soften it as they would, their hearts were lighter. The children's faces, hushed and clustered round to hear what they so little understood, were brighter; and it was a happier house for this man's death! The only emotion that the Ghost could show him, caused by the event, was one of pleasure.

"Let me see some tenderness connected with a death," said Scrooge; "or that dark chamber, Spirit, which we left just now, will be forever present to me."

The Ghost conducted him through several streets familiar to his feet; and as they went along, Scrooge looked here and there to find himself, but nowhere was he to be seen. They entered poor Bob Cratchit's house; the dwelling he had visited before; and found the mother and children seated round the fire.

Quiet. Very quiet. The noisy little Cratchits were as still as statues in one corner, and sat

---

14. **dominion** (də·min'yən): place of supreme authority or rule.

15. **creditor:** person to whom money is owed.

looking up at Peter, who had a book before him. The mother and her daughters were engaged in sewing. But surely they were very quiet!

" 'And he took a child, and set him in the midst of them.' "[16]

Where had Scrooge heard those words? He had not dreamed them. The boy must have read them out as he and the Spirit crossed the threshold. Why did he not go on?

The mother laid her work upon the table, and put her hand up to her face.

"The color hurts my eyes," she said.

The color? Ah, poor Tiny Tim!

"They're better now again," said Cratchit's wife. "It makes them weak by candlelight; and I wouldn't show weak eyes to your father when he comes home for the world. It must be near his time."

"Past it rather," Peter answered, shutting up his book. "But I think he has walked a little slower than he used, these few last evenings, mother."

They were very quiet again. At last she said, and in a steady, cheerful voice, that only faltered once:

"I have known him walk with—I have known him walk with Tiny Tim upon his shoulder very fast indeed."

"And so have I," cried Peter. "Often."

"And so have I," exclaimed another. So had all.

"But he was very light to carry," she resumed, intent upon her work, "and his father loved him so, that it was no trouble, no trouble. And there is your father at the door!"

She hurried out to meet him; and little Bob in his comforter—he had need of it, poor fellow—came in. His tea was ready for him on the hob, and they all tried who should help him to it most. Then the two young Cratchits got upon his knees, and laid, each child, a little cheek against his face, as if they said, "Don't mind it, father. Don't be grieved!"

Bob was very cheerful with them, and spoke pleasantly to all the family. He looked at the work upon the table, and praised the industry and speed of Mrs. Cratchit and the girls. They would be done long before Sunday, he said.

"Sunday! You went today, then, Robert?" said his wife.

"Yes, my dear," returned Bob. "I wish you could have gone. It would have done you good to see how green a place it is. But you'll see it often.

I promised him that I would walk there on a Sunday. My little, little child!" cried Bob. "My little child!"

He broke down all at once. He couldn't help it. If he could have helped it, he and his child would have been farther apart, perhaps, than they were.

He left the room, and went upstairs into the room above, which was lighted cheerfully, and hung with Christmas. There was a chair set close beside the child, and there were signs of someone having been there lately. Poor Bob sat down in it, and when he had thought a little and composed himself, he kissed the little face. He was reconciled to what had happened, and went down again quite happy.

They drew about the fire, and talked, the girls and mother working still. Bob told them of the extraordinary kindness of Mr. Scrooge's nephew, whom he had scarcely seen but once, and who, meeting him in the street that day, and seeing that he looked a little—"just a little down, you know," said Bob, inquired what had happened to distress him. "On which," said Bob, "for he is the pleasantest-spoken gentleman you ever heard, I told him. 'I am heartily sorry for it, Mr. Cratchit,' he said, 'and heartily sorry for your good wife.' By-the-by, how he ever knew *that* I don't know."

"Knew what, my dear?"

"Why, that you were a good wife," replied Bob.

"Everybody knows that," said Peter.

"Very well observed, my boy!" cried Bob. "I hope they do. 'Heartily sorry,' he said, 'for your good wife. If I can be of service to you in any way,' he said, giving me his card, 'that's where I live. Pray come to me.' Now, it wasn't," cried Bob, "for the sake of anything he might be able to do for us, so much as for his kind way, that this was quite delightful. It really seemed as if he had known our Tiny Tim, and felt with us."

"I'm sure he's a good soul!" said Mrs. Cratchit.

"You would be sure of it, my dear," returned Bob, "if you saw and spoke to him. I shouldn't be at all surprised—mark what I say!—if he got Peter a better situation."

"Only hear that, Peter," said Mrs. Cratchit.

"And then," cried one of the girls, "Peter will be keeping company with someone, and setting up for himself."

"Get along with you!" retorted Peter, grinning.

"It's just as likely as not," said Bob, "one of these days; though there's plenty of time for that, my dear. But, however and whenever we part from one another, I am sure we shall none of us forget poor Tiny Tim—shall we—or this first parting that there was among us?"

"Never, father!" cried they all.

---

16. " 'And . . . them' ": quotation from the Bible (Mark 9:36). Dickens indirectly compares Tiny Tim to the child Christ gives the twelve disciples.

"And I know," said Bob, "I know, my dears, that when we recollect how patient and how mild he was, although he was a little, little child, we shall not quarrel easily among ourselves, and forget poor Tiny Tim in doing it."

"No, never, father!" they all cried again.

"I am very happy," said little Bob, "I am very happy!"

Mrs. Cratchit kissed him, his daughters kissed him, the two young Cratchits kissed him, and Peter and himself shook hands. Spirit of Tiny Tim, thy childish essence was from God!

"Specter," said Scrooge, "something informs me that our parting moment is at hand. I know it but I know not how. Tell me what man that was whom we saw lying dead?"

The Ghost of Christmas Yet to Come conveyed him, as before—though at a different time, he thought: Indeed there seemed no order in these latter visions, save that they were in the Future—into the resorts of businessmen, but showed him not himself. Indeed, the Spirit did not stay for anything, but went straight on, as to the end just now desired, until besought by Scrooge to tarry[17] for a moment.

"This court," said Scrooge, "through which we hurry now, is where my place of occupation is, and has been for a length of time. I see the house. Let me behold what I shall be in days to come."

The Spirit stopped; the hand was pointed elsewhere.

"The house is yonder," Scrooge exclaimed. "Why do you point away?"

The inexorable[18] finger underwent no change.

Scrooge hastened to the window of his office, and looked in. It was an office still, but not his. The furniture was not the same, and the figure in the chair was not himself. The Phantom pointed as before.

He joined it once again, and, wondering why and whither he had gone, accompanied it until they reached an iron gate. He paused to look round before entering.

A churchyard. Here, then, the wretched man, whose name he had now to learn, lay underneath the ground. It was a worthy place. Walled in by houses; overrun by grass and weeds, the growth of vegetation's death, not life; choked up with too much burying; fat with repleted[19] appetite. A worthy place!

The Spirit stood among the graves, and pointed down to one. He advanced toward it trembling.

The Phantom was exactly as it had been, but he dreaded that he saw new meaning in its solemn shape.

"Before I draw nearer to that stone to which you point," said Scrooge, "answer me one question. Are these the shadows of the things that Will be, or are they shadows of the things that May be only?"

Still the Ghost pointed downward to the grave by which it stood.

"Men's courses will foreshadow certain ends, to which, if persevered in, they must lead," said Scrooge. "But if the courses be departed from, the ends will change. Say it is thus with what you show me!"

The Spirit was immovable as ever.

Scrooge crept toward it, trembling as he went; and, following the finger, read upon the stone of the neglected grave his own name, EBENEZER SCROOGE.

"Am *I* that man who lay upon the bed?" he cried upon his knees.

The finger pointed from the grave to him, and back again.

"No, Spirit! Oh no, no!"

The finger still was there.

"Spirit!" he cried, tightly clutching at its robe, "hear me! I am not the man I was. I will not be the man I must have been but for this intercourse.[20] Why show me this, if I am past all hope?"

For the first time the hand appeared to shake.

"Good Spirit," he pursued, as down upon the ground he fell before it, "your nature intercedes for me, and pities me. Assure me that I yet may change these shadows you have shown me by an altered life?"

The kind hand trembled.

"I will honor Christmas in my heart, and try to keep it all the year. I will live in the Past, the Present, and the Future. The Spirits of all Three shall strive within me. I will not shut out the lessons that they teach. Oh, tell me I may sponge away the writing on this stone!"

In his agony he caught the spectral hand. It sought to free itself, but he was strong in his entreaty, and detained it. The Spirit stronger yet, repulsed him.

Holding up his hands in a last prayer to have his fate reversed, he saw an alteration in the Phantom's hood and dress. It shrunk, collapsed, and dwindled down into a bedpost.

---

17. **tarry:** wait.
18. **inexorable** (in·ek′sə·rə·b'l): inflexible; relentless.
19. **repleted:** well-filled.

20. **intercourse:** here, Scrooge's experiences with the three spirits.

Responding to the Novel

Analyzing Stave Four

Identifying Facts

1. Describe the Ghost of Christmas Yet to Come. What aspect of the Ghost's behavior scares Scrooge the most?
2. Tell what Scrooge overhears the merchants at the Exchange discussing. Who in particular does Scrooge hope to see there?
3. List the four people at the junk dealer's shop. What are three of them trying to sell? Where and from whom did they get the goods? Tell how Scrooge reacts to what he witnesses at the shop.
4. Explain why the young man and his wife Caroline feel relieved that the unnamed businessman has died. What is Scrooge's reaction to this scene?
5. List three details that alert you to the fact that Tiny Tim has died. In what ways has Scrooge's nephew shown ''extraordinary kindness'' to the Cratchit family?

6. What does Scrooge finally discover in the churchyard? What assurance does he beg the Ghost to give him? What resolution does Scrooge make?

Interpreting Meanings

7. Readers usually realize the dead business-man's identity before Scrooge does. This kind of contrast between the reader's knowledge and a character's is called **dramatic irony.** Find at least three clues before the scene in the churchyard that alert you to the dead man's identity. Explain the effect this dramatic irony had as you read Stave Four.
8. The **climax** of a story is the point when the main character's conflict reaches an intense turning point. Identify the climax of *A Christmas Carol.* What is the result, or resolution, of Scrooge's conflict?
9. At the end of Stave Four, Scrooge pleads to learn whether he can alter the future that the Ghost has shown him. The Ghost does not answer in words, but gives a sign. Identify this sign, and explain what you think it means.
10. In this stave you encountered a slang meaning for the word *screw.* Do you think Dickens had this meaning in mind when he chose a name for the main character of *A Christmas Carol?*

Writing About Stave Four

A Creative Response

1. **Anticipating the Novel's Conclusion.** At the end of Stave Four, Scrooge resolves to honor Christmas all the year and to "live in the Past, the Present, and the Future." Considering the previous staves, list three or four specific things Scrooge could do on Christmas Day to put his resolutions into action. Then write a paragraph Scrooge might have composed, in which he expresses his plans for Christmas. Write from the first-person point of view, using the pronoun *I.*

A Critical Response

2. **Analyzing a Meaningful Passage.** The following passage appears early in Stave Four.

"Ghost of the Future!" [Scrooge] exclaimed, "I fear you more than any specter I have seen. But as I know your purpose is to do me good, and as I hope to live to be another man from what I was, I am prepared to bear your company, and do it with a thankful heart. Will you not speak to me?"

By studying this passage you can gather some of your thoughts about *A Christmas Carol.* Answer the following questions about the passage in a short paragraph each.

a. Why does Scrooge fear the Ghost of the Future more than any other Ghost?
b. Why does Scrooge think the Ghost's purpose is to do him good?
c. Why is Scrooge unsure of what will occur in the future?
d. Why does the Ghost of the Future not speak to Scrooge?

Analyzing Language and Vocabulary

Synonyms

One way Dickens tries to keep you interested in the story is by using synonyms. **Synonyms** are words whose meanings are similar but not exactly the same. Instead of constantly repeating an important word, such as *ghost,* Dickens uses many synonyms for the word that have different shades of meaning. This adds variety to the text.

1. Look up the following words in a dictionary. Which synonyms have the most general meaning? Which have frightening **connotations,** or associations, in addition to their general meaning?

ghost	specter	apparition
phantom	goblin	supernatural visitor
shade	spirit	unearthly visitor

2. In Stave One, Scrooge's nephew tells him not to be so *dismal* and *morose.* Later, Scrooge spends the evening by himself. Locate the paragraph on page 624 that begins, "Scrooge took his melancholy dinner. . . ." Find five or six words in the paragraph that have the same general meaning as *dismal* and *morose.* Explain what these synonyms add to your understanding of Scrooge and his way of life.
3. Locate the description of the Ghost of Christmas Present in the paragraph on page 643 beginning, "Scrooge reverently did so." List five words from the paragraph that are synonyms for *happy.* Considering what you know about Scrooge's house, explain why this Ghost's characteristics are a startling contrast.

Stave Five:
The End of It

Yes! and the bedpost was his own. The bed was his own, the room was his own. Best and happiest of all, the Time before him was his own, to make amends in!

"I will live in the Past, the Present, and the Future!" Scrooge repeated as he scrambled out of bed. "The Spirits of all Three shall strive within me. O Jacob Marley! Heaven and the Christmas Time be praised for this! I say it on my knees, old Jacob; on my knees!"

He was so fluttered and so glowing with his good intentions, that his broken voice would scarcely answer to his call. He had been sobbing violently in his conflict with the Spirit, and his face was wet with tears.

"They are not torn down," cried Scrooge, folding one of his bed-curtains in his arms. "They are not torn down, rings and all. They are here—I am here—the shadows of the things that would have been may be dispelled. They will be. I know they will!"

His hands were busy with his garments all this time: turning them inside out, putting them on upside down, tearing them, mislaying them, making them parties to every kind of extravagance.

"I don't know what to do!" cried Scrooge, laughing and crying in the same breath, and making a perfect Laocoön[1] of himself with his stockings. "I am as light as a feather, I am as happy as an angel, I am as merry as a schoolboy, I am as giddy as a drunken man. A merry Christmas to everybody! A happy New Year to all the world! Hallo here! Whoop! Hallo!"

He had frisked into the sitting room, and was now standing there, perfectly winded.

"There's the saucepan that the gruel was in!" cried Scrooge, starting off again, and going round the fireplace. "There's the door by which the Ghost of Jacob Marley entered! There's the corner where the Ghost of Christmas Present sat! There's the window where I saw the wandering Spirits! It's all right, it's all true, it all happened. Ha, ha, ha!"

Really, for a man who had been out of practice for so many years, it was a splendid laugh, a most illustrious laugh. The father of a long, long line of brilliant laughs!

"I don't know what day of the month it is," said Scrooge. "I don't know how long I have been among the Spirits. I don't know anything. I'm quite a baby. Never mind. I don't care. I'd rather be a baby. Hallo! Whoop! Hallo here!"

He was checked up in his transports[2] by the churches ringing out the lustiest peals he had ever heard. Clash, clash, hammer; ding, dong, bell! Bell, dong, ding; hammer, clash, clash! Oh, glorious, glorious!

Running to the window, he opened it, and put out his head. No fog, no mist; clear, bright, jovial, stirring, cold; cold, piping for the blood to dance to; golden sunlight; heavenly sky; sweet fresh air; merry bells. Oh, glorious! Glorious!

"What's today?" cried Scrooge, calling downward to a boy in Sunday clothes, who perhaps had loitered in to look about him.

"Eh?" returned the boy with all his might of wonder.

"What's today, my fine fellow?" said Scrooge.

"Today!" replied the boy. "Why, Christmas Day."

"It's Christmas Day!" said Scrooge to himself. "I haven't missed it. The Spirits have done it all in one night. They can do anything they like. Of course they can. Of course they can. Hallo, my fine fellow!"

"Hallo!" returned the boy.

"Do you know the poulterer's in the next street but one, at the corner?" Scrooge inquired.

"I should hope I did," replied the lad.

"An intelligent boy!" said Scrooge. "A remarkable boy! Do you know whether they've sold the prize turkey that was hanging up there? Not the little prize turkey: the big one?"

"What! the one as big as me?" returned the boy.

"What a delightful boy!" said Scrooge. "It's a pleasure to talk to him. Yes, my buck!"

"It's hanging there now," replied the boy.

"Is it?" said Scrooge. "Go and buy it."

"Walk-er!"[3] exclaimed the boy.

"No, no," said Scrooge. "I am in earnest. Go and buy it, and tell 'em to bring it here, that I may give them the directions where to take it. Come back with the man, and I'll give you a shilling. Come back with him in less than five minutes, and I'll give you half-a-crown!"

The boy was off like a shot. He must have had a steady hand at a trigger who could have got a shot off half as fast.

---

1. **Laocoön** (lā·äk′ə·wän′): priest of Troy in ancient Asia Minor who, with his two sons, was destroyed by two huge sea serpents.

2. **checked in his transports:** halted in his ecstasy.
3. **"Walk-er!":** slang word expressing disbelief, equivalent to "You're kidding!"

"I'll send it to Bob Cratchit's," whispered Scrooge, rubbing his hands, and splitting with a laugh. "He shan't know who sends it. It's twice the size of Tiny Tim. Joe Miller[4] never made such a joke as sending it to Bob's will be!"

The hand in which he wrote the address was not a steady one; but write it he did, somehow, and went downstairs to open the street door, ready for the coming of the poulterer's man. As he stood there, waiting his arrival, the knocker caught his eye.

"I shall love it as long as I live!" cried Scrooge, patting it with his hand. "I scarcely ever looked at it before. What an honest expression it has in its face! It's a wonderful knocker! Here's the turkey. Hallo! Whoop! How are you! Merry Christmas!"

It *was* a turkey! He never could have stood upon his legs, that bird. He would have snapped 'em short off in a minute, like sticks of sealing wax.

"Why, it's impossible to carry that to Camden Town," said Scrooge. "You must have a cab."

The chuckle with which he said this, and the chuckle with which he paid for the turkey, and the chuckle with which he paid for the cab, and the chuckle with which he recompensed[5] the boy, were only to be exceeded by the chuckle with which he sat down breathless in his chair again, and chuckled till he cried.

Shaving was not an easy task, for his hand continued to shake very much; and shaving requires attention, even when you don't dance while you are at it. But if he had cut the end of his nose off, he would have put a piece of sticking-plaster[6] over it, and been quiet satisfied.

He dressed himself "all in his best," and at last got out into the streets. The people were by this time pouring forth, as he had seen them with the Ghost of Christmas Present; and, walking with his hands behind him, Scrooge regarded everyone with a delighted smile. He looked so irresistibly pleasant, in a word, that three or four good-humored fellows said, "Good morning, sir! A merry Christmas to you!" And Scrooge said often afterwards that, of all the blithe sounds he had ever heard, those were the blithest in his ears.

He had not gone far when, coming on toward him, he beheld the portly gentleman who had walked into his countinghouse the day before, and said, "Scrooge and Marley's, I believe?" It sent a pang across his heart to think how this old gen-tleman would look upon him when they met; but he knew what path lay straight before him, and he took it.

"My dear sir," said Scrooge, quickening his pace, and taking the old gentleman by both his hands, "how do you do? I hope you succeeded yesterday. It was very kind of you. A merry Christmas to you, sir!"

"Mr. Scrooge?"

"Yes," said Scrooge. "That is my name, and I fear it may not be pleasant to you. Allow me to ask your pardon. And will you have the good-ness—" Here Scrooge whispered in his ear.

"Lord bless me!" cried the gentleman, as if his breath were taken away. "My dear Mr. Scrooge, are you serious?"

"If you please," said Scrooge. "Not a farthing[7] less. A great many back payments are included in it, I assure you. Will you do me that favor?"

"My dear sir," said the other, shaking hands with him, "I don't know what to say to such munifi—"[8]

"Don't say anything, please," retorted Scrooge. "Come and see me. Will you come and see me?"

"I will!" cried the old gentleman. And it was clear he meant to do it.

"Thankee," said Scrooge. "I am much obliged to you. I thank you fifty times. Bless you!"

He went to church, and walked about the streets, and watched the people hurry to and fro, and patted the children on the head, and questioned beggars, and looked down into the kitchens of houses, and up to the windows; and found that everything could yield him pleasure. He had never dreamed that any walk—that anything—could give him so much happiness. In the afternoon he turned his steps toward his nephew's house.

He passed the door a dozen times before he had the courage to go up and knock. But he made a dash and did it.

"Is your master at home, my dear?" said Scrooge to the girl. "Nice girl! Very."

"Yes, sir."

"Where is he, my love?" said Scrooge.

"He's in the dining room, sir, along with mistress. I'll show you upstairs, if you please."

"Thankee. He knows me," said Scrooge, with his hand already on the dining room lock. "I'll go in here, my dear."

He turned it gently, and sidled his face in round the door. They were looking at the table (which was spread out in great array); for these young

---

4. **Joe Miller:** famous English comedian.
5. **recompensed** (rek′əm·pens′′d): rewarded.
6. **sticking-plaster:** adhesive bandage.

7. **farthing:** former British coin equal to one fourth of a penny.
8. The uncompleted word is *munificence* (myo͞o·nif′ə·sens), which means great generosity.

housekeepers are always nervous on such points, and like to see that everything is right.

"Fred!" said Scrooge.

Dear heart alive, how his niece by marriage started! Scrooge had forgotten, for the moment, about her sitting in the corner with the footstool, or he wouldn't have done it on any account.

"Why, bless my soul!" cried Fred, "who's that?"

"It's I. Your uncle Scrooge. I have come to dinner. Will you let me in, Fred?"

Let him in! It is a mercy he didn't shake his arm off. He was at home in five minutes. Nothing could be heartier. His niece looked just the same.

So did Topper when *he* came. So did the plump sister when *she* came. So did everyone when *they* came. Wonderful party, wonderful games, won-derful unanimity,[9] won-der-ful happiness!

But he was early at the office next morning. Oh, he was early there! If he could only be there first, and catch Bob Cratchit coming late! That was the thing he had set his heart upon.

And he did it; yes, he did! The clock struck nine. No Bob. A quarter past. No Bob. He was full eighteen minutes and a half behind his time.

---

9. **unanimity** (yōō·nə·nim′ə·tē): complete agreement.

Scrooge sat with his door wide open, that he might see him come into the tank.

His hat was off before he opened the door; his comforter too. He was on his stool in a jiffy, driving away with his pen, as if he were trying to overtake nine o'clock.

"Hallo!" growled Scrooge in his accustomed voice as near as he could feign it. "What do you mean by coming here at this time of day?"

"I am very sorry, sir," said Bob. "I *am* behind my time."

"You are!" repeated Scrooge. "Yes, I think you are. Step this way, sir, if you please."

"It's only once a year, sir," pleaded Bob, appearing from the tank. "It shall not be repeated. I was making rather merry yesterday, sir."

"Now, I'll tell you what, my friend," said Scrooge. "I am not going to stand this sort of thing any longer. And therefore," he continued, leaping from his stool, and giving Bob such a dig in the waistcoat that he staggered back into the tank again—"and therefore I am about to raise your salary!"

Bob trembled, and got a little nearer to the ruler. He had a momentary idea of knocking Scrooge down with it, holding him, and calling to the people in the court for help and a strait-waistcoat.[10]

"A merry Christmas, Bob!" said Scrooge, with an earnestness that could not be mistaken, as he clapped him on the back. "A merrier Christmas, Bob, my good fellow, than I have given you for many a year! I'll raise your salary, and endeavor to assist your struggling family, and we will discuss your affairs this very afternoon, over a Christmas bowl of smoking bishop,[11] Bob! Make up the fires and buy another coal-scuttle before you dot another i, Bob Cratchit!"

Scrooge was better than his word. He did it all, and infinitely more; and to Tiny Tim, who did *not* die, he was a second father. He became as good a friend, as good a master, and as good a man as the good old City knew, or any other good old city, town, or borough in the good old world. Some people laughed to see the alteration in him, but he let them laugh, and little heeded them; for he was wise enough to know that nothing ever happened on this globe, for good, at which some people did not have their fill of laughter in the outset; and knowing that such as these would be blind anyway, he thought it quite as well that they should wrinkle up their eyes in grins as have the malady in less attractive forms. His own heart laughed, and that was quite enough for him.

He had not further intercourse with Spirits, but lived upon the Total-Abstinence Principle[12] ever afterward; and it was always said of him that he knew how to keep Christmas well, if any man alive possessed the knowledge. May that be truly said of us, and all of us! And so, as Tiny Tim observed, God bless Us, Every One!

---

10. **strait-waistcoat:** strait-jacket.

11. **bishop:** hot, spiced port wine.
12. **Total-Abstinence** (ab'stə·nəns) **Principle:** completely giving up alcoholic spirits. Dickens is punning here—he means ghostly "spirits."

Responding to the Novel

Analyzing Stave Five

Identifying Facts

1. What does Scrooge conclude when he sees that his bed-curtains have not been torn down? What day is it when he wakes up?
2. What errand does Scrooge hire a boy to do?
3. Scrooge meets the "portly gentleman" who visited his office in Stave One. In your own words, explain what Scrooge tells this man.
4. Tell how Scrooge is welcomed at his nephew's house. What four wonderful things does Scrooge enjoy there?
5. What joke does Scrooge play on Bob Cratchit? What is Bob's first reaction to the new Scrooge? What does Scrooge do to make up for how he has treated Bob in the past?
6. Explain how Scrooge's relationship with the Cratchit family changes. Tell what happens to Tiny Tim.

Interpreting Meanings

7. In Stave One, the **atmosphere** in Scrooge's house is dark and gloomy. What is the atmosphere like in the house in Stave Five? Include two or three details from the stave to support your analysis.

8. At the end of Stave Five, Scrooge does not mind that some people laugh at him for being generous. What does this attitude tell you about how deep his change of heart is?

Applying Meanings

9. Scrooge's personality changes a lot over the course of *A Christmas Carol.* Do you think many people in real life undergo such great changes after enduring very emotional experiences? Or do people usually stay pretty much the same?

Analyzing the Novel as a Whole

Interpreting Meanings

1. Summarize the plot of *A Christmas Carol.* Try to be as concise as possible, using no more than fifteen sentences. Be sure to answer the following questions in your summary.

   a. What is the **basic situation** at the opening of the novel?

   b. What is Scrooge's main **external conflict,** or conflict with other characters?

   c. What is Scrooge's main **internal conflict,** or conflict between opposing feelings and emotions in his own mind?

   d. What **complications** arise as the story unfolds?

   e. What is the **climax** of the story, its most exciting point and the moment where the outcome is decided?

   f. What is the **resolution** of the story, that is, how are the novel's problems solved and the story brought to an end?

2. List what you consider the novel's ten most important characters. Then describe the distinctive traits of each in two or three sentences per character.

3. In a novel, a character can remain pretty much the same or it can change over the course of the story. Which of the characters in *A Christmas Carol* is most clearly a **dynamic character**—one who changes over the course of the novel? Which are some of the **static characters**—characters

Scrooge extinguishes the first of the Three Spirits. Etching by John Leech for an 1843 edition of *A Christmas Carol.*

who stay essentially the same throughout the novel? Quote passages from the text in explaining your answer.

4. A good novel creates a special world all its own. This world may resemble the real world, but important features are made up. When you discuss the novel, you have to deal with the made-up world, not the real world. Based on the world Dickens creates in *A Christmas Carol,* do you think Scrooge really traveled with the Ghosts of Christmas Past, Present, and Future? Or do you think it possible that Scrooge dreamed everything while he slept? Is there perhaps another explanation? Quote details from the novel to support your interpretation.

5. Dickens is noted for his ability to describe a **setting,** the time and place in which the action of a story takes place. *A Christmas Carol* takes place in several settings. Which of these settings left the deepest impression on you? Identify one or more such settings and tell why it affected you more than the other settings.

6. Were you surprised by the ending of *A Christmas Carol?* If you were, explain why you expected a different ending. If you were not surprised, identify and discuss the elements of the story that lead you to expect the ending.

Writing About the Novel

A Creative Response

1. **Writing a Letter.** Choose a character from Scrooge's present, such as Bob Cratchit, Fred, the portly gentleman collecting money for the poor, or the boy Scrooge hires on Christmas Day. Pretend you are this character, and write a letter of one or two paragraphs. Address it to a friend or relative who has not yet met the "new" Scrooge. Describe the changes you have seen with your own eyes. Use specific details to show your friend or relative that Scrooge really is a different man.

A Critical Response

2. **Identifying a Novel's Central Theme.** The **central theme** is the main idea expressed in a literary work. A novel may have several minor themes in addition to the central theme. Themes can be about almost any subject. Usually, however, they make a statement about an important aspect of human life—such as love, happiness, work, and death. A theme typically is not stated directly. The reader must think about all elements of the literary work and then make an educated guess in determining its theme or themes. In a composition of two or three paragraphs, state what you believe is the central theme of *A Christmas Carol.* Support your opinion by quoting passages from several staves.

Analyzing Language and Vocabulary

Figurative Language in Prose

Dickens uses two figures of speech that are commonly found in poetry—similes and metaphors. Each of these figures of speech makes a comparison between basically dissimilar things. **Similes** make a comparison by using connective words such as *like* or *as:* Scrooge's "mind flew back again, like a strong spring released." **Metaphors** often imply the comparison rather than use a connecting word: Scrooge "thought such another creature . . . might have called him father, and been a springtime in the haggard winter of his life." Such comparisons make Dickens's prose lively and colorful. They stir the reader's imagination to see ordinary things in startlingly fresh ways.

1. Identify each of the following quotations from *A Christmas Carol* as either a simile or a metaphor. Then explain what things are being compared.

    a. "Marley's face . . . had a dismal light about it, like a bad lobster in a dark cellar."
    b. Scrooge "was endeavoring to pierce the darkness with his ferret eyes. . . ."
    c. "In came a fiddler with a music book, and went up to the lofty desk, . . . and tuned like fifty stomachaches."
    d. ". . . you [Scrooge] are more worthless and less fit to live than millions like this poor man's child. O God! to hear the insect on the leaf pronouncing on the too much life among his hungry brothers in the dust!"
    e. "Alleys and archways, like so many cesspools, disgorged their offenses of smell and dirt. . . ."

2. Identify at least five other similes or metaphors in *A Christmas Carol.*

Scrooge and Bob Cratchit. Etching by John Leech for an 1843 edition of *A Christmas Carol.*

The Pearl

The Pearl is a morality set to music.

—Joseph Fontenrose

On the surface, John Steinbeck's novel *The Pearl* is a rather simple, straightforward tale of what happens to an Indian family in Mexico after Kino, the husband, finds a very valuable pearl. As you poke beneath the surface, however, you'll find a rich assortment of subjects to think about. Some of the subjects will connect directly with your own life. Some will be open to a variety of interpretations, and you'll enjoy the excitement of discussing them with persons who hold different interpretations.

The Setting of the Novel

At the time of the story, around 1900, villages like the one in *The Pearl* still reflected the social structure set up at the time of the Spanish *conquistadores*. These were the explorers who had conquered the Mexican Indians about 400 years earlier.

At the top of village society were people of Spanish background. They included large landowners, priests and other officials of the Roman Catholic church, and higher military officers. In the middle were people of mixed Spanish and Indian background. At the very bottom were the Indians, *los Indios,* the descendants of the original inhabitants of the area. Most Indians lived pretty much the way their ancestors had. They were very attached to their villages.

The religion of the Indians was a mixture of Roman Catholicism and traditional beliefs. In *The Pearl,* the word *God* refers to Christian beliefs; the word *gods* refers to the Indians' traditional beliefs. As you read, note how Kino goes back and forth in thinking of "God" and "the gods."

Thinking About the Novel's Themes

Most novels have two or more **themes.** Some themes are expressed openly. But usually you'll have to think about a variety of elements in the story and then make an **inference,** or educated guess, about how they fit together to express an idea about life. You'll then have to check to see whether anything else in the novel contradicts your inference. If you find something contradictory, you may need to restate the theme—or even scrap it entirely. Or you may decide the contradiction is so minor that the theme holds true.

A theme says something about a subject. The following questions are about subjects that readers have found in *The Pearl.*

1. What makes some people act in evil ways?
2. Can we control our lives, or are our lives determined by luck and by other forces we cannot control?
3. Can good luck bring happiness?

Indian Woman Holding Baby by Diego Rivera (1927). Pencil.

Worcester Art Museum, Worcester, Massachusetts.

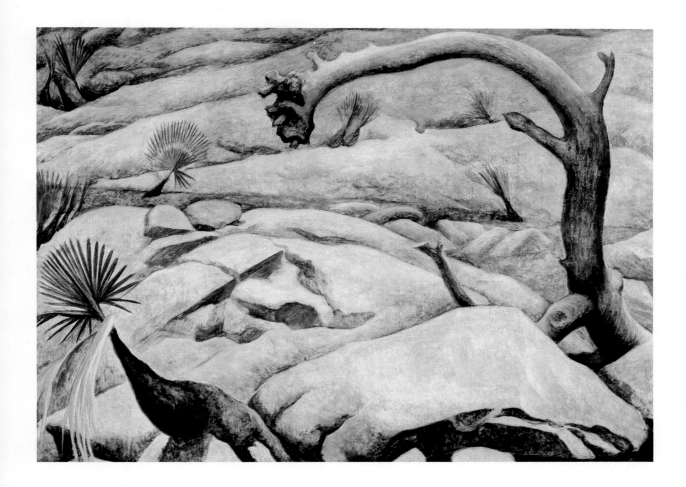

John Steinbeck (1902–1968)

John Steinbeck was born in 1902 in Salinas, California. Several of his books deal with the fish canneries and farms of the area. He attended Stanford University, but left in 1925 without earning a degree.

Steinbeck won a wide following after the publication in 1937 of *Of Mice and Men* and *The Red Pony*. Perhaps his greatest novel, *The Grapes of Wrath,* appeared in 1939. It tells the moving story of the Joad family, forced to leave Oklahoma and travel to California in search of work during the Great Depression of the 1930's.

The Pearl was published in book form in 1947. Steinbeck's later works include the novel *East of Eden* (1952) and *Travels with Charley in Search of America* (1962), a nonfiction account.

Steinbeck received many honors before his death in 1968. In accepting the 1962 Nobel Prize for literature, he said,

> The writer is delegated to declare and to celebrate man's proven capacity for greatness of heart and spirit—for gallantry in defeat, for courage, compassion, and love. In the endless war against weakness and despair, these are the bright rally flags of hope and of emulation.

Tecalpexco by Diego Rivera (1937). Tempera on board.

Amherst College, Mead Art Museum, Amherst, Massachusetts. Bequest of Mrs. Phillip Youtz, 1975.

THE PEARL

John Steinbeck

In the town they tell the story of the great pearl—how it was found and how it was lost again. They tell of Kino, the fisherman, and of his wife, Juana, and of the baby, Coyotito. And because the story has been told so often, it has taken root in every man's mind. And, as with all retold tales that are in people's hearts, there are only good and bad things and black and white things and good and evil things and no in-between anywhere.

If this story is a parable, perhaps everyone takes his own meaning from it and reads his own life into it. In any case, they say in the town that . . .

I

Kino awakened in the near dark. The stars still shone and the day had drawn only a pale wash of light in the lower sky to the east. The roosters had been crowing for some time, and the early pigs were already beginning their ceaseless turning of twigs and bits of wood to see whether anything to eat had been overlooked. Outside the brush house in the tuna clump, a covey of little birds chittered and flurried with their wings.

Kino's eyes opened, and he looked first at the lightening square which was the door and then he looked at the hanging box where Coyotito slept. And last he turned his head to Juana, his wife, who lay beside him on the mat, her blue head shawl over her nose and over her breasts and around the small of her back. Juana's eyes were open too. Kino could never remember seeing them closed when he awakened. Her dark eyes made little reflected stars. She was looking at him as she was always looking at him when he awakened.

Kino heard the little splash of morning waves on the beach. It was very good—Kino closed his eyes again to listen to his music. Perhaps he alone did this and perhaps all of his people did it. His people had once been great makers of songs so that everything they saw or thought or did or

heard became a song. That was very long ago. The songs remained; Kino knew them, but no new songs were added. That does not mean that there were no personal songs. In Kino's head there was a song now, clear and soft, and if he had been able to speak it, he would have called it the Song of the Family.

His blanket was over his nose to protect him from the dank air. His eyes flicked to a rustle beside him. It was Juana arising, almost soundlessly. On her hard bare feet she went to the hanging box where Coyotito slept, and she leaned over and said a little reassuring word. Coyotito looked up for a moment and closed his eyes and slept again.

Juana went to the fire pit and uncovered a coal and fanned it alive while she broke little pieces of brush over it.

Now Kino got up and wrapped his blanket about his head and nose and shoulders. He slipped his feet into his sandals and went outside to watch the dawn.

Outside the door he squatted down and gathered the blanket ends about his knees. He saw the specks of Gulf clouds flame high in the air. And a goat came near and sniffed at him and stared with its cold yellow eyes. Behind him Juana's fire leaped into flame and threw spears of light through the chinks of the brush-house wall and threw a wavering square of light out the door. A late moth blustered in to find the fire. The Song of the Family came now from behind Kino. And the rhythm of the family song was the grinding stone where Juana worked the corn for the morning cakes.

The dawn came quickly now, a wash, a glow, a lightness, and then an explosion of fire as the sun arose out of the Gulf. Kino looked down to cover his eyes from the glare. He could hear the pat of the corncakes in the house and the rich smell of them on the cooking plate. The ants were busy on the ground, big black ones with shiny bodies, and little dusty quick ants. Kino watched with the detachment of God while a dusty ant frantically tried to escape the sand trap an ant lion had dug for him. A thin, timid dog came close and, at a soft word from Kino, curled up, arranged its tail neatly over its feet, and laid its chin delicately on the pile. It was a black dog with yellow-gold spots where its eyebrows should have been. It was a morning like other mornings and yet perfect among mornings.

Kino heard the creak of the rope when Juana took Coyotito out of his hanging box and cleaned him and hammocked him in her shawl in a loop that placed him close to her breast. Kino could see these things without looking at them. Juana

sang softly an ancient song that had only three notes and yet endless variety of interval. And this was part of the family song too. It was all part. Sometimes it rose to an aching chord that caught the throat, saying this is safety, this is warmth, this is the *Whole*.

Across the brush fence were other brush houses, and the smoke came from them too, and the sound of breakfast, but those were other songs, their pigs were other pigs, their wives were not Juana. Kino was young and strong and his black hair hung over his brown forehead. His eyes were warm and fierce and bright and his mustache was thin and coarse. He lowered his blanket from his nose now, for the dark poisonous air was gone and the yellow sunlight fell on the house. Near the brush fence two roosters bowed and feinted at each other with squared wings and neck feathers ruffled out. It would be a clumsy fight. They were not game chickens. Kino watched them for a moment, and then his eyes went up to a flight of wild doves twinkling inland to the hills. The world was awake now, and Kino arose and went into his brush house.

As he came through the door Juana stood up from the glowing fire pit. She put Coyotito back in his hanging box and then she combed her black hair and braided it in two braids and tied the ends with thin green ribbon. Kino squatted by the fire pit and rolled a hot corncake and dipped it in sauce and ate it. And he drank a little pulque[1] and that was breakfast. That was the only breakfast he had ever known outside of feast days and one incredible fiesta on cookies that had nearly killed him. When Kino had finished, Juana came back to the fire and ate her breakfast. They had spoken once, but there is not need for speech if it is only a habit anyway. Kino sighed with satisfaction—and that was conversation.

The sun was warming the brush house, breaking through its crevices in long streaks. And one of the streaks fell on the hanging box where Coyotito lay, and on the ropes that held it.

It was a tiny movement that drew their eyes to the hanging box. Kino and Juana froze in their positions. Down the rope that hung the baby's box from the roof support a scorpion moved slowly. His stinging tail was straight out behind him, but he could whip it up in a flash of time.

Kino's breath whistled in his nostrils and he opened his mouth to stop it. And then the startled look was gone from him and the rigidity from his body. In his mind a new song had come, the Song

---

1. **pulque** (pōōl′kē): fermented drink made from the juice of the agave plant.

of Evil, the music of the enemy, of any foe of the family, a savage, secret, dangerous melody, and underneath, the Song of the Family cried plaintively.

The scorpion moved delicately down the rope toward the box. Under her breath Juana repeated an ancient magic to guard against such evil, and on top of that she muttered a Hail Mary between clenched teeth. But Kino was in motion. His body glided quickly across the room, noiselessly and smoothly. His hands were in front of him, palms down, and his eyes were on the scorpion. Beneath it in the hanging box Coyotito laughed and reached up his hand toward it. It sensed danger when Kino was almost within reach of it. It stopped, and its tail rose up over its back in little jerks and the curved thorn on the tail's end glistened.

Kino stood perfectly still. He could hear Juana whispering the old magic again, and he could hear the evil music of the enemy. He could not move until the scorpion moved, and it felt for the source of the death that was coming to it. Kino's hand went forward very slowly, very smoothly. The thorned tail jerked upright. And at that moment the laughing Coyotito shook the rope and the scorpion fell.

Kino's hand leaped to catch it, but it fell past his fingers, fell on the baby's shoulder, landed and struck. Then, snarling, Kino had it, had it in his fingers, rubbing it to a paste in his hands. He threw it down and beat it into the earth floor with his fist, and Coyotito screamed with pain in his box. But Kino beat and stamped the enemy until it was only a fragment and a moist place in the dirt. His teeth were bared and fury flared in his eyes and the Song of the Enemy roared in his ears.

But Juana had the baby in her arms now. She found the puncture with redness starting from it already. She put her lips down over the puncture and sucked hard and spat and sucked again while Coyotito screamed.

Kino hovered; he was helpless, he was in the way.

The screams of the baby brought the neighbors. Out of their brush houses they poured—Kino's brother Juan Tomás and his fat wife Apolonia and their four children crowded in the door and blocked the entrance, while behind them others tried to look in, and one small boy crawled among legs to have a look. And those in front passed the word back to those behind—"Scorpion. The baby has been stung."

Juana stopped sucking the puncture for a moment. The little hole was slightly enlarged and its edges whitened from the sucking, but the red swelling extended further around it in a hard lymphatic[2] mound. And all of these people knew about the scorpion. An adult might be very ill from the sting, but a baby could easily die from the poison. First, they knew, would come swelling and fever and tightened throat, and then cramps in the stomach, and then Coyotito might die if enough of the poison had gone in. But the stinging pain of the bite was going away. Coyotito's screams turned to moans.

Kino had wondered often at the iron in his patient, fragile wife. She, who was obedient and respectful and cheerful and patient, she could arch her back in child pain with hardly a cry. She could stand fatigue and hunger almost better than Kino himself. In the canoe she was like a strong man. And now she did a most surprising thing.

"The doctor," she said. "Go to get the doctor."

The word was passed out among the neighbors where they stood close packed in the little yard behind the brush fence. And they repeated among themselves, "Juana wants the doctor." A wonderful thing, a memorable thing, to want the doctor. To get him would be a remarkable thing. The doctor never came to the cluster of brush houses. Why should he, when he had more than he could do to take care of the rich people who lived in the stone and plaster houses of the town.

"He would not come," the people in the yard said.

"He would not come," the people in the door said, and the thought got into Kino.

"The doctor would not come," Kino said to Juana.

She looked up at him, her eyes as cold as the eyes of a lioness. This was Juana's first baby—this was nearly everything there was in Juana's world. And Kino saw her determination and the music of the family sounded in his head with a steely tone.

"Then we will go to him," Juana said, and with one hand she arranged her dark blue shawl over her head and made of one end of it a sling to hold the moaning baby and made of the other end of it a shade over his eyes to protect him from the light. The people in the door pushed against those behind to let her through. Kino followed her. They went out of the gate to the rutted path and the neighbors followed them.

The thing had become a neighborhood affair. They made a quick soft-footed procession into the center of the town, first Juana and Kino, and behind them Juan Tomás and Apolonia, her big

---

2. **lymphatic** (lim·fat′ik): containing lymph, a clear, yellowish body fluid given off by inflamed body tissues.

stomach jiggling with the strenuous pace, then all the neighbors with the children trotting on the flanks. And the yellow sun threw their black shadows ahead of them so that they walked on their own shadows.

They came to the place where the brush houses stopped and the city of stone and plaster began, the city of harsh outer walls and inner cool gardens where a little water played and the bougainvillea³ crusted the walls with purple and brick-red and white. They heard from the secret gardens the singing of caged birds and heard the splash of cooling water on hot flagstones. The procession crossed the blinding plaza and passed in front of the church. It had grown now, and on the outskirts the hurrying newcomers were being softly informed how the baby had been stung by a scorpion, how the father and mother were taking it to the doctor.

And the newcomers, particularly the beggars from the front of the church who were great experts in financial analysis, looked quickly at Juana's old blue skirt, saw the tears in her shawl, appraised the green ribbon on her braids, read the age of Kino's blanket and the thousand washings of his clothes, and set them down as poverty people and went along to see what kind of drama might develop. The four beggars in front of the church knew everything in the town. They were students of the expressions of young women as they went into confession, and they saw them as they came out and read the nature of the sin. They knew every little scandal and some very big crimes. They slept at their posts in the shadow of the church so that no one crept in for consolation without their knowledge. And they knew the doctor. They knew his ignorance, his cruelty, his avarice,⁴ his appetites, his sins. They knew his clumsy abortions and the little brown pennies he gave sparingly for alms. They had seen his corpses go into the church. And, since early Mass was over and business was slow, they followed the procession, these endless searchers after perfect knowledge of their fellow men, to see what the fat lazy doctor would do about an indigent⁵ baby with a scorpion bite.

The scurrying procession came at last to the big gate in the wall of the doctor's house. They could hear the splashing water and the singing of caged birds and the sweep of the long brooms on the flagstones. And they could smell the frying of good bacon from the doctor's house.

Kino hesitated a moment. This doctor was not of his people. This doctor was of a race which for nearly four hundred years had beaten and starved and robbed and despised Kino's race, and frightened it too, so that the indigene⁶ came humbly to the door. And as always when he came near to one of this race, Kino felt weak and afraid and angry at the same time. Rage and terror went together. He could kill the doctor more easily than he could talk to him, for all of the doctor's race spoke to all of Kino's race as though they were simple animals. And as Kino raised his right hand to the iron ring knocker in the gate, rage swelled in him, and the pounding music of the enemy beat in his ears, and his lips drew tight against his teeth—but with his left hand he reached to take off his hat. The iron ring pounded against the gate. Kino took off his hat and stood waiting. Coyotito moaned a little in Juana's arms and she spoke softly to him. The procession crowded close, the better to see and hear.

After a moment the big gate opened a few inches. Kino could see the green coolness of the garden and little splashing fountain through the opening. The man who looked out at him was one of his own race. Kino spoke to him in the old language. "The little one—the first born—has been poisoned by the scorpion," Kino said. "He requires the skill of the healer."

The gate closed a little, and the servant refused to speak in the old language. "A little moment," he said. "I go to inform myself," and he closed the gate and slid the bolt home. The glaring sun threw the bunched shadows of the people blackly on the white wall.

In his bed chamber the doctor sat up in his high bed. He had on his dressing gown of red watered silk that had come from Paris, a little tight over the chest now if it was buttoned. On his lap was a silver tray with a silver chocolate pot and a tiny cup of eggshell china, so delicate that it looked silly when he lifted it with his big hand, lifted it with the tips of thumb and forefinger and spread the other three fingers wide to get them out of the way. His eyes rested in puffy little hammocks of flesh and his mouth drooped with discontent. He was growing very stout, and his voice was hoarse with the fat that pressed on his throat. Beside him on a table was a small Oriental gong and a bowl of cigarettes. The furnishings of the room were heavy and dark and gloomy. The pictures were religious, even the large tinted photograph of his

---

3. **bougainvillea** (boo′gən·vil′ē·ə): woody tropical vines.
4. **avarice** (av′ər·is): greed for riches.
5. **indigent** (in′di·jənt): poor.

6. **indigene:** (in′di·jēn′): person whose ancestors have lived in an area for a long time.

Old Church of Michoacan, Mexico
by Millard Sheets (1981). Watercolor.

Courtesy Kennedy Galleries Inc.,
New York City.

dead wife, who, if Masses willed and paid for out of her own estate could do it, was in Heaven. The doctor had once for a short time been a part of the great world and his whole subsequent life was memory and longing for France. "That," he said, "was civilized living"—by which he meant that on a small income he had been able to keep a mistress and eat in restaurants. He poured his second cup of chocolate and crumbled a sweet biscuit in his fingers. The servant from the gate came to the open door and stood waiting to be noticed.

"Yes?" the doctor asked.

"It is a little Indian with a baby. He says a scorpion stung it."

The doctor put his cup down gently before he let his anger rise.

"Have I nothing better to do than cure insect bites for 'little Indians'? I am a doctor, not a veterinary."

"Yes, Patron," said the servant.

"Has he any money?" the doctor demanded. "No, they never have any money. I, I alone in the world am supposed to work for nothing—and I am tired of it. See if he has any money!"

At the gate the servant opened the door a trifle and looked out at the waiting people. And this time he spoke in the old language.

"Have you money to pay for the treatment?"

Now Kino reached into a secret place somewhere under his blanket. He brought out a paper folded many times. Crease by crease he unfolded it, until at last there came to view eight small misshapen seed pearls, as ugly and gray as little ulcers, flattened and almost valueless. The servant took the paper and closed the gate again, but this time he was not gone long. He opened the gate just wide enough to pass the paper back.

"The doctor has gone out," he said. "He was called to a serious case." And he shut the gate quickly out of shame.

And now a wave of shame went over the whole procession. They melted away. The beggars went back to the church steps, the stragglers moved off, and the neighbors departed so that the public shaming of Kino would not be in their eyes.

For a long time Kino stood in front of the gate with Juana beside him. Slowly he put his suppliant[7] hat on his head. Then, without warning, he struck the gate a crushing blow with his fist. He looked down in wonder at his split knuckles and at the blood that flowed down between his fingers.

---

7. **suppliant** (sup′lē·ənt): humble; asking humbly; entreating in a much and unproud way.

Responding to the Novel

Analyzing Chapter I

Identifying Facts

1. Briefly describe the songs Kino hears in Chapter I. What is the significance of the songs?
2. Describe Kino and Juana's morning routine. What do they eat? What do they talk about?
3. Describe how the scorpion attacks Coyotito.
4. According to the servant, why can't the doctor treat Coyotito? What is the real reason?

Interpreting Meanings

5. **Setting** plays an important role in *The Pearl*.

   a. Describe the **physical setting** of the story: Where is the village located and how, roughly, is it laid out?
   b. Describe the **social setting** of the story: Who are the two main social groups in Chapter I? What are some of the differences in the way members of each group live?

6. **Conflict**—a struggle between opposing forces—is a key element in any novel. Describe the conflict between Kino, Juana, and the doctor.
7. The story is told from the **omniscient point of view.** This allows us to learn about the thoughts of all the characters. How might the story be different if it were told in the first person from Kino's point of view?
8. **Compare** and **contrast** Kino and Juana. In what ways are they similar, in what ways different? (You will gain some insight by examining closely what each does in the moments after Coyotito is stung.)
9. At the end of the chapter Kino strikes the gate outside the doctor's house. What emotions do you think he is feeling? Would you react similarly if you were in the same situation?
10. In the Preface, Steinbeck says: "as with all retold tales that are in people's hearts, there are only good and bad things and black and white things and good and evil things and no in-between anywhere." Do you think this is true so far in the story of Kino and Juana and Coyotito? Is it true in fairy tales and children's stories? Is it true in real life?

Analyzing Language and Vocabulary

Sensory Details

A writer uses sensory details to add color and life to a description. **Sensory details** contain descriptive words that appeal to our senses of sight, taste, touch, smell, and hearing. For example, a sensory detail might help us to *hear* Kino's songs, or to *feel* the heat of the sun as it shines upon the town.

1. For each of the following quotations from *The Pearl* identify the sense or senses to which the quotation appeals—sight, touch, hearing, smell, or taste. What specific words appeal to the senses you named for each quotation?

   a. "The roosters had been crowing for some time, and . . . a covey of little birds chittered and flurried with their wings."
   b. "Behind him Juana's fire leaped into flame and threw spears of light through the chinks of the brush-house wall and threw a wavering square of light out the door."
   c. "His eyes were warm and fierce and bright and his mustache was thin and coarse."
   d. "Kino squatted by the fire pit and rolled a hot corncake and dipped it in sauce and ate it."
   e. "His body glided quickly across the room, noiselessly and smoothly."
   f. "Then, snarling, Kino had it, had it in his fingers, rubbing it to a paste in his hands. He threw it down and beat it into the earth floor with his fist, and Coyotito screamed with pain . . ."
   g. "The scurrying procession . . . could hear the splashing water and the singing of caged birds and the sweep of the long brooms on the flagstones. And they could smell the frying of good bacon . . ."

2. Read the paragraph on page 676 which begins "The dawn came quickly now . . ." Divide a sheet of paper into five columns labeled *sight, hearing, touch, taste,* and *smell.* Then go through the paragraph and list the passages that appeal to each sense. (Some may appeal to more than one sense.)

II

The town lay on a broad estuary,[1] its old yellow plastered buildings hugging the beach. And on the beach the white and blue canoes that came from Nayarit were drawn up, canoes preserved for generations by a hard shell-like waterproof plaster whose making was a secret of the fishing people. They were high and graceful canoes with curving bow and stern and a braced section midships where a mast could be stepped to carry a small lateen sail.[2]

The beach was yellow sand, but at the water's edge a rubble of shell and algae took its place. Fiddler crabs bubbled and sputtered in their holes in the sand, and in the shallows little lobsters popped in and out of their tiny homes in the rubble and sand. The sea bottom was rich with crawling and swimming and growing things. The brown algae waved in the gentle currents and the green eelgrass swayed and little sea horses clung to its stems. Spotted botete, the poison fish, lay on the bottom in the ellgrass beds, and the bright-colored swimming crabs scampered over them.

On the beach the hungry dogs and the hungry pigs of the town searched endlessly for any dead fish or sea bird that might have floated in on a rising tide.

Although the morning was young, the hazy mirage was up. The uncertain air that magnified some things and blotted out others hung over the whole Gulf so that all sights were unreal and vision could not be trusted; so that sea and land had the sharp clarities and the vagueness of a dream. Thus it might be that the people of the Gulf trust things of the spirit and things of the imagination, but they do not trust their eyes to show them distance or clear outline or any optical exactness. Across the estuary from the town one section of mangroves stood clear and telescopically defined, while another mangrove clump was a hazy black-green blob. Part of the far shore disappeared into a shimmer that looked like water. There was no certainty in seeing, no proof that what you saw was there or was not there. And the people of the Gulf expected all places were that way, and it was not strange to them. A copper haze hung over the water, and the hot morning sun beat on it and made it vibrate blindingly.

The brush houses of the fishing people were back from the beach on the right-hand side of the town, and the canoes were drawn up in front of this area.

Kino and Juana came slowly down to the beach and to Kino's canoe, which was the one thing of value he owned in the world. It was very old. Kino's grandfather had brought it from Nayarit, and he had given it to Kino's father, and so it had come to Kino. It was at once property and source of food, for a man with a boat can guarantee a woman that she will eat something. It is the bulwark[3] against starvation. And every year Kino refinished his canoe with the hard shell-like plaster by the secret method that had also come to him from his father. Now he came to the canoe and touched the bow tenderly as he always did. He laid his diving rock and his basket and the two ropes in the sand by the canoe. And he folded his blanket and laid it in the bow.

Juana laid Coyotito on the blanket, and she placed her shawl over him so that the hot sun could not shine on him. He was quiet now, but the swelling on his shoulder had continued up his neck and under his ear and his face was puffed and feverish. Juana went to the water and waded in. She gathered some brown seaweed and made a flat damp poultice[4] of it, and this she applied to the baby's swollen shoulder, which was as good a remedy as any and probably better than the doctor could have done. But the remedy lacked his authority because it was simple and didn't cost anything. The stomach cramps had not come to Coyotito. Perhaps Juana had sucked out the poison in time, but she had not sucked out her worry over her first-born. She had not prayed directly for the recovery of the baby—she had prayed that they might find a pearl with which to hire the doctor to cure the baby, for the minds of people are as unsubstantial as the mirage of the Gulf.

Now Kino and Juana slid the canoe down the beach to the water, and when the bow floated, Juana climbed in, while Kino pushed the stern in and waded beside it until it floated lightly and trembled on the little breaking waves. Then in coordination Juana and Kino drove their double-bladed paddles into the sea, and the canoe creased the water and hissed with speed. The other pearlers were gone out long since. In a few moments Kino could see them clustered in the haze, riding over the oyster bed.

Light filtered down through the water to the bed where the frilly pearl oysters lay fastened to the rubbly bottom, a bottom strewn with shells of

---

1. **estuary** (es'choo·werlē): inlet of the sea.
2. **lateen sail:** triangular sail attached to a short mast.
3. **bulwark** (bool'wərk): strong defense or protection.
4. **poultice** (pōl'tis): hot, soft, moist mass, as of flour, herbs, or mustard, applied to an inflamed part of the body.

broken, opened oysters. This was the bed that had raised the King of Spain to be a great power in Europe in past years, had helped to pay for his wars, and had decorated the churches for his soul's sake. The gray oysters with ruffles like skirts on the shells, the barnacle-crusted oysters with little bits of weed clinging to the skirts and small crabs climbing over them. An accident could happen to these oysters, a grain of sand could lie in the folds of muscle and irritate the flesh until in self-protection the flesh coated the grain with a layer of smooth cement. But once started, the flesh continued to coat the foreign body until it fell free in some tidal flurry or until the oyster was destroyed. For centuries men had dived down and torn the oysters from the beds and ripped them open, looking for the coated grains of sand. Swarms of fish lived near the bed to live near the oysters thrown back by the searching men and to nibble at the shining inner shells. But the pearls were accidents, and the finding of one was luck, a little pat on the back by God or the gods or both.

Kino had two ropes, one tied to a heavy stone and one to a basket. He stripped off his shirt and trousers and laid his hat in the bottom of the canoe. The water was oily smooth. He took his rock in one hand and his basket in the other, and he slipped feet first over the side and the rock carried him to the bottom. The bubbles rose behind him until the water cleared and he could see. Above, the surface of the water was an undulating mirror of brightness, and he could see the bottoms of the canoes sticking through it.

Kino moved cautiously so that the water would not be obscured with mud or sand. He hooked his foot in the loop on his rock and his hands worked quickly, tearing the oysters loose, some singly, others in clusters. He laid them in his basket. In some places the oysters clung to one another so that they came free in lumps.

Now, Kino's people had sung of everything that happened or existed. They had made songs to the fishes, to the sea in anger and to the sea in calm, to the light and the dark and the sun and the moon, and the songs were all in Kino and in his people— every song that had ever been made, even the ones forgotten. And as he filled his basket the song was in Kino, and the beat of the song was his pounding heart as it ate the oxygen from his held breath, and the melody of the song was the gray-green water and the little scuttling animals and the clouds of fish that flitted by and were gone. But in the song there was a secret little inner song, hardly perceptible, but always there, sweet and secret and clinging, almost hidden in the counter-melody and this was the Song of the Pearl That Might Be, for every shell thrown in the basket might contain a pearl. Chance was against it, but luck and the gods might be for it. And in the canoe above him Kino knew that Juana was making the magic of prayer, her face set rigid and her muscles hard to force the luck, to tear the luck out of the gods' hands, for she needed the luck for the swollen shoulder of Coyotito. And because the need was great and the desire was great, the little secret melody of the pearl that might be was stronger this morning. Whole phrases of it came clearly and softly into the Song of the Undersea.

Kino, in his pride and youth and strength, could remain down over two minutes without strain, so that he worked deliberately, selecting the largest shells. Because they were disturbed, the oyster shells were tightly closed. A little to his right a

hummock of rubbly rock stuck up, covered with young oysters not ready to take. Kino moved next to the hummock, and then, beside it, under a little overhang, he saw a very large oyster lying by itself, not covered with its clinging brothers. The shell was partly open, for the overhang protected this ancient oyster, and in the lip-like muscle Kino saw a ghostly gleam, and then the shell closed down. His heart beat out a heavy rhythm and the melody of the maybe pearl shrilled in his ears. Slowly he forced the oyster loose and held it tightly against his breast. He kicked his foot free from the rock loop, and his body rose to the surface and his black hair gleamed in the sunlight. He reached over the side of the canoe and laid the oyster in the bottom.

Then Juana steadied the boat while he climbed in. His eyes were shining with excitement, but in decency he pulled up his rock, and then he pulled up his basket of oysters and lifted them in. Juana sensed his excitement, and she pretended to look away. It is not good to want a thing too much. It sometimes drives the luck away. You must want it just enough, and you must be very tactful with God or the gods. But Juana stopped breathing. Very deliberately Kino opened his short strong knife. He looked speculatively at the basket. Perhaps it would be better to open *the* oyster last. He took a small oyster from the basket, cut the muscle, searched the folds of flesh, and threw it in the water. Then he seemed to see the great oyster for the first time. He squatted in the bottom of the canoe, picked up the shell and examined it. The flutes were shining black to brown, and only a few

small barnacles adhered to the shell. Now Kino was reluctant to open it. What he had seen, he knew, might be a reflection, a piece of flat shell accidentally drifted in or a complete illusion. In this Gulf of uncertain light there were more illusions than realities.

But Juana's eyes were on him and she could not wait. She put her hand on Coyotito's covered head. "Open it," she said softly.

Kino deftly slipped his knife into the edge of the shell. Through the knife he could feel the muscle tighten hard. He worked the blade lever-wise and the closing muscle parted and the shell fell apart. The lip-like flesh writhed up and then subsided. Kino lifted the flesh, and there it lay, the great pearl, perfect as the moon. It captured the light and refined it and gave it back in silver incandescence.[5] It was as large as a seagull's egg. It was the greatest pearl in the world.

Juana caught her breath and moaned a little. And to Kino the secret melody of the maybe pearl

---

5. **incandescence** (in′kən·des′′ns): brilliant shine or gleam.

broke clear and beautiful, rich and warm and lovely, glowing and gloating and triumphant. In the surface of the great pearl he could see dream forms. He picked the pearl from the dying flesh and held it in his palm, and he turned it over and saw that its curve was perfect. Juana came near to stare at it in his hand, and it was the hand he had smashed against the doctor's gate, and the torn flesh of the knuckles was turned grayish white by the sea water.

Instinctively Juana went to Coyotito where he lay on his father's blanket. She lifted the poultice of seaweed and looked at the shoulder. "Kino," she cried shrilly.

He looked past his pearl, and he saw that the swelling was going out of the baby's shoulder, the poison was receding from its body. Then Kino's fist closed over the pearl and his emotions broke over him. He put back his head and howled. His eyes rolled up and he screamed and his body was rigid. The men in the other canoes looked up, startled, and then they dug their paddles into the sea and raced toward Kino's canoe.

Responding to the Novel

Analyzing Chapter II

Identifying Facts

1. Describe the **setting** of Chapter II. What is the beach like? What is the atmosphere over the estuary like? What are the villagers doing?
2. Describe the "secret little inner song" that Kino hears.
3. Why is the canoe important to Kino?
4. Describe the way a pearl is created.
5. How does Kino find the large pearl? What two **similes** does the narrator use to describe the appearance and size of the pearl?

Interpreting Meanings

6. Early in the chapter the narrator says Juana's homemade poultice is probably a better treatment for Coyotito's illness than what the doctor

could come up with. Yet Juana prays that she and Kino can get enough money to pay the doctor to treat Coyotito. What point do you think the writer is making about Juana's feelings about herself and about money? What do these feelings reveal about the ways the Europeans control the Indians?

7. Near the end of the chapter, as Juana and Kino examine the pearl, the narrator reminds us of what happened to Kino at the end of Chapter I. Why do you think the narrator reminds us of the earlier event?

Applying Meanings

8. Do you think a stroke of good fortune, such as winning a lottery or finding something very valuable, has to change a person's life?

III

A town is a thing like a colonial animal.[1] A town has a nervous system and a head and shoulders and feet. A town is a thing separate from all other towns, so that there are no two towns alike. And a town has a whole emotion. How news travels through a town is a mystery not easily to be solved. News seems to move faster than small boys can scramble and dart to tell it, faster than women can call it over the fences.

Before Kino and Juana and the other fishers had come to Kino's brush house, the nerves of the town were pulsing and vibrating with the news—Kino had found the Pearl of the World. Before panting little boys could strangle out the words, their mothers knew it. The news swept on past the brush houses, and it washed in a foaming wave into the town of stone and plaster. It came to the priest walking in his garden, and it put a thoughtful look in his eyes and a memory of certain repairs necessary to the church. He wondered what the pearl would be worth. And he wondered whether he had baptized Kino's baby, or married him for that matter. The news came to the shopkeepers, and they looked at men's clothes that had not sold so well.

The news came to the doctor where he sat with a woman whose illness was age, though neither she nor the doctor would admit it. And when it was made plain who Kino was, the doctor grew stern and judicious at the same time. "He is a client of mine," the doctor said. "I'm treating his child for a scorpion sting." And the doctor's eyes rolled up a little in their fat hammocks and he thought of Paris. He remembered the room he had lived in there as a great and luxurious place, and he remembered the hard-faced woman who had lived with him as a beautiful and kind girl, although she had been none of these three. The doctor looked past his aged patient and saw himself sitting in a restaurant in Paris and a waiter was just opening a bottle of wine.

The news came early to the beggars in front of the church, and it made them giggle a little with pleasure, for they knew that there is no almsgiver in the world like a poor man who is suddenly lucky.

Kino has found the Pearl of the World. In the town, in little offices, sat the men who bought pearls from the fishers. They waited in their chairs until the pearls came in, and then they cackled and fought and shouted and threatened until they reached the lowest price the fisherman would stand. But there was a price below which they dared not go, for it had happened that a fisherman in despair had given his pearls to the church. And when the buying was over, these buyers sat alone and their fingers played restlessly with the pearls, and they wished they owned the pearls. For there were not many buyers really—there was only one, and he kept these agents in separate offices to give a semblance of competition. The news came to these men, and their eyes squinted and their fingertips burned a little, and each one thought how the patron could not live forever and someone had to take his place. And each one thought how with some capital he could get a new start.

All manner of people grew interested in Kino—people with things to sell and people with favors to ask. Kino had found the Pearl of the World. The essence of pearl mixed with essence of men and a curious dark residue was precipitated.[2] Every man suddenly became related to Kino's pearl, and Kino's pearl went into the dreams, the speculations, the schemes, the plans, the futures, the wishes, the needs, the lusts, the hungers, of everyone, and only one person stood in the way and that was Kino, so that he became curiously every man's enemy. The news stirred up something infinitely black and evil in the town; the black distillate[3] was like the scorpion, or like hunger in the smell of food, or like loneliness when love is withheld. The poison sacks of the town began to manufacture venom, and the town swelled and puffed with the pressure of it.

But Kino and Juana did not know these things. Because they were happy and excited they thought everyone shared their joy. Juan Tomás and Apolonia did, and they were the world too. In the afternoon, when the sun had gone over the mountains of the Peninsula to sink in the outward sea, Kino squatted in his house with Juana beside him. And the brush house was crowded with neighbors. Kino held the great pearl in his hand, and it was warm and alive in his hand. And the music of the pearl had merged with the music of the family so that one beautified the other. The

---

1. **colonial animal:** group of simple organisms that work together to function as a larger organism.

2. In chemistry, mixing together certain substances will cause the solid part of one substance to precipitate, or separate from the liquid it was dissolved in.
3. **distillate:** something removed from a mixture by evaporating and then condensing.

neighbors looked at the pearl in Kino's hand and they wondered how such luck could come to any man.

And Juan Tomás, who squatted on Kino's right hand because he was his brother, asked, "What will you do now that you have become a rich man?"

Kino looked into his pearl, and Juana cast her eyelashes down and arranged her shawl to cover her face so that her excitement could not be seen. And in the incandescence of the pearl the pictures formed of the things Kino's mind had considered in the past and had given up as impossible. In the pearl he saw Juana and Coyotito and himself standing and kneeling at the high altar, and they were being married now that they could pay. He spoke softly, "We will be married—in the church."

In the pearl he saw how they were dressed—Juana in a shawl stiff with newness and a new skirt, and from under the long skirt Kino could see that she wore shoes. It was in the pearl—the picture glowing there. He himself was dressed in new white clothes, and he carried a new hat—not of straw but of fine black felt—and he too wore shoes—not sandals but shoes that laced. But Coyotito—he was the one—he wore a blue sailor suit from the United States and a little yachting cap such as Kino had seen once when a pleasure boat put into the estuary. All of these things Kino saw in the lucent[4] pearl and he said, "We will have new clothes."

And the music of the pearl rose like a chorus of trumpets in his ears.

Then to the lovely gray surface of the pearl came the little things Kino wanted: a harpoon to take the place of one lost a year ago, a new harpoon of iron with a ring in the end of the shaft; and—his mind could hardly make the leap—a rifle—but why not, since he was so rich. And Kino saw Kino in his pearl, Kino holding a Winchester carbine. It was the wildest daydreaming and very pleasant. His lips moved hesitantly over this— "A rifle," he said. "Perhaps a rifle."

It was the rifle that broke down the barriers. This was an impossibility, and if he could think of having a rifle whole horizons were burst and he could rush on. For it is said that humans are never satisfied, that you give them one thing and they want something more. And this is said in disparagement, whereas it is one of the greatest talents the species has and one that has made it superior to animals that are satisfied with what they have.

The neighbors, close pressed and silent in the

---

4. **lucent** ($\overline{loo}$'s'nt): giving off light; shining.

house, nodded their heads at his wild imaginings. And a man in the rear murmured, "A rifle. He will have a rifle."

But the music of the pearl was shrilling with triumph in Kino. Juana looked up, and her eyes were wide at Kino's courage and at his imagination. And electric strength had come to him now the horizons were kicked out. In the pearl he saw Coyotito sitting at a little desk in a school, just as Kino had once seen it through an open door. And Coyotito was dressed in a jacket, and he had on a white collar and a broad silken tie. Moreover, Coyotito was writing on a big piece of paper. Kino looked at his neighbors fiercely. "My son will go to school," he said, and the neighbors were hushed. Juana caught her breath sharply. Her eyes were bright as she watched him, and she looked quickly down at Coyotito in her arms to see whether this might be possible.

But Kino's face shone with prophecy. "My son will read and open the books, and my son will write and will know writing. And my son will make numbers, and these things will make us free because he will know—he will know and through him we will know." And in the pearl Kino saw himself and Juana squatting by the little fire in the brush hut while Coyotito read from a great book. "This is what the pearl will do," said Kino. And he had never said so many words together in his life. And suddenly he was afraid of his talking. His hand closed down over the pearl and cut the light away from it. Kino was afraid as a man is afraid who says, "I will," without knowing.

Now the neighbors knew they had witnessed a great marvel. They knew that time would now date from Kino's pearl, and that they would discuss this moment for many years to come. If these things came to pass, they would recount how Kino looked and what he said and how his eyes shone, and they would say, "He was a man transfigured. Some power was given to him, and there it started. You see what a great man he has become, starting from that moment. And I myself saw it."

And if Kino's planning came to nothing, those same neighbors would say, "There it started. A foolish madness came over him so that he spoke foolish words. God keep us from such things. Yes, God punished Kino because he rebelled against the way things are. You see what has become of him. And I myself saw the moment when his reason left him."

Kino looked down at his closed hand and the knuckles were scabbed over and tight where he had struck the gate.

Now the dusk was coming. And Juana looped her shawl under the baby so that he hung against her hip, and she went to the fire hole and dug a coal from the ashes and broke a few twigs over it and fanned a flame alive. The little flames danced on the faces of the neighbors. They knew they should go to their own dinners, but they were reluctant to leave.

The dark was almost in, and Juana's fire threw shadows on the brush walls when the whisper came in, passed from mouth to mouth. "The Father is coming—the priest is coming." The men uncovered their heads and stepped back from the door, and the women gathered their shawls about their faces and cast down their eyes. Kino and Juan Tomás, his brother, stood up. The priest came in—a graying, aging man with an old skin and a young sharp eye. Children, he considered these people, and he treated them like children.

"Kino," he said softly, "thou art named after a great man—and a great Father of the Church." He made it sound like a benediction.[5] "Thy namesake tamed the desert and sweetened the minds of thy people, didst thou know that?[6] It is in the books."

Kino looked quickly down at Coyotito's head, where he hung on Juana's hip. Some day, his mind said, that boy would know what things were in the books and what things were not. The music had gone out of Kino's head, but now, thinly, slowly, the melody of the morning, the music of evil, of the enemy sounded, but it was faint and weak. And Kino looked at his neighbors to see who might have brought this song in.

But the priest was speaking again. "It has come to me that thou hast found a great fortune, a great pearl."

Kino opened his hand and held it out, and the priest gasped a little at the size and beauty of the pearl. And then he said, "I hope thou wilt remember to give thanks, my son, to Him who has given thee this treasure, and to pray for guidance in the future."

Kino nodded dumbly, and it was Juana who spoke softly. "We will, Father. And we will be married now. Kino has said so." She looked at the neighbors for confirmation, and they nodded their heads solemnly.

The priest said, "It is pleasant to see that your first thoughts are good thoughts. God bless you, my children." He turned and left quietly, and the people let him through.

But Kino's hand had closed tightly on the pearl

---

5. **benediction** (ben′ə·dik′shən): blessing.
6. Eusebio Kino was an explorer and Jesuit missionary in the Gulf region (present-day Arizona and Mexico) from the 1680's to his death in 1711.

again, and he was glancing about suspiciously, for the evil song was in his ears, shrilling against the music of the pearl.

The neighbors slipped away to go to their houses, and Juana squatted by the fire and set her clay pot of boiled beans over the little flame. Kino stepped to the doorway and looked out. As always, he could smell the smoke from many fires, and he could see the hazy stars and feel the damp of the night air so that he covered his nose from it. The thin dog came to him and threshed itself in greeting like a wind-blown flag, and Kino looked down at it and didn't see it. He had broken through the horizons into a cold and lonely outside. He felt alone and unprotected, and scraping crickets and shrilling tree frogs and croaking toads seemed to be carrying the melody of evil. Kino shivered a little and drew his blanket more tightly against his nose. He carried the pearl still in his hand, tightly closed in his palm, and it was warm and smooth against his skin.

Behind him he heard Juana patting the cakes before she put them down on the clay cooking sheet. Kino felt all the warmth and security of his family behind him, and the Song of the Family came from behind him like the purring of a kitten. But now, by saying what his future was going to be like, he had created it. A plan is a real thing, and things projected are experienced. A plan once made and visualized becomes a reality along with other realities—never to be destroyed but easily to be attacked. Thus Kino's future was real, but having set it up, other forces were set up to destroy it, and this he knew, so that he had to prepare to meet the attack. And this Kino knew also—that the gods do not love men's plans, and the gods do not love success unless it comes by accident. He knew that the gods take their revenge on a man if he be successful through his own efforts. Consequently Kino was afraid of plans, but having made one, he could never destroy it. And to meet the attack, Kino was already making a hard skin for himself against the world. His eyes and his mind probed for danger before it appeared.

Standing in the door, he saw two men approach; and one of them carried a lantern which lighted the ground and the legs of the men. They turned in through the opening of Kino's brush fence and came to his door. And Kino saw that one was the doctor and the other the servant who had opened the gate in the morning. The split knuckles on Kino's right hand burned when he saw who they were.

The doctor said, "I was not in when you came this morning. But now, at the first chance, I have come to see the baby."

Kino stood in the door, filling it, and hatred raged and flamed in back of his eyes, and fear too, for the hundreds of years of subjugation were cut deep in him.

"The baby is nearly well now," he said curtly.

The doctor smiled, but his eyes in their little lymph-lined hammocks did not smile.

He said, "Sometimes, my friend, the scorpion sting has a curious effect. There will be apparent improvement, and then without warning—pouf!" He pursed his lips and made a little explosion to show how quick it could be, and shifted his small black doctor's bag about so that the light of the lamp fell upon it, for he knew that Kino's race love the tools of any craft and trust them. "Sometimes," the doctor went on in a liquid tone, "sometimes there will be a withered leg or a blind eye or a crumpled back. Oh, I know the sting of the scorpion, my friend, and I can cure it."

Kino felt the rage and hatred melting toward fear. He did not know, and perhaps this doctor did. And he could not take the chance of putting his certain ignorance against this man's possible knowledge. He was trapped as his people were always trapped, and would be until, as he had said, they could be sure that the things in the books were really in the books. He could not take a chance—not with the life or with the straightness of Coyotito. He stood aside and let the doctor and his man enter the brush hut.

Juana stood up from the fire and backed away as he entered, and she covered the baby's face with the fringe of her shawl. And when the doctor went to her and held out his hand, she clutched the baby tight and looked at Kino where he stood with the fire shadows leaping on his face.

Kino nodded, and only then did she let the doctor take the baby.

"Hold the light," the doctor said, and when the servant held the lantern high, the doctor looked for a moment at the wound on the baby's shoulder. He was thoughtful for a moment and then he rolled back the baby's eyelid and looked at the eyeball. He nodded his head while Coyotito struggled against him.

"It is as I thought," he said. "The poison has gone inward and it will strike soon. Come look!" He held the eyelid down. "See—it is blue." And Kino, looking anxiously, saw that indeed it was a little blue. And he didn't know whether or not it was always a little blue. But the trap was set. He couldn't take the chance.

The doctor's eyes watered in their little hammocks. "I will give him something to try to turn the poison aside," he said. And he handed the baby to Kino.

Then from his bag he took a little bottle of white powder and a capsule of gelatine. He filled the capsule with the powder and closed it, and then around the first capsule he fitted a second capsule and closed it. Then he worked very deftly. He took the baby and pinched its lower lip until it opened its mouth. His fat fingers placed the capsule far back on the baby's tongue, back of the point where he could spit it out, and then from the floor he picked up the little pitcher of pulque and gave Coyotito a drink, and it was done. He looked again at the baby's eyeball and he pursed his lips and seemed to think.

At last he handed the baby back to Juana, and he turned to Kino. "I think the poison will attack within the hour," he said. "The medicine may save the baby from hurt, but I will come back in an hour. Perhaps I am in time to save him." He took a deep breath and went out of the hut, and his servant followed him with the lantern.

Now Juana had the baby under her shawl, and she stared at it with anxiety and fear. Kino came to her, and he lifted the shawl and stared at the baby. He moved his hand to look under the eyelid, and only then saw that the pearl was still in his hand. Then he went to a box by the wall, and from it he brought a piece of rag. He wrapped the pearl in the rag, then went to the corner of the brush house and dug a little hole with his fingers in the dirt floor, and he put the pearl in the hole and covered it up and concealed the place. And then he went to the fire where Juana was squatting, watching the baby's face.

The doctor, back in his house, settled into his chair and looked at his watch. His people brought him a little supper of chocolate and sweet cakes and fruit, and he stared at the food discontentedly.

In the houses of the neighbors the subject that would lead all conversations for a long time to come was aired for the first time to see how it would go. The neighbors showed one another with their thumbs how big the pearl was, and they made little caressing gestures to show how lovely it was. From now on they would watch Kino and Juana very closely to see whether riches turned their heads, as riches turn all people's heads. Everyone knew why the doctor had come. He was not good at dissembling[7] and he was very well understood.

Out in the estuary a tight woven school of small fishes glittered and broke water to escape a school of great fishes that drove in to eat them. And in the houses the people could hear the swish of the small ones and the bouncing splash of the great ones as the slaughter went on. The dampness

---

7. **dissembling** (di·sem'b'liŋ): disguising; pretending.

arose out of the Gulf and was deposited on bushes and cacti and on little trees in salty drops. And the night mice crept about on the ground and the little night hawks hunted them silently.

The skinny black puppy with flame spots over his eyes came to Kino's door and looked in. He nearly shook his hind quarters loose when Kino glanced up at him, and he subsided when Kino looked away. The puppy did not enter the house, but he watched with frantic interest while Kino ate his beans from the little pottery dish and wiped it clean with a corncake and ate the cake and washed the whole down with a drink of pulque.

Kino was finished and was rolling a cigarette when Juana spoke sharply. "Kino." He glanced at her and then got up and went quickly to her for he saw fright in her eyes. He stood over her, looking down, but the light was very dim. He kicked a pile of twigs into the fire hole to make a blaze, and then he could see the face of Coyotito. The baby's face was flushed and his throat was working and a little thick drool of saliva issued from his lips. The spasm of the stomach muscles began, and the baby was very sick.

Kino knelt beside his wife. "So the doctor knew," he said, but he said it for himself as well as for his wife, for his mind was hard and suspicious and he was remembering the white powder. Juana rocked from side to side and moaned out the little Song of the Family as though it could ward off the danger, and the baby vomited and writhed in her arms. Now uncertainty was in Kino, and the music of evil throbbed in his head and nearly drove out Juana's song.

The doctor finished his chocolate and nibbled the little fallen pieces of sweet cake. He brushed his fingers on a napkin, looked at his watch, arose, and took up his little bag.

The news of the baby's illness traveled quickly among the brush houses, for sickness is second only to hunger as the enemy of poor people. And some said softly, "Luck, you see, brings bitter friends." And they nodded and got up to go to Kino's house. The neighbors scuttled with covered noses through the dark until they crowded into Kino's house again. They stood and gazed, and they made little comments on the sadness that this should happen at a time of joy, and they said, "All things are in God's hands." The old women squatted down beside Juana to try to give her aid if they could and comfort if they could not.

Then the doctor hurried in, followed by his man. He scattered the old women like chickens. He took the baby and examined it and felt its head. "The poison it has worked," he said. "I think I can defeat it. I will try my best." He asked for water, and in the cup of it he put three drops of ammonia, and he pried open the baby's mouth and poured it down. The baby spluttered and screeched under the treatment, and Juana watched him with haunted eyes. The doctor spoke a little as he worked. "It is lucky that I know about the poison of the scorpion, otherwise—" and he shrugged to show what could have happened.

But Kino was suspicious, and he could not take his eyes from the doctor's open bag, and from the bottle of white powder there. Gradually the spasms subsided and the baby relaxed under the doctor's hands. And then Coyotito sighed deeply and went to sleep, for he was very tired with vomiting.

The doctor put the baby in Juana's arms. "He will get well now," he said. "I have won the fight." And Juana looked at him with adoration.

The doctor was closing his bag now. He said, "When do you think you can pay this bill?" He said it even kindly.

"When I have sold my pearl I will pay you," Kino said.

"You have a pearl? A good pearl?" the doctor asked with interest.

And then the chorus of the neighbors broke in. "He has found the Pearl of the World," they cried, and they joined forefinger with thumb to show how great the pearl was.

"Kino will be a rich man," they clamored. "It is a pearl such as one has never seen."

The doctor looked surprised. "I had not heard of it. Do you keep this pearl in a safe place? Perhaps you would like me to put it in my safe?"

Kino's eyes were hooded now, his cheeks were drawn taut. "I have it secure," he said. "Tomorrow I will sell it and then I will pay you."

The doctor shrugged, and his wet eyes never left Kino's eyes. He knew the pearl would be buried in the house, and he thought Kino might look toward the place where it was buried. "It would be a shame to have it stolen before you could sell it," the doctor said, and he saw Kino's eyes flick involuntarily to the floor near the side post of the brush house.

When the doctor had gone and all the neighbors had reluctantly returned to their houses, Kino squatted beside the little glowing coals in the fire hole and listened to the night sound, the soft sweep of the little waves on the shore and the distant barking of dogs, the creeping of the breeze through the brush house roof and the soft speech of his neighbors in their houses in the village. For these people do not sleep soundly all night; they awaken at intervals and talk a little and then go to sleep again. And after a while Kino got up and went to the door of his house.

He smelled the breeze and he listened for any foreign sound of secrecy or creeping, and his eyes searched the darkness, for the music of evil was sounding in his head and he was fierce and afraid. After he had probed the night with his senses he went to the place by the side post where the pearl was buried, and he dug it up and brought it to his sleeping mat, and under his sleeping mat he dug another little hole in the dirt floor and buried his pearl and covered it up again.

And Juana, sitting by the fire hole, watched him with questioning eyes, and when he had buried his pearl she asked, "Who do you fear?"

Kino searched for a true answer, and at last he said, "Everyone." And he could feel a shell of hardness drawing over him.

After a while they lay down together on the sleeping mat, and Juana did not put the baby in his box tonight, but cradled him in her arms and covered his face with her head shawl. And the last light went out of the embers in the fire hole.

But Kino's brain burned, even during his sleep, and he dreamed that Coyotito could read, that one of his own people could tell him the truth of things. And in his dream, Coyotito was reading from a book as large as a house, with letters as big as dogs, and the words galloped and played on the book. And then darkness spread over the page, and with the darkness came the music of evil again, and Kino stirred in his sleep; and when he stirred, Juana's eyes opened in the darkness. And then Kino awakened, with the evil music pulsing in him, and he lay in the darkness with his ears alert.

Then from the corner of the house came a sound so soft that it might have been simply a thought, a little furtive[8] movement, a touch of a foot on earth, the almost inaudible purr of controlled breathing. Kino held his breath to listen, and he knew that whatever dark thing was in his house was holding its breath too, to listen. For a time no sound at all came from the corner of the brush house. Then Kino might have thought he had imagined the sound. But Juana's hand came creeping over to him in warning, and then the sound came again! The whisper of a foot on dry earth and the scratch of fingers in the soil.

And now a wild fear surged in Kino's breast, and on the fear came rage, as it always did. Kino's hand crept into his breast where his knife hung on a string, and then he sprang like an angry cat, leaped striking and spitting for the dark thing he knew was in the corner of the house. He felt cloth, struck at it with his knife and missed, and struck again and felt his knife go through cloth, and then his head crashed with lightning and exploded with pain. There was a soft scurry in the doorway, and running steps for a moment, and then silence.

Kino could feel warm blood running down from his forehead, and he could hear Juana calling to him. "Kino! Kino!" And there was terror in her voice. Then coldness came over him as quickly as the rage had, and he said, "I am all right. The thing has gone."

He groped his way back to the sleeping mat. Already Juana was working at the fire. She uncovered an ember from the ashes and shredded little pieces of cornhusk over it and blew a little flame into the cornhusks so that a tiny light danced through the hut. And then from a secret place Juana brought a little piece of consecrated[9] candle and lighted it at the flame and set it upright on a fireplace stone. She worked quickly, crooning[10] as she moved about. She dipped the end of her head shawl in water and swabbed the blood from Kino's bruised forehead. "It is nothing," Kino said, but his eyes and his voice were hard and cold and a brooding hate was growing in him.

Now the tension which had been growing in Juana boiled up to the surface and her lips were thin. "This thing is evil," she cried harshly. "This pearl is like a sin! It will destroy us," and her voice rose shrilly. "Throw it away, Kino. Let us break it between stones. Let us bury it and forget the place. Let us throw it back into the sea. It has brought evil. Kino, my husband, it will destroy us." And in the firelight her lips and eyes were alive with her fear.

But Kino's face was set, and his mind and his will were set. "This is our one chance," he said. "Our son must go to school. He must break out of the pot that holds us in."

"It will destroy us all," Juana cried. "Even our son."

"Hush," said Kino. "Do not speak any more. In the morning we will sell the pearl, and then the evil will be gone, and only the good remain. Now hush, my wife." His dark eyes scowled into the little fire, and for the first time he knew that his knife was still in his hands, and he raised the blade and looked at it and saw a little line of blood on the steel. For a moment he seemed about to wipe the blade on his trousers but then he plunged the knife into the earth and so cleansed it.

---

8. **furtive** (fur′tiv): sneaky.

9. **consecrated** (kän′sə·krāt′id): set apart as holy or sacred.
10. **crooning**: singing or humming in a low tone.

The distant roosters began to crow and the air changed and the dawn was coming. The wind of the morning ruffled the water of the estuary and whispered through the mangroves, and the little waves beat on the rubbly beach with an increased tempo. Kino raised the sleeping mat and dug up his pearl and put it in front of him and stared at it.

And the beauty of the pearl, winking and glimmering in the light of the little candle, cozened[11] his brain with its beauty. So lovely it was, so soft, and its own music came from it—its music of promise and delight, its guarantee of the future, of comfort, of security. Its warm lucence promised a poultice against illness and a wall against insult. It closed a door on hunger. And as he stared at it Kino's eyes softened and his face relaxed. He could see the little image of the consecrated candle reflected in the soft surface of the pearl, and he heard again in his ears the lovely music of the undersea, the tone of the diffused green light of the sea bottom. Juana, glancing secretly at him, saw him smile. And because they were in some way one thing and one purpose, she smiled with him.

And they began this day with hope.

---

11. **cozened:** deceived.

Responding to the Novel

Analyzing Chapter III

Identifying Facts

1. The news that Kino has found the Pearl of the World spreads quickly in the village. How do the following characters react to the news.

   a. The priest
   b. The doctor
   c. The beggars
   d. The pearl buyers

2. How do Kino and Juana feel about their future right after the pearl is found? What does Kino plan to do with the money after he sells the pearl?

3. How does Kino feel after the visit of the priest?

4. Describe the first and second visits of the doctor. From evidence in the chapter, can you tell for sure whether the doctor, on his first visit, gave Coyotito something to make him sick?

5. What happens in the family's home in the night?

Interpreting Meanings

6. At the beginning of the chapter, the narrator compares a town to a colonial animal whose parts are very closely linked. How do events in the chapter support this description of a town.

7. Describe the **inner conflict** Kino has to resolve in this chapter about the doctor. Why does he decide to let the doctor treat Coyotito?

8. Describe Kino's **external conflict** with the doctor. What does the doctor want from Kino?

9. A **dynamic character** changes as a result of a story's events. How do Juana's feelings about the great pearl change in this chapter? What causes the change?

10. A **symbol** is an object that stands for something outside of, or broader than, itself. How do the concluding paragraphs of the chapter suggest that the pearl is a symbol? What do you think the pearl may symbolize at this stage of the story?

11. Kino say that in the morning he and Juana will sell the pearl, and then the evil will be gone. But certain comments by other characters and the narrator suggest that things will not work out as Kino hopes. What obstacles do you think Kino and Juana will have to face in the next chapter.

IV

It is wonderful the way a little town keeps track of itself and of all its units. If every single man and woman, child and baby, acts and conducts itself in a known pattern and breaks no walls and differs with no one and experiments in no way and is not sick and does not endanger the ease and peace of mind or steady unbroken flow of the town, then that unit can disappear and never be heard of. But let one man step out of the regular thought or the known and trusted pattern, and the nerves of the townspeople ring with nervousness and communication travels over the nerve lines of the town. Then every unit communicates to the whole.

Thus, in La Paz, it was known in the early morning through the whole town that Kino was going to sell his pearl that day. It was known among the neighbors in the brush huts, among the pearl fishermen; it was known among the Chinese grocery-store owners; it was known in the church, for the altar boys whispered about it. Word of it crept in among the nuns; the beggars in front of the church spoke of it, for they would be there to take the tithe[1] of the first fruits of the luck. The little boys knew about it with excitement, but most of all the pearl buyers knew about it, and when the day had come, in the offices of the pearl buyers, each man sat alone with his little black velvet tray, and each man rolled the pearls about with his fingertips and considered his part in the picture.

It was supposed that the pearl buyers were individuals acting alone, bidding against one another for the pearls the fishermen brought in. And once it had been so. But this was a wasteful method, for often, in the excitement of bidding for a fine pearl, too great a price had been paid to the fishermen. This was extravagant and not to be countenanced. Now there was only one pearl buyer with many hands, and the men who sat in their offices and waited for Kino knew what price they would offer, how high they would bid, and what method each one would use. And although these men would not profit beyond their salaries, there was excitement among the pearl buyers, for there was excitement in the hunt, and if it be a man's function to break down a price, then he must take joy and satisfaction in breaking it as far down as possible. For every man in the world functions to the best of his ability, and no one does less than his best, no matter what he may think about it. Quite apart from any reward they might get, from any word of praise, from any promotion, a pearl buyer was a pearl buyer, and the best and happiest pearl buyer was he who bought for the lowest prices.

The sun was hot yellow that morning, and it drew the moisture from the estuary and from the Gulf and hung it in shimmering scarves in the air so that the air vibrated and vision was insubstantial. A vision hung in the air to the north of the city—the vision of a mountain that was over two hundred miles away, and the high slopes of this mountain were swaddled with pines and a great stone peak arose above the timber line.

And the morning of this day the canoes lay lined up on the beach; the fishermen did not go out to dive for pearls, for there would be too much happening, too many things to see when Kino went to sell the great pearl.

In the brush houses by the shore Kino's neighbors sat long over their breakfasts, and they spoke of what they would do if they had found the pearl. And one man said that he would give it as a present to the Holy Father in Rome. Another said that he would buy Masses for the souls of his family for a thousand years. Another thought he might take the money and distribute it among the poor of La Paz; and a fourth thought of all the good things one could do with the money from the pearl, of all the charities, benefits, of all the rescues one could perform if one had money. All of the neighbors hoped that sudden wealth would not turn Kino's head, would not make a rich man of him, would not graft onto him the evil limbs of greed and hatred and coldness. For Kino was a well-liked man; it would be a shame if the pearl destroyed him. "That good wife Juana," they said, "and the beautiful baby Coyotito, and the others to come. What a pity it would be if the pearl should destroy them all."

For Kino and Juana this was the morning of mornings of their lives, comparable only to the day when the baby was born. This was to be the day from which all other days would take their arrangement. Thus they would say, "It was two years before we sold the pearl," or, "It was six weeks after we sold the pearl." Juana, considering the matter, threw caution to the winds, and she dressed Coyotito in the clothes she had prepared for his baptism, when there would be money for his baptism. And Juana combed and braided her hair and tied the ends with two little bows of red ribbon, and she put on her marriage skirt and

---

1. **tithe** (tīth): one tenth of one's income or wealth, paid as a tax or as a contribution to a church.

Old Colonial Bridge, Mexico by Millard Sheets
(1981). Watercolor.

Courtesy Kennedy Galleries,
Inc., New York.

waist.[2] The sun was quarter high when they were ready. Kino's ragged white clothes were clean at least, and this was the last day of his raggedness. For tomorrow, or even this afternoon, he would have new clothes.

The neighbors, watching Kino's door through the crevices in their brush houses, were dressed and ready too. There was no self-consciousness about their joining Kino and Juana to go pearl selling. It was expected, it was an historic moment, they would be crazy if they didn't go. It would be almost a sign of unfriendship.

---

2. **waist:** here, blouse.

Juana put on her head shawl carefully, and she draped one end under her right elbow and gathered it with her right hand so that a hammock hung under her arm, and in this little hammock she placed Coyotito, propped up against the head shawl so that he could see everything and perhaps remember. Kino put on his large straw hat and felt it with his hand to see that it was properly placed, not on the back or side of his head, like a rash, unmarried, irresponsible man, and not flat as an elder would wear it, but tilted a little forward to show aggressiveness and seriousness and vigor. There is a great deal to be seen in the tilt of a hat on a man. Kino slipped his feet into his sandals and pulled the thongs up over his heels. The great pearl was wrapped in an old soft piece of deerskin and placed in a little leather bag, and the leather bag was in a pocket in Kino's shirt. He folded his blanket carefully and draped it in a narrow strip over his left shoulder, and now they were ready.

Kino stepped with dignity out of the house, and Juana followed him, carrying Coyotito. And as they marched up the freshet[3]-washed alley toward the town, the neighbors joined them. The houses belched people; the doorways spewed out children. But because of the seriousness of the occasion, only one man walked with Kino, and that was his brother, Juan Tomás.

Juan Tomás cautioned his brother. "You must be careful to see they do not cheat you," he said.

And, "Very careful," Kino agreed.

"We do not know what prices are paid in other places," said Juan Tomás. "How can we know what is a fair price, if we do not know what the pearl buyer gets for the pearl in another place."

"That is true," said Kino, "but how can we know? We are here, we are not there."

As they walked up toward the city the crowd grew behind them, and Juan Tomás, in pure nervousness, went on speaking.

"Before you were born, Kino," he said, "the old ones thought of a way to get more money for their pearls. They thought it would be better if they had an agent who took all the pearls to the capital and sold them there and kept only his share of the profit."

Kino nodded his head. "I know," he said. "It was a good thought."

"And so they got such a man," said Juan Tomás, "and they pooled the pearls, and they started him off. And he was never heard of again and the pearls were lost. Then they got another man, and they started him off, and he was never heard of again. And so they gave the whole thing up and went back to the old way."

"I know," said Kino. "I have heard our father tell of it. It was a good idea, but it was against religion, and the Father made that very clear. The loss of the pearl was a punishment visited on those who tried to leave their station. And the Father made it clear that each man and woman is like a soldier sent by God to guard some part of the castle of the Universe. And some are in the ramparts[4] and some far deep in the darkness of the walls. But each one must remain faithful to his post and must not go running about, else the castle is in danger from the assaults of Hell."

---

3. **freshet** (fresh′it): stream or rush of fresh water.
4. **ramparts**: structures built up to protect a castle, fort, etc.

"I have heard him make that sermon," said Juan Tomás. "He makes it every year."

The brothers, as they walked along, squinted their eyes a little, as they and their grandfathers and their great-grandfathers had done for four hundred years, since first the strangers came with arguments and authority and gunpowder to back up both. And in the four hundred years Kino's people had learned only one defense—a slight slitting of the eyes and a slight tightening of the lips and a retirement. Nothing could break down this wall, and they could remain whole within the wall.

The gathering procession was solemn, for they sensed the importance of this day, and any children who showed a tendency to scuffle, to scream, to cry out, to steal hats and rumple hair, were hissed to silence by their elders. So important was this day that an old man came to see, riding on the stalwart shoulders of his nephew. The procession left the brush huts and entered the stone and plaster city where the streets were a little wider and there were narrow pavements beside the buildings. And as before, the beggars joined them as they passed the church; the grocers looked out at them as they went by; the little saloons lost their customers and the owners closed up shop and went along. And the sun beat down on the streets of the city and even tiny stones threw shadows on the ground.

The news of the approach of the procession ran ahead of it, and in their little dark offices the pearl buyers stiffened and grew alert. They got out papers so that they could be at work when Kino appeared, and they put their pearls in the desks, for it is not good to let an inferior pearl be seen beside a beauty. And word of the loveliness of Kino's pearl had come to them. The pearl buyers' offices were clustered together in one narrow street, and they were barred at the windows, and wooden slats cut out the light so that only a soft gloom entered the offices.

A stout slow man sat in an office waiting. His face was fatherly and benign, and his eyes twinkled with friendship. He was a caller of good mornings, a ceremonious shaker of hands, a jolly man who knew all jokes and yet who hovered close to sadness, for in the midst of a laugh he could remember the death of your aunt, and his eyes could become wet with sorrow for your loss. This morning he had placed a flower in a vase on his desk, a single scarlet hibiscus, and the vase sat beside the black velvet-lined pearl tray in front of him. He was shaved close to the blue roots of his beard, and his hands were clean and his nails polished. His door stood open to the morning, and he hummed under his breath while his right hand practiced legerdemain.[5] He rolled a coin back and forth over his knuckles and made it appear and disappear, made it spin and sparkle. The coin winked into sight and as quickly slipped out of sight, and the man did not even watch his own performance. The fingers did it all mechanically, precisely, while the man hummed to himself and peered out the door. Then he heard the tramp of feet of the approaching crowd, and the fingers of his right hand worked faster and faster until, as the figure of Kino filled the doorway, the coin flashed and disappeared.

"Good morning, my friend," the stout man said. "What can I do for you?"

Kino stared into the dimness of the little office, for his eyes were squeezed from the outside glare. But the buyer's eyes had become as steady and cruel and unwinking as a hawk's eyes, while the rest of his face smiled in greeting. And secretly, behind his desk, his right hand practiced with the coin.

"I have a pearl," said Kino. And Juan Tomás stood beside him and snorted a little at the understatement. The neighbors peered around the doorway, and a line of little boys clambered on the window bars and looked through. Several little boys, on their hands and knees, watched the scene around Kino's legs.

"You have a pearl," the dealer said. "Sometimes a man brings in a dozen. Well, let us see your pearl. We will value it and give you the best price." And his fingers worked furiously with the coin.

Now Kino instinctively knew his own dramatic effects. Slowly he brought out the leather bag, slowly took from it the soft and dirty piece of deerskin, and then he let the great pearl roll into the black velvet tray, and instantly his eyes went to the buyer's face. But there was no sign, no movement, the face did not change, but the secret hand behind the desk missed in its precision. The coin stumbled over a knuckle and slipped silently into the dealer's lap. And the fingers behind the desk curled into a fist. When the right hand came out of hiding, the forefinger touched the great pearl, rolled it on the black velvet; thumb and forefinger picked it up and brought it near to the dealer's eyes and twirled it in the air.

Kino held his breath, and the neighbors held their breath, and the whispering went back through the crowd. "He is inspecting it—No price

has been mentioned yet—They have not come to a price."

Now the dealer's hand had become a personality. The hand tossed the great pearl back to the tray, the forefinger poked and insulted it, and on the dealer's face there came a sad and contemptuous smile.

"I am sorry, my friend," he said, and his shoulders rose a little to indicate that the misfortune was no fault of his.

"It is a pearl of great value," Kino said.

The dealer's fingers spurned the pearl so that it bounced and rebounded softly from the sides of the velvet tray.

"You have heard of fool's gold," the dealer said. "This pearl is like fool's gold. It is too large. Who would buy it? There is no market for such things. It is a curiosity only. I am sorry. You thought it was a thing of value, and it is only a curiosity."

Now Kino's face was perplexed and worried. "It is the Pearl of the World," he cried. "No one has ever seen such a pearl."

"On the contrary," said the dealer, "it is large and clumsy. As a curiosity it has interest; some museum might perhaps take it to place in a collection of seashells. I can give you, say, a thousand pesos.[6]"

Kino's face grew dark and dangerous. "It is worth fifty thousand," he said. "You know it. You want to cheat me."

And the dealer heard a little grumble go through the crowd as they heard his price. And the dealer felt a little tremor of fear.

"Do not blame me," he said quickly. "I am only an appraiser. Ask the others. Go to their offices and show your pearl—or better let them come here, so that you can see there is no collusion.[7] Boy," he called. And when his servant looked through the rear door, "Boy, go to such a one, and such another one and such a third one. Ask them to step in here and do not tell them why. Just say that I will be pleased to see them." And his right hand went behind the desk and pulled another coin from his pocket, and the coin rolled back and forth over his knuckles.

Kino's neighbors whispered together. They had been afraid of something like this. The pearl was large, but it had a strange color. They had been suspicious of it from the first. And after all, a thousand pesos was not to be thrown away. It was

---

5. **legerdemain** (lej′ər·di·mān′): tricks requiring manual skill.

6. **thousand pesos:** eighty dollars. At the time, a peso was worth about eight cents.

7. **collusion** (kə·lōō′zhən): secret agreement for an illegal or deceitful purpose.

comparative wealth to a man who was not wealthy. And suppose Kino took a thousand pesos. Only yesterday he had nothing.

But Kino had grown tight and hard. He felt the creeping of fate, the circling of wolves, the hover of vultures. He felt the evil coagulating[8] about him, and he was helpless to protect himself. He heard in his ears the evil music. And on the black velvet the great pearl glistened, so that the dealer could not keep his eyes from it.

The crowd in the doorway wavered and broke and let the three pearl dealers through. The crowd was silent now, fearing to miss a word, to fail to see a gesture or an expression. Kino was silent and watchful. He felt a little tugging at his back, and he turned and looked in Juana's eyes, and when he looked away he had renewed strength.

The dealers did not glance at one another nor at the pearl. The man behind the desk said, "I have put a value on this pearl. The owner here does not think it fair. I will ask you to examine this—this thing and make an offer. Notice," he said to Kino, "I have not mentioned what I have offered."

The first dealer, dry and stringy, seemed now to see the pearl for the first time. He took it up, rolled it quickly between thumb and forefinger, and then cast it contemptuously back into the tray.

"Do not include me in the discussion," he said dryly. "I will make no offer at all. I do not want it. This is not a pearl—it is a monstrosity." His thin lips curled.

Now the second dealer, a little man with a shy soft voice, took up the pearl, and he examined it carefully. He took a glass from his pocket and inspected it under magnification. Then he laughed softly.

"Better pearls are made of paste," he said. "I know these things. This is soft and chalky, it will lose its color and die in a few months. Look—" He offered the glass to Kino, showed him how to use it, and Kino, who had never seen a pearl's surface magnified, was shocked at the strange-looking surface.

The third dealer took the pearl from Kino's hands. "One of my clients likes such things," he said. "I will offer five hundred pesos, and perhaps I can sell it to my client for six hundred."

Kino reached quickly and snatched the pearl from his hand. He wrapped it in the deerskin and thrust it inside his shirt.

The man behind the desk said, "I'm a fool, I know, but my first offer stands. I still offer one thousand. What are you doing?" he asked, as Kino thrust the pearl out of sight.

"I am cheated," Kino cried fiercely. "My pearl is not for sale here. I will go, perhaps even to the capital."

Now the dealers glanced quickly at one another. They knew they had played too hard; they knew they would be disciplined for their failure, and the man at the desk said quickly, "I might go to fifteen hundred."

But Kino was pushing his way through the crowd. The hum of talk came to him dimly, his rage blood pounded in his ears, and he burst through and strode away. Juana followed, trotting after him.

When the evening came, the neighbors in the brush houses sat eating their corncakes and beans, and they discussed the great theme of the morning. They did not know, it seemed a fine pearl to them, but they had never seen such a pearl before, and surely the dealers knew more about the value of pearls than they. "And mark this," they said. "Those dealers did not discuss these things. Each of the three knew the pearl was valueless."

"But suppose they had arranged it before?"

"If that is so, then all of us have been cheated all of our lives."

Perhaps, some argued, perhaps it would have been better if Kino took the one thousand five hundred pesos. That is a great deal of money, more than he has ever seen. Maybe Kino is being a pigheaded fool. Suppose he should really go to the capital and find no buyer for his pearl. He would never live that down.

And now, said other fearful ones, now that he had defied them, those buyers will not want to deal with him at all. Maybe Kino has cut off his own head and destroyed himself.

And others said, Kino is a brave man, and a fierce man; he is right. From his courage we may all profit. These were proud of Kino.

In his house Kino squatted on his sleeping mat, brooding. He had buried his pearl under a stone of the fire hole in his house, and he stared at the woven tules[9] of his sleeping mat until the crossed design danced in his head. He had lost one world and had not gained another. And Kino was afraid. Never in his life had he been far from home. He was afraid of strangers and of strange places. He was terrified of that monster of strangeness they called the capital. It lay over the water and through the mountains, over a thousand miles, and every strange terrible mile was frightening. But

---

8. **coagulating** (kō·ag′yōō·lāt′iŋ): becoming a solid mass; clotting.

9. **tules:** large bulrushes, or marsh plants, with long stems.

Kino had lost his old world and he must clamber on to a new one. For his dream of the future was real and never to be destroyed, and he had said "I will go," and that made a real thing too. To determine to go and to say it was to be halfway there.

Juana watched him while he buried his pearl, and she watched him while she cleaned Coyotito and nursed him, and Juana made the corncakes for supper.

Juan Tomás came in and squatted down beside Kino and remained silent for a long time, until at last Kino demanded, "What else could I do? They are cheats."

Juan Tomás nodded gravely. He was the elder, and Kino looked to him for wisdom. "It is hard to know," he said. "We do know that we are cheated from birth to the overcharge on our coffins. But we survive. You have defied not the pearl buyers, but the whole structure, the whole way of life, and I am afraid for you."

"What have I to fear but starvation?" Kino asked.

But Juan Tomás shook his head slowly. "That we must all fear. But suppose you are correct—suppose your pearl is of great value—do you think then the game is over?"

"What do you mean?"

"I don't know," said Juan Tomás, "but I am afraid for you. It is new ground you are walking on, you do not know the way."

"I will go. I will go soon," said Kino.

"Yes," Juan Tomás agreed. "That you must do. But I wonder if you will find it any different in the capital. Here, you have friends and me, your brother. There, you will have no one."

"What can I do?" Kino cried. "Some deep outrage is here. My son must have a chance. That is what they are striking at. My friends will protect me."

"Only so long as they are not in danger or discomfort from it," said Juan Tomás. He arose, saying, "Go with God."

And Kino said, "Go with God," and did not even look up, for the words had a strange chill in them.

Long after Juan Tomás had gone Kino sat brooding on his sleeping mat. A lethargy[10] had settled on him, and a little gray hopelessness. Every road seemed blocked against him. In his head he heard only the dark music of the enemy. His senses were burningly alive, but his mind went back to the deep participation with all things, the

_____
10. **lethargy** (leth′ər·jē): great lack of energy; sluggishness.

gift he had from his people. He heard every little sound of the gathering night, the sleepy complaint of settling birds, the love agony of cats, the strike and withdrawal of little waves on the beach, and the simple hiss of distance. And he could smell the sharp odor of exposed kelp from the receding tide. The little flare of the twig fire made the design on his sleeping mat jump before his entranced eyes.

Juana watched him with worry, but she knew him and she knew she could help him best by being silent and by being near. And as though she too could hear the Song of Evil, she fought it, singing softly the melody of the family, of the safety and warmth and wholeness of the family. She held Coyotito in her arms and sang the song to him, to keep the evil out, and her voice was brave against the threat of the dark music.

Kino did not move nor ask for his supper. She knew he would ask when he wanted it. His eyes were entranced, and he could sense the wary, watchful evil outside the brush house; he could feel the dark creeping things waiting for him to go out into the night. It was shadowy and dreadful, and yet it called to him and threatened him and challenged him. His right hand went into his shirt and felt his knife; his eyes were wide; he stood up and walked to the doorway.

Juana willed to stop him; she raised her hand to stop him, and her mouth opened with terror. For a long moment Kino looked out into the darkness and then he stepped outside. Juana heard the little rush, the grunting struggle, the blow. She froze with terror for a moment, and then her lips drew back from her teeth like a cat's lips. She set Coyotito down on the ground. She seized a stone from the fireplace and rushed outside, but it was over by then. Kino lay on the ground, struggling to rise, and there was no one near him. Only the shadows and the strike and rush of waves and the hiss of distance. But the evil was all about, hidden behind the brush fence, crouched beside the house in the shadow, hovering in the air.

Juana dropped her stone, and she put her arms around Kino and helped him to his feet and supported him into the house. Blood oozed down from his scalp and there was a long deep cut in his cheek from ear to chin, a deep, bleeding slash. And Kino was only half conscious. He shook his head from side to side. His shirt was torn open and his clothes half pulled off. Juana sat him down on his sleeping mat and she wiped the thickening blood from his face with her skirt. She brought him pulque to drink in a little pitcher, and still he shook his head to clear out the darkness.

"Who?" Juana asked.

"I don't know," Kino said. "I didn't see."

Now Juana brought her clay pot of water and she washed the cut on his face while he stared dazed ahead of him.

"Kino, my husband," she cried, and his eyes stared past her. "Kino, can you hear me?"

"I hear you," he said dully.

"Kino, this pearl is evil. Let us destroy it before it destroys us. Let us crush it between two stones. Let us—let us throw it back in the sea where it belongs. Kino, it is evil, it is evil!"

And as she spoke the light came back in Kino's eyes so that they glowed fiercely and his muscles hardened and his will hardened.

"No," he said. "I will fight this thing. I will win over it. We will have our chance." His fist pounded the sleeping mat. "No one shall take our good fortune from us," he said. His eyes softened then and he raised a gentle hand to Juana's shoulder. "Believe me," he said. "I am a man." And his face grew crafty.

"In the morning we will take our canoe and we will go over the sea and over the mountains to the capital, you and I. We will not be cheated. I am a man."

"Kino," she said huskily, "I am afraid. A man can be killed. Let us throw the pearl back into the sea."

"Hush," he said fiercely. "I am a man. Hush." And she was silent, for his voice was command. "Let us sleep a little," he said. "In the first light we will start. You are not afraid to go with me?"

"No, my husband."

His eyes were soft and warm on her then, his hand touched her cheek. "Let us sleep a little," he said.

Responding to the Novel

Analyzing Chapter IV

Identifying Facts

1. Describe the way the pearl buyers do business.
2. Juan Tomás tells Kino of a method used in the past by the villagers to get more money for their pearls. What was this method? How did the priest explain its lack of success?
3. What do the buyers say about Kino's pearl? How does Kino end the bargaining?
4. What happens to Kino in the evening? Describe the contrasting reactions of Kino and Juana.

Interpreting Meanings

5. As the plot of *The Pearl* unfolded in the first three chapters we learned about the **basic situation** of the characters. We also saw how Kino became involved in **conflicts** after finding the great pearl. In Chapter IV a major **complication** develops in the plot. What is this complication? How must it change the course of the story?
6. Juan Tomás can be seen as **symbolizing** traditional ways in the village. Kino can be seen as representing a desire for change. How does their discussion after Kino's experience with the pearl buyers demonstrate this contrast? Which character do you agree with?
7. What does the description of the stout pearl buyer's trick with the coin suggest about his motives and personality? How does the trick **foreshadow** the result of his meeting with Kino?

Applying Meanings

8. The narrator tells us that people had different opinions about Kino's actions. Some thought he might be a pigheaded fool. Others thought he was a brave man. What do you think? If you had been negotiating to sell the pearl, would you have accepted the buyer's final offer?

V

The late moon arose before the first rooster crowed. Kino opened his eyes in the darkness, for he sensed movement near him, but he did not move. Only his eyes searched the darkness, and in the pale light of the moon that crept through the holes in the brush house Kino saw Juana arise silently from beside him. He saw her move toward the fireplace. So carefully did she work that he heard only the lightest sound when she moved the fireplace stone. And then like a shadow she glided toward the door. She paused for a moment beside the hanging box where Coyotito lay, then for a second she was back in the doorway, and then she was gone.

And rage surged in Kino. He rolled up to his feet and followed her as silently as she had gone, and he could hear her quick footsteps going toward the shore. Quietly he tracked her, and his brain was red with anger. She burst clear of the brush line and stumbled over the little boulders toward the water, and then she heard him coming and she broke into a run. Her arm was up to throw when he leaped at her and caught her arm and wrenched the pearl from her. He struck her in the face with his clenched fist and she fell among the boulders, and he kicked her in the side. In the pale light he could see the little waves break over her, and her skirt floated about and clung to her legs as the water receded.

Kino looked down at her and his teeth were bared. He hissed at her like a snake, and Juana stared at him with wide unfrightened eyes, like a sheep before the butcher. She knew there was murder in him, and it was all right; she had accepted it, and she would not resist or even protest. And then the rage left him and a sick disgust took its place. He turned away from her and walked up the beach and through the brush line. His senses were dulled by his emotion.

He heard the rush, got his knife out and lunged at one dark figure and felt his knife go home, and then he was swept to his knees and swept again to the ground. Greedy fingers went through his clothes, frantic fingers searched him, and the pearl, knocked from his hand, lay winking behind a little stone in the pathway. It glinted in the soft moonlight.

Juana dragged herself up from the rocks on the edge of the water. Her face was a dull pain and her side ached. She steadied herself on her knees for a while and her wet skirt clung to her. There was no anger in her for Kino. He had said, "I am a man," and that meant certain things to Juana. It meant that he was half insane and half god. It meant that Kino would drive his strength against a mountain and plunge his strength against the sea. Juana, in her woman's soul, knew that the mountain would stand while the man broke himself; that the sea would surge while the man drowned in it. And yet it was this thing that made him a man, half insane and half god, and Juana had need of a man; she could not live without a man. Although she might be puzzled by these differences between man and woman, she knew them and accepted them and needed them. Of course she would follow him, there was no question of that. Sometimes the quality of woman, the reason, the caution, the sense of preservation, could cut through Kino's manness and save them all. She climbed painfully to her feet, and she dipped her cupped palms in the little waves and washed her bruised face with the stinging salt water, and then she went creeping up the beach after Kino.

A flight of herring clouds had moved over the sky from the south. The pale moon dipped in and out of the strands of clouds so that Juana walked in darkness for a moment and in light the next. Her back was bent with pain and her head was low. She went through the line of brush when the moon was covered, and when it looked through she saw the glimmer of the great pearl in the path behind the rock. She sank to her knees and picked it up, and the moon went into the darkness of the clouds again. Juana remained on her knees while she considered whether to go back to the sea and finish her job, and as she considered, the light came again, and she saw two dark figures lying in the path ahead of her. She leaped forward and saw that one was Kino and the other a stranger with dark shiny fluid leaking from his throat.

Kino moved sluggishly, arms and legs stirred like those of a crushed bug, and a thick muttering came from his mouth. Now, in an instant, Juana knew that the old life was gone forever. A dead man in the path and Kino's knife, dark bladed beside him, convinced her. All of the time Juana had been trying to rescue something of the old peace, of the time before the pearl. But now it was gone, and there was no retrieving it. And knowing this, she abandoned the past instantly. There was nothing to do but to save themselves.

Her pain was gone now, her slowness. Quickly she dragged the dead man from the pathway into the shelter of the brush. She went to Kino and sponged his face with her wet skirt. His senses were coming back and he moaned.

"They have taken the pearl. I have lost it. Now it is over," he said. "The pearl is gone."

Juana quieted him as she would quiet a sick child. "Hush," she said. "Here is your pearl. I found it in the path. Can you hear me now? Here is your pearl. Can you understand? You have killed a man. We must go away. They will come for us, can you understand? We must be gone before the daylight comes.''

"I was attacked," Kino said uneasily. "I struck to save my life."

"Do you remember yesterday?" Juana asked. "Do you think that will matter? Do you remember the men of the city? Do you think your explanation will help?"

Kino drew a great breath and fought off his weakness. "No," he said. "You are right." And his will hardened and he was a man again.

"Go to our house and bring Coyotito," he said, "and bring all the corn we have. I will drag the canoe into the water and we will go."

He took his knife and left her. He stumbled toward the beach and he came to his canoe. And when the light broke through again he saw that a great hole had been knocked in the bottom. And a searing rage came to him and gave him strength. Now the darkness was closing in on his family; now the evil music filled the night, hung over the mangroves, skirled[1] in the wave beat. The canoe of his grandfather, plastered over and over, and a splintered hole broken in it. This was an evil beyond thinking. The killing of a man was not so evil as the killing of a boat. For a boat does not have sons, and a boat cannot protect itself, and a wounded boat does not heal. There was sorrow in Kino's rage, but this last thing had tightened him beyond breaking. He was an animal now, for hiding, for attacking, and he lived only to preserve himself and his family. He was not conscious of the pain in his head. He leaped up the beach, through the brush line toward his brush house, and it did not occur to him to take one of the canoes of his neighbors. Never once did the thought enter his head, any more than he could have conceived breaking a boat.

The roosters were crowing and the dawn was not far off. Smoke of the first fires seeped out through the walls of the brush houses, and the first smell of cooking corncakes was in the air. Already the dawn birds were scampering in the bushes. The weak moon was losing its light and the clouds thickened and curdled to the southward. The wind blew freshly into the estuary, a nervous, restless wind with the smell of storm on its breath, and there was change and uneasiness in the air.

Kino, hurrying toward his house, felt a surge of exhilaration. Now he was not confused, for there was only one thing to do, and Kino's hand went first to the great pearl in his shirt and then to his knife hanging under his shirt.

He saw a little glow ahead of him, and then without interval a tall flame leaped up in the dark with a crackling roar, and a tall edifice[2] of fire lighted the pathway. Kino broke into a run; it was his brush house, he knew. And he knew that these houses could burn down in a very few moments. And as he ran a scuttling figure ran toward him— Juana, with Coyotito in her arms and Kino's shoulder blanket clutched in her hand. The baby moaned with fright, and Juana's eyes were wide and terrified. Kino could see the house was gone, and he did not question Juana. He knew, but she said, "It was torn up and the floor dug—even the baby's box turned out, and as I looked they put the fire to the outside."

The fierce light of the burning house lighted Kino's face strongly. "Who?" he demanded.

"I don't know," she said. "The dark ones."

The neighbors were tumbling from their houses now, and they watched the falling sparks and stamped them out to save their own houses. Suddenly Kino was afraid. The light made him afraid. He remembered the man lying dead in the brush beside the path, and he took Juana by the arm and drew her into the shadow of a house away from the light, for light was danger to him. For a moment he considered and then he worked among the shadows until he came to the house of Juan Tomás, his brother, and he slipped into the doorway and drew Juana after him. Outside, he could hear the squeal of children and the shouts of the neighbors, for his friends thought he might be inside the burning house.

The house of Juan Tomás was almost exactly like Kino's house; nearly all the brush houses were alike, and all leaked light and air, so that Juana and Kino, sitting in the corner of the brother's house, could see the leaping flames through the wall. They saw the flames tall and furious, they saw the roof fall and watched the fire die down as quickly as a twig fire dies. They heard the cries of warning of their friends, and the shrill, keening cry of Apolonia, wife of Juan Tomás. She, being the nearest woman relative, raised a formal lament for the dead of the family.

Apolonia realized that she was wearing her second-best head shawl and she rushed to her house to get her fine new one. As she rummaged in a box by the wall, Kino's voice said quietly, "Apolonia, do not cry out. We are not hurt."

"How do you come here?" she demanded.

"Do not question," he said. "Go now to Juan Tomás and bring him here and tell no one else. This is important to us, Apolonia."

---

1. **skirled:** sounded out in shrill, piercing tones.

2. **edifice** (ed′ə·fis): building.

She paused, her hands helpless in front of her, and then, "Yes, my brother-in-law," she said.

In a few moments Juan Tomás came back with her. He lighted a candle and came to them where they crouched in a corner and he said, "Apolonia, see to the door, and do not let anyone enter." He was older, Juan Tomás, and he assumed the authority. "Now, my brother," he said.

"I was attacked in the dark," said Kino. "And in the fight I have killed a man."

"Who?" asked Juan Tomás quickly.

"I do not know. It is all darkness—all darkness and shape of darkness."

"It is the pearl," said Juan Tomás. "There is a devil in this pearl. You should have sold it and passed on the devil. Perhaps you can still sell it and buy peace for yourself."

And Kino said, "Oh, my brother, an insult has been put on me that is deeper than my life. For on the beach my canoe is broken, my house is burned, and in the brush a dead man lies. Every escape is cut off. You must hide us, my brother."

And Kino, looking closely, saw deep worry come into his brother's eyes and he forestalled him in a possible refusal. "Not for long," he said quickly. "Only until a day has passed and the new night has come. Then we will go."

"I will hide you," said Juan Tomás.

"I do not want to bring danger to you," Kino said. "I know I am like a leprosy.[3] I will go tonight and then you will be safe."

"I will protect you," said Juan Tomás, and he called, "Apolonia, close up the door. Do not even whisper that Kino is here."

They sat silently all day in the darkness of the house, and they could hear the neighbors speaking of them. Through the walls of the house they could watch their neighbors raking the ashes to find the bones. Crouching in the house of Juan Tomás, they heard the shock go into their neighbors' minds at the news of the broken boat. Juan Tomás went out among the neighbors to divert their suspicions, and he gave them theories and ideas of what had happened to Kino and to Juana and to the baby. To one he said, "I think they have gone south along the coast to escape the evil that was on them." And to another, "Kino would never leave the sea. Perhaps he found another boat." And he said, "Apolonia is ill with grief."

And in that day the wind rose up to beat the Gulf and tore the kelps and weeds that lined the shore, and the wind cried through the brush houses and no boat was safe on the water. Then Juan Tomás told among the neighbors, "Kino is gone. If he went to the sea, he is drowned by now." And after each trip among the neighbors Juan Tomás came back with something borrowed. He brought a little woven straw bag of red beans and a gourd[4] full of rice. He borrowed a cup of dried peppers and a block of salt, and he brought in a long working knife, eighteen inches long and heavy, as a small ax, a tool and a weapon. And when Kino saw this knife his eyes lighted up, and he fondled the blade and his thumb tested the edge.

The wind screamed over the Gulf and turned the water white, and the mangroves plunged like frightened cattle, and a fine sandy dust arose from the land and hung in a stifling cloud over the sea. The wind drove off the clouds and skimmed the sky clean and drifted the sand of the country like snow.

Then Juan Tomás, when the evening approached, talked long with his brother. "Where will you go?"

"To the north," said Kino. "I have heard that there are cities in the north."

"Avoid the shore," said Juan Tomás. "They are making a party to search the shore. The men in the city will look for you. Do you still have the pearl?"

"I have it," said Kino. "And I will keep it. I might have given it as a gift, but now it is my misfortune and my life and I will keep it." His eyes were hard and cruel and bitter.

Coyotito whimpered and Juana muttered little magics over him to make him silent.

"The wind is good," said Juan Tomás. "There will be no tracks."

They left quietly in the dark before the moon had risen. The family stood formally in the house of Juan Tomás. Juana carried Coyotito on her back, covered and held in by her head shawl, and the baby slept, cheek turned sideways against her shoulder. The head shawl covered the baby, and one end of it came across Juana's nose to protect her from the evil night air. Juan Tomás embraced his brother with the double embrace and kissed him on both cheeks. "Go with God," he said, and it was like a death. "You will not give up the pearl?"

"This pearl has become my soul," said Kino. "If I give it up I shall lose my soul. Go thou also with God."

---

3. **leprosy** (lep′rə·sē): infectious disease that attacks the skin and nerves. The disease causes bodily deformities, and leaves scabs and ulcers on the skin.

4. **gourd:** here, the dried, hollowed out shell of an inedible fruit used as a cup, dipper, sack, etc. The fruit is related to the squash family.

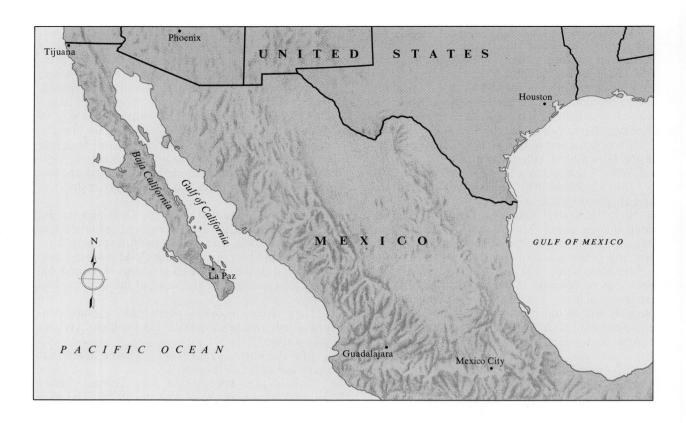

Responding to the Novel

Analyzing Chapter V

Identifying Facts

1. What is Juana attempting to do as the chapter opens? How does Kino stop her?
2. What happens to Kino as he returns from the beach?
3. Juana gives Kino first aid, and they make a decision. Why can't they act on the decision?
4. Why do Kino and Juana go to Juan Tomás's house? How does Juan Tomás help them?

Interpreting Meanings

5. In Chapter III the narrator said a town was like a colonial animal, with all parts very closely tied to each other. What three major events in Chapter V break Kino's ties with the town and make him an outsider? Do you think he could become part of the town again in the future?

6. Exlain in your own words why Juana has no anger for Kino, despite the way he has treated her. Do you agree with her attitude?
7. Did the violent conflict between Kino and Juana in this chapter surprise you? Or did passages in earlier chapters suggest that it might occur? Explain your answer.
8. At the end of the chapter Kino says, "This pearl has become my soul. . . . If I give it up I shall lose my soul." Explain what he means. Does the statement represent a change in Kino's feelings from earlier chapters?

Applying Meanings

9. Kino says the "pearl has become my soul." Do you think some people have similar feelings today? What objects today might play a role similar to the role of Kino's pearl?

VI

The wind blew fierce and strong, and it pelted them with bits of sticks, sand, and little rocks. Juana and Kino gathered their clothing tighter about them and covered their noses and went out into the world. The sky was brushed clean by the wind and the stars were cold in a black sky. The two walked carefully, and they avoided the center of town where some sleeper in a doorway might see them pass. For the town closed itself in against the night, and anyone who moved about in the darkness would be noticeable. Kino threaded his way around the edge of the city and turned north, north by the stars, and found the rutted sandy road that led through the brushy country toward Loreto where the miraculous Virgin has her station.[1]

Kino could feel the blown sand against his ankles and he was glad, for he knew there would be no tracks. The little light from the stars made out for him the narrow road through the brushy country. And Kino could hear the pad of Juana's feet behind him. He went quickly and quietly, and Juana trotted behind him to keep up.

Some ancient thing stirred in Kino. Through his fear of dark and the devils that haunt the night, there came a rush of exhilaration; some animal thing was moving in him so that he was cautious and wary and dangerous; some ancient thing out of the past of his people was alive in him. The wind was at his back and the stars guided him. The wind cried and whisked in the brush, and the family went on monotonously, hour after hour. They passed no one and saw no one. At last, to their right, the waning[2] moon arose, and when it came up the wind died down, and the land was still.

Now they could see the little road ahead of them, deep cut with sand-drifted wheel tracks. With the wind gone there would be footprints, but they were a good distance from the town and perhaps their tracks might not be noticed. Kino walked carefully in a wheel rut, and Juana followed in his path. One big cart, going to the town in the morning, could wipe out every trace of their passage.

All night they walked and never changed their pace. Once Coyotito awakened, and Juana shifted him in front of her and soothed him until he went to sleep again. And the evils of the night were about them. The coyotes cried and laughed in the brush, and the owls screeched and hissed over their heads. And once some large animal lumbered away, crackling the undergrowth as it went. And Kino gripped the handle of the big working knife and took a sense of protection from it.

The music of the pearl was triumphant in Kino's head, and the quiet melody of the family underlay it, and they wove themselves into the soft padding of sandaled feet in the dusk. All night they walked, and in the first dawn Kino searched the roadside for a covert[3] to lie in during the day. He found his place near to the road, a little clearing where deer might have lain, and it was curtained thickly with the dry brittle trees that lined the road. And when Juana had seated herself and had settled to nurse the baby, Kino went back to the road. He broke a branch and carefully swept the footprints where they had turned from the roadway. And then, in the first light, he heard the creak of a wagon, and he crouched beside the road and watched a heavy two-wheeled cart go by, drawn by slouching oxen. And when it had passed out of sight, he went back to the roadway and looked at the rut and found that the footprints were gone. And again he swept out his traces and went back to Juana.

She gave him the soft corncakes Apolonia had packed for them, and after a while she slept a little. But Kino sat on the ground and stared at the earth in front of him. He watched the ants moving, a little column of them near to his foot, and he put his foot in their path. Then the column climbed over his instep and continued on its way, and Kino left his foot there and watched them move over it.

The sun arose hotly. They were not near the Gulf now, and the air was dry and hot so that the brush cricked with heat and a good resinous smell came from it. And when Juana awakened, when the sun was high, Kino told her things she knew already.

"Beware of that kind of tree there," he said, pointing. "Do not touch it, for if you do and then touch your eyes, it will blind you. And beware of the tree that bleeds. See, that one over there. For if you break it the red blood will flow from it, and it is evil luck." And she nodded and smiled a little at him, for she knew these things.

"Will they follow us?" she asked. "Do you think they will try to find us?"

"They will try," said Kino. "Whoever finds us will take the pearl. Oh, they will try."

---

1. A shrine to the Virgin Mary is situated in the city of Loreto.
2. **waning** (wān'iη): growing gradually smaller.

3. **covert:** shelter or protected place.

And Juana said, "Perhaps the dealers were right and the pearl has no value. Perhaps this has all been an illusion."

Kino reached into his clothes and brought out the pearl. He let the sun play on it until it burned in his eyes. "No," he said, "they would not have tried to steal it if it had been valueless."

"Do you know who attacked you? Was it the dealers?"

"I do not know," he said. "I didn't see them."

He looked into his pearl to find his vision. "When we sell it at last, I will have a rifle," he said, and he looked into the shining surface for his rifle, but he saw only a huddled dark body on the ground with shining blood dripping from its throat. And he said quickly, "We will be married in a great church." And in the pearl he saw Juana with her beaten face crawling home through the night. "Our son must learn to read," he said frantically. And there in the pearl Coyotito's face, thick and feverish from the medicine.

And Kino thrust the pearl back into his clothing, and the music of the pearl had become sinister in his ears and it was interwoven with the music of evil.

The hot sun beat on the earth so that Kino and Juana moved into the lacy shade of the brush, and small gray birds scampered on the ground in the shade. In the heat of the day Kino relaxed and covered his eyes with his hat and wrapped his blanket about his face to keep the flies off, and he slept.

But Juana did not sleep. She sat quiet as a stone and her face was quiet. Her mouth was still swollen where Kino had struck her, and big flies buzzed around the cut on her chin. But she sat as still as a sentinel,[4] and when Coyotito awakened she placed him on the ground in front of her and watched him wave his arms and kick his feet, and he smiled and gurgled at her until she smiled too. She picked up a little twig from the ground and tickled him, and she gave him water from the gourd she carried in her bundle.

Kino stirred in a dream, and he cried out in a guttural[5] voice, and his hand moved in symbolic fighting. And then he moaned and sat up suddenly, his eyes wide and his nostrils flaring. He listened and heard only the cricking heat and the hiss of distance.

"What is it?" Juana asked.

"Hush," he said.

"You were dreaming."

"Perhaps." But he was restless, and when she gave him a corncake from her store he paused in his chewing to listen. He was uneasy and nervous; he glanced over his shoulder; he lifted the big knife and felt its edge. When Coyotito gurgled on the ground Kino said, "Keep him quiet."

"What is the matter?" Juana asked.

"I don't know."

He listened again, an animal light in his eyes. He stood up then, silently; and crouched low, he threaded his way through the brush toward the road. But he did not step into the road; he crept into the cover of a thorny tree and peered out along the way he had come.

And then he saw them moving along. His body stiffened and he drew down his head and peeked out from under a fallen branch. In the distance he could see three figures, two on foot and one on horseback. But he knew what they were, and a chill of fear went through him. Even in the distance he could see the two on foot moving slowly along, bent low to the ground. Here, one would pause and look at the earth, while the other joined him. They were the trackers, they could follow the trail of a bighorn sheep in the stone mountains. They were as sensitive as hounds. Here, he and Juana might have stepped out of the wheel rut, and these people from the inland, these hunters, could follow, could read a broken straw or a little tumbled pile of dust. Behind them, on a horse, was a dark man, his nose covered with a blanket, and across his saddle a rifle gleamed in the sun.

Kino lay as rigid as the tree limb. He barely breathed, and his eyes went to the place where he had swept out the track. Even the sweeping might be a message to the trackers. He knew these inland hunters. In a country where there is little game they managed to live because of their ability to hunt, and they were hunting him. They scuttled over the ground like animals and found a sign and crouched over it while the horseman waited.

The trackers whined a little, like excited dogs on a warming trail. Kino slowly drew his big knife to his hand and made it ready. He knew what he must do. If the trackers found the swept place, he must leap for the horseman, kill him quickly and take the rifle. That was his only chance in the world. And as the three drew nearer on the road, Kino dug little pits with his sandaled toes so that he could leap without warning, so that his feet would not slip. He had only a little vision under the fallen limb.

Now Juana, back in her hidden place, heard the pad of the horse's hoofs, and Coyotito gurgled. She took him up quickly and put him under her

---

4. **sentinel** (sen′ti·n′l): person or animal set to guard a group.
5. **guttural** (gut′ər·əl): harsh raspy sound produced in the throat.

shawl and gave him her breast and he was silent.

When the trackers came near, Kino could see only their legs and only the legs of the horse from under the fallen branch. He saw the dark horny feet of the men and their ragged white clothes, and he heard the creak of leather of the saddle and the clink of spurs. The trackers stopped at the swept place and studied it, and the horseman stopped. The horse flung his head up against the bit and the bit-roller clicked under his tongue and the horse snorted. Then the dark trackers turned and studied the horse and watched his ears.

Kino was not breathing, but his back arched a little and the muscles of his arms and legs stood out with tension and a line of sweat formed on his upper lip. For a long moment the trackers bent over the road, and then they moved on slowly, studying the ground ahead of them, and the horseman moved after them. The trackers scuttled along, stopping, looking, and hurrying on. They would be back, Kino knew. They would be circling and searching, peeping, stooping, and they would come back sooner or later to his covered track.

He slid backward and did not bother to cover his tracks. He could not; too many little signs were there, too many broken twigs and scuffed places and displaced stones. And there was a panic in Kino now, a panic of flight. The trackers would find his trail, he knew it. There was no escape, except in flight. He edged away from the road and went quickly and silently to the hidden place where Juana was. She looked up at him in question.

"Trackers," he said. "Come!"

And then a helplessness and a hopelessness swept over him, and his face went black and his eyes were sad. "Perhaps I should let them take me."

Instantly Juana was on her feet and her hand lay on his arm. "You have the pearl," she cried hoarsely. "Do you think they would take you back alive to say they had stolen it?"

His hand strayed limply to the place where the pearl was hidden under his clothes. "They will find it," he said weakly.

"Come," she said. "Come!"

And when he did not respond, "Do you think they would let me live? Do you think they would let the little one here live?"

Her goading struck into his brain; his lips snarled and his eyes were fierce again. "Come," he said. "We will go into the mountains. Maybe we can lose them in the mountains."

Frantically he gathered the gourds and the little bags that were their property. Kino carried a bun-dle in his left hand, but the big knife swung free in his right hand. He parted the brush for Juana and they hurried to the west, toward the high stone mountains. They trotted quickly through the tangle of the undergrowth. This was panic flight. Kino did not try to conceal his passage as he trotted, kicking the stones, knocking the telltale leaves from the little trees. The high sun streamed down on the dry creaking earth so that even veg-etation ticked in protest. But ahead were the na-ked granite mountains, rising out of erosion rubble and standing monolithic[6] against the sky. And Kino ran for the high place, as nearly all animals do when they are pursued.

This land was waterless, furred with the cacti which could store water and with the great-rooted brush which could reach deep into the earth for a little moisture and get along on very little. And underfoot was not soil but broken rock, split into small cubes, great slabs, but none of it water-rounded. Little tufts of sad dry grass grew be-tween the stones, grass that had sprouted with one single rain and headed, dropped its seed, and died. Horned toads watched the family go by and turned their little pivoting dragon heads. And now and then a great jackrabbit, disturbed in his shade, bumped away and hid behind the nearest rock. The singing heat lay over this desert country, and ahead the stone mountains looked cool and wel-coming.

And Kino fled. He knew what would happen. A little way along the road the trackers would become aware that they had missed the path, and they would come back, searching and judging, and in a little while they would find the place where Kino and Juana had rested. From there it would be easy for them—these little stones, the fallen leaves and the whipped branches, the scuffed places where a foot had slipped. Kino could see them in his mind, slipping along the track, whining a little with eagerness, and behind them, dark and half disinterested, the horseman with the rifle. His work would come last, for he would not take them back. Oh, the music of evil sang loud in Kino's head now, it sang with the whine of heat and with the dry ringing of snake rattles. It was not large and overwhelming now, but secret and poisonous, and the pounding of his heart gave it undertone and rhythm.

The way began to rise, and as it did the rocks grew larger. But now Kino had put a little distance between his family and the trackers. Now, on the first rise, he rested. He climbed a great boulder

---

6. **monolithic** (măn′ə·lith′ic): large and unyielding like a single huge block of stone.

and looked back over the shimmering country, but he could not see his enemies, not even the tall horseman riding through the brush. Juana had squatted in the shade of the boulder. She raised her bottle of water to Coyotito's lips; his little dried tongue sucked greedily at it. She looked up at Kino when he came back; she saw him examine her ankles, cut and scratched from the stones and brush, and she covered them quickly with her skirt. Then she handed the bottle to him, but he shook his head. Her eyes were bright in her tired face. Kino moistened his cracked lips with his tongue.

"Juana," he said, "I will go on and you will hide. I will lead them into the mountains, and when they have gone past, you will go north to Loreto or to Santa Rosalia. Then, if I can escape them, I will come to you. It is the only safe way."

She looked full into his eyes for a moment. "No," she said. "We go with you."

"I can go faster alone," he said harshly. "You will put the little one in danger if you go with me."

"No," said Juana.

"You must. It is the wise thing and it is my wish," he said.

"No," said Juana.

He looked then for weakness in her face, for fear or irresolution,[7] and there was none. Her eyes were very bright. He shrugged his shoulders helplessly then, but he had taken strength from her. When they moved on it was no longer panic flight.

The country, as it rose toward the mountains, changed rapidly. Now there were long outcroppings of granite with deep crevices between, and Kino walked on bare unmarkable stone when he could and leaped from ledge to ledge. He knew

---

7. **irresolution** (i·rez′ə·lōo′shən): wavering in purpose; indecision.

that wherever the trackers lost his path they must circle and lose time before they found it again. And so he did not go straight for the mountains any more; he moved in zigzags, and sometimes he cut back to the south and left a sign and then went toward the mountains over bare stone again. And the path rose steeply now, so that he panted a little as he went.

The sun moved downward toward the bare stone teeth of the mountains, and Kino set his direction for a dark and shadowy cleft[8] in the range. If there were any water at all, it would be there where he could see, even in the distance, a hint of foliage. And if there were any passage through the smooth stone range, it would be by this same deep cleft. It had its danger, for the trackers would think of it too, but the empty water bottle did not let that consideration enter. And as the sun lowered, Kino and Juana struggled wearily up the steep slope toward the cleft.

High in the gray stone mountains, under a frowning peak, a little spring bubbled out of a rupture in the stone. It was fed by shade-preserved snow in the summer, and now and then it died completely and bare rocks and dry algae were on its bottom. But nearly always it gushed out, cold and clean and lovely. In the times when the quick rains fell, it might become a freshet and send its column of white water crashing down the mountain cleft, but nearly always it was a lean little spring. It bubbled out into a pool and then fell a hundred feet to another pool, and this one, overflowing, dropped again, so that it continued, down and down, until it came to the rubble of the upland, and there it disappeared altogether. There wasn't much left of it then anyway, for every time it fell over an escarpment[9] the thirsty air drank it, and it splashed from the pools to the dry vegetation. The animals from miles around came to drink from the little pools, and the wild sheep and the deer, the pumas and raccoons, and the mice—all came to drink. And the birds which spent the day in the brushland came at night to the little pools that were like steps in the mountain cleft. Beside this tiny stream, wherever enough earth collected for root-hold, colonies of plants grew, wild grape and little palms, maidenhair fern, hibiscus, and tall pampas grass with feathery rods raised above the spike leaves. And in the pool lived frogs and water-skaters, and water-worms crawled on the bottom of the pool. Everything that loved water came to these few shallow places. The cats took their prey there, and strewed feathers and lapped water through their bloody teeth. The little pools were places of life because of the water, and places of killing because of the water, too.

The lowest step, where the stream collected before it tumbled down a hundred feet and disappeared into the rubbly desert, was a little platform of stone and sand. Only a pencil of water fell into the pool, but it was enough to keep the pool full and to keep the ferns green in the underhang of the cliff, and wild grape climbed the stone mountain and all manner of little plants found comfort here. The freshets had made a small sandy beach through which the pool flowed, and bright green watercress grew in the damp sand. The beach was cut and scarred and padded by the feet of animals that had come to drink and to hunt.

The sun had passed over the stone mountains when Kino and Juana struggled up the steep broken slope and came at last to the water. From this step they could look out over the sunbeaten desert to the blue Gulf in the distance. They came utterly weary to the pool, and Juana slumped to her knees and first washed Coyotito's face and then filled her bottle and gave him a drink. And the baby was weary and petulant,[10] and he cried softly until Juana gave him her breast, and then he gurgled and clucked against her. Kino drank long and thirstily at the pool. For a moment, then, he stretched out beside the water and relaxed all his muscles and watched Juana feeding the baby, and then he got to his feet and went to the edge of the step where the water slipped over, and he searched the distance carefully. His eyes set on a point and he became rigid. Far down the slope he could see the two trackers; they were little more than dots or scurrying ants and behind them a larger ant.

Juana had turned to look at him and she saw his back stiffen.

"How far?" she asked quietly.

"They will be here by evening," said Kino. He looked up the long steep chimney of the cleft where the water came down. "We must go west," he said, and his eyes searched the stone shoulder behind the cleft. And thirty feet up on the gray shoulder he saw a series of little erosion caves. He slipped off his sandals and clambered up to them, gripping the bare stone with his toes, and he looked into the shallow caves. They were only a few feet deep, wind-hollowed scoops, but they sloped slightly downward and back. Kino crawled into the largest one and lay down and knew that he could not be seen from the outside. Quickly he went back to Juana.

---

8. **cleft:** crack or opening.
9. **escarpment:** steep slope or cliff.

10. **petulant** (pech′o͞o·lənt): impatient or irritable.

"You must go up there. Perhaps they will not find us there," he said.

Without question she filled her water bottle to the top, and then Kino helped her up to the shallow cave and brought up the packages of food and passed them to her. And Juana sat in the cave entrance and watched him. She saw that he did not try to erase their tracks in the sand. Instead, he climbed up the brush cliff beside the water, clawing and tearing at the ferns and wild grape as he went. And when he had climbed a hundred feet to the next bench, he came down again. He looked carefully at the smooth rock shoulder toward the cave to see that there was no trace of passage, and last he climbed up and crept into the cave beside Juana.

"When they go up," he said, "we will slip away, down to the lowlands again. I am afraid only that the baby may cry. You must see that he does not cry."

"He will not cry," she said, and she raised the baby's face to her own and looked into his eyes and he stared solemnly back at her.

"He knows," said Juana.

Now Kino lay in the cave entrance, his chin braced on his crossed arms, and he watched the blue shadow of the mountain move out across the brushy desert below until it reached the Gulf, and the long twilight of the shadow was over the land.

The trackers were long in coming, as though they had trouble with the trail Kino had left. It was dusk when they came at last to the little pool. And all three were on foot now, for a horse could not climb the last steep slope. From above they were thin figures in the evening. The two trackers scurried about on the little beach, and they saw Kino's progress up the cliff before they drank. The man with the rifle sat down and rested himself, and the trackers squatted near him, and in the evening the points of their cigarettes glowed and receded. And then Kino could see that they were eating, and the soft murmur of their voices came to him.

Then darkness fell, deep and black in the mountain cleft. The animals that used the pool came near and smelled men there and drifted away again into the darkness.

He heard a murmur behind him. Juana was whispering, "Coyotito." She was begging him to be quiet. Kino heard the baby whimper, and he knew from the muffled sounds that Juana had covered his head with her shawl.

Down on the beach a match flared, and in its momentary light Kino saw that two of the men were sleeping, curled up like dogs, while the third watched, and he saw the glint of the rifle in the match light. And then the match died, but it left a picture on Kino's eyes. He could see it, just how each man was, two sleeping curled and the third squatting in the sand with the rifle between his knees.

Kino moved silently back into the cave. Juana's eyes were two sparks reflecting a low star. Kino crawled quietly close to her and he put his lips near to her cheek.

"There is a way," he said.

"But they will kill you."

"If I get first to the one with the rifle," Kino said, "I must get to him first, then I will be all right. Two are sleeping."

Her hand crept out from under her shawl and gripped his arm. "They will see your white clothes in the starlight."

"No," he said. "And I must go before moonrise."

He searched for a soft word and then gave it up. "If they kill me," he said, "lie quietly. And when they are gone away, go to Loreto."

Her hand shook a little, holding his wrist.

"There is no choice," he said. "It is the only way. They will find us in the morning."

Her voice trembled a little. "Go with God," she said.

He peered closely at her and he could see her large eyes. His hand fumbled out and found the baby, and for a moment his palm lay on Coyotito's head. And then Kino raised his hand and touched Juana's cheek, and she held her breath.

Against the sky in the cave entrance Juana could see that Kino was taking off his white clothes, for dirty and ragged though they were they would show up against the dark night. His own brown skin was a better protection for him. And then she saw how he hooked his amulet[11] neck-string about the horn handle of his great knife, so that it hung down in front of him and left both hands free. He did not come back to her. For a moment his body was black in the cave entrance, crouched and silent, and then he was gone.

Juana moved to the entrance and looked out. She peered like an owl from the hole in the mountain, and the baby slept under the blanket on her back, his face turned sideways against her neck and shoulder. She could feel his warm breath against her skin, and Juana whispered her combination of prayer and magic, her Hail Marys and her ancient intercession,[12] against the black unhuman things.

---

11. **amulet** (am′yə·lit): charm worn on the body because of its supposed magic against injury or evil.
12. **intercession:** pleading or prayer in behalf of others.

The night seemed a little less dark when she looked out, and to the east there was a lightening in the sky, down near the horizon where the moon would show. And, looking down, she could see the cigarette of the man on watch.

Kino edged like a slow lizard down the smooth rock shoulder. He had turned his neck-string so that the great knife hung down from his back and could not clash against the stone. His spread fingers gripped the mountain, and his bare toes found support through contact, and even his chest lay against the stone so that he would not slip. For any sound, a rolling pebble or a sigh, a little slip of flesh on rock, would rouse the watcher below. Any sound that was not germane to the night would make them alert. But the night was not silent; the little tree frogs that lived near the stream twittered like birds, and the high metallic ringing of the cicadas[13] filled the mountain cleft. And Kino's own music was in his head, the music of the enemy, low and pulsing, nearly asleep. But the Song of the Family had become as fierce and sharp and feline as the snarl of a female puma. The family song was alive now and driving him down on the dark enemy. The harsh cicada seemed to take up its melody, and the twittering tree frogs called little phrases of it.

And Kino crept silently as a shadow down the smooth mountain face. One bare foot moved a few inches and the toes touched the stone and gripped, and the other foot a few inches, and then the palm of one hand a little downward, and then the other hand, until the whole body, without seeming to move, had moved. Kino's mouth was open so that even his breath would make no sound, for he knew that he was not invisible. If the watcher, sensing movement, looked at the dark place against the stone which was his body, he could see him. Kino must move so slowly he would not draw the watcher's eyes. It took him a long time to reach the bottom and to crouch behind a little dwarf palm. His heart thundered in his chest and his hands and face were wet with sweat. He crouched and took slow long breaths to calm himself.

Only twenty feet separated him from the enemy now, and he tried to remember the ground between. Was there any stone which might trip him in his rush? He kneaded his legs against cramp and found that his muscles were jerking after their long tension. And then he looked apprehensively to the east. The moon would rise in a few moments now, and he must attack before it rose. He could

see the outline of the watcher, but the sleeping men were below his vision. It was the watcher Kino must find—must find quickly and without hesitation. Silently he drew the amulet string over his shoulder and loosened the loop from the horn handle of his great knife.

He was too late, for as he rose from his crouch the silver edge of the moon slipped above the eastern horizon, and Kino sank back behind his bush.

It was an old and ragged moon, but it threw hard light and hard shadow into the mountain cleft, and now Kino could see the seated figure of the watcher on the little beach beside the pool. The watcher gazed full at the moon, and then he lighted another cigarette, and the match illumined his dark face for a moment. There could be no waiting now; when the watcher turned his head, Kino must leap. His legs were as tight as wound springs.

And then from above came a little murmuring cry. The watcher turned his head to listen and then he stood up, and one of the sleepers stirred on the ground and awakened and asked quietly, "What is it?"

"I don't know," said the watcher. "It sounded like a cry, almost like a human—like a baby."

The man who had been sleeping said, "You can't tell. Some coyote bitch with a litter. I've heard a coyote pup cry like a baby."

The sweat rolled in drops down Kino's forehead and fell into his eyes and burned them. The little cry came again and the watcher looked up the side of the hill to the dark cave.

"Coyote maybe," he said, and Kino heard the harsh click as he cocked the rifle.

"If it's a coyote, this will stop it," the watcher said as he raised the gun.

Kino was in mid-leap when the gun crashed and the barrel-flash made a picture on his eyes. The great knife swung and crunched hollowly. It bit through neck and deep into chest, and Kino was a terrible machine now. He grasped the rifle even as he wrenched free his knife. His strength and his movement and his speed were a machine. He whirled and struck the head of the seated man like a melon. The third man scrabbled away like a crab, slipped into the pool, and then he began to climb frantically, to climb up the cliff where the water penciled down. His hands and feet threshed in the tangle of the wild grapevine, and he whimpered and gibbered as he tried to get up. But Kino had become as cold and deadly as steel. Deliberately he threw the lever of the rifle, and then he raised the gun and aimed deliberately and fired. He saw his enemy tumble backward into the pool,

---

13. **cicados** (si·kā′dəs): large flylike insects with transparent wings.

and Kino strode to the water. In the moonlight he could see the frantic frightened eyes, and Kino aimed and fired between the eyes.

And then Kino stood uncertainly. Something was wrong, some signal was trying to get through to his brain. Tree frogs and cicadas were silent now. And then Kino's brain cleared from its red concentration and he knew the sound—the keening, moaning, rising hysterical cry from the little cave in the side of the stone mountain, the cry of death.

Everyone in La Paz remembers the return of the family; there may be some old ones who saw it, but those whose fathers and whose grandfathers told it to them remember it nevertheless. It is an event that happened to everyone.

It was late in the golden afternoon when the first little boys ran hysterically in the town and spread the word that Kino and Juana were coming back. And everyone hurried to see them. The sun was settling toward the western mountains and the shadows on the ground were long. And perhaps that was what left the deep impression on those who saw them.

The two came from the rutted country road into the city, and they were not walking in single file, Kino ahead and Juana behind, as usual, but side by side. The sun was behind them and their long shadows stalked ahead, and they seemed to carry two towers of darkness with them. Kino had a rifle across his arm and Juana carried her shawl like a sack over her shoulder. And in it was a small limp heavy bundle. The shawl was crusted with dried blood, and the bundle swayed a little as she walked. Her face was hard and lined and leathery with fatigue and with the tightness with which she fought fatigue. And her wide eyes stared inward on herself. She was as remote and as removed as Heaven. Kino's lips were thin and his jaws tight, and the people say that he carried fear with him, that he was as dangerous as a rising storm. The people say that the two seemed to be removed from human experience; that they had gone through pain and had come out on the other side; that there was almost a magical protection about them. And those people who had rushed to see them crowded back and let them pass and did not speak to them.

Kino and Juana walked through the city as though it were not there. Their eyes glanced neither right nor left nor up nor down, but stared only straight ahead. Their legs moved a little jerkily, like well-made wooden dolls, and they carried pillars of black fear about them. And as they walked through the stone and plaster city brokers peered at them from barred windows and servants put one eye to a slitted gate and mothers turned the faces of their youngest children inward against their skirts. Kino and Juana strode side by side through the stone and plaster city and down among the brush houses, and the neighbors stood back and let them pass. Juan Tomás raised his hand in greeting and did not say the greeting and left his hand in the air for a moment uncertainly.

In Kino's ears the Song of the Family was as fierce as a cry. He was immune and terrible, and his song had become a battle cry. They trudged past the burned square where their house had been without even looking at it. They cleared the brush that edged the beach and picked their way down the shore toward the water. And they did not look toward Kino's broken canoe.

And when they came to the water's edge they stopped and stared out over the Gulf. And then Kino laid the rifle down, and he dug among his clothes, and then he held the great pearl in his hand. He looked into its surface and it was gray and ulcerous. Evil faces peered from it into his eyes, and he saw the light of burning. And in the surface of the pearl he saw the frantic eyes of the man in the pool. And in the surface of the pearl he saw Coyotito lying in the little cave with the top of his head shotaway. And the pearl was ugly; it was gray, like a malignant[14] growth. And Kino heard the music of the pearl, distorted and insane. Kino's hand shook a little, and he turned slowly to Juana and held the pearl out to her. She stood beside him, still holding her dead bundle over her shoulder. She looked at the pearl in his hand for a moment and then she looked into Kino's eyes and said softly, "No, you."

And Kino drew back his arm and flung the pearl with all his might. Kino and Juana watched it go, winking and glimmering under the setting sun. They saw the little splash in the distance, and they stood side by side watching the place for a long time.

And the pearl settled into the lovely green water and dropped toward the bottom. The waving branches of the algae called to it and beckoned to it. The lights on its surface were green and lovely. It settled down to the sand bottom among the fern-like plants. Above, the surface of the water was a green mirror. And the pearl lay on the floor of the sea. A crab scampering over the bottom raised a little cloud of sand, and when it settled the pearl was gone.

And the music of the pearl drifted to a whisper and disappeared.

---

14. **malignant** (mə·lig′nənt): dangerous; very harmful.

Responding to the Novel

Analyzing Chapter VI

Identifying Facts

1. Describe the first part of Kino and Juana's flight. Where do they stop to rest?
2. As they rest, what vision does Kino see in the pearl?
3. Describe the trackers. Why are they following Kino and Juana?
4. What route do Kino and Juana take to try to lose the trackers? Where do they decide to spend the night?
5. Where do the trackers camp, and what happens to them?
6. What happens to Coyotito?
7. Describe Kino and Juana's return to La Paz.

Interpreting Meanings

8. Why do you think Juana and Kino throw the pearl back into the sea?
9. **Foreshadowing** is when a writer hints at what will happen later in the story. Identify two passages in this chapter in which Coyotito's fate is foreshadowed.
10. Kino and Juana could have done a number of things after the encounter with the trackers. What else could they have done? Why do you think they decide to return to La Paz? Does Coyotito's fate aid their decision?
11. Do you think the novel ends on an optimistic note? That is, does the future look brighter for the couple after the awful events of the preceding days? Have they gained something valuable from their experience? Or is the ending pessimistic, showing the couple pretty much defeated by events?

Analyzing the Novel as a Whole

1. Review the six chapters of *The Pearl.* Then write a short **summary** of the novel's plot. Be sure to include the following elements in your summary:

   a. The **basic situation** as the novel opens
   b. The main **conflicts** that lend energy to the story

   c. Major **complications** that make the conflicts more difficult to resolve
   d. The **climax,** or most exciting point of the story
   e. The **resolution,** or how the story is closed

2. How does the relationship between Kino and Juana change over the course of the story? Refer to a specific event or passage to show each important change in their relationship.
3. What different things does the pearl seem to symbolize, or stand for, at different stages of the novel? Be sure to explain what you think the pearl symbolizes in the very last paragraphs of the final chapter.
4. In **irony,** a sharp contrast exists between what is expected to happen (or what would be appropriate) and what actually does happen. What did Kino hope and expect the pearl would do for him and his family? Ironically, what did it do to his family instead?
5. Readers of *The Pearl* have interpreted Kino's experiences in several ways. The following are three such interpretations. Which interpretation makes the most sense to you? (Substitute another interpretation if you are not satisfied with any of these.)

   a. Kino is a decent, honest man who learns that the desire for money can be destructive.
   b. Kino is destroyed by his own greed.
   c. Kino learns that he can't escape his fate of being an Indian in Mexico.

6. The preface says the novel might be seen as a **parable,** that is a short, fairly simple story that teaches a moral lesson. What would you say is the main moral lesson presented in *The Pearl*? Do you agree with the lesson?
7. The preface also says that "perhaps everyone takes his own meaning from [the story] and reads his own life into it." Do you agree? Or do you think the story has only one meaning, which readers must try to discover?
8. Do you think the story has something to say to people whose lives are very different from those of Kino and Juana?

9. The story of *The Pearl* is set in Mexico around 1900. Do you think a similar chain of events could occur in the United States today? Give specific reasons to support your answer.

10. Suppose you were designing the cover for a new edition of *The Pearl*. Which scene from the novel would you choose as the most important or most interesting to use as an illustration for the cover? Explain why you chose the scene.

Writing About the Novel

A Creative Response

1. **Dramatizing a Scene.** Working in groups, choose a scene from *The Pearl* and dramatize it in a script that could be used for radio broadcast. A **radio script** usually will have a narrator who sets the scene and occasionally comments on the action. Most of the story, however, is presented in dialogue and sound effects. Use dialogue from the novel and make up more as needed. In the script, sound effects should be italicized and placed in parentheses. Descriptions of the actors' tone of voice are usually printed the same way. You might want to dramatize one of the following scenes.

    a. Kino and Juana taking Coyotito to the doctor's house
    b. Kino dealing with the pearl buyers
    c. Kino and Juana walking through the village to the shore at the end of the story

2. **Extending the Story.** Several loose ends are left dangling at the end of *The Pearl.* Unanswered questions include the following:

    a. Will Kino be punished for his wrongdoing?
    b. Will Kino and Juana rejoin the Indian community in La Paz?
    c. How will Kino and Juana get along with each other? With Juan Tomás? With the doctor and the priest and the other inhabitants of the village?
    d. Will Kino resume diving for pearls or will he seek a new way of making a living?

    Write down any other important questions you feel are not answered in the novel's **resolution.** Then extend the story for a few days or weeks, and show how the loose ends could be tied up. Call your composition "Chapter VII."

A Critical Response

3. **Looking at a Biblical Parable.** One of the parables in the Bible concludes with this passage:

> Lay not up for yourselves treasures upon earth, where moth and rust doth corrupt, and where thieves break through and steal:
>
> But lay up for yourselves treasures in heaven, where neither moth nor rust doth corrupt, and where thieves do not break through nor steal:
>
> For where your treasure is, there will your heart be also.
>
> —Matthew 6: 19-21

In the first of two paragraphs, explain in your own words the lesson of this Biblical parable. In the second paragraph discuss whether Kino at the end of *The Pearl* would agree with the lesson. Give at least three reasons to support your interpretation of Kino's thoughts.

4. **Discussing Themes.** A **theme** is what a writer says about an important subject. Most works of literature have two or more themes, one often stands out as the principal theme. The following are some of the subjects readers have found to be important in *The Pearl.*

    a. The struggle between good and evil.
    b. The degree to which people can control their own lives.
    c. The difference between what appears to be real or true and what actually is real or true.
    d. The relationship of Indians and people of European background; in Mexico around 1900.
    e. Similarities between humans and animals.

    Pick two of the subjects and explain what the novel says about them. Write a paragraph about each theme.

5. **Comparing Stories.** Steinbeck drew inspiration for *The Pearl* from a story he heard while in Mexico. The story is printed in Focusing on Background on page 716. To see how a writer can keep and change aspects of a story, **compare** and **contrast** the story heard in Mexico and *The Pearl.* As your first step, before you write, draw a chart like the following on a sheet of paper. Leave enough room in the columns to write in information.

	Story heard in Mexico	*The Pearl*
Setting.		
Main characters.		
Who finds pearl.		
What finder wants to do with money from selling pearl.		
What happens when finder tries to sell pearl.		
What finder does with people who cause trouble.		
What happens to pearl.		
Mood at end of story.		

In the first two paragraphs of an essay discuss the similarities and differences in the two stories. In the third paragraph, explain what you think about the way Steinbeck changed the story.

Analyzing Language and Vocabulary

Imagery and Figures of Speech

Images are words or phrases that create vivid pictures in the reader's mind. Most images appeal to our sense of sight, but images may also appeal to our senses of hearing, taste, touch, and smell.

Figures of speech are expressions which are not literally true. Figures of speech create powerful and imaginative effects through unusual comparisons between things that are not essentially alike at all. Some of the most common figures of speech are similes, metaphors, and personifications. A **simile** is a direct comparison using words such as *like, as, than,* or *resembles.* (*Lil is like a diamond.*) A **metaphor** omits the words of comparison and directly identifies the two unlike things. (*Lil is a diamond.*) **Personification** is a kind of metaphor or simile in which an ~~~~~~~~~~ or emotic~~~~ The fol~~~~ swer the ~~~~

Day of the Dead/The Offering by Diego Rivera (1923–1924). Fresco, Court of Fiestas, Secretariat of Public Education, Mexico City.

Courtesy Bob Schalkwijk.

1.

"The dawn came quickly now, a wash, a glow, a lightness, and then an explosion of fire as the sun arose out of the Gulf. Kino looked down to cover his eyes from the glare. He could hear the pat of the corncakes in the house and the rich smell of them on the cooking plate. The ants were busy on the ground, big black ones with shiny bodies, and ····le dusty quick ants."

Identify five **images** in this passage. What sense does each one appeal to?
What phrase is a **metaphor?**

2.

". . . the buyer's eyes had become as steady and cruel and unwinking as a hawk's eyes, while the rest of his face smiled in greeting."

a. What kind of figure of speech compares the pearl buyer's eyes to a hawk's?

b. Why do you think Steinbeck chose a hawk for the comparison, rather than a parrot, sparrow, or seagull?

3.

"The wind screamed over the Gulf and turned the water white, and the mangroves plunged like frightened cattle, and a fine sandy dust arose from the land and hung in a stifling cloud over the sea."

a. Where can you find **personification**?

b. Think of words that could be substituted for the words *screamed, plunged, frightened,* and *stifling,* and would change the passage's feeling.

Focusing on Background
Where did the story come from?

John Steinbeck heard a story about a great pearl while in Mexico. The story became the basis for *The Pearl.*

The Pearl of La Paz

"The Gulf and Gulf ports have always been unfriendly to colonization. Again and again attempts were made before a settlement would stick. Humans are not much wanted on the Peninsula.[1] But at La Paz the pearl oysters drew men from all over the world. And, as in all concentrations of natural wealth, the terrors of greed were let loose on the city again and again. An event which happened at La Paz in recent years is typical of such places. An Indian boy by accident found a pearl of great size, an unbelievable pearl. He knew its value was so great that he need never work again. In his one pearl he had the ability to be drunk as long as he wished, to marry any one of a number of girls, and to make many more a little happy too. In his great pearl lay salvation, for he could in advance purchase masses sufficient to pop him out of Purgatory[2] like a squeezed watermelon seed. In addition he could shift a number of dead relatives a little nearer to Paradise. He went to La Paz with his pearl in his hand and his future clear into eternity in his heart. He took his pearl to a broker and was offered so little that he grew angry, for he knew he was cheated. Then he carried his pearl to another broker and was offered the same amount. After a few more visits he came to know that the brokers were only the many hands of one head and that he could not sell his pearl for more. He took it to the beach and hid it under a stone, and that night he was clubbed into unconsciousness and his clothing was searched. The next night he slept at the house of a friend and his friend and he were injured and bound and the whole house searched. Then he went inland to lose his pursuers and he was waylaid[3] and tortured. But he was very angry now and he knew what he must do. Hurt as he was he crept back to La Paz in the night and he skulked like a hunted fox to the beach and took out his pearl from under the stone. Then he cursed it and threw it as far as he could into the channel. He was a free man again with his soul in danger and his food and shelter insecure. And he laughed a great deal about it.

"This seems to be a true story, but it is so much like a parable that it almost can't be. This Indian boy is too heroic, too wise. He knows too much and acts on his knowledge. In every way, he goes contrary to human direction. The story is probably true, but we don't believe it; it is far too reasonable to be true."

—from *The Sea of Cortez,* John Steinbeck

---

1. **the Peninsula:** Baja California, a long peninsula in Mexico that is connected to the state of California.

2. **Purgatory:** in the Roman Catholic religion, a place where souls must spend time atoning for sins before moving to heaven.

3. **waylaid:** attacked by ambush.

TONE

Whenever you read a novel or a short story, you should give some attention to the writer's tone. **Tone** refers to the writer's attitude toward characters, setting, and events. The writer's tone might be cheerful or depressing, optimistic or pessimistic, sympathetic, sarcastic, or impersonal.

I

Here is the opening passage of a novel in which tone plays a vital part. How do you think the writer wants you to feel about the **character** and the **setting** of his novel?

It was a quiet morning, the town covered over with darkness and at ease in bed. Summer gathered in the weather, the wind had the proper touch, the breathing of the world was long and warm and slow. You had only to rise, lean from your window, and know that this indeed was the first real time of freedom and living, this was the first morning of summer.

Douglas Spaulding, twelve, freshly wakened, let summer idle him on its early-morning stream. Lying in this third-story cupola bedroom, he felt the tall power it gave him, riding high in the June wind, the grandest tower in town. At night, when the trees washed together, he flashed his gaze like a beacon from this lighthouse in all directions over swarming seas of elm and oak and maple. Now . . .

"Boy," whispered Douglas.

A whole summer ahead to cross off the calendar, day by day. Like the goddess Siva in the travel books, he saw his hands jump everywhere, pluck sour apples, peaches, and midnight plums. He would be clothed in trees and bushes and rivers. He would freeze, gladly, in the hoarfrosted ice-house door. He would bake, happily, with ten thousand chickens, in Grandma's kitchen.

But now—a familiar task awaited him.

One night each week he was allowed to leave his father, his mother, and his younger brother Tom asleep in their small house next door and run here, up the dark spiral stairs to his grandparents' cupola, and in this sorcerer's tower sleep with thunders and visions, to wake before the crystal jingle of milk bottles and perform his ritual magic.

He stood at the open window in the dark, took a deep breath and exhaled.

The street lights, like candles on a black cake, went out. He exhaled again and again and the stars began to vanish.

Douglas smiled. He pointed a finger.

There, and there. Now over here, and here . . .

Yellow squares were cut in the dim morning earth as house lights winked slowly on. A sprinkle of windows came suddenly alight miles off in dawn country.

"Everyone yawn. Everyone up."

The great house stirred below.

—from *Dandelion Wine,*
Ray Bradbury

In this opening passage, Bradbury's tone is positive, upbeat, maybe even joyful. He wants his readers to share the happiness that Douglas feels as he anticipates a summer filled with pleasures.

Bradbury establishes this tone by filling his opening passage with positive details. In the first paragraph, for example, these phrases suggest a feeling of contentment:

1. a quiet morning
2. at ease in bed
3. the wind had the proper touch
4. the breathing of the world was long and warm and slow
5. the first real time of freedom and living

What words or phrases can you find in the rest of the passage that help to create this positive, joyful tone?

Do any details suggest that something sinister might happen next?

II

The following passage describes the effects of a dust storm in the American Southwest during the 1930's. As you read, try to decide what this writer's attitude is toward his subject.

The dawn came, but no day. In the gray sky a red sun appeared, a dim red circle that gave a little light, like dusk; and as that day advanced, the dusk slipped back toward darkness, and the wind cried and whimpered over the fallen corn.

Men and women huddled in their houses, and they tied handkerchiefs over their noses when they went out, and wore goggles to protect their eyes.

When the night came again it was black night, for the stars could not pierce the dust to get down, and the window lights could not even spread beyond their own yards. Now the dust was evenly mixed with the air, an emulsion of dust and air. Houses were shut tight, and cloth wedged around doors and windows, but the dust came in so thinly that it could not be seen in the air, and it settled like pollen on the chairs and tables, on the dishes. The people brushed it from their shoulders. Little lines of dust lay at the door sills.

In the middle of that night the wind passed on and left the land quiet. The dust-filled air muffled sound more completely than fog does. The people, lying in their beds, heard the wind stop. They awakened when the rushing wind was gone. They lay quietly and listened deep into the stillness. Then the roosters crowed and their voices were muffled, and the people stirred restlessly in their beds and wanted the morning. They knew it would take a long time for the dust to settle out of the air. In the morning the dust hung like fog, and the sun was as red as ripe new blood.

—from *The Grapes of Wrath,*
John Steinbeck

1. Steinbeck's description does not include any direct comments on the effects of the dust storm.

Yet, his description creates feelings in the reader. How does he want you to feel about the people in his story, and the storm that has hit them?

2. Find the two references to the sun in the excerpt. What effect do these descriptions have on Steinbeck's **tone**? What effect do they have on you?

3. In this passage, the wind and the dust seem more like characters than the people do. Explain how Steinbeck accomplishes this effect. What kind of characters are they?

4. How does Steinbeck seem to feel about the people and their hostile surroundings?

5. Compare the two excerpts you have just read. What kind of story do you predict each novel will probably tell? Which novel do you think might tell a more personal story? What makes you think so?

6. Does the writer make you want to go on reading either story? Why, or why not?

Writing

1. **Analyzing a Writer's Tone.** Select a passage from any novel or short story you have read, either in this book or elsewhere. Write a paragraph analyzing the writer's **tone,** or attitude. In your paragraph, identify the title of the story or book the passage is taken from, identify the author, and explain what you think the writer's tone is. Then include several quotations from the passage to support your opinion.

2. **Creating Tone.** Think of a character or a setting you would like to write about. Then write two different paragraphs describing this person or setting. Use descriptive words to create a positive **tone** in the first paragraph; use other words to create a negative tone in the second paragraph.

Exercises in Critical Thinking and Writing

ANALYZING CAUSE AND EFFECT

Writing Assignment
Write an essay in which you analyze the causes of Scrooge's transformation in *A Christmas Carol.*

Background
Recognizing Cause and Effect
In a well-written novel or story, events don't all happen by chance. Some events **cause** other events to happen or cause characters to react in a certain way. The result, or consequence, of a cause is called an **effect.** You should be able to recognize causes and their effects in a novel or short story.

Characters in a novel should behave in a way that seems believable. Figuring out characters' **motivations** (the reasons why they act the way they do) requires analyzing causes and effects, as in the following questions about *A Christmas Carol*:

1. What caused Belle to break off her engagement to the young Scrooge? What was the effect on Scrooge?
2. What were the probable causes that made Scrooge become the unpleasant, miserly man we meet when the novel opens?
3. What effect does Scrooge's miserliness have on the Cratchit family?
4. At the end of the novel, what has caused Scrooge to change?
5. How does the change in Scrooge's character and behavior cause a change in the lives of the Cratchit family?

Making Inferences
To answer some of these questions, you will have to make **inferences.** That is, you will have to make an educated guess based on what you know about the characters and their situations. For example, look at the second part of Question 1. Dickens does not directly state how the broken engagement affected Scrooge, but you can make a good guess based on what you know about Scrooge's later life and character. Scrooge was probably determined not to get romantically involved again and so devoted himself entirely to work and making money.

Try to answer all of the above questions. Which ones require that you make an inference?

Prewriting
Complete the following chart to help you summarize the effect each ghost's visit has on Scrooge. You will have to make some **inferences** when you fill in the column on effects.

	Causes What the Ghost Shows Scrooge	**Effects** What Scrooge Realizes
The Ghost of Christmas Past		
The Ghost of Christmas Present		
The Ghost of Christmas Yet to Come		

A sample entry might look like this:

	Causes	**Effects**
The Ghost of Christmas Past	Scrooge sees his lonely life as a young man. He sees the joy at Fezziwig's. He sees how he neglected his fiancée and ruined his changes for a family.	Scrooge realizes how much he's been focusing on raising money at the expense of human relationships.

Writing

Use your completed chart for details for your essay. Follow this plan:

Paragraph 1: Introductory paragraph cites title and author, summarizes plot very briefly, and mentions the visit of Jacob Marley's ghost.

Paragraphs 2–4: For each of the three ghosts (Past, Present, and Future), discuss what the ghost showed Scrooge and how the visit affected Scrooge. Devote a paragraph to each ghost's visit.

Paragraph 5: Summarize your main ideas.

The following model shows how each paragraph of your essay might begin. You may either use these sentences, or make up your own.

In *A Christmas Carol*, Charles Dickens uses four ghosts as a means of changing the miserly and cold-hearted Scrooge into a generous, warm man who loves Christmas. When we first see Scrooge, ...

Later that night, Scrooge is visited by his dead partner's ghost, who tells him . . .

The first ghost, the Ghost of Christmas Past, shows Scrooge . . .

The second ghost, the Ghost of Christmas Present, takes Scrooge into the world of festivities about to take place. . . .

The third ghost, the Ghost of Christmas Yet to Come, is the ghost Scrooge fears the most. . . .

By seeing his past, present, and future, Scrooge realizes that . . .

Revision and Proofreading Self-Check

1. Does the essay describe each ghost's visit and discuss the effects on Scrooge? Does it explain the cause of Scrooge's transformation?
2. Have I included details and examples to support my ideas?
3. Does the essay have a strong introduction and conclusion?
4. Have I expressed my ideas clearly?
5. Are words spelled correctly? Are sentences punctuated correctly?

Partner Check

1. Are there any spelling errors? Are sentences punctuated correctly?
2. Does the essay describe each ghost's visit and the effects on Scrooge?
3. Does the writer give enough supporting details and examples?
4. Does the essay have introductory and concluding paragraphs?
5. What do I like best about this paper?
6. What do I think needs improvement?

WRITING ABOUT LITERATURE

The Writing Process

In English class, your teacher will ask you to express various responses to what you read. You might be asked to analyze a poem, to compare two short stories, to show how two characters differ from each other, or to give your opinion of something you have read. Because many of your responses will be in writing, you should know the steps to take in writing a good essay.

A good essay, like any other superior product, doesn't come about by accident. It's the result of thought, planning, attention to detail, revision, and last-minute polishing. Good writers think of writing as a *process*—a series of steps that will lead to a finished product they are pleased with.

The writing process is made up of three main stages: **prewriting, writing,** and **revising.** If you give careful attention to each stage of the process, you're likely to find that writing good essays is not as difficult as you thought.

Prewriting

During the **prewriting** stage, your first goal is to come up with ideas. You might discuss the assignment with someone in your class. Or you might work alone, jotting down everything that comes to mind as you think about the assignment. The next step during this stage is to narrow your topic. It will help to write several **thesis statements**—sentences that could serve as the main idea of the essay you are planning. You will eventually decide to use only one of these statements in your essay.

Writing

The prewriting material becomes the basis of what you do during the **writing** stage. First, choose the thesis statement you think best. It is likely to become a key part of your essay and will help keep you from wandering away from your topic. Second, concentrate on getting your ideas on paper. Don't worry too much about grammar, spelling, or punctuation. Just say all that you want to say as clearly as possible.

Revising

During the third stage—**revising**—your job is to mold the essay into final form. This is the time to look for errors in spelling, punctuation, capitalization, and sentence structure. It is also the time to decide whether you have said everything you wanted to say and have used the clearest possible language. When you have rewritten your essay with all necessary changes, you have finished the last stage of the writing process.

This whole process doesn't have to take a lot of time. In some cases, for example, you will know at once what you want to say in your essay. The prewriting stage could then take only a few minutes. The time you spend on each stage is up to you. The key thing to understand is the importance of going through all three steps.

The following material will help you apply the three steps in the writing process to typical assignments in English class. You'll probably find the material helpful for assignments in other classes as well.

Writing Answers to Essay Questions

There are two keys to writing a good answer to an essay question. First, you must understand exactly what the question asks you to do. Second, you must complete the three stages of the writing process.

Understanding Essay Questions

Before you begin the prewriting stage, think about the question and figure out what you are being asked to do. In most questions, the most important word is the verb. The following verbs appear in many essay questions. If you understand them, your answers are likely to be good.

● **Analyze.** When you analyze something, you take it apart to see how it works. If a question asks you to analyze a whole literary work, try to focus on the elements of the work. Sometimes a question will ask you to analyze just one element. In this case, you'll have to show how the element affects the selection as a whole.

Question: Analyze the use of the pearl as a symbol in *The Pearl*.

Possible Strategy: Go through the novel and find places where the pearl is described. Then review the ways the pearl is used in the plot. Finally, think about what the pearl means to Juana and Kino at different stages of the story. Write down several things the pearl might symbolize. Which seems to apply to the novel most exactly?

● **Compare.** When you compare two things, you show how they are alike. If a question asks you to compare two pieces of writing, look for as many similarities as you can find. *Note:* Sometimes when a question asks you to compare, it also expects you to mention important differences. Your teacher will clarify this for you.

Question: Compare the style of Lincoln's ''Gettysburg Address'' with that of King's ''I Have a Dream.''

Possible Strategy: Reread both speeches carefully. Then make a list of all the elements the speeches have in common. Think about such things as each speaker's purpose, his audience, his feeling about his subject matter, and his use of language. (Look for repetition, alliteration, and phrases meant to stir the audience.)

● **Contrast.** When you contrast two things, you show how they differ from each other. If a question asks you to contrast two pieces of writing, look for as many differences as you can find.

Question: Contrast the character of Scrooge with the character of Bob Cratchit in *A Christmas Carol*.

Possible Strategy: Make two lists, one labeled *Scrooge* and one labeled *Bob*. Then supply details from the novel telling what each character is like. Remember all the ways character is revealed: by appearance, speech, actions, thoughts, responses of other characters, and direct comments by the writer.

● **Describe.** When you describe something or someone, you paint a picture with words. Description is usually based mostly on details that someone can see. However, you could also include details that appeal to the senses of hearing, smell, taste, and touch.

Question: Describe the three ghosts in *A Christmas Carol*.

Possible Strategy: Reread the paragraphs of the novel where Dickens describes each ghost. Write down the specific details that help you to see and hear each spirit. Use these details in your essay.

● **Discuss.** When you discuss a topic, you examine it in a general way and make comments on it.

Question: Discuss Poe's creation of atmosphere in ''The Raven.''

Possible Strategy: Begin by thinking of some general words that will describe the mood you felt in reading the poem. Then list all the details in the poem that contribute to that mood.

● **Evaluate.** When you evaluate a work of literature, you make a judgment about how effective it is. An evaluation is an expression of opinion backed up by references to details in the work.

Question: In an essay, write your evaluation of the short story ''Bargain.''

Possible Strategy: First, review the elements of the short story. Next, decide how these elements are used in ''Bargain.'' Finally, make notes describing your responses to the way the elements are used in the story.

● **Explain.** When you explain something, you make it more understandable by giving reasons telling why or how something is a certain way. Explanations often use words and expressions like *first, second, therefore, as a result.*

Question: Explain how Daniel Webster wins the courtroom debate in ''The Devil and Daniel Webster.''

Possible Strategy: Begin by explaining what the debate is all about. Then summarize the ways in which Webster convinces the jury that his arguments are stronger than those of the Devil.

● **Illustrate.** When you illustrate something, you provide examples that support a certain position.

Question: How does Thayer use sounds to create humor in ''Casey at the Bat''? Use examples from the poem to illustrate your answer.

Possible Strategy: First review all the ways a poet can use sound effects. Next, see which ones apply to this poem. Finally, list those sound effects that are especially funny.

Writing Essays About Literature

Prewriting

Choosing a Topic. If you are planning an essay that responds to a question, your topic has already been chosen. Sometimes, however, your teacher will ask you to choose a topic. In that case, keep three things in mind. (1) You can always find a topic if you think about the elements of literature you've studied in this book. (2) Library research is also a good way to find topics to write about. (3) The narrower and more specific your topic is, the easier it will be to write about.

Gathering Information. If you do library research, the prewriting stage should include taking notes about what you read. Most people use index cards, with only one piece of information on each card. Each notecard should also include the title of the work where you found the information, its publisher and copyright date, and the number of the page on which the information appears.

If you are working on an assigned topic, prewriting might consist of anything that will help you get some ideas on paper. For example, you might make a list of everything you think of as you reread the literary work. (See the reader's notes in the sections called "Responding" in the front of several units in this book.) You might talk to a friend who has read the work and discuss some ideas about it. You might even simply begin writing, putting down anything that comes into your head. This is called **free writing,** and some people find it an effective way of discovering ideas to write about.

Writing a Thesis Statement. A thesis statement is a sentence (or more) that states the central idea of your essay. There are two good reasons for having a thesis statement by the start of the writing stage. First, the thesis statement will almost certainly appear in the early part of the essay you are planning. Second, the thesis statement can help you stick to your topic. *Note:* It often will be helpful to start by writing several thesis statements. Look them over and choose the best one for your essay.

Writing

There are many ways to organize an essay; when you are more experienced at writing, you may want to experiment with different methods of organization. For now, though, it would be a good idea to write all your essays according to the following three-part plan.

Introduction. The first paragraph of your essay should mention the title and author of the work you are writing about. It should also tell what your essay will be about. In most cases, the best way to do that is by using the thesis statement you have already written. The introduction might also mention some important details you will refer to in supporting the thesis statement.

Body. The body of your essay should be *at least* one paragraph long. Each paragraph should include one or more examples to support your thesis statement. A paragraph consists of a topic sentence and evidence that supports that sentence. Wherever possible, use quotations from the work you are writing about.

Conclusion. The last paragraph of your essay might do one of three things: It could (1) restate the thesis statement in other words; (2) summarize the main points of the essay; or (3) give your personal response to the work.

Revising

Revising means making changes in the first draft of an essay. There are several kinds of changes you might make. Because of this, some writers read their essays several times. During each reading, they concentrate on only one kind of change.

Reading for Content. During one reading of your essay, you should think about nothing but content. Did you include a thesis statement? Does it say what you want it to say? Does each paragraph in the body of the essay support your thesis statement? Does your concluding paragraph end your essay as you intended it to?

Reading for Style. You should also reread your essay to see if you can improve the writing style. Does your essay read as smoothly as you want it to? Would some long sentences be easier to understand if they were broken into two or three shorter sentences? Should some short sentences be combined into longer ones? Do you find unnecessary words or phrases that could be cut? Are your ideas clear and easy to follow?

Proofreading for Errors. Proofreading involves looking for mistakes in grammar, spelling, punctuation, capitalization, and sentence structure. During this reading, remember that the title of a poem, a short story, or an essay mentioned in your essay should be enclosed in quotation marks; the title of a play, a novel, or any other book should be in italics. (In handwriting and typing, you underline anything that should be in italics.)

Use the following proofreader's symbols to correct errors in spelling, capitalization, and punctuation.

Symbol	Meaning of Symbol	Explanation
≡	Capitalize a lowercase letter.	John updike
/	Change a capital letter to lower case.	"To Build A Fire"

∧	Insert a word or phrase.	"Lincoln Shot"	Is
⟨delete⟩	Delete (take out) one or more letters and close up the space.	"Tar Maan"	
∧	Insert a letter.	James Thuber	
⊙	Add a period.	N Scott Momaday	
⌃	Add a comma.	Sandburg, Sexton and Alvarez	
⌄⌄	Insert quotation marks.	"Raymond's Run"	
___	Set in italics.	A Christmas Carol	
∽	Change the order of the letters.	"Plnating the Gate"	
¶	Begin a new paragraph.	¶This poem has a lot of vivid images.	

A Model Essay

The following is an essay based on library research. The essay includes revisions the writer made during the final stage of the writing process.

Why Is "Casey at the Bat" So Popular?

INTRODUCTION
Gives title and author.

by Ernest Lawrence Thayer
"Casey at the Bat" is one of the most popular poem in America. It has been the subject of two silent movies, a cartoon, several paintings,

Identifies source of information.

and one opera (Gardner, pages 10–15). Why is Casey at the Bat so

States thesis.

popular? I think its because of its subject matter, its humor and its early history.

BODY
One paragraph for each item in thesis statement.

"Casey at the Bat"
The subject matter of the poem is very American. Baseball has

States topic sentence.

more than
been called "the national pastime for over one hundred years. More

Adds supporting details.

to any sporting evento
families go to baseball games than other sports. Baseball is a subject

most
that all Americans know about and Americans love.

The humor in the poem is also appealing. Thayer uses fun rhymes and rhythm *He also uses* and fancy language that is way out of place in describing a baseball game *In addition,* and he makes a joke out of the crowd's hero-worship, *by having* as Casey ends up as a failure. ~~It is really a neat poem to recite aloud.~~

States another topic sentence.

Adds supporting details.

The early history of the poem might also ~~have~~ *has* something to do with *its popularity.* ~~being popular.~~ The poem was first published in a newspaper in 1988, and it was reprinted in a few other newspapers, and then it disappeared. Not long after that, a popular comedian named William De Wolf Hopper was looking for something to perform ~~in a theater~~ before an audience of baseball people. A friend of his gave him a copy of "Casey at the Bat," and Hoper *p* recited it for his audience. It was such a hit that he made it a perm*a*nent part of his act. Because of Hopper, people all over the country got to hear "Casey At the Bat" read aloud (Gardner pages 1-9).

States another topic sentence.

Adds supporting details.

Identifies source of information.

CONCLUSION

Gives personal response.

I think "Casey At the Bat" deserves the popularity which it has gotten over the years. Baseball is one of my favorite sports, and the poem is really funny. I especially like the *fancy* language, because it reminds me of some bad sportscasters I've heard of. The next time I have to recite a poem in class, I think I'll choose "Casey at the Bat."

Identifying Your Sources

Whenever you do research for an essay, identify your sources of information. (In the essay you just read, there are two references, with page numbers, to a writer named Gardner.) At the end of your essay, include a bibliography—a list of books and articles used in writing the essay. List your sources alphabetically by the authors' last names. Here is a sample bibliography.

Cerf, Bennett. *An Encyclopedia of Modern American Humor* (Garden City, NY: Doubleday and Co., 1954).

Gardner, Martin. *Casey at the Bat* (Chicago: University of Chicago Press, 1984).

A HANDBOOK OF LITERARY TERMS

You will find more information about the entries in this Handbook at the pages given at the ends of the entries. To learn more about **Alliteration,** for example, turn to pages 373–374, 443–444, and 656 in this book.

Cross-references at the ends of the entries refer to other entries in the Handbook containing closely related information. For instance, at the end of **Allegory** you are referred to **Symbol.**

ALLEGORY A story or poem in which the characters and settings and events stand for other people or events or ideas. An allegory is used to teach a lesson or to explain something (such as a moral principle). An allegory has at least two meanings. Its literal meaning is the one a reader gets from the surface story. Its symbolic meaning is the one that lies beneath the surface. Some readers believe *The Pearl* (page 672) is an allegory intended to teach a lesson about the dangers of seeking material success.

See also *Symbol.*

ALLITERATION The repetition of the same, or very similar, consonant sounds in words that are close together. Alliteration occurs mostly in poetry, though prose writers use it from time to time. While alliteration usually occurs at the beginning of words, it can also occur within or at the end of words. Alliteration can do many things, such as help establish a mood, emphasize words, and serve as a memory aid. In the following stanza, notice the repeated *s, m,* and *b* sounds.

> The sun was shining on the sea,
>   Shining with all his might:
> He did his very best to make
>   The billows smooth and bright—
> And this was odd, because it was
>   The middle of the night.
>
> —from "The Walrus and the Carpenter,"
> Lewis Carroll

See pages 373–374, 443–444, 656.

ALLUSION A reference to someone or something that is known from literature, history, religion, mythology, politics, sports, or some other field most people are familiar with. Allusions enrich the reading experience. Writers expect readers to recognize allusions and to think almost at the same time about the literary work and the allusions contained in it. "Little Miss Muffet" (page 416) alludes to a well-known nursery rhyme. If a reader does not understand that allusion, the poem is not as meaningful as it is intended to be.

See pages 40, 50, 413, 545, 608.

ANECDOTE A brief story told to illustrate a point. Anecdotes are frequently found in biographies and autobiographies. "Green Gulch" (page 464) is made up mostly of an anecdote.

ASSONANCE The repetition of similar vowel sounds in words close together. Assonance occurs mostly in poetry. "Wolves" (page 392), for example, contains several words with long and short *o* sounds to suggest the sound of howling wolves.

ATMOSPHERE The overall mood or feeling of a work of literature. A work's atmosphere can often be described in one or two adjectives, such as scary, happy, sad, or nostalgic. Atmosphere is created through a writer's use of words to create images, sounds, and descriptions that convey a particular feeling. "The Raven" (page 385) is noted for its gloomy atmosphere.

See also *Diction, Mood.*

AUTOBIOGRAPHY An account of the writer's own life, or part of it. "The Cold Wave" (page 455) is an example of autobiographical writing.

See pages 451, 493–494.
See also *Biography.*

BALLAD A song or poem that tells a story. Ballads usually tell sensational stories of tragedy or adventure, using simple language with a great deal of repetition. They also usually have regular rhythm and rhyme patterns, which make them easy to memorize. "The Cowboy's Lament" (page 419) is an example of a ballad.

See also *Lyric Poem.*

BIOGRAPHY An account of a person's life, or part of it, written or told by another person. Biographies are among the most popular forms of contemporary literature. You can find biographies of a wide variety of people in libraries and bookstores. "Lincoln Is Shot" (page 29) is a biographical selection that tells about the final hours of Abraham Lincoln.

CHARACTER A person or an animal in a story, play, or other literary work. In some works, such as myths and tall tales, a character might be an animal. In stories such as fairy tales, a part of nature, such as the ocean, might be a character. In most cases, though, a character is an ordinary human being. Almost all good stories have interesting characters.

Characters can be classified as static or dynamic. A **static character** is one who does not change much in the course of a work. Johnny in "The Ransom of Red Chief" is a static character. By contrast, a **dynamic character** changes as a result of the story's events. Squeaky in "Raymond's Run" (page 152) is a dynamic character.

See pages 221, 337–338.
See also *Characterization.*

CHARACTERIZATION The way a writer reveals the personality of a character. A writer may simply tell readers that a character is amusing, evil, dull, brave, or something else. This method is called **direct characterization.** Most often, though, writers use **indirect characterization,** revealing personality in one or more of the following ways:

1. through the words of the character
2. through description of the character's looks and clothing
3. through the character's thoughts and feelings
4. through comments made about the character by other characters in the story
5. through the character's action and behavior

When a writer uses indirect characterization, we must use our own judgment to decide what the character is like, based on the evidence the writer gives us.

CHRONOLOGICAL ORDER An arrangement of events in the order in which they occurred. Most stories are told in chronological order. Sometimes, however, a writer will interrupt the chronological order to depict something that happened in the past or that will happen in the future. *The Diary of Anne Frank* (page 222), for example, begins in 1945, when Mr. Frank arrives at the hiding place. The main story, however, takes place from 1942 to 1944.

See also *Flashback.*

CLIMAX The point in a story that has the greatest suspense or interest for the reader. The outcome of a story's main conflict is usually decided at the climax.

See also *Plot.*

COMEDY In general, a story that ends happily. Comedies may include several scenes that make us smile or laugh. The comic effect is often produced through exaggeration, irony, or understatement. The character's problems usu-ally are not treated very seriously in a comedy. Many comedies end with a wedding.

See pages 57, 89–90, 91–92.
See also *Exaggeration, Irony, Tragedy, Understatement.*

COMPARISON Showing similarities between two or more things. You could, for example, compare "To Build a Fire" (page 6) with "The Cold Wave" (page 455) by showing how each describes extremely cold conditions.

See pages 611–612.
See also *Contrast.*

CONFLICT A struggle between opposing characters or between opposing forces. In an **external conflict,** a character struggles with some outside force. This outside force might be another character, society as a whole, or a natural force. In "Stickeen" (page 40), for instance, John Muir and Stickeen struggle with a natural obstacle while on a glacier. By contrast, an **internal conflict** takes place within the character's own mind. It is a struggle between opposing needs or desires or emotions. In "Stickeen" the dog Stickeen has an internal conflict as it decides whether to try to cross the sliver bridge.

See page 3.
See also *Resolution.*

CONNOTATION A meaning, association, or emotion suggested by a word, aside from its dictionary definition, or denotation. Some words have very similar meanings, but widely different connotations. Suppose, for example, you wanted to describe someone who rarely changes plans in the face of opposition. You could say the person was either *determined* or *pigheaded.* The two words have very similar definitions. But *determined* has positive connotations and *pigheaded* has negative connotations.

See pages 389, 437, 465, 467.

CONTEXT The words and sentences that surround a word in a piece of writing. You can often use clues in the context to make an educated guess about the meaning of an unfamiliar word or phrase. Think about the word in italics in the following sentence, for example.

He swung the *mace* over his head, causing his enemies to run for shelter.

Even if you have never seen the word *mace* before, you should be able to tell that it is some sort of weapon. The sentence—which forms the context for the word—allows you to draw that conclusion.

See pages 82, 369, 524.

CONTRAST Showing differences between two or more things. You might, for example, show a contrast between the outcome of the struggle with nature in "To Build a Fire" (page 6) and "Stickeen" (page 40).

> See pages 611–612.
> See also *Comparison*.

DENOTATION The dictionary definition of a word or expression.

> See also *Connotation*.

DESCRIPTION Writing intended to create a mood or emotion or to recreate a person, a place, a thing, an event, or an experience. Description works through images that appeal to the senses of sight, smell, taste, hearing, or touch. Writers use description in all forms of fiction, nonfiction, and poetry. "The Legend of Sleepy Hollow" (page 580) is noted for its descriptive writing.

> See pages 463, 621.

DIALECT A way of speaking characteristic of a certain geographical area or a certain group of people. Dialects may have a distinct vocabulary, pronunciation system, and grammar. In a sense, we all speak dialects. One dialect usually becomes dominant in a country or culture, however, and is accepted as the standard way of speaking and writing. In the United States, for example, the formal written language is known as Standard English. (You usually hear it spoken by newscasters on television.) Writers often reproduce regional dialects, or those that reveal a person's economic or social class, in order to give a story local color. The poem "Sisters" (page 356) contains dialect.

> See pages 159, 357, 548, 553, 574, 579.

DIALOGUE Conversation between two or more characters. Most stage dramas consist entirely of dialogue, together with stage directions. (Screenplays and television dramas sometimes also include an unseen narrator.) The dialogue in a drama must move the plot along and reveal character almost single-handedly. Dialogue is also an important element in most stories and novels, as well as in some poems and nonfiction. It is one of the most effective ways for a writer to show what a character is like. Dialogue can also add realism and humor.

In the written form of a play, dialogue appears without quotation marks. In prose or poetry, however, dialogue is normally enclosed in quotation marks.

A **monologue,** or **soliloquy,** is a part of a drama in which one character speaks alone.

> See pages 219, 335–336.

DICTION The choice of words of a writer or speaker. People use different types of words depending on the audience they are addressing, the subject they are discussing, and the effect they are trying to produce. For example, slang words that would be suitable to a humorous piece like "The Ransom of Red Chief" (page 66) would not be suitable to a serious essay like "A Tragedy Revealed: A Heroine's Last Days" (page 481). Diction is an essential element of a writer's style. Diction has a tremendous effect on the tone of a piece of writing.

> See page 75.
> See also *Connotation, Style, Tone*.

DRAMA A work of literature meant to be performed by actors for an audience. (A drama can be appreciated and enjoyed in written form, however.) The actors work from a script, which includes dialogue and stage directions. The script of a drama written for the screen is called a **screenplay** and it also includes camera directions. The action of a drama is usually driven by a character who wants something very much and takes steps to get it. The main stages of a drama are often described as **introduction, complications, climax,** and **resolution.**

> See pages 219–221, 286.

END-STOPPED LINE A line of poetry in which a pause occurs naturally at the end of the line. The pause usually is signaled by a period, comma, or semicolon, but it may simply be a natural pause between words. The following excerpt contains three end-stopped lines and two **run-on lines** (lines with no pause at the end).

> The sea is calm tonight,
> The tide is full, the moon lies fair
> Upon the straits;—on the French coast the light
> Gleams and is gone; the cliffs of England stand,
> Glimmering and vast, out in the tranquil bay.
>
> —from "Dover Beach,"
> Matthew Arnold

EPIC A long narrative poem that tells of the deeds of a heroic character. The hero usually embodies the values of a particular society. Most epics include elements of myth, legend, folktale, and history. Their tone is serious and their language is grand. Most epic heroes undertake quests of tremendous value to themselves or their people. Homer's *Iliad* and *Odyssey* are the best known epics in Western civilization. The great epic of ancient Rome is Virgil's *Aeneid,* which, like the *Iliad* and *Odyssey,* is based on events that happened during and after the Trojan War.

The English-speaking people have two major epics. *Beowulf* is about a hero who saves a people from two monsters who are threatening the stability of their kingdom. *Paradise Lost,* written by John Milton in the seventeenth century, is an epic that retells the story of the creation and fall of the human race. The great French national epic is *The Song of Roland,* about a knight of Charlemagne's. The great Spanish national epic is the story of a knight called El Cid.

The Song of Hiawatha (page 509) is an American epic about the Mohawk leader Hiawatha, who lived around 1450.

ESSAY A short piece of nonfiction prose. It typically examines a single subject from a limited and usually personal point of view. Most essays can be categorized as either personal or formal. Personal essays are also called informal or familiar essays.

The **personal essay** generally reveals a great deal about the writer's personality and tastes. Its tone is often conversational, sometimes even humorous, and there may be no attempt to be objective. In fact, in a personal essay we are interested in the writer's feelings and response to an experience.

The **formal essay** is usually serious, objective, and impersonal in tone. Its purpose is to inform its readers about some topic of interest or to convince them to accept the writer's views. The statements in a formal essay should be supported by facts and logic.

Essays are included in Unit Seven of this book.

See page 451.

EXAGGERATION Overstating something, usually for the purpose of creating a comic effect. Much of the humor in "The Ransom of Red Chief" (page 66), for example, comes from exaggeration.

See pages 56, 58–59.

EXPOSITION The kind of writing that explains or gives information. Exposition is common in essays, which call for facts or examples to back up personal opinions. In fiction, exposition refers to the part of a story in which the reader is given background information. For example, look at the early paragraphs of "Bargain" (page 20). The story begins with action and dialogue. Then the action is interrupted for two paragraphs of exposition, beginning with "Three of us worked there regularly. . . ."

FABLE A brief story told in prose or poetry that teaches a moral or a practical lesson about how to get along in life. The characters of most fables are animals that speak and behave like people. Some of the most popular fables are those attributed to Aesop, who supposedly was a slave in ancient Greece. Well-known Aesop's fables include "The Fox and the Grapes" and "The Tortoise and the Hare."

FANTASY Imaginative writing that carries the reader into an invented, unrealistic world. In fantasy worlds, supernatural forces are often at play. Characters may wave magic wands, cast magical spells, or appear and disappear at will. These characters may seem almost like ordinary human beings—or they may be witches, Martians, elves, giants, or fairies. To take characters or readers into a fantasy world, the writer often uses some kind of magic carpet—a time machine, a magical looking glass, a mysterious door, even a Kansas tornado. Some of the oldest fantasy stories are called **fairy tales.** A newer type of fantasy, which deals with the changes that science may bring in the future, is called **science fiction.** The selections in Unit Three of this book are fantasies.

See page 95.
See also *Science Fiction.*

FICTION A prose account that is basically made-up rather than factually true. The term fiction usually refers to novels and short stories. Fiction may be based on a writer's actual experiences or on historical events, but characters, events, or other details are altered or added by the writer to create a desired effect. "Bargain" (page 20) is almost entirely made-up. "Ninki" (page 60), on the other hand, is based to some extent on the writer's actual experiences.

See also *Nonfiction.*

FIGURE OF SPEECH A word or phrase that describes one thing in terms of another and is not meant to be understood as literally true. Figures of speech always involve some sort of imaginative comparison between seemingly unlike things.

Some 250 different types of figures of speech have been identified. The most common by far are the **simile** ("The sun was like a ball of fire"), the **metaphor** ("He has a sunny disposition"), and **personification** ("The sun smiled down on the bathers").

See pages 20, 28, 398–401, 443–444, 675, 715–716.
See also *Metaphor, Personification, Simile.*

FLASHBACK Interruption in the present action of a plot to flash backward and tell what happened at an earlier time. A flashback breaks the normal movement of the narrative from one point in time forward to another point. A flashback can also be placed at the very beginning of a work. It usually gives background information needed to understand the present action. The first scene of *The Diary of Anne Frank* (page 222) takes place about one year after the main action of the play. Almost the entire play, then, is a flashback to an earlier time. Flashbacks are common in stories, novels, and movies and sometimes appear in stage plays and poems.

A break in the movement of a plot to jump to an episode in the future is known as a **flash-forward.**

FOLKTALE A story with no known author, which originally was passed on from one generation to another by word of mouth. Most folktales reflect the values of the society that preserves them. Folktales generally differ from myths in that they are not about gods. "The Tar Man" (page 569) is a folktale.

See pages 499–500.
See also *Fable, Legend, Myth.*

FOIL A character in a story who serves as a contrast to another character. A writer uses a foil to accentuate and clarify the distinct qualities of two characters. In "The First Rose of Summer" (page 165) the narrator's brother serves as a foil for the narrator.

FORESHADOWING The use of clues or hints suggesting events that will occur later in the plot. Foreshadowing is used to build suspense or anxiety in the reader or viewer. In a drama, a gun found in a bureau drawer in Act I is likely to foreshadow violence later in the play. Details in the early part of "To Build a Fire" (page 6) foreshadow what happens to the man as he trudges in the Yukon cold.

FREE VERSE Poetry without a regular meter or a rhyme scheme. Poets writing in free verse try to capture the natural rhythms of ordinary free speech. Free verse may use internal rhyme, repetition, alliteration, onomatopoeia, and other musical devices. Free verse also frequently makes use of vivid imagery and striking metaphors and similes. The following poem in free verse includes vivid images and an extended metaphor.

Mother to Son

Well, son, I'll tell you:
Life for me ain't been no crystal stair.
It's had tacks in it,
And splinters,
And boards torn up,
And places with no carpet on the floor—
Bare.
But all the time
I'se been a-climbin' on,
And reachin' landin's,
And turnin' corners,
And sometimes goin' in the dark

Where there ain't been no light.
So boy, don't you turn back.
Don't you set down on the steps
'Cause you finds it's kinder hard.
Don't you fall now—
For I'se still goin', honey,
I'se still climbin',
And life for me ain't been no crystal stair.

—Langston Hughes

See page 345.
See also *Meter, Rhyme.*

IMAGERY Language that appeals to the senses. Most images are visual—that is, they create pictures in the reader's mind by appealing to the sense of sight. Images can also appeal to the senses of sound, touch, taste, or smell, or even to several senses at once. While imagery is an element in all types of writing, it is especially important in poetry. The following poem contains images that appeal to our senses of sight, sound, and touch.

Those Winter Sundays

Sundays too my father got up early
and put his clothes on in the blueblack cold,
then with cracked hands that ached
from labor in the weekday weather made
banked fires blaze. No one ever thanked him.

I'd wake and hear the cold splintering, breaking.
When the rooms were warm, he'd call,
and slowly I would rise and dress,
fearing the chronic angers of that house,

Speaking indifferently to him,
who had driven out the cold
and polished my good shoes as well.
What did I know, what did I know
of love's austere and lonely offices?

—Robert Hayden

See pages 103, 194, 390–391, 476, 641, 680, 715.

INFERENCE A conclusion that can be drawn from hints, clues, or other information. Many modern writers do not directly tell readers everything there is to know about their characters. Instead, writers expect readers to be alert for information on which inferences, or educated guesses, can be based. For example, the narrator of "Calling Home" (page 174) leaves important points of the story unsaid. As a reader, you have to use what the narrator does say to piece together the full picture of what happened.

IRONY A contrast between expectation and reality. Irony can create powerful effects, ranging from humor to strong emotion.

The following terms refer to three common types of irony.

1. **Verbal irony** involves a contrast between what is said or written and what is really meant. If you call a baseball player who has just struck out "slugger," you are using verbal irony.

2. **Situational irony** occurs when what happens is very different from what we expected would happen. The situation that develops in "The Ransom of Red Chief" (page 66) is ironic—you would not expect a kidnap victim to gain control over his kidnappers.

3. **Dramatic irony** occurs when the audience or the reader knows something a character does not know. *The Diary of Anne Frank* (page 222) is filled with dramatic irony. We know the terrible fate of the people in the secret annex, and they do not. Note the irony in the following words spoken by Mr. Frank to Mr. Van Daan. "Didn't you hear what Miep said? The invasion has come! We're going to be liberated! This is a time to celebrate." (Act One, Scene 3)

See pages 57, 223.

LEGEND A story of extraordinary deeds that is handed down from one generation to the next. Legends are based to some extent on fact.

See pages 499–500, 501, 525.
See also *Fable, Folktale, Myth, Tall Tale.*

LIMERICK A humorous poem of five lines with a rhyme scheme of *aabba*. Here is an example of a limerick:

A handsome young actor named Sammy
Was often described as quite hammy.
    He'd cry out in pain
    Onstage up in Maine,
And wake up the folks in Miami.

LYRIC POEM A poem that expresses the personal feelings or thoughts of a speaker. Lyric poems can express a wide range of emotions, from the deep affection of "The Secret Heart" (page 353) to the mild annoyance of "Sonic Boom" (page 376). They do not tell a story and usually are short and musical.

See page 418.
See also *Narrative Poem.*

METAMORPHOSIS A marvelous change from one shape or form to another one. In myths and other stories, the change is usually from human or god to animal, from animal to human, or from human to plant. Greek and Roman myths contain many examples of metamorphosis. The myth of Narcissus, for example, tells how the vain youth Narcissus pines away for love of his own reflection, and is finally changed into a flower. Metamorphosis is also found in many fairy tales. For instance, a frog may be transformed into a handsome prince. Other kinds of fantasy may also contain metamorphosis. For example, "Story from Bear Country" (page 100) involves the metamorphosis of people into bears.

METAPHOR A comparison between two unlike things in which one thing becomes another thing. A metaphor is an important type of figure of speech. Metaphors are used in all forms of writing and are common in ordinary speech. When you say someone has "a heart of stone," you do not mean the person's heart is made of rock. You mean the person is cold and uncaring.

Metaphors differ from similes, which use specific words (notably *like, as, than,* and *resembles*) to state comparisons. William Wordsworth's famous comparison, "I wandered lonely as a cloud," is a simile because it uses *as*. If Wordsworth had written, "I was a lonely, wandering cloud," he would have been using a metaphor.

An **extended metaphor** is a metaphor that is extended, or developed, over several lines of writing or even throughout an entire poem. The following famous poem, which mourns the death of President Abraham Lincoln, contains an extended metahor in which the United States is compared to a ship. Lincoln is compared to the captain of the ship.

O Captain! My Captain!

O Captain! my Captain! our fearful trip is done,
The ship has weathered every rack, the prize we
        sought is won,
The port is near, the bells I hear, the people all
        exulting,
While follow eyes the steady keel, the vessel grim
        and daring;
    But O heart! heart! heart!
        O the bleeding drops of red,
            Where on the deck my Captain lies,
                Fallen cold and dead.

O Captain! my Captain! rise up and hear the bells;
Rise up—for you the flag is flung—for you the bugle
        trills,
For you bouquets and ribboned wreaths—for you the
        shores a-crowding,
For you they call, the swaying mass, their eager faces
        turning;
        Here Captain! dear father!

This arm beneath your head!
    It is some dream that on the deck
      You've fallen cold and dead.

My Captain does not answer, his lips are pale and
    still,
My father does not feel my arm, he has no pulse nor
    will,
The ship is anchored safe and sound, its voyage
    closed and done,
From fearful trip the victor ship comes in with object
    won;
    Exult O shores! and ring O bells!
      But I with mournful tread
        Walk the deck my Captain lies,
          Fallen cold and dead.

—Walt Whitman

See pages 359, 399–400, 572.
See also *Figure of Speech, Simile.*

METER A pattern of stressed and unstressed syllables in poetry. It is a common practice to show this pattern in writing by using two symbols. The symbol ′ indicates a stressed syllable. The symbol ‿ indicates an unstressed syllable. Indicating the metrical pattern of a poem in this way is called **scanning** the poem. The following lines by William Shakespeare are scanned in part. (The lines make up the speech of the mischiefmaker Puck, or Robin Goodfellow, at the end of the comedy *A Midsummer Night's Dream.* "Reprehend" means criticize; "serpent's tongue" means hissing; "Give me your hands" means clap.)

If we shadows have offended,
Think but this, and all is mended,
That you have but slumbered here
While these visions did appear,
And this weak and idle theme,
No more yielding but a dream,
Gentles, do not reprehend.
If you pardon, we will mend.
And, as I am an honest Puck,
If we have unearnèd luck
Now to scape the serpent's tongue,
We will make amends ere long,
Else the Puck a liar call.
So, good night unto you all.
Give me your hands, if we be friends,
And Robin shall restore amends.

—from *A Midsummer Night's Dream,*
  William Shakespeare

See pages 344–345.

MOTIVATION The reasons a character behaves in a certain way. Among the many reasons for a person's behavior are feelings, desires, experiences, and commands by others. It often is not easy to pinpoint a character's motivation. The main motivation of the man in "To Build a Fire" (page 6), however, is clear—he wants to survive the extreme cold.

MYTH A story that explains something about the world and typically involves gods or other supernatural beings. Myths reflect the traditions and beliefs of the culture that produced them. Almost every culture has **creation myths,** stories that explain how the world came to exist or how human beings were created. "Sky Woman" (page 502) is an example. Myths may also explain many other aspects of life and the natural world. The ancient Greek myths, for instance, tell how Prometheus secured for men the gift of fire. Most myths are very old and were handed down orally before being put in written form. The exact origin of most myths is not known.

See pages 499–500, 501.
See also *Fable, Folktale, Legend.*

NARRATION The kind of writing that tells a story. Narration is the main tool of writers of fiction. It is also used in nonfiction, whenever a series of events are related in the order in which they happened.

See also *Exposition, Fiction, Nonfiction.*

NARRATIVE POEM A poem that tells a story. "The Cowboy's Lament" (page 419) and "Paul Revere's Ride" (page 346) are narrative poems.

See page 418.
See also *Lyric Poem.*

NONFICTION Prose writing that deals with real people, events, and places without changing facts. Popular forms of nonfiction are the autobiography, the biography, and the essay. Other examples of nonfiction include newspaper stories, magazine articles, historical writing, scientific reports, and even personal diaries and letters. Unit Seven of this book includes several types of nonfiction.

See pages 449–451.
See also *Autobiography, Biography, Fiction.*

NOVEL A long fictional story, whose length is normally somewhere between one hundred and five hundred book pages. A novel uses all the elements of storytelling—plot, character, setting, theme, and point of view. It usually has more characters, settings, and themes and a more complex plot than a short story. Modern writers sometimes do not pay much attention to one or more of the novel's traditional elements. Some novels today are basically character studies, with only the barest story lines. Other novels don't probe much below the surface of their characters and concentrate instead on plot and setting. A novel can deal with almost anything. One novel in this book—*A Christmas Carol* (page 617)—contains elements of fantasy. The other novel—*The Pearl* (page 672)—is a gripping tale that seems to deal with actual events.

See pages 615–616.

ONOMATOPOEIA The use of a word whose sound imitates or suggests its meaning. Onomatopoeia is so natural to us that we begin using it instinctively at a very early age. *Buzz, rustle, boom, tick-tock, tweet,* and *bark* are all examples of onomatopoeia. Onomatopoeia is an important element in creating the music of poetry. In the following lines, the poet suggests the sound of sleigh bells in the cold night air by using onomatopoeic words.

> Hear the sledges with the bells—
> Silver bells!
> What a world of merriment their melody foretells!
> How they tinkle, tinkle, tinkle,
> In the icy air of night!
> While the stars that oversprinkle
> All the Heavens, seem to twinkle
> With a crystalline delight.

> —from "The Bells,"
> Edgar Allan Poe

See pages 373, 377, 656.
See also *Alliteration.*

PERSONIFICATION A figure of speech in which an object or animal is given human feelings, thoughts, or attitudes. In "Silver" (page 395), for example, the poet speaks of the moon as though it were a person.

> Slowly, silently, now the moon
> Walks the night in her silver shoon;
> This way, and that, she peers and sees
> Silver fruit upon silver trees.

> —from "Silver,"
> Walter de la Mare

See page 401.
See also *Figure of Speech.*

PERSUASION A kind of writing intended to convince a reader to think or act in a certain way. Examples of persuasive writing are found in newspaper editorials, in speeches, and in many essays and articles. The tech-

niques of persuasion are used in all kinds of advertising. Persuasion can use language that appeals to the emotions, or it can use logic to appeal to reason. When persuasive writing appeals to reason and not to the emotions, it is called **argument.** The speeches by Abraham Lincoln, Red Cloud, and Martin Luther King, Jr. (pages 600–608) are examples of persuasive writing.

PLOT The series of related events that make up a story. Plot is what happens in a short story, novel, play, or narrative poem. Most plots are built on these bare bones: An **introduction,** or **exposition,** tells us who the characters are and, usually, what their conflict is. **Complications** arise as the characters take steps to resolve the conflict. Eventually, the plot reaches a **climax,** the most exciting moment in the story, when the outcome is decided one way or another. The final part of a story is the **resolution.** This is when the story's problems are solved and the story is closed.

Not all works of fiction or drama have a traditional plot structure. Modern writers often experiment with plot, eliminating at times some or nearly all of the parts of a traditional plot in order to focus on other elements, such as character, point of view, or mood.

See pages 220–221.

POETRY A kind of rhythmic, compressed language that uses figures of speech and imagery designed to appeal to our emotions and imaginations. Poetry is usually arranged in lines. It often has a regular pattern of rhythm, and may have a regular rhyme scheme. Free verse is poetry that has no regular pattern of rhythm or rhyme, though it generally is arranged in lines. The major forms of poetry are the **lyric,** the **epic,** and the **ballad.** Beyond this, it is difficult to define poetry, though many readers feel it is easy to recognize. Emily Dickinson once explained how she recognized poetry:

> If I read a book and it makes my whole body so cold that no fire can ever warm me, I know that it is poetry. If I feel physically as if the top of my head were taken off, I know that it is poetry.

> —Emily Dickinson

See pages 341–342, 445–446.
See also *Ballad, End-Stopped Line, Figure of Speech, Free Verse, Imagery, Limerick, Lyric Poem, Meter, Narrative Poem, Refrain, Rhyme, Rhythm, Run-On Line, Speaker.*

POINT OF VIEW The vantage point from which a story is told. The most common points of view are the omniscient, the third-person limited, and the first person.

1. In the **omniscient, or all-knowing, point of view,** the narrator knows everything about the characters and their problems. This all-knowing narrator can tell us about the past, the present, and the future of the characters. This narrator can even tell us what the characters are thinking. The narrator can also tell us what is happening in other places or parts of the world. But the narrator is not in the story. Rather, this kind of narrator stands above the action like a god. The omniscient is a very familiar point of view; we hear it in fairy tales from the time we are very young. "The Legend of Sleepy Hollow" (page 580) is told from the omniscient point of view.

2. In the **third-person limited point of view,** the narrator focuses on the thoughts and feelings of just one character. With this point of view, we feel we are observing the action through the eyes and with the feelings of only one of the characters in the story. "Calling Home" (page 174) is told from the third-person limited point of view.

3. In the **first-person point of view,** one of the characters is actually telling the story, using the personal pronoun "I." We become very familiar with the narrator, but we can know only what this person knows, observe only what this person observes. All our information about the story must come from this one person. The information can be incorrect. "Raymond's Run" (page 152) is told from the first-person point of view.

PROSE Any writing that is not poetry. Essays, short stories, novels, newspaper articles, and letters are all written in prose. As a rule, prose is straightforward language that does not call attention to itself, as the language of poetry usually does.

See also *Poetry.*

PROTAGONIST The main character in a work of literature. The protagonist is involved in the work's central conflict. If there is another character opposing the protagonist, that character is called the **antagonist.** In "The Legend of Sleepy Hollow" (page 580) Ichabod Crane is the protagonist and Brom Van Brunt (Brom Bones) is the antagonist.

PUN A play (1) on the multiple meanings of a word or (2) on two words that sound alike but have different meanings. Most often puns are used for their humorous effects; they turn up in jokes all the time. *"Where does an elephant put suitcases?" Answer: "In its trunk."* This pun is called a **homographic pun;** it is based on a word (*trunk*) that has two meanings ("the long proboscis of an elephant" and "a compartment in an automobile"). *"Is Swiss cheese good for you?" Answer: "Yes, it's holesome."* This pun is called a **homophonic pun;** it is based on words that sound alike but are spelled differently and have different meanings (*hole* and *whole*).

See page 65.

REFRAIN A repeated sound, word, phrase, line, or group of lines. Refrains are usually associated with songs and poems, but are also used in speeches and other forms of literature. Refrains are most often used to build rhythm, but they may also provide emphasis or commentary, create suspense, or help hold a work together. Refrains may be repeated with small variations in a work in order to fit a particular context or to create a special effect. The line "I loved my friend" serves as a refrain in "Poem" (page 383).

See pages 374–375.

RHYME The repetition of accented vowel sounds and all sounds following them, in words that are close together in a poem. *Mean* and *screen* are rhymes, as are *crumble* and *tumble.* The many purposes of rhyme in poetry include building rhythm, lending a songlike quality, emphasizing ideas, organizing the poem (for instance, into stanzas or couplets), providing humor or delight for the reader, and aiding memory.

End-rhymes are rhymes at the ends of lines. In the following poem, *breaking/aching* form end-rhymes, as do *vain/pain/again/vain.*

> If I can stop one heart from breaking,
> I shall not live in vain;
> If I can ease one life the aching,
> Or cool one pain,
> Or help one fainting robin
> Unto his nest again,
> I shall not live in vain.
>
> —Emily Dickinson

Internal rhymes are rhymes within a line. The following line has an internal rhyme (*turning/burning*):

> Back into the chamber turning, all my soul within me burning
>
> —from "The Raven," Edgar Allan Poe

Rhyming sounds need not be spelled the same way: *gear/here,* for instance, form a rhyme. Rhymes can involve more than one syllable or more than one word; *poet/know it* is an example. Rhymes involving sounds that are similar but not exactly the same are called **approximate rhymes** (or **near rhymes** or **slant rhymes**). *Leave/live* is an example of an approximate rhyme. Poets writing in English often use approximate rhymes because English is not a very rhymable language. It has many words that rhyme with no other word, or just one other word (*mountain/fountain,* for instance). Poets interested in how a poem looks on the printed page sometimes use **eye rhymes,** or **visual rhymes**—"rhymes" involving words that are spelled similarly but pronounced differently. *Tough/cough* is an eye rhyme. (*Tough/rough* is a "real" rhyme.)

The pattern of end-rhymes in a poem is called a **rhyme scheme.** To indicate the rhyme scheme of a poem, use a separate letter of the alphabet for each rhyme. For example, the rhyme scheme of the Dickinson poem on page 734 is *ababcbb.*

See pages 360–362, 366, 443–444.

RHYTHM A musical quality produced by the repetition of stressed and unstressed syllables or by the repetition of certain other sound patterns. Rhythm occurs in all languages—written and spoken—but is particularly important in poetry.

The most obvious kind of rhythm is the regular repetition of stressed and unstressed syllables found in some poetry. In the following lines describing a cavalry charge, the rhythm echoes the galloping of the attacking horses.

The Assyrian came down like the wolf on the fold,
And his cohorts were gleaming in purple and gold;
And the sheen of their spears was like stars on the sea,
When the blue wave rolls nightly on deep Galilee.

—from "The Destruction of Sennacherib,"
George Gordon, Lord Byron

Marking the stressed (′) and unstressed (◡) syllables in a line is called **scanning** the line. Byron's lines are scanned for you, showing that they have a rhythm pattern in which two unstressed syllables are followed by a stressed syllable. Read the lines aloud and listen to this rhythmic pattern. Also notice how the poem's end-rhymes help create the rhythm.

Writers can also create rhythm by repeating words and phrases, or even by repeating whole lines and sentences. The following passage by Walt Whitman is written in free verse and does not follow a regular pattern of rhythm or rhyme. Yet the lines are rhythmical because of Whitman's use of repetition:

I hear the sound I love, the sound of the human voice,
I hear all sounds running together, combined, fused, or following,
Sounds of the city and sounds out of the city, sounds of the day and night,
Talkative young ones to those that like them, the loud laugh of work-people at their meals . . .

—from "Song of Myself,"
Walt Whitman

See page 344.

RUN-ON LINE A line of poetry in which there is no natural pause at the end of the line.

See also *End-Stopped Line.*

SCIENCE FICTION A kind of fantasy usually based on changes that science may bring in the future. Some science fiction deals with the past, especially prehistoric times. While science fiction creates imaginary worlds—often on other planets or in Earth's future—it typically makes use of physical laws as we know them. It is realistic, except that it is set in another place or time and presents imaginary scientific discoveries or developments. Classic early science fiction novels include Jules Verne's *Twenty Thousand Leagues Under the Sea* and H. G. Wells's *The War of the Worlds.* "The Ruum" (page 120) is a science fiction story.

See also *Fantasy.*

SETTING The time and place of a story, play, or narrative poem. Most often the setting is described early in the story. For example, the story "Calling Home" (page 174) begins, "In August, after two months in the bush, the platoon returned to Chu Lai for a week's stand down." Setting often contributes to a work's emotional effect. "The Raven" (page 385) is an example. Setting frequently plays an important role in a story's plot, especially when a conflict is between a character and nature. In "To Build a Fire" (page 6), for instance, a man struggles against the Yukon cold.

See pages 335–336.

SHORT STORY A short fictional prose narrative that usually takes up about ten to twenty book pages. Short stories were first written in the nineteenth century. Early short-story writers include Sir Walter Scott and Edgar Allan Poe. Short stories are usually built on a plot that consists of at least these bare bones: the **introduction** or **exposition, complications, climax,** and **resolution.** Short stories are more limited than novels. They usually have only one or two major characters and one important setting.

See pages 145–148.

SIMILE A comparison between two unlike things, using a word such as *like, as, than,* or *resembles.* The simile is an important type of figure of speech. In "Trades" (page 410) the poet compares a tool to a tongue.

With the claws of my hammer glistening
Like the tongue of a snake.

—from "Trades,"
Amy Lowell

See pages 398–399.
See also *Figure of Speech, Metaphor.*

SPEAKER The voice talking to us in a poem. The speaker may be the poet, but you should not assume that it always is. It is best to think of the voice in a poem as belonging to a character the poet has created. The character may be a child, a woman, a man, an animal, or even an object like a chair.

STANZA A group of consecutive lines in a poem that form a single unit. A stanza in a poem is something like a paragraph in prose; it often expresses a unit of thought. A stanza may consist of one line, or two, three, four, or any number of lines beyond that. The word *stanza* is an Italian word for "stopping place" or "place to rest." In some poems each stanza has the same rhyme scheme.

STYLE The way in which a writer uses language. All writers have their own ways of saying things in writing. Style has to do with word choice, sentence structure, and tone. One writer's style might include many figures of speech, for example; another writer might prefer straightforward language with few figures of speech.

See pages 132, 138.
See also *Diction, Tone.*

SUSPENSE The uncertainty or anxiety a reader feels about what will happen next in a story. Any kind of writing that has a plot also involves some degree of suspense.

See pages 3, 51–52, 53–54.
See also *Plot.*

SYMBOL A person, place, thing, or event that has meaning in itself and also stands for something beyond itself. Some symbols are so well-known that we sometimes forget they are symbols. The bald eagle, for example, is a symbol of the United States, the star of David is a symbol of Judaism, and the cross stands for Christianity. In literature, symbols are often personal and surprising. In "The Runaway" (page 406), for example, the horse symbolizes human fear.

See page 401.

TALL TALE An exaggerated, far-fetched story that is obviously untrue, but is told as though it should be believed. Most tall tales, like the stories about Paul Bunyan (page 549), are intended as amusement and are funny. Some writers, though, have used the tall tale to convey a serious message. "The Devil and Daniel Webster" (page 534) is an example of a tall tale with a serious intent.

See page 557.

THEME A main idea in a work of literature. A theme is not the same as a subject. The subject of a work can usually be expressed in a word or two: love, childhood, death. The theme is the idea the writer wishes to convey *about* that subject. The theme must be expressed in a statement or sentence. A theme of "The Circuit" (page 165) might be stated, "The system of migratory farm labor in California in the 1950's prevented children from developing their abilities." A work can have more than one theme. A work's themes usually are not stated directly. Most often, the reader has to think about all the elements of the work and use them to make an inference, or educated guess, about what the themes are.

See pages 495–496, 672–673.

TONE The attitude a writer takes toward a literary work, its characters, the events it tells about, and its audience. A writer's tone can be unemotional, as in "To Build a Fire" (page 6), or passionate and involved, as In "The First Rose of Summer" (page 180). When you speak, your tone of voice gives added meaning to what you say. Writers are skillful at using written language to achieve effects similar to those people achieve with their voices.

See pages 57, 717–718.

TRAGEDY A play, novel, or other narrative, dealing with serious and important events, in which the main character comes to an unhappy end. In a tragedy, the main character is usually dignified and courageous. This character's downfall may be caused by a character flaw, or it may result from forces beyond his or her control. The tragic hero or heroine usually wins some self-knowledge and wisdom, even though he or she suffers defeat, perhaps even death.

See also *Comedy.*

UNDERSTATEMENT A statement that says less than what is meant. Understatement is the opposite of exaggeration, and it is usually used for comic effect. If you say the Grand Canyon is a nice little hole in the ground, you are using understatement.

See page 57.
See also *Exaggeration.*

GLOSSARY

The glossary below is an alphabetical list of words found in the selections in this book. Use this glossary just as you use a dictionary—to find out the meanings of unfamiliar words. (A few technical, foreign, or more obscure words in this book are not listed here but are defined instead for you in the footnotes that accompany each selection.)

Many words in the English language have more than one meaning. This glossary gives the meanings that apply to the words as they are used in the selections in this book. Words closely related in form and meaning are usually listed together in one entry (*appease* and *appeasingly*), and the definition is given for the first form.

The following abbreviations are used:

adj., adjective   **n.**, noun   **v.**, verb
adv., adverb   **pl.**, plural form

Unless a word is very simple to pronounce, its pronunciation is given in parentheses. A guide to the pronunciation symbols appears at the bottom of each righthand glossary page.

For more information about the words in this glossary, or about words not listed here, consult a dictionary.

abate (ə·bāt′) *v.* To make less in amount or degree.
abominable (ə·bäm′ə·nə·b'l) *adj.* Highly unpleasant; very bad.
abrupt (ə·brupt′) *adj.* Sudden.
absent minded (ab′s'nt mīn′did) *adj.* So dreamy or lost in thought as not to pay attention to what one is doing or what is going on around one.
abyss (ə·bis′) *n.* A deep crack in the earth.
accrue (ə·krōō′) *v.* **1.** To come as a natural growth or right. **2.** To be added periodically, as an increase.
accumulate (ə·kyōōm′yə·lāt′) *v.* To pile up or collect.
accustomed (ə·kus′təmd) *adj.* Usual.
acquaint (ə·kwānt′) *v.* To give knowledge to; make familiar with.

acquit (ə·kwit′) *v.* To clear someone of a charge.
acute (ə·kyōōt′) *adj.* Sharp; sensitive.
adduce (ə·dōōs′) *v.* To give as reason or proof.
adjacent (ə·jā′sənt) *adj.* Nearby.
advert (ad·vurt′) *v.* To call attention to or refer to.
affability (af′ə·bil′ə·tē) *n.* Friendliness.
affront (ə·frunt′) *n.* An intentional insult.
agitation (aj′ə·tā′shən) *n.* Emotional excitement.
allay (ə·lā′) *v.* To lessen or relieve.
allegiance (ə·lē′jəns) *n.* **1.** Loyalty. **2.** Duty; obligation.
aloof (ə·lōōf′) *adj.* At a distance; removed.
amiable (ā′mē·ə·b'l) *adj.* Having a pleasant and friendly manner.
amorous (am′ər·əs) *adj.* Showing love or desire.
animation (an′ə·mā′shən) *n.* Liveliness.
annihilation (ə·nī′ə·lā′shən) *n.* Murder; destruction.
anonymity (an′ə·nim′ə·tē) *n.* The condition of having no individual identity.
apathetic (ap′ə·thet′ik) *adj.* **1.** Feeling little or no emotion. **2.** Listless.
appalled (ə·pôl′'d) *adj.* Shocked; horrified.
appease (ə·pēz′) *v.* To satisfy or relieve. —**appeasingly** *adv.*
appendage (ə·pen′dij) *n.* Anything affixed or added.
apprehension (ap′rə·hen′shən) *n.* An anxious feeling.
apt *adj.* Likely.
arrant (ar′ənt) *adj.* Roving; wandering.
array (ə·rā′) *n.* An orderly grouping or arrangement.
ascot (as′kət) *n.* A type of necktie or scarf with very wide ends hanging one over the other from the knot.
askew (ə·skyōō′) *adv.* To one side; crookedly.
assuage (ə·swāj′) *v.* To calm.
assurance (ə·shoor′əns) *n.* Self-confidence.
astride (ə·strīd′) *adv.* With a leg on either side.
atone (ə·tōn′) *v.* To make up for wrongdoing.
audacity (ô·das′ə·tē) *n.* Boldness; daring.
audible (ô′də·b'l) *adj.* Loud enough to be heard.
authenticate (ô·then′tə·kāt′) *v.* To make valid. —**authentication** *n.*
authoritative (ə·thôr′ə·tāt′iv) *adj.* Bossy.
avarice (av′ə·ris) *n.* Greed.

---

fat, āpe, cär; ten, ēven; is, bīte; gō, hôrn, tōōl, look; oil, out; up, fʉr; get; joy; yet; chin; she; thin, *th*en; zh, leisure; ŋ, ring; ə for *a* in *ago, e* in *agent, i* in *sanity, o* in *comply, u* in *focus;* ′ as in *able* (ā′b'l).

avert (ə·vʉrt′) *v.* To ward off; prevent.

awe (ô) *n.* A feeling of reverence, fear, and wonder caused by something majestic or sacred.

baffle (baf′′l) *v.* To confuse or puzzle.

ballast (bal′əst) *n.* Anything heavy carried in a ship or vehicle to give it stability.

battlement (bat′′l·mənt) *n.* A low wall with open spaces for shooting, built on top of a castle, tower, or fort.

bay *v.* To bark; howl.

beguile (bi·gīl′) *v.* To charm or delight.

belfry (bel′frē) *n.* A bell tower, usually at the top of a building.

benediction (ben′ə·dik′shən) *n.* A blessing.

benevolence (bə·nev′ə·ləns) *n.* Kindliness.

bestow (bi·stō′) *v.* To give or present.

betray (bi·trā′) *v.* **1.** To reveal secret information. **2.** To deceive or break faith with.

blissful (blis′fəl) *adj.* Joyous; very happy.

bluffly (bluf′lē) *adv.* In a rough but kind manner.

bore (bôr) *v.* To make a hole as if by drilling.

borne (bôrn) *v.* Carried; transported.

bout *n.* A struggle; contest or match.

brandish (bran′dish) *v.* To wave or exhibit in a challenging or exultant way.

brier (brī′ər) *n.* Any prickly or thorny bush.

brimstone (brim′stōn′) *n.* Sulfur, a chemical element that burns with a stifling odor.

brine (brīn) *n.* **1.** Sea water. **2.** Water full of salt.

bristle (bris′′l) *n.* Any short, stiff, prickly hair of a plant or animal.—*v.* To have the bristles become stiff in fear or irritation.

brood (brood) *v.* To keep thinking about something in a troubled way; worry.

brusque (brusk′) *adj.* Rough and abrupt in manner.

burrow (bʉr′ō) *v.* To hide in a hole or shelter dug in the ground. —*n.* A hole or tunnel dug in the ground.

caliber (kal′ə·bər) *n.* Worth or value; quality.

canopy (kan′ə·pē) *n.* A drapery, awning, or other rooflike covering, usually placed over a bed or window.

capacious (kə·pā′shəs) *adj.* Roomy; spacious.

capitulation (kə·pich′ə·lā′shən) *n.* Surrender.

caprice (kə·prēs′) *n.* An impulsive change in the way one acts; whim.

capricious (kə·prish′əs) *adj.* Tending to change abruptly and without apparent reason.

capsize (kap′sīz) *v.* To overturn or upset, especially a boat.

carcass (kär′kəs) *n.* The dead body of an animal.

carillon (kar′ə·län′) *n.* A set of bells, each producing a single tone of the chromatic scale.

cascade (kas·kād′) *n.* A small, steep waterfall.

celestial (sə·les′chəl) *adj.* Of the heavens or the sky.

character (kar′ik·tər) *n.* **1.** Basic quality or nature. **2.** Pattern of behavior; personality.

characteristic (kar′ik·tə·ris′tik) *adj.* Typical; distinctive.

chasm (kaz′′m) *n.* A deep crack in the earth's surface.

chastisement (chas·tīz′mənt) *n.* Punishment.

cherish (cher′ish) *v.* **1.** To take good care of; foster. **2.** To hold dear.

clamber (klam′bər) *v.* To climb clumsily.

cleave (klēv) *v.* To divide by a blow; split.

coax (kōks) *v.* To persuade by using soothing words, agreeable manner, etc.—**coaxingly** *adv.*

coeducational (kō′ej·ə·kā′shən·əl) *adj.* Having students of both sexes attending classes together.

collaborate (kə·lab′ə·rāt′) *v.* To work together on some undertaking.

collate (kä·lāt′) *v.* **1.** To compare critically in order to note similarities and differences. **2.** To gather together in the proper order for assembling, as the pages of a book.

collusion (kə·loo′zhən) *n.* A secret agreement for dishonest or illegal purposes; conspiracy.

communal (käm·yoon′′l) *adj.* Belonging to the community; shared; public.

compact (käm′pakt) *n.* A small cosmetic case usually containing face powder and a mirror.

compel (kəm·pel′) *v.* To force, as to do something. —**compellingly** *adv.*

compliance (kəm·plī′əns) *n.* In accordance with a request, a wish, or a demand.

composure (kəm·pō′zhər) *n.* Calmness of mind or manner.

comprehend (käm′prə·hend′) *v.* To understand.

conceal (kən·sēl′) *v.* To keep out of sight; hide.

condescension (kän′də·sen′shən) *n.* A proud or haughty manner.

conduct (kən·dukt′) *v.* To manage, control, or direct.

confidence (kän′fə·dəns) *n.* **1.** Full trust. **2.** Self-reliance. **3.** A secret.

conflagration (kän′flə·grā′shən) *n.* Fire.

conscientious (kän′shē·en′shəs) *adj.* Showing care and precision.

conscious (kän′shəs) *adj.* Aware.

consecrated (kän′sə·krāt′id) *adj.* **1.** Set apart for service to God. **2.** Entirely devoted.

consequence (kän′sə·kwens′) *n.* Importance in terms or outcome or result.

consolatory (kən·sol′ə·tôr′ē) *adj.* Comforting.

console (kän′sōl) *n.* An instrument panel containing controls for operating equipment.

conspicuous (kən·spik′yoo·wəs) *adj.* Obvious.

conspirator (kən·spir′ə·tər) *n.* A person who takes part in a secret plot that is usually harmful.

consult (kən·sult′) *v.* To ask an opinion of or seek advice from.

consume (kən·sōōm′) *v.* **1.** To use up. **2.** To destroy. **3.** To eat or drink; devour.

contemptuous (kən·temp′choo·wəs) *adj.* Scornful. —**contemptuously** *adv.*

contraband (kän′trə·band′) *adj.* Forbidden by law to be imported or exported.

contrary (kän′trer·ē) *adj.* **1.** Opposite in nature, order, direction, etc. **2.** Inclined to oppose stubbornly.

contretemps (kōn′trə·tän′) *n.* An unfortunate happening.

conviction (kən·vik′shən) *n.* The state or appearance of being convinced, as of the truth of a belief.

countenance (koun′tə·nəns) *n.* **1.** The look on a person's face that shows the person's nature or feelings. **2.** The face. —*v.* To approve; tolerate.

courteous (kur′tē·əs) *adj.* Polite.

courtesy (kur′tə·sē) *n.* Gracious politeness.

covert (kuv′ərt) *n.* A covered place; shelter.

cozen (kuz′′n) *v.* To deceive; trick.

creed (krēd) *n.* A statement of belief or principle.

cunning (kun′iŋ) *adj.* **1.** Skillful in deception. **2.** Pretty in a delicate way.

curio (kyoor′ē·ō′) *n.* Any unusual or rare article.

curriculum (kə·rik′yə·ləm) *n.* All of the courses of study offered in a school or on a particular subject.

cynical (sin′i·k′l) *adj.* **1.** Denying the sincerity of people's motives and actions. **2.** Sarcastic; sneering.

daft (daft) *adj.* **1.** Silly; foolish. **2.** Crazy; insane.

dank (daŋk) *adj.* Damp and chilly.

dastardly (das′tərd·lē) *adj.* Cowardly.

daunt (dônt) *v.* To make afraid.

decapitate (di·kap′ə·tāt′) *v.* To cut off the head of.

deception (di·sep′shən) *n.* The act of misleading or trying to make a person believe what is not true.

decry (di·krī′) *v.* To speak strongly and openly against.

defensive (di·fen′siv) *adj.* Self-protective.

deft (deft) *adj.* Skillful in a quick, sure, and easy way, especially with the hands.

deign (dān) *v.* To lower oneself voluntarily from what one regards as a superior station in order to give something.

deliverance (di·liv′ər·əns) *n.* A setting free; rescue.

demeanor (di·mēn′ər) *n.* Behavior; conduct.

demented (di·ment′id) *adj.* Insane; mad.

denunciation (di·nun′sē·ā′shən) *n.* A public accusation or speech condemning someone or something.

deport (di·pôrt′) *v.* To carry away; banish.

deprecation (dep′rə·kā′shən) *n.* Protesting or pleading against; disapproval.

depreciation (di·prē′shē·ā′shən) *n.* A decrease in value.

depredation (dep′rə·dā′shən) *n.* The act of robbing, plundering, or destroying.

derisively (di·rī′siv·lē) *adv.* In a manner that shows a lack of respect and that ridicules.

desperation (des′pə·rā′shən) *n.* The state of being driven by a loss of hope.

despotic (de·spät′ik) *adj.* Like a tyrant.

destitute (des′tə·tōōt′) *adj.* Being without; lacking.

devotion (di·vō′shən) *n.* **1.** Dedication of oneself to an activity, purpose, or person. **2.** Worship.

dexterous (dek′strəs) *adj.* Having skill in the use of the hands or body.

diabolical (dī′ə·bäl′ik·əl) *adj.* Cruel; fiendish.

diagonal (dī·ag′ə·n′l) *adj.* At an angle. —**diagonally** *adv.*

diatribe (dī′ə·trīb′) *n.* A bitter, abusive criticism.

dictate (dik′tāt) *n.* A command.

diffuse (di·fyōōz′) *v.* To spread or scatter.

dignified (dig′nə·fīd′) *adj.* Showing proper pride and self-respect.

dilate (dī′lāt) *v.* To become wider or larger.

discernible (di·surn′ə·b′l) *adj.* Able to be seen or made out clearly.

discourse (dis′kôrs) *n.* Conversation; talk.

discreet (dis·krēt′) *adj.* Careful about what one says or does. —**discreetly** *adv.*

discriminate (dis·krim′ə·nāt′) *v.* To see the difference between things.

discrimination (dis·krim′ə·nā′shən) *n.* The act of seeing differences.

disgruntled (dis·grun′t′ld) *adj.* Discontented and sulky.

disheveled (di·shev′′ld) *adj.* Untidy; rumpled.

dismal (diz′m′l) *adj.* Causing gloom or misery; dreary.

disparagement (dis·par′ij·mənt) *n.* A show of disrespect; putting someone down.

dispatch (dis·pach′) *v.* To send out or away.

dissemble (di·sem′b′l) *v.* To conceal under a false appearance; disguise.

distinction (dis·tiŋk′shən) *n.* The quality that makes one seem superior or worthy of special recognition.

distinctness (dis·tiŋk′nəs) *n.* Clarity; sharpness.

dither (di*th*′ər) *n.* A state of nervous excitement or confusion.

diverse (dī·vurs′) *adj.* Varied.

divert (də·vurt′) *v.* To distract the attention of.

divine (də·vīn′) *v.* To guess. —*adj.* Of or like God.

dogged (dôg′id) *adj.* Stubborn. —**doggedly** *adv.*

dole (dōl) *v.* To give sparingly.

domestic (də·mes′tik) *adj.* Having to do with the home, housekeeping, or the family.

dreary (drir′ē) *adj.* Gloomy; cheerless.

---

fat, āpe, cär; ten, ēven; is, bīte; gō, hôrn, tōōl, look; oil, out; up, fur; get; joy; yet; chin; she; thin, *th*en; zh, leisure; ŋ, ring; ə for *a* in *ago, e* in *agent, i* in *sanity, o* in *comply, u* in *focus;* ′ as in *able* (ā′b′l).

drone (drōn) *n.* An idle person who lives by the work of others; parasite.

dubious (dōō′bē·əs) *adj.* Causing or feeling doubt. —**dubiously** *adv.*

dunce (duns) *n.* A dull, ignorant person.

dynamic (dī·nam′ik) *adj.* Active; energetic.

edict (ē′dikt) *n.* Order; decree.

eloquence (el′ə·kwəns) *n.* Speech or writing that is vivid, forceful, graceful, and persuasive.

elucidation (i·loo′sə·dā′shən) *n.* Clarification; explanation.

embodiment (im·bäd′ē·mənt) *n.* The concrete expression of a quality or an idea.

emerge (i·mʉrj′) *v.* To come forth into view.

emigration (em′ə·grā′shən) *n.* The act of leaving one place, as a country or region, to settle in another.

enchantment (in·chant′mənt) *n.* A magic spell or charm.

endurance (in·door′əns) *n.* The ability to continue.

ensue (in·sōō′) *v.* To come afterward; follow.

entanglement (in·taŋ′g′l·mənt) *n.* State or condition of being tangled or caught, as in a vine or net.

enterprising (en′tər·prī′ziŋ) *adj.* Full of energy and having the ability and the willingness to think and act on one's own, without being urged.

entreaty (in·trēt′ē) *n.* An earnest request.

epitaph (ep′ə·taf′) *n.* An inscription on a tombstone in memory of the person buried there.

equity (ek′wət·ē) *n.* Fairness; justice.

ethical (eth′i·k′l) *adj.* Having to do with standards of conduct and moral judgment; in keeping with principles of right and wrong.

excruciating (iks·krōō′shē·āt′iŋ) *adj.* Causing intense physical or mental pain.

excursion (ik·skʉr′zhən) *n.* A short journey.

execrable (ek′si·krə·b′l) *adj.* Abominable; detestable.

exhilarate (ig·zil′ə·rāt′) *v.* To make cheerful or lively.

exhorter (ig·zôrt′ər) *n.* One who argues by advising or warning.

extent (ik·stent′) *n.* The space, amount, or degree that a thing covers; size.

extravagant (ik·strav′ə·gənt) *adj.* Ornate and showy.

extremities (ik·strem′ə·tēz) *n. pl.* The hands and feet.

extrude (ik·strōōd′) *v.* To push or force out.

exultant (ig·zult′′nt) *adj.* Joyful; rejoicing.

falter (fôl′tər) *v.* To stumble in action or speech.

familiar (fə·mil′yər) *adj.* Too friendly, intimate, or bold.

fancy (fan′sē) *v.* To imagine.

farce (färs) *n.* **1.** An exaggerated comedy based on humorous and unlikely characters. **2.** Something absurd or ridiculous.

fatalist (fāt′′l·ist) *n.* One who believes that all events are determined by fate and so cannot be avoided.

fatigue (fə·tēg′) *n.* Physical or mental tiredness.

feign (fān) *v.* To pretend.

feint (fānt) *n.* **1.** A pretense; false show. **2.** A pretended attack, to put an opponent off guard.

ferule (fer′əl) *n.* A flat stick or ruler used to punish children.

fervor (fʉr′vər) *n.* Great warmth of emotion.

fillip (fil′əp) *n.* Something that stimulates or livens up.

finicky (fin′i·kē) *adj.* Fussy; overly particular.

flay (flā) *v.* To criticize or scold without mercy.

flounder (floun′dər) *v.* To struggle awkwardly to move, speak, or act.

foray (fôr′ā) *n.* A sudden attack or raid in order to seize or steal things.

foreboding (fôr·bōd′iŋ) *n.* A prediction or feeling of something that is to come, especially something bad.

forlorn (fər·lôrn′) *adj.* **1.** Abandoned or deserted. **2.** In pitiful condition; miserable.

formidable (fôr′mə·də·b′l) *adj.* Awe-inspiring.

fortify (fôr′tə·fī′) *v.* To strengthen.

fortitude (fôr′tə·tōōd′) *n.* The strength to bear misfortune; courage.

frailty (frāl′tē) *n.* The condition of being fragile, delicate, or weak.

fraudulent (frô′jə·lənt) *adj.* Based on deceit, trickery, or cheating.

furtive (fʉr′tiv) *adj.* Sneaky.

futility (fyoo·til′ə·tē) *n.* The quality of being useless or hopeless.

gape (gāp) *v.* To stare with open mouth.

garrulous (gar′ə·ləs) *adj.* Talkative.

genial (jēn′yəl) *adj.* Cheerful; friendly.

gesticulation (jes·tik′yə·lā′shən) *n.* Motions, especially of the hands and arms, as in adding force or meaning to one's speech or as signals in the place of speech.

gesture (jes′chər) *n.* A movement of the body or part of the body to express or emphasize an idea or a feeling.

giddy (gid′ē) *adj.* Dazed; dizzy; lightheaded.

gingerly (jin′jər·lē) *adv.* In a delicate or cautious way.

glockenspiel (gläk′ən·spēl) *n.* A percussion instrument with flat metal bars set in a frame, producing bell-like tones when struck with small hammers.

glower (glou′ər) *n.* An angry stare; scowl.

grapple (grap′′l) *v.* To struggle in hand-to-hand combat; wrestle.

grievous (grē′vəs) *adj.* Causing suffering; hard to bear.

grim (grim) *adj.* Hard; stern.

gulf (gulf) *n.* **1.** A deep, wide gap in the earth's surface. **2.** A large area of ocean reaching into land.

Hades (hā′dēz) *n.* **1.** The home of the dead beneath the earth. **2.** Hell.

hallow (hal′ō) *v.* To bless.

haunch (hônch) *n.* The part of the body that includes the hip, buttock, and thickest part of the thigh.

headland (hed′lənd) *n.* A point of land reaching out into the water.

hearse (hʉrs) *n.* A vehicle used for carrying a corpse.

heartrending (härt′ren′diŋ) *adj.* Causing much grief or mental anguish.

hew (hyōō) *v.* To cut or chop.

hollow (häl′ō) *n.* A cavity; a hole. —*adj.* Having an empty space.

horizontal (hôr′ə·zän′t′l) *adj.* Parallel to the horizon; not up and down.

hostile (häs′t′l) *adj.* Cold, hard, and unwelcoming.

humiliated (hyoo·mil′ē·āt′id) *adj.* Ashamed; mortified.

hunch (hunch) *v.* **1.** To move forward jerkily. **2.** To form an arch or a hump with the body.

hypocritical (hip′ə·krit′i·k′l) *adj.* False; pretending something that is not so.

hysterical (his·ter′i·k′l) *adj.* Emotionally uncontrolled.

illuminate (i·lōō′mə·nāt′) *v.* To give light to.

immaculate (i·mak′yə·lit) *adj.* **1.** Perfectly clean. **2.** Perfectly correct; flawless.

immense (i·mens′) *adj.* Very large; vast; huge.

immortality (i·môr·tal′ə·tē) *n.* The condition of living or lasting forever.

impede (im·pēd′) *v.* To bar or hinder the progress of.

impediment (im·ped′ə·mənt) *n.* Something that gets in the way of the progress of.

impel (im·pel′) *v.* To push, drive, or propel forward.

imperceptible (im′per·sep′tə·b′l) *adj.* Not plain or clear to the senses; so small or subtle that it is difficult to perceive.

impetuous (im·pech′oo·wəs) *adj.* Done suddenly; impulsive.

implacable (im·plak′ə·b′l) *adj.* That cannot be satisfied; relentless.

implement (im′plə·mənt) *v.* To carry into effect; accomplish.

imposing (im·pō′ziŋ) *adj.* Impressive.

impractical (im·prak′tə·k′l) *adj.* Not workable or useful.

improvise (im′prə·vīz′) *v.* To make or do with the tools or materials on hand, usually to fill a need that was not foreseen.

impudent (im′pyōō·dənt) *adj.* Shamelessly bold or disrespectful.

impunity (im·pyōō′nə·tē) *n.* Freedom from punishment, penalty, or harm.

inaccessible (in′ək·ses′ə·b′l) *adj.* Impossible to reach.

inarticulate (in′är·tik′yə·lit) *adj.* Unable to speak, as from strong emotion.

inaudible (in·ô′də·b′l) *adj.* Unable to be heard.

incoherent (in′kō·hir′ənt) *adj.* Not logically connected; disjointed; having disconnected speech that is difficult to understand.

incontinent (in·känt′′n·ənt) *adj.* Unable to be restrained or contained. —**incontinently** *adv.*

incredulity (in′krə·dōō′lə·tē) *n.* Unwillingness or inability to believe; doubt.

indecisive (in′di·sī′siv) *adj.* Having regular difficulty making decisions; hesitating. —**indecisively** *adv.*

indifference (in·dif′ər·əns) *n.* Lack of interest, concern, or feeling.

indigene (in′di·jēn′) *n.* A native plant, animal, or person.

indigent (in′di·jənt) *adj.* Poor; needy.

indignant (in·dig′nənt) *adj.* Feeling or expressing anger, especially at injustice or meanness. —**indignantly** *adv.*

indignation (in′dig·nā′shən) *n.* Anger or scorn resulting from injustice, ingratitude, or meanness.

indulge (in·dulj′) *v.* **1.** To give way to one's own desires; do what one likes. **2.** To go easy with; be lenient. —**indulgent** *adj.* —**indulgence** *n.*

industrious (in·dus′trē·əs) *adj.* Hard-working. —**industriously** *adv.*

ineffable (in·ef′ə·b′l) *adj.* Too overwhelming to be described or expressed.

ineffectual (in′i·fek′choo·wəl) *adj.* Not successful; not effective.

inert (in·ʉrt′) *adj.* Without power to move or act.

inexorable (in·ek′sər·ə·b′l) *adj.* That cannot be moved or influenced by persuasion; unrelenting.

inexplicable (in·eks′pli·kə·b′l) *adj.* That cannot be explained or understood.

infernal (in·fʉr′n′l) *adj.* Hellish; fiendish.

inflection (in·flek′shən) *n.* Any change in tone or pitch of the voice.

injudicious (in′jōō·dish′əs) *adj.* Showing poor judgment.

inlet (in′let) *n.* A narrow strip of water extending into a body of land.

innumerable (i·nōō′mər·ə·b′l) *adj.* Too numerous to be counted; a great many.

insufferable (in·suf′ər·ə·b′l) *adj.* Unbearable.

insurmountable (in′sər·moun′tə·b′l) *adj.* That cannot be passed over or overcome.

intangible (in·tan′jə·b′l) *adj.* That cannot be touched; not physical or solid.

intent (in·tent′) *adj.* **1.** Firmly directed or fixed; intense. **2.** Totally involved.

interminable (in·tʉr′mi·nə·b′l) *adj.* Endless.

interposition (in′tər·pə·zish′ən) *n.* The disputed teaching or belief that a state may reject a federal order that it considers to be trespassing on its rights.

---

fat, āpe, cär; ten, ēven; is, bīte; gō, hôrn, tōōl, look; oil, out; up, fʉr; get; joy; yet; chin; she; thin, *th*en; **zh,** leisure; **ŋ,** ring; ə for *a* in *ago, e* in *agent, i* in *sanity, o* in *comply, u* in *focus;* ' as in *able* (ā′b′l).

intimate (in′tə·mit) *adj.* Closely acquainted; very familiar.

intolerable (in·täl′ər·ə·b′l) *adj.* Unbearable; too severe or painful to be endured.

intricate (in′tri·kit) *adj.* Full of elaborate detail.

intrusive (in·trōō′siv) *adj.* Forcing oneself into a position where one is not welcome.

intuition (in′too·wish′ən) *n.* The ability to understand or know things without conscious reasoning; immediate understanding.

invariable (in·ver′ē·ə·b′l) *adj.* Not changing; constant.

invincible (in·vin′sə·b′l) *adj.* That cannot be overcome; unconquerable.

ironical (ī·rän′i·k′l) *adj.* Having the quality of irony; being the opposite of what is or might be expected.

itinerant (ī·tin′ər·ənt) *adj.* Traveling from place to place.

jocund (jäk′ənd) *adj.* Cheerful; gay.

jowl *n.* 1. Jaw, especially the lower jaw with the cheeks. 2. The fleshy, hanging part under the lower jaw.

judicious (jōō·dish′əs) *adj.* Wise and careful.

keen (kēn) *v.* To wail; cry.

kerosene (ker′ə·sēn′) *n.* A thin oil distilled from petroleum or shale oil.

knoll (nōl) *n.* A small hill; mound.

labored (lā′bərd) *adj.* Done with great effort; strained.

labyrinth (lab′ə·rinth′) *n.* A complicated and confusing arrangement.

lackadaisical (lak′ə·dā′zi·k′l) *adj.* Showing lack of interest or spirit; listless.

lament (lə·ment′) *v.* To feel or express deep sorrow for; mourn or grieve for. —**lamentation** *n.*

languid (laŋ′gwid) *adj.* Sluggish; slow.

larynx (lar′iŋks) *n.* The structure in the throat containing the vocal cords and serving as the organ of voice.

laud (lôd) *v.* To praise.

lethargy (leth′ər·jē) *n.* Lack of energy; dullness.

linger (liŋ′gər) *v.* To continue to stay; delay.

loathe (lōth) *v.* To dislike intensely; detest.

lofty (lôf′tē) *adj.* Very high.

longitudinal (län′jə·tōōd′′n·əl) *adj.* Running or placed lengthwise.

lout *n.* A clumsy, stupid fellow; a rude, ill-mannered person.

luminous (lōō′mə·nəs) *adj.* Shining; bright.

lunge (lunj) *n.* A sudden plunge forward.

lurch *v.* To roll, pitch, or sway suddenly forward or to one side.

macabre (mə·käb′rə) *adj.* Gruesome; horrible; ghastly.

majestic (mə·jes′tik) *adj.* Very grand or dignified.

makeshift (māk′shift′) *adj.* That will do for a while as a substitute.

malignancy (mə·lig′nən·sē) *n.* An abnormal growth, as a tumor, that can be life-threatening.

manifest (man′ə·fest′) *adj.* Apparent; obvious.

manifestation (man′ə·fes·tā′shən) *n.* Anything made evident, shown clearly, or revealed.

manipulate (mə·nip′yə·lāt′) *v.* To work, operate, or treat with or as with the hand or hands. —**manipulation** *n.*

margin (mär′jən) *n.* A border, edge, or limit.

martyr (mär′tər) *n.* A person who chooses to suffer or die rather than give up his or her beliefs.

matted (mat′id) *adj.* Closely tangled together in a dense mass.

meditate (med′ə·tāt) *v.* To think deeply; ponder.

melancholy (mel′ən·käl′ē) *adj.* Sad; gloomy.

menace (men′is) *v.* To threaten. —*n.* Anything threatening harm or evil.

merciless (mur′si·lis) *adj.* pitiless; cruel.

mercurial (mər·kyoor′ē·əl) *adj.* Highly changeable.

methodical (mə·thäd′i·k′l) *adj.* Orderly; systematic. —**methodically** *adv.*

meticulous (mə·tik′yoo·ləs) *adj.* Overly careful about details; finicky; fussy. —**meticulously** *adv.*

mincing (min′siŋ) *adj.* Characterized by short steps or artificial daintiness. —**mincingly** *adv.*

minimize (min′ə·mīz′) *v.* 1. To reduce to a minimum. 2. To make appear to be of the least possible amount.

mitigate (mit′ə·gāt′) *v.* To make less severe.

molestation (mō′les·tā′shən) *n.* Interference or meddling with the intention of causing trouble or harm.

mollify (mäl′ə·fī′) *v.* To soften; make less stern or violent.

monotonous (mə·nät′′n·əs) *adj.* Having little or no variation. —**monotonously** *adv.*

morose (mə·rōs′) *adj.* Gloomy; sullen. —**morosely** *adv.*

mortal (môr′t′l) *adj.* 1. That must eventually die. 2. Causing death; deadly; fatal.

mortician (môr·tish′ən) *n.* Undertaker; funeral director.

multitude (mul′tə·tōōd′) *n.* A large number of persons or things.

nettled (net′′ld) *adj.* Annoyed; irritated.

niche (nich) *n.* 1. A hollow in a wall. 2. The specific space occupied by an organism in its habitat.

nominally (näm′i·n′l·ē) *adv.* Slightly; to a small degree.

nonchalance (nän′shə·läns′) *n.* Indifference; lack of concern.

nullification (nul′ə·fi·kā′shən) *n.* In U.S. history, the refusal of a state to recognize or enforce any federal law believed to interfere with the power of the state.

oblivious (ə·bliv′ē·əs) *adj.* Forgetful or unmindful.

odious (ō′dē·əs) *adj.* Hateful; disgusting; offensive.

offal (ôf′′l) *n.* The waste parts, especially the inner parts such as the guts and intestines, of a butchered animal.

ominous (äm′ə·nəs) *adj.* Serving as an omen, especially an evil one; threatening.

onerous (än′ər·əs) *adj.* Burdensome.

onslaught (än′slôt′) *n.* Attack.

oppression (ə·presh′ən) *n.* Tyranny; harsh rule; being kept down by cruel and unjust powers. —**oppressive** *adj.*

opulence (äp′yə·ləns) *n.* Abundance; richness.

ostentatious (äs′tən·tā′shəs) *adj.* A showy manner.

pacify (pas′ə·fī′) *v.* To calm; appease.

palatable (pal′it·ə·b′l) *adj.* Acceptable to the taste; fit to be eaten.

pall (pôl) *n.* A dark or gloomy covering.

pallid (pal′id) *adj.* Pale; wan.

palpable (pal′pə·b′l) *adj.* **1.** Able to be touched or felt; tangible. **2.** Easily perceived by the senses.

parry (par′ē) *v.* To turn aside, as by a clever reply or remark; evade.

patron (pā′trən) *n.* A person, usually wealthy, who supports some activity or institution.

paunch (pônch) *n.* A protruding abdomen or belly. —**paunchy** *adj.*

pedagogue (ped′ə·gäg′) *n.* A teacher, often a stern and exacting one.

peevish (pē′vish) *adj.* **1.** Hard to please; irritable. **2.** Showing ill humor or impatience.

penance (pen′əns) *n.* An act of self-punishment to show sorrow or remorse for a wrongdoing.

pendulous (pen′joo·ləs) *adj.* Hanging loosely; hanging so as to swing.

pensive (pen′siv) *adj.* **1.** Thinking deeply. **2.** Expressing deep thoughtfulness, often with some sadness.

perception (pər·sep′shən) *n.* **1.** The ability to understand or become aware of, especially through the senses. **2.** An idea or understanding gained through the senses; awareness or insight.

perennial (pə·ren′ē·əl) *adj.* **1.** Active throughout the whole year. **2.** Returning year after year.

peril (per′əl) *n.* Something that may cause harm.

perpetual (pər·pech′oo·wəl) *adj.* Permanent; endless.

perplexed (pər·plekst′) *adj.* Filled with doubt or uncertainty; confused.

persevere (pur′sə·vir′) *v.* To stick patiently with a task; persist. —**perseverance** *n.*

persistent (pər·sis′tənt) *adj.* Continuing, without stopping.

pervade (pər·vād′) *v.* **1.** To spread throughout. **2.** To fill.

pessimistic (pes′ə·mis′tik) *adj.* Expecting the worst; looking on the dark side; cynical.

petulant (pech′oo·lənt) *adj.* Impatient or irritable, especially over small annoyances.

philosopher (fi·läs′ə·fər) *n.* A person who is learned in philosophy, the study of the principles underlying conduct, thought, knowledge, and the nature of the universe.

philosophic (fil′ə·säf′ik) *adj.* **1.** Sensibly composed or calm; rational. **2.** Of or according to a philosopher.

physique (fi·zēk′) *n.* The structure, health, strength, form, or appearance of the body.

pillion (pil′yən) *n.* A cushion attached behind a saddle for an extra rider.

pinion (pin′yən) *v.* **1.** To keep from moving by binding the arms. **2.** To confine.

pious (pī′əs) *adj.* **1.** Having or showing religious devotion. **2.** Seemingly good and virtuous, but often assuming that manner hypocritically.

pique (pēk) *v.* To pride oneself.

placid (plas′id) *adj.* Undisturbed; calm; quiet.

plausible (plô′zə·b′l) *adj.* Acceptable; reasonable.

pliability (plī′ə·bil′ə·tē) *n.* Flexibility.

poignant (poin′yənt) *adj.* **1.** Sharply painful to the feelings. **2.** Emotionally touching. —**poignancy** *n.*

poise (poiz) *n.* **1.** Balance. **2.** Ease of manner; self-assurance; composure.

ponderous (pän′dər·us) *adj.* **1.** Very heavy. **2.** Massive.

porous (pôr′əs) *adj.* Full of tiny openings through which air, fluids, or light may pass.

portal (pôr′t′l) *n.* Doorway; entrance.

portentous (pôr·ten′təs) *adj.* Warning of some event about to occur, especially an evil one; ominous.

potent (pōt′′nt) *adj.* Effective or powerful in action.

precarious (pri·ker′ē·əs) *adj.* Uncertain; dependent upon chance. —**precariously** *adv.*

precede (pri·sēd′) *v.* To be, come, or go before in time, place, order, rank, or importance.

precipitate (pri·sip′ə·tāt′) *v.* To cause; to bring on.

predominant (pri·däm′ə·nənt) *adj.* Having authority or dominating influence over others; superior. —**predominance** *n.*

preen (prēn) *v.* To adorn or trim oneself carefully.

premonition (prē′mə·nish′ən) *n.* A feeling that something is going to happen, especially something bad.

pretext (prē′tekst) *n.* A false reason to hide the real one; excuse.

prevalence (prev′ə·ləns) *n.* Wide or common occurrence; great number.

---

fat, āpe, cär; ten, ēven; is, bīte; gō, hôrn, tōōl, look; oil, out; up, fur; get; joy; yet; chin; she; thin, *th*en; zh, leisure; η, ring; ə for *a* in *ago, e* in *agent, i* in *sanity, o* in *comply, u* in *focus;* ′ as in *able* (ā′b′l).

prodigy (präd′ə·jē) *n.* A wonderfully extraordinary person, thing, or act, especially a child of highly unusual talent or genius.

profound (prə·found′) *adj.* **1.** Very deep or low. **2.** Deeply or intensely felt. —**profoundly** *adv.*

prompt (prämpt) *adj.* On time; ready; punctual.

propagate (präp′ə·gāt′) *v.* To reproduce or multiply, as a plant or animal.

protuberance (prō·tōō′bər·əns) *n.* A thing or a part that bulges or swells out.

providence (präv′ə·dəns) *n.* The care or guidance of God or nature.

purify (pyoor′ə·fī′) *v.* To rid of impurities or pollution; cleanse.

pursuit (pər·sōōt′) *n.* The act of chasing.

quandary (kwän′drē) *n.* A state of uncertainty.

query (kwir′ē) *n.* A question.

ravenous (rav′ə·nəs) *adj.* Very hungry.

recess (rē′ses) *n.* **1.** A hollow, inner place. **2.** A break from work.

reclamation (rek′lə·mā′shən) *n.* A reclaiming or recovery.

recoil (ri·koil′) *v.* To start or shrink back in fear, surprise, or disgust.

redeem (ri·dēm′) *v.* To get back; recover; save.

refrain (ri·frān′) *v.* To hold back.

reiterate (rē·it′ə·rāt′) *v.* To repeat something done or said.

reminiscence (rem′ə·nis′′ns) *n.* An account, written or spoken, of remembered experiences.

remorse (ri·môrs′) *n.* A deep sense of guilt over a wrong one has done.

remote (ri·mōt′) *adj.* **1.** Distant. **2.** Slight.

render (ren′dər) *v.* To give or present.

repose (ri·pōz′) *n.* Calm; peace; restfulness.

repudiate (ri·pyōō′dē·āt′) *v.* To refuse to have anything to do with; push aside or disown publicly.

requisition (rek′wə·zish′ən) *n.* A formal request. —*v.* To demand or take, as by authority.

resent (ri·zent′) *v.* To feel bitter and upset about an act or toward a person, from a sense of feeling personally injured or offended.

respite (res′pit) *n.* A delay; an interval of relief or rest.

restorative (ri·stôr′ə·tiv) *adj.* Capable of restoring, especially health, strength, etc.

restrain (ri·strān′) *v.* **1.** To hold back from action. **2.** To keep under control.

revile (ri·vīl′) *v.* To use harsh and abusive language in speaking to or about; call bad names.

revulsion (ri·vul′shən) *n.* **1.** A sudden, complete, and violent change of feeling. **2.** Extreme disgust.

rigid (rij′id) *adj.* Stiff and hard; not bending.

ritual (rich′oo·wəl) *n.* A set form or system of rights, religious or otherwise.

rout (rout) *n.* A disorderly crowd or flight.

saffron (saf′rən) *n.* **1.** An aromatic plant used for coloring and flavoring foods. **2.** An orange-yellow color.

sagacity (sə·gas′ə·tē) *n.* The quality or an instance of showing sound judgment, foresight, etc.

sage (sāj) *n.* A very wise man. —*adj.* Having wisdom and good judgment. —**sagely** *adv.*

saunter (sôn′tər) *v.* To walk about idly; stroll.

savor (sā′vər) *v.* To dwell on with delight; enjoy.

scandalous (skan′d′l·əs) *adj.* Not considered decent or moral; offensive.

secretion (si·krē′shən) *n.* A substance released by an organism for a special use within the organism or for waste.

secure (si·kyoor′) *v.* To get possession of; acquire.

seethe (sē*th*) *v.* To be violently disturbed.

sequestered (si·kwes′tərd) *adj.* Secluded; removed from others.

serene (sə·rēn′) *adj.* Calm; peaceful.

settee (se·tē′) *n.* A small or medium-sized sofa.

shrewd (shrōōd) *adj.* Clever; sharp-minded.

sidle (sī′d′l) *v.* To move sideways in a shy or sneaky manner.

silhouette (sil′oo·wet′) *n.* The outline of a figure.

simultaneous (sī′m′l·tā′nē·əs) *adj.* Occurring or done at the same time.

smite (smīt) *v.* To hit or punish.

sobered (sō′bərd) *adj.* Made serious.

solicitude (sə·lis′ə·tōōd′) *n.* Care; concern.

soliloquy (sə·lil′ə·kwē) *n.* Lines in a drama in which a character reveals his thoughts to the audience, but not to the other characters, as if speaking to himself.

somber (säm′bər) *adj.* Solemn; serious.

sparse (spärs) *adj.* Thinly spread; not crowded.

spasmodic (spaz·mäd′ik) *adj.* Characterized by sudden, fitful, involuntary muscular contractions.

speculation (spek′yə·lā′shən) *n.* A thought; meditation. —**speculative** *adj.* —**speculatively** *adv.*

spiral (spī′rəl) *adj.* Circling around a central point; coiled. —*v.* To move in a continuous, widening increase (or decrease); spin.

staid (stād) *adj.* Settled and steady.

static (stat′ik) *n.* Electrical discharges in the atmosphere that interfere with radio and television reception.

stealthy (stel′thē) *adj.* Secret; sly. —**stealthily** *adv.*

stifle (stī′f′l) *v.* To hold back; suppress; stop.

stout *adj.* Fat.

stow (stō) *v.* To pack or store.

straddle (strad′′l) *v.* To place oneself with a leg on either side of.

straits (strāts) *n. pl.* Difficulty.

strident (strīd′′nt) *adj.* Harsh-sounding; shrill.

stupefied (stoo′pə·fīd′) *adj.* **1.** Stunned. **2.** Amazed.

subdue (səb·doo′) *v.* **1.** To make less intense. **2.** To control.

subjugate (səb′jə·gāt′) *v.* To conquer.

subtle (sut′′l) *adj.* Delicately suggestive; not obvious.

sufficient (sə·fish′′nt) *adj.* As much as is needed; enough.

sullen (sul′ən) *adj.* Sulky; glum. **—sullenly** *adv.*

summon (sum′ən) *v.* To call for.

sundry (sun′drē) *adj.* Various; miscellaneous.

supplication (sup′lə·kā′shən) *n.* A humble request or sincere appeal. **—suppliant** *adj.*

surmount (sər·mount′) *v.* To conquer; overcome.

surreptitious (sur′əp·tish′əs) *adj.* Done in a secret way. **—surreptitiously** *adv.*

sustain (sə·stān′) *v.* **1.** To provide for the support of. **2.** To strengthen the spirits; comfort; encourage. **—sustenance** *n.*

swain (swān) *n.* A young lover; man who is polite and attentive to a woman.

swathe (swā*th*) *v.* To wrap or bind.

sympathy (sim′pə·thē) *n.* Understanding between people that arises from sameness of feeling.

tableau (tab·lō′) *n.* A representation of a scene by a group of people posing silently and without moving.

tarry (tar′ē) *v.* **1.** To linger. **2.** To stay for a time longer than was intended.

temperamental (tem′prə·men′t′l) *adj.* **1.** Pertaining to one's frame of mind or nature. **2.** Easily upset.

tenacious (tə·nā′shəs) *adj.* Holding firmly.

terrestrial (tə·res′trē·əl) *adj.* Of this world; earthly.

thrash (thrash) *v.* To move violently; beat.

throng *n.* A crowd.

throttle (thrät′′l) *v.* To choke; strangle.

tithe (tī*th*) *n.* One-tenth of the annual produce of one's land or of one's income, contributed to support a church or its clergy.

tolerance (täl′ər·əns) *n.* Ability to bear up or put up with.

torrent (tôr′ənt) *n.* A very heavy and violent flow, especially of water.

totem (tōt′əm) *n.* Among primitive peoples, an animal or natural object taken by a family or clan as its symbol.

totter (tät′ər) *v.* To rock unsteadily as if about to fall.

tranquillity (traŋ·kwil′ə·tē) *n.* Peacefulness; calmness.

transfixed (trans·fikst′) *adj.* Absolutely still; motionless.

transparent (trans·per′ənt) *n.* **1.** So fine as to be seen through. **2.** Open; not hidden; obvious.

treacherous (trech′ər·əs) *adj.* Characterized by disloyalty; untrustworthy.

tremulous (trem′yoo·ləs) *adj.* **1.** Trembling. **2.** Fearful.

tribute (trib′yoot) *n.* Something given, done, or said, as a gift showing respect, honor, or praise.

trice (trīs) *n.* A very short time; an instant; a moment.

trifle (trī′f′l) *n.* Something of little value.

tumult (too′mult) *n.* **1.** Noisy commotion, as the roar of a crowd. **2.** Confusion; disturbance. **—tumultuous** *adj.*

turmoil (tur′moil) *n.* Commotion; uproar; confusion.

tyranny (tir′ə·nē) *n.* **1.** Oppressive and unjust government. **2.** Cruel and unjust power.

ubiquitous (yoo·bik′wə·təs) *adj.* Present, or seeming to be present, everywhere at the same time.

unabashed (un′ə·basht′) *adj.* Not embarrassed; poised.

unalterable (un·ôl′tər·ə·b′l) *adj.* Not able to be changed.

undaunted (un·dôn′tid) *adj.* Not hesitating or stopping because of fear or discouragement.

undulation (un′joo·lā′shən) *n.* A wavy motion.

unwavering (un·wā′vər·iŋ) *adj.* Steady; showing no doubt.

vehement (vē′ə·mənt) *adj.* Having or demonstrating intense feeling or passion. **—vehemently** *adv.*

venerable (ven′ər·ə·b′l) *adj.* Worthy of respect because of age, dignity, character, etc.

vengeful (venj′fəl) *adj.* Desiring or seeking revenge.

vermilion (vər·mil′yən) *n.* A bright red or scarlet.

vex (veks) *v.* To irritate; annoy; distress.

vigil (vij′əl) *n.* A purposeful watch during the usual hours of sleep.

vigilance (vij′ə·ləns) *n.* Watchfulness.

vile (vīl) *adj.* Repulsive; disgusting; distasteful.

vista (vis′tə) *n.* A view.

wallow (wäl′ō) *v.* **1.** To roll about, as in mud or water. **2.** To indulge oneself fully in (a particular activity).

wary (wer′ē) *adj.* Cautious.

waver (wā′vər) *v.* To move unsteadily.

whorl (hwôrl) *n.* A thing with a coiled or spiral appearance.

wistful (wist′fəl) *adj.* Showing vague longings.

wretched (rech′id) *adj.* Of poor quality.

writhe (rī*th*) *v.* To make turning or twisting movements.

wrought (rôt) *adj.* Formed; made.

wry (rī) *adj.* **1.** Made by twisting or distorting the features. **2.** Distorted in meaning; ironic.

zeal (zēl) *n.* Enthusiasm; devotion.

---

fat, āpe, cär; ten, ēven; is, bīte; gō, hôrn, tool, look; oil, out; up, fur; get; joy; yet; chin; she; thin, *th*en; zh, leisure; ŋ, ring; ə for a in ago, e in agent, i in sanity, o in comply, u in focus; ′ as in able (ā′b′l).

INDEX OF SKILLS

CRITICAL THINKING SKILLS

The page numbers in italics refer to critical thinking skills covered in the Exercises in Critical Thinking and Writing.

Analysis

AN ORGANIZATION OF CONTENTS BY THEME

INDEX OF AUTHORS AND TITLES